Grace Abounding

The Core Knowledge Anthology of African-American Literature, Music, and Art

Executive Editor
Robert D. Shepherd

Senior Editor
Michael L. Ford

Contributing Editors
Corey Carter
Amy S. Miller
Milton L. Welch

Core Knowledge Foundation
Charlottesville, VA

Grace Abounding

Consultants and Contributing Writers

Joel Baumgart
Ewa Beaujon
Mary Kathryn Hassett
Marilyn Shepherd
Gerald Terrell

Design and Typesetting

Kazuko Ashizawa
Kelley Anne Gable

ISBN: 1-933486-02-3

Second Edition.

4 5 6 7 8 9 10 15 14 13 12 11

Cover: "The Creation," by Aaron Douglas, 1927.
Reproduced by permission of the Howard University Gallery of Art.

www.coreknowledge.org

Acknowledgments: "All Stories Are Anansi's" from *The Hat-Shaking Dance and Other Ashanti Tales from Ghana* by Harold Courlander with Albert Kofi Prempeh. © 1957, 1985 by Harold Courlander. Reprinted by permission of Michael Courlander and Erika Courlander.
(Cont. on page 838.)

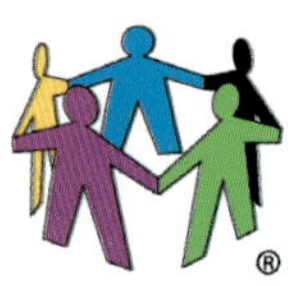

To the children,
those of African descent and otherwise,
who will become tomorrow's
Jacob Lawrences, Maya Angelous,
John Coltranes, and Kathryn Dunhams.

Watch out for them, world.
What you see in this book
is just the beginning.

The Core Knowledge Foundation would like to thank the following individuals and institutions for their contributions to this anthology:

Michael S. Harper

Rita Dove

Donna VanDerZee

E. D. Hirsch, Jr.

Schomburg Center for Research in Black Culture

Eileen Johnston of the Howard University Gallery of Art

University of North Carolina Library (Documenting the American South)

W. E. B. Du Bois Library, University of Massachusetts at Amherst

The National Archives

University of Virginia Library

Library of Congress Photo Duplications Department

Judy Ladendorf and Lynn Tews of the Permissions Group

Paul R. Jones Gallery

Mrs. Coni Porter Uzelac

Diana Brewster

Sam Sheng

Becky Ottesen

Matthew Davis

Diane Perkins Castro

J. Henry Baker

Mike Przyuski

Erin Kist

Amy Tucker

Jackie Beilhart

About Grace Abounding

Grace Abounding: The Core Knowledge Anthology of African-American Literature, Art, and Music presents a story that spans hundreds of generations, crisscrossing continents and oceans, from roots in ageless proverbial wisdom and ancient rhythms to the expansive universe of modern poetry and the unbounded, glorious craziness of "free jazz." In short, *Grace Abounding* surveys the astonishing contributions that African Americans have made to American and world culture. Within these pages you will find history, literature, art, music, and dance—products of unconquerable creativity, faith, wisdom, and kinship. For hundreds of years, from the songs and stories that helped to maintain hope and dignity in the dark days of slavery to the most fruitful and vibrant arts and socio-political movements of the twentieth century, works by African Americans have contributed immeasurably to the development of American culture, though the creators of these works have often labored without thanks or even token recognition and were often subject to (but never resigned to) appalling oppression and abuse.

African-American literature and arts cannot and will not be lumped together under a single, definable aesthetic and treat no single theme or set of themes. As artists whose expressions are born, first and foremost, out of personal experience, African Americans must, of course, tell their personal stories, but many have also felt compelled to tell the story of a people who endured oppression and injustice of a kind no one should have to endure, of a people who suffered but triumphed. The aim of this book is not to assert a definitive definition of what African-American art is; nor do the editors and authors of this text seek to set forth a fixed, conclusive body of works to be separated as an "other" art, to be viewed or interpreted apart from the works from other cultural traditions. Rather, this book simply presents, in a tantalizing, inviting manner, scores of American artists whose works are already recognized as truly great. This book presents masterpiece after masterpiece, and its primary aim is to introduce these works to students and to point students toward those other masterpieces that do not appear in this book but are waiting to be explored (and created) by their eager minds.

This book is filled with what one might call "household names," ones that should be familiar to people all over the world. The Reverend Dr. Martin Luther King, Jr., would perhaps be first among those names. Langston Hughes and Maya Angelou, Frederick Douglass and Harriet Tubman—these names have been fixed in textbooks for at least forty years, and so they will remain. These are some of the most talented and courageous Americans who ever lived, and so it is right that they be remembered and celebrated. Others are familiar, as well—bold social movers and great thinkers like W. E. B. Du Bois, Booker T. Washington, and Malcolm X. Their names continue to stir both controversy and adoration. Their underlying philosophies differed, yet each had the same basic goal, which was to obtain no more and no less than what was pursued and promised by America's Founders. And there are many others whose works have already made a profound and permanent impact on American culture. They are not new "discoveries"—their names are known, but not known well enough by those of us living today in the world they helped to form. Frances Harper, James Whitfield, Ida B. Wells-Barnett, Fannie Coppin, Countee Cullen, Paul Laurence Dunbar, James Weldon Johnson, Claude McKay, Jean Toomer, Helene Johnson, Sterling Brown, Arna Bontemps, Richard Wright, Margaret Walker, Robert Hayden, Derek Walcott—these are but a few of the great African Americans whom every American needs to know.

To the Student

This is the beginning of an extraordinary journey, but one that far too few students have ever taken. Every time you begin one of the literary selections in *Grace Abounding*—from the proverbs and folktales to the essays and poems—you will be dipping your bucket into a fresh well of knowledge and wisdom. Drink it in. Help yourself. The pages of this book contain great works of literature and art that have already had a tremendous impact on your life, whether you realize it or not. And these great works have been carefully framed by the editors of this book with you, the student, in mind. All the necessary tools and keys to understanding have been built into every page. At first, you might be surprised by the sheer number of vocabulary words and footnotes in this book, as well as by the wealth of information presented in the Prereading and Delving Deeper sections that accompany every literary selection. These are not intended to overwhelm you with information; they are there to guide you and to show that there is often much, much more to a work of literature than first meets the eye. Take your time with each work and you will be rewarded.

In literature, in art, and in music, history is reborn. History and the arts are inseparable, and few artistic and cultural traditions, especially in America, are more closely tied to history than those of African Americans. Perhaps no body of literature can provide a more accurate reflection of the American experience, with all of its rights and wrongs, joys and sorrows. The American experience is unique in human history, but it is a part of human history nonetheless. And as much as humans are capable of loving and helping one another, so too we are guilty of inflicting great wrongs upon one another. This book will not shield you from raw truths about our history. But this book is not supposed to make you mad. It is not supposed to make you pessimistic or angry about the world. Rather, it should make you aware, and curious, and much wiser about the forces at work in society, both good and bad, that every person in our society has a responsibility to recognize and respond to. When bad, unjust, and even evil things occur, it is the individuals who have committed themselves to knowledge and understanding who must step forward, bring communities together, and make things right, no matter who is to blame or how hopeless the situation might seem.

Everything else that could be said in this message has already been printed on the pages of this book. Let these great writers, artists, thinkers, and activists speak for themselves. Go! Thumb through these pages. Glance at the vivid illustrations and, when you find one that really catches your eye, go ahead and start reading. These pages will excite your imagination and your desire to learn and leave you with the supreme knowledge that absolutely nothing in this world can suppress human creativity and expression, *yours* as well as *theirs*.

To the Teacher

Grace Abounding in the Classroom. This anthology can be used, in whole or in part, in any language arts or history program, grades K-12, whether or not a school or district specifically mandates a course in African-American Studies. Understanding the Selection and Delving Deeper pages, end-of-unit skills sections, and Prereading discussions throughout the book, as well as the Handbook of Literary Terms and Glossary, cover the full gamut of reading, writing, speaking, and listening skills common in most states' learning standards; indeed, as a whole, the range of literary selections and the number of skills covered in *Grace Abounding* represent far more information than the most ambitious curriculum would expect or hope to cover in a single year.

Organizing a skills program. The indexes in this book and the teacher guides, activities, tests, and other supplemental materials available online provide all the necessary tools for teachers and curriculum coordinators who seek to align *Grace Abounding* with specific learning standards or curriculum guidelines.

About the Literary Selections. *Grace Abounding* presents a comprehensive survey of African-American literature. It is the most extensive collection of African-American literature, art, and music available to primary or secondary schools. Still, the literary and art selections herein present only a small, carefully chosen sampling of the enormous wealth of African-American material available in libraries, recordings, galleries, and, increasingly, on the Internet. This book is a doorway into a vast and ever-evolving literary and arts tradition, and it is the hope of the authors and editors that students will come away from *Grace Abounding* with a newfound interest in all literature, all art, all music, all culture, as well as an understanding of the profound degree to which history, the future, and human creativity are intertwined. Taken as a whole, the literary selections included in *Grace Abounding* provide ample exposure to the literary forms, styles, and genres with which students should be familiar as they approach and proceed through high school.

Reading Level and Age Appropriateness. Each of the four units of this book contains selections that are suitable for younger readers, grades K–6, including folktales, autobiographical narratives, poems, and short stories. Everything in the book is suitable for readers in grade 7 and up. However, certain essays and poems may be deemed too challenging or unnecessary for certain reading levels and age groups. A list of suggested reading levels is available online, though teachers and administrators are the best judges with regard to which selections will be required reading. That said, all literary selections, activities, accompanying illustrations, and music and art selections have been carefully selected and designed with the understanding that young readers, whether assigned certain readings or not, are likely to read independently any given page in the book.

Study Apparatus

Every literary selection in *Grace Abounding* contains elements designed to maximize the student's learning experience. Here are some components of the study apparatus in this text:

Prereadings. At the beginning of each literary selection you will find a Prereading page that provides crucial background information about the author's purpose and style and the historical context in which the piece was written. Prereadings also provide helpful strategies for reading the text in question.

Guided Reading Questions. These appear only in short stories and essays, particularly complex or lengthy pieces, and are placed to ensure that students maintain focus and do not overlook key points in the readings.

Vocabulary in Place. The blue boxes on the bottom of the page contain clear, concise definitions, in language easy for students to understand, of words every student ought to know. The Glossary in the back of the book and the online vocabulary materials will help teachers make the most of the wealth of vocabulary words in this book.

Footnotes. Footnotes appear in just about every literary selection and are used to interpret or shed light on many elements of the texts: commonly used phrases, sayings, and quotations (e.g., from scripture or from historical documents); interpretations or definitions of archaic, unusual, or specialized terms, usages, and spellings; allusions and references to other writers and literary works; major historical events and figures; and relations to other selections in *Grace Abounding*. Teachers and students will be surprised by the comprehensiveness of the footnotes in *Grace Abounding*. In fact, this book presents an innovative and exciting approach to teaching literature. Footnotes open doors to essential knowledge; each entry represents a key to cultural awareness and literacy and so to advanced reading comprehension. It is our hope that students will gain wisdom from the care with which these notes were prepared, that they will learn that knowledge and the continued quest for knowledge leads one to expansive and previously unimagined worlds. Don't underestimate what one can learn from reference materials. Remember what Malcolm X learned from studying dictionaries! Footnotes will not obstruct or stifle a young reader's progress; on the contrary, they should reinforce the idea that when reading, **it is OK to stop and think!** That is what good readers do. With a little practice, students will learn to use these extensive footnotes (and the other study apparatus) to gain the most from their reading. Train students to use their fingers or a pen (with the cap on!) to hold a place in the text so they can easily return to their spot after reading, and considering, a footnote. Every footnote brings a student one step closer to becoming an expert reader.

Understanding the Selection. After every selection there are Recalling, Interpreting, and Synthesizing questions (arranged according to Bloom's Taxonomy of Educational Objectives). These may be used as either discussion or short-answer questions. More often than not, students will be expected, and should be encouraged, to refer directly to the text whenever necessary. Teachers may use these questions as the basis for tests and quizzes, though materials more suited to this purpose are also available online.

Delving Deeper. The final page of every selection features writing, research, or discussion activities in the categories of Understanding Literature, History Connections, Speaking and Listening, and Writing. Also, after certain poems, entries entitled A Reading of the Selection present interpretations that will give young readers unprecedented insight into how expert readers approach poetry and why poetry is so necessary.

End-of-Unit Activities. At the ends of the units are additional writing, speaking, and listening activities designed to cover, comprehensively, the essential skills in these areas. These activities also encourage additional reflection upon essential ideas presented in the unit.

Please visit www. graceabounding.coreknowledge.org

About Core Knowledge

The Core Knowledge Foundation is dedicated to preserving and transmitting to future generations the knowledge and cultural traditions that are central to the American experience. From its beginning, the Foundation has attempted to reflect in its curricula the ethnic and cultural diversity that is our greatest asset as a nation. Dedicated to excellence and fairness in education, the Foundation is an independent, nonprofit, nonpartisan organization founded by E. D. Hirsch, Jr., professor emeritus of education and humanities at the Unversity of Virginia. The Foundation derives its mission from ideas first presented in Dr. Hirsch's best-selling book *Cultural Literacy: What Every American Needs to Know* (1987) and further elaborated in *The Schools We Need* (1996) and *The Knowledge Deficit* (2006). A leader in the national school reform movement, the Foundation holds that for the sake of academic excellence and in order to achieve higher literacy rates, schools need to teach a solid, specific, sequenced, and shared body of knowledge. A carefully worked-out sequence of grade-by-grade content, based on what America's children need to know to become literate citizens, is detailed in such publications as the *Core Knowledge Sequence (K–8)* and the *Core Knowledge Preschool Sequence.*

Core Knowledge curricula are currently being taught in schools throughout the United States. The *Core Knowledge Sequence* has been aligned with state standards, thereby enabling students to meet state testing and NCLB requirements. Even to schools that do not follow its curricula to the letter, the Core Knowledge Foundation offers models of curricula designed to ensure that American students learn what they need to learn in order to become good readers, learners, and citizens.

Gerald L. Terrell, Sr., VP, K–8 Schools, Core Knowledge
www.coreknowledge.org

Table of Contents

Unit 1 Origin: Out of Africa

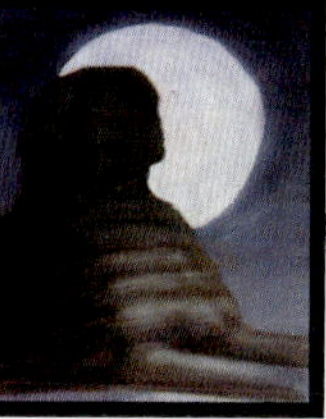

Unit 2 Let My People Go, 1619–1865

Literature

Poetry

The Novel

Unit 3 Up from Bondage, 1866–1939

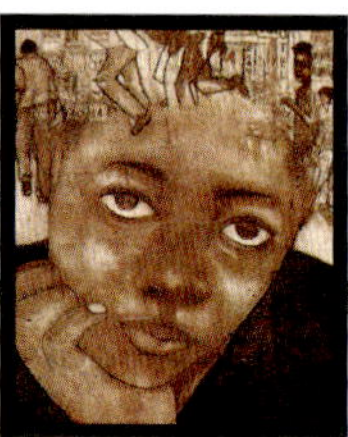

Unit 4 Civil Rights and Beyond, 1939–Present

Poetry

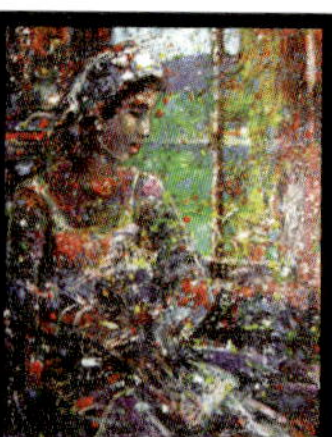

A Gallery of African-American Art

Appendices

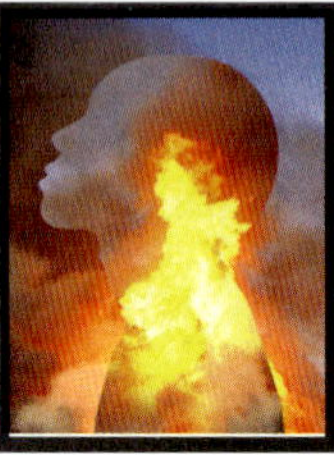

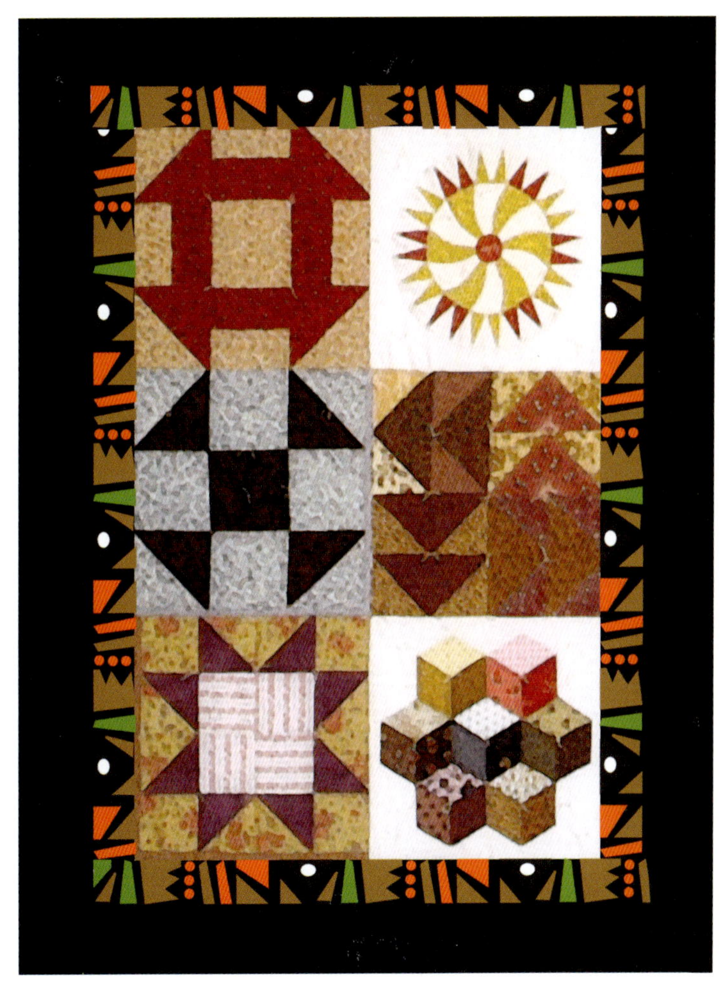

The Oral Tradition
AKHENATEN
The Fable
The Folktale
The Proverb
The Oral Epic
EQUIANO
CALL AND RESPONSE
Equiano
THE PRAISE POEM
The Proverb
Call and Response
The Oral Epic
The Oral Tradition
The Praise Poem
Akhenaten
The Fable

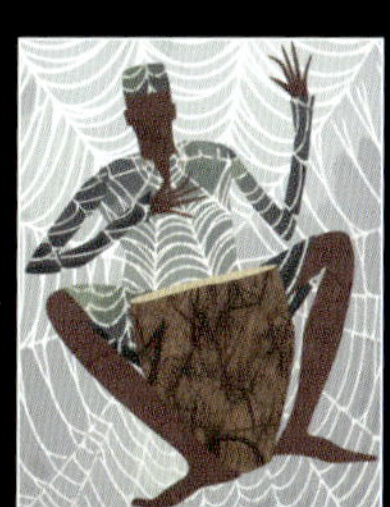

Unit 1

Origin: Out of Africa

"For Africa to me . . .
is more than a glamorous fact.
It is a historical truth.
No man can know
where he is going
unless he knows exactly
where he has been."

—Maya Angelou

Unit 1 Introduction

Out of Africa

Something in Africa invites us all to its embrace.
If you were to visit this continent, you too would feel—in some subtle, deep-rooted sense—that you were at home.

That is because you have already been to Africa. At least a part of you has.

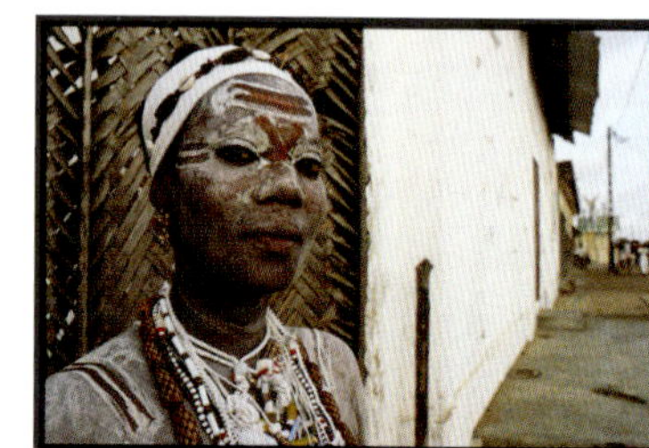

Inside human cells, there is genetic material, called **DNA,** which determines individual hereditary characteristics. DNA exists both within the nucleus and outside the nucleus in tiny organelles called **mitochondria.** Mitochondrial DNA is passed down solely from mothers to their children. By studying the mitochondrial DNA of human beings, scientists have figured out that every person on the planet is descended from a single woman who lived somewhere on the vast continent of Africa about 200,000 years ago. Every person now alive, therefore, is distantly related. This is a well-established scientific fact. Scientists call the mother from whom all people descended **Mitochondrial Eve.**

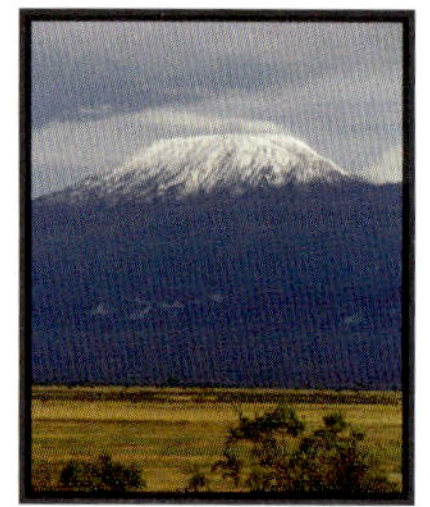

Perhaps she lived in East Africa, in modern-day Tanzania, which is home to majestic Mount Kilimanjaro, as well as to Olduvai Gorge, where three-million-year-old bones of prehistoric ancestors were unearthed in the 1970s.

Perhaps her children's children first ventured from the ancestral home, across the grassy savanna teeming with wildlife, to the rainforests of West Africa. Some, we know, traveled up the Nile River Valley and then onward in all directions, crossing rivers, seas, and oceans. Mitochondrial Eve's descendants made their own families, whose children and children's children formed into tribes, villages, nations, and empires.

Their hands built all the nations of the earth, and their tongues invented all of its languages. They waged war and learned to make peace. They made music, and they danced. They learned to follow the stars, they established trade routes, and they mapped the earth. They became queens and kings, prophets and philosophers, liberators and enslavers, heroes and villains, explorers, traders, conquerors, builders, composers, painters, and poets. They became everyone who ever lived.

They became *you*.

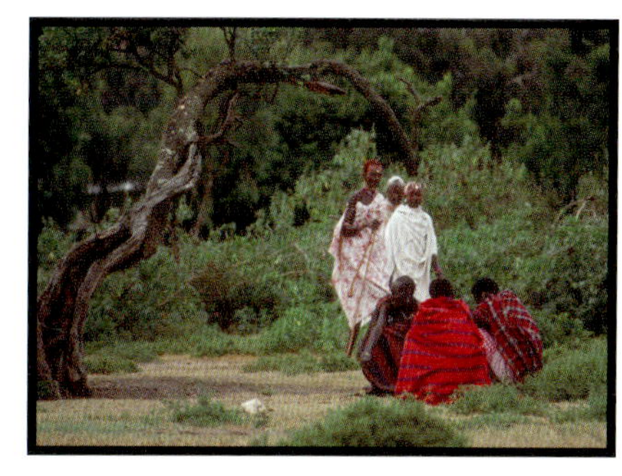

If you were to travel over the whole of Africa, you would hear as many as 2,000 languages spoken by literally thousands of ethnic groups, including the Ashanti, Berbers, Wolof, Senufo, Yoruba, Zulu, Pygmies, Maasai, Fulani, Bushmen, and Bambara. Most of these peoples do not have a written history or literary record that goes back more than a century or two. However, their oral stories and histories may go all the way back to the dawn of human time. Certainly, African (and African-American) folklore and mythology have deep roots in the past. Both were preserved thanks to the **oral tradition,** through which information, stories, poems, and songs were passed verbally from one generation to the next, not as books are passed, not with a single telling or forced memorization, but by steady, consistent retelling and repetition, the addition of colorful details and the loss of others, day by day, story by story, over centuries and millennia.

That which is entrusted to the oral tradition of a culture becomes second nature to the people of that culture. Such material endures as long as someone is willing to tell and someone else is ready to listen.

For many Africans, however, the natural passage of stories from one generation to the next was brutally and utterly disrupted in the early 1500s with the beginning of the transatlantic slave trade. (See the Historical Background: Slavery and the Slave Trade on page 88.) Enslaved Africans took little in the way of possessions to the New World, but they had untold riches stored in their memories. Africans who were enslaved in the Americas never lost their desire to tell stories, to make music, to sing, and to dance as a way to ease their troubles, share with loved ones, and cement the bonds of community. Often, they were willing to risk everything just to make music and to worship as they pleased. In most cases, enslaved Africans were forbidden to practice their native religions or even to speak in their native tongues. This made it all the more difficult for them to preserve their heritage. Still, elements of the African story tradition survived. Even after an exhausting day's labor, there was still time, sometimes, for telling stories.

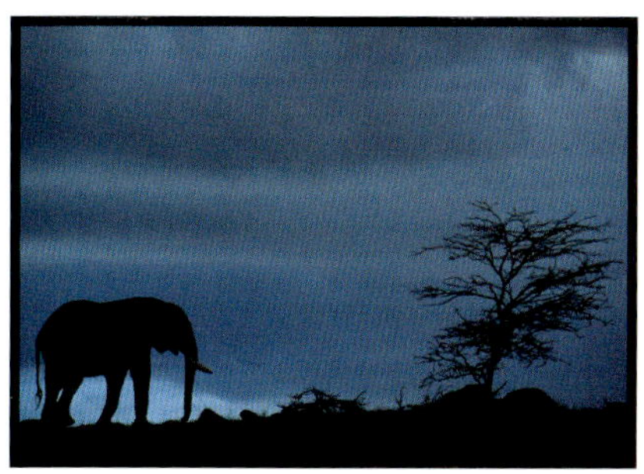

And with the telling of these stories, a new story began. African tales, proverbs, and poems were gradually adapted to the realities of life in America. In recent decades, at last, these stories have appeared in written form. And what wonderful stories they are! The ancient stories will last for as long as there are stories to be told.

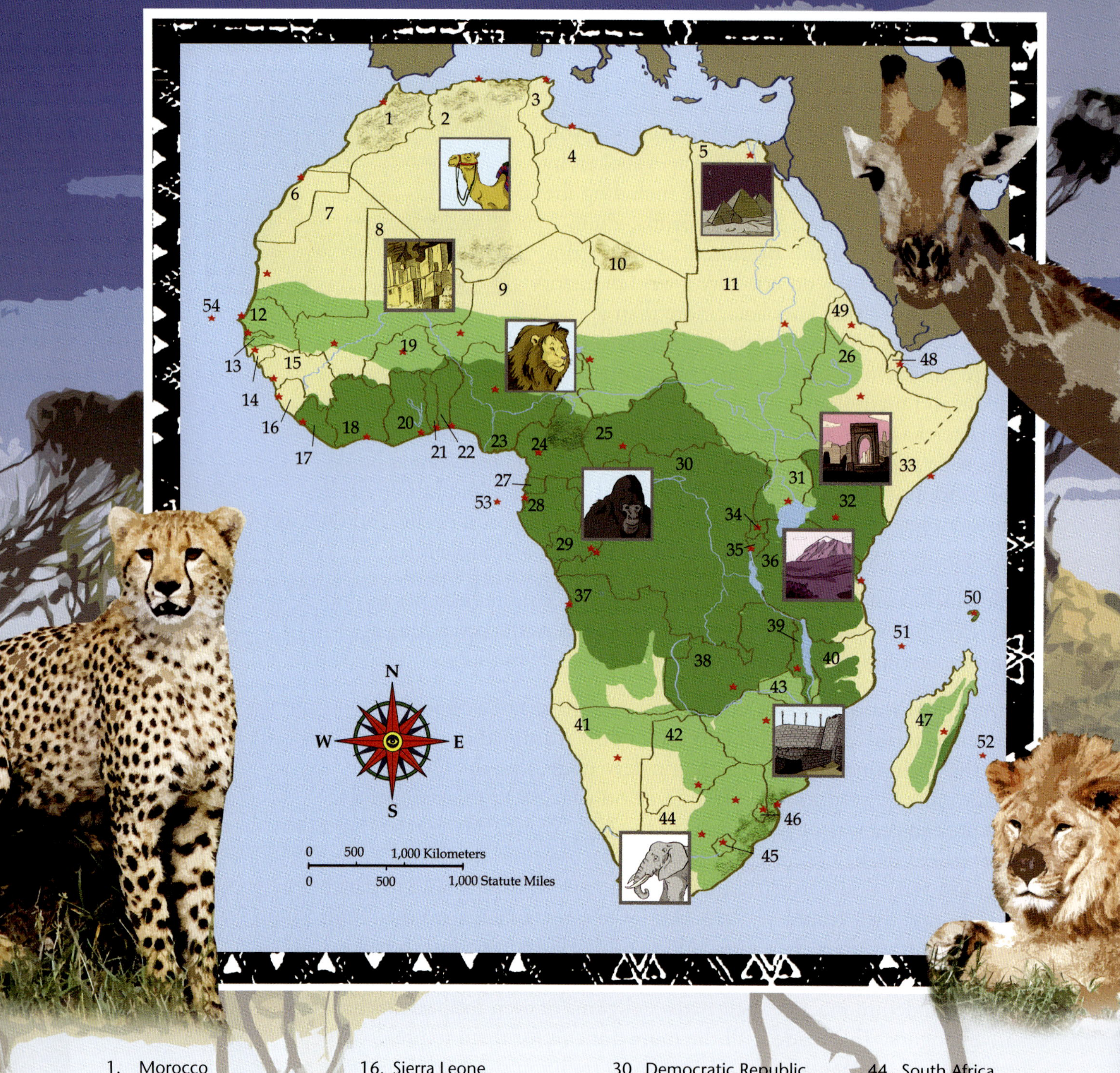

1. Morocco
2. Algeria
3. Tunisia
4. Libya
5. Egypt
6. Western Sahara
7. Mauritania
8. Mali
9. Niger
10. Chad
11. Sudan
12. Senegal
13. The Gambia
14. Guinea-Bissau
15. Guinea
16. Sierra Leone
17. Liberia
18. Ivory Coast/ Côte D'Ivoire
19. Burkina Faso
20. Ghana
21. Togo
22. Benin
23. Nigeria
24. Cameroon
25. Central African Republic
26. Ethiopia
27. Equatorial Guinea
28. Gabon
29. Congo
30. Democratic Republic of Congo
31. Uganda
32. Kenya
33. Somalia
34. Rwanda
35. Burundi
36. Tanzania
37. Angola
38. Zambia
39. Malawi
40. Mozambique
41. Namibia
42. Botswana
43. Zimbabwe
44. South Africa
45. Lesotho
46. Swaziland
47. Madagascar
48. Djibouti
49. Eritrea
50. Seychelles
51. Comoros
52. Mauritius
53. São Tomé & Principe
54. Cape Verde

Africa is…

… the second largest continent in the world. Only Asia is bigger.

… almost an island. The tiny Sinai Peninsula is its only link to other land.

… four times the size of the U.S.

Africa has…

… five principal geographic regions: North Africa, Southern Africa, East Africa, Central Africa, West Africa.

… an estimated 840 million people.

… seven general climatic regions:

The **Sahara Desert** region encompasses most of North Africa and is the largest desert in the world (other than Antarctica). It covers roughly 3.5 million square miles. Temperatures there can rise to 136°F (57.7°C).

The **Maghreb** region of northwest Africa includes the Mediterranean coastlands and the Atlas Mountains.

The **Sahel** region covers a belt of grasslands south of the Sahara stretching from Senegal to Sudan.

The **Sudan** region lies just below the Sahel but is slightly more moist and arable.

The **Guinea** region contains lush rainforests and runs along the Atlantic coast from Guinea to Nigeria.

The **Congo** is the rainforest region of the Congo River Basin.

The **Great Lakes** region is distinguished by five major lakes (Albert, Edward, Kivu, Tanganyika, and Victoria) in and around the Great Rift Valley.

… reserves of many natural resources, including petroleum, iron ore, gold, copper, tin, uranium, diamonds, salt, phosphates, manganese, coal, and zinc.

… Mt. Kilimanjaro, one of world's tallest mountains, with an elevation of 19,336 ft.

Africa's People…

… make up the world's most physically diverse population.

… speak more than 2,000 different languages. Some languages are spoken by millions of people, while others are spoken by only a few.

… grow, harvest, and sell a rich array of food, spices, and other agricultural resources such as cassava, rice, wheat, millet, beans, okra, eggplant, coconuts, lentils, ginger, sorghum, garlic, onions, nutmeg, sugarcane, bananas, vanilla, cocoa, cumin, curry, clove, spinach, tamarind, plantains, olives, dates, citrus fruits, pepper, cashews, maize, parsley, cinnamon, groundnuts, coffee, yams, tea, palm oil, timber, rubber, and cotton.

Did You Know?

… A giraffe's tongue is blue and can extend more than 16 inches (40.6 cm). Each giraffe has its own unique pattern of coat markings.

… The black rhinoceros grows to 14 ft (4.3 m) in length and weighs up to 3,900 lbs (1,769 kg), or more than three fully mature beef cattle. Despite its size, it can run at speeds of up to 35 mph.

… African elephants live longer than any land mammal except for humans.

… Despite a weight of up to 1,500 lbs (680 kg) and a shoulder-height of up to 8 ft (2.4 m), the eland can jump nearly 7 ft in the air.

… A hippopotamus can weigh 3.5 tons (3,175 kg) and can gallop at speeds up to 18 mph (29 km/h). Hippos are responsible for more human deaths than any other animal in Africa.

… The lion is the largest African carnivore.

… The cheetah is the fastest land animal, with a top speed of over 70 mph (113 km/h).

Africanisms in the English Language

Joseph E. Holloway and **Winifred K. Vass,** in their fascinating book *The African Heritage of American English,* published by the Indiana University Press, recount the wealth of language, including words, phrases, and place names, inherited from African sources. The study of the origins of words and phrases is known as **etymology.** Below are a few of the many examples to be found in the work of Holloway and Vass. Please note that etymology is not an exact science, and often words have multiple origins. Note also that some of the etymologies given below are controversial. Readers are referred to the superb work of Holloway and Vass for more detailed information about these and other words and phrases of African origin. Note that ***Fula, Tshiluba, Yoruba,*** and ***Wolof*** are all names of African languages and peoples. ***Bantu*** and ***Mandingo*** are names of groups of related African languages.

banana, from the Wolof word for the fruit

banjo, from the Kimbundu word *mbanza,* a stringed instrument

booboo, meaning a blunder or error, from the Bantu word *mbubu,* meaning stupid or blundering

bozo, a big, strong, stupid fellow, from the Bantu suffix *-boza,* indicating someone who knocks things over in passing

chigger, a small biting insect, from the Wolof word *jiga* for the same thing

dashiki, a loose pullover garment, from the Yoruba word for such a garment, *danshiki*

goober, peanut, from the Bantu word for the peanut, *nguba*

guff, meaning empty or foolish talk, from the Bantu word *nkufukila,* meaning made-up stories

gumbo, a soup made with okra, from the Bantu word for okra, *kingumbo*

hulla-balloo, meaning a noise or uproar, from the Bantu *halua balualua* for the same thing

jambalaya, a dish containing seasoned rice usually cooked with sausage, shrimp, or oysters, from the Bantu word *tshimbolebole,* meaning a dish of cooked corn

jazz, a type of music, from the Bantu suffix *-jaja,* meaning to make someone dance

jitterbug, a type of dance, from the Mandingo word *ji-to*, meaning frightened or cowardly

jive, meaning insincere talk, from the Bantu word *tshivuma,* meaning loud voices or noise, or possibly from the Wolof *jev,* meaning to talk about someone in his or her absence

juba, a name given to a skilled dancer, from the Bantu *juba, jiouba,* or *diubu,* meaning to beat out a rhythm

juke joint, a place of entertainment, from the Wolof word *dzug,* meaning to misbehave or to behave in a disorderly manner

mojo, a spell or charm, from the Fula word *moca,* to cast a magic spell by spitting

moolah, money, from the Bantu word *mulambo,* meaning receipts or tax money

palooka, a bad prizefighter or an oafish person, from the Bantu *-paluka tshiseke,* to have a fit or spasm

rootin-tootin, meaning noisy or boisterous, from the Wolof *rutu-tuti,* meaning a rapid drumming sound

yackety-yak, to chatter, from the Bantu word *yakula-yakula,* meaning to gab or chatter

yam, an edible tuber, from the Wolof word *nyam,* food, to eat, or Bambara *nyambu,* manioc

zombi, a walking corpse, from the Kimbund word *nzambi,* ghost, phantom

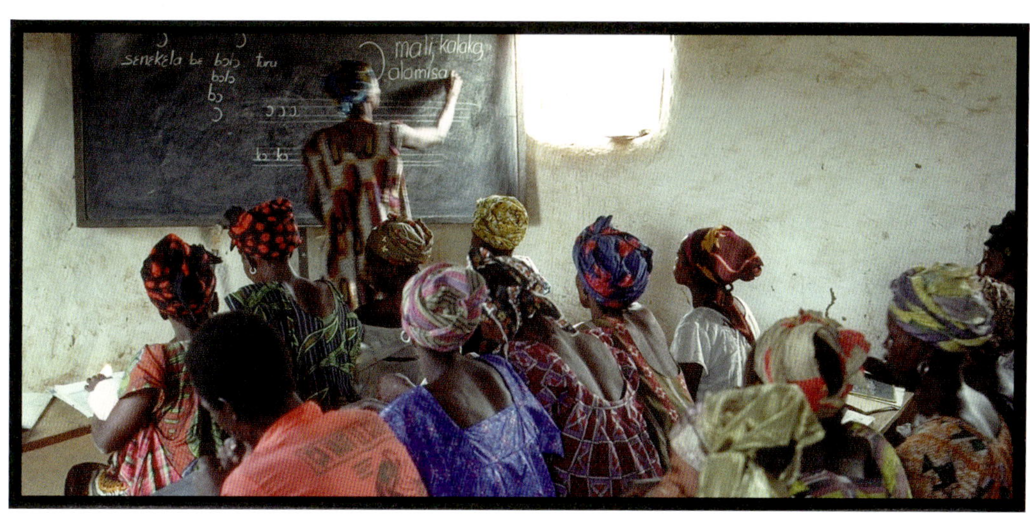

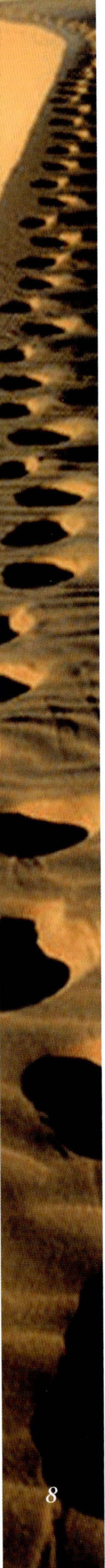

Prereading

A Sampling of African Proverbial Wisdom

Traditional

What is wisdom? How does one become wise? What must one do to gain wisdom? Must one learn wisdom on one's own, or can it be learned from others? Can all people become wise, or are some people born with that potential and others not?

Ask ten people and you will probably hear ten different answers for each of the questions above. By one common definition, wisdom is simply the ability to judge what is true or right. Some people call it common sense. You have learned over the course of your life that when the sky fills with dark clouds, and when you hear a rustling in the trees, then it is a good time either to go indoors or to take out an umbrella (unless you happen to like rain, in which case you might take off your shoes and dance). The fact that you recognize the signs of rain and then act accordingly shows that you possess wisdom with regard to the weather.

But there is more to the word *wisdom* than that. The word is also used to refer to the entire body of learning or knowledge possessed by a specific culture or group of people. Parents share their wisdom with children, neighbors with neighbors, and elders with anyone wise enough to listen. Sometimes, this wisdom is passed along in the form of **proverbs,** which are short sayings that express a basic truth or, well, a bit of wisdom. In order to qualify as a true proverb, the saying must be in widespread use so that most people in a given region or community are familiar with it.

A bunch of shepherds standing around laughing at a friend whose flock had run away for the second time probably invented the saying, "He is a fool whose sheep run away twice." But this saying by no means pertains only to people who herd sheep. The point of this Ashanti proverb is that only a fool makes the same careless, easily preventable mistake twice.

Pay attention, and these bits of wisdom might keep you out of trouble. Proverbs are the cornerstone of African oral traditions and more: they are the means by which everyone can revisit the origins of language, story, and wisdom!

The Origin of African Proverbial Wisdom

Traditional (Ashanti). Retold by William Lewis.

Once upon a time, Kwaku[1] Anansi, the spider, possessed all the wisdom in the world. Perhaps his father, the sky god, Nyame, gave Anansi all of this wisdom in order that he might share it with everyone else. But the spider was a greedy, tricky fellow in those days, and he wished to keep all the wisdom for himself. So Anansi decided to stuff all of the wisdom into his big clay jug and hide it in the biggest tree he could find. He fastened a rope to the jug and set off toward the forest early one morning, before anyone else was awake.

Anansi's son, Ntikuma, was a light sleeper. Hearing his father tiptoe past, Ntikuma followed, for he did not want his father to hide all the wisdom.

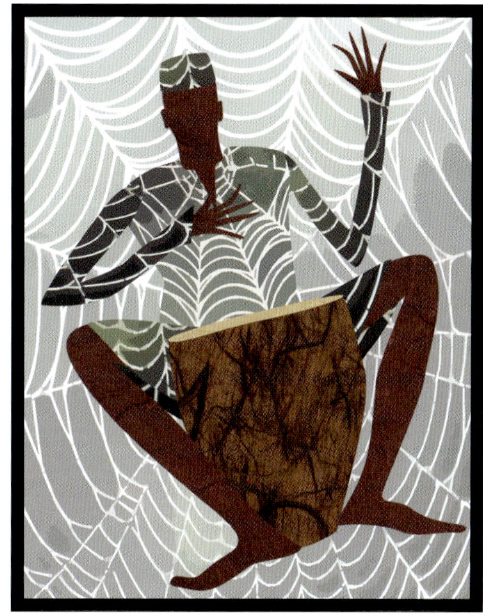

Anansi dragged the jug over the grassy savanna and across the river until he finally reached the deep, dark forest. He found a mighty baobab tree in which to hide his wisdom, but he had a terribly hard time climbing the tree while holding the heavy jug snug against his belly.

Ntikuma watched with amusement as his father struggled in the baobab tree, until finally he could stand it no more. "Father," the child called, "Why don't you carry the jug on your back instead of on your belly? Then maybe you can climb the tree!"

Well, Anansi nearly fell right out of that tree, jug and all! He was angry that his son had followed and spied on him. Moreover, Anansi was angry (and not a little bit embarassed) that his son had made such a wise suggestion, especially since Anansi possessed all the wisdom. But the truth is that all creatures have some little bit of wisdom that they are born with, and sometimes this is enough.

Furious, Anansi hurled the jug at his son, who ducked safely aside. The jug crashed to the forest floor, and all the wisdom was flung around the world. It spread over all the animals, under every rock, and into the sky, the grasses, the waters, and even the people. Ever since then, people have collected those bits of wisdom and used them to make proverbs. ■

1 **Kwaku.** The word *Kwaku* means, literally, "Uncle."

A Sampling of African Proverbial Wisdom

Traditional

Botswana (Tswana)	"He flees from the roaring lion to the crouching lion."
Ghana (Ashanti)	"He is a fool whose sheep run away twice."
	"If nothing touches the palm-leaves, they do not rustle."
Nigeria (Efik)	"His opinions are like water in the bottom of a canoe, going from side to side."
Nigeria (Yoruba)	"The man who has bread does not appreciate the severity of famine."
	"The pot-lid is always badly off: the pot gets all the sweet, the lid nothing but steam."
(Zar)	"One should not prepare leather for a battle shield on the day of the fight."
Ethiopia	"The best of mankind is a farmer; the best food is fruit."
Kenya (Luyia)	"The dog knows the places he is thrown food."
	"A messenger should not be beaten."
Kenya (Kalenjin)	"A hyena cannot smell its own stench."
	"Do not follow the person who is running away."
Sierra Leone	"Do not tell the man carrying you that he smells bad."
Somalia	"A man who dictates to others separates himself from them."
Tanzania (Sukuma)	"That which is good is never finished."

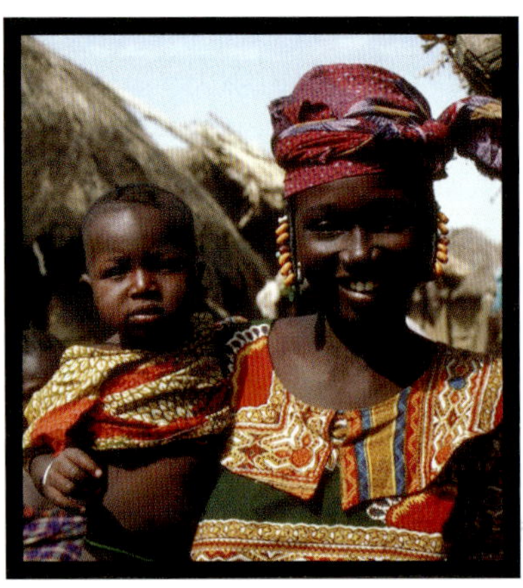

Other African Proverbs

"It takes a whole village to raise a child."

"A wise man who knows proverbs settles disputes."

"He who learns teaches."

"The fool speaks; the wise man listens."

"Do not look where you fell but where you slipped."

"If you don't stand for something, you will fall for something."

"It is the calm and silent water that drowns a man."

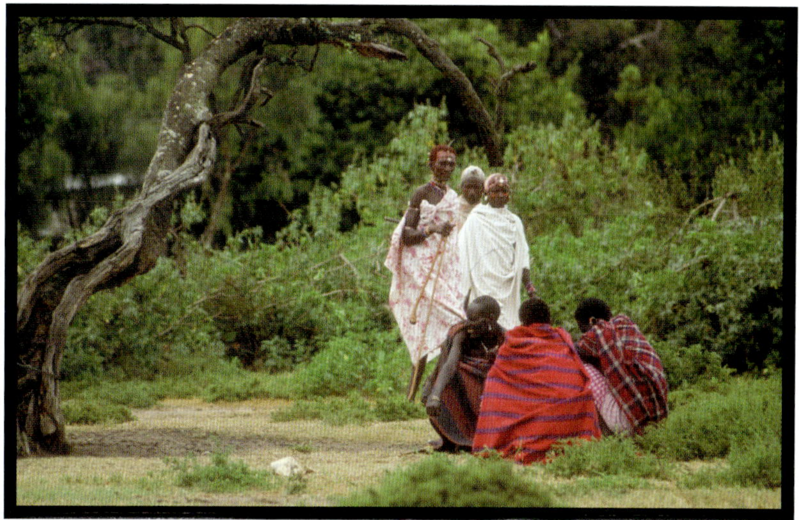

"When the music changes, so does the dance."

"When a needle falls into a deep well, many people will look into the well, but few will be ready to go down after it."

"He who cannot dance will say that the drum is bad."

"He who asks questions cannot avoid answers."

"To try and to fail is not laziness."

"There are forty kinds of lunacy, but only one kind of common sense."

"Smooth seas do not make skillful sailors."

"It is not what you are called, but what you answer to."

"If you run after two hares, you will catch neither."

"Tomorrow belongs to those who prepare for today."

"Only a fool tests the depths of the water with both feet."

"If you offend, ask for a pardon; if offended, forgive."

"If you climb up a tree, you must climb down the same tree."

"A stream cannot rise above its source."

"It is not work that kills, but worry."

"Seeing is different than being told."

"If you're not part of the solution, you're part of the problem."

"Do not call to a dog with a whip in your hand."

"Wood already touched by fire is not hard to set alight."

"He who is being carried does not realize how far the town is."

"Rain does not fall on one roof alone."

"Knowledge is like a garden: if it is not cultivated, it cannot be harvested." ■

Understanding the Selection

Recalling

1. What is wisdom? What is a proverb?
2. Why do people use proverbs?
3. What characteristic(s) must a saying have in order for it to qualify as a proverb?
4. Why is Anansi so angry at his son?
5. What happens to all the wisdom in Anansi's jug?
6. According to the proverbs, what does it take to raise a child?

Interpreting

1. How does a person get wisdom? Are proverbs based on things that really happened?
2. Why might the use of a proverb be a more effective teaching tool than simply telling people what they should or should not do?
3. If your grandmother often tells you a story about an important lesson she learned as a child, is she telling you a proverb?
4. Does Anansi put his wisdom to good use? Is it enough to simply possess wisdom?
5. How can the Anansi story be used to explain the origin of proverbs?
6. What wisdom is this proverb supposed to offer its listeners?

Synthesizing

1. What can a proverb teach you about a specific country or region of the world? Select three proverbs and explain, in your own words, what each proverb suggests about its place of origin. Can one culture's proverb be useful to someone from another culture? For example, can a person from the United States sensibly make use of a proverb about hyenas?

Delving Deeper

Understanding Literature

Proverbs in Literature. Every human society has its own body of **proverbs,** short sayings that express traditional wisdom. It is not difficult to imagine that the development of proverbial wisdom occurred naturally, and fairly rapidly, after the development of spoken language. Sometimes a proverb is simply the best way to express an idea or the easiest way to remember an important lesson. Occasionally, a proverb is simply humorous or interesting.

Technically, proverbs are not literature; definitions of *literature* usually stress the written word, whereas proverbs are generally spoken. Proverbs are a kind of **orature,** imaginative art employing language that is passed down orally from one generation to the next. However, proverbs do play an important role in the development and study of a particular culture's body of literature (and art).

Writing is simply one way to tell a story and to preserve it for future generations. The vast majority of African cultures have told and preserved stories by different means. Among certain African peoples, dancers and drummers tell tales of love, heroism, and disaster. A design sewn into a blanket or painted on a clay jug might tell a story about the creation of the world. In West Africa, there are storytellers known as **griots** who preserve local oral tradition by singing the great stories of their ancestors. (See *Sunjata,* page 47.) There are stories everywhere in Africa and, like proverbs, most of them are spoken, not written.

Keep the African proverbs in mind as you work your way through this anthology. You will see that ancient proverbial wisdom—the thoughts of those who lived hundreds or thousands of years ago—remains at the foundation of many modern stories and poems. A writer can use a proverb as the basis of a story's plot or theme; a poet can wrap a proverb in silk with a few well-chosen lines. In modern times (with modern media), proverbs as orature may be less common in our daily lives. However, thanks to writers, cultural anthropologists, the printing press, and the Internet, entire bodies of proverbial wisdom have been preserved.

Bear in mind, as well, the countless voices that have spoken these proverbs through the millennia and the countless minds that have benefited from the proverbs' eternal wisdom. Set aside a notebook or a section of your writing journal and title it, "Traces of the African Oral Tradition and Proverbial Wisdom in African-American Literature." Add entries as you see fit. Someday, you may find that this is a great subject for an essay or a thesis or that proverbs can stimulate you to produce creative writing of your own.

Prereading

"All Stories Are Anansi's"

Anonymous

Africa is the birthplace of humanity. It is a delightful accident, then, that the continent of Africa is shaped roughly like the profile of a human head or skull. **West Africa,** located on the Atlantic Coast (at the base of the back of the skull), runs from the Sahara Desert in the north to the Gulf of Guinea in the south. The majority of enslaved people brought to the Americas came from this region, and, therefore, the stories carried to the New World by the slaves were largely West African.

Anansi the Spider is a major character in West African folklore. This character is believed to have originated in the myths and legends of the Ashanti (or Asante) people, heirs to a major state, the **Ashanti Confederacy,** that flourished from 1570 to 1900 in the area of modern-day Ghana. The central figure in traditional Ashanti religion is Nyame, the sky god. Anansi the Spider is Nyame's son and is the main character in hundreds of wonderful tales told throughout West Africa. Anansi stories are also common among the descendants of West Africans in Jamaica, Suriname, and the Netherlands Antilles.

Like many **myths,** the stories about Anansi often explain the origins of natural or cultural phenomena. Anansi, for example, is sometimes identified as the one who brings rain to put out fires. Anansi is an example of a stock character of myth and legend known as the **trickster.** He loves to play tricks and often bends or breaks the rules. As you read the following story, ask yourself these questions:

1. What tricks does Anansi carry out?
2. Of what things does this story explain the origins?

All Stories Are Anansi's[1]

Anonymous

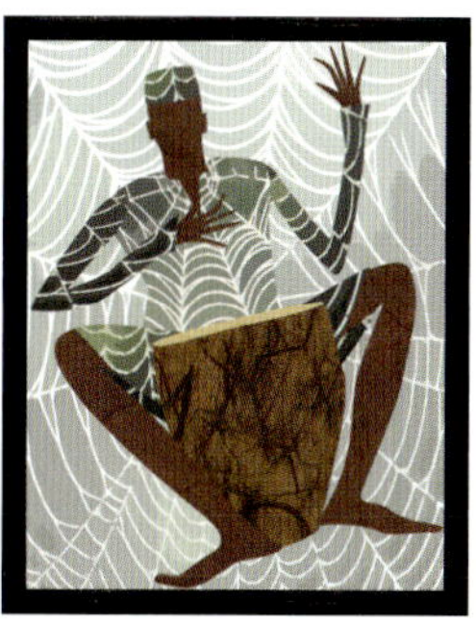

In the beginning, all tales and stories belonged to Nyame,[2] the Sky God. But Kwaku[3] Anansi, the spider, yearned to be the owner of all the stories known in the world, and he went to Nyame and offered to buy them.

What does Anansi the Spider want? Who has what he wants?

The Sky God said: "I am willing to sell the stories, but the price is high. Many people have come to me offering to buy, but the price was too high for them. Rich and powerful families have not been able to pay. Do you think you can do it?"

Anansi replied to the Sky God: "I can do it. What is the price?"

"My price is three things," the Sky God said. "I must first have Mmoboro,[4] the hornets. I must then have Onini,[5] the great python. I must then have Osebo,[6] the leopard. For these things I will sell you the right to tell all stories."

Anansi said: "I will bring them."

He went home and made his plans. He first cut a gourd from a vine and made a small hole in it. He took a large **calabash,** and filled it with water. He went to the tree where the hornets lived. He poured some of the water over himself, so that he was dripping. He threw some water over the hornets, so that they too were dripping. Then he put the calabash on his head, as though to protect himself from a storm, and called out to the hornets: "Are you foolish people? Why do you stay in the rain that is falling?"

The hornets answered: "Where shall we go?"

"Go here, in this dry gourd," Anansi told them.

The hornets thanked him and flew into the gourd through the small hole. When the last of them had entered, Anansi plugged the hole with a ball of grass, saying: "Oh, yes, but you are really foolish people!"

In what way have the hornets been foolish?

He took his gourd full of hornets to Nyame, the Sky God. The Sky God accepted them. He said: "There are two more things."

Anansi returned to the forest and cut a long bamboo pole and some strong vines. Then he walked toward the house of Onini, the python, talking to himself. He said: "My wife is stupid. I say he is longer and stronger. My wife says he is shorter and weaker. I give

VOCABULARY IN PLACE

- **calabash,** ***n.*** A large gourd used as a vessel, jar, or bowl

[1] **Anansi.** The name is variously spelled in written versions of the stories. Common variants include *Ananzi* and *Ananse.*

[2] **Nyame.** The chief god in traditional Ashanti religion, who, like Zeus in Greek mytholgy, is identified as both a sky god and as the great father. The name is pronounced NYAH-meh.

[3] **Kwaku.** The word *Kwaku* means, literally, "Uncle."

[4] **Mmoboro.** Pronounced mmoh-BOH-roh

[5] **Onini.** Pronounced oh-NEE-nee

[6] **Osebo.** Pronounced oh-SAY-boh

him more respect. She gives him less respect. Is she right or am I right? I am right, he is longer. I am right, he is stronger."

When Onini, the python, heard Anansi talking to himself, he said: "Why are you arguing this way with yourself?"

The spider replied: "Ah, I have had a dispute with my wife. She says you are shorter and weaker than this bamboo pole. I say you are longer and stronger."

What does Anansi pretend to have been arguing about?

Onini said: "It's useless and silly to argue when you can find out the truth. Bring the pole and we will measure."

So Anansi laid the pole on the ground, and the python came and stretched himself out beside it.

"You seem a little short," Anansi said.

The python stretched further.

"A little more," Anansi said.

"I can stretch no more," Onini said.

"When you stretch at one end, you get shorter at the other end," Anansi said. "Let me tie you at the front so you don't slip."

He tied Onini's head to the pole. Then he went to the other end and tied the tail to the pole. He wrapped the vine all around Onini, until the python couldn't move.

"Onini," Anansi said, "it turns out that my wife was right and I was wrong. You are shorter than the pole and weaker. My opinion wasn't as good as my wife's. But you were even more foolish than I, and you are now my prisoner."

Anansi carried the python to Nyame, the Sky God, who said: "There is one thing more."

Osebo, the leopard, was next. Anansi went into the forest and dug a deep pit where the leopard was accustomed to walk. He covered it with small branches and leaves and put dust on it, so that it was impossible to tell where the pit was. Anansi went away and hid. When Osebo came prowling in the black of night, he stepped into the trap Anansi had prepared and fell to the bottom. Anansi heard the sound of the leopard falling, and he said: "Ah, Osebo, you are half-foolish!"

What do you think will happen to the leopard?

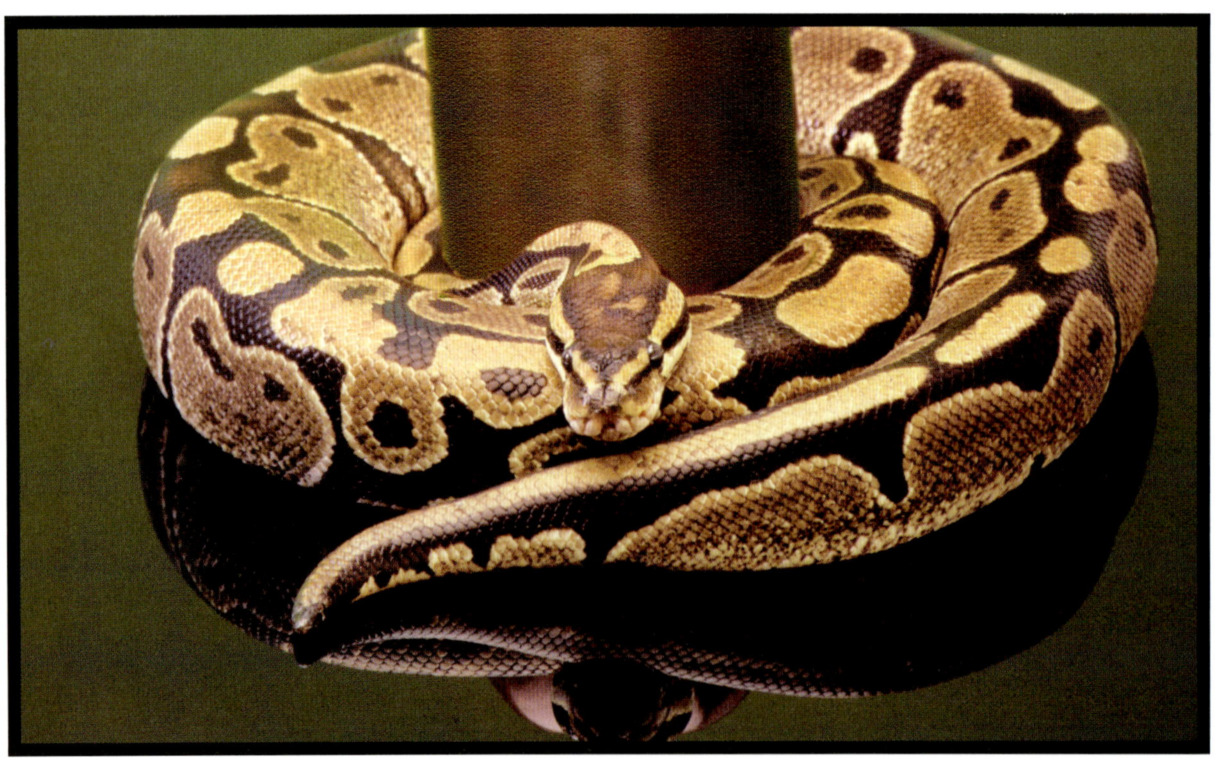

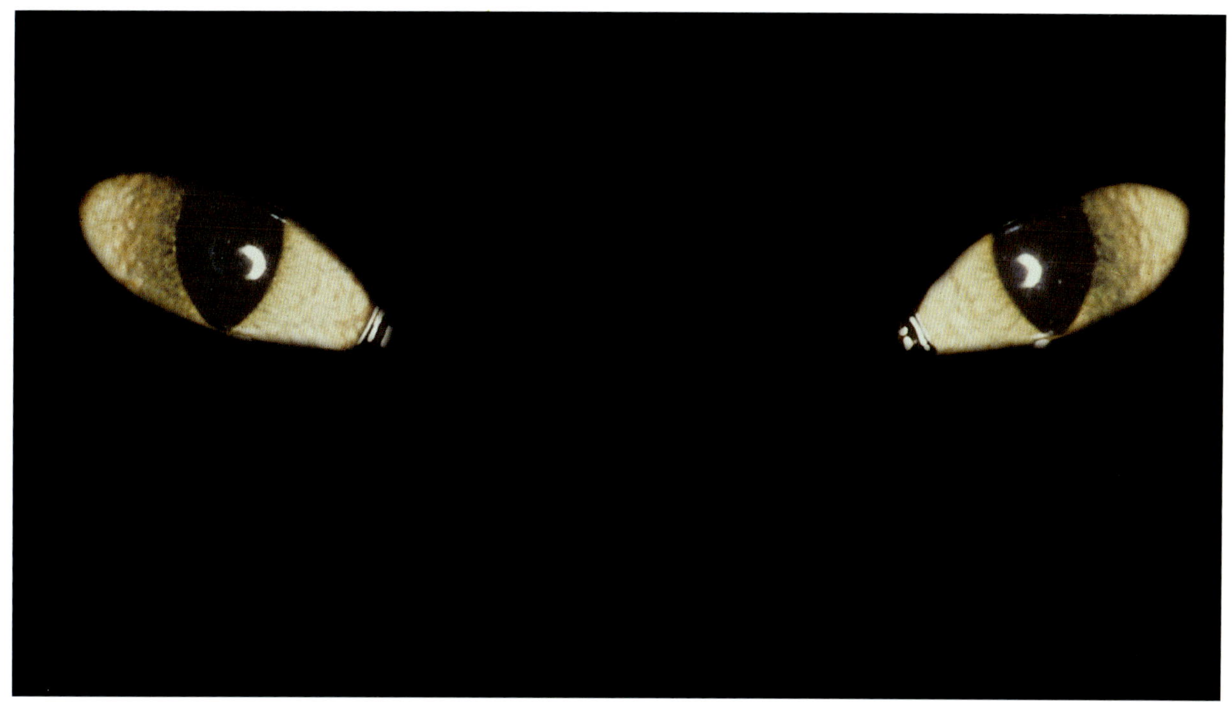

When morning came, Anansi went to the pit and saw the leopard there.

"Osebo," he asked, "what are you doing in this hole?"

"I have fallen into a trap," Osebo said. "Help me out."

"I would gladly help you," Anansi said. "But I'm sure that if I bring you out, I will have no thanks for it. You will get hungry, and later on you will be wanting to eat me and my children."

"I swear it won't happen!" Osebo said.

"Very well. Since you swear it, I will take you out," Anansi said.

He bent a tall green tree toward the ground, so that its top was over the pit, and he tied it that way. Then he tied a rope to the top of the tree and dropped the other end of it into the pit.

"Tie this to your tail," he said.

Osebo tied the rope to his tail.

"Is it well tied?" Anansi asked.

"Yes, it is well tied," the leopard said.

"In that case," Anansi said, "you are not merely half-foolish, you are all-foolish."

And he took his knife and cut the other rope, the one that held the tree bowed to the ground. The tree straightened up with a snap, pulling Osebo out of the hole. He hung in the air head downward, twisting and turning. And while he hung this way, Anansi killed him with his weapons.

Then he took the body of the leopard and carried it to Nyame, the Sky God, saying: "Here is the third thing. Now I have paid the price."

What does Anansi mean when he says that he has paid the price?

Nyame said to him: "Kwaku Anansi, great warriors and chiefs have tried, but they have been unable to do it. You have done it. Therefore, I will give you the stories. From this day onward, all stories belong to you. Whenever a man tells a story, he must acknowledge that it is Anansi's tale."

In this way Anansi, the spider, became the owner of all stories that are told. To Anansi all these tales belong. ■

Understanding the Selection

Recalling

1. According to this story, who originally owned all the stories in the world? How much are the stories worth?
2. What three things must someone do in order to win the stories?
3. How does Anansi capture the hornets, the python, and the leopard?
4. Who, according to Nyame, has tried to win the stories in the past?
5. Why, according to this story, are there so many Anansi stories in the world?

Interpreting

1. Why are stories so valuable?
2. What makes these tasks so difficult?
3. What do Anansi's actions toward the hornets, the python, and the leopard reveal about him? What kind of fellow is Anansi?
4. What characteristics or qualities does Anansi have that warriors and chiefs evidently do not have in such abundance? What does this story tell about the value of strength and wealth versus wisdom or intelligence?
5. What does this origin myth tell us about the nature of storytelling?

Synthesizing

1. Anansi is sometimes referred to as a trickster and sometimes as a god of wisdom. In what ways does he reveal these qualities in this story? Why do you suppose Anansi is a spider? (Hint: think about what "tricks" spiders play.)
2. In West African folklore and mythology, Anansi is considered the god who brought practical arts to the people. What art does he bring to the people in this story?

Delving Deeper

Understanding Literature

Trickster Tales. In the mythologies of many cultures around the globe, there are gods or heroes who are associated with cleverness and cunning. These characters are known as **tricksters.** Greek mythology has Hermes, who stole the cattle of the sun god, and Prometheus, who stole fire and brought it to humans. Native Americans of the Southwest tell stories about such tricksters as Coyote and Hare. People in the Appalachian region of the U.S. tell of the trickster Jack. Natives of the Pacific Northwest tell stories about the trickster Raven. In Japanese myths, there are tricksters such as Badger, Tengu, and Kitsune. Often, tricksters are comic, mischievous characters who cause trouble, pull pranks on others, and act selfishly but end up bringing about good. Anansi, for instance, intends to keep all wisdom to himself but accidentally breaks the jar he has stored it in, scattering wisdom around the world. Many trickster stories explain origins. The story you have just read, for example, explains why there are so many Anansi stories. In Polynesian mythology, there is a trickster named Maui who created the Polynesian islands by fishing them up from the bottom of the sea. Often, tricksters are associated with invention and with bringing practical arts, such as farming or language, to the people. Africans brought trickster stories with them to the Americas, and these developed into popular stories such as the tales of Br'er Rabbit. (See page 160.) What trickster tales do you know?

About the Author

The Oral Tradition. The story that you have just read does not have a particular author. Instead, it comes out of the oral tradition. The **oral tradition** is all the stories, poems, songs, proverbs, and other materials within a particular culture that are passed down by word of mouth from generation to generation. In a sense, a story like "All Stories Are Anansi's" has had hundreds of authors—people who tell the story over the generations, probably changing the story in little ways each time they tell it. On pages 8–11, you learned about proverbs and the important role that they play in African cultures. Stories have also played very important roles in Africa, for it is through the retelling of stories that African peoples have traditionally kept alive their religious beliefs, their histories, and their customs.

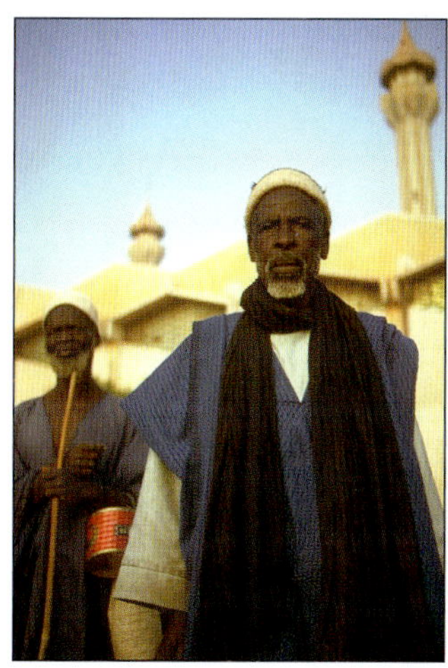

Prereading

"How Many Spots Does a Leopard Have?"

Retold by Julius Lester

In the United States, parents often take their children to movie theaters to see blockbuster animated films that feature talking animals. These films typically use state-of-the-art, high-tech digital animation and special effects. But stories with talking animals are not a new creation. They are as old as human history.

In the traditional, native religions of Africa, Animism and Totemism play a large role. **Animism** is the belief that all things in nature, including plants and animals, are inhabited by spirits. **Totemism** is the belief that individuals or groups of people, such as clans or tribes, have a special spiritual connection to particular animals. Thus, members of a particular clan might associate themselves with the lion. Under the influence of imported religions, especially Islam and Christianity, traditional Animism and Totemism have declined in Africa, but hints of the former, older beliefs remain alive in the form of thousands of animal stories that are told all over the continent.

The story of how Anansi the spider brought wisdom to the world is an example of a **myth.** It is a story that tells of the actions of gods and that explains natural phenomena. The story that you are about to read is an example of a folktale. A **folktale** is any story that is known among the people and that does not deal with the actions of gods or goddesses. Folktales tend to have human or animal characters. This story is a particular kind of folktale known as a fable. A **fable** has animal characters and teaches a **moral,** or lesson. Fables with talking animals probably grew out of older, Animistic stories about animal gods or animal spirits.

As you read the following story, ask yourself these questions:

1. What characteristics do the various animals in the story have?
2. What lesson or lessons does the story teach?

How Many Spots Does a Leopard Have?

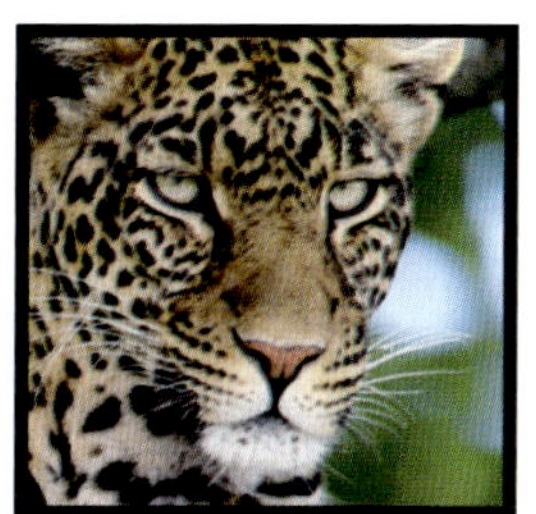

Retold by Julius Lester

One morning Leopard was doing what he enjoyed doing most. He was looking at his reflection in the lake. How handsome he was! How magnificent was his coat! And, ah! The spots on his coat! Was there anything in creation more **superb?**

What does Leopard think of himself?

Leopard's **rapture** was broken when the water in the lake began moving. Suddenly Crocodile's ugly head appeared above the surface.

Leopard jumped back. Not that he was afraid. Crocodile would not bother him. But then again, one could never be too sure about Crocodile.

"Good morning, Leopard," Crocodile said. "Looking at yourself again, I see. You are the most **vain** creature in all of creation."

Leopard was not embarrassed. "If you were as handsome as I am, if you had such beautiful spots, you, too, would be vain."

"Spots! Who needs spots? You're probably so in love with your spots that you spend all your time counting them."

Now there was an idea that had not occurred to Leopard. "What a wonderful idea!" he exclaimed. "I would very much like to know how many spots I have." He stopped. "But there are far too many for me to count myself."

The truth was that Leopard didn't know how to count. "Perhaps you will count them for me, Crocodile?"

"Not on your life!" answered Crocodile. "I have better things to do than count spots." He slapped his tail angrily and dove beneath the water.

Leopard chuckled. "Crocodile doesn't know how to count, either."

Leopard walked along the lakeshore until he met Weasel. "Good morning, Weasel. Would you count my spots for me?"

"Who? Me? Count? Sure. One-two-three-four."

"Great!" exclaimed Leopard. "You can count."

Weasel shook his head. "But I can't. What made you think that I could?"

"But you just did. You said, 'One-two-three-four.' That's counting."

Weasel shook his head again. "Counting is much more difficult than that. There is something that comes after four, but I don't know what it is."

"Oh," said Leopard. "I wonder who knows what comes after four."

"Well, if you ask at the lake when all the animals come to drink, you will find someone who can count."

How well do you think the animals will do at counting?

"You are right, Weasel! And I will give a grand prize to the one who tells me how many spots I have."

VOCABULARY IN PLACE

- **superb,** ***adj.*** Magnificent; impressive
- **rapture,** ***n.*** Joy
- **vain,** ***adj.*** Excessively proud of one's appearance

"What a great idea!" Weasel agreed.

That afternoon all the animals were gathered at the lake to drink. Leopard announced that he would give a magnificent prize to the one who could count his spots.

Elephant said he should be first since he was the biggest and the oldest.

"One-two-three-four-five-six-seven-eight-nine-ten," Elephant said very loudly and with great speed. He took a deep breath and began again. "One-two-three-four-five-si— "

"No! No! No!" the other animals interrupted. "You've already counted to ten once."

Why does Elephant look down his trunk at the other animals?

Elephant looked down his long trunk at the other animals. "I beg your pardon. I would appreciate it if you would not interrupt me when I am counting. You made me forget where I was. Now, where was I? I know I was somewhere in the second ten."

"The second ten?" asked Antelope. "What's that?"

"The numbers that come after the first ten, of course. I don't much care for those 'teen' things, thirteen, fourteen, and what have you. It is **eminently** more sensible to count ten twice and that makes twenty. That is multiplication."

None of the other animals knew what Elephant was talking about.

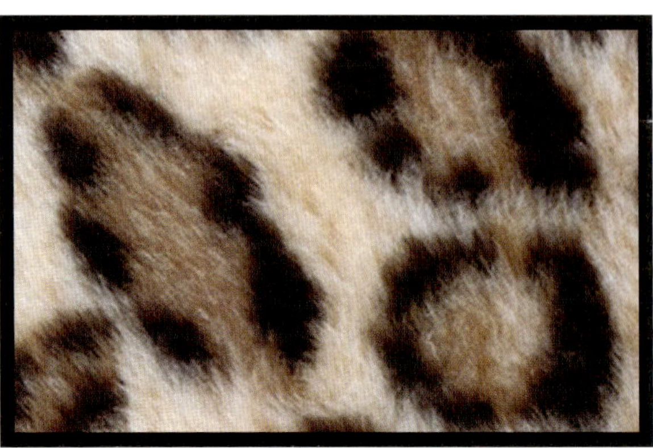

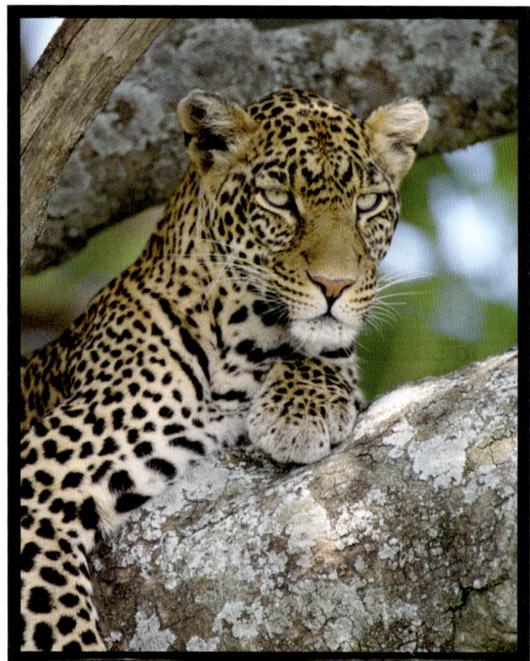

"Why don't you start over again?" suggested Cow.

Elephant began again and he counted ten twice and stopped. He frowned and looked very confused. Finally he said, "Leopard has more than twenty spots."

"How many more than twenty?" Leopard wanted to know.

Elephant frowned more. "A lot." Then he brightened. "In fact, you have so many more spots than twenty that I simply don't have time to count them now. I have an important engagement I mustn't be late for." Elephant started to walk away.

"Ha! Ha! Ha!" laughed Mule. "I bet Elephant doesn't know how to count higher than twenty."

Mule was right.

"Can *you* count above twenty?" Leopard asked Mule.

VOCABULARY IN PLACE

- **eminently,** *adv.* Remarkably, to an unusual degree

"Who? Me? I can only count to four because that's how many legs I have."

Leopard sighed. "Can anyone count above twenty?" he asked **plaintively.**

Bear said, "Well, once I counted up to fifty. Is that high enough?"

Leopard shrugged. "I don't know. It might be. Why don't you try and we will see."

Bear agreed. "I'll start at your tail. One-two-three-four-five-six . . . Hm. Is that one spot or two spots?"

All the animals crowded around to get a close look. They argued for some time and finally agreed that it should only count as one.

"So, where was I?" asked Bear.

"Five," answered Turkey.

"It was six, you turkey," said Chicken.

"Better start again," suggested Cow.

Bear started again and got as far as eleven.

What causes Bear to lose count?

"Eleven. That's a beautiful spot right there, Leopard."

"Which one?" Leopard wanted to know.

"Right there. Oh, dear. Or was it that spot there? They're both **exquisite.** My, my. I don't know where I left off counting. I must start again."

Bear counted as far as twenty-nine this time and then stopped suddenly. "Now, what comes after twenty-nine?"

"I believe thirty does," offered Turtle.

"That's right!" exclaimed Bear. "Now, where did I leave off?"

"You were still on the tail," offered Lion.

"Yes, but was that the twenty-ninth spot, or was it this one here?"

The animals started arguing again.

"You'd better start again," suggested Cow.

"Start what again?" asked Rabbit who had just arrived.

The animals explained to Rabbit about the difficulty they were having in counting Leopard's spots.

"Is that all?" Rabbit said. "I know the answer to that."

"You do?" all the animals, including Leopard, exclaimed at once.

"Certainly. It's really quite simple." Rabbit pointed to one of Leopard's spots. "This one is dark." He pointed to another. "This one is light. Dark, light, dark, light, dark, light." Rabbit continued in this way until he had touched all of Leopard's spots.

"It's simple," he concluded. "Leopard has only two spots—dark ones and light ones."

All the animals remarked on how smart Rabbit was, all of them, that is, except Leopard. He knew something was wrong with how Rabbit counted, but unless he learned to count for himself, he would never know what it was.

Leopard had no choice but to give Rabbit the magnificent prize. What was it? What else except a picture of Leopard himself! ■

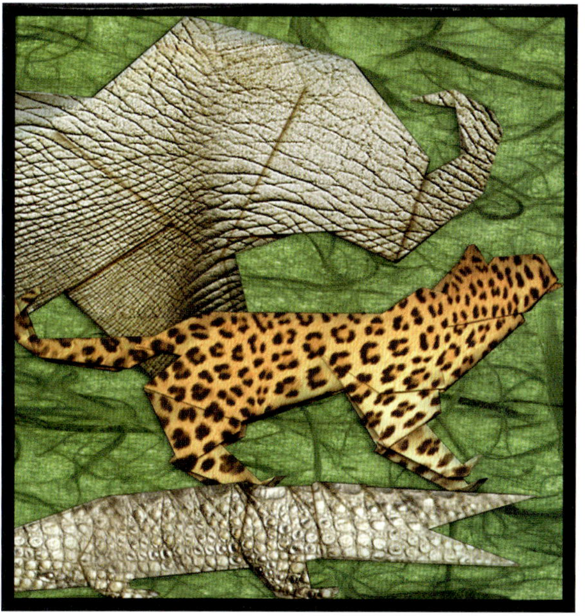

VOCABULARY IN PLACE

- **plaintively,** ***adv.*** In a sad or distressed manner
- **exquisite,** ***adj.*** Lovely, especially in an unusually fine or delicate way

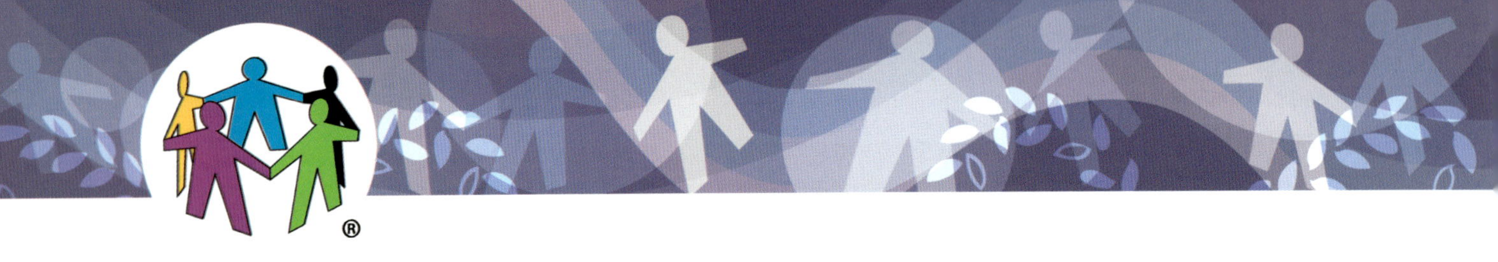

Understanding the Selection

Recalling

1. Who gives Leopard the idea of counting his spots?
2. How do Leopard and Crocodile avoid having to try counting the spots?
3. Why do Weasel and Elephant stop counting the spots?
4. What are some reactions of the other animals while Bear is trying to count the spots?
5. How many spots does Rabbit say that Leopard has?

Interpreting

1. Why does Leopard want to know how many spots he has?
2. What character trait is shared by Leopard and Crocodile?
3. What character trait is shared by Weasel and Elephant?
4. What do these reactions reveal about the other animals? Are they helping Bear to succeed?
5. Why doesn't Leopard challenge Rabbit's method of counting?

Synthesizing

1. What is humorous about the "prize" that Leopard gives in the end? At what character trait does this story poke fun? (Hint: several of the animals share this trait.)
2. If the leopard were the totem for a particular clan, what characteristics might that clan value?

Delving Deeper

Understanding Literature

Fables and Character Education. As you learned in the Prereading section, a **fable** is a story with animal characters that teaches a lesson. Sometimes, this lesson is stated in so many words as a **moral,** or lesson, at the end of the story. For example, there is an ancient African fable called "The White Man and the Snake" that goes like this:

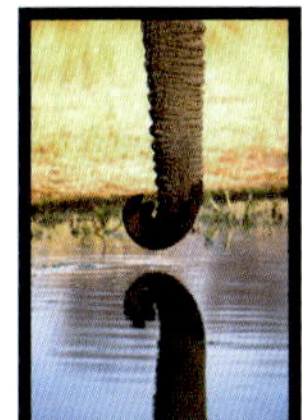

A white man, while traveling in Africa, came upon Snake, on whom a rock had fallen.

"Help me," cried Snake. The man, being kind-hearted, lifted the rock off Snake.

The snake then said, "Now that I am free, I shall bite you."

The man was horrified. "That would not be fair," he said, "not after I went out of my way to help you."

"Certainly it is fair," said Snake, "for biting people is what snakes do. Even a white man knows that."

"I tell you what," said the white man. "We do not agree about this, you and I. Suppose that we go to find an impartial judge who will tell us whether your biting me is fair and just. Who is the wisest of the animals?"

"That would be Elephant," said the snake. So, the two went off in search of Elephant. When they found him, they explained the whole situation.

"The white man is puny," said Elephant. "I doubt that he could even lift the rock. I won't believe it until I see this with my own eyes. Can you take me to the place and show me the whole thing from the beginning?"

So, the white man, Snake, and Elephant all went back to the place where the rock was. "Now," said Elephant. "Let's see the whole thing from the beginning. Snake, you lie there, and white man, put the rock back on the snake." This they did. When Snake was once again under the rock, Elephant said, "OK. Now leave Snake there. He was ungrateful, and that is a grave sin. From this point on, let him help himself." The moral of this story is, of course, that people should show gratitude for the kind actions of others.

Fables are found worldwide. Some famous fables include those told by the ancient Greek Aesop and by the French writer La Fontaine. Look up these writers on the Internet or in a library to find some of their delightful fables.

All fables teach a lesson. Fables are used to build character by educating children in moral values and virtues. What is the moral of the fable "How Many Spots Does a Leopard Have"?

Prereading

"Tug of War"

Anonymous

People love to root for the underdog. When someone who is ordinarily thought of as weaker and less capable pulls through and succeeds, the accomplishment seems all the more wonderful because it is unlikely.

"Tug of War" is a traditional African folktale. Like the stories of Anansi the Spider, this is a **trickster tale** in which a clever creature outwits ones much bigger and stronger than he. Stories about Turtle the trickster are very common in Africa, as are stories about the trickster Hare (a creature similar to a rabbit). It is interesting, of course, that all of these creatures are small. The idea is that a small but intelligent creature can sometimes prevail over a creature who is large but not as intelligent.

The title of this story comes, of course, from the familiar game in which two people or two teams of people stand at either end of a rope and attempt to pull one another past a line in the middle. Ordinarily, a tug of war is a game of brute physical strength. Not so in this story, as you will see.

As you read the following story, think about these questions:

1. Who is the **protagonist,** or central character?
2. What **characteristics,** or qualities, does this central character have?
3. Who are the **minor characters** in the story?
4. What characteristics do these minor characters have?
5. What **motivates** the central character? In other words, what causes him to act as he does? What does he want, and how does he set about getting it?
6. What is the **theme,** or message, of this story?

Tug of War

Anonymous

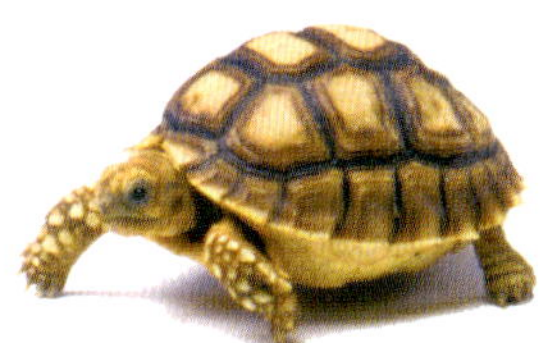

Turtle was small, but he talked big. He loved to boast and brag and say things like, "I'm as powerful as the biggest animals around here, indeed I am. And that includes Elephant and Hippopotamus. That's right: Elephant and Hippopotamus call me 'friend' because I'm as powerful as they are."

Of what does Turtle boast? Do you think that Turtle is right?

One day Elephant and Hippopotamus happened to hear from some of the other animals what Turtle was going around saying. Elephant and Hippopotamus laughed. "So," they said, "Turtle says we call him 'friend'? That's the silliest thing we've ever heard. We don't call him 'friend.' He's so little we don't think of him at all."

And when the animals told Turtle what Elephant and Hippopotamus said, Turtle got mad, very mad. "So, they do not think of me because I'm so small? They do not call me 'friend'? Well, I'll show them who is really

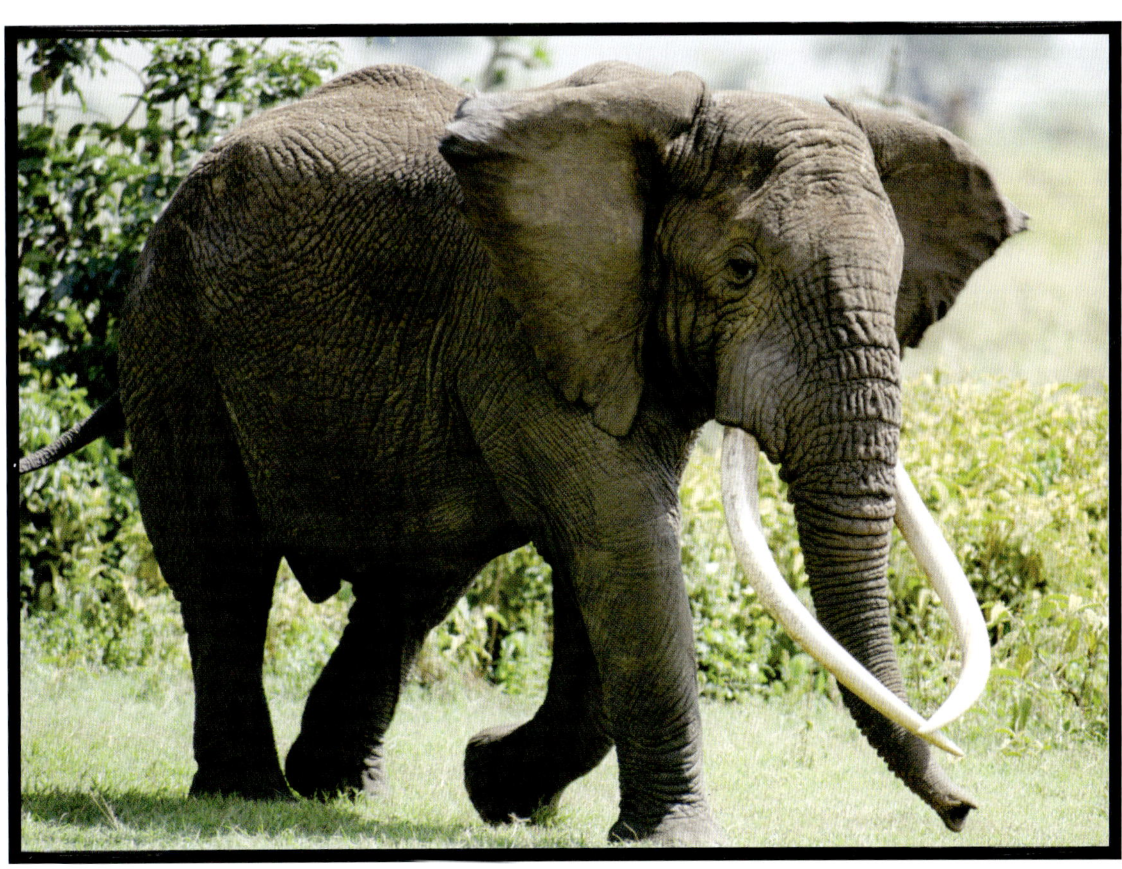

powerful. And they will call me 'friend,' just you wait and see!" Then Turtle set off to find Elephant and Hippopotamus.

He found Elephant lying down in the forest. Elephant was big as a mountain; his trunk was long as a river. But Turtle was bold. He walked right up and shouted, "Hey, friend, get up and say hello to your friend."

Elephant looked all around to see where the voice could be coming from. Finally he looked down—*way* down—and spotted Turtle. "Oh, it's you, is it?" said Elephant. "Go away, you small animal of no importance. And watch out who you call 'friend.'"

"I call *you* 'friend' because that's what you are—right, Elephant?"

"Wrong!" rumbled Elephant. "And what is this foolishness I hear, that you claim to be as powerful as I am? Do you dare to think of yourself as equal to me? Don't be stupid, little creature."

"Now, Elephant," said Turtle, "just listen. Yes, I call you 'friend,' and yes, I say we are equal. You think that because you're so much bigger than me, that makes you better. Well, let's have a tug of war to find out."

What relationship does Turtle say that he has to Elephant?

"A tug of war?" said Elephant. He laughed so hard the earth shook for miles around. "Why," he said to Turtle, "you haven't got a chance."

"Maybe not, maybe so," said Turtle. "But if you're so sure, what have you got to lose?"

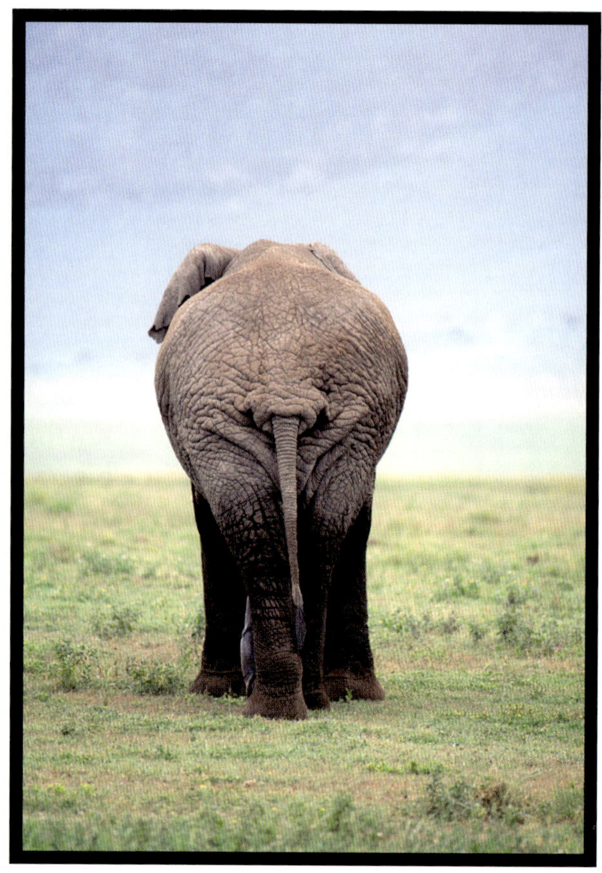

Then Turtle cut a very long vine and gave one end to Elephant. "Here," said Turtle. "Now, if I pull you down, I am greater. If you pull me down, you are greater. We won't stop tugging until one of us pulls the other over or the vine breaks. And if the vine breaks, we are equal and will call each other 'friend.'"

And Turtle walked off with the other end of the long, long vine until, some time later, he found Hippopotamus bathing in the river.

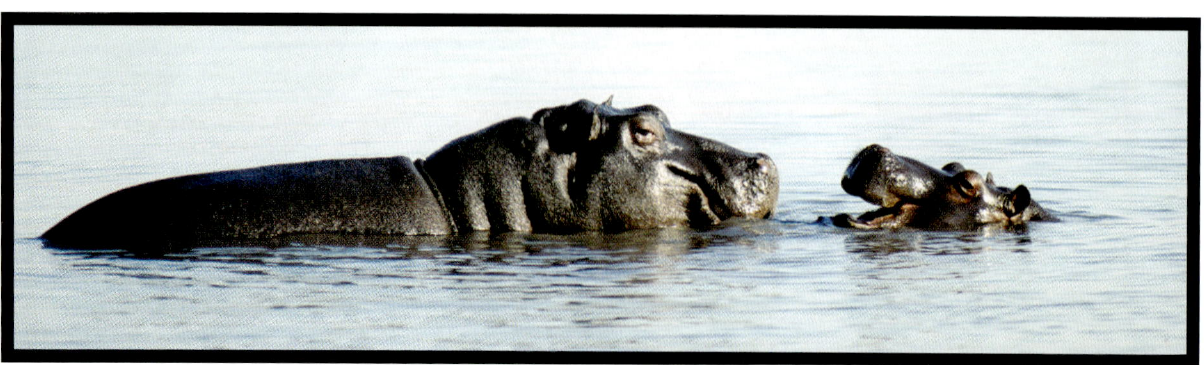

"Oh, friend, I'm here!" shouted Turtle. "Come out of the water and give your friend a proper greeting, why don't you?"

Hippopotamus could hardly believe his ears. "Don't call *me* 'friend,' you little good-for-nothing!" he bellowed.

"Now hold on, friend Hippo," said Turtle. "You think that because you're so much bigger than me, that makes you better. Well, let's have a tug of war to find out. Whoever pulls the other down is greater. We will keep pulling until one of us wins or the vine breaks. And if the vine breaks, we are equal and will call each other 'friend.'"

"You silly turtle, you must have no brain in that little head," said Hippopotamus. "I'll pull you down before you can blink."

"Well, let us see," said Turtle, and he gave Hippopotamus the other end of the long, long vine. "Now I'll go pick up my end," said Turtle, "and when you feel me start tugging, you tug back."

What is Turtle's plan? How does he intend to outwit Elephant and Hippopotamus?

Turtle walked into the forest and picked up the middle of the vine. He gave it a good hard shake. When Hippopotamus felt this, he started to tug. When Elephant felt the tug, he tugged back.

Elephant and Hippopotamus both tugged so mightily that the vine stretched tight. Turtle settled into a comfortable spot and watched for a while as the vine moved just a little bit one way, then just a little the other way. He took out his lunch and munched on his food very slowly, enjoying every bite. Then he yawned and fell asleep.

He woke a couple of hours later, feeling very refreshed from his nap. He looked to see the vine still stretched tight, and he smiled. Yes, Elephant and Hippopotamus were still pulling with all their might. Neither one could pull the other over.

"I suppose it's about time," said Turtle, and he cut the vine.

When the vine broke, both Elephant and Hippopotamus tumbled down, *WHUMP BUMPITY-BUMP BAM BOOM!*

Turtle went to see Elephant and found him sprawled on the ground, rubbing his head. "Turtle," said Elephant, "you *are* powerful. You were right; we are equal. I guess that bigger doesn't mean better after all, my, uh, my—*friend.*"

Then Turtle went to see Hippopotamus, who was also sprawled on the ground, rubbing his head.

"So, Turtle," said Hippopotamus, "we are equal after all. You were right, my *friend.*"

From then on, whenever the animals held a meeting, there at the front sat Elephant, Hippopotamus, and Turtle. And they always called each other "friend."

They are friends, yes—but tell me, do you think they are equal? ■

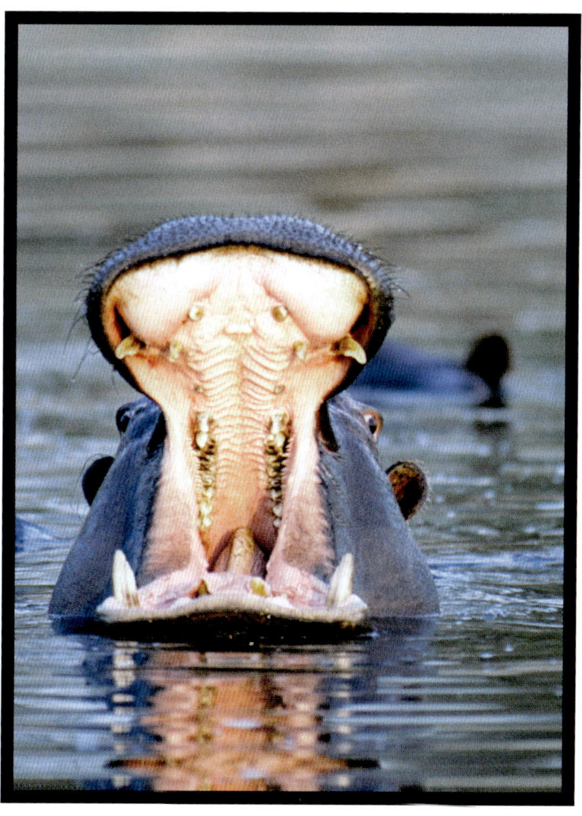

Understanding the Selection

Recalling

1. What does Turtle boast of in the first paragraph?
2. How do Elephant and Hippopotamus respond when Turtle addresses them as "friend"?
3. How do Elephant and Hippopotamus respond when Turtle suggests a tug of war?
4. What happens to the vine?

Interpreting

1. Why would a small creature like Turtle boast that his friends are big and powerful?
2. What does this response reveal about Elephant and Hippopotamus? What are they like?
3. Again, what does this response reveal about Elephant and Hippopotamus?
4. What do Elephant and Hippopotamus think happened to the vine?

Synthesizing

1. In what way is Turtle more than the equal of Elephant and Hippopotamus?
2. Why might it be good for the animals to have someone like Turtle at the head of the group when they are meeting to decide important issues or to deal with important problems? What makes Turtle special?

Delving Deeper

Understanding Literature

The Elements of a Story. Even though "Tug of War" is a simple folktale and fable, it nonetheless has many of the elements of a sophisticated short story. The following are some common elements of stories:

Setting. The time and place of the story and all the details that help to convey this time and place. Some stories have more than one setting.

Protagonist. The main character in the story.

Antagonist. The person, persons, or force against which the main character struggles.

Motivation. What moves a character to act as he or she does.

Central Conflict. The main struggle that the main character is involved in.

Plot. The series of events in a story.

Inciting Incident. The event that introduces the conflict of the story.

Resolution. The event that ends, or resolves, the conflict of the story.

Theme. The main idea, or lesson, that the story teaches. In a fable, the theme is a moral lesson that the story teaches.

Work with other students to answer the following questions about "Tug of War":

1. What is the setting of the story? Where does it take place?
2. Who is the protagonist of the story, and what is he like? Why is he considered a "trickster"?
3. Who are the antagonists in the story?
4. What motivates the protagonist? How does he want to be thought of? How would you answer the question posed in the last line of the story?
5. What is the central conflict in this story? For what does Turtle struggle?
6. What is the inciting incident in the story? In other words, what happens to set the conflict in motion?
7. How is the conflict in the story finally ended, or resolved? Who prevails, or succeeds, in the end—the protagonist or the antagonists? What characteristic makes it possible for this character to prevail?
8. What lesson does this story teach? Why would parents tell this story to their children, in addition to wanting to entertain them?

Prereading

"Talk"

Anonymous

"Talk" is a folktale from the Ashanti people (also called Asante), who live in West Africa, in what is now the country of Ghana. Many Ashanti are farmers, and their major crops include cacao (the main ingredient in chocolate) and, as you'll see in the story, yams. Here is a bit of background information that will become meaningful to you when you read the story: traditionally, almost every Ashanti man and woman owned an elaborately carved wooden stool, a prized and very personal possession.

Not surprisingly for a story called "Talk," this story contains quite a lot of **dialogue,** or words spoken by the characters. As you read, pay attention to the conventions for presenting dialogue:

1. Notice that a writer places dialogue in quotation marks.
2. Dialogue is usually accompanied by **speaker's tags** such as "he said" or "she replied."
3. A writer begins a new paragraph for each new speaker.

Stories like this one come out of the oral tradition and were originally told, not written down. Part of the fun of such a story would be hearing it performed by a talented storyteller. A good storyteller would try to come up with different, appropriate voices for each of the characters in the story. Try to imagine, as you read this story, what would be appropriate voices for the various speakers in it. The story contains talking yams and dogs, for example. What would talking yams and dogs sound like?

Talk

Anonymous Ashanti Tale
Retold by Harold Courlander and George Herzog

Once, not far from the city of Accra[1] on the Gulf of Guinea, a country man went out to his garden to dig for some yams to take to market. While he was digging, one of the yams said to him:

The man starts out to do an ordinary thing. Then, what extraordinary thing happens?

"Well, at last you're here. You never weeded me, but now you come around with your digging stick. Go away and leave me alone!"

The farmer turned around and looked at his cow in amazement. The cow was chewing her cud[2] and looking at him.

"Did you say something?" he asked.

The cow kept on chewing and said nothing, but the man's dog spoke up.

"It wasn't the cow who spoke to you," the dog said. "It was the yam. The yam says leave him alone."

The man became angry because his dog had never talked before, and he didn't like his **tone** besides. So he took his knife and cut a branch from a palm tree to whip his dog. Just then the palm tree said:

"Put that branch down!"

The man was getting very upset about the way things were going, and he started to throw the palm branch away, but the palm branch said:

"Man, put me down softly!"

He put the branch down gently on a stone, and the stone said:

"Hey, take that thing off me!"

This was enough, and the frightened

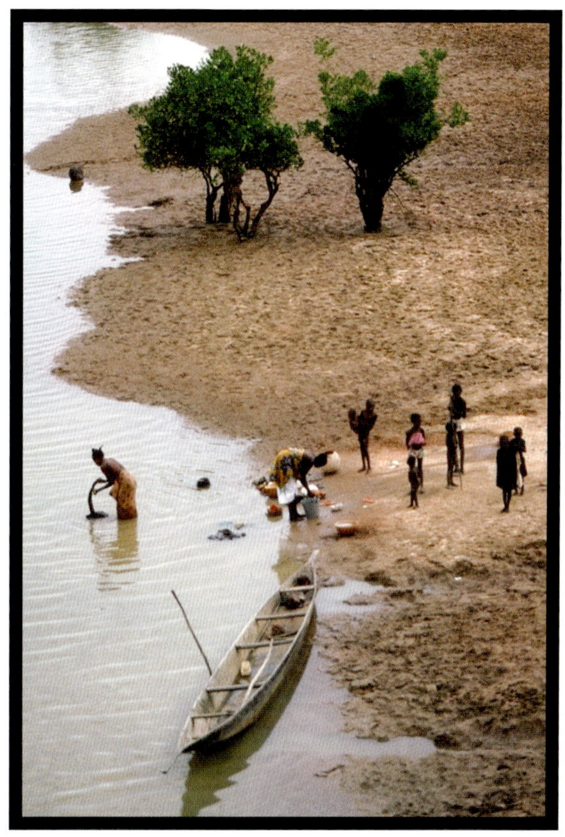

1 **Accra.** Capital of Ghana, West Africa, and a seaport town on the Gulf of Guinea

2 **cud.** Mouthful of previously swallowed food, which a cow regurgitates and then chews slowly for a long time

VOCABULARY IN PLACE

• **tone,** ***n.*** Manner or style of speaking

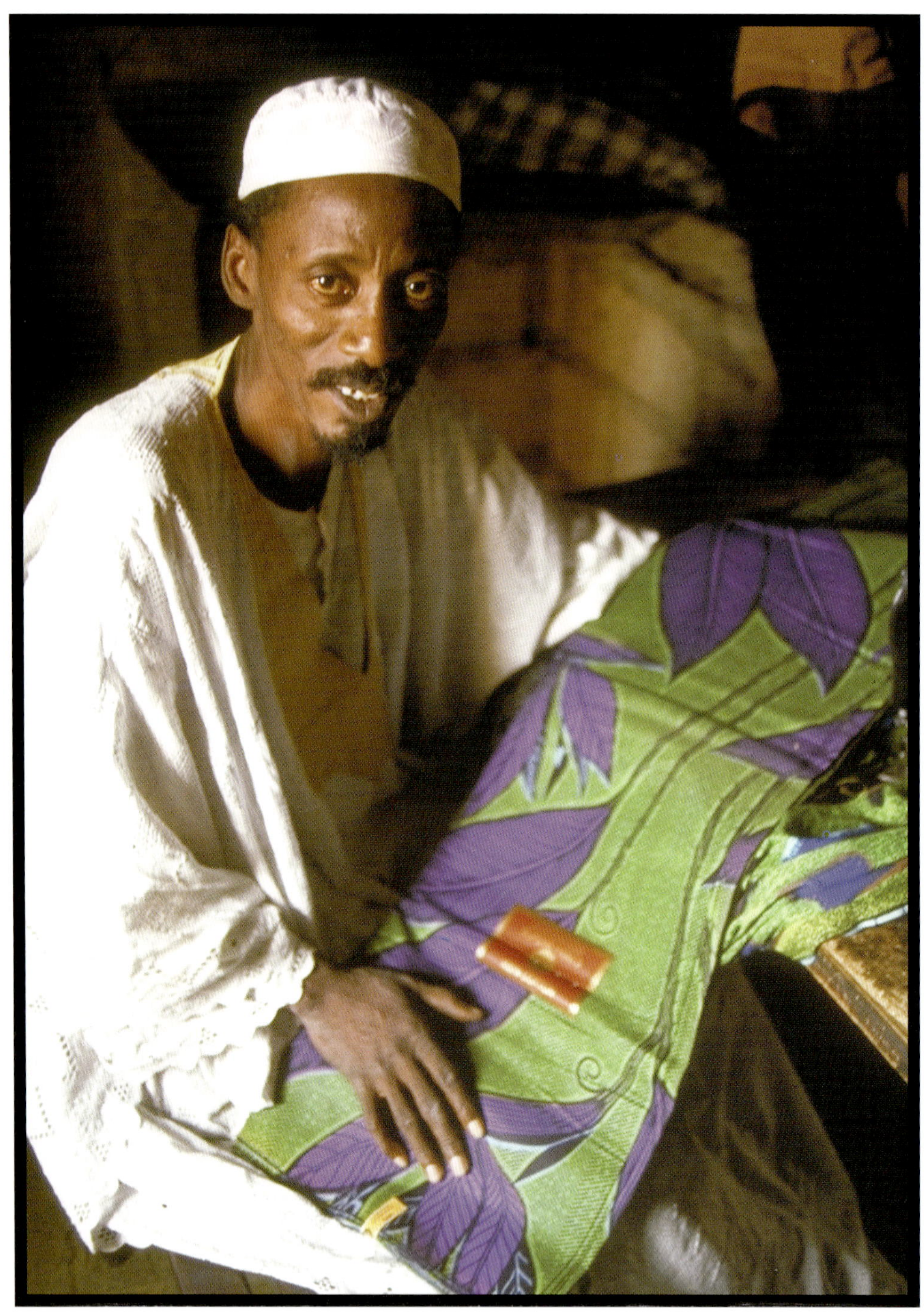

farmer started to run for his village. On the way he met a fisherman going the other way with a fish trap on his head.

"What's the hurry?" the fisherman asked.

"My yam said, 'Leave me alone!' Then the dog said, 'Listen to what the yam says!' When I went to whip the dog with a palm branch the tree said, 'Put that branch down!' Then the palm branch said, 'Do it softly!' Then the stone said, 'Take that thing off me!'"

"Is that all?" the man with the fish trap asked. "Is that so frightening?'"

"Well," the man's fish trap said, "did he take it off the stone?"

"Wah!" the fisherman shouted. He threw the fish trap on the ground and began to run with the farmer, and on the trail they met a **weaver** with a bundle of cloth on his head.

"Where are you going in such a rush?" he asked them.

"My yam said, 'Leave me alone!'" the farmer said. "The dog said, 'Listen to what the yam says!' The tree said, 'Put that branch down!' The branch said, 'Do it softly!' And the stone said, 'Take that thing off me!'"

"And then," the fisherman continued, "the fish trap said, 'Did he take it off?'"

"That's nothing to get excited about," the weaver said, "no reason at all."

"Oh yes it is," his bundle of cloth said. "If it happened to you, you'd run too!"

"Wah!" the weaver shouted. He threw his bundle on the trail and started running with the other men. They came panting to the **ford** in the river and found a man bathing.

"Are you chasing a **gazelle?**" he asked them.

Why would the man in the river think that the men were chasing a gazelle?

The first man said breathlessly:

"My yam talked at me and it said, 'Leave me alone!' And my dog said, 'Listen to your yam!' And when I cut myself a branch, the tree said, 'Put that branch down!' And the branch said, 'Do it softly!' And the stone said, 'Take that thing off me!'"

The fisherman panted:

"And my trap said, 'Did he?'"

The weaver **wheezed:**

"And my bundle of cloth said, 'You'd run too!'"

"Is that why you're running?" the man in the river asked.

"Well, wouldn't you run if you were in their position?" the river said.

The man jumped out of the water and began to run with the others. They ran down the main street of the village to the house of the chief. The chief's servants brought his stool out, and he came and sat on it to listen to their complaints. The men began to recite their troubles.

"I went out to my garden to dig yams," the farmer said, waving his arms. "Then everything began to talk! My yam said, 'Leave me alone!' My dog said, 'Pay attention to your yam!' The tree said, 'Put that branch down!' The branch said, 'Do it softly!' And the stone said, 'Take it off me!'"

"And my fish trap said, 'Well, did he take it off?'" the fisherman said.

"And my cloth said, 'You'd run too!'" the weaver said.

"And the river said the same," the bather said hoarsely, his eyes bulging.

The chief listened to them patiently, but he couldn't **refrain** from **scowling.**

"Now this is really a wild story," he said at last. "You'd better all go back to your work before I punish you for disturbing the peace."

What disturbs the chief about the men's statements?

So the men went away, and the chief shook his head and mumbled to himself, "Nonsense like that upsets the community."

"Fantastic, isn't it?" his stool said. "Imagine, a talking yam!" ■

VOCABULARY IN PLACE

- **weaver,** ***n.*** A person who makes cloth or rugs for a living
- **ford,** ***n.*** The shallow part of a body of water
- **gazelle,** ***n.*** A small, swift antelope
- **wheeze,** ***v.*** To breathe with difficulty, making a hoarse sound
- **refrain,** ***v.*** To prevent oneself from doing something
- **scowling,** ***ger.*** The act of making a face that shows extreme dissatisfaction

Understanding the Selection

Recalling

1. What does the man set out to do in his garden? What unusual thing happens?
2. What does the yam say to the man?
3. What do the palm tree and the branch say to the man?
4. What is the weaver's initial reaction on hearing what happened to the farmer and to the fisherman?
5. What is the chief's initial reaction on hearing the men's story?

Interpreting

1. How do you know, at the very beginning, that this is a fanciful, imaginative, lighthearted tale? Give examples from the text to support your answer.
2. What is the **tone,** or manner of speaking, of the yam?
3. In what ways do people treat plants and nonliving things differently than they typically treat other people? Why do people act differently toward other people?
4. Why does the weaver change his attitude? What makes this change humorous?
5. How do you know that the chief does not really believe the men at first?

Synthesizing

1. Is it possible that this is a true story? Why, or why not? How does one recognize a piece of fanciful literature, which is technically known as **fantasy?**
2. Imagine if the nonliving or nonspeaking things in your life started talking to you. What would they say? Pick three objects, such as your shoes or desk, and write one sentence of dialogue that each object would say to you.

Delving Deeper

Speaking and Listening

Storytelling. From the dawn of human history, people gathered with other members of their group, or clan, in the evening. Throughout most of history, people did not have televisions and music players and computers and other means for entertaining themselves. In many traditional cultures and societies, even today, such items are still rare.

What did people do when they gathered around their campfires in the evening, long, long ago? They told stories, sang songs, drummed, and danced. In every culture around the globe, there are ancient stories and poems and songs that have been passed down from generation to generation.

Storytelling is an important art form. The oldest form of storytelling is **dramatic interpretation** in which a solo performer tells the story, varying his or her voice for the different characters. With the invention of writing, stories were written down, and a new way of telling stories became possible: **reader's theater,** in which several people read different parts. One person might read the part of the **narrator,** the voice telling the main parts of the story, and various people might read the dialogue of the various characters in the story. Stories can also, of course, be acted out, or presented as **drama.**

Whether a story is told as a dramatic interpretation, as reader's theater, or as drama, there are several techniques that can be used to make the story come alive for the audience. Here is a list of points to keep in mind when telling a story:

1. Vary your **pitch,** how high or low your voice is.
2. Vary your **volume,** the loudness or softness of your voice.
3. Vary your **tone,** the manner in which you speak, to convey different emotions. If you are reading a sad passage, try to read it in a sad voice. If you are reading a bit of dialogue, try to imagine what the character is feeling and to convey that emotion in your voice. Is the character angry, scared, joyful, worried, scornful, or lazy? Let your audience hear that in your voice.
4. Vary your **pace,** how quickly you say the words, to fit the action and emotion in different parts of the story. If something exciting is happening, speak more quickly and excitedly.
5. Vary the **quality** of your voice to suit each character. Try to express the character's tone. If the character is big and strong, use a deep voice. If the character is young, use a more high-pitched voice.

Practice telling this story alone and with others. See if you can make it an exciting, fun piece for others to listen to.

Prereading

"Great Hymn to the Aten"

by Pharaoh Amenhotep IV (Akhenaten)

Amenhotep IV ruled Egypt during the Eighteenth Dynasty, from approximately 1391 to 1353 BCE. Before his reign, Egyptians were **polytheists,** people who worshipped a number of gods. The chief among these gods was Re, or Ra. Perhaps in order to challenge the power of the priests of the traditional Egyptian religion, or perhaps because of his own faith, Amenhotep IV declared that there was only one god, the Aten, whom he identified with the sun. Amenhotep changed his name to *Akhenaten,* which means "servant of the Aten," and composed a beautiful hymn to the glory of the single god. Because he taught that there was one god, Akhenaten is remembered for introducing **monotheism** to Egypt.

A **hymn** is a song of worship or praise. "The Great Hymn to the Aten" is also an example of an ancient African literary type known as the **praise song,** in which a hero or god is celebrated. As you read Akhenaten's praise song, ask yourself the following questions:

1. Given the Egyptians' former belief in many gods, what makes this song revolutionary?
2. What, according to the speaker, are the accomplishments of the Aten? What has the Aten done for the world and for humankind?
3. What, according to the song, is the relationship between the Aten and the Pharaoh?

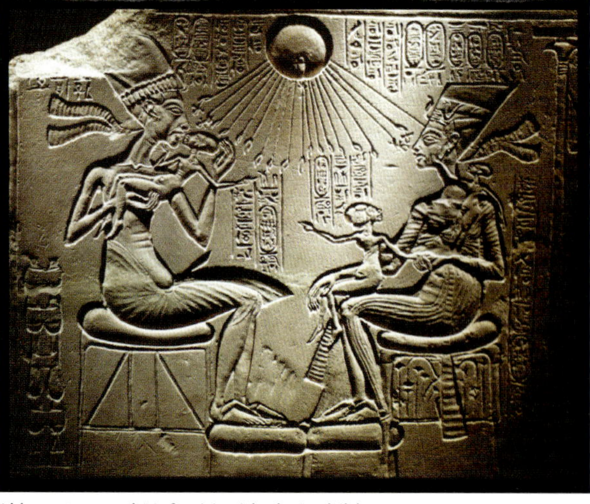

Akhenaten and Nefertiti with their children.

The "Great Hymn to the Aten" is presented here in a brilliant translation. The beauty of the translation becomes particularly evident when it is read aloud.

Great Hymn to the Aten[1]

by Pharaoh Amenhotep IV (Akhenaten),
translated by Wim van den Dungen

I. The Aten as Re[2] with His Course[3]
Morning Beauty

Splendid You rise in the lightland of the sky,
O living Aten, creator of life!
You have dawned in the eastern lightland.
You fill every land with your beauty.

Noon Dominion

You are beauteous, mighty and **radiant.**
Risen high over every land,
your rays embrace the lands,
to the limit of all that You made.
Being Re, You reach their end.
You bend them for your beloved son.
Though You are far, your rays are on Earth.
Though seen by them, your course is unknown.

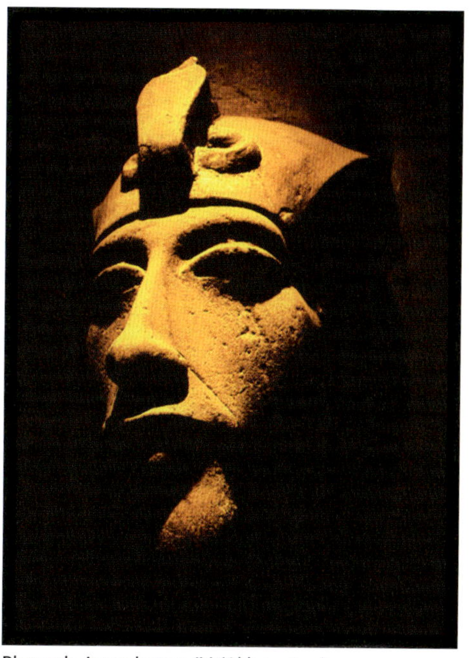
Pharaoh Amenhotep IV (Akhenaten)

[1] **Aten.** Sun. *Aten* was the Egyptian word for sun, and so, in English, it is written "the Aten," just as we would say "the sun."

[2] **Re.** The primary god of the Egyptians, identified during the reign of Amenhotep IV with the Aten who was formerly a lesser entity

[3] **Course.** The path that the sun appears to take across the sky

VOCABULARY IN PLACE

- **radiant,** ***adj.*** Giving off rays (of light)

Night Chaos

When You set in the western lightland,
Earth is in darkness, as if death.
The sleepers are in their **chambers,** heads covered,
no eye seeing the other.
One could steal their goods from under their heads,
they would not notice it.
Every lion comes from its den.
The serpents bite.
Darkness **hovers,** Earth is silent
For its creator rests in the lightland.

Dawn Rebirth

At dawn You have risen in the lightland.
To shine as the Aten of daytime!
You **dispel** the dark and cast your rays.
The Two Lands[4] celebrate daily.
Awake they stand on their feet.
You have made them get up.
They wash and dress, their arms raised
in **adoration** to your appearance.
The entire land sets out to work.
All cattle are satisfied with their fodder.[5]
The trees and the grass become green.
Birds fly from their nests, their wings praising your Ka.[6]
All game animals **frisk** on their hooves, all that fly and flutter,
live when You dawn for them.
Ships **fare** downstream and back upstream,
roads lie open when You rise.
The fish in the river **dart** before You.
Your rays penetrate the Great Green deep.

---

[4] **Two Lands.** Nubia and Egypt, over both of which Akhenaten ruled

[5] **fodder.** Food for animals, such as dried grasses

[6] **Ka.** In ancient Egyptian religion, the life force, or spirit, within a person or god

VOCABULARY IN PLACE

- **chaos,** ***n.*** Confusion, disarray
- **chamber,** ***n.*** Room
- **hover,** ***v.*** To hang in the air
- **dispel,** ***v.*** Drive away
- **adoration,** ***n.*** Profound love or regard, worship
- **frisk,** ***v.*** To move briskly and playfully
- **fare,** ***v.*** To move toward a goal
- **dart,** ***v.*** To move about quickly

II. Works and Nature of the Aten

The Child

O You, who make the seed grow in women,
who create people from seed,
who feed the son in his mother's womb,
who soothe him to still his tears.
You nurse in the womb!
Giver of breath to **nourish** all creatures.
When the child emerges from the womb
to breathe on the day of his birth,
You open wide his mouth to supply his needs.

The Chicken[7]

The chick in the egg, chirping in the shell,
You give it breath within to **sustain** its life.
When it is complete, it breaks out from the egg.
It emerges from the egg, to say it is complete.
Walking on its legs when emerging.

The Aten as Doer: Un-saying, Solitary, Omnipotent[8]

How many are your deeds,
though hidden from sight.
O sole God without equal!
You made the Earth as You desired, You alone.
With people, cattle, and all creatures.
With everything upon Earth that walks on legs,
and all that is on high and flies with its wings.

Monotheism did not survive Akhenaten. One of the most famous of Egyptian pharaohs, pictured at right, was Ramses II, who ruled from 1279 to 1212 BCE during the Nineteenth Dynasty. His name is derived from that of Ra, the chief god of the traditional polytheistic religion of Egypt.

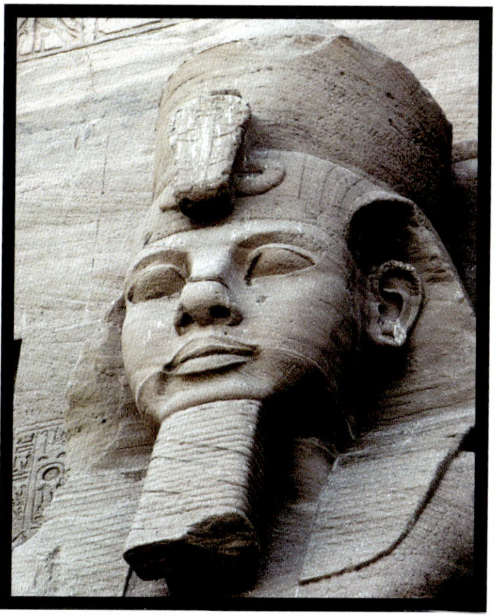

[7] **The Chicken.** The passage suggests that nothing is so lowly that the Aten has no part in its being.

[8] **Un-saying, Solitary, Omnipotent.** The meaning of "un-saying" here is unclear. It may refer to the fact that the Aten is ultimately unknowable or to the Aten's power to undo as well as to create. The Aten is solitary in the sense of being the one god and in the sense of having no equals. He is also omnipotent, or all-powerful.

VOCABULARY IN PLACE

- **nourish,** *v.* To feed and otherwise provide for
- **sustain,** *v.* To maintain or keep in existence

The Two Niles:[9] the Aten as National, International, and Transnational[10] Governor

The foreign lands of Syria and Nubia,[11] and the land of Egypt,
You set all in their places and supply their needs.
They all have their food, and their lifetimes are counted.
Tongues differ in speech, their characters as well.[12]
Their skins are **distinct**, for You distinguished the peoples.

You made the Nile in the Netherworld.[13]
You bring it up when You will,
to keep those of Egypt alive,
for You have created them for yourself.

Lord of All who **toils** for them.
Lord of All Lands who shines for them.
O Aten of daytime, great in glory!

All distant lands, You make them live.
You made a heavenly Nile **descend** for them.
With waves beating on the mountains like the sea,
To **drench** their fields and their towns.

How excellent are your ways, O Lord of Eternity!
The Nile from heaven for foreign peoples
and all land-creatures that walk on legs.
For Egypt the Nile from the Netherworld.

III. Theology of the Aten

Life-giving Nature of the Aten

Your rays nurse all fields.
When You shine they live, they grow for You.
You made the seasons,
So that all that You made may come to life.
Winter cools them, and heat makes them sense You.

---

9 **The Two Niles.** The Nile River and its source, the Blue Nile

10 **Transnational.** Between nations

11 **Syria and Nubia.** Other ancient Middle Eastern empires. Ancient *Syria,* located in southwest Asia on the Mediterranean coast, included Lebanon, most of present-day Israel and Jordan, and part of Iraq and Saudi Arabia. *Nubia* was an ancient kingdom of the Nile River Valley, located in southern Egypt and northern Sudan.

12 **Tongues . . . as well.** The people speak and write (make characters) in different languages.

13 **Netherworld.** The underground abode of the dead

VOCABULARY IN PLACE

- **distinct,** ***adj.*** Clearly differing from one another
- **toil,** ***v.*** To work
- **descend,** ***v.*** To come down from a higher place to a lower one
- **drench,** ***v.*** To wet thoroughly

The Aten Is Sole Witness, Sole Creator, and Sole Presence

You created the sky far away in order to **ascend** to it,
to witness everything You created.
You are alone, shining in your form of the living Aten.
Risen, radiant, distant and near.
You made millions of forms from yourself alone:
cities, towns, fields, the river's course.
All eyes see You above them
as the Aten of the daytime on high.
When You are gone, (. . .) your eye is gone (. . .)
which You have made (?) {for their sake}[14]

Pharaoh as the Exclusive Mediator of the Aten[15]

But even then You are in my heart
And there is no other who knows You,
only your son, *Nefer-kheperu-Re, Sole-one-of-Re,*[16]
whom You have taught your ways and your might.

The ones on Earth come into being by your hand,
in the way You made them.
When You rise, they live.
When You set, they die.
You yourself are lifetime itself,
one lives through You.
All eyes rest on beauty until You set.
All labor ceases when You rest in the West.

When You rise, You make all arms firm for the King,
every leg is on the move since You founded the Earth.
You **rouse** them for our son, who emerged from your body.
The King who lives by Maat,[17]
the Lord of the Two Lands:
Nefer-kheperu-Re, Sole-one-of-Re,
the Son of Re who lives by Maat,
the Lord of Crowns, *Akhenaten,* great in his lifetime.
And the great Queen whom he loves,
the Lady of the Two Lands:
Nefer-neferu-Aten Nefertiti,[18]
who lives and is **rejuvenated** forever and ever."

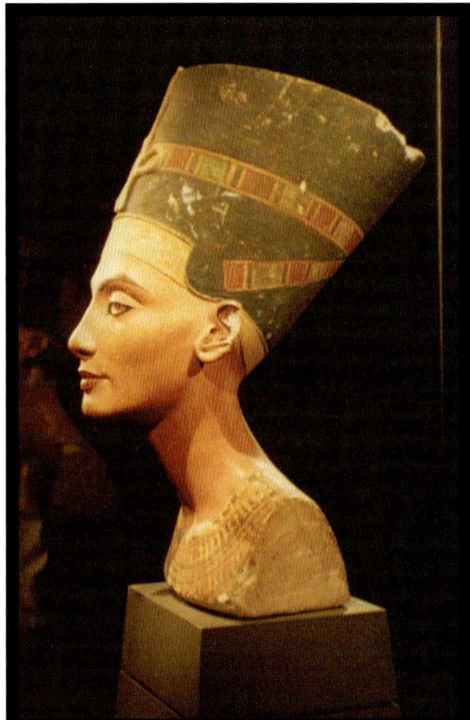

Queen Nefertiti

VOCABULARY IN PLACE

- **ascend,** *v.* To move upward, rise up
- **rouse,** *v.* To awaken; also, to excite to action
- **rejuvenated,** *past part.* Refreshed or reborn

14 **You are gone . . . sake.** In this section of the hymn, parts of the text are missing or the hieroglyphs are difficult to decipher.

15 **Exclusive Mediator of the Aten.** Akhenaten considered himself to be the only, or exclusive, one who could communicate the will of the Aten to the people. He thus set himself up against and above the traditional Egyptian priesthood.

16 ***Nefer-kheperu-Re, Sole-one-of-Re.*** This was Akhenaten's *praenomen,* or throne name. In addition, he had the *nomen,* or birth name Amenhotep IV, which he changed to Akhenaten as part of his attempt to establish the Aten as the sole deity in Egypt.

17 **Maat.** Universal truth, law, and order

18 ***Nefer-neferu-Aten Nefertiti.*** Queen Nefertiti, the wife of Akhenaten. *Nefer-neferu-Aten* means "beautiful is the beauty of the Aten."

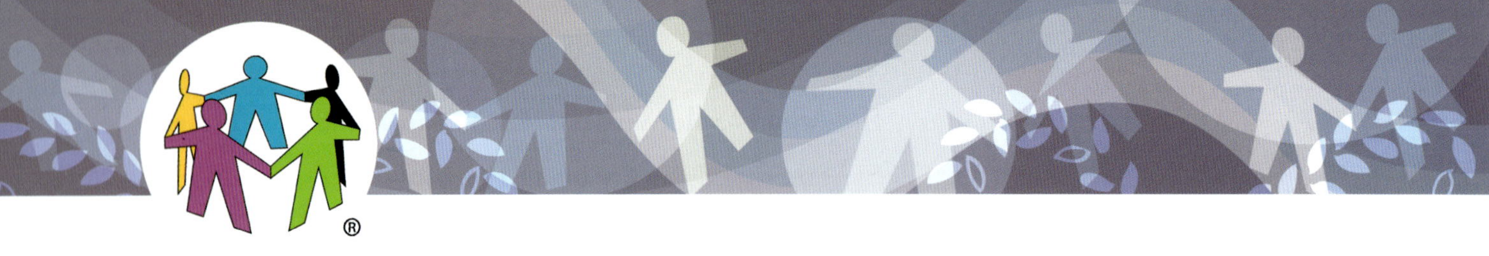

Understanding the Selection

Recalling

1. According to line 2 of the poem, what does the Aten create?
2. According to the "Night Chaos" section of the poem, what terrible things can happen in the night?
3. According to the "Dawn Rebirth" section of the poem, what happens when the Aten shines again?
4. What, according to the poem, makes possible the birth and growth of children and chickens?
5. What river is mentioned repeatedly on page 42 ?
6. Who, according to the poem, is the only one who knows the Aten?

Interpreting

1. Is there any scientific truth to this claim? How does life on Earth depend upon the sun?
2. Why is the day, when the Aten is present, better?
3. According to the poem, the Aten is responsible for what specific, good, purposeful activities? What general point is being made about the Aten?
4. How much of a debt, according to the poem, do people owe to the Aten?
5. Who directs the river? Why is the river so important?
6. Why do you think Akhenaten wanted people to believe this?

Synthesizing

1. Mahatma Gandhi, the great Indian spiritual and political leader, once said that there is one God, but He has many names. Would Akhenaten agree? Why, or why not?
2. What are some of the many ways, according to the poem, in which people are dependent upon the Aten?

Delving Deeper

Understanding Literature

Praise Songs and Hymns. As you learned in the Prereading, a **praise song** is a traditional African song form in which a person (often a hero) or god is celebrated. Commonly, in a praise song, the subject is given many special names that tell of his or her attributes. Often, in West Africa, praise songs are performed by **griots,** or traditional storytellers, who accompany themselves on a traditional 21-stringed instrument called the **kora.**

Hymns are songs of worship or praise of God. As you will learn in chapters to come, hymns, especially in the form of spirituals and gospel songs, have played a very important role in African-American culture. You can see from this selection that the singing of hymns, the urge to lift one's voice in praise, has deep roots in African heritage.

About the Author

Amenhotep IV (Akhenaten). Amenhotep IV ruled Egypt from approximately 1391 to 1353 BCE. His chief wife was Nefertiti, widely admired today for her beauty because of the famous bust of her that appears on page 43. In the third year of his reign, Amenhotep IV held a Sed festival, a celebration of the divine power of the Pharaoh, an unusual move because such festivals were usually held late in a Pharaoh's reign. It was in this year that Amenhotep started a revolution by proclaiming the Aten, previously a fairly obscure deity, the supreme god, a belief that he emphasized by changing his own name to *Akhenaten,* or "servant of the Aten." In his fifth year as Pharaoh, he started to build a new capital for Egypt, which he called Akhetaten, and he built a number of temple complexes to the deity. In his ninth year as Pharaoh, he proclaimed the Aten the one god and himself and his queen the sole interpreters of the will of the Aten to the people. The last years of Akhenaten's reign were troubled, with rebellions throughout the Egyptian empire. After his death, subsequent Pharaohs returned to the ancient religion and attempted to erase Akhenaten's memory.

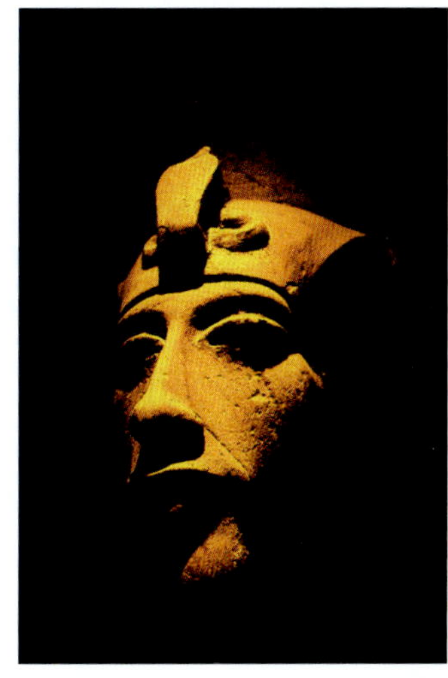

Prereading

from *Sunjata*

by Bamba Suso

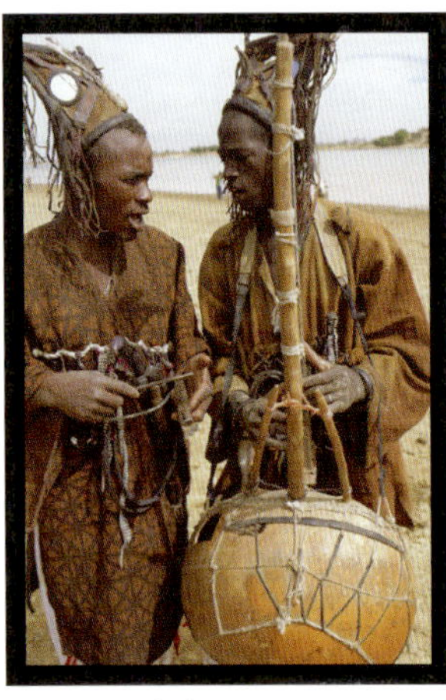
Griots with *koras*

According to legend, **Sunjata** (also **Sundiata) Keita,** whose name means "**the lion king,**" was one of seven sons of a chief of the Mande people in West Africa. He did not seem destined for greatness. In fact, for the first seven years of his life, he was unable to walk and could only pull himself up to a standing position by enormous strength of will. The Mande were ruled at the time by their Sudanese neighbors, the Susu (or Soso). When Sunjata miraculously learned to walk, the Susu leader, Sumanguru, fearing the newly strong chief's son would take over his throne, banished Sunjata and his mother from the kingdom. However, from exile, Sunjata was able to draw together an army. Around the year 1230, he overthrew the Susu and established what was to become the mighty empire of **Mali.** The story of Sunjata's struggle against Sumanguru is told and retold in West Africa by professional singers and storytellers known as **jalis** (the Mande term for **griots**). Jalis typically accompany their songs with instruments such as the **balafon,** or xylophone; the **ngoni,** or **xalam,** a small lute; and the **kora,** a 21-string harp-like instrument.

The story of Sunjata has a special place in West African culture. Sunjata is a widely revered hero, and his story is one of the great oral epics of the world. An **epic** is a long poem that tells a story about heroes and/or gods and that embodies and portrays the way of life of a people. No two tellings of the Sunjata story are ever exactly alike. The selection presented here comes from a performance by a griot named Bamba Suso and was recorded by a scholar named Gordon Innes in the 1970s. Bamba Suso performed before an audience that was familiar with the story's cultural references and narrative structure. Readers should not feel discouraged if they find the story difficult to follow; remember, the story is meant to be *told,* so it is a good idea to read passages aloud and perhaps have fun "performing" certain scenes.

This selection from the story tells how Nyakhaleng Juma Suukho, one of Sunjata's sisters who has been married off to Sumanguru, tricks Sumanguru into giving up the secret to his power. It is similar to the Biblical story of Samson and Delilah. As you read, ask yourself the following questions:

1. What is the secret to the main character's strength?
2. How does Sunjata's sister learn this secret?

from Sunjata

by Bamba Suso

When it was evening, Sunjata's sister came to him—Nyakhaleng Juma Suukho—
And said, "To be sure, hot water kills a man,
But cold water too kills a man.
Leave the smith[1] and me together."
She was the best-looking woman in both Susu[2] and Manding.[3]
When she had got herself ready,
She left the land of Manding and went to the land of Susu.
When the woman had gone some distance she reached Susu,
She reached Susu Sumanguru.
The gates of his **fortified** town. . . .

They took her to Susu Sumanguru.
When Susu Sumanguru saw her,
He greatly desired the woman.
He welcomed her to the house,
And gave her every kind of hospitality.
Night fell,
And he and the woman were in his house. . . .
They were chatting,
Till the smith's mind turned in a certain
    direction,
And then she said to him, "I am a guest;
I have come to you—
Don't be impatient."
She said to him, "There is something that
    greatly puzzles me;
Any army which comes to this town of yours
    is destroyed."
Susu Sumanguru said to her,
"Ah, my father was a jinn."[4]
When he said that, his mother heard it,

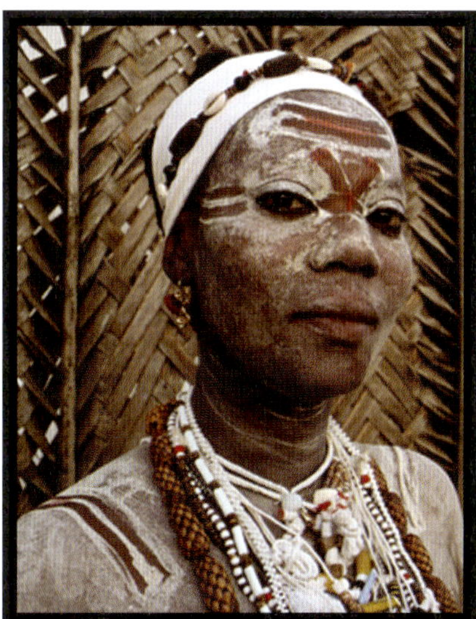

[1] **the smith.** The blacksmith. Sunjata's rival, Susu Sumanguru, the king who was ruling over the Mande people and whom Sunjata wished to overthrow, belonged to this traditional occupational group.

[2] **Susu.** The native land of Susu Sumanguru

[3] **Manding.** Sunjata's native land, which Sumanguru took over and, at this point in the story, was part of the Susu empire

[4] **jinn.** A wizard or sorcerer, a genie

VOCABULARY IN PLACE

- **fortified,** ***adj.*** Surrounded by walls and trenches and/or protected by armed guards for security reasons

Because Susu Sumanguru's
Mother was a human being,
But his father was a jinn.
Two women had **conceived** him;[5]
As you may know, the griots[6] praise smiths in terms of this,
Saying, ***"Between Susuo and Dabi,[7] take suck from two mothers."***
Two women had conceived him;
When he was inside one of them,
She was fit, and people saw her going about
For a week or ten days, and the other one was ill;
When he returned to the other one,
The one he came out of became ill.
He would return inside her
For a week or ten days and people saw her around too.
That is why they called him ***Between Susuo and Dabi, take suck from two mothers.***
But when these events were taking place,
Dabi was still alive.
When Sumanguru said to Sunjata's sister, "My father is a jinn,"
The old lady[8] appeared,
And said to him, "Don't give away all your secrets to a one-night woman."
When Susu Sumanguru's mother said that, the woman[9] got up and said to him,
"I'm going, because your mother is driving me away."
He said, "Wait!"
He went and gave his mother some palm wine,
And she drank it, became drunk and fell asleep.
He said to Sunjata's sister, "Let us continue with our chat.
She is an old lady."
They were chatting,
And she said to him, "Did you say that your father was a jinn?"
He said, "My father is a jinn, and he lives on this hill.
This jinn has seven heads.
So long as he is alive, war will never damage this country."
She said to him, "Your father,
How can he be killed?"

[5] **two women . . . him.** This is an example of the many miraculous elements of this story. According to tradition, Sumanguru had, when he was yet unborn, switched back and forth between the wombs of two mothers.

[6] **griots.** A *griot* is a traditional singer/storyteller from West Africa. The *Sunjata* story is one that was traditionally told by griots. Often, the stories of the griots incorporated elaborate praises for the characters in those stories or for the ancestors of those hearing the stories.

[7] ***Susuo and Dabi.*** Sumanguru's two mothers

[8] **the old lady.** Dabi

[9] **the woman.** Sunjata's sister, Nyakhaleng Juma Suukho

VOCABULARY IN PLACE

- **conceive,** ***v.*** To become pregnant with

He said, "You must go and find a white chicken,
Then they must remove the spur of the white chicken,
They must pick the leaves of self-seeded[10] guinea-corn,
They must put *korte*[11] powder in it.
If they put that on the tip of an arrow,
And shoot it at this hill,
They will kill my father.
That is the only thing that will kill him."
She asked him, "Supposing they kill him?"
He replied, "If war came, this country would be destroyed."
She asked, "Supposing this land were destroyed, what would happen to you?"
He said, "I would become a whirlwind."[12]
She said, "Supposing people went into the whirlwind with swords?"
He said, "I would become an African fan-palm."
She said to him, "What if people were about to **fell** the palm?"
He said, "I would become an ant-hill."
She asked, "Supposing people were about to scatter the ant-hill?"
He said, "I would become a Senegalese cou–"
His heart **palpitated,**
And he fell silent.
The woman said to him, "Wait,
I am going to the wash-place, . . ."
(AMADU:[13] That "Senegalese cou–"
—what was it he cut short there?
BAMBA:[14] He had cut short the name
"Senegalese coucal."[15]
Even today, if you fire at a Senegalese
coucal in the bush,

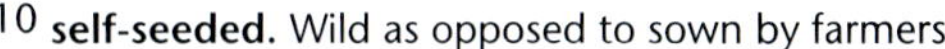

[10] **self-seeded.** Wild as opposed to sown by farmers

[11] ***korte.*** A traditional concoction, made from various roots, that was used in sorcery

[12] **I would . . . a whirlwind.** This is another magical element of the story. Sumanguru explains how he would attempt to escape from his enemies through various magical transformations.

[13] **AMADU.** The accompanist of Bamba Suso, the griot telling this story

[14] **BAMBA.** Bamba Suso, the griot telling this story

[15] **Senegalese coucal.** A species of bird found throughout much of Africa

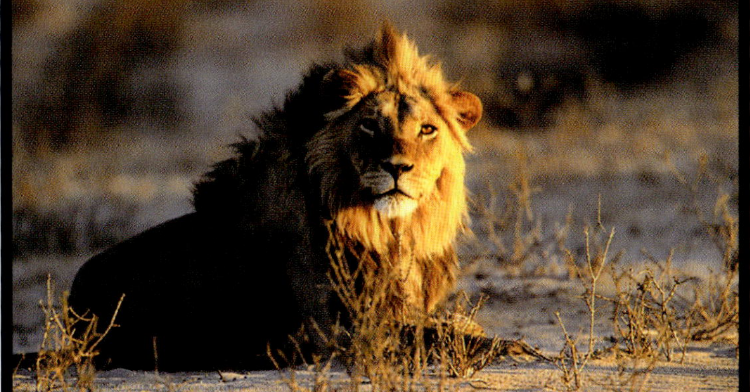

VOCABULARY IN PLACE

- **fell,** *v.* To cut down
- **palpitate,** *v.* Throb

Quite often the gun will shatter in your hands.)[16]
Nyakhaleng Juma[17] was in the wash-place,
And Susu Sumanguru was in bed inside the house.
After some time, he would say to her,
"Aren't you coming back today?"
At that time in Manding
They had a *korte* ring,[18]
And when they laid it down,
And the person for whom it had been laid down spoke,
It would answer him.
It did not answer everybody,
But it would answer the person for whom it had been laid down.
She took off that *korte* ring
And threw it into the pot of ablution water.[19]
When Sumanguru said, "Aren't you coming?"
It would say to him, "Wait;
Such is this fort of yours
That a guest who comes to you
Is completely in your hands.
You are king;
Why are you so impatient?"[20]
When she had thrown the ring in there,
She climbed over the wall of the fort and off she went.
When she had gone, Sumanguru lay for a long time,
He had a short nap,
Then he awoke with a start
And went and looked inside the wash-place.
He said, "I think there is more to this than just a visit to the wash-place."
He did not find anyone there.
At length he came upon the *korte* ring,
But he did not see anyone.
He wept.
She reached Sunjata,
And she told him all that Sumanguru had said.
They went and found a white cock,
They found self-seeded guinea-corn,
They found *korte* powder.

[16] **if you fire . . . hands.** For unknown reasons, it was traditionally believed that it was dangerous to shoot at this particular bird.

[17] **Nyakhaleng Juma.** Sunjata's sister

[18] ***korte* ring.** Enchanted rings are a common element, or motif, in folk stories around the world.

[19] **ablution water.** Water used for ritual bathing

[20] **And the person . . . so impatient.** Sunjata's sister tricks Sumanguru by leaving a magic ring that speaks to him as though it were her. He thinks that she is still in the wash-place, but she has actually escaped.

That is why the members of the Kante family do not eat white chicken.
When they had prepared this arrow,
They gave it to Sankarang Madiba Konte.
It was Sankarang Madiba Konte who fired the arrow.
That is why the griots say, "***The head and neck of an arrow both with red* mananda,**[21]
Arrow on the forehead Faa Ganda."[22]
It was he who slew the jinn on the hill [Susu Sumanguru's father].
When he had slain the jinn on the hill in Susu,
The griots called him ***The red arrow firer of Manding.***
Next morning the army rose up and flung itself against the fortified town;
It was not yet two o'clock when they smashed it. ■

---

21 ***red* mananda.** The meaning of this phrase is unknown, but it may refer to the magic poison, prepared from the spur of a white cock, guinea-corn, and *korte* powder, that was applied to the arrow tip.

22 ***Faa Ganda.*** Another name of Sankarang Madiba Konte, the person who fired the arrow that killed Sumanguru's father

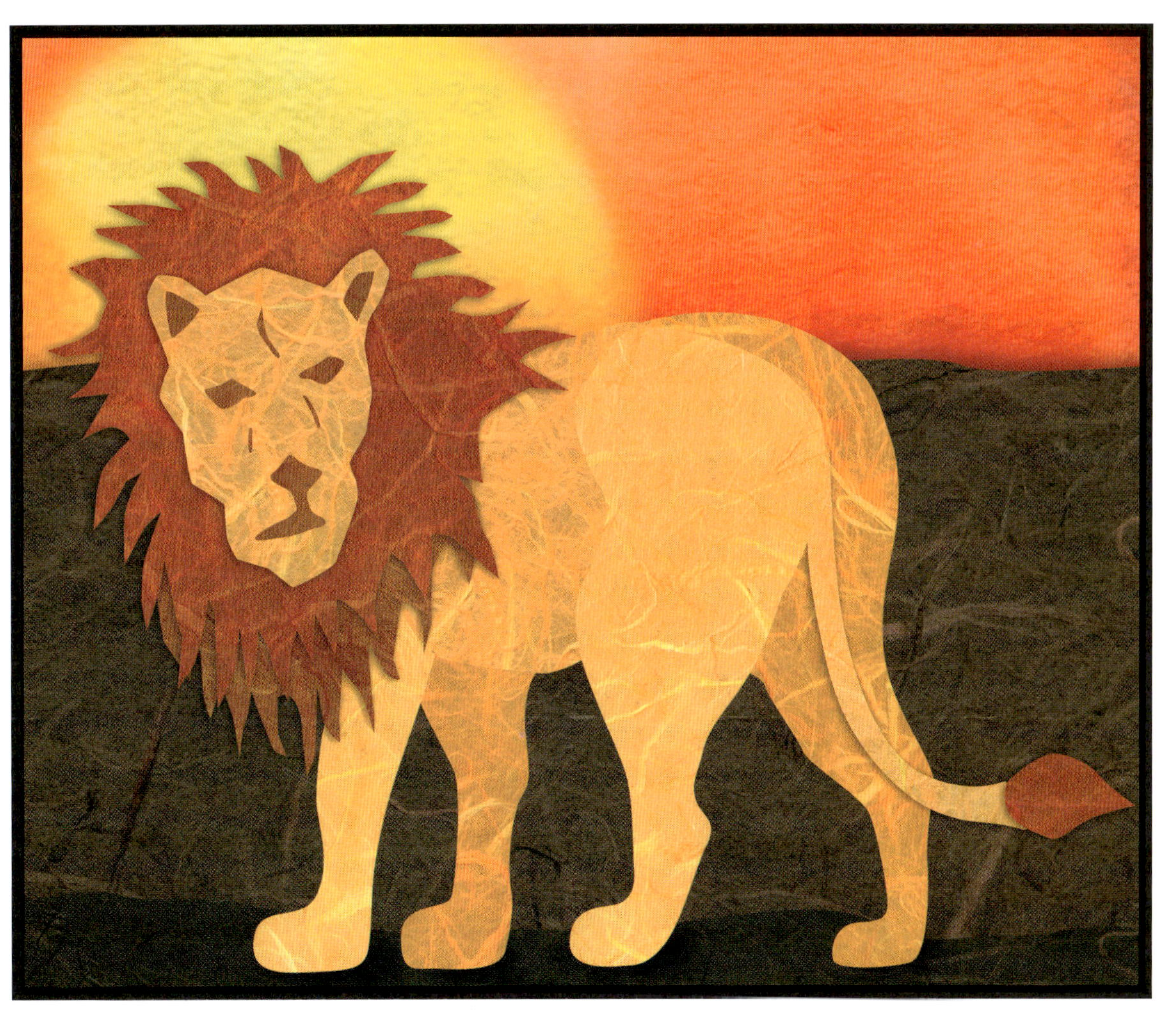

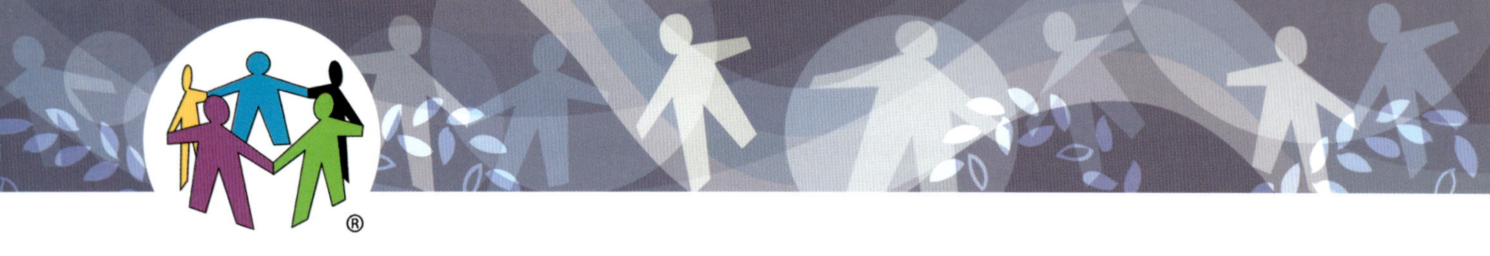

Understanding the Selection

Recalling

1. What proverb does Sunjata's sister quote at the beginning of the selection?
2. What sort of person was Sumanguru's father?
3. Of what does Sumanguru's mother warn him?
4. Sumanguru describes the magical transformations he would undergo if he were personally attacked. What things does he say he would turn into?
5. What ingredients are gathered by Sunjata and his sister?
6. What happens to Sumanguru's father?

Interpreting

1. If battle against Sunjata is the "hot water" that might kill Sumanguru, what is the "cold water"?
2. What importance does this fact have with regard to Sunjata's battle against Sumanguru?
3. Does Sumanguru heed his mother's warning? Explain.
4. Why does Sumanguru stop in the middle of saying "a Senegalese coucal"? Why does his heart start to palpitate?
5. Why do they gather these ingredients? What use do they have for them?
6. What happens to Sumanguru's village as a result?

Synthesizing

1. There is an ancient tradition of tales about the hero or warrior whose downfall is caused by a beautiful woman. The Samson and Delilah story from the Bible is one example. What deception is carried out in this story?
2. Myths and epic poems often contain supernatural elements. What supernatural elements are present in this story?

Delving Deeper

Understanding Literature

Epic. As you learned in the Prereading, an **epic** is a long poem that tells a story about heroes or gods and that embodies and portrays the way of life of a people. What heroes appear in the selection you have read from the oral epic poem *Sunjata?* What supernatural elements occur in the story? What did you learn from the selection about life in West Africa in ancient times?

Often, epics tell the stories of ancient, legendary heroes. The *Odyssey,* for example, tells the story of the legendary hero Odysseus. The *Aeneid,* by the Roman poet Virgil, tells the story of a hero named Aeneas and how he came to found the city of Rome. The selection you have just read is from an **oral epic** that tells the story of Sunjata, the legendary founder of the empire of Mali.

Interestingly, in this epic, the downfall of the **antagonist,** the enemy of the main character, or **protagonist,** is not brought about, for the most part, by the actions of the hero. Who brings about Sumanguru's downfall? How does she do this? How does this course of events prove the proverb that says, "Hot water kills a man, but cold water too kills a man"? Why might the people of Mali be interested in hearing this story? Why would it be important to them that the griots keep this story alive through frequent retelling?

About the Author

Bamba Suso. Bamba Suso was a master **jali** (the Gambian word for griot) from The Gambia. He was recorded in the early 1970s by the English scholar Gordon Innes. Suso's parents came from Galen, in western Mali, and so he had an historical connection to the Sunjata legend. Suso became a renowned authority on Sunjata Keita and other heroes of the Mande people. At the time when he was recorded by Innes, Suso was considered a **ngara,** or master musician. However, in keeping with tradition, a musician of his advanced stature did not sing the traditional epic songs, as did younger musicians. Instead, as a master of the craft, he spoke out the words of the song in a strong, clear voice while being accompanied by the superb kora player Amadu Bansang Jebate.

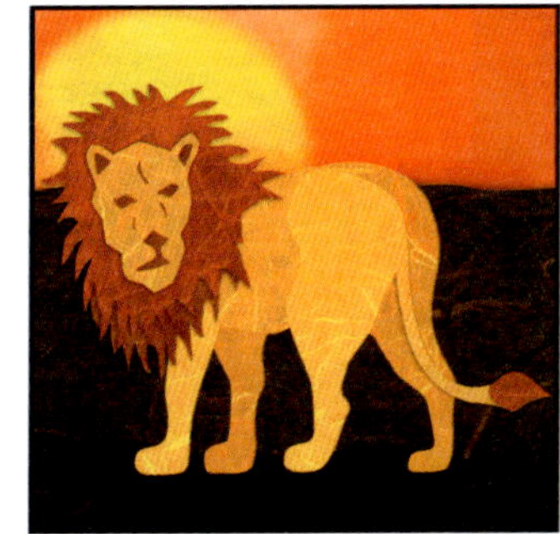

Prereading

"My Early Life" from *The Interesting Narrative of the Life of Olaudah Equiano*

by Olaudah Equiano

The work of Olaudah Equiano is remarkable and noteworthy for several reasons. He published the following narrative while residing in England in 1789, the year the U.S. Constitution was ratified, when the wounds of the Revolutionary War were still fresh and the Abolitionist (antislavery) Movement was still in its infancy. His autobiography helped to make Abolitionism a mainstream movement. It was among the first published autobiographical works by a person of African descent, and it provides valuable, first-hand insight into traditional African life and the brutality of the slave trade.

In recent years, there has been increased attention on Equiano as a result of controversial evidence put forth by researcher Vincent Carretta, who suggests that Equiano was actually born in South Carolina, and not in Guinea, as is stated in the following pages. Later events in Equiano's life after age ten have been irrefutably confirmed through historical records such as ships' logs. All scholars agree, as well, that regardless of whether Equiano was African-born, his account of life in Guinea is accurate and reliable. Equiano would have had little motive to invent his depiction of Guinea, and since his perspective is that of a young boy, it is likely that most of what he knew about the place was learned from other enslaved Africans, from the many books he read, and from his extensive travels in later life.

No scholar has ever suggested that Equiano's portrayal of everyday life in Guinea is inaccurate. In fact, all agree that it is extraordinary, not because it was written by a former slave, but because it was written at all. Equiano anticipates a certain amount of controversy or skepticism in his somewhat apologetic opening paragraphs.

Take your time with this historic **memoir**, for the language and style might challenge you at times, but it is worth understanding every word!

from The Interesting Narrative of the Life of Olaudah Equiano

by Olaudah Equiano

I believe it is difficult for those who publish their own memoirs[1] to escape the **imputation** of vanity. Nor is this the only disadvantage under which they labour: it is also their misfortune that whatever is uncommon is rarely, if ever, believed, and from what is obvious we are apt to turn with disgust, and to charge the writer of it with **impertinence.**

People generally think those memoirs only worthy to be read or remembered which abound in great or striking events, those, in short, which in a high degree excite either admiration or pity: all others they **consign** to contempt and oblivion. It is therefore, I confess, not a little hazardous in a private and obscure individual, and a stranger too, thus to solicit the indulgent attention of the public; especially when I own I offer here the history of neither a saint, a hero, nor a tyrant. I believe there are few events in my life, which have not happened to many: it is true the incidents of it are numerous; and, did I consider myself an European, I might say my sufferings were great: but when I compare my lot with that of most of my countrymen, I regard myself as a particular favourite of Heaven, and acknowledge the mercies of Providence[2] in every occurrence of my life. If then the following narrative does not appear sufficiently interesting to engage general attention, let my motive be some excuse for its publication. I

How did Equiano feel compared to other Africans?

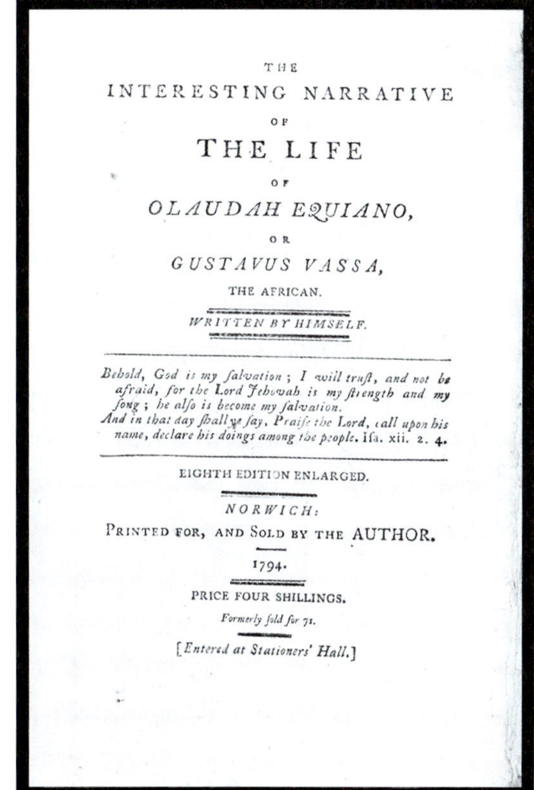

THE
INTERESTING NARRATIVE
OF
THE LIFE
OF
OLAUDAH EQUIANO,
OR
GUSTAVUS VASSA,
THE AFRICAN.

WRITTEN BY HIMSELF.

Behold, God is my salvation; I will trust, and not be afraid, for the Lord Jehovah is my strength and my song; he also is become my salvation.
And in that day shall ye say, Praise the Lord, call upon his name, declare his doings among the people. Isa. xii. 2. 4.

EIGHTH EDITION ENLARGED.

NORWICH:
PRINTED FOR, AND SOLD BY THE AUTHOR.

1794.

PRICE FOUR SHILLINGS.
Formerly sold for 7s.

[Entered at Stationers' Hall.]

Frontispiece and title page from *Olaudah Equiano.* Library of Congress, LC-USZ62-54026

1 **memoir.** An autobiography; an account of the author's personal experiences

2 **Providence.** God; care or control exercised by a deity

VOCABULARY IN PLACE

- **imputation,** ***n.*** A suggestion or accusation
- **impertinence,** ***n.*** Rudeness
- **consign,** ***v.*** To give to the care of another; transfer

am not so foolishly vain as to expect from it either immortality or literary reputation. If it affords any satisfaction to my numerous friends, at whose request it has been written,[3] or in the smallest degree promotes the interests of humanity, the ends for which it was undertaken will be fully attained, and every wish of my heart gratified. Let it therefore be remembered, that, in wishing to avoid censure, I do not aspire to praise.

That part of Africa, known by the name of Guinea, to which the trade for slaves is carried on, extends along the coast above 3400 miles, from Senegal to Angola, and includes a variety of kingdoms. Of these the most considerable is the kingdom of Benin, both as to extent and wealth, the richness and cultivation of the soil, the power of its king, and the number and warlike disposition of the inhabitants. It is situated nearly under the line, and extends along the coast about 170 miles, but runs back into the interior part of Africa to a distance hitherto[4] I believe unexplored by any traveler; and seems only terminated at length by the empire of Abyssinia, near 1500 miles from its beginning. This kingdom is divided into many provinces or districts: in one of the most remote and fertile of which, called Eboe, I was born, in the year 1745, in a charming fruitful vale,[5] named Essaka. The distance of the province from the capital of Benin and the sea coast must be very considerable; for I had never heard of white men or Europeans, nor of the sea: and our subjection to the king of Benin was little more than nominal; for every transaction of the government, as far as my slender observation extended, was conducted by the chiefs or elders of the place. The manners and government of a people who have little commerce with other countries are generally very simple; and the history of what passes in one family or village may serve as a specimen of a nation. My father was one of those elders or chiefs I have spoken of, and was styled Embrenche; a term, as I remember, importing the highest distinction, and signifying in our language a mark of grandeur.[6] This mark is conferred on the person entitled to it, by cutting the skin across at the top of the forehead, and drawing it down to the eye-brows; and while it is in this situation applying a warm hand, and rubbing it until it shrinks up into a thick weal[7] across the lower part of the forehead. Most of the judges and senators were thus marked; my father had long borne it: I had seen it conferred on one of my brothers, and I was also destined to receive it by my parents. Those Embrenche, or chief men, decided disputes and punished crimes; for which purpose they always assembled together. The proceedings were generally short; and in most cases the law of retaliation prevailed. I remember a man was brought before my father, and the other judges, for kidnapping a boy; and, although he was the son of a chief or senator, he was condemned to make recompense by a man or woman slave. Adultery, however, was sometimes punished with slavery or death; a punishment which I believe is inflicted on it throughout most of the nations of Africa: so sacred among them is the honour of the marriage bed, and so jealous are they of the fidelity of their wives. Of this I recollect an instance: —a woman was convicted before

Who was in charge of day-to-day legal and commercial affairs in the kingdom?

Was Equiano's father an important man?

---

[3] **at whose . . . written.** Equiano raised money for publishing his autobiography by selling advance or subscription-only copies to friends and supporters.

[4] **hitherto.** Until now, up to this point

[5] **fruitful vale.** A fertile river valley

[6] **grandeur.** Magnificence, majesty

[7] **weal.** A welt or raised lump

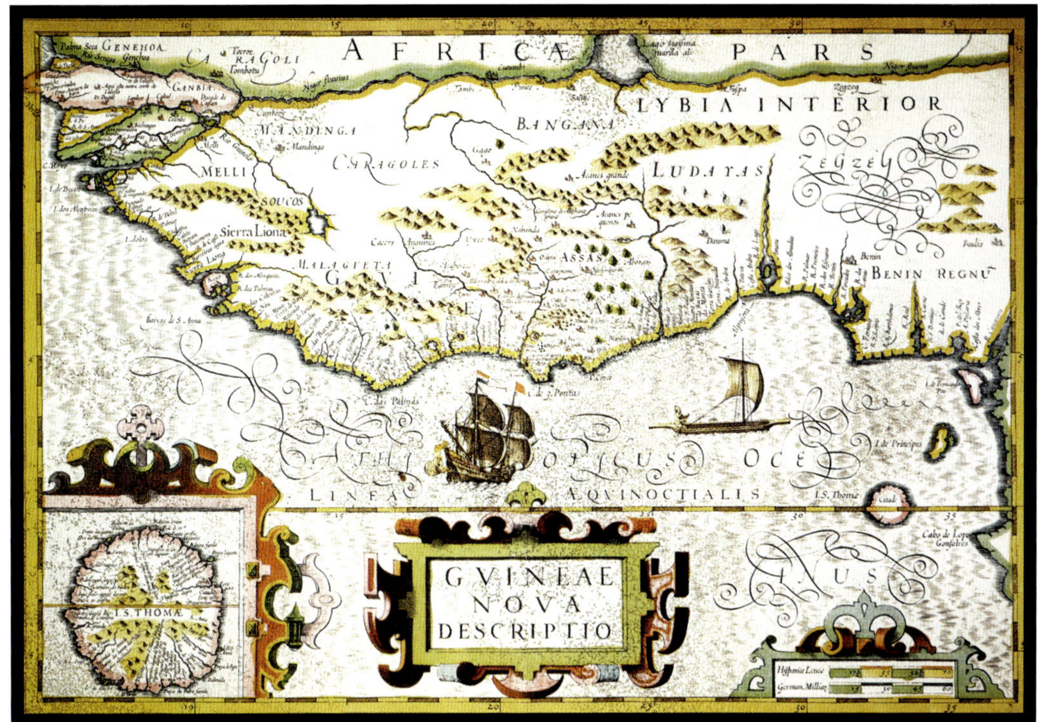

West African map, 1606. Jodocus Hondius's 1606 map of the West African coast from Senegal to Cape Lopez on the Gulf of Guinea.

the judges of adultery, and delivered over, as the custom was, to her husband to be punished. Accordingly he determined to put her to death: but it being found, just before her execution, that she had an infant at her breast; and no woman being **prevailed** on to perform the part of a nurse, she was spared on account of the child. The men, however, do not preserve the same constancy to their wives, which they expect from them; for they indulge in a plurality, though seldom in more than two. Their mode of marriage is thus: —both parties are usually **betrothed** when young by their parents, (though I have known the males to betroth themselves). On this occasion a feast is prepared, and the bride and bridegroom stand up in the midst of all their friends, who are assembled for the purpose, while he declares she is thenceforth to be looked upon as his wife, and that no other person is to pay any addresses to her. This is also immediately proclaimed in the **vicinity,** on which the bride retires from the assembly. Some time after she is brought home to her husband, and then another feast is made, to which the relations of both parties are invited: her parents then deliver her to the bridegroom, accompanied with a number of blessings, and at the same time they tie round her waist a cotton string of the thickness of a goose-quill, which none but married women are permitted to wear: she is now considered as completely his wife; and at this time the **dowry** is given to the new married pair, which generally consists of portions of land, slaves, and cattle, household goods, and implements of husbandry. These are offered by the friends of both parties; besides which

VOCABULARY IN PLACE

- **prevail,** *v.* To persuade someone to do something
- **betroth,** *v.* To promise to marry or give in marriage
- **vicinity,** *n.* Immediately adjacent area, nearby place
- **dowry,** *n.* Money or property brought by a bride to her marriage

the parents of the bridegroom present gifts to those of the bride, whose property she is looked upon before marriage; but after it she is esteemed the sole property of her husband. The ceremony being now ended the festival begins, which is celebrated with bonfires, and loud acclamations of joy, accompanied by music and dancing.

We are almost a nation of dancers, musicians, and poets. Thus every great event, such as a triumphant return from battle, or other cause of public rejoicing, is celebrated in public dances, which are accompanied with songs and music suited to the occasion. The assembly is separated into four divisions, which dance either apart or in succession, and each with a character peculiar to itself. The first division contains the married men, who in their dances frequently exhibit feats of arms, and the representation of a battle. To these succeed the married women, who dance in the second division. The young men occupy the third; and the maidens the fourth. Each represents some interesting scene of real life, such as a great achievement, domestic employment, a pathetic story, or some rural sport; and as the subject is generally founded on some recent event, it is therefore ever new. This gives our dances a spirit and variety which I have scarcely seen elsewhere.[8] We have many musical instruments, particularly drums of different kinds, a piece of music which resembles a guitar, and another much like a stickado.[9] These last are chiefly used by betrothed virgins, who play on them on all grand festivals.

What did the people of Guinea do to mark important events?

As our manners are simple, our luxuries are few. The dress of both sexes is nearly the same. It generally consists of a long piece of calico, or muslin,[10] wrapped loosely round the body, somewhat in the form of a highland plaid. This is usually dyed blue, which is our favourite colour. It is extracted from a berry, and is brighter and richer than any I have seen in Europe. Besides this, our women of distinction wear golden ornaments; which they **dispose** with some **profusion** on their arms and legs. When our women are not employed with the men in **tillage,** their usual occupation is spinning and weaving cotton, which they afterwards dye and make it into garments. They also manufacture earthen vessels, of which we have many kinds. Among the rest tobacco pipes, made after the same fashion, and used in the same manner, as those in Turkey.

Our manner of living is entirely plain; for as yet the natives are unacquainted with those refinements in cookery which debauch[11] the taste: bullocks, goats, and poultry supply the greatest part of their food. These constitute likewise the principal wealth of the country, and the chief articles of its commerce. The flesh is

Were people in Guinea accustomed to luxury? What were the country's most valuable resources?

---

8 **scarcely seen elsewhere.** [This footnote appeared in Equiano's original text.] When I was in Smyrna I have frequently seen the Greeks dance after this manner.

9 **stickado.** A reference to the Italian instrument *sticcado pastorale,* which is similar to a xylophone

10 **calico, or muslin.** A coarse, colorful cotton fabric

11 **debauch.** Corrupt or ruin

VOCABULARY IN PLACE

- **dispose,** *v.* To arrange
- **profusion,** *n.* Abundance or extravagance
- **tillage,** *n.* The cultivation of land

usually stewed in a pan; to make it savoury we sometimes use also pepper, and other spices, and we have salt made of wood ashes. Our vegetables are mostly plantains, eadas, yams, beans, and Indian corn. The head of the family usually eats alone; his wives and slaves have also their separate tables. Before we taste food we always wash our hands: indeed our cleanliness on all occasions is extreme; but on this it is an indispensable ceremony. After washing, libation[12] is made, by pouring out a small portion of the food, in a certain place, for the spirits of departed relations, which the natives suppose to preside over their conduct, and guard them from evil. They are totally unacquainted with strong or spirituous liquours; and their principal beverage is palm wine. This is gotten from a tree of that name by tapping it at the top, and fastening a large gourd to it; and sometimes one tree will yield three or four gallons in a night. When just drawn it is of a most delicious sweetness; but in a few days it acquires a tartish and more spirituous flavour: though I never saw any one intoxicated by it. The same tree also produces nuts and oil. Our principal luxury is in perfumes; one sort of these is an odoriferous wood of delicious fragrance: the other a kind of earth; a small portion of which thrown into the fire diffuses a most powerful odour.[13] We beat this wood into powder, and mix it with palm oil; with which both men and women perfume themselves.

In our buildings we study convenience rather than ornament. Each master of a family has a large square piece of ground, surrounded with a moat or fence, or enclosed with a wall made of red earth tempered; which, when dry, is as hard as brick. Within this are his houses to accommodate his family and slaves; which, if numerous, frequently present the appearance of a village. In the middle stands the principal building, appropriated to the sole use of the master, and consisting of two apartments; in one of which he sits in the day with his family, the other is left apart for the reception of his friends. He has besides these a distinct apartment in which he sleeps, together with his male children. On each side are the apartments of his wives, who have also their separated day and night houses. The habitations of the slaves and their families are distributed throughout the rest of the enclosure. These houses never exceed one story in height: they are always built of wood, or stakes driven into the ground, crossed with wattles,[14] and neatly plastered within, and without. The roof is thatched with reeds. Our day-houses are left open at the sides; but those in which we sleep are always covered, and plastered in the inside, with a composition mixed with cow-dung, to keep off the different insects, which annoy us during the night. The walls and floors also of these are generally covered with mats. Our beds consist of a platform, raised three or four feet from the ground, on which are laid skins, and different parts of a spongy tree called plaintain. Our covering is calico or muslin, the same as our dress. The usual seats are a few logs of wood; but we have benches, which are generally perfumed, to accommodate strangers: these compose the greater part of our household furniture. Houses so constructed and furnished require

Were their buildings decorated in order to show off their wealth?

[12] **libation.** The pouring of a liquid as part of a religious ritual

[13] **powerful odour.** [This footnote appeared in Equiano's original text.] When I was in Smyrna I saw the same kind of Earth, and brought some of it with me to England; it resembles musk in strength, but is more delicious in scent, and is not unlike the smell of a rose.

[14] **wattles.** Sticks or reeds

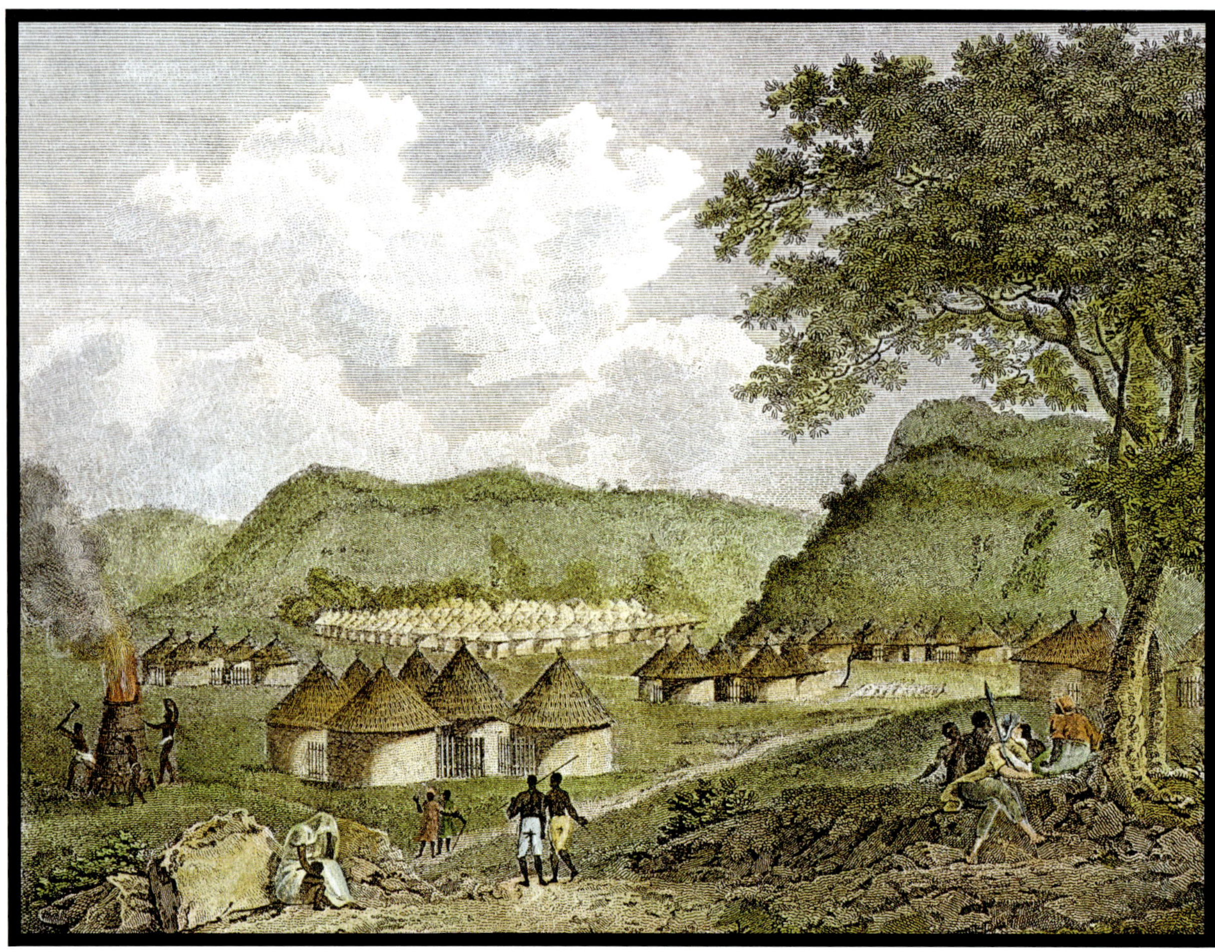

View of Kamalia, West Africa, 1799.

but little skill to erect them. Every man is a sufficient architect for the purpose. The whole neighbourhood afford their unanimous assistance in building them and in return receive, and expect no other recompense than a feast.

As we live in a country where nature is prodigal[15] of her favours, our wants are few and easily supplied; of course we have few manufactures. They consist for the most part of calicoes, earthen ware, ornaments, and instruments of war and **husbandry.** But these make no part of our commerce, the principal articles of which, as I have observed, are provisions. In such a state money is of little use; however we have some small pieces of coin, if I may call them such. They are made something like an anchor; but I do not remember either their value or denomination. We have also markets, at which I have been frequently with my mother. These are sometimes visited by stout mahogany-coloured men from the south west of us: we call them Oye-Eboe, which term signifies red men living at a distance. They generally bring us fire-arms, gunpowder, hats, beads,

[15] **prodigal.** Extravagant; very generous

VOCABULARY IN PLACE

- **husbandry,** *n.* The practice or act of breeding and raising livestock

and dried fish. The last we esteemed a great rarity, as our waters were only brooks and springs. These articles they barter with us for odoriferous woods and earth and our salt of wood ashes. They always carry slaves through our land; but the strictest account is exacted of their manner of **procuring** them before they are suffered to pass. Sometimes indeed we sold slaves to them, but they were only prisoners of war, or such among us as had been convicted of kidnapping, or adultery, and some other crimes, which we esteemed **heinous.** This practice of kidnapping induces me to think, that, notwithstanding all our strictness, their principal business among us was to trepan[16] our people. I remember too they carried great sacks along with them, which not long after I had an opportunity of fatally seeing applied to that infamous purpose.

Did Equiano's people care where the Oye-Eboe had procured their slaves? What did the Oye-Eboe want to do to Equiano's people?

Our land is uncommonly rich and fruitful, and produces all kinds of vegetables in great abundance. We have plenty of Indian corn, and vast quantities of cotton and tobacco.[17] Our pineapples grow without culture; they are about the size of the largest sugar-loaf, and finely flavoured. We have also spices of different kinds, particularly pepper; and a variety of delicious fruits which I have never seen in Europe; together with gums of various kinds and honey in abundance. All our industry is exerted to improve those blessings of nature. Agriculture is our chief employment; and every one, even the children and women, are engaged in it. Thus we are all **habituated** to labour from our earliest years. Every one contributes something to the common stock; and as we are unacquainted with **idleness,** we have no beggars. The benefits of such a mode of living are obvious. The West India planters[18] prefer the slaves of Benin or Eboe to those of any other part of Guinea, for their hardiness, intelligence, integrity, and zeal. Those benefits are felt by us in the general healthiness of the people, and in their vigour and activity; I might have added too in their **comeliness.** Deformity is indeed unknown amongst us, I mean that of shape. Numbers of the natives of Eboe now in London might be brought in support of this assertion: for, in regard to complexion, ideas of beauty are wholly relative. I remember while in Africa to have seen three negro children, who were tawny,[19] and another quite white, who were universally regarded by myself, and the natives in general, as far as related to their complexions, as deformed. Our women too were in my eyes at least uncommonly graceful, alert, and modest to a degree of bashfulness; nor do I remember to have ever heard of an instance of **incontinence** amongst them before marriage.

Why did plantation owners prefer enslaved workers from Benin or Eboe?

16 **trepan.** Ensnare, trap, trick

17 **Indian corn . . . cotton and tobacco.** All of these goods originated in the Americas, which means that Guineans traded for and transplanted New World plants.

18 **West India planters.** Plantation owners in the West Indies, or the islands of the Caribbean

19 **tawny.** Brownish-orange to light brown

VOCABULARY IN PLACE

- **procure,** ***v.*** To obtain or acquire
- **heinous,** ***adj.*** Shockingly evil; abominable
- **habituated,** ***past part.*** Accustomed to
- **idleness,** ***n.*** Laziness
- **comeliness,** ***n.*** Attractiveness
- **incontinence,** ***n.*** The act of being unfaithful or unchaste; lack of restraint

They are also remarkably cheerful. Indeed cheerfulness and **affability** are two of the leading characteristics of our nation.

Our tillage is exercised in a large plain or common, some hours walk from our dwellings, and all the neighbours resort thither in a body. They use no beasts of husbandry; and their only instruments are hoes, axes, shovels, and beaks, or pointed iron to dig with. Sometimes we are visited by locusts, which come in large clouds, so as to darken the air, and destroy our harvest. This however happens rarely, but when it does, a famine is produced by it. I remember an instance or two wherein this happened. This common is often the theatre of war; and therefore when our people go out to till their land, they not only go in a body, but generally take arms with them for fear of a surprise; and when they apprehend an invasion they guard the avenues to their dwellings, by driving sticks into the ground, which are so sharp at one end as to pierce the foot, and are generally dipt[20] in poison. From what I can recollect of these battles, they appear to have been irruptions of one little state or district on the other, to obtain prisoners or booty.[21] Perhaps they are incited to this by those traders who brought the European goods I mentioned amongst us. Such a mode of obtaining slaves in Africa is common; and I believe more are procured this way, and by kidnapping, than any other. When a trader wants slaves, he applies to a chief for them, and tempts him with his wares. It is not extraordinary, if on this occasion he yields to the temptation with as little firmness, and accepts the price of his fellow creature's liberty with as little reluctance as the enlightened merchant. Accordingly he falls on his neighbours, and a desperate battle ensues. If he prevails and takes prisoners, he gratifies his **avarice** by selling them; but, if his party be vanquished, and he falls into the hands of the enemy, he is put to death: for, as he had been known to **foment** their quarrels, it is thought dangerous to let him survive, and no ransom can save him, though all other prisoners may be redeemed. We have firearms, bows and arrows, broad two edged swords and javelins: we have shields also which cover a man from head to foot. All are taught the use of these weapons; even our women are warriors, and march boldly out to fight along with the men. Our whole district is a kind of militia: on a certain signal given, such as the firing of a gun at night, they all rise in arms and rush upon their enemy. It is perhaps something remarkable, that when our people march to the field a red flag or banner is borne before them. I was once a witness to a battle in our common. We had been all at work in it one day as usual, when our people were suddenly attacked. I climbed a tree at some distance, from which I beheld the fight. There were many women as well as men on both sides; among others my mother was there, and armed with a broad sword. After fighting for a considerable time with great fury, and after many had been killed our people obtained the victory, and took their enemy's Chief prisoner. He was carried off in great triumph, and, though he offered a large

What was usually the cause of wars or battles between various groups of people?

Were men the only ones who fought in these wars?

[20] **dipt.** Dipped

[21] **booty.** Treasure gotten by illicit or illegal means

VOCABULARY IN PLACE

- **affability,** *n.* The state of being easy and pleasant to speak to
- **avarice,** *n.* Greed, a great desire for wealth
- **foment,** *v.* To promote the growth of; incite

ransom for his life, he was put to death. A virgin of note among our enemies had been slain in the battle, and her arm was exposed in our market-place, where our trophies were always exhibited. The spoils were divided according to the merit of the warriors. Those prisoners which were not sold or redeemed we kept as slaves: but how different was their condition from that of the slaves in the West Indies! With us they do no more work than other members of the community, even their masters; their food, clothing and lodging were nearly the same as theirs, (except that they were not permitted to eat with those who were free-born): and there was scarce any other difference between them, than a superior degree of importance which the head of a family possesses in our state, and that authority which, as such, he exercises over every part of his household. Some of these slaves have even slaves under them as their own property, and for their own use.

How were conditions for enslaved people in Equiano's community as compared to those of slaves in the West Indies?

As to religion, the natives believe that there is one Creator of all things, and that he lives in the sun, and is girted[22] round with a belt that he may never eat or drink; but, according to some, he smokes a pipe, which is our own favourite luxury. They believe he governs events, especially our deaths or captivity; but, as for the doctrine of eternity, I do not remember to have ever heard of it: some however believe in the transmigration[23] of souls in a certain degree. Those spirits, which are not transmigrated, such as our dear friends or relations, they believe always attend them, and guard them from the bad spirits or their foes. For this reason they always before eating, as I have observed, put some small portion of the meat, and pour some of their drink, on the ground for them; and they often make oblations[24] of the blood of beasts or fowls at their graves. I was very fond of my mother, and almost constantly with her. When she went to make these oblations at her mother's tomb, which was a kind of small solitary thatched house, I sometimes attended her. There she made her libations, and spent most of the night in cries and **lamentations.** I have been often extremely terrified on these occasions. The loneliness of the place, the darkness of the night, and the ceremony of libation, naturally awful and gloomy, were heightened by my mother's lamentations; and these, concurring with the cries of **doleful** birds, by which these places were frequented, gave an inexpressible terror to the scene.

We compute the year from the day on which the sun crosses the line,[25] and on its setting that evening there is a general shout throughout the land; at least I can speak from my own knowledge throughout our vicinity. The people at the same time make a great noise with rattles, not unlike the basket rattles used by children here, though much larger, and hold up their hands to heaven for a blessing. It is then the greatest offerings are made; and those children whom our wise men foretell will be fortunate are then presented to different people. I remember many used to come to

What did they do to celebrate the start of a new year?

22 **girted.** Encircled

23 **transmigration.** Passage into another body after death

24 **oblations.** Offerings

25 **sun crosses the line.** Probably the summer solstice, when the sun is farthest from the equator

VOCABULARY IN PLACE

- **lamentations,** ***n. pl.*** Sounds of grief or mourning, wails or cries expressing great sorrow
- **doleful,** ***adj.*** Full of grief, sad

see me, and I was carried about to others for that purpose. They have many offerings, particularly at full moons; generally two at harvest before the fruits are taken out of the ground: and when any young animals are killed, sometimes they offer up part of them as a sacrifice. These offerings, when made by one of the heads of a family, serve for the whole. I remember we often had them at my father's and my uncle's, and their families have been present. Some of our offerings are eaten with bitter herbs. We had a saying among us to any one of a cross temper, "That if they were to be eaten, they should be eaten with bitter herbs."

We practiced circumcision like the Jews, and made offerings and feasts on that occasion in the same manner as they did. Like them also, our children were named from some event, some circumstance, or fancied foreboding[26] at the time of their birth. I was named Olaudah, which, in our language, signifies **vicissitude** or fortune also; one favoured, and having a loud voice and well spoken.

What did the name Olaudah *mean?*

I remember we never polluted the name of the object of our adoration; on the contrary, it was always mentioned with the greatest reverence; and we were totally unacquainted with swearing, and all those terms of abuse and **reproach** which find their way so readily and **copiously** into the languages of more civilized people. The only expressions of that kind I remember were "May you rot, or may you swell, or may a beast take you."

I have before remarked that the natives of this part of Africa are extremely cleanly. This necessary habit of decency was with us a part of religion, and therefore we had many purifications and washings; indeed almost as many, and used on the same occasions, if my recollection does not fail me, as the Jews. Those that touched the dead at any time were obliged to wash and purify themselves before they could enter a dwelling-house. Every woman too, at certain times, was forbidden to come into a dwelling-house, or touch any person, or any thing we ate. I was so fond of my mother I could not keep from her, or avoid touching her at some of those periods, in consequence of which I was obliged to be kept out with her, in a little house made for that purpose, till offering was made, and then we were purified.

In what way was cleanliness "a part of religion"?

Though we had no places of public worship, we had priests and magicians, or wise men. I do not remember whether they had different offices, or whether they were united in the same persons, but they were held in great reverence by the people. They calculated our time, and foretold events, as their name imported, for we called them *Ah-affoe-way-cah,* which signifies calculators or yearly men, our year being called *Ah-affoe.* They wore their beards, and when they died they were succeeded by their sons. Most of their implements and things of value were **interred** along with them. Pipes and tobacco were also put into the grave with the corpse, which was always perfumed and ornamented, and animals were offered in sacrifice to them. None accompanied their funerals but those

26 **fancied foreboding.** A vision of the future. *Foreboding* generally refers to a vision of impending evil.

VOCABULARY IN PLACE

- **vicissitude,** ***n.*** A sudden or unexpected change in life
- **reproach,** ***n.*** Criticism, disapproval
- **copiously,** ***adv.*** Plentifully
- **interred,** ***past part.*** Placed in a grave or tomb; buried

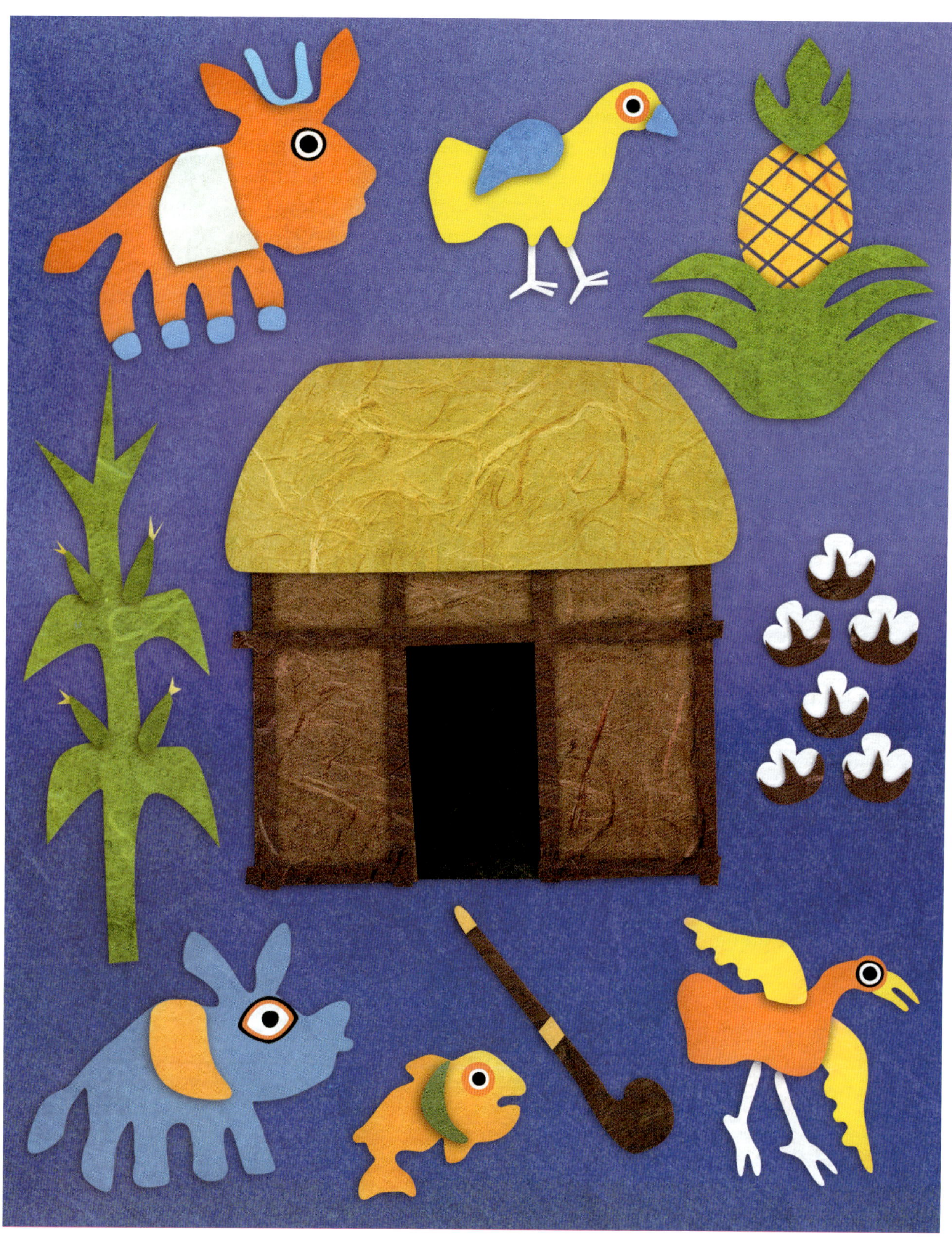

of the same profession or tribe. These buried them after sunset, and always returned from the grave by a different way from that which they went.

These magicians were also our doctors or physicians. They practiced bleeding by cupping;[27] and were very successful in healing wounds and expelling poisons. They had likewise some extraordinary method of discovering jealousy, theft, and poisoning; the success of which no doubt they derived from their unbounded influence over the **credulity** and superstition of the people. I do not remember what those methods were, except that as to poisoning: I recollect an instance or two, which I hope it will not be deemed **impertinent** here to insert, as it may serve as a kind of specimen of the rest, and is still used by the negroes in the West Indies. A virgin had been poisoned, but it was not known by whom; the doctors ordered the corpse to be taken up by some persons, and carried to the grave. As soon as the bearers had raised it on their shoulders, they seemed seized with some sudden impulse, and ran to and fro unable to stop themselves. At last, after having passed through a number of thorns and prickly bushes unhurt, the corpse fell from them close to a house, and defaced it in the fall; and, the owner being taken up, he immediately confessed the poisoning.

To what did Equiano attribute the doctors' success in discovering jealously and solving crimes?

The natives are extremely cautious about poison. When they buy any eatable the seller kisses it all round before the buyer, to shew him it is not poisoned; and the same is done when any meat or drink is presented, particularly to a stranger. We have serpents of different kinds, some of which are esteemed **ominous** when they appear in our houses, and these we never molest. I remember two of those ominous snakes, each of which was as thick as the calf of a man's leg, and in colour resembling a dolphin in the water, crept at different times into my mother's night-house, where I always lay with her, and coiled themselves into folds, and each time they crowed like a cock. I was desired by some of our wise men to touch these, that I might be interested in the good omens, which I did, for they were quite harmless, and would tamely suffer themselves to be handled; and then they were put into a large open earthen pan, and set to one side of the highway. Some of our snakes, however, were poisonous: one of them crossed the road one day when I was standing on it, and passed between my feet without offering to touch me, to the great surprise of many who saw it; and these incidents were accounted by the wise men, and therefore by my mother and the rest of the people, as remarkable omens in my favour.

Such is the imperfect sketch my memory has furnished me with of the manners and customs of a people among whom I first drew my breath.

[Editor's note: At this point Equiano draws a comparison between "the manners and customs of my countrymen and those of the

[27] **cupping.** A treatment in which glass cups are applied to the skin in order to draw blood toward or through the surface

VOCABULARY IN PLACE

- **credulity,** ***n.*** The tendency to believe too readily; gullibility
- **impertinent,** ***adj.*** Exceeding the limits of good manners
- **ominous,** ***adj.*** Foreshadowing evil

Jews, before they reached the Land of Promise, and particularly the patriarchs while they were yet in the pastoral state which is described in Genesis." This kind of analogy with the release of Israel from bondage became a common theme of African-American literature, particularly in the slave narratives and spiritual songs. Equiano went so far as to suggest that his people may have been originally Hebrew. He drew this conclusion based on the many cultural similarities between the two peoples; he also cites several scholars from the eighteenth century who made the same argument. Equiano goes on to point out that the color of a person's skin is simply the result of natural processes, as was shown (according to Equiano) by the fact that the skin complexions of Spanish settlers in the New World darkened over time.]

These instances, and a great many more which might be **adduced,** while they shew how the complexions of the same persons vary in different climates, it is hoped may tend also to remove the prejudice that some conceive against the natives of Africa on account of their colour. Surely the minds of the Spaniards did not change with their complexions! Are there not cases enough to which the apparent inferiority of an African may be **ascribed,** without limiting the goodness of God, and supposing he forbore to stamp understanding on certainly his own image, because "carved in ebony." Might it not naturally be ascribed to their situation? When they come among Europeans, they are ignorant of their language, religion, manners, and customs. Are any pains taken to teach them these? Are they treated as men? Does not slavery itself depress the mind, and extinguish all its fire and every noble sentiment? But, above all, what advantages do not a refined people possess over those who are rude and uncultivated. Let the polished and **haughty** European recollect that his ancestors were once, like the Africans, uncivilized, and even barbarous. Did Nature make them inferior to their sons? And should they too have been made slaves? Every rational mind answers, No. Let such reflections as these melt the pride of their superiority into sympathy for the wants and miseries of their **sable** brethren, and compel them to acknowledge, that understanding is not confined to feature or colour. If, when they look round the world, they feel **exultation,** let it be tempered with **benevolence** to others, and gratitude to God, "who hath made of one blood all nations of men for to dwell on all the face of the earth;and whose wisdom is not our wisdom, neither are our ways his ways."[28]

What did Equiano hope to prove with regard to prejudice against skin color?

What is Equiano's main point here?

[28] **who hath . . . earth.** The first part of this quotation is a reference to the Bible, Acts 17:26. The second part is a paraphrase of Isaiah 55:8.

VOCABULARY IN PLACE

- **adduce,** *v.* To give as an example or proof
- **ascribe,** *v.* To attribute to a specified cause
- **haughty,** *adj.* Scornfully or condescendingly proud
- **sable,** *adj.* Dark, black
- **exultation,** *n.* Great joy
- **benevolence,** *n.* Kindness, generosity

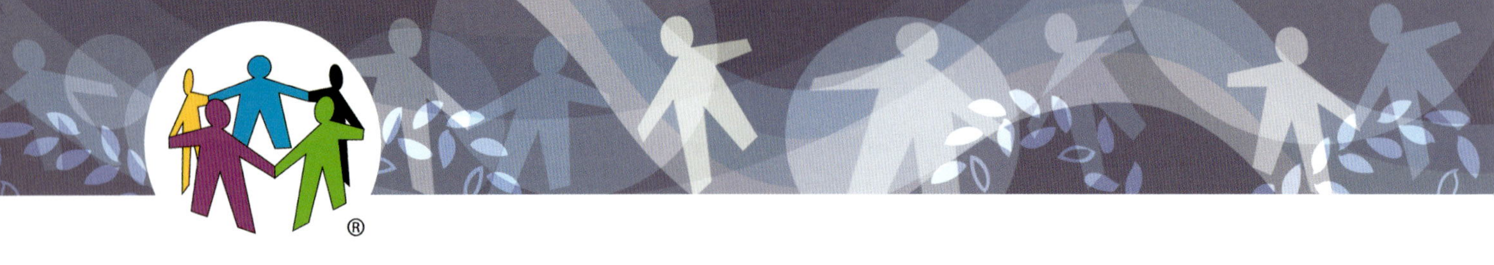

Understanding the Selection

Recalling

1. In what kingdom did Equiano say he was born?
2. What special term was used to refer to Equiano's father? What special mark did a person who was so called also receive?
3. Into what groups were the dancers at public events divided? What kinds of things did the dances usually represent?
4. Into what parts was the principal building belonging to the master of a family divided? What were the purposes of these apartments?
5. From what part of the world, according to Equiano, did the West Indian planters like to get their slaves?

Interpreting

▶ 1. Why was Equiano unfamiliar with white men, Europeans, and the sea?

▶ 2. What did the special term mean? Of what class of men was Equiano's father?

▶ 3. What, according to Equiano, kept the dances "ever new"?

▶ 4. How did the organization of the family compound reflect the status of the people living in the family?

▶ 5. What made people from this part of the world so valuable to slave owners?

Synthesizing

1. Who, according to Equiano, was made in "certainly his [God's] own image"?
2. At the time when Equiano's book was written, some racist white Europeans believed that only Europeans were civilized and that other races were "savages." What proofs does Equiano offer of a high degree of civilization among his people?

Delving Deeper

Understanding Literature

Autobiography and Cultural Studies. As you know, an **autobiography** is the story of a person's life, as told by that person. By reading an autobiography, you can extend the range of your experience. In other words, you can imagine what it would be like to experience things that haven't happened to you personally.

A **culture** is the sum of all the things that people create and pass down from one generation to another, including homes, ways of finding and preparing food, beliefs, stories, proverbs, and social hierarchies and relationships. Reading an autobiography by someone from a very different, foreign culture can be particularly interesting because much of that culture will be new to you, and thinking about the differences between your culture and that of the autobiographer can be revealing. Look back over this selection and make a list of ten ways in which the culture of the West African Ibo people described by Equiano is different from the culture in which you live.

About the Author

Olaudah Equiano (circa 1745–1797) became famous for his autobiography, an account of an extraordinary life full of difficulties, successes, and astonishing adventures. According to his account, he was born among the Ibo people in what is today Nigeria. In his autobiography he described how he and his sister were kidnapped when he was eleven years old and how he endured the notorious "Middle Passage" and was transported to the West Indies. There he was purchased and enslaved by a British naval officer, Michael Pascal, who renamed him Gustavus Vassa.

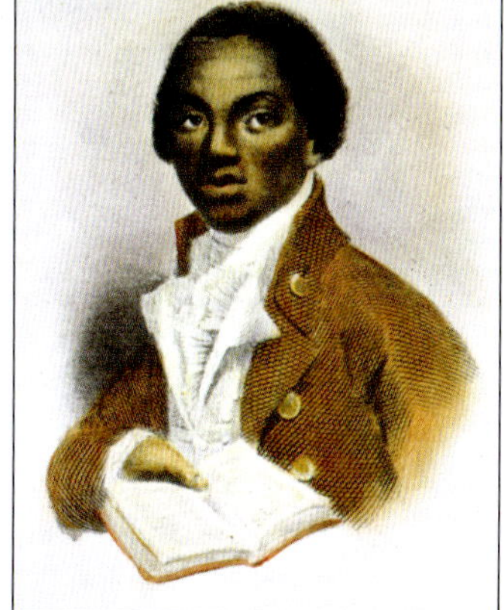

During the Seven Years War, Equiano served as a seaman on ships in Canada and in the Mediterranean and participated in several naval battles. Pascal took him to England, where he learned to read and write and became a Christian. In 1763, he was sold to an American Quaker merchant. He worked for this man as a seaman and trader and was able to buy his own freedom in 1766. In his later life, he worked as an Abolitionist. His autobiography, published in 1789 in Great Britain, became an enormous success and was translated into many languages.

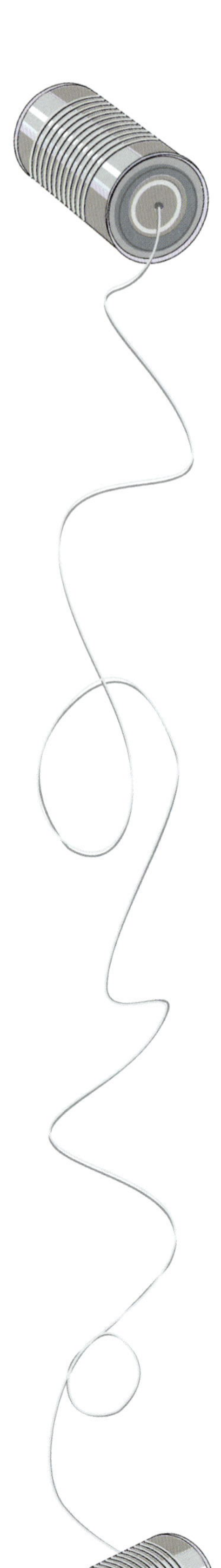

Unit 1

Speaking and Listening Skills: Guidelines for Discussion

The Communications Triangle. Every act of communication involves certain parts that can be seen clearly in a diagram known as the **communications triangle.** Here's one version of that diagram:

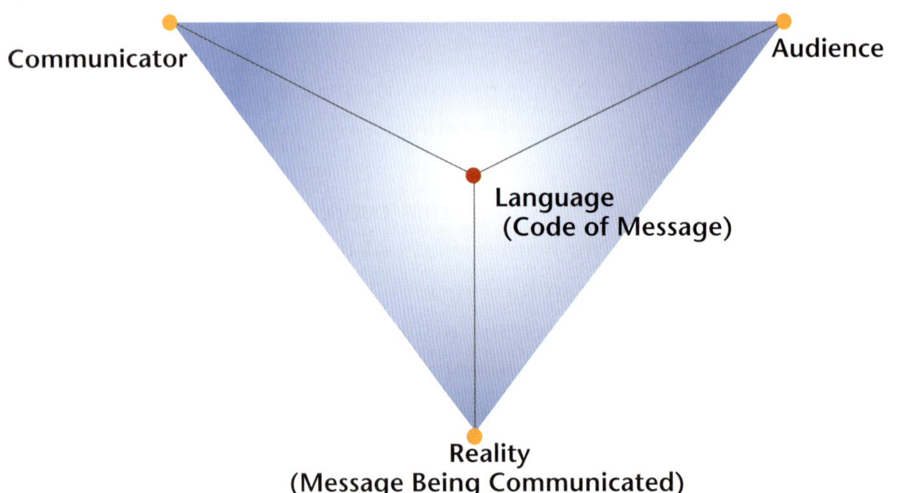

So, for example, when a ship blows a horn to signal its presence, the communicator is the captain of the ship. The audience is other ships or boats in the vicinity. The reality, or message being communicated, is "I'm here." And the code of the message is the sound of the horn. Any communications situation, from a radio address by the president to a love note written in skywriting by an airplane, can be analyzed in terms of the communications triangle.

Communications problems can arise because of problems between any of the parts of this triangle. For example, miscommunication can happen when a speaker uses language that doesn't properly describe the reality. So, for example, suppose that the largest forest fire in history were occurring in the western United States and that a federal official were to refer to the fire as "our little problem out West." This would be miscommunication because such language understates the situation and so does not correspond to the reality. If a speaker assumes background knowledge that the audience doesn't have, that, too, can cause miscommunication. If the audience is not familiar with the reality, that can cause misunderstanding and puts the burden on the speaker to explain what the reality is. Communication can also fail if the message cannot be heard by the audience because the channel along which it travels is too noisy or because the message is not loud enough or forceful enough to be heard. Thinking about the ways in which communication can break down between the parts of the communications triangle can help you to improve your ability to communicate well in any situation, from classroom discussion to public speaking.

Discussion is the art of talking about a subject with others in such a way as to learn from one another. It's a standard part of many human interactions, in classrooms, for example, and in businesses, and in meetings at all levels of government, from those of the local school board to those that take place in the United Nations.

It's one thing to hold a discussion. It's another thing altogether to hold a great discussion—one that is interesting and valuable for all involved. Here are some general guidelines to follow when moderating or participating in a discussion:

1. **Stick to the topic.** Make sure that the topic or subject of discussion is clearly articulated at the beginning. For some discussions, it is a good idea to make up an **agenda** beforehand—a list of the topics to be discussed.

2. **Be respectful and pay attention when others are speaking.** Look at the speaker and show by your body language and facial expressions that you are interested in what is being said. It's a good idea to take notes as others are speaking to keep track of the main points being made. If you don't agree with what someone else has said, remain respectful and avoid attacking the person. State your differing opinion, but do so with tact and without excessive emotionalism in your voice.

3. **Wait your turn to speak.** If you wish to speak, put your hand up and wait for the moderator of the discussion to call on you. You may want to make notes to yourself about what you want to say when your turn to speak comes.

4. **Make use of Rogerian listening.** Carl Rogers was a psychologist who taught a superb way to facilitate communication between speakers. When one speaker wants to respond to what a previous speaker has said, he or she begins by repeating, in other words, what was said by that previous speaker. So, for example, a speaker might begin his or her response by saying, "What I heard Sally say was that. . . . Did I get what you were saying, Sally?" The speaker would then give Sally a chance to respond and only then say what he or she has to say.

5. **Participate actively in the discussion.** Don't simply sit and listen. Take part. If you don't have anything of your own to add to the discussion, you can still play a role by reiterating or agreeing with what others have said or by asking questions (see the next point). If you are the moderator of a discussion, try to get participation from the entire group. Don't let one or two people monopolize the conversation.

6. **Ask clarifying questions.** A great way to keep a discussion moving forward is to ask questions to clarify what other speakers have said. So, for example, one might ask speakers to define terms that they have used or to elaborate on points that they have made or to provide supporting evidence.

7. **Sum up what has been said.** At the end of the discussion, the moderator, or someone called upon to do so by the moderator, should summarize the discussion. If the discussion is about some plan of action to be undertaken, then the summary should describe exactly what those actions will be and who is going to do them.

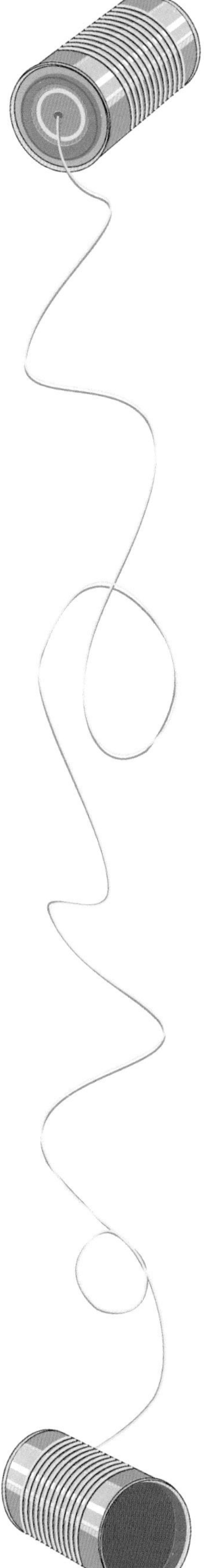

Assignment: Choose one of the following topics for a small group discussion:

Equiano's description of life in an Ibo village and how that life differs from life in the United States today

The question of whether reparations should be paid to the descendants of enslaved persons

The role of orature (proverbs, stories, jokes, nursery rhymes, campfire stories, family histories, bedtime stories, sermons, and so on) in contemporary culture. Is orature a dead form today? What examples of orature are still to be found in society today?

As a group, choose one student to serve as a moderator of the discussion. Have that student work up some questions to pose to the group, and have all the members of the group prepare for the discussion by doing some personal research beforehand. Then, hold the discussion in class and try to follow the guidelines for discussion described above. The moderator should keep a scorecard and mark pluses and minuses beside each participant's name to indicate when he or she is following or not following the guidelines. For example, a student might get a plus for saying something and so participating in the discussion but a minus for speaking without being called upon. At the end of the discussion, discuss as a group what went well in the discussion and what went badly. Try to come to a consensus about how the discussion could have been improved.

Unit 1 Writing

Critical and Expository Writing

1. **A Paragraph about Proverbial Wisdom.** Choose a proverb from "A Sampling of African Proverbial Wisdom," on page 8. Write a long paragraph on the subject addressed by the proverb. Plan your **paragraph** by first determining what the subject of the proverb is and by **paraphrasing,** or putting into your own words, what the proverb says about that subject. Then, decide whether you agree or disagree with the proverb and why. Come up with **evidence** in the form of examples or brief stories (anecdotes) to support your position. Outline a paragraph to present your point of view. The paragraph should begin by stating the proverb and then an opinion regarding it. The paragraph should then support the opinion expressed.

2. **Collection of Traditional Sayings.** Interview some adults whom you know and ask them to think about and share with you some traditional sayings (otherwise known as **proverbs** or **aphorisms**). When asking adults for these, make sure to give them time to think about the question and to come up with some good ones from their memories. Work with other students in your class to compile a little **booklet of traditional sayings** from your community.

3. **Description of a Rite of Passage.** A **rite of passage** is a ceremony or ritual that is held to mark a major transition in life. Olaudah Equiano describes how dances were often held to mark rites of passage in West Africa. Write an essay in which you describe in detail some rite of passage that occurs in your culture in the United States. For example, you might write about weddings or funerals or the prom or high-school graduation ceremonies or christenings or bar mitzvahs. Write as though you were explaining the ceremony or ritual to someone who knows nothing about it. Use lots of specific detail, and make sure to explain the significance of the items and actions involved in the rite of passage.

Creative Writing

1. **A Praise Poem.** A **praise poem** is a traditional African poem that is written to tell about the accomplishments and characteristics of an exceptional or noteworthy person. Choose someone about whom you would like to write a **praise poem**. Make a list of that person's outstanding qualities, or characteristics. Then come up with a list of **praise names,** or phrases that could be used to describe the person in a laudatory way. You can choose, if you like, to write in free verse, but try to earn some extra credit (and praise) by writing your praise poem in rhymed verse.

2. **Drama.** Rewrite a passage from the *Sunjata,* on page 47, as a **one-scene stage play.** Use stage directions and dialogue. Follow the format of the selection from *A Raisin in the Sun* on page 677. You may want to add a narrator to your list of characters in order to have someone to relate those events that do not translate easily to the stage.

3. **Fable**. A **fable** is a story with animal characters that teaches a moral. "A Tug of War," on page 27, is an example of a fable. Usually, fables confer traditional characteristics on the animals involved. For example, mice are usually meek and furtive. Elephants and owls are wise. Foxes are sly and wise. Snakes are devious and mean, and so on. Write a **fable** in which one of the animals does not live up to these traditional associations. For example, you might write about a snake who turns out to be unexpectedly kind-hearted. Make sure that your fable has a **central conflict,** or struggle, and that it teaches a moral lesson.

Unit 1

Focus on: Traditional African Music

Introduction: A Worldwide Music

The Role of Music in Traditional African Culture

The Rhythmical Complexity of Traditional African Music

The Communal Role of Dance in Traditional African Culture

The Call-and-Response Tradition

Traditional African Instruments

Musical Traditions That Survived the African Diaspora

Focus on: Traditional African Music

Introduction: A Worldwide Music

From Tokyo to Lagos, from Amsterdam to São Paulo, from Reykjavik to Jakarta—almost wherever you go on planet Earth at the dawn of the twenty-first century, you will hear American popular music and its derivatives—local music heavily influenced by American pop. The popular music of America—blues, jazz, rock, R & B, and hip hop in particular—has conquered the world. That much is obvious. What isn't as readily obvious and as widely recognized is the extent to which this music was the creation of African Americans, for as we shall see in the music sections that follow each unit in this book, it was African Americans who gave what is now the world's popular music its distinctive qualities and form.

A mere one hundred and fifty years ago, Americans of African descent barely subsisted. They were beaten and starved and forced to toil from daybreak to well past dusk so that their so-called "masters" could wear fine clothing and sip tea on verandas. They were stripped of their heritage—forced to make new lives without their languages and customs and stories and histories and family ties. They were caricatured and humiliated in minstrel shows. Who would have thought, back then, that today, only a century and a half later, the music created by this once subject people would be heard in clubs in Beijing and St. Petersburg and Ramallah and Buenos Aires? It is an altogether astonishing accomplishment—one of the most astonishing in the history of human culture. And it is a great testament to the human spirit—to the ability of a people to prevail over the worst that can befall them.

When different musical cultures collide and create a new kind of music that blends elements of both, that new music has resulted from a process that musicologists call **fusion.** Visit the continent of Africa today and you will hear, from Algiers in the far north to Cape Town in the far south, the sounds of **Afro-Pop.** This music blends elements of American jazz and rock with traditional African and sometimes Islamic music to produce some of the most exciting sounds that the world has ever heard. And oddly enough, the jazz and rock that came back to Africa to influence the creation of Afro-Pop was itself largely the creation of people of African descent, half a world away. The music left Africa in chains and returned triumphant.

To understand the music of the world in the twenty-first century, you must go back to the roots of that music. And those roots, like the roots of the human race itself, are to be found under African skies.

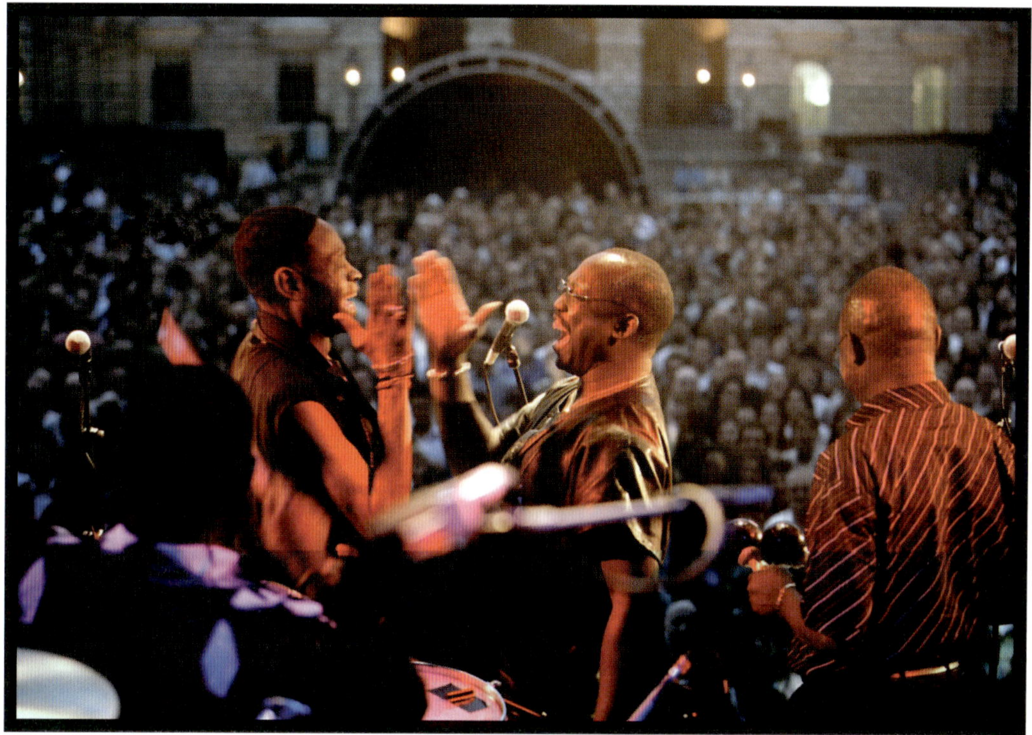

Orchestre Baobab at Live Concert. Popular Afro-Pop band in performance.

The Role of Music in Traditional African Culture

In the United States today, we tend to think of music as a form of recreation and entertainment and not as something created with some specific purpose in mind. Prior to the modern age, however, in traditional cultures like those of Africa, music has generally played a useful role. Lullabies were sung to comfort babies. Proverbs were put to music to teach young children and to train them for adult life. In West Africa, stories were often chanted or spoken by traditional storytellers, or **griots,**[1] accompanied by music played on instruments such as the **kora,** the **balafon,** and the **ngoni.** (See the descriptions of these on page 81.) Typically, the stories told by griots were tribal or family histories and included **praise songs**—songs that presented a series of elaborate names for a person and told about that person's family history, place of origin, accomplishments, and so on. Music was an important part of many rituals and ceremonies. There were wedding songs, hunting songs, war chants, and funeral dirges, to name a few. In most African cultures, music has always been an integral part of life, not something separate, not something merely ornamental.

[1] **griot.** For an example of a traditional story told by a West African griot, see the selection from *Sunjata* on page 47.

Although there is no one unifying musical tradition in a massive continent like Africa, there are some features common to its many cultures that can be found in American music from its very beginnings.

The Rhythmical Complexity of Traditional African Music

The rhythms of sub-Saharan Africa, particularly those of West Africa, can be heard in almost all forms of American popular music, including blues, jazz, and rock 'n' roll. Sub-Saharan African music is characterized by a high level of rhythmic sophistication. Using drums and a variety of other percussion instruments, such as shakers, bells, and rattles, traditional African musicians would often create complex rhythmical patterns known as polyrhythms. A **polyrhythm** occurs when two or more different rhythmical patterns are played simultaneously. For example, one performer might beat a pattern in 2/4 time, while another would beat a pattern in 3/4 time, as follows:

1 / / 2 / / 1 / / 2 / /

1 / 2 / 3 / 1 / 2 / 3 /

Another hallmark of West African music was **syncopation.** Syncopation occurs when normally weak beats (off beats) are accented. Both polyrhythms and syncopation were carried to the New World by enslaved persons and found their way, eventually, into sophisticated modern musical forms such as jazz and bossa nova.

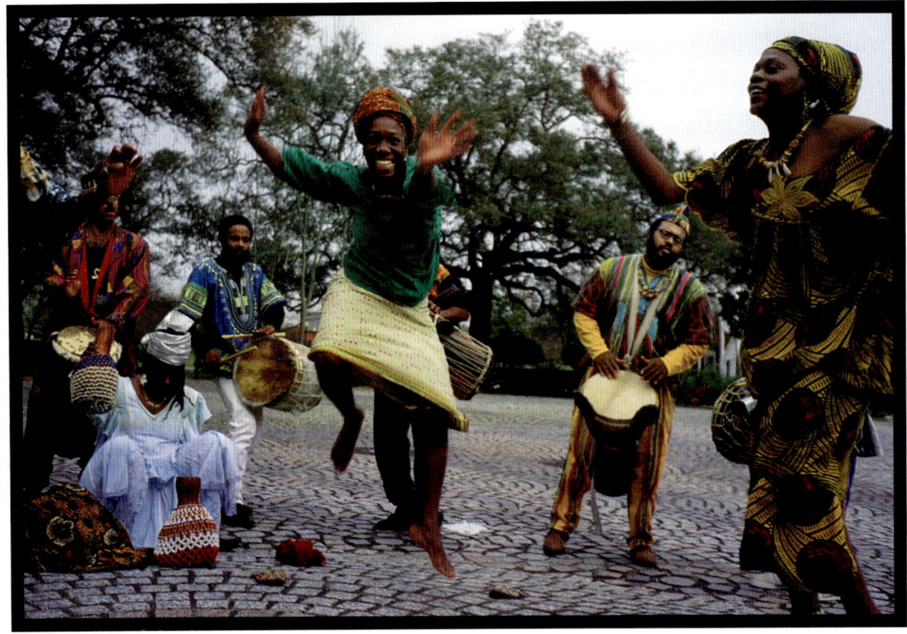

African Dance Group at Congo Square, New Orleans. The musical group Percussion Inc. teaches children about African culture.

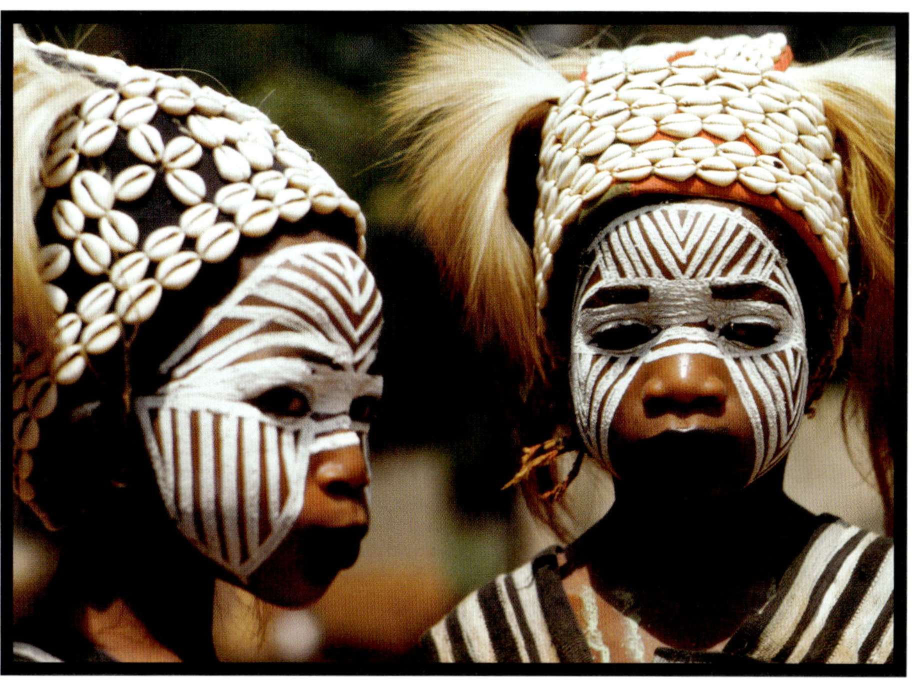

Ivory Coast girls wear ritual dance headdresses.

The Communal Role of Dance in Traditional African Culture

Olaudah Equiano, who was born in Nigeria, captured by slave traders, and transported to the New World, wrote in his autobiography in 1789:

> We are almost a nation of dancers, musicians, and poets. Thus every great event, such as a triumphant return from battle or other cause of public rejoicing, is celebrated in public dances which are accompanied with songs and music suited to the occasion.[2]

As Equiano pointed out, dance played a central role in traditional African community life. The integral relationship between dance and music reflects its communal nature. On most occasions, percussion, in the form of drums, handclapping, and foot stomping, accompanied the movement, providing direction for the dancers through rhythmical phrases. Often, both the musicians and dancers improvised, entering into a sort of conversation of movement and rhythm. Dances were not merely for entertainment, but typically served social purposes. Dances might be performed to celebrate weddings and anniversaries, to train young warriors, to mark important life events such as entry into adulthood, to welcome visitors, to summon spirits, to ward off disease or bad luck, to honor ancestors, or as part of ceremonies held to choose husbands and wives. Some dances were very elaborate, involving, for example, imitation of animals or spirits; costumes,

---

[2] **We are . . . occasion.** For more from Olaudah Equiano's fascinating autobiography, see the selections on pages 55 and 97.

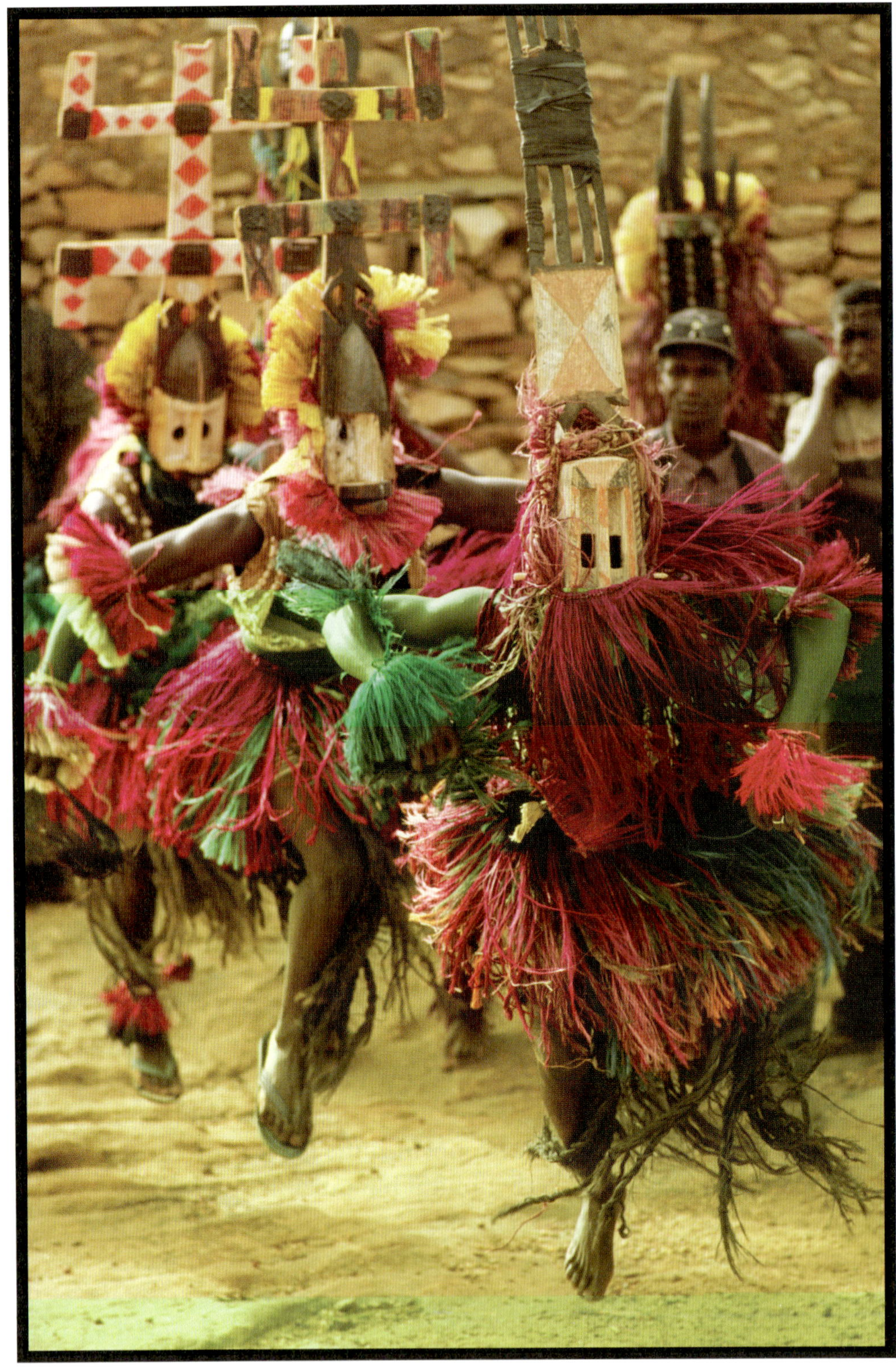

Dama Dancers in Mali. Costumed dancers perform the Dama, a ritual dance to help the deceased cross over to the spirit world.

masks, headdresses, and body paint; traditional body movements, gestures, and facial expressions with symbolic meaning; and multiple rhythms occurring simultaneously. Sometimes dances involved individual performers, but typically they were collective, group efforts, with little separation between performers and audience. Dancers performed various kinds of group movement, for example in circular, linear, serpentine, or columnar formations. Characteristics of West African dance that greatly influenced popular dance styles in the United States include energetic percussiveness; striking the ground with a flat foot; gliding, dragging, or shuffling steps; a crouching stance; a center of motion based on the stomach and hips; a rhythmic, swinging quality; syncopated movement; and **improvisation,** or on-the-spot invention.

The Call-and-Response Tradition

Africans who left their native countries, both as enslaved people and as willing immigrants, brought with them a rich heritage of music and dance that reinforced community. Often, a dance or music leader invited participation by others in a pattern known as **call and response.** The leader or soloist sang or chanted a particular line, and the group or chorus would respond to the leader in unison. West African slaves brought their tradition of call and response with them to the New World, where it influenced African-American religious worship and a wide variety of musical forms. So, for example, in many African-American churches, the minister or choir leader spoke or sang a line, and the congregation or choir responded in unison.

Or, to give another example, in a typical blues lyric, one line (the call) was repeated twice, followed by an answering line (the response):

> Wake up, Mama, turn your lamp down low,
> Wake up, Mama, turn your lamp down low,
> Have you got the nerve to drive
> Papa McTell from your do'?

Traditional African Instruments

It would be impossible in any brief survey to give a full account of the richness and variety of traditional African instruments. Africans showed remarkable ingenuity in using materials found in nature to create percussion, string, and wind instruments. Here is a small sample of the richness of African instrumentation:

The **djembe** is a popular West African drum, with a head of animal hide, a wooden body, and a goblet-like shape. The tone of the drum can be varied by striking the head near the center for a lower tone or near the rim for a higher tone.

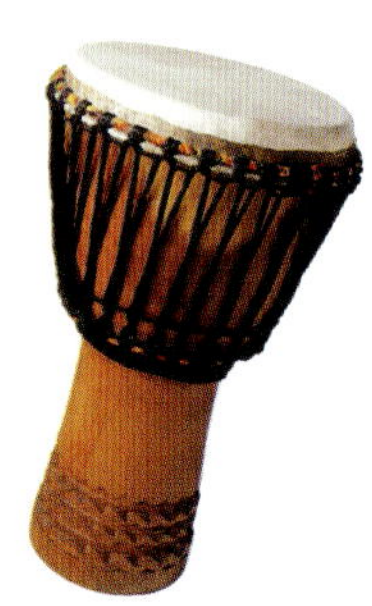

The **kalangu** is a drum shaped like an hourglass. It has an animal hide top to which are attached tensioning cords. The drum is struck with a wooden mallet. By pressing on the tensioning cords, the player can vary the pitch of the drum and thus imitate the changing pitches of the human voice. Because it was used to imitate the human voice, the kalangu and its relatives are sometimes referred to as **talking drums.** Talking drums were often used to communicate messages over long distances. They were also used in ceremonies to communicate traditional proverbs.

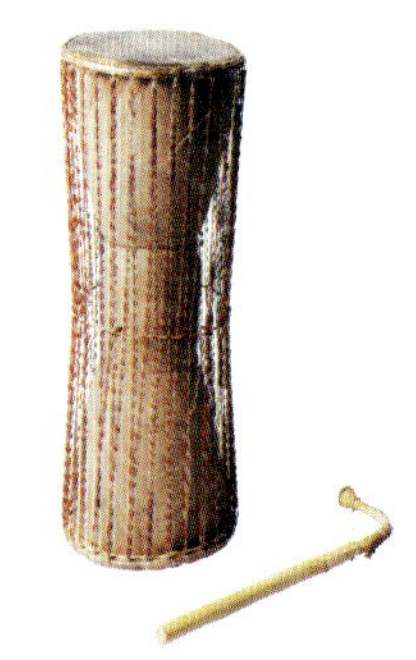

The **mbira, or kalimba,** consists of a wooden board attached to a resonator (a sound chamber), such as a gourd, with plucked metal keys of differing lengths. This instrument is also commonly referred to as a **thumb piano.**

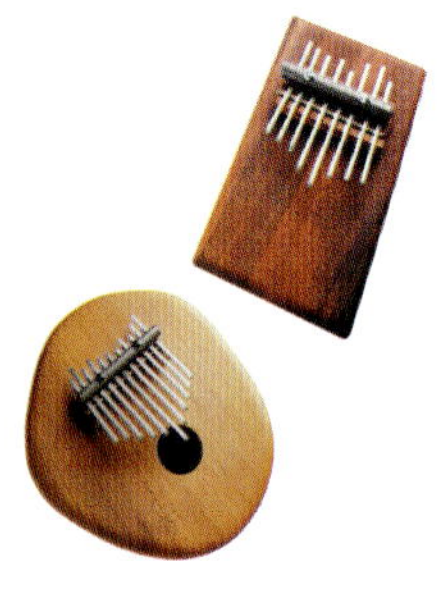

The **shekere** is a rattle made of a gourd, covered with a network of beads.

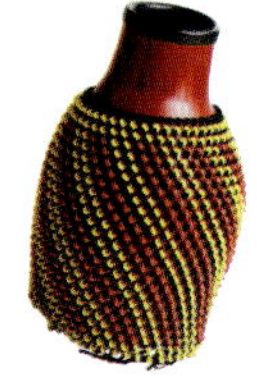

The **udu pot** is a percussion instrument made of fired clay pottery and containing two openings, one at the top and one on the side.

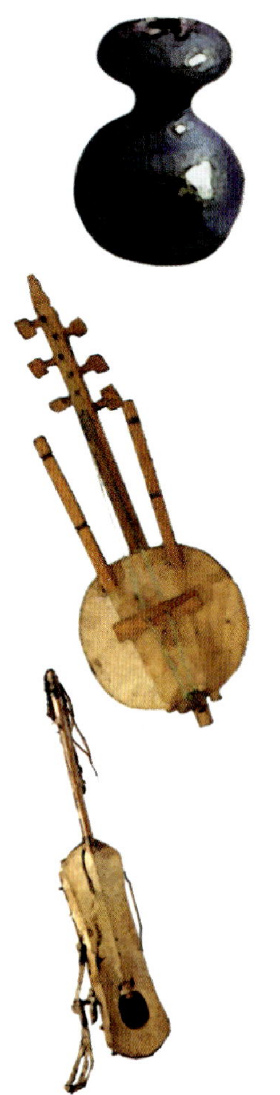

The **kora** is a harp-lute with twenty-one strings that is used to accompany traditional storytelling. It has a resonator made of a large **calabash** (a kind of gourd), one side of which is removed and covered with animal hide. It has a notched bridge and a hardwood neck. The strings are attached to leather straps that are turned in order to tune the strings.

The **ngoni,** or **xalam,** is a small lute with a wooden handle and body. The body is covered with cowhide. The strings, which are usually made of fishing line, are attached to the neck with leather straps that are moved for tuning, as on the kora.

The **balaphone** is a type of xylophone, similar to a **marimba** (a Latin American instrument derived from the balaphone and its relatives). It has rosewood keys and a bamboo frame. Under this frame are resonators of various sizes made of gourds containing small holes covered with paper made from the egg sacks of spiders. This instrument is played by striking the wooden keys with mallets.

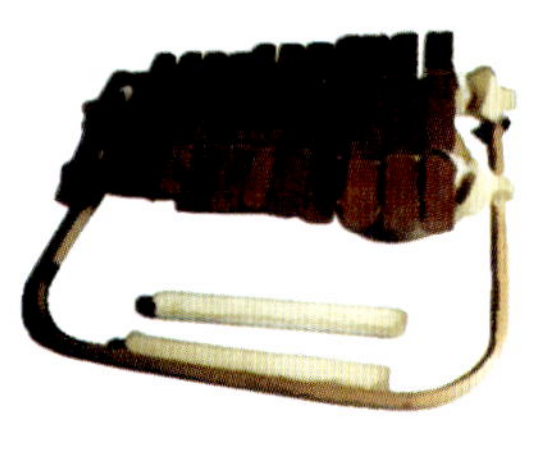

The **umuduri** (related to the Brazilian **berimbau**) is a musical bow made of a single string attached to a bowed wooden stick. A gourd is attached as a resonator. Across the continent of Africa, there are many such bowed instruments. One of them, known as the **earth bow,** uses a hole in the ground as a resonating chamber.

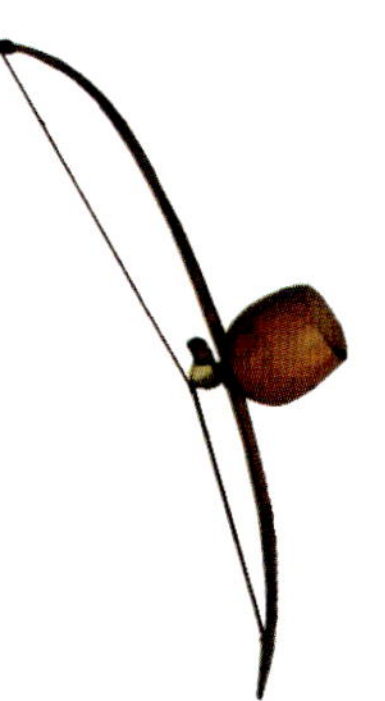

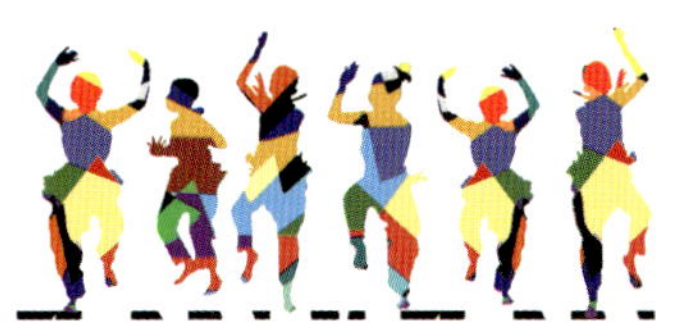

Musical Traditions That Survived the African Diaspora

The slave trade from West Africa to the New World, which lasted from the fifteenth to the nineteenth century and was often referred to as the **African Diaspora,** wreaked havoc on the traditional cultures of the enslaved. Enslaved Africans nonetheless managed to keep elements of their traditions alive.

In the Americas, enslaved craftsmen continued to manufacture traditional drums, and hide-covered instruments with resonators, like the kora and the ngoni, evolved into the banjo.

As we have seen, call-and-response forms were kept alive in African-American religious ceremonies and music, and polyrhythms and syncopation found their way into new musical forms such as the blues and jazz.

In addition, throughout the dark period of American slavery, men, women, and children of African descent would, from time to time, escape from their labors to sing and dance, often in secret in the deep woods, away from the prying eyes of slave owners and overseers. As you will learn in the music section following Unit 2, the elements of traditional West African musical culture remembered by slaves in the Americas were like a tiny flame, kept burning over centuries, that set fire to the musical imaginations of subsequent generations. Or, to use another metaphor, one might say that these seeds from African music eventually blossomed into the many varieties of music that we think of as essentially American. ■

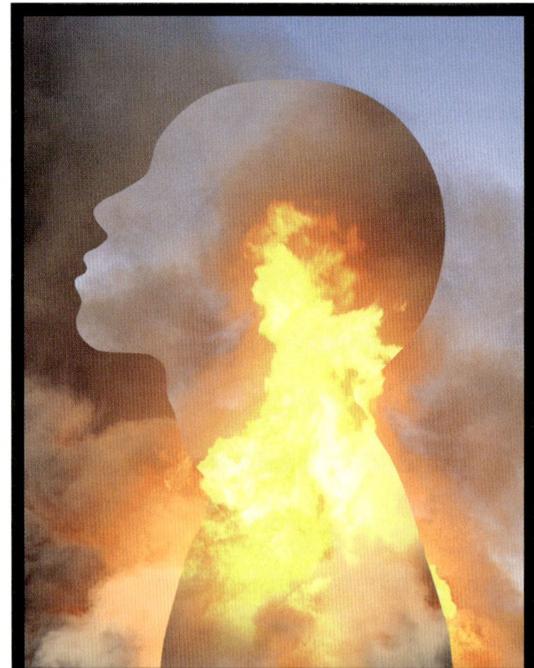

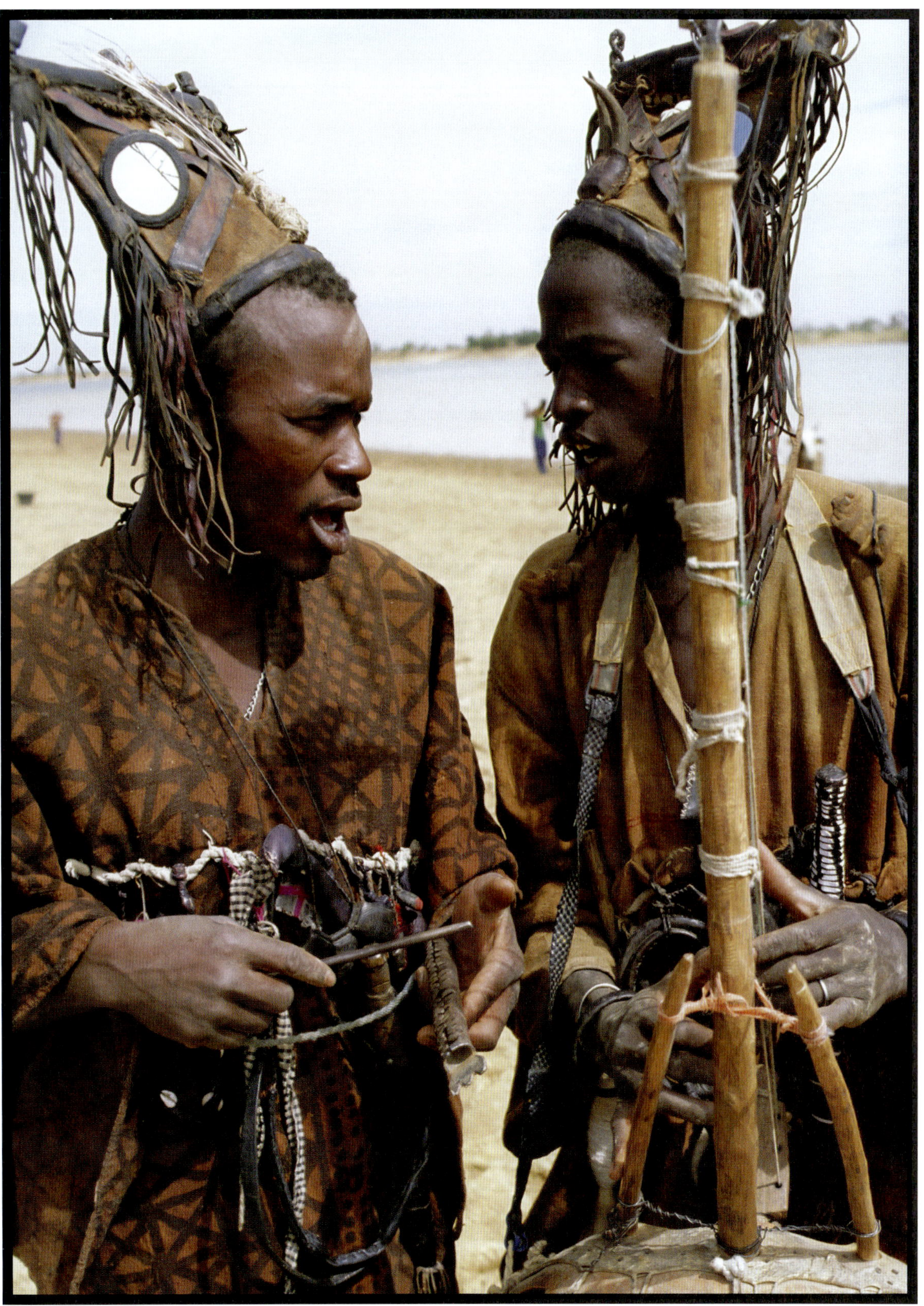

Griots, traditional musicians, Sofara, Mali, Africa. The griot on the right is holding a kora.

Frances Watkins Harper

Olaudah Equiano

James Whitfield Nat Turner

FREDERICK DOUGLASS

BENJAMIN BANNEKER

Sojourner Truth

Frances Watkins Harper

Olaudah Equiano

Jupiter Hammon Harriet Jacobs

WILLIAM WELLS BROWN

James Whitfield **W. E. B. Du Bois**

Frances Watkins Harper

James Whitfield SOJOURNER TRUTH

Nat Turner Harriet Jacobs

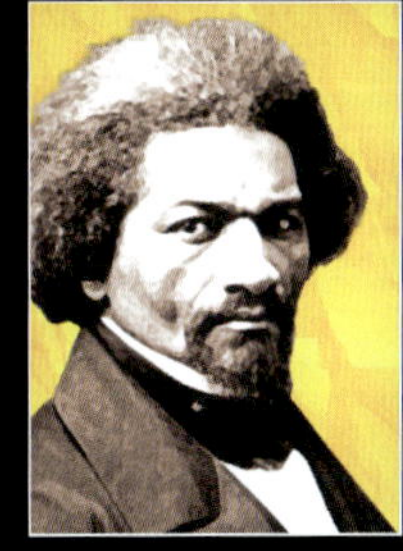

Unit 2

et My People Go

"For it is not light
that is needed, but fire;
it is not the gentle shower,
but thunder.
We need the storm,
the whirlwind,
and the earthquake."

—Frederick Douglass

Unit 2 Introduction

Let my People Go

The first ships carrying enslaved Africans arrived in the Americas in the 1520s and the slave trade, thus begun, lasted almost four hundred years, during which time an estimated 12 million West Africans were kidnapped, shackled, packed into cargo holds, and removed from their homes to a continent far across a treacherous sea. Those who survived the journey, some 10 million, were displayed in markets from Brazil to Boston, where they were sold as property, human chattel, slaves. This was the **African Diaspora**, the forced dispersal of a people from their homeland. In the United States, the sweat and blood of enslaved Africans helped to create and build a new and mighty nation, but for generations, that nation would not accept them as citizens.

The enslaved Africans were allowed no possessions, but each carried a priceless treasure, tucked in the very core of his or her heart: stories. These stories, bearing ancient wisdom and accompanied by ageless, vital rhythm and dance, remained with the people as they made their way in the new and hostile land. These same stories helped to guide them through four hundred years of enslavement, and these stories, churned and changed by the American experience, came forth once again in new forms, as naturally as light from the sun, from people who could not help but tell stories.

How could something like this happen? Greed, that basic human trait, was the driving force: greed among the plantation owners in the Americas who sought to maximize production through minimal labor costs; greed among the auctioneers and merchants who counted human heads as though they were heads of cattle; greed among stakeholders in the international trading companies that owned the slave ships; greed among the traders who swapped guns and trinkets to equally greedy African chieftains willing to trade their captured enemies and neighbors. *Greed* is one of the first words that should come to mind when one considers the exploration and settlement of the New World.

Of course, other words that should come to mind include *liberty, freedom,* and *justice*. These words are forever cemented into the foundation of American history and appear in nearly every important document associated with the founding of the United States. But for enslaved Africans—in a strange land, stripped of their personal and communal histories—these words were not supposed to mean anything. For the enslaved, *liberty, freedom,* and *justice* were not supposed to matter.

It did not take long, however, for these essential words to take root in the earliest written works by African Americans. Jupiter Hammon and Phillis Wheatley, the earliest black poets, did not openly speak out against slavery—not like later writers such as Frederick Douglass and Frances Harper. Hammon and Wheatley both expressed a certain resignation to, or acceptance of, their condition, for enslavement was the only life that either ever knew. But the desire for freedom is as basic as the desire for food or water, and these early poets found their outlets in religion and in writing.

The second unit of this anthology contains far fewer selections than those that follow. The fact is that there were few published African-American writers prior to the Civil War. Those who *were* published saw the authenticity of their work questioned again and again. Frederick Douglass, whose writing ranks among the finest of the English language, confronted doubters at every turn in his public life. Shockingly, few whites in those days could believe that African Americans were capable of reading and writing with skill.

It was not enough that the man clawed his way up from slavery, teaching himself to read and write along the way. It was not enough that he knew—despite the deep well of anger, sadness, and resentment in his heart—that the best way to change the world was patiently, painstakingly to put down that anger and sadness between the covers of a book.

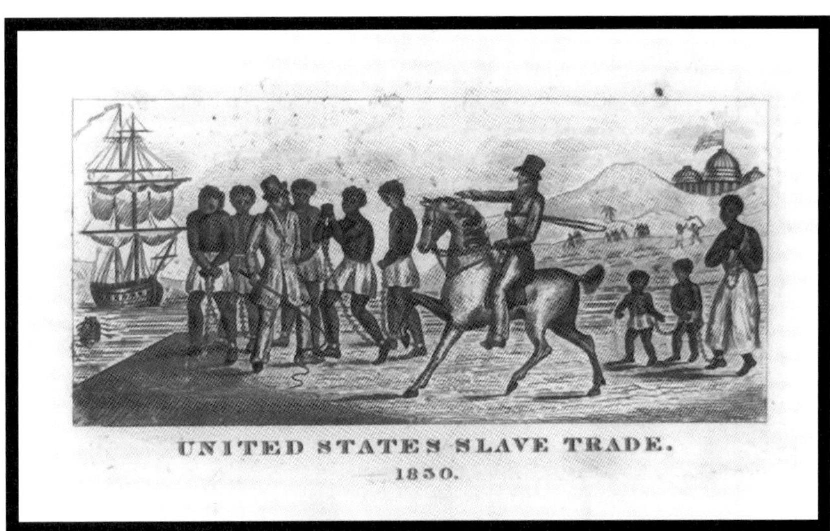

"The United States Slave Trade, 1830." Engraving. Library of Congress, LC-USZ62-89701.

The only way to get the majority of the nineteenth-century reading public to buy a book by an African-American writer was to preface it with letters of guarantee from prominent white citizens who were willing to attest to the fact that the writer was really the writer. Such prejudice and doubt can hold sway for a while, but the truth—and the stories and poems that carry it from generation to generation—always finds a way around and beyond such obstacles.

The early voices of African-American literature are a prelude—the opening notes in a suite that was finally heard in full force a half-century after the Civil War, when the works of the Harlem Renaissance, featured in Unit 3 of *Grace Abounding*, began to resonate throughout the land.

Historical Background: Slavery and the Slave Trade

What Is Slavery?

*We were all ranked together. . . . Men and women,
old and young, married and single, were ranked with horses,
sheep, and swine. There were horses and men, cattle and women,
pigs and children, all holding the same rank in the scale of being.*

—Frederick Douglass

The above quotation offers some sense of the dehumanizing effects of slavery, a practice that is older than human civilization and that continues in some parts of the world to this day, despite its extreme barbarity. Slavery in the United States had its own particular characteristics, but all forms of slavery are the same in that one group of people essentially exercises unrestricted control over another.

One of the most conspicuous aspects of slavery is its sheer physical brutality. As Douglass pointed out in *Narrative of the Life of Frederick Douglass, An American Slave,* even when slave "masters" began their careers with relatively generous natures, they themselves became dehumanized—the institution made them increasingly cruel. Speaking of one of his "mistresses," Mrs. Hughes, Douglass wrote that under slavery's influence, "the tender heart became stone, and the lamblike disposition gave way to one of tiger-like fierceness." Why? Because absolute power corrupts absolutely.

Of course, people do not remain in bondage of their own free will, and so they have to be forced. The desire of slave owners to maintain their dominance gave rise to a multitude of dreadful torture devices and perverse practices. The whip was the most common tool of the master or overseer; its shrill crack echoed in the ears of victims and witnesses for years afterward. Whipping left the skin permanently scarred and sometimes led to death.

Physical punishment was but one of the tortures inflicted upon slaves. The mere memory of a severe beating (or witnessing the beating of another) haunted the enslaved for the rest of their lives, dulled their emotions and senses, and sometimes left them mere shells of human beings. Constant hard labor, lack of decent food, and poor living conditions also had emotional, physical, and spiritual impacts. Then there was separation from family and friends and uncertainty as to what hardship the next day might bring. Given the toll that slavery usually took on its victims, it is altogether an astonishing testament to the human spirit that so many could endure its worst and still emerge strong, free, and rational.

The Transatlantic Slave Trade

Slavery began in the Western Hemisphere in the early 1500s, as soon as Spanish adventurers began combing the New World for its expected caches of gold, silver, and other riches. Early Spanish settlers in the Caribbean and South America exploited native Arawak and Carib Indian populations in order to satisfy their labor needs, and these groups were rapidly annihilated by disease and hardship. By the early 1520s, the Spanish turned to Africa, where Portuguese traders had long before established ties to existing slave markets along that continent's western coast.

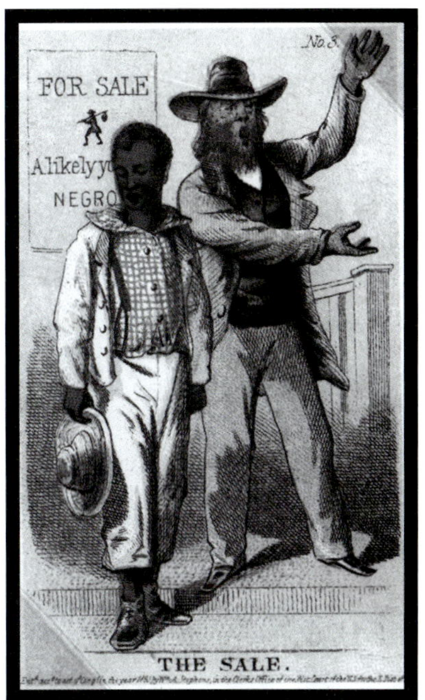

The Sale, by Henry Louis Stephens, circa 1863, Library of Congress. LC-USZ62-41837.

Large-scale transatlantic shipment of African slaves increased sharply in the late sixteenth century with the development of sugar and tobacco plantations in Brazil, Jamaica, and St. Domingue.[1] Later, Cuba was also home to an immense plantation system, as were other parts of the British and French West Indies. Through the mid-1800s, however, Brazil would prove to be by far the single largest importer of African slaves, absorbing more than 60 percent of all forced migrants from Africa to the Western Hemisphere.

Slave traders developed a route known as the **Triangle Trade,** wherein African slaves were traded in the Americas for raw materials (sugar, molasses, timber, and later, tobacco and cotton), which in turn were shipped to Europe for consumption or processed into manufactured goods. These goods were used to purchase more slaves in Africa, completing the triangle and beginning the process anew. (See map on the next page.)

Many slaves were prisoners of war or victims of raids perpetrated by rival tribes (and sometimes Portuguese traders), who swapped their human commodities for textiles, guns, and other European goods. By the end of the transatlantic slave trade in the mid-nineteenth century, as many as 12 million Africans had been sold into slavery and transported to the Western Hemisphere. Of these, approximately 10 million survived the wretched journey across the Atlantic.

[1] **St. Domingue.** Modern Hispaniola, the island shared by Haiti and the Dominican Republic

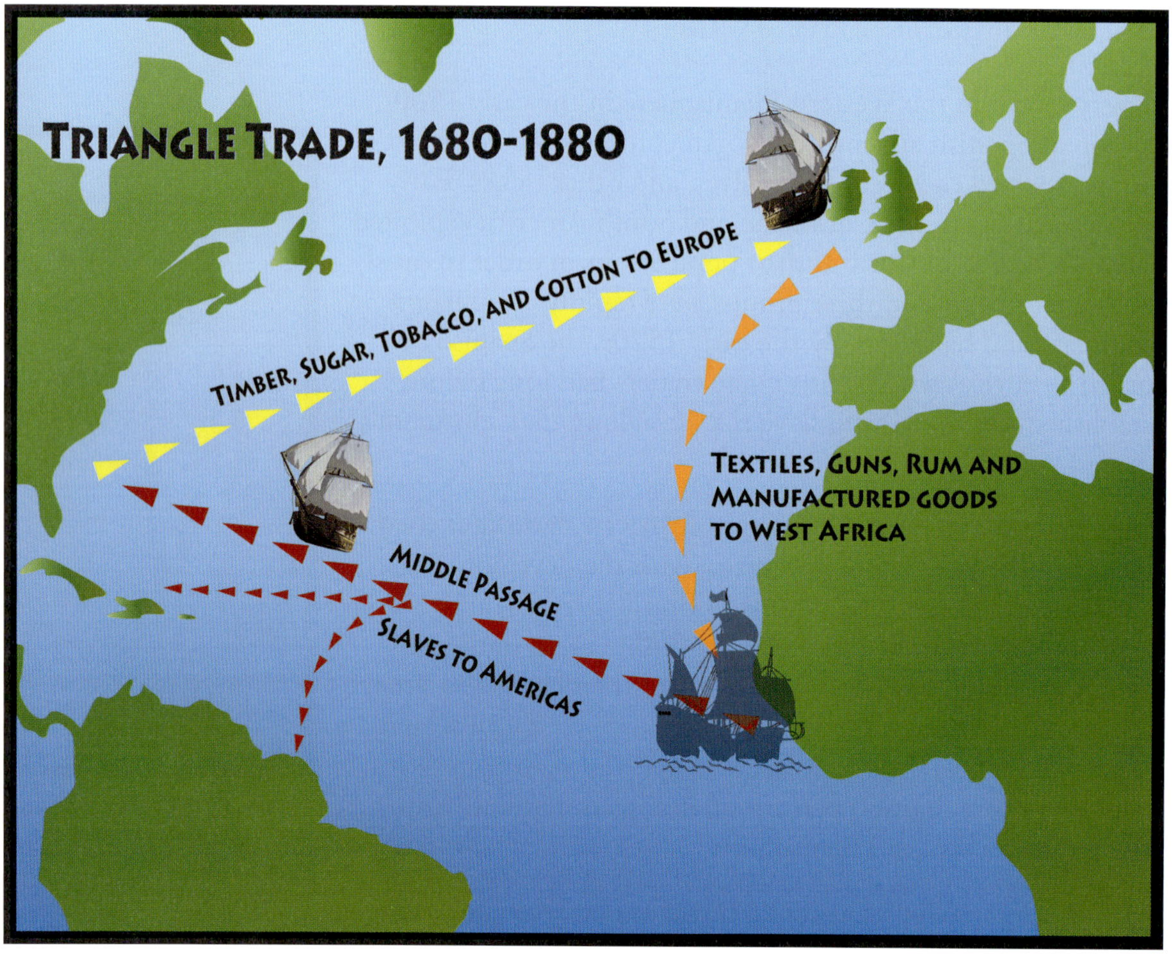

The Triangle Trade. Slaves were bartered for, purchased, or captured in West Africa and brought to the Americas. Raw materials and other commodities were purchased in the Americas and brought back to Europe. Finished goods such as textiles and guns were then taken to West Africa for bartering.

Known commonly as the **Middle Passage,** the trip from Africa to the Americas lasted anywhere from a few weeks to months depending on the point of embarkation and the final destination. Most slave ships were relatively small merchant vessels that transported one hundred to three hundred slaves, but large ships capable of carrying as many as one thousand slaves were not unusual. Violent mutiny was a constant threat aboard any slave ship, and history records hundreds of such events. Crews took every precaution to prevent uprisings and visited swift and severe punishment on rebellious slaves.

The conditions aboard a slave vessel—especially one of the very large ones—are virtually unimaginable for modern minds. Slaves were usually kept in the cargo hold, where chains were available for the unruly, if not for the entire population. Traders often modified their cargo holds in order to use every inch of space, allowing perhaps four feet of headroom for the slaves. Thus slaves led a nightmarish existence in the dark, stuffy cargo holds, awash in human waste, blood, and general misery. As the journey wore on, supplies on board the ships dwindled, and sickness became rampant, resulting in increased death rates among slaves and crew alike.

Slavery in the English Colonies and United States

The English colonies, and later the United States, imported only about 5 percent of all African slaves. Early on, the English relied on indentured servants in colonies like Virginia and Barbados. These were usually young men who agreed to work (essentially as slaves) for several years in return for passage, housing, and food. As riches from the New World were transferred overseas, the economies and opportunities in Europe improved, and the pool of willing indentured servants dried up. This development, together with a soaring worldwide demand for sugar and cotton, caused planters in the English colonies to follow the lead of their counterparts in the Caribbean and South America to meet their labor needs.

The typical landowner in North America also differed fundamentally from his counterparts in Brazil, Cuba, and St. Domingue. Normally, an English settler did not come to the New World intent on making quick riches and returning to Europe to live out his days as an absentee landlord. Instead, the English colonist made his new home in the Americas and had an interest in making sure that his slaves were in relatively good health. By comparison, landowners further south often had little direct contact with their plantations and cared little for the slave population as long as profits remained high. Even in the English colonies, however, and in the southern United States thereafter, privation was common.

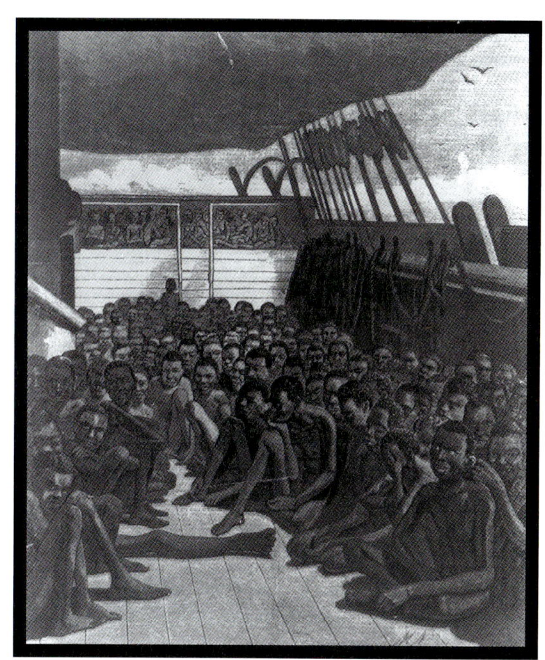

The Slave Deck of the Bark Wildfire, Brought into Key West on April 30, 1860. Wood engraving illustration from *Harper's Weekly,* June 2, 1860.

The aftermath of the American Revolutionary War (1775–83) brought the beginning of the Abolitionist Movement, as well as the seeds of division that would eventually lead to the Civil War. The Revolution sparked new ways of thinking among Americans, many of whom were uncomfortable with the presence of human bondage in a nation that proclaimed to the rest of the world that "all men are created equal."

Slavery was abolished or gradually phased out in the northern states during the late eighteenth and early nineteenth centuries. In New York, Delaware, and Pennsylvania, laws were passed whereby slaves would be freed within a certain number of years or once they reached a certain age. Furthermore, significant antislavery measures were enacted by Congress, including the Northwest Ordinance of 1787, which prohibited slavery in northwestern territories, and a law in 1808 that finally put an end to the importation of African slaves.

At the same time, slave ownership was considered a sacred property right by second- and third-generation slave owners living in the southern states, where roughly 90 percent of slaves were held. In northern states, slave owners normally owned no more than five slaves, who worked as house servants, drivers, handymen, and the like. In the South, however, slaves were the backbone of the agrarian economy. Slave owners often paternally viewed themselves not only as owners but as divinely appointed guardians of their enslaved workers. Some believed not only in the inferiority of the African race but also in the inherent responsibility of slave owners to see at least to the minimum subsistence needs of their human "property."

Plantation Life in the United States

The average plantation in Georgia, South Carolina, and other southern states held about fifty slaves, though this number could range from just a few to several hundred. Large-scale insurrections were rare, in part because of the tight restrictions placed on the movements of slaves and on communication between neighboring plantations.

Although most slave owners did not believe themselves to be overtly abusive, the established system was nonetheless cruel and inhumane. Slave owners employed a variety of methods, but whipping was the most common mode of punishment and torture. Punishments and practices varied from plantation to plantation; whereas twelve lashes of the whip might be sufficient to one "master," another "master" might see fit to administer a hundred or more for the same offense.

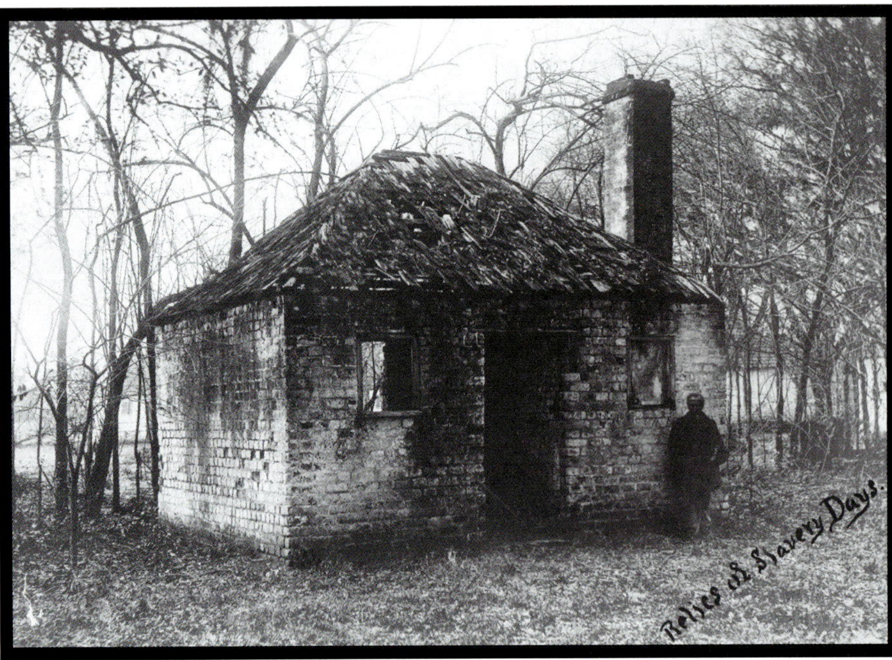

Relics of Slavery Days, Slave Quarters at the Hermitage Plantation outside of Savannah, Georgia. Photograph, circa 1900. Library of Congress, LC-USZ62-103293.

A slave family's "quarters" normally consisted of dirt floors, thin walls, and a leaky roof. Enslaved people worked all day, most every day, though in most places they were afforded time off on the Sabbath and on certain holidays. Food was basic, with most slaves receiving a paltry breakfast and an evening meal, which they were often too exhausted to prepare or consume.

A slave could sometimes earn wages or make a little money by plying a trade or performing odd jobs. Occasionally, if the "master" was willing, a slave could even afford to buy his or her own freedom. Such opportunities were uncommon, however, in the southern states. Perhaps the cruelest aspect of the southern slavery system was the fact that entire families were often the sole property of the plantation owner and could be separated and sold at the "master's" discretion. This practice was especially brutal because the family was a slave's major refuge from the hardships of life. The importation of slaves from Africa decreased, but the demand for slaves continued to rise, especially with the establishment of western slave states like Louisiana and Mississippi. Thus slave owners and traders became more intent on increasing the number of American-born slaves and less likely to allow slaves to purchase their own freedom.

With the enlargement of the American-born slave population came the development of a distinct culture, which included religion, music, and folklore, all of which provided some refuge for slaves. Though families were split and separated, these elements of culture remained and were passed down through the generations to become vital, enduring components of American civilization.

The Rise of Abolitionism

By the early nineteenth century, major powers in Europe had abolished slavery, as had most of the northern United States. The growth of the Abolitionist Movement fueled further insurrections and escape attempts in the South. Thanks to the efforts of staunch white Abolitionists and of freed or escaped slaves like Harriet Tubman, Frederick Douglass, and Sojourner Truth, the **Underground Railroad,** a network of safe houses, provided refuge for fugitive slaves as they sought haven in the free states.

But freedom was not guaranteed, even once a fugitive reached a state where slavery itself had been abolished. In ***Dred Scott v. Sanford,*** the Supreme Court of the United States sided with the precedent that a black person had no rights

> *which the white man was bound to respect; and that the Negro might justly and lawfully be reduced to slavery for his benefit. He was bought and sold and treated as an ordinary article of merchandise and traffic, whenever profit could be made by it.*

Dred Scott, despite having been transported in and out of "free" states, would remain the property of another man. Similarly, the **Fugitive Slave Act of 1850** and other laws protected the rights of southern slaveholders to reclaim their property and required that law enforcement officials in northern states do their part to return fugitive slaves to their "rightful" owners.

Such laws enraged Abolitionists and helped to increase popular support for their movement. In his newspaper, *The Liberator*, Abolitionist leader William Lloyd Garrison wrote, "Enslave the liberty of but one human being and the liberties of the world are put in peril." Garrison spoke for all opponents of slavery who saw the institution as a threat to the cause of liberty around the world. By themselves, however, the Abolitionists were unable to bring an end to slavery. Achieving this would come at a cost of 600,000 lives, the wounding of hundreds of thousands of people, and the destruction of cities and towns throughout the South in the bloodiest conflict ever to occur on American soil: the **Civil War.**

Politics was among the chief obstacles to freedom for the slaves. Even at the height of the Civil War, President Lincoln was reluctant to free the slaves for fear of offending "border" states where slavery was allowed but whose armies remained loyal to the United States. Lincoln's order freeing slaves in the rebellious states, the **Emancipation Proclamation,** became law on January 1, 1863. Only after the terrible Battle of Gettysburg, later that year, did the Union Army begin liberating slaves *en masse.* Still, thousands of African Americans remained enslaved until the end of the war, unaware or unable to take advantage of Lincoln's decree that "all persons held as slaves within any State or designated part of a State, the people whereof shall then be in rebellion against the United States, shall be then, thenceforward, and forever free."

Two years later, in 1865, Congress formally ended slavery in the United States with the ratification of the Thirteenth Amendment to the Constitution. In 1888, Brazil became the last country in the Western Hemisphere to abolish the evil that had begun there nearly four centuries before in the name of gold, sugar, and profit. ■

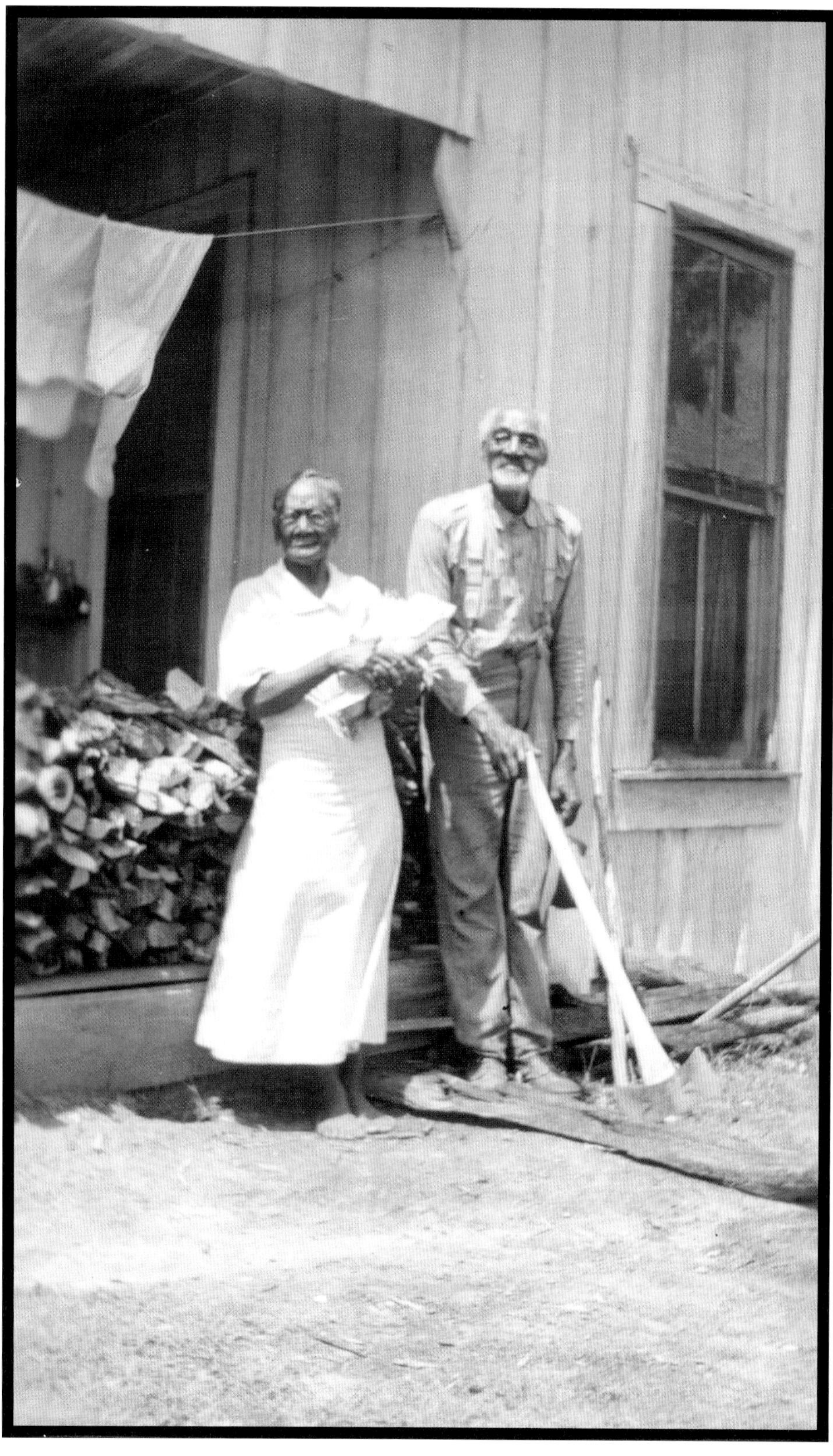

Minerva and Edgar Bendy, Formerly Enslaved Persons.
Photograph, part of Portraits of African-American Ex-Slaves from the U.S. Works Progress Administration, Federal Writers' Project Slave Narratives Collections. Library of Congress, LC-USZ62-125169.

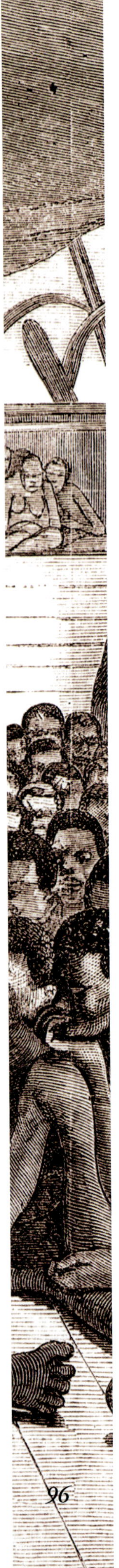

Prereading

"Horrors of a Slave Ship" from *The Interesting Narrative of the Life of Olaudah Equiano*

by Olaudah Equiano

One of the great values of Olaudah Equiano's outstanding autobiography is its detailed first-hand account of the **Middle Passage,** which was the name given to the wretched journey endured by enslaved Africans on their way to the Americas. This voyage could last anywhere from a few weeks to months. Conditions aboard the vessels were abominable, as traders sought to maximize profits by cramming as much human cargo as possible below decks, often in chains, and by offering their prisoners only enough food, water, and daylight to survive. Many slaves died before reaching America's slave auctions. As Equiano revealed in his narrative, terror and hardship for the enslaved African began in Africa, when he or she was captured in battle or simply kidnapped by traders from rival tribes. Slavery is as old as human history, but the transatlantic slave trade brought the cruelty of slavery to a new level.

Equiano experienced enslavement firsthand when, at the young age of eleven, he and his sister were kidnapped from their home in what is now Nigeria. For seven months, he was forcibly marched to the west coast, enduring a heart-wrenching separation from his sister and serving as a slave for several different masters before finally being sold to sea merchants upon his arrival at the coast. The following selection begins with Equiano's first sighting of the Atlantic Ocean and the enormous slave ship he was soon to board—a prelude to the harrowing journey to follow.

As you read Equiano's account, ask yourself the following questions:

1. What motivated the people who perpetrated these deeds?

2. Why did Equiano write this piece, and what effect do you think it might have had on readers of his time?

from The Interesting Narrative of the Life of Olaudah Equiano

by Olaudah Equiano

The first object which saluted my eyes when I arrived on the coast was the sea, and a slave ship, which was then riding at anchor, and waiting for its cargo. These filled me with astonishment, which was soon converted into terror when I was carried on board. I was immediately handled and tossed up to see if I were sound,[1] by some of the crew; and I was now persuaded that I had gotten into a world of bad spirits, and that they were going to kill me. Their complexions, too, differing so much from ours, their long hair, and the language they spoke (which was very different from any I had ever heard) united to confirm me in this belief. Indeed such were the horrors of my views and fears at the moment, that, if ten thousand worlds had been my own, I would have freely parted with them all to have exchanged my condition with that of the meanest slave in my own country. When I looked round the ship too, and saw a large furnace of copper boiling, and a multitude of black people of every description chained together, every one of their **countenances** expressing dejection and sorrow, I no longer doubted of my fate; and, quite overpowered with horror and anguish, I fell motionless on the deck and fainted. When I recovered a little, I found some black people about me, whom I believed were some of those who brought me on board, and had been receiving their pay; they talked to me in order to cheer me, but all in vain. I asked them if we were not to be eaten by those white men with horrible looks, red faces, and long hair. They told me I was not, and one of the crew brought me a small portion of spirituous liquor in a wine glass; but being afraid of him, I would not take it out of his hand. One of the blacks, therefore, took it from him and gave it to me, and I took a little down my palate,[2] which, instead of reviving me, as they thought it would, threw me into the greatest **consternation** at the strange feeling it produced, having never tasted any such liquor before. Soon after this the blacks who brought me on board went off, and left me abandoned in despair.

Why did the white men frighten him so much?

I now saw myself deprived of all chance of returning to my native country, or even the least glimpse of hope of gaining the shore, which I now considered as friendly; and I even wished for my former slavery[3] in preference to my present situation, which was filled with horrors of every kind, still heightened by my ignorance of what I was to undergo. I was not long suffered to indulge my grief; I was soon put down under the decks, and there I received such a **salutation** in my nostrils as I had never experienced in

[1] **sound.** Strong, healthy

[2] **took . . . palate.** Drank a little

[3] **former slavery.** Equiano refers here to the seven-month period between his kidnapping and his arrival at the coast, during which time he served as a slave for several different African masters.

VOCABULARY IN PLACE

- **countenance,** ***n.*** Facial expression
- **consternation,** ***n.*** Paralyzing dismay or fear
- **salutation,** ***n.*** Greeting

my life; so that, with the **loathsomeness** of the stench, and crying together, I became so sick and low that I was not able to eat, nor had I the least desire to taste anything. I now wished for the last friend, death, to relieve me; but soon, to my grief, two of the white men offered me eatables; and, on my refusing to eat, one of them held me fast by the hands, and laid me across, I think, the windlass,[4] and tied my feet, while the other flogged me severely. I had never experienced anything of this kind before, and, although not being used to the water, I naturally feared that element the first time I saw it, yet, nevertheless, could I have got over the nettings, I would have jumped over the side, but I could not; and besides, the crew used to watch us very closely who were not chained down to the decks, lest we should leap into the water; and I have seen some of these poor African prisoners most severely cut, for attempting to do so, and hourly whipped for not eating. This indeed was often the case with myself. In a little time after, amongst the poor chained men, I found some of my own nation, which in a small degree gave ease to my mind. I inquired of these what was to be done with us? They gave me to understand, we were to be carried to these white people's country to work for them. I then was a little revived, and thought, if it were no worse than working, my situation was not so desperate; but still I feared I should be put to death, the white people looked and acted, as I thought, in so savage a manner; for I had never seen among any people such instances of brutal cruelty; and this not only shown towards us blacks, but also to some of the whites themselves. One white man in particular I saw, when we were permitted to be on deck, flogged so unmercifully with a large rope near the foremast,[5] that he died in consequence of it; and they tossed him over the side as they would have done a **brute.** This made me fear these people the more; and I expected nothing less than to be treated in the same manner. I could not help expressing my fears and apprehensions to some of my countrymen; I asked them if these people had no country, but lived in this hollow place (the ship)? They told me they did not, but came from a distant one. "Then," said I, "how comes it in all our country we never heard of them?" They told me because they lived so very far off. I then asked where were their women? Had they any like themselves? I was told they had. "And why," said I, "do we not see them?" They answered, because they were left behind. I asked how the vessel could go? They told me they could not tell; but that there were cloths put upon the masts by the help of the ropes I saw, and then the vessel went on; and the white men had some spell or magic they put in the water when they liked, in order to stop the vessel. I was exceedingly amazed at this account, and really thought they were spirits. I therefore wished much to be from amongst them, for I expected they would sacrifice me; but my wishes were **vain**—for we were so quartered that it was impossible for any of us to make our escape.

What did young Equiano learn from his countrymen?

While we stayed on the coast I was mostly on deck; and one day, to my great astonishment, I saw one of these vessels coming in with the sails up. As soon as the

4 **windlass.** A device with a crank used to lift an anchor

5 **foremast.** A mast is a large pole to which sails are rigged. The foremast, which in Equiano's time would have been made of wood, is the mast closest to the front, or bow, of the sailing vessel.

VOCABULARY IN PLACE

- **loathsomeness,** ***n.*** Nastiness
- **brute,** ***n.*** Animal
- **vain,** ***adj.*** Pointless; to no avail

whites saw it, they gave a great shout, at which we were amazed; and the more so, as the vessel appeared larger by approaching nearer. At last, she came to an anchor in my sight, and when the anchor was let go, I and my countrymen who saw it, were lost in astonishment to observe the vessel stop—and were now convinced it was done by magic. Soon after this the other ship got her boats out, and they came on board of us, and the people of both ships seemed very glad to see each other. Several of the strangers also shook hands with us black people, and made motions with their hands, signifying I suppose, we were to go to their country, but we did not understand them.

Why was Equiano astonished?

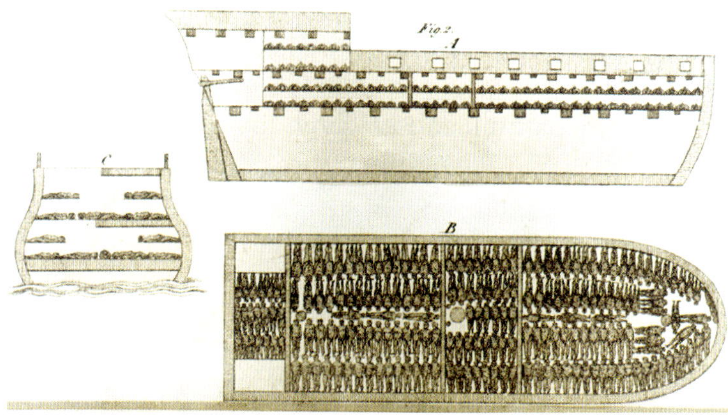

Slave Ship, Eighteenth Century

At last, when the ship we were in had got in all her cargo, they made ready with many fearful noises, and we were all put under deck, so that we could not see how they managed the vessel. But this disappointment was the least of my sorrow. The stench of the hold while we were on the coast was so intolerably loathsome, that it was dangerous to remain there for any time, and some of us had been permitted to stay on the deck for the fresh air; but now that the whole ship's cargo were confined together, it became absolutely **pestilential.** The closeness[6] of the place, and the heat of the climate, added to the number in the ship, which was so crowded that each had scarcely room to turn himself, almost suffocated us. This produced **copious** perspiration, so that the air soon became unfit for respiration, from a variety of loathsome smells, and brought on a sickness among the slaves, of which many died—thus falling victims to the improvident avarice,[7] as I may call it, of their purchasers. This wretched situation was again aggravated by the galling[8] of the chains, now became insupportable, and the filth of the necessary tubs,[9] into which the children often fell, and were almost suffocated. The shrieks of the women, and the groans of the dying, rendered the whole a scene of horror almost inconceivable. Happily perhaps, for myself, I was soon reduced so low here that it was thought necessary to keep me almost always on deck; and from my extreme youth I was not put in fetters. In this situation I expected every hour to share the fate of my companions, some of whom were almost daily brought upon deck at the point of death, which I began to hope would soon put an end to my miseries. Often did I think many of the inhabitants of the deep much more happy than myself. I envied them the freedom they enjoyed, and as often wished I

Who were the "inhabitants of the deep"?

6 **closeness.** Tightness, smallness

7 **improvident avarice.** *Avarice* is greed. *Improvident avarice* is greed so consuming that it causes people to act rashly, not thriftily, so as to hurt their own economic interests.

8 **galling.** Rubbing that causes a sore or wound

9 **necessary tubs.** Vessels for elimination of bodily waste

VOCABULARY IN PLACE

- **pestilential,** ***adj.*** Infected with contagious disease; deadly
- **copious,** ***adj.*** Plentiful

could change my condition for theirs. Every circumstance I met with served only to render my state more painful, and heighten my apprehensions, and my opinion of the cruelty of the whites.

One day they had taken a number of fishes; and when they had killed and satisfied themselves with as many as they thought fit, to our astonishment who were on deck, rather than give any of them to us to eat, as we expected, they tossed the remaining fish into the sea again, although we begged and prayed for some as well as we could, but in vain; and some of my countrymen, being pressed by hunger, took an opportunity, when they thought no one saw them, of trying to get a little privately; but they were discovered, and the attempt procured them some very severe floggings. One day, when we had a smooth sea and moderate wind, two of my wearied countrymen who were chained together (I was near them at the time), preferring death to such a life of misery, somehow made through the nettings and jumped into the sea; immediately, another quite **dejected** fellow, who, on account of his illness, was suffered to be out of irons,[10] also followed their example; and I believe many more would very soon have done the same if they had not been prevented by the ship's crew who were instantly alarmed. Those of us that were the most active, were in a moment put down under the deck; and there was such a noise and confusion amongst the people of the ship as I never heard before, to stop her, and get the boat out to go after the slaves. However, two of the wretches were drowned, but they got the other, and afterwards flogged him unmercifully, for thus attempting to prefer death to slavery. In this manner we continued to undergo more hardships than I can now relate, hardships which are inseparable from this accursed trade. Many a time we were near suffocation from the want of fresh air, which we were often without for whole days together. This, and the stench of the necessary tubs, carried off many.

What did the sailors do with the leftover fish?

During our passage I first saw flying fishes, which surprised me very much; they used frequently to fly across the ship, and many of them fell on the deck. I also now first saw the use of the quadrant;[11] I had often with astonishment seen the **mariners** make observations with it, and I could not think what it meant. They at last took notice of my surprise; and one of them, willing to increase it, as well as to gratify my curiosity, made me one day look through it. The clouds appeared to me to be land, which disappeared as they passed along. This heightened my wonder; and I was now more persuaded than ever, that I was in another world, and that every thing about me was magic. At last we came in sight of the island of Barbadoes, at which the whites on board gave a great shout, and made many signs of joy to us. We did not know what to think of this; but as the vessel drew nearer, we plainly saw the harbor, and other ships of different kinds and sizes, and we soon anchored amongst them, off Bridgetown. Many merchants and planters[12] now came on board, though it was in the evening. They put us in separate parcels, and examined us attentively. They also made us jump, and pointed to the land, signifying we were to go there. We thought by this, we should be eaten by these ugly men, as they appeared to us, and, when soon after we were all put down under the deck again, there was much

[10] **irons.** Metal restraints, especially chains attached to metal cuffs

[11] **quadrant.** A device, also called a *sextant,* used in navigation

[12] **planters.** Wealthy plantation owners

VOCABULARY IN PLACE

- **dejected,** *past part.* Extremely sad, despairing
- **mariner,** *n.* Sailor

dread and trembling among us, and nothing but bitter cries to be heard all the night from these apprehensions, insomuch that at last the white people got some old slaves from the land to **pacify** us. They told us we were not to be eaten, but to work, and were soon to go on land, where we should see many of our country people. This report eased us much. And sure enough, soon after we were landed, there came to us Africans of all languages.

We were conducted immediately to the merchant's yard, where we were all pent up together, like so many sheep in a fold, without regard to sex or age. As every object was new to me, everything I saw filled me with surprise. What struck me first was that the houses were built with stories, and in every other respect different from those in Africa; but I was still more astonished on seeing people on horseback. I did not know what this could mean; and indeed I thought these people were full of nothing but magical arts. While I was in this astonishment one of my fellow prisoners spoke to a countryman of his, about the horses, who said they were the same kind they had in their country. I understood them, though they were from a distant part of Africa, and I thought it odd I had not seen any horses there; but afterwards, when I came to converse with different Africans, I found they had many horses amongst them, and much larger than those I then saw. We were not many days in the merchant's custody before we were sold after their usual manner, which is this: On a signal given, (as the beat of a drum), the buyers rush at once into the yard where the slaves are confined, and make choice of that parcel they like best. The noise and clamour with which this is attended, and the eagerness visible in the countenances of the buyers, serve not a little to increase the apprehensions of the terrified Africans, who may well be supposed to consider them as the ministers of that destruction to which they think themselves devoted. In this manner, without **scruple,** are relations and friends separated, most of them never to see each other again. I remember in the vessel in which I was brought over, in the men's apartment, there were several brothers, who, in the sale, were sold in different lots; and it was very moving on this occasion, to see and hear their cries at parting. O, ye **nominal** Christians! might not an African ask you—learned you this from your God, who says unto you, Do unto all men as you would men should do unto you? Is it not enough that we are torn from our country and friends to toil for your luxury and lust of gain? Must every tender feeling be likewise sacrificed to your avarice? Are the dearest friends and relations, now **rendered** more dear by their separation from their **kindred,** still to be parted from each other, and thus prevented from cheering the gloom of slavery, with the small comfort of being together, and mingling their sufferings and sorrows? Why are parents to lose their children, brothers their sisters, or husbands their wives? Surely this is a new **refinement** in cruelty, which, while it has no advantage to **atone** for it, thus aggravates distress, and adds fresh horrors even to the wretchedness of slavery. ■

What surprises Equiano about the houses?

VOCABULARY IN PLACE

- **pacify,** *v.* Restore calm or establish peace in
- **scruple,** *n.* An uneasy feeling arising from conscience; qualm
- **nominal,** *adj.* In name only; half-hearted, uncommitted
- **render,** *v.* To make
- **kindred,** *n.* Relations, family members, or, metaphorically, others of the same tribe or community
- **refinement,** *n.* Sophistication; improvement
- **atone,** *v.* To make amends for

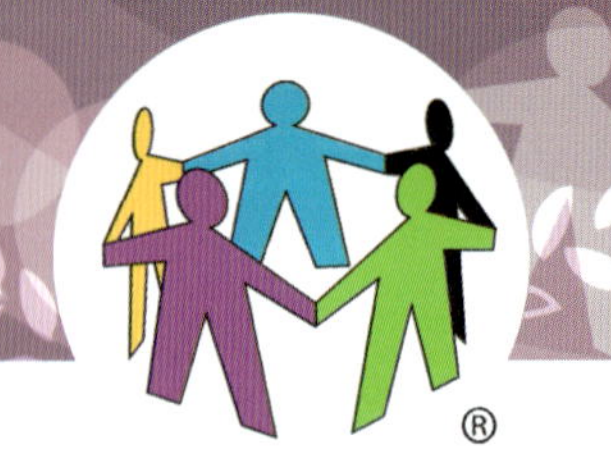

Understanding the Selection

Recalling

1. What did Equiano first see when he came to the coast? How did he react to the sight?

2. What did Equiano experience once he was taken below decks?

3. How did Equiano react when the boat stopped? To what did he attribute the motion of the boat?

4. What happened to Equaino and the others once they arrived in Barbados?

Interpreting

1. Why might Equiano have had such a reaction? Had he had any similar experience before?

2. Why did enslaved prisoners on board the ship get sick so often? Why did many of them die?

3. What impressions did Equiano form of the white sailors upon seeing them stop the vessel?

4. What, in particular, horrified Equiano about the nature of slavery as practiced in the Americas and in the Caribbean?

Synthesizing

1. Millions of Africans endured the unthinkable suffering of the Middle Passage. What were the circumstances that led to its development? What motivated slave traders to carry out such brutality? How do you suppose they justified their horrific acts?

Delving Deeper

Understanding Literature

Writing, Purpose, and Social Justice. People write to achieve many different goals, or **purposes**. Some writing is done purely **to express** the writer's feelings or opinions. Some is done simply **to entertain.** A lot of writing, such as the writing that you find in textbooks, news stories, newspapers, and on the Internet, is done **to inform.** One particularly important purpose served by some writing is **to persuade** others to adopt a point of view or take some action.

Equiano's autobiography certainly served all of these purposes. However, perhaps the most important purpose that it served was a persuasive one. The autobiography became one of the most important documents of the **Abolitionist Movement** because it graphically portrayed some of the worst evils of slavery. Discuss with your classmates this aspect of the selection. Pose this question: What details from Equiano's narrative most convincingly put forward the case that slavery and the slave trade were evil?

Speaking and Listening Project

The Oral Report. The following are some topics related to slavery and the slave trade. Do some research on one of these topics and prepare a brief oral report for your class.

1. The revolt aboard the slave ship *Amistad* (1839)
2. The *Amistad* hearing before the Supreme Court (1841)
3. The film *Amistad,* directed by Stephen Spielberg (1997)
4. The life of John Newton, author of the song "Amazing Grace"
5. Goree Island, Senegal, West Africa
6. Elmina Castle, in Ghana, West Africa
7. Slavery in Western Europe, as compared to the United States
8. Slavery in Brazil, Cuba, or Haiti
9. Early Portuguese slave traders
10. Slavery in other time periods or geographic regions

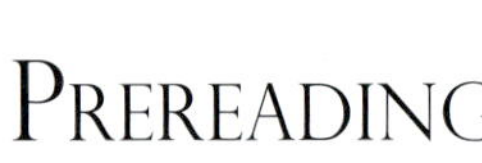

Prereading

from "The Confessions of Nat Turner"

as Recorded by Thomas R. Gray

The following graphic, matter-of-fact confession was made voluntarily by Nat Turner and recorded in jail. It is a tragic and chilling story. Turner's confession reveals the depth of anger and desire for revenge that slavery instilled in its victims.

All his life, Nat Turner felt that he was destined to do something extraordinary. In August, 1831, he witnessed a rare solar eclipse, which he took as a final sign that it was time to launch the slave rebellion that he and a few others had been planning for months.

Turner's raid lasted about forty-eight hours and became the bloodiest and most well-known slave rebellion in American history. When it was over, about sixty whites—men, women, and children—had been murdered. Most of Turner's comrades (at least forty in all) were captured and killed, and more than a hundred other innocent black people were later massacred, solely out of revenge.

Turner managed to elude capture for two months until October 30, 1831, when a single man with a shotgun cornered him in a hole in the ground just a few miles from the farm where the raid began. Turner was imprisoned and tried. On November 11, he was hanged.

Turner's court-appointed lawyer, Thomas R. Gray, made no serious attempt to mount a defense on his client's behalf. Gray did, however, take the time to record Turner's entire confession and, for this, later generations owe Gray a certain debt. Were it not for his pen, we would not have these pages.

The Confessions of Nat Turner was originally published with Gray's own notes, which are not included here, except for the occasional question from Gray. Note that due to the graphic nature of this material, it has been excerpted and not given in its entirety.

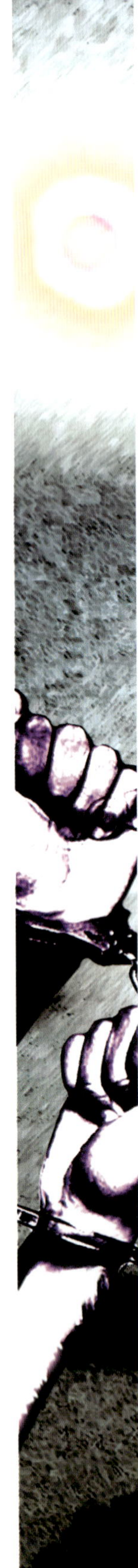

from The Confessions of Nat Turner

As Recorded by Thomas R. Gray

Sir,—You have asked me to give a history of the motives which **induced** me to undertake the late **insurrection,** as you call it—To do so I must go back to the days of my infancy, and even before I was born. I was thirty-one years of age the second of October last, and born the property of Benjamin Turner, of this county. In my childhood a circumstance occurred which made an **indelible** impression on my mind, and laid the ground work of that enthusiasm which has terminated so fatally to many, both white and black, and for which I am about to **atone** at the gallows. It is here necessary to relate this circumstance. **Trifling** as it may seem, it was the commencement of that belief which has grown with time, and even now, sir, in this dungeon, helpless and forsaken as I am, I cannot **divest** myself of. Being at play with other children, when three or four years old, I was telling them something, which my mother, overhearing, said it had happened before I was born—I stuck to my story, however, and related some things which went, in her opinion, to confirm it. Others being called on were greatly astonished, knowing that these things had happened, and caused them to say, in my hearing, I surely would be a prophet, as the Lord had shown me things that had happened before my birth. And my mother and grandmother strengthened me in this my first impression, saying, in my presence, I was intended for some great purpose, which they had always thought from certain marks on my head and breast.

Why did Turner's parents believe that he was "intended for some great purpose"?

My grandmother, who was very religious, and to whom I was much attached—my master, who belonged to the church, and

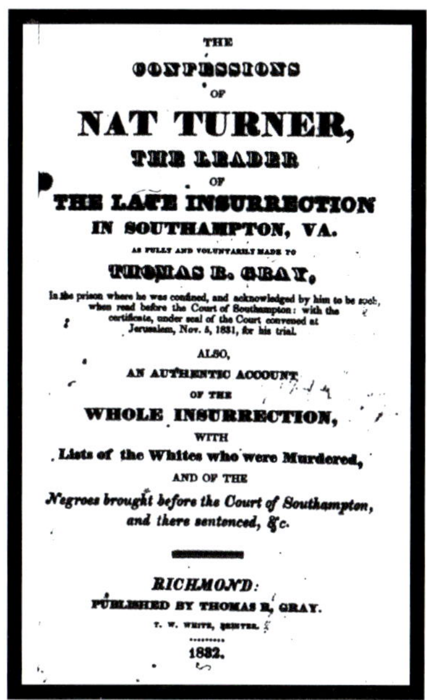
THE
CONFESSIONS
OF
NAT TURNER,
THE LEADER
OF
THE LATE INSURRECTION
IN SOUTHAMPTON, VA.
AS FULLY AND VOLUNTARILY MADE TO
THOMAS R. GRAY,
In the prison where he was confined, and acknowledged by him to be such, when read before the Court of Southampton: with the certificate, under seal of the Court convened at Jerusalem, Nov. 5, 1831, for his trial.
ALSO,
AN AUTHENTIC ACCOUNT
OF THE
WHOLE INSURRECTION,
WITH
Lists of the Whites who were Murdered,
AND OF THE
Negroes brought before the Court of Southampton, and there sentenced, &c.
RICHMOND:
PUBLISHED BY THOMAS R. GRAY.
T. W. WHITE, PRINTER.
1832.

Frontispiece, Library of Congress, LC-USZ62-58152

VOCABULARY IN PLACE

- **induce,** *v.* To cause or lead to
- **insurrection,** *n.* Open revolt against government
- **indelible,** *adj.* Permanent
- **atone,** *v.* To show remorse or regret; make amends
- **trifling,** *adj.* Insignificant
- **divest,** *v.* To free of, rid

other religious persons who visited the house, and whom I often saw at prayers, noticing the **singularity** of my manners, I suppose, and my uncommon intelligence for a child, remarked I had too much sense to be raised, and, if I was, I would never be of any service to any one as a slave. To a mind like mine, restless, **inquisitive**, and observant of every thing that was passing, it is easy to suppose that religion was the subject to which it would be directed; and, although this subject principally occupied my thoughts, there was nothing that I saw or heard of to which my attention was not directed. The manner in which I learned to read and write, not only had great influence on my own mind, as I acquired it with the most perfect ease,—so much so, that I have no recollection whatever of learning the alphabet—but, to the astonishment of the family, one day, when a book was shown me to keep me from crying, I began spelling the names of different objects. This was a source of wonder to all in the neighborhood, particularly the blacks—and this learning was constantly improved at all opportunities. When I got large enough to go to work, while employed, I was reflecting on many things that would present themselves to my imagination, and whenever an opportunity occurred of looking at a book, when the schoolchildren were getting their lessons, I would find many things that the **fertility** of my own imagination had depicted to me before. All my time, not devoted to my master's service, was spent either in prayer, or in making experiments in casting different things in moulds made of earth, in attempting to make paper, gunpowder, and many other experiments, that, although I could not perfect, yet convinced me of its practicability if I had the means.[1]

What sort of a child was Nat Turner? What did others think about him when he was a child?

What did young Nat Turner do in his spare time?

I was not addicted to stealing in my youth, nor have ever been; yet such was the confidence of the negroes in the neighborhood, even at this early period of my life, in my superior judgment, that they would often carry me with them when they were going on any **roguery**, to plan for them. Growing up among them with this confidence in my superior judgment, and when this, in their opinions, was perfected by Divine inspiration, from the circumstances already alluded to in my infancy, and which belief was ever afterwards **zealously inculcated** by the **austerity** of my life and manners, which became the subject of remark by white and black; having soon discovered to be great, I must appear so, and therefore studiously avoided mixing in society, and wrapped myself in mystery, devoting my time to fasting and prayer.

By this time, having arrived to man's estate,[2] and hearing the Scriptures

1 When questioned as to the manner of manufacturing those different articles, he was found well informed on the subject. (This footnote appears in the original text.)

2 **having arrived . . . estate.** Having reached manhood

VOCABULARY IN PLACE

- **singularity,** ***n.*** Uniqueness
- **inquisitive,** ***adj.*** Questioning and reflective
- **fertility,** ***n.*** Ability to produce (ideas)
- **roguery,** ***n.*** Mischief
- **zealously,** ***adv.*** With enthusiastic devotion
- **inculcate,** ***v.*** To impress on the mind through repetition
- **austerity,** ***n.*** The quality of being stern or disciplined

commented on at meetings, I was struck with that particular passage which says, "Seek ye the kingdom of Heaven, and all things shall be added unto you." I reflected much on this passage, and prayed daily for light on this subject. As I was praying one day at my plough, the Spirit spoke to me, saying "Seek ye the kingdom of heaven and all things shall be added unto you."

Who spoke to Nat while he was ploughing? What did the voice tell him?

Question. What do you mean by the Spirit?

Answer. The Spirit that spoke to the prophets in former days,—and I was greatly astonished, and for two years prayed continually, whenever my duty would permit; and then again I had the same revelation, which fully confirmed me in the impression that I was **ordained** for some great purpose in the hands of the Almighty. Several years rolled round, in which many events occurred to strengthen me in this my belief. At this time I reverted in my mind to the remarks made of me in my childhood, and the things that had been shown me; and as it had been said of me in my childhood, by those by whom I was taught to pray, both white and black, and in whom I had the greatest confidence, that I had too much sense to be raised, and if I was I would never be of any use to any one as a slave; now finding I had arrived at man's estate, and was a slave, and these revelations being made known to me, I began to direct my attention to this great object, to fulfill the purpose for which, by this time, I felt assured I was intended. Knowing the influence I had obtained over the minds of my fellow-servants—(not by the means of **conjuring** and such-like tricks—for them I always spoke of such things with contempt), but by the **communion** of the Spirit, whose revelations I often communicated to them, and they believed and said my wisdom came from God,—I now began to prepare them for my purpose, by telling them something was about to happen that would terminate in fulfilling the great promise that had been made to me.

How had Turner gained influence "over the minds of [his] fellow-servants"? What did he tell them about the future?

About this time I was placed under an overseer, from whom I ran away, and after remaining in the woods thirty days, I returned, to the astonishment of the Negroes on the plantation, who thought I had made my escape to some other part of the country, as my father had done before. But the reason of my return was, that the Spirit appeared to me and said I had my wishes directed to the things of this world, and not to the kingdom of heaven, and that I should return to the service of my earthly master—"For he who knoweth his Master's will, and doeth it not, shall be beaten with many stripes, and thus have I **chastened** you."[3] And the Negroes found fault, and murmured against me, saying that if they had my sense they would not serve any master in the world. And about this time I had a vision—and I saw white spirits and black spirits engaged in battle, and the sun was darkened—the thunder rolled in the heavens, and blood flowed in streams—and I heard a voice saying, "Such is your luck, such you are called to see; and let it come rough or smooth, you must surely bear it."

[3] **For he . . . chastened you.** From Luke 12:47

VOCABULARY IN PLACE

- **ordained,** *past part.* Predestined
- **conjure,** *v.* To evoke by means of a magic spell
- **communion,** *n.* A joining together
- **chasten,** *v.* To punish

I now withdrew myself as much as my situation would permit from the intercourse of my fellow-servants, for the **avowed** purpose of serving the Spirit more fully; and it appeared to me, and reminded me of the things it had already shown me, and that it would then reveal to me the knowledge of the elements, the revolution of the planets, the operation of tides, and changes of the seasons. After this revelation in the year 1825, and the knowledge of the elements being made known to me, I sought more than ever to obtain true holiness before the great day of judgment should appear, and then I began to receive the true knowledge of faith. And from the first steps of righteousness until the last, was I made perfect; and the Holy Ghost was with me, and said, "Behold me as I stand in the Heavens." And I looked and saw the forms of men in different attitudes; and there were lights in the sky, to which the children of darkness gave other names than what they really were; for they were the lights of the Saviour's hands, stretched forth from east to west, even as they were extended on the cross on Calvary[4] for the redemption of sinners. And I wondered greatly at these miracles, and prayed to be informed of a certainty of the meaning thereof; and shortly afterwards, while laboring in the field, I discovered drops of blood on the corn, as though it were dew from heaven; and I communicated it to many, both white and black, in the neighborhood—and I then found on the leaves in the woods hieroglyphic[5] characters and numbers, with the forms of men in different attitudes, portrayed in blood, and representing the figures I had seen before in the heavens. And now the Holy Ghost had revealed itself to me, and made plain the miracles it had shown me; for as the blood of Christ had been shed on this earth, and had ascended to heaven for the salvation of sinners, and was now returning to earth again in the form of dew,—and as the leaves on the trees bore the impression of the figures I had seen in the heavens,—it was plain to me that the Saviour was about to lay down the yoke he had borne for the sins of men, and the great day of judgment was at hand.

What did Nat see on the corn?

How did Nat interpret the signs that he saw?

About this time I told these things to a white man, (Etheldred T. Brantley), on whom it had a wonderful effect; and he ceased from his wickedness, and was attacked immediately with a **cutaneous** eruption, and blood oozed from the pores of his skin, and after praying and fasting nine days, he was healed. And the Spirit appeared to me again, and said, as the Saviour had been baptized, so should we be also; and when the white people would not let us be baptized by the church, we went down into the water together, in the sight of many who **reviled** us, and were baptized by the Spirit. After this I rejoiced greatly, and gave thanks to God. And on the 12th of May, 1828, I heard a loud noise in the heavens, and the Spirit instantly appeared to me and said the Serpent[6] was loosened, and Christ had laid down the yoke he had borne for the sins of men, and that I should take it on and fight against the Serpent, for the time was fast approaching when the first should be last and the last should be first.[7]

4 **Calvary.** In the New Testament, the location where Jesus Christ was crucified

5 **hieroglyphic.** Ancient form of writing (Egyptian)

6 **the Serpent.** A traditional way of referring to Satan, as in the Book of Genesis

7 **the first . . . be first.** A paraphrase of Mark 10:31

VOCABULARY IN PLACE

- **avowed,** ***past part.*** Stated, expressed, proclaimed
- **cutaneous,** ***adj.*** Having to do with the skin
- **revile,** ***v.*** To abuse verbally

Question. Do you not find yourself mistaken now?

Answer. Was not Christ crucified? And by signs in the heavens that it would make known to me when I should commence the great work, and until the first sign appeared I should conceal it from the knowledge of men; and on the appearance of the sign (the eclipse of the sun, last February), I should arise and prepare myself, and slay my enemies with their own weapons. And immediately on the sign appearing in the heavens, the seal was removed from my lips, and I communicated the great work laid out for me to do, to four in whom I had the greatest confidence (Henry, Hark, Nelson, and Sam). It was intended by us to have begun the work of death on the 4th July last. Many were the plans formed and rejected by us, and it affected my mind to such a degree that I fell sick, and the time passed without our coming to any determination how to commence—still forming new schemes and rejecting them, when the sign appeared again, which determined me not to wait longer.

What final sign did Turner look for?

Since the commencement of 1830 I had been living with Mr. Joseph Travis, who was to me a kind master, and placed the greatest confidence in me; in fact, I had no cause to complain of his treatment to me. On Saturday evening, the 20th of August, it was agreed between Henry, Hark, and myself, to prepare a dinner the next day for the men we expected, and then to concert[8] a plan, as we had not yet determined on any. Hark, on the following morning, brought a pig, and Henry brandy; and being joined by Sam, Nelson, Will, and Jack, they prepared in the woods a dinner, where, about three o'clock, I joined them.

Question. Why were you so backward in joining them?

Answer. The same reason that has caused me not to mix with them for years before, I saluted them on coming up, and asked Will how came he there. He answered, his life was worth no more than others, and his liberty as dear to him. I asked him if he thought to obtain it. He said he would, or lose his life. This was enough to put him in full confidence. Jack, I knew, was only a tool in the hands of Hark. It was quickly agreed we should commence at home (Mr. J. Travis') on that night; and until we had armed and equipped ourselves, and gathered sufficient force, neither age nor sex was to be spared—which was invariably adhered to. We remained at the feast until about two hours in the night, when we went to the house and found Austin. They all went to the cider press and drank, except myself.

On returning to the house, Hark went to the door with an axe, for the purpose of breaking it open, as we knew we were strong enough to murder the family, if they were awaked by the noise; but reflecting that it might create an alarm in the neighborhood, we determined to enter the house secretly, and murder them whilst sleeping. Hark got a ladder and set it against the chimney, on which I ascended, and hoisting a window, entered and came down stairs, unbarred the door, and removed the guns from their places. It was then observed that I must spill the first blood.

[Editor's note: At this point in his confession, Nat Turner described in graphic detail how he and his followers moved from house to house killing white men, women, and children and recruiting additional enslaved persons to join in the revolt.]

[8] **concert.** Work together to develop

We again divided, a part going to Mr. Richard Porter's, and from thence to Nathaniel Francis', the others to Mr. Howell Harris', and Mr. T. Doyles'. On my reaching Mr. Porter's, he had escaped with his family. I understood there, that the alarm had already spread, and I immediately returned to bring up those sent to Mr. Doyles', and Mr. Howell Harris'; the party I left going on to Mr. Francis', having told them I would join them in that neighborhood. I met these sent to Mr. Doyles' and Mr. Harris' returning, having met Mr. Doyles on the road and killed him; and learning from some who joined them, pursued the course taken by the party gone on before. But knowing they would complete the work of death and pillage, at Mr. Francis' before I could get there, I went to Mr. Peter Edwards', expecting to find them there, but they had been here also. I then went to Mr. John T. Barrow's, they had been here and murdered him. I pursued on their track to Capt. Newit Harris', where I found the greater part mounted, and ready to start. The men now amounting to about forty, shouted and hurraed as I rode up; some were in the yard, loading their guns, others drinking. They said Captain Harris and his family had escaped; the property in the house they destroyed, robbing him of money and other valuables. I ordered them to mount and march instantly. This was about nine or ten o'clock, Monday morning. I proceeded to Mr. Levi Waller's, two or three miles distant.

I took my station in the rear, and as it was my object to carry terror and devastation wherever we went, I placed fifteen or twenty of the best armed and most to be relied on in front, who generally approached the houses as fast as their horses could run. This was for two purposes—to prevent their escape, and strike terror to the inhabitants; on this account I never got to the houses, after leaving Mrs. Whitehead's, until the murders were committed, except in one case. I sometimes got in sight in time to see the work of death completed, viewed the mangled bodies as they lay, in silent satisfaction, and immediately started in quest of other victims.

[Editor's note: At this point Turner described additional murders and a confrontation with a group of eighteen armed white men. In the skirmish, several of Turner's men were wounded.]

After trying in vain to collect a sufficient force to proceed to Jerusalem, I determined to return, as I was sure they would make back to their old neighborhood, where they would rejoin me, make new recruits, and come down again. On my way back, I called at Mrs. Thomas's, Mrs. Spencer's, and several other places. The white families having fled, we found no more victims to gratify our thirst for blood. We stopped at Maj. Ridley's quarter for the night, and being joined by four of his men, with the recruits made since my defeat, we mustered now about forty strong. After placing out **sentinels**, I laid down to sleep, but was quickly roused by a great racket; starting up, I found some mounted, and others in great confusion; one of the sentinels having given the alarm that we were about to be attacked, I ordered some to ride round and **reconnoiter**, and on their return the others being more alarmed, not knowing who they were, fled in different ways, so that I was reduced to about twenty again.

With this I determined to attempt to recruit, and proceed on to rally in the neighborhood I had left. Dr. Blunt's was the nearest house, which we reached just before day. On riding up the yard, Hark fired a gun.

VOCABULARY IN PLACE

- **sentinel,** *n.* Guard
- **reconnoiter,** *v.* To inspect or check an area

We expected Dr. Blunt and his family were at Maj. Ridley's, as I knew there was a company of men there. The gun was fired to ascertain if any of the family were at home; we were immediately fired upon and retreated, leaving several of my men. I do not know what became of them, as I never saw them afterwards. Pursuing our course back and coming in sight of Captain Harris', where we had been the day before, we discovered a party of white men at the house, on which all deserted me but two, (Jacob and Nat), we concealed ourselves in the woods until near night, when I sent them in search of Henry, Sam, Nelson, and Hark, and directed them to rally all they could, at the place we had had our dinner the Sunday before, where they would find me, and I accordingly returned there as soon as it was dark and remained until Wednesday evening, when discovering white men riding around the place as though they were looking for some one, and none of my men joining me, I concluded Jacob and Nat had been taken, and compelled to betray me.

What happened to all of Turner's men?

On this I gave up all hope for the present; and on Thursday night, after having supplied myself with provisions from Mr. Travis's, I scratched a hole under a pile of fence-rails in a field, where I concealed myself for six weeks, never leaving my hiding-place but for a few minutes in the dead of night to get water, which was very near. Thinking by this time I could venture out, I began to go about in the night, and eavesdrop the houses in the neighborhood; pursuing this course for about a fortnight,[9] and gathering little or no intelligence, afraid of speaking to any human being, and returning every morning to my cave before the dawn of day. I know not how long I might have led this life, if accident had not betrayed me. A dog in the neighborhood passing by my hiding-place one night while I was out, was attracted by some meat I had in my cave, and crawled in and stole it, and was coming out just as I returned. A few nights after, two Negroes having started to go hunting with the same dog, and passed that way, the dog came again to the place, and having just gone out to walk about, discovered me and barked; on which thinking myself discovered, I spoke to them to beg concealment. On making myself known, they fled from me. Knowing then they would betray me, I immediately left my hiding place, and was pursued almost incessantly, until I was taken, a fortnight afterwards, by Mr. Benjamin Phipps, in a little hole I had dug out with my sword, for the purpose of concealment, under the top of a fallen tree.

On Mr. Phipps' discovering the place of my concealment, he cocked his gun and aimed at me, I requested him not to shoot and I would give up, upon which he demanded my sword. I delivered it to him, and he brought me to prison. During the time I was pursued, I had many hair-breadth escapes, which your time will not permit you to relate. I am here loaded with chains, and willing to suffer the fate that awaits me. ■

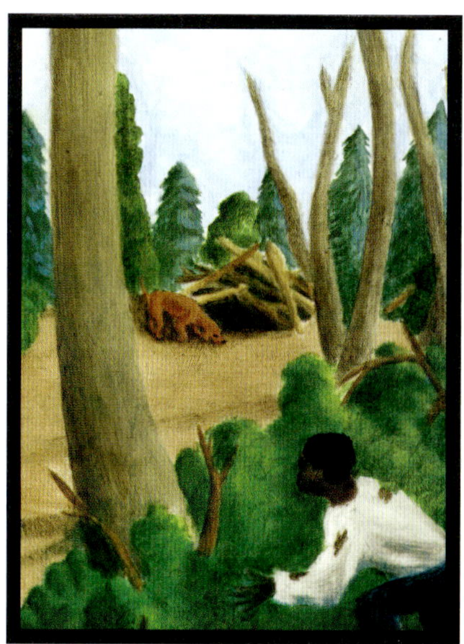

[9] **fortnight.** Two weeks

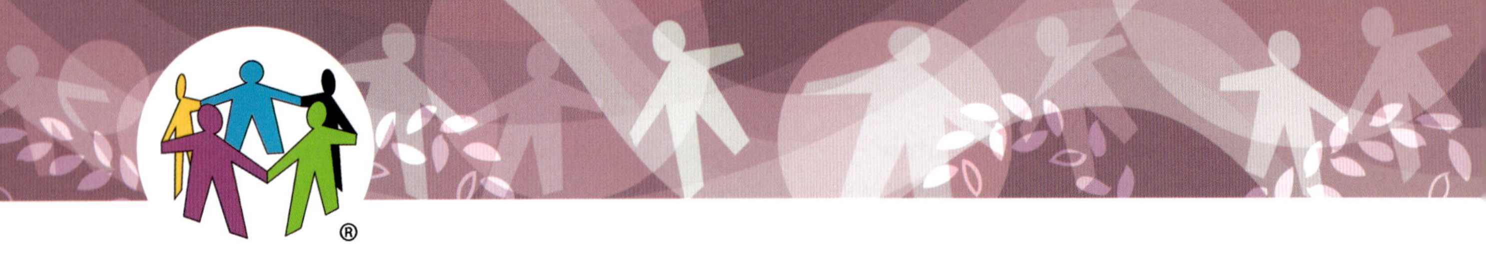

Understanding the Selection

Recalling

1. What did Nat's mother overhear him saying to other children when Nat was three or four years old?
2. What happened to Nat one day while he was ploughing?
3. After his return to the plantation from which he ran away, Nat had a vision. What did he see?
4. What signs did Nat see in the sky, on the corn, and on the leaves of trees?
5. Did Turner have many accomplices?

Interpreting

1. How did the people around young Nat react to what his mother overheard?
2. How did Nat's perceptions differ from those of most people?
3. What did Nat come to believe was the "great purpose" for which he was "ordained"?
4. How did Nat interpret these signs? How did other slaves react to his visions?
5. Why did so many people join him over the course of his raid?

Synthesizing

1. What motivated Nat Turner to carry out this raid? Why was he "willing to suffer the fate that await[ed]" him? Cite several examples from the text.
2. Why did Turner paraphrase the scriptural passage, "But many [that are] first shall be last; and the last first"?

Delving Deeper

Understanding Literature

Oral History. An **oral history** is an autobiographical account told to someone else who then writes it down. Fortunately for later historians, the lawyer Thomas R. Gray met with Nat Turner after his capture and recorded a first-hand account of this most famous of slave uprisings. From oral histories, as from autobiographies, one can learn how individuals from the past viewed themselves and the world in which they lived. Why do some people need to dictate their own history? What makes an oral history different from a written one?

If you have an elder relative, friend, or neighbor, take a few hours one day to record some of his or her oral history. Doing such an assignment can be fascinating, for an older person is a time machine (as the short-story writer Ray Bradbury once put it). Compose a list of questions to help "break the ice." It makes people happy to know that others are listening to their stories and recording them. And those who listen always stand to gain a great deal of wisdom and understanding in return.

About the Author

Nat Turner (1800–1831) was born on a plantation in Southhampton County, Virginia. He was deeply inculcated with religious belief from an early age. From youth, he saw visions and heard voices that led him to believe that he was destined for great things. In 1821, Turner escaped enslavement, as had his father before him, but after receiving a vision telling him to lead a slave rebellion, Turner returned to the plantation, began preaching to congregations of African Americans throughout the surrounding county, and started to plan his rebellion. Turner originally planned to mount his revolt on Independence Day, 1831, but illness caused him to postpone the date to August 22. He and his small band of followers moved from house to house, killing all whites whom they encountered and recruiting additional rebels. Dozens of people joined with Turner, who was headed toward the arsenal in Jerusalem, Virginia. The two-day rebellion led to the deaths of about sixty whites and was ended by an attack by local militia in which over 100 innocent blacks were killed. Turner himself was captured on October 30, tried, and sentenced to death.

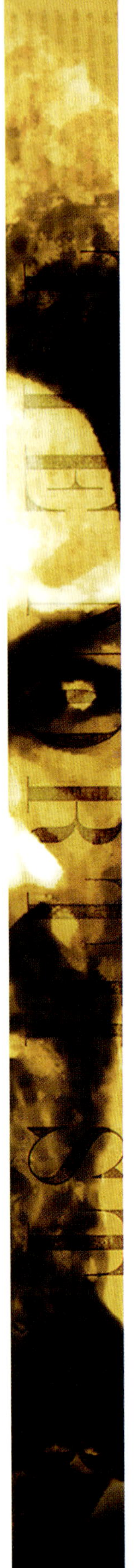

Prereading

from *Narrative of the Life of Frederick Douglass, an American Slave*
by Frederick Douglass

The *Narrative of the Life of Frederick Douglass, an American Slave,* is universally acknowledged to be one of the greatest of the so-called **slave narratives,** autobiographical accounts written by enslaved persons or formerly enslaved persons that tell about their experiences under the brutal system that prevailed in much of the United States before the Civil War. A moving testament to the human spirit, Douglass's *Narrative* tells how he was born into slavery in Maryland, escaped from bondage, and found his way to the North and freedom.

In the selection from the *Narrative* reprinted here, Douglass tells how he taught himself to read. In many parts of the South during the slavery era, teaching a slave to read was a crime. Keeping slaves ignorant was one way in which white slave owners perpetuated the myth of racial inferiority. Nonetheless, many slaves, Douglass among them, struggled against the odds to master reading and writing. Douglass mastered these arts so well, in fact, that after his escape, he founded one of the nation's most important Abolitionist newspapers, *The North Star,* and became one of the country's leading writers and orators (speakers) for the anti-slavery cause. As you read the selection from the *Narrative,* think about these questions:

1. What negative effects did slavery have on slaveholders?
2. Why did slaveholders not want slaves to learn to read?
3. What did learning to read enable Douglass to do that he would not otherwise have been able to do?

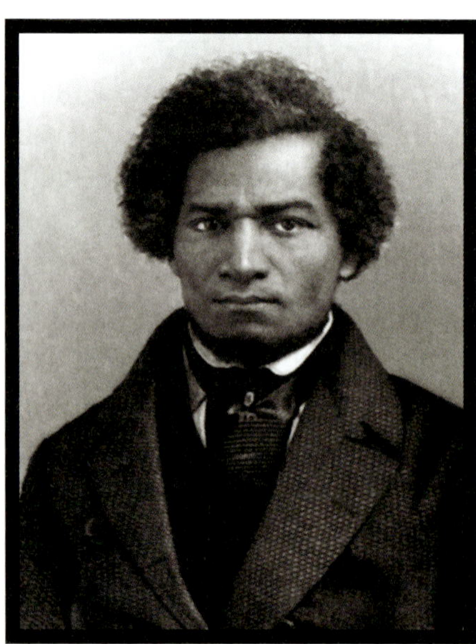

Frederick Douglass

from Narrative of the Life of Frederick Douglass

by Frederick Douglass

I lived in Master Hugh's family about seven years. During this time, I succeeded in learning to read and write. In accomplishing this, I was compelled to resort to various **stratagems**. I had no regular teacher. My mistress,[1] who had kindly commenced to instruct me, had, in **compliance** with the advice and direction of her husband, not only ceased to instruct, but had set her face against my being instructed by any one else. It is due, however, to my mistress to say of her, that she did not adopt this course of treatment immediately. She at first lacked the **depravity** indispensable to shutting me up in mental darkness. It was at least necessary for her to have some training in the exercise of irresponsible power, to make her equal to the task of treating me as though I were a brute.[2]

My mistress was, as I have said, a kind and tender-hearted woman; and in the simplicity of her soul she commenced, when I first went to live with her, to treat me as she supposed one human being ought to treat another. In entering upon the duties of a slaveholder, she did not seem to perceive that I sustained to her the relation of a mere **chattel,** and that for her to treat me as a human being was not only wrong, but dangerously so. Slavery proved as injurious to her as it did to me. When I went there, she was a pious, warm, and tender-hearted woman. There was no sorrow or suffering for which she had not a tear. She had bread for the hungry, clothes for the naked, and comfort for every mourner that came within her reach.

Slavery soon proved its ability to **divest** her of these heavenly qualities. Under its influence, the tender heart became stone, and the lamblike disposition gave way to one of tiger-like fierceness. The first step in her downward course was in her ceasing to instruct me. She now commenced to practice her husband's precepts. She finally became even more violent in her opposition than her husband himself. She was not satisfied with simply doing as well as he had commanded; she seemed anxious to do better.

How did Mrs. Auld change? What caused this change in her?

---

1 **mistress.** The slave owner, Mrs. Auld. She had begun teaching young Douglass to read but abruptly ended the lessons at her husband's insistence.

2 **brute.** An animal

VOCABULARY IN PLACE

- **stratagem,** *n.* A clever, underhanded scheme for achieving an objective
- **compliance,** *n.* Acquiescence, act of yielding to the will of another person
- **depravity,** *n.* Moral corruption
- **chattel,** *n.* An article of movable personal property, such as a cow or wagon
- **divest,** *v.* To deprive or rid oneself of, as of rights or property

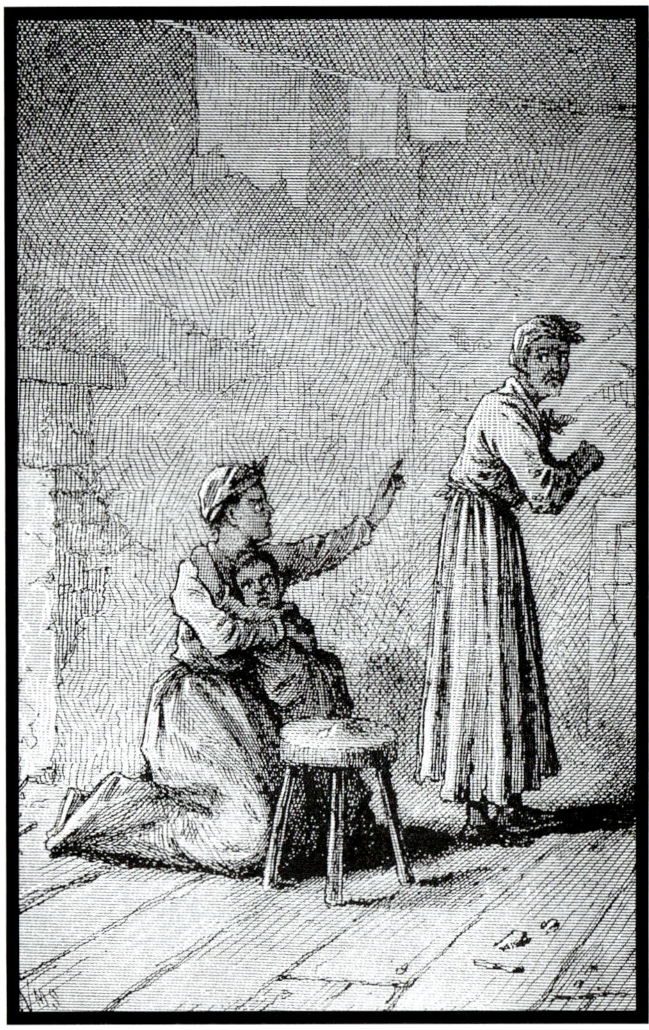

An image from one of Frederick Douglass's autobiographies

Nothing seemed to make her more angry than to see me with a newspaper. She seemed to think that here lay the danger. I have had her rush at me with a face made all up of fury, and snatch from me a newspaper, in a manner that fully revealed her **apprehension.** She was an **apt** woman; and a little experience soon demonstrated, to her satisfaction, that education and slavery were incompatible with each other.

From this time I was most narrowly watched. If I was in a separate room any considerable length of time, I was sure to be suspected of having a book, and was at once called to give an account of myself. All this, however, was too late. The first step had been taken. Mistress, in teaching me the alphabet, had given me the INCH, and no precaution could prevent me from taking the ELL.[3]

The plan which I adopted, and the one by which I was most successful, was that of making friends of all the little white boys whom I met in the street. As many of these as I could, I converted into teachers. With their kindly aid, obtained at different times and in different places, I finally succeeded in learning to read. When I was sent on errands, I always took my book with me, and by going one part of my errand quickly, I found time to get a lesson before my return. I used also to carry bread with me, enough of which was always in the house, and to which I was always welcome; for I was much better off in this regard than many of the poor white children in our neighborhood. This bread I used to bestow upon the hungry little **urchins,** who, in return, would give me that more valuable bread of knowledge. I am strongly tempted to give the names of two or three of those little boys, as a testimonial of the gratitude and affection I bear them; but **prudence** forbids;—not that it would injure me, but it might embarrass them; for

What did the little boys do for young Douglass?

[3] **ELL.** An English measurement equal to 45 inches

VOCABULARY IN PLACE

- **apprehension,** ***n.*** Fearful anticipation of the future
- **apt,** ***adj.*** Quick to learn and understand
- **urchin,** ***n.*** Mischievous, playful youngster
- **prudence,** ***n.*** The exercise of good judgment

it is almost an unpardonable offence to teach slaves to read in this Christian country. It is enough to say of the dear little fellows, that they lived on Philpot Street, very near Durgin and Bailey's shipyard. I used to talk this matter of slavery over with them. I would sometimes say to them, I wished I could be as free as they would be when they got to be men. "You will be free as soon as you are twenty-one, BUT I AM A SLAVE FOR LIFE![4] Have not I as good a right to be free as you have?" These words used to trouble them; they would express for me the liveliest sympathy, and **console** me with the hope that something would occur by which I might be free.

I was now about twelve years old, and the thought of being A SLAVE FOR LIFE began to bear heavily upon my heart. Just about this time, I got hold of a book entitled "The Columbian Orator."[5] Every opportunity I got, I used to read this book. Among much of other interesting matter, I found in it a dialogue between a master and his slave. The slave was represented as having run away from his master three times. The dialogue represented the conversation which took place between them, when the slave was retaken the third time. In this dialogue, the whole argument in behalf of slavery was brought forward by the master, all of which was disposed of by the slave. The slave was made to say some very smart as well as impressive things in reply to his master—things which had the desired though unexpected effect; for the conversation resulted in the voluntary emancipation of the slave on the part of the master.

What selections in The Columbian Orator *were of particular interest to Douglass?*

In the same book, I met with one of Sheridan's[6] mighty speeches on and in behalf of Catholic emancipation. These were choice documents to me. I read them over and over again with **unabated** interest. They gave tongue to interesting thoughts of my own soul, which had frequently flashed through my mind, and died away for want of utterance. The moral which I gained from the dialogue was the power of truth over the conscience of even a slaveholder. What I got from Sheridan was a bold denunciation of slavery, and a powerful vindication of human rights. The reading of these documents enabled me to utter my thoughts, and to meet the arguments brought forward to sustain slavery; but while they relieved me of one difficulty, they brought on another even more painful than the one of which I was relieved. The more I read, the more I was led to **abhor** and detest my enslavers. I could regard them in no other light than a band of successful robbers, who had left their homes, and gone to Africa, and stolen us from our homes, and in a strange land reduced us to slavery. I **loathed** them as being the meanest as well as the most wicked of men. As I read and contemplated the subject, behold! that very discontentment which Master Hugh

---

[4] **You will be free . . . SLAVE FOR LIFE.** At twenty-one, the white children would become adults, with the full rights of citizens.

[5] **The Columbian Orator.** A popular book edited by Caleb Bingham, a Massachusetts educator, containing selected essays and speeches, along with rules of speech-making (oratory)

[6] **Sheridan.** Richard Brinsley Sheridan, a British playwright of the eighteenth century who supported Irish independence from Great Britain. Douglass saw many similarities between the subjugation of the Irish by the British and slavery in the United States.

VOCABULARY IN PLACE

- **console,** *v.* To comfort
- **unabated,** *adj.* Continued at full strength or force
- **abhor,** *v.* To regard with horror or hatred
- **loathe,** *v.* To dislike greatly

had predicted would follow my learning to read had already come, to torment and sting my soul to unutterable anguish. As I writhed under it, I would at times feel that learning to read had been a curse rather than a blessing. It had given me a view of my wretched condition, without the remedy. It opened my eyes to the horrible pit, but to no ladder upon which to get out. In moments of agony, I envied my fellow-slaves for their stupidity. I have often wished myself a beast. I preferred the condition of the meanest reptile to my own. Any thing, no matter what, to get rid of thinking! It was this everlasting thinking of my condition that tormented me. There was no getting rid of it. It was pressed upon me by every object within sight or hearing, animate or inanimate. The silver trump[7] of freedom had roused my soul to eternal wakefulness. Freedom now appeared, to disappear no more forever. It was heard in every sound, and seen in every thing. It was ever present to torment me with a sense of my **wretched** condition. I saw nothing without seeing it, I heard nothing without hearing it, and felt nothing without feeling it. It looked from every star, it smiled in every calm, breathed in every wind, and moved in every storm.

I often found myself regretting my own existence, and wishing myself dead; and but for the hope of being free, I have no doubt but that I should have killed myself, or done something for which I should have been killed. While in this state of mind, I was eager to hear any one speak of slavery. I was a ready listener. Every little while, I could hear something about the abolitionists. It was some time before I found what the word meant. It was always used in such connections as to make it an interesting word to me. If a slave ran away and succeeded in getting clear, or if a slave killed his master, set fire to a barn, or did any thing very wrong in the mind of a slaveholder, it was spoken of as the fruit of ABOLITION. Hearing the word in this connection very often, I set about learning what it meant. The dictionary afforded me little or no help. I found it was "the act of abolishing;" but then I did not know what was to be abolished. Here I was perplexed. I did not dare to ask any one about its meaning, for I was satisfied that it was something they wanted me to know very little about. After a patient waiting, I got one of our city papers, containing an account of the number of petitions from the north, praying for the abolition of slavery in the District of Columbia, and of the slave trade between the States. From this time I understood the words ABOLITION and ABOLITIONIST, and always drew near when that word was spoken, expecting to hear something of importance to myself and fellow-slaves. The light broke in upon me by degrees. I went one day down on the wharf of Mr. Waters; and seeing two Irishmen unloading a scow[8] of stone, I went, unasked, and helped them. When we had finished, one of them came to me and asked me if I were a slave. I told him I was. He asked, "Are ye a slave for life?" I told him that I was. The good Irishman seemed to be deeply affected by the statement. He said to the other that it was a pity so fine a little fellow as myself should be a slave for life. He said it was a shame to hold me. They both advised me to run away to the north; that I should find friends there,

How did Douglass figure out the meaning of the word abolition*? What does it mean?*

[7] **trump.** Trumpet

[8] **scow.** A large, flat-bottomed boat with square ends, used for transporting freight

VOCABULARY IN PLACE

- **wretched,** ***adj.*** Miserable, unhappy, distressed

and that I should be free. I pretended not to be interested in what they said, and treated them as if I did not understand them; for I feared they might be **treacherous.** White men have been known to encourage slaves to escape, and then, to get the reward, catch them and return them to their masters. I was afraid that these seemingly good men might use me so; but I nevertheless remembered their advice, and from that time I resolved to run away. I looked forward to a time at which it would be safe for me to escape. I was too young to think of doing so immediately; besides, I wished to learn how to write, as I might have occasion to write my own pass. I consoled myself with the hope that I should one day find a good chance. Meanwhile, I would learn to write.

Why did Douglass want to learn how to write?

The idea as to how I might learn to write was suggested to me by being in Durgin and Bailey's shipyard, and frequently seeing the ship carpenters, after hewing, and getting a piece of timber ready for use, write on the timber the name of that part of the ship for which it was intended. When a piece of timber was intended for the larboard side, it would be marked thus—"L." When a piece was for the starboard side, it would be marked thus—"S." A piece for the larboard side forward, would be marked thus—"L. F." When a piece was for starboard side forward, it would be marked thus—"S. F." For larboard aft, it would be marked thus—"L. A." For starboard aft, it would be marked thus—"S. A."[9] I soon learned the names of these letters, and for what they were intended when placed upon a piece of timber in the shipyard. I immediately commenced copying them, and in a short time was able to make the four letters named. After that, when I met with any boy who I knew could write, I would tell him I could write as well as he. The next word would be, "I don't believe you. Let me see you try it." I would then make the letters which I had been so fortunate as to learn, and ask him to beat that. In this way I got a good many lessons in writing, which it is quite possible I should never have gotten in any other way. During this time, my copy-book[10] was the board fence, brick wall, and pavement; my pen and ink was a lump of chalk. With these, I learned mainly how to write. I then commenced and continued copying the Italics in Webster's Spelling Book,[11] until I could make them all without looking on the book. By this time, my little Master Thomas had gone to school, and learned how to write, and had written over a number of copy-books. These had been brought home, and shown to some of our near neighbors, and then laid aside. My mistress used to go to class meeting at the Wilk Street meetinghouse every Monday afternoon, and leave me to take care of the house. When left thus, I used to spend the time in writing in the spaces left in Master Thomas's copy-book, copying what he had written. I continued to do this until I could write a hand very similar to that of Master Thomas. Thus, after a long, tedious effort for years, I finally succeeded in learning how to write. ■

[9] **When a piece . . . marked thus—"S. A."** *Larboard* refers to the left side of the boat, and *starboard* to the right. *Forward* and *aft* refer to the front and rear, respectively.

[10] **copy-book.** A popular way of teaching writing was to have the student copy the stories and speeches written by famous people into a blank notebook.

[11] **Webster's Spelling Book.** *The American Spelling Book,* by Noah Webster, an enormously popular nineteenth-century reference book

VOCABULARY IN PLACE

- **treacherous,** ***adj.*** Untrustworthy, dangerous, unreliable

Understanding the Selection

Recalling

1. What did Douglass learn to do in the seven years during which he lived with the Aulds?
2. How did Mrs. Auld try to prevent Douglass from learning how to read?
3. What were two of Douglass's favorite selections from *The Columbian Orator?*
4. What is an abolitionist?

Interpreting

1. Why did Douglass say that slavery did as much to harm the slaveholder as it did to harm the slave?
2. How did Douglass feel about the white boys who helped him learn how to read?
3. What did the enslaved people of the United States and the Catholics of Ireland have in common?
4. How did the word *abolitionism* save Frederick Douglass's life?

Synthesizing

1. Explain the following statement: "Mistress, in teaching me the alphabet, had given me the INCH, and no precaution could prevent me from taking the ELL." Why was Douglass so intent on learning to read well?
2. Why did Douglass become more discontent with being a "slave for life" the more he read? Why do you think slave owners discouraged teaching slaves to read?

Delving Deeper

History Connection

The Abolitionist Movement. In the 1820s, a Protestant evangelical movement swept the northern United States. This movement, known as the **Second Great Awakening,** created in many intellectuals and religious activists the desire to see morality prevail in the political and social spheres. Evangelicalism led to the **Temperance Movement,** which sought to ban alcohol; the **Women's Suffrage Movement,** which sought to give women the vote; and the **Abolitionist Movement,** which sought to free African Americans from slavery. Of these three movements, the last was the first to achieve success in its major goal.

In 1831, delegates from throughout the United States met in Philadelphia, the birthplace of the Constitution, to form the **American Anti-Slavery Society,** which produced books and pamphlets and lobbied Congress to end slavery once and for all. Reaction to the Abolitionist Movement was fierce and extreme. There were anti-Abolitionist riots in several cities and murders of Abolitionist leaders. Nonetheless, the Abolitionists pressed on. Among their many accomplishments was the founding of institutions of higher education for black men and women, including Knox College, the Oneida Institute, and the racially integrated Oberlin College.

By the 1850s, tensions over the issue of slavery had reached a boiling point. The country was deeply divided. **The Fugitive Slave Law of 1850** required federal marshalls to arrest escaped slaves or face stiff fines. **The Kansas-Nebraska Act of 1854** repealed the **Missouri Compromise** (which outlawed slavery north of the 40th parallel) and allowed people in the Kansas and Nebraska territories to vote to accept or reject slavery. In 1857, the Supreme Court ruled in ***Dred Scott v. Sanford*** that slaves were property and could not sue in court. Abolitionists had worked to organize a series of safe houses from the South to the North—the **Underground Railroad**—to help enslaved persons to escape to freedom, but the Dred Scott Decision threatened to undo that great work, for if slaves were property, then slave owners could sue for their return. In 1859, Abolitionist John Brown led an attack on a federal armory at Harpers Ferry, Virginia, in hopes of sparking a slave uprising. Brown was defeated and hanged. It took a civil war to settle the question of slavery for good. The **Thirteenth Amendment to the Constitution,** ratified on December 6, 1865, stated unequivocally and for all time that "Neither slavery nor involuntary servitude, except as a punishment for crime whereof the party shall have been duly convicted, shall exist within the United States, or any place subject to their jurisdiction."

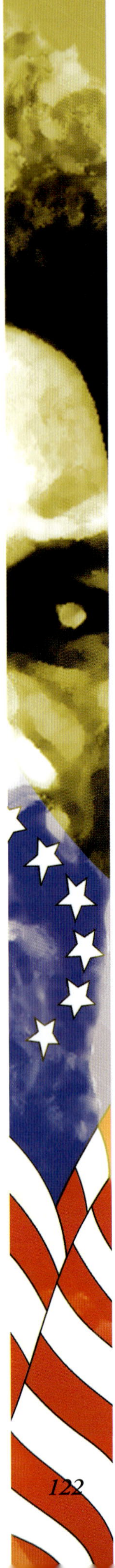

Prereading

from "What to the Slave Is the Fourth of July?"

by Frederick Douglass

Douglass delivered this speech to an audience of 600 white Northerners at a meeting of the Rochester Ladies Antislavery Society in his adopted hometown of Rochester, New York, on the 5th of July, 1852. The speech is justly famous for its commitment to the ideals of liberty as espoused by the Founding Fathers and for its indictment of a country that had failed to extend the promise of liberty to those of African heritage.

At the time of this speech, the Abolitionist Movement in the United States was extremely active, and debate raged throughout the country over the subject of slavery. Two years earlier, a series of laws had been passed by Congress to attempt to deal with the divisive issue of slavery. Called the **Compromise of 1850**, these laws represented, to the Abolitionists, an unacceptable attempt to make peace on both sides while allowing slavery to continue. The laws admitted California to the Union as a free state, admitted the territory of New Mexico (which included what are now Arizona and Utah) without prohibiting slavery there, did away with the slave trade in Washington, D.C., and required citizens to help return runaway, or fugitive, slaves to their owners. It is the fourth directive—requiring the apprehension of fugitives—that, for slaves and Abolitionists, made the Compromise of 1850 more of a disaster than an acceptable series of trade-offs.

Frederick Douglass himself had escaped from slavery in 1838, and after his escape, he lived, at first, in Massachusetts. Then, during a lecture tour, he was befriended by two Quakers, Isaac and Amy Post, who lived in Rochester and influenced him to settle there. Douglass traveled frequently, giving lectures and speeches about slavery and abolition. He also founded an Abolitionist newspaper, *The North Star,* and wrote the first of his memoirs, excerpted in the previous selection. The following selection will give you some idea of the power of Frederick Douglass's oratory and of his impressive command of the English language, all the more astonishing because he was largely self-taught. He was a man of undeniable genius and courage. He was not afraid of surprising or otherwise offending his audience in his effort to lay bare the truth about slavery in America. What meaning did the Fourth of July, American Independence Day, have for a person like Douglass, an escaped slave? What meaning did it have for the slaves who were still, at the time of this speech, in bondage?

from What to the Slave Is the Fourth of July?

by Frederick Douglass

Fellow-citizens, pardon me, allow me to ask, why am I called upon to speak here today?

What have I, or those I represent,[1] to do with your national independence? Are the great principles of political freedom and of natural justice, **embodied** in that Declaration of Independence, extended to us? and am I, therefore, called upon to bring our humble offering to the national altar, and to confess the benefits and express **devout** gratitude for the blessings resulting from your independence to us?

Why did Douglass speak of "your national independence" and not of "our national independence"?

Would to God, both for your sakes and ours, that an **affirmative** answer could be truthfully returned to these questions! Then would my task be light, and my burden easy and delightful.

For *who* is there so cold, that a nation's sympathy could not warm him? Who so **obdurate** and dead to the claims of gratitude, that would not thankfully acknowledge such priceless benefits?

Who so **stolid** and selfish, that would not give his voice to swell the hallelujahs of a nation's **jubilee**, when the chains of **servitude** had been torn from his limbs? I am not that man. In a case like that, the dumb might eloquently speak, and the "lame man leap as an hart."[2]

But, such is not the state of the case. I say it with a sad sense of the **disparity** between us. I am not included within the pale[3] of this glorious anniversary! Your high independence only reveals the immeasurable distance between us. The blessings in which you, this day, rejoice, are not enjoyed in common. The rich inheritance of justice, liberty, prosperity and independence, bequeathed by your fathers, is shared by you, not by me. The sunlight that brought life and healing to you, has brought stripes[4] and death to me. This Fourth [of]

What did the Independence Day celebration reveal about the differences between blacks and whites?

1 **those I represent.** Enslaved African Americans. Frederick Douglass was born into slavery and escaped to the North.

2 **hart.** A *hart* is a deer. Douglass is saying that it is impossible for him to join wholeheartedly in the American Fourth of July celebration.

3 **pale.** A bounded area

4 **stripes.** Wounds or scars from whipping

VOCABULARY IN PLACE

- **embodied,** ***past part.*** Given form and substance
- **devout,** ***adj.*** Worshipful, pious
- **affirmative,** ***adj.*** Positive, supportive
- **obdurate,** ***adj.*** Hardened in wickedness
- **stolid,** ***adj.*** Showing or feeling little emotion
- **jubilee,** ***n.*** A festival or celebration
- **servitude,** ***n.*** The state of being a servant or slave
- **disparity,** ***n.*** Differences

July is *yours*, not *mine*. *You* may rejoice, *I* must mourn. To drag a man in fetters[5] into the grand illuminated temple of liberty, and call upon him to join you in joyous **anthems**, were inhuman mockery and sacrilegious irony.[6] Do you mean, citizens, to mock me, by asking me to speak today? If so, there is a parallel to your conduct. And let me warn you that it is dangerous to copy the example of a nation whose crimes, towering up to heaven, were thrown down by the breath of the Almighty, burying that nation in irrecoverable ruin! I can today take up the **plaintive lament** of a peeled and woe-smitten people!

"By the rivers of Babylon, there we sat down. Yea! we wept when we remembered Zion. We hanged our harps upon the willows in the midst thereof. For there, they that carried us away captive, required of us a song; and they who wasted us required of us mirth, saying, Sing us one of the songs of Zion. How shall we sing the Lord's song in a strange land? If I forgot thee, O Jerusalem, let my right hand forget her cunning. If I do not remember thee, let my tongue cleave to the roof of my mouth."[7]

Why did Douglass choose to quote this passage?

Fellow-citizens; above your national, **tumultuous** joy, I hear the mournful wail of millions! whose chains, heavy and grievous yesterday, are, today, rendered more **intolerable** by the jubilee shouts that reach them. If I do forget, if I do not faithfully remember those bleeding children of sorrow this day, "may my right hand forget her cunning, and may my tongue cleave to the roof of my mouth!"[8] To forget them, to pass lightly over their wrongs, and to **chime in** with the popular theme, would be treason most scandalous and shocking, and would make me a **reproach** before God and the world.

My subject, then fellow-citizens, is AMERICAN SLAVERY. I shall see, this day, and its popular characteristics, from the slave's point of view. Standing there, identified with the American bondman,[9] making his wrongs mine, I do not hesitate to declare, with all my soul, that the character and conduct of this nation never looked blacker to me than on the 4th of July! Whether we turn to the declarations of the past, or to the professions of the present, the conduct of the nations of the past, or to the professions of the present, the conduct of the nation seems equally hideous and revolting. America is false to the past, false to the present, and solemnly binds herself to be false to the future. Standing with God and the crushed and bleeding slave on this occasion, I will, in the name of humanity which is outraged, in the name of liberty which is fettered, in the name of

5 **fetters.** Chains

6 **inhuman mockery and sacrilegious irony.** It is unjust, cruel, and blasphemous (offensive to God) for white Americans to expect slaves to join in Fourth of July festivities.

7 **By the rivers of Babylon . . . my mouth.** From Psalm 137:1–6. This beautiful and moving psalm tells of an event that occurred after the fall of Jerusalem to the invading Babylonians in 586 BCE.

8 **may my . . . mouth.** Another reference to Psalm 137:1–6. The singer of the psalm says that if he forgets Jerusalem, may these things happen to him.

9 **bondman.** Enslaved person, one held in bonds

VOCABULARY IN PLACE

- **anthem,** *n.* A song of praise
- **plaintive,** *adj.* Expressing sadness or regret
- **lament,** *n.* Expression of grief
- **tumultuous,** *adj.* Noisy and disorderly
- **intolerable,** *adj.* Unbearable
- **chime in,** *v.* To join in to a conversation
- **reproach,** *n.* Disapproval, disgrace

the Constitution and the Bible, which are disregarded and trampled upon, dare to call in question and to denounce, with all the emphasis I can command, everything that serves to **perpetuate** slavery—the great sin and shame of America! "I will not **equivocate;** I will not excuse"; I will use the severest language I can command; and yet not one word shall escape me that any man, whose judgment is not blinded by prejudice, or who is not at heart a slaveholder, shall not confess to be right and just.

But I fancy I hear someone of my audience say, it is just in this circumstance that you and your brother abolitionists fail to make a favorable impression on the public mind. Would you argue more, and denounce less, would you persuade more, and **rebuke** less, your cause would be much more likely to succeed. But, I submit, where all is plain there is nothing to be argued. What point in the anti-slavery creed would you have me argue? On what branch of the subject do the people of this country need light? Must I undertake to prove that the slave is a man? That point is **conceded** already. Nobody doubts it. The slaveholders themselves acknowledge it in the enactment of laws for their government. They acknowledge it when they punish disobedience on the part of the slave. There are seventy-two crimes in the State of Virginia, which if committed by a black man, (no matter how ignorant he be), subject him to the punishment of death; while only two of the same crimes will subject a white man to the like punishment. What is this but the acknowledgement that the slave is a moral, intellectual and responsible being? The manhood of the slave is conceded. It is admitted in the fact that Southern statute books are covered with enactments forbidding, under severe fines and penalties, the teaching of the slave to read or to write. When you can point to any such laws, in reference to the beasts of the field, then I may consent to argue the manhood of the slave. When the dogs in your streets, when the fowls of the air, when the cattle on your hills, when the fish of the sea, and the reptiles that crawl, shall be unable to distinguish the slave from a brute,[10] then will I argue with you that the slave is a man!

What evidence did Douglass use to show that the slave was already considered a man?

For the present, it is enough to **affirm** the equal manhood of the negro race. Is it not astonishing that, while we are ploughing, planting and reaping, using all kinds of mechanical tools, erecting houses, constructing bridges, building ships, working in metals of brass, iron, copper, silver and gold; that, while we are reading, writing and ciphering,[11] acting as clerks, merchants and secretaries, having among us lawyers, doctors, ministers, poets, authors, editors, **orators** and teachers; that, while we are engaged in all manner of enterprises common to other men, digging gold in California, capturing the whale in the Pacific,[12] feeding sheep and

10 **brute.** Animal

11 **ciphering.** Doing mathematics

12 **digging gold . . . the Pacific.** A reference to the Gold Rush, which began in 1849, and to whale hunting. Both were potentially lucrative, but dangerous, businesses.

VOCABULARY IN PLACE

- **perpetuate,** *v.* To cause to continue; uphold
- **equivocate,** *v.* To falsify; avoid a direct, straightforward, or complete statement
- **rebuke,** *v.* To criticize sharply
- **concede,** *v.* To agree to
- **affirm,** *v.* To declare to be true
- **orator,** *n.* Public speaker

cattle on the hill-side, living, moving, acting, thinking, planning, living in families as husbands, wives and children, and above all, confessing and worshipping the Christian's God, and looking hopefully for life and immortality beyond the grave, we are called upon to prove that we are men!

Would you have me argue that man is entitled to liberty? That he is the rightful owner of his own body? You have already declared it. Must I argue the wrongfulness of slavery? Is that a question for Republicans? Is it to be settled by the rules of logic and argumentation, as a matter beset with great difficulty, involving a doubtful application of the principle of justice, hard to be understood? How should I look today, in the presence of Americans, dividing, and subdividing a **discourse,** to show that men have a natural right to freedom? speaking of it relatively, and positively, negatively, and affirmatively. To do so, would be to make myself ridiculous, and to offer an insult to your understanding. There is not a man beneath the canopy of heaven, that does not know that slavery is wrong *for him.*

What, am I to argue that it is wrong to make men brutes, to rob them of their liberty, to work them without wages, to keep them ignorant of their relations to their fellow men, to beat them with sticks, to **flay** their flesh with the lash, to load their limbs with irons, to hunt them with dogs, to sell them at auction, to **sunder** their families, to knock out their teeth, to burn their flesh, to starve them into obedience and submission to their masters? Must I argue that a system thus marked with blood, and stained with pollution, is *wrong?* No! I will not. I have better employments for my time and strength, than such arguments would imply.

What, then, remains to be argued? Is it that slavery is not divine; that God did not establish it; that our doctors of divinity are mistaken? There is blasphemy in the thought. That which is inhuman, cannot be divine! *Who* can reason on such a proposition? They that can, may; I cannot.

The time for such argument is past.

At a time like this, scorching irony, not convincing argument, is needed. O! had I the ability, and could I reach the nation's ear, I would, today, pour out a fiery stream of biting ridicule, blasting reproach, **withering** sarcasm, and stern **rebuke.** For it is not light that is needed, but fire; it is not the gentle shower, but thunder. We need the storm, the whirlwind, and the earthquake. The feeling of the nation must be quickened; the conscience of the nation must be **roused;** the **propriety** of the nation must be startled; the hypocrisy of the nation must be exposed; and its crimes against God and man must be proclaimed and denounced.

What did Douglass mean when he said, "we need the storm"?

What, to the American slave, is your 4th of July? I answer: a day that reveals to him, more than all other days in the year, the gross injustice and cruelty to which he is the constant victim.

VOCABULARY IN PLACE

- **discourse,** *n.* Speech
- **flay,** *v.* To cut
- **sunder,** *v.* To divide or separate
- **withering,** *v.* Shriveling
- **rebuke,** *n.* Scolding, reprimand
- **rouse,** *adj.* To excite to anger or to action
- **propriety,** *n.* Appropriateness; sense of what is proper

To him, your celebration is a **sham;** your boasted liberty, an unholy license; your national greatness, swelling vanity; your sounds of rejoicing are empty and heartless; your **denunciations** of tyrants, brass fronted **impudence;** your shouts of liberty and equality, hollow mockery; your prayers and hymns, your sermons and thanksgivings, with all your religious parade, and solemnity, are, to him, mere **bombast,** fraud, deception, impiety, and hypocrisy—a thin veil to cover up crimes which would disgrace a nation of savages. There is not a nation on the earth guilty of practices, more shocking and bloody, than are the people of these United States, at this very hour.

Go where you may, search where you will, roam through all the **monarchies** and **despotisms** of the world, travel through South America, search out every abuse, and when you have found the last, lay your facts by the side of the everyday practices of this nation, and you will say with me, that, for revolting barbarity and shameless hypocrisy, America **reigns** without a rival. ■

History Connection

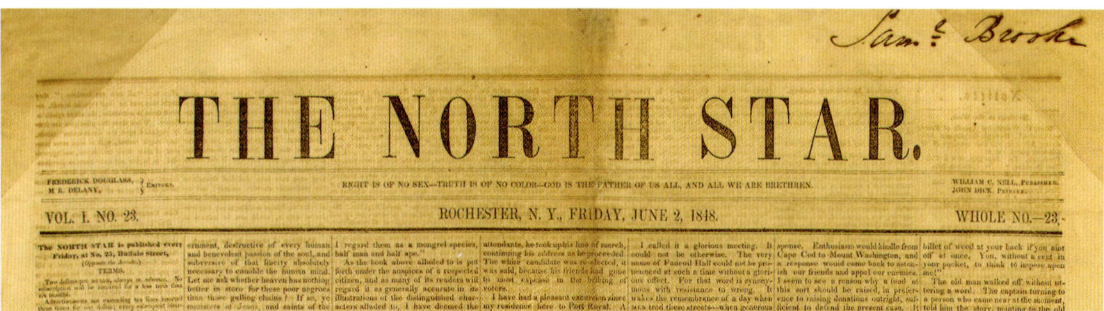

THE NORTH STAR.

FREDERICK DOUGLASS, M. R. DELANY, EDITORS.

RIGHT IS OF NO SEX—TRUTH IS OF NO COLOR—GOD IS THE FATHER OF US ALL, AND ALL WE ARE BRETHREN.

WILLIAM C. NELL, PUBLISHER. JOHN DICK, PRINTER.

VOL. I. NO. 23. ROCHESTER, N. Y., FRIDAY, JUNE 2, 1848. WHOLE NO.—23.

Front page image of *The North Star,* Frederick Douglass's Abolitionist newspaper, published in Rochester, New York, 1848. Library of Congress.

The North Star. Douglass used writing and publishing as his most effective weapons in the war against slavery. Soon after escaping to freedom he began writing for William Lloyd Garrison's *The Liberator* and other Abolitionist newspapers. *The North Star,* as well as *Frederick Douglass' Paper,* gained wide readership throughout the North and contributed greatly to the increase in Abolitionist sentiments during the run-up to the Civil War.

VOCABULARY IN PLACE

- **sham,** ***n.*** Something that is not genuine, a fake
- **denunciation,** ***n.*** Condemnation, censure
- **impudence,** ***n.*** Disrespectfulness, shamelessness
- **bombast,** ***n.*** Pompous speech
- **monarchy,** ***n.*** Nation ruled by a king or queen
- **despotism,** ***n.*** Nation ruled by a tyrant, someone with absolute power and authority
- **reign,** ***v.*** To rule or govern

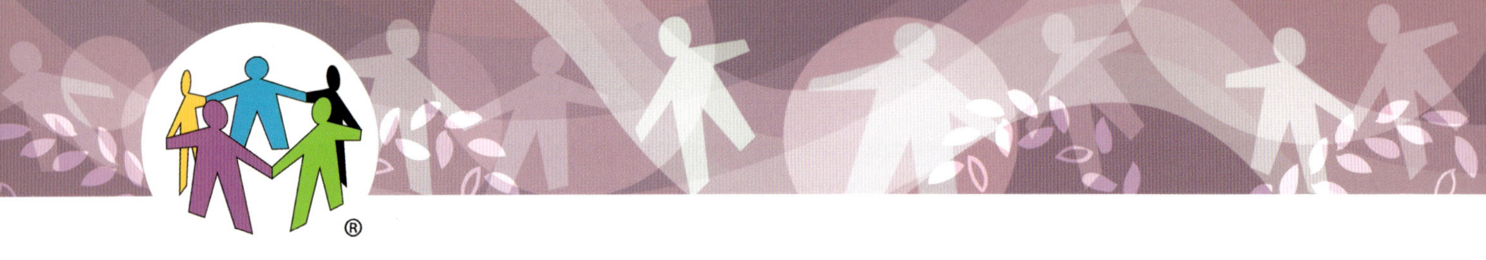

Understanding the Selection

Recalling

1. What question did Douglass pose at the beginning of this selection?
2. According to Douglass, to whom did the Fourth of July belong? To whom did it not belong?
3. What religious scripture did Douglass quote in this selection?
4. What point did Douglass say was "conceded," or agreed upon, already? Identify one example that he used to support this claim.
5. How did Douglass answer his opening question?

Interpreting

1. Why would it seem somewhat strange to have an ex-slave and representative of enslaved people speak at an Independence Day celebration?
2. Why did Douglass feel that the Fourth of July was not his holiday? Why did he say "I must mourn"?
3. What similarity is there between the Jews being asked by the Babylonians to sing one of their songs and Frederick Douglass being asked to speak at a Fourth of July celebration?
4. How did laws against teaching a slave to read effectively prove that slave owners "conceded" that "slaves [were] men"?
5. What was the slave's perspective on Independence Day?

Synthesizing

1. How would you describe the language that Douglass used at the end of this section of his speech to describe the Independence Day celebration of 1852? What did he think of celebrating independence given the circumstances of the times?

Delving Deeper

Understanding Literature

Allusion. An **allusion** is a reference in a literary work to some external source, such as another literary work. In this section from his famous speech, Douglass makes an allusion to Psalm 137:1–6. This psalm tells the story of an event that occurred after the Babylonians sacked Jerusalem in 586 BC. In the **psalm,** or hymn, a group of Jewish slaves are encamped with their Babylonian captors "by the rivers of Babylon," probably the Tigris and Euphrates rivers. The Babylonians ask the Jews to "Sing us one of the songs of Zion." Zion is the hill near Jerusalem on which Solomon's Temple was built and is symbolic of Israel as a whole. The singer of the psalm answers, "How can we sing the Lord's song in a strange land?" Douglass uses this allusion to point out that he, too, has a difficult time, as an escaped slave, feeling mirth and "singing" at an Independence Day celebration.

About the Author

Frederick Douglass (circa 1818–1895) was born into slavery in Talbot County, Maryland. Early in his life, he was separated from his mother, his brothers, and his sister. After escaping from slavery in 1838, disguised as a merchant seaman, he headed north. A brilliant speaker and an extraordinary **autodidact,** or self-educated man, Douglass became one of the greatest champions of the Abolitionist Movement, the attempt to rid the country of slavery. Douglass founded two newspapers, *The North Star* and *Frederick Douglass' Paper,* set up his home in Rochester as a station on the Underground Railroad, grew famous due to his moving autobiographical writings, and became a personal friend of President Abraham Lincoln. After the Civil War, Douglass served as a bank president and a U.S. Marshal, lectured widely, and campaigned tirelessly for voting rights for blacks and women. Near the end of his life, he served as U.S. Consul General to the country of Haiti. These were altogether astonishing accomplishments for a man born into slavery who had to teach himself how to read and write. Those of us who are born into more privileged circumstances have much to learn from this exceptional man and his unconquerable spirit.

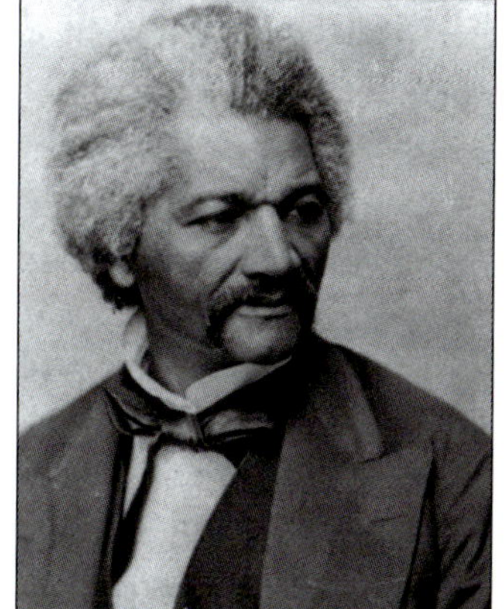

Prereading

from *Incidents in the Life of a Slave Girl*

by Harriet Jacobs

This is the first slave narrative published by an African-American woman. Few of the hundreds of other published slave narratives portray so effectively and eloquently the brutality and injustice of slavery.

In *Incidents,* Jacobs calls herself "Linda Brent," which is also the penname under which she published. She also changed the names of other characters in order to protect their identities. Published in 1860, *Incidents* consists of forty-one chapters. The author's original preface and three of these chapters are here included in their entirety, along with an excerpt from the final, poignant chapter, "Free at Last."

In 1825, at the age of twelve, Jacobs was purchased by a sinister man named Dr. James Norcum (called Dr. Flint in the text), who tormented her for ten years. Jacobs suffered tremendously due to the wickedness of this man and his jealous wife. She also feared that Dr. Norcum would sell her children and send her to a plantation. Jacobs finally resolved to escape.

Perhaps the most remarkable episode in Jacobs's narrative involves the seven years during which she hid in a tiny makeshift hideout in the corner of a storage shed. During this time, Jacobs could see and hear her own children through a peephole but could not risk communicating with them in any way. Such a painful, heart-rending experience no parent should have to endure.

Despite fleeing the horrid conditions in the Norcum household, Jacobs remained far from freedom. It wasn't until 1842 that she finally escaped to the North.

from Incidents in the Life of a Slave Girl

by Harriet Jacobs

Preface by the Author

Reader, be assured this narrative is no fiction. I am aware that some of my adventures may seem incredible; but they are, nevertheless, strictly true. I have not exaggerated the wrongs inflicted by Slavery; on the contrary, my descriptions fall far short of the facts. I have concealed the names of places, and given persons fictitious names. I had no motive for secrecy on my own account, but I deemed it kind and considerate towards others to pursue this course.

Why did Jacobs change the names of the people in her account?

I wish I were more **competent** to the task I have undertaken. But I trust my readers will excuse **deficiencies** in consideration of circumstances. I was born and reared in Slavery; and I remained in a Slave State twenty-seven years. Since I have been at the North, it has been necessary for me to work diligently for my own support, and the education of my children. This has not left me much **leisure** to make up for the loss of early opportunities to improve myself, and it has compelled me to write these pages at irregular intervals, whenever I could snatch an hour from household duties.

When I first arrived in Philadelphia, Bishop Paine advised me to publish a sketch of my life, but I told him I was altogether incompetent to such an undertaking. Though I have improved my mind somewhat since that time, I still remain of the same opinion; but I trust my motives will excuse what might otherwise seem **presumptuous.** I have not written my experiences in order to attract attention to myself—, on the contrary, it would have been more pleasant to me to have been silent about my own history. Neither do I care to excite sympathy for my own sufferings. But I do earnestly desire to arouse the women of the North to a realizing sense of the condition of two millions of women at the South, still in bondage, suffering what I suffered, and most of them far worse. I want to add my testimony to that of abler pens to convince the people of the Free States what Slavery really is. Only by experience can any one realize how deep, and dark, and foul is that pit of **abominations.** May the blessing of God rest on this imperfect effort in behalf of my persecuted people!

What was Jacobs's motive for sharing her story?

LINDA BRENT
[Penname of Harriet Jacobs]

VOCABULARY IN PLACE

- **competent,** ***adj.*** Adequate for the purpose; capable
- **deficiency,** ***n.*** Incompleteness or inadequacy
- **leisure,** ***n.*** Free time
- **presumptuous,** ***adj.*** Boldly arrogant or offensive
- **abomination,** ***n.*** Detestable or loathsome thing or act

Chapter 1: Childhood

I was born a slave; but I never knew it till six years of happy childhood had passed away. My father was a carpenter, and considered so intelligent and skilful in his trade, that, when buildings out of the common line[1] were to be erected, he was sent for from long distances, to be head workman. On condition of paying his mistress[2] two hundred dollars a year, and supporting himself, he was allowed to work at his trade, and manage his own affairs. His strongest wish was to purchase his children; but, though he several times offered his hard earnings for that purpose, he never succeeded. In complexion my parents were a light shade of brownish yellow, and were termed mulattoes. They lived together in a comfortable home; and, though we were all slaves, I was so fondly shielded that I never dreamed I was a piece of merchandise, trusted to them for safe keeping, and liable to be demanded of them at any moment. I had one brother, William, who was two years younger than myself—a bright, affectionate child. I had also a great treasure in my **maternal** grandmother, who was a remarkable woman in many respects. She was the daughter of a planter in South Carolina, who, at his death, left her mother and his three children free, with money to go to St. Augustine,[3] where they had relatives. It was during the Revolutionary War; and they were captured on their passage, carried back, and sold to different purchasers. Such was the story my grandmother used to tell me; but I do not remember all the particulars. She was a little girl when she was captured and sold to the keeper of a large hotel. I have often heard her tell how hard she fared[4] during childhood. But as she grew older she **evinced** so much intelligence, and was so faithful, that her master and mistress could not help seeing it was for their interest to take care of such a valuable piece of property. She became an **indispensable** personage in the household, officiating[5] in all capacities, from cook and wet nurse to seamstress. She was much praised for her cooking; and her nice crackers became so famous in the neighborhood that many people were desirous of obtaining them. In consequence of numerous requests of this kind, she asked permission of her mistress to bake crackers at night, after all the household work was done; and she obtained leave to do it, provided she would clothe herself and her children from the profits. Upon these terms, after working hard all day for her mistress, she began her midnight bakings, assisted by her two oldest children. The business proved profitable; and each year she laid by a little, which was saved for a fund to purchase her children. Her master died, and the property was divided among his heirs. The widow had her dower[6] in the hotel which she continued to keep open.

1 **buildings . . . common line.** Buildings and houses that were not ordinary; he specialized in unusual projects

2 **mistress.** Female slave owner

3 **St. Augustine.** A city in Florida

4 **how hard she fared.** What a difficult time she had

5 **officiating.** Performing duties associated with a position of authority

6 **dower.** The estate a widow inherits upon her husband's death

VOCABULARY IN PLACE

- **maternal,** ***adj.*** From the mother's side of the family
- **evince,** ***v.*** To show or determine clearly
- **indispensable,** ***adj.*** Essential, necessary

My grandmother remained in her service as a slave; but her children were divided among her master's children. As she had five, Benjamin, the youngest one, was sold, in order that each heir might have an equal portion of dollars and cents. There was so little difference in our ages that he seemed more like my brother than my uncle. He was a bright, handsome lad, nearly white; for he inherited the complexion my grandmother had derived from Anglo-Saxon[7] ancestors. Though only ten years old, seven hundred and twenty dollars were paid for him. His sale was a terrible blow to my grandmother, but she was naturally hopeful, and she went to work with renewed energy, trusting in time to be able to purchase some of her children. She had laid up three hundred dollars, which her mistress one day begged as a loan, promising to pay her soon. The reader probably knows that no promise or writing given to a slave is legally binding; for, according to Southern laws, a slave, being property, can hold no property. When my grandmother lent her hard earnings to her mistress, she trusted solely to her honor. The honor of a slaveholder to a slave!

Why was Benjamin sold? How did Harriet's grandmother react?

What happened to her grandmother's money?

To this good grandmother I was indebted for many comforts. My brother Willie and I often received portions of the crackers, cakes, and preserves, she made to sell; and after we ceased to be children we were indebted to her for many more important services.

Such were the unusually fortunate circumstances of my early childhood. When I was six years old, my mother died; and then, for the first time, I learned, by the talk around me, that I was a slave. My mother's mistress was the daughter of my grandmother's mistress. She was the foster sister of my mother; they were both nourished at my grandmother's breast. In fact, my mother had been weaned at three months old, that the babe of the mistress might obtain sufficient food. They played together as children; and, when they became women, my mother was a most faithful servant to her whiter foster sister. On her death-bed her mistress promised that her children should never suffer for any thing; and during her lifetime she kept her word. They all spoke kindly of my dead mother, who had been a slave merely in name, but in nature was noble and womanly. I grieved for her, and my young mind was troubled with the thought of who would now take care of me and my little brother. I was told that my home was now to be with her mistress; and I found it a happy one. No toilsome or disagreeable duties were **imposed** on me. My mistress was so kind to me that I was always glad to do her bidding, and proud to labor for her as much as my young years would permit. I would sit by her side for hours, sewing **diligently**, with a heart as free from care as that of any free-born white child. When she thought I was tired, she would send me out to run and jump; and away I bounded, to gather berries or flowers to decorate her room. Those were happy days—too happy to last. The slave child had

[7] **Anglo-Saxon.** Of English ancestry

VOCABULARY IN PLACE

- **impose,** *v.* To force something upon someone else
- **diligently,** *adv.* In an attentive and thorough manner

no thought for the morrow;[8] but there came that **blight,** which too surely waits on every human being born to be a chattel.[9]

When I was nearly twelve years old, my kind mistress sickened and died. As I saw the cheek grow paler, and the eye more glassy, how earnestly I prayed in my heart that she might live! I loved her; for she had been almost like a mother to me. My prayers were not answered. She died, and they buried her in the little churchyard, where, day after day, my tears fell upon her grave.

I was sent to spend a week with my grandmother. I was now old enough to begin to think of the future; and again and again I asked myself what they would do with me. I felt sure I should never find another mistress so kind as the one who was gone. She had promised my dying mother that her children should never suffer for any thing; and when I remembered that, and recalled her many proofs of attachment to me, I could not help having some hopes that she had left me free. My friends were almost certain it would be so. They thought she would be sure to do it, on account of my mother's love and faithful service. But, alas! we all know that the memory of a faithful slave does not **avail** much to save her children from the auction block.

What did Harriet Jacobs think her mistress would do? What really happened?

After a brief period of suspense, the will of my mistress was read, and we learned that she had **bequeathed** me to her sister's daughter, a child of five years old. So vanished our hopes. My mistress had taught me the precepts of God's Word: "Thou shalt love thy neighbor as thyself." "Whatsoever ye would that men should do unto you, do ye even so unto them." But I was her slave, and I suppose she did not recognize me as her neighbor. I would give much to blot out from my memory that one great wrong.

As a child, I loved my mistress; and, looking back on the happy days I spent with her, I try to think with less bitterness of this act of injustice. While I was with her, she taught me to read and spell; and for this privilege, which so rarely falls to the lot of a slave, I bless her memory.

She possessed but few slaves; and at her death those were all distributed among her relatives. Five of them were my grandmother's children, and had shared the same milk that nourished her mother's children. Notwithstanding my grandmother's long and faithful service to her owners, not one of her children escaped the auction block. These God-breathing machines are no more, in the sight of their masters, than the cotton they plant, or the horses they tend.

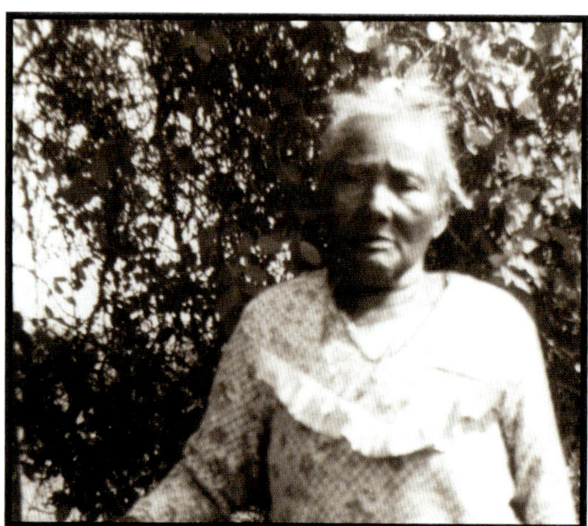

Callie Shepard, age 84, a formerly enslaved person. Photo taken as part of a project for the Works Progress Administration. Library of Congress, LC-USZ62-125297.

[8] **morrow.** Next day

[9] **chattel.** Moveable personal property, such as livestock or wagons

VOCABULARY IN PLACE

- **blight,** *n.* Something that impairs growth or withers hopes and ambitions
- **avail,** *v.* To be of use or advantage; to help
- **bequeath,** *v.* To leave or give personal property

Chapter XVII: The Flight

Mr. Flint was hard pushed for house servants, and rather than lose me he had restrained his **malice.** I did my work faithfully, though not, of course, with a willing mind. They were evidently afraid I should leave them. Mr. Flint wished that I should sleep in the great house instead of the servants' quarters. His wife agreed to the proposition, but said I mustn't bring my bed into the house, because it would scatter feathers on her carpet. I knew when I went there that they would never think of such a thing as furnishing a bed of any kind for me and my little ones. I therefore carried my own bed, and now I was forbidden to use it. I did as I was ordered. But now that I was certain my children were to be put in their power, in order to give them a stronger hold on me, I resolved to leave them that night. I remembered the grief this step would bring upon my dear old grandmother, and nothing less than the freedom of my children would have induced me to disregard her advice. I went about my evening work with trembling steps. Mr. Flint twice called from his chamber door to inquire why the house was not locked up. I replied that I had not done my work. "You have had time enough to do it," said he. "Take care how you answer me!"

Why did Harriet Jacobs decide to run away at that moment?

I shut all the windows, locked all the doors, and went up to the third story, to wait till midnight. How long those hours seemed, and how **fervently** I prayed that God would not forsake me in this hour of utmost need! I was about to risk every thing on the throw of a die;[10] and if I failed, O what would become of me and my poor children? They would be made to suffer for my fault.

At half past twelve I stole softly down stairs. I stopped on the second floor, thinking I heard a noise. I felt my way down into the parlor, and looked out of the window. The night was so intensely dark that I could see nothing. I raised the window very softly and jumped out. Large drops of rain were falling, and the darkness **bewildered** me. I dropped on my knees, and breathed a short prayer to God for guidance and protection. I groped my way to the road, and rushed towards the town with almost lightning speed. I arrived at my grandmother's house, but dared not see her. She would say, "Linda, you are killing me;" and I knew that would unnerve me.

I tapped softly at the window of a room, occupied by a woman, who had lived in the house several years. I knew she was a faithful friend, and could be trusted with my secret. I tapped several times before she heard me. At last she raised the window, and I whispered, "Sally, I have run away. Let me in, quick." She opened the door softly, and said in low tones, "For God's sake, don't. Your grandmother is trying to buy you and de chillern.[11] Mr. Sands was here last week. He tole her he was going away on business, but he wanted her to go ahead about buying you and de

Why didn't her grandmother want her to run away?

10 **die.** The singular form of *dice*

11 **de chillern.** The children

VOCABULARY IN PLACE

- **malice,** ***n.*** A desire to harm others or to see others suffer
- **fervently,** ***adv.*** In a manner that shows great emotion
- **bewilder,** ***v.*** Confuse

chillern, and he would help her all he could. Don't run away, Linda. Your grandmother is all bowed down wid trouble now."

I replied, "Sally, they are going to carry my children to the plantation tomorrow; and they will never sell them to any body so long as they have me in their power. Now, would you advise me to go back?'

"No, chile, no," answered she. "When dey finds you is gone, dey won't want de plague ob de chillern; but where is you going to hide? Dey knows ebery inch ob dis house."

I told her I had a hiding-place, and that was all it was best for her to know. I asked her to go into my room as soon as it was light, and take all my clothes out of my trunk, and pack them in hers; for I knew Mr. Flint and the **constable** would be there early to search my room. I feared the sight of my children would be too much for my full heart; but I could not go into the uncertain future without one last look. I bent over the bed where lay my little Benny and baby Ellen. Poor little ones! fatherless and motherless! Memories of their father came over me. He wanted to be kind to them; but they were not all to him, as they were to my womanly heart. I knelt and prayed for the innocent little sleepers. I kissed them lightly, and turned away.

How would Harriet Jacobs's escape prevent her children from being brought to Mr. Flint's plantation?

As I was about to open the street door, Sally laid her hand on my shoulder, and said, "Linda, is you gwine all alone? Let me call your uncle."

"No, Sally," I replied, "I want no one to be brought into trouble on my account."

I went forth into the darkness and rain. I ran on till I came to the house of the friend who was to conceal me.

Early the next morning Mr. Flint was at my grandmother's inquiring for me. She told him she had not seen me, and supposed I was at the plantation. He watched her face narrowly, and said, "Don't you know any thing about her running off?" She assured him that she did not. He went on to say, "Last night she ran off without the least **provocation.** We had treated her very kindly. My wife liked her. She will soon be found and brought back. Are her children with you?" When told that they were, he said, "I am very glad to hear that. If they are here, she cannot be far off. If I find out that any of my n— have had any thing to do with this damned business, I'll give 'em five hundred lashes." As he started to go to his father's, he turned round and added, persuasively, "Let her be brought back, and she shall have her children to live with her."

The tidings made the old doctor rave and storm at a furious rate. It was a busy day for them. My grandmother's house was searched from top to bottom. As my trunk was empty, they concluded I had taken my clothes with me. Before ten o'clock every vessel northward bound was thoroughly examined, and the law against harboring fugitives[12] was read to all on board. At night a watch was set over the town. Knowing how distressed my grandmother would be, I wanted to send her a message; but it could not be done. Every one who went in or out of her house was closely watched. The doctor said he would take my children, unless she became responsible for them; which of course she willingly did.

12 **harboring fugitives.** Sheltering escaped slaves

VOCABULARY IN PLACE

- **constable,** *n.* A police officer
- **provocation,** *n.* The act of inciting anger or resentment

The next day was spent in searching. Before night, the following advertisement was posted at every corner, and in every public place for miles round:

$300 REWARD! Ran away from the subscriber, an intelligent, bright, mulatto girl, named Linda, 21 years of age. Five feet four inches high. Dark eyes, and black hair inclined to curl; but it can be made straight. Has a decayed spot on a front tooth. She can read and write, and in all probability will try to get to the Free States. All persons are forbidden, under penalty of law, to harbor or employ said slave. $150 will be given to whoever takes her in the state, and $300 if taken out of the state and delivered to me, or lodged in jail.

Dr. Flint.

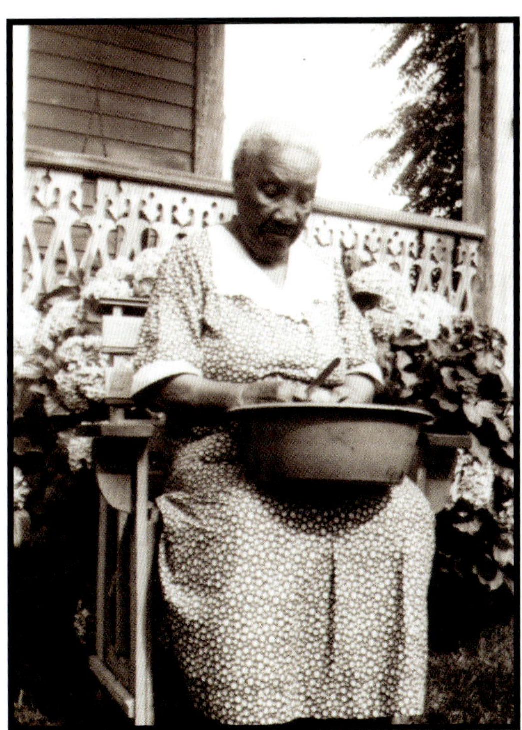

Betty Simmons, a formerly enslaved person. Photo taken as part of a project for the Works Progress Administration. Library of Congress, LC-USZ62-125348.

Chapter XXI: The Loophole of Retreat

A small shed had been added to my grandmother's house years ago. Some boards were laid across the joists[13] at the top, and between these boards and the roof was a very small garret,[14] never occupied by any thing but rats and mice. It was a pent[15] roof, covered with nothing but shingles, according to the southern custom for such buildings. The garret was only nine feet long and seven wide. The highest part was three feet high, and sloped down abruptly to the loose board floor. There was no admission for either light or air. My uncle Phillip, who was a carpenter, had very skillfully made a concealed trap-door, which communicated with the storeroom. He had been doing this while I was waiting in the swamp. The storeroom opened upon a piazza.[16] To this hole I was **conveyed** as soon as I entered the house. The air was stifling; the darkness total. A bed had been spread on the floor. I could sleep quite comfortably on one side; but the slope was so sudden that I could not turn on my other without hitting the roof. The rats and mice ran over my bed; but I was

In what kind of place did Jacobs hide?

13 **joists.** Wooden beams set parallel from wall to wall to support a floor or ceiling

14 **garret.** A room under a pitched roof; an attic

15 **pent.** Penned or shut up; closely confined

16 **piazza.** A veranda; a porch extending alongside a building covered by a roof

VOCABULARY IN PLACE

- **convey,** *v.* To transport

weary, and I slept such sleep as the wretched may, when a **tempest** has passed over them. Morning came. I knew it only by the noises I heard; for in my small den day and night were all the same. I suffered for air even more than for light. But I was not comfortless. I heard the voices of my children. There was joy and there was sadness in the sound. It made my tears flow. How I longed to speak to them! I was eager to look on their faces; but there was no hole, no crack, through which I could peep. This continued darkness was oppressive. It seemed horrible to sit or lie in a cramped position day after day, without one gleam of light. Yet I would have chosen this, rather than my lot as a slave, though white people considered it an easy one; and it was so compared with the fate of others. I was never cruelly overworked; I was never **lacerated** with the whip from head to foot; I was never so beaten and bruised that I could not turn from one side to the other; I never had my heel-strings cut to prevent my running away; I was never chained to a log and forced to drag it about, while I toiled in the fields from morning till night; I was never branded with hot iron, or torn by bloodhounds. On the contrary, I had always been kindly treated, and tenderly cared for, until I came into the hands of Dr. Flint. I had never wished for freedom till then. But though my life in slavery was comparatively devoid of hardships, God pity the woman who is compelled to lead such a life!

How did Harriet's experiences compare to those of other slaves?

My food was passed up to me through the trap-door my uncle had **contrived;** and my grandmother, my uncle Phillip, and aunt Nancy would seize such opportunities as they could, to mount up there and chat with me at the opening. But of course this was not safe in the daytime. It must all be done in darkness. It was impossible for me to move in an erect position, but I crawled about my den for exercise. One day I hit my head against something, and found it was a gimlet.[17] My uncle had left it sticking there when he made the trap-door. I was as rejoiced as Robinson Crusoe[18] could have been at finding such a treasure. It put a lucky thought into my head. I said to myself, "Now I will have some light. Now I will see my children." I did not dare to begin my work during the daytime, for fear of attracting attention. But I groped round; and having found the side next the street, where I could frequently see my children, I stuck the gimlet in and waited for evening. I bored three rows of holes, one above another; then I bored out the interstices[19] between. I thus succeeded in making one hole about an inch long and an inch broad. I sat by it till late into the night, to enjoy the little whiff of air that floated in. In the morning I watched for my children. The first person I saw in the street was Dr. Flint. I had a shuddering, superstitious feeling that it was a bad omen. Several familiar faces passed by. At last I heard the merry laugh of children, and presently

[17] **gimlet.** A small hand tool used for boring holes

[18] **Robinson Crusoe.** Title character and hero of the adventure novel by Daniel Defoe, published in 1719

[19] **interstices.** The spaces between the holes

VOCABULARY IN PLACE

- **tempest,** *n.* A violent windstorm, frequently accompanied by rain, snow, or hail
- **lacerate,** *v.* To tear, wound
- **contrive,** *v.* To plan with cleverness; devise

two sweet little faces were looking up at me, as though they knew I was there, and were conscious of the joy they imparted. How I longed to *tell* them I was there!

What torments did Jacobs experience while hiding? What made her able to bear this suffering?

My condition was now a little improved. But for weeks I was tormented by hundreds of little red insects, fine as a needle's point, that pierced through my skin, and produced an **intolerable** burning. The good grandmother gave me herb teas and cooling medicines, and finally I got rid of them. The heat of my den was intense, for nothing but thin shingles protected me from the scorching summer's sun. But I had my **consolations.** Through my peeping-hole I could watch the children, and when they were near enough, I could hear their talk. Aunt Nancy brought me all the news she could hear at Dr. Flint's. From her I learned that the doctor had written to New York to a colored woman, who had been born and raised in our neighborhood, and had breathed his contaminating atmosphere. He offered her a reward if she could find out any thing about me. I know not what was the nature of her reply; but he soon after started for New York in haste, saying to his family that he had business of importance to transact. I peeped at him as he passed on his way to the steamboat. It was a satisfaction to have miles of land and water between us, even for a little while; and it was a still greater satisfaction to know that he believed me to be in the Free States. My little den seemed less dreary than it had done. He returned, as he did from his former journey to New York, without obtaining any satisfactory information. When he passed our house next morning, Benny was standing at the gate. He had heard them say that he had gone to find me, and he called out, "Dr. Flint, did you bring my mother home? I want to see her." The doctor stamped his foot at him in a rage, and exclaimed, "Get out of the way, you little damned rascal! If you don't, I'll cut off your head."

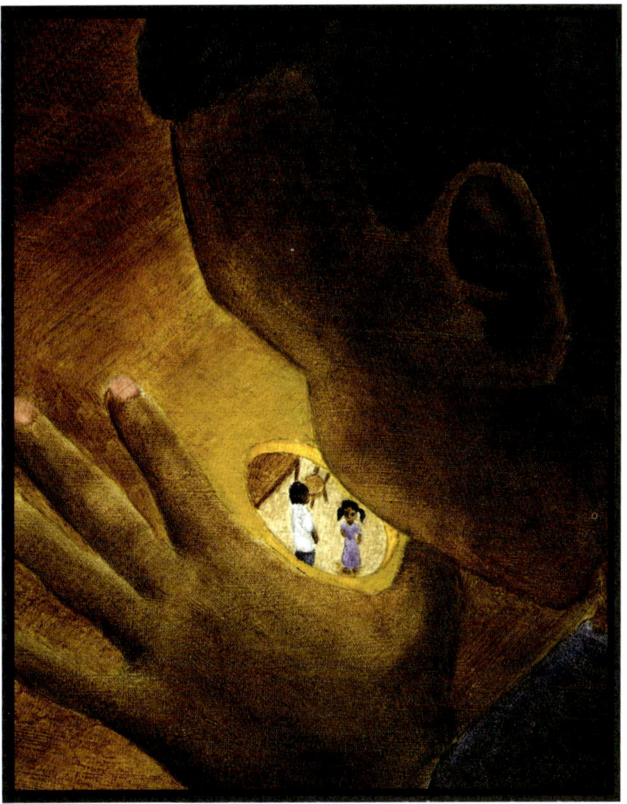

VOCABULARY IN PLACE

- **intolerable,** ***adj.*** Unbearable
- **consolation,** ***n.*** Something that makes up for grief or loss

Benny ran terrified into the house, saying, "You can't put me in jail again. I don't belong to you now." It was well that the wind carried the words away from the doctor's ear. I told my grandmother of it, when we had our next conference at the trap-door, and begged of her not to allow the children to be **impertinent** to the **irascible** old man.

Autumn came, with a pleasant abatement[20] of heat. My eyes had become accustomed to the dim light, and by holding my book or work in a certain position near the aperture[21] I contrived to read and sew. That was a great relief to the **tedious monotony** of my life. But when winter came, the cold penetrated through the thin shingle roof, and I was dreadfully chilled. The winters there are not so long, or so severe, as in northern latitudes;[22] but the houses are not built to shelter from cold, and my little den was peculiarly comfortless. The kind grandmother brought me bedclothes and warm drinks. Often I was obliged to lie in bed all day to keep comfortable; but with all my **precautions,** my shoulders and feet were frostbitten. O, those long, gloomy days, with no object for my eye to rest upon, and no thoughts to occupy my mind, except the dreary past and the uncertain future! I was thankful when there came a day sufficiently mild for me to wrap myself up and sit at the loophole to watch the passers by. Southerners have the habit of stopping and talking in the streets, and I heard many conversations not intended to meet my ears. I heard slave-hunters planning how to catch some poor fugitive. Several times I heard allusions to Dr. Flint, myself, and the history of my children, who, perhaps, were playing near the gate. One would say, "I wouldn't move my little finger to catch her, as old Flint's property." Another would say, "I'll catch any n— for the reward. A man ought to have what belongs to him, if he is a damned brute." The opinion was often expressed that I was in the Free States. Very rarely did any one suggest that I might be in the **vicinity.** Had the least suspicion rested on my grandmother's house, it would have been burned to the ground. But it was the last place they thought of. Yet there was no place, where slavery existed, that could have afforded me so good a place of concealment.

What kind of news did Jacobs hear from her hideout?

Dr. Flint and his family repeatedly tried to coax and bribe my children to tell something they had heard said about me. One day the doctor took them into a shop, and offered them some bright little silver pieces and **gay** handkerchiefs if they would tell where their mother was. Ellen shrank away from him, and would not speak; but Benny spoke up, and said, "Dr. Flint, I don't know where my mother is. I guess she's in New York; and when you go there again, I wish you'd ask her to come home, for I want to see her; but if you put her in jail, or tell her you'll cut her head off, I'll tell her to go right back." ■

---

20 **abatement.** Reduction, lessening

21 **aperture.** Opening

22 **northern latitudes.** Northern regions

VOCABULARY IN PLACE

- **impertinent,** ***adj.*** Fresh; bad-mannered
- **irascible,** ***adj.*** Easily angered
- **tedious,** ***adj.*** Extremely tiresome
- **monotony,** ***n.*** Sameness
- **precaution,** ***n.*** An action taken in advance to protect against danger
- **vicinity,** ***n.*** An area nearby
- **gay,** ***adj.*** Delightful; lovely

Timeline of Harriet Jacob's Life

1819 Mother dies and Harriet realizes that she is a slave

1825 Becomes the property of Dr. Flint's daughter

1826 Grandmother is given her freedom. Father dies.

1829 Moves in with her grandmother after the birth of her son (by a "Mr. Sands")

1831 Daughter by "Mr. Sands" is born

1835 Goes into hiding in her grandmother's house, where she remains through 1841

1842 Escapes to New York. Gains employment as a nursemaid for an English couple, Mr. and Mrs. Willis.

1844 Reunited with her children in Boston for the first time in nine years

1845 Learns the true meaning of freedom when she travels to England with Mr. Willis

1849 Moves to Rochester, New York. Her previous "owner," Dr. Flint's daughter, continues to look for her.

1850 Moves back to New York City

1852 Cornelia Willis, her employer, buys Harriet's freedom for $300. She no longer needs to fear her former owners.

1853 Grandmother dies. Harriet publishes anonymous letters about her experiences as a slave and begins to write her book, *Incidents in the Life of a Slave Girl.*

1858 Travels to England to try to sell the manuscript of her book

1861 *Incidents in the Life of a Slave Girl* is published under the pseudonym Linda Brent

1863 Moves with daughter to Alexandria, Virginia, to assist African-American refugees emerging into freedom from the South. Harriet establishes The Jacobs Free School in Alexandria, where black teachers are employed to help the refugees.

1865 Moves to Savannah, Georgia, to continue relief efforts

1877 Moves to Washington, D.C., and continues as a civil rights activist for the rest of her life

1897 Dies in Washington, D.C.

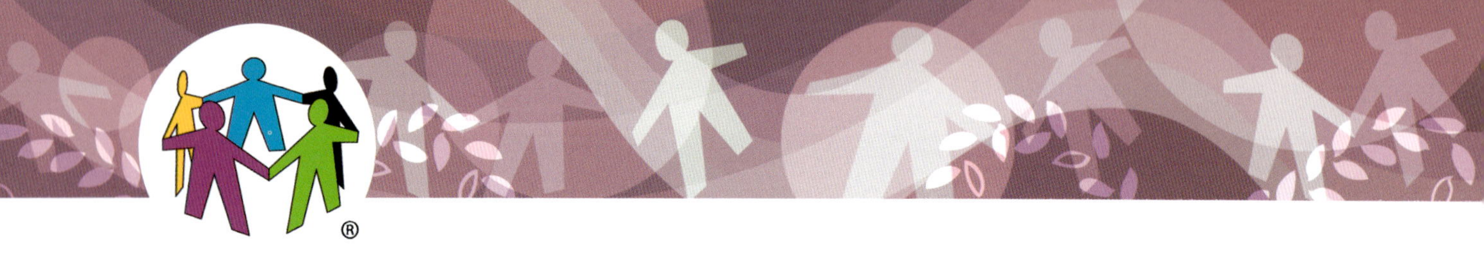

Understanding the Selection

Recalling

1. What was the purpose of Harriet Jacobs's narrative, according to the last paragraph of her preface?
2. Why did Harriet's grandmother save money?
3. What hope did Harriet have for herself on the death of her "kind mistress"?
4. What tool did Harriet find in her attic space? What did she use it for and why?
5. What were her "consolations" while she lived in the attic? How did she pass the time?

Interpreting

1. Who did she hope would read her narrative? Why did she say that her narrative was "imperfect"?
2. Why was it a bad idea for Harriet's grandmother to loan money to her "mistress"?
3. What lesson did Harriet learn from her dashed hopes?
4. What was most horrifying about the conditions in which she found herself while she was hiding in the attic?
5. How badly did Dr. Flint want to find her? Why didn't she want her children to be ill-mannered toward the old man?

Synthesizing

1. Review the preface to Harriet Jacobs's autobiography. Given her stated purpose in writing this work, do you think, based on what you have read, that she succeeded? Would reading this work move people to oppose slavery? What aspects of the slaves' condition were particularly terrible and likely to incite anger and opposition? Provide specific examples from the text.

Delving Deeper

Understanding Literature

Catalogue. A **catalogue** is a literary device that consists of a list, as of names of warriors or ships. Often, in a **rhetorical** work, written to move and persuade an audience, this literary device is used to enumerate grievances or wrongs. For example, the Declaration of Independence contains a long catalogue of grievances of the American colonies against King George III of England. Reread the catalogue of mistreatments of slaves given by Jacobs on page 138 of this selection. Notice that these were abuses of a physical kind. Jacobs also suffered horrible physical abuse at the hands of Dr. Flint, but the worst of the abuse that she suffered in the selection you've just read was of the emotional or psychological kind. Discuss this with your classmates. What physical abuse did Harriet suffer? What emotional abuse? What effect would reading about Jacobs's ordeal have had on the intended audience for the book?

About the Author

Harriet Jacobs (1813–1897), Abolitionist and writer, was born in Edenton, North Carolina. She was the first African-American woman to publish her autobiography. As in slave narratives by such distinguished authors as Frederick Douglass and William Wells Brown, Jacobs exposed the horrors of slavery even as she revealed profound courage and determination to be free.

Incidents in the Life of a Slave Girl is valued for its vivid portrayal of the particular sufferings of black women during slavery. Jacobs was encouraged to compose her autobiography by her friend and fellow Abolitionist Amy Post, while living in Rochester, New York, and working in an antislavery reading room above the offices of Frederick Douglass's newspaper, *The North Star.* Publication of Jacobs's narrative, however, proved difficult; two publishers went bankrupt before publishing her work, with one requiring that her writings be prefaced by a white Abolitionist and editor, Lydia Maria Child. (The work was often dismissed as fiction or attributed to Child's editorial expertise until the 1980s, when scholar Jean Fagan Yellin, through careful research into North Carolina records, identified the characters in *Incidents,* thereby confirming the historical truth behind Jacobs's compelling account.) After the Civil War, Jacobs moved around the South assisting newly-freed African Americans before settling in Washington, D.C., where she remained active in civil rights and women's suffrage causes for her remaining days.

Prereading

"Ar'n't I a Woman" Speech at the Akron Convention

by Sojourner Truth

This selection features Sojourner Truth's famous "Ar'n't I a Woman" speech, one of the earliest of great speeches by American women. Students are encouraged to read or perform the speech aloud but not to make light of what may appear to be unusual language. This is a serious speech, and it had a serious impact on American history!

Sojourner Truth could neither read nor write, but she did not lack strength of intellect. She commanded attention every time she opened her mouth, partly thanks to her heavy Dutch accent, the result of having been enslaved much of her life by a Dutch family in upstate New York, but mostly because of her ability to state a strong moral argument in clear, unequivocal, memorable language. Be sure to read the biography of her long and fascinating life at the end of the selection. Also, the brief but fascinating *Narrative of the Life of Sojourner Truth* (which Truth dictated to writer Olive Gilbert) is highly recommended to all students of American history.

Frances Gage, a white Abolitionist, Women's Rights activist, and Truth's close friend, provided this mostly accurate (though incomplete) account of the famous speech. The **vernacular** language (everyday language specific to a certain social group) that Gage used was partly an attempt to demonstrate how Truth's unique speaking style transfixed her audiences. Many opponents and enemies of Sojourner Truth were impressed—if not swayed to her beliefs—after hearing her for the first time. In this excerpt from Gage's personal **memoirs**, the author sets the scene for Truth's speech with wonderful, colorful, insightful writing. Gage also intersperses helpful, revealing comments throughout the speech.

This speech was delivered at a Women's Rights convention in Akron, Ohio. As Gage points out, Truth's speech is also remarkable because—in those days—few women were willing or encouraged to stand up and speak publicly about anything, much less in as forthright a manner as Sojourner Truth spoke. She took the podium after several men had delivered long, degrading speeches, explaining various reasons why women should not be entitled to the same rights as men. But there is only one speech that history remembers from that day, for Sojourner Truth stole the show!

"Ar'n't I a Woman" Speech at the Akron Convention, Akron, Ohio, May 28–29, 1851

from *Reminiscences by Frances D. Gage of Sojourner Truth*

The leaders of the movement trembled on seeing a tall, **gaunt** black woman in a gray dress and white turban, surmounted with an **uncouth** sun-bonnet, march deliberately into the church, walk with the air of a queen up the aisle, and take her seat upon the pulpit steps. A buzz of **disapprobation** was heard all over the house, and there fell on the listening ear, "An abolition affair!" "Woman's rights and niggers!" "I told you so!" "Go it, darkey!"

How did the crowd react when Truth entered the church? Why?

I chanced on that occasion to wear my first laurels[1] in public life as president of the meeting. At my request order was restored, and the business of the convention went on. Morning, afternoon, and evening exercises came and went. Through all these sessions old Sojourner, quiet and **reticent** . . . sat crouched against the wall on the corner of the pulpit stairs, her sun-bonnet shading her eyes, her elbows on her knees, her chin resting upon her broad, hard palms. At intermission she was busy selling the "Life of Sojourner Truth," a narrative of her own strange and adventurous life. Again and again, **timorous** and trembling ones came to me and said, with earnestness, "don't let her speak, Mrs. Gage, it will ruin us. Every newspaper in the land will have our cause mixed up with abolition and niggers, and we shall be utterly denounced." My only answer was, "We shall see when the time comes."

Why did the conference attendees complain about Sojourner Truth?

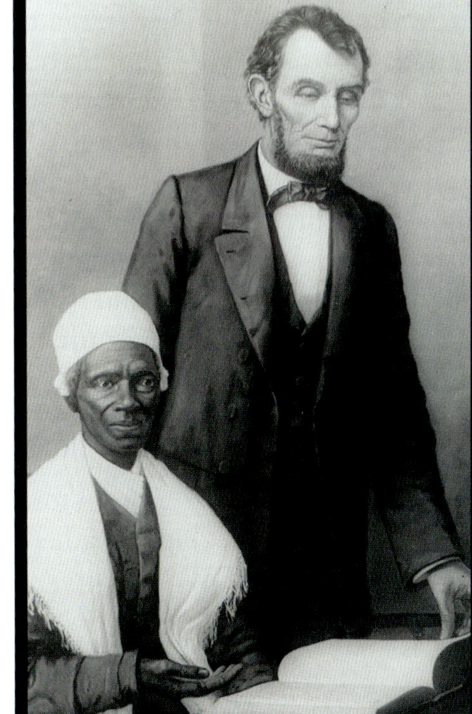

Sojourner Truth with President Abraham Lincoln. Library of Congress, LC-USZ62-16225.

[1] **laurels.** In ancient Greece, champions wore a wreath made of branches from the laurel tree. Gage did not literally wear laurels, but writers sometimes refer to any accomplished person as "wearing laurels."

VOCABULARY IN PLACE

- **gaunt,** ***adj.*** Thin and bony; haggard
- **uncouth,** ***adj.*** Crude, unrefined
- **disapprobation,** ***n.*** Condemnation; moral disapproval
- **reticent,** ***adj.*** Restrained in expression; shy
- **timorous,** ***adj.*** Nervous

My second day the work waxed warm.[2] Methodist, Baptist, Episcopal, Presbyterian, and Universalist ministers came in to hear and discuss the resolutions presented. One claimed superior rights and privileges for man, on the ground of "superior intellect"; another, because of the "manhood of Christ; if God had desired the equality of woman, He would have given some token of His will through the birth, life, and death of the Saviour." Another gave us a theological view of the "sin of our first mother."[3]

There were very few women in those days who dared to "speak in meeting"; and the **august** teachers of the people were seemingly getting the better of us, while the boys in the galleries, and the sneerers among the pews, were hugely enjoying the **discomfiture**, as they supposed, of the "strong-minded."[4] Some of the tender-skinned friends were on the point of losing dignity, and the atmosphere **betokened** a storm. When, slowly from her seat in the corner rose Sojourner Truth, who, till now, had scarcely lifted her head. "Don't let her speak!" gasped half a dozen in my ear. She moved slowly and solemnly to the front, laid her old bonnet at her feet, and turned her great speaking eyes to me. There was a hissing sound of disapprobation above and below. I rose and announced "Sojourner Truth," and begged the audience to keep silence for a few moments.

What was the atmosphere like in the church before Truth took the stage?

The **tumult** subsided at once, and every eye was fixed on this almost Amazon form,[5] which stood nearly six feet high, head erect, and eyes piercing the upper air like one in a dream. At her first word there was a profound hush. She spoke in deep tones, which, though not loud, reached every ear in the house, and away through the **throng** at the doors and windows.

"Wall, chilern, whar dar is so much racket dar must be somethin' out o' kilter.[6] I tink dat 'twixt de niggers of de Souf and de womin at de Norf, all talkin' 'bout rights, de white men will be in a fix pretty soon. But what's all dis here talkin' 'bout?

"Dat man ober dar say dat womin needs to be helped into carriages, and lifted ober ditches, and to hab de best place everywhar. Nobody eber helps me into carriage, or ober mud-puddles, or gibs me any best place!" And raising herself to her full height, and her voice to a pitch like rolling thunder, she asked. "And ar'n't I a woman? Look at me! Look at my arm! (and she bared her right arm to the shoulder, showing her tremendous muscular

2 **waxed warm.** Became more intense; increased

3 **sin of our first mother.** A reference to Eve's actions in the Garden of Eden, from the Old Testament book of Genesis

4 **august teachers . . . "strong-minded."** The ministers and other speakers were turning the women's rights convention into an anti-women's rights convention by controlling the podium and making jokes. *Strong-minded* is Gage's term for the women's rights advocates who, though losing ground, were determined to accomplish their goal.

5 **Amazon form.** The Amazons were a legendary tribe of warrior women mentioned originally in Greek legends that were based upon the fighting culture of an actual ancient race called the Scythians (of modern-day Iran). The word *amazon* is sometimes used to refer to an "aggressive, tall, strong-willed woman," but it is generally not polite or politically correct to address or refer to a person as such.

6 **out o' kilter.** Not in proper form or condition

VOCABULARY IN PLACE

- **august,** ***adj.*** Inspiring awe or admiration
- **discomfiture,** ***n.*** Frustration, disappointment, or embarrassment
- **betoken,** ***v.*** To give a sign of
- **tumult,** ***n.*** Disturbance, racket
- **throng,** ***n.*** A crowd of people

power). I have ploughed, and planted, and gathered into barns, and no man could head me![7] And ar'n't I a woman? I could work as much and eat as much as a man—when I could get it—and bear de lash[8] as well! And a'n't I a woman? I have borne thirteen chilern, and seen 'em mos' all sold off to slavery, and when I cried out with my mother's grief, none but Jesus heard me! And ar'n't I a woman?

What did Sojourner Truth mean when she asked "ar'n't I a woman?" Did she expect the audience to answer?

"Den dey talks 'bout dis ting in de head; what dis dey call it?" ("Intellect," whispered some one near.) "Dat's it, honey. What's dat got to do wid womin's rights or nigger's rights? If my cup won't hold but a pint, and yourn holds a quart, wouldn't ye be mean not to let me have my little half measure full?" And she pointed her significant finger, and sent a keen glance at the minister who had made the argument. The cheering was long and loud.

How did the crowd respond during her speech?

"Den dat little man in black dar, he say women can't have as much rights as men, 'cause Christ wan't a woman! Whar did your Christ come from?" Rolling thunder couldn't have stilled that crowd, as did those deep, wonderful tones, as she stood there with outstretched arms and eyes of fire. Raising her voice still louder, she repeated, "Whar did your Christ come from? From God and a woman! Man had nothin' to do wid Him." Oh, what a **rebuke** that was to that little man.

Turning again to another objector, she took up the defense of Mother Eve. I can not follow her through it all. It was pointed, and witty, and solemn; **eliciting** at almost every sentence deafening applause; and she ended by asserting: "If de fust woman God ever made was strong enough to turn de world upside down all alone, dese women togedder (and she glanced her eye over the platform) ought to be able to turn it back, and get it right side up again! And now dey is asking to do it, de man better let 'em." Long-continued cheering greeted this. "'Bleeged[9] to ye for hearin' on me, and now ole Sojourner han't got nothin' more to say."

Why did Sojourner Truth single out certain men in the audience? How did those men feel about this?

Amid roars of applause, she returned to her corner, leaving more than one of us with streaming eyes and hearts beating with gratitude . . . and carried us safely over the slough[10] of difficulty turning the whole tide in our favor. I have never in my life seen anything like the magical influence that subdued the mobbish spirit of the day, and turned the sneers and jeers of an excited crowd into notes of respect and admiration. Hundreds rushed up to shake hands with her, and congratulate the glorious old mother, and bid her God-speed on her mission of "testifyin' agin concerning the wickedness of this 'ere people." ■

---

[7] **head me.** Outdo or outwork me

[8] **bear the lash.** Endure whipping

[9] **'Bleeged.** Obliged; thank you

[10] **slough.** A depression or pit

VOCABULARY IN PLACE

- **rebuke,** ***n.*** Sharp criticism
- **elicit,** ***v.*** To draw out

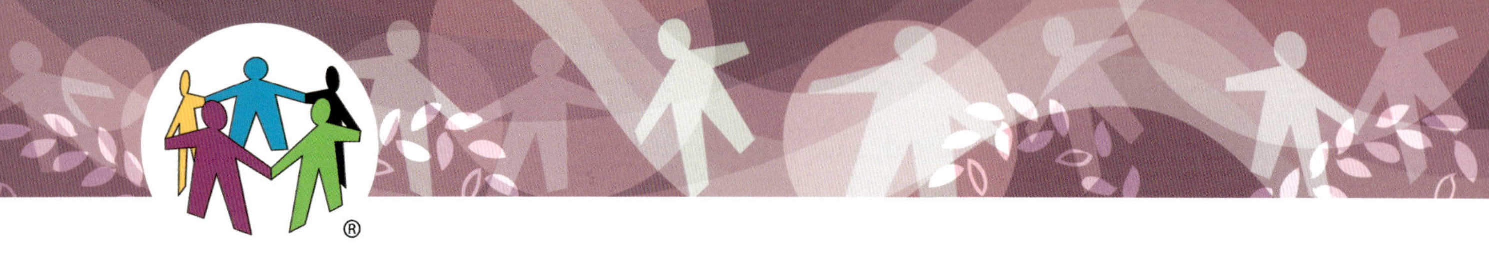

Understanding the Selection

Recalling

1. What did the other attendees at the conference—including fellow women's rights advocates—say to Francis Gage about Sojourner Truth?
2. Who were the women's opponents at this convention?
3. What was the atmosphere at the convention just before Truth took the pulpit?
4. What did Sojourner Truth say about her own physical abilities and life experiences?

Interpreting

1. Why did Frances Gage allow Sojourner Truth to speak despite the objections?
2. What did these opponents say about women's rights? What reasoning and examples did they use?
3. How did Sojourner Truth's physical presence and the sound of her voice transform the mood of the convention when she began to speak?
4. Through her powerful words about her own life, what did Sojourner Truth say about women in general?

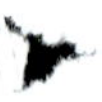

Synthesizing

1. Sojourner Truth took the pulpit at a very tense moment during the Akron Convention as the debate had turned strongly in favor of several men who spoke against women's rights. How did Sojourner Truth knock down her opponents' arguments? Why did she win the crowd with her speech, and what were the strongest parts of her speech? Use examples from the text to support your answer.

Delving Deeper

About the Author

Sojourner Truth (1797–1883) lived a long and fascinating life, by the end of which she had been invited to the White House twice to meet two presidents, Lincoln and Grant, and had risen to national prominence as an orator and activist.

Born Isabella Baumfree to Dutch slave owners in upstate New York, she escaped from slavery in the 1820s. She went to New York City, where—in a time when religious zealots stood on virtually every corner preaching about the end of the world—she became deeply involved in a cult led by the self-proclaimed "Prophet Matthias." In her autobiography, *Narrative of the Life of Sojourner Truth* (1850), she recounted tales of murder, adultery, fraud, and other scandals that eventually landed her in court against other members of the cult. She won this court case, as well as another in which she sued for her son Peter's freedom from slavery. This makes Sojourner Truth the first black woman in American history to win not one but two court cases against white people.

In 1843 Isabella Baumfree experienced a spiritual revelation. Soon after, she changed her name to Sojourner Truth. A *sojourner* is a traveler; Sojourner Truth intended to travel the country preaching "God's truth and plan for salvation." Her travels soon brought her into contact with members of the Abolitionist Movement, which was also closely tied to several Christian groups. She met and worked closely with such notable Abolitionists as William Lloyd Garrison, Frederick Douglass, and Olive Gilbert (to whom Truth dictated her *Narrative*).

During the Civil War, Truth lobbied for the formation and continued support of all-black units in the Union Army. After the enactment of the Emancipation Proclamation, she became a prominent figure fighting for the rights of inhabitants in the "Freedmen's Villages"—the squalid tent-cities in Washington, D.C., that were home to tens of thousands of African-American refugees recently freed from the South. She also petitioned Congress to grant land in the West to former slaves.

Truth later became active in the Women's Rights and Suffrage Movements, through which she worked with important activists such as Elizabeth Cady Stanton and Lucretia Mott. By the end of her long public life, Sojourner Truth had met, worked, struggled with, and was an inspiration to practically every great American who shared her cause and her time in history, as well as to countless others whose names are forgotten.

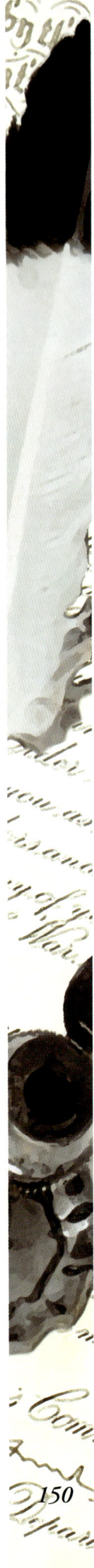

Prereading

Letter to Thomas Jefferson

by Benjamin Banneker

Banneker was a remarkable man. When he was 21 years old, a traveling salesman gave him a pocketwatch. With no formal training—having received only a rudimentary education, but spending most of his childhood working on the family farm—Banneker took the watch home, disassembled it, and carved a precise, large-scale, wooden replica that continued to strike on the hour for more than forty years.

Banneker developed a passion for astronomy late in life. At 58 he learned everything he could on the subject by reading and figuring things out for himself. He published the first edition of *Benjamin Banneker's Pennsylvania, Delaware, Maryland, and Virginia Almanac* in 1792. It featured his own astronomical calculations for predicting lunar and solar eclipses, as well as an **ephemeris** (a table or chart providing the coordinates of celestial bodies, such as the sun, moon, and planets, during specified times).

Shortly before he published his almanac, Banneker sat down to write a letter to then Secretary of State Thomas Jefferson. Banneker was certainly not the last person ever to criticize Jefferson, however politely, for penning the famous phrase "all men are created equal" as his very own slaves toiled in his fields. However, Banneker was among the *first* to raise the issue.

Banneker hoped that his almanac and letter would work to disprove theories claiming that those descended from Africa were intellectually inferior to other peoples. (Such theories were used as justifications for slavery and have long since been abandoned by the scientific community.) Jefferson was well-known for his intellect thanks to his many writings and works in areas from philosophy and astronomy to botany and architecture. (Indeed, though Banneker could not have known at the time, Jefferson's rough draft of the Declaration of Independence included references to the immorality of the slave trade, though the clause was removed due to political pressure from the southern colonies, including Jefferson's Virginia.)

The letter to Thomas Jefferson provides an impressive display of early-American **rhetoric** (the art of persuasion). As in other writings of the period, certain sentence structures, vocabulary, and the generally florid eighteenth-century style will be challenging to some readers, but Banneker's main point should be quite clear. Be sure to read Jefferson's reply on page 155.

Letter to Thomas Jefferson

by Benjamin Banneker

Maryland, Baltimore County
August 19, 1791

SIR,

I am fully sensible of the greatness of that freedom, which I take with you on the present occasion; a liberty which seemed to me scarcely allowable, when I reflected on that distinguished and dignified station in which you stand, and the almost general prejudice and prepossession,[1] which is so prevalent in the world against those of my complexion.

Is it socially acceptable for Banneker to write to Jefferson?

I suppose it is a truth too well attested to you, to need a proof here, that we are a race of beings, who have long labored under the abuse and **censure** of the world; that we have long been looked upon with an eye of contempt; and that we have long been considered rather as **brutish** than human, and scarcely capable of mental **endowments**.

Sir, I hope I may safely admit, in consequence of that report which hath reached me, that you are a man far less inflexible in sentiments of this nature, than many others; that you are measurably friendly, and well disposed towards us; and that you are willing and ready to lend your aid and assistance to our relief, from those many distresses, and numerous calamities, to which we are reduced. Now Sir, if this is founded in truth, I apprehend you will embrace every opportunity, to **eradicate** that train of absurd and false ideas and opinions, which so generally prevails with respect to us; and that your **sentiments** are **concurrent** with mine, which are, that one universal Father hath given being to us all; and that he hath not only made us all of one flesh, but that he hath also, without partiality, afforded us all the same sensations and endowed us all with the same faculties; and that however variable we may be in society or religion, however diversified in situation or color, we are all of the same family, and stand in the same relation to him.

Sir, if these are sentiments of which you are fully persuaded, I hope you cannot but acknowledge, that it is the indispensable duty of those, who maintain for themselves the rights of human nature, and who possess the obligations of Christianity, to extend their power and influence to the relief of every part of the human race, from whatever burden or oppression they may unjustly labor under; and this, I apprehend, a full conviction of the truth and obligation of these principles should lead all to. Sir, I have long been convinced, that if your love for yourselves, and for those

What should have been the duty of Jefferson and others who claimed natural rights for themselves?

[1] **prejudice and prepossession.** Judgments or opinions formed without knowledge or examination of the facts

VOCABULARY IN PLACE

- **censure,** ***n.*** Expression of strong disapproval; harsh criticism
- **brutish,** ***adj.*** Uncivilized, primitive, beastly
- **endowment,** ***n.*** A natural gift, ability, or quality
- **eradicate,** ***v.*** To tear up by the roots; wipe out
- **sentiments,** ***n. pl.*** Feelings
- **concurrent,** ***adj.*** In accordance with; in harmony with

inestimable laws, which preserved to you the rights of human nature, was founded on sincerity, you could not but be **solicitous**, that every individual, of whatever rank or distinction, might with you equally enjoy the blessings thereof; neither could you rest satisfied short of the most active effusion of your exertions,[2] in order to their promotion from any state of degradation, to which the unjustifiable cruelty and barbarism of men may have reduced them.

Sir, I freely and cheerfully acknowledge, that I am of the African race, and in that color which is natural to them of the deepest dye; and it is under a sense of the most profound gratitude to the Supreme Ruler of the Universe, that I now confess to you, that I am not under that state of tyrannical thraldom,[3] and inhuman captivity, to which too many of my brethren are doomed, but that I have abundantly tasted of the fruition[4] of those blessings, which proceed from that free and unequalled liberty with which you are favored; and which, I hope, you will willingly allow you have mercifully received, from the immediate hand of that Being, from whom proceedeth every good and perfect Gift.

Was Banneker a slave?

Sir, suffer me to recall to your mind that time, in which the arms and tyranny of the British crown were exerted,[5] with every powerful effort, in order to reduce you to a state of servitude: look back, I entreat you, on the variety of dangers to which you were exposed; reflect on that time, in which every human aid appeared unavailable, and in which even hope and fortitude wore the aspect of inability to the conflict, and you cannot but be led to a serious and grateful sense of your miraculous and **providential** preservation; you cannot but acknowledge, that the present freedom and tranquility which you enjoy you have mercifully received, and that it is the peculiar blessing of Heaven.

This, Sir, was a time when you clearly saw into the injustice of a state of slavery, and in which you had just apprehensions of the horrors of its condition. It was now that your **abhorrence** thereof was so excited, that you publicly held forth this true and invaluable doctrine, which is worthy to be recorded and remembered in all succeeding ages: "We hold these truths to be self-evident, that all men are created equal; that they are endowed by their Creator with certain unalienable rights, and that among these are, life, liberty, and the pursuit of happiness." Here was a time, in which your tender feelings for yourselves had engaged you thus to declare, you were then impressed with proper ideas of the great violation of liberty, and the free possession of those blessings, to which you were entitled by nature; but, Sir, how **pitiable** is it to reflect, that although you were so fully convinced of the benevolence of the Father of Mankind,

Why did Banneker remind Jefferson of pre-Revolutionary days?

---

2 **effusion of your exertions.** Disbursement (or distribution) of your effort

3 **tyrannical thraldom.** Enslaved by tyranny (absolute rule, e.g., by a king)

4 **fruition.** Completion, realization

5 **that time . . . were exerted.** A reference to the Colonial period prior to the Revolutionary War (1775–1783), when Britain ruled the 13 colonies

VOCABULARY IN PLACE

- **inestimable,** ***adj.*** Of immeasurable value; priceless
- **solicitous,** ***adj.*** Full of desire; eager
- **providential,** ***adj.*** As if through divine intervention
- **abhorrence,** ***n.*** Loathing, hatred
- **pitiable,** ***adj.*** Arousing or deserving of pity, pathetic

and of his equal and impartial distribution of these rights and privileges, which he hath conferred upon them, that you should at the same time counteract his mercies, in detaining by fraud and violence so numerous a part of my brethren, under groaning captivity and cruel oppression, that you should at the same time be found guilty of that most criminal act, which you professedly detested[6] in others, with respect to yourselves.

I suppose that your knowledge of the situation of my brethren, is too extensive to need a recital here; neither shall I presume to prescribe methods by which they may be relieved, otherwise than by recommending to you and all others, to wean[7] yourselves from those narrow prejudices which you have **imbibed** with respect to them, and as Job[8] proposed to his friends, "put your soul in their souls' stead;" thus shall your hearts be enlarged with kindness and benevolence towards them; and thus shall you need neither the direction of myself or others, in what manner to proceed herein. And now, Sir, although my sympathy and affection for my brethren hath caused my enlargement[9] thus far, I ardently hope, that your **candor** and generosity will plead with you in my behalf, when I make known to you, that it was not originally my design; but having taken up my pen in order to direct to you, as a present, a copy of an Almanac, which I have calculated for the succeeding year, I was unexpectedly and unavoidably led thereto.

This calculation[10] is the production of my arduous study, in this my advanced stage of life; for having long had unbounded desires to become acquainted with the secrets of nature, I have had to gratify my curiosity herein, through my own **assiduous** application to Astronomical Study, in which I need not recount to you the many difficulties and disadvantages, which I have had to encounter.

And although I had almost declined to make my calculation for the ensuing year, in consequence of that time which I had allotted therefore, being taken up at the Federal Territory, by the request of Mr. Andrew Ellicott, yet finding myself under several engagements to Printers of this state, to whom I had communicated my design, on my return to my place of residence, I industriously applied myself thereto, which I hope I have accomplished with correctness and accuracy; a copy of which I have taken the liberty to direct to you, and which I humbly request you will favorably receive; and although you may have the opportunity of **perusing** it after its publication, yet I choose to send it to you in manuscript previous thereto, that thereby you might not only have an earlier inspection, but that you might also view it in my own hand writing.

And now, Sir, I shall conclude, and subscribe myself, with the most profound respect,

Your most obedient humble servant,

BENJAMIN BANNEKER. ■

---

6 **professedly detested.** Claimed to despise

7 **wean.** To detach from a habit; quit

8 **Job.** In the Bible, an upright man whose faith in God survived the test of repeated misfortunes

9 **enlargement.** Stepping outside of accepted social boundaries. Once again, Banneker refers to the liberty he is taking as a black man writing to a white man.

10 **calculation.** Banneker refers here to his astronomical calculations, a major part of his almanac.

VOCABULARY IN PLACE

- **imbibe,** *v.* To absorb into the mind
- **candor,** *n.* Sincerity and openness
- **assiduous,** *adj.* Diligent, unceasing, persistent
- **peruse,** *v.* To read or examine with care

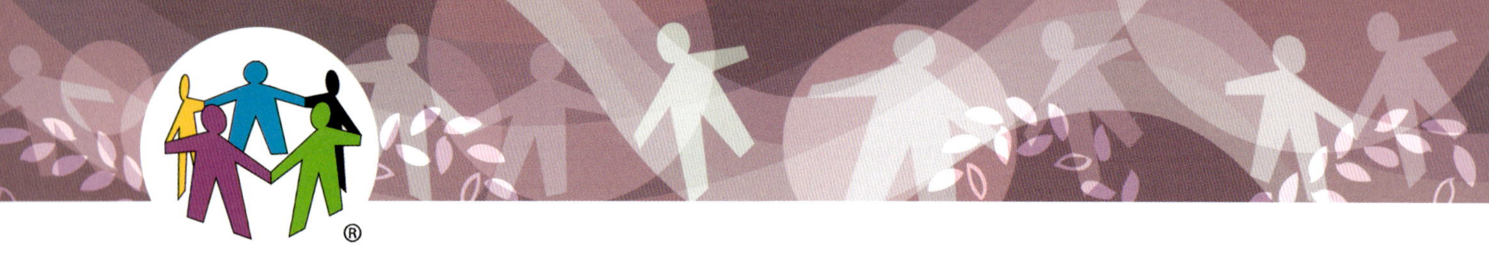

Understanding the Selection

Recalling

1. As far as he had heard, what type of man did Banneker think Jefferson was?
2. What document, written by Jefferson, did Banneker quote?
3. To what was Banneker referring when he said "the situation of my brethren"?
4. Toward the end of the letter, what did Banneker announce that he was giving Jefferson?
5. For what two reasons did Banneker send his almanac to Jefferson?

Interpreting

1. What did Banneker hope to accomplish with this letter? What did he want Jefferson to do?
2. What effect did he hope that the quotation would have on Jefferson?
3. Why would Jefferson have had "extensive" knowledge in this area? Why did Banneker suggest that Jefferson's knowledge of slavery was "too extensive to need a recital"?
4. What "difficulties and disadvantages" do you think Banneker encountered?
5. Why did Banneker think it was important that Jefferson see the almanac in his own handwriting?

Synthesizing

1. What is Banneker's main purpose in writing the letter? Do you think he makes a convincing argument? Why, or why not?
2. Find at least one passage in which Banneker acknowledges his inferior social status. Is he apologetic? Does he write to Jefferson as a second-class citizen or as an equal? Use a quotation from the text to support your answer.

Delving Deeper

History Alive!

Jefferson's Reply. Thomas Jefferson's short reply to Banneker's letter is printed here in its entirety:

August 30, 1791

SIR,

I THANK you, sincerely, for your letter of the 19th instant, and for the Almanac it contained. No body wishes more than I do, to see such proofs as you exhibit, that nature has given to our black brethren talents equal to those of the other colors of men; and that the appearance of the want of them, is owing merely to the degraded condition of their existence, both in Africa and America. I can add with truth, that no body wishes more ardently to see a good system commenced, for raising the condition, both of their body and mind, to what it ought to be, as far as the imbecility of their present existence, and other circumstances, which cannot be neglected, will admit.

I have taken the liberty of sending your Almanac to Monsieur de Condozett, Secretary of the Academy of Sciences at Paris, and Member of the Philanthropic Society, because I considered it as a document, to which your whole color had a right for their justification, against the doubts which have been entertained of them.

I am with great esteem, Sir, Your most obedient Humble Servant,

THOMAS JEFFERSON.

How do you think Banneker felt when he read this letter? Did Jefferson address the issues raised in Banneker's letter? Do you think he took Banneker seriously? Why or why not?

About the Author

Benjamin Banneker (1731–1806), African-American publisher and astronomer, was born in Maryland. His mother was a white woman from England who freed and married one of her slaves. Banneker received basic reading and arithmetic instruction but spent most of his childhood working on the family farm. A self-taught clockmaker, Banneker was hired once by a surveyor to create a highly precise instrument which would allow his client to make calculations based on the stars. Thereafter, beginning at age 58, Banneker became an avid astronomer. He published his almanac from 1792 to 1797 and became known as the Sable (black) Astronomer.

Prereading

"The Knee-High Man"

Anonymous, Retold by Julius Lester

There are many reasons for telling stories. One reason is to pass down wisdom from generation to generation. In those traditional societies in which reading and writing are unknown, stories are especially important as vehicles for communication of ideas from one generation to the next. The following story is an example of an African-American folktale that comes out of the **oral tradition.** The tale is interesting because it deals with a character who is unhappy with who and what he is. In the course of the story, this character learns that his unhappiness is based on misconceptions. He learns this from an owl, a bird traditionally associated with wisdom (probably because of its big eyes and its tendency to sit quietly and observe).

Folktales tend to have elements that occur again and again in story after story. These elements are known as **motifs.** Here are some common folktale motifs to look for as you read "The Knee-High Man":

1. A character who is unusually short or small
2. A character who sets out to find an answer
3. Things that appear or happen in sets of three (the so-called "Rule of Threes")
4. Animals that talk to people

The motif of the small person occurs, for example, in such classic folktales as "Thumbelina" and "Tom Thumb." The motif of the character who sets out to find an answer occurs in such tales as "Why the Sea Is Salt" and the tale collected by the Brothers Grimm known as "The White Snake." The motif of things that happen in threes occurs in most stories, as, for example, when Goldilocks tastes porridge from three bowls and tries three beds. The motif of talking animals appears in thousands and thousands of tales, such as "The White Snake" and "The Bremen Town Musicians."

The Knee-High Man

Anonymous, Retold by Julius Lester

Once upon a time there was a knee-high man. He was no taller than a person's knees. Because he was so short, he was very unhappy. He wanted to be big like everybody else.

One day he decided to ask the biggest animal he could find how he could get big. So he went to see Mr. Horse. "Mr. Horse, how can I get big like you?"

Mr. Horse said, "Well, eat a whole lot of corn. Then run around a lot. After a while you'll be as big as me."

The knee-high man did just that. He ate so much corn that his stomach hurt. Then he ran and ran and ran until his legs hurt. But he didn't get any bigger. So he decided that Mr. Horse had told him something wrong. He decided to go ask Mr. Bull.

"Mr. Bull? How can I get big like you?"

Mr. Bull said, "Eat a whole lot of grass. Then bellow and bellow as loud as you can. The first thing you know, you'll be as big as me."

So the knee-high man ate a whole field of grass. That made his stomach hurt. He bellowed and bellowed and bellowed all day and all night. That made his throat hurt. But he didn't get any bigger. So he decided that Mr. Bull was all wrong, too.

Now he didn't know anyone else to ask. One night he heard Mr. Hoot Owl hooting, and he remembered that Mr. Owl knew everything. "Mr. Owl? How can I get big like Mr. Horse and Mr. Bull?"

"What do you want to be big for?" Mr. Hoot Owl asked.

"I want to be big so that when I get into a fight, I can whip everybody," the knee-high man said.

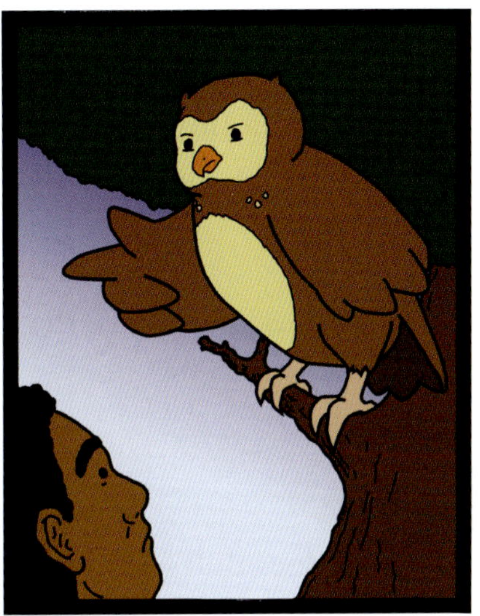

Mr. Owl hooted. "Anybody ever try to pick a fight with you?"

The knee-high man thought a minute. "Well, now that you mention it, nobody ever did try to start a fight with me."

Mr. Owl said, "Well, you don't have any reason to fight. Therefore, you don't have any reason to be bigger than you are."

"But, Mr. Owl," the knee-high man said, "I want to be big so I can see far into the distance."

Mr. Hoot Owl hooted. "If you climb a tall tree, you can see into the distance from the top."

The knee-high man was quiet for a minute. "Well, I hadn't thought of that."

Mr. Hoot Owl hooted again. "And that's what's wrong, Mr. Knee-High Man. You hadn't done any thinking at all. I'm smaller than you, and you don't see me worrying about being big. Mr. Knee-High Man, you wanted something that you didn't need." ■

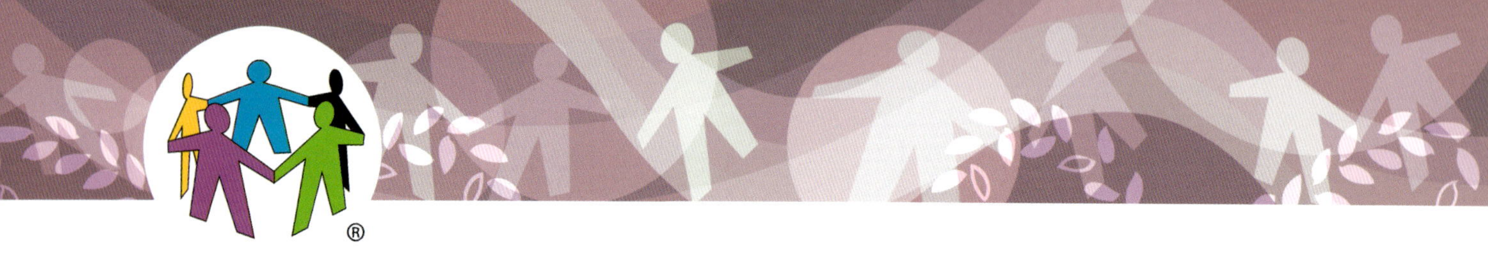

Understanding the Selection

Recalling

1. Why is the man in this story unhappy? What does he want?
2. What advice does Horse give the man?
3. What advice does Bull give the man?
4. Owl does not give the man advice. Instead, he asks questions. What questions does Owl ask?

Interpreting

1. What does the man decide to do in order to deal with his unhappiness?
2. Why would Horse give the man this advice? Does the advice make sense for a horse? Does it make sense for a man? Explain.
3. Why would Bull give the man this advice? Does this advice make sense for a bull? Does it make sense for a man? Explain.
4. In what way does Owl show his wisdom?

Synthesizing

1. What lesson does this story teach us about our desires? Do we always know what is best for us?
2. What lesson does this story teach us about comparing ourselves to other people? Have you ever heard the expression "The grass is always greener on the other side of the fence"? How does "Knee-High Man" illustrate this saying?

Delving Deeper

Understanding Literature

Understanding Motifs. As you have learned, a **motif** is an element that appears again and again in a literary work or in a group of literary works. For example, the idea of the poor child who is actually a prince or a princess is a motif that appears in many folktales around the world. In folktales, jokes, oral poetry, songs, and other works in the oral tradition, things often happen in groups of three. This organizational principle in stories is often called the "Rule of Threes." In a typical story, a character will encounter three different characters or obstacles and get something or learn something from each one. In the story from the Brothers Grimm called "The White Snake," the main character befriends three groups of animals, and each later helps him to perform one of three tasks that he has to perform in order to win the hand of a princess. Does "Knee-High Man" make use of the "Rule of Threes" motif? Why, or why not? Work with a partner to come up with your own folktale that involves a series of three events. Incorporate at least one additional common motif into your story. (Refer to the Prereading for more ideas.)

About the Author

Julius Lester (b.1939) grew up in the Midwest and the South. He was the son of a Methodist minister and later converted to Judaism. He received a Bachelor of Arts degree in English from Fisk University in 1960, and after graduation he became involved in the Civil Rights Movement. He collaborated with a number of famous folk musicians, including Pete Seeger and Judy Collins, and wrote a book on playing the guitar in the style of the African-American blues musician Huddie William Ledbetter (Leadbelly). He teaches Judaic and Near Eastern Studies at the University of Massachusetts at Amherst and has published widely for both adults and children. His works include nonfiction, children's books, poetry, and novels. He received the Newbery Honor Medal in 1969 for *To Be a Slave* and the Randolph Caldecott Honor Medal in 1995 for *John Henry.* Other works by Lester include *Ackamarackus: Julius Lester's Sumptuously Silly Fantastically Funny Fables* (2001), *The Blues Singers: Ten Who Rocked the World* (2001), *From Slave Ship to Freedom Road* (1998), and *Why Heaven Is Far Away* (2002).

Prereading

"Tar Baby"

Anonymous

As you have learned in previous lessons, African Americans who were brought to the New World as slaves carried with them a rich oral tradition that included **trickster tales**—stories about mischievous animals who enjoyed playing tricks on others. Such tales are told all over the world and, of course, all over the continent of Africa. Like fables, these stories typically contain talking animals. Common African tricksters include Anansi the Spider, Turtle, and Hare.

In the United States, African tales about the trickster hare developed into a delightful series of Rabbit stories, including the following famous story about Rabbit and Tar Baby. Tar is a dark, sticky, oily substance produced from coal, wood, or other organic matter. It was traditionally used for such purposes as coating boat hulls or roofing materials to make them waterproof.

The story of Rabbit and Tar Baby was collected from African-American storytellers in the late nineteenth century by Robert Roosevelt, uncle of President Theodore Roosevelt, and by a white writer named Joel Chandler Harris, who retold stories that he heard from an African-American source on a plantation in Georgia. Harris's versions of these tales contained an African-American storyteller character named Uncle Remus. Those versions were immensely popular in the late nineteenth and early twentieth centuries, but are now considered by many to be racist because of their condescending treatment of African Americans. The popularity of such tales among white and black audiences alike nonetheless demonstrates the extraordinary vitality, inventiveness, and wit to be found in the African-American oral tradition.

In many versions of this story, including Roosevelt's and Harris's retellings, animals address one another as "Br'er," or brother. This, too, is a survival of a traditional West African form of address.

The story of "The Tar Baby and the Briar Patch" is given here in a version from southern Kentucky. As in other trickster tales, this one contains a couple of **reversals,** or surprising changes of fortune for the central character.

Tar Baby

Anonymous

Now Rabbit he had a way of gettin' hisself in trouble 'cause the only animal he cared much about wuz hisself. Truth be told, some of t'other animals would just as soon Fox caught up to Rabbit and had 'im for dinner. That was 'specially true after all the trouble they had with Rabbit over the well.

Here's how it all got started: One mornin' Bear an' Fox an' Rabbit an' Possum an' all the other critters that lives in the woods this side o' Greezy Creek was meetin' in a clearin' and talkin' a whole lot a biznis, when Rabbit up and said they oughta all throw in together an' build a well. "Who wants to drink ole Greezy Creek water when you kin have nice, fresh, sweet water from a deep, dark well," said Rabbit, all musical-like.

"So who, 'zactly, gonna dig this well?" asked Bear, who was big and strong and tired of always doin' more than his share of the heavy labor. Rabbit answered him back all earnest-like that "'course all the animals would do their share."

Well, if you know Rabbit, I 'spect you know what happened next. When the day come to build the well, Possum come 'round to Rabbit's hole and called, "Rabbit, git ta movin'; everbody's waitin'. Today's when we're going to build that well."

"Can't dig no wells, today, Sister Possum," said Rabbit. "I got a baaad case o' the Lassitudes. Better get away quick before you catch it, too."

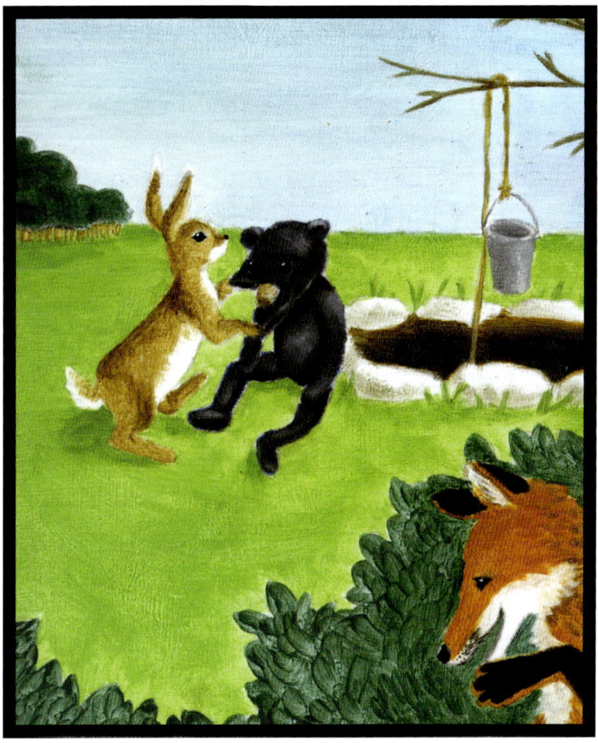

Of course, none of the other animals wuz fooled, except Possum, who kept asking if the Lassitudes wuz catchin'.[1] So, all of the animals worked, laboring hard in the hot sun, diggin' that well, while Rabbit laid in the cool shade of his rabbit hole, doin' a whole lot o' nuthin'.

The next morning, all the animals come to the well to get a drink, but when they got there, they saw they wuz already rabbit tracks goin' up to the well and comin' back from it.

---

1 **catchin'**. Contagious (dialectical)

"Why that sneaky little varmit," said Bear. "We ought to go pull him up outten that hole and feed him to Br'er Fox here."

"Not a bad idea," said Fox. "But who's going to catch him?" Now, this was a problem, because Rabbit wuz lazy, but he wuz also fast.

"Wait a minute! I got an idea," said Fox. Now Fox's idea wuz this: They carved a perfect little man out of wood and covered him all over with tar. Fox called the little man his "Tar Baby."

Then, that evenin', they propped the Tar Baby up against the wall of the well and waited for Rabbit to show up. Sho' enough, along come Rabbit an' when he saw they wuz someone else at the well, he stopped up short and said, "Good evenin'. Come ta hep yoreself at this well, have you? I tell you what, as a repreesentative of the animals hereabouts, I have th'authority ta let you use this here well for a very small and reasonable recompense" (by which Rabbit meant that the little Tar Baby could pay him for the privilege of gittin' some water).

'Course, the Tar Baby didn't say nary a word.

"I say, do you hear me talking to you?" said Rabbit. "I expect maybe you is so stuck up you thinks you is too proud ta talk ta no rabbits."

Still, the Tar Baby didn't say a word.

"Well, I never!" said Rabbit, turning away from the Tar Baby. He wuz all ready jis to grab some water and go off in a huff. But the more he thought about that stuck-up little fella, the madder he got. He turned back to the Tar Baby and said, all hurt an' everythin', "I think you owe me an apology."

The Tar Baby didn't say a word.

"If you don't apologize to me this instant," said Rabbit, "I'll make you wish you did."

The Tar Baby didn' say a word.

"All right," said Rabbit. "You asked for it." And he hauled off to smack that Tar Baby in the cheek, and of course, when he hit the Tar Baby, his paw just got stuck there.

"Let go," said Rabbit. "Let me go this instant, or I'll hit you with my other paw." But, of course, when he hit the Tar Baby with his other paw, it stuck, too. So then Rabbit decided he'd kick the Tar Baby, first with one foot and then the other, and in that way he got all four o' his paws stuck to that Tar Baby like a fly to fly paper.

The other animals peeked out through the bushes and watched as Fox walked up to Rabbit.

"Looks like you got yourself in a pretty pickle, Br'er Rabbit," said Fox. "Maybe I'll just help you free and have you over to my house for a little rabbit stew."

"Rabbit stew," said Rabbit, "Oh, that would be bad, bad, bad. But anything's OK, long's you don't throw me in no briar patch."

"Why don't you want to be throwd in the briar patch, Rabbit?" asked the Fox.

"Oh, boil me in hot water, set me on fire, throw me from the top o' the tallest tree, but please, please, please don't throw me in no briar patch. Them briars would poke out my eyes and scratch me all over and put me in misery I jus' couldn't stan'. So please, please, do with me as you will. But please don' throw me in no briar patch."

Well, the moment he heard that, Fox grabbed Rabbit by the ears and tossed him right into that briar patch and said, "There you go, Rabbit. And it serves you right."

But it was Rabbit who got the last laugh. He went skipping and ducking in and around them briars, saying, "Silly ol' Fox. I wuz borned and raised in the briar patch."

Which didn't please that old Br'er Fox one bit. ■

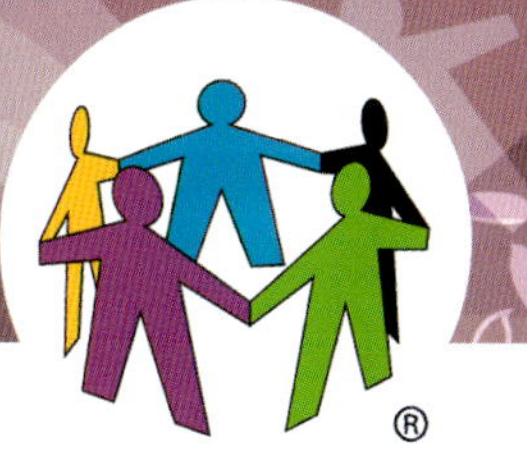

Understanding the Selection

Recalling

1. According to the first line of this story, which animal does Rabbit care most about?
2. What does Rabbit suggest that the animals do? What objection does Bear raise?
3. What illness does Rabbit claim to have?
4. What do the other animals discover when they come to the well in the morning?
5. Why does Rabbit get mad at the Tar Baby? What happens to Rabbit when he strikes the Tar Baby?
6. What does Fox threaten to do to Rabbit?

Interpreting

1. What does this fact tell you about the character of Rabbit?
2. Why might Bear raise this objection? What does this fact suggest about Bear's opinion of Rabbit?
3. Is this a real illness? How do you know?
4. Why are the other animals upset at Rabbit? What do they decide to do to get even?
5. Why does Rabbit demand an apology from the Tar Baby? Does this fit in with what you know about Rabbit's personality?
6. How does Rabbit outwit Fox in the end?

Synthesizing

1. What lesson do the other animals mean to teach Rabbit? Are they successful?
2. Stories serve many different purposes. For example, they can be told to entertain and to instruct. What aspects of this story serve these two different purposes?

Prereading

"The Headless Hant"

Anonymous

"The Headless Hant" is an example of the type of folktale known as the **ghost story.** Collected in North Carolina, this story is told in an evocative, beautiful rural dialect.

Everyone from kids around a campfire to elderly folks sitting on front porches loves a good ghost story, and this is a fine example of the genre. One amusing aspect of the story is that the characters seem to take the appearance of the horrid ghost in stride, as if such appearances occurred all the time and weren't much to remark upon. In addition to some typical ghost story elements, this tale contains more than a little bit of wish fulfillment. One can imagine it being told by someone who didn't have much in the way of earthly goods and who liked to imagine life being easier. One thing that rural folk did have, of course, was their imaginations, and it is to such richness of imagination that we owe the rich tradition of African-American folktale.

The Headless Hant[1]

Anonymous

A man and his wife was going along the big road. It was cold and the road was muddy and sticky red, and their feet was mighty nigh froze off, and they was hungry, and it got pitch dark before they got where they was going.

'Twan't long before they came to a big fine house with smoke coming outen the chimley and a fire shining through the winder. It was the kin' of a house rich folks lives in, so they went round to the back porch and knocked on the back door. Somebody say, "Come in!" They went in but they didn't see nobody.

They looked all up and down and all round, but still they didn't see nobody. They saw the fire on the hearth[2] with the skillets setting in it all ready for supper to be cooked in'em. They saw there was meat and flour and lard and salsody[3] and a pot of beans smoking and a rabbit a-biling[4] in a covered pot.

Still they didn't see nobody, but they saw everything was ready for somebody. The woman took off her wet shoes and stockings to warm her feet at the fire, and the man took the bucket and lit out for the springhouse[5] to get fresh water for the coffee. They 'lowed they was going to have them brown beans and that molly cottontail[6] and that cornbread and hot coffee in three shakes.

The woman was toasting her feet when right through the shut door in walks a man and he don't have no head. He had on his britches and his shoes and his galluses[7] and his vest and his coat and his shirt and his collar, but he don't have no head. Jcs raw neck and bloody stump.

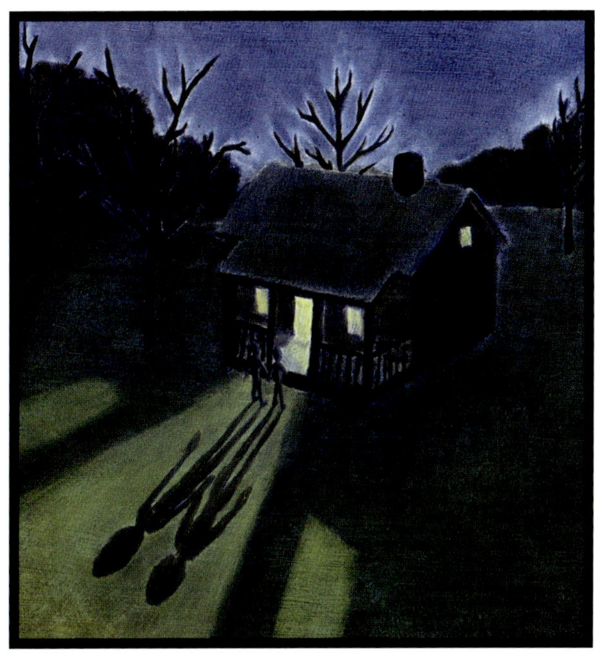

And he started to tell the woman, without no mouth to tell her with, how come he happened to come in there that a-way. She mighty nigh jumped outen her skin, but

[1] **hant.** Ghost (dialectical, related to the word *haunt)*

[2] **hearth.** Literally, the floor of a fireplace and the extension of that floor into the room; figuratively, the fireplace itself

[3] **salsody.** Sal soda, or sodium carbonate, is a chemical used in making washing powders; alternatively, this might be a reference to sodium bicarbonate, or baking soda, which is used to make bread rise when baked (dialectical).

[4] **a-biling.** Boiling (dialectical)

[5] **springhouse.** An enclosure built above a spring, or water source, in order to protect that source

[6] **molly cottontail.** A rabbit

[7] **galluses.** Suspenders

she said, "What in the name of the Lord do you want?" So he said he's awful misery, being dead and buried in two pieces. He said somebody kilt him for his money and took him to the cellar and buried him in two pieces, his head in one place and his corpse in'nother. He said them robbers dug all round trying to find his money, and when they didn't find it they went off and left him in two pieces, so now he hankers[8] to be put back together so's to get rid of his misery.

Then the hant said some other folks had been there and asked him what he wanted but they didn't say in the name of the Lord, and 'cause she did is how come he could tell her 'bout his misery.

'Bout that time the woman's husband came back from the springhouse with the bucket of water to make coffee with and set the bucket on the shelf before he saw the hant. Then he saw the hant with the bloody joint of his neck sticking up and he come nigh jumping outen his skin.

Then the wife told the hant who her husband is, and the hant begun at the start and told it all over again 'bout how come he is the way he is. He told'em if they'd come down into the cellar and find his head and bury him all in one grave he'd make'em rich.

They said they would and that they'd get a torch.

The hant said, "Don't need no torch." And he went up to the fire and stuck his front finger in it and it blazed up like a lightwood knot[9] and he led the way down to the cellar by the light.

They went a long way down steps before they came to the cellar. Then the hant say, "Here's where my head's buried and over here's where the rest of me's buried. Now yo' all dig right over yonder where I throw this spot of light and dig till you touch my barrels of gold and silver money."

So they dug and dug and sure 'nough they found the barrels of money he'd covered up with the thick cellar floor. Then they dug up the hant's head and histed the thing on the spade.[10] The hant jes reached over and picked the head offen the spade and put it on his neck. Then he took off his burning finger and stuck it in a candlestick on a box, and still holding on his head, he crawled back into the hole that he had come out of.

And from under the ground they heard him a-saying, "Yo' all can have my land, can have my house, can have all my money and be as rich as I was, 'cause you buried me in one piece together, head and corpse."

Then they took the candlestick blazing with the hant's finger and went back upstairs and washed themselves with lye soap.[11] Then the woman made up the cornbread with the spring water and greased the skillet with hogmeat and put in the hoecake[12] and lifted the lid on with the tongs and put coals on fire on top of the lid and round the edges of the skillet, and cooked the hoecake done. Her man put the coffee and water in the pot and set it on the trivet[13] to boil. Then they et that supper of them beans and that rabbit and that hoecake and hot coffee. And they lived there all their lives and had barrels of money to buy vittels[14] and clothes with. And they never heard no more 'bout the man that came upstairs without no head where his head ought to be. ■

---

8 **hankers.** Longs, fervently desires (dialectical)

9 **lightwood knot.** *Lightwood* is a regional term for kindling, wood used to start fires; a knot is a dense deformation in wood; the density makes the wood ideal for use in a torch.

10 **histed . . . on the spade.** Hoisted, or picked up, the thing on the shovel

11 **lye soap.** A soap that contains the active ingredient lye, which is made by leaching water through wood ash

12 **hoecake.** Cornbread

13 **trivet.** A stand in a fireplace on which cooking is done

14 **vittels.** Victuals, or food (dialectical)

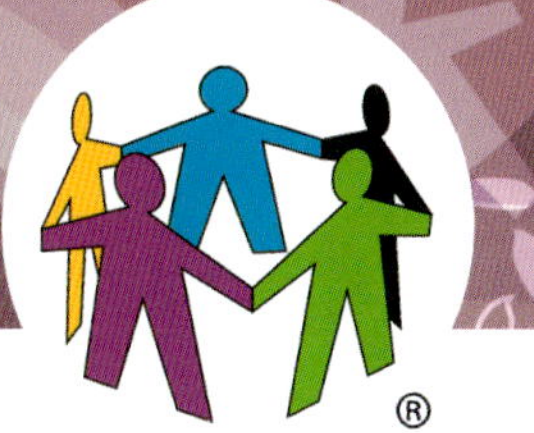

Understanding the Selection

Recalling

1. How are the two people feeling at the beginning of the story?
2. What do they find when they go into the house?
3. Where does the man go and for what purpose? What happens after he leaves? What does the woman ask her visitor?
4. How does the hant, or ghost, come to be missing his head? What does the hant want the people to do for him?
5. With what does the hant light the way down to the cellar? What does he do to leave a light for the man and the woman?

Interpreting

1. What evidence does the story provide that these are people who do not have much?
2. Why is it odd that they should find these things? What is missing?
3. What is the special significance of the woman's question? What does this question allow the visitor to do?
4. A common motif in folktales is that of the **grateful dead**—dead people who are thankful for something done for them by living people. What example of this motif does the story provide?
5. What is your emotional reaction to this detail in the story? Why might the storyteller have included it?

Synthesizing

1. A good ghost story is supposed to elicit chills from its audience. Do you think that this story would have that effect on a young audience or a superstitious one? Why, or why not?
2. In what way might this story be an example of wish fulfillment on the part of a storyteller who does not, himself or herself, have a lot of earthly wealth?

PREREADING

"The Signifying Monkey"

Anonymous

"The Signifying Monkey" is perhaps the most famous of a genre of African-American oral works known as toasts. A **toast** is a long poem that is acted out. It is generally in **rhymed couplets,** or pairs of lines with four beats per line. Because they are meant to be performed, toasts often contain enormous variety—exciting situations, multiple characters and voices, action, and commentary. The variety provides fuel for the performer to display not only his or her verbal brilliance but also his or her skill as an entertainer. Typically, toasts contain lots of humor and ironic or surprising endings.

The "Signifying Monkey" originated as a trickster character in West African folklore. The adjective *signifying* tells us that the monkey is engaged in a particular kind of speech, known as **signification**. When **signifying,** a character or person uses humor and wit to put down another character or person, sometimes to his or her face and sometimes to a third character or to an audience. Signification always involves humor, and the humor makes use of all the tricks in the book—**puns (double meanings), implication, association, repetition, parallelism, onomatopoeia, catalogs of abuse,** and so on. To the extent that a signification is verbally brilliant and devastating, it is successful. A variety of signification popular since the mid-twentieth century is the verbal sparring known as "playing the dozens," in which two people trade insults, often about one another's nearest and dearest relatives. One also finds many examples of signification in contemporary rap music and slam poetry.

A number of scholars have pointed out that signification has deeper meanings than simply its entertainment value. Signification is subtle and indirect persuasion. It is hip, sophisticated, and ironic. It shows irreverence for conventional, unjust authority and power. The great scholar **Henry Louis Gates, Jr.**, has made signification the basis of a new variety of criticism that views the African-American literary tradition as "double-voiced," involving ironic interpretations and transmutations (changes). For example, the spirituals ironically appropriated white religious concepts to express subtle, subversive messages about freedom and resistance.

The Signifying Monkey

Anonymous

The Monkey and the Lion
Got to talking one day.
Monkey looked down and said, Lion,
I hear you's king in every way.
But I know somebody
Who do not think that is true—
He told me he could whip
The living daylights out of you.
Lion said, Who?
Monkey said, Lion,
He talked about your mama
And talked about your grandma, too,
And I'm too polite to tell you
What he said about you.
Lion said, Who said what? Who?
Monkey in the tree,
Lion on the ground.
Monkey kept on signifying
But he didn't come down.
Monkey said, His name is Elephant—
He stone sure is not your friend.
Lion said, He don't need to be
Because today will be his end.
Lion took off through the jungle
Lickity-split,
Meaning to grab Elephant
And tear him bit to bit. Period!
He come across Elephant copping[1] a
righteous nod
Under a fine cool shady tree.
Lion said, You big old no-good
so-and-so,
It's either you or me.
Lion let out a solid roar
And bopped Elephant with his paw.

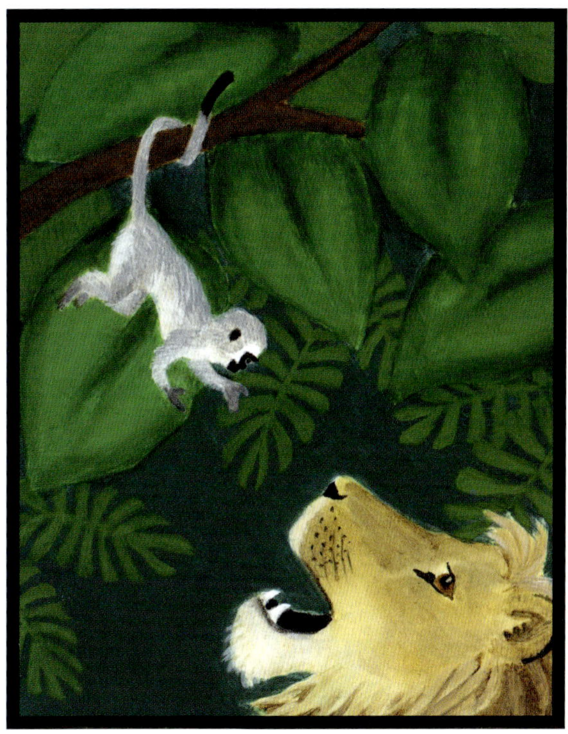

Elephant just took his trunk
And busted old Lion's jaw.
Lion let out another roar,
Reared up six feet tall.
Elephant just kicked him in the belly
And laughed to see him drop and fall.
Lion rolled over,
Copped Elephant by the throat.

[1] **copping.** Getting, taking (slang)

VOCABULARY IN PLACE

- **righteous,** *adj.* Upright, important
- **nod** *n.* Nap

Elephant just shook him loose
And butted him like a goat,
Then he tromped him and he stomped
him
Till the Lion yelled, Oh, no!
And it was near-nigh sunset
When the Elephant let Lion go.
The signifying Monkey
Was still setting in his tree
When he looked down and saw the Lion.
Said, Why, Lion, who can that there be?
Lion said, It's me.
Monkey rapped, "Why, Lion,
You look more dead than alive!
Lion said, Monkey, I don't want
To hear your jive-end jive.[2]
Monkey just kept on signifying
Lion, you for sure caught hell—
Mister Elephant's done whipped you
To a fare-thee-well!
Why, Lion, you look like to me
You been in the precinct[3] station
And had the third-degree,
You ain't no king to me.
Facts, I don't think that you
Can even as much as roar—
And if you try I'm liable
To come down out of this tree and
Whip your tail some more.
The Monkey started laughing
And jumping up and down.
But he jumped so hard the limb broke
And he landed—bam!—on the ground.
When he went to run, his foot slipped
And he fell flat down.
Grr-rrr-rr-r! The Lion was on him
With his front feet and his hind.
Monkey hollered, Ow!
I didn't mean it, Mister Lion!
Lion said, You little flea-bag you!
Why, I'll eat you up alive.
I wouldn't a-been in this fix a-tall
Wasn't for your signifying jive.
Please, said Monkey, Mister Lion,
If you'll just let me go,
I got something to tell you, please,
I think you ought to know.
Lion let the Monkey loose
To see what his tale could be —
And Monkey jumped right back on up
Into his tree.
What I was gonna tell you, said Monkey,
Is you square[4] old so-and-so,
If you fool with me I'll get
Elephant to whip your head some
more.
Monkey, said the Lion,
Beat to his unbooted knees,
You and all your signifying children
Better stay up in them trees.
Which is why today
Monkey does his signifying
A-way-up out of the way. ■

[2] **jive.** Falsehoods uttered in a lively, convincing manner

[3] **precinct.** Police

[4] **square.** Not hip; conventional and boring (a term borrowed from the slang of jazz musicians)

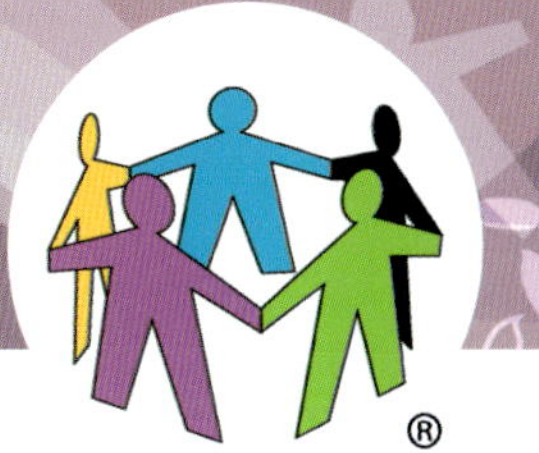

Understanding the Selection

Recalling

1. What does Monkey tell Lion at the beginning of the story?
2. What does Lion do as a result of listening to Monkey? What happens to Lion as a result?
3. What happens to Lion when he goes to the Elephant?
4. What happens to Monkey as a result of jumping up and down on the limb?
5. What does Monkey promise Lion if Lion will let him go?
6. What warning does Lion give to Monkey at the end of the poem?

Interpreting

1. Do you think that what Monkey says is true? Why, or why not?
2. Does Lion try to verify what Monkey said? What does this fact tell you about Lion?
3. Does Lion deserve what happens to him? Why, or why not?
4. Why is this a problem for Monkey?
5. Has Lion learned from his experience with Monkey? What does this tell you about Lion?
6. What fact in nature does this poem explain?

Synthesizing

1. What makes "The Signifying Monkey" an example of a trickster tale?
2. What elements of "The Signifying Monkey" suggest that it has deeper origins than simply being a story told for entertainment? (Hint: Think about myths and what functions they perform. What similar function is carried out by this poem?)

Prereading

The Poetry of Jupiter Hammon and Phillis Wheatley

The poets Jupiter Hammon (1711–1806) and Phillis Wheatley (1754–1784) had a great deal in common. Both achieved "firsts" in American publishing: Hammon was the first African American, and Wheatley the first African-American woman, to publish a poem. Both were slaves—Hammon for his entire life, Wheatley for most of hers. They were devout Christians, as well. Hammon considered himself to be more of a preacher than a poet. In his writings and speeches, he expressed the belief that slavery was God's will and that justice would be served in heaven. (See About the Author for more biographical information.)

Wheatley was not quite as accepting of slavery, though this fact is reflected more in her personal letters than in her poems, which tend to be in keeping with the popular topics and style of her day. She was widely read and received much support in America and Europe, but the American Anti-Slavery Movement did not gain widespread support until the mid-1800s. In Wheatley's time, most white readers thought of slavery as a normal, perhaps unfortunate, fact of life.

There is no such thing as "good" slavery—both poets were other people's property—but neither Hammon nor Wheatley personally experienced the worst of the brutality and suffering that generally accompanied this station in life. These poets *did* overcome many of the immense barriers created by their social status. Wheatley's original collection of poems included a disclaimer from the publisher insisting that these really were "written by Phillis, a young Negro Girl, who was but a few years since, brought an uncultivated Barbarian from Africa," which was followed by signatures of prominent Boston citizens who were willing to attest to this fact. At the time, many people believed that Africans were simply incapable of intellectual achievement. Wheatley and Hammon, and countless others since, proved them wrong.

The first poem in this section contains selected stanzas from Hammon's "Address to Phillis Wheatley, Ethiopian Poetess," encouraging Wheatley to maintain her religious faith. The next poem is Wheatley's "On Being Brought from Africa to America," in which she expresses, subtly, the fact that people of African descent are as capable of spiritual development as anyone else. The third reading is a selection from Wheatley's "To S. M., A Young African Painter, On Seeing His Works."

from An Address to Miss Phillis Wheatley, Ethiopian Poetess[1]

by Jupiter Hammon

I

O come you **pious** youth! Adore
The wisdom of thy God,
In bringing thee from distant shore,
To learn His holy word.

II

Thou mightst been left behind
Amidst a dark **abode**;
God's tender mercy still combin'd,
Thou hast the holy word.

III

Fair wisdom's ways are paths of peace,
And they that walk therein,
Shall **reap** the joys that never cease,
And Christ shall be their king.

IV

God's tender mercy brought thee here;
Tost o'er the raging main;[2]
In Christian faith thou hast a share,
Worth all the gold of Spain.

V

While thousands tossed by the sea,
And others settled down,
God's tender mercy set thee free,
From dangers that come down.

VII

The blessed Jesus, who came down,
Unvail'd[3] his sacred face,
To cleanse the soul of every wound,
And give repenting grace.

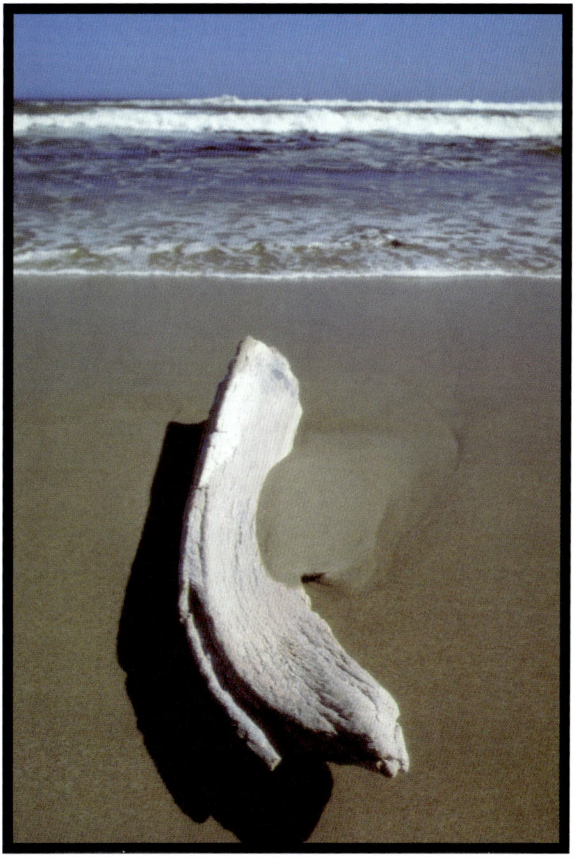

1 **Ethiopian Poetess.** Wheatley was not Ethiopian, but West African. Slaves in America did not come from Ethiopia. However, in the eighteenth century, *Ethiopian* was a label commonly given to all people of African descent. A *poetess* is a female poet.

2 **tost o'er the raging main.** *Tost o'er* means *tossed over. Main* refers to the ocean, across which captives were brought from Africa.

3 **Unvail'd.** Removed the veil from

VOCABULARY IN PLACE

- **pious,** ***adj.*** Deeply religious; devout
- **abode,** ***n.*** A dwelling-place; house
- **reap,** ***v.*** To gather or harvest

IX

Come you, Phillis, now aspire,
And seek the living God,
So step by step thou mayst go higher,
Till perfect in the word.

XIV

The **bounteous** mercies of the Lord,
Are hid beyond the sky,
And holy souls that love His word,
Shall taste them when they die.

XVII

While thousands muse with earthly toys;[4]
And **range** about the street,
Dear Phillis, seek for heaven's joys,
Where we do hope to meet.

XVIII

When God shall send his **summons** down,
And number saints together,[5]
Blest angels chant, (triumphant sound),
Come live with me forever.

XXI

Now glory be to the Most High,[6]
United praises given,
By all on earth, **incessantly**,
And all the host of heav'n.[7]

---

[4] **muse with earthly toys.** Become absorbed with material possessions

[5] **number . . . together.** Group together or count as one. This is a reference to Judgment Day.

[6] **the Most High.** God

[7] **host of heav'n.** Angels, saints, and other heavenly beings

VOCABULARY IN PLACE

- **bounteous,** ***adj.*** Abundant or overflowing
- **range,** ***v.*** To wander or roam over a large area
- **summons,** ***n.*** A call from an authority to appear or do
- **incessantly,** ***adv.*** Continuously, without stopping

On Being Brought from Africa to America

by Phillis Wheatley

'Twas mercy brought me from my Pagan land,[1]
Taught my **benighted** soul to understand
That there's a God, that there's a Saviour[2] too:
Once I redemption neither sought nor knew.
Some view our **sable** race with scornful eye,
"Their colour is a **diabolic** die."[3]
Remember, Christians, Negroes, black as Cain,[4]
May be **refin'd**, and join th' angelic train.

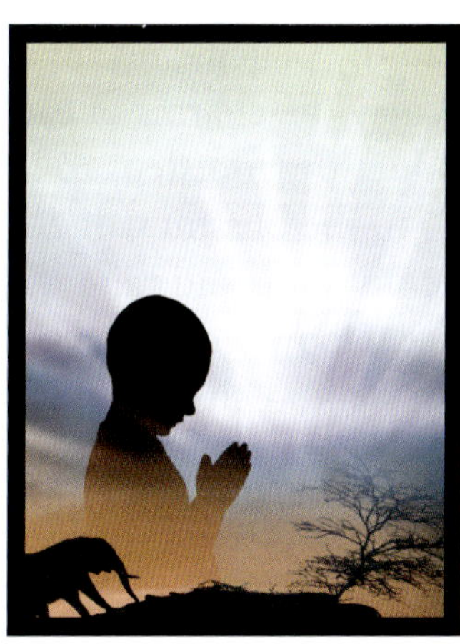

[1] **Pagan land.** A land where people worship multiple gods, a place without Christianity

[2] **Saviour.** Jesus Christ

[3] **die.** Dye

[4] **Cain.** In the Bible, the eldest son of Adam and Eve, who murdered his brother Abel out of jealousy

VOCABULARY IN PLACE

- **benighted,** ***adj.*** Intellectually or morally ignorant
- **sable,** ***adj.*** Black
- **diabolic,** ***adj.*** Devilish, characteristic of the devil
- **refined,** ***past part.*** Purified

from To S. M.,[1] a Young African Painter, on Seeing His Works

by Phillis Wheatley

To show the lab'ring bosom's deep intent,
And thought in living characters to paint,
When first thy pencil did those beauties give,
And breathing figures learnt from thee to live,[2]
How did those prospects give my soul delight,
A new creation rushing on my sight?[3]
Still, wond'rous youth! Each noble path pursue,
On deathless glories fix thine **ardent** view:
Still may the painter's and the poet's fire
To aid thy pencil, and thy verse **conspire**!
And may the charms of each seraphic theme
Conduct thy footsteps to immortal fame![4]
High to the blissful wonders of the skies
Elate thy soul, and raise thy wishful eyes.
Thrice happy, when exalted to survey
That splendid city, crown'd with endless day,
Whose twice six gates on radiant hinges ring:
Celestial Salem blooms in endless spring.[5]

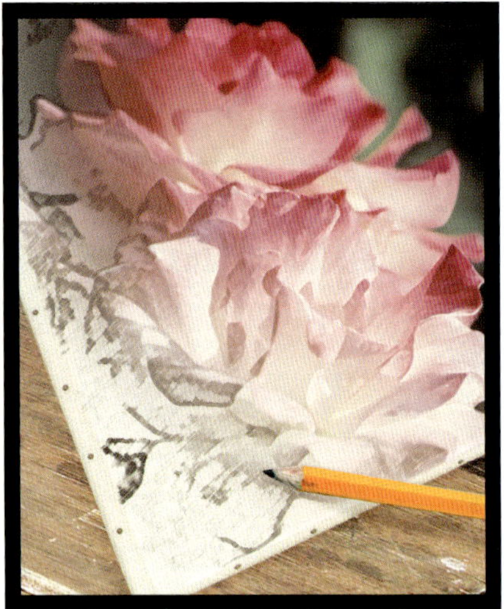

1 **S. M.** Scipio Moorhead, enslaved by the Reverend John Moorhead of Boston. The Reverend was one of the signers in the opening letter of Wheatley's book, which verified the "authenticity" of her work.

(The following notes should serve as paraphrase to help students through the challenging language and style of this example of eighteenth-century poetry. Students should read the lines, read the paraphrase, and then reread the lines)

2 **Lines 1–4.** These lines praise the artist's talent: line 1, *bosom* refers to the heart's desires, which the artist skillfully portrays; line 2, the figures in the paintings are lifelike; lines 3–4, the artist gave life to the figures with his brush.

3 **Line 5–6.** A *prospect* is something presented to the eye; one might refer to a pretty scene as "a pleasant prospect." The poet wonders how it is possible that these painted scenes could "delight" her so much.

4 **Lines 7–12.** Lines 7–8, the speaker calls on the painter to continue to create great works; lines 9–10, the speaker hopes that the artist will continue (still) to express poetry through his painting; lines 11–12, *seraphic* means angelic; the poet hopes that angels will lead the artist to eternal fame.

5 **Lines 15–18.** These lines describe the joy that he will feel when, through the glory of his work, he is led to the twelve gates of the Holy City.

VOCABULARY IN PLACE

- **ardent,** *adj.* Passionate; displaying strong enthusiasm
- **conspire,** *v.* To join or act together
- **elate,** *v.* To make proud or joyful

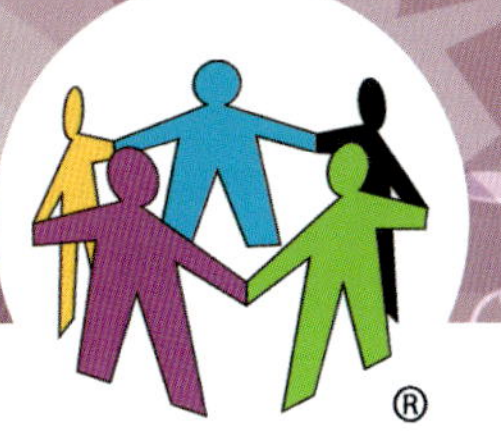

Delving Deeper

About the Author

Jupiter Hammon (1711–circa 1800) was born into slavery to the powerful Lloyd family of Long Island, New York. He lived in the Lloyds' house and went to school with their children, who called him "brother Jupiter." Hammon worked alongside Henry Lloyd, traveling and negotiating trade agreements for him. The Lloyd family encouraged Hammon to write and publish. He often wrote about his belief that a better life awaited his fellow slaves and him in heaven. His writing is almost all religious, and he may have thought of himself primarily as a preacher rather than as a poet. He published his first poem, "An Evening Prayer," in 1761. He is also remembered as an orator, particularly for his "Address to the Negroes of the State of New York," published in 1787, in which he said,

There are some things very encouraging in God's word for such . . . creatures as we are, for God has not chosen the rich of this world. Not many rich, not many nobles are called, but God hath chosen the weak things of this world. . . . Most of us are cut off from comfort and happiness here in this world. . . . Why should we not take care to be happy after death?

Hammon's last years were spent living with the great-grandson of Henry Lloyd.

About the Author

Phillis Wheatley (1754–1784) was the first African American, the first slave, and the third woman in the United States to publish a book of poetry. Wheatley came to Boston as a captured slave from West Africa in 1761, on board the slave ship *Phillis.* John Wheatley, a tailor, bought her as an assistant for his wife, Susannah. Because young Wheatley was only seven, in poor health, and liked so much by her mistress, she was taught reading and writing. She learned quickly, and the Wheatleys never trained her as a servant or asked her to do servant work. Instead, they allowed her to study classic literature and philosophy.

Her first poem appeared in 1767 in the *Mercury* of Newport, Rhode Island, the nation's oldest newspaper. In 1763 her book, *Poems on Various Subjects,* was published in England. Her "master" emancipated her that same year.

In 1774 Phillis wrote to her longtime friend Samson Occum, a Mohegan Indian poet and ordained minister, praising him for a letter he had written that criticized ministers who were slaveholders. She pointed out in this letter, as she did in some of her poems, the hypocrisy on the part of colonists who demanded freedom from Britain yet held onto their slaves. Wheatley was well received at home and abroad and met both George Washington and Voltaire, the famous French philosopher.

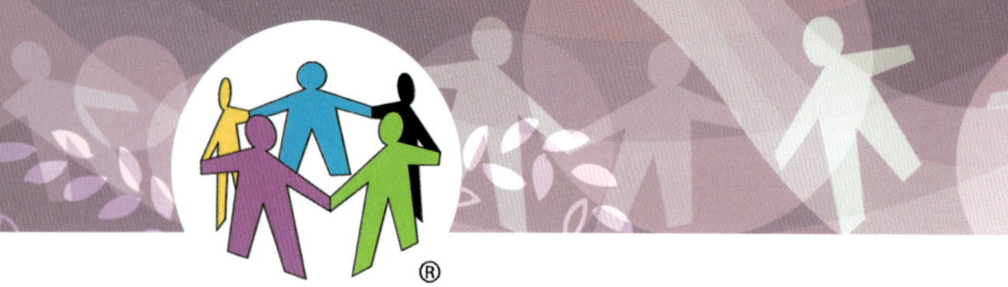

Understanding the Selection

Recalling

1. Who is the "pious youth" addressed in the first line of Hammon's poem?
2. In the fifth stanza of "To Phillis Wheatley," to whom might the "thousands tossed by the sea" refer?
3. In "On Being Brought from Africa," what does the speaker say she gained by being brought to America? How does America differ from her native land?
4. How did the artist's work affect the soul of the speaker in "To S. M." ?
5. What does the speaker want the artist to do? Explain using at least two examples from the poem.

Interpreting

1. In Hammon's poem, what is the speaker's tone? Does he sound hopeful or gloomy? Provide examples to support your answer.
2. What does the speaker mean when he tells Wheatley that she was "set free," even though she was enslaved at the time?
3. Is the speaker glad to be in America? What does she want her readers (white Christians) to understand about the black race?
4. What motivated the speaker to write to S. M.? How did his work affect her?
5. Is the speaker worried that S. M. might lose his inspiration or motivation to create great work? Why, or why not?

Synthesizing

1. Hammon and Wheatley often focused on spirituality and Christianity. What might Hammon have liked about Wheatley's poems? Identify one line or phrase in each of Wheatley's poems with which Hammon would have agreed.
2. Did Hammon and Wheatley consider themselves "free" in any way, despite the fact that they were enslaved? Use evidence from the poems to support your answer.

Delving Deeper

Understanding Literature

Unintended Irony. We find irony in literature and in everyday life. An **irony** is a difference between appearance and reality. There are several kinds of irony. **Dramatic irony** exists when the audience knows something that the characters do not. **Verbal irony** is an expression that is intended to have a meaning opposite to the literal meaning of the words or one in which the words are ambiguous and contradictory. If you show up an hour late and your friend says, "You're right on time, as usual," then your friend's jab is ironic because on a literal level it means the opposite of what it is intended to mean. Beethoven, arguably the greatest composer of all time, went deaf at the height of his career. It is ironic that one who composed music should lose his hearing. Writers also like to point out the ironies of everyday life: Frederick Douglass and William Wells Brown both wrote about the irony of the fact that so many slave owners claimed to be very religious.

There is a bit of irony in Verse IV of Jupiter Hammon's "Address to Phillis Wheatley." Spain did have a lot of gold in the 1600s, but not so much during the 1700s. In Hammon's lifetime, Spain's treasury rapidly declined, partly due to war in Europe but also due to losses caused by war and hurricanes on the *Spanish Main,* the route traveled by Spanish treasure fleets returning from South America. Looking back, we find truth in the poet's statement that faith was more valuable than gold, at least as it relates to the gold in Spain. Hammon would not be surprised to know that Spain is no longer known for its vast wealth in gold. This drives home the point that Hammon was trying to make to Wheatley: "earthly toys" are only temporary, but there is something more important and permanent to be found.

Do you think this irony was intentional? Was the irony simply the result of the poet's trying for a convenient rhyme? Or was Hammon aware that Spain's gold was in fact running out and that it could no longer protect a crumbling empire?

Writing

An Address to . . . You might have noticed that two out of three of the poems in this section are personal messages to specific people. These days, if you want to praise the work of an artist or celebrity, you might write him or her a fan letter. In the literary world—and especially during the 1700s when Wheatley and Hammon were writing—it was quite common for writers to express praise (and sometimes criticism) of other artists through poems such as these. After reading Wheatley's "Address to S. M.," try your hand at writing a poetic "address" to a friend or to a favorite musical artist, athlete, or other celebrity. Be positive and polite.

Prereading

"Bury Me in a Free Land" and "The Slave Auction"

by Frances E. W. Harper

Here is a writer, political and social activist, and intellectual whose poetic work—as well as her life's work—deserve long-overdue recognition. After her death, Frances Harper was essentially brushed aside by literary critics from both sides of America's racial divide. Many viewed her writing style as unsophisticated and sentimental (overly emotional). Indeed, the voice in Harper's verse and prose stands in sharp contrast to that in the writing of her contemporaries, whose poems and stories often used a more flowery style and more complex structures.

Interestingly, it is exactly Harper's popular, open, and communicative style that makes her work so enduring and accessible for twenty-first century readers. Her poetry remains as moving and elegant today as it was when it achieved its early commercial and critical success in the 1850s.

Harper made a modest fortune from the sales of her early poems, articles, and stories. She was widely read for her journalistic work in newspapers and journals and has been called the mother of African-American journalism. However, writing was only one tool with which she carried out her life's work.

All of her life, Harper was witness to the evils of slavery and racial bigotry. Though born to free parents, her freedom was never guaranteed, especially after the passage of the Fugitive Slave Act of 1850, which led to a rash of kidnappings of free blacks; and like all African Americans after the Civil War, she lived under threat of lynching and the inequities of Jim Crow laws. She was one of the few souls able to express the sorrow, pain, and hopes of an oppressed and abused people.

Bury Me in a Free Land

by Frances E. W. Harper

Make me a grave where'er you will,
In a lowly plain, or a lofty hill;
Make it among earth's humblest graves,
But not in a land where men are slaves.

I could not rest if around my grave
I heard the steps of a trembling slave;
His shadow above my silent tomb
Would make it a place of fearful gloom.

I could not rest if I heard the tread
Of a coffle gang[1] to the **shambles** led,
And the mother's shriek of wild despair
Rise like a curse on the trembling air.

I could not sleep if I saw the lash
Drinking her blood at each fearful gash,
And I saw her babes torn from her breast,
Like trembling doves from their parent nest.

I'd shudder and start if I heard the bay
Of bloodhounds seizing their human prey,
And I heard the captive plead in vain
As they bound afresh his **galling** chain.

---

[1] **coffle gang.** A group of prisoners chained together

VOCABULARY IN PLACE

- **shambles,** ***n. pl.*** A scene of bloodshed or carnage; a butcher's shop (archaic)
- **galling,** ***adj.*** Causing irritation or pain

If I saw young girls from their mothers' arms
Bartered and sold for their youthful charms,
My eye would flash with a mournful flame,
My death-paled cheek grow red with shame.

I would sleep, dear friends, where bloated might
Can rob no man of his dearest right;
My rest shall be calm in any grave
Where none can call his brother a slave.

I ask no monument, proud and high,
To arrest the gaze of the passers-by;
All that my **yearning** spirit craves,
Is bury me not in a land of slaves. ■

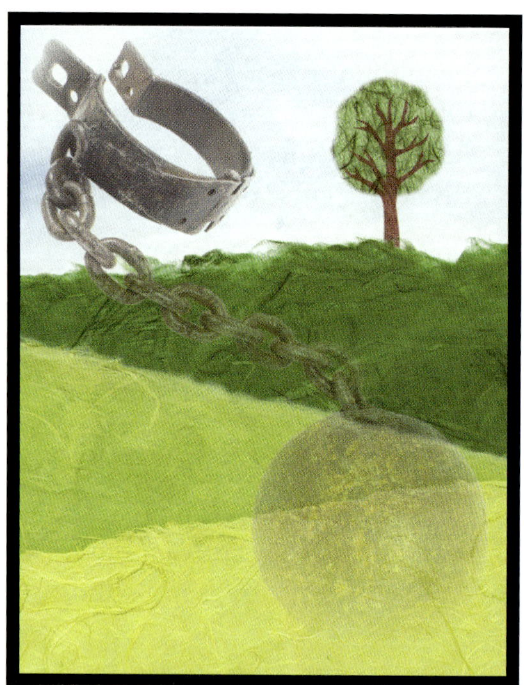

VOCABULARY IN PLACE

- **yearning,** ***part.*** Feeling a strong desire for something one does not have

The Slave Auction

by Frances E. W. Harper

The sale began—young girls were there,
    Defenceless in their wretchedness,
Whose stifled sobs of deep despair
    Revealed their anguish and distress.

And mothers stood with streaming eyes,
    And saw their dearest children sold;
Unheeded rose their bitter cries,
    While tyrants bartered them for gold.[1]
And woman, with her love and truth—
    For these in sable[2] forms may dwell—
Gaz'd on the husband of her youth,
    With anguish none may paint or tell.

And men, whose sole crime was their hue,[3]
    The impress of their Maker's hand,
And frail and shrinking children, too,
    Were gathered in that mournful band.

Ye who have laid your love to rest,
    And wept above their lifeless clay,[4]
Know not the anquish of that breast
    Whose lov'd are rudely torn away.

Ye may not know how **desolate**
    Are bosoms[5] rudely forced to part,
And how a dull and heavy weight
    Will press the life-drops from the heart. ■

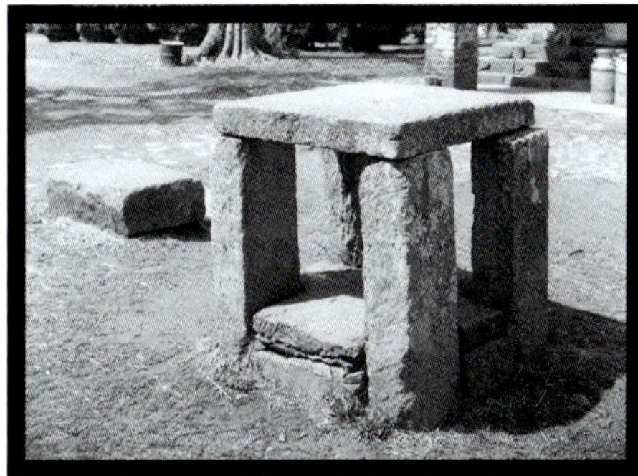

Slave Auction Block, Greenhill Plantation, Campbell County, Virginia. Library of Congress. HABS, VA, 16-LONI.V, 1J.

1 **tyrants bartered . . . gold.** Cruel men traded people for gold

2 **sable.** Black

3 **hue.** The color of their skin

4 **clay.** Body

5 **bosoms.** Chests; the hearts of loved ones

VOCABULARY IN PLACE

• **desolate,** ***adj.*** Empty; devoid of life

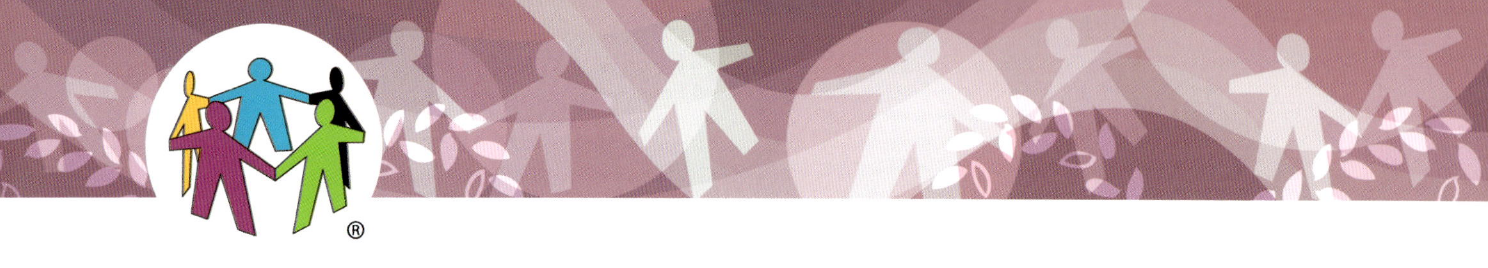

Understanding the Selection

Recalling

1. In "Bury Me in a Free Land," where does the speaker want her grave to be?
2. What would disturb the speaker's sleep? List three phrases or images from the poem.
3. In the first verse of "The Slave Auction," who is said to be crying and in deep despair?
4. According to the speaker, who or what is responsible for the hue of a man's skin? Why are these men being punished?
5. To what does the speaker compare the separation of families?

Interpreting

1. Why does it matter to the speaker where she is buried?
2. Why doesn't the speaker want a monument? What would she like instead?
3. What did the mothers see? Why were their "sobs of despair" unheeded?
4. What does the speaker want readers to understand about the families at this auction?
5. Why can't those who have buried loved ones fully appreciate the pain of being separated through slavery?

Synthesizing

1. Identify and discuss important images and methods that Frances Harper uses in these poems in order to (a) express the evils of slavery and (b) encourage readers to take up the cause of abolition. Would these poems have inspired you if you lived in Harper's day? Explain.
2. What do both of these poems have to do with the act of mourning?

Delving Deeper

History Connection

Research. As was mentioned in the Prereading section, Frances Harper's accomplishments were largely overlooked by twentieth-century historians and critics. With your help, that is now going to change.

Choose one of the following questions about Harper's accomplishments. Use the school library or Internet to answer the question, and write a short paragraph explaining what you learned. You might have to "dig deep" to find your answers!

1. What was Harper's connection to Frederick Douglass?
2. What was Harper's connection to John Brown?
3. Why is Harper called the "mother" of African-American journalism? Be specific.
4. With what famous women's rights pioneers did Harper work?
5. What was Harper's connection to the African-American Unitarian Church?

About the Author

Frances Ellen Watkins Harper (1825–1911) was a poet, novelist, and short-story writer who changed the shape of American history through her literary works and social activism. One of the most prolific writers of her time, Harper used her literary talents to speak out against the injustice and pain of slavery and to champion such social reform movements as the Abolitionist, Women's Suffrage, and Temperance Movements. Harper holds the distinction of being the first African-American woman to publish a short story. She also published four novels, numerous stories, essays, letters, and many volumes of poetry, including *Poems on Miscellaneous Subjects* (1854) and *Sketches of Southern Life* (1872). In addition to being an accomplished writer, she was also an extremely successful orator who moved audiences with her skill in poetry-reading and her passionate lectures. During her time, Harper was acclaimed not for the technical beauty of her poetry but for her excellence in delivery and her ability to move people. Through her commitment to literature as a vehicle for social reform, Harper inspired a new generation of poets and gave rise to the tradition of African-American protest poetry.

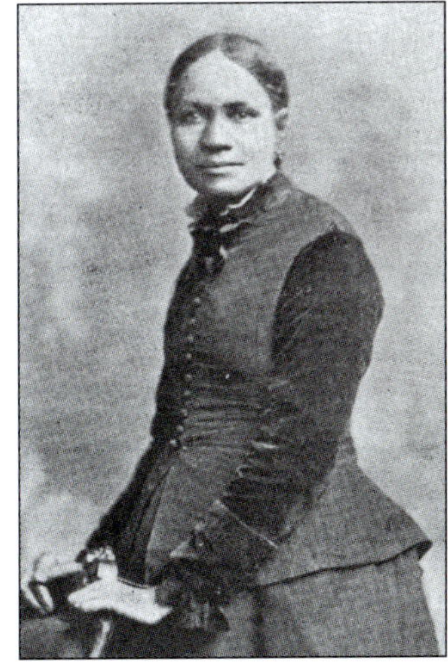

Prereading

"Self-Reliance"

by James Whitfield

Frederick Douglass is credited with "discovering" James Whitfield, who in 1850 was working as a barber in Buffalo, New York. Over the next two years, Douglass published several of Whitfield's anti-slavery poems in his newspaper *The North Star*. Whitfield's work received immediate praise, and many, including Douglass, thought Whitfield should and would be counted alongside famous names like Edgar Allan Poe and John Greenleaf Whittier.

But Whitfield encountered an obstacle that confronts most poets, regardless of race or gender: it is very difficult to make a living selling poems. Whitfield continued to toil as a barber in order to support his family, even though his book, *America and Other Poems* (1853), was well received. Today, Whitfield is often looked upon as an example of a literary genius whose potential was never realized because he never had enough time to write.

However, that is not to say that James Whitfield was a failure. His unusually direct, passionate, and angry anti-slavery poems were widely read. Thus, he had an important impact on his era by helping to sway readers to the Abolitionist cause. Most importantly, though, Whitfield will *always* be first among great African-American poets—not the first to write or publish poetry, but at least one of the first to write and publish *great* poetry.

Self-Reliance. This poem consists of one hundred beautiful lines about personal values, responsibility, and simply doing the right thing. The poem's language is in keeping with the style of his time, but Whitfield's distinct voice still sings to us today; he still invites us, with his glowing images and effortless rhythm, into the soul of the poet-philosopher-barber who had so very much to share with the world.

Whitfield's poetry was meant to be read aloud. His ideas and sentences may seem complex, but it is well worth the effort to follow them closely from beginning to end. The bulk of the poem is printed here in two columns, which means there is twice as much text per page as in most other poems, so do not be intimidated by the number of vocabulary entries. Read the poem slowly, and then read it at least once more for clarity before moving on.

Self-Reliance

by James Whitfield

I love the man whose **lofty** mind
On God and its own strength relies;
Who seeks the welfare of his kind,[1]
And dare be honest though he dies;
Who cares not for the world's applause,
But, to his own fixed purpose true,
The path which God and nature's laws
Point out, doth earnestly pursue.
When **adverse** clouds around him lower,
And stern oppression bars his way,
When friends desert in trial's hour,
And hope sheds but a feeble ray;
When all the powers of the earth and hell
Combine to break his spirit down,
And strive, with their terrific yell,
To crush his soul beneath their frown—
When numerous friends, whose cheerful tone
In happier hours once cheered him on,
With visions that full brightly shone,
But now, alas! Are dimmed and gone!

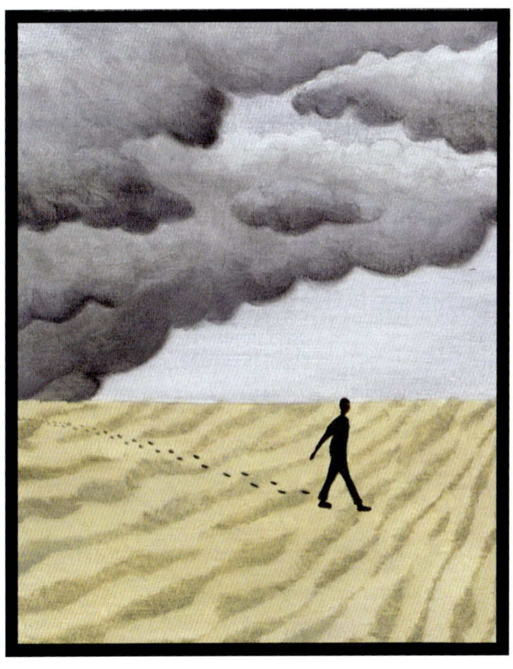

[1] **his kind.** People of his race or family

VOCABULARY IN PLACE

- **lofty,** ***adj.*** Elevated in character; exalted or dignified
- **adverse,** ***adj.*** Harmful or unfavorable

When love, which in his bosom burned
With all the fire of **ardent** youth,
And which he fondly thought returned
With equal purity and truth,
Mocking his hopes, falls to the ground,
Like some false vision of the night,
Its vows a hollow, empty sound,
Scathing his heart with deadly **blight**,
Choking that welling spring of love,
Which lifts the soul to God above,
In bonds mysterious to unite
The finite with the infinite;
And draw a blessing from above,
Of infinite on finite love.[2]
When hopes of better, fear of worse,
Alike are fled, and naught remains
To stimulate him on his course:
No hope of bliss, no fear of pains
Fiercer than what already **rend**,
With tortures keen, his inmost heart,
Without a hope, without a friend,
With nothing to **allay** the smart
From blighted love, affections broken,
From blasted hopes and **cankering** care,
When every thought, each word that's spoken
Urges him onward to despair.
When through the opening vista round,
Shines on him no pellucid[3] ray,
Like beam of early morning found,
The **harbinger** of perfect day;
But like the midnight's darkening frown,
When stormy **tempests** rear on high,
When pealing thunder shakes the ground,
And **lurid** lightning rends the sky!
When clothed in more than midnight gloom,
Like some foul specter[4] from the tomb,

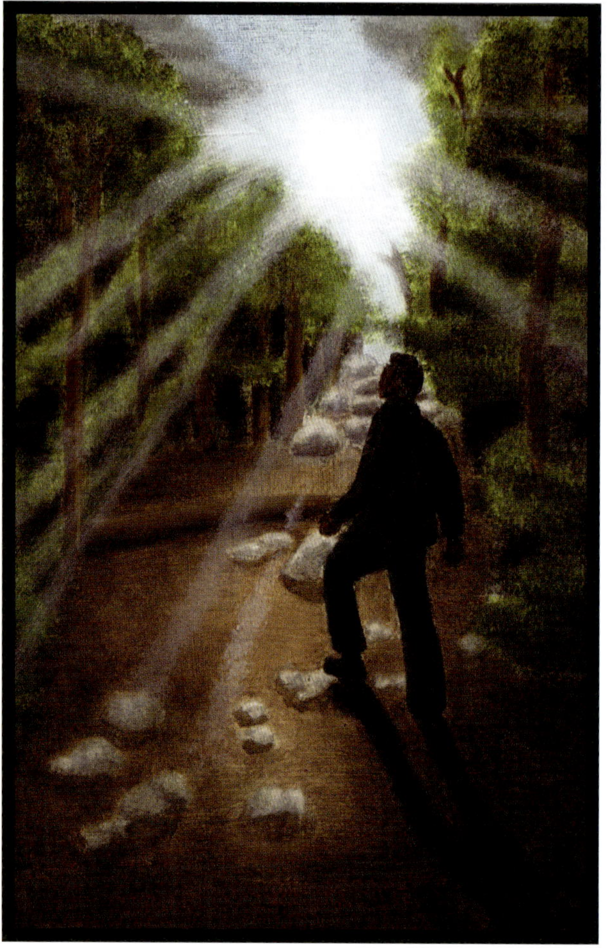

[2] **The finite . . . finite love.** Human love is finite (has an end) because people are mortal. But such love reminds us of God and His love, which is infinite.

[3] **pellucid.** Transparent

[4] **specter.** Ghost

VOCABULARY IN PLACE

- **ardent,** *adj.* Passionate; characterized by strong enthusiasm
- **blight,** *n.* Disease
- **rend,** *v.* To tear apart violently, to shred
- **allay,** *v.* To relieve
- **canker,** *v.* To infect with corruption or decay
- **harbinger,** *n.* One that signals the approach of something
- **tempest,** *n.* A violent storm
- **lurid,** *adj.* Shining with the glare of fire

Despair, with stern and fell control,
Sits brooding o'er his inmost soul—
'Tis then the faithful mind is proved,
That, true alike to man and God,
By all the ills of life unmoved,
Pursues its straight and narrow road.
For such a man the siren song[5]
Of pleasure hath no lasting charm;
Nor can the mighty and the strong
His spirit tame with powerful arm.
His pleasure is to wipe the tear
Of sorrow from the mourner's cheek,
The **languid**, fainting heart to cheer,
To **succor** and protect the weak.
When the bright face of fortune smiles
Upon his path with cheering ray,
And pleasure, with **alluring wiles**,
Flatters, to lead his heart astray,
His soul in conscious virtue strong,
And armed with **innate rectitude**,
Loving the right, detesting wrong,
And seeking the eternal good
Of all alike, the high or low,
His dearest friend, or **direst** foe,
Seeks out the brave and faithful few,
Who, to themselves and Maker true,
Dare, in the name and fear of God,
To spread the living truth abroad!
Armed with the same sustaining power,
Against adversity's dark hour,
And from the deep deceitful **guile**
Which lurks in pleasure's hollow smile,
Or from the false and fitful beam
That marks ambition's meteor fire,
Or from the dark and lurid gleam
Revealing passion's deadly **ire.**
His steadfast soul fearing no harm,
But trusting in the aid of Heaven,
And wielding, with **unfaltering** arm,
The utmost power which God has given—
Conscious that the Almighty power
Will nerve the faithful soul with might,
Whatever storms may round him lower,
Strikes boldly for the true and right. ■

[5] **siren song.** In Greek mythology, the Sirens were sea nymphs (minor female goddesses) who lured sailors to destruction with their beautiful songs.

VOCABULARY IN PLACE

- **languid,** *adj.* Lacking energy; weak
- **succor,** *v.* To give assistance
- **alluring,** *adj.* Inviting or tempting
- **wile,** *n.* A trick intended to deceive or ensnare
- **innate,** *adj.* Possessed at birth; inborn
- **rectitude,** *n.* Moral uprightness; righteousness
- **dire,** *adj.* Threatening or terrible
- **guile,** *n.* Skillful deceit; cunning
- **ire,** *n.* Anger; wrath
- **unfaltering,** *adj.* Steady in purpose or action; confident

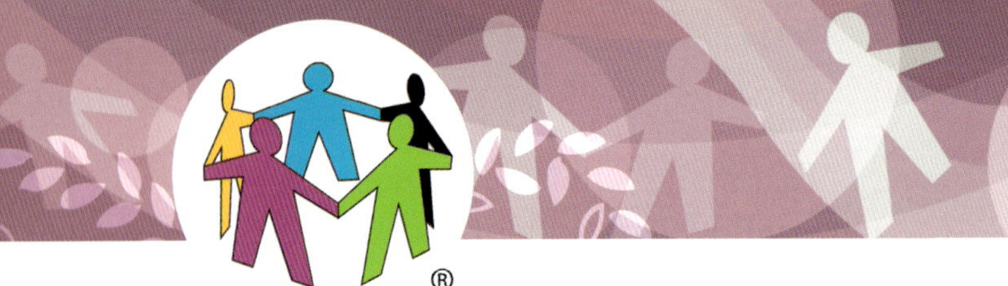

Understanding the Selection

Recalling

1. According to the poem's speaker, on what should a mind rely (lines 1–4)?
2. Does the self-reliant man care for the "world's applause"? What should he care about instead?
3. Has the self-reliant man ever been in love? What happens to his heart if his love is not returned? Use a quotation from the text to support your answer.
4. Is a self-reliant man tempted by the "siren song" (lines 63–64)?
5. Provide two examples from the poem in which the self-reliant man is described as helping other people.

Interpreting

1. What kind of man does the speaker "love"?
2. How might caring about "the world's applause" affect a person's action or behavior?
3. How does the self-reliant man react when his heart is broken?
4. Can force be used to "tame" the self-reliant man's spirit? Explain your answer using evidence from the text.
5. Why would the self-reliant man take pleasure in wiping tears "of sorrow from the mourner's cheek"?

Synthesizing

1. According to the poem's speaker, how important is God in the life and mind of a self-reliant person? Use at least two quotations from the text to support your answer.
2. Do you think that a self-reliant person, as described in this poem, would be difficult to find? Why or why not?

Delving Deeper

Writing

Opinion Essay. Should a person care about the "world's applause"? Address this question in a one-page **opinion essay** in which you present your opinion and evidence to support it. Evidence can include facts from the news, from history, or from your personal experiences. You may want to give examples of people who did or did not worry about others' opinions.

Here's one way you might approach writing this essay: Start by making a list of at least twenty celebrities or well-known people, living or dead, such as politicians, leaders of important organizations, athletes, singers, artists, and writers. From this list, select two people, one of whom is the type of person who, in your opinion, seeks the world's applause, and the other the type who carries out his or her work without caring for the world's applause.

Write a descriptive paragraph about each person in which you present evidence as to why he or she does or does not "care for the world's applause." Then, give your opinion of each person and explain whether he or she would fit James Whitfield's model of self-reliance. Use at least two quotations from Whitfield's poem in your essay.

About the Author

James Monroe Whitfield (1822–1871) was born to free parents in Exeter, New Hampshire. Later, he moved to Boston and then to Buffalo, New York, where he worked in a basement barbershop. He published the collection *America and Other Poems* in 1853, and though it met with critical and commercial success, he continued to work as a barber in order to make a living.

Frederick Douglass first urged Whitfield to publish his poems, which originally appeared in Lloyd Garrison's *The Liberator* and in Douglass's newspapers, *The North Star* and *Frederick Douglass' Paper*. Whitfield became active in the Abolitionist Movement and was also strongly influenced by writer Martin Delany, a black nationalist who argued that African Americans should emigrate to South America in search of equality and justice.

Whitfield is often called an orator-poet, as his poems were intended to be read aloud. He moved to San Francisco in 1861 and lived the rest of his days there, writing and performing his poetry and continuing to work as a barber.

Prereading

from *Clotelle: A Tale of the Southern States*

by William Wells Brown, M.D.

The passage you are about to read is from the first novel ever published by an African-American writer. However, William Wells Brown's original novel was published in England, and so it is not the first such novel by an African American published in the United States. That honor belongs to Harriet Wilson's *Our Nig* (1859).

The history of Brown's novel is rather complicated. In fact, there were four different versions of the book published between 1853 and 1867, all under different titles.

The following passage, "Chapter II: The Negro Sale," is taken from the third version of the novel. Through it, readers will come to understand the dehumanizing brutality of slavery, which William Wells Brown experienced firsthand. The desire to expose this brutality motivated much of his writing. Many episodes in this novel mirror true experiences from his amazing life.

Readers should be familiar with the following list of important characters in this chapter. There is more about the origins of the novel (particularly, the real story behind the character of Mr. Graves, the old slave owner) in the Understanding Literature section on page 197.

1. **Henry Linwood** is a local aristocrat and slave owner who has come to the auction of Mr. Graves's estate.
2. **Isabella** is Linwood's lover and the main character in this chapter.
3. **Agnes** is Isabella's mother; **Marion** is Isabella's sister.
4. **Clotelle**, the novel's heroine (female hero), is Linwood and Isabella's daughter, but has not yet been born.

from Clotelle: A Tale of the Southern States
Chapter II: The Negro Sale

by William Wells Brown, M.D.

As might have been expected, the day of sale brought an unusually large number together to compete for the property to be sold. Farmers, who make a business of raising slaves for the market, were there, and slave-traders, who make a business of buying human beings in the slave-raising States and taking them to the far South, were also in attendance. Men and women, too, who wished to purchase for their own use, had found their way to the slave sale.

In the midst of the throng was one who felt a deeper interest in the result of the sale than any other of the bystanders. This was young Linwood.[1] True to his promise, he was there with a blank bank-check in his pocket, awaiting with impatience to enter the list as a bidder for the beautiful slave.

It was indeed a **heart-rending** scene to witness the **lamentations** of these slaves, all of whom had grown up together on the old homestead of Mr. Graves, and who had been treated with great kindness by that gentleman, during his life. Brothers and sisters were torn from each other, and mothers saw their children for the last time on earth.

It was late in the day, and when the greatest number of persons were thought to be present, when Agnes and her daughters were brought out to the place of sale. The mother was first put upon the auction-block, and sold to a noted Negro trader named Jennings. Marion was next ordered to **ascend** the stand, which she did with a trembling step, and was sold for $1200.

How does the crowd react to Isabella's appearance? Why?

All eyes were now turned on Isabella, as she was led forward by the auctioneer. The appearance of the handsome quadroon[2] caused a deep sensation among the crowd. There she stood, with a skin as fair as most white women, her features as beautifully regular as any of her sex of pure Anglo-Saxon[3] blood, her long black hair done up in the neatest manner, her form tall and graceful, and her whole appearance indicating one superior to her condition.

---

[1] **Linwood.** A local slave owner. He and the main character, Isabella, are in love.

[2] **quadroon.** This was a common word for a biracial (specifically one-quarter black) person in the mid-nineteenth century.

[3] **Anglo-Saxon.** Of or descended from the Germanic peoples—the Angles, the Saxons, and the Jutes—who settled in Britain in the fifth century

VOCABULARY IN PLACE

- **heart-rending,** ***adj.*** Causing anguish or deep distress (**rend,** ***v.*** To tear apart)
- **lamentation,** ***n.*** The act of expressing grief; mourning
- **ascend,** ***v.*** To go or move up; to climb

The auctioneer commenced by saying that Miss Isabella was fit to **deck** the drawing-room[4] of the finest mansion in Virginia.

"How much, gentlemen, for the real Albino![5]—fit fancy-girl for any one! She enjoys good health, and has a sweet temper. How much do you say?"

"Five hundred dollars."

"Only five hundred for such a girl as this? Gentlemen, she is worth a deal more than that sum. You certainly do not know the value of the article you are bidding on. Here, gentlemen, I hold in my hand a paper certifying that she has a good moral character."

"Seven hundred."

"Ah, gentlemen, that is something like. This paper also states that she is very intelligent."

"Eight hundred."

"She was first sprinkled, then immersed, and is now warranted to be a devoted Christian, and perfectly trustworthy."[6]

"Nine hundred dollars."

"Nine hundred and fifty."

"One thousand."

"Eleven hundred."

Here the bidding came to a dead stand. The auctioneer stopped, looked around, and began in a rough manner to relate some **anecdote** connected with the sale of the slaves, which he said had come under his own observation.

At this **juncture** the scene was indeed a most striking one. The laughing, joking, swearing, smoking, spitting, and talking kept up a continual hum and confusion among the crowd, while the slave-girl stood with tearful eyes, looking alternately at her mother and sister and toward the young man whom she hoped would become her purchaser.

Who does Isabella hope will purchase her?

"The **chastity** of this girl," now continued the auctioneer, "is pure. She has never been from under her mother's care. She is virtuous, and as gentle as a dove."

The bids here took a fresh start, and went on until $1800 was reached. The auctioneer once more resorted to his jokes, and concluded by assuring the company that Isabella was not only pious, but that she could make an excellent prayer.

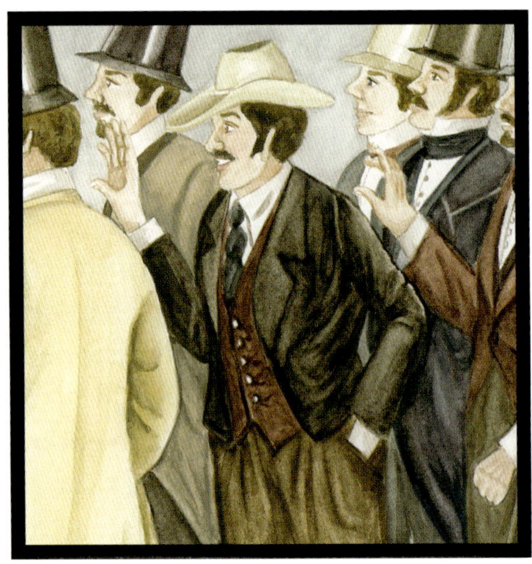

4 **drawing-room.** A large room in which guests are entertained

5 **Albino.** An *albino* is a person or animal lacking normal skin pigmentation; the result is that the skin is especially white. True albinos also have abnormally white hair, and their eyes have pink irises and red pupils. Isabella is not a true albino; this is the auctioneer's distasteful attempt at humor.

6 **sprinkled . . . devoted Christian.** She has gradually been converted to Christianity and is considered to be a true believer.

VOCABULARY IN PLACE

- **deck,** *v.* To decorate
- **anecdote,** *n.* A short account of an interesting or funny event
- **juncture,** *n.* A point in time, especially a critical point
- **chastity,** *n.* Innocence, purity

"Nineteen hundred dollars."

"Two thousand."

This was the last bid, and the quadroon girl was struck off, and became the property of Henry Linwood.

This was a Virginia slave-auction, at which the bones, sinews, blood, and nerves of a young girl of eighteen were sold for $500; her moral character for $200; her superior intellect for $100; the benefits supposed to **accrue** from her having been sprinkled and immersed, together with a warranty of her devoted Christianity, for $300; her ability to make a good prayer for $200; and her chastity for $700 more. This, too, in a city thronged with churches, whose tall spires look like so many signals pointing to heaven, but whose ministers preach that slavery is a God ordained institution!

Why does the narrator emphasize the fact that there are so many churches in this town?

The slaves were speedily separated, and taken along by their respective masters. Jennings, the slave-speculator, who had purchased Agnes and her daughter Marion, with several of the other slaves, took them to the county prison, where he usually kept his human cattle after purchasing them, previous to starting for the New Orleans market.[7]

Linwood had already provided a place for Isabella, to which she was taken. The most trying moment for her was when she took leave of her mother and sister. The "Good-by" of the slave is unlike that of any other class in the community. It is indeed a farewell forever. With tears streaming down their cheeks, they embraced and commended each other to God, who is no respecter of persons, and before whom master and slave must one day appear. ■

[7] **New Orleans market.** This was the worst place an enslaved person could be sent because, in all likelihood, it meant that he or she would be sold to a large plantation in the Deep South, where conditions were worse than anywhere else. The expression "sold down the river" means that one has been sent to a terrible place. The expression comes from the fact that slaves headed for the Deep South were usually transported down the Mississippi River.

VOCABULARY IN PLACE

- **accrue**, *v.* To increase or accumulate

About the Author

William Wells Brown, M.D. (1816–1884) was born in Lexington, Kentucky, to a slave mother and a slave-owning father. He escaped slavery in 1834, adopting the name of the man who aided his escape (Wells Brown). Brown was almost entirely self-educated. He became an active Abolitionist and published the successful *Narrative of William Wells Brown, A Fugitive Slave* (1847). He is best known as the first African American to publish a novel. In addition to the *Clotelle* series of novels, he wrote a play entitled *The Escape: or, A Leap to Freedom,* which was the first play published by an African American; he also wrote the first travel book by a black American, *Three Years in Europe* (1852). He became active in the medical field during the 1860s and opened a doctor's office in Boston in 1865. He lectured throughout the U.S. and published another comprehensive history book entitled *The Rising Son; or, The Antecedents and Advancement of the Colored Race* (1874), in which he profiled 110 important African Americans.

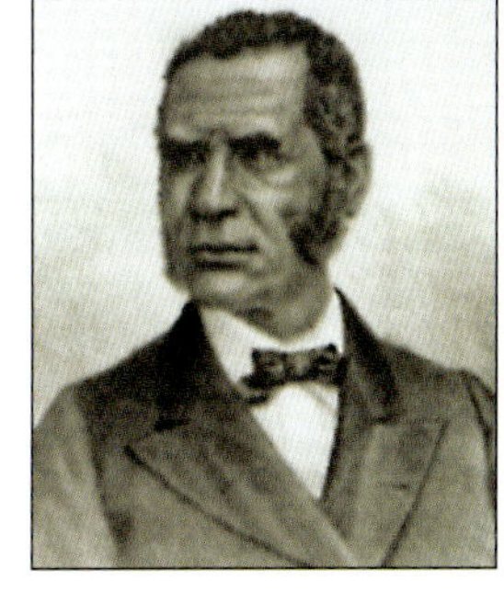

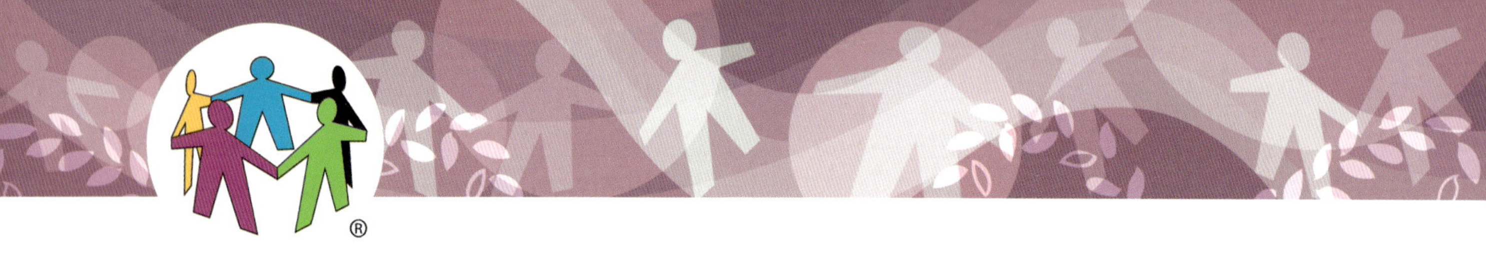

Understanding the Selection

Recalling

1. What happened to Mr. Graves? What is happening to his slaves?
2. Who is Linwood? Who loves him?
3. What happens to Isabella's mother and sister?
4. Describe the auctioneer's attitude. Does he think that Isabella will bring a high price?
5. Who wins the bidding for Isabella?

Interpreting

1. Why were Mr. Graves's slaves so sad about his death?
2. What will happen to Isabella if Linwood does not win the auction?
3. Will she see either of them again?
4. Why does the auctioneer try to be humorous? How do his comments make Isabella feel? Use evidence from the text to support your answer.
5. Why is Isabella so sad in the end, even though the auction ended as well as she could have hoped?

Synthesizing

1. Near the end of this chapter, the narrator divides the final sale price for Isabella into several categories. What statement did the author or narrator intend to make with regard to the nature of slavery and the slave trade?
2. Separation from family is one of the most important recurring themes in nearly all literature about slavery and the slave trade. How is this theme addressed in *Clotelle?*

Delving Deeper

Understanding Literature

The Politics of Publishing. The story behind *Clotelle* is interesting and somewhat complex, but it is worthy of extra study and important if you are interested in the "hows" and "whys" of publishing. Authors and their editors at publishing houses must make decisions if they want to sell books.

William Wells Brown's *Clotelle* was published in four different versions between 1853 and 1867. The first version was titled *Clotel: Or, the President's Daughter.* The next three versions were published in the United States, beginning with *Miralda, or The Beautiful Quadroon: A Romance of American Slavery Founded on Fact* (published in serialized form in New York City), followed by *Clotelle: A Tale of the Southern States* (1864) and *Clotelle; or, The Colored Heroine* (1867).

The basic plot of the original novel centers around the daughters and granddaughters of Thomas Jefferson. This would have raised quite a stir in the United States at the time. Modern DNA tests have shown that Jefferson, or a close relative of his, fathered children with a slave named Sally Hemmings. But for Brown, a black man, to criticize Jefferson openly might have been enough to have the book effectively banned in U.S. markets. The basic plot remains the same in later versions, but only the first version, published in England, actually mentions the third President of the United States by name. Thereafter, the president's character is replaced by a generic "southern planter" (Mr. Graves in the third version). Many details vary from version to version. Sometimes, it seems that even Brown could not keep them all straight; thus critics have used such words as "messy" and "jumbled" to describe the various versions. However, Brown's gift for expressing the horrors of slavery is obvious throughout his work.

The series presents a good story, but it is not *outstanding* literature, and it is not representative of Brown's best writing, nor would the writer have wanted it to be remembered as such. The novel carries important messages in protest of slavery, and in that regard it did help to stir Abolitionist sentiments. Brown intended to expose hypocrisy in American society. That is why he pointed out the number of churches in the town in "Chapter 2: The Negro Sale," and that is why he focused on Jefferson, whom Brown viewed as the prime example of hypocrisy in action: the same man who penned the phrase "all men are created equal" was himself a slave owner!

Remember a few things about this book and its author. First, Brown escaped from slavery and was self-educated. Sometimes, a writer (or his publisher) just needs to sell books. In this case, Brown sculpted his work according to the demands of his readership. That is probably why Jefferson's name was removed; deep research would be needed to determine whether it was Brown or his editor who first suggested such changes.

- Why was Brown's original novel changed to satisfy readers in the United States?
- Do you think things like this still happen in the literary marketplace today?

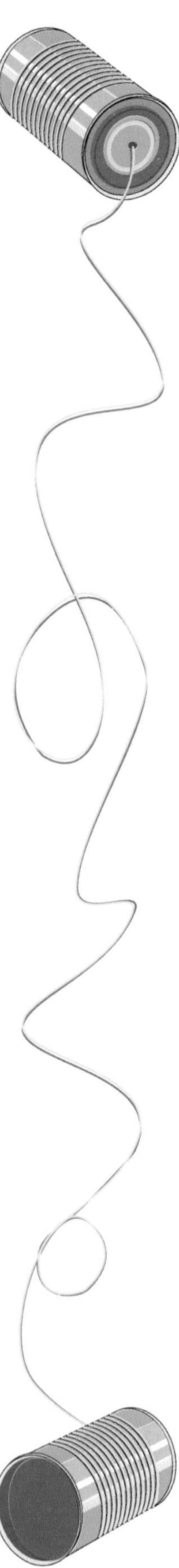

Unit 2

Speaking and Listening Skills: Dramatic Interpretation and Reader's Theater

Dramatic interpretation is the art of reading a literary work aloud and making it come alive for your listeners. The West African griots such as Bamba Suso, the author of the selection from the *Sunjata* in Unit 1, were and are masters of dramatic interpretation. **Reader's theater** is a form of dramatic performance in which people read aloud parts on stage but do not move about. In essence, reader's theater is a kind of dramatic interpretation done with a number of actors and/or characters.

To read a literary work aloud and do it well, you must prepare the piece very carefully. Begin by reading the piece (a poem or song or selection from a play or story) several times silently, until you know it very well. As you read, think about the speaker of the poem or song or about the characters in the play or story. What are they like? How would they look? How would they sound? How old are they? What are their backgrounds? What tone of voice would they use, and what mood would be conveyed? Practice reading the piece, varying each of the following:

1. **Pitch.** When people speak, their voices naturally vary in **pitch** from high to low. For example, say these two sentences aloud:

   I'm going to the library.
   Are you?

   Notice that when you ask a question, your voice naturally rises in pitch toward the end of the sentence. Whenever people speak, they naturally vary their pitch within sentences. Say the two sentences above once more. This time, try to exaggerate the pitches used. Whenever you are speaking in front of an audience, you should slightly exaggerate the natural variations in pitch.

2. **Volume.** One way to add interest to any speaking that is done in public is to vary the volume, or loudness, of your speech. Again, people naturally vary their volume a bit when they speak conversationally, but in public speaking situations, it pays to speak louder than usual and to vary the volume more than is usual.

3. **Pace.** Pace refers to how quickly a person speaks. In conversation, we can get away with speaking very, very quickly. In a public speaking situation, however, one should slow down enough to ensure that the audience can hear every word. To add interest, a good public speaker varies his or her pace quite a bit—sometimes speaking very, very slowly to emphasize a point and sometimes speaking more quickly to convey emotion.

4. **Timbre, or Vocal Quality.** Listen to a bunch of different musical instruments. A single note—a middle C, for example—sounds different if played on a flute than if played on a trumpet or a guitar. The difference in sound of each instrument is a difference in **timbre.** Human voices, like the voices of instruments, also differ from one another in timbre. A child's voice sounds different, for example, than the voice of an elderly person, and a large person's voice sounds different from a small person's. Experiment with trying to create different vocal qualities. Can you speak like an elderly person? Like an infant? Like an adult man or woman?

5. **Stress.** The words in a sentence are naturally **stressed** (given emphasis) or **unstressed** (not given emphasis). One notices these stresses, particularly, in poetry, which is often written using particular patterns of stress. For example, consider this line:

   Is this the face that launched a thousand ships?

   Every other word in this sentence receives a strong stress. Now turn to some piece of prose in this book and read a line or two aloud. As you read, pay attention to the natural rhythms, or patterns of stresses, in the lines. As you read the lines aloud, try to exaggerate, just a bit, the stresses. A good public speaker does exactly that. Good public speakers also occasionally stress individual words especially strongly in order to emphasize them. Think, for example, about the difference of meaning depending on which of the words in the following sentence is stressed, or emphasized:

   Are you going to the prom with Jim?
   Are **you** going to the prom with Jim?
   Are you going to the **prom** with Jim?
   Are you going to the prom with **Jim**?

   Stress can be an important determinant of meaning. So, when you read a work aloud, pay attention to which words you stress and which you don't.

6. **Proximity.** In many public speaking situations, you have the ability to move around, to get closer or further away from your audience. Good speakers often vary the **proximity**, or closeness, to their audience, moving or leaning closer to emphasize an important point, for example.

7. **Facial Expressions and Body Language.** Good speakers also make sure that their facial expressions (the emotions communicated by their faces) and their body language (the emotions communicated by how they hold or move their bodies) mirror what they are saying. If a speaker is making an impassioned call to action, for example, he or she might have a furrowed brow and a look of determination. He or she might also gesticulate or even pound on a lectern to add particular emphasis.

8. **Tone.** One's **tone** is the emotional quality in one's voice. For example, a voice might convey sadness, triumph, despair, anger, joy, wistfulness, nostalgia, hope, determination, or loss. Again, good speakers match the tone of the voice to the content of what is being said.

   Assignment: Read the music section on page 201, and review the slave narratives on pages 114 and 130. Then choose one of the following topics:

   The Spirituals
   Slave Narratives
   The Blues

   Work with a group of students to write a short (twenty- to thirty-minute) piece of reader's theater that presents a number of works read by various actors. Choose the works that you want to include. You will find some works in the music sections of this book. You will also want to do some additional research in the library or on the Internet to find additional works. Then write a part for a narrator who introduces the genre at the beginning of the piece and then introduces each of the pieces. Once you have a script that includes the narrator's part and the works that you are going to present, get together with your group and rehearse your reader's theater presentation. Choose one person in your group to act as a director, giving advice to everyone else on how to vary the elements of the voice to make the pieces and the narration come alive for the audience. Don't be shy! Work to put together an exciting, electrifying, emotionally moving performance.

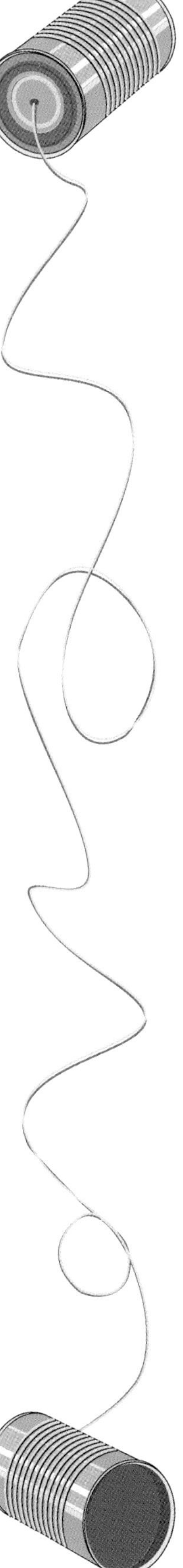

Unit 2 Writing

Critical and Expository Writing

1. **An Oral History**. "The Confessions of Nat Turner" is an example of an **oral history.** Collect an oral history yourself. Find an older person in your family who might have an interesting story to tell about some time in the distant past. Such a person (as the short-story writer Ray Bradbury once suggested) can be a time machine to take you back to another world. Interview this person to collect the story. Then retell the story, in writing, to the best of your memory as you heard it. Share the story you collected with the rest of your class.

2. **A Personal Essay.** The autobiographical narrative, like those written by Frederick Douglass and Harriet Jacobs, is closely related to another form, the **personal essay.** In a personal essay, you write about an experience that you had and then tell what you learned from the experience. Think of an event that occurred in your life that taught you an important lesson. Make a list of the parts of the event and another list of concrete sensory details that you can use to make your retelling of the event vivid for your readers. Then, write an introductory paragraph that sets up the story and suggests what its subject or theme will be. The body of your essay should tell the story in the **first person**, using pronouns like *I, me,* and *we*. The conclusion should derive the lesson or moral from your story.

3. **A Letter to a Person in Power**. Reread Benjamin Banneker's moving letter to Thomas Jefferson. Then, take a cue from Mr. Banneker and write your own **letter** to a person in a position of power and authority. You might write, for example, to your school principal or to your state governor. Choose an issue that you care about and that the person to whom you are writing can address. Tell the person how you feel about the issue and why. Present evidence to support your opinion. In your letter, be respectful and ask the addressee to take some particular action with regard to the issue.

4. **Analysis of the Code in a Set of Spirituals.** The spirituals were often written in what is known as the code. On a literal level, they were about events and characters from the Bible. On a metaphorical level, they were about the situation of the singers. Do some research on the Internet or in the library to find a few spirituals to analyze. Then write an **essay** in which you explain the dual meanings of the spirituals that you find. (See The Spirituals on pages 202–206.)

Creative Writing

1. **A Campfire Story.** Kids love to tell scary stories around a campfire. "The Headless Hant," in this unit, is an example of such a story. Write your own scary **campfire story.** Begin by coming up with a central character and a conflict or struggle that the character faces. Then make a list of events that introduce the conflict, build the suspense, and eventually resolve the conflict. Make a list of details that you can include in your story to make it creepy and spine-tingling. After you have written your draft and revised it a few times, try it out loud with a bunch of your fellow students.

2. **A Speech for a Piece of Historical Fiction.** Sojourner Truth was very eloquent, but she was not literate. She could not read and write. We have her fine speech "Ar'n't I a Woman" because someone in her audience wrote the speech down from memory. Writers of historical fiction often have to do something similar. They invent conversation and speeches that might have been given at the time and try to make these as authentic as possible. Choose a historical event related to African-American history. See the timelines on pages 229 and 480 for ideas. Do some research on this event. Then, write an invented **speech** that might have been given to a group of high-school students by someone who was an eyewitness to these events. To do this, you will have to invent a character and his or her role in the event. In other words, you will have to think like a writer of historical fiction.

Unit 2

Focus on: African-American Music to the Reconstruction Era

The Spirituals

from "Didn't My Lord Deliver Daniel"

from "Sometimes I Feel like a Motherless Child"

from "Swing Low, Sweet Chariot"

from "Go Down, Moses"

"Follow the Drinking Gourd"

from *The Souls of Black Folk,* W. E. B. Du Bois

Work Songs and Field Hollers

from "Well, My Hammer"

"Long John"

"Lawd, I'm Goin' to Take My Time"

from "Mama's Gonna Buy You a Mockin' Bird"

"John Henry"

Outlaw Songs

"Po' Lazarus"

African-American Dance in the Slavery and Reconstruction Eras

Focus on: African-American Music to the Reconstruction Era

The Spirituals

Didn't my Lord deliver Daniel,[1]
Deliver Daniel, deliver Daniel,
Didn't my Lord deliver Daniel,
An' why not every man?

—from "Didn't My Lord Deliver Daniel,"
traditional African-American Spiritual

As the lyrics above suggest, many enslaved African Americans felt like the Biblical character Daniel—trapped and longing to be delivered, or rescued. In the Americas, people of African descent found themselves removed from their homelands, their tribes, their kinsmen and loved ones. One can only imagine the loneliness and loss that these people felt, and that loneliness and loss was expressed in the music that they created:

Sometimes I feel like a motherless child.
Sometimes I feel like a motherless child.
Sometimes I feel like a motherless child.
Long way from my home.

—from "Sometimes I Feel like a Motherless Child,"
traditional African-American Spiritual

When slaves came to the New World, they were exposed to Christianity and to traditional Protestant church music. The hymns that they heard and the Bible stories that they learned provided material for the music that the enslaved would use in their own worship, which combined elements of traditional African spirituality with the new Christian teachings. Denied the opportunity to express themselves openly in spiritually meaningful ways, some slaves formed an "invisible institution," holding religious services in secret. These **camp meetings,** or **bush meetings,** took place away from supervision in creek beds, in forests, or in slave quarters at night, where they would hold services

[1] **Daniel.** Biblical prophet enslaved in Babylon and rescued by God from a den of lions

that included such elements of traditional African religion as ring dances and ecstatic entrancement. Traditional African religions were either Islamic or Animist. In Animist religions, the world is perceived as being filled with spirits, and both priests and worshippers believe themselves capable of experiencing entrancement, or possession by these spirits. This idea of entrancement became connected, in early African-American religious practice, to the Christian idea of possession by the Holy Ghost, accompanied by ecstatic movements and vocalizations referred to as "speaking in tongues." As part of their worship, enslaved African Americans created a new kind of music that fused traditional African melodies and rhythms with new Christian ideas and stories. This sacred folk music came to be known as the **jubilee,** or **spiritual.**

Sung both at religious gatherings and as work songs in the fields, the spirituals were passed down orally through the generations. Often, these songs contained **call-and-response elements,** in which a leader would sing one line, and the group would respond.

Call: I looked over Jordan and what did I see.
Response: Comin' for to carry me home.
Call: A whole host of angels a comin' after me.
Response: Comin' for to carry me home.

—from "Swing Low, Sweet Chariot,"
traditional African-American Spiritual

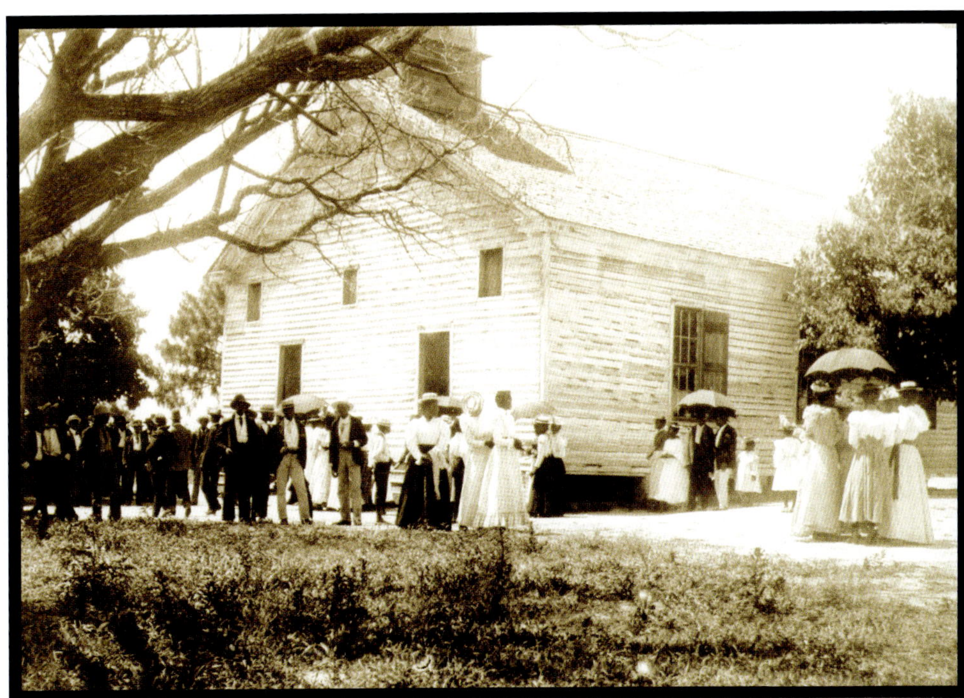

Members of an African-American church in Georgia, circa 1899. Image collected by W. E. B. Du Bois. Library of Congress, LC-USZ62-118809

The call-and-response form helped to reinforce bonds of community among people who had very little but one another. This dependence on one another was an early example of the truth expressed by Nikki Giovanni in a poem, over a century later, that "Black / love is Black wealth." Self-expression was not unknown, however, in the secretive camp meetings, as many slaves preached and gave improvised, heartfelt testimony or took turns acting as song leaders.

Significantly, the spirituals served a political as well as a spiritual purpose, for many of them were written in a secret language that has come to be known as **the code.** Biblical stories were adapted in the songs to express secret messages about resistance and escape. Of particular interest to enslaved Africans was the story of the enslavement of the Jews in Egypt, as told in the books of Genesis and Exodus in the Bible. According to this story, the Jews, or people of Israel, were taken captive and forced to labor for their Egyptian masters until, eventually, they were led by Moses to freedom in a Promised Land, Canaan, that lay beyond the River Jordan. In the code of the spirituals, all of these elements took on secondary meanings. The people of Israel stood for enslaved African Americans. The Egyptian leader, the Pharaoh, stood for slave owners and overseers. Egypt stood for the Southern slave states. Moses stood for "conductors" on the **Underground Railroad,** the series of safe houses organized by abolitionists to ferry slaves to freedom. The most famous of these conductors, Harriet Tubman, came to be known as "the Moses of her people" (see the selection on page 232). The Promised Land stood for free states in the North, or for Canada, in which slavery was forbidden by law. The River Jordan became associated with the Mississippi and Ohio Rivers, which separated the free North from the slave-owning South.

> When Israel was in Egypt's land,
> Let my people go.
> Oppressed so hard they could not stand,
> Let my people go.
>
> Go down, Moses,
> Way down in Egypt's land.
> Tell ole Pharaoh,
> Let my people go.
>
> —from "Go Down, Moses,"
> traditional African-American Spiritual

In the lines from the spiritual "Swing Low, Sweet Chariot" mentioned above, the *chariot* and the *host of angels* both refer, as well, to conductors on the Underground Railroad. In perhaps the most famous of the spirituals, "Follow the Drinking Gourd," the Drinking Gourd is the Big Dipper Constellation, which points to the North Star. By looking for the North Star, runaway slaves could orient themselves and make sure that they were heading north, toward freedom. The song contains coded instructions for escape along one of the paths of the Underground Railroad. It was taught to slaves by one of the most famous of the Underground Railroad conductors, a man named Peg Leg Joe:

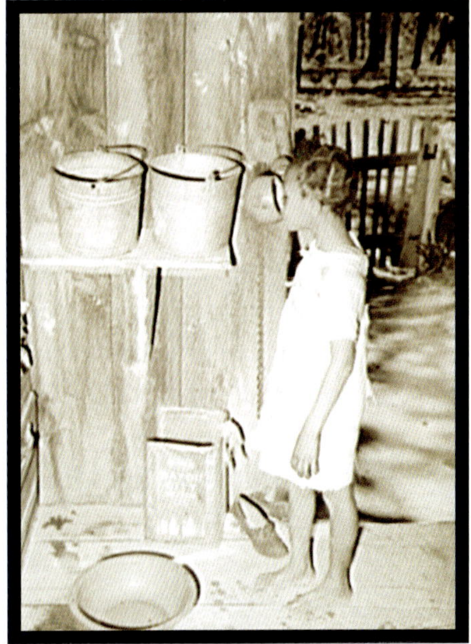

A child drinks from a drinking gourd. Library of Congress, LC-USF34-032707.

Follow the Drinking Gourd

Follow the Drinking Gourd.
Follow the Drinking Gourd.
For the old man is a-waitin' for to carry you to
 freedom
If you follow the Drinking Gourd.

When the sun comes up and the first quail calls,[2]
Follow the Drinking Gourd.
For the old man is a-waitin' for to carry you to
 freedom
If you follow the Drinking Gourd.

The riverbank[3] makes a very good road.
The dead trees will show you the way.
Left foot, peg foot, traveling on,
Follow the Drinking Gourd.

The river ends between two hills.
Follow the Drinking Gourd.[4]
There's another river on the other side.
Follow the Drinking Gourd.

[2] **When the sun . . . calls.** A reference to the beginning of winter, when the sun starts climbing higher in the sky and the quail, a kind of bird, begins to migrate.

[3] **riverbank.** A reference to the Tombigbee River, which runs through Mississippi and Alabama. Runaway slaves are directed by this verse to follow the river and the markings left on dead trees by Peg Leg Joe.

[4] **The river . . . Drinking Gourd.** This verse directs the runaway to come to the end of the Tombigbee River to head north to yet another river, the Tennessee, and then to head north again along the banks of the Tennessee River.

Where the great big river meets the little river,
Follow the Drinking Gourd.
The old man is a-waitin' for to carry you to freedom.
Follow the Drinking Gourd.[5]

In the spirituals we see how enslaved peoples found consolation in religion but also adapted it to their needs. They developed their own variety of **liberation theology** and sought not only spiritual freedom but physical, political freedom as well.

The spirituals are sometimes referred to as the **sorrow songs** because, of course, they often expressed great sadness.

> Nobody knows the trouble I've seen.
> Nobody knows but Jesus.
> Nobody knows the trouble I've seen.
> Great Glory, Hallelujah!
>
> —from "Nobody Knows the Trouble I've Seen,"
> traditional African-American Spiritual

In his great autobiography, the newspaper editor and Abolitionist leader Frederick Douglass, himself a former slave, wrote, "To those songs I trace my first glimmering conception of the dehumanizing character of slavery. . . . Every tone was a testimony against slavery, and a prayer to God for deliverance from chains." Remarkably, however, the songs were not just about sorrow. As the great intellectual leader W. E. B. Du Bois wrote in his book *The Souls of Black Folk:*

> Through all the sorrow of the Sorrow Songs there breathes a hope—a faith in the ultimate justice of things. The minor cadences of despair change often to triumph and calm confidence.[6] Sometimes it is faith in life, sometimes a faith in death, sometimes assurance of boundless justice in some fair world beyond. But whichever it is, the meaning is always clear: that sometime, somewhere, men will judge men by their souls and not by their skins. Is such a hope justified? Do the Sorrow Songs sing true?
>
> —from *The Souls of Black Folk,*
> W. E. B. Du Bois (1868–1963)

[5] **where the great . . . Drinking Gourd.** This verse tells the runaway to come to the place where the Tennessee River meets the big river, the Ohio, where an Underground Railroad conductor will be waiting.

[6] **despair . . . confidence.** See, for example, the lines from "Nobody Knows the Trouble I've Seen," quoted above.

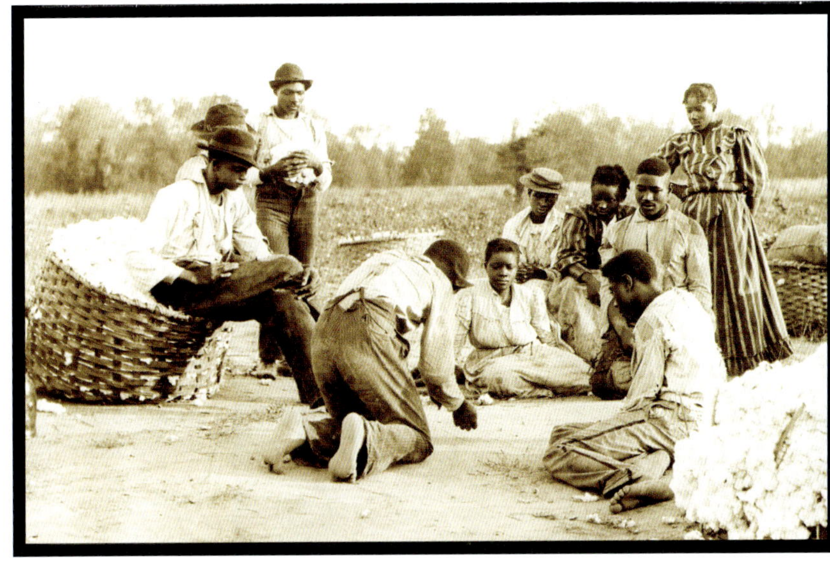

Cotton field workers. Library of Congress, LC-USZ62-118809.

Work Songs and Field Hollers

The motivating force behind slavery was, of course, greed. Africans were enslaved in the New World in order to provide labor for raising crops such as sugar cane, tobacco, and cotton and to do other sorts of manual work, such as building, clearing land, or laying railroad lines. To deal with their boredom and pain and to ease their work, enslaved laborers and, later, African-American convicts working on prison plantations would sing, both individually and collectively. Often, their songs took the form of communal **work songs**, call-and-response pieces in which a leader would sing the main text and the rest of the workers would answer, as in this example:[7]

Leader	**Chorus**
Well, my hammer.	Hammer ring.
Got a ten-pound hammer.	Hammer ring.
Cap'n went to Houston.	Hammer ring.
To git me a hammer.	Hammer ring.
Way down in de bottom.	Hammer ring.
Hew out a live oak.	Hammer ring.
Son, you got a fever.	Hammer ring.
Don't you see you got a fever.	Hammer ring.

—from "Well, My Hammer,"
traditional African-American Work Song

[7] Though collected in the early twentieth century, this song is derived from and probably indicative of the pre-Civil War African-American work songs, most of which have been lost because they existed only in the oral tradition, were not written down, and were sung in a time before mechanical recording devices.

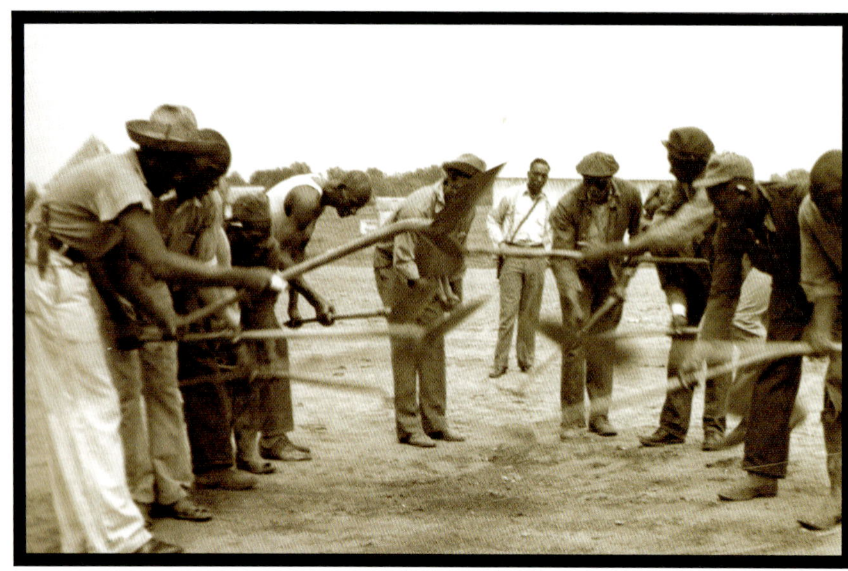

African-American convicts working with shovels, Cummins State Farm, Gould, Arkansas. Library of Congress, LC-USZ62-38540.

The work songs were generally highly rhythmical and performed in time with the work being done, such as swinging a hammer or an axe. Sometimes, the work songs expressed the desire to escape, as in this famous example, called "Long John." Note that in performance, all the lines of this song would be sung by the leader and repeated by the chorus, in call-and-response fashion:

Long John

It's a long John,
He's a long gone,
Like a turkey through the corn,
Through the long corn.

Well, my John said,
In the ten chap' ten,
"If a man die,
He will live again."

Well, they crucified Jesus,
And they nailed him to the cross.
Sister Mary cried,
"My child is lost."

Well-a two, three minutes,
Let me catch my wind.
In-a two, three minutes,
I'm gone again.

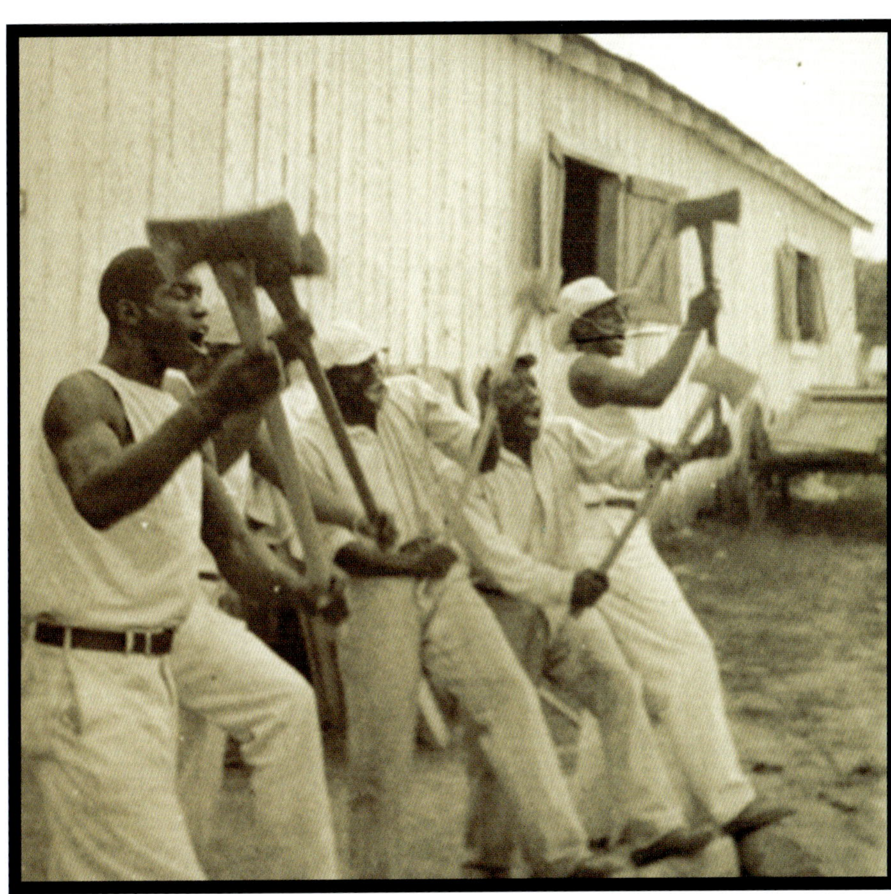

"Lightnin'" Washington, an African-American prisoner, singing with his group in the woodyard at Darrington State Farm, Texas. Library of Congress, LC-USZ62-23008.

Well, long John,
He's long gone.
With his long clothes on,
Just a-skippin' through the corn.

He's long gone.
He's long gone.
He's long gone.
It's a long John.

Sometimes a single worker would be inspired to produce a spontaneous piece of his own. Such pieces, performed by individuals as they worked, were known as **field hollers.** Often these were beautiful, plaintive, moving pieces containing bent or slurred notes that eventually became the basis of the melodies of blues songs. Here is an example:

Sung: Oh! Oh! Captain keep on hollerin', "Hurry!"
Lawd, I'm goin' to take my time.
Spoken: Godalmighty, yonder he comes. Where? Right there.
Sung: Captain say, "Hurry!" Boss say, "Run!"

Got two or three notions. Can't do nary one.
Oh, if you see Vandella, tell her this for me,
Got a long holdover and never go free.

—traditional African-American Field Holler[8]

In addition to working in the fields, African Americans also worked in homes as servants and nursemaids, and African-American women doing enforced childcare produced lullabies, including this humorous African-American variant of a well-known Scots-Irish lullaby with a haunting melody:

Hush, little baby, don't say a word.
Mama's gonna buy you a mockin' bird.
An' if that mockin' bird don't sing,
Mama's gonna whip you' bom-bom-bing.

—from "Mama's Gonna Buy You a Mockin' Bird,"
traditional African-American Scots-Irish Lullaby

Work songs and field hollers led, eventually, to the blues, and they also spawned a popular genre of work-related folk songs that include such well-known pieces as "Casey Jones" (which tells the story of a famous railroad engineer) and "Boll Weevil" (which is the story of an insect infestation that destroyed cotton crops throughout the South in the early part of the twentieth century). Perhaps the most famous of these folk songs about work and workers was "John Henry," which was being passed around in the oral tradition as early as the 1870s. The real John Henry was a African-American man who was born a slave in the mid-nineteenth century. Like many other African Americans, after the Civil War John Henry took a job working for one of the railroad companies that were at the time laying track in various parts of the United States. As a steel driver for the C & O Railroad, John Henry's job was to break rocks by using a hammer to drive steel spikes into them. Each driver worked with a second man, the shaker, whose job was to turn the spike after it was struck. According to legend, an attempt was made to introduce a steam-driven machine to do drilling, and John Henry, a giant of a man known for his enormous strength, undertook to race the machine to prove that he could outperform it, which he did. However, as a result of his exertions, he died shortly thereafter, perhaps of a stroke. A song about this great duel between man and machine swept the country and has been a part of the American folk tradition ever since. The song exists in many versions, but this is one of the earliest:

8 Again, this field holler was collected in the early twentieth century, but it is derived from and probably indicative of pre-Civil War field hollers now lost to scholarship.

John Henry

John Henry was a railroad man,
He worked from six 'till five,
"Raise 'em up bullies and let 'em drop down,
I'll beat you to the bottom or die."

John Henry said to his captain:
"You are nothing but a common man,
Before that steam drill shall beat me down,
I'll die with my hammer in my hand."

John Henry said to the shakers:
"You must listen to my call,
Before that steam drill shall beat me down,
I'll jar these mountains till they fall."

John Henry's captain said to him:
"I believe these mountains are caving in."
John Henry said to his captain: "Oh, Lord!
That's my hammer you hear in the wind."

John Henry he said to his captain:
"Your money is getting mighty slim,
When I hammer through this old mountain,
Oh Captain will you walk in?"

John Henry's captain came to him
With fifty dollars in his hand,
He laid his hand on his shoulder and said:
"This belongs to a steel driving man."

John Henry was hammering on the right side,
The big steam drill on the left,
Before that steam drill could beat him down,
He hammered his fool self to death.

They carried John Henry to the mountains,
From his shoulder his hammer would ring,
She caught on fire by a little blue blaze
I believe these old mountains are caving in.

John Henry was lying on his death bed,
He turned over on his side,
And these were the last words John Henry said
"Bring me a cool drink of water before I die."

John Henry had a little woman,
Her name was Pollie Ann,
He hugged and kissed her just before he died,
Saying, "Pollie, do the very best you can."

John Henry's woman heard he was dead,
She could not rest on her bed,
She got up at midnight, caught that No. 4 train,
"I am going where John Henry fell dead."

They carried John Henry to that new burying ground
His wife all dressed in blue,
She laid her hand on John Henry's cold face,
"John Henry I've been true to you."

Outlaw Songs

It is natural, of course, for people who are enslaved or imprisoned to react against their oppressors, and such reaction sometimes took the form, in early African-American music, of songs that celebrated those brave enough to run away, as in "Long John," above, or those who challenged authority. Thus was born a genre of outlaw songs. The following example, "Po' Lazarus," was often sung as a work song, particularly among convicts:

Po' Lazarus

Well, the high sheriff he told his deputy,
Want you go out and bring me Lazarus

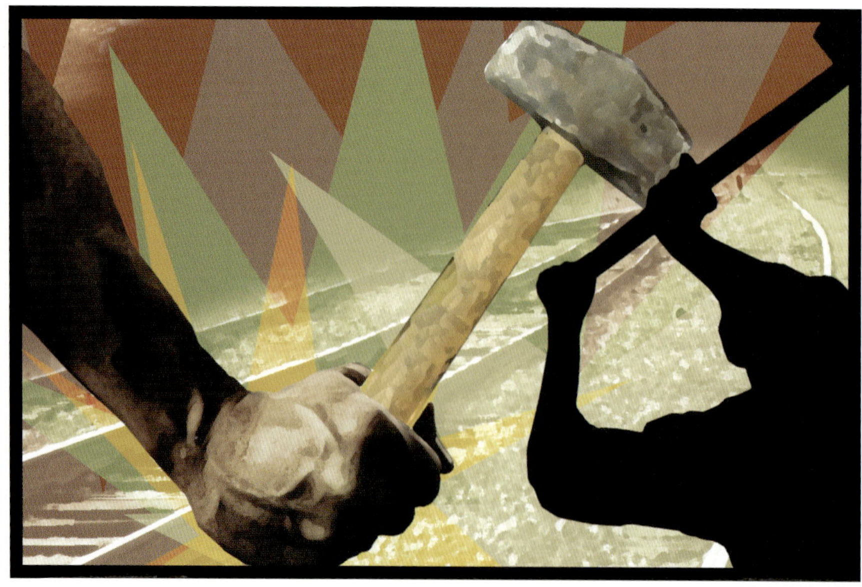

Well, the high sheriff told his deputy
I want you go out and bring me Lazarus
Bring him dead or alive,
Lawd, Lawd
Bring him dead or alive

Well the deputy he told the high sheriff
I ain't gonna mess with Lazarus
Well the deputy he told the high sheriff
Says I ain't gonna mess with Lazarus
Well he's a dangerous man
Lawd, Lawd
He's a dangerous man

Well then the high sheriff, he found Lazarus
He was hidin' in the chill of a mountain
Well the high sheriff, found Lazarus
He was hidin' in the chill of the mountain
With his head hung down
Lawd, Lawd
With his head hung down

Well then the high sheriff, he told Lazarus
He says Lazarus I come to arrest you
Well the high sheriff, told Lazarus
Says Lazarus I come to arrest you
And bring ya dead or alive
Lawd, Lawd
Bring you dead or alive

Well then Lazarus, he told the high sheriff
Says I never been arrested
Well Lazarus, told the high sheriff
Says I never been arrested
By no one man
Lawd, Lawd
By no one man

And then the high sheriff, he shot Lazarus
Well, he shot him mighty big number
Well the high sheriff, shot Lazarus
Well he shot him with a mighty big number
With a forty five
Lawd, Lawd
With a forty five

Well then they take old Lazarus
Yes they laid him on the commissary gallery
Well they taken poor Lazarus
And the laid him on the commissary gallery
He said my wounded side
Lawd, Lawd
My wounded side

African-American Dance in the Slavery and Reconstruction Eras

The rhythms and dances of Africa survived the horrors of the Middle Passage and the desperate lives of enslaved peoples to become the bedrock of music in the New World. African traditions had to overcome many obstacles, however. Many Protestants in the United States, in a holdover from the Puritan Era, considered dancing immoral, and so it was often prohibited among slaves. Drums, so central to African music making, were widely outlawed after they were used in a slave revolt, the Stono Rebellion, in 1739.

Since showy dancing often was considered licentious or immoral, slaves executed a **ring dance**, or **ring shout**, itself derived from African sources, that was less likely to offend since the feet shuffled in a sliding step and hardly left the ground. The ring shout, described by legendary

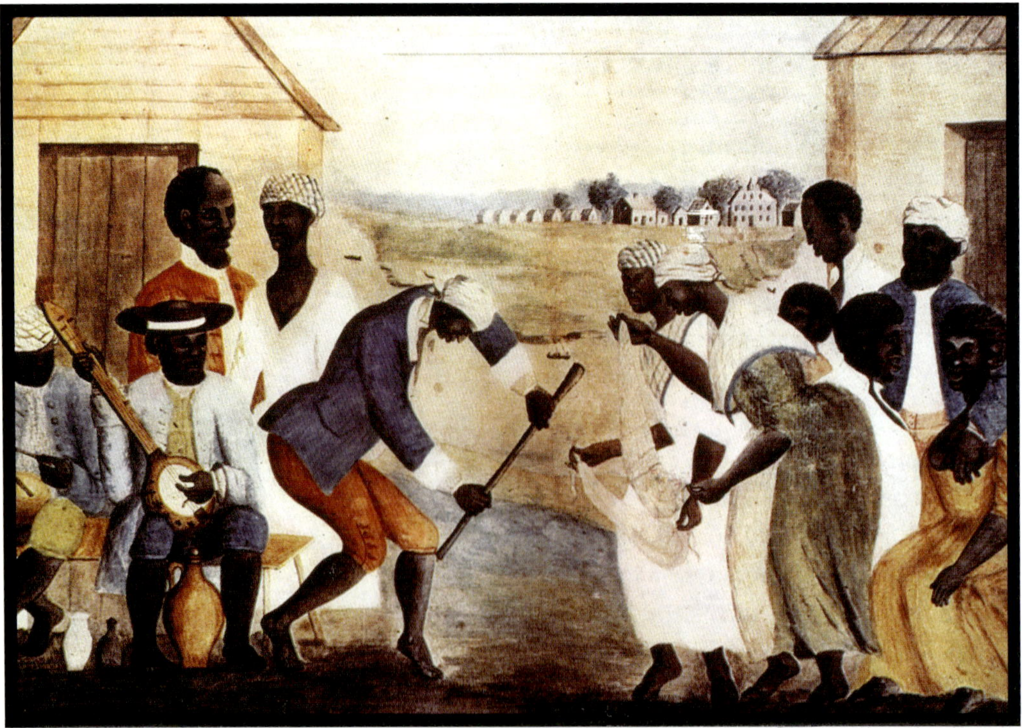

The Old Plantation, 18th century, watercolor, American.

African-American writer Ralph Ellison as "America's first choreography," is a counterclockwise circle dance. In keeping with communal spiritual practices in West Africa, the ring dance had no audience—everyone participated by singing and using hand claps to keep tight rhythmic coordination. In addition to the shuffle of the ring dance, enslaved African Americans developed other popular steps, like **breakdowns** and the **strut,** featuring remarkable improvisations. One innovation was the **cakewalk,** a style of dance that developed among African-American slaves to lampoon, or make fun of, the airs put on by slave owners. The cakewalk featured exaggerated body language and combined several formal European dance patterns with traditional African steps, especially dance in a linear, often serpentine fashion. Many slave owners found the comic antics of the cakewalk fascinating and organized regular contests among the dancers. It was customary for a cake, or pieces of cake, to be awarded as a prize for the best dancers, hence the name of the dance. The name *cakewalk* also underlies the modern idioms "takes the cake" and "piece of cake." The syncopated dancing tradition of the cakewalk continued among African Americans in the South after the Civil War and gradually spread northward until finally becoming a nationwide sensation at the close of the nineteenth century.

Unfortunately, in the **minstrel shows** of the late nineteenth and early twentieth century, such forms of African-American dance as the cakewalk were themselves exaggerated and lampooned, often by white performers wearing blackface makeup and perpetuating, in their extreme antics, not only racist stereotypes but also the myth that the enslaved peoples of the South were always singing and dancing and thus happy with their lot. There is a terrible irony here: The cakewalk originated as a form of subtle, ironic protest, but this subtlety and irony was lost on the white audiences of the minstrel shows.

The influence of African Americans on New World dance was not limited to preserving and incorporating the traditions of African dance. African Americans were also responsible for many innovations and for blending African rhythms with the various European traditions they were newly encountering. One such innovator was **William Henry Lane** (1825–1852), better known as **Master Juba.** Long before the Civil War, he performed in the Five Points neighborhood of New York, a famously tough neighborhood composed primarily of Irish immigrants and free blacks. Master Juba is credited with blending elements of the Irish jig with African shuffle to form a dance style called the **buck and wing,** which is now known as **American tap dance.** In the arts, this blending of cultural traditions is called *syncretism,* from a Greek word meaning "to unite or fuse."

Ann Petry Harriet Tubman

BOOKER T. WASHINGTON

MARCUS GARVEY W. E. B. Du Bois

Ida B. Wells-Barnett

Arthur Schomburg

Fenton Johnson Langston Hughes

Paul Laurence Dunbar

Angelina Weld Grimke

Waverly Turner Carmichael

ALICE DUNBAR NELSON

Georgia Douglas Johnson

Langston Hughes Anne Spencer

Zora Neale Hurston Helene Johnson

Charles W. Chesnutt

Claude McKay Jean Toomer

COUNTEE CULLEN

Sterling Brown Arna Bontemps

Francis Jackson Coppin

NELLA LARSEN Gwendolyn Bennett

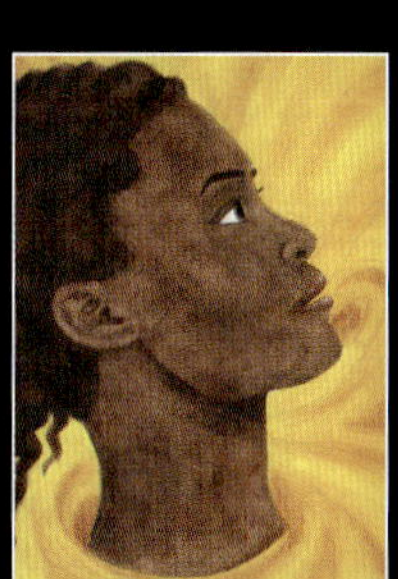

Unit 3
Up from Bondage

"There is in this world no such force as the force of a person determined to rise. The human soul cannot be permanently chained."

—W. E. B. Du Bois

Unit 3 Introduction

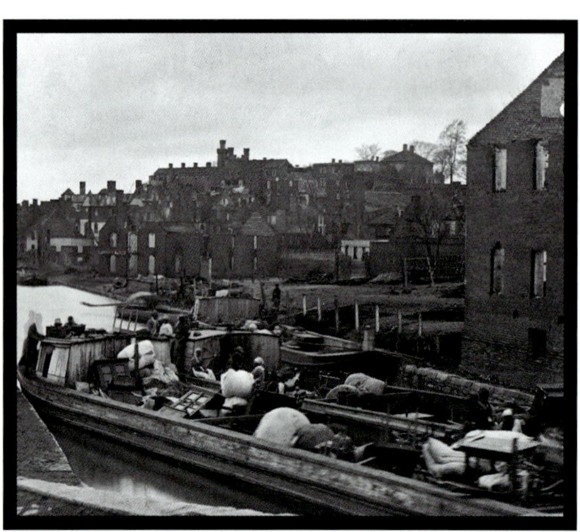

Richmond, Va. Barges with African Americans on the Canal; ruined buildings beyond. June, 1865. Photograph. Library of Congress, LC-DIG-cwpt-04079.

Up from Bondage, 1866–1939

The American Civil War left more than 600,000 dead soldiers in its wake and transformed the nation. For 4 million African Americans, the end of the war meant the beginning of the slow march to equal rights and freedom. The war destroyed the old plantation economy and devastated cities in the South. In the North, by contrast, the war actually spurred industrial growth, and though families would long mourn their lost sons and fathers, the northern economy flourished during and after the war. Naturally, many African Americans in the South were eager to seek new lives in the prosperous North, but the political, social, and economic conditions around the country made it difficult for many people to start again.

In the South, the end of the war marked the start of the period known as **Reconstruction.**[1] Much of the South was occupied and governed by Federal troops. Emancipated African Americans sought assistance from the newly formed **Freedmen's Bureau** and hoped to find jobs in the North. Many others stayed behind, near the crumbling plantations, perhaps to receive their "forty acres and a mule" under a program administered by the Freedmen's Bureau. There was hope for the future, but uncertainty was really the order of the day.

Social conditions deteriorated once the euphoria of war's end had passed: political momentum was lost with Lincoln's assassination; the next president, the ill-fated Andrew Johnson, was actually sympathetic to the defeated rebels, who in turn transformed the South into a nightmarish place for black Americans; next came eight tumultuous, fruitless years with the able general

[1] **Reconstruction.** This and many other key terms from the post-Civil War, Jim Crow, and early Civil Rights eras will be detailed in the essay on page 222 and the glossary on page 224.

but poor president Ulysses S. Grant at the helm of the executive branch; these were followed by the contentious election of Rutherford B. Hayes, who forged the disastrous **Compromise of 1877,** effectively trading the hopes and rights of millions of American citizens for his seat in the Oval Office. By the late 1800s, many African Americans—whether they had moved north or remained in the South—were seriously questioning whether they had truly been emancipated.

The last three decades of the nineteenth century were a troubled time in the African-American story. The Ku Klux Klan initiated its brutal, depraved reign of terror. Blacks were deprived of their voting rights, exploited by politicians, and ignored or abused by the legal system. **Jim Crow laws** and the doctrine of **separate but equal** public facilities created for the newly emancipated a status as second-class citizens and deferred their dreams.

But all the injustice and racism could not undo the essential liberties set forth by the First Amendment to the U.S. Constitution. Armed with these rights and little else, black activists and leaders, along with their allies in government, the press, and the business world, used the mandates of Congress and the Supreme Court to their advantage. Political activists, writers, artists, scholars, philosophers, educators, entrepreneurs, and entertainers of this era gradually lighted the way for their counterparts in the second half of the twentieth century.

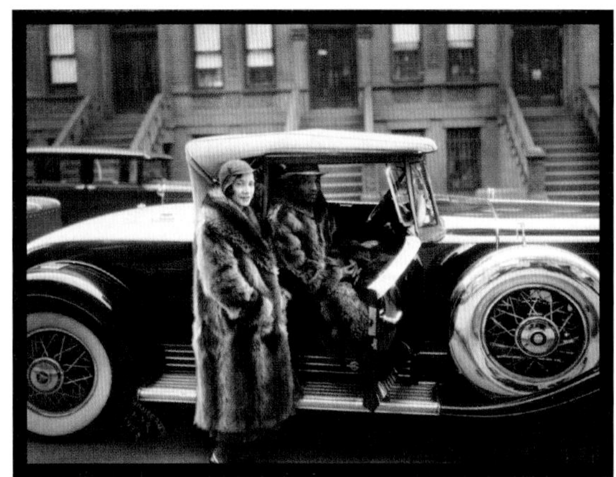

Couple in Raccoon Coats, 1925. This well-to-do couple was ready for a night on the town in Harlem, exactly 60 years after the end of the Civil War. Photograph by James VanDerZee.

Nearly 90 percent of African Americans remained in the South until the early 1900s. The outbreak of the First World War (1914–18) created incredible demand for labor in the industrial North; at the same time, the infestation of the beetle known as the **boll weevil** devastated cotton crops upon which the South's economy was fully dependent, even in the early twentieth century. The war and the boll weevil were mixed blessings: farmers in the South experienced the deepest imaginable poverty, but opportunities abounded in cities like New York, Detroit, and Chicago—cities to which African Americans moved by the hundreds of thousands between 1914 and the 1940s in what soon came to be known as the **Great Migration.**

A new story now unfolds: from the ruins of war, along the trail of the newly freed refugees and the millions migrating toward new lives, to the glitter of **Harlem Renaissance** nights and the troubles of the **Great Depression**—Unit 3 of *Grace Abounding* presents some of the finest literature to emerge in America during this period of constant change and ongoing struggle, when a people became divided once again, and artists searched for their own souls and those of their people.

A Tour of Harlem, circa 1926

The **Harlem Renaissance** reached its peak during an exciting and fascinating decade in American history. The end of the First World War ushered in a new wave of social change: the stock market soared; Prohibition was in full effect; daredevils and airshows were all the rage; Al Capone ruled Chicago, and Charlie Chaplin ruled the silver screen; the automobile became a fixed part of American life, and jazz was born. Most Americans did not fully share in the economic prosperity of the times, but there was a universal sense of optimism and enthusiasm—imaginations everywhere were unbound. So began an extraordinary outpouring of literature, ideas, art, and music from the hearts and minds of African Americans all over the country. And the community of Harlem was the center of it all.

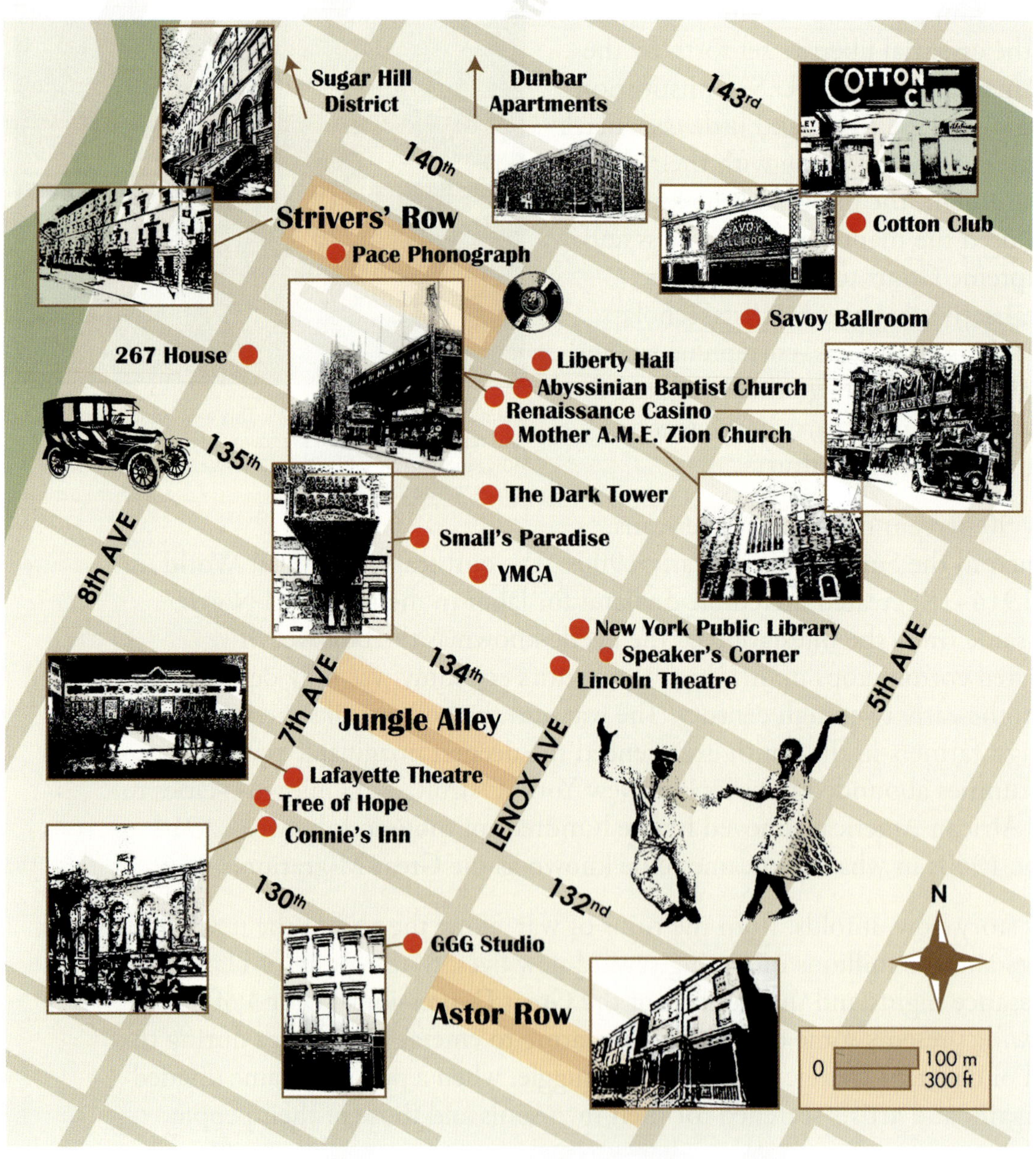

A Few Landmarks of the Harlem Renaissance

Savoy Ballroom. A popular dance club from 1926–1958, best known as the home of a wildly popular dance known as the "Lindy Hop"

The Cotton Club. A famous Prohibition-era nightclub in the heart of Harlem where greats like Duke Ellington, Fletcher Anderson, Cab Calloway, and Ethel Waters got their start. Ironically, the club's owner denied admission to these performers' African-American fans.

The Apollo Theater. (Not pictured on map. Located at 253 W. 125 St.) Grew to prominence during the 1920s and is still the place "where stars are born and legends are made."

Strivers' Row. A residential area popular among black professionals. The two rows of 1890s brownstones on 138th and 139th Streets were originally built for middle-class families, but by the 1920s the area attracted wealthy and influential African Americans.

Abyssinian Baptist Church. Keeper of the Harlem gospel music tradition

The New York Public Library and Speaker's Corner. Home of the library's Division of Negro Literature, History, and Prints, a major research center. Black scholar Arthur Schomburg's collection was the cornerstone of the division. The 135th St. Branch was also a cultural and literary center in Harlem, where poets could often be heard reciting their works on the street corner outside the building.

The Dark Tower. A'lelia Walker, daughter of Madame C. J. Walker, dubbed her inherited Harlem mansion after poet Countee Cullen's column of the same name in *Opportunity* magazine. The Dark Tower became the cultural nexus of Harlem, drawing scholars, travelers, and musicians of every race to all-night marathons of dance, drink, and conversation. James Weldon Johnson and Zora Neale Hurston, among others, were regular attendees.

Lincoln Theater. This theater, founded in 1915, was one of the only places where African Americans were allowed to watch movies, which were silent in those days. Theaters hired musicians to provide musical accompaniment. One of the Lincoln's first pianists was future jazz great Fats Waller, who started playing in the 1,000-seat theater when he was 12 years old.

Jungle Alley. The best of New York's nightlife—a block-long stretch of nightclubs and cabarets. where anything could happen on a Saturday night, including an appearance by young, brilliant Duke Ellington, and others.

See what you can find out about other Harlem hotspots. Select a place that most interests you and do a creative project describing a night in the life of a Harlem resident, circa 1926. You can write a poem, story, essay, play, journal entry, newspaper article, or letter. Or, use your location as the basis of a visual arts or music project.

[Editor's Note: Key historical terms appear below in boldface and are defined in the glossary that follows. Readers should be familiar with these terms and events before proceeding with Unit 3.]

Historical Background: Reconstruction and Segregation 1865–1938

Now will the poets sing,—
Their cries go thundering
Like blood and tears
Into the nation's ears
—Countee Cullen

The Civil War ended—despite the horrific loss of life—with the best possible outcome: the Union was intact, and slavery was abolished. One might hope or even assume that peace, prosperity, and reconciliation would soon follow, and signs everywhere did point to improvement. African Americans who remained in the South lost no time in establishing their own institutions, including schools, churches, and communities, and they voted in great numbers. Emancipation was the law everywhere, but systematic separation of the races soon became reality under what came to be known as the **Jim Crow** system. Following the war, legislatures in the South immediately enacted **Black Codes** and other laws intended to force racial **segregation** and ensure the **disenfranchisement** of black voters. The Confederacy was defeated, but a new brand of racist oppression was forming. Fortunately, the United States Congress, with a mandate from the American people, established **Congressional Reconstruction**, including the **Fourteenth and Fifteenth Amendments**, the **Civil Rights Acts of 1866 and 1875**, and associated **Enforcement Acts.** For a little more than a decade, African Americans were free to vote and to build new lives.

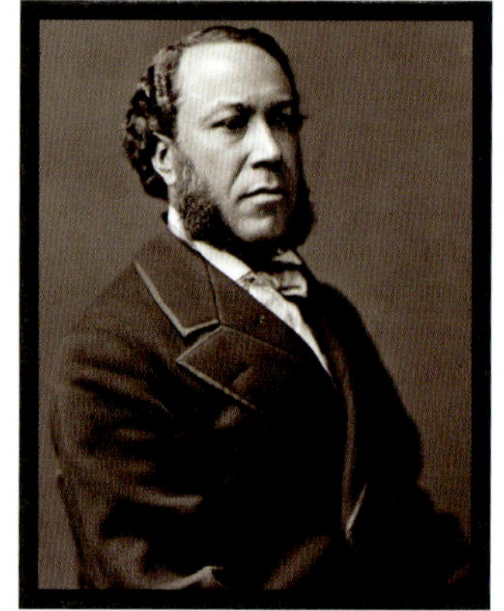

Joseph H. Rainey (1832–1887). First African American elected to the U.S. House of Representatives (1870–1879). Library of Congress, LC-DIG-cwpbh-04424.

But with every law passed by Congress and with every African American voted into the legislature, resentment and stubborn hatred brewed along many Main Streets, in church and civic meetings, and in the courthouses of the South. And it was during the decade of Reconstruction that the fanatic **Ku Klux Klan** crept from the shadows to terrorize the South's African-American population. With the **Compromise of 1877**, the fundamental gains of the past decade began to unravel. Shortly after 1877, black politicians like Joseph H. Rainey were abruptly voted out of office. At Southern voting polls, black Americans encountered new obstacles in the form of literacy tests, poll taxes, and various forms of fraud from vote rigging to vote stealing. In cities and small towns alike, a **color line** was established whereby black people were physically separated from whites in most public places, be it at the water fountain, the department store, or at school.

Through a deliberate and ruthless policy of oppression, white elites made life a nightmare for many blacks in the South. The **sharecropping** system—originally envisioned as the legal means by which blacks could claim a rightful stake in the economy—proved to be a trap in which people found themselves hopelessly in debt to landlords and merchants. Black men by

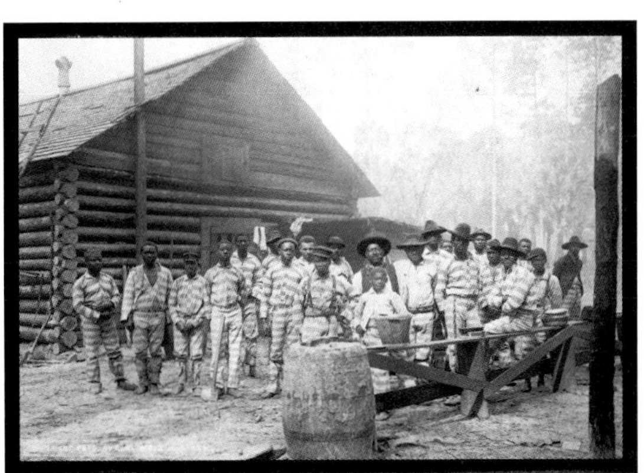

A Chain Gang, circa 1898. Photograph by Carl Weis. Library of Congress, LC-USZ6-1848.

the thousands found themselves incarcerated on prison farms, where they worked on brutal **chain gangs,** often leased out as cheap labor for local government contractors or friends of the warden. **Miscegenation laws** were also imposed in order to prohibit interracial marriages. Worst of all, the rate of racist intimidation and murder at the hands of the Ku Klux Klan increased dramatically beginning in the 1880s. The horror of lynching, an evil suffered by roughly 5,000 African Americans (between 1882 and 1968), is not possible to describe adequately in decent terms. The history of lynching is well documented, in writing and photographically; indeed, drugstores in southern towns used to sell souvenir postcards of lynchings featuring photos and flippant, degrading captions or poems. The act often involved a large mob of white people and at least one, often several, black victims. Sometimes the victims were accused of terrible crimes, and sometimes they were bound, tortured, and hung with little or no justification other than racist hatred.

Just before the turn of the century, in 1896, the Supreme Court ruled in the case of ***Plessy v. Ferguson*** that racially segregated railroad cars (and, by extension, all public facilities) were legal as long as they were of equal quality. The policy of "separate but equal" was applied to nearly all public institutions and facilities, but it was in the schools that the policy was revealed as a disaster and a sham. All-black public schools were systematically starved of funds and resources, with predictable results.

Of course, African Americans were by no means defenseless or helpless during these troubled years. The people fighting for the rights of African Americans following the Civil War were many of the same people from the Abolition Movement, including Frederick Douglass, Harriet Tubman, Sojourner Truth, and Frances Harper. These experienced, influential activists were joined by new voices—Booker T. Washington, Ida B. Wells-Barnett, W. E. B. Du Bois, and others who helped light the way for the movers and shakers of the twentieth century. One way to counter the inequities of "separate but equal" public facilities was for black people to build their own separate institutions independent from local and state governments. Scores of **African-American colleges and universities** emerged, including Tuskegee Institute, Howard University, and Hampton Institute. Gradually, with the dawning of the twentieth century, African Americans made steady progress on the road to equality, creating and fortifying the institutions and grass-roots organizations that would eventually become powerful groups like the **National Association for the Advancement of Colored People (NAACP).**

But America's racial divide was deep. Every positive action by or on behalf of African Americans was countered by racist reaction. The incredible success of the movie ***The Birth of a Nation*** (1915), which shamelessly smeared African Americans by exploiting every conceivable negative and degrading racial stereotype, shows the sort of challenges and obstacles faced by African-American writers, intellectuals, artists, and activists of the early-twentieth century.

A Glossary of Key Terms and Events from The History of Jim Crow

By Dr. Ronald L. F. Davis

Jim Crow: A term describing the American racist culture against blacks, it originated as a derogatory way of depicting black people in the minstrel shows of early nineteenth-century America. Thomas Dartmouth "Daddy" Rice popularized the term by marking his face with burned cork or a charcoal paste (known as blackface), dressing in sloppy clothes, and dancing a silly jig while grinning broadly. Historian Charles Reagan Wilson, director of the Center for the Study of Southern Culture at the University of Mississippi, claims that Rice was inspired by the performance he had seen in Louisville, Kentucky, by an elderly slave owned by a Mr. Crow. By 1860, the term was a common part of the nation's vocabulary. Abolitionist speakers used the term in the 1840s to describe segregated railroad cars for blacks and whites: the northern black cars were Jim Crow cars. On the eve of the Civil War, the universal image of the silly Jim Crow minstrel character provided southern whites with one of many stereotypical images of black inferiority that were a fundamental component of white popular culture. By the 1890s, the term had come to mean the separation of blacks from whites and the general customs and laws that subordinated blacks as an inferior people. Historians have used the term in reference to the process of segregation or setting the races apart—sometimes meaning customary or informal segregation and sometimes meaning legal or codified segregation.

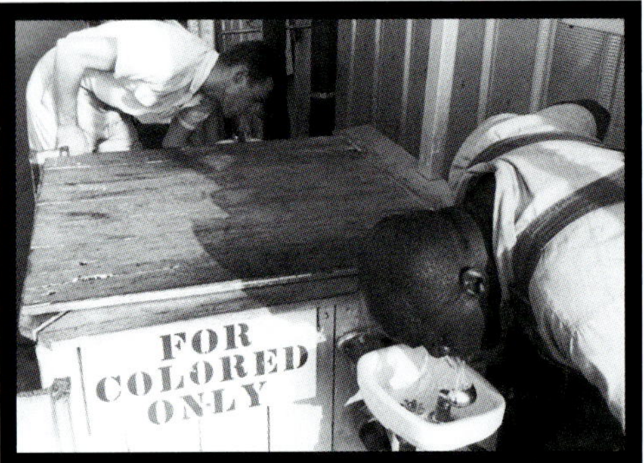

Segregated drinking fountain in use in the American South, circa 1950.

Disenfranchisement: The move by militant southern Democrats in 1890 to systematically and legally end black voting. To circumvent the 15th Amendment—which explicitly forbids the denial of votes on "account of race, color, or previous condition of servitude" —white racists rewrote state constitutions by adopting complex voting requirements that—without mentioning race—disfranchised black voters. Mississippi set the pace in 1890 with a set of disfranchisement measures that required proof of residency, payment of a poll tax, no criminal convictions, and literacy tests, which whites were allowed to pass if they understood the State Constitution when read to them. Louisiana introduced the grandfather clause in 1898, which stated that only men who had been eligible to vote before 1867, or whose fathers or grandfathers had been eligible to vote prior to that year, were qualified to vote. This obviously excluded virtually all black males. Some states also passed the so-called "white primary," which limited voting in the Democratic Party primaries to whites. These measures taken together eliminated the black vote from southern politics.

Black Codes: (1865–1867) Laws and proclamations restricting the civil rights of the formerly enslaved African Americans that were passed in most southern states at the end of the Civil War. The harshest provisions used vagrancy and apprenticeship laws to bind the freedmen to the land, limiting their personal freedom and relegating them to a status similar to serfs in Eastern Europe. The U.S. Congress reacted to these laws by imposing military rule over the South and passing civil rights legislation. The Codes also energized the drive for the 14th and 15th Amendments to the U.S. Constitution, extending citizenship to all African Americans and suffrage to black males.

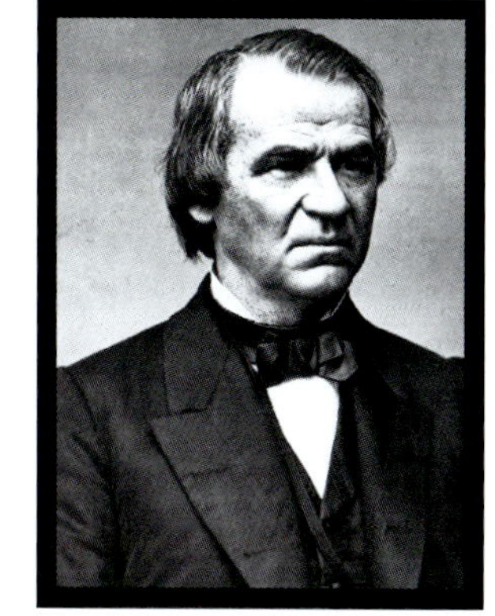

Andrew Johnson (1808–1875), U.S. President 1865–1869. Escaped impeachment by one vote. Library of Congress, LC-USZ62-13017.

Congressional Reconstruction: (1866–1876) A plan imposed on southern states by the U.S. Congress out of anger over white attacks on African Americans, the passage of so-called "Black Codes" limiting freedom for blacks, and President Andrew Johnson's mild program of Reconstruction. According to this plan, Congress refused to accept senators and representatives elected from southern states; passed the 14th Amendment to the U.S. Constitution, granting citizenship to African Americans and ensuring that they were counted in the population for representation in the House of Representatives; restricted supporters of the Confederacy in state and Federal government from holding office; and made accepting the 14th Amendment a prerequisite to congressional recognition of a state's representatives and senators. Initially, all the southern state legislatures except Tennessee voted against the amendment, but it finally passed in 1868. To enforce its authority, Congress placed military commanders with Federal troops in charge of the former Confederate states. It also required the former Confederate states to rewrite their constitutions so as to protect the civil rights of blacks, and it passed the 15th Amendment to the U.S. Constitution, which guaranteed suffrage for African-American males. This amendment was ratified by the states in 1870.

Civil Rights Act of 1866: The law bestowing citizenship upon African Americans and passed over President Andrew Johnson's veto. It spelled out the civil rights granted to all persons born in the U.S. (except Native Americans), including the right to make and enforce contracts, to sue and give evidence, and to inherit, purchase, and convey real and personal property. It did not apply, however, to state segregation statutes. Nor did it mention the state rights of blacks regarding public education or public accommodations. Due to the racial violence, the Ku Klux Klan, and the political upheaval of the era, it failed to protect the civil rights of the formerly enslaved people of the South.

Civil Rights Act of 1875: A law passed on March 1, 1875, that guaranteed equal rights for blacks in public places and made illegal the exclusion of African Americans from jury duty. However, the Supreme Court declared this act invalid in 1883 because it protected social rather than political rights. The court also argued that the 14th Amendment prohibited the states from depriving individuals of their civil rights but did not protect the abuse of individuals' civil rights by other individuals. This ruling ended Federal protection of African Americans against discrimination by private persons.

Enforcement Acts: In response to the terrorist attacks by whites, such as those by the Ku Klux Klan, on black and white Republicans in the South during Reconstruction, Congress passed a set of three laws known as the Enforcement Acts on May 31, 1870; February 28, 1871; and April 20, 1871. These acts made illegal the intimidation of voters, "going in disguise upon the public highway" with the intent of denying a citizen his constitutional rights, and the failure to perform one's duty as an election officer. The third Act provided for Federal supervision of elections in both northern and southern cities with a population of over 20,000. Thousands of people were arrested under the provisions of these acts, but the conviction rates were small—for instance, less than 15 percent of the 1,500 people arrested in South Carolina. Moreover, sentences were usually mild. In the end, these Acts did help break up the Klan; however, most scholars contend that there was little need for the Klan after 1876 when Reconstruction ended because disfranchisement could be obtained by economic, political, and legal intimidation in the open and in broad daylight.

Ku Klux Klan: A secret society whose ultimate goal is to establish white supremacy. Founded in 1866 in Pulaski, Tennessee, the Ku Klux Klan intimidated, assaulted, and murdered African Americans and white Republicans (carpetbaggers and Union League members).

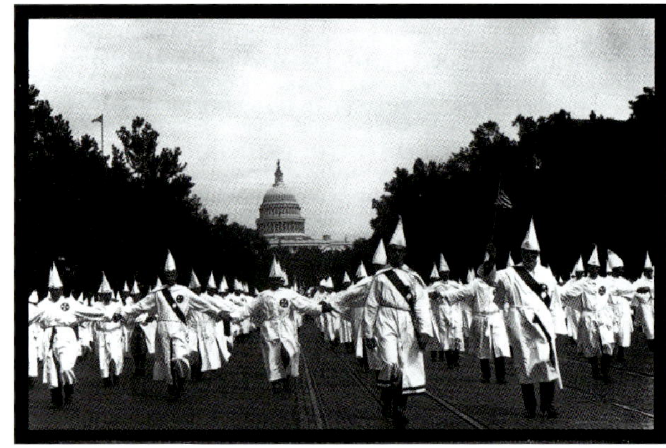

Members of the Ku Klux Klan, a hate group, hold a march in Washington, D.C., on August 9, 1925.

Compromise of 1877: A deal regarding the presidency in the election of 1876. In the election, neither of the two presidential candidates, Rutherford B. Hayes (Republican) and Samuel J. Tilden (Democrat), won the required majority of the Electoral College vote. Tilden held the majority of the popular vote (4,282,020 to 4,036,572) as well as a 20-vote lead in the Electoral College (184 to 165). Twenty votes were in dispute because of fraud and violence in Florida, Louisiana, and South Carolina. (Oregon's electoral eligibility left that state's vote uncounted as well.) Tilden needed one vote and Hayes needed 20 to achieve the necessary majority. In absence of a constitutional provision for resolving the dilemma, Congress created an Electoral Commission consisting of five members each from the House, Senate, and Supreme Court. Behind-the-scenes negotiations produced congressional approval of an eight-to-seven vote (along party lines) in favor of Hayes. According to the informal terms of the deal, the South would accept Hayes as President; the appointment of Republican James A. Garfield as Speaker of the House; protection of black civil rights in return for Federal aid to create internal improvements in the South; the patronage appointment of Democrats to Federal offices; and the return of home rule to the white South . . . meaning the end of Reconstruction. Although Garfield was defeated as Speaker of the House, all Federal troops were withdrawn from the former states of the Confederacy. In a brief time, all the remaining Republican governments in the South collapsed and the "Solid Democratic South" emerged—allowing, thereafter, for the disfranchisement of black voters by means of law and violence.

Sharecropping: (1866–1955) When the federal government refused to confiscate and redistribute the lands of ex-Confederates to the formerly enslaved, a new system of agricultural labor emerged known as sharecropping. Landless farmers contracted to work the land for a share of the crop as their wages, using the remaining shares to pay rent and supplies. In time, most southern states passed "crop lien" laws that gave the merchant suppliers first claim to the crops of those working on shares over the claims of landlords. This crop lien enabled merchants to ensnare black sharecroppers and tenants into a system of debt and high interest rates from which there was virtually no escape. Those croppers who fled from their debts to the merchants rather than carrying over the debt to the next crop could be prosecuted in criminal courts. Black farmers who rented the land, called tenants, also became entrapped in the debt system because they had to give crop liens in order to obtain credit for seed, mules, tools and supplies. Most "furnishing merchants" insisted that sharecroppers and tenants grow only cotton on their lands rather than cultivating less lucrative food crops.

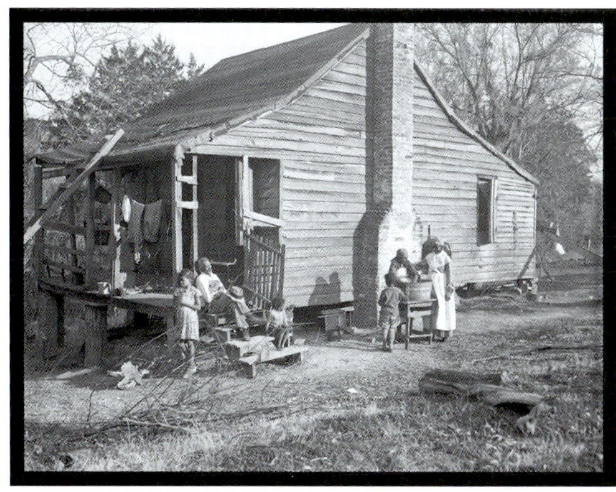

An African-American family in the yard of a former slave shack, 1938. The two women are washing clothes. Former slave Horace Bailey, age 85, rests on the porch.

Chain Gangs and Convict Leasing: Practices used by the states to put prisoners to work and, at times, save money. Toward the end of Reconstruction, nearly every state in the former Confederacy turned to leasing out prisoners convicted of property crimes to private businesses, such as railroads, planters, mine owners, and lumber yards. These unregulated convict farms and gangs were the scenes of horrible inhumanity. And, the barbarities in such camps were tolerated principally because those who were abused were black. The death rate in the camps was staggering. Historian Joel Williamson notes that in Texas, the rate of death per 1,000 prisoners stood at 250 in the timber camps, compared to 25 per 1,000 in the nation as a whole. Some states and county governments worked the convicts in chain gangs on roads, bridges, and other public projects. This system provided the state with the maximum amount of punishment at the lowest possible cost.

Color Line: A barrier or non-physical wall, usually created by custom or economic differences, to separate nonwhite persons from white persons. In the 1890s, this customary barrier in the southern states of America became a legal line of separation with laws stating clearly where blacks could and could not go in public spaces. By the turn of the century, African Americans were confronted with "colored" signs on doors, water fountains, bathrooms, and in bus and train stations telling them where they could or could not stand, sit, eat, or walk. The "colored" sign was the most visible mark of inferiority imposed upon African Americans by the Jim Crow laws. The color line also existed in the midwestern and northeastern states, but it was not so clearly marked and was seldom enforced by law.

Miscegenation: A term referring to the intermarriage of persons of different races. Local and state laws often forbade interracial marriages in the antebellum South, and custom strongly frowned upon any such relationships between the races. Census enumerators usually listed light-skinned slaves and free blacks as mulattoes, meaning the offspring of white and black parents. The number of mulattoes in the South was very high on the eve of the Civil War, perhaps the majority of slaves in some regions. Many of these people were the children of light-skinned slaves and dark-skinned slaves; many were the offspring of mulatto parents; and many were the products of interracial relations. After the Civil War, the term *miscegenation* started being used as a derogatory word covering the whole range of mixed racial offspring, and the word *mulatto* was dropped from the vocabulary and from the census. Instead, census takers listed any and all light-skinned African Americans as simply "Negro." The Reconstruction governments removed the bans on interracial marriages, but many southern states reinstated these laws after 1876, and some states even wrote anti-miscegenation provisions into their state constitutions.

Plessy v. Ferguson: The 1896 Supreme Court case in which the Court upheld a Louisiana law requiring segregated railroad facilities as long as such facilities were equal to each other. The Court essentially ruled that segregation did not constitute discrimination, thus establishing the "separate but equal" doctrine that was practiced until the *Brown v. Board* decision in 1954.

African-American Colleges and Universities: Institutions of higher education established for African Americans. Many were established from Reconstruction to 1900, including Howard University in Washington, D.C., Fisk University, Atlanta University, Clark University, Alcorn State University, Bethune-Cookman College, Hampton Institute, Richmond Theological Seminary, Tuskegee Institute, and Langston University in Oklahoma. Most of these were vocational schools such as teachers' colleges and schools of agriculture. They also offered some courses in the sciences and the liberal arts. In general, the so-called "Tuskegee Model" of industrial education, endorsed by Booker T. Washington, competed with a more academically oriented curriculum for blacks at the turn of the century. W. E. B. Du Bois, one of the critics of the industrial model within the African-American community, argued that the industrial model failed to educate blacks as leaders because it did not educate them in the liberal arts, sciences, and professional disciplines.

The Birth of a Nation: A silent film released in 1915 by D. W. Griffith, widely acclaimed as a cinematic masterpiece, it stands today as a symbol of extreme racism. It depicted the domination of the South during the Reconstruction years by an immoral and ignorant black population unfit for freedom. The Ku Klux Klan saved the day by rescuing white women from the debauchery of crazed black troops. The film won wide audience approval, grossing $18 million ($300 million in 2006 dollars). President Wilson praised the film, while the NAACP condemned it. In some communities, white filmgoers attacked blacks after seeing the film.

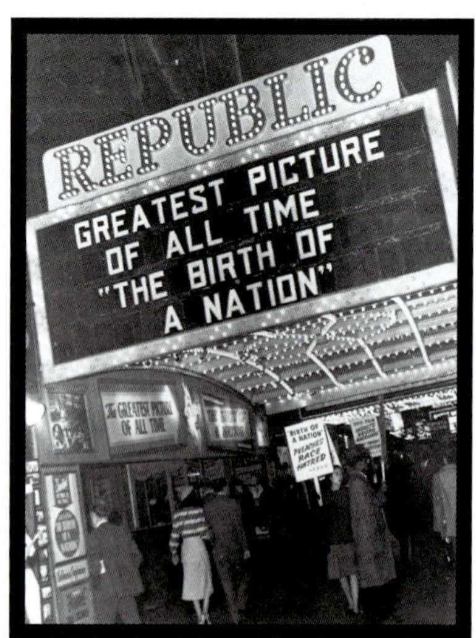

NAACP picket outside theatre protesting movie *The Birth of a Nation,* 1947.

After a decade of hopeful improvements following the Civil War, economic, social, and political conditions rapidly deteriorated for African Americans, particularly in the South. However, in the rest of the country, from the North to California, the period from 1870 to the 1900s was a time of great prosperity. Indeed, such vast fortunes were made—particularly by "captains of industry" like John D. Rockefeller, J. P. Morgan, and Andrew Carnegie, and their many business associates—that Mark Twain called it the Gilded Age, during which the nation experienced extraordinary economic, industrial, territorial, and population growth. African Americans migrated in huge numbers, mainly to urban centers in the North, "toward the larger and the more democratic chance," as Alain Locke wrote in his preface to *The New Negro* (see page 290). By the 1920s, many cities in the North were home to vibrant, thriving African-American communities.

Major Events, 1863–1936

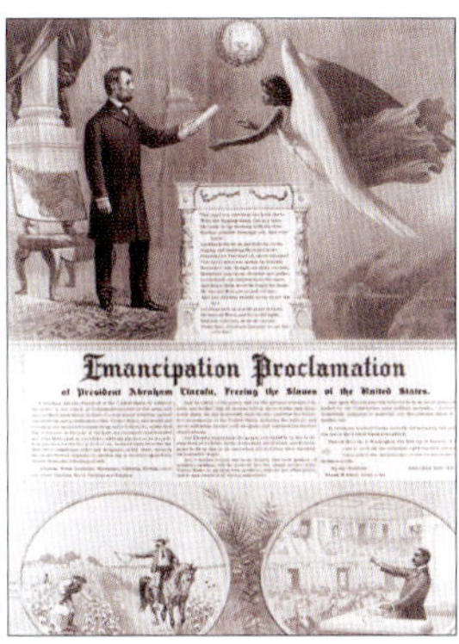

1863

- **The Emancipation Proclamation.** Lincoln's document legally frees slaves in states in rebellion against the United States.
- **New York City Draft Riots.** Hundreds of black Americans killed or injured during riots protesting inequities in draft laws, as many recent European immigrants protest having to fight a war on behalf of black people and the ability of rich people to buy their way out of service.
- **Sergeant William H. Carney** of the all-black 54th Massachusetts Infantry Regiment becomes the first African American to receive the Congressional Medal of Honor for heroic deeds during the assault on Fort Wagner, South Carolina.

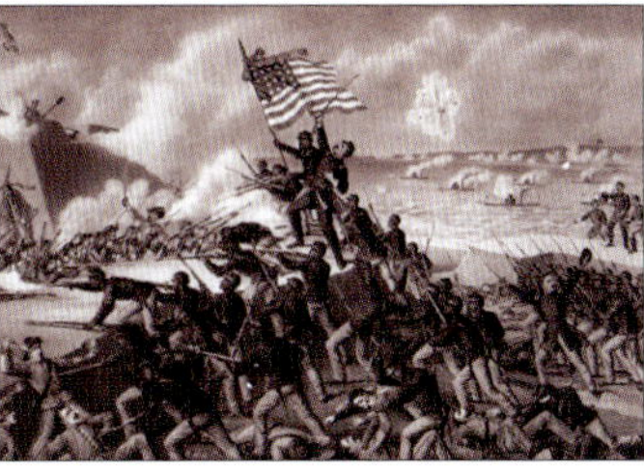

1865

- April 7, the Civil War ends when **General Robert E. Lee** surrenders to **Ulysses S. Grant** at **Appomattox Court House**, Virginia.
- December 18, Congress ratifies the **Thirteenth Amendment** to the Constitution, outlawing slavery.
- **Black Codes** are passed, restricting the rights of newly freed African Americans.
- The **Freedmen's Bureau** is established to provide assistance to emancipated slaves.

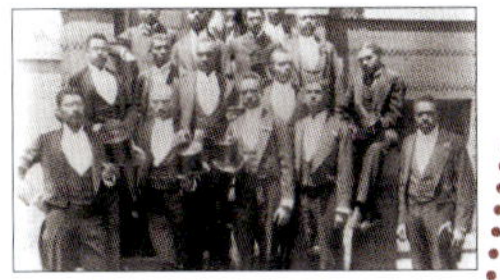

1867

- **Howard University** is founded in Washington, D.C., to provide education for newly emancipated slaves.

1870

- **Fifteenth Amendment** to the Constitution is ratified, prohibiting the use of race, color, or previous enslavement as a voting qualification.

1863 1864 1865 1866 1867 1869 1870 1877

1864

- ***The New Orleans Tribune***, one of the first daily newspapers produced by African Americans, begins publication.

1866

- **The Fourteenth Amendment** to the Constitution is ratified, granting citizenship to freed slaves and providing due process and equal protection under the law to all citizens.

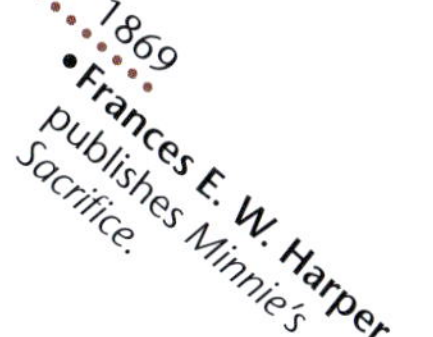

1869

- **Frances E. W. Harper** publishes *Minnie's Sacrifice.*

1877

- **The Compromise of 1877.** Promising to withdraw federal troops from the South in exchange for the presidency, Rutherford B. Hayes ends Reconstruction and federal efforts to protect African Americans' civil rights.

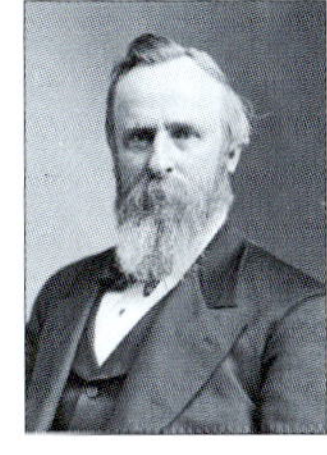

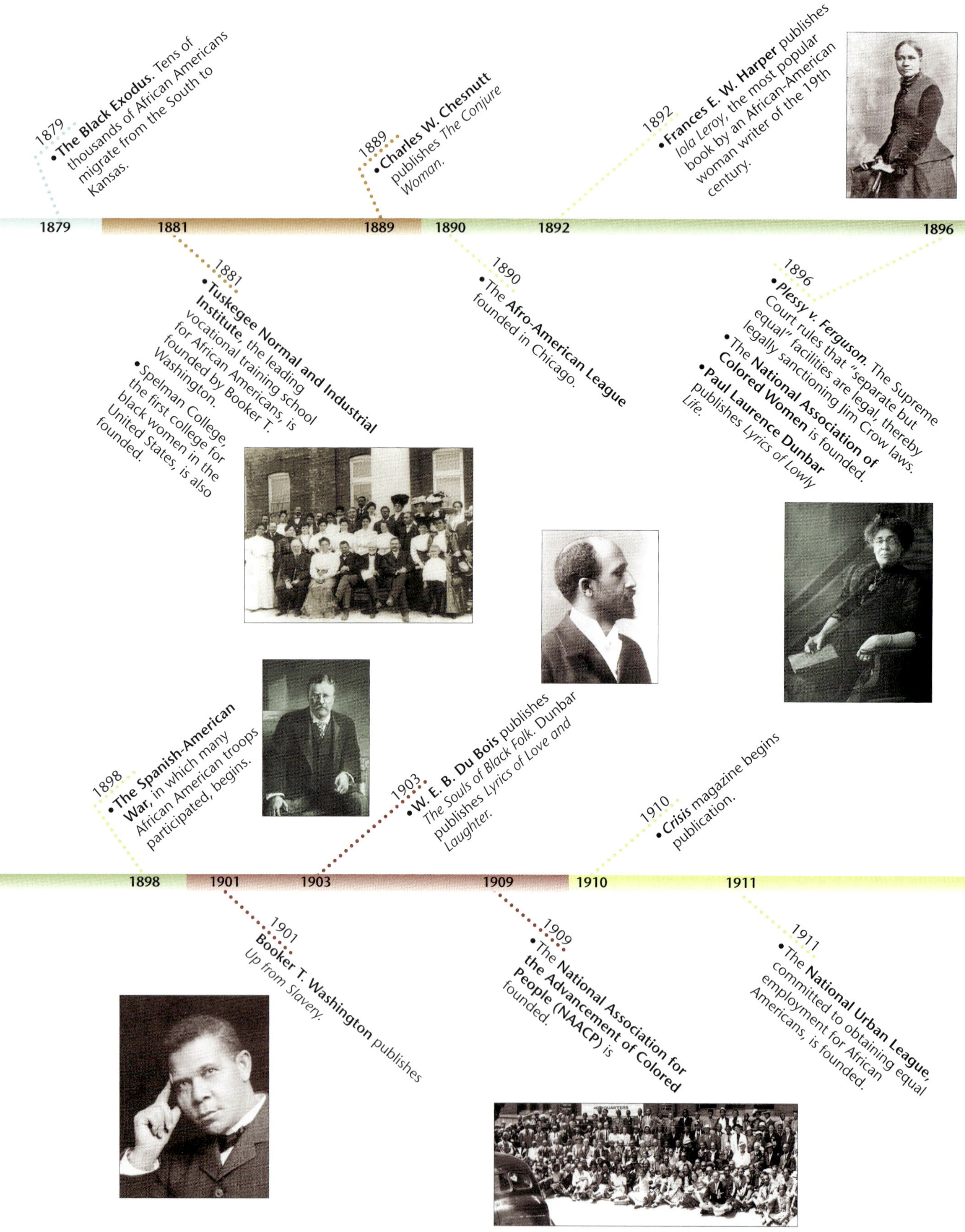

1879
1881
1889
1890
1892
1896
1879
• **The Black Exodus.** Tens of thousands of African Americans migrate from the South to Kansas.
1881
• **Tuskegee Normal and Industrial Institute**, the leading vocational training school for African Americans, is founded by Booker T. Washington.
• Spelman College, the first college for black women in the United States, is also founded.
1889
• **Charles W. Chesnutt** publishes *The Conjure Woman.*
1890
• The **Afro-American League** founded in Chicago.
1892
• **Frances E. W. Harper** publishes *Iola Leroy*, the most popular book by an African-American woman writer of the 19th century.
1896
• ***Plessy v. Ferguson.*** The Supreme Court rules that "separate but equal" facilities are legal, thereby legally sanctioning Jim Crow laws.
• The **National Association of Colored Women** is founded.
• **Paul Laurence Dunbar** publishes *Lyrics of Lowly Life.*
1898
1901
1903
1909
1910
1911
1898
• **The Spanish-American War,** in which many African American troops participated, begins.
1901
Booker T. Washington publishes *Up from Slavery.*
1903
• **W. E. B. Du Bois** publishes *The Souls of Black Folk.* Dunbar publishes *Lyrics of Love and Laughter.*
1909
• The **National Association for the Advancement of Colored People (NAACP)** is founded.
1910
• ***Crisis*** magazine begins publication.
1911
• The **National Urban League,** committed to obtaining equal employment for African Americans, is founded.

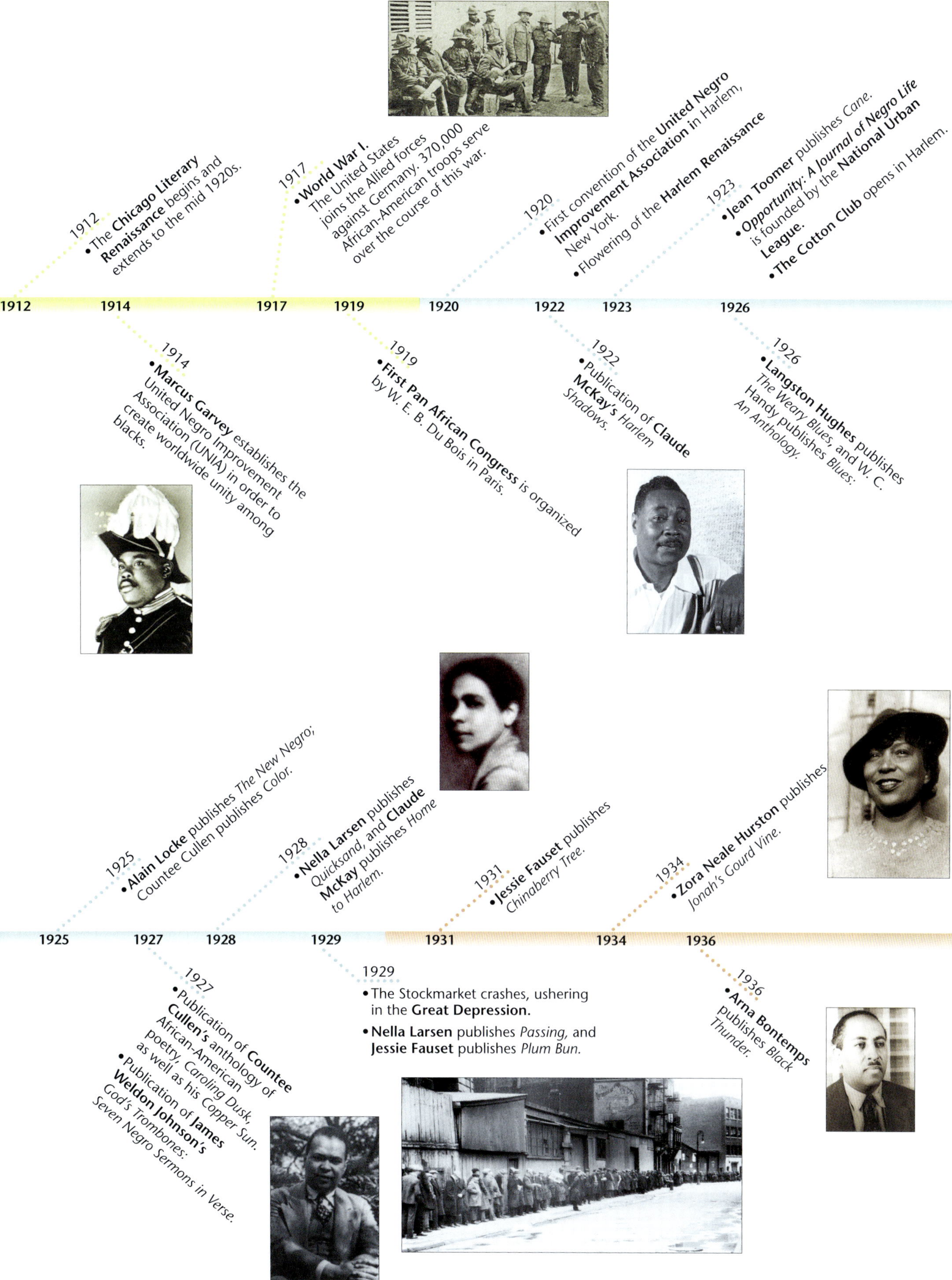

1912
- The **Chicago Literary Renaissance** begins and extends to the mid 1920s.

1914
- **Marcus Garvey** establishes the United Negro Improvement Association (UNIA) in order to create worldwide unity among blacks.

1917
- **World War I.** The United States joins the Allied forces against Germany. 370,000 African-American troops serve over the course of this war.

1919
- **First Pan African Congress** is organized by W. E. B. Du Bois in Paris.

1920
- First convention of the **United Negro Improvement Association** in Harlem, New York.
- Flowering of the **Harlem Renaissance**

1922
- Publication of **Claude McKay's** *Harlem Shadows.*

1923
- **Jean Toomer** publishes *Cane.*
- ***Opportunity: A Journal of Negro Life*** is founded by the **National Urban League.**
- **The Cotton Club** opens in Harlem.

1926
- **Langston Hughes** publishes *The Weary Blues*, and W. C. Handy publishes *Blues: An Anthology.*

1912 1914 1917 1919 1920 1922 1923 1926

1925
- **Alain Locke** publishes *The New Negro;* Countee Cullen publishes *Color.*

1927
- Publication of **Countee Cullen's** anthology of African-American poetry, *Caroling Dusk,* as well as his *Copper Sun.*
- Publication of **James Weldon Johnson's** *God's Trombones: Seven Negro Sermons in Verse.*

1928
- **Nella Larsen** publishes *Quicksand*, and **Claude McKay** publishes *Home to Harlem.*

1929
- The Stockmarket crashes, ushering in the **Great Depression.**
- **Nella Larsen** publishes *Passing*, and **Jessie Fauset** publishes *Plum Bun.*

1931
- **Jessie Fauset** publishes *Chinaberry Tree.*

1934
- **Zora Neale Hurston** publishes *Jonah's Gourd Vine.*

1936
- **Arna Bontemps** publishes *Black Thunder.*

1925 1927 1928 1929 1931 1934 1936

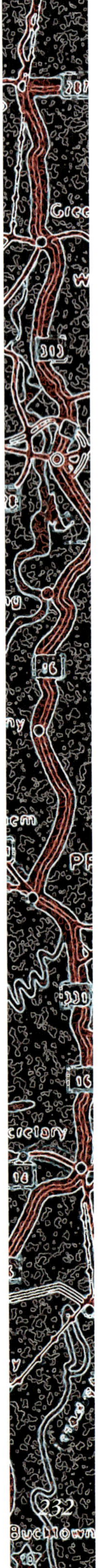

Prereading

from *Harriet Tubman: Conductor on the Underground Railroad*

by Ann Petry

The following selection is "Chapter 5: The Flight," from a historical novel—or biographical narrative—that Ann Petry wrote about the amazing life of **Harriet Tubman** (1820–1913). (See the Understanding Literature on page 239 for more information about historical novels and biographical narratives.)

Published in 1955 and intended for adolescent readers, Petry's novel tells the story of Tubman's entire life. All the major events in the book are true, yet it is a fictionalized account of Tubman's life because the author invented certain elements, such as dialogue and details of the setting, in order to make the novel exciting and informative for a young audience. Indeed, the book is a true "page-turner" because Tubman led such an exciting life. The job of a historical novelist is to do such thorough research that he or she can portray the historical time and place accurately.

Most readers are probably familiar with Harriet Tubman. She was the most famous conductor on the **Underground Railroad**—a network formed by Abolitionists in order to help enslaved persons escape to freedom in the North. After her own escape to freedom in 1849, Tubman quickly became active on the Underground Railroad. She made her first expedition in 1851, and by the start of the Civil War, she had helped roughly 300 slaves escape to freedom, including her own parents! She was never caught, despite enormous rewards placed on her head by slave owners.

The selection you are about to read provides a window into Harriet Tubman's early life. In a later chapter of the book, Petry penned the following passage to describe Tubman's reputation:

The slaves said that she could see in the dark like a mule, that she could smell danger down the wind like a fox, that she could move through the thick underbrush without making a sound, like a field mouse. They said, voice muted, awed, that she talked every day with God, just like Moses.

Little wonder it is, then, that Tubman was called "The Moses of Her People," after the Biblical patriarch who led the Israelites out of bondage in Egypt.

Chapter 5: The Flight

by Ann Petry

Every night in the quarter,[1] after the children were asleep, Old Rit and Ben talked about Harriet. Old Rit started the conversation.

"What's going to happen to Minty?"[2] she asked.

Ben stirred under the ragged quilt, and then turned over. "You have to trust in the Lord, Rit. He'll take care of her."

Rit ignored his reply. "Here she is back on the plantation again. She's seven years old and she hasn't learned anything special. You know the Master isn't going to keep her around here, just kicking up her heels and eating her head off. What'll happen to her?"

How do they know that things are not going well on the plantation? Why is the trader's presence a bad sign?

This time Ben did not answer. They both knew things weren't going well with the master. He needed money. He was hiring out more and more of his slaves. He was selling more and more of them each year. The plantation was beginning to have a ragged, uncared for look. The fences were down. Honeysuckle and bull briar were slowly taking over the big fields. The outbuildings needed repair.

Rit touched Ben on the arm, lightly, to attract his attention. Then she whispered, "The trader's back in Cambridge again. He's got the big front room at the tavern. Less than two months and he's back again. He didn't used to come so often."

She waited for Ben to say something, to reassure her. He knew just as she did that when the trader got ready to leave, some of the master's prime hands were sure to go with him. Well, not exactly with him. They'd go with the chain gang, walking down that long, terrible road that ended in New Orleans or Natchez, chained two by two, and another chain down through the middle of the group, and each slave chained to that, too. She'd heard the white folks call it a coffle or drove, but to her it was always simply the chain gang.

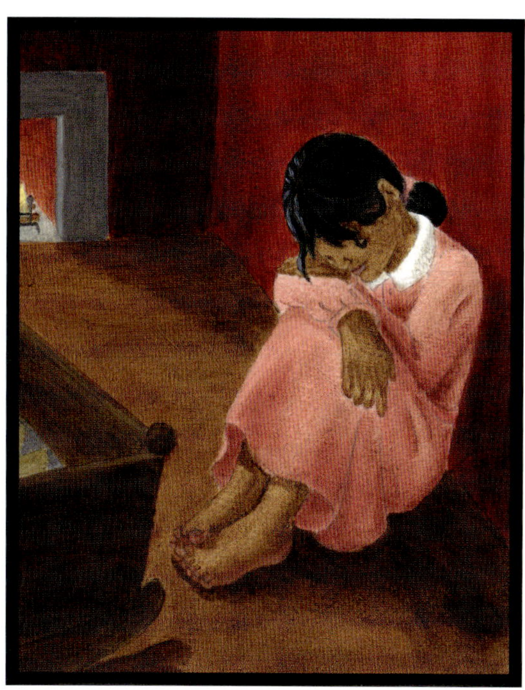

[1] **the quarter.** Short for *slave quarters,* where the enslaved workers lived

[2] **Minty.** Harriet's nickname

"Nothing's going to happen to Minty," Old Ben said, sharply. "I'll see that it don't."

The sharpness in his voice told her that he was thinking about the chain gang too, and remembering their two little ones, just about the size of Minty, who had gone away like that. One minute they had been carrying water to the field hands, and the next minute they were in a lot with the other slaves that had been sold, sort of thrown in for good measure, and then—gone—gone with the chain gang.

But there's nothing Ben can do, she thought. He can try, of course. But the trader had a reputation for driving a hard bargain, and if the master needed the money, and one extra child meant a slightly better price for the lot—why, even Ben wouldn't be able to stop the sale.

Rit gave a long sigh. "I wish the old days were back again. The days when the Master was rich and just raised tobacco, just nothing but tobacco. And everybody worked. Even the little slaves helped squash those fat juicy hornworms that get on the backside of the tobacco leaves. And everybody had plenty to eat and we all felt safe. In the old days the Master never sold off any of his slaves. Everybody knew that and—"

Were Rit and Ben enslaved in the "old days"? Why were things better then?

Ben agreed with her. "Yes," he said slowly, "things was better then. It seems like they seesaw more now. He grows a little cotton, and he grows a little wheat, and he grows a little corn. Then maybe there's too much rain, or maybe not enough rain, so the crop's no good. Now he's selling the big timber off to the shipbuilders. Pretty soon there won't be any more of them big stands of oaks. We keep hacking 'em down, day after day we're hacking 'em down. What's he going to do when his timber's gone?"

"You know what he's going to do," Rit said impatiently. "He's going to keep on raising slaves and selling them off. He gets enough money just from that. He don't have to bother to have his land worked any more. He's just living off his slaves."

Living off his slaves, she thought, and little Minty doesn't know how to cook or sew, and the slave trader is in Cambridge—and maybe tomorrow he'll be riding out here.

What does Rit mean when she says that the "master" is "living off his slaves"? Why is this bad for a girl like Minty?

"Oh Ben," she said, "What's going to happen to Minty?"

"I guess maybe we just better pray to the good Lord to look out for her," he said. "We just better pray—"

A few days later, Harriet was hired out again, as a child's nurse. Rit said, "May the Lord be praised, it's an answer to my prayer, to my prayer. May the Lord be praised."

Once again, Harriet, the small girl in the tow-linen[3] shirt, barefooted, feet not touching the floor of the wagon, sat listening to the clop-clop of horses' hoofs, listening to the creak of a wagon that was carrying her farther and farther away from home.

Her forehead was wrinkled by a frown because she kept thinking: Where am I going this time? How long will it take to get there? Why do I have to go anywhere?

Suppose she didn't like the people. What could she do about it? She wouldn't know how to get back home.

Finally the wagon stopped in front of a big house. She never did know where it was located, near what town, how far away from

[3] **tow-linen.** A coarse form of cloth, woven from flax and, in the case of slave clothing, left unbleached

the Brodas plantation. But she soon knew what she was supposed to do. She looked after Miss Susan's baby and helped with the housework, too. It wasn't a big family, just Miss Susan and her husband, and the baby, and Miss Emily, a sister of Miss Susan's who was visiting.

That first morning, Miss Susan told her to go and sweep the parlor and dust it. Harriet was awed by the room. There was a thick carpet on the floor, soft and springy under her feet, like walking on layers of pine needles, and there were so many different kinds of chairs and tables, and the wood around the fireplace was carved into a pattern. She'd never seen anything like it.

She swept as hard as she could, and then immediately dusted all the dark shiny wood of the furniture.

Miss Susan said, "Have you finished?" and came in to run her fingers over the shiny surface of the chairs and tables. Her fingers were coated with dust. "Do it again," she snapped. "Are you just plain stupid? Why, you haven't dusted in here at all. You do it right—or—"

Harriet swept again, and then dusted, getting more and more frightened. Miss Susan said it wasn't done properly and went and got a whip and kept whipping her and shouting at her; and Harriet screamed.

She heard a voice calling, "Susan! Susan! What are you doing? What is the matter?"

Miss Emily had heard the screams and came downstairs, protesting, "Why do you whip the child, Susan, for not doing what she has never been taught to do? Leave her to me a few minutes, and you will see that she will soon learn how to sweep and dust a room."

Why does Miss Emily interfere? How does Susan usually treat Harriet?

Harriet learned how to clean the house. She looked after the baby, too. In later life, she said, "I was so little that I had to sit on the floor and have the baby put in my lap. That baby was always in my lap except when it was asleep or its mother was feeding it."

Miss Susan said that the baby mustn't be allowed to cry. Harriet had to keep rocking it so it wouldn't cry. Every night the same thing happened. She sat on the floor and rocked the cradle back and forth, back and forth, until the baby went to sleep. Then her head dropped, her eyelids closed, her hand started slipping, slipping, slipping away from the dark polished wood of the cradle. Finally she slept, on the floor, by the cradle.

Then the baby would wail, suddenly, a thin, high, piercing sound. Miss Susan would wake up, furious, and reach for the whip she kept on a little shelf behind her bed.

Harriet finally reached a point in exhaustion where she was past needing sleep, where she snatched it in brief moments, head nodding, eyes closed, and yet not really asleep, prepared to start rocking the cradle before the baby woke up and cried.

Even so, sometimes she went sound asleep, to be awakened by the wailing of the baby. She was whipped so often that the back of her neck was covered with scars, crisscrossed with scars, so deep that they would be visible for the rest of her life. Finally she learned to sleep without really going to sleep, learned to listen while still asleep, head nodding, eyes closed, but all her senses alerted to the slightest movement from the cradle, listening, listening, and yet asleep. So that if the baby stirred she started rocking the cradle.

How does Harriet manage to sleep and listen for the baby at the same time? Why does she have to do this?

She thought of running away, and didn't. She did not know how to reach the Brodas plantation, did not know in which direction to walk, assuming that she could have got away from the house. She had no idea how far it was. It had seemed an **interminable** journey when the overseer brought her to Miss Susan's in a wagon.

Sometimes Miss Susan and her husband went out to parties. Then there were **plumes** on Miss Susan's bonnet, and she wore a silk dress, soft, swishy, and embroidered petticoats[4] underneath, making a rustling sound when she walked. She smelled of orrisroot.[5] And the master would smile at Miss Susan, and toy with his watch chain.

On those nights, the baby cried and cried, while Harriet slept. Harriet slept and yet she was listening. Sound asleep but listening. Not for the baby. Ears straining, even in sleep, for the sound of footsteps on the stairs, not even footsteps, just the creak of the stairs, and she was awake, because it meant Miss Susan was coming home. Thus she learned to stay alert even though she was deeply, restfully asleep.

During the day, she toyed with the idea of running away. Then she would thrust the thought from her as impossible.

Yet she did run away. Years afterward, she described what happened in these words: "One morning, after breakfast, Miss Susan had the baby, and I stood by the table waiting until I was to take it; near me was a bowl of lumps of white sugar. My mistress got into a great quarrel with her husband; she had an awful temper, and she would scold and storm and call him all kinds of names.

"Now you know, I never had anything good, no sweet, no sugar; and that sugar, right by me, did look so nice, and my mistress's back was turned to me while she was fighting with her husband, so I just put my fingers in the sugar bowl to take one lump and maybe she heard me for she turned and saw me.

"The next minute she had the rawhide down. I give one jump out of the door and I saw that they came after me, but I just flew and they didn't catch me. I ran and I ran and I passed many a house, but I didn't dare to stop for they all knew my mistress and they would send me back."

She ran until she was exhausted. She kept looking over her shoulder. After a while she didn't see Miss Susan and her husband. She decided that they must have got tired and stopped chasing her. She slowed her pace, then at the thought of having to go back to Miss Susan and whatever form of punishment she and her husband would have devised, she started running again.

She said, "By and by when I was almost tuckered out, I came to a great big pigpen. There was an old sow there, and perhaps eight or ten little pigs. I was too little to climb into it, but I tumbled over the high part and fell in on the ground; I was so beaten out that I could not stir.

"And there I stayed from Friday until the next Tuesday, fighting with those little pigs for the potato peelings and the other scraps that came down in the trough. The old sow would push me away when I tried to get her children's food, and I was awfully afraid of her. By Tuesday I was so starved I knew I had to go back to my mistress. I didn't have anywhere else to go, even though I knew what was coming. So I went back." ■

How does Harriet survive after she runs away? Why does she finally return to Miss Susan?

---

[4] **embroidered petticoats.** A *petticoat* is a special garment that a woman wore beneath her skirt or dress to give it a fashionable shape. *Embroidery* is fancy needlework.

[5] **orrisroot.** *Orris* is a variety of *iris* flower; its fragrant roots are commonly used in perfumes.

VOCABULARY IN PLACE

- **interminable,** ***adj.*** Endless; being or seeming to be without end
- **plume,** ***n.*** A feather, especially a large showy one

History Connection

A Letter from a Formerly Enslaved Person to His Former "Master"

[*Editor's Note: The following letter, written in Dayton, Ohio, on August 7, 1865, after the end of the Civil War, was reprinted in the* New York Tribune *on August 22 of that same year. The letter was written by Jourdon Anderson, a former slave, to his former master, P. H. Anderson of Big Spring, Tennessee. In this letter Anderson mentions the sum of $11,680. By one measure, that sum is equal to $1,218,103 in 2004 dollars.*]

Sir:

I got your letter and was glad to find you had not forgotten Jourdon, and that you wanted me to come back and live with you again, promising to do better for me than anybody else can. I have often felt uneasy about you. I thought the Yankees would have hung you long before this for harboring Rebs they found at your house. I suppose they never heard about your going to Col. Martin's to kill the Union soldier that was left by his company in their stable. Although you shot at me twice before I left you, I did not want to hear of your being hurt, and am glad you are still living. It would do me good to go back to the dear old home again and see Miss Mary and Miss Martha and Allen, Esther, Green, and Lee. Give my love to them all, and tell them I hope we will meet in the better world, if not in this. I would have gone back to see you all when I was working in the Nashville hospital, but one of the neighbors told me Henry intended to shoot me if he ever got a chance.

As to my freedom, which you say I can have, there is nothing to be gained on that score, as I got my free-papers in 1864 from the Provost-Marshal-General of the Department of Nashville. Mandy says she would be afraid to go back without some proof that you are sincerely disposed to treat us justly and kindly—and we have concluded to test your sincerity by asking you to send us our wages for the time we served you. This will make us forget and forgive old scores, and rely on your justice and friendship in the future. I served you faithfully for thirty-two years and Mandy twenty years. At $25 a month for me, and $2 a week for Mandy, our earnings would amount to $11,680. Add to this the interest for the time our wages has been kept back and deduct what you paid for our clothing and three doctor's visits to me, and pulling a tooth for Mandy, and the balance will show what we are in justice entitled to. Please send the money by Adams Express, in care of V. Winters, esq, Dayton, Ohio. If you fail to pay us for faithful labors in the past we can have little faith in your promises in the future. We trust the good Maker has opened your eyes to the wrongs which you and your fathers have done to me and my fathers, in making us toil for you for generations without recompense. Here I draw my wages every Saturday night, but in Tennessee there was never any pay day for the Negroes any more than for the horses and cows. Surely there will be a day of reckoning for those who defraud the laborer of his hire.

In answering this letter please state if there would be any safety for my Milly and Jane, who are now grown up and both good-looking girls. You know how it was with Matilda and Catherine. I would rather stay here and starve and die if it comes to that than have my girls brought to shame by the violence and wickedness of their young masters. You will also please state if there has been any schools opened for the colored children in your neighborhood, the great desire of my life now is to give my children an education, and have them form virtuous habits.

P.S.—Say howdy to George Carter, and thank him for taking the pistol from you when you were shooting at me.

From your old servant, Jourdon Anderson

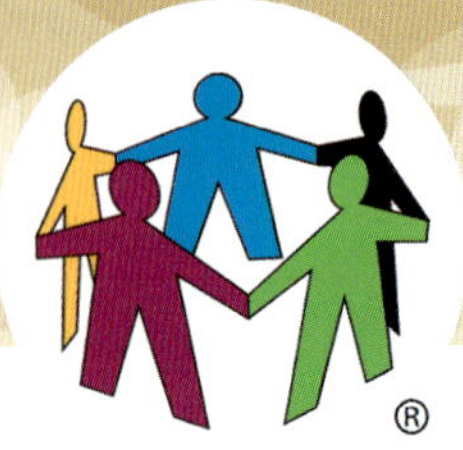

Understanding the Selection

Recalling

1. What are the signs that the plantation is in bad shape? How is the "master" managing to get the money he needs?
2. To whom is Harriet hired out?
3. Why does Miss Susan first whip Harriet?
4. What are some of the things that Harriet learns to do in order to get the sleep she needs without being whipped?
5. What finally prompts Harriet to run away? Where does she go, and how does she survive?

Interpreting

1. How do Rit and Ben know that the "master" does not intend to keep Harriet around? What are they afraid he will do?
2. Is Harriet accustomed to being hired out to other families?
3. What sort of person is Miss Susan? How does she treat Harriet?
4. What effect might a lack of sleep and constant mistreatment have on the personality and physical well-being of a seven-year-old girl?
5. Why does Harriet decide to return to Miss Susan in the end of the chapter? What do you think that Miss Susan does when Harriet returns?

Synthesizing

1. Why do Harriet's parents, Rit and Ben, have so much reason to worry about their daughter's future? Give at least two examples from the text to support your answer.
2. How might Harriet's experiences as a little girl have affected her later in life, both physically and mentally?

Delving Deeper

Understanding Literature

Historical Fiction. Historical fiction has become increasingly popular among readers and writers in recent years. The writer begins with a true event or historical period; often, at least some of the characters (whether major or minor, famous or obscure) are actual historical figures. The writer must then conduct research in order to portray accurately the story's setting and the characters' personalities. Then, creating dialogue and character actions to flesh out the "true" events and characters, the writer makes history come alive. Historical fiction takes the reader into the scene, alongside heroes and villains. It recreates the sights, sounds, smells, and the very thoughts of people who made their mark long ago. Try writing your own historical short story or a scene from a novel. Select a historical period or event, write **sketches** (brief descriptions) of your characters (real and fictional), and do some research into the type of furniture, clothing, and other details relevant to the times. Don't worry—you do not have to become an expert historian. Use your imagination and have fun!

About the Author

Ann Petry (1908–1997) is known for her novels and stories about strong, independent women. Her work often features humor and sensitive descriptions of place and character. Her masterpiece, *The Street* (1946), is about a mother struggling to raise a son. Petry received numerous awards for her writing, and her books have been translated into twelve languages. Petry was born to one of the few middle-class African-American families in Old Saybrook, Connecticut. Receiving her pharmacy degree from the Connecticut College of Pharmacy, she worked in her family's drugstores prior to marrying and moving to Harlem in 1938. After serving as a journalist for two Harlem newspapers, *The Amsterdam News* and *The People's Voice,* she launched a successful writing career.

In addition to narratives and short stories for adults, Petry composed four books for children. Concerned with the lack of books for young black children, she wrote such works as *Harriet Tubman* and *Tituba of Salem Village.* She once said of her characters: "These are people. Look at them, listen to them; watch Harriet Tubman in the nineteenth century, a heroic woman, a rescuer of other slaves. Look at Tituba in the seventeenth century, a slave involved in the witchcraft trials of Salem Village. . . . Remember for what a long, long time black people have been in this country, have been a part of America: a sturdy, indestructible, wonderful part of America, woven into its heart and into its soul."

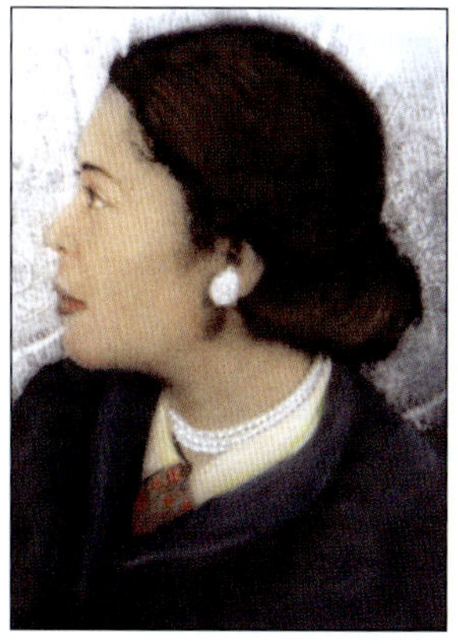

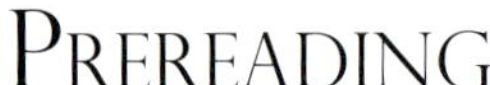

Prereading

"The Struggle for an Education"
from *Up From Slavery*
by Booker T. Washington

This is the third chapter from Booker T. Washington's famous autobiography, *Up from Slavery*. Washington is remembered for many things, but the field of education is where he made his most important impact on American history.

Washington was born into slavery in Franklin County, Virginia. Later, recalling the days when he carried books to school for his "master's" daughter, Washington wrote, "I had the feeling that to get into a schoolhouse and study would be about the same as getting into paradise." This same sentiment motivated him to make the journey from the coal mines of West Virginia—where his family moved after the Civil War—to Hampton Normal and Agricultural Institute on Virginia's eastern shore.

The Hampton Institute opened its doors in 1868 during a pivotal period in American history. The Civil War was over, but wounds to the landscape and social fabric of the United States were still fresh. For blacks, the struggle toward prosperity, much less equality, had only begun. Millions of black Americans were free from enslavement and searching for new futures, but they were cut off, socially and legally, from most tools by which one might achieve the American Dream.

Booker T. Washington helped lay the groundwork for the Great Migration, when African Americans moved *en masse* from the South, seeking industrial jobs in northern and midwestern cities such as Detroit, Chicago, New York, Cleveland, and Philadelphia.

Washington always believed that civil rights and equality would be gained only after black Americans had achieved economic independence. To Washington, education was the only key to economic freedom and would lead inevitably to social equality and justice. For an alternative view see W. E. B. Du Bois, pages 269 and 279.

This excerpt should give you an appreciation for the following:

1. The obstacles faced by all African Americans in the late nineteenth century
2. Washington's belief in the importance of education
3. The efforts of whites and blacks alike to improve the opportunities available to all African Americans
4. The importance of education in your own life

The Struggle for an Education

by Booker T. Washington

One day, while at work in the coal-mine, I happened to overhear two miners talking about a great school for coloured people somewhere in Virginia. This was the first time that I had ever heard anything about any kind of school or college that was more **pretentious** than the little coloured school in our town.

In the darkness of the mine[1] I noiselessly crept as close as I could to the two men who were talking. I heard one tell the other that not only was the school established for the members of my race, but that opportunities were provided by which poor but worthy students could work out all or part of the cost of board, and at the same time be taught some trade or industry.

As they went on describing the school, it seemed to me that it must be the greatest place on earth, and not even Heaven presented more attractions for me at that time than did the Hampton Normal and Agricultural Institute[2] in Virginia, about which these men were talking. I resolved at once to go to that school, although I had no idea where it was, or how many miles away, or how I was going to reach it; I remembered only that I was on fire constantly with one ambition, and that was to go to Hampton. This thought was with me day and night.

After hearing of the Hampton Institute, I continued to work for a few months longer in the coal-mine. While at work there, I heard of

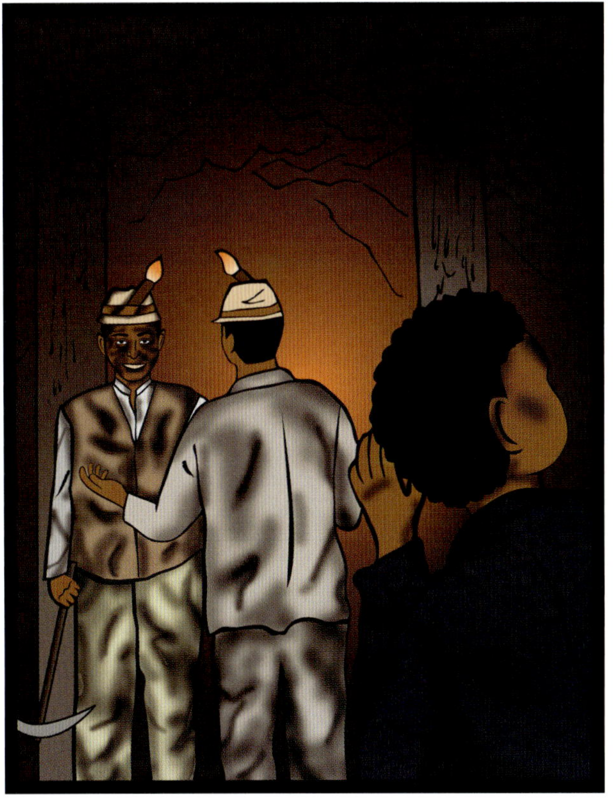

[1] **mine.** Washington worked in the coal and salt mines in West Virginia starting at age 10.

[2] **Hampton Normal and Agricultural Institute.** Known today as Hampton University, the school was founded in Hampton, Virginia, in 1868. (See the History Connection on page 251.)

VOCABULARY IN PLACE

- **pretentious,** ***adj.*** Claiming or demanding a position of merit, usually unjustified. (This word is normally used to describe a negative trait, like snobbery or showiness. Washington, however, would not have used our modern sense of this word to describe Hampton. His intended meaning was closer to the word *prestigious.*)

a vacant position in the household of General Lewis Ruffner, the owner of the salt-furnace and coal-mine. Mrs. Viola Ruffner, the wife of General Ruffner, was a "Yankee" woman from Vermont. Mrs. Ruffner had a reputation all through the **vicinity** for being very strict with their servants, and especially with the boys who tried to serve her. Few of them remained with her more than two or three weeks. They all left with the same excuse: she was too strict. I decided, however, that I would rather try Mrs. Ruffner's house than remain in the coal-mine, and so my mother applied to her for the vacant position. I was hired at a salary of $5 per month.

I had heard so much about Mrs. Ruffner's severity that I was almost afraid to see her, and trembled when I went into her presence. I had not lived with her many weeks, however, before I began to understand her. I soon began to learn that, first of all, she wanted everything kept clean about her, that she wanted things done promptly and systematically, and that at the bottom of everything she wanted absolute honesty and frankness. Nothing must be sloven or slipshod;[3] every door, every fence, must be kept in repair.

I cannot now recall how long I lived with Mrs. Ruffner before going to Hampton, but I think it must have been a year and a half. At any rate, I here repeat what I have said more than once before, that the lessons that I learned in the home of Mrs. Ruffner were as valuable to me as any education I have ever gotten anywhere since. Even to this day I never see bits of paper scattered around a house or in the street that I do not want to pick them up at once. I never see a filthy yard that I do not want to clean it, a paling[4] off of a fence that I do not want to put it on, an unpainted or unwhitewashed house that I do want to paint or whitewash it, or a button off one's clothes, or a grease-spot on them or on a floor, that I do not want to call attention to it.

How did Washington learn to deal with Mrs. Ruffner? How did Washington differ from other boys?

From fearing Mrs. Ruffner I soon learned to look upon her as one of my best friends. When she found that she could trust me she did so **implicitly.** During the one or two winters that I was with her she gave me an opportunity to go to school for an hour in the day during a portion of the winter months, but most of my studying was done at night, sometimes alone, sometimes under some one whom I could hire to teach me. Mrs. Ruffner always encouraged and sympathized with me in all my efforts to get an education. It was while living with her that I began to get together my first library. I secured a dry-goods box, knocked out one side of it, put some shelves in it, and began putting into it every kind of book that I could get my hands upon, and called it my "library."

Did Washington regularly attend school while working for Mrs. Ruffner? What did she encourage him to do?

Notwithstanding my success at Mrs. Ruffner's I did not give up the idea of going to the Hampton Institute. In the fall of 1872 I determined to make an effort to get there, although, as I stated, I had no idea of the direction in which Hampton was, or what it would cost to go there. I do not think that any one thoroughly sympathized with me in

3 **sloven or slipshod.** Disorderly or messy. Perhaps a common expression in Washington's day. *Sloven* is a noun meaning "a person who is careless in personal appearance or work." The word *slovenly* is an adjective meaning "untidy or disordered." *Slipshod* is an adjective meaning "marked by carelessness; haphazard."

4 **paling.** A single part of the *pale,* the upright row of pointed boards that make a fence

VOCABULARY IN PLACE

- **vicinity,** ***n.*** A nearby, surrounding, or adjoining place; a neighborhood
- **implicitly,** ***adv.*** Without doubt, unquestioningly

my ambition to go to Hampton unless it was my mother, and she was troubled with a grave fear that I was starting out on a "wild-goose chase." At any rate, I got only a half-hearted consent from her that I might start. The small amount of money that I had earned had been consumed by my stepfather and the remainder of the family, with the exception of a very few dollars, and so I had very little with which to buy clothes and pay traveling expenses. My brother John helped me all that he could, but of course that was not a great deal. For his work was in the coal-mine, where he did not earn much, and most of what he did earn went in the direction of paying the household expenses.

Perhaps the thing that touched and pleased me most in connection with my starting for Hampton was the interest that many of the older coloured people took in the matter. They had spent the best days of their lives in slavery, and hardly expected to live to see the time when they would see a member of their race leave home to attend a boarding-school. Some of these older people would give me a nickel, others a quarter, or a handkerchief.

Did Washington's family and community support his dream of attending Hampton?

Finally the great day came, and I started for Hampton. I had only a small, cheap satchel that contained what for articles of clothing I could get. My mother at the time was rather weak and broken in health. I hardly expected to see her again, and thus our parting was all the more sad. She, however, was very brave through it all. At that time there were no through trains connecting that part of West Virginia with eastern Virginia. Trains ran only a portion of the way, and the remainder of the distance was traveled by stage-coaches.

The distance from Malden to Hampton is about five hundred miles. I had not been away from home many hours before it began to grow painfully evident that I did not have enough money to pay my fare to Hampton. One experience I shall long remember. I had been traveling over the mountains most of the afternoon in an old-fashion stage-coach, when, late in the evening, the coach stopped for the night at a common unpainted house called a hotel. All the other passengers except myself were whites. In my ignorance I supposed that the little hotel existed for the purpose of accommodating the passengers who traveled on the stage-coach. The difference that the colour of one's skin would make I had not thought anything about. After all the other passengers had been shown rooms and were getting ready for supper, I shyly presented myself before the man at the desk. It is true I had practically no money in my pocket with which to pay for bed or food, but I had hoped in some way to beg my way into the good graces of the landlord, for at that season in the mountains of Virginia the weather was cold, and I wanted to get indoors for the night. Without asking as to whether I had any money, the man at the desk firmly refused to even consider the matter of providing me with food or lodging. This was my first experience in finding out what the colour of my skin meant. In some way I managed to keep warm by walking about, and so got through the night. My whole soul was so bent upon reaching Hampton that I did not have time to cherish any bitterness toward the hotel-keeper.

What happened when he tried to get a hotel room?

By walking, begging rides both in wagons and in the cars, in some way, after a number of days, I reached the city of Richmond, Virginia, about eighty-two miles from Hampton. When I reached there, tired, hungry, and dirty, it was late in the night. I had never been in a large city, and this rather added to my misery. When I reached Richmond, I was completely out of money.

I had not a single acquaintance in the place, and, being unused to city ways, I did not know where to go. I applied at several places for lodging, but they all wanted money, and that was what I did not have. Knowing nothing else better to do, I walked the streets. In doing this I passed by many food stands where fried chicken and half-moon apple pies were piled high and made to present a most tempting appearance. At that time it seemed to me that I would have promised all that I expected to possess in the future to have gotten ahold of one of those chicken legs or one of those pies. But I could not get either of these, nor anything else to eat.

I must have walked the streets till after midnight. At last I became so exhausted that I could walk no longer. I was tired, I was hungry, I was everything but discouraged. Just about the time when I reached extreme physical exhaustion, I came upon a portion of a street where the board sidewalk was considerably elevated. I waited for a few minutes, till I was sure that no passers-by could see me, and then crept under the sidewalk and lay for the night upon the ground, with my satchel of clothing for a pillow. Nearly all night I could hear the tramp of feet over my head. The next morning I found myself refreshed, but I was extremely hungry, because it had been a long time since I had had sufficient food. As soon as it became light enough for me to see my surroundings I noticed that I was near a large ship, and that this ship seemed to be unloading a cargo of pig iron. I went at once to the vessel and asked the captain to permit me to help unload the vessel in order to get money for food. The captain, a white man, who seemed to be kind-hearted, consented. I worked long enough to earn money for my breakfast, and it seems to me, as I remember it now, to have been about the best breakfast that I have ever eaten.

My work pleased the captain so well that he told me if I desired I could continue working for a small amount per day. This I was very glad to do. I continued working on this vessel for a number of days. After buying food with the small wages I received there was not much left to add to the amount I must get to pay my way to Hampton. In order to economize in every way possible, so as to be sure to reach Hampton in a reasonable time, I continued to sleep under the same sidewalk that gave me shelter the first night I was in Richmond. Many years after that the coloured citizens of Richmond very kindly tendered me a reception at which there must have been two thousand people present. This reception was held not far from the spot where I slept the first night I spent in that city, and I must confess that my mind was more upon the sidewalk that first gave me shelter than upon the reception, agreeable and cordial as it was.

Why was this sidewalk so important to Washington in later years?

When I had saved what I considered enough money with which to reach Hampton, I thanked the captain of the vessel for his kindness, and started again. Without any unusual occurrence I reached Hampton, with a surplus of exactly fifty cents with which to begin my education. To me it had been a long, eventful journey; but the first sight of the large, three-story, brick school building seemed to have rewarded me for all that I had undergone in order to reach the place. If the people who gave the money to provide that building could appreciate the influence the sight of it had upon me, as well as upon thousands of other youths, they would feel all the more encouraged to make such gifts. It seemed to me to be the largest and most beautiful building I had ever seen. The sight of it seemed to give me new life. I felt that a new kind of existence had now begun—that life would now have a new meaning. I felt that I had reached the promised land, and I resolved to let no obstacle prevent me from putting forth the highest effort to fit myself to accomplish the most good in the world.

As soon as possible after reaching the grounds of the Hampton Institute, I presented myself before the head teacher for assignment to a class. Having been so long without proper food, a bath and change of clothing, I did not, of course, make a very favourable impression upon her, and I could see at once that there were doubts in her mind about the wisdom of admitting me as a student. I felt that I could hardly blame her if she got the idea that I was a worthless loafer or tramp. For some time she did not refuse to admit me, neither did she decide in my favour, and I continued to linger about her, and to impress her in all the ways I could with my worthiness. In the meantime I saw her admitting other students, and that added greatly to my discomfort, for I felt, deep down in my heart, that I could do as well as they, if I could only get a chance to show what was in me.

After some hours had passed, the head teacher said to me: "The adjoining recitation-room needs sweeping. Take the broom and sweep it."

It occurred to me at once that here was my chance. Never did I receive an order with more delight. I knew that I could sweep, for Mrs. Ruffner had thoroughly taught me how to do that when I lived with her.

I swept the recitation-room three times. Then I got a dusting-cloth and I dusted it four times. All the woodwork around the walls, every bench, table, and desk, I went over four times with my dusting-cloth. Besides, every piece of furniture had been moved and every closet and corner in the room had been thoroughly cleaned. I had the feeling that in a large measure my future depended upon the impression I made upon the teacher in the cleaning of that room. When I was through, I reported to the head teacher. She was a "Yankee" woman who knew just where to look for dirt. She went into the room and inspected the floor and closets; then she took her handkerchief and rubbed it on the woodwork about the walls, and over the table and benches. When she was able to find no bit of dirt on the floor, or a particle of dust on any of the furniture, She quietly remarked, "I guess you will do to enter this institution."

How did the head teacher "test" whether Washington was worthy of entering Hampton? Did Washington prove himself?

I was one of the happiest souls on earth. The sweeping of that room was my college examination, and never did any youth pass an examination for entrance into Harvard or Yale that gave him more genuine satisfaction. I have passed several examinations since then,

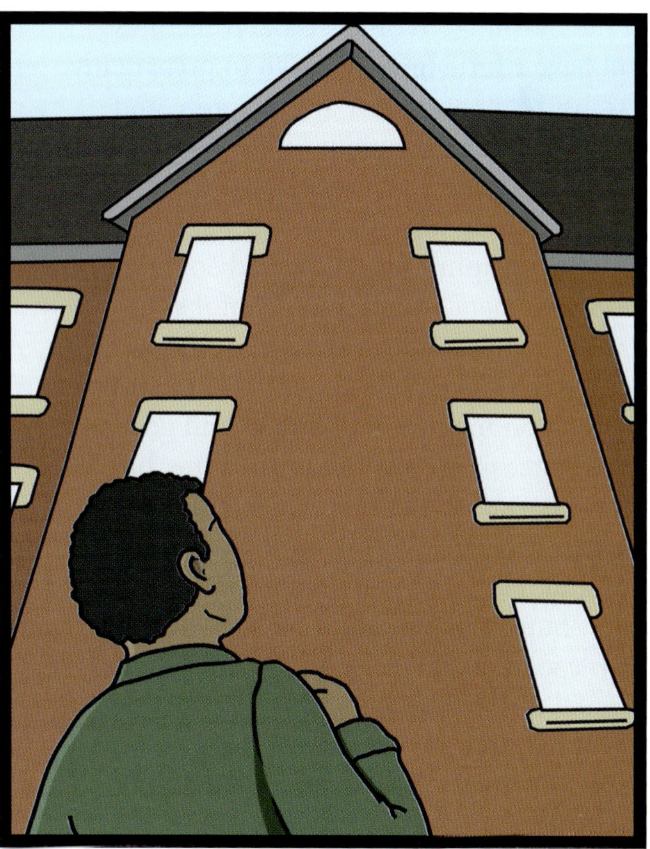

but I have always felt that this was the best one I ever passed.

I have spoken of my own experience in entering the Hampton Institute. Perhaps few, if any, had anything like the same experience that I had, but about that same period there were hundreds who found their way to Hampton and other institutions after experiencing something of the same difficulties that I went through. The young men and women were determined to secure an education at any cost.

The sweeping of the recitation-room in the manner that I did it seems to have paved the way for me to get through Hampton. Miss Mary F. Mackie, the head teacher, offered me a position as janitor. This, of course, I gladly accepted, because it was a place where I could work out nearly all the cost of my board. The work was hard and taxing, but I stuck to it. I had a large number of rooms to care for, and had to work late into the night, while at the same time I had to rise by four o'clock in the morning, in order to build the fires and have a little time in which to prepare my lessons. In all my career at Hampton, and ever since I have been out in the world, Miss Mary F. Mackie, the head teacher to whom I have referred, proved one of my strongest and most helpful friends. Her advice and encouragement were always helpful and strengthening to me in the darkest hour.

I have spoken of the impression that was made upon me by the buildings and general appearance of the Hampton Institute, but I have not spoken of that which made the greatest and most lasting impression upon me, and that was a great man—the noblest, rarest human being that it has ever been my privilege to meet. I refer to the late General Samuel C. Armstrong.

It has been my fortune to meet personally many of what are called great characters, both in Europe and America, but I do not hesitate to say that I never met any man who, in my estimation, was the equal of General Armstrong. Fresh from the degrading influences of the slave plantation and the coal-mines, it was a rare privilege for me to be permitted to come into direct contact with such a character as General Armstrong. I shall always remember that the first time I went into his presence he made the impression upon me of being a perfect man: I was made to feel that there was something about him that was superhuman. It was my privilege to know the General personally from the time I entered Hampton till he died, and the more I saw of him the greater he grew in my estimation. One might have removed from Hampton all the buildings, classrooms, teachers, and industries, and given the men and women there the opportunity of coming into daily contact with General Armstrong, and that alone would have been a liberal education.[5] The older I grow, the more I am convinced that there is no education which one can get from books and costly apparatus that is equal to that which can be gotten from contact with great men and women. Instead of studying books so constantly, how I wish that our schools and colleges might learn to study men and things!

General Armstrong spent two of the last six months of his life in my home at Tuskegee. At that time he was paralyzed to the extent that he had lost control of his body and voice in a very large degree. Notwithstanding his affliction, he worked almost constantly night and day for the cause to which he had given his life. I never saw a man who so completely

---

[5] **liberal education.** The word *liberal* is derived from the Latin word for *free*. In Roman times, slaves were allowed to study the practical arts, such as engineering, but not subjects such as literature, history, natural sciences, philosophy, and languages (commonly known today as the liberal arts). The latter subjects constituted the education believed proper to a free person.

lost sight of himself. I do not believe he ever had a selfish thought. He was just as happy in trying to assist some other institution in the South as he was when working for Hampton. Although he fought the Southern white man in the Civil War, I never heard him utter a bitter word against him afterward. On the other hand, he was constantly seeking to find ways by which he could be of service to the Southern whites.

It would be difficult to describe the hold that he had upon the students at Hampton, or the faith they had in him. In fact, he was worshipped by his students. It never occurred to me that General Armstrong could fail in anything that he undertook. There is almost no request that he could have made that would not have been complied with. When he was a guest at my home in Alabama, and was so badly paralyzed that he had to be wheeled about in an invalid's chair, I recall that one of the General's former students had occasion to push his chair up a long, steep hill that taxed his strength to the utmost. When the top of the hill was reached, the former pupil, with a glow of happiness on his face, exclaimed, "I am so glad that I have been permitted to do something that was real hard for the General before he dies!" While I was a student at Hampton, the dormitories became so crowded that it was impossible to find room for all who wanted to be admitted. In order to help remedy the difficulty the General conceived the plan of putting up tents to be used as rooms. As soon as it became known that General Armstrong would be pleased if some of the older students would live in the tents during the winter, nearly every student in school volunteered to go.

I was one of the volunteers. The winter that we spent in those tents was an intensely cold one, and we suffered severely—how much I am sure General Armstrong never knew, because we made no complaints. It was enough for us to know that we were making it possible for an additional number of students to secure an education. More than once, during a cold night, when a stiff gale would be blowing, our tent was lifted bodily, and we would find ourselves in the open air. The General would usually pay a visit to the tents early in the morning, and his earnest, cheerful, encouraging voice would **dispel** any feeling of **despondency.**

I have spoken of my admiration for General Armstrong, and yet he was but a type of that Christlike body of men and women who went into the Negro schools at the close of the war by the hundreds to assist in lifting up my race. The history of the world fails to show a higher, purer, and more unselfish class of men and women than those who found their way into those Negro schools.

Life at Hampton was a constant revelation to me; was constantly taking me into a new world. The matter of having meals at regular hours, of eating on a tablecloth, using a napkin, the use of the bathtub and of the toothbrush, as well as the use of sheets upon the bed, were all new to me.

I sometimes feel that almost the most valuable lesson I got at the Hampton Institute was in the use and value of the bath. I learned there for the first time some of its value, not only in keeping the body healthy, but in inspiring self-respect and promoting virtue. In all my travels in the South and elsewhere since leaving Hampton I have always in some way sought my daily bath. To get it sometimes when I have been the guest of my own people in a single-roomed cabin has not always been

VOCABULARY IN PLACE

- **dispel,** *v.* To rid one's mind of
- **despondency,** *n.* Depression from loss of hope or confidence

easy to do, except by slipping away to some stream in the woods. I have always tried to teach my people that some provision for bathing should be a part of every house.

For some time, while a student at Hampton, I possessed but a single pair of socks, but when I had worn these till they became soiled, I would wash them at night and hang them by the fire to dry, so that I might wear them again the next morning.

The charge for my board at Hampton was ten dollars per month. I was expected to pay a part of this in cash and to work out the remainder. To meet this cash payment, as I have stated, I had just fifty cents when I reached the institution. Aside from a very few dollars that my brother John was able to send me once in a while, I had no money with which to pay my board. I was determined from the first to make my work as janitor so valuable that my services would be **indispensable**. This I succeeded in doing to such an extent that I was soon informed that I would be allowed the full cost of my board in return for my work. The cost of tuition was seventy dollars a year. This, of course, was wholly beyond my ability to provide. If I had been compelled to pay the seventy dollars for tuition, in addition to providing for my board, I would have been compelled to leave the Hampton school. General Armstrong, however, very kindly got Mr. S. Griffitts Morgan, of New Bedford, Mass., to **defray** the cost of my tuition during the whole time that I was at Hampton. After I finished the course at Hampton and had entered upon my lifework at Tuskegee, I had the pleasure of visiting Mr. Morgan several times.

After having been for a while at Hampton, I found myself in difficulty because I did not have books and clothing. Usually, however, I got around the trouble about books by borrowing from those who were more fortunate than myself. As to clothes, when I reached Hampton I had practically nothing. Everything that I possessed was in a small hand satchel. My anxiety about clothing was increased because of the fact that General Armstrong made a personal inspection of the young men in ranks, to see that their clothes were clean. Shoes had to be polished, there must be no buttons off the clothing, and no grease-spots. To wear one suit of clothes continually, while at work and in the schoolroom, and at the same time keep it clean, was rather a hard problem for me to solve. In some way I managed to get on till the teachers learned that I was in earnest and meant to succeed, and then some of them were kind enough to see that I was partly supplied with second-hand clothing that had been sent in barrels from the North. These barrels proved a blessing to hundreds of poor but deserving students. Without them I question whether I should ever have gotten through Hampton.

When I first went to Hampton I do not recall that I had ever slept in a bed that had two sheets on it. In those days there were not many buildings there, and room was very precious. There were seven other boys in the same room with me; most of them, however, students who had been there for some time. The sheets were quite a puzzle to me. The first night I slept under both of them, and the second night I slept on top of both of them; but by watching the other boys I learned my lesson in this, and have been trying to follow it ever since and to teach it to others.

I was among the youngest of the students who were in Hampton at that time. Most of the students were men and women—some as

VOCABULARY IN PLACE

- **indispensable,** ***adj.*** Absolutely necessary, essential
- **defray,** ***v.*** To undertake the payment of; to pay

old as forty years of age. As I now recall the scene of my first year, I do not believe that one often has the opportunity of coming into contact with three or four hundred men and women who were so tremendously in earnest as these men and women were. Every hour was occupied in study or work. Nearly all had had enough actual contact with the world to teach them the need for education. Many of the older ones were, of course, too old to master the text-books very thoroughly, and it was often sad to watch their struggles; but they made up in earnestness much of what they lacked in books. Many of them were as poor as I was, and, besides having to wrestle with their books, they had to struggle with a poverty which prevented their having the necessities of life. Many of them had aged parents who were dependent upon them, and some of them were men who had wives whose support in some way they had to provide for.

The great and prevailing idea that seemed to take possession of every one was to prepare himself to lift up the people at his home. No one seemed to think of himself. And the officers and teachers, what a rare set of human beings they were! They worked for the students night and day, in season and out of season. They seemed happy only when they were helping the students in some manner. Whenever it is written—and I hope it will be—the part that the Yankee teachers played in the education of the Negroes immediately after the war will make one of the most thrilling parts of the history of this country. The time is not far distant when the whole South will appreciate this service in a way that it has not yet been able to do. ■

What motivated the students at Hampton Institute? Why were they so determined to succeed?

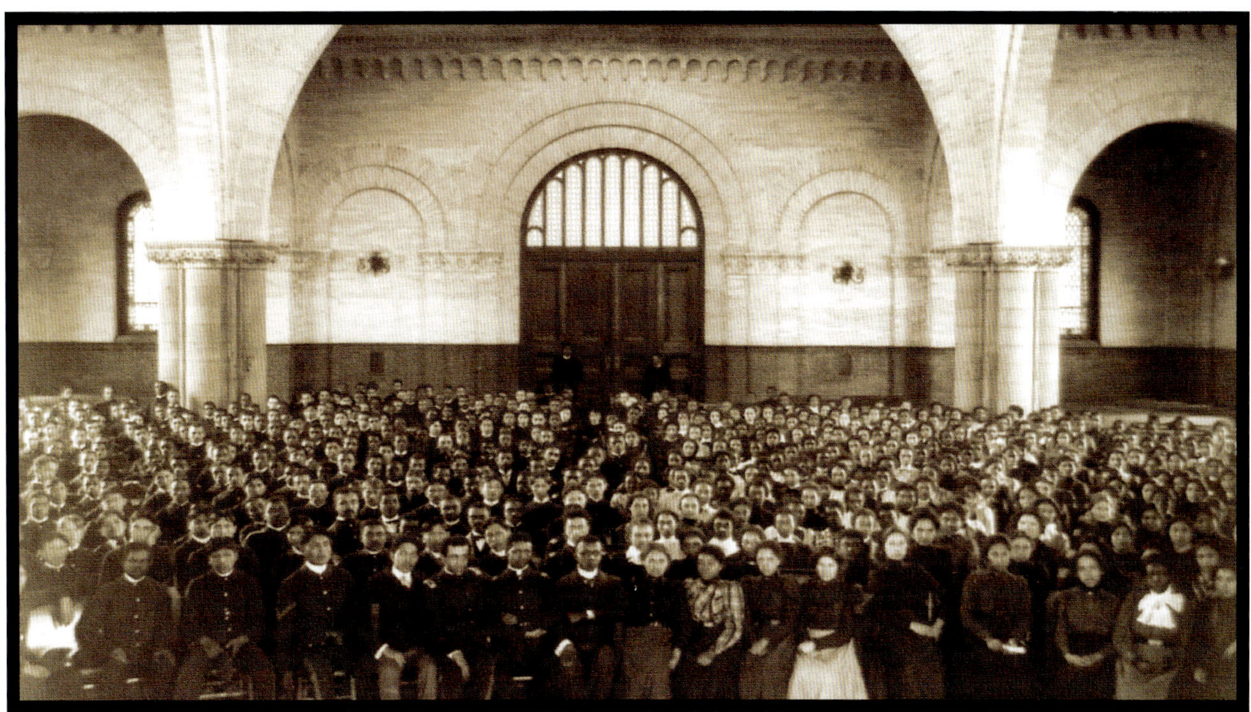

School Assembly at Hampton Institute, Hampton, Virginia, circa 1899. Library of Congress, LC-USZ62-94863.

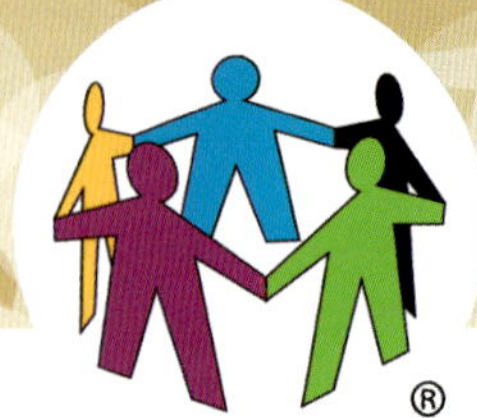

Understanding the Selection

Recalling

1. How did Booker T. Washington find out about Hampton Institute?
2. What was Mrs. Ruffner's reputation among those who had worked for her?
3. While working for Mrs. Ruffner, did Washington go to school? How did he learn to read?
4. How did Washington get money to travel to Hampton? Was his family very supportive?
5. Was Washington accepted at the school right away? How did he gain admittance?
6. Why did the students have to live in tents? Whose idea was this?

Interpreting

1. Why was this such exciting news for him? Were there many schools like this at the time?
2. Why did Washington say that the lessons he learned from Mrs. Ruffner were "as valuable to me as any education"?
3. Was Washington enthusiastic about learning and reading? Provide a quotation from the text to support your answer.
4. Why did people in Washington's neighborhood help? How did he feel about receiving their support?
5. Why did the teacher decide that Washington should be accepted into the Hampton Institute?
6. Why didn't they complain about living in the tents?

Synthesizing

1. These days, most students simply walk out the door and climb on the bus in order to get to school, whether they want to or not. It has not always been so easy. Summarize three obstacles, or difficulties, that Washington overcame on his way to gaining admittance to the Hampton Institute. Were these sorts of obstacles common to African Americans at the time? How have things changed since?

Delving Deeper

History Connection

Hampton Normal and Agricultural Institute. A "normal" school was a school that trained teachers by setting the "norms," or standards, by which teachers were expected to work. Hampton Institute was founded in 1868 to train African-American teachers to assist the thousands of former slaves in search of new lives following Emancipation.

The institute's unofficial motto was "Learning by Doing," which illustrates the stress placed on the development of practical vocational skills. Hampton Institute did not neglect "book learning," but the ultimate goal was to provide students with concrete skills that would help them to earn money. Booker T. Washington carried this philosophy with him to the Tuskegee Institute, and for the rest of his life he encouraged African Americans to focus first on achieving economic freedom, after which civil rights and equality would follow.

Using the Internet or library, research the Hampton Institute and answer the following:

- What did General Samuel Armstrong do during the Civil War? How did he raise the money to found the Hampton Institute?
- What is the Emancipation Oak? What happened there in 1861 and 1863?
- Why were American Indians enrolled in the Hampton Institute?
- Does the Hampton Institute still exist? If so, how has it changed?

About the Author

Booker Taliaferro Washington (1856–1915) was born into slavery but grew up to become one of the most prominent social activists of his time, a celebrated educator, a famous author, and an advisor to two U.S. presidents.

Washington was born on the farm of James Burroughs in Franklin County, Virginia. Following Emancipation, Washington's family moved to West Virginia, where, starting at age ten, he worked in salt and coal mines. When he was sixteen, he journeyed 500 miles to enroll at the Hampton Normal and Agricultural Institute, where he later taught.

In 1881, Washington became the first principal of the Tuskegee Institute in Alabama. His controversial "Atlanta Compromise" speech in 1895 catapulted him into the national political spotlight, earning him an invitation to work as an advisor to Presidents Roosevelt and Taft. That year he also published his famous autobiography, *Up From Slavery.*

Prereading

from *Reminiscences of School Life*

by Fanny Jackson Coppin

This selection contains two samples from Fanny Coppin's autobiography. The first excerpt is from the opening chapter, entitled "Autobiography: A Sketch," from which students will learn of the challenges Coppin faced along the road to becoming one of the first highly educated black women in the country and a major participant in the effort to educate African Americans after the Civil War.

The second sample, "Good Manners," is the seventh chapter in her book. It will give students a sense of Coppin's overall philosophy regarding **pedagogy** (the art of teaching). This single page represents the entire chapter. Do not be fooled by the brief nature of this passage, for manners were of the utmost importance to Coppin. Her advice on the subject gets right to the point: good manners lead to good things; bad manners lead nowhere.

The author had two goals in mind when she wrote this book. First, she aimed to tell her impressive story for the same reasons that drove Frederick Douglass, Booker T. Washington, and scores of others to write and publish their narratives: to expose the wrongfulness and brutality of slavery. Second, the book served as a textbook in teacher-training institutes, for Coppin devoted much of her career to teacher education.

Later in her story, Coppin wrote of her "deep-seated purpose to get an education and become a teacher to [her] people." The opening pages of Coppin's book reveal the personal and intellectual strengths that helped her to achieve her stated purpose.

Autobiography: A Sketch

by Fanny Jackson Coppin

There are some few points in my life which, "some **forlorn** and shipwrecked brother seeing, may take heart again."

We used to call our grandmother "mammy," and one of my earliest recollections—I must have been about three years old—is, I was sent to keep my mammy company. It was in a little one-room cabin. We used to go up a ladder to the loft where we slept.

Mammy used to make a long prayer every night before going to bed; but not one word of all she said do I remember except the one word "offspring." She would ask God to bless her offspring. This word remained with me, for, I wondered what offspring meant.

Mammy had six children, three boys and three girls. One of these, Lucy, was my mother. Another one of them, Sarah, was purchased by my grandfather, who first saved money and bought himself, then four of his children. Sarah went to work at six dollars a month, saved one hundred and twenty-five dollars, and bought little Frances, having taken a great liking to her, for on account of my birth, my grandfather refused to buy my mother; and so I was left a slave in the District of Columbia, where I was born. . . .

When my aunt had finally saved up the hundred and twenty-five dollars, she bought me and sent me to New Bedford, Mass., where another aunt lived, who promised to get me a place to work for my board, and get a little education if I could. She put me out to work, at a place where I was allowed to go to school when I was not at work. But I could not go on wash day, nor ironing day, nor cleaning day, and this interfered with my progress. There were no Hamptons,[1] and no night schools then.

How did Fanny Coppin gain her freedom?

Finally, I found a chance to go to Newport with Mrs. Elizabeth Orr, an aunt by marriage, who offered me a home with her and a better chance at school. I went with her, but I was not satisfied to be a burden on her small resources. I was now fourteen years old, and felt that I ought to take care of myself. So I found a permanent place[2] in the family of Mr. George H. Calvert, a great grandson of Lord Baltimore, who settled Maryland. His wife was Elizabeth Stuart, a descendant of Mary, Queen of Scots.[3] Here I had one hour every other afternoon in the week to take some private lessons, which I did. . . . After that, I attended for a few months the public colored school. . . . I thus prepared myself to enter the examination for the Rhode Island

1 **Hamptons.** A reference to Hampton Normal and Agricultural Institute, established in Virginia in 1868 for the purpose of training African-American teachers

2 **permanent place.** A position as a live-in house servant

3 **Mary, Queen of Scots.** Mary Stuart (1542–1587), the most famous Scottish monarch

VOCABULARY IN PLACE

- **forlorn,** ***adj.*** Sad or lonely from being deserted or abandoned

State Normal School[4]. . . . The school was then located at Bristol, R.I. Here, my eyes were first opened on the subject of teaching. I said to myself, is it possible that teaching can be made so interesting as this! But, having finished the course of study there, I felt that I had just begun to learn; and, hearing of Oberlin College, I made up my mind to try to get there. I had learned a little music while at Newport, and had mastered the elementary studies of the piano and guitar. My aunt in Washington still helped me, and I was able to pay my way to Oberlin, the course of study there being the same as that at Harvard College. Oberlin was then the only College in the United States where colored students were permitted to study.

The faculty did not forbid a woman to take the gentleman's course, but they did not advise it. There was plenty of Latin and Greek in it, and as much mathematics as one could shoulder. Now, I took a long breath and prepared for a delightful contest. All went smoothly until I was in the junior year in College. Then, one day, the Faculty sent for me—**ominous** request—and I was not slow in obeying it. It was a custom in Oberlin that forty students from the junior and senior classes were employed to teach the preparatory classes.[5] As it was now time for the juniors to begin their work, the Faculty informed me that it was their purpose to give me a class, but I was to distinctly understand that if the pupils rebelled against my teaching, they did not intend to force it. Fortunately for my training at the normal school, and my own dear love of teaching, tho there was a little surprise on the faces of some when they came into class, and saw the teacher, there were no signs of rebellion. The class went on increasing in numbers until it had to be divided, and I was given both divisions. One of the divisions ran up again, but the Faculty decided that I had as much as I could do, and it would not allow me to take any more work.

Why did Coppin refer to her education as a "delightful contest"? What sort of person was Coppin?

Why were Coppin's students surprised when they first saw her?

When I was within a year of graduation, an application came from a Friends' school[6] in Philadelphia for a colored woman who could teach Greek, Latin, and higher mathematics. The answer returned was: "We have the woman, but you must wait a year for her."

Then began a correspondence with Alfred Cope, a saintly character, who, having found out what my work in college was, teaching my classes in college, besides sixteen private music scholars, and keeping up my work in the senior class, immediately sent me a check for eighty dollars, which wonderfully lightened my burden as a poor student.

I shall never forget my obligation to Bishop Daniel A. Payne, of the African Methodist Episcopal Church, who gave me a scholarship of nine dollars a year upon entering Oberlin.

My obligation to the dear people of Oberlin can never be measured in words. When President Finney met a new student, his first words were: "Are you a Christian? And if not, why not?" He would follow you up with

[4] **Normal School.** A teacher-training school where teachers were taught the "norms," or standards, of teaching

[5] **preparatory classes.** Introductory classes for first-year students

[6] **Friends' school.** One of a network of schools established by Quakers. Quakers are members of the Society of Friends, a Christian denomination, so called because of an early leader's command that believers should "tremble [quake] at the word of the Lord." Quakers are pacifists, and were avid Abolitionists. After the Civil War, Quakers continued to be allies to African Americans in the quest for civil equality.

VOCABULARY IN PLACE

- **ominous**, ***adj.*** Menacing; threatening

an intelligent **persistence** that could not be resisted, until the question was settled.

When I first went to Oberlin I boarded in what was known as the Ladies' Hall, and although the food was good, yet, I think, that for lack of variety I began to run down in health. About this time I was invited to spend a few weeks in the family of Professor H. E. Peck, which ended in my staying a few years, until the independence of the Republic of Hayti[7] was recognized, under President Lincoln, and Professor Peck was sent as the first U.S. Minister to that interesting country; then the family was broken up, and I was invited by Professor and Mrs. Charles H. Churchill to spend the remainder of my time, about six months, in their family. The influence upon my life in these two Christian homes, where I was regarded as an honored member of the family circle, was a **potent** factor in forming the character which was to stand the test of the new and strange conditions of my life in Philadelphia. I had been so long in Oberlin that I had forgotten about my color, but I was sharply reminded of it when, in a storm of rain, a Philadelphia street car conductor forbid my entering a car that did not have on it "for colored people," so I had to wait in the storm until one came in which colored people could ride. This was my first unpleasant experience in Philadelphia. Visiting Oberlin not long

How did the Churchill family treat her? What impact did this treatment have on her life?

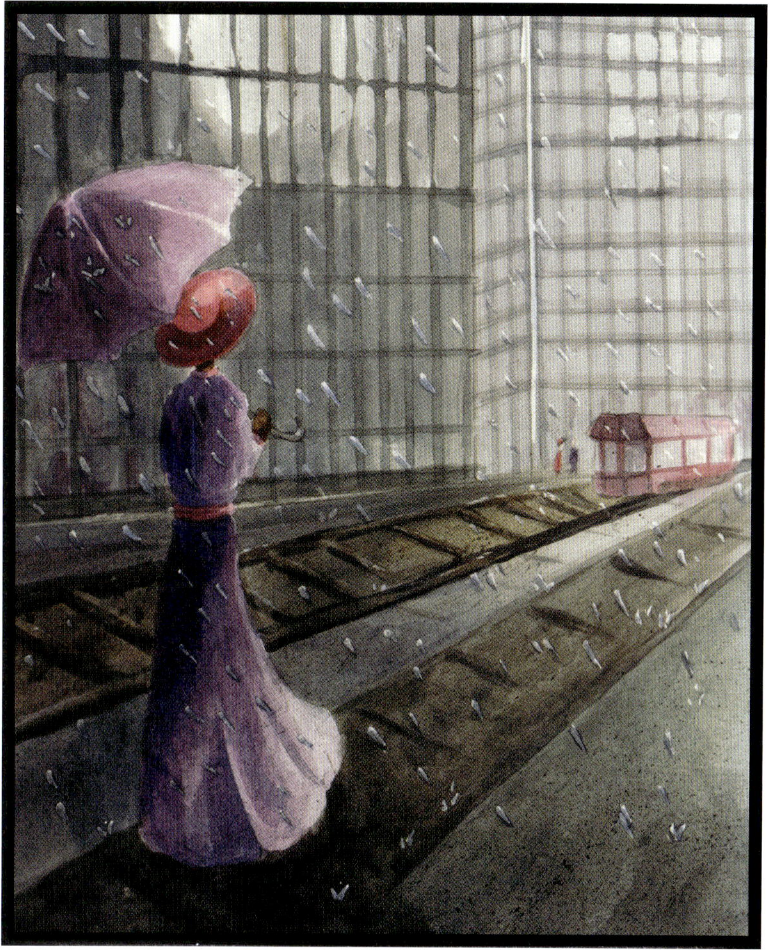

[7] **Republic of Hayti.** Modern-day Haiti gained its independence from France in 1804. This was the first nation founded by self-liberated slaves. Western nations, including the United States, refused for decades to recognize Haiti as an independent nation, partly out of the fear that doing so would incite or encourage American slaves to rebel.

VOCABULARY IN PLACE

- **persistence,** ***n.*** The state or quality of holding firmly to a purpose or goal despite obstacles or setbacks
- **potent,** ***adj.*** Possessing strength; powerful

after my work began in Philadelphia, President Finney asked me how I was growing in grace;[8] I told him that I was growing as fast as the American people would let me. When told of some of the conditions which were meeting me, he seemed to think it **unspeakable.**

At one time, at Mrs. Peck's, when we girls were sitting on the floor getting out our Greek, Miss Sutherland, from Maine, suddenly stopped, and, looking at me, said: "Fanny Jackson, were you ever a slave?" I said yes; and she burst into tears. Not another word was spoken by us. But those tears seemed to wipe out a little of what was wrong.

I never rose to recite in my classes at Oberlin but I felt that I had the honor of the whole African race upon my shoulders. I felt that, should I fail, it would be ascribed to the fact that I was colored. At one time, when I had quite a signal triumph in Greek, the Professor of Greek concluded to visit the class in mathematics and see how we were getting along. I was particularly anxious to show him that I was as safe in mathematics as in Greek.

I, indeed, was more anxious, for I had always heard that my race was good in the languages, but stumbled when they came to mathematics. Now, I was always fond of a demonstration, and happened to get in the examination the very proposition that I was well acquainted with; and so went that day out of the class with flying colors. ■

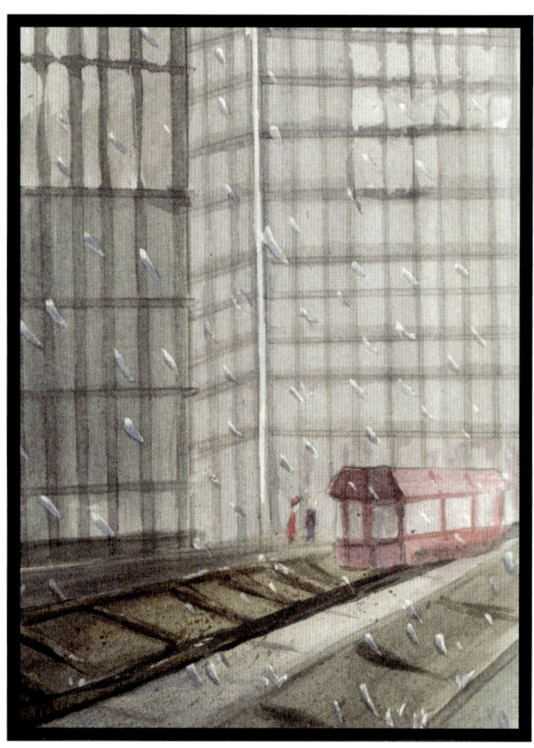

8 **growing in grace.** Grace is forgiveness or mercy extended regardless of a person's merit. To grow in grace could mean either to experience increasingly the grace of God in one's own life or to grow increasingly able to forgive and sympathize with others.

VOCABULARY IN PLACE

- **unspeakable,** ***adj.*** Beyond description; inexpressibly bad

Good Manners

by Fanny Jackson Coppin

The teaching of good manners in the home, is of the highest importance. The little child is taught to say, if you please, and thank you, not only to mother and father, but to brothers and sisters; and I know of nothing that **conduces** more to the happiness of the home than the manner of speaking to each other by all the members of the family. Some people seem to think that good manners need only be exercised toward our superiors or toward strangers, but this is a great mistake. A gentleman can always be told by the way he speaks to those that he thinks are his inferiors in some respect. His equals he does not wish to offend, his superiors he does not dare to offend, and of those whom he considers his inferiors he would be all the more considerate.

It is a very unsafe thing to graduate our politeness to what we suppose to be the position of the person we are addressing. I have heard of a car conductor who was very impolite to an old gentleman on his train because he was rather shabbily dressed; and he made many inquiries as to how he came by his rate book,[1] with other unnecessary questions, which did not concern him. A short time after, when he was released from his position, he was astonished to find that he had been talking to the president of the road. Good manners will often take people where neither money nor education will take them.

If we could follow many serious evils in life to their sources, we should find that many of them sprang from what we should regard as very insignificant matters. The girl who could not hold her tongue in school, but was always ready with a smart reply, may trace her broken household some day to that same fluency in speech. For it is indeed true that one word brings on another and the word that is brought on is generally not such as to help matters. We do well to remember that a soft answer turneth away **wrath**, but **grievous** words stir up anger.[2] Words, words, how they can make or mar our lives! The temper must be curbed, must be held in if necessary with "bit and bridle"[3] until it yields to control. ■

1 **rate book.** Possibly a book containing the railway rates

2 **a soft . . . anger.** See Proverbs 15:1.

3 **bit and bridle.** Implements used in horse training; the *bridle* is a harness attached to an animal's head; the *bit* is a mouthpiece used to control the animal.

VOCABULARY IN PLACE

- **conduce,** ***v.*** To contribute to or lead to a specific result
- **wrath,** ***n.*** Forceful, often vindictive anger; vengeance
- **grievous,** ***adj.*** Causing or characterized by severe pain, suffering, or sorrow

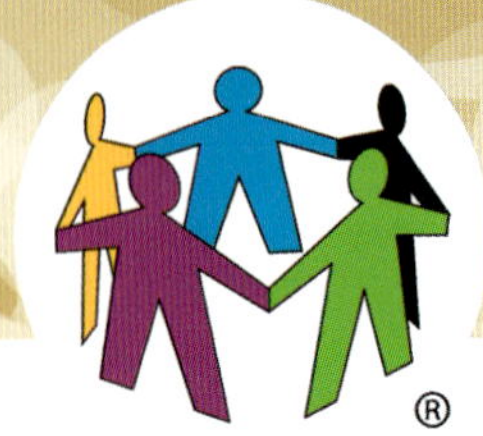

Understanding the Selection

Recalling

1. How did Fanny Coppin gain her freedom? How did she learn to read and write?
2. Who gave Coppin a scholarship to help with school?
3. Why did the faculty at Oberlin send for her? Why was this summons "ominous" to her?
4. How did the class react to her?
5. What in Philadelphia reminded Coppin of her skin color?
6. Why did the conductor lose his job?

Interpreting

1. When and why did Fanny decide that gaining an education and becoming a teacher would be her most important goals?
2. In what way did this support impact her desire to succeed?
3. Why might the students have rebelled? What did the faculty plan to do if the students rebelled?
4. How was she able to cope with challenges in the classroom?
5. Why did she feel that the "honor" of her race was on her shoulders?
6. How would good manners have helped him keep his job?

Synthesizing

1. *Determination* and *courage* are two adjectives one might use to describe Fanny Coppin's personal characteristics. Find one example in the excerpt from "Autobiography: A Sketch" in which she exhibits each of these qualities.
2. Do you think Fanny Coppin would have made a good teacher? Why? Explain using two quotations from the text to support your answer.

Delving Deeper

Writing

Good Manners. People in the nineteenth century placed a lot of emphasis on good manners. For American children, this usually meant never speaking unless spoken to, always respecting elders, taking great care to be polite and well-behaved, and generally never calling attention to themselves by being noisy or rude. In the 1800s, Americans were simply far more concerned with displaying good manners than most people are today; there were strict written and unwritten codes by which men, women, and children lived and interacted. Today, many people would argue that parents and teachers do not place enough emphasis on the teaching of good manners.

Write a short personal essay or story in which you answer the following questions: Do you think that you have good manners? Do you think that your friends have good manners? When did you first learn about manners? Who taught you about good manners, and how did he or she teach you?

About the Author

Frances (Fanny) Jackson Coppin (1837–1913) was an educator, missionary, and pioneer of teacher and vocational training for African Americans.

She was born into slavery (as Francis Marion Jackson) in Washington, D.C., and as a girl was bought and freed by an aunt. She spent her childhood in Massachusetts and Rhode Island and later moved to Ohio, where she attended Oberlin College, one of the only colleges at the time to admit black people. She also became one of the first African-American women to receive a degree from a major college. After graduating in 1865, Coppin taught Latin, Greek, and math at the Institute for Colored Youth in Philadelphia, where she became principal in 1869.

Fanny Coppin believed that job training was as important as academics for African Americans trying to find employment in an era of racial discrimination. During her long career in education, she designed numerous courses of study dealing with teaching and with various other trades.

Coppin left the U.S. in 1902 to do missionary work with her husband in Cape Town, South Africa. Coppin's autobiography and philosophy of education, *Reminiscences of School Life, and Hints on Teaching,* was published in 1913.

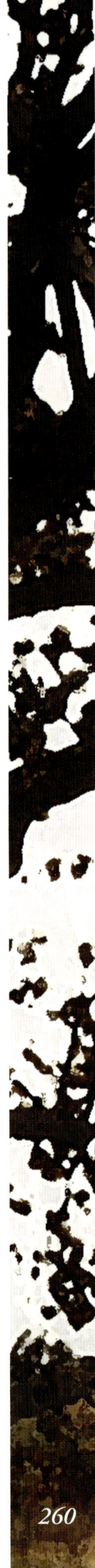

Prereading

from "Southern Horrors: Lynch Law in All Its Phases" and *A Red Record*

by Ida B. Wells-Barnett

One of the greatest of American civil rights and women's rights advocates, Ida B. Wells-Barnett worked as a newspaper editor and journalist for much of her life. She earned fame as one of the first **muckrakers**—journalists who use the power of the press and other media to campaign against injustice. Wells-Barnett led the charge against a terrible scourge that swept the United States from the Reconstruction Era (just after the Civil War) well into the twentieth century—lynching. A **lynching** is violence, usually a murder by hanging, perpetrated against someone for an imagined or real offense, usually by a group or mob, but always outside the ordinary legal system. The word *lynching* comes from ***lynch law,*** an ironic term referring to what is actually an unlawful act. Lynch law is judgment and punishment carried out by people who have no proper, governmentally instituted authority to act.

Before the Civil War, the lynching of criminals, such as horse thieves, was a fairly common occurrence in the South and the West. In the last two decades of the nineteenth century, however, lynching increasingly became used in the United States as a tool for carrying out violence against people not belonging to the white, Anglo-Saxon, Christian majority. During the Reconstruction Era, the United States Congress passed laws to protect the rights of black Americans, and states in the South responded with harsh Jim Crow laws that kept blacks from voting, holding public office, using public accommodations, and serving on juries. Many racist white Americans also responded by carrying out lynchings. According to reliable estimates, nearly 5,000 people were lynched by mobs between 1882 and 1968. Lynching was a kind of terrorism conducted by racist whites, including members of the Ku Klux Klan, against black people and their supporters in order to keep blacks down and to reinforce the imagined superiority and prerogatives of white people.

Few people who carried out lynchings were ever prosecuted for their crimes. After three of her friends were lynched in 1892, Ida B. Wells-Barnett began a campaign against lynching and produced two great works on the subject: "Southern Horrors: Lynch Law in All Its Phases" (1892) and *A Red Record: Tabulated Statistics and Alleged Causes of Lynching in the United States, 1892–1893–1894* (1895).

from Southern Horrors and A Red Record

by Ida B. Wells-Barnett

from "Southern Horrors: Lynch Law in All Its Phases"

Nothing is more definitely settled than that he [the Afro-American] must act for himself. I have shown how he may employ the **"boycott," emigration,** and the Press; and I feel that by a combination of all these agencies Lynch Law—the last relic of barbarism and slavery—can be effectually stamped out. "The gods help those who help themselves."[1] . . .

The following details of lynching from 1882 to 1891 inclusive, is proof of all that has been said, in the preceding pages. During these years the South has had full control of the political, legislative, judicial, and executive machinery. With the judges, juries, and prosecuting attorneys with all Southern white men, no Negro has ever been known to escape the penalty of the law for any crime he commits. It is only the wealthy white man, with money and influence, who fails of conviction for his crimes. There is not, and never has been, any fear by the mob that a Negro would not receive full punishment for all crimes of which he is convicted. But if this state of affairs did prevail, . . . clearly the laws or those who are paid to enforce them are at fault. Hence, those who make such inoperative laws, or the officials who fail to do their duty, and not the criminals, should be lynched. But the reverse is true. The gaols,[2] penitentiaries, and convict farms are filled with race criminals who are too poor and

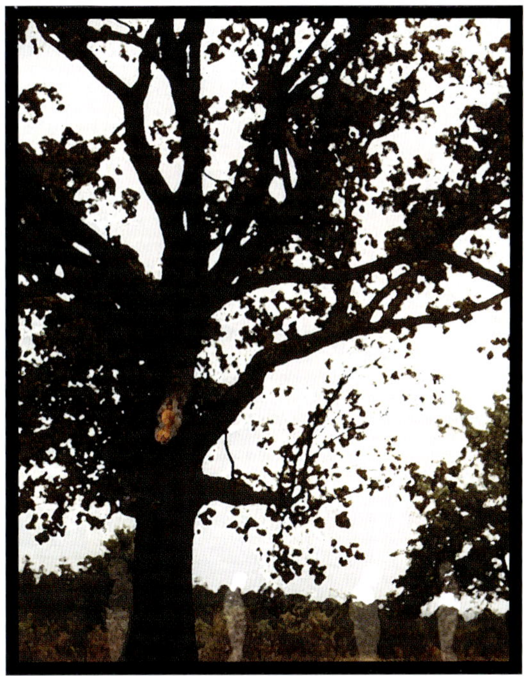

[1] **The gods . . . themselves.** Although the origin of this phrase is debated, some attribute it to Aesop's fable "Hercules and the Wagoner." In this tale, a wagoner's wheel becomes stuck, and he prays to Hercules for help. The god appears, tells the wagoner to put his own shoulder to the wheel, and then utters this famous phrase.

[2] **gaols.** Jails

VOCABULARY IN PLACE

- **boycott,** *n.* Concerted action to keep from using or buying some product or dealing with some organization in order to bring about change
- **emigration,** *n.* Movement out of one country or area in transit to another

weak to **avert** such a fate. Yet of this race there were lynched in—

1882–52	1886–73	1889–95
1883–39	1887–70	1890–100
1884–53	1888–72	1891–169
1885–77		

Of this number only 269 were charged with outrage[3]; 253 with murder; 44 with robbery; 37 with **incendiarism;** 32 with reasons unstated (not necessary to give a reason for lynching a Negro); 27 with "race prejudice"; 13 with quarreling with white men; 10 with making threats; 7 with rioting; 5 with **miscegenation;** 4 with burglary. ■

Are these capital offenses, ones equal to the punishment?

from *A Red Record: Tabulated Statistics and Alleged Causes of Lynching in the United States, 1892–1893–1894*

Hanged for Stealing Hogs

Details are very meagre of a lynching which occurred near Knox Point, La., on the twenty-fourth of October, 1893. Upon one point, however, there was no uncertainty, and that is, that the persons lynched were Negroes. It was claimed that they had been stealing hogs, but even this claim had not been subjected to the investigation of a court. That matter was not considered necessary. A few of the neighbors who had lost hogs suspected these men were responsible for their loss, and made up their minds to furnish an example for others to be warned by. The two men were secured by a mob and hanged.

Lynched for No Offense

Perhaps the most characteristic feature of this record of lynch law for the year 1893, is the remarkable fact that five human beings were lynched and that the matter was considered of so little importance that the powerful press bureaus of the country did not consider the matter of enough importance to ascertain the causes for which they were hanged. It tells the world, with perhaps greater emphasis than any other feature of the record, that Lynch Law has become so common in the United States that the finding of the dead body of a Negro, suspended between heaven and earth to the limb of a tree, is of so slight importance that neither the civil authorities[4] nor press agencies consider the matter worth investigating. July 21, in Shelby County, Tenn., a colored man by the name of Charles Martin was lynched. July 30, at Paris, Mo., a colored man named William Steen shared the same fate. December 28, Mack Segars was announced to have been lynched at Brantley, Alabama. August 31, at Yarborough, Texas, and on September 19, at Houston, a colored man was found lynched, but so little attention was paid to the matter that not only was no record made as to why these last two men were lynched, but even their names were not given. The **dispatches**

[3] **outrage.** An extreme offense against public sensibilities

[4] **civil authorities.** Government authorities, such as mayors, police officers, district attorneys, judges, and legislators

VOCABULARY IN PLACE

- **avert,** *v.* To turn aside
- **incendiarism,** *n.* Arousing anger or causing riot
- **miscegenation,** *n.* Cohabitation, marriage, or such relations between people of different races
- **dispatch,** *n.* A story sent out by reporters or news services

simply stated that an unknown Negro was found lynched in each case.

There are friends of humanity who feel their souls shrink from any compromise with murder, but whose deep and abiding reverence for womanhood causes them to hesitate in giving their support to this crusade against Lynch Law, out of fear that they may encourage **miscreants** whose deeds are worse than murder. But to these friends it must appear certain that these five men could not have been guilty of any terrible crime. They were simply lynched by parties of men who had it in their power to kill them, and who chose to avenge some fancied wrong by murder, rather than submit their grievances to court.

Lynched because They Were ***Saucy***

At Moberly, Mo., February 18, and at Fort Madison, S.C., June 2, both in 1892, a record was made in the line of lynching which should certainly appeal to every humanitarian who has any regard for the sacredness of human life. John Hughes, of Moberly, and Isaac Lincoln, of Fort Madison, and Will Lewis in Tullahome, Tenn., suffered death for no more serious charge than that they "were saucy to white people." In the days of slavery it was held to be a very serious matter for a colored person to fail to yield the sidewalk at the demand of a white person, and it will not be surprising to find some evidence of this intolerance existing in the days of freedom. But the most that could be expected as a penalty for acting or speaking saucily to a white person would be a slight physical **chastisement** to make the Negro "know his place" or an arrest and fine. But Missouri, Tennessee and South Carolina chose to make precedents[5] in their cases and as a result both men, after being charged with their offense and **apprehended,** were taken by a mob and lynched. The civil authorities, who in either case would have been very quick to satisfy the aggrieved white people had they complained and brought prisoners to court, by imposing proper penalty upon them, did not feel it their duty to make any investigation after the Negroes were killed. They were dead and out of the way and as no one would be called upon to render an account for their taking off,[6] the matter was dismissed from the public mind.

Lynched for a Quarrel

One of the most notable instances of lynching for the year 1893, occurred about the twentieth of September. It was notable for the fact that the mayor of the city exerted every available power to protect the victim of the lynching from the mob. In his splendid endeavor to uphold the law, the mayor called out the troops, and the result was a deadly fight between the militia and mob, nine of the mob being killed. The trouble occurred at Roanoke, Va. It is frequently claimed that lynchings occur only in sparsely settled districts, and, in fact, it is a favorite plea of governors and reverend apologists to couple two **arrant** falsehoods, stating that lynchings

---

[5] **precedent.** An action by a governmental authority, especially a court, that sets a model to be followed in later, similar circumstances. There are two kinds of law. *Statutory law* consists of laws passed by legislators. *Common law,* by contrast, consists entirely of *precedents*—rulings made by previous courts and interpretations of those rulings.

[6] **taking off.** Killing (archaic)

VOCABULARY IN PLACE

- **miscreant,** ***n.*** Wrong-doer
- **saucy,** ***adj.*** Insolent, flippant
- **chastisement,** ***n.*** Punishment
- **apprehend,** ***v.*** To capture
- **arrant,** ***adj.*** Completely such; thoroughgoing

occur only because of assaults upon white women, and that these assaults occur and the lynchings follow in thinly inhabited districts where the power of the law is entirely inadequate to meet the emergency. This Roanoke case is a double refutation, for it not only disproves the alleged charge that the Negro assaulted a white woman, as was telegraphed all over the country at the time, but it also shows conclusively that even in one of the largest cities of the old state of Virginia, one of the original thirteen colonies, which prides itself on being the mother of presidents, it was possible for a lynching to occur in broad daylight under circumstances of revolting savagery.

When the news first came from Roanoke of the contemplated lynching, it was stated that a big **burly** Negro had assaulted a white woman, that he had been apprehended and that the citizens were determined to summarily dispose of his case. Mayor Trout was a man who believed in maintaining the majesty of the law, and who at once gave notice that no lynching would be permitted in Roanoke, and that the Negro, whose name was Smith, being in the custody of the law, should be dealt with according to law; but the mob did not pay any attention to the brave words of the mayor. It evidently thought that it was only another case of **swagger,** such as frequently characterizes lynching episodes. Mayor Trout, finding immense crowds gathering about the city, and fearing an attempt to lynch Smith, called out the militia and stationed them at the jail.

What does Wells-Barnett seem to appreciate about Mayor Trout?

It was known that the woman refused to accuse Smith of assaulting her, and that his offense consisted in quarreling with her about the change of money in a **transaction** in which he bought something from her market booth. Both parties lost their temper, and the result was a **row** from which Smith had to make his escape. At once the old cry was sounded that the woman had been assaulted, and in a few hours all the town was wild with people thirsting for the assailant's blood. . . .

The next day the mob grew in numbers and its rage increased in its intensity. There was no longer any doubt that Smith, innocent as he was of any crime, would be killed, for with the mayor out of the city and the governor of the state using no effort to control the mob, it was only a question of a few hours when the assault would be repeated and its victim put to death. . . .

Suspected, Innocent and Lynched

Five persons, Benjamin Jackson, his wife, Mahala Jackson, his mother-in-law, Lou Carter, Rufus Bigley, were lynched near Quincy, Miss., the charge against them being suspicion of well poisoning. It appears from the newspaper dispatches at that time that a family by the name of Woodruff was taken ill in September of 1892. As a result of their illness one or more of the family are said to have died, though that matter is not stated definitely. It was suspected that the cause of their illness was the existence of poison in the water, some miscreant having placed poison in the well. Suspicion pointed to a colored man named Benjamin Jackson who was at

VOCABULARY IN PLACE

- **burly,** ***adj.*** Strong, massive
- **swagger,** ***n.*** Literally, a cocky walk; figuratively, an expression of excessive self-assuredness
- **transaction,** ***n.*** An interchange, especially one involving a purchase or barter
- **row,** ***n.*** An altercation or fight (rhymes with cow)

once arrested. With him also were arrested his wife and mother-in-law and all were held on the same charge.

The matter came up for judicial investigation, but as might have been expected, the white people concluded it was unnecessary to wait the result of the investigation—that it was preferable to hang the accused first and try him afterward. By this method of procedure, the desired result was always obtained—the accused was hanged. Accordingly Benjamin Jackson was taken from the officers by a crowd of about two hundred people, while the inquest was being held and hanged. After the killing of Jackson, the inquest was continued to **ascertain** the possible connection of the other persons charged with the crime. Against the wife and mother-in-law of the unfortunate man there was not the slightest evidence and the **coroner's** jury was fair enough to give them their liberty. They were declared innocent and returned to their homes. But this did not protect the women from the demands of the Christian white people of that section of the country. In any other land and with any other people, the fact that these two accused persons were women would have pleaded in their favor for protection and fair play, but that had no weight with the Mississippi Christians nor the further fact that a jury of white men had declared them innocent. The hanging of one victim on an unproven charge did not begin to satisfy the mob in its bloodthirsty demands and the result was that even after the women had been discharged, they were at once taken in charge by a mob, which hung them by the neck until they were dead.

Still the mob was not satisfied. During the coroner's investigation the name of a fourth person, Rufus Bigley, was mentioned. He was acquainted with the Jacksons and that fact, together with some testimony **adduced** at the **inquest,** prompted the mob to decide that he should die also. Search was at once made for him and the next day he was apprehended. He was not given over into the hands of the civil authorities for trial nor did the coroner's inquest find that he was guilty, but the mob was quite sufficient in itself. After finding Bigley, he was strung up to a tree and his body left hanging, where it was found next day. It may be remarked here in passing that this instance of the moral degradation of the people of Mississippi did not excite any interest in the public at large. American Christianity heard of this awful affair and read of its details and neither press nor pulpit[7] gave the matter more than a passing comment. Had it occurred in the wilds of interior Africa, there would have been an outcry from the humane people of this country against the savagery which would so mercilessly put men and women to death. But it was an evidence of American civilization to be passed by unnoticed, to be denied or condoned as the requirements of any future emergency might determine. ■

[7] **pulpit.** A raised stand used for conducting religious services. Here the word refers to religious leaders. This use of an associated thing (a pulpit) in place of the thing itself (religious leaders) is an example of a literary technique known as **synecdoche.**

VOCABULARY IN PLACE

- **ascertain,** *v.* To determine
- **coroner,** *n.* A public officer whose job it is to investigate the causes of people's deaths
- **adduce,** *v.* To cite as evidence or proof
- **inquest,** *n.* A formal inquiry by a public official or institution, such as a grand jury or a legislative committee

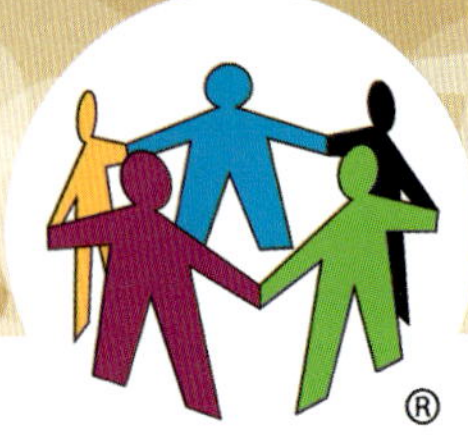

Understanding the Selection

Recalling

1. According to the first paragraph of the selection from "Southern Horrors," what three tools can people use against lynch law?
2. According to Wells-Barnett's investigation in *A Red Record,* why were people lynched in Knox Point, Louisiana, in 1893?
3. Why were people lynched in Moberly, Missouri, and Madison, South Carolina, in 1892? What does the word *saucy* mean?
4. Of what was the African American in Roanoke, Virginia, accused?
5. Of what were Benjamin Jackson and others accused?

Interpreting

1. Why would Ida Wells-Barnett be described, if she lived today, as an "activist"?
2. Was the legal system used to determine whether a crime had been committed? Even if the crime had been committed, was the punishment suited to the crime?
3. What made those lynchings particularly unwarranted?
4. What actually occurred between this African American and the woman at the market?
5. What evidence existed against Jackson and the others?

Synthesizing

1. In what ways are the so-called "crimes" described by Wells-Barnett in *A Red Record* similar to one another?
2. The Constitution of the United States guarantees to citizens the rights to due process of the law and trial by jury. In what ways did lynch law violate the Constitution? Why are due process and trial by jury so very important?

Delving Deeper

Writing

Etymology and Eponyms. **Etymology** is the study of the origins of words. For instance, the word *hippopotamus* comes from the Greek words *hippos,* meaning "horse," and *potamus,* meaning "river." Thus, *hippopotamus* literally means a "river horse." An **eponym** is a person whose name has become a word. The term *lynching* comes from the phrase *lynch law.* Scholars are divided about the origin of the latter term. Some believe it comes from the name of Colonel Charles Lynch, a Virginian who in 1782 set up a vigilante committee to try and punish supporters of the British during the American Revolution. Others believe that the term comes from the name of William Lynch, a plantation owner from the West Indies who visited Virginia and gave a speech about how to maintain control over slaves. Either Charles Lynch or William Lynch is probably the eponym of the word *lynching.* Similarly, the word *boycott* comes from the name of Charles C. Boycott (1832–1897), an English landlord who was socially and economically isolated by local citizens when he defied a new Irish land reform policy. Use a dictionary to find the origins of these words: *sandwich, bloomers, quisling,* and *guillotine.*

About the Author

Ida B. Wells-Barnett (1862–1931) was a civil rights advocate who became an anti-lynching activist. She worked as a newspaper editor and journalist and was also a defender of women's rights. Ida Bell Wells was born into slavery in Holly Springs, Mississippi, though she and her family were freed six months after her birth. After graduating from nearby Rusk College, she went to work as a teacher in Memphis, Tennessee.

In Memphis, Wells became an editor and journalist at an African-American newspaper called *The Free Speech and Headlight* for which she wrote articles about racial discrimination and African Americans' civil rights. In 1892, after three of her friends were lynched for defending their property from rioting whites, Wells wrote articles criticizing lynching and violence against blacks.

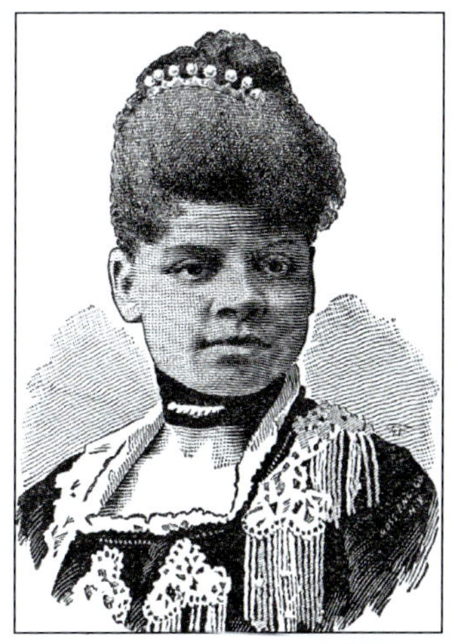

Wells eventually settled in Chicago, where in 1895 she married a well-known lawyer, Ferdinand Barnett. She continued to work for the anti-lynching and civil rights causes and in 1909 helped found the National Association for the Advancement of Colored People (NAACP).

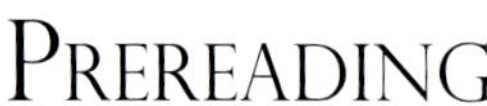

Prereading

"Of Our Spiritual Strivings"

by W. E. B. Du Bois

[*The range of references and advanced language of this selection make it difficult for younger readers. Teachers should direct younger students to key passages or provide a synopsis.*]

The Souls of Black Folk is a collection of essays and letters in which W. E. B. Du Bois examines the development of African-American culture, the meaning of emancipation, and the roles and responsibilities of African-American leaders.

The first chapter of the book, "Of Our Spiritual Strivings," provides one of the keys to understanding the fundamental differences between the philosophies of Du Bois and Booker T. Washington. (See page 241.) The latter stressed the importance of vocational education and improvement through economic gain. Du Bois disagreed with Washington's basic premise and instead encouraged blacks to separate culturally and economically from whites.

In later life, Du Bois became so disenchanted by racial prejudice and social injustice in America that he moved to Ghana. When this book was published in 1903, however, he was approaching the height of his power and influence as a leading black intellectual and activist. His work helped to inspire the poets, artists, and thinkers of the Harlem Renaissance.

Du Bois is defined by his willingness to lay bare, unabashedly, the truth about social injustice and racism. This he accomplished with brilliant writing. His defiant, confrontational tone resulted in his being labeled a radical, and he was ostracized by many of his contemporaries. But Du Bois could not be dismissed as a fanatic or mere rabble-rouser; this is because he was a highly-educated, well-traveled, and courageous individual. He said what few had dared to think, and he exposed harsh truths that could not be ignored.

Readers are encouraged to take their time with this excerpt from one of the most important books of the early twentieth century. They should approach Du Bois's work with patience and a desire to uncover the subtleties of his argument.

Of Our Spiritual Strivings
from The Souls of Black Folk

by W. E. B. Du Bois

O water, voice of my heart, crying in the sand,
All night long crying with a mournful cry,
As I lie and listen, and cannot understand
The voice of my heart in my side or the voice of the sea,
O water, crying for rest, is it I, is it I?
All night long the water is crying to me.

Unresting water, there shall never be rest
Till the last moon drop and the last tide fail,
And the fire of the end begin to burn in the west;
And the heart shall be weary and wonder and cry like the sea,
All life long crying without avail,
As the water all night long is crying to me.

ARTHUR SYMONS

Between me and the other world there is ever an unasked question: unasked by some through feelings of delicacy; by others through the difficulty of rightly framing it. All, nevertheless, flutter round it. They approach me in a half-hesitant sort of way, eye me curiously or compassionately, and then, instead of saying directly, How does it feel to be a problem? they say, I know an excellent colored man in my town; or, I fought at Mechanicsville;[1] or, Do not these Southern outrages make your blood boil? At these I smile, or am interested, or reduce the boiling to a simmer, as the occasion may require. To the real question, How does it feel to be a problem? I answer seldom a word.

And yet, being a problem is a strange experience,—peculiar even for one who has never been anything else, save perhaps in babyhood and in Europe. It is in the early days of rollicking boyhood that the revelation first bursts upon one, all in a day, as it were. I remember well when the shadow swept across me. I was a little thing, away up in the hills of New England, where the dark Housatonic winds between Hoosac and Taghkanic[2] to the sea. In a wee wooden schoolhouse, something

[1] **Mechanicsville.** Near Richmond, Virginia, Mechanicsville was the site of a Civil War battle in 1862.

[2] **Housatonic . . . Taghkanic.** The Housatonic River begins in Du Bois's native state of Massachusetts and flows through Connecticut to the Long Island Sound. The Hoosac and Taghkanic are mountain ranges in Massachusetts.

put it into the boys' and girls' heads to buy gorgeous visiting-cards—ten cents a package—and exchange. The exchange was merry, till one girl, a tall newcomer, refused my card,—refused it **peremptorily,** with a glance. Then it dawned upon me with a certain suddenness that I was different from the others; or like, mayhap, in heart and life and longing, but shut out from their world by a vast veil. I had thereafter no desire to tear down that veil, to creep through; I held all beyond it in common contempt, and lived above it in a region of blue sky and great wandering shadows. That sky was bluest when I could beat my mates at examination-time, or beat them at a foot-race, or even beat their stringy heads. Alas, with the years all this fine contempt began to fade; for the words I longed for, and all their dazzling opportunities, were theirs, not mine. But they should not keep these prizes, I said; some, all, I would wrest from them. Just how I would do it I could never decide: by reading law, by healing the sick, by telling the wonderful tales that swam in my head,—some way. With other black boys the strife was not so fiercely sunny: their youth shrunk into tasteless **sycophancy,** or into silent hatred of the pale world about them and mocking distrust of everything white; or wasted itself in a bitter cry, why did God make me an outcast and a stranger in mine own house? The shades of the prison-house closed round about us all: walls strait and stubborn to the whitest, but relentlessly narrow, tall, and unscalable to sons of night who must plod darkly on in resignation, or beat **unavailing** palms against the stone, or steadily, half hopelessly, watch the streak of blue above.

After the Egyptian and Indian, the Greek and Roman, the Teuton and Mongolian, the Negro is a sort of seventh son, born with a veil, and gifted with second-sight[3] in this American world,—a world which yields him

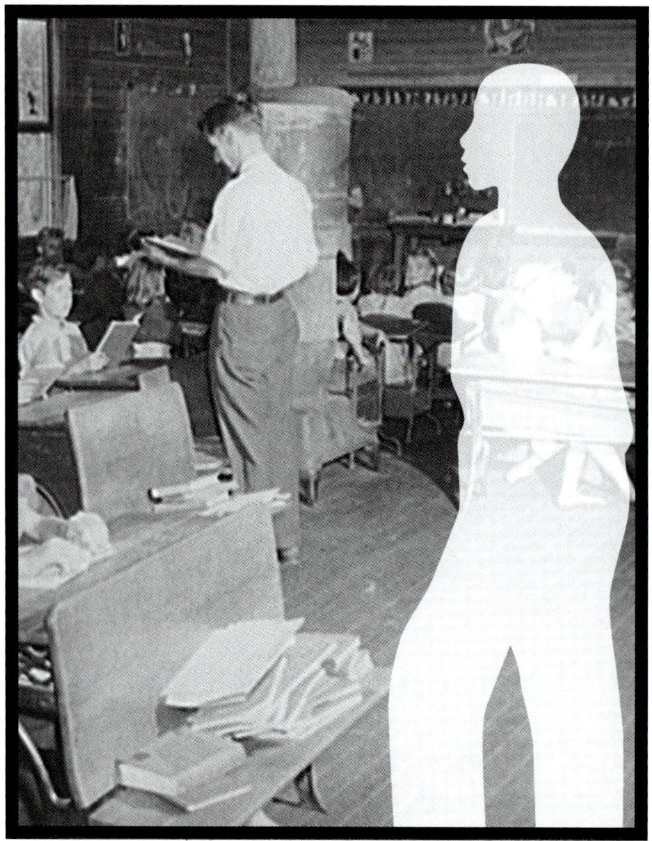

[3] **Egyptian . . . second-sight.** The six other cultures mentioned represent civilizations that made major impacts on human history. According to European folklore, anyone born as the seventh son (usually "seventh son of a seventh son") possesses special powers. Often *second-sight* (the power to see things that cannot be detected by the five senses) is one of these powers. To be a seventh son was considered both a blessing and a curse, because despite having these powers, seventh sons were traditionally viewed with suspicion.

VOCABULARY IN PLACE

- **peremptorily,** ***adv.*** In an abrupt and conclusive manner that allows for no contradiction or refusal
- **sycophancy,** ***n.*** Servile flattery. A *sycophant* is a person who attempts to win favor by flattering influential people.
- **unavailing,** ***adj.*** Ineffectual or useless; futile

no true self-consciousness, but only lets him see himself through the revelation of the other world. It is a peculiar sensation, this double-consciousness, this sense of always looking at one's self through the eyes of others, of measuring one's soul by the tape of a world that looks on in amused contempt and pity.

Who feels a "twoness" and why?

One ever feels his twoness,—an American, a Negro; two souls, two thoughts, two unreconciled strivings; two warring ideals in one dark body, whose **dogged** strength alone keeps it from being torn asunder.

The history of the American Negro is the history of this strife,—this longing to attain self-conscious manhood, to merge his double self into a better and truer self. In this merging he wishes neither of the older selves to be lost. He would not Africanize America, for America has too much to teach the world and Africa. He would not bleach his Negro soul in a flood of white Americanism, for he knows that Negro blood has a message for the world. He simply wishes to make it possible for a man to be both a Negro and an American, without being cursed and spit upon by his fellows, without having the doors of Opportunity closed roughly in his face.

According to Du Bois, what does the "American Negro" want, and what does he not want?

This, then, is the end of his striving: to be a coworker in the kingdom of culture, to escape both death and isolation, to husband and use his best powers and his **latent** genius. These powers of body and mind have in the past been strangely wasted, dispersed, or forgotten. The shadow of a mighty Negro past flits through the tale of Ethiopia the Shadowy and of Egypt the Sphinx. Through history, the powers of single black men flash here and there like falling stars, and die sometimes before the world has rightly gauged their brightness. Here in America, in the few days since Emancipation, the black man's turning hither and thither in hesitant and doubtful striving has often made his very strength to lose effectiveness, to seem like absence of power, like weakness. And yet it is not weakness,—it is the contradiction of double aims. The double-aimed struggle of the black artisan—on the one hand to escape white contempt for a nation of mere hewers of wood and drawers of water, and on the other hand to plough and nail and dig for a poverty-stricken horde—could only result in making him a poor craftsman, for he had but half a heart in either cause. By the poverty and ignorance of his people, the Negro minister or doctor was tempted toward **quackery** and demagogy;[4] and by the criticism of the other world, toward ideals that made him ashamed of his lowly tasks. The would-be black **savant** was confronted by the paradox that the knowledge his people needed was a twice-told tale to his white neighbors, while the knowledge which would teach the white world was Greek to his own flesh and blood. The innate love of harmony and beauty that set the ruder souls of his people a-dancing and a-singing raised but confusion and doubt in the soul of the black

[4] **demagogy.** The character or practices of a *demagogue,* a leader who obtains power by means of impassioned appeals to the emotions or prejudices of a populace

VOCABULARY IN PLACE

- **dogged,** ***adj.*** Stubbornly determined; tenacious
- **latent,** ***adj.*** Present and potential but not evident or active
- **quackery,** ***n.*** The act of pretending to have credentials or knowledge that one does not have, as when an untrained person dispenses medicine
- **savant,** ***n.*** A learned person; a scholar

artist; for the beauty revealed to him was the soul-beauty of a race which his larger audience despised, and he could not articulate the message of another people. This waste of double aims, this seeking to satisfy two unreconciled ideals, has wrought sad havoc with the courage and faith and deeds of ten thousand thousand people,—has sent them often wooing false gods and invoking false means of salvation, and at times has even seemed about to make them ashamed of themselves.

Why did his people's cultural heritage raise "confusion and doubt" in the artist?

Away back in the days of bondage they thought to see in one divine event the end of all doubt and disappointment; few men ever worshipped Freedom with half such unquestioning faith as did the American Negro for two centuries. To him, so far as he thought and dreamed, slavery was indeed the sum of all villainies, the cause of all sorrow, the root of all prejudice; Emancipation was the key to a promised land of sweeter beauty than ever stretched before the eyes of wearied Israelites. In song and exhortation swelled one refrain—Liberty; in his tears and curses the God he implored had Freedom in his right hand. At last it came,—suddenly, fearfully, like a dream. With one wild carnival of blood and passion came the message in his own plaintive cadences:[5]—

"Shout, O children!
Shout, you're free!
For God has bought your liberty!"

Years have passed away since then,—ten, twenty, forty; forty years of national life, forty years of renewal and development, and yet the swarthy spectre[6] sits in its accustomed seat at the Nation's feast. In vain do we cry to this our vastest social problem:—

"Take any shape but that, and my
firm nerves
Shall never tremble!"[7]

The Nation has not yet found peace from its sins; the freedman has not yet found in freedom his promised land. Whatever of good may have come in these years of change, the shadow of a deep disappointment rests upon the Negro people,—a disappointment all the more bitter because the unattained ideal was unbounded save by the simple ignorance of a lowly people.

The first decade was merely a prolongation of the vain search for freedom, the boon that seemed ever barely to elude their grasp,—like a tantalizing will-o'-the-wisp,[8]—maddening and misleading the headless host. The holocaust of war, the terrors of the Ku-Klux Klan, the lies of carpet-baggers,[9] the disorganization of industry, and the contradictory advice of

5 **plaintive cadences.** Du Bois refers to the sorrowful *(plaintive)* rhythms *(cadences)* with which the "American Negro" sang of freedom.

6 **swarthy spectre.** A dark-complexioned ghost or spirit

7 **Take any shape . . . tremble!** This citation comes from William Shakespeare's *Macbeth,* Act 3, Scene 4. Because of his excessive guilt, Macbeth imagines that he sees the ghost of someone whom he has caused to be murdered. Du Bois is making the point that the race problem is the most frightening and difficult problem facing America's citizens, just as guilt is the most frightening and difficult problem that Macbeth faces.

8 **will-o'-the-wisp.** A light that flashes or hovers at night over marshes and bogs. This light is the subject of many folktales, especially in Ireland, where it was sometimes said to mark treasure. However, the light sometimes led travelers to doom by drowning or to getting lost. Modern science has revealed that the light is caused by gases released by decaying matter.

9 **carpet-bagger.** A politician or other outsider who seeks a position of power in a new locality. This term originated after the Civil War when northern politicians moved southward and appealed to black voters in order to gain elected office but often failed to deliver on their campaign promises.

friends and foes, left the bewildered **serf** with no new watchword beyond the old cry for freedom. As the time flew, however, he began to grasp a new idea. The ideal of liberty demanded of its attainment powerful means, and these the Fifteenth Amendment gave him. The ballot, which before he had looked upon as a visible sign of freedom, he now regarded as the chief means of gaining and perfecting the liberty with which war had partially endowed him. And why not? Had not votes made war and emancipated millions? Had not votes enfranchised the freedmen? Was anything impossible to a power that had done all this? A million black men started with renewed zeal to vote themselves into the kingdom. So the decade flew away, then revolution of 1876[10] came, and left the half-free serf weary, wondering, but still inspired. Slowly but steadily, in the following years, a new vision began gradually to replace the dream of political power,—a powerful movement, the rise of another ideal to guide the unguided, another pillar of fire by night after a clouded day. It was the ideal of "book-learning"; the curiosity, born of compulsory ignorance, to know and test the power of the **cabalistic** letters of the white man, the longing to know. Here at last seemed to have been discovered the mountain path to Canaan;[11] longer than the highway of Emancipation and law, steep and rugged, but straight, leading to heights high enough to overlook life.

How was "book-learning" expected to help? What was Du Bois's attitude toward this?

Up the new path the advance guard toiled, slowly, heavily, doggedly; only those who have watched and guided the faltering feet, the misty minds, the dull understandings, of the dark pupils of these schools know how faithfully, how piteously, this people strove to learn. It was weary work. The cold statistician wrote down the inches of progress here and there, noted also where here and there a foot had slipped or some one had fallen. To the tired climbers, the horizon was ever dark, the mists were often cold, the Canaan was always dim and far away. If, however, the vistas disclosed as yet no goal, no resting-place, little but flattery and criticism, the journey at least gave leisure for reflection and self-examination; it changed the child of Emancipation to the youth with dawning self-consciousness, self-realization, self-respect. In those somber forests of his striving his own soul rose before him, and he saw himself,—darkly as through a veil; and yet he saw in himself some faint revelation of his power, of his mission. He began to have a dim feeling that, to attain his place in the world, he must be himself, and not another. For the first time he sought to analyze the burden he bore upon his back, that dead-weight of social degradation partially masked behind a half-named Negro problem. He felt his poverty; without a cent, without a home, without land, tools, or savings, he had entered into competition with rich, landed, skilled neighbors. To be a poor man is hard, but to be a poor race in a land of dollars is the very bottom of hardships. He felt the weight of his ignorance,—not simply of letters, but of life, of business, of the humanities; the accumulated sloth and shirking and

10 **revolution of 1876.** Please see the History Connection, page 277.

11 **Canaan.** Promised Land of the Israelites. An ancient region made up of Palestine or the part of Palestine between the Jordan River and the Mediterranean Sea.

VOCABULARY IN PLACE

- **serf,** ***n.*** An agricultural worker
- **cabalistic,** ***adj.*** Having a secret or hidden meaning; occult

awkwardness of decades and centuries shackled his hands and feet. Nor was his burden all poverty and ignorance. The red stain of bastardy, which two centuries of systematic legal defilement of Negro women had stamped upon his race, meant not only the loss of ancient African chastity, but also the hereditary weight of a mass of corruption from white adulterers, threatening almost the obliteration of the Negro home.

Who felt "the weight of his ignorance" and what was the result?

A people thus handicapped ought not to be asked to race with the world, but rather allowed to give all its time and thought to its own social problems. But alas! while sociologists gleefully count his bastards and his prostitutes, the very soul of the toiling, sweating black man is darkened by the shadow of a vast despair. Men call the shadow prejudice, and learnedly explain it as the natural defence of culture against crime, the "higher" against the "lower" races. To which the Negro cries Amen! and swears that to so much of this strange prejudice as is founded on just homage to civilization, culture, righteousness, and progress, he humbly bows and meekly does **obeisance.** But before that nameless prejudice that leaps beyond all this he stands helpless, dismayed, and well-nigh speechless; before that personal disrespect and mockery, the ridicule and systematic humiliation, the distortion of fact and wanton license of fancy,[12] the cynical ignoring of the better and the boisterous welcoming of the worse, the all-pervading desire to **inculcate** disdain for everything black, from Toussaint[13] to the devil,—before this there rises a sickening despair that would disarm and discourage any nation save that black host to whom "discouragement" is an unwritten word.

But the facing of so vast a prejudice could not but bring the inevitable self-questioning, self-disparagement, and lowering of ideals which ever accompany repression and breed in an atmosphere of contempt and hate. Whisperings and **portents** came borne upon the four winds: Lo! we are diseased and dying, cried the dark hosts; we cannot write, our voting is vain; what need of education, since we must always cook and serve? And the Nation echoed and enforced this self-criticism, saying: Be content to be servants, and nothing more; what need of higher culture for halfmen? Away with the black man's ballot, by force or fraud,—and behold the suicide of a race! Nevertheless, out of the evil came something of good,—the more careful adjustment of education to real life, the clearer perception of the Negroes' social responsibilities, and the sobering realization of the meaning of progress.

So dawned the time of *Sturm und Drang*:[14] storm and stress today rocks our little boat on the mad waters of the world-sea; there is within and without the sound of

[12] **wanton license of fancy.** Reckless presentation of fiction as truth. *Wanton* means reckless; *fancy* refers to imagination or fantasy.

[13] **Toussaint.** Toussaint L'Ouverture (1743–1803), Haitian military and political leader who led a successful slave insurrection (1791–1793) and helped the French expel the British from Haiti in 1798

[14] ***Sturm und Drang.*** A late-eighteenth-century German romantic literary movement typified by works that depicted the struggles of a highly emotional individual against conventional society

VOCABULARY IN PLACE

- **obeisance,** *n.* A gesture of the body, such as a curtsy, that expresses deference or homage
- **inculcate,** *v.* To impress upon the mind of another by frequent instruction or repetition
- **portent,** *n.* An indication of something important or calamitous about to occur; an omen

conflict, the burning of body and rending of soul; inspiration strives with doubt, and faith with vain questionings. The bright ideals of the past,—physical freedom, political power, the training of brains and the training of hands,—all these in turn have waxed and waned, until even the last grows dim and overcast. Are they all wrong,—all false? No, not that, but each alone was over-simple and incomplete,—the dreams of a **credulous** race-childhood, or the fond imaginings of the other world which does not know and does not want to know our power. To be really true, all these ideals must be melted and welded into one. The training of the schools we need today more than ever,—the training of deft hands, quick eyes and ears, and above all the broader, deeper, higher culture of gifted minds and pure hearts. The power of the ballot we need in sheer self-defence,—else what shall save us from a second slavery? Freedom, too, the long-sought, we still seek,—the freedom of life and limb, the freedom to work and think, the freedom to love and aspire. Work, culture, liberty,—all these we need, not singly but together, not successively but together, each growing and aiding each, and all striving toward that vaster ideal that swims before the Negro people, the ideal of human brotherhood, gained through the unifying ideal of Race; the ideal of fostering and developing the traits and talents of the Negro, not in opposition to or contempt for other races, but rather in large conformity to the greater ideals of the American Republic, in order that some day on American soil two world-races may give each to each those characteristics both so sadly lack. We the darker ones come even now not altogether empty-handed: there are today no truer exponents of the pure human spirit of the Declaration of Independence than the American Negroes; there is no true American music but the wild sweet melodies of the Negro slave; the American fairy tales and folk-lore are Indian and African; and, all in all, we black men seem the sole oasis of simple faith and reverence in a dusty desert of dollars and smartness. Will America be poorer if she replace her brutal **dyspeptic** blundering with light-hearted but determined Negro humility? or her coarse and cruel wit with loving jovial good-humor? Or her vulgar music with the soul of the Sorrow Songs?

How could the "power of the ballot," or voting, save blacks from a second slavery?

Merely a concrete test of the underlying principles of the great republic is the Negro Problem, and the spiritual striving of the freedmen's sons is the **travail** of souls whose burden is almost beyond the measure of their strength, but who bear it in the name of an historic race, in the name of this the land of their fathers' fathers, and in the name of human opportunity.

And now what I have briefly sketched in large outline let me on coming pages tell again in many ways, with loving emphasis and deeper detail, that men may listen to the striving in the souls of black folk. ■

VOCABULARY IN PLACE

- **credulous,** ***adj.*** Ready to believe, especially on slight or uncertain evidence
- **dyspeptic,** ***adj.*** Displaying a sullen disposition
- **travail,** ***n.*** Work, especially of a painful or laborious nature; toil

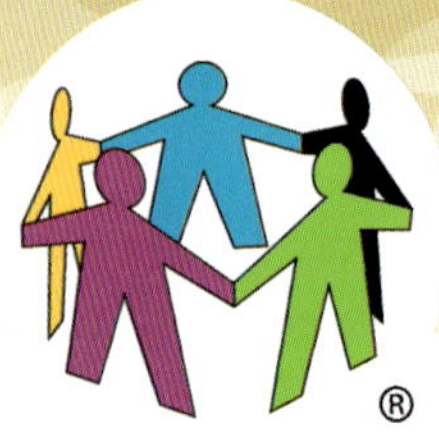

Understanding the Selection

Recalling

1. According to Du Bois, what "unasked question" do white people want to ask black people?

2. Which people are "gifted with second-sight in this American world"?

3. Locate and reread the fourth paragraph of the chapter, which begins "The history of the American Negro is the history of this strife." What caused this strife?

4. By Du Bois's account, what happened in the decade following the Civil War and since Emancipation?

5. What is the "double-aimed struggle" of the black artisan?

6. What "bright ideals of the past" have "waxed and waned"?

Interpreting

1. Why do you think that he seldom answers this question?

2. Why do these same people feel a "twoness"?

3. What is the main idea of this paragraph? Write one or two sentences, in your own words, to summarize the author's main point.

4. Did emancipation from slavery bring African Americans true freedom? Support your answer with a quotation from the text.

5. What effect does this struggle have upon the artisan's skills?

6. Why must these ideals be "melted and welded into one"?

Synthesizing

1. While Booker T. Washington encouraged blacks to learn practical, vocational skills, Du Bois promoted academic and intellectual development. Did Du Bois think that Washington was totally wrong? How did Du Bois propose to change things?
2. Why was Du Bois such a controversial figure? Find at least one of Du Bois's ideas that might have alarmed both blacks and whites in 1903.

Delving Deeper

History Connection

Revolution of 1876. This is a historical period that altered the course of American history but receives little mention in most history books. After ten years of efforts by the federal government to "reconstruct" the South, members of the old white aristocracy led a movement to reverse the policies enacted on behalf of freed blacks in the first decade following the war. Whites reclaimed most of the land, and blacks were virtually reduced to slavery as exploited, powerless sharecroppers. The Ku Klux Klan became much more prominent in 1876, as well; thereafter—and for decades to come—lynchings were an everyday threat, and the Jim Crow laws became the law of the land throughout the South.

Research Topics: 1) How did everyday life change for African Americans after 1876? 2) How are the following related: President Rutherford B. Hayes, the Compromise of 1877, Congressional Reconstruction, and the political revolution of 1876?

About the Author

W. E. B. Du Bois (1868–1963) was a writer, a sociologist, a civil rights activist, and an important African-American leader of the early twentieth century. Born William Edward Burghardt Du Bois in Great Barrington, Massachusetts, he was raised by his mother, who encouraged him to study. He attended Fisk University in Nashville, Tennessee. In 1896 he became one of the first African Americans to receive a Ph.D. from Harvard University.

Du Bois taught at the University of Pennsylvania and Atlanta University, where he published his most famous work, *The Souls of Black Folk* (1903). In 1905, he founded the Niagara Movement, a group dedicated to battling racial segregation. He was also a founding member of the National Association for the Advancement of Colored People (NAACP), for which he served as director of publications and as editor of its influential journal, *Crisis.*

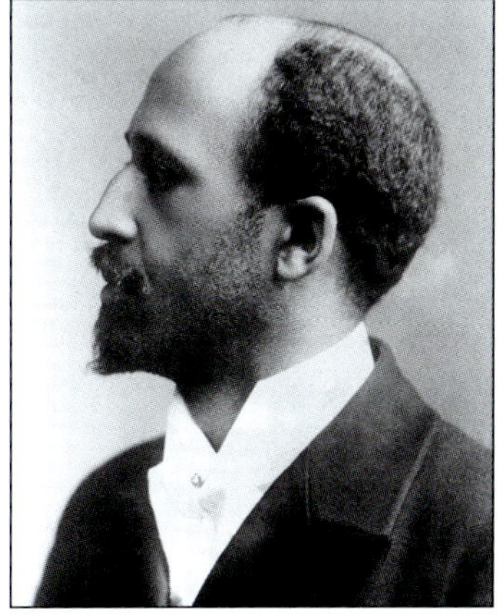

In 1934 Du Bois went back to teach at the University of Atlanta, and in 1940 he published his autobiography, *Dusk of Dawn.* Other works include *John Brown* (1909), *The Negro* (1915), *Darkwater: Voices from within the Veil* (1920), and *Black Reconstruction* (1935). He later moved to Ghana, where he became a citizen shortly before his death in 1963.

Prereading

"Address to the Country"

by W. E. B. Du Bois

In early 1905, W. E. B. Du Bois and twenty-six businessmen, educators, and political activists held a meeting at a house in Buffalo, New York, just down the road from Niagara Falls. Led by Du Bois, these individuals resolved to fight—by peaceful means—for the basic rights, freedoms, and privileges that every American deserves but that had been systematically denied to most African Americans. A few months later, the group issued its "Declaration of Principles" to members of the newly founded Niagara Movement. These principles detailed 18 essential areas in which blacks had been deprived their due rights. (See the History Connection on page 283.)

The group held its first convention at Niagara Falls and used this landmark as a symbol of the "tides of protest" they intended to unleash upon American society. For several years, the Niagara Movement published pamphlets and lobbied various politicians, including President Theodore Roosevelt, to put an end to Jim Crow laws and to address a host of other civil rights issues.

The following speech, Du Bois's "Address to the Country," was delivered at the organization's second convention, which was staged at another symbolic location, Harper's Ferry, Virginia, site of abolitionist John Brown's famous raid. Perhaps the speech had little immediate, measurable impact on civil rights, but Du Bois's words resounded around the country. This speech, along with his book, *The Souls of Black Folk,* made Du Bois one of the most recognized leaders of the early Civil Rights Movement.

Slow growth and poor organization led to the disbanding of the Niagara Movement in 1910, but not before Du Bois and other leaders founded a new organization, The National Association for the Advancement of Colored People (NAACP), which continues its mission to this day and whose contribution to the history of the twentieth century has been immeasurable.

This is a piece that begs to be read aloud. Remember: this is a speech, not an essay or story, so try to imagine listening to Du Bois deliver these words himself.

Address to the Country
Speech at the Second Convention of the Niagara Movement

by W. E. B. Du Bois

The men of the Niagara Movement[1] coming from the toil of the year's hard work and pausing a moment from the earning of their daily bread turn toward the nation and again ask in the name of ten million the privilege of a hearing. In the past year the work of the Negro hater has flourished in the land. Step by step the defenders of the rights of American citizens have retreated. The work of stealing the black man's ballot[2] has progressed and the fifty and more representatives of stolen votes still sit in the nation's capital. Discrimination in travel and public accommodation has so spread that some of our weaker brethren are actually afraid to thunder against color discrimination as such and are simply whispering for ordinary decencies.

Against this the Niagara Movement eternally protests. We will not be satisfied to take one jot or tittle[3] less than our full manhood rights. We claim for ourselves every single right that belongs to a freeborn American, political, civil and social; and until we get these rights we will never cease to protest and **assail** the ears of America. The battle we wage is not for ourselves alone but for all true Americans. It is a fight for ideals, lest this, our common fatherland, false to its founding, become in truth the land of the thief and the home of the Slave—a by-word and a hissing among the nations for its sounding **pretensions** and pitiful accomplishment.

What "ideals" was Du Bois speaking about here?

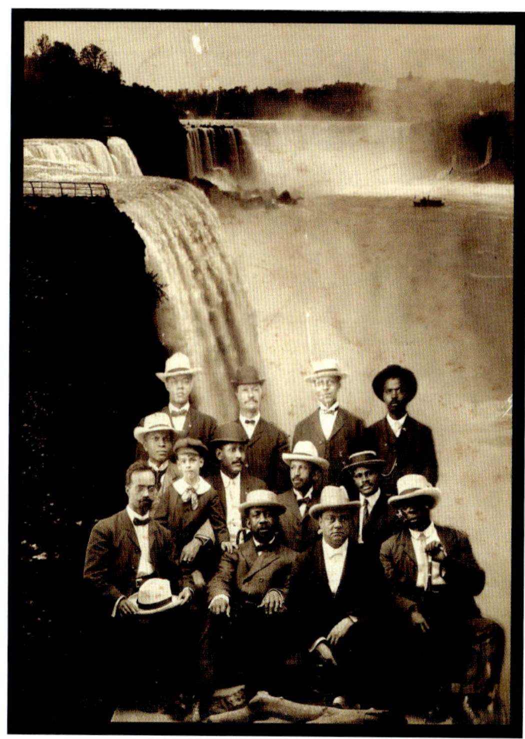

"Founders of the Niagara Movement." Du Bois is seated in the middle with the white hat. Daguerreotype. University of Massachusetts Library.

[1] **Niagara Movement.** Founded by Du Bois and others in 1905, this organization was the forerunner of the National Association for the Advancement of Colored People (NAACP).

[2] **stealing the black man's ballot.** Poll taxes and other oppressive tactics were used to prevent blacks from voting.

[3] **jot or tittle.** Small bit

VOCABULARY IN PLACE

- **assail,** *v.* To attack verbally, as with ridicule or censure
- **pretension,** *n.* Unjustified claim

Never before in the modern age has a great and civilized folk threatened to adopt so cowardly a creed in the treatment of its fellow-citizens born and bred on its soil. Stripped of **verbiage** and **subterfuge** and in its naked nastiness the new American creed says: Fear to let black men even try to rise lest they become the equals of the white. And this is the land that professes to follow Jesus Christ. The blasphemy of such a course is only matched by its cowardice.

In detail our demands are clear and **unequivocal**. First, we would vote; with the right to vote goes everything: Freedom, manhood, the honor of your wives, the chastity of your daughters, the right to work, and the chance to rise, and let no man listen to those who deny this.

We want full manhood suffrage, and we want it now, henceforth and forever.

Second. We want discrimination in public accommodation to cease. Separation in railway and street cars, based simply on race and color, is un-American, un-democratic, and silly. We protest against all such discrimination.

Third. We claim the right of freemen to walk, talk, and be with them that wish to be with us. No man has a right to choose another man's friends, and to attempt to do so is an **impudent** interference with the most fundamental human privilege.

Fourth. We want the laws enforced against rich as well as poor; against Capitalist as well as Laborer; against white as well as black. We are not more lawless than the white race, we are more often arrested, convicted and mobbed. We want justice even for criminals and outlaws. We want the Constitution of the country enforced. We want Congress to take charge of Congressional elections. We want the Fourteenth amendment[4] carried out to the letter and every State dis-franchised in Congress which attempts to disfranchise its rightful voters. We want the Fifteenth amendment[5] enforced and No State allowed to base its franchise simply on color.

The failure of the Republican Party in Congress at the session just closed to redeem its pledge of 1904 with reference to suffrage conditions at the South seems a plain, deliberate, and premeditated breach of promise, and stamps that party as guilty of obtaining votes under false pretense.

Fifth. We want our children educated. The school system in the country districts of the South is a disgrace and in few towns and cities are the Negro schools what they ought to be. We want the national government to step in and wipe out illiteracy in the South. Either the United States will destroy ignorance or ignorance will destroy the United States.

And when we call for education we mean real education. We believe in work. We ourselves are workers, but work is not necessarily education. Education is the development of power and ideal. We want our children trained as intelligent human beings should be, and we will fight for

[4] **Fourteenth amendment.** Prevents states from discriminating against any United States citizen (reverses the judgment of the infamous *Dred Scott* case)

[5] **Fifteenth amendment.** States that the right to vote cannot be denied on the grounds of race

VOCABULARY IN PLACE

- **verbiage,** *n.* An excess of words; wordiness
- **subterfuge,** *n.* A deceptive stratagem or device; a trick
- **unequivocal,** *adj.* Admitting no doubt; unambiguous
- **impudent,** *adj.* Marked by contemptuous boldness or disregard for others

all time against any proposal to educate black boys and girls simply as servants and underlings, or simply for the use of other people. They have a right to know, to think, to aspire.

These are some of the chief things which we want. How shall we get them? By voting where we may vote, by persistent, unceasing **agitation;** by hammering at the truth, by sacrifice and work.

We do not believe in violence, neither in the despised violence of the raid nor the lauded violence of the soldier, nor the barbarous violence of the mob, but we do believe in John Brown, in that **incarnate** spirit of justice, that hatred of a lie, that willingness to sacrifice money, reputation, and life itself on the altar of right. And here on the scene of John Brown's **martyrdom** we **reconsecrate** ourselves, our honor, our property to the final emancipation of the race which John Brown died to make free.

Our enemies, triumphant for the present, are fighting the stars in their courses. Justice and humanity must prevail. We live to tell these dark brothers of ours—scattered in counsel,[6] wavering and weak—that no bribe of money or notoriety, no promise of wealth or fame, is worth the surrender of a peoples' manhood or the loss of a man's self-respect. We refuse to surrender the leadership of this race to cowards and bucklers. We are men; we will be treated as men. On this rock we have planted our banners. We will never give up, though the trump of doom[7] find us still fighting.

And we shall win. The past promised it, the present foretells it. Thank God for John Brown! Thank God for Garrison and Douglass! Sumner and Phillips, Nat Turner and Robert Gould Shaw,[8] and all the hallowed dead who died for freedom! Thank God for all those today, few though their voices be, who have not forgotten the divine brotherhood of all men white and black, rich or poor, fortunate and unfortunate.

We appeal to the young men and women of this nation, to those whose nostrils are not yet befouled by greed and snobbery and racial narrowness: Stand up for the right, prove yourselves worthy of your heritage and whether born north or south dare to treat men as men. Cannot the nation that has absorbed ten million foreigners into its political life without catastrophe absorb ten million Negro Americans into that same political life at less cost than their unjust and illegal exclusion will involve?

Courage brothers! The battle for humanity is not lost or losing. All across the skies sit signs of promise. The Slav is raising in his might, the yellow millions are tasting liberty, the black Africans are writing toward the light, and everywhere the laborer,[9] with ballot in his hand, is voting open the gates of Opportunity and Peace. The morning breaks over blood-stained hills. We must not falter, we may not shrink. Above are the everlasting stars. ■

---

6 **scattered in counsel.** Unable to agree or overwhelmed by advice *(counsel)* from others

7 **trump of doom.** In other words, the last trumpet sounded at the end of time. See I Thessalonians 4:16 and Revelation 8:2–11:15.

8 **Garrison . . . Shaw.** Abolitionists and civil-rights activists

9 **everywhere the laborer.** A reference to political activists who organized labor unions in the early twentieth century

VOCABULARY IN PLACE

- **agitation,** ***n.*** The stirring up of public interest
- **incarnate,** ***adj.*** Embodied in human form
- **martydom,** ***n.*** The act of dying for a cause
- **reconsecrate,** ***v.*** To solemnly rededicate to a service or goal

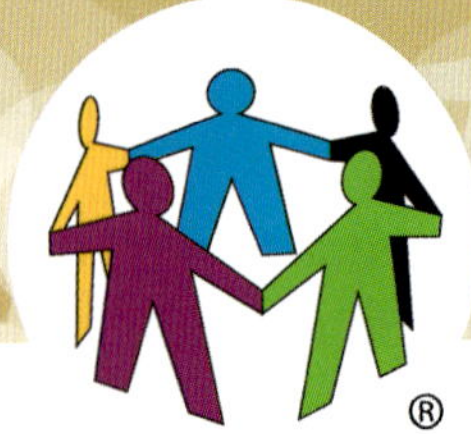

Understanding the Selection

Recalling

1. What hardships or injustices did Du Bois mention in the opening of his speech? Find at least three examples.
2. What was the basic, fundamental demand of the Niagara Movement?
3. According to Du Bois, what would happen to the United States if it did not destroy ignorance?
4. Did members of the Niagara Movement believe that violence could be an effective tool?
5. According to Du Bois, what did the past promise? What did the present foretell?

Interpreting

1. According to Du Bois, what result had discrimination had on the "weaker brethren"?
2. Why, according to Du Bois, was theirs a battle for all "true Americans"?
3. What kind of education did Du Bois desire? How did it differ from other types of education, such as that promoted by Booker T. Washington?
4. How did Du Bois justify his attitude toward violence while simultaneously hailing John Brown and Nat Turner as heroes?
5. Why was Du Bois so confident in this assertion?

Synthesizing

1. Summarize Du Bois's overall tone and mood in the speech. How might the crowd have reacted? How do you think other Americans, white and black, might have reacted? Use examples from the text to support your answer.
2. How did Du Bois try to appeal to all Americans, black and white? Do you think that the reasoning behind his argument is convincing? Why, or why not?

Delving Deeper

History Connection

Niagara Movement. This is a photo of the Niagara Movement's original Declaration of Principles, which each member had to sign. There are thirteen additional principal issues, grievances, or concerns set forth in the original document: Courts, Public Opinion, Health, Employers and Labor Unions, Protest, Color Line, "Jim Crow" Cars, [African-American] Soldiers, War Amendments, Oppression, the Church, Agitation, Help.

The final "principle" details each member's "Duties":

1. The duty to vote
2. The duty to respect the rights of others
3. The duty to work
4. The duty to obey the laws
5. The duty to be clean and orderly
6. The duty to send our children to school
7. The duty to respect ourselves, even as we respect others

Working in pairs or small groups, discuss and write short answers to the following questions. Be prepared to present your ideas to the class.

- Why were these "duties" important to the members?
- How would these duties help the members to address their principal concern?
- What mood does the opening of the document convey? Are the members optimistic or pessimistic about the future? Use evidence from the document to support your answer.

THE NIAGARA MOVEMENT

Declaration of Principles
1905

The members of the conference, known as the Niagara Movement, assembled in annual meeting at Buffalo, July 11th, 12th and 13th, 1905, congratulate the Negro-Americans on certain undoubted evidences of progress in the last decade, particularly the increase of intelligence, the buying of property, the checking of crime, the uplift in home life, the advance in literature and art, and the demonstration of constructive and executive ability in the conduct of great religious, economic and educational institutions.

Progress

At the same time, we believe that this class of American citizens should protest emphatically and continually against the curtailment of their political rights. We believe in manhood suffrage; we believe that no man is so good, intelligent or wealthy as to be entrusted wholly with the welfare of his neighbor.

Suffrage

We believe also in protest against the curtailment of our civil rights. All American citizens have the right to equal treatment in places of public entertainment according to their behavior and deserts.

Civil Liberty

We especially complain against the denial of equal opportunities to us in economic life; in the rural districts of the South this amounts to peonage and virtual slavery; all over the South it tends to crush labor and small business enterprises; and everywhere American prejudice, helped often by iniquitous laws, is making it more difficult for Negro-Americans to earn a decent living.

Economic Opportunity

Common school education should be free to all American children and compulsory. High school training should be adequately provided for all, and college training should be the monopoly of no class or race in any section of our common country. We believe that, in defense of our own institutions, the United States should aid common school education, particularly in the South, and we especially recommend concerted agitation to this end.

Education

Prereading

Telegram Sent to the Disarmament Conference

by Marcus Garvey

> *I am not advising you to arm now with the things they have, I am asking you to arm through organization; arm through preparedness. . . . I am saying to the Negro People of the world, get armed with organization; get armed by coming together 400,000,000 strong. That is your weapon. Their weapon in the past has been big guns and explosive shells; your weapon must be universal organization.*

The above lines are from a speech that Marcus Garvey delivered in Liberty Hall, New York City, one week before he sent the following telegram. In the speech, Garvey encouraged Africans and people of African descent all over the world to unite around their common causes. He also criticized all major world leaders who had taken part in a recent series of peace and international policy conferences around the world.

Participants in the **Paris Peace Conference of 1919** hammered out the **Treaty of Versailles,** which formally ended World War I. Part I of the treaty established the **League of Nations,** the international organization whose mission was to ensure lasting world peace. Member states held numerous conferences on everything from human trafficking to military disarmament. (Clearly, peace in Europe was fleeting, as World War II broke out within two decades. Who or what was to blame for the rise of the abominable Adolph Hitler will be debated for years to come.)

The Treaty of Versailles demanded that Germany abandon its colonial interests in Africa, which was subsequently divided into several large territories and placed under the administration of "Mandatory Powers" (as termed in Article 22 of the Covenant of the League of Nations) such as France and Britain. Marcus Garvey and others were angered by the notion that Africa and its people should be divided up as spoils of war.

Following the text of the telegram is a special section of quotations from Marcus Garvey's writings and speeches that will help to shed light on his philosophy and legacy. These great words inspired future leaders, especially Malcolm X and other participants in the **Black Power** and **Black Arts Movements** of the 1960s and '70s. (See Unit 4 of *Grace Abounding.*) Garvey was a major advocate of **Black nationalism,** a political and social movement that celebrated African heritage and culture and sought to unify Africans "at home and abroad" to develop their own economic and cultural institutions rather than assimilate into white society.

Telegram Sent to the Disarmament Conference[1]

by Marcus Garvey

NOVEMBER 11, 1921
President and Members of the International Conference on Disarmament,

Care of Secretary of Conference,
Pan-American Building,
Washington, D.C.

HONORABLE GENTLEMEN:
I salute you in the name of Democracy, and for the cause of Justice on behalf of the four hundred million Negroes of the world. Your Honorable Conference now sitting in Washington has a purpose that has been announced and advertised to the world for several months. You were called together by the President to the Democratic Republic of the United States of America to discuss the problem of armaments, the settlement of which you believe will ensure the perpetual peace of the world. As the elected spokesman of the Negro peoples of the world who desire freedom, politically, industrially, educationally, socially and religiously, as well as a full enjoyment of world democracy and a national independence all our own on the continent of Africa, it is for me to inform you of a little **slight** that has been shown to four hundred million Negroes who form a part of this world's population. At the Versailles Peace Conference, the statesmen who gathered there made the awful mistake of legislating for the **disposition** of other people's lands (especially in Africa) without taking them into consideration, believing that a world peace could have been established after such a conference. The mistake is now apparent. There can be no peace among us mortals so long as the strong of humanity oppresses the weak, for in due process of time and through

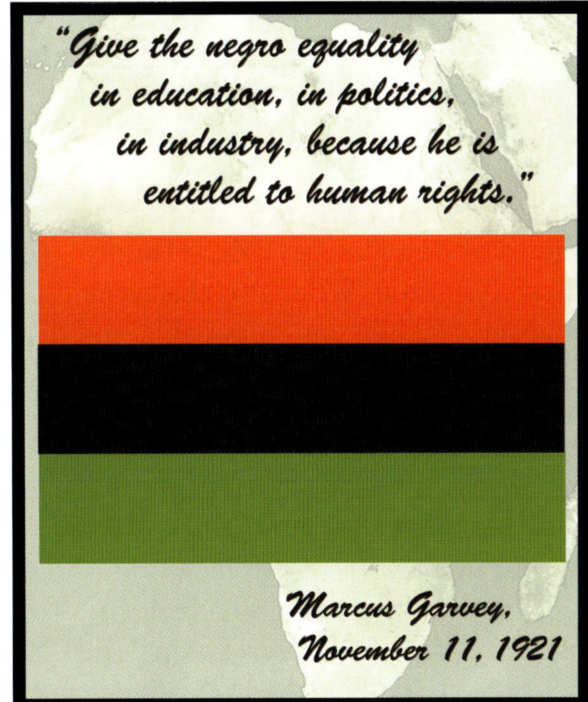

The UNIA (Universal Negro Improvement Association) flag

1 **Disarmament Conference.** One of many conferences held following World War I through which nations sought to ensure peace by limiting or regulating military power around the world

VOCABULARY IN PLACE

- **slight,** *n.* A deliberate discourtesy; the act of treating something as if it has little importance
- **disposition,** *n.* A bestowal or transfer to another

evolution the weak will one day turn, even like the worm, and then humanity's hope of peace will be shattered. All men have brains; some use their abilities for inventing destructive elements of warfare, such as guns, gun-powder, gas,[2] and other destructive chemicals. The Negro for hundreds of years has attempted nothing destructive to the peace and good-will of humanity; in fact, he has not even made an attempt to make the world know that he is alive; nevertheless, like the worm, the Negro will one day turn.[3] I humbly ask you therefore that your Honorable Conference act, not like the one at Versailles, but that you realize and appreciate the fact that the Negro is a man, and that there can be no settlement of world affairs without proper consideration being given to him with his rights. President Harding of America has but recently sounded the real cry of Democracy. He says to his own country, and I think it should be an advice to the world, "Give the Negro equality in education, in politics, in industry, because he is entitled to human rights." I humbly beg to recommend to your Honorable Conference those quoted words of President Harding. Negroes have blood, they have souls, and for the cause of Liberty they feel that the conduct of men like Alexander, Hannibal, Caesar, Napoleon, Wellington, Lafayette, Garabaldi, Washington,[4] is **imitable,** and that peace not founded on real human justice will only be a mockery of the divine **invocation,** "Peace, perfect peace." I trust your Honorable Conference will not fail to take into consideration, therefore, that there are four hundred million Negroes in the world who demand Africa as their rightful heritage, even as the European claims Europe, and the Asiatic Asia. I pray that your Conference will not only be one of disarmament, but that it will be a congregation of the "Bigger Brotherhood," through which Europe will see the rights of Asia, Asia and Europe see the rights of Africa, and Africa and Asia see the rights of Europe and accordingly give every race and nation their due, and let there be peace indeed. On behalf of the four hundred million Negroes of the world not represented at your Honorable Conference,

According to Garvey, what had "Negro" people done for "hundreds of years"?

I have the honor to be

Your obedient servant,

MARCUS GARVEY,
President General of the Universal Negro Improvement Association and First Provisional President of Africa, New York City.

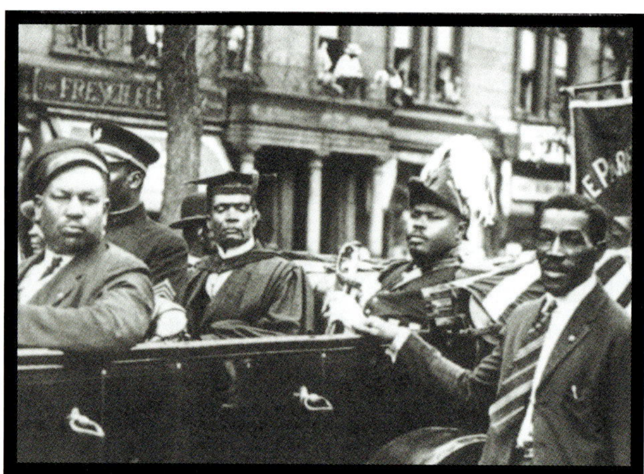

Marcus Garvey, second from right.
Photograph by James VanDerZee

[2] **gas.** A reference to mustard gas and other lethal gases that were widely used to horrible effect during World War I

[3] **one day turn.** Meaning black people will one day be empowered to gain what is rightly theirs

[4] **Alexander . . . Washington.** Famous historical figures. (See History Connection, page 289.)

VOCABULARY IN PLACE

- **imitable,** ***adj.*** Worthy of imitation
- **invocation,** ***n.*** A prayer or other saying used to seek guidance or inspiration from a higher power

Selected Quotations from the Speeches and Writings of Marcus Garvey

- "Liberate the minds of men and ultimately you will liberate the bodies of men."

- "All of us may not live to see the higher accomplishment of an African Empire—so strong and powerful, as to compel the respect of mankind, but we in our lifetime can so work and act as to make the dream a possibility within another generation."

- "God and nature first made us what we are, and then out of our own created genius we make ourselves what we want to be. Follow always that great law. Let the sky and God be our limit and Eternity our measurement."

- "There is no force like success, and that is why the individual makes all effort to surround himself throughout life with the evidence of it; as of the individual, so should it be of the nation."

- "The only protection against INJUSTICE in man is POWER—physical, financial, and scientific."

- "Progress is the attraction that moves humanity."

- "A race without authority and power is a race without respect."

- "The whole world is run on bluff."

- "Chance has never yet satisfied the hope of a suffering people. Action, self-reliance, the vision of self and the future have been the only means by which the oppressed have seen and realized the light of their own freedom."

- "If you have no confidence in self you are twice defeated in the race of life. With confidence you have won even before you have started."

- "Be as proud of your race today as your fathers were in days of yore. We have a beautiful history, and we shall create another in the future that will astonish the world."

- "Education is the medium by which a people are prepared for the creation of their own particular civilization, and the advancement and glory of their own race."

- "What you do today that is worthwhile, inspires others to act at some future time."

- "Men who are in earnest are not afraid of consequences."

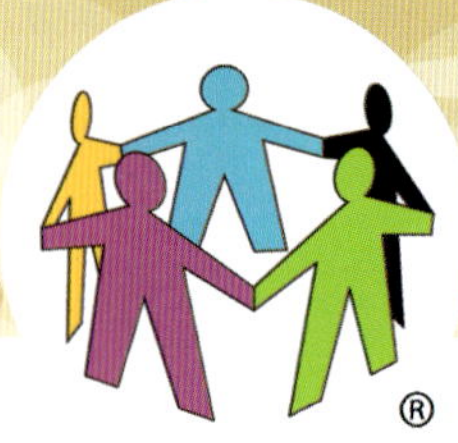

Understanding the Selection

Recalling

1. What did the attendees of the conference hope to accomplish by settling the "problem of armaments"?
2. According to Garvey, what "slight" was shown to the people of Africa and to people of African descent by the designers of the Treaty of Versailles?
3. What does Garvey want the conference attendees to realize about African Americans?
4. According to President Harding, why did black people deserve "equality in education, in politics, in industry"?

Interpreting

1. Did Garvey agree that peace is dependent on controlling armaments alone?
2. Why did Garvey say that the "mistake is now apparent" with regard to the Treaty of Versailles? What warning was Garvey sending to the conference?
3. Why did Garvey want the conference attendees to think about African Americans, even though "the Negro" was not part of the "problem of armaments"?
4. What did Garvey mean when he said that President Harding had "sounded the real cry of democracy"?

Synthesizing

1. Why did Marcus Garvey decide to send this letter to the Disarmament Conference, even though, presumably, the agenda for the meeting had little or nothing to do with Africa or with people of African descent?
2. Choose at least three of Garvey's Select Quotations and explain why each is still relevant or useful to people today.

Delving Deeper

History Connection

Working individually or in small groups, use your school library or the Internet to research the important historical figures mentioned by Garvey (see footnote 4). All of these men have in common the fact that they were famous military, social, and political leaders. Select three of these names and answer the following questions. Present your findings to the class.

What did this man accomplish militarily? What important social or legal policies did he establish? Why might a leader like Garvey think that this man's deeds were "imitable"?

About the Author

Marcus Mosiah Garvey (1887–1940) was a social activist and Black Nationalist leader. He founded the Universal Negro Improvement Association (UNIA), which started the "Back to Africa" movement in the 1920s, and he was influential to a later generation of African-American leaders.

Garvey was born in Saint Ann's Bay, Jamaica. He left school to work at the age of 14 and eventually gained employment with a printing company in Kingston, Jamaica. In 1907, he helped organize a strike to campaign for higher wages for workers. Garvey traveled to Central America, where he edited newspapers, and later moved to England to live with his sister. He founded the UNIA in 1914, following his return to Jamaica.

In 1916, Garvey moved the UNIA headquarters to Harlem, New York, and started the *Negro World,* a newspaper that he used to promote black pride and nationalism. Through the newspaper and his powerful speaking style, Garvey urged African Americans that the best way to avoid the racial segregation, discrimination, and lynching that were rampant in parts of the U.S. was to leave the country and go "Back to Africa." He often wore military regalia to lend seriousness to his message and inspire Black pride.

During the campaign, Garvey bought steamships to transport the people who had signed up. He received huge financial support, but he was not known as a good businessman and his money soon ran out. He was arrested, charged with fraud, and spent two years in jail.

Garvey wrote several speeches, articles, and other works during his lifetime. His published works include *Philosophy and Opinions of Marcus Garvey* (1923) and *The Tragedy of White Injustice* (1935). After his release from jail, he was deported back to Jamaica and eventually settled in London before his death in 1940.

Prereading

Preface to *The New Negro*

by Alain Locke

Like so many educators, philosophers, and editors, Alain Locke's impact on history and culture may be immeasurable, in the sense that it is both profound and difficult to calculate. Those who simply ponder and convey the fruits of human intellect and creativity do not often themselves become the emblems of great cultural movements. Locke is unusual in this respect. His name will be remembered, thanks in part to the fact that he coined the term ***Harlem Renaissance,*** and was the first to recognize and articulate the profound cultural "metamorphosis" taking place all around him.

This essay, the forward to his anthology *The New Negro,* established Locke as the philosophical (and editorial) muscle behind the great Harlem Renaissance. The works featured in his renowned anthology are essential contributions by the new generation of "enlightened" individuals, who replaced the "protective social mimicry" inherent in such degrading characterizations as Jim Crow with the same "self-reliance and self-respect" that had always been present in Negro spirituals, folk art, and lore. (See the History Connection on page 303 for more on *The New Negro.*)

As a philosopher, Locke was concerned first and foremost with logical reasoning as the means to satisfy his love and pursuit of wisdom. In his essay, Locke rejects **sentimentalism**—basing thoughts and ideas on emotions instead of reason—and leads his readers down an elegant, logical path to reveal a radical but exquisitely, undeniably truthful interpretation of the African-American cultural heritage, an interpretation that ran counter to what most people had been led to believe.

Locke appeals to all American intellectuals, black and white, in making the point that African-American art does not need to be accepted, judged, or even defined. It simply needs to be displayed and recognized for what it is—an integral and evolving facet of American life. He begins by overturning common assumptions regarding the tremendous northward migration of African Americans during the opening decades of the twentieth century, stating that, regardless of obvious economic and social factors, the main cause of the migration was simply the desire to seize a "new vision of opportunity."

preface to The New Negro

by Alain Locke

In the last decade something beyond the watch and guard of statistics has happened in the life of the American Negro and the three norns who have traditionally presided over the Negro problem have a changeling[1] in their laps. The Sociologist, the Philanthropist, the Race-leader[2] are not unaware of the New Negro, but they are at a loss to account for him. He simply cannot be swathed in their formulae.[3] For the younger generation is vibrant with a new psychology; the new spirit is awake in the masses, and under the very eyes of the professional observers is transforming what has been a **perennial** problem into the **progressive** phases of contemporary Negro life.

Could such a **metamorphosis** have taken place as suddenly as it has appeared to? The answer is no; not because the New Negro is not here, but because the Old Negro had long become more of a myth than a man. The old Negro, we must remember, was a creature of moral debate and historical controversy. His has been a stock figure perpetuated as an historical fiction partly in innocent sentimentalism,[4] partly in deliberate reactionism. The Negro himself has contributed his share to this through a sort of protective social mimicry[5] forced upon him by the adverse circumstances of dependence. So for generations in the mind of America, the Negro has been more of a formula than a human being—a something to be argued about, condemned or defended, to be "kept down," or "in his place," or "helped up," to be worried with or worried over, harassed or patronized, a social bogey or a social burden. The thinking Negro even has been induced to share the same general attitude, to focus his attention on controversial issues, to see himself in the **distorted** perspective of a social problem. His shadow, so to speak, has

1 **three norns . . . changeling.** In Norse mythology, the Norns are the three goddesses of fate (past, present, and future). A *changeling,* also from European folklore, is a child that has been secretly exchanged for another. Locke introduces the "New Negro" as an individual who can no longer adhere to or be defined by commonly accepted, harmful misconceptions.

2 **Sociologist . . . Race-leader.** Activists, white or black, who work closely with the black community. A *philanthropist* is one who gives money to charitable causes.

3 **swathed . . . formulae.** Defined in conventional terms. (*Swath* means to wrap. *Formulae* is a plural form of *formula.*)

4 **sentimentalism.** The practice of basing one's thoughts on emotion as opposed to reason or logic. Rejecting sentimentalism is key to Locke's approach as a philosopher and is referred to frequently in the essay as the means to true progress.

5 **mimicry.** The act of *mimicking,* imitating another so as to ridicule. Locke exposes the negative effects caused by degrading depictions of black people in minstrel shows and elsewhere.

VOCABULARY IN PLACE

- **perennial,** ***adj.*** Enduring; recurring
- **progressive,** ***adj.*** Advancing toward better conditions
- **metamorphosis,** ***n.*** Transformation
- **distorted,** ***past part.*** False; misrepresented

been more real to him than his personality. Through having had to appeal from the unjust stereotypes of his oppressors and traducers[6] to those of his liberators, friends and benefactors he has had to subscribe to the traditional positions from which his case has been viewed. Little true social or self-understanding has or could come from such a situation.

Why was the Negro unable to gain true "social or self-understanding"?

But while the minds of most of us, black and white, have thus burrowed in the trenches of the Civil War and Reconstruction, the actual march of development has simply flanked these positions, necessitating a sudden reorientation of view. We have not been watching in the right direction; set North and South on a sectional axis, we have not noticed the East till the sun has us blinking.[7]

Recall how suddenly the Negro spirituals revealed themselves; suppressed for generations under the stereotypes of Wesleyan hymn harmony,[8] secretive, half-ashamed, until the courage of being natural brought them out—and behold, there was folk-music. Similarly the mind of the Negro seems suddenly to have slipped from under the tyranny of social intimidation and to be shaking off the psychology of imitation and implied inferiority. By shedding the old chrysalis[9] of the Negro problem[10] we are achieving something like a spiritual emancipation. Until recently, lacking self-understanding, we have been almost as much of a problem to ourselves as we still are to others. But the decade that found us with a problem has left us with only a task. The multitude perhaps feels as yet only a strange relief and a new vague urge, but the thinking few know that in the reaction the vital inner grip of prejudice has been broken.

How was the "grip of prejudice" broken?

With this renewed self-respect and self-dependence, the life of the Negro community is bound to enter a new dynamic phase, the buoyancy from within compensating for whatever pressure there may be of conditions from without. The migrant masses, shifting from country-side to city, hurdle several generations of experience at a leap, but more important, the same thing happens spiritually in the life-attitudes and self-expression of the Young Negro, in his poetry, his art, his education and his new outlook, with the additional advantage, of course, of the poise and greater certainty of knowing what it is all about. From this comes the promise and warrant of a new leadership. As one of them has discerningly put it:

> We have tomorrow
> Bright before us
> Like a flame.
>
> Yesterday, a night-gone thing
> A sun-down name.
>
> And dawn today
> Broad arch above the road we came.
> We march![11]

---

6 **traducer.** One who causes humiliation or disgrace by making false and malicious statements

7 **But while . . . blinking.** In this paragraph Locke introduces his idea that while most people were thinking of issues related to the Civil War and Reconstruction, Negro culture had moved on to a new plane.

8 **Wesleyan hymn harmony.** Charles Wesley (1707–1788), famous for the many hymns he wrote during the Methodist movement. Wesley was a staunch Abolitionist and believed that singing (which many Protestants considered sinful) was the ultimate expression of faith. Ironically, however, many whites who sang Wesley's songs did not approve of the Negro spirituals, which were wrongly labeled as being unrefined or vulgar.

9 **chrysalis.** The protective casing that covers the butterfly pupa in its final stage of development

10 **Negro problem.** A general term widely used by writers and activists during the late nineteenth and early twentieth centuries to describe the divide in American society over issues of race

11 **We have . . . We march!** This is an early poem by Langston Hughes entitled "Youth." Compare this with Sonia Sanchez's "We Can Be"on page 584.

This is what, even more than any "most creditable record of fifty years of freedom," requires that the Negro of today be seen through other than the dusty spectacles of past controversy. The day of "aunties," "uncles" and "mammies" is equally gone. Uncle Tom and Sambo have passed on, and even the "Colonel" and "George" play barnstorm roles from which they escape with relief when the public spotlight is off. The popular melodrama has about played itself out, and it is time to scrap the fictions, garret the bogeys and settle down to a realistic facing of facts.

First we must observe some of the changes which since the traditional lines of opinion were drawn have rendered these quite obsolete. A main change has been, of course, that shifting of the Negro population which has made the Negro problem no longer exclusively or even predominantly Southern. Why should our minds remain sectionalized, when the problem itself no longer is? Then the trend of migration has not only been toward the North and the Central Midwest, but city-ward and to the great centers of industry—the problems of adjustment are new, practical, local and not peculiarly racial. Rather they are an integral part of the large industrial and social problems of our present-day democracy. And finally, with the Negro rapidly in process of class differentiation, if it ever was warrantable to regard and treat the Negro *en masse*[12] it is becoming with every day less possible, more unjust and more ridiculous.

Why was it "unjust" to "treat the Negro en masse*"?*

In the very process of being transplanted, the Negro is becoming transformed.

The tide of Negro migration, northward and city-ward, is not to be fully explained as a blind flood started by the demands of war industry coupled with the shutting off of foreign migration, or by the pressure of poor crops coupled with increased social terrorism in certain sections of the South and Southwest. Neither labor demand, the boll weevil nor the Ku Klux Klan is a basic factor, however contributory any or all of them may have been. The wash and rush of this human tide on the beach line of the northern city centers is to be explained primarily in terms of a new vision of opportunity, of social and economic freedom, of spirit to seize, even in the face of an extortionate[13] and heavy toll, a chance for the improvement of conditions. With each successive wave of it, the movement of the Negro becomes more and more a mass movement toward the larger and the more democratic chance—in the Negro's case a deliberate flight not only from countryside to city, but from medieval America to modern.

Did Locke agree with the common theories as to the causes of "Negro migration"?

Take Harlem as an instance of this. Here in Manhattan is not merely the largest Negro community in the world, but the first concentration in history of so many diverse elements of Negro life. It has attracted the African, the West Indian, the Negro American; has brought together the Negro of the North and the Negro of the South; the man from the city and the man from the town and village; the peasant, the student, the business man, the professional man, artist, poet, musician, adventurer and worker, preacher and criminal, exploiter and social outcast. Each group has come with its own separate motives and for its own special ends, but their greatest experience has been the finding of one another. Proscription[14] and prejudice have thrown these dissimilar

---

12 ***en masse.*** All together (French)

13 **extortionate.** Characterized by *extortion,* the act of obtaining by coercion or intimidation

14 **proscription.** The act of banning or outlawing. African Americans were barred from many public facilities and opportunities during the Jim Crow era.

elements into a common area of contact and interaction. Within this area, race sympathy and unity have determined a further fusing of sentiment and experience. So what began in terms of segregation becomes more and more, as its element mix and react, the laboratory of a great race-welding. Hitherto, it must be admitted that American Negroes have been a race more in name than in fact, or to be exact, more in sentiment than in experience. The chief bond between them has been that of a common condition rather than a common consciousness; a problem in common rather than a life in common. In Harlem, Negro life is seizing upon its first chances for group expression and self-determination.[15]

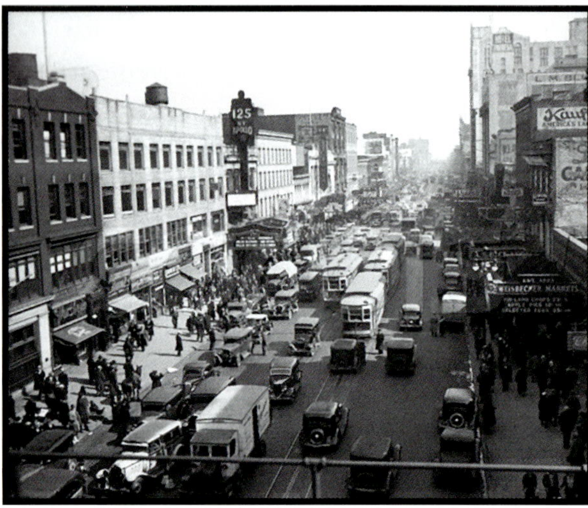

Harlem was a bustling community, circa 1930, as documented in this scene of 125th Street. The marquee of the Apollo Theater appears on the left side of the street.

It is—or promises at least to be—a race capital. That is why our comparison is taken with those **nascent** centers of folk-expression and self-determination which are playing a creative part in the world today. Without pretense to their political significance, Harlem has the same role to play for the New Negro as Dublin has had for the New Ireland or Prague for the New Czechoslovakia.

Harlem, I grant you, isn't typical—but it is significant, it is prophetic. No sane observer, however sympathetic to the new trend, would contend that the great masses are **articulate** as yet, but they stir, they move, they are more than physically restless. The challenge of the new intellectuals among them is clear enough—the "race radicals" and realists who have broken with the old epoch of philanthropic guidance,[16] sentimental appeal and protest. But are we after all only reading into the stirrings of a sleeping giant the dreams of an agitator? The answer is in the migrating peasant. It is the "man farthest down" who is most active in getting up. One of the most characteristic symptoms of this is the professional man, himself migrating to recapture his constituency after a vain effort to maintain in some Southern corner what for years back seemed an established living and clientele. The clergyman following his errant flock, the physician or lawyer trailing his clients, supply the true clues. In a real sense it is the rank and file who are leading, and the leaders who are following. A transformed and transforming psychology permeates the masses.

Why was Harlem so special?

15 **Hitherto . . . self-determination.** *Hitherto* means "until now." One cannot overstate the importance of this paragraph with regard to the essay as a whole. Locke recognized that a social and cultural phenomenon was taking place, the creation of a center of African-American culture.

16 **old epoch . . . guidance.** An *epoch* is a particular period in history. The author refers to the period, especially between Reconstruction and the 1920s, when many white activists and charities—despite good intentions—fostered, according to Locke, an atmosphere of dependence and low self-respect.

VOCABULARY IN PLACE

- **nascent,** ***adj.*** Emerging; coming into existence
- **articulate,** ***adj.*** Capable of clear expression

When the racial leaders of twenty years ago[17] spoke of developing race-pride and stimulating race-consciousness, and of the desirability of race solidarity, they could not in any accurate degree have anticipated the abrupt feeling that has surged up and now pervades the awakened centers. Some of the recognized Negro leaders and a powerful section of white opinion identified with "race work" of the older order have indeed attempted to discount this feeling as a "passing phase," an attack of "race nerves" so to speak, an "aftermath of the war," and the like. It has not **abated,** however, if we are to gauge by the present tone and temper of the Negro press, or by the shift in popular support from the officially recognized and **orthodox** spokesmen to those of the independent, popular, and often radical type who are unmistakable symptoms of a new order. It is a social disservice to blunt the fact that the Negro of the Northern centers has reached a stage where **tutelage,** even of the most interested and well-intentioned sort, must give place to new relationships, where positive self-direction must be reckoned with in ever increasing measure. The American mind must reckon with a fundamentally changed Negro.

What were the "tone and temper of the Negro press," according to Locke?

The Negro too, for his part, has idols of the tribe to smash.[18] If on the one hand the white man has erred in making the Negro appear to be that which would excuse or **extenuate** his treatment of him, the Negro, in turn, has too often unnecessarily excused himself because of the way he has been treated. The intelligent Negro of today is resolved not to make discrimination an extenuation for his shortcomings in performance, individual or collective; he is trying to hold himself at par, neither inflated by sentimental allowances nor depreciated by current social discounts. For this he must know himself and be known for precisely what he is, and for that reason he welcomes the new scientific rather than the old sentimental interest. Sentimental interest in the Negro has ebbed. We used to lament this as the falling off of our friends; now we rejoice and pray to be delivered both from self-pity and condescension. The mind of each racial group has had a bitter weaning, apathy or hatred on one side matching disillusionment or resentment on the other; but they face each other today with the possibility at least of entirely new mutual attitudes.

It does not follow that if the Negro were better known, he would be better liked or better treated. But mutual understanding is basic for any subsequent cooperation and adjustment. The effort toward this will at least have the effect of remedying in large part what has been the most unsatisfactory feature of our present stage of race relationships in America, namely the fact that the more intelligent and representative elements of the two race groups have at so many points got quite out of vital touch with one another.

Did Locke express hope for the future? Why, or why not?

---

17 **racial leaders . . . years ago.** For example, Booker T. Washington and W. E. B. Du Bois

18 **idols . . . to smash.** The philosopher Francis Bacon (1561–1629), in his work *Novum Organum,* coined the term *idols of the tribe* to describe false beliefs resulting from natural human tendencies.

VOCABULARY IN PLACE

- **abate,** *v.* Lessen; decrease in intensity
- **orthodox,** *adj.* Adhering to accepted or traditional beliefs
- **tutelage,** *n.* The activity of a guardian or tutor
- **extenuate,** *v.* To lessen the magnitude or seriousness of

The fiction is that the life of the races is separate, and increasingly so. The fact is that they have touched too closely at the unfavorable and too lightly at the favorable levels.

While inter-racial councils have sprung up in the South, drawing on forward elements of both races, in the Northern cities manual laborers may brush elbows in their everyday work, but the community and business leaders have experienced no such interplay or far too little of it. These segments must achieve contact or the race situation in America becomes desperate. Fortunately this is happening. There is a growing realization that in social effort the co-operative basis must supplant long-distance philanthropy, and that the only safeguard for mass relations in the future must be provided in the carefully maintained contacts of the enlightened minorities of both race groups. In the intellectual realm a renewed and keen curiosity is replacing the recent apathy; the Negro is being carefully studied, not just talked about and discussed. In art and letters, instead of being wholly caricatured, he is being seriously portrayed and painted.

Who needed to work together in order to improve the "race situation"?

To all of this the New Negro is keenly responsive as an **augury** of a new democracy in American culture. He is contributing his share to the new social understanding. But the desire to be understood would never in itself have been sufficient to have opened so completely the protectively closed portals of the thinking Negro's mind. There is still too much possibility of being snubbed or patronized for that. It was rather the necessity for fuller, truer self-expression, the realization of the unwisdom of allowing social discrimination to segregate him mentally, and a counter-attitude to cramp and fetter his own living—and so the "spite-wall" that the intellectuals built over the "color-line"[19] has happily been taken down. Much of this re-opening of intellectual contacts has centered in New York and has been richly fruitful not merely in the enlarging of personal experience, but in the definite enrichment of American art and letters and in the clarifying of our common vision of the social tasks ahead.

The particular significance in the re-establishment of contact between the more advanced and representative classes is that it promises to offset some of the unfavorable reactions of the past, or at least to re-surface race contacts somewhat for the future. Subtly the conditions that are molding a New Negro are molding a new American attitude.

However, this new phase of things is delicate; it will call for less charity but more justice; less help, but infinitely closer understanding. This is indeed a critical stage of race relationships because of the likelihood, if the new temper is not understood, of engendering sharp group antagonism and a second crop of more calculated prejudice. In some quarters, it has already done so.

Having weaned the Negro, public opinion cannot continue to paternalize.[20] The Negro today is inevitably moving forward under the control largely of his own objectives. What

19 **"spite-wall" . . . "color-line".** The *color line* was a name given to the practice of racial segregation, particularly in the South. The "spite-wall" was a psychological and emotional barrier that some black intellectuals built in order to try to ignore the color line, which in turn isolated them further from their white counterparts.

20 **paternalize.** The practice of treating or governing people in a fatherly manner, especially by providing for their needs without giving them rights or responsibilities

VOCABULARY IN PLACE

- **augury,** *n.* Omen; a sign of something coming

are these objectives? Those of his outer life are happily already well and finally formulated, for they are none other than the ideals of American institutions and democracy. Those of his inner life are yet in process of formation, for the new psychology at present is more of a consensus of feeling than of opinion, of attitude rather than of program. Still some points seem to have crystallized.

Did the Negro's basic goals differ from those of other Americans, according to Locke?

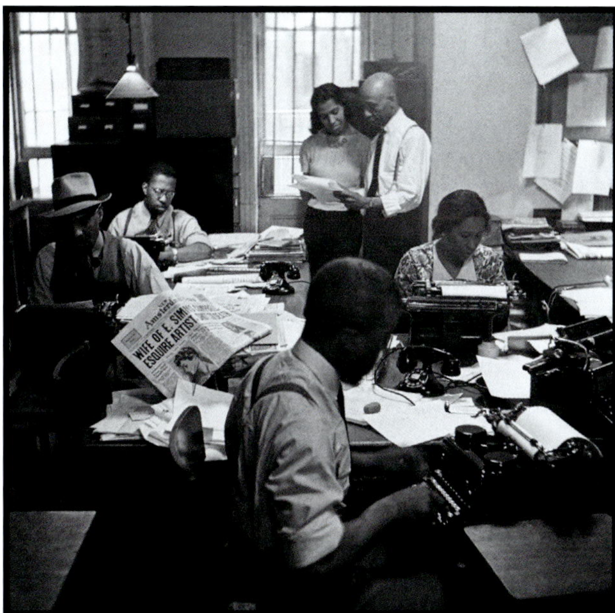

The newsroom of the *New York Amsterdam News.* Founded in Harlem in 1909, this paper had—by the late 1940s—the largest circulation in the Negro press.

Up to the present one may adequately describe the Negro's "inner objectives" as an attempt to repair a damaged group psychology and reshape a warped social perspective. Their realization has required a new mentality for the American Negro. And as it matures we begin to see its effects; at first, negative, **iconoclastic,** and then positive and constructive. In this new group psychology we note the lapse of sentimental appeal, then the development of a more positive self-respect and self-reliance; the repudiation of social dependence, and then the gradual recovery from hyper-sensitiveness and "touchy" nerves, the repudiation of the double standard of judgment with its special philanthropic allowances and then the sturdier desire for objective and scientific appraisal; and finally the rise from social disillusionment to race pride, from the sense of social debt to the responsibilities of social contribution, and offsetting the necessary working and commonsense acceptance of restricted conditions, the belief in ultimate esteem and recognition. Therefore the Negro today wishes to be known for what he is, even in his faults and shortcomings, and scorns a **craven** and precarious survival at the price of seeming to be what he is not. He resents being spoken of as a social **ward** or minor, even by his own, and to being regarded a chronic patient for the sociological clinic, the sick man of American Democracy. For the same reasons, he himself is through with those social nostrums and panaceas,[21] the so-called "solutions" of his "problem," with which he and the country have been so liberally dosed in the past. Religion, freedom, education, money—in turn, he has ardently hoped for and peculiarly trusted these things; he still believes in them, but not in blind trust that they alone will solve his life-problem.

Each generation, however, will have its creed, and that of the present is the belief

21 **nostrums and panaceas.** A *nostrum* is a medicine whose effectiveness is unproved; a *panacea* is a remedy for all diseases.

VOCABULARY IN PLACE

- **iconoclastic,** ***adj.*** Seeking to overthrow traditional ideas
- **craven,** ***adj.*** Characterized by abject fear; cowardly
- **ward,** ***n.*** A person under the care or protection of another

in the **efficacy** of collective effort, in race cooperation. This deep feeling of race is at present the mainspring of Negro life. It seems to be the outcome of the reaction to proscription and prejudice; an attempt, fairly successful on the whole, to convert a defensive into an offensive position, a handicap into an incentive. It is radical in tone, but not in purpose and only the most stupid forms of opposition, misunderstanding or persecution could make it otherwise. Of course, the thinking Negro has shifted a little toward the left with the world-trend, and there is an increasing group who affiliate with radical and liberal movements.[22] But fundamentally for the present the Negro is radical on race matters, conservative on others, in other words, a "forced radical," a social protestant rather than a genuine radical. Yet under further pressure and injustice iconoclastic thought and motives will inevitably increase. Harlem's **quixotic** radicalisms call for their ounce of democracy today lest to-morrow they be beyond cure.

The Negro mind reaches out as yet to nothing but American wants, American ideas. But this forced attempt to build his Americanism on race values is a unique social experiment, and its ultimate success is impossible except through the fullest sharing of American culture and institutions. There should be no delusion about this. American nerves in sections unstrung with race hysteria are often fed the opiate that the trend of Negro advance is wholly separatist, and that the effect of its operation will be to encyst the Negro as a benign foreign body in the body politic.[23] This cannot be—even if it were desirable. The racialism of the Negro is no limitation or reservation with respect to American life; it is only a constructive effort to build the obstructions in the stream of his progress into an efficient dam of social energy and power. Democracy itself is obstructed and **stagnated** to the extent that any of its channels are closed. Indeed they cannot be selectively closed. So the choice is not between one way for the Negro and another way for the rest, but between American institutions frustrated on the one hand and American ideals progressively fulfilled and realized on the other.

According to Locke, what could cause American democracy to stagnate?

There is, of course, a warrantably comfortable feeling in being on the right side of the country's professed ideals. We realize that we cannot be undone without America's undoing. It is within the **gamut** of this attitude that the thinking Negro faces America, but with variations of mood that are if anything more significant than the attitude itself. Sometimes we have it taken with the defiant ironic challenge of McKay:[24]

---

22 **the left . . . radical movements.** Following the First World War and the early success of the Russian (Bolshevik) Revolution of 1917, there was an upsurge in the number of Socialist and Communist parties worldwide. Such groups generally comprised the most radical elements of the politically liberal Left (as opposed to the conservative Right).

23 **American nerves . . . body politic.** Locke suggested that Americans (especially where there was severe racial strife) were led to believe that black activists desired complete separation from white society, and would therefore become a benign (unthreatening) segment outside of the political mainstream.

24 **Claude McKay.** (1889–1948), African-American poet. See page 349.

VOCABULARY IN PLACE

- **efficacy,** ***n.*** Effectiveness, usefulness
- **quixotic,** ***adj.*** Impulsive; idealistic without regard to practicality (from *Don Quixote,* hero of the romance by Cervantes)
- **stagnated,** ***past part.*** Ceased development or progress; motionless
- **gamut,** ***n.*** A complete range or extent; course

Mine is the future grinding down today
Like a great landslip moving to the sea,
Bearing its freight of debris far away
Where the green hungry waters restlessly
Heave mammoth pyramids, and
break and roar
Their eerie challenge to the crumbling
shore.

Sometimes, perhaps more frequently as yet, it is taken in the fervent and almost **filial** appeal and counsel of Weldon Johnson's:[25]

O Southland, dear Southland!
Then why do you still cling
To an idle age and a musty page,
To a dead and useless thing?

But between defiance and appeal, midway almost between **cynicism** and hope, the prevailing mind stands in the mood of the same author's *To America*, an attitude of sober **query** and **stoical** challenge:

How would you have us, as we are?
Or sinking 'neath the load we bear,
Our eyes fixed forward on a star,
Or gazing empty at despair?

Rising or falling? Men or things?
With dragging pace or footsteps
fleet?
Strong, willing sinews in your wings,
Or tightening chains about your
feet?

More and more, however, an intelligent realization of the great discrepancy between the American social creed and the American social practice forces upon the Negro the taking of the moral advantage that is his. Only the steadying and sobering effect of a truly characteristic gentleness of spirit prevents the rapid rise of a definite cynicism and counter-hate and a defiant superiority feeling. Human as this reaction would be, the majority still deprecate its advent,[26] and would gladly see it forestalled by the speedy **amelioration** of its causes. We wish our race pride to be a healthier, more positive achievement than a feeling based upon a realization of the short-comings of others. But all paths toward the attainment of a sound social attitude have been difficult; only a relatively few enlightened minds have been able as the phrase puts it "to rise above" prejudice. The ordinary man has had until recently only a hard choice between the alternatives of **supine** and humiliating submission and stimulating but hurtful counter-prejudice. Fortunately from some inner, desperate resourcefulness has recently sprung up the simple expedient of fighting prejudice by mental passive resistance, in other words by trying to ignore it. For the few, this manna[27] may perhaps be effective, but the masses cannot thrive upon it.

Who was able "to rise above" prejudice? How were they able to do this while many others could not?

25 **Weldon Johnson.** James Weldon Johnson (1871–1938), African-American poet. See page 329.

26 **deprecate its advent.** Denounce or condemn its arrival

27 **manna.** Spiritual nourishment of divine origin; something of value received unexpectedly. (From the Bible, the food that was provided for the Israelites during their flight from Egypt.)

VOCABULARY IN PLACE

- **filial,** ***adj.*** In the manner of a child to a parent
- **cynicism,** ***n.*** An attitude of jaded negativity and distrust
- **query,** ***n.*** Question, inquiry
- **stoical,** ***adj.*** Unaffected by pain or pleasure; impassive
- **amelioration,** ***n.*** The act of making better or fixing
- **supine,** ***adj.*** Lying on the back; passive

Fortunately there are constructive channels opening out into which the **balked** social feelings of the American Negro can flow freely.

Without them there would be much more pressure and danger than there is.

According to Locke, what would African Americans do with respect to Africa?

These compensating interests are racial but in a new and enlarged way. One is the consciousness of acting as the advance-guard of the African peoples in their contact with Twentieth Century civilization; the other, the sense of a mission of rehabilitating the race in world esteem from that loss of prestige for which the fate and conditions of slavery have so largely been responsible. Harlem, as we shall see, is the center of both these movements; she is the home of the Negro's "Zionism."[28] The pulse of the Negro world has begun to beat in Harlem. A Negro news-paper carrying news material in English, French and Spanish, gathered from all quarters of America, the West Indies and Africa has maintained itself in Harlem for over five years. Two important magazines, both edited from New York, maintain their news and circulation consistently on a **cosmopolitan** scale. Under American **auspices** and backing, three pan-African congresses have been held abroad for the discussion of common interests, colonial questions and the future cooperative development of Africa. In terms of the race question as a world problem, the Negro mind has leapt, so to speak, upon the parapets of prejudice and extended its cramped horizons. In so doing it has linked up with the growing group consciousness of the dark-peoples and is gradually learning their common interests. As one of our writers has recently put it: "It is imperative that we understand the white world in its relations to the non-white world." As with the Jew, persecution is making the Negro international.

As a world phenomenon this wider race consciousness is a different thing from the much asserted rising tide of color. Its inevitable causes are not of our making. The consequences are not necessarily damaging to the best interests of civilization. Whether it actually brings into being new Armadas of conflict or argosies of cultural exchange and enlightenment can only be decided by the attitude of the dominant races in an era of critical change. With the American Negro, his new internationalism is primarily an effort to recapture contact with the scattered peoples of African derivation. Garveyism[29] may be a **transient**, if spectacular, phenomenon, but the possible role of the American Negro in the future development of Africa is one of the most constructive and universally helpful missions that any modern people can lay claim to.

Constructive participation in such causes cannot help giving the Negro valuable group incentives, as well as increased prestige at home and abroad. Our greatest rehabilitation

---

28 **Zionism.** A Jewish movement that arose in the late nineteenth century in response to growing anti-Semitism and that sought to establish a Jewish homeland in Palestine

29 **Garveyism.** Named after Marcus Garvey (1887–1940), leader of a Black Nationalist Movement that called on people of African descent worldwide to return to Africa. Garvey was a popular though controversial figure; he greatly influenced fellow black leaders and thinkers, though Locke and others recognized that, in practice, Garvey's plan was not a realistic solution to America's race issues. (See page 284 for more on Garvey.)

VOCABULARY IN PLACE

- **balked,** ***past part.*** Hindered; blocked as if by an obstacle
- **cosmopolitan,** ***n.*** Relevant to the whole world
- **auspices,** ***n.pl.*** Protection or support; patronage
- **transient,** ***adj.*** Remaining in place only a brief time

may possibly come through such channels, but for the present, more immediate hope rests in the revaluation by white and black alike of the Negro in terms of his artistic **endowments** and cultural contributions, past and prospective. It must be increasingly recognized that the Negro has already made very substantial contributions, not only in his folk-art, music especially, which has always found appreciation, but in larger, though humbler and less acknowledged ways. For generations the Negro has been the peasant matrix[30] of that section of America which has most undervalued him, and here he has contributed not only materially in labor and in social patience, but spiritually as well. The South has unconsciously absorbed the gift of his folk-temperament. In less than half a generation it will be easier to recognize this, but the fact remains that a leaven of humor, sentiment, imagination and tropic **nonchalance** has gone into the making of the South from a humble, unacknowledged source. A second crop of the Negro's gifts promises still more largely. He now becomes a conscious contributor and lays aside the status of a beneficiary and ward for that of a collaborator and participant in American civilization. The great social gain in this is the releasing of our talented group from the **arid** fields of controversy and debate to the productive fields of creative expression. The especially cultural recognition they win should in turn prove the key to that revaluation of the Negro which must precede or accompany any considerable further betterment of race relationships.

What did Locke say would be easier to recognize "in less than a half a generation"?

But whatever the general effect, the present generation will have added the motives of self-expression and spiritual development to the old and still unfinished task of making material headway and progress. No one who understandingly faces the situation with its substantial accomplishment or views the new scene with its still more abundant promise can be entirely without hope. And certainly, if in our lifetime the Negro should not be able to celebrate his full initiation into American democracy, he can at least, on the **warrant** of these things, celebrate the attainment of a significant and satisfying new phase of group development, and with it a spiritual Coming of Age. ■

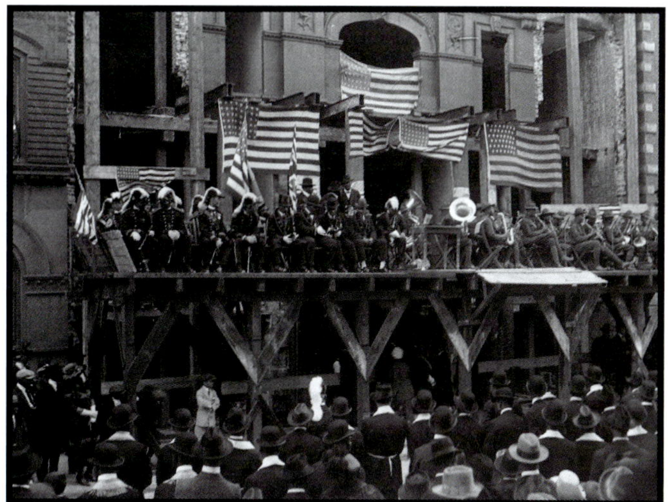

Harlem, 1920. Members of many prominent civic groups and other local residents gather for a ceremony to lay the cornerstone for a new Baptist church on 129th Street.

30 **matrix.** Locke is using a now-common sense of the word *matrix:* a substance or situation in which something else develops. A womb is a matrix. Locke pointed out that African Americans were, for generations, the source of the South's development in both economic and spiritual terms.

VOCABULARY IN PLACE

- **endowments,** ***n.pl.*** Natural gifts, abilities, or qualities
- **nonchalance,** ***n.*** Casual lack of concern
- **arid,** ***adj.*** Lifeless and dull
- **warrant,** ***n.*** Justification for an action or belief; grounds

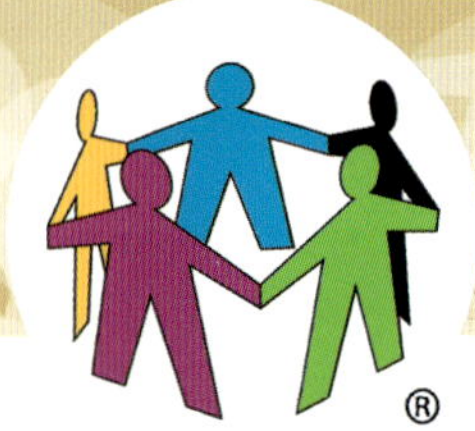

Delving Deeper

Recalling

1. Whom did Alain Locke say had undergone a "metamorphosis"?
2. What "past controversies" and other negative aspects of life since Reconstruction did Locke want African Americans to shed?
3. To what did most Americans attribute the mass migration of African Americans from the South to the North? Did Locke agree?
4. To which specific community did Locke point as a prime example of the cultural transformation that was occurring?
5. Did Locke say that African Americans wanted the same things as other Americans?
6. Did Locke see a role for African Americans in the future of Africa?

Interpreting

1. Did Locke assume that many people were aware of this metamorphosis?
2. According to Locke, what happened in the black community as a result of a lack of "self-understanding"? Did he think this would change?
3. According to Locke, what was the real, fundamental reason that black people moved northward? Use a quotation to support your answer.
4. What did Locke mean when he said "Negroes have been a race more in name than in fact"? What were they "seizing upon" for the first time?
5. What evidence did he put forth to support this idea? Did he think that black "radicals" were the same as other social radicals of the time?
6. What "common interests" did "dark-peoples" worldwide share?

Synthesizing

1. What aspects of the "old world" did Locke consider dead or dying? What positive changes occurred in black communities as a result of post-Civil War migration?
2. How important was the folk tradition to Locke? Find at least two examples in the essay in which he mentions folk culture and discuss its relevance in the overall essay.
3. Why was Harlem special to Locke?

Delving Deeper

History Connection

Notable Names. Locke's anthology, *The New Negro,* established his reputation as the leading expert on African-American culture. It also introduced to the world outside Harlem such soon-to-be famous names as Langston Hughes, Countee Cullen, and Jean Toomer. Several other writers and thinkers included in *The New Negro* are definitely worth getting to know, although their works do not appear in *Grace Abounding.* **Jessie Fauset** was known for her fiction, essays, and poetry, but she is best remembered as the editor of *Crisis* magazine. Known as the "Midwife of the Harlem Renaissance," she was one of the most important driving forces behind the careers of poets like Hughes, Cullen, and Toomer. Editor and essayist **Charles S. Johnson** was one of the era's most influential editors and cultural historians. **Robert R. Moton** was an educator who succeeded Booker T. Washington as principal of Tuskegee Institute, which gained national college accreditation under his leadership. He was influential in national and international race relations, and served as an advisor to President Wilson and to other political figures. Other notable writers in *The New Negro* include fiction writers **Eric Walrond, Bruce Nugent,** and **Rudolph Fisher.**

About the Author

Alain Locke (1886–1954) was one of the preeminent scholars and philosophers of his time. Key to his thought was the idea of *cultural pluralism,* the placing of high value on the diverse traditions that come together creatively in an open, democratic state. Born in Philadelphia, Locke graduated *magna cum laude* from Harvard, was elected to Phi Beta Kappa, and was the first African American to win Harvard's Bowdoin Prize. He was also the first African American to be named a Rhodes Scholar. He studied at Oxford University in England for two years. He then went to the University of Berlin to complete advanced doctoral work in philosophy. Returning to the United States in 1912, Locke had trouble finding a teaching position despite his academic achievements. By 1918 he found his place in Howard University's philosophy department, which he chaired until 1953. *The New Negro* (1925) established Locke as the early-twentieth century's authority on modern African-American culture. He served as mentor to some of the finest writers and artists of his time, and it is fair to say that the Harlem Renaissance would not have been interpreted in the same way by people in the 1920s or by people today if it had not been for Alain Locke's work.

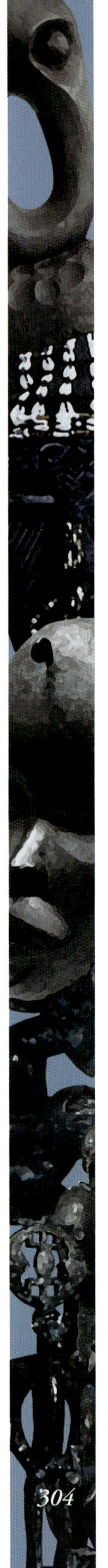

Prereading

"The Negro Digs Up His Past"

by Arthur Schomburg

Arthur Schomburg was a great collector who scoured the earth in search of anything and everything associated with his cultural heritage. But Schomburg was not obsessive or compulsive; he simply wanted to quench his thirst for knowledge about Africans, for ever since he was a child, people had been telling him that black people had no history, no culture, and no true heroes.

The quest for knowledge led him to the conclusion that recovering and reconstructing history was the best way to fight racial prejudice. Why was this the only way? Schomburg did not place blame on any single group or event, but he did state that the cultural heritage of people of African descent had been largely ignored or dismissed by Westerners. Great black achievers—especially scholars, scientists, and historians—were forgotten or ignored by history. Only by recovering the lost pieces of history could he and other scholars reverse the tide of racism in America.

It all began with a few books, and Schomburg soon realized that collecting would be his life's pursuit. By the time the New York Public Library purchased his collection and hired him as the curator of its Division of Negro Literature, History, and Prints, Schomburg had collected over 10,000 books, letters, manuscripts, prints, paintings, sculptures, posters, and playbills produced by the hands and minds of Africa's children.

"The Negro Digs Up His Past" presents a window into Schomburg's world. In addition to presenting Schomburg's basic belief in the need to uproot the cultural stereotypes that feed racism, this essay presents a mini-encyclopedia of African and African-American achievement. Indeed, there is almost too much information to contain within the bounds of such a brief essay.

Readers should not be intimidated by the sheer volume of information in this essay or by Schomburg's scholarly writing style. Schomburg wanted to inspire others to dig methodically and passionately into history, for history's finest gems are often buried deeply.

Concentration will be key to understanding this essay fully. Do not worry about remembering specific names and events; focus instead on the heart of Schomburg's argument.

The Negro Digs Up His Past

by Arthur Schomburg

The American Negro must remake his past in order to make his future. Though it is **orthodox** to think of America as the one country where it is unnecessary to have a past, what is a luxury for the nation as a whole becomes a prime social necessity for the Negro. For him, a group tradition must supply compensation for persecution, and pride of race the **antidote** for prejudice. History must restore what slavery took away, for it is the social damage of slavery that the present generations must repair and offset. So among the rising democratic millions we find the Negro thinking more collectively, more **retrospectively** than the rest, and apt out of the very pressure of the present to become the most enthusiastic **antiquarian** of them all.

According to Schomburg, why are history and cultural tradition so important for "the Negro"?

Vindicating evidences of individual achievement have as a matter of fact been gathered and treasured for over a century: Abbé Grégoire's liberal-minded book[1] on Negro notables in 1808 was the pioneer effort; it has been followed at intervals by less known and often less discriminating **compendiums** of exceptional men and women of African stock. But this sort of

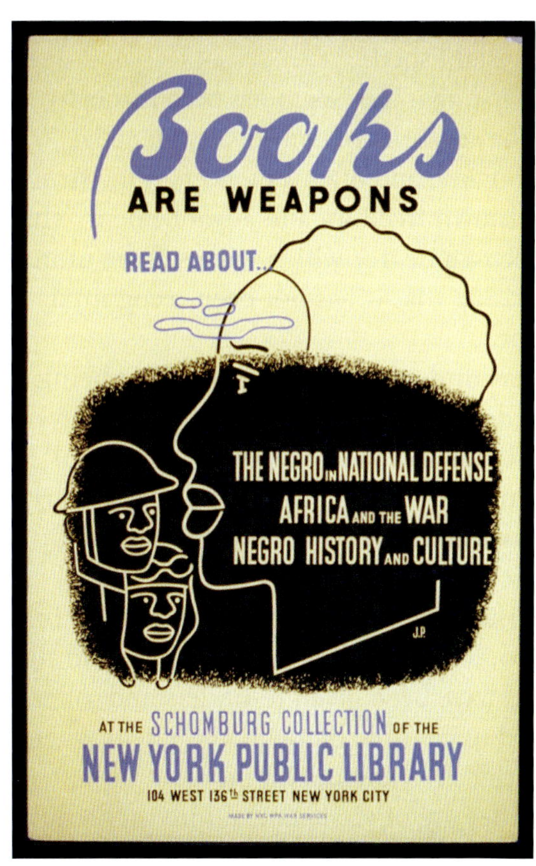

Poster encouraging citizens to use the resources of the Schomburg Collection. Library of Congress, LC-USZC2-1124.

[1] **Abbé Grégoire's . . . book.** Henri (Abbé) Grégoire (1750–1831). A leader of the French Revolution, Roman Catholic priest, Abolitionist, and early advocate of racial equality. His book *De La Littérature Des Nègres (On the Literature of the Negroes)* presented research into the "intellectual faculties" and scientific and artistic accomplishments of persons of African descent.

VOCABULARY IN PLACE

- **orthodox,** ***adj.*** Standard or traditional
- **antidote,** ***n.*** A cure, usually for poison
- **retrospectively,** ***adv.*** In a way that contemplates the past
- **antiquarian,** ***n.*** A scholar or lover of old things
- **vindicate,** ***v.*** To provide justification or support for
- **compendium,** ***n.*** A collection or brief summary

thing was on the whole pathetically over-corrective, ridiculously over-**laudatory**; it was apologetics[2] turned into biography. A true historical sense develops slowly and with difficulty under such circumstances. But today, even if for the ultimate purpose of group justification, history has become less a matter of argument and more a matter of record. There is the definite desire and determination to have a history, well documented, widely known at least within race circles, and administered as a stimulating and inspiring tradition for the coming generations.

What is meant by the phrase "true historical sense"? Does "the Negro" have one, according to Schomburg?

Gradually as the study of the Negro's past has come out of the vagaries of rhetoric and propaganda[3] and become systematic and scientific, three outstanding conclusions have been established:

First, that the Negro has been throughout the centuries of controversy an active collaborator, and often a pioneer, in the struggle for his own freedom and advancement. This is true to a degree which makes it the more surprising that it has not been recognized earlier.

Second, that by virtue of their being regarded as something "exceptional," even by friends and well-wishers, Negroes of **attainment** and genius have been unfairly **disassociated** from the group, and group credit lost accordingly.

Third, that the remote racial origins of the Negro, far from being what the race and the world have been given to understand, offer a record of credible group achievement when scientifically viewed, and more important still, that they are of vital general interest because of their bearing upon the beginnings and early development of human culture.

With such crucial truths to document and establish, an ounce of fact is worth a pound of controversy. So the Negro historian today digs under the spot where his predecessor stood and argued. Not long ago, the Public Library of Harlem housed a special exhibition of books, pamphlets, prints and old engravings, that simply said, to skeptic and believer alike, to scholar and school-child, to proud black and astonished white, "Here is the evidence." Assembled from the rapidly growing collections of the leading Negro book-collectors and research societies, there were in these cases, materials not only for the first true writing of Negro history, but for the rewriting of many important paragraphs of our common American history. Slow though it be, historical truth is no exception to the proverb.

Here among the rarities of early Negro Americana was Jupiter Hammon's[4] Address to the Negroes of the State of New York, edition of 1787, with the first American Negro poet's famous "If we should ever get to Heaven, we shall find nobody to reproach us for being black, or for being slaves." Here was Phillis Wheatley's Mss. Poem of 1767[5] addressed to the students of Harvard, her spirited

---

[2] **apologetics.** Formal argumentation in defense of something. Schomburg was criticizing the fact that the creative and intellectual achievements of Africans had been passed down as the work of a few exceptional individuals.

[3] **the vagaries of rhetoric and propaganda**. A *vagary* is a whimsical idea or action. *Rhetoric,* here, means insincere language. Schomburg refers to a time when African-American history is no longer mere words or mere allegations with no proof.

[4] **Jupiter Hammon.** African-American poet (1711–1806). See page 173.

[5] **Phillis Wheatley's Mss. Poem of 1767.** African-American poet (1753–1784). *Mss.* refers to the handwritten manuscript of "To the University of Cambridge." See page 175.

VOCABULARY IN PLACE

- **laudatory,** ***adj.*** Expressing praise
- **attainment,** ***n.*** Achievement
- **disassociate,** ***v.*** To separate out; disunite

encomiums[6] upon George Washington and the Revolutionary Cause, and John Marrant's[7] St. John's Day eulogy to the "Brothers of African Lodge No. 459" delivered at Boston in 1789. Here too were Lemuel Haynes'[8] Vermont commentaries on the American Revolution and his learned sermons to his white congregation in Rutland, Vermont, and the sermons of the year 1808 by the Rev. Absalom Jones of St. Thomas Church, Philadelphia, and Peter Williams of St. Philip's, New York, pioneer Episcopal rectors who spoke out in daring and influential ways on the Abolition of the Slave Trade. Such things and many others are more than mere items of curiosity: they educate any receptive mind.

Reinforcing these were still rarer items of Africana and foreign Negro interest, the volumes of Juan Latino, the best Latinist[9] of Spain in the reign of Philip V, incumbent of the chair of Poetry at the University of Granada and author of Poems printed there in 1573 and a book on the Escurial published 1576; the Latin and Dutch treatises of Jacobus Eliza Capitein, a native of West Coast Africa and graduate of the University of Leyden, Gustavus Vassa's[10] celebrated autobiography that supplied so much of the evidence in 1796 for Granville Sharpe's attack on slavery in the British colonies, Julien Raymond's Paris exposé of the disabilities of the free people of color in the then (1791) French colony of Hayti, and Baron de Vastey's *Cry of the Fatherland,* the famous **polemic** by the secretary of Christophe[11] that **precipitated** the Haytian struggle for independence. The cumulative effect of such evidences of scholarship and moral **prowess** is too weighty to be dismissed as exceptional.

Why does Schomburg include so many historical examples? How does this support the main idea of the essay?

But weightier surely than any evidence of individual talent and scholarship could ever be, is the evidence of important collaboration and significant pioneer initiative in social service and reform, in the efforts toward race emancipation, colonization and race betterment. From neglected and rust-spotted pages comes testimony to the black men and women who stood shoulder to shoulder in courage and

What is "weightier than individual talent and scholarship"? Why?

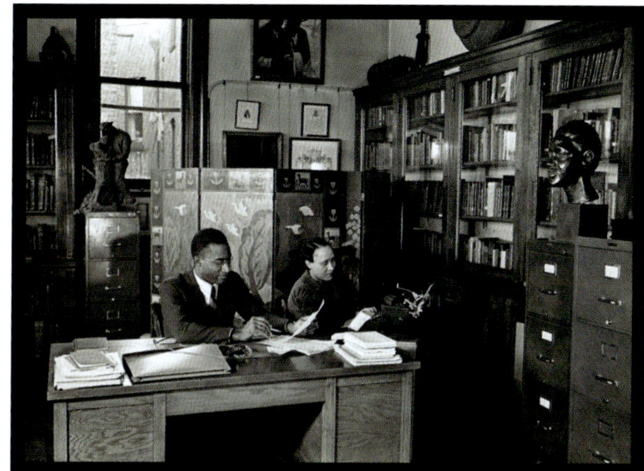

Researchers in the reading room known as the Schomburg Collection of Negro Literature.

6 **encomium.** A formal expression of praise; a tribute

7 **John Marrant.** Marrant (1755–1791), a traveling preacher, has often been called "America's first black preacher." Here Schomburg refers to Marrant's famous "A Sermon Preached on the 24th Day of June 1789, Being the Festival of St. John the Baptist."

8 **Lemuel Haynes.** American patriot (1753–1833) credited with being the first black minister to preach to a white congregation

9 **Latinist.** A specialist in Latin translation and interpretation

10 **Gustavus Vassa.** Also known as Olaudah Equiano. See page 55 and page 97.

11 **Christophe.** Henry Christophe (1767–1820), Haitian revolutionary leader and King Henry I of Haiti, 1807–1820

VOCABULARY IN PLACE

- **polemic,** ***n.*** An aggressive attack on someone else's opinions
- **precipitate,** ***v.*** To cause or bring on abruptly
- **prowess,** ***n.*** Superior skill or ability

zeal, and often on a **parity** of intelligence and talent, with their notable white benefactors. There was the already cited work of Vassa that aided so materially the efforts of Granville Sharpe; the record of Paul Cuffee, the Negro colonization pioneer, associated so importantly with the establishment of Sierra Leone as a British colony for the occupancy of free people of color in West Africa; the dramatic and history-making exposé of John Baptist Phillips, African graduate of Edinburgh, who compelled through Lord Bathhurst in 1824 the enforcement of the articles of **capitulation** guaranteeing freedom to the blacks of Trinidad. There is the record of the pioneer colonization project of Rev. Daniel Coker in conducting a voyage of ninety expatriates to West Africa in 1820, of the missionary efforts of Samuel Crowther in Sierra Leone, first Anglican bishop of his diocese, and that of the work of John Russwurm, a leader in the work and foundation of the American Colonization Society.

When we consider the facts, certain chapters of American history will have to be reopened. Just as black men were influential factors in the campaign against the slave trade, so they were among the earliest **instigators** of the abolition movement. Indeed there was a dangerous calm between the agitation for the suppression of the slave trade and the beginning of the campaign for emancipation. During that interval colored men were very influential in arousing the attention of public men who in turn aroused the conscience of the country. Continuously between 1808 and 1845, men like Prince Saunders, Peter Williams, Absalom Jones, Nathaniel Paul, and Bishops Varick and Richard Allen, the founders of the two wings of African Methodism, spoke out with force and initiative, and men like Denmark Vesey (1822), David Walker (1828) and Nat Turner (1831)[12] advocated and organized schemes for direct action. This culminated in the generally ignored but important conventions of Free People of Color[13] in New York, Philadelphia and other centers, whose platforms and efforts are to the Negro of as great significance as the nationally cherished memories of Faneuil and Independence Halls.[14] Then with Abolition comes the better documented and more recognized collaboration of Samuel R. Ward, William Wells Brown, Henry Highland Garnett, Martin Delaney, Harriet Tubman, Sojourner Truth, and Frederick Douglass[15] with their great colleagues, Tappan, Phillips, Sumner, Mott, Stowe and Garrison.[16]

But even this latter group who came within the limelight of national and international notice, and thus into open comparison with the best minds of their

---

12 **Denmark Vesey . . . Nat Turner.** Walker was a free black abolitionist. Vesey and Turner led slave rebellions. For Nat Turner, see page 105.

13 **Free People of Color.** In New York and Philadelphia during the late 1700s, this well-organized network of activists lobbied, often successfully, for equal rights regarding education and other public services.

14 **Faneuil and Independence Halls.** Faneuil Hall is a meeting place in Boston and the site of many important historical events. Independence Hall in Philadelphia is the site of the signing of the Declaration of Independence, July 4, 1776, and the drafting and signing of the U.S. Constitution in 1787.

15 **Samuel R. Ward . . . Frederick Douglass.** Ward (1817–1866) was an escaped slave and Abolitionist. For Brown (1814–1884), see page 193. Garnett and Delaney were Abolitionists and proponents of mass African-American emigration to Africa. Tubman, Truth, and Douglass were escaped slaves and Abolitionists. (See Unit 2.)

16 **Tappan . . . Garrison.** Prominent white Abolitionists

VOCABULARY IN PLACE

- **zeal,** ***n.*** Enthusiastic devotion to a cause
- **parity,** ***n.*** Equality
- **capitulation,** ***n.*** Surrender
- **instigator,** ***n.*** A person who stirs others to action

generation, the public too often regards as a group of inspired illiterates, eloquent echoes of their Abolitionist sponsors. For a true estimate of their ability and scholarship, however, one must go with the antiquarian to the files of the *Anglo-African Magazine*, where page by page comparisons may be made. Their writings show Douglass, McCune Smith,[17] Wells Brown, Delaney, Wilmot Blyden and Alexander Crummell[18] to have been as scholarly and versatile as any of the noted publicists with whom they were associated. All of them labored internationally in the cause of their fellows; to Scotland, England, France, Germany and Africa, they carried their brilliant offensive of debate and propaganda, and with this came instance upon instance of signal foreign recognition, from academic, scientific, public and official sources. Delaney's *Principia of Ethnology* won public reception from learned societies, Pennington's **discourses** an honorary doctorate from Heidelberg, Wells Brown's three year mission the entrée of[19] the salons of London and Paris, and the tours of Frederick Douglass, receptions second only to Henry Ward Beecher's.[20]

What is meant by the term "inspired illiterates"?

Have African-American scholars received public recognition for their work? What does this prove, according to Schomburg?

After this great era of public interest and discussion, it was Alexander Crummell, who, with the reaction already setting in, first organized Negro brains defensively through the founding of the American Negro Academy in 1897 at Washington. A New York boy whose zeal for education had suffered a rude shock when refused admission to the Episcopal Seminary by Bishop Onderdonk, he had been befriended by John Jay[21] and sent to Cambridge University, England, for his education and ordination. On his return, he was beset with the idea of promoting race scholarship, and the Academy was the final result. It has continued ever since to be one of the **bulwarks** of our intellectual life, though unfortunately its members have had to spend too much of their energy and effort answering detractors and disproving popular fallacies. Only gradually have the men of this group been able to work toward pure scholarship. Taking a slightly different start, The Negro Society for Historical Research was later organized in New York, and has succeeded in stimulating the collection from all parts of the world of books and documents dealing with the Negro. It has also brought together for the first time co-operatively in a single society African, West Indian and Afro-American scholars. Direct offshoots of this same effort are the extensive private collections of Henry P. Slaughter of Washington, the Rev. Charles

What is the significance of the American Negro Academy?

[17] **McCune Smith.** (1813–1865) The first professionally trained African-American physician

[18] **Wilmot Blyden and Alexander Crummell.** Blyden (1832–1912) was a Liberian clergyman and educator; in his time he was the foremost advocate of Pan-Africanism, the belief that all people of African descent share common bonds and must work together in order to achieve prosperity and cultural independence. Crummell (1819–1898) was an African-American Episcopalian priest, teacher, and missionary.

[19] **the entrée of.** Entry into

[20] **Henry Ward Beecher.** (1813–1887) American clergyman and Abolitionist; brother of Harriet Beecher Stowe (author of *Uncle Tom's Cabin*)

[21] **John Jay.** (1745–1829) American patriot, political theorist, and first Chief Justice of the Supreme Court

VOCABULARY IN PLACE

- **discourse,** *n.* A formal, lengthy discussion of a subject
- **bulwark,** *n.* Something serving as a defense or safeguard

D. Martin of Harlem, of Arthur Schomburg of Brooklyn, and of the late John E. Bruce, who was the enthusiastic and far-seeing pioneer of this movement. Finally and more recently, the Association for the Study of Negro Life and History has extended these efforts into a scientific research project of great achievement and promise. Under the direction of Dr. Carter G. Woodson, it has continuously maintained for nine years the publication of the learned quarterly, *The Journal of Negro History*, and with the assistance and recognition of two large educational foundations has maintained research and published valuable monographs[22] in Negro history. Almost keeping pace with the work of scholarship has been the effort to popularize the results, and to place before Negro youth in the schools the true story of race **vicissitude,** struggle and accomplishment. So that quite largely now the ambition of Negro youth can be nourished on its own milk.

Such work is a far cry from the **puerile** controversy and petty **braggadocio** with which the effort for race history first started. But a general as well as a racial lesson has been learned. We seem lately to have come at last to realize what the truly scientific attitude requires, and to see that the race issue has been a plague on both our historical houses,[23] and that history cannot be properly written with either bias or counter-bias. The blatant Caucasian racialist with his theories and assumptions of race superiority and dominance has in turn bred his Ethiopian counterpart—the rash and rabid amateur who has **glibly** tried to prove half of the world's geniuses to have been Negroes and to trace the pedigree of nineteenth century Americans from the Queen of Sheba. But fortunately today there is on both sides of a really common cause less of the sand of controversy and more of the dust of digging.

What is "bias"? Why does bias affect the way history is written?

Of course, a racial motive remains—legitimately compatible with scientific method and aim. The work our race students now regard as important, they undertake very naturally to overcome in part certain handicaps of **disparagement** and **omission** too well-known to particularize. But they do so not merely that we may not wrongfully be deprived of the spiritual nourishment of our cultural past, but also that the full story of human collaboration and interdependence may be told and realized. Especially is this likely to be the effect of the latest and most fascinating of all of the attempts to open up the closed Negro past, namely the important study of African cultural origins and sources. The bigotry of civilization which is the taproot[24] of intellectual prejudice begins far back and must be corrected at its source. Fundamentally it has come about from the depreciation of Africa which has sprung up

22 **monograph.** A lengthy, scholarly piece of writing on a specific, often limited subject

23 **plague on both our historical houses.** The phrase is an allusion, or reference, to Shakespeare's *Romeo and Juliet,* wherein the dying Mercutio curses Romeo and Juliet's respective families, saying, "A plague o' both your houses."

24 **taproot.** The primary root of a plant; the source

VOCABULARY IN PLACE

- **vicissitude,** ***n.*** A change or variation, often sudden
- **puerile,** ***adj.*** Childish and silly
- **braggadocio,** ***n.*** Exaggerated boasting
- **glibly,** ***adv.*** Showing little thought, preparation, or concern
- **disparagement,** ***n.*** A lowering of esteem; belittlement
- **omission,** ***n.*** Something left out or not included

What is the "bigotry of civilization," and why must it be corrected?

from ignorance of her true role and position in human history and the early development of culture. The Negro has been a man without a history because he has been considered a man without a worthy culture. But a new notion of the attainment and potentialities of the African stocks has recently come about, partly through the corrective influence of the more scientific study of African institutions and early cultural history, partly through growing appreciation of the skill and beauty and in many cases the historical priority of the African native crafts, and finally through the signal recognition which first in France and Germany, but now very generally, the astonishing art of the African sculptures has received. Into these fascinating new vistas, with limited horizons lifting in all directions, the mind of the Negro has leapt forward faster than the slow clearings of scholarship will yet safely permit. But there is no doubt that here is a field full of the most intriguing and inspiring possibilities. Already the Negro sees himself against a reclaimed background, in a perspective that will give pride and self-respect ample scope, and make history yield for him the same values that the treasured past of any people affords. ■

Why does Schomburg think that native African sculpture is important?

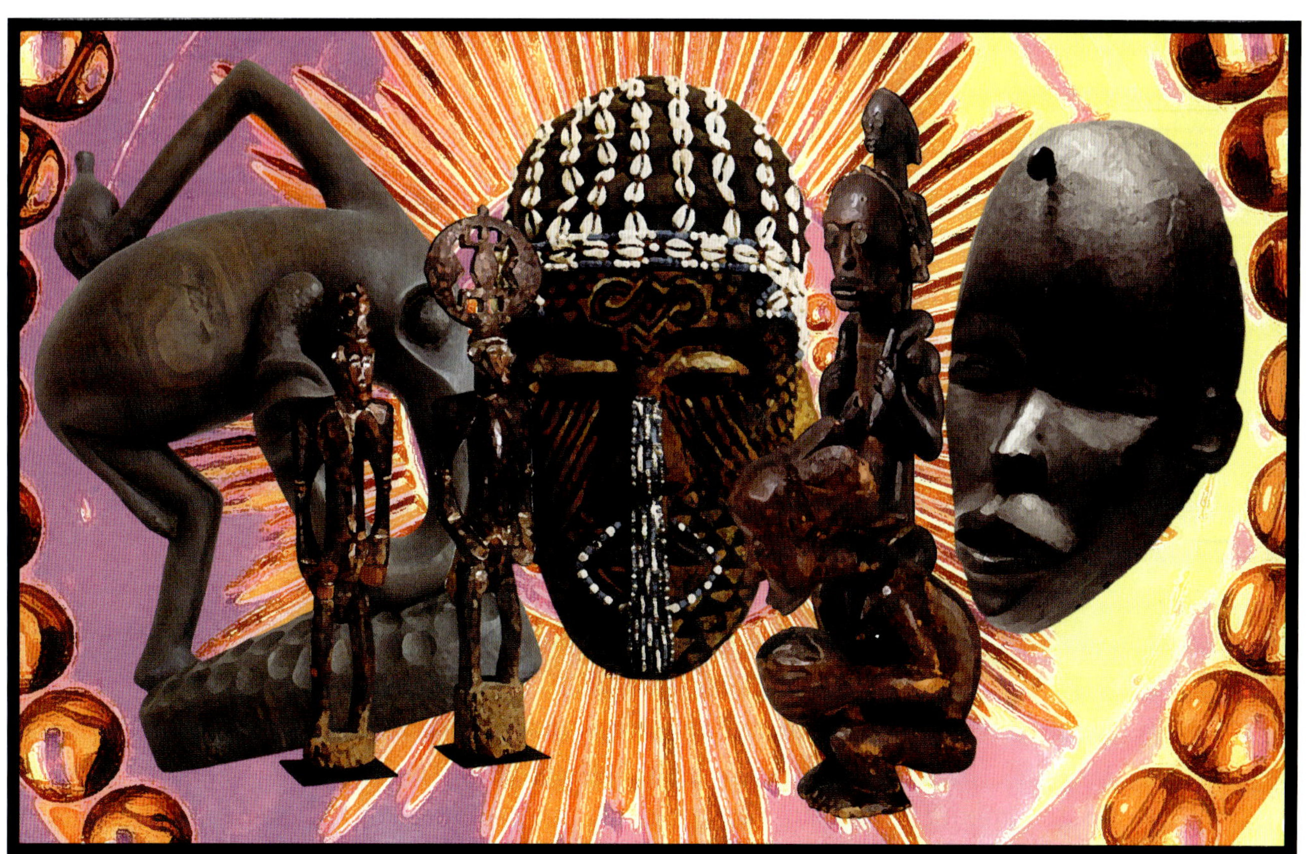

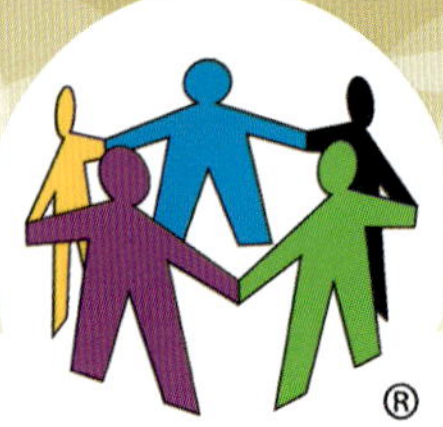

Understanding the Selection

Recalling

1. According to Schomburg, what is a "luxury for most Americans," but "a prime social necessity for the Negro"?
2. Review the "three outstanding conclusions" mentioned on page 306. Write one sentence to summarize each of these conclusions in your own words.
3. What kind of exhibit was housed at the Public Library of Harlem?
4. What, according to Schomburg, is "weightier surely than any evidence of individual talent"?
5. What academy did Alexander Crummell found and why?
6. Why has the Negro been considered "a man without history"?

Interpreting

1. How will African Americans change their future by remaking the past?
2. How have these conclusions been established? What impact has each of these conclusions had on the "Negro historian"?
3. Why were white people "astonished" by this exhibit?
4. How might this factor set African Americans apart from other American ethnic or racial groups?
5. Why has scholarly work in this academy been stifled?
6. How have African native crafts and sculpture helped to change this false notion?

Synthesizing

1. What does Schomburg mean when he calls for African Americans to remake their "group tradition"? How will this provide an "antidote for prejudice"?
2. What was Schomburg's main purpose in writing this essay?
3. Does Schomburg seem optimistic about the future of African-American scholarship? Provide examples from the text to support your answer.

Delving Deeper

Writing

Names Worthy of Remembrance. Arthur Schomburg cites at least 50 historical figures in his essay "The Negro Digs Up His Past." Take out references to major figures like George Washington, King Philip V, and the Queen of Sheba, and you are left with dozens of notable people, every one of whom contributed directly to the world as you know it today.

This is a three-part project:

1. Working in small groups or as a class, compile a complete list of every single name mentioned by Schomburg in his entire essay, beginning with Abbé Grégoire. If you do not find at least 45 names, then look again. Once the list is complete, divide the names equally among workgroups or individual students.
2. Using your library and the Internet, create a short biography for each name to which you are assigned. If possible, include the person's lifespan, birthplace, education, major accomplishments, and a one-sentence synopsis of any important publications or speeches. A basic Internet search may not provide adequate resources for many of the names on the list. Prepare to dig deep!
3. Assemble the final drafts in a single packet. Make copies so that everyone in the class will have a reminder that we must all work to preserve and interpret our cultural heritage.

About the Author

Arturo (Arthur) Schomburg (1874–1938), writer, historian, **bibliophile** (lover and collector of books), and curator, was born in Puerto Rico. He moved to New York City in 1891, where he finished his high-school education.

Schomburg became active in several fraternal organizations, including the Black Freemasons, where he befriended fellow bibliophiles and scholars. He soon became intensely interested in collecting evidence of black cultural heritage. His vast collection was purchased for the New York Public Library in 1926, but Schomburg continued to work as a curator and collector for the rest of his life.

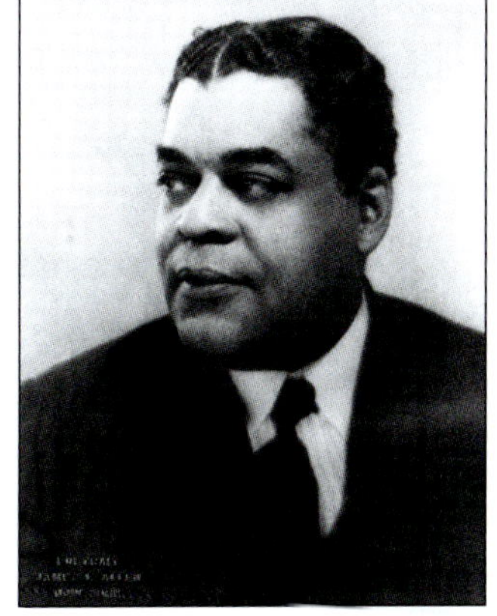

Schomburg published numerous articles in scholarly and literary journals, befriended and influenced nearly every major figure of the Harlem Renaissance, and belonged to more than 30 organizations, including the NAACP and the Urban League.

Prereading

"The Negro Artist and the Racial Mountain"
by Langston Hughes

In June of 1926, George Samuel Schuyler, an African-American journalist, published in the *Nation* magazine an article called "Negro-Art Hokum." In this article, Schuyler argued against having African-American artists work toward creating a racially identified art. Schuyler asserted that "it is sheer nonsense to talk about 'racial differences' as between the American black man and the American white man." He asserted that such talk about differences was racist and that because there were no significant differences between the two groups, it made no sense to talk about a particularly "Negro" art. In Schuyler's own words,

> On this baseless premise, so flattering to the white mob, that the blackamoor [person of African descent] is inferior and fundamentally different, is erected the postulate that he must needs be peculiar; and when he attempts to portray life through the medium of art, it must of necessity be a peculiar art. While such reasoning may seem conclusive to the majority of Americans, it must be rejected with a loud guffaw by intelligent people.

The same issue of the *Nation* carried Langston Hughes's famous reply to Schuyler, "The Negro Artist and the Racial Mountain." In this essay, Hughes explains why he believes that the African-American experience provides distinct material for a distinctly African-American art. He also attacks what he calls the "Racial Mountain," the desire that he saw in one young artist to "run away spiritually from his race" and to accept "American standardization." As you read this piece, remember to place it in the context of its time. In the 1920s, many African Americans were struggling mightily as sharecroppers in the South and as newly arrived, low-wage workers in the North. Many African Americans were subjected to continual degradation; they were treated day in and day out as inferior. A common reaction to oppression, oddly enough, is identification with the oppressor. Such identification sometimes happens, for example, in the minds of prisoners of war and of hostages. Writing before the Black Arts Movement of the 1960s and '70s, Langston Hughes critiqued blacks' overidentification with white culture and called for art celebrating a distinct African-American heritage. The early date of this essay makes the point of view that it expresses seem astonishingly forward-thinking.

The Negro Artist and the Racial Mountain

by Langston Hughes

One of the most promising of the young Negro poets said to me once, "I want to be a poet—not a Negro poet," meaning, I believe, "I want to write like a white poet"; meaning **subconsciously,** "I would like to be a white poet"; meaning behind that, "I would like to be white." And I was sorry the young man said that, for no great poet has ever been afraid of being himself. And I doubted then that, with his desire to run away spiritually from his race, this boy would ever be a great poet. But this is the mountain standing in the way of any true Negro art in America—this urge within the race toward whiteness, the desire to pour racial individuality into the mold of American standardization, and to be as little Negro and as much American as possible.

What is the "racial mountain" of Hughes's title?

But let us look at the immediate background of this young poet. His family is of what I suppose one would call the Negro middle class: people who are by no means rich yet never uncomfortable nor hungry—**smug,** contented, respectable folk, members of the Baptist church. The father goes to work every morning. He is a chief steward[1] at a large white club. The mother sometimes does fancy sewing or supervises parties for the rich families of the town. The children go to a mixed school. In the home they read white papers and magazines. And the mother often says "Don't be like niggers" when the children are bad. A frequent phrase from the father is, "Look how well a white man does things." And so the word *white* comes to be unconsciously a symbol of all the virtues. It holds for the children beauty, morality, and money. The whisper of "I want to be white" runs silently through their minds. This young poet's home is, I believe, a fairly typical home of the colored middle class. One sees immediately how difficult it would be for an artist born in such a home to interest himself in interpreting the beauty of his own people. He is never taught to see that beauty. He is taught rather not to see it, or if he does, to be ashamed of it when it is not according to Caucasian[2] patterns.

For racial culture the home of a self-styled "high-class" Negro has nothing better to offer. Instead there will perhaps be more aping of things white than in a less cultured or less wealthy home. The father is perhaps a doctor, lawyer, landowner, or politician. The mother may be a social worker, or a teacher, or she may do nothing and have a

1 **chief steward.** One who is in charge of the practical affairs of a club, hotel, or resort

2 **Caucasian.** Of or related to the white "race"

VOCABULARY IN PLACE

- **subconsciously,** ***adv.*** In a manner not readily recognized because the thought wells up from the depths of the mind; not readily available to conscious inspection
- **smug,** ***adj.*** Showing excessive self-satisfaction

maid. Father is often dark but he has usually married the lightest woman he could find. The family attend a fashionable church where few really colored faces are to be found. And they themselves draw a color line. In the North they go to white theatres and white movies. And in the South they have at least two cars and a house "like white folks." Nordic[3] manners, Nordic faces, Nordic hair, Nordic art (if any), and an Episcopal[4] heaven. A very high mountain indeed for the would-be racial artist to climb in order to discover himself and his people.

But then there are the low-down folks, the so-called common element, and they are the majority—may the Lord be praised! The people who have their nip of gin on Saturday nights and are not too important to themselves or the community, or too well fed, or too learned to watch the lazy world go round. They live on Seventh Street in Washington, off State Street in Chicago and they do not particularly care whether they are like white folks or anybody else. Their joy runs, bang! into **ecstasy.** Their religion soars to a shout. Work maybe a little today, rest a little tomorrow. Play awhile. Sing awhile. O, let's dance! These common people are not afraid of spirituals, as for a long time their more intellectual **brethren** were, and jazz is their child. They furnish a wealth of colorful, distinctive material for any artist because they still hold their own individuality in the face of American standardizations. And perhaps these common people will give to the world its truly great Negro artist, the one who is not afraid to be himself. Whereas the better-class Negro would tell the artist what to do, the people at least let him alone when he does appear. And they are not ashamed of him—if they know he exists at all. And they accept what beauty is their own without question.

Certainly there is, for the American Negro artist who can escape the restrictions the more advanced among his own group would put upon him, a great field of unused material ready for his art. Without going outside his race, and even among the better classes with their "white" culture and conscious American manners, but still Negro enough to be different, there is sufficient matter to furnish a black artist with a lifetime of creative work. And when he chooses to touch on the relations between Negroes and whites in this country with their innumerable overtones and undertones surely, and especially for literature and the drama, there is an inexhaustible supply of themes at hand. To these the Negro artist can give his racial individuality, his heritage of rhythm and warmth, and his **incongruous** humor that so often, as in the Blues, becomes **ironic** laughter mixed with tears. But let us look again at the mountain.

A prominent Negro clubwoman in Philadelphia paid eleven dollars to hear Raquel Meller sing Andalusian[5] popular songs. But she told me a few weeks before she would not think of going to hear "that woman," Clara Smith, a great black artist, sing Negro folksongs. And many an upper-

[3] **Nordic.** Of or related to Scandinavian peoples of Northern Europe or, by extension, to others of similar physical type

[4] **Episcopal.** Of or related to the Episcopal church, widely attended in the early twentieth century in the United States by upper-class whites of Anglo-Saxon descent

[5] **Andalusian.** Having to do with Anadalusia, a region of Southern Spain on the Mediterranean Sea, the Strait of Gibraltar, and the Atlantic Ocean

VOCABULARY IN PLACE

- **ecstasy,** *n.* Extreme joy
- **brethren,** *n.* Brothers (poetic)
- **incongruous,** *adj.* Contradictory, incompatible
- **ironic,** *adj.* Contradictory in a surprising or humorous way

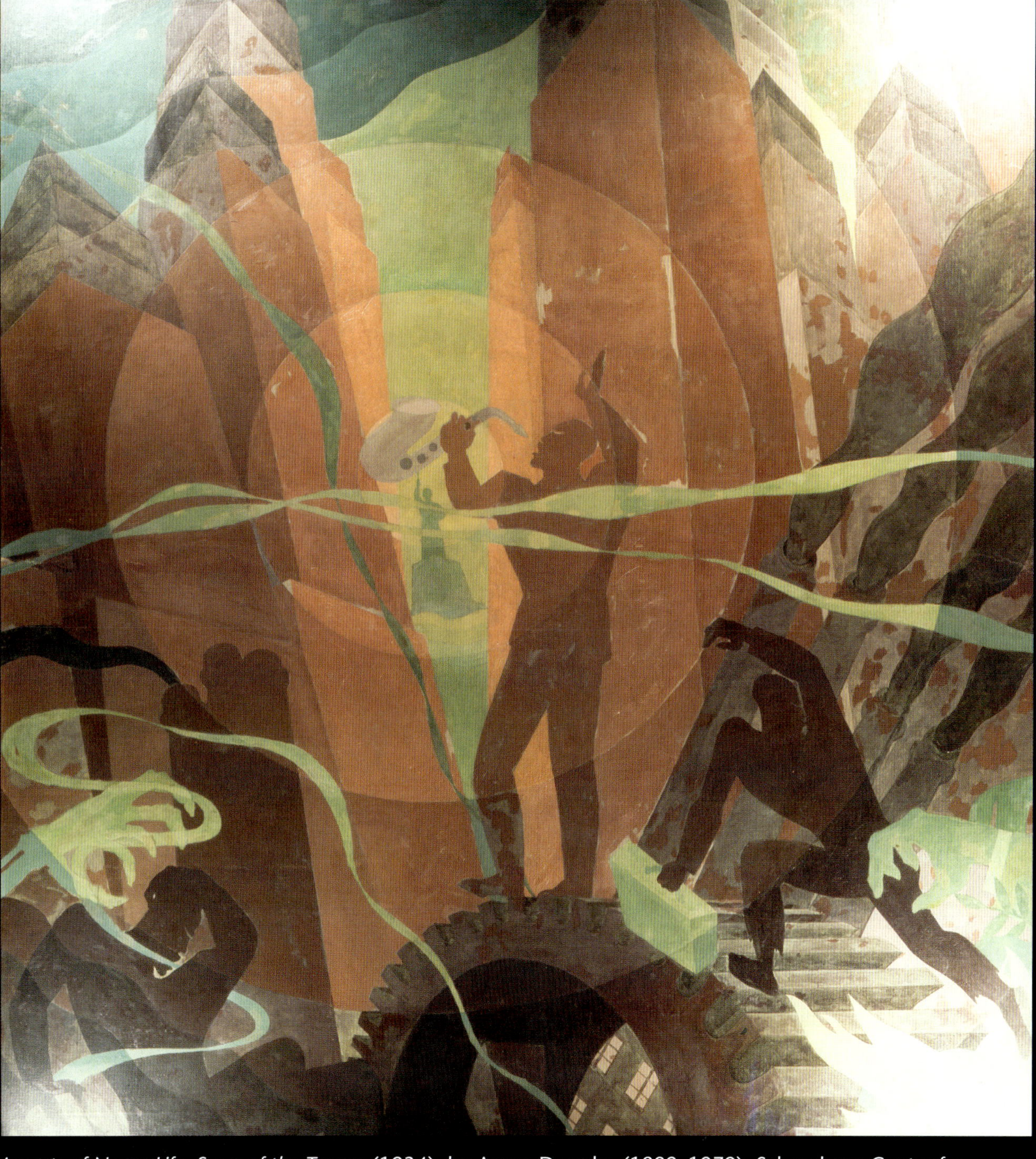

Aspects of Negro Life: Song of the Towers (1934), by Aaron Douglas (1899–1979). Schomburg Center for Research in Black Culture.

class Negro church, even now, would not dream of employing a spiritual in its services. The drab melodies in white folks' hymnbooks are much to be preferred. "We want to worship the Lord correctly and quietly. We don't believe in 'shouting.' Let's be dull like the Nordics," they say, in effect.

The road for the serious black artist, then, who would produce a racial art is most certainly rocky and the mountain is high. Until recently he received almost no encouragement for his work from either white or colored people. The fine novels of Chesnutt[6] go out of print with neither race noticing their passing. The quaint charm and humor of Dunbar's[7] dialect verse brought to him, in his day, largely the same kind of encouragement that one would give a sideshow freak (A colored man writing poetry! How odd!) or a clown (How amusing!).

The present **vogue** in things Negro, although it may do as much harm as good for the budding colored artist, has at least done this: it has brought him forcibly to the attention of his own people among whom for so long, unless the other race had noticed him beforehand, he was a prophet with little honor.[8] I understand that Charles Gilpin acted for years in Negro theatres without any special **acclaim** from his own, but when Broadway gave him eight curtain calls, Negroes, too, began to beat a tin pan in his honor. I know a young colored writer, a manual worker by day, who had been writing well for the colored magazines for some years, but it was not until he recently broke into the white publications and his first book was accepted by a prominent New York publisher that the "best" Negroes in his city took the trouble to discover that he lived there. Then almost immediately they decided to give a grand dinner for him. But the society ladies were careful to whisper to his mother that perhaps she'd better not come. They were not sure she would have an evening gown.

The Negro artist works against an undertow of sharp criticism and misunderstanding from his own group and unintentional bribes from the whites. "Oh, be respectable, write about nice people, show how good we are," say the Negroes. "Be stereotyped, don't go too far, don't shatter our illusions about you, don't amuse us too seriously. We will pay you," say the whites. Both would have told Jean Toomer not to write *Cane*. The colored people did not praise it. The white people did not buy it. Most of the colored people who did read *Cane* hate it. They are afraid of it. Although the critics gave it good reviews the public remained indifferent. Yet (excepting the work of Du Bois[9]) *Cane* contains the finest prose written by a Negro in America. And like the singing of Robeson,[10] it is truly racial.

But in spite of the Nordicized Negro **intelligentsia** and the desires of some white editors we have an honest American Negro literature already with us. Now I await the

[6] **Chesnutt.** Charles W. Chesnutt. See the selection from Chesnutt's work and the biography on page 425.

[7] **Dunbar's.** Paul Laurence Dunbar. See the selections from Dunbar's work and the biography on page 327.

[8] **prophet with little honor.** A reference to Mark 6:4. Jesus tells the people of Nazareth, his home town, that "A prophet is not without honor, save in his own country," meaning that his own people will not honor him, perhaps because familiarity breeds contempt.

[9] **Du Bois.** W. E. B. Du Bois. See page 269.

[10] **Robeson.** Paul Robeson (1898–1976), a famous African-American singer and actor

VOCABULARY IN PLACE

- **vogue,** ***n.*** Fashion
- **acclaim,** ***n.*** Fame
- **intelligentsia,** ***n.*** Members of the intellectual elite

rise of the Negro theatre.[11] Our folk music, having achieved worldwide fame, offers itself to the genius of the great individual American composer who is to come. And within the next decade I expect to see the work of a growing school of colored artists who paint and model the beauty of dark faces and create with new technique the expressions of their own soul-world. And the Negro dancers who will dance like flame and the singers who will continue to carry our songs to all who listen—they will be with us in even greater numbers tomorrow.

Most of my own poems are racial in theme and treatment, derived from the life I know. In many of them I try to grasp and hold some of the meaning and rhythms of jazz. I am as sincere as I know how to be in these poems and yet after every reading I answer questions like these from my own people: Do you think Negroes should always write about Negroes? I wish you wouldn't read some of your poems to white folks. How do you find anything interesting in a place like a cabaret?[12] Why do you write about black people? You aren't black. What makes you do so many jazz poems?

But jazz to me is one of the **inherent** expressions of Negro life in America; the eternal tom-tom[13] beating in the Negro soul—the tom-tom of revolt against weariness in a white world, a world of subway trains, and work, work, work; the tom-tom of joy and laughter, and pain swallowed in a smile. Yet the Philadelphia club-woman is ashamed to say that her race created it and she does not like me to write about it. The old subconscious "white is best" runs through her mind. Years of study under white teachers, a lifetime of white books, pictures, and papers, and white manners, morals, and Puritan standards made her dislike the spirituals. And now she turns up her nose at jazz and all its **manifestations**—likewise almost everything else distinctly racial. She doesn't care for the Winold Reiss portraits of Negroes because they are "too Negro." She does not want a true picture of herself from anybody. She wants the artist to flatter her, to make the white world believe that all Negroes are as smug and as near white in soul as she wants to be. But, to my mind, it is the duty of the younger Negro artist, if he accepts any duties at all from outsiders, to change through the force of his art that old whispering "I want to be white," hidden in the **aspirations** of his people, to "Why should I want to be white? I am a Negro—and beautiful!"

So I am ashamed for the black poet who says, "I want to be a poet, not a Negro poet," as though his own racial world were not as interesting as any other world. I am ashamed, too, for the colored artist who runs from the painting of Negro faces to the painting of sunsets after the manner of the **academicians** because he fears the strange un-whiteness of his own features. An artist must be free to choose what he does, certainly, but he must also never be afraid to do what he might choose. ■

---

11 **Negro theatre.** Langston Hughes himself became one of the leading lights of American theater. See his biography on page 371.

12 **cabaret.** A restaurant or club in which music, generally vocal music accompanied by a band, is played

13 **tom-tom.** A type of drum

VOCABULARY IN PLACE

- **inherent,** ***adj.*** Essential, built-in, inborn
- **manifestation,** ***n.*** Outward show
- **aspiration,** ***n.*** Hope, dream
- **academician,** ***n.*** Teacher in a university, professor

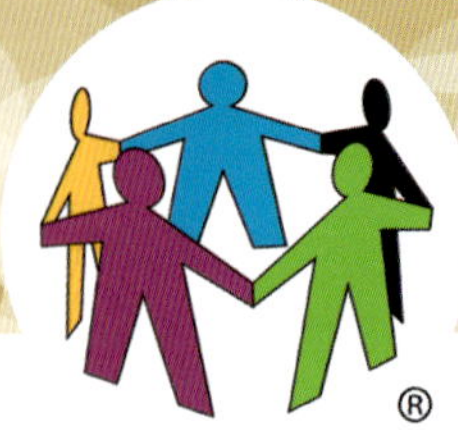

Understanding the Selection

Recalling

1. What did "One of the most promising of the young Negro poets" say to Hughes?
2. According to Hughes, what had the word *white* become a symbol of?
3. Who, according to Hughes, made up the majority of blacks in America at the time this essay was written?
4. What did Hughes state that the black artist can find "without going outside his race"?
5. From what music did Hughes say he drew his inspiration?

Interpreting

1. Do you agree with Hughes's reading of what the young poet said? Is any other interpretation possible?
2. What did he say led black middle-class families to adopt such an attitude?
3. What do such people provide to the black artist who is able to retain his or her "individuality in the face of American standardizations"?
4. What kinds of things did Hughes want black artists to deal with in their work?
5. Why did this music, in particular, appeal to Hughes?

Synthesizing

1. What, according to Hughes, is the "racial mountain"? Why did he think black artists needed to climb, or conquer, this mountain?
2. Do you agree with Hughes that artists who are also people of color should focus their work on their own unique histories and experiences, or do you think, instead, that an artist is an artist, irrespective of his or her race or ethnicity? Explain.

Delving Deeper

Understanding Literature

Essay Form. Langston Hughes's "The Negro Artist and the Racial Mountain" provides a good example of essay form. An **essay** should have a clear introduction, body, and conclusion. The **introduction** should capture the reader's attention and state a main idea, or **thesis.** The **body** should support that thesis. The **conclusion** should restate the thesis in other words. In the introduction to this essay, Hughes captures the reader's attention by quoting a young African-American poet of his acquaintance. He then states his main idea:

> But this [running away from one's racial identity] is the mountain standing in the way of any true Negro art in America—this urge within the race toward whiteness, the desire to pour racial individuality into the mold of American standardization, and to be as little Negro and as much American as possible.

Hughes then uses the body of his essay to support his thesis. He does so by providing examples of how people at the time were running away from their racial identity (the typical middle-class father, the prominent Negro clubwoman from Philadelphia), by talking about the possibilities for African-American art based upon the experiences of the "low-down" folks (the so-called common element) and by discussing some examples of great African-American art and artists (Toomer, Dunbar, Du Bois, Robeson). He then explains why he considers his own work "racial in theme and treatment."

Finally, Hughes concludes his essay by returning to the question raised by the young poet's comment—the question of whether there can be or should be a specifically "Negro" art. Reread his conclusion and note the subtle way in which Hughes restates and reaffirms his thesis.

Try your hand at writing your own essay on the topic of what young artists of today should treat as their subject matter. You can define the term *artist* very broadly to include pop musicians, writers, film makers, video producers, and others. Begin by grabbing your reader's attention and stating a thesis. Write several paragraphs to support your thesis. Then end with a strong conclusion that restates your main idea in a different way.

About the Author

See the biography of Langston Hughes on page 371.

Prereading

"We Wear the Mask" and "Sympathy"

by Paul Laurence Dunbar

Paul Laurence Dunbar once said, "I hope there is something worthy in my writings and not merely the novelty of a black face associated with the power to rhyme that has attracted attention."

Anyone who reads a Dunbar poem and fails to recognize the worthiness—the worlds of emotion, suffering, hope, and faith—behind Dunbar's rhymes simply needs to read the poem again.

Still, Dunbar was expressing a common sentiment among black writers of his time. Fortunately, he never seemed to care what others thought about his work. He simply wrote of the things he felt and knew. He toured Europe and the United States reciting his poems, undoubtedly enchanting his audiences with his powerful, precise images. Many of his works were influenced by or written completely in African-American dialect, and his words and tone are always elegant and lyrical, yet direct and to the point.

Can a poet speak for an entire group of people? If that group's shared experiences are deeply engrained enough, and that poet listens hard and long enough, then yes, the collective thoughts and memory of a people can be absorbed by the poet's senses and returned—in elegant, pure, and eloquent style—at the end of the poet's pen. Most poets are lucky to have one such poem that is truly worthy of remembrance. Dunbar penned them by the dozen.

In "We Wear the Mask" and "Sympathy," Dunbar has chosen two familiar symbols—a caged bird and a mask—in order to express two basic things that most African Americans felt in the decades that followed the Civil War and Emancipation. Slavery was dead but its weight remained. For generations to come, black Americans would continue to fight, step by step, from plantation roots toward equality, oppressed all the way by racist laws, terrified by lynch mobs, and degraded and insulted from every side. Dunbar's work reflects on that hard journey but never fails to leave hope for a future when that journey will be done.

We Wear the Mask

by Paul Laurence Dunbar

We wear the mask that grins and lies,
It hides our cheeks and shades our eyes,—
This debt we pay to human **guile;**[1]
With torn and bleeding hearts we smile,
And mouth with myriad subtleties.[2]

Why should the world be overwise,
In counting all our tears and sighs?[3]
Nay, let them only see us, while
We wear the mask.

We smile, but, O great Christ, our cries
To thee from tortured souls arise.
We sing, but oh the clay is **vile**
Beneath our feet, and long the mile;
But let the world dream otherwise,
We wear the mask! ■

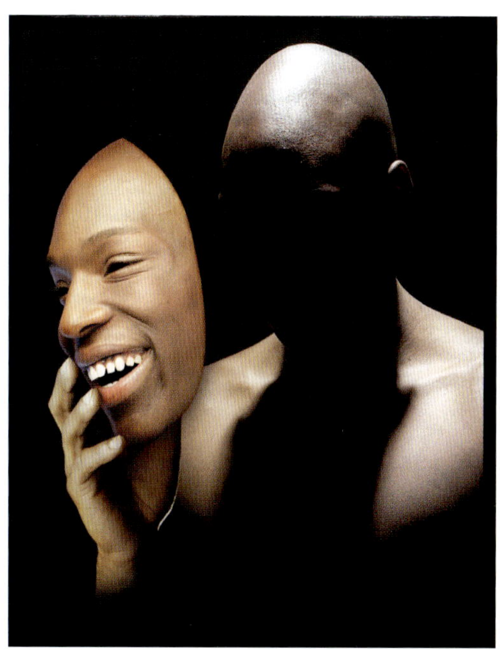

1 **human guile.** A reference to the cruel legacy of slavery as well as to fraud and other injustices suffered since slavery's end

2 **mouth with myriad subtleties.** *Myriad* means a large number; *subtleties* are restrained or hidden details. In other words, our smiles mask the complexities of our true feelings.

3 **Why should . . . tears and sighs.** Why should we bother the world with our troubles all the time?

VOCABULARY IN PLACE

- **guile,** ***n.*** Sinister cunning in attaining a goal; artful deception
- **vile,** ***adj.*** Unpleasant or objectionable; disgusting

Sympathy

by Paul Laurence Dunbar

I know what the caged bird feels, alas!
When the sun is bright on the upland slopes;
When the wind stirs soft through the springing grass,
And the river flows like a stream of glass;
When the first bird sings and the first bud opes,[1]
And the faint perfume from its chalice[2] steals—
I know what the caged bird feels!

I know why the caged bird beats his wing
Till its blood is red on the cruel bars;
For he must fly back to his perch and cling
When he **fain** would be on the bough a-swing;[3]
And a pain still throbs in the old, old scars
And they pulse again with a **keener** sting—
I know why he beats his wing!

I know why the caged bird sings, ah me,
When his wing is bruised and his bosom sore,—
When he beats his bars and he would be free;
It is not a carol of joy or glee;
But a prayer that he sends from his heart's deep core,
But a plea, that upward to Heaven he flings—
I know why the caged bird sings!

---

[1] **opes.** Opens

[2] **chalice.** A cup or goblet, especially one used in ceremonies or rituals. Here, the chalice is a metaphor for the flower bud.

[3] **When he . . . bough a-swing.** He wishes he were swinging in a *bough*, or tree branch.

VOCABULARY IN PLACE

- **fain,** ***adv.*** Happily or gladly
- **keen,** ***adj.*** Intense, piercing

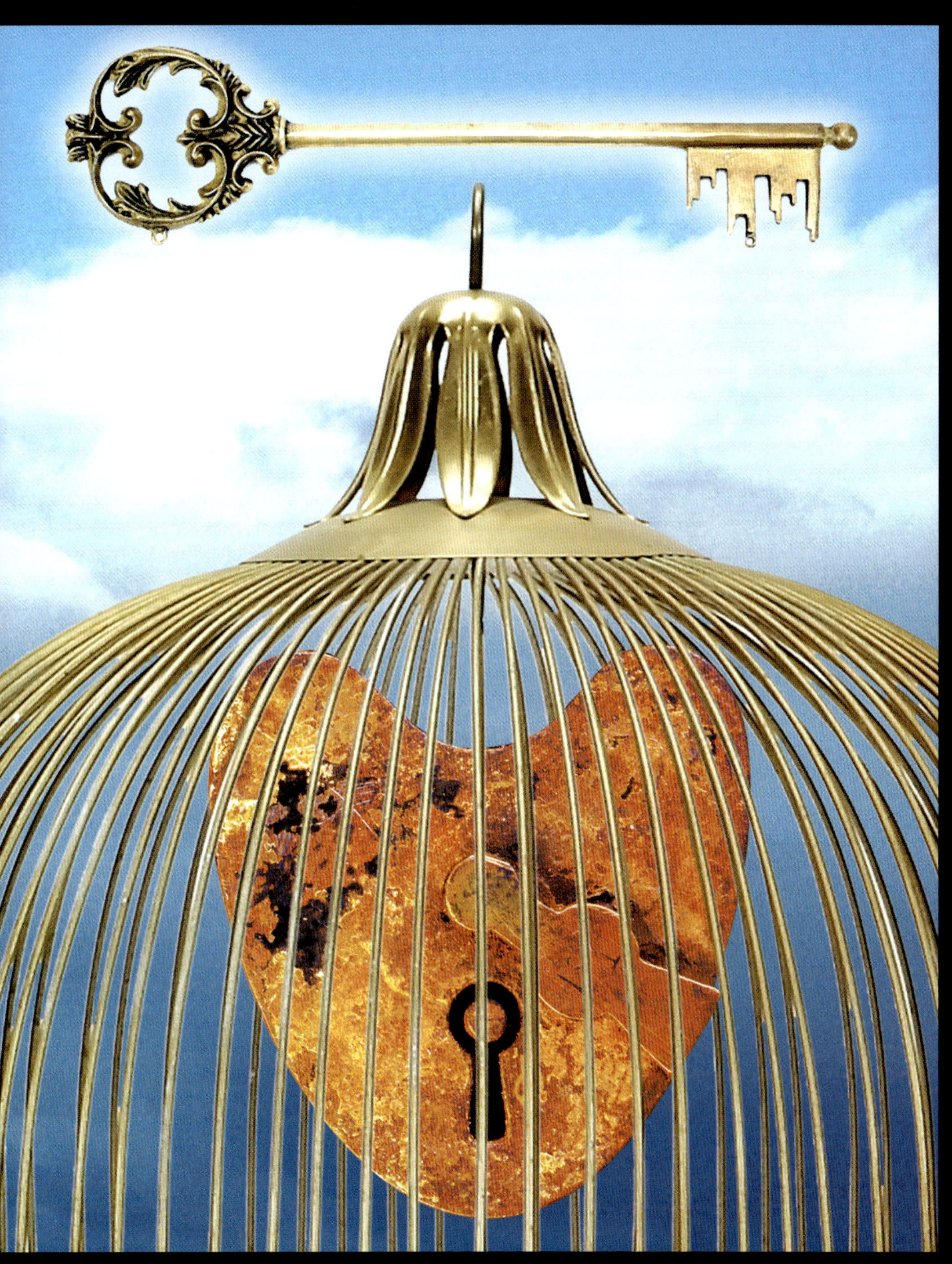

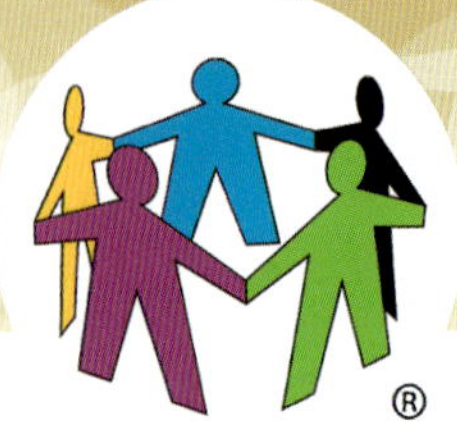

Understanding the Selection

Recalling

1. What does the mask do to people's faces?
2. What question does the speaker of "We Wear the Mask" ask?
3. Identify four images or scenes from lines 1–7 of "Sympathy" that the bird sees from its cage.
4. What causes pain to the bird in the second stanza? Find two examples.
5. What does the caged bird fling up to heaven?

Interpreting

1. To whom does the word "we" in the line "we wear the mask" refer?
2. Why does the speaker want the "tears and sighs" to be hidden from the world?
3. How does the caged bird feel, and why does it feel that way?
4. To what might the phrase "old scars" refer? Are there any similar references in this stanza?
5. To a person who does not "know," what emotions might the caged bird's song suggest? What does the speaker know about the song that others might not know?

Synthesizing

1. In "We Wear the Mask," does the speaker think that it is important to wear the mask? Do you think that he *wants* to wear it? What is the alternative?
2. What thematic similarity can you find in the last stanza of "We Wear the Mask" and the last stanza of "Sympathy?"

Delving Deeper

Writing

Who wears the mask? Write a one-page essay on the following topic: Do people in today's world wear masks?

To organize your thoughts, write brief (one sentence), informal answers to the following questions. If necessary, review your notes from your reading of "We Wear the Mask":

- What is the "mask," according to Dunbar? Why did African Americans wear it?
- Are African Americans the only people who might wear the "mask"?
- Why might someone feel the need to hide his or her true thoughts and feelings?

The questions above, or your answers to them, should serve as the topics for at least three paragraphs in your essay. It will help if you develop a detailed outline before you start writing. Use the outline to organize the points, or evidence, that you will present in the essay. Find at least one quotation from the poem to use somewhere in your essay. (The most likely place for it will be in the introductory paragraph.) Also, incorporate into your essay at least two examples from your own experiences or from stories you have heard.

About the Author

Paul Laurence Dunbar (1872–1906) was born in Dayton, Ohio. His mother, who raised her children alone, taught Paul to read and encouraged his love of literature. He was the only black student to attend his high school, where he became president of the literary society. Later, with the help of former classmates Orville and Wilbur Wright, he published the African-American newsletter *The Dayton Tattler.*

In his short life, Dunbar published seven collections of poetry, in addition to several novels, essays, and short stories. He published his first collection, *Oak and Ivory,* in 1892. Three years later, with *Majors and Minors,* he was recognized as a rising star. His early works incorporated humor and dialect, but there were always deep issues at heart.

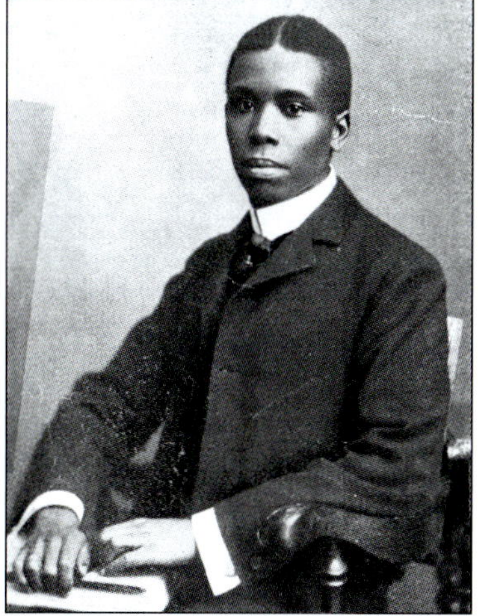

Dunbar had widespread success in 1896 with *Lyrics of Lowly Life,* which carried him on a tour of England. He married shortly after returning, but he also developed tuberculosis, which plagued him the rest of his life.

The creative vision exhibited in both the form and content of Paul Dunbar's poetry greatly influenced the generation of poets who shaped the Harlem Renaissance.

Prereading

The Poetry of James Weldon Johnson

James Weldon Johnson was among the most influential and innovative poets of the early twentieth century. He is sometimes called the "elder statesman" or father figure of the Harlem Renaissance, especially in relation to Langston Hughes, Claude McKay, and many others whom he inspired.

The Creation. The book *God's Trombones*—which consists of seven sermons and was more than a decade in the making—made an enormous impact on the African-American literary scene in 1927, and "The Creation" was widely viewed as the book's centerpiece.

Johnson is known for his **free verse** poetry, which does not rely on strict **meters** (pattern of rhythms) or **rhyme scheme** (pattern of rhymes). Instead, his poetry depends upon the rhythms of natural speech but artfully finds the music in these rhythms. Johnson avoided the popular style of writing in **dialect.** However, if you imagine a black evangelical preacher reciting the poem, then it becomes apparent that Johnson was actually writing in the **vernacular** (in ordinary speech rather than in a formal literary style). (See Delving Deeper on page 335 for analysis of the boldfaced terms in this paragraph.)

The poem appears very simple in terms of vocabulary, structure, and theme. That is where the simplicity ends and the real poetry begins. Consider the following points before you read the poem:

1. Johnson generally wrote using Standard English, in part to appeal to a wider audience and also to avoid compounding negative stereotypes about black culture.
2. Despite preferring to compose free verse poetry, Johnson created verse that was highly musical.
3. The poem roughly parallels the first two chapters of the Book of Genesis in its imagery and narrative style.
4. Johnson intended for this poem to be read aloud.

Lift Ev'ry Voice and Sing. This is actually a song that Johnson wrote much earlier in his career. So popular was the song that it came to be known as the black national anthem. To the poet's surprise, the song swept the nation, and to this day it remains popular in church choirs.

The Awakening. This fine little love poem, published in *50 Years and Other Poems* (1917), reveals Johnson's versatility as a poet.

The Creation

by James Weldon Johnson

And God stepped out on space,
And he looked around and said:
I'm lonely—
I'll make me a world.

And far as the eye of God could see
Darkness covered everything,
Blacker than a hundred midnights
Down in a cypress swamp.[1]

Then God smiled,
And the light broke,
And the darkness rolled up on one side,
And the light stood shining on the other,
And God said: That's good!

Then God reached out and took the light in his hands,
And God rolled the light around in his hands
Until he made the sun;
And he set that sun a-blazing in the heavens.
And the light that was left from making the sun
God gathered it up in a shining ball
And flung it against the darkness,
Spangling[2] the night with the moon and stars.
Then down between

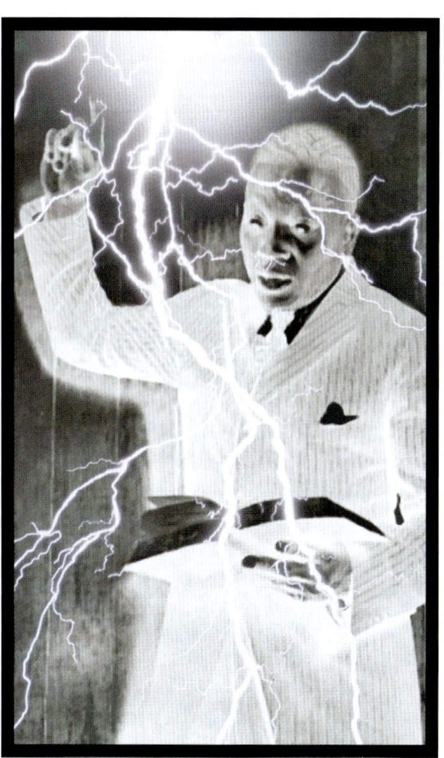

---

1 **cypress swamp.** The *cypress* is a type of evergreen tree common in swamps in the deep South.

2 **Spangling.** Randomly sprinkling

The darkness and the light
He hurled the world;
And God said: That's good!

Then God himself stepped down—
And the sun was on his right hand,
And the moon was on his left;
The stars were clustered about his head,
And the earth was under his feet.
And God walked, and where he trod
His footsteps hollowed the valleys out
And bulged the mountains up.

Then he stopped and looked and saw
That the earth was hot and barren.
So God stepped over to the edge of the world
And he spat out the seven seas—
He batted his eyes, and the lightnings flashed—
He clapped his hands, and the thunders rolled—
And the waters above the earth came down,
The cooling waters came down,

Then the green grass sprouted,
And the little red flowers blossomed,
The pine tree pointed his finger to the sky,
And the oak spread out his arms,
The lakes cuddled down in the hollows of the ground,
And the rivers ran down to the sea;
And God smiled again,
And the rainbow appeared,
And curled itself around his shoulder.

Then God raised his arm and he waved his hand
Over the sea and over the land,
And he said: Bring forth! Bring forth!
And quicker than God could drop his hand,
Fishes and fowls
And beasts and birds
Swam the rivers and the seas,
Roamed the forests and the woods,
And split the air with their wings.
And God said: That's good!

Then God walked around,
And God looked around
On all that he had made.
He looked at his sun,
And he looked at his moon,
And he looked at his little stars;
He looked on his world
With all its living things,
And God said: I'm lonely still.

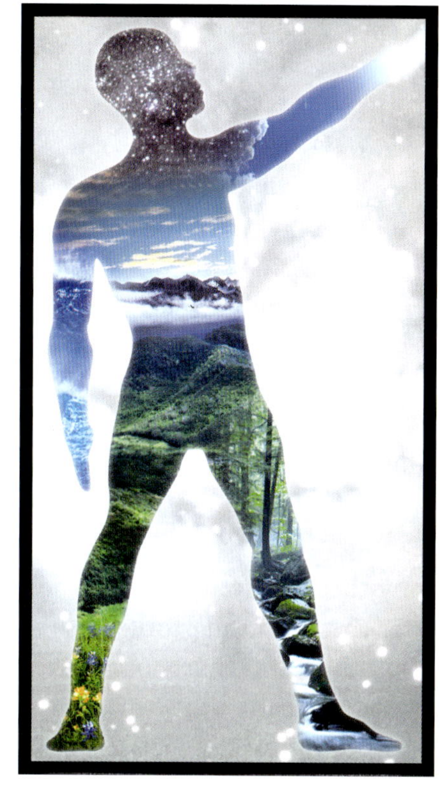

Then God sat down—
On the side of a hill where he could think;
By a deep, wide river he sat down;
With his head in his hands,
God thought and thought,
Till he thought: I'll make me a man!

Up from the bed of the river
God scooped the clay;
And by the bank of the river
He kneeled him down;
And there the great God Almighty
Who lit the sun and fixed it in the sky,
Who flung the stars to the most far corner of the night,
Who rounded the earth in the middle of his hand;
This Great God,
Like a mammy bending over her baby,
Kneeled down in the dust
Toiling over a lump of clay
Till he shaped it in his own image;

Then into it he blew the breath of life,
And man became a living soul.
Amen. Amen. ■

Lift Ev'ry Voice and Sing

by James Weldon Johnson

Lift ev'ry voice and sing,
Till earth and heaven ring,
Ring with the harmonies of Liberty;
Let our rejoicing rise
High as the list'ning skies,
Let it resound loud as the rolling sea.
Sing a song full of the faith that the dark past has taught us,
Sing a song full of the hope that the present has brought us;
Facing the rising sun of our new day begun,
Let us march on till victory is won.

Stony the road we trod,
Bitter the chast'ning rod,[1]
Felt in the days when hope unborn had died;
Yet with a steady beat,
Have not our weary feet
Come to the place for which our fathers sighed?
We have come over a way that with tears has been watered,
We have come, treading our path through the blood of the slaughtered,
Out from the gloomy past,
Till now we stand at last
Where the white gleam of our bright star is cast.

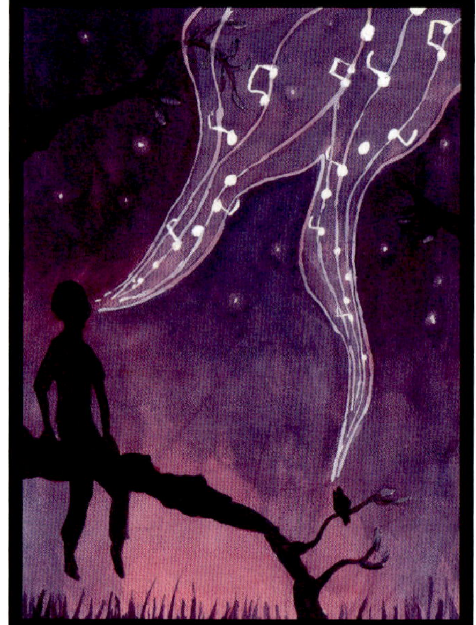

God of our weary years,
God of our silent tears,
Thou who hast brought us thus far on the way;
Thou who hast by Thy might,
Led us into the light,
Keep us forever in the path, we pray.
Lest our feet stray from the places, our God, where we met Thee,
Lest our hearts, drunk with the wine of the world, we forget Thee;
Shadowed beneath Thy hand,
May we forever stand,
True to our God,
True to our native land. ■

[1] **chast'ning rod.** A club or whip (used to punish an enslaved person). *To chasten* means "to correct by punishment."

The Awakening

by James Weldon Johnson

I dreamed that I was a rose
That grew beside a lonely way,
Close by a path none ever chose,
And there I lingered day by day.
Beneath the sunshine and the show'r
I grew and waited there apart,
Gathering perfume hour by hour,
And storing it within my heart,
Yet, never knew,
Just why I waited there and grew.

I dreamed that you were a bee
That one day gaily flew along,
You came across the hedge to me,
And sang a soft, love-burdened song.
You brushed my petals with a kiss,
I woke to gladness with a start,
And yielded up to you in bliss
The treasured fragrance of my heart;
And then I knew
That I had waited there for you. ■

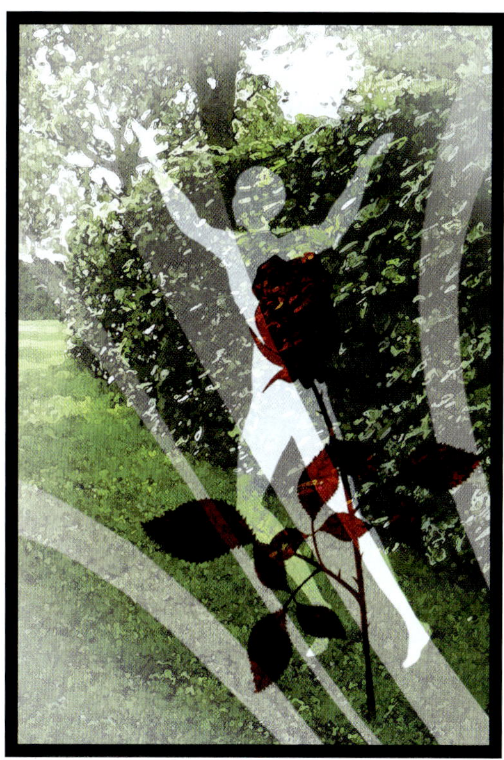

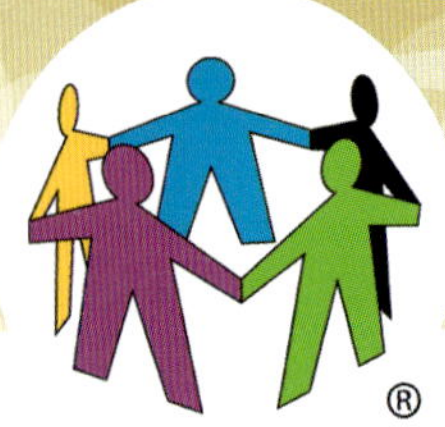

Understanding the Selection

Recalling

1. Why does God decide to make the world in "The Creation"? What does he do to make light?
2. What words are repeated at the end of lines 40 and 41?
3. To **personify** is to represent a nonliving thing as having human characteristics. Identify at least three examples of **personification** in "The Creation."
4. What is the last thing that God created? Why did he create it?
5. To what two things does the speaker of "Lift Ev'ry Voice and Sing" wish to remain true?
6. For what was the rose waiting in "The Awakening"?

Interpreting

1. What do these actions suggest about God as a character? What impression of God does the speaker present to listeners?
2. What is the purpose of this repetition? What is the speaker's tone?
3. What single adjective would you use to summarize the overall mood created by lines 42–60? How does the speaker create this mood?
4. Is the image of God as a "mammy" consistent with other images or descriptions of God in this poem? Why or why not?
5. To what place, specifically, do you think the speaker is referring in the last line of the poem?
6. What is the significance of the poem's title?

Synthesizing

1. How does Johnson capture the voice of an African-American preacher in "The Creation"? What specific language and imagery does he use to echo or reflect the everyday language (vernacular) of some African Americans?
2. How do these three poems differ from one another in style, structure, and language? What do these differences show you about Johnson as a poet?

Delving Deeper

Understanding Literature

Free Verse Poetry. A **free verse** poem does not necessarily lack structure or complexity; the poet does not simply throw words on the paper and let them land where they may. Free verse poetry breaks from traditional forms, such as the **sonnet,** in which the lines follow a set rhyme scheme and meter (measured by the number of syllables and stresses per line). To achieve a musical effect, the free verse poet relies instead on devices of sound such as alliteration and the natural rhythms of language.

Critics condemned **Walt Whitman** (1819–1892)—the first great American free verse poet—saying that his work lacked proper discipline and structure and was, therefore, unworthy of serious consideration. But Whitman's work *was* structured: he was heavily influenced by the ancient Hebrew tradition of non-rhyming verse. More importantly, his work celebrated the American spirit and revealed new horizons to poets. Free verse poetry spawned the development of a rich, uniquely American poetic style. To write good free verse poetry still requires deep reflection, hard work, and creativity. James Weldon Johnson combined Whitman's style with black vernacular. Today, most scholars agree that Johnson did the same for African-American poetry that Whitman did for American poetry as a whole.

About the Author

James Weldon Johnson (1871–1938), poet, educator, diplomat, and civil rights activist, was born in Jacksonville, Florida. He graduated from Atlanta University in 1896 and worked as a teacher and principal, but his career took a dramatic turn with the successful publication of the song "Lift Ev'ry Voice and Sing." Johnson then moved to New York to pursue literary interests. He obtained a degree from Columbia University and, seeking new experiences, joined the Foreign Service, serving as consul to Nicaragua from 1909 to 1913.

After returning to the United States, Johnson served as an editorial writer for the *New York Age* and later took a job at the NAACP, where he became general secretary in 1920. This job absorbed much of his time and energy. Johnson wrote a well-known preface to *The Book of American Negro Poetry* and contributed to several other important anthologies and publications. He published two collections of poetry, *Fifty Years and Other Poems* (1917) and *God's Trombones* (1927). He also published *Black Manhattan* (1930), a book about black life in New York; an autobiography, *Along This Way* (1933); and *Negro Americans, What Now?* (1934).

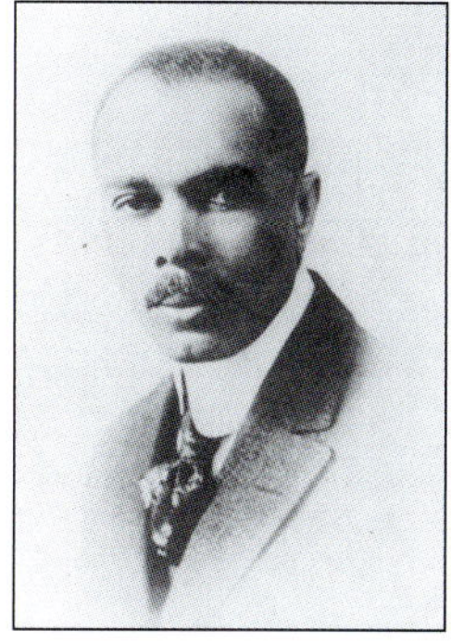

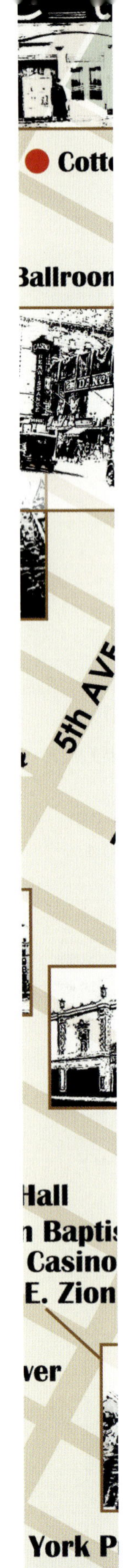

Prereading

The Poetry of Fenton Johnson, Anne Spencer, and Waverly Turner Carmichael

These three poets came from very different backgrounds, yet grouped together they help to illustrate the diversity of voices and personalities that sparked the Harlem Renaissance. Of course, there had always been black American writers and artists, but it was during those years when Harlem blossomed that those artists came together, literally and figuratively, to form a community of ideas and hope.

The Banjo Player. Fenton Johnson led the Chicago version of the Harlem Renaissance. Following in the footsteps of Paul Laurence Dunbar, Johnson became well versed in traditional poetic forms but was also eager, in the early twentieth century, to break new ground in style and content. His work, both experimental and traditional, had a profound influence on the poets of the 1920s and '30s and appeared in many anthologies. "The Banjo Player" looks more like a paragraph than a poem, but the cadence and stark beauty of Johnson's language reveal his gifts as a poet.

White Things. The voice of protest and anger in Anne Spencer's "White Things" is far different from the voice in most of her other poetry, which tends to focus on nature and romance. Spencer penned this poem in response to a particularly heinous lynching, and in it she exposes and condemns white people's apparent obsession with controlling all colorful things. Readers should pay close attention to the last four lines, which—as graphic and intense as they are—deliver the essential meaning of the poem as a whole.

Keep Me, Jesus, Keep Me. Waverly Turner Carmichael will be unfamiliar to most readers. He was one of numerous young, talented writers inspired by the nationwide arts and civil rights movements. We know little about him, but his biography is interesting nonetheless. (See About the Author, page 341.) Clearly, the words he put to paper were genuine and raw, reflecting the dialect and faithful prayers that he heard in Alabama during his poverty-stricken childhood. "Keep Me, Jesus, Keep Me" is a ***hymn***, or religious song. Perhaps Carmichael first penned (or prayed) these words in a trench on some awful battlefield during the First World War.

The Banjo Player

by Fenton Johnson

There is music in me, the music of a peasant people.
I wander through the levee,[1] picking my banjo and singing my songs of the cabin and the field.
At the Last Chance Saloon I am as welcome as the violets in March;
there is always food and drink for me there, and the dimes of those who love honest music.
Behind the railroad tracks the little children clap their hands and love me as they love Kris Kringle.[2]
But I fear that I am a failure. Last night a woman called me a troubadour.
What is a troubadour?[3] ■

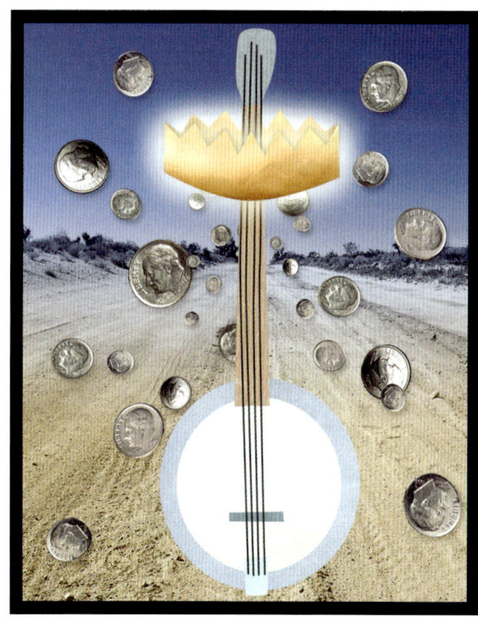

[1] **levee.** An embankment used to prevent flooding and by extension the community living on and near this embankment

[2] **Kris Kringle.** Another name for Santa Claus

[3] **What is a troubadour?** The poem's speaker is a folk hero in his community. He is a recorder and transmitter of his community's identity and cultural traditions. A *troubadour* was a traveling musician, poet, and storyteller in France during the Middle Ages. Troubadours, like this banjo player, were much more than simply entertainers. It is ironic, therefore, that the banjo player should fear that he has been slighted. This irony underscores his connection to the common people.

White Things[1]

by Anne Spencer

Most things are colorful things—the sky, earth, and sea.
Black men are most men; but the white are free!
White things are rare things; so rare, so rare
They **stole** from out a silvered world—somewhere.
Finding earth-plains **fair** plains, save[2] greenly grassed,
They strewed white feathers of cowardice, as they passed;
The golden stars with lances fine,
The hills all red and darkened pine,
They blanched with their wand of power;
And turned the blood in a ruby rose
To a poor white poppy-flower.

They pyred[3] a race of black, black men,
And burned them to ashes white; then,
Laughing, a young one claimed a skull,
For the skull of a black is white, not dull,
But a glistening awful thing
Made, it seems, for the ghoul to swing
In the face of God with all his might,
And swear by the hell that sired[4] him:
"Man-maker, make white!" ■

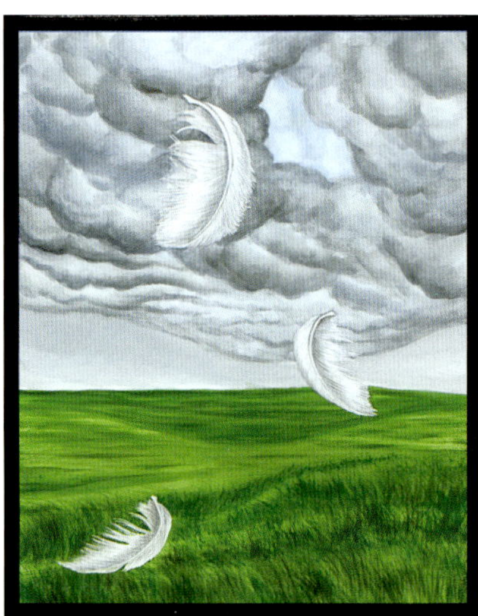

[1] **White Things.** Spencer wrote this poem after hearing of a horrific lynching, the details of which are too graphic to describe in these pages. This is a protest poem against lynching in general.

[2] **save.** With the exception of

[3] **pyred.** Put them on a funeral **pyre** (a heap of wood used for burning a body during a funeral rite)

[4] **sired.** Brought into being

VOCABULARY IN PLACE

- **steal,** *v.* To sneak quietly; to creep
- **fair,** *adj.* Of light color

Keep Me, Jesus, Keep Me

by Waverly Turner Carmichael

Keep me[1] 'neath Thy mighty wing,
Keep me, Jesus, keep me;
Help me praise Thy Holy name,
Keep me, Jesus, keep me.
O my Lamb,[2] come, my Lamb,
O my good Lamb,
Save me, Jesus, save me.

Hear me as I cry to Thee;
Keep me, Jesus, keep me;
May I that bright glory see;
Keep me, Jesus, keep me.
O my Lamb, my good Lamb,
O my good Lamb,
Keep me, Jesus, keep me. ■

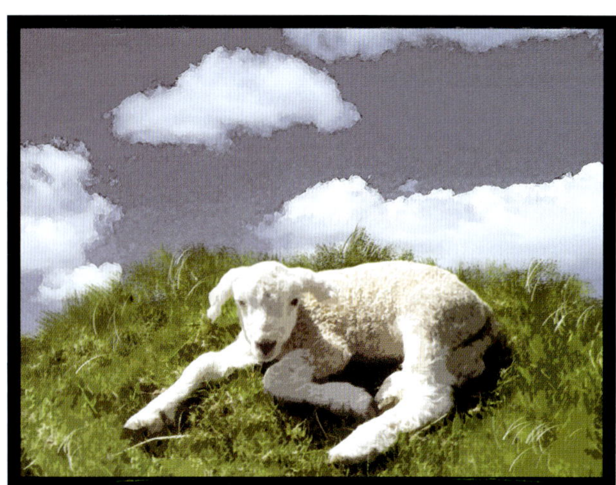

1 **Keep me.** Protect me

2 **Lamb.** "Lamb of God" is one of the titles given to Jesus Christ in the New Testament. The sacrificial lamb is a common symbol throughout the Bible.

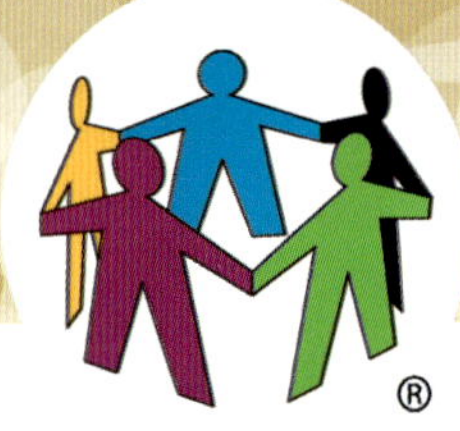

Understanding the Selection

Recalling

1. What kind of music does the speaker of "The Banjo Player" play? What are his songs about?
2. How does the banjo player make a living? What do the children do when he plays? How much do the children like him?
3. According to the speaker in "White Things," what color are most men?
4. What did the "white things" find?
5. Who is the "young one" (line 14)? Who is the "ghoul" (line 17)?
6. Find the beat to "Keep me, Jesus, Keep Me" by clapping or stomping a foot as you read. There are four beats in the first line. How many are in the second?

Interpreting

1. To or for whom does he play his music? How do others feel about his music? Support your answer with evidence from the poem.
2. Why do they love him so much, and do you think he likes to play for them, even if they do not pay him? Why, or why not?
3. Are white things common in nature? Where did "white things" come from? Use a quote from the poem to support your answer.
4. What did they do to the land?
5. What did the white man do to the black man?
6. What pattern do the beats in each line follow? Is the pattern the same throughout the poem? Where does it vary, and what effect does this have on the poem?

Synthesizing

1. What is a troubadour? Why does the speaker "fear that [he is] a failure"?
2. Why is "White Things" called a **protest poem**? What was Spencer protesting against? Can either of the other poems in this section be called protest poems?
3. Which of these poems is the most interesting or meaningful to you? Why?

About the Author

Fenton Johnson (1888–1958), considered one of the most influential forebears of the Harlem Renaissance, was one of the first black poets to write poetry in dialect, and some of his works are considered revolutionary in terms of theme and style. He founded and published two literary journals, including *Favorite Magazine* (1918–1920), out of his native Chicago. Johnson's major works focus on racial issues and the deteriorating living conditions throughout black communities in America. His major poetry collections are *A Little Dreaming* (1913), *Visions of the Dusk* (1915), and *Songs of the Soil* (1916). While his earlier work reveals the influence of Paul Laurence Dunbar and the Romantic Poets, Johnson became increasingly involved in exploring African-American folk forms, such as spirituals and blues—characteristics that link him with the early stirrings of the Harlem Renaissance.

About the Author

Anne Spencer (1882–1975), poet, civil rights activist, and beloved hostess during the Harlem Renaissance was born in Henry County, Virginia. She lived much of her life in Lynchburg, Virginia, where she maintained a famous garden and hosted many black literary and artistic personalities in her home. "White Things" was first published in *Crisis,* the magazine of the NAACP. Her work was published in several major anthologies of her day, including ten poems in *Caroling Dusk* and five in *The Book of African Poetry.* Other notable poems include "Before the Feast at Shushan" and "Lady, Lady." Spencer was also active in the early Civil Rights Movement.

About the Author

Waverly Turner Carmichael (1895–*unknown*) was born in Alabama and brought up in a life of poverty and constant toil. Fortunately, he was able to enroll in the Snow Hill Institute, an excellent all-black boarding school near his home. In 1915, Carmichael enrolled in a few summer courses at Harvard University. Shortly after, he enlisted with the 367th Infantry Regiment, "The Buffaloes," an all-black unit that fought with distinction in France in 1918. It is likely that he lived in Harlem after the war. In 1920, he published a volume of poetry entitled *From the Heart of a Folk; a Book of Songs,* and two of his poems were published in James Weldon Johnson's anthology *The Book of Negro Poetry* (1922). Little is known of his life thereafter.

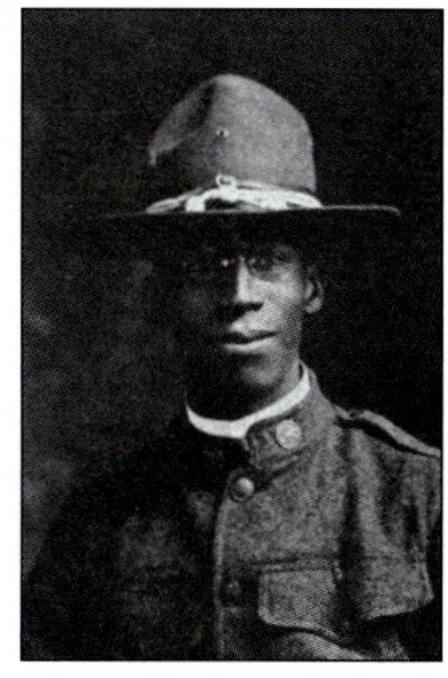

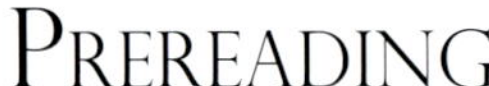

Prereading

The Poetry of Alice Dunbar Nelson, Georgia Douglas Johnson, and Angelina Weld Grimké

These poets, all of whom were friends, addressed the issues confronting women in the early 1900s. Women's lives were governed by strict social expectations: they were expected to stay home and were discouraged from seeking financial, intellectual, or political independence. As African-American women, therefore, these three writers had to conquer *two* mountains of inequality.

I Sit and Sew. Thanks to her mixed heritage and her upbringing in culturally diverse New Orleans, Alice Dunbar Nelson was fully aware of the challenges and issues related to race relations. However, as a writer, she preferred to avoid the subjects of race and racism and chose instead to address primarily women's and domestic issues. The poem "I Sit and Sew" was written at the height of America's involvement in the First World War; the speaker in the poem expresses feelings of frustration and powerlessness in wartime. Dunbar Nelson's poetry is traditional in form, but the imagery she used and the themes she explored were—in the first decades of the twentieth century—revolutionary for a female poet. As a result, she is counted as a mother figure among Harlem Renaissance poets.

The Heart of a Woman. Georgia Douglas Johnson is also counted among the pioneers of twentieth-century African-American as well as women's writing. She gave voice to many women, black and white alike, who felt smothered by the roles they were expected to play in society and were frustrated—artistically, intellectually, and politically—in a world largely controlled by men. "The Heart of a Woman" was also the title of Johnson's first book, which focuses on the issues that prevented her from achieving her full potential as an artist.

The Black Finger. Angelina Weld Grimké did address racial issues in some poems, but the bulk of her work, like that of the two poets above, revolved around other themes. Grimké focused on sexism, death, and lost love, and her poems often spoke in a voice of despair or isolation. "The Black Finger" is an exception to much of her work in that it does deal with race. However, it is typical of Grimké's work in terms of its form and length: often her poems were direct (to the point), inspired by a single moment's perception that she expressed using strong, crisp images.

I Sit and Sew

by Alice Dunbar Nelson

I sit and sew—a useless task it seems,
My hands grown tired, my head weighed down with dreams—
The **panoply** of war, the **martial** tred of men,
Grim-faced, stern-eyed, gazing beyond the **ken**
Of lesser souls, whose eyes have not seen Death
Nor learned to hold their lives but as a breath—
But—I must sit and sew.

I sit and sew—my heart aches with desire—
That pageant terrible,[1] that fiercely pouring fire
On wasted fields, and writhing grotesque things
Once men. My soul in pity flings
Appealing cries, yearning only to go
There in that **holocaust** of hell, those fields of woe—
But—I must sit and sew.

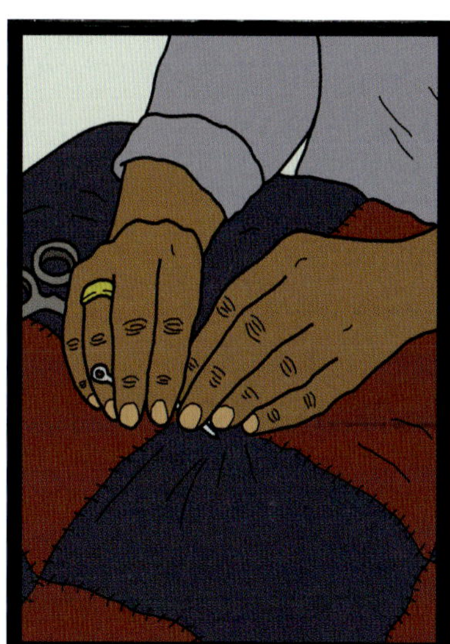

The little useless seam, the idle patch;
Why dream I here beneath my homely thatch,[2]
When there they lie in sodden mud and rain,
Pitifully calling me, the quick[3] ones and the slain?
You need me, Christ! It is no **roseate** dream
That beckons me—this pretty **futile** seam,
It stifles me—God, must I sit and sew? ■

1 **pageant terrible.** A terrible display or presentation

2 **homely thatch.** Unattractive thatched roof

3 **quick.** Living

VOCABULARY IN PLACE

- **panoply,** ***n.*** The arms and armor of a warrior
- **martial,** ***adj.*** Warlike
- **ken,** ***n.*** Range of vision
- **holocaust,** ***n.*** Great destruction resulting in the extensive loss of life, especially by fire
- **roseate,** ***adj.*** Rose-colored
- **futile,** ***adj.*** Useless; having no useful result

The Heart of a Woman

by Georgia Douglas Johnson

The heart of a woman goes forth with the dawn,
As a lone bird, soft winging, so restlessly on,
Afar o'er life's turrets and vales[1] does it roam
In the wake of those echoes the heart calls home.

The heart of a woman falls back with the night,
And enters some alien cage in its plight,
And tries to forget it has dreamed of the stars,
While it breaks, breaks, breaks on the sheltering bars. ■

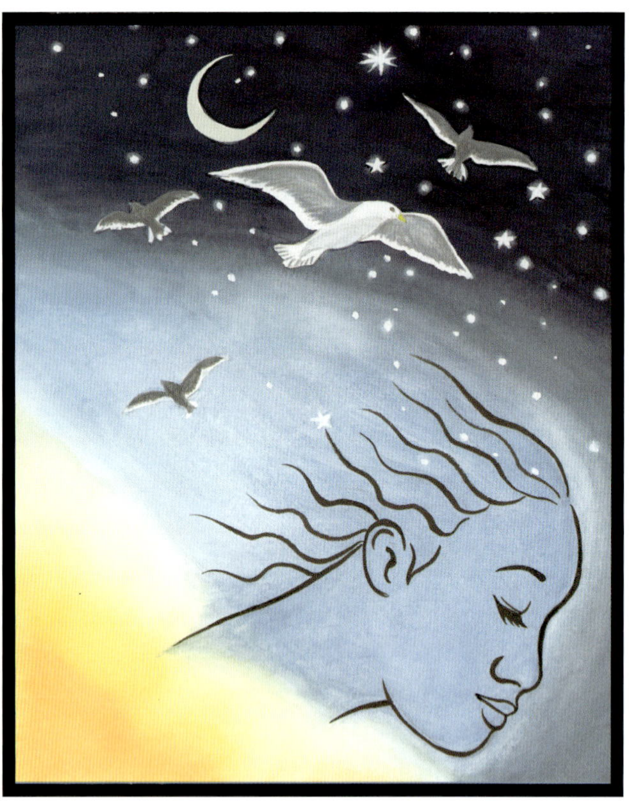

[1] **turrets and vales.** A metaphor for life's ups and downs. A *turret* is a tower, and a *vale* is a valley.

The Black Finger

by Angelina Weld Grimké

I have just seen a beautiful thing
    Slim and still,
Against a gold, gold sky,
    A straight cypress,[1]
    Sensitive
    Exquisite,
A black finger
Pointing upwards.
Why, beautiful, still finger are you black?
And why are you pointing upwards? ■

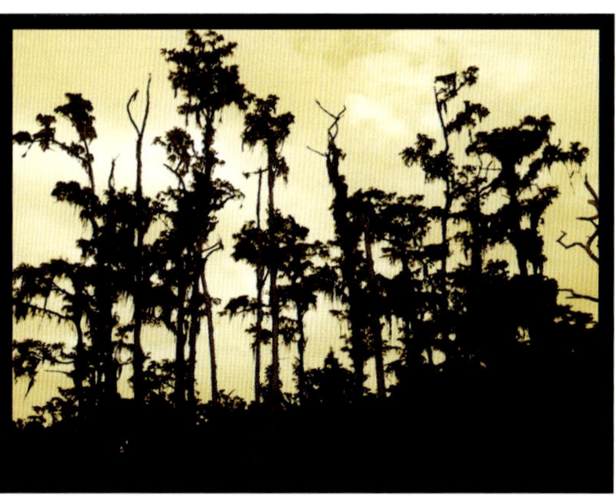

Cypress Trees in South Carolina. Library of Congress, LC-B811-3569

[1] **cypress.** A large family of evergreen trees. The trees are common in the Deep South, where they take root in swamps and can grow to impressive heights.

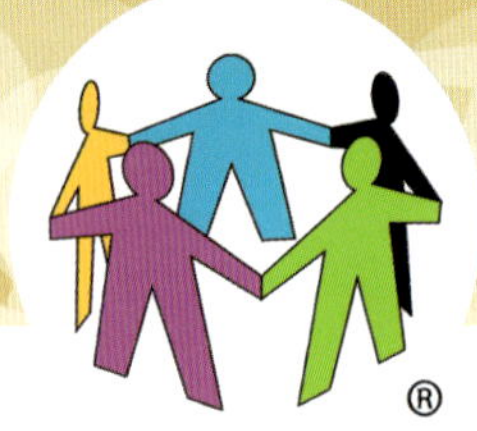

Understanding the Selection

Recalling

1. What is the speaker in "I Sit and Sew" thinking about while she is sewing?
2. Who is "pitifully calling" the speaker of "I Sit and Sew"?
3. According to the first stanza of "The Heart of a Woman," what is the heart, and what does it do?
4. What does the heart do when it returns at night?
5. To what does the speaker of "The Black Finger" compare the finger?
6. What two questions does the speaker of "The Black Finger" ask, and to whom does she ask them?

Interpreting

1. What words or phrases would you use to describe the speaker's mood? Why does she feel this way?
2. Why does she think that they need her?
3. How does the heart's action in the second stanza contrast with its actions in the first stanza?
4. What do the "sheltering bars" symbolize in a woman's life?
5. Why might the cypress tree be an important or familiar symbol to African Americans?
6. Does she expect an answer to her questions? What, in your opinion, is the answer to the question in line 10?

Synthesizing

1. In the poem "I Sit and Sew," why does the speaker feel that her work is useless?
2. In terms of theme, main idea, or overall mood, which two out of these three poems have the most in common? Explain your choice using evidence from the text.
3. Why does the speaker of "The Black Finger" describe the finger as being beautiful?

About the Author

Alice Dunbar Nelson (1875–1935), poet, fiction writer, journalist, educator, political organizer, and women's and civil rights activist, was born of mixed African, white, and American Indian ancestry. She published her first book, *Violets,* at the age of 20, followed by a major collection of short stories, *The Goodness of St. Rocque and Other Stories,* in 1899, one year after marrying poet Paul Laurence Dunbar. She continued to use the name Dunbar even after the marriage collapsed. Dunbar Nelson was frustrated throughout her career by editors who insisted that she modify the language, dialogue, and even the plot of her stories to fit white readers' expectations of African-American writing. She was also an accomplished columnist and editor for many newspapers, literary journals, and other publications. Many writers of the Harlem Renaissance era viewed her as a mother figure or mentor.

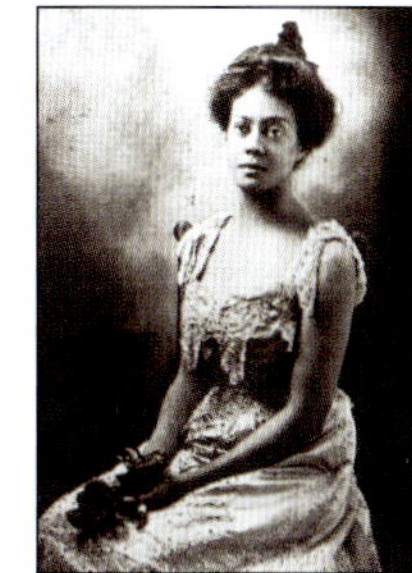

About the Author

Georgia Douglas Johnson (1880–1966) was born and educated in Atlanta and lived for much of her adult life in Washington, D.C. She was known both for her artistic and intellectual pursuits and for her hospitable and gracious nature. Her home became a weekly gathering place for young artists, including many famous people who visited from Harlem, and her door was always open to artists in need. Principal collections of her poetry include *The Heart of a Woman* (1918), *Bronze* (1922), *An Autumn Love Cycle* (1928), and *Share My World* (1962). She was also a prolific playwright and short-story writer, though, unfortunately, much of her life's work remains missing or lost.

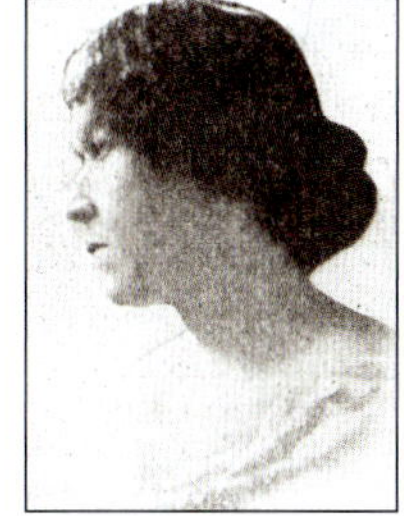

About the Author

Angelina Weld Grimké (1880–1958), poet and journalist, was born in Boston, Massachusetts. Her great-aunts were the famous white Abolitionists Sarah and Angelina Grimké. Her father served as vice president of the NAACP and was the second African American to graduate from Harvard Law School. Despite her relatively small body of work, Grimké was a prominent poet during the Harlem Renaissance. Her most famous poems include "Trees" and "The Eyes of My Regret," and her poems appeared in such prominent publications as *The Crisis, Opportunity,* and *The New Negro.* She also published a play, *Rachel* (1920), which was produced (on behalf of the NAACP) in an effort to rally support against the movie *The Birth of a Nation* and its derogatory depictions of African Americans.

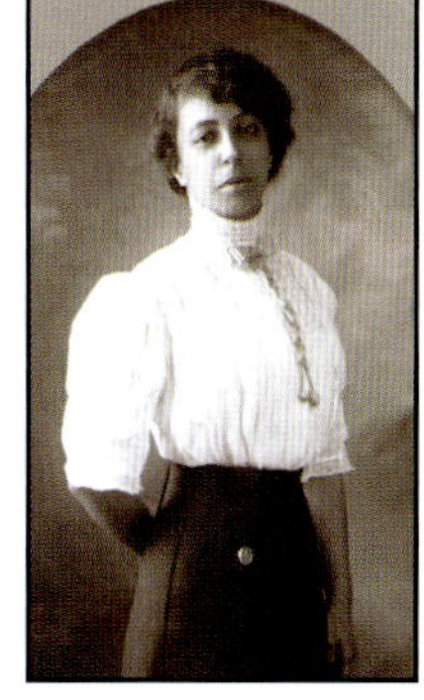

Prereading

The Poetry of Claude McKay

In the preface to *The Book of American Negro Poetry* (1922), the famous poet and editor James Weldon Johnson praised McKay, who "though still quite a young man" had "already demonstrated his power, breadth and skill as a poet."

McKay's "power" as a poet lies in his ability to expose raw truths about race and racism. The word *breadth* refers to the fact that he wrote on a wide variety of themes; among his works one will find as many poems protesting racism as there are poems about love, nature, the seasons, and his Jamaican homeland.

As for McKay's "skill," he was recognized throughout England and America as a great **lyricist** (one who composes deeply emotional, song-like verses, which typically follow a specific rhyme and meter), and he wrote some of the best **sonnets** of the twentieth century. (For a definition of the sonnet, please see the Handbook of Literary Terms.) However, his mastery of the English literary tradition is not the only reason he inspired poetry's greats like Langston Hughes and Countee Cullen. McKay's name endures as a leader among twentieth-century black poets because he was one of the first to lay bare the truth and speak directly to people of African descent, rather than trying to cater to a white literary market.

If We Must Die. This work is the best-known display of McKay's "power, breadth, and skill as a poet." It is about the awful "Red Summer" of 1919, when more than twenty violent race riots shook cities across the United States. As the great publisher and editor of *Pearson's Magazine,* Frank Harris, remarked upon first reading the poem, "[This] is a great poem, authentic fire and blood; blood pouring from a bleeding heart." Winston Churchill helped immortalize the poem when he recited it to all of England during the worst days of the Second World War.

The Tropics in New York. Another display of McKay's extraordinary skill. It illustrates the way in which a poet can control the reader's sense of setting. Pay attention to the shift in setting and tone between the first two stanzas, as the speaker reveals a world of lush, delicious memory, triggered by a simple fruit-stand outside his window.

Outcast. McKay returns to his favorite form, the sonnet, and proves once again his ability to mingle the traditions of English-language poetry with the pressing themes of race and cultural heritage that fueled the Harlem Renaissance.

If We Must Die

by Claude McKay

If we must die, let it not be like hogs
Hunted and penned in an **inglorious** spot,
While round us bark the mad and hungry dogs,
Making their mock at our accursed lot.[1]
If we must die, O let us nobly die,
So that our precious blood may not be shed
In vain; then even the monsters we defy
Shall be **constrained** to honor us though dead!
O kinsmen! we must meet the common foe![2]
Though far outnumbered let us show us brave,
And for their thousand blows deal one death blow!
What though before us lies the open grave?[3]
Like men we'll face the murderous, cowardly pack,
Pressed to the wall, dying, but fighting back! ■

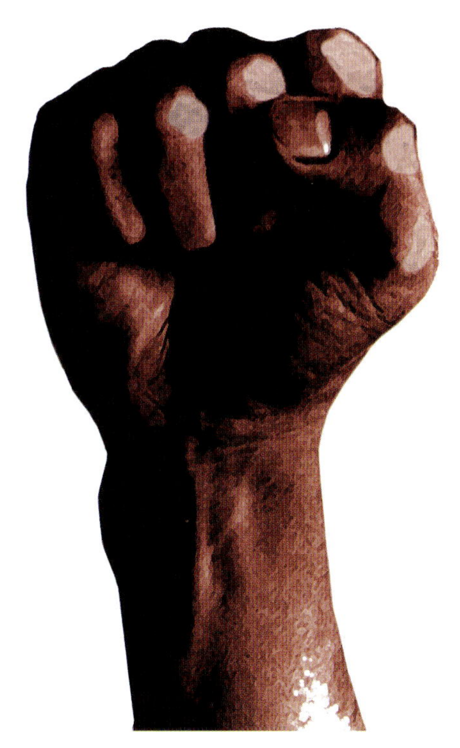

[1] **Making their mock at our accursed lot.** Humiliating our already suffering people

[2] **common foe.** Shared enemy

[3] **what though . . . open grave.** Whichever path we choose leads to death.

VOCABULARY IN PLACE

- **inglorious,** ***adj.*** Not famous; obscure; shameful
- **constrain,** ***v.*** To require or compel

The Tropics in New York

by Claude McKay

Bananas ripe and green, and ginger-root,
Cocoa in pods and alligator pears,[1]
And tangerines and mangoes and grape fruit,
Fit for the highest prize at parish[2] fairs,

Set in the window, bringing memories
Of fruit-trees laden by low-singing rills,[3]
And dewy dawns, and mystical blue skies
In **benediction** over nun-like hills.

My eyes grew dim, and I could no more gaze;
A wave of longing through my body swept,
And, hungry for the old, familiar ways,
I turned aside and bowed my head and wept. ■

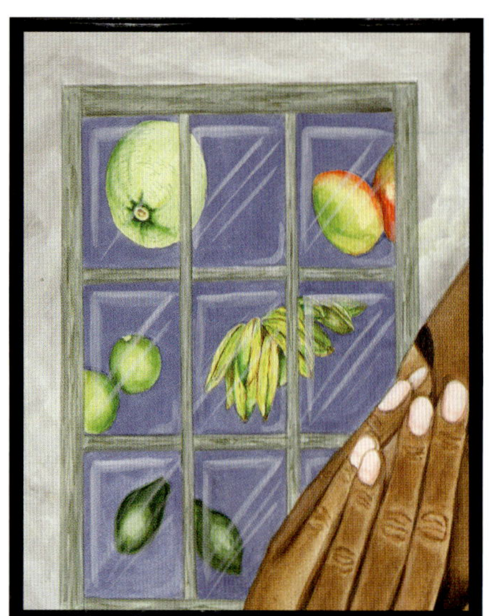

[1] **alligator pear.** Avocado (Jamaica)

[2] **parish.** County. Specifically, an administrative division in Britain or in one of its colonies or former colonies, such as Jamaica.

[3] **rills.** Creeks or streams

VOCABULARY IN PLACE

• **benediction,** ***n.*** A blessing; an expression of good will

Outcast

by Claude McKay

For the dim regions whence my fathers came
My spirit, bondaged by the body, longs.
Words felt, but never heard, my lips would frame;
My soul would sing forgotten jungle songs.
I would go back to darkness and to peace,
But the great western world[1] holds me in fee,[2]
And I may never hope for full release
While to its alien gods I bend my knee.
Something in me is lost, forever lost,
Some vital thing has gone out of my heart,
And I must walk the way of life a ghost
Among the sons of earth, a thing apart;
For I was born, far from my native clime,[3]
Under the white man's menace, out of time.[4] ■

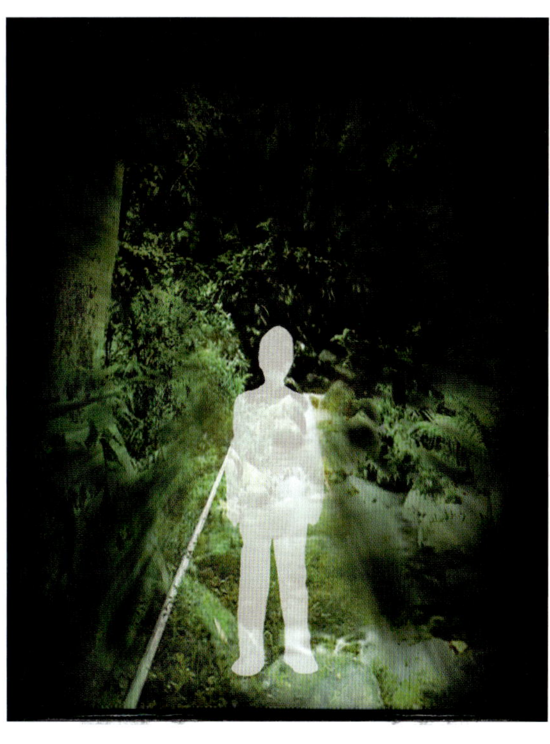

[1] **great western world.** Europe, the British Isles, and the United States; those cultures that trace their roots to Greco-Roman civilization

[2] **in fee.** In absolute and legal possession

[3] **clime.** Climate

[4] **out of time.** Outside of or apart from the desired place or time

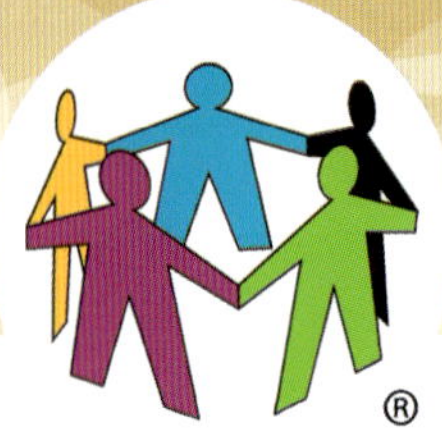

Understanding the Selection

Recalling

1. In the poem "If We Must Die," how does the speaker not want those referred to as "we" to die?
2. What question does the speaker ask in line 12?
3. What is the fruit "fit for" in the first stanza of "The Tropics in New York"?
4. Where does the speaker see the fruit?
5. What does the poet do in the last stanza? What is he longing for?
6. In "Outcast," where does the speaker want to go?
7. Where was the speaker born?

Interpreting

1. Why is it better to die in the manner described in lines 5-6 rather than that described in lines 1–4? What effect will resistance have on "the common foe"?
2. Of what does the speaker not want his audience to be afraid?
3. What tells the reader that the speaker longs for a place outside the United States?
4. What effect has the sight of the fruit had on the poem's speaker?
5. What does the speaker mean by "old, familiar ways" (line 11)? Why can't he find these things in a city?
6. What "vital thing" has gone out of his heart? Why is he "a ghost"?
7. Is he referring to Jamaica or Africa?

Synthesizing

1. McKay's success lay in the fact that he appealed to two fundamentally different types of readers: those who believed that black writers should focus on race and use poetry to reveal social truths and those who said that black poets should strive, instead, to produce great English-language poems. Select one of McKay's poems and explain, in your own words, how it might satisfy both types of readers.

Delving Deeper

Understanding Literature

Words Reserved for Poets? Have you ever asked yourself, "What is the *real* difference between a poem and a paragraph?" How about, "If I write a paragraph and 'break it up' into irregular lines, will it then be a poem?"

Rhythm and meter are important parts of a poem. Most lines in a typical **sonnet** are in the **iambic pentameter** form, consisting of five alternating weak and strong stresses per line. If you clap your hands to the beat (on the stressed syllables) in a McKay sonnet, you should clap five times in every line.

A piece of writing does not have to have a regular meter or rhyme scheme to qualify as a poem. In the end, the quality of the poem is determined purely by the poet's use of language. Fortunately for the poet, the English language is really an immense, ever-expanding trove of borrowings from other languages, from dialects, and from a variety of cultural traditions.

Sometimes, it seems that certain words or phrases that we encounter in poems were invented simply for the sake of writing a poem. In Shakespeare's case, this is literally true: he is credited with having invented at least 1,700 words. Claude McKay did not invent the word *rill,* but it is certainly not common in everyday English. What other words or phrases in McKay's poem "The Tropics in New York" seem to be reserved for poetry? What words or phrases in this poem seem to be especially poetic?

About the Author

Claude McKay (1889–1948), poet, journalist, and political activist, was born and raised in Jamaica. Although he had known racism in Jamaica, it was not until he arrived in Alabama to study at the Tuskegee Institute that he was introduced to Jim Crow and the horror of lynching, and he began to realize the extent of racist bigotry in the United States.

Prior to moving to the U.S., McKay published two collections of poetry in his native Jamaica, but he received little critical attention. In America, he published several poems and wrote for magazines; but it was not until 1919, when he visited England, that he finally gained the recognition he deserved, including from such notables as George Bernard Shaw. In England, McKay also became an active socialist.

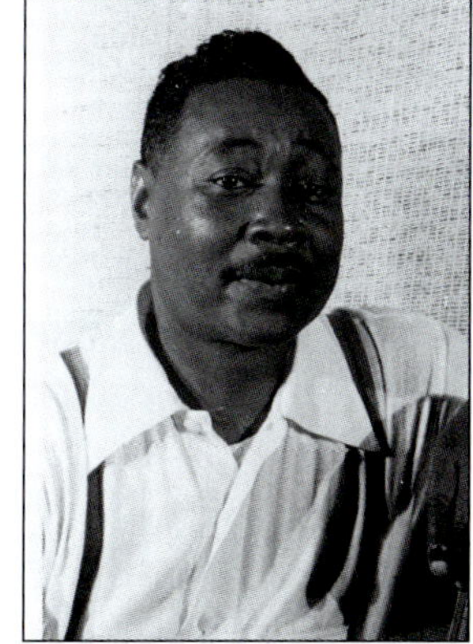

McKay's best-known poetry collection is *Harlem Shadows* (1922). He was also a gifted novelist, publishing at least five major titles, including *Home to Harlem* (1928), which made him the first black writer to publish a bestselling novel. James Weldon Johnson once wrote, "Claude McKay's poetry was one of the greatest forces in bringing about [the Harlem Renaissance]."

Prereading

"The Negro Speaks of Rivers," "Mother to Son," "Dream Variations," and "Dreams"

by Langston Hughes

As he argued persuasively in his essay "The Negro Artist and the Racial Mountain," Langston Hughes felt that African Americans have a distinct heritage and unique spirit worthy of celebration. Though he wrote numerous plays, essays, translations, and short stories, two novels, and an autobiography, Hughes thought of himself primarily as a poet—and that is how most remember him to this day. He once called poetry "the human soul entire, squeezed like a lemon or a lime, drop by drop, into atomic words."

The three well-known poems in this section vary in terms of style, voice, and central theme; each, however, reflects Hughes's pride in his people.

The Negro Speaks of Rivers. Hughes's explosive impact on the world of poetry began in 1921, when, at the young age of 19, he published his first poem, "The Negro Speaks of Rivers," in *Crisis* magazine. As Hughes later wrote in his autobiography, *The Big Sea* (1940), he composed this poem while traveling by train to see his father, who lived in Mexico. Viewing the muddy waters of the Mississippi flowing to the South, he thought of slaves past—for whom being "sold down the river" meant a terrible fate—and then of other rivers intertwined with the history of black people. And so, with this poem, he launched a deep admiration for African Americans that flows throughout his writings.

Mother to Son. The speaker in this poem projects a loving yet sobering tone intended to warn her child of life's realities while encouraging him not to give up hope. "Mother to Son" provides valuable advice to any reader, but in itself, the advice is not profound or original; the poem's true significance lies in the strength, weariness, and cultural heritage of the speaker's voice.

Dream Variations. One of Hughes's most famous poems, this piece contains language as simple and unadorned as that of any poem ever written. But under the pen of a fine poet, *simple* becomes *elegant,* and *unadorned* becomes *refined.* The poem's two stanzas are nearly parallel in both structure and language, and there is a similar, dramatic mood shift after the fourth line of each stanza.

Dreams. Of what importance is holding onto one's dreams? This recurring theme in Hughes's work gets a graceful, simple treatment in this famous poem.

The Negro Speaks of Rivers

by Langston Hughes

I've known rivers:
I've known rivers ancient as the world and older than the
flow of human blood in human veins.

My soul has grown deep like the rivers.

I bathed in the Euphrates[1] when dawns were young.
I built my hut near the Congo[2] and it **lulled** me to sleep.
I looked upon the Nile and raised the pyramids above it.
I heard the singing of the Mississippi when Abe Lincoln
went down to New Orleans,[3] and I've seen its muddy
bosom turn all golden in the sunset.
I've known rivers:
Ancient, **dusky** rivers.

My soul has grown deep like the rivers. ■

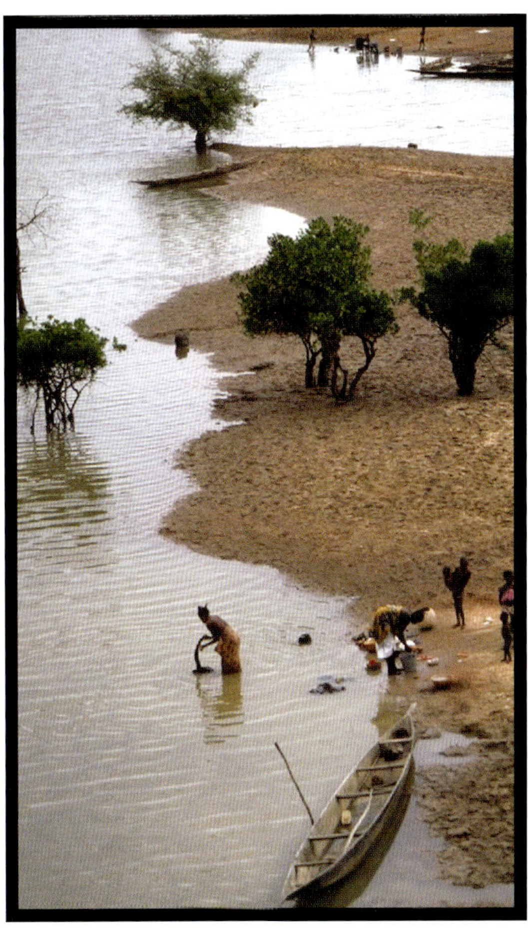

1 **Euphrates.** A river in southwestern Asia that flows into the Persian Gulf; it was important in the development of several great civilizations in ancient Mesopotamia.

2 **Congo.** A river in central Africa that flows about 2,900 miles and empties into the Atlantic Ocean

3 **when Abe . . . Orleans.** In 1830, at the age of 22, Abe Lincoln took a flatboat trip to New Orleans. There, it is believed, he witnessed a slave auction that left a significant impression on him.

VOCABULARY IN PLACE

- **lull,** *v.* To cause to sleep or rest; to soothe
- **dusky,** *adj.* Dark in color

Mother to Son

by Langston Hughes

Well, son, I'll tell you:
Life for me ain't been no crystal stair.
It's had tacks in it,
And splinters,
And boards torn up,
And places with no carpet on the floor–
Bare.
But all the time
I'se been a-climbin' on,
And reachin' landin's,
And turnin' corners,
And sometimes goin' in the dark
Where there ain't been no light.
So boy, don't you turn back.
Don't you set[1] down on the steps
'Cause you finds it's kinder[2] hard.
Don't you fall now–
For I'se still goin', honey,
I'se still climbin',
And life for me ain't been no crystal stair. ■

---

1 **set.** Sit

2 **kinder.** Kind of; sort of

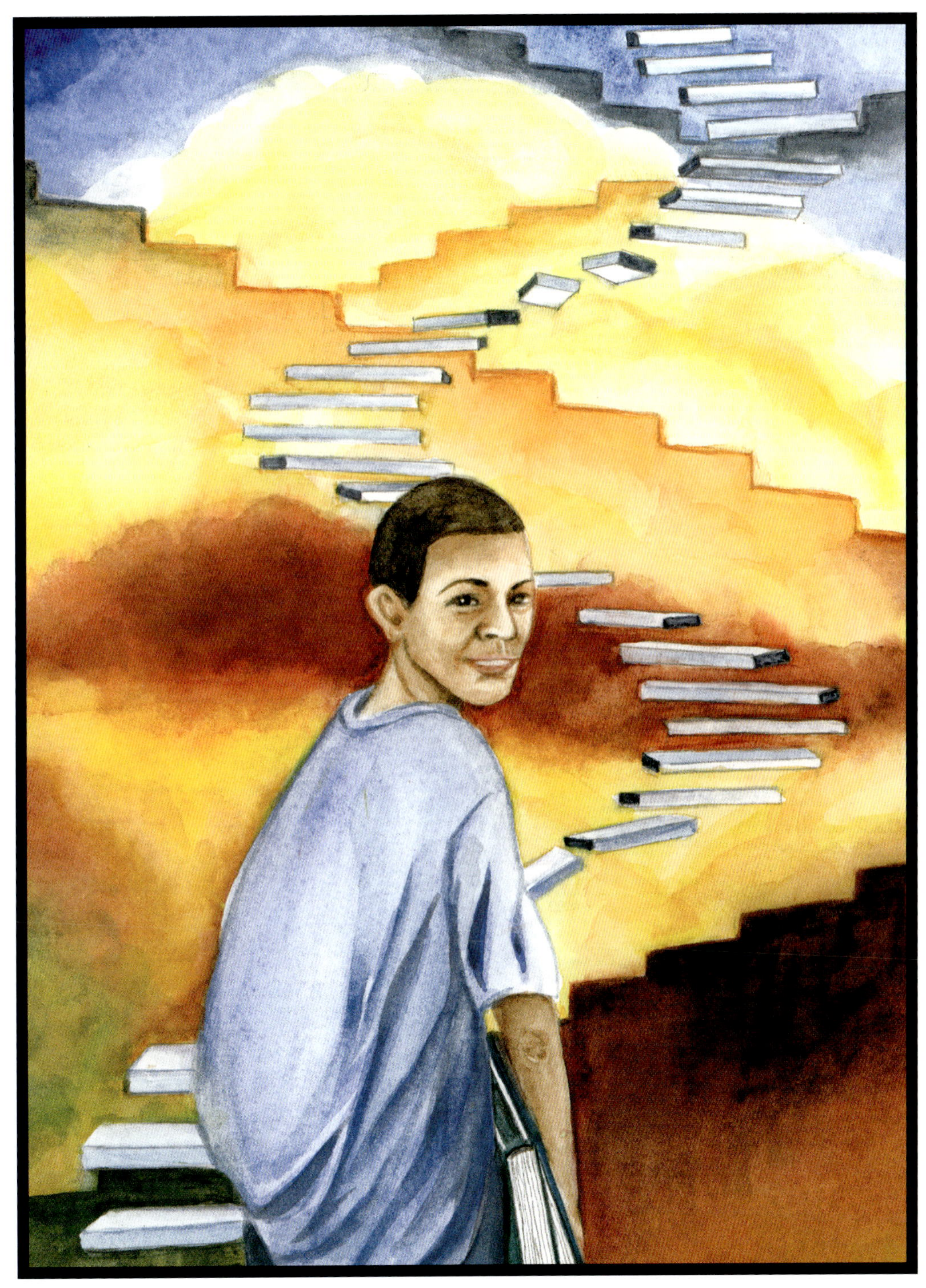

Dream Variations[1]

by Langston Hughes

To fling my arms wide
In some place of the sun,
To whirl and to dance
Till the white day is done.
Then rest at cool evening
Beneath a tall tree
While night comes on gently,
    Dark like me—
That is my dream!

To fling my arms wide
In the face of the sun,
Dance! Whirl! Whirl!
Till the quick day is done.
Rest at pale evening . . .
A tall, slim tree . . .
Night coming tenderly
    Black like me. ■

Dreams

by Langston Hughes

Hold fast to dreams
For if dreams die
Life is a broken-winged bird
That cannot fly.
Hold fast to dreams
For when dreams go
Life is a barren field
Frozen with snow. ■

1 **Variations.** In music, variations are alternative versions of one theme. Improvised variations are a defining feature of jazz music.

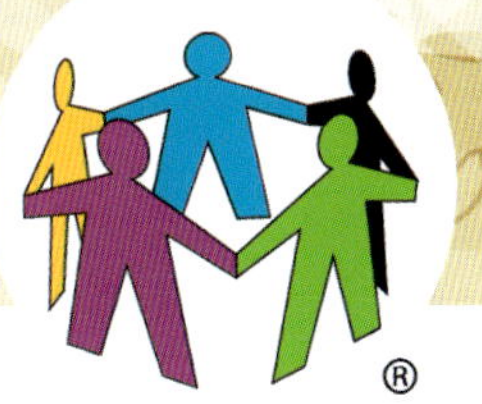

Understanding the Selection

Recalling

1. To what rivers does the speaker of "The Negro Speaks of Rivers" refer?
2. What phrases does he use to describe the rivers he has "known"?
3. What is the refrain, or chorus, in the poem "Mother to Son"?
4. What kinds of images does "mother" use to describe her life?
5. How does the night come on? What color or shade is it?

Interpreting

1. What historical events or themes are associated with each of these rivers? Why does Hughes choose these particular rivers? How is this tied to African-American history?
2. What does he say about his soul and the soul of his people through these images?
3. How does "mother" characterize her own life? What does she mean when she says that she's been "a climbin' on"?
4. What kind of woman is "mother," and what is she trying to teach her son?
5. How does the speaker's behavior differ during the day as compared to the night? What does his behavior have to do with the color of his skin?

Synthesizing

1. Poets often imaginatively embody other people. For whom does Hughes speak in "The Negro Speaks of Rivers"? Whose voice does he seemingly embody in "Mother to Son"? How do these voices differ?
2. Despite these differences, what similarities do the poems share in terms of talking about African-American history and heritage?

Prereading

"April Rain Song," "Jazzonia," "The Weary Blues," and "Harlem [2]"

by Langston Hughes

Langston Hughes has often been hailed as the "Poet Laureate of Harlem." This is, perhaps, ironic given that he was a transient artist, meaning that rather than settling in a single location, he enjoyed moving about from place to place like a nomad. In his childhood, he lived in Missouri, Kansas, Illinois, and Ohio and visited his father in Mexico. In his early twenties, he joined ships' crews and ventured to Africa and Europe. Upon his return, he lived in Washington, D.C., was educated at Lincoln University in Pennsylvania, and toured the South. During the 1930s, he traveled to Haiti, the Soviet Union, and Central Asia. It was not until the 1940s that Harlem became his permanent home.

Yet, from his early twenties, Hughes kept his finger on the pulse of Harlem. He interacted with and befriended many artists and intellectuals connected with the Harlem Renaissance, from Arna Bontemps and Gwendolyn Bennett to Zora Neale Hurston. Harlem provided the setting for much of his work. Indeed, though well-traveled, he was concerned with this African-American section of New York and identified with its people, writing that "their problems and interests are my problems and interests."

As you will see in the following four selections, Hughes had many views of Harlem.

April Rain Song. This early Hughes poem was included in *The Dream-Keeper and Other Poems* (1932), a volume of poetry for children. It conveys a sense of Harlem as a place of quiet contentment, where dreams are nourished.

Jazzonia and Weary Blues. In "Jazzonia" and "The Weary Blues," Hughes not only displays his gift for capturing a scene, but also reveals one of his most distinctive talents—weaving the folk forms and rhythms of African-American music into poetry. "The Weary Blues," which contains the first blues he heard growing up in Lawrence, Kansas, won Hughes first prize in *Opportunity* magazine's poetry contest in 1925.

Harlem [2]. This is one part of a book-length poem entitled *Montage of a Dream Deferred* (1951). The undercurrent of grief in his earlier portraits of vibrant cabaret life gives way here to bitter questioning and an expression of Harlem's urban desperation.

April Rain Song

by Langston Hughes

Let the rain kiss you.
Let the rain beat upon your head with silver liquid drops.
Let the rain sing you a lullaby.

The rain makes still pools on the sidewalk.
The rain makes running pools in the gutter.
The rain plays a little sleep-song on our roof at night—

And I love the rain. ■

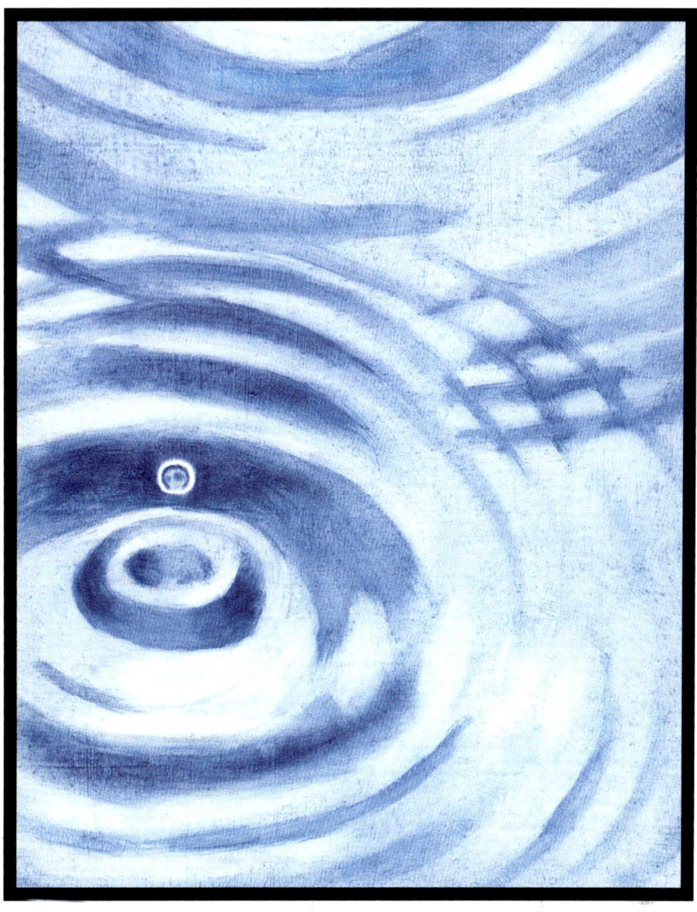

Jazzonia

by Langston Hughes

Oh, silver tree!
Oh, shining rivers of the soul!

In a Harlem cabaret
Six long-headed jazzers play.
A dancing girl whose eyes are bold
Lifts high a dress of silken gold.

Oh, singing tree!
Oh, shining rivers of the soul!

Were Eve's eyes
In the first garden
Just a bit too bold?
Was Cleopatra gorgeous
In a gown of gold?

Oh, shining tree!
Oh, silver rivers of the soul!

In a whirling cabaret
Six long-headed jazzers play. ■

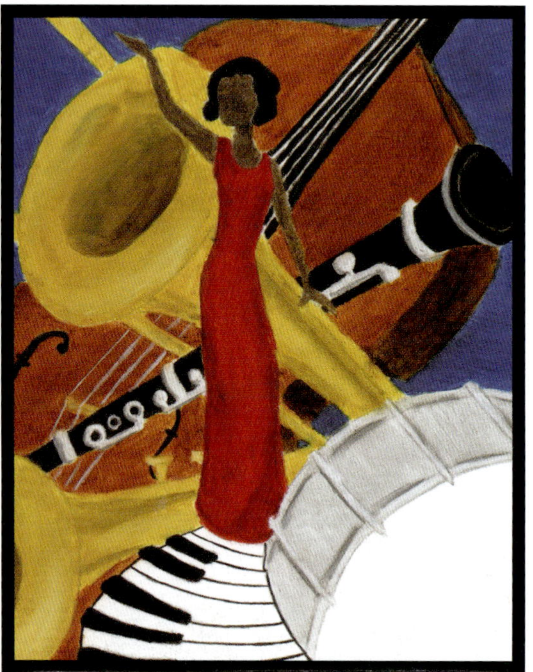

The Weary Blues

by Langston Hughes

Droning a drowsy **syncopated** tune,
Rocking back and forth to a mellow **croon,**
I heard a Negro play.
Down on Lennox Avenue[1] the other night
By the pale dull **pallor** of an old gas light
He did a lazy sway. . . .
He did a lazy sway. . . .
To the tune o' those Weary Blues.
With his ebony hands on each ivory key
He made that poor piano moan with melody.
O Blues!
Swaying to and fro on his rickety stool
He played that sad raggy tune like a
musical fool.
Sweet Blues!
Coming from a black man's soul.
O Blues!
In a deep song voice with a melancholy tone
I heard that Negro sing, that old piano moan—
"Ain't got nobody in all this world,
Ain't got nobody but ma self.
I's gwine to quit ma frownin'
And put ma troubles on the shelf."
Thump, thump, thump, went his foot on
the floor.
He played a few chords then he sang some
more—
"I got the Weary Blues
And I can't be satisfied.
Got the Weary Blues
"And I can't be satisfied—
I ain't happy no mo'
And I wish that I had died."
And far into the night he crooned that tune.
The stars went out and so did the moon.
The singer stopped playing and went to bed
While the Weary Blues echoed through his
head.
He slept like a rock or a man that's dead. ■

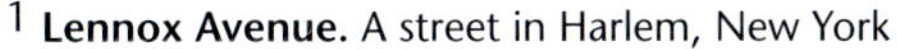

[1] **Lennox Avenue.** A street in Harlem, New York

VOCABULARY IN PLACE

- **syncopated,** ***past part.*** Containing accented beats that are outside or not in keeping with the overall rhythmical pattern, as, for example, a 3/4 time rhythm superimposed over a 4/4 time rhythm
- **croon,** ***n.*** Song, especially a plaintive one
- **pallor,** ***n.*** Unnatural paleness

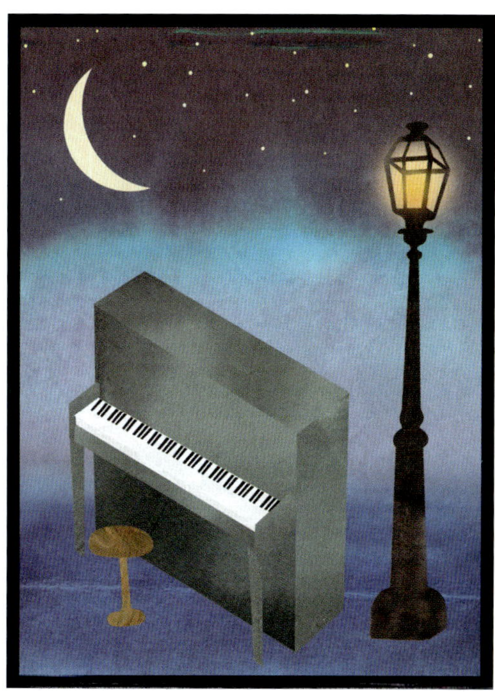

Harlem [2]

by Langston Hughes

What happens to a dream **deferred?**
Does it dry up
like a raisin in the sun?
Or **fester** like a sore—
And then run?
Does it stink like rotten meat?
Or crust and sugar over—
like a syrupy sweet?

Maybe it just sags
like a heavy load

Or does it explode? ■

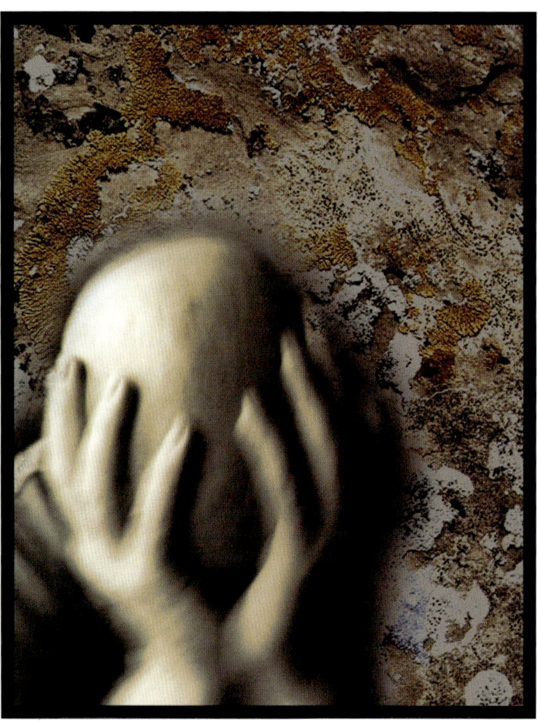

VOCABULARY IN PLACE

- **deferred, past part.** Put off
- **fester,** *v.* To become infected or filled with pus

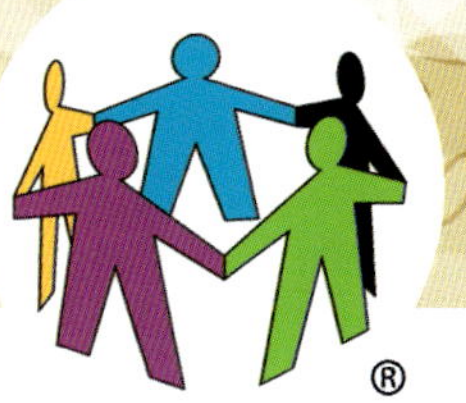

Understanding the Selection

Recalling

1. What sorts of images does Hughes use in "April Rain Song" to describe what the rain does?

2. In "Jazzonia," to whom does Hughes compare the women dancing?

3. What is the refrain in "Jazzonia"? What images does this refrain use?

4. In "The Weary Blues," Hughes employs blues-influenced poetry to frame a blues singer's lyrics. What kinds of words and images does he use to describe the music scene he experienced "the other night"? What words describe the blues singer himself?

Interpreting

1. How does Hughes personify the rain? In other words, how does he describe rain as if it were a person? What impact does this have upon the poem?

2. What similarities do you see between the second and fourth stanzas? What does the comparison with Eve and Cleopatra suggest about these dancers and their impact upon the poet's gaze?

3. If Eve ate from the forbidden tree and Cleopatra was famous for floating down the Nile, how does this refrain connect this Harlem cabaret scene to the past? What kind of place is "Jazzonia," this city of jazz?

4. How do words like *rickety* and *melancholy* contribute to the overall mood of the poem? What is the singer's state of mind, and how can you tell? How does this scene differ from the Jazz cabaret of "Jazzonia"?

Synthesizing

1. What kind of rhyme scheme is used in "The Weary Blues"? What effect do this rhyming and the poem's rhythms have upon the poem?
2. What different views of life in Harlem docs Hughes present in these poems?

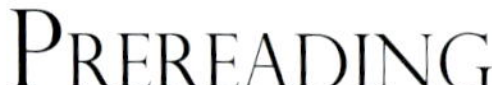

Prereading

"Daybreak in Alabama," "Song for a Dark Girl," and "I, Too"

by Langston Hughes

Langston Hughes has been called the "poet of the people," not only for his democratic approach to poetry—his attempts to write in a nonpretentious, accessible manner—but also for his portrayals of the lives of those whom he affectionately called the "low-down folk." At a time when depicting the lives of middle- and upper-class people was the fashion, Hughes populated his poetry with laborers, alcoholics, musicians, and dancers. Embracing the lives of such "common people," he reflected upon and gave voice to a broader spectrum comprising the rich heritage of African-American life.

As did other artists of the Harlem Renaissance, Hughes also wrote some of his poetry as a social protest against racial injustice. Despite their differences in tone and style, each of the following poems speaks to racial prejudice in some way.

Daybreak in Alabama. In a style reminiscent of Walt Whitman, a poet whom he deeply admired, Hughes connects his poet's voice with nature and communicates a dream of a world beyond racial prejudice.

Song for a Dark Girl. Composed in a lyrical blues style, this poem cries out against the tragic pain of lynching in a haunting, wrenching, and extremely memorable way. Along with the Billie Holiday song "Strange Fruit" (see page 467), this may be one of the two greatest expressions of the tragedy of lynching in America.

I, Too. Hughes composed this poem while stranded in Genoa, Italy. His wallet and passport had been stolen and, though he attempted to join ships' crews to earn his way back to America, white crews refused to work alongside a black man. Some have speculated that Hughes responds in this poem to Walt Whitman's "I Hear America Singing," a poem celebrating the many voices—boatman, shoemaker, wood-cutter, mother—that comprise America's "song." Whether or not this is the case, "I, Too" envisions a day when African Americans will take their rightful place and have a full chance at achieving the American dream.

Daybreak in Alabama

by Langston Hughes

When I get to be a composer
I'm gonna write me some music about
Daybreak in Alabama
And I'm gonna put the purtiest[1] songs in it
Rising out of the ground like a swamp mist
And falling out of heaven like soft dew.
I'm gonna put some tall tall trees in it
And the scent of pine needles
And the smell of red clay after rain
And long red necks
And poppy colored[2] faces
And big brown arms
And the field daisy eyes[3]
Of black and white black white black people
And I'm gonna put white hands
And black hands and brown and yellow hands
And red clay earth hands in it
Touching everybody with kind fingers
And touching each other natural as dew
In that dawn of music when I
Get to be a composer
And write about daybreak
In Alabama. ■

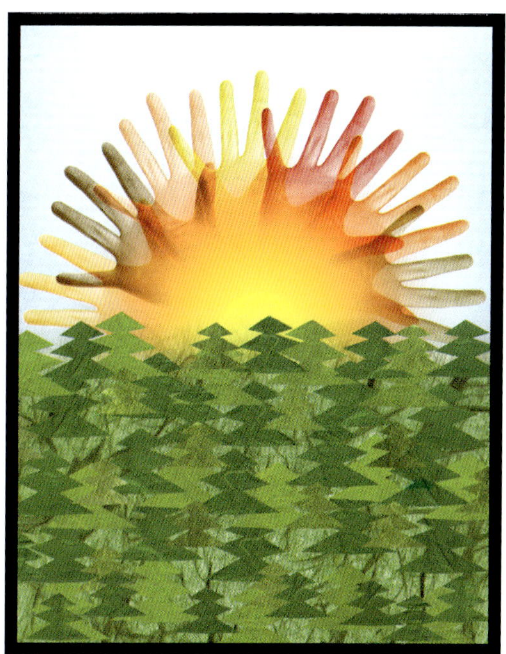

1 **purtiest.** Prettiest (dialectical)

2 **poppy colored.** The poppy flower is orange-red.

3 **field daisy eyes.** The daisy, a common flower, has white petals and a dark brown center.

Song for a Dark Girl

by Langston Hughes

Way Down South in Dixie[1]
(Break the heart of me)
They hung my black young lover
To a cross roads tree.

Way Down South in Dixie
(Bruised body high in air)
I asked the white Lord Jesus
What was the use of prayer.

Way Down South in Dixie
(Break the heart of me)
Love is a naked shadow
On a **gnarled** and naked tree. ■

1 **Dixie.** The South. The line "Way down south in Dixie" comes from the song "Dixie's Land," which may have been written by Daniel Decatur Emmett. The song contains a clearly racist story about a freed slave pining for the good life back on the plantation. It was widely considered to be the anthem of the Confederacy. Hughes's use of this line is, therefore, ironic. The "Song of the Dark Girl" is in stark contrast to the song "Dixie's Land" that the poem quotes.

VOCABULARY IN PLACE

- **gnarled,** ***adj.*** Bent, twisted

I, Too

by Langston Hughes

I, too,[1] sing America.

I am the darker brother.
They send me to eat in the kitchen
When company comes,
But I laugh,
And eat well,
And grow strong.

Tomorrow,
I'll be at the table
When company comes.
Nobody'll dare
Say to me,
"Eat in the kitchen,"
Then.

Besides,
They'll see how beautiful I am
And be ashamed—

I, too, am America. ■

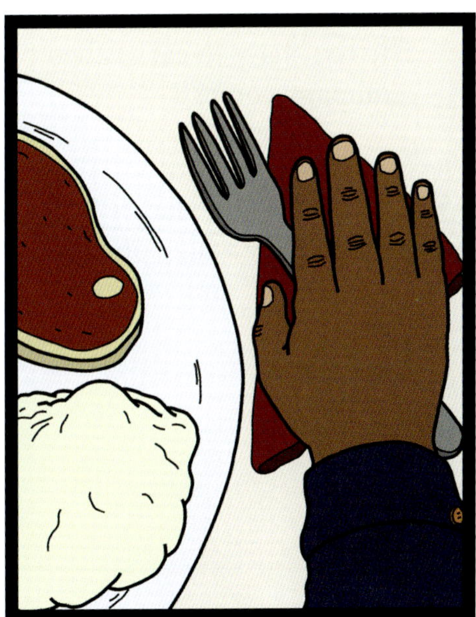

[1] **I, too.** Perhaps a reference to the white poet Walt Whitman, who wrote the magnificent poem "I Hear America Singing," which features the voices of varied people and celebrates the diversity of the country

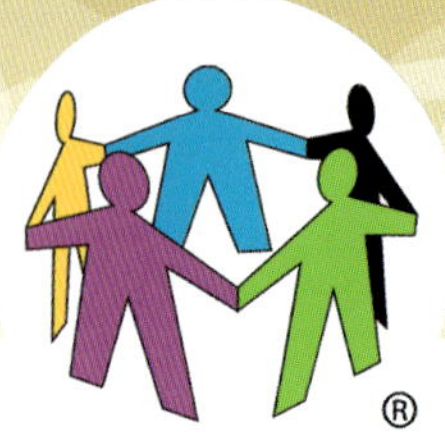

Understanding the Selection

Recalling

1. What are the colors of the hands described in "Daybreak in Alabama," and what are the hands doing?
2. What event is described in the first stanza of "Song for a Dark Girl"?
3. What question does the girl pose in stanza 2?
4. Where does the speaker of "I, Too" have to eat "When company comes"?
5. What does the "darker brother" say will happen "tomorrow," and why?

Interpreting

▶ 1. Why would these various hands "touching everybody with kind fingers" be a kind of "Daybreak in Alabama"?

▶ 2. What is the speaker's response to this event?

▶ 3. What mood does this question reveal?

▶ 4. Why would he have to eat there? Does he let this fact get him down or keep him down? How do you know?

▶ 5. Is this a literal tomorrow? Explain.

Synthesizing

1. "Daybreak in Alabama" begins with a physical description of the beauty of daybreak in that part of the country. What kind of daybreak is described in the second part of the poem? In what way is that daybreak beautiful?
2. Both "Song for a Dark Girl" and "I, Too" deal with terrible consequences of racism. How do the feelings of the speaker differ and why?

Delving Deeper

Understanding Literature

Stanza and Quatrain. A **stanza** is a group of lines in a poem, generally a group that has a set rhyme scheme. A **quatrain** is a four-line stanza. "Song for a Dark Girl" is written in quatrains. What is the rhyme scheme of these quatrains?

One of the reasons for the power of "Song for a Dark Girl" is that Hughes describes one of the most wrenching, awful, difficult experiences that a person could possibly face but uses a simple, highly formal form. The contrast between the form and the subject makes the statement of the poem all the more powerful.

About the Author

Langston Hughes (1902–1967) was one of the greatest American writers of the twentieth century and a leading voice of the Harlem Renaissance. Born James Langston Hughes in Joplin, Missouri, he was the great-great-grandson of John Mercer Langston, the first African American ever elected to public office. After some time spent at Columbia University in New York, Hughes traveled, settling eventually in Washington, D.C., where he worked busing tables until his first collection of poetry, *The Weary Blues* (1926), was published. After graduating from Pennsylvania's Lincoln University in 1929, he published his debut novel, *Not without Laughter* (1930), which received excellent reviews.

Hughes was known for his insight into the lives of ordinary Americans, his proud description of black culture, and his comments on politics and race. After discovering the worlds of jazz and blues, he began to create poetry with unique, distinct rhythms influenced by those varieties of music. He said, "I tried to write poems like the songs they sang on Seventh Street. . . . [These songs] had the pulse beat of the people who keep on going."

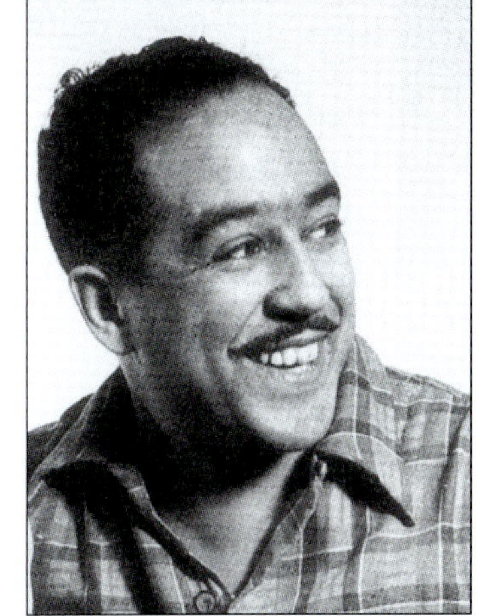

A prolific writer, Hughes produced sixteen books of poetry, two novels, and twenty plays, winning many literary awards and other honors. His works include *The Dream Keeper and Other Poems* (1932), *Montage of a Dream Deferred* (1951), and the plays *Mulatto* (1935), *Soul Gone Home* (1937), and *Simply Heavenly* (1957).

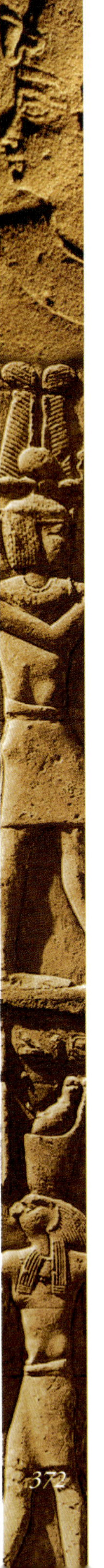

Prereading

"Heritage" and "Fantasy"

by Gwendolyn Bennett

Gwendolyn Bennett is an important writer who, during the latter half of the twentieth century, received little critical or historical recognition. Today, however, she is correctly remembered as a key figure of the Harlem Renaissance in her own right. Through her creative versatility and wide-ranging interests as a painter and graphic designer, journalist, poet, educator, and administrator, Bennett was a living embodiment of the energy and enthusiasm that blossomed in Harlem during the 1920s.

Heritage. Like its creator, this poem has become emblematic of the Harlem Renaissance. It has appeared in virtually every comprehensive anthology or academic study of African-American poetry since the 1920s, and it neatly encapsulates one of the driving themes of the Harlem Renaissance.

"Heritage" takes up a theme that was common among poets of the Harlem Renaissance era: the longing to experience Africa as the ancestors experienced it. For all five senses to be somehow immersed in African cultural heritage was, and remains, a strong desire for many African-American artists. Perhaps, by breathing the ancestors' same air and tasting their water, the soul of a people might be cleansed of its collective sadness.

Fantasy. Here Bennett uses the precise, vivid language of a skilled poet to reveal a colorful world as seen through the eyes of a painter. This poem is as much a display of Bennett's artistic abilities as it is an expression of the African heritage that constantly tugged at her imagination.

Heritage

by Gwendolyn Bennett

I want to see the slim palm-trees,
Pulling at the clouds
With little pointed fingers. . . .

I want to see **lithe** Negro girls,
Etched dark against the sky
While sunset lingers.

I want to hear the silent sands,
Singing to the moon
Before the Sphinx-still face. . . .

I want to hear the chanting
Around a **heathen** fire
Of a strange black race.

I want to breathe the Lotus flow'r,
Sighing to the stars
With tendrils drinking at the Nile. . . .

I want to feel the surging
Of my sad people's soul
Hidden by a minstrel-smile.[1] ■

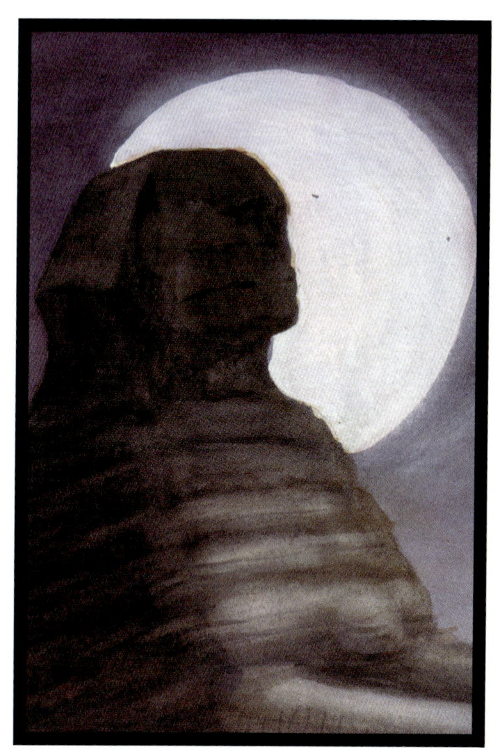

[1] **minstrel-smile.** A *minstrel*, in the traditional or medieval sense, is a traveling musician or lyrical poet. Bennett refers, here, to black minstrels who, as objects of entertainment for white society, used outward smiles that concealed their true feelings. The minstrel's smile is, therefore, used as a metaphor for the "mask" that African Americans wear in their daily lives in order to conceal their true feelings about the past and/or society. (See Paul Laurence Dunbar, "We Wear the Mask," page 323.)

VOCABULARY IN PLACE

- **lithe,** ***adj.*** Marked by effortless grace; also, supple or flexible
- **heathen,** ***n.*** A person or group that is considered uncivilized, irreligious, or unenlightened

Fantasy

by Gwendolyn Bennett

I sailed in my dreams to the Land of Night
Where you were the dusk-eyed queen,
And there in the **pallor** of moon-veiled light
The loveliest things were seen . . .

A slim-necked peacock **sauntered** there
In a garden of lavender hues,
And you were strange with your purple hair
As you sat in your amethyst[1] chair
With your feet in your hyacinth[2] shoes.

Oh, the moon gave a bluish light
Through the trees in the land of dreams and night.
I stood behind a bush of yellow-green
And whistled a song to the dark-haired queen . . . ■

---

1 **amethyst.** Dark purple, or the color of the semi-precious gemstone *amethyst*

2 **hyacinth.** A type of flowering plant

VOCABULARY IN PLACE

- **pallor,** ***n.*** Extreme or unnatural paleness
- **saunter,** ***v.*** To walk at a leisurely pace; stroll

History Connection

Renaissance Woman. Gwendolyn Bennett is most often cited as a poet of the Harlem Renaissance, but her real influence cannot be measured in terms of literary achievement or awards. Perhaps Bennett's most important contribution involved her work as an activist and organizer, and as a versatile, vibrant personality, bursting with creativity and purpose. Poet, short-story writer, columnist, journalist, illustrator, graphic artist, arts educator, teacher, and administrator on the New York City Works Progress Administration Federal Art Project—Gwendolyn Bennett was eager to try just about everything. This was partly because, as demonstrated in the photo below and in her poetry, she was good at everything she set her mind to.

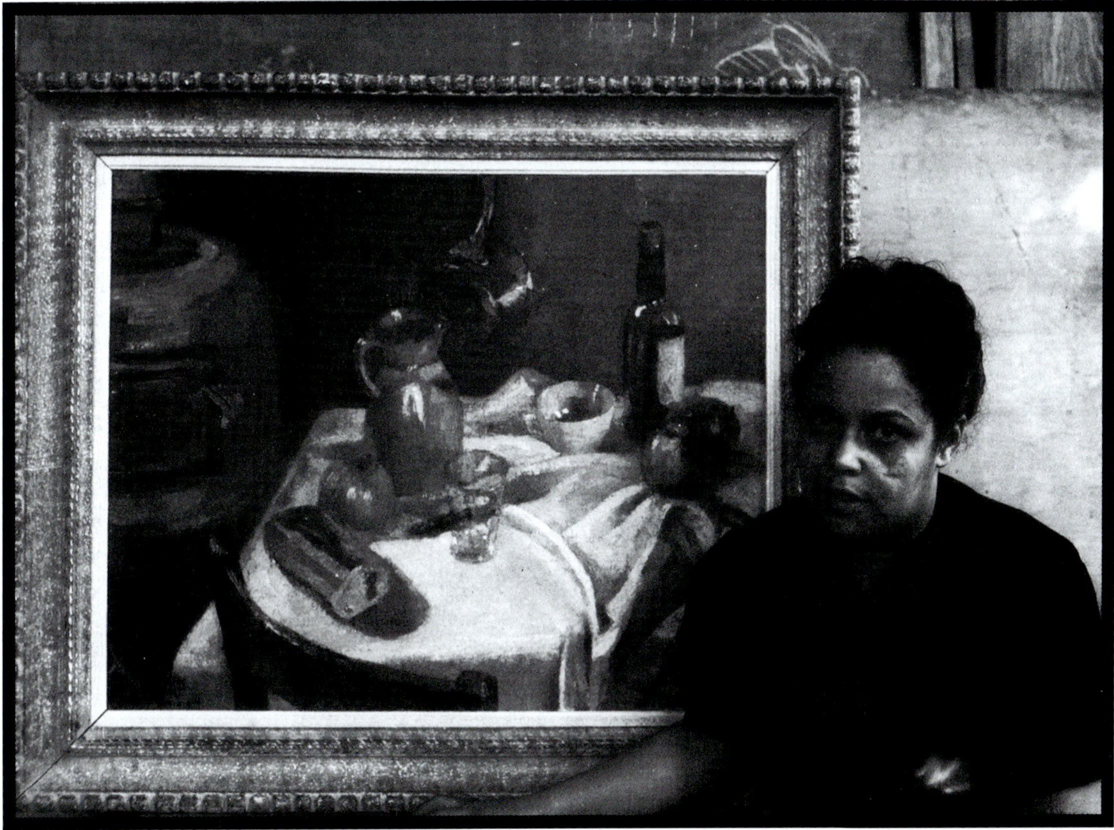

A Renaissance man or woman is someone who has broad intellectual interests and excels in areas of both arts and sciences. The term was coined during the Renaissance, the revival of arts and learning that originated in Italy during the fourteenth century. **Leonardo da Vinci** (1452–1519), a painter, engineer, musician, and scientist, is the most famous Renaissance man in history. Can you think of anyone else in history who might qualify as a Renaissance man or woman? Do you have a friend or family member who has lots of interests and seems to succeed at everything he or she attempts? Do you think that someone can decide to become a Renaissance man or woman, or is it something that simply develops over time?

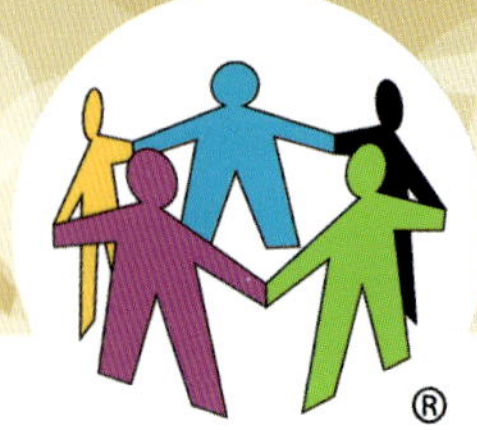

Understanding the Selection

Recalling

1. What sounds does the speaker in "Heritage" want to hear in the vicinity of the Sphinx?
2. In "Heritage," what does the speaker want to feel? Who are the "sad people" to whom she refers in the last stanza?
3. How does the speaker in "Fantasy" describe the queen's eyes?
4. Where does the speaker in "Fantasy" go in her dreams?
5. What does the speaker do while she is in this strange land?

Interpreting

1. What does the speaker mean in saying that "silent sands" can sing to the moon?
2. How will the things that she sees, hears, and breathes in Africa cause these people's souls to surge?
3. With regard to color and overall mood, what characteristics do you associate with the time of day called "dusk"?
4. What is the speaker's mood in this poem? Support your answer with at least one quotation from the text.
5. Whom might the speaker be addressing in line 2 of "Fantasy"?

Synthesizing

1. Bennett is known for her ability to "paint a picture" using a minimal number of words. Select two short (3–5 words) lines or phrases in each poem that you think are especially strong or effective images. Be prepared to explain your choices.

Delving Deeper

Writing

Personification. If you enjoy writing stories and poems, then you probably know that sometimes you can really get stuck trying to figure out exactly how to express an idea or feeling. Sometimes, the words just aren't there. No matter what you are writing, one of the first things you should do when you come to such an impasse—when you are trying to think of the best, most direct way to explain a complicated idea—is to think about things to which your readers will easily relate. The idea is to express your complex idea in terms that will allow your reader to conjure a clear mental image. Writers, poets, and storytellers use **personification**—the representation of nonliving, inanimate objects as having "living" characteristics or abilities—in order to help readers make sense of something unfamiliar. For instance, Bennett personifies the palm trees in the first stanza of "Heritage" by having them pull on the clouds as though they have hands or arms. In fact, trees cannot and do not pull on anything (especially clouds), but the image makes the reader imagine that she is lying on her back, looking up at the leaves of these tall trees.

What other two nonliving things does Bennett personify in "Heritage"?

Look around the classroom and choose an object about which to write a short poem or verse. Personify this object's characteristics in order to describe its function or appearance.

About the Author

Gwendolyn Bennett (1902–1981) was born in Giddings, Texas, but her family did not find a true home until settling in Brooklyn, New York. She showed early interest in the arts as she joined the literary society, took part in art and drama clubs, and won a citywide art contest.

She published 26 poems in prominent literary journals and was recognized by her peers as a skilled poet (though she never published a collection of her own). Bennett was also a journalist and columnist, and she was always on the lookout for anyone willing to purchase, print, or otherwise share in her visual art and graphic design work.

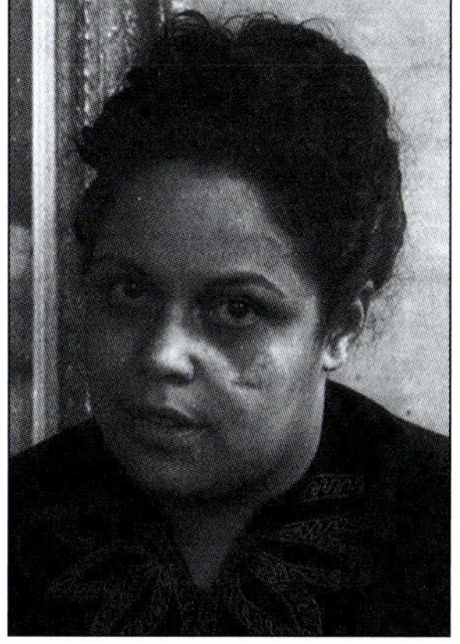

Bennett's close circle of friends during the 1920s included such notables as Langston Hughes, Helene Johnson, and Countee Cullen. These friendships led to continued arts-based activism during the 1930s, when she founded the Harlem Artists' Guild and performed invaluable work for the Works Progress Administration's Federal Art Project.

Prereading

"Incident" and "Heritage"

by Countee Cullen

The following poems were written by a man who was for a few years during the 1920s the most popular and well-known African-American poet in the United States. Countee Cullen is seen by many as a defining voice of the Harlem Renaissance. The details of his early life are clouded by uncertainty, and Cullen himself never made much effort to clear up the facts. He wanted his poems to stand on their own, not as works of a great African-American poet but simply as works of a great poet.

In fact, Cullen never wanted to be known as a "Negro poet" *per se.* Although he did not shy away from race as a subject, in terms of his style and technique Cullen did not wish to be singled out for being black any more than his hero, English poet John Keats, would be singled out for being white.

Readers will find in "Incident" and "Heritage" a poet who clearly had race and racism on his mind, but it is the masterful construction of the poems—his style, technique, and the layers of meaning that he wove with his images and symbols—that earned him praise from almost every corner of the literary world. In a time when American society was sharply divided, Countee Cullen was admired as a "crossover" poet, with fans on both sides of the racial divide.

Incident. In "Incident," Cullen masterfully captures a theme that many black writers have touched upon: that moment, when as children, they first realized that racism existed. Reliving this moment from the point of view of a child reminds us powerfully of how unnatural, how artificial, how violently and unnecessarily thrust upon people racism is.

Heritage. This long narrative poem delves into another important theme as the speaker ponders his rich African heritage, describing (or imagining) the "scenes his fathers loved." Yet the speaker is disconnected from this heritage and essentially trapped in a culture that he does not feel is his. The Reading of the Selection on page 382 will help you make sense of this fascinating poem. You should read this poem once, study the "reading," and then reread it at least once more for clarity.

Incident

by Countee Cullen

Once riding in old Baltimore,
    Heart-filled, head-filled with **glee,**
I saw a Baltimorean
    Keep looking straight at me.

Now I was eight and very small,
    And he was no whit[1] bigger,
And so I smiled, but he poked out
    His tongue and called me, "Nigger."

I saw the whole of Baltimore
    From May until December:
Of all the things that happened there
    That's all that I remember. ■

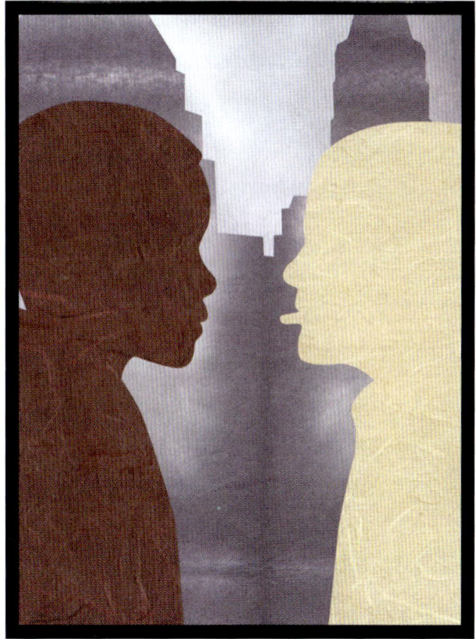

1 **whit.** A particle or iota (possibly a play on the word *white*)

VOCABULARY IN PLACE

- **glee,** ***n.*** Joy; jubilant delight

Heritage

by Countee Cullen

What is Africa to me:
Copper sun or scarlet sea,
Jungle star or jungle track,
Strong bronzed men, or regal black
Women from whose loins I sprang
When the birds of Eden sang?
One three centuries removed
From the scenes his fathers loved,
Spicy grove, cinnamon tree,
What is Africa to me?

So I lie, who all day long
Want no sound except the song
Sung by wild **barbaric** birds
Goading massive jungle herds,
Juggernauts of flesh that pass
Trampling tall defiant grass
Where young forest lovers lie,
Plighting troth[1] beneath the sky.
So I lie, who always hear,
Though I cram against my ear
Both my thumbs, and keep them there,
Great drums throbbing through the air.
So I lie, whose fount of pride,
Dear distress, and joy allied,
Is my somber flesh and skin,
With the dark blood dammed within
Like great pulsing tides of wine
That, I fear, must burst the fine
Channels of the chafing net[2]
Where they surge and foam and fret.

Africa? A book one thumbs
Listlessly, till slumber comes.
Unremembered are her bats
Circling through the night, her cats
Crouching in the river reeds,
Stalking gentle flesh that feeds

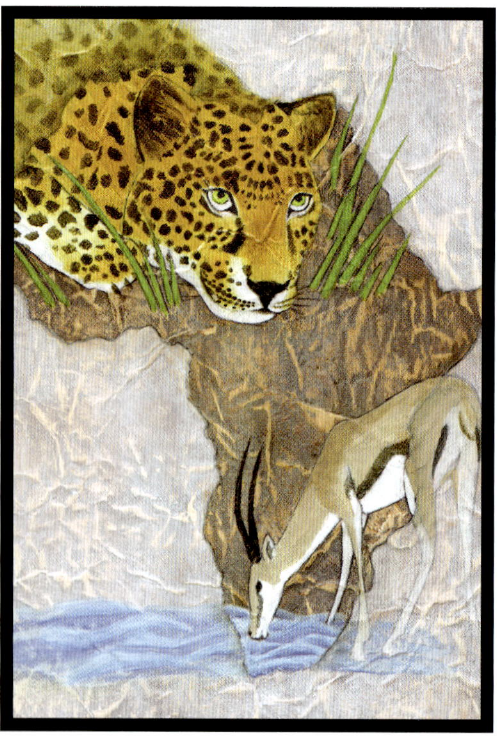

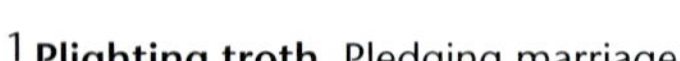

[1] **Plighting troth.** Pledging marriage

[2] **chafing net.** The net is a symbol of (white) society and traditions to which the narrator is expected to conform; he feels that some day his African heritage (the "dark blood") will burst forth and easily overwhelm the limitations placed upon him by white society.

VOCABULARY IN PLACE

- **barbaric,** ***adj.*** Uncivilized
- **goad,** ***v.*** To prod or urge
- **juggernaut,** ***n.*** An overwhelming, advancing force that seems to crush everything in its path
- **listlessly,** ***adv.*** Unenergetically

By the river brink; no more
Does the bugle-throated roar
Cry that monarch claws[3] have leapt
From the scabbards[4] where they slept.
Silver snakes that once a year
Doff the lovely coats you wear,
Seek no covert in your fear
Lest a mortal eye should see;
What's your nakedness to me?[5]
Here no leprous flowers rear
Fierce corollas in the air;[6]
Here no bodies sleek and wet,
Dripping mingled rain and sweat,
Tread the savage measures of
Jungle boys and girls in love.
What is last year's snow to me,
Last year's anything? The tree
Budding yearly must forget
How its past arose or set—
Bough and blossom, flower, fruit,
Even what shy bird with mute
Wonder at her **travail** there,
Meekly labored in its hair.
One three centuries removed
From the scenes his fathers loved,
Spice grove, cinnamon tree,
What is Africa to me?

So I lie, who find no peace
Night or day, no slight release
From the **unremittent** beat
Made by cruel padded feet
Walking through my body's street.
Up and down they go, and back,
Treading out a jungle track.
So I lie, who never quite
Safely sleep from rain at night—
I can never rest at all
When the rain begins to fall;
Like a soul gone mad with pain
I must match its weird refrain;
Ever must I twist and squirm,
Writhing like a baited worm,
While its primal measures drip[7]
Through my body, crying, "Strip!
Doff[8] this new **exuberance.**
Come and dance the Lover's Dance!"
In an old remembered way
Rain works on me night and day.

Quaint, **outlandish heathen** gods
Black men fashion out of rods,
Clay, and brittle bits of stone,
In a likeness like their own,
My conversion came high-priced;
I belong to Jesus Christ,
Preacher of humility;
Heathen gods are **naught** to me.

[3] **monarch claws.** The lion's claws. The lion is the king (monarch) of the jungle.

[4] **scabbards.** Sheaths in which swords or daggers are kept

[5] **Silver snakes . . . nakedness to me.** Snakes are a traditional symbol of power in Africa. Here, the narrator addresses the snakes directly. *Doff* means to "take off" (snakes shed their skin). A *covert* is a hiding place. *Lest* means "for fear that." The narrator pretends, through his question, not to care about the power of the snake or other important symbols of African heritage. But, of course, this pretense is ironic. He cares deeply.

[6] **Here no . . . in the air.** *Leprous* refers to something that has leprosy (a tropical disease). A *corolla* is the group of petals on a flower. The image of a flower shedding its petals is a metaphor for the love described in the next four lines (48–51).

[7] **primal measures drip.** If something is *primal* it is "first in time, original," or "of great importance." When the narrator hears the rain in the city, he is reminded of the torrential annual rains to which much of Africa is subject. To him, the sound of rain evokes a sense of the dawn of human time.

[8] **doff.** Discard, remove

VOCABULARY IN PLACE

- **travail,** ***n.*** Labor, work
- **unremittent,** ***adj.*** Unceasing, persistent
- **exuberance,** ***n.*** A feeling of unrestrained joy
- **outlandish,** ***adj.*** Bizarre, strikingly unfamiliar
- **heathen,** ***adj.*** Non-Christian; also, uncivilized or barbaric
- **naught,** ***n.*** Nothing

Father, Son, and Holy Ghost,
So I make an idle boast;
Jesus of the twice-turned cheek,[9]
Lamb of God, although I speak
With my mouth thus, in my heart
Do I play a double part.
Ever at Thy glowing altar
Must my heart grow sick and falter,
Wishing He I served were black,
Thinking then it would not lack
Precedent of pain to guide it,
Let who would or might deride it;
Surely then this flesh would know
Yours had borne a kindred woe.
Lord I fashion dark gods, too,
Daring even to give You
Dark despairing features where,
Crowned with dark rebellious hair,
Patience wavers just so much as
Mortal grief compels, while touches
Quick and hot, of anger, rise
To smitten cheek and weary eyes.
Lord, forgive me if my need
Sometimes shapes a human creed.

All day long and all night through,
One thing only I must do:
Quench my pride and cool my blood,
Lest I perish in the flood.
Lest a hidden ember set
Timber that I thought was wet
Burning like the dryest flax,[10]
Melting like the merest wax,
Lest the grave restore its dead,
Not yet has my heart or head
In the least way realized
They and I are civilized. ■

[9] **Jesus of the twice-turned cheek.** A reference to Jesus's Sermon on the Mount, in which he instructed his followers to "turn the other cheek" if they were struck

[10] **flax.** A widely cultivated fibrous plant

A Reading of the Selection

Heritage. This poem is divided into seven stanzas, each with its own primary theme:

1. The poem begins with several distinct, vivid images linked to Africa. In lines 7–10, the narrator introduces himself as one who has never been to Africa (line 7) and poses the poem's fundamental question (line 10).
2. The narrator is essentially trapped in white culture, but he craves the culture of his ancestors. He lies around his city apartment but longs for sounds of birds and herds. The desire tortures him; he holds his ears (lines 20–21), but still he hears the ancient drums.
3. He presents all of Africa as a single reference book, as it is presented in the culture in which he is trapped. But the images of Africa—bats, cats, snakes, lovers (lines 33–51)—overwhelm him no matter how he tries to ignore them. He pretends not to care about any of this, and explains (via the image of the budding tree) that society expects him to forget his past and conform to its system (lines 53–59).
4. He evokes the rhythms of Africa, primarily through the torrential rains to which much of the continent is subjected annually. The sound of rain in the city truly tortures him and he longs to escape to his ancient, ancestral land.
5. He has converted to Christianity.
6. (Line 101) He is troubled by depictions of Jesus Christ as a white man, for the white face does not reflect the "pain" (line 103) that black people (and Jesus) have endured.
7. He knows that he must try to ignore these echoes and constant reminders of his African heritage or he will "perish" (line 120). To survive he must adapt to the culture that this society has forced upon him, for if he dwells on the images of Africa, he will eventually be overwhelmed.

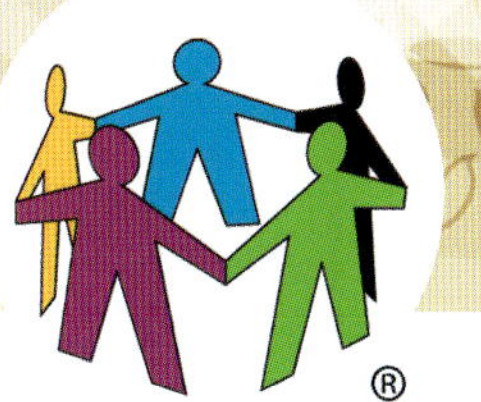

Understanding the Selection

Recalling

1. How does the poem's speaker feel in the first stanza of "Incident?" Who is looking at him?
2. What does the white boy do?
3. What question does the speaker of "Heritage" want to answer?
4. What sounds does the speaker want to hear?
5. To what does the speaker of "Heritage" compare Africa in the third stanza?
6. Is the speaker able to rest or find peace? Identify two lines in the poem that support your answer.
7. Is the speaker religious?

Interpreting

1. Why does he smile at the white boy? What reaction does he expect from the boy?
2. Why is this the only thing that the speaker remembers about the months he spent in Baltimore?
3. What is his connection to Africa? Has he ever been there?
4. Why does he cover his ears?
5. Does the speaker really think that Africa is a boring book? Why or why not?
6. What does the rain remind him of? Why does he feel that he must "doff this new exuberance"?
7. Is he satisfied with his religion? How would he like to change it?

Synthesizing

1. How do the poems "Incident" and "Heritage" show that Countee Cullen did not feel accepted or welcomed by American society?
2. Does the speaker of "Heritage" express much hope for the future? What does he think will eventually happen to him? Use quotations from the text to support your answer.

Prereading

"Yet Do I Marvel," "A Song of Praise," and "Scottsboro, Too, Is Worth Its Song"

by Countee Cullen

Yet Do I Marvel. This is one of Cullen's best-known poems. The first two **quatrains** of this **Shakespearean sonnet** (see explanation on page 389) present examples of contradictions or injustices that appear in the world. In the third quatrain, the poet admits that God's ways are simply too difficult for a person to understand, and the concluding **couplet** (last two lines) presents another contradiction or dilemma, this one related to the poet himself. There are several issues within this poem that have for years kept readers and scholars debating the poet's true intent. The discussion questions in Understanding the Selection will help shed light on the poem.

A Song of Praise. This is Cullen's ode to African-American women. The language of this poem conveys the anger and frustration that Cullen felt about the foul treatment—physical abuse, verbal insults, and social discrimination—leveled at African-American women during and after slavery.

Scottsboro, Too, Is Worth Its Song. Cullen appeals to poets everywhere to take up an important social cause. Nine black teenage boys in Scottsboro, Alabama, were accused, convicted, and sentenced to death for raping two white women. As it turned out, the charges were entirely fabricated—the rape never actually occurred, according to one of the alleged victims—but the Alabama Supreme Court nevertheless upheld the conviction. Cullen's appeal to poets (and the public in general) did help to galvanize public support for the boys. Fortunately, a terrible injustice was averted: the convictions were eventually overturned, and the boys were freed.

Yet Do I Marvel

by Countee Cullen

I doubt not God is good, well-meaning, kind,
And did He stoop to **quibble** could tell why
The little buried mole continues blind,
Why flesh that mirrors Him must some day die,
Make plain the reason tortured Tantalus[1]
Is baited by the fickle fruit, declare
If merely brute **caprice** dooms Sisyphus[2]
To struggle up a never-ending stair.
Inscrutable His ways are, and immune
To catechism[3] by a mind too strewn
With petty cares to slightly understand
What awful brain compels His awful hand.[4]
Yet do I marvel at this curious thing:
To make a poet black, and bid him sing!

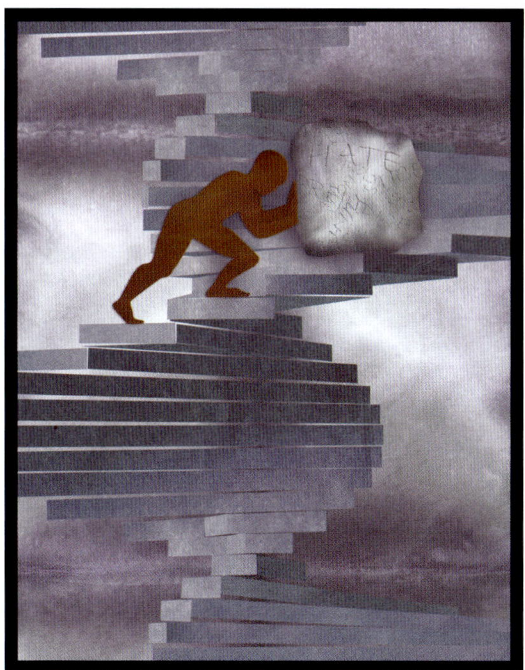

[1] **Tantalus.** In Greek mythology, a king who for his crimes was condemned to stand in water that receded when he tried to drink it and with fruit hanging above him that disappeared when he reached for it. (This is the source of the word *tantalize,* which means "to excite by exposing something desirable but keeping it out of reach.")

[2] **Sisyphus.** In Greek mythology, a king who for his crimes was condemned to roll a huge stone up a hill only to have it roll back down when he neared the top

[3] **catechism.** A close questioning or examination

[4] **awful brain . . . awful hand.** The poet employs both meanings of *awful:* the common definition, "extremely bad or unpleasant" and the second, less common, older definition, "commanding or inspiring awe."

VOCABULARY IN PLACE

- **quibble,** *v.* To evade the essential aspects of an issue by raising trivial distinctions and objections
- **caprice,** *n.* An inclination to change one's mind impulsively
- **inscrutable,** *adj.* Difficult to understand; unfathomable

A Song of Praise
(For One Who Praised His Lady's Being Fair)

by Countee Cullen

You have not heard my love's dark throat,
    Slow-**fluting** like a reed,
Release the perfect golden note
    She caged there for my need.

Her walk is like the replica
    Of some barbaric dance
Wherein the soul of Africa
    Is **winged** with arrogance.

And yet so light she steps across
    The ways her sure feet pass,
She does not dent the smoothest moss
    Or bend the thinnest grass.

My love is dark as yours is fair,
    Yet lovelier I hold her
Than **listless** maids with **pallid** hair,
    And blood that's thin and colder.

You-proud-and-to-be-pitied one,
    Gaze on her and despair;
Then seal your lips until the sun
    Discovers one as fair. ■

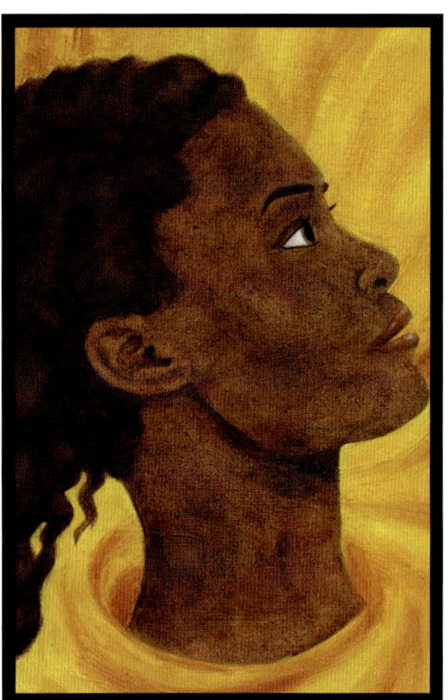

VOCABULARY IN PLACE

- **flute,** *v.* To produce a flutelike tone
- **winged,** *adj.* As if with wings; elevated or sublime
- **listless,** *adj.* Lacking energy or disinclined to exert effort
- **pallid,** *adj.* Pale; lacking intensity of color

Scottsboro,[1] Too, Is Worth Its Song
(A Poem to American Poets)

by Countee Cullen

I said:
Now will the poets sing,—
Their cries go thundering
Like blood and tears
Into the nation's ears,
Like lightning dart
Into the nation's heart.
Against disease and death and all things fell,[2]
And war,
Their strophes[3] rise and swell
To jar[4]
The foe smug in his citadel.[5]

Remembering their sharp and pretty
Tunes for Sacco and Vanzetti,[6]
I said:
Here too's a cause divinely spun
For those whose eyes are on the sun,
Here in epitome[7]
Is all disgrace
And epic wrong,
Like wine to brace
The minstrel heart, and blare it into song.

Surely, I said,
Now will the poets sing.
    But they have raised no cry.
    I wonder why ■

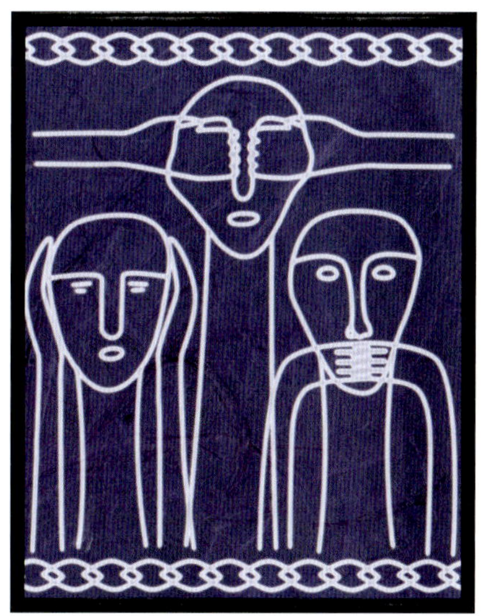

[1] **Scottsboro.** See Prereading, page 384.

[2] **fell.** Of an inhumanely cruel nature; fierce

[3] **strophes.** Metrical phrases

[4] **jar.** Jolt, startle

[5] **citadel.** Fortress

[6] **Sacco and Vanzetti.** Anarchists (political activists who believe rulers or government are unnecessary) who were arrested for murder, tried, and executed in Massachusetts in 1927. Their conviction sparked worldwide protests and rioting throughout Europe. Many celebrities and prominent figures took up the two Italian immigrants' cause, including Dorothy Parker, Upton Sinclair, George Bernard Shaw, H. G. Wells, Albert Einstein, and the Pope. The U.S. Supreme Court denied Sacco and Vanzetti's appeals. The case continues to spark debate to this day.

[7] **epitome.** A typical or ideal example

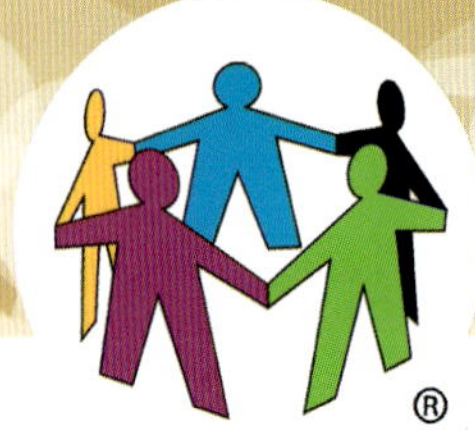

Understanding the Selection

Recalling

1. What four things in lines 1–9 of "Yet Do I Marvel" would the poem's speaker like for God to explain?
2. At what "curious thing" does the speaker marvel?
3. In the second stanza of "A Song of Praise," how does the speaker describe his love's walk?
4. Who is the "proud-and-to-be-pitied" person to whom the speaker refers in line 17?
5. For whom did Cullen write "Scottsboro, Too, is Worth Its Song"? What did he expect them to do?
6. To what historical event does the speaker refer?

Interpreting

1. Will God will ever "stoop" to explain these things? Use a quotation from the poem to support your answer.
2. What is your interpretation of the poem's final line? Does the poet want to sing? Is he able to sing?
3. Does the description in the third stanza contradict the one in the second stanza? Why is this significant?
4. What will cause this person to "despair" (line 18)?
5. Have the poets done what Cullen wanted them to do? What will happen if they do?
6. Why do you think events in Scottsboro did not receive much attention?

Synthesizing

1. What similarities or common themes exist between these three poems? Explain, using evidence from the poems to support your answer.
2. Notice the two subtitles that Cullen included with "A Song of Praise" and "Scottsboro, Too, Is Worth Its Song." Why might a poet include subtitles with his poem?

Delving Deeper

Understanding Literature

Discussing Poetry. From time to time in the poetry sections of *Grace Abounding* readers will find A Reading of the Selection. A **reading** is simply an interpretation of a literary work; some poems contain lines upon whose meaning scholars will probably never agree. Truly, some poems or lines mean different things to different people.

You might be surprised to find just how much you can discuss or debate the details of a good poem. In discussing "Scottsboro, Too, Is Worth Its Song," you might start with the poem's **structure.** How many parts or stanzas does the poem contain, and how do these parts differ structurally? Does each part convey a unique **mood** or **theme** or is the speaker's **voice** consistent throughout the poem? How do **rhyme scheme** and **rhythm** affect the **tone** and mood? Try to come to some consensus as to how closely the poem's structure is related to the speaker's overall mood and meaning. Next, discuss specific lines, phrases, and words that you think are especially significant, confusing, interesting, or simply well written. For example, why does the speaker repeat "I said" three times? Why does the speaker mention Sacco and Vanzetti? Why isn't there a period at the end of the poem?

About the Author

Countee Cullen (1903–1946) did little to clear up the many uncertainties surrounding his biography. He was probably born in Louisville, Kentucky, but early in his life he moved to New York City where he was raised mainly by adoptive parents, Reverend Frederick and Carolyn Cullen. His first published poem, "I Have a Rendezvous with Life," won a city-wide contest when Cullen was seventeen years old. The title of this poem was inspired by World War I soldier Alan Seeger's famous "I Have a Rendezvous with Death" (1917). Cullen most admired and emulated the lyrical, romantic style of John Keats.

Cullen's first book of poetry, *Color* (1925), established his reputation as a skilled, visionary poet. He earned a master's degree from Harvard University that same year and soon became one of the most nationally recognized voices of the Harlem Renaissance. In addition to two books of children's poetry, he published two more poetry collections, *Ballad of the Brown Girl* and *Copper Sun*. He also wrote *One Way to Heaven* (1934), a novel about the Harlem Renaissance.

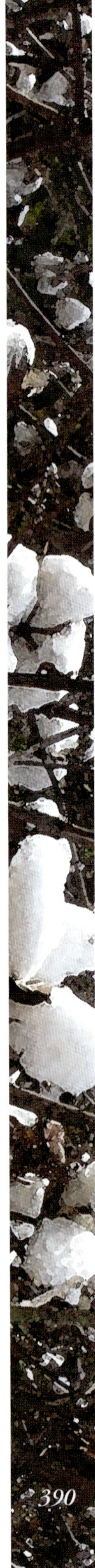

Prereading

"November Cotton Flower" and "Cotton Song"

by Jean Toomer

"King Cotton" was historically a major source of revenue in the southern United States. In the days of slavery, and for decades thereafter, large numbers of African Americans labored in cotton fields. The failure of a cotton crop could be disastrous for families and communities. A crop could fail due to drought, mismanagement of the soil, or insect infestations. Beginning in the early 1900s, cotton farmers in the U.S. found themselves facing a formidable enemy in the boll weevil, an insect that had spread north from Mexico. A boll weevil infestation, followed by insufficient rain, would be enough to destroy a crop and ruin the local economy.

November Cotton Song. This is a **sonnet**, a fourteen-line poem. Sonnets can have any of a number of different rhyme schemes. Often, in a sonnet, the first eight lines (the **octave**) present a situation, and the next six lines (the **sestet**) comment upon that situation.

As you read Toomer's poem "November Cotton Song," do the following:

1. Read the poem aloud once. Then, read it silently a few times. Try to picture in your mind's eye the scene described in the first eight lines. What do the cotton-stalks look like? What has happened to the "branch," or creek, and to the soil?
2. Think about how people who depend upon cotton for their livelihood might feel to see their fields in this condition.
3. A healthy cotton flower has brown spots on it. The plant flowers early in the year. Ask yourself, what is unusual about the flowering in this poem? How do the old people react to it? What do they think it looks like and means?

Cotton Song. In order to deal with the harsh reality of life in the fields, slaves and, later on, sharecroppers, often sang as they worked. Their **work songs** were often highly rhythmical, in keeping with the rhythms of repetitive work, and they often included examples of **onomatopoeia**, words that mimicked the grunts, groans, and other noises made by workers. In this poem, Toomer imitates the style of a traditional work song. As you read the poem, ask yourself these questions: "What can a person do when faced with adversity, such as having to work long hours in the fields?" and "How do the work songs show the indomitable spirit of African Americans?"

November Cotton Flower

by Jean Toomer

Boll-weevil's coming, and the winter's cold,[1]
Made cotton-stalks look rusty, seasons old,[2]
And cotton, scarce as any southern snow,
Was vanishing; the branch, so pinched and slow,
Failed in its function as the autumn rake;[3]
Drouth[4] fighting soil had caused the soil to take
All water from the streams; dead birds were found
In wells a hundred feet below the ground[5]
Such was the season when the flower bloomed.
Old folks were startled, and it[6] soon assumed
Significance. **Superstition** saw
Something it had never seen before:
Brown eyes that loved without a trace of fear,
Beauty so sudden for that time of year. ■

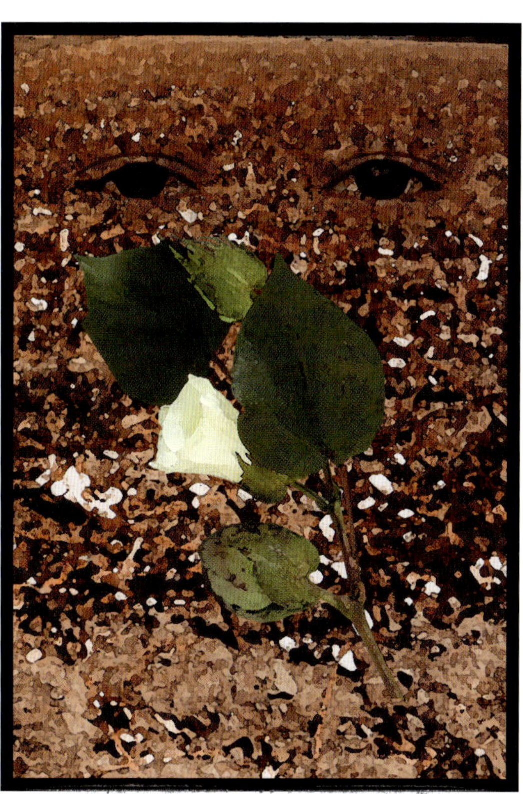

[1] **Boll-weevil's . . . cold.** The coming of the boll-weevils earlier in the year, followed by the cold of winter

[2] **seasons old.** As though they were many seasons old

[3] **autumn rake.** In a normal year, the branch, or stream, would carry off debris, cleaning the land.

[4] **Drouth.** Alternative spelling of *drought,* a period without rain

[5] **dead birds . . . ground.** The birds died trying to find water in deep wells.

[6] **it.** The flower

VOCABULARY IN PLACE

- **superstition,** ***n.*** A belief that is not based in reason or scientific understanding, especially one that involves magic or the supernatural

Cotton Song[1]

by Jean Toomer

Come, brother, come. Lets lift it;
Come now, hewit![2] roll away!
Shackles fall upon the Judgment Day
But lets not wait for it.

God's body's got a soul,
Bodies like to roll the soul,
Cant blame God if we dont roll,

Come, brother, roll, roll!
Cotton **bales** are the fleecy way
Weary sinner's bare feet trod,
Softly, softly to the throne of God,
"We aint agwine t wait until th Judgment

Nassur;[3] nassur,
Hump.
Eoho, eoho, roll away!
We aint agwine t wait until th Judgment

God's body's got a soul,
Bodies like to roll the soul,
Cant blame God if we dont roll,
Come, brother, roll, roll! ■

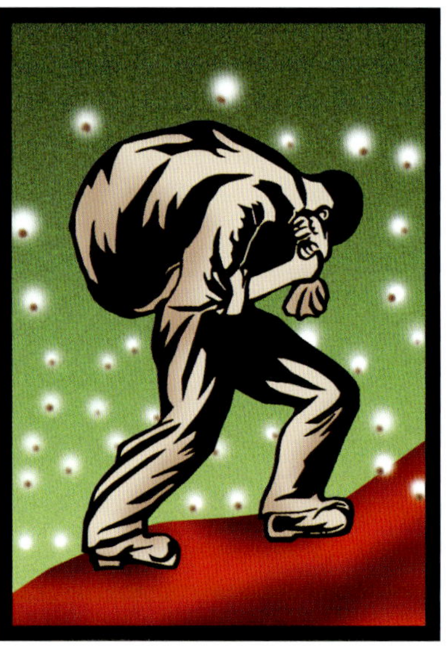

[1] **Cotton Song.** This poem is based upon traditional work songs sung by workers in fields.

[2] **hewit.** Heave it.

[3] **Nassur.** No sir

VOCABULARY IN PLACE

- **shackles,** ***n.*** Manacles and chains
- **bales,** ***n.*** Bundles

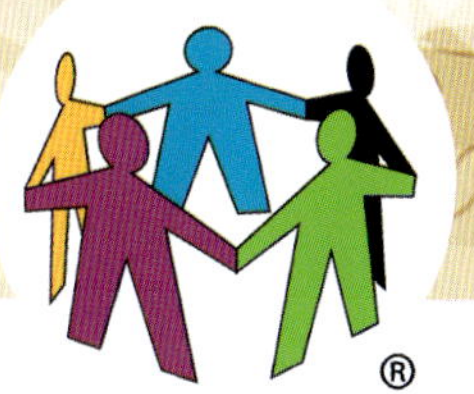

Understanding Literature

Rhyme Scheme and Couplets. A **rhyme scheme** is a pattern of rhymes at the ends of the lines in a poem. A rhyme scheme is labeled using letters of the alphabet, as follows:

The weevil's got a long, thin nose (*a*)
An' sticks it in where it don' belong (*b*)
He causes blight where the cotton grows (*a*)
And does the po' farmer wrong. (*b*)

We would refer to the rhyme scheme in the poem above as *abab*.

Exercise A. Answer the following questions.

1. What is the rhyme scheme of Jean Toomer's sonnet?
2. What happens when you get to lines 11 and 12?

In Standard English, the words *saw* and *before* in lines 11 and 12 do not rhyme. However, in some dialects of English in the Southern United States, the consonant sound spelled *re* in the word *before* is barely pronounced. When the word *before* is pronounced in that way (that is, as /bĕfŏ/), then it almost rhymes with the word *saw*.

A **couplet** is a pair of rhyming lines that expresses a complete thought. Jean Toomer's poem is made of seven couplets. The final couplet, as in many sonnets, sums up the main idea of the sonnet as a whole.

Exercise B. Complete one of the following couplets by writing a line that rhymes with the line provided. Possible rhymings are provided in parentheses.

These things I wish to do before I die:	(lie, try, sigh, cry, fly, why, pie)
A true friend's worth is measured by his deeds.	(needs, leads, bleeds, succeeds, creeds, pleads)
How few the days we spend beneath the sun	(run, fun, everyone, done, won)

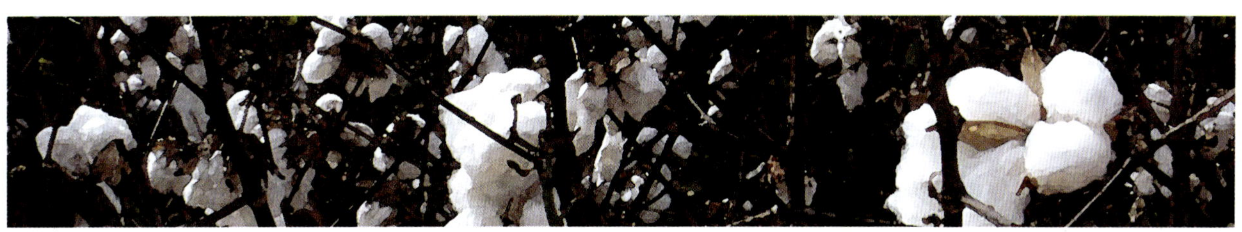

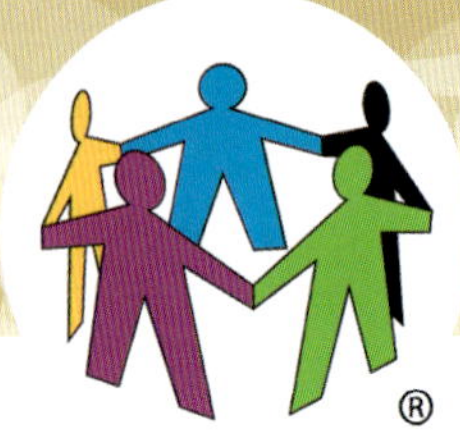

Understanding the Selection

Recalling

1. According to the second line of "November Cotton Song," what do the cotton-stalks look like?
2. To what does the speaker compare the cotton in line 3 of "November Cotton Song"?
3. In "November Cotton Song," where are the dead birds found?
4. When does the cotton flower bloom?
5. How do the old folks react to the blooming of the flower?
6. In "Cotton Song," when do the shackles fall off?

Interpreting

1. What caused the cotton-stalks to look this way?
2. What do "southern snow" and the cotton crop this year have in common?
3. What caused the birds to go there? Why might they have died?
4. How would you characterize this season? What is unusual about the flower blooming at this time?
5. What does the flower look like to the superstitious old people?
6. What can people do in the meantime?

Synthesizing

1. Superstitious people often draw irrational conclusions based upon accidental similarities. In what ways are a cotton flower and a human face alike? How were the people probably feeling before they saw the cotton flower? How did the cotton flower make them feel?
2. In "Cotton Song," people are not going to wait until the Judgment Day to do what?

Delving Deeper

Understanding Literature

Meter, Rhyme Scheme, and Free Verse. The **meter** of a poem is its rhythmical pattern. Traditionally, poems in English have had regular rhythmical patterns. Line 8 of "November Cotton Song" has such a pattern. It is in **iambic pentameter.** That is, it has five **poetic feet** made up of an **unstressed syllable** followed by a **stressed syllable,** as follows:

˘ / ˘ / ˘ / ˘ / ˘ /
In wells a hundred feet above the ground

As you learned in the Prereading, "November Cotton Flower" is a **sonnet,** a fourteen-line poem that usually has one of a number of traditional **rhyme schemes.** This sonnet is a bit unusual in that it consists entirely of paired rhyming lines with the rhyme scheme *aa bb cc dd ee ff gg.* The eleventh and twelfth lines rhyme in dialect. "Cotton Song," in contrast, is a **free verse** poem, one without a regular meter and rhyme scheme. Nonetheless, the poem is extremely musical. Read the poem aloud. Then think about the elements that make it so.

About the Author

Jean Toomer (1894–1967) received wide acclaim for his novel *Cane,* published in 1925. He also wrote many short stories, poems, articles, and plays. A deeply spiritual person, his aim was to help build a world without divisions between races or between God and humanity.

Toomer was born in Washington, D.C., the only child of a white planter and the daughter of the first black governor in the United States, Governor Pinckney Pinchback of Louisiana. As a biracial child, Jean had confusing experiences in both black and white schools. As an adult, he rejected racial categories and chose to define himself simply as American. Toomer said, "I wrote a poem called 'The First American,' the idea of which was that here in America we are in the process of forming a new race . . . not European, not African, not Asiatic—but American."

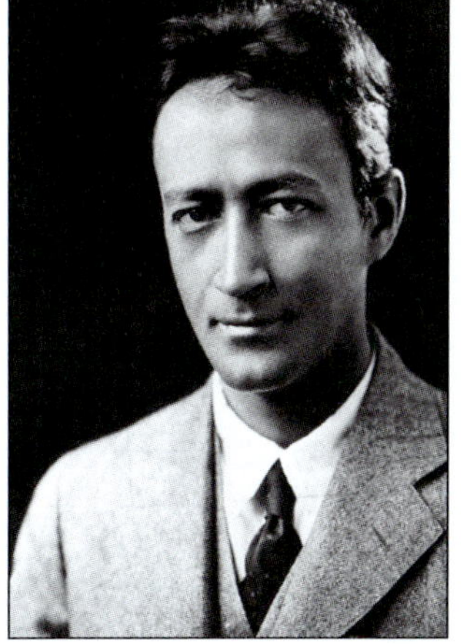

Toomer's main interest was in philosophy, especially in the teachings of mystic Georges Ivanovich Gurdjieff. In 1942, he formed a cooperative called "Friends of Being," a group of idealists who lived and worked together in an effort to overcome racial and spiritual separateness.

Prereading

"Magalu" and "Sonnet to a Negro in Harlem"

by Helene Johnson

At the height of the Harlem Renaissance, Helene Johnson was recognized as one of the most gifted, brightest young stars on the poetry scene, but her name is seldom included among the great American poets. Perhaps that is because she published relatively few poems in her brief career, which began in 1925 when she received the first in a string of literary awards. She did not publish any poems after the late 1930s, instead focusing her energy on raising her daughter. This proved to be a great loss to the literary world. Thankfully, virtually every poem that she did publish was a gem. Helene Johnson's enormous talent is reflected in every word she wrote.

Magalu. The poem "Magalu" is set in Africa (probably West Africa, judging from the types of animals and plants). The speaker in the poem is addressing a native named "Magalu" and trying to discourage her from being tempted by the words of a missionary. Helene Johnson felt that African heritage is the true heritage of African Americans, and in this poem, the speaker is concerned that Magalu will trade all the beauty and harmony of her natural world for a foreign culture that will actually erase joy and splendor from her life.

Sonnet to a Negro in Harlem. The speaker in this poem also addresses another person, but the poem creates a very different mood. The subject of the poem—a proud, arrogant, yet admirable man—represents the overall confidence, energy, and hope that enveloped Harlem during the 1920s, as a young generation of African Americans, the children and grandchildren of formerly enslaved people, expressed a newfound identity and community through their art, literature, music, political activism, and social unity.

Magalu

by Helene Johnson

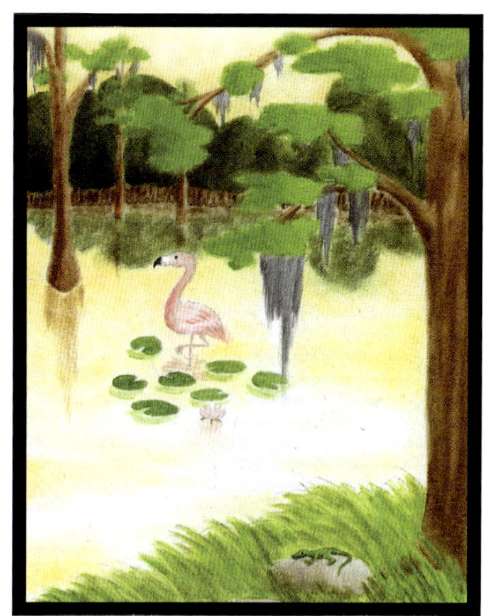

Summer comes
The ziczac[1] hovers
'Round the greedy-mouthed crocodile.
A vulture bears away a foolish jackal.
The flamingo is a dash of pink
Against dark green mangroves,[2]
Her slender legs rivalling her slim neck.
The laughing lake gurgles delicious music in its throat
And lulls to sleep the lazy lizard,
A **nebulous** being on a sun-scorched rock.
In such a place,
In this pulsing, riotous gasp of color,
I met Magalu, dark as a tree at night,
Eager-lipped, listening to a man with a white collar
And a small black book with a cross on it.
Oh Magalu, come! Take my hand and I will read you poetry,
Chromatic[3] words,
Seraphic[4] symphonies,
Fill up your throat with laughter and your heart with song.
Do not let him lure you from your laughing waters,
Lulling lakes, **lissome** winds.
Would you sell the colors of your sunset and the fragrance
Of your flowers, and the passionate wonder of your forest
For a **creed** that will not let you dance? ■

---

1 **ziczac.** A type of fly

2 **mangrove.** A species of tree that grows along riverbanks and wetlands with extensive root systems that extend above ground

3 **Chromatic.** This adjective can refer either to music (i.e., the chromatic scale) or to colors.

4 **Seraphic.** Angelic; specifically, a reference to the Seraphic Choir, which, according to the Christian tradition, is the highest order of angels

VOCABULARY IN PLACE

- **nebulous,** ***n.*** Cloudy, misty; lacking definite form
- **lissome,** ***adj.*** Easily bent, supple
- **creed,** ***n.*** A system of belief

Sonnet to a Negro in Harlem

by Helene Johnson

You are **disdainful** and magnificent—
Your perfect body and your **pompous** gait,[1]
Your dark eyes flashing solemnly with hate,
Small wonder that you are incompetent
To imitate those whom you so despise—
Your shoulders towering high above the throng,
Your head thrown back in rich, barbaric song,
Palm trees and mangoes stretched before your eyes.
Let others toil and sweat for labor's sake
And wring from grasping hands their meed of gold.[2]
Why urge ahead your **supercilious** feet?
Scorn will **efface** each footprint that you make.
I love your laughter arrogant and bold.
You are too splendid for this city street!

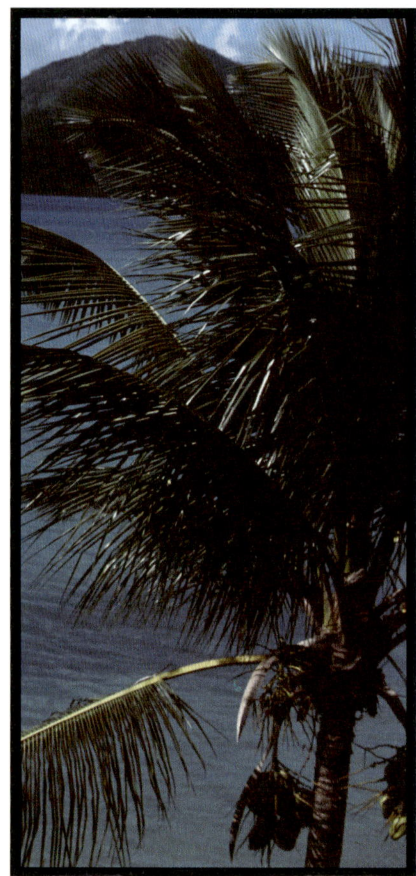

[1] **gait.** Manner of walking

[2] **meed of gold.** Payment or wages in the form of gold. *Meed* is a sweet wine made from fermented honey.

VOCABULARY IN PLACE

- **disdainful,** *n.* Treating others with contempt; proud
- **pompous,** *adj.* Characterized by excessive self-esteem; showy
- **supercilious,** *adj.* Feeling or showing disdain or disapproval
- **efface,** *v.* To rub or wipe out; erase

Understanding Literature

Sonnet. A **sonnet** is a fourteen-line poem that follows any of a number of different rhyme schemes. The **Elizabethan,** or **Shakespearean,** sonnet is made up of four parts. The first three are **quatrains,** or groups of four lines. The last part is a **couplet,** or a pair of lines. The rhyme scheme of a typical Elizabethan sonnet is as follows: *abab cdcd efef gg.*

An **Italian,** or **Petrarchan,** sonnet, named after the Italian poet Francésco Petrarch, (1304–1374), has two parts, an **octave,** with eight lines, and a **sestet,** with six. A typical Petrarchan rhyme scheme is *abbaabba cdecde.*

The rhyme scheme of a sonnet is usually a significant clue to the arrangement of its ideas. Helene Johnson's poem is Petrarchan in form. Reread the poem carefully and think about these questions:

1. What is the rhyme scheme of the octave, or first eight lines?
2. What is the rhyme scheme of the sestet, or final six lines?
3. What is said in the octave? (Summarize it in your own words.)
4. What is said in the sestet? (Summarize it in your own words.)

Traditionally, sonnets are love poems. Petrarch wrote a beautiful series of poems to his beloved Laura—poems that inspired a tradition of poems about unrequited love for an impossibly distant, unattainable, perfect beloved. In what ways does Helene Johnson play ironically with this Petrarchan tradition in her "Sonnet to a Negro in Harlem"? In what ways is the object of the affections expressed by the speaker in Johnson's poem far from the perfect object of platonic love immortalized by Petrarch?

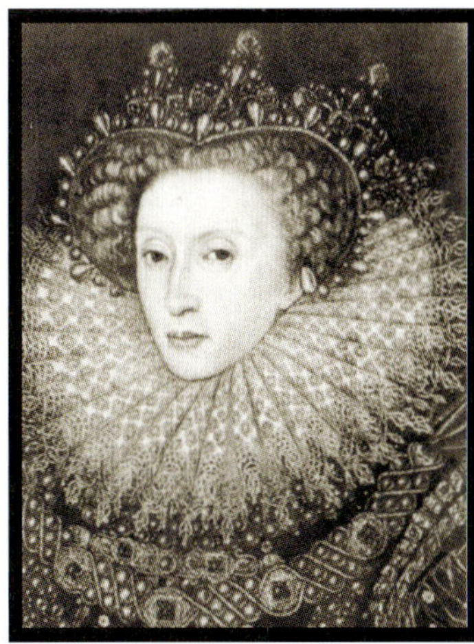

Elizabeth I (1533–1603), Queen of England and Ireland (1558–1603). Library of Congress, LC-USZ62-47605.

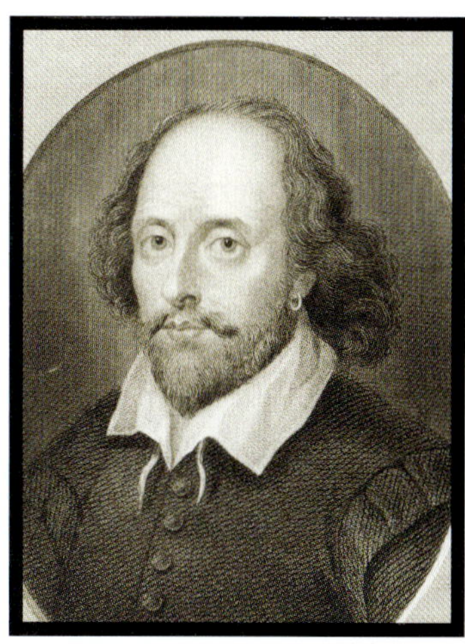

William Shakespeare (1564–1616), English poet and playwright. Library of Congress, LC-USZ62-104495.

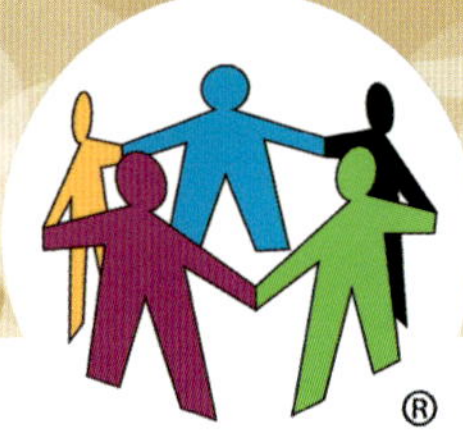

Understanding the Selection

Recalling

1. Reread lines 1–10 and identify three sounds that Magalu might hear and three interesting things that Magalu might see in this setting.
2. Who is the man with the white collar and black book?
3. What does the speaker want to give to Magalu?
4. What important characteristics distinguish the subject in "Sonnet to a Negro in Harlem" from other people in the crowd?
5. How does the speaker feel about the main character in this sonnet?

Interpreting

1. What sort of scene is the speaker trying to establish in the first 10 lines of "Magalu"? What does the speaker want readers to understand about this place?
2. Does the speaker want Magalu to listen to this man? Explain your answer.
3. How might the speaker's offer differ from what the man with the white collar is telling Magalu?
4. Is the subject in "Sonnet to a Negro in Harlem" presented as a friendly person? Does he care what other people think about him?
5. What does *splendid* mean? In what sense is this character splendid?

Synthesizing

1. Reread line 8 of "Sonnet to a Negro in Harlem." The palm trees and mangoes are in this man's memory or imagination—not really on the Harlem streets. Where do these things really exist? How does this image connect him to "Magalu"?
2. Do you think that the main character in "Sonnet to a Negro in Harlem" would listen to the man with the white collar in "Magalu"? Why, or why not?

Delving Deeper

Understanding Literature

Antithesis. An **antithesis** is a statement that directly contradicts another statement. In what way is the "creed that will not let you dance" the antithesis of the whole world described by Johnson in the poem "Magalu"? Think of the astonishingly vivid **imagery** of the speaker's descriptions in that poem, the appeals to all the senses: touch, taste, sight, sound, and smell. Make a chart in which you classify the images in the poem and tell what senses they appeal to. Then think about why the creed mentioned in the last line is out of place in the world of the poem.

About the Author

Helene Johnson (1907–1995) was a major poet of the Harlem Renaissance. Appearing in magazines such as *Opportunity, Fire!,* and *Vanity Fair,* her poetry covered a range of themes, including the beauty of the natural world, pride in the African heritage, and racist oppression.

Born in Boston to Ella and William Johnson, Helene attended public schools and Boston University. At 19 years old, already having received numerous praises for her earliest works, she and her cousin novelist Dorothy West moved to Harlem. Befriending such other literary greats as Zora Neale Hurston and Gwendolyn Bennett, Johnson continued to publish her poetry and won several honors and awards through *Opportunity* contests. Her poetry also appeared in Countee Cullen's anthology *Caroling Dusk* (1927) and in James Weldon Johnson's *Book of American Negro Poetry* (1931).

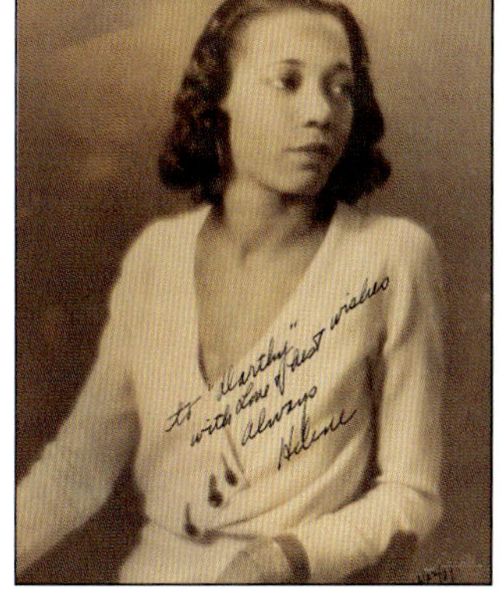

Despite receiving such critical acclaim early on, by the 1940s Johnson had faded from view, presumably to focus on her home life. Among the youngest of the Harlem Renaissance Poets, Johnson made a small, yet powerful contribution.

Prereading

"Ma Rainey"

by Sterling Brown

The origins of blues music are mysterious. The music draws upon African roots and is related to the spirituals and work songs of the slavery era, but this music is also entirely original in many ways. The term *blues* represents both a musical style and a subject matter. Musically, blues is based on taking a five-note, or pentatonic, scale; flatting the third and seventh tones; and adding an augmented fourth. (See pages 438–443.) These changes in the scale create so-called **blue notes** and give the music its distinctive sound. Blues also often involves slurring or bending of notes in imitation of the human voice, particularly of a plaintive cry. Blues songs are unusual in that the **tonic,** or base chord, is usually a dominant seventh. In the most common form of blues, so-called twelve-bar blues, a verse consists of three four-measure lines, the first of which is repeated.

> The mailman passed but he didn't leave no news.
> The mailman passed but he didn't leave no news.
> I'll tell the world he left me with those Gulf Coast blues.
>
> —"Gulf Coast Blues," Clarence Williams (1923)

The subject matter of the blues, of course, is usually some trouble, worry, or hard time. Indeed, "having the blues" means feeling sad or otherwise unhappy. The blues, a folk music invented by anonymous men and women in the era just after the Civil War, became enormously popular in the 1920s and '30s and has remained so since.

One of the earliest of the professional blues singers was **Gertrude Pridget "Ma" Rainey,** often referred to as "The Mother of the Blues." Ma Rainey was born in Columbus, Georgia, and became a vaudeville performer at an early age. She made her first recordings in 1923, became a great star, and helped to train and make successful another great early blues singer, **Bessie Smith.** A stout, heavy woman who dressed in a flashy style, she sang in a booming, soulful voice. Her memory is powerfully evoked in this poem by Sterling Brown. Readers are encouraged to compare this poem to Robert Hayden's "Homage to the Empress of the Blues" on page 543.

Ma Rainey[1]

by Sterling Brown

I

When Ma Rainey
Comes to town,
Folks from anyplace
Miles aroun',
From Cape Girardeau,[2]
Poplar Bluff,[3]
Flocks in to hear
Ma do her stuff;
Comes flivverin'[4] in,
Or ridin' mules,
Or packed in trains,
Picknickin' fools. . . .
That's what it's like,
Fo' miles on down,
To New Orleans **delta**
An' Mobile[5] town,
When Ma hits
Anywheres aroun'.

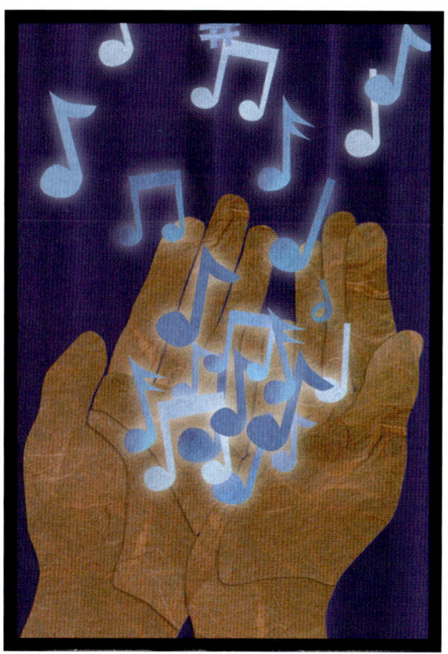

[1] **Ma Rainey.** Celebrated blues singer (1886–1939)

[2] **Cape Girardeau.** A city and county in southeastern Missouri

[3] **Poplar Bluff.** The seat of Butler County, in southeastern Missouri

[4] **flivverin'.** Riding in a flivver, a small, cheap automobile

[5] **Mobile.** A seaport in Alabama

VOCABULARY IN PLACE

- **delta,** ***n.*** A triangular area of land created by alluvial deposits (materials carried downstream) left at the mouth of a river

II

Dey comes to hear Ma Rainey from de little river settlements,
From blackbottom[6] cornrows and from lumber camps;
Dey stumble in de hall, jes a-laughin' an' a-cacklin',
Cheerin' lak roarin' water, lak wind in river swamps.

An' some jokers keeps deir laughs a-goin' in de crowded aisles,
An' some folks sits dere waitin' wid deir aches an' miseries,
Till Ma comes out before dem, a-smilin' gold-toofed smiles
An' Long Boy ripples minors on de black an' yellow keys.[7]

III

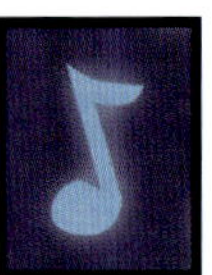

O Ma Rainey,
Sing yo' song;
Now you's back
Whah you belong,
Git way inside us,
Keep us strong. . . .
O Ma Rainey,
Li'l an' low;
Sing us 'bout de hard luck
Roun' our do';
Sing us 'bout de lonesome road
We mus' go. . . .

[6] **blackbottom.** Land with dark, rich, fertile soil located in the bottomland around a river or stream

[7] **ripples minors . . . yellow keys.** Plays minor scales, arpeggio, or improvisations on the black and white (yellowish) keys of a piano

IV

I talked to a fellow, an' the fellow say,
"She jes' catch hold of us, somekindaway.
She sang Backwater Blues one day:

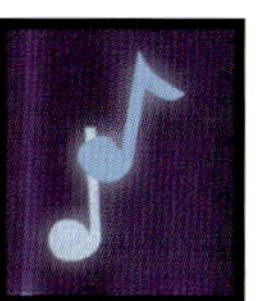

'It rained fo' days an' de skies was dark as night,
Trouble taken place in de lowlands at night.

'Thundered an' lightened an' the storm begin to roll
Thousan's of people ain't got no place to go.

'Den I went an' stood upon some high ol' lonesome hill,
An' looked down on the place where I used to live.'

An' den de folks, dey natchally bowed dey heads an' cried,
Bowed dey heavy heads, shet dey moufs up tight an' cried,
An' Ma lef' de stage, an' followed some de folks outside."

Dere wasn't much more de fellow say:
She jes' gits hold of us dataway. ■

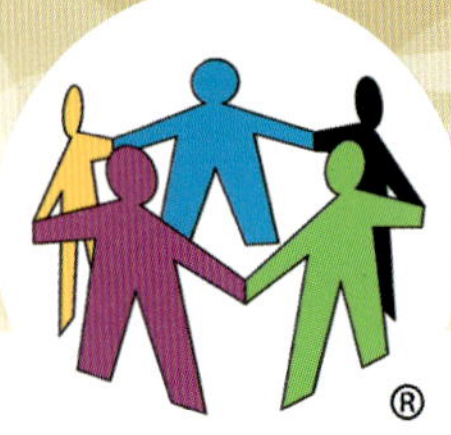

Understanding the Selection

Recalling

1. What happens, according to the first section of the poem, when Ma Rainey comes to town?
2. What areas of the country do the people come from in parts I and II of the poem?
3. What does Ma Rainey do, according to part III of the poem?
4. What happens in the selection from "Backwater Blues" quoted in part IV of this poem?
5. How do the people react when Ma Rainey sings "Backwater Blues"?

Interpreting

1. What effect does her presence have?
2. Is this sophisticated, big-city music? Explain.
3. Are the lives of the people for whom she sings easy? Why might this music be so important to them?
4. What sort of feeling is evoked by these lines from the blues song?
5. Why would people want to listen to music that makes them react in this way?

Synthesizing

1. What makes Ma Rainey's music so appealing to the people for whom she sings? What does she sing about? Why does her music get "hold of" them "dataway"?
2. What purpose is served by blues music? Why are people able to relate to it? Why does it ease their "aches an' miseries"?

Delving Deeper

Understanding Literature

Speaker and Dialect. The **speaker** of a poem is the voice assumed by the writer. It is the voice that speaks the poem. A **dialect** is a variety of language that is spoken in a region of the country or by a subgroup of a population. Two dialects of the same language can differ in pronunciation, grammar, word choice, and other ways. The best writers of contemporary poetry, fiction, and drama are able to give their work authenticity by capturing, accurately, the dialects spoken by their characters. In Sterling Brown's "Ma Rainey," both the speaker of the poem and the fellow to whom the speaker talks in part IV use a Southern rural dialect that, for example, violates usual subject/verb agreement, as in "Folks . . . flocks in" and pronounces "then" as "Den." Read through the poem again and find as many examples of dialectical usages as you can.

About the Author

Sterling Brown (1901–1989) was a professor of English, poet, and essayist. He taught literature at Howard University for forty years, and he published two books of poetry: *Southern Road* (1932) and *The Last Ride of Wild Bill and Eleven Narrative Poems* (1975). Brown is best known for his nonfiction works on literary topics, such as *The Negro in American Fiction.* Born into a middle-class community in Washington, D.C., Brown graduated at the top of his high-school class, received a Bachelor's degree with honors from Williams College, and earned a Master's degree in literature from Harvard University. He taught at Virginia Seminary, married, and had one child.

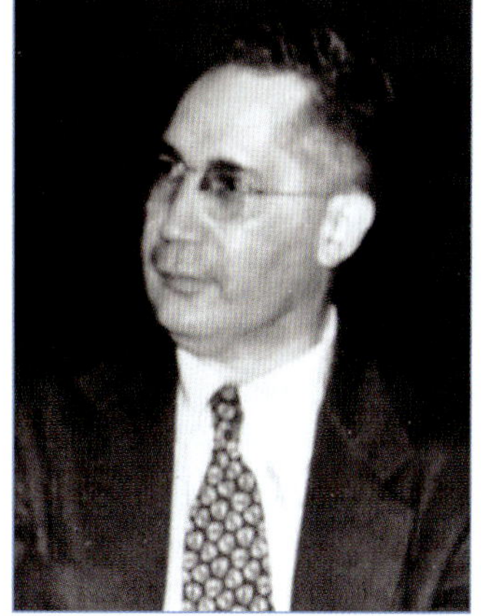

Brown's poetry was inspired by the works of early modern masters, including Robert Frost and Zora Neale Hurston, who used ordinary, conversational language in their work. In a 1942 speech, Brown said, "I was first attracted by certain qualities that I thought the speech of the people had, and I wanted to get for my own writing a flavor, a color, a pungency of speech. . . . Then later, I came to something more important—I wanted to get an understanding of people." (See also "Br'er Sterling and the Rocker," by Michael Harper, page 613.)

Prereading

Poems by Arna Bontemps

In a quiet, measured, reflective voice, the poet Arna Bontemps wrote about human aspirations. Throughout his life, Bontemps had enormous concern for African-American children and hoped to give them dreams for their own futures. For that reason, he worked as a librarian; wrote inspiring biographies of such notable African Americans as George Washington Carver, Althea Gibson, and Jackie Robinson; and created children's books with African-American characters and themes.

The Day-Breakers. The subtlety of this poem lies in the many meanings of its title. One sense of the word *break* is to "break soil," that is, to chop at the earth to loosen it in order to do planting. So, in that sense, a *day-breaker* might be someone who goes out during the day to do hard labor. *Day-break* also means, of course, the moment when the sun comes up. A *day-breaker* would be, then, someone who makes the sun come up. In what sense might people "make the sun come up"? Think about this as you read the poem.

Southern Mansion. Throughout the Old South, one finds surviving plantation houses, often abandoned or, increasingly, preserved as museums. These buildings are stark reminders of a system of privilege that provided luxurious living for a few on the backs of the labor of others—the slaves who tended the fields, nursed the children, and carried out innumerable other tasks so that their white "masters" could live genteel lives. In this poem, Bontemps powerfully evokes the past during a walk around such a mansion, a surviving relic of the **antebellum** (pre-war) South.

A Black Man Talks of Reaping. As with "The Day-Breakers," Bontemps uses an agricultural metaphor in this poem in order to comment upon African-American life. Yet, whereas the former poem ends on a note of strength and determination, "A Black Man Talks of Reaping" communicates anguish over a history of African Americans laboring without receiving their just rewards. The poem's speaker also laments the fact that blacks have been unable to leave a legacy for future generations.

The Day-Breakers

by Arna Bontemps

We are not come to wage a strife[1]
With swords[2] upon this hill.
It is not wise to waste the life
Against a stubborn will.
Yet would we die as some have done.
Beating a way for the rising sun.[3] ■

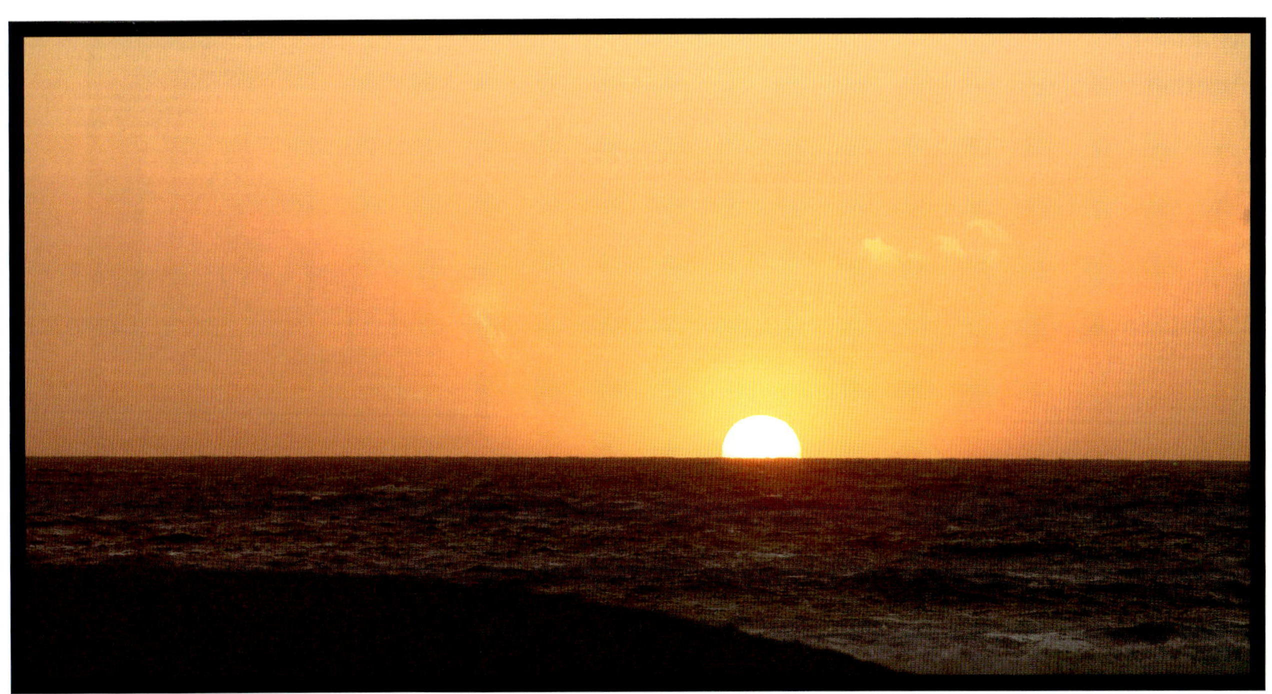

[1] **wage a strife.** Carry out a fight

[2] **swords.** People are gathered on a hill but are not carrying swords. This word suggests that they might be carrying other implements, such as picks and hoes—consistent with the interpretation of day-breakers as agricultural laborers.

[3] **rising sun.** The sun is a traditional poetic symbol of power, authority, and accomplishment.

Southern Mansion

by Arna Bontemps

Poplars[1] are standing there still as death
And ghosts of dead men
Meet their ladies walking
Two by two beneath the shade[2]
And standing on the marble steps.

There is a sound of music echoing
Through the open door
And in the field there is
Another sound tinkling in the cotton:
Chains of bondmen[3] dragging on the ground.

The years go back with an iron clank,
A hand is on the gate,
A dry leaf trembles on the wall.
Ghosts are walking.
They have broken roses[4] down
And poplars stand there still as death. ■

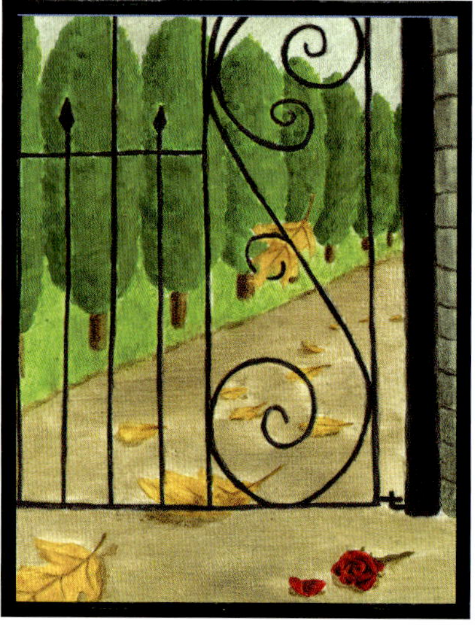

[1] **Poplars.** Poplar trees are tall and straight, with light gray, whitish bark. They quiver in the wind and are traditionally associated with weeping. Their wood is often used in the construction of coffins. Poplars are often planted along paths and roadways.

[2] **shade.** The word *shade* has a double meaning: it refers to a place sheltered from sunlight and it also means "ghost," as in "the shades of departed heroes." The poplars make shade and are, figuratively, shades.

[3] **bondmen.** Slaves, who often wore chains to keep them from escaping

[4] **roses.** Roses are traditional symbols of love and beauty.

A Black Man Talks of Reaping[1]

by Arna Bontemps

I have sown beside all waters[2] in my day.
I planted deep, within my heart the fear
That wind or **fowl** would take the grain away.
I planted safe against[3] this **stark,** lean year.

I scattered seed enough to plant the land
In rows from Canada to Mexico
But for my reaping only what the hand
Can hold at once is all that I can show.

Yet what I sowed and what the orchard yields
My brother's sons[4] are gathering stalk and root,
Small wonder then my children glean in fields
They have not sown, and feed on bitter fruit. ■

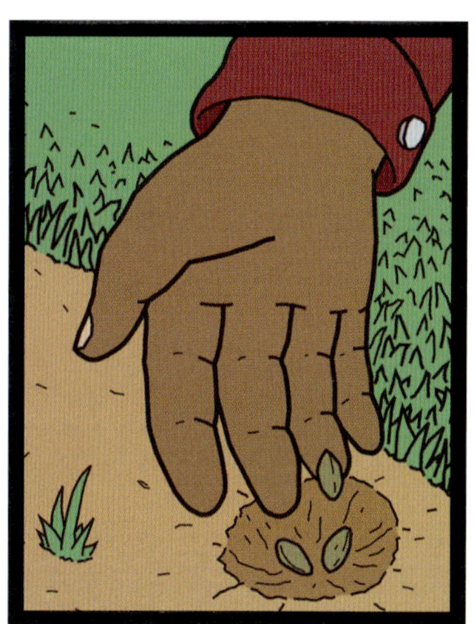

[1] **Reaping.** This is a poetic word for harvesting, or collecting the results of one's labors.

[2] **all waters.** Traditionally, human habitations have been built near water so that people could drink and irrigate their crops. Compare with Langston Hughes's "The Negro Speaks of Rivers," on page 355.

[3] **planted safe against.** Planted in such a way as to ensure that I would have it later in a time of need

[4] **brother's sons.** Probably a reference to the white "brother"

VOCABULARY IN PLACE

- **fowl,** ***n.*** Bird
- **stark,** ***adj.*** Harsh, unadorned, not fruitful, meager

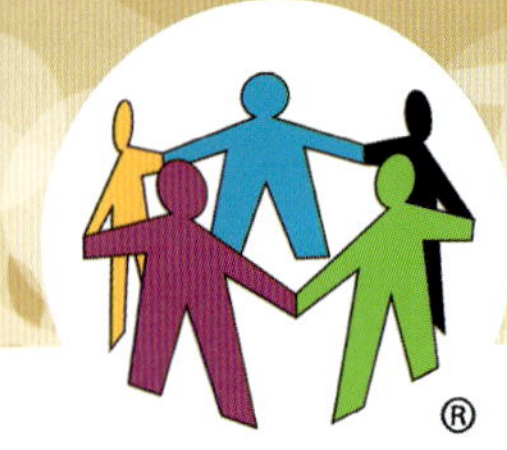

Understanding the Selection

Recalling

1. What have the people in "The Day-Breakers" not come to do?
2. Why is it not wise to "wage a strife," according to lines 3 and 4 of "The Day-Breakers"?
3. What does the speaker imagine hearing and seeing while viewing the "Southern Mansion"?
4. What has the speaker in "A Black Man Talks of Reaping" done? What has he gained as a result?
5. What are the "brother's sons" doing in "A Black Man Talks of Reaping"?

Interpreting

1. What kind of warfare or strife might the speaker of the poem be talking about?
2. What could "The Day-Breakers" expect if they did engage in strife? What would they confront?
3. To what era do the things that the speaker imagines belong? How do these imagined things make the speaker and the reader feel? What is creepy about the mansion?
4. If the sowing refers to any kind of work in the world, and the reaping refers to receiving the results of one's labors, what, then, is the speaker saying about his condition?
5. What is particularly terrible about pulling up the stalks and roots of the plants that were sown?

Synthesizing

1. Often poetry is written to create a **mood**, or feeling, in the reader. What elements contribute to the overall mood of "Southern Mansion"?
2. "The Day-Breakers" and "A Black Man Talks of Reaping" deal with the same theme—expectations for the future. How do they differ in their attitudes and conclusions?

Delving Deeper

Understanding Literature

Symbolism. A **symbol** is an image that stands both for itself and for something beyond itself. For example, the dove is a traditional symbol of peace. Arna Bontemps makes frequent use of traditional symbols. In "The Day-Breakers," the rising sun is a symbol for rising fortune and accomplishment. The poem suggests that by not warring now, but by working hard, people can bring about a better future. Poplars are traditionally associated with ghosts and death. Iron is associated with bondage because of the manacles that were made of iron. Dry or autumn leaves are associated with death and decay because they appear in autumn, at the end of the summer. Roses are traditional symbols of love and beauty. Think about what all these symbols might mean in the poem "Southern Mansion." Then think about what the waters, the planting, the seeds, the reaping, and the bitter fruit might symbolize in "A Black Man Talks of Reaping."

About the Author

Arna Bontemps (1902–1973) was born in Alexandria, Louisiana, to a brick mason and a teacher, who lived in a mixed white, African-American, and Creole community. He got his bachelor's degree in southern California and then moved to Harlem, New York, where he became a teacher.

In New York, Bontemps wrote poetry and worked within the same artistic community as Langston Hughes and Zora Neale Hurston, during the period known as the Harlem Renaissance.

In 1931, Bontemps left Harlem for a teaching job in Alabama and began to write children's books. Bontemps is remembered for his love of children and for his desire to create literature for black children. He wrote at least sixteen books for children, including *Popo and Filina: Children of Haiti* (1932), which he co-wrote with Langston Hughes.

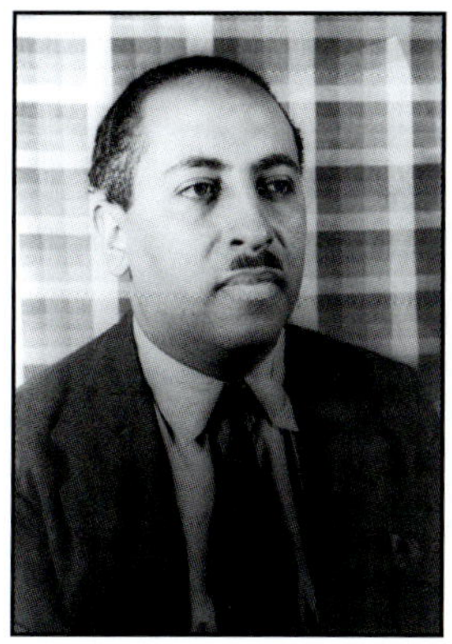

Bontemps received a master's degree in library science at the University of Chicago; served as head librarian at Fisk Univeristy in Nashville, Tennessee; wrote numerous biographies of famous African Americans; worked as a professor at the University of Illinois and at Yale; and returned to Fisk late in life to serve as a writer-in-residence.

Prereading

"The Bouquet"

by Charles W. Chesnutt

This writer is often cited as the first "great" African-American novelist. While there were several successful and accomplished novelists before him, he was the first who consistently produced masterful works of literature. He was also a great short-story writer who could expose truth and injustice in the simple, everyday actions of his beautifully composed characters.

Charles W. Chesnutt was born and raised during a pivotal time in American history—the Reconstruction era—and spent much of his life frustrated by the mistreatment of black people all around the United States. Chesnutt's perspective on racial matters is somewhat unusual because a person passing him on the street might easily have assumed that he was white. He never pretended to be white, but his physical features made the reality of racism in America all the more acute and painful to him.

The following background information and analysis will help you get the most out of this masterpiece of American fiction:

1. "The Bouquet" is set in North Carolina shortly after the Civil War. Mary Myrover and her mother are descended from a long line of wealthy slave owners.
2. Most of Chesnutt's stories centered on racial themes. Pay attention to details in the story related to racial discrimination.
3. Analyze this exemplary model of the short story form. Examine the ways in which a writer can use details and carefully chosen actions to reveal the essence of a character, setting, or historical era. Make an informal character chart in your notebook, and jot down important details and quotations, along with page and paragraph citations, to assist in a later analysis of short-story elements.
4. The word *juxtapose* means "to place side by side, especially for comparison or contrast." As you read, pay attention to the way in which the writer juxtaposes Sophy (the main character) and Prince (the dog).

The Bouquet

by Charles W. Chesnutt

1

Mary Myrover's friends were somewhat surprised when she began to teach a colored school. Miss Myrover's friends are mentioned here, because nowhere more than in a Southern town is public opinion a force which cannot be lightly **contravened.** Public opinion, however, did not oppose Miss Myrover's teaching colored children; in fact, all the colored public schools in town—and there were several — were taught by white teachers, and had been so taught since the State had undertaken to provide free public instruction for all children within its boundaries. Previous to that time, there had been a Freedmen's Bureau[1] school and a Presbyterian missionary school, but these had been withdrawn when the need for them became less pressing. The colored people of the town had been for some time **agitating** their right to teach their own schools, but as yet the claim had not been conceded.

The reason Miss Myrover's course created some surprise was not, therefore, the fact that a Southern white woman should teach a colored school; it lay in the fact that up to this time no woman of just her quality had taken up such work. Most of the teachers of colored schools were not of those who had constituted the aristocracy of the old regime;[2] they might be said rather to represent the new order of things, in which labor was in time to become honorable, and men were after a somewhat longer time, to depend, for their place in society, upon themselves rather than upon their ancestors. Mary Myrover belonged to one of the proudest of the old families. Her ancestors had been people of distinction in Virginia before a collateral branch of the main stock had settled in North Carolina. Before the war, they had been able to live up to their **pedigree;** but the war brought sad changes. Miss Myrover's father— the Colonel Myrover who led a gallant but desperate charge at Vicksburg[3]— had fallen on the battlefield, and his tomb in the white cemetery was a shrine for the family. On the Confederate Memorial Day, no other grave was so profusely decorated with flowers, and, in the oration pronounced, the name of Colonel Myrover was always used to illustrate the highest type of patriotic devotion and self-sacrifice. Miss Myrover's brother, too, had fallen in the conflict; but his bones lay in some unknown trench, with those of a thousand others who had fallen on the same

On which side did the Myrovers fight during the Civil War?

VOCABULARY IN PLACE

- **contravene,** *v.* To act or be counter to; violate
- **agitate,** *v.* To arouse interest in
- **pedigree,** *n.* A line of ancestors; a lineage

1 **Freedmen's Bureau.** A bureau established by the U.S. War Department in 1865 to manage the needs of emancipated slaves

2 **old regime.** The former system. Prior to the Civil War, the aristocracy (wealthy plantation owners) controlled most of the South's resources and political institutions.

3 **Vicksburg.** The Battle or Siege of Vicksburg (Mississippi), May 18–July 4, 1863, resulted in a combined total of nearly 20,000 Union and Confederate casualties. Victory at Vicksburg gave the North command over the Mississippi River.

field. Ay, more, her lover, who had hoped to come home in the full tide of victory and claim this bride as a reward for gallantry, had shared the fate of her father and brother. When the war was over, the remnant of the family found itself involved in the common ruin,—more deeply involved, indeed, than some others; for Colonel Myrover had believed in the ultimate triumph of his cause, and had invested most of his wealth in Confederate bonds,[4] which were now only so much waste paper.

There had been a little left. Mrs. Myrover was thrifty, and had laid by a few hundred dollars, which she kept in the house to meet unforeseen **contingencies.** There remained, too, their home, with an ample garden and a well-stocked orchard, besides a considerable tract of country land, partly cleared, but productive of very little revenue.

With their shrunken resources, Miss Myrover and her mother were able to hold up their heads without embarrassment for some years after the close of the war. But when things were adjusted to the changed conditions, and the stream of life began to flow more vigorously in the new channels, they saw themselves in danger of dropping behind, unless in some way they could add to their meager income. Miss Myrover looked over the field of employment, never very wide for women in the South, and found it occupied. The only available positions she could be supposed prepared to fill, and which she could take without distinct loss of **caste,** was that of a teacher, and there was no vacancy except in one of the colored schools. Even teaching was a doubtful experiment; it was not what she would have preferred, but it was the best that could be done.

Why does Miss Myrover have to find a job?

"I don't like it, Mary," said her mother. "It's a long step from owning such people to teaching them. What do they need with education? It will only make them unfit for work."

"They're free now, mother, and perhaps they'll work better if they're taught something. Besides, it's only a business arrangement, and doesn't involve any closer contact than we have with our servants."

Why doesn't Mrs. Myrover want her daughter to teach black students?

"Well, I should say not!" sniffed the old lady. "Not one of them will ever dare to presume on your position to take any liberties with us. *I'll* see to that."

Miss Myrover began her work as a teacher in the autumn, at the opening of the school year. It was a **novel** experience at first. Though there had always been Negro servants in the house, and though on the streets colored people were more numerous than those of her own race, and though she was so familiar with their dialect that she might almost be said to speak it, barring certain characteristic grammatical inaccuracies, she had never been brought in personal contact with so many of them at once as when she confronted the fifty or sixty faces—of colors ranging from a white almost as clear as her own to the darkest livery of the sun—which were gathered in the schoolroom on the morning when she began her duties. Some of the inherited prejudice

[4] **Confederate bonds.** A bond is a certificate of debt issued by a government guaranteeing payment of the original investment plus interest. Bonds issued by the Confederate government became worthless when the South crumbled.

VOCABULARY IN PLACE

- **contingency,** ***n.*** An unforeseen event or condition
- **caste,** ***n.*** A social class separated from others according to hereditary rank, profession, or wealth
- **novel,** ***adj.*** Strikingly new; unusual

of her caste, too, made itself felt, though she tried to repress any outward sign of it; and she could perceive that the children were not altogether responsive; they, likewise, were not entirely free from **antagonism.** The work was unfamiliar to her. She was not physically very strong, and at the close of the first day went home with a splitting headache. If she could have resigned then and there without causing comment or annoyance to others, she would have felt it a privilege to do so. But a night's rest banished her headache and improved her spirits, and the next morning she went to her work with renewed vigor, fortified by the experience of the first day.

Miss Myrover's second day was more satisfactory. She had some natural talent for organization, though **hitherto** unaware of it, and in the course of the day she got her classes formed and lessons under way. In a week or two she began to classify her pupils in her own mind, as bright or stupid, mischievous or well behaved, lazy or industrious, as the case might be, and to regulate her discipline accordingly. That she had come of a long line of ancestors who had exercised authority and mastership was perhaps not without its effect upon her character, and enabled her more readily to maintain good order in the school. When she was fairly broken in, she found the work rather to her liking, and derived much pleasure from such success as she achieved as a teacher.

It was natural that she should be more attracted to some of her pupils than to others. Perhaps her favorite—or, rather, the one she liked best, for she was too fair and just for conscious favoritism—was Sophy Tucker. Just the ground for the teacher's liking for Sophy might not at first be apparent. The girl was far from the whitest of Miss Myrover's pupils; in fact, she was one of the darker ones. She was not the brightest in intellect, though she always tried to learn her lessons. She was not the best dressed, for her mother was a poor widow, who went out washing and scrubbing for a living. Perhaps the real tie between them was Sophy's intense devotion to the teacher. It had manifested itself almost from the first day of the school, in the rapt look of admiration Miss Myrover always saw on the little black face turned toward her. In it there was nothing of envy, nothing of regret; nothing but worship for the beautiful white lady—she was not especially handsome, but to Sophy her beauty was almost divine—who had come to teach her. If Miss Myrover

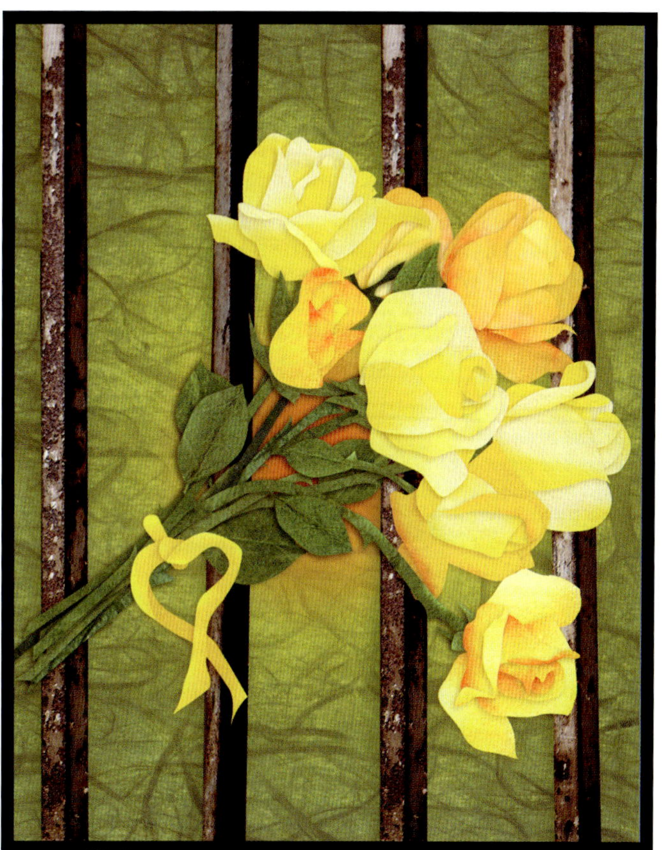

VOCABULARY IN PLACE

- **antagonism,** ***n.*** Actively-expressed opposition, or hostility
- **hitherto,** ***adv.*** Up to this time

dropped a book, Sophy was the first to spring and pick it up; if she wished a chair moved, Sophy seemed to anticipate her wish; and so of all the numberless little services that can be rendered in a schoolroom.

Miss Myrover was fond of flowers, and liked to have them about her. The children soon learned of this taste of hers, and kept the vases on her desk filled with blossoms during their season. Sophy was perhaps the most active in providing them. If she could not get garden flowers, she would make excursions to the woods in the early morning, and bring in great dew-laden bunches of bay, or jasmine, or some other fragrant forest flower which she knew the teacher loved.

"When I die, Sophy," Miss Myrover said to the child one day, "I want to be covered with roses. And when they bury me, I'm sure I shall rest better if my grave is banked with flowers, and roses are planted at my head and at my feet."

Miss Myrover was at first amused at Sophy's devotion; but when she grew more accustomed to it, she found it rather to her liking. It had a sort of flavor of the old regime, and she felt, when she bestowed her kindly notice upon her little black attendant, some of the feudal condescension[5] of the mistress toward the slave. She was kind to Sophy, and permitted her to play the role she had assumed, which caused sometimes a little jealousy among the other girls. Once she gave Sophy a yellow ribbon which she took from her own hair. The child carried it home, and cherished it as a priceless treasure, to be worn only on the greatest occasions.

How did Miss Myrover feel about Sophy's devotion?

Sophy had a rival in her attachment to the teacher, but the rivalry was altogether friendly. Miss Myrover had a little dog, a white spaniel, answering to the name of Prince. Prince was a dog of high degree, and

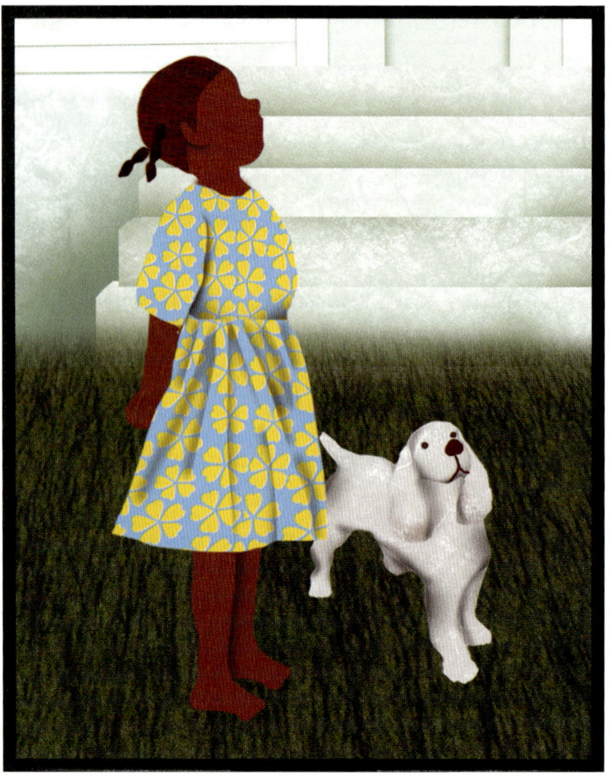

would have very little to do with the children of the school; he made an exception, however, in the case of Sophy, whose devotion for his mistress he seemed to comprehend. He was a clever dog, and could fetch and carry, sit up on his haunches, extend his paw to shake hands, and possessed several other canine accomplishments. He was very fond of his mistress, and always, unless shut up at home, accompanied her to school, where he spent most of his time lying under the teacher's desk, or, in cold weather, by the stove, except when he would go out now and then and chase an imaginary rabbit round the yard, presumably for exercise.

At school Sophy and Prince vied with each other in their attentions to Miss Myrover. But when school was over, Prince went away with her, and Sophy stayed

5 **feudal condescension.** She is "stooping" or lowering herself to the level of those with inferior social status. The word *feudal* here refers to the relationship between lord and serf in medieval Europe.

behind; for Miss Myrover was white and Sophy was black, which they both understood perfectly well. Miss Myrover taught the colored children, but she could not be seen with them in public. If they occasionally met her on the street, they did not expect her to speak to them, unless she happened to be alone and no other white person was in sight. If any of the children felt slighted, she was not aware of it, for she intended no slight; she had not been brought up to speak to Negroes on the street, and she could not act differently from other people. And though she was a woman of sentiment and capable of deep feeling, her training had been such that she hardly expected to find in those of darker hue than herself the same susceptibility—varying in degree, perhaps, but yet the same in kind—that gave to her own life the alternations of feeling that made it most worth living.

Why can't Sophy and Miss Myrover walk together in public?

Once Miss Myrover wished to carry home a parcel of books. She had the bundle in her hand when Sophy came up.

"Lemme tote yo' bundle fer yer, Miss Ma'y?" she asked eagerly. "I'm gwine yo' way."

"Thank you, Sophy," was the reply. "I'll be glad if you will."

Sophy followed the teacher at a respectful distance. When they reached Miss Myrover's home, Sophy carried the bundle to the doorstep, where Miss Myrover took it and thanked her.

Mrs. Myrover came out on the piazza as Sophy was moving away. She said, in the child's hearing, and perhaps with the intention that she should hear: "Mary, I wish you wouldn't let those little darkeys follow you to the house. I don't want them in the yard. I should think you'd have enough of them all day."

"Very well, mother," replied her daughter. "I won't bring any more of them. The child was only doing me a favor."

Mrs. Myrover was an invalid, and opposition or irritation of any kind brought on nervous paroxysms[6] that made her miserable, and made life a burden to the rest of the household, so that Mary seldom crossed her whims. She did not bring Sophy to the house again, nor did Sophy again offer her services as porter.

One day in spring Sophy brought her teacher a bouquet of yellow roses.

"Dey come off'n my own bush, Miss Ma'y," she said proudly, "an' I didn't let nobody e'se pull 'em, but saved 'em all fer you, 'cause I know you likes roses so much. I'm gwine bring 'em all ter you as long as dey las'."

"Thank you, Sophy," said the teacher; "you are a very good girl."

2

For another year Mary Myrover taught the colored school, and did excellent service. The children made rapid progress under her tuition, and learned to love her well; for they saw and appreciated, as well as children could, her **fidelity** to a trust that she might have slighted, as some others did, without much fear of criticism. Toward the end of her second year she sickened, and after a brief illness died.

Old Mrs. Myrover was **inconsolable.** She ascribed her daughter's death to her labors as teacher of Negro children. Just how

[6] **paroxysms.** Seizures; sudden spasms

VOCABULARY IN PLACE

- **fidelity**, ***n.*** Loyalty, faithfulness
- **inconsolable**, ***adj.*** Impossible or difficult to comfort

the color of the pupils had produced the fatal effects she did not stop to explain. But she was too old, and had suffered too deeply from the war, in body and mind and estate, ever to reconcile herself to the changed order of things following the return of peace; and, with an unsound yet perfectly explainable logic, she visited some of her displeasure upon those who had profited most, though passively, by her losses.

"I always feared something would happen to Mary," she said. "It seemed unnatural for her to be wearing herself out teaching little Negroes who ought to have been working for her. But the world has hardly been a fit place to live in since the war, and when I follow her, as I must before long, I shall not be sorry to go."

She gave strict orders that no colored people should be admitted to the house. Some of her friends heard of this, and **remonstrated.** They knew the teacher was loved by the pupils, and felt that sincere respect from the humble would be a worthy tribute to the proudest. But Mrs. Myrover was **obdurate.**

Whom does Mrs. Myrover blame for her daughter's death?

"They had my daughter when she was alive," she said, "and they've killed her. But she's mine now, and I won't have them come near her. I don't want one of them at the funeral or anywhere around."

For a month before Miss Myrover's death Sophy had been watching her rosebush—the one that bore the yellow roses—for the first buds of spring, and, when these appeared, had awaited impatiently their gradual unfolding. But not until her teacher's death had they become full-blown roses. When Miss Myrover died, Sophy determined to pluck the roses and lay them on her coffin. Perhaps, she thought, they might even put them in her hand or on her breast. For Sophy remembered Miss Myrover's thanks and praise when she had brought her the yellow roses the spring before.

On the morning of the day set for the funeral, Sophy washed her face until it shone, combed and brushed her hair with painful conscientiousness, put on her best frock, plucked her yellow roses, and, tying them with the treasured ribbon her teacher had given her, set out for Miss Myrover's home.

She went round to the side gate—the house stood on a corner—and stole up the path to the kitchen. A colored woman, whom she did not know, came to the door.

"W'at yer want, chile?" she inquired.

"Kin I see Miss Ma'y?" asked Sophy timidly.

"I don't know, honey. Ole Miss Myrover say she don't want no cullud folks roun' de house endyoin' di fun'al. I'll look an' see if she's roun' de front room, whar de co'pse is. You sed down heah an' keep still, an' ef she's upstairs maybe I kin git yer in dere a minute. Ef I can't, I kin put yo' bokay 'mongs' de res', whar she won't know nuthin' erbout it."

A moment after she had gone, there was a step in the hall, and old Mrs. Myrover came into the kitchen.

"Dinah!" she said in a **peevish** tone; "Dinah!"

Receiving no answer, Mrs. Myrover peered around the kitchen, and caught sight of Sophy.

"What are you doing here?" she demanded.

VOCABULARY IN PLACE

- **remonstrate,** ***v.*** To plead in protest; present an objection
- **obdurate,** ***adj.*** Not giving in to persuasion
- **peevish,** ***adj.*** Discontented or querulous; annoyed

"I—I'm-m waitin' ter see de cook, ma'am," stammered Sophy.

"The cook isn't here now. I don't know where she is. Besides, my daughter is to be buried today, and I won't have any one visiting the servants until the funeral is over. Come back some other day, or see the cook at her own home in the evening."

She stood waiting for the child to go, and under the keen glance of her eyes, Sophy, feeling as though she had been caught in some disgraceful act, hurried down the walk and out of the gate, with her bouquet in her hand.

"Dinah," said Mrs. Myrover, when the cook came back, "I don't want any strange people admitted here today. The house will be full of our friends, and we have no room for others."

"Yas'm," said the cook. She understood perfectly what her mistress meant, and what the cook thought about her mistress was a matter of no consequence.

The funeral services were held at St. Paul's Episcopal Church, where the Myrovers had always worshiped. Quite a number of Miss Myrover's pupils went to the church to attend the services. The building was not a large one. There was a small gallery at the rear, to which colored people were admitted, if they chose to come, at ordinary services; and those who wished to be present at the funeral supposed that the usual custom would prevail. They were therefore surprised, when they went to the side entrance by which colored people gained access to the gallery stairs, to be met by an usher who barred their passage.

"I'm sorry," he said, "but I have had orders to admit no one until the friends of the family have all been seated. If you wish to wait until the white people have all gone in, and there's any room left, you may be able to get into the back part of the gallery. Of course I can't tell yet whether there'll be any room or not."

Now the statement of the usher was a very reasonable one; but, strange to say, none of the colored people chose to remain except Sophy. She still hoped to use her floral offering for its destined end, in some way, though she did not know just how. She waited in the yard until the church was filled with white people, and a number who could not gain admittance were standing about the doors. Then she went round to the side of the church, and, depositing her bouquet carefully on an old mossy gravestone, climbed up on the projecting sill of a window near the chancel.[7] The window was of stained glass, of somewhat

[7] **chancel.** The space around the altar in a church

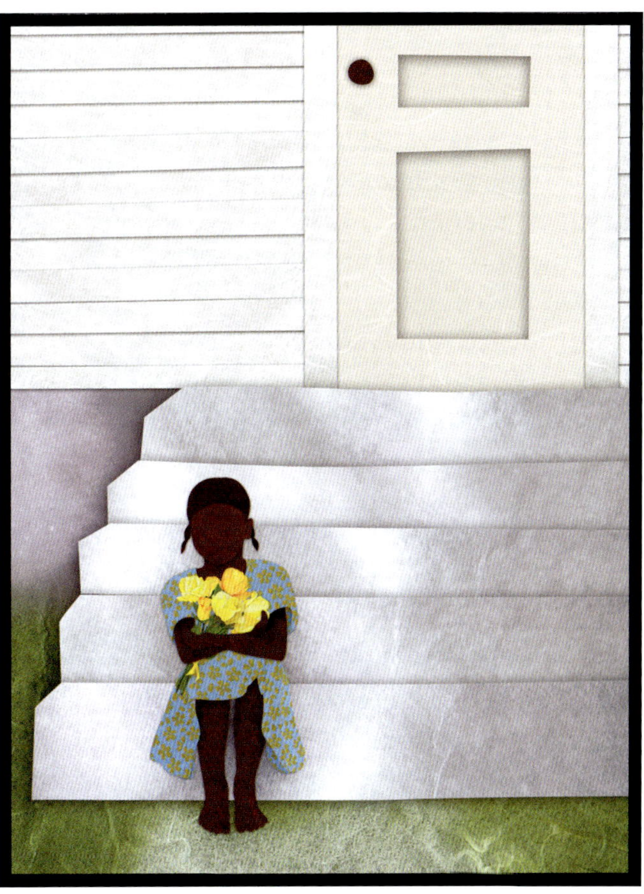

ancient make. The church was old, had indeed been built in colonial times, and the stained glass had been brought from England. The design of the window showed Jesus blessing little children. Time had dealt gently with the window, but just at the feet of the figure of Jesus a small triangular piece of glass had been broken out. To this **aperture** Sophy applied her eyes, and through it saw and heard what she could of the services within.

Before the chancel, on trestles draped in black, stood the somber casket in which lay all that was mortal of her dear teacher. The top of the casket was covered with flowers; and lying stretched out underneath it she saw Miss Myrover's little white dog, Prince. He had followed the body to the church, and, slipping in unnoticed among the mourners, had taken his place, from which no one had the heart to remove him.

The white-robed rector[8] read the solemn service for the dead, and then delivered a brief address, in which he dwelt upon the uncertainty of life, and, to the believer, the certain blessedness of eternity. He spoke of Miss Myrover's kindly spirit, and, as an illustration of her love and self-sacrifice for others, referred to her labors as a teacher of the poor ignorant Negroes who had been placed in their midst by an all-wise Providence, and whom it was their duty to guide and direct in the station in which God had put them. Then the organ pealed, a prayer was said, and the long cortege[9] moved from the church to the cemetery, about half a mile away, where the body was to be interred.

When the services were over, Sophy sprang down from her perch, and, taking her flowers, followed the procession. She did not walk with the rest, but at a proper and respectful distance from the last mourner. No one noticed the little black girl with the bunch of yellow flowers, or thought of her as interested in the funeral.

The cortege reached the cemetery and filed slowly through the gate; but Sophy stood outside, looking at a small sign in white letters on a black background:—

"*Notice.* This cemetery is for white people only. Others please keep out."

Sophy, thanks to Miss Myrover's painstaking instruction, could read this sign very distinctly. In fact, she had often read it before. For Sophy was a child who loved beauty, in a blind, groping sort of way, and had sometimes stood by the fence of the cemetery and looked through at the green mounds and shaded walks and blooming flowers within, and wished that she might walk among them. She knew, too, that the little sign on the gate, though so courteously worded, was no mere formality; for she had heard how a colored man, who had wandered into the cemetery on a hot night and fallen asleep on the flat top of a tomb, had been arrested as a vagrant and fined five dollars, which he had worked out on the streets, with a ball-and-chain attachment, at twenty-five cents a day. Since that time the cemetery gate had been locked at night.

So Sophie stayed outside, and looked through the fence. Her poor bouquet had begun to droop by this time, and the yellow ribbon had lost some of its freshness. Sophy could see the rector standing by the grave, the mourners gathered round; she could faintly distinguish the solemn words with which ashes were committed to ashes, and dust to

8 **rector.** A cleric in charge of a parish

9 **cortege.** Funeral procession

VOCABULARY IN PLACE

- **aperture,** ***n.*** An opening, such as a hole, gap, or slit

dust. She heard the hollow thud of the earth falling on the coffin; and she leaned against the iron fence, sobbing softly, until the grave was filled and rounded off, and the wreaths and other floral pieces were disposed upon it. When the mourners began to move toward the gate, Sophy walked slowly down the street, in a direction opposite to that taken by most of the people who came out.

When they had all gone away, and the sexton[10] had come out and locked the gate behind him, Sophy crept back. Her roses were faded now, and from some of them the petals had fallen. She stood there irresolute, loath to leave with her heart's desire unsatisfied, when as her eyes sought again the teacher's last resting-place, she saw lying beside the new-made grave what looked like a small bundle of white wool. Sophy's eyes lighted up with a sudden glow.

"Prince! Here Prince!" she called.

The little dog rose, and trotted down to the gate. Sophy pushed the poor bouquet between the iron bars. "Take that ter Miss Ma'y, Prince," she said, "that's a good doggie."

The dog wagged his tail intelligently, took the bouquet carefully in his mouth, carried it to his mistress's grave, and laid it among the other flowers. The bunch of roses was so small that from where she stood Sophy could see only a dash of yellow against the white background of the mass of flowers.

When Prince had performed his mission he turned his eyes toward Sophy inquiringly, and when she gave him a nod of approval lay down and resumed his watch by the graveside. Sophy looked at him a moment with a feeling very much like envy, and then turned and moved slowly away. ■

---

[10] **sexton.** An employee or officer of a church who is responsible for upkeep of church property and sometimes for ringing bells and digging graves

Understanding Literature

Conflict. This is the perhaps the most important element of a *good* short story. **Conflict** is any opposition faced by the main character; it can be **internal** (an emotional or psychological issue within the main charcater) or **external** (character vs. character, character vs. society, or character vs. nature or fate). Conflict is the driving force behind the plot—it keeps events moving from one to the next. "The Bouquet" contains three sets of external conflict: Sophy vs. Prince, Sophy vs. Mrs. Myrover (Mary's mother), Mary Myrover vs. her mother. What other conflicts, internal and external, exist in the story? How do internal and external conflicts help drive the story's plot? How does conflict affect your understanding of the story's setting, characters, and events?

Foreshadowing. Fiction writers often plant clues early on about what is going to happen later in a story. This narrative device is called **foreshadowing,** and it is used to create interesting layers and richness. Foreshadowing can build suspense and expectations; some writers use it to mislead readers, especially in mystery or detective stories. The suggestion of future events helps establish the mood and provides insight into a character's personality. Did you notice Chestnutt's use of foreshadowing in Part 1? (Hint, review page 418.) Why did Chesnutt choose to use suspense in the early part of the story? How does this help to cxplain Sophy's determination to deliver the bouquet at the end?

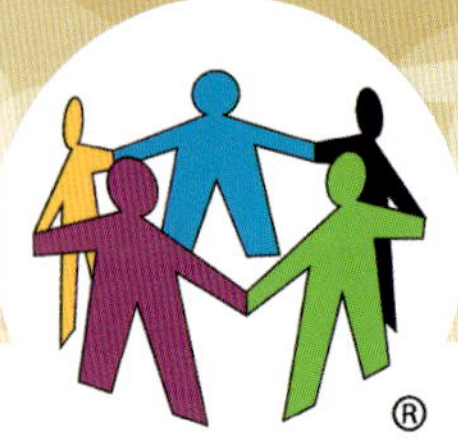

Understanding the Selection

Recalling

1. What was the financial and social status of the Myrover family prior to the Civil War? What is their status at the beginning of the story?

2. How does Mrs. Myrover react when Mary gets a teaching job? Using evidence from the text, provide two reasons that Mrs. Myrover objected to Mary's job.

3. Who is Miss Myrover's favorite student?

4. Who is Sophy's rival? What is he allowed to do after school that Sophy is not allowed to do?

5. Whom does Mrs. Myrover blame for her daughter's death?

Interpreting

1. Who has a harder time adjusting to post-Civil War society, Mary or her mother? Provide two examples from the story to support your answer.

2. Does Mary agree with her mother? What does the narrator mean by the phrase "the inherited prejudice of her caste"? (See pages 416–417.)

3. Why is this student so enamored of Miss Myrover?

4. Why is this rivalry described as "altogether friendly"?

5. In what way does Sophy suffer as a result of Mrs. Myrover's prejudice?

Synthesizing

1. What is the turning point in the plot of the story? Why did the author choose to separate the story into two parts?
2. What statement did the author intend to make when he juxtaposed Sophy and Prince in the end of the story?
3. How have things changed, or not changed, since this story was published in 1899?

Delving Deeper

Understanding Literature

Short Story Elements. A writer attends to three major elements in developing a short story: **setting** (time and place), **characterization** (representation of the characters' personalities and/or personal development), and **plot** (how events influence characters and vice versa). Continue to analyze Chesnutt's story-building technique by completing the following exercises in your notebook:

1. Summarize the setting by identifying five key passages or quotes that reveal details with regard to the time or location in which the story takes place.
2. Explain how the war changed each character's social and financial status and how each character adapted (or failed to adapt) to life after the war.
3. Outline the major events in the story and explain, using evidence from the text, how the author uses these events to reveal important information about the characters.

About the Author

Charles W. Chesnutt (1858–1932), novelist and short-story writer, is known not only as a great writer but also as a great black writer who had a large white readership, which was rare in those days. He was born in Cleveland, Ohio, in 1858 to free black parents who had been forced to flee from North Carolina. His family moved back to Fayetteville, North Carolina, several years after the war, and Chesnutt grew up to witness the hardship, discrimination, and broken promises of the Reconstruction period.

Charles Chesnutt started his adult life as an educator, first as a teacher in all-black schools and later as a principal at a normal (teacher-training) school.

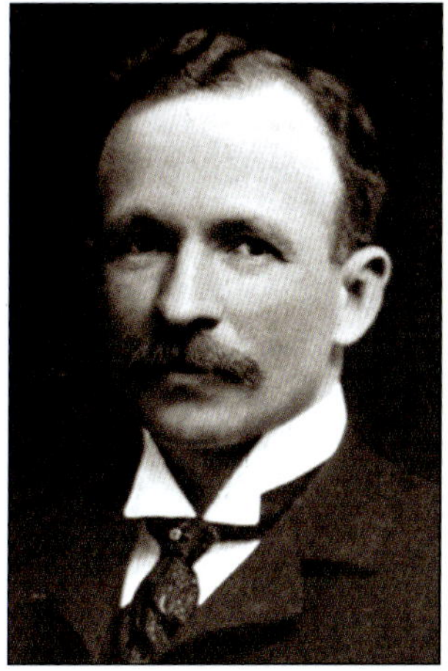

Writing was a background hobby for many years until Chesnutt published his first short story, "Uncle Peter's House," in 1885. Soon after, publication in the *Atlantic Monthly* put him on the road to success and a lasting reputation as a great storyteller. Houghton Mifflin published his first major story collection, *The Conjure Woman.* Chesnutt's other major works include *The House Behind the Cedars* (a novel), *Frederick Douglass: A Biography,* and *The Marrow of Tradition* (a story collection).

Prereading

from Their Eyes Were Watching God

by Zora Neale Hurston

When it was first published in 1937, *Their Eyes Were Watching God* met with strong criticism. In recent decades, however, it has been recognized as a stunning achievement, not only in the African-American literary tradition but in American letters has a whole. At first, it was rejected for being a love story rather than a political protest novel. It was also criticized for depicting rural blacks as relatively happy rather than embittered. Almost seven decades later, however, its portrait of a strong female controlling her own destiny is seen as an example of feminism far ahead of its time. Its faithful rendering of dialect is seen as belonging to the great tradition of Mark Twain and other masters of the vernacular.

Before the events of Chapter 12, which is presented here, we see the main character, born Janie Crawford, telling her life story to her trusted friend, Pheoby. Part of the story concerns her being married off by her grandmother to a much older man, Logan Killick. Unhappy beyond endurance, she runs off with Joe Starks, an ambitious man, who takes her to a black town in Florida where he runs the general store and serves as mayor.

As in her first marriage, in this one Janie is trapped inside her husband's vision of what a wife should be. In her first marriage, she was treated as a workhorse; in her second, as a fine lady suited only for porch-sitting and entertaining. After the death of Joe Starks, Janie finds someone to suit her own vision of happiness, someone with whom she can be completely herself. Society, however, doesn't see this person, colorfully named Tea Cake, as a suitable choice. He is too young and too likely to be only after her money. In this chapter we see how Janie stands up for herself and defends her choice. Although the remainder of the novel records many setbacks and one tragic flood, it also testifies to the rightness of Janey's choice.

One of the exciting aspects of Zora Neale Hurston's writing is its use of authentic rural Southern dialectical speech. Some passages may be slow reading because of the invented spellings that Hurston uses to render this dialect, but try reading these passages aloud to yourself. Doing so should help you to hear what is being said.

from Their Eyes Were Watching God

by Zora Neale Hurston

Chapter 12

It was after the picnic that the town began to notice things and got mad. Tea Cake and Mrs. Mayor Starks! All the men that she could get, and fooling with somebody like Tea Cake! Another thing, Joe Starks hadn't been dead but nine months and here she goes **sashaying** off to a picnic in pink linen. Done quit attending church, like she used to. Gone off to Sanford in a car with Tea Cake and her all dressed in blue! It was a shame. Done took to high heel slippers and a ten dollar hat! Looking like some young girl, always in blue because Tea Cake told her to wear it. Poor Joe Starks. Bet he turns over in his grave every day. Tea Cake and Janie gone fishing. Tea Cake and Janie gone to Orlando to the movies. Tea Cake and Janie gone to a dance. Tea Cake making flower beds in Janie's yard and seeding the garden for her. Chopping down that tree she never did like by the dining room window. All those signs of possession. Tea Cake and Janie playing checkers; playing coon-can;[1] playing Florida flip[2] on the store porch all afternoon as if nobody else was there. Day after day and week after week.

"Pheoby," Sam Watson said one night as he got in the bed, "Ah b'lieve yo' buddy is all tied up with dat Tea Cake shonough. Didn't b'lieve it at first."

"Aw she don't mean nothin' by it. Ah think she's sort of stuck on dat undertaker up at Sanford."

"It's somebody 'cause she looks might good dese days. New dresses and her hair combed a different way nearly every day. You got to have something to comb hair over. When you see uh woman doin' so much rakin' in her head, she's combin' at some man or 'nother."

"'Course she kin do as she please, but dat's uh good chance she got up a Sanford. De man's wife died and he got uh lovely place tuh take her to—already furnished. Better'n her house Joe left her."

"You better sense her intuh things then 'cause Tea Cake can't do nothin' but help her spend whut she got. Ah reckon dat's whut he's after. Throwin' away whut Joe Starks worked hard tuh git tuhgether."

"Dat's de way it looks. Still and all, she's her own woman. She oughta know by now whut she wants tuh do."

"De men wuz talkin' 'bout it in de grove tuhday and givin' her and Tea Cake both de devil. Dey figger he's spendin' on her now in order tuh make her spend on him later."

"Umph! Umph! Umph!"

"Oh dey got it all figgered out. Maybe it ain't as bad as they say, but they talk it and make it sound real bad on her part."

---

1 **coon-can.** A card game for two players, an early version of rummy

2 **Florida flip.** A gambling game of some sort

VOCABULARY IN PLACE

- **sashay,** *v.* To walk, move, or proceed easily or nonchalantly

"Dat's jealousy and **malice**. Some uh dem very mens wants tuh do whut dey claim deys skeered Tea Cake is doin'."

"De Pastor claim Tea Cake don't 'low her tuh come tuh church only once in awhile 'cause he want dat change tuh buy gas wid. Just draggin' de woman away from church. But anyhow, she's yo' bosom friend, so you better go see 'bout her. Drop uh lil hint here and dere and if Tea Cake is tryin' tuh rob her she kin see and know. Ah laks de woman and Ah sho would hate tuh see her come up lak Mis' Tyler."

"Aw mah God, naw! Reckon Ah better step over dere tomorrow and have some chat wid Janie. She jus' ain't thinkin' whut she doin', dat's all."

The next morning Pheoby picked her way over to Janie's house like a hen to a neighbor's garden. Stopped and talked a little with everyone she met, turned aside momentarily to pause at a porch or two—going straight by walking crooked. So her firm intention looked like an accident and she didn't have to give her opinion to folks along the way.

Janie acted glad to see her and after a while Pheoby **broached** her with, "Janie, everybody's talkin' 'bout how dat Tea Cake is draggin' you round tuh places you ain't used tuh. Baseball games and huntin' and fishin'. He don't know you'se useter uh more high time crowd than dat. You always did class off."

Why might the people in the town be upset that Janie is spending time with Tea Cake?

"Jody classed me off. Ah didn't. Naw, Pheoby, Tea Cake ain't draggin' me off nowhere Ah don't want tuh go. Ah always did want tuh git round uh whole heap, but Jody wouldn't 'low me tuh. When Ah wasn't in de store he wanted me tuh jes sit wid folded hands and sit dere. And Ah'd sit dere wid de walls creepin' up on me and squeezin' all de life outa me. Pheoby, dese educated women got uh heap of things to sit down and consider. Somebody done tole 'em what to set down for. Nobody ain't told poor me, so sittin' still worries me. Ah wants tuh utilize mah-self all over."

"But, Janie, Tea Cake, whilst he ain't no jail-bird, he ain't got uh dime tuh cry. Ain't you skeered he's jes after yo' money—him bein' younger than you?"

"He ain't never ast de first penny from me yet, and if he love property he ain't no different from all de rest of us. All dese ole men dat's settin' round me is after de same thing. They's three mo' wider women in town, how come dey don't break dey neck after dem? 'Cause dey ain't got nothin', dat's why."

"Folks seen you out in colors and dey thinks you ain't payin' de right amount uh respect tuh yo' dead husband."

What color would a widow be expected to wear? What social convention is Janie violating?

"Ah ain't grievin' so why do Ah hafta mourn? Tea Cake love me in blue, so Ah wears it. Jody ain't never in his life picked out no color for me. De world picked out black and white for mournin', Joe didn't. So Ah wasn't wearin' it for him. Ah was wearin' it for de rest of y'all."

"But anyhow, watch yo'self, Janie, and don't be took advantage of. You know how dese young men is wid older women. Most of de time dey's after whut dey kin git, then dey's gone lak uh turkey through de corn."

"Tea Cake don't talk dat way. He's aimin' tuh make hisself permanent wid me. We done made up our mind tuh marry."

"Janie, you'se yo' own woman, and Ah hope you know whut you doin'. Ah sho hope you ain't lak uh possum—de older you gits, de less sense yuh got. Ah'd feel uh whole heap

VOCABULARY IN PLACE

- **malice,** *n.* Desire to harm others or see others harmed
- **broach,** *v.* To bring up as a subject for discussion

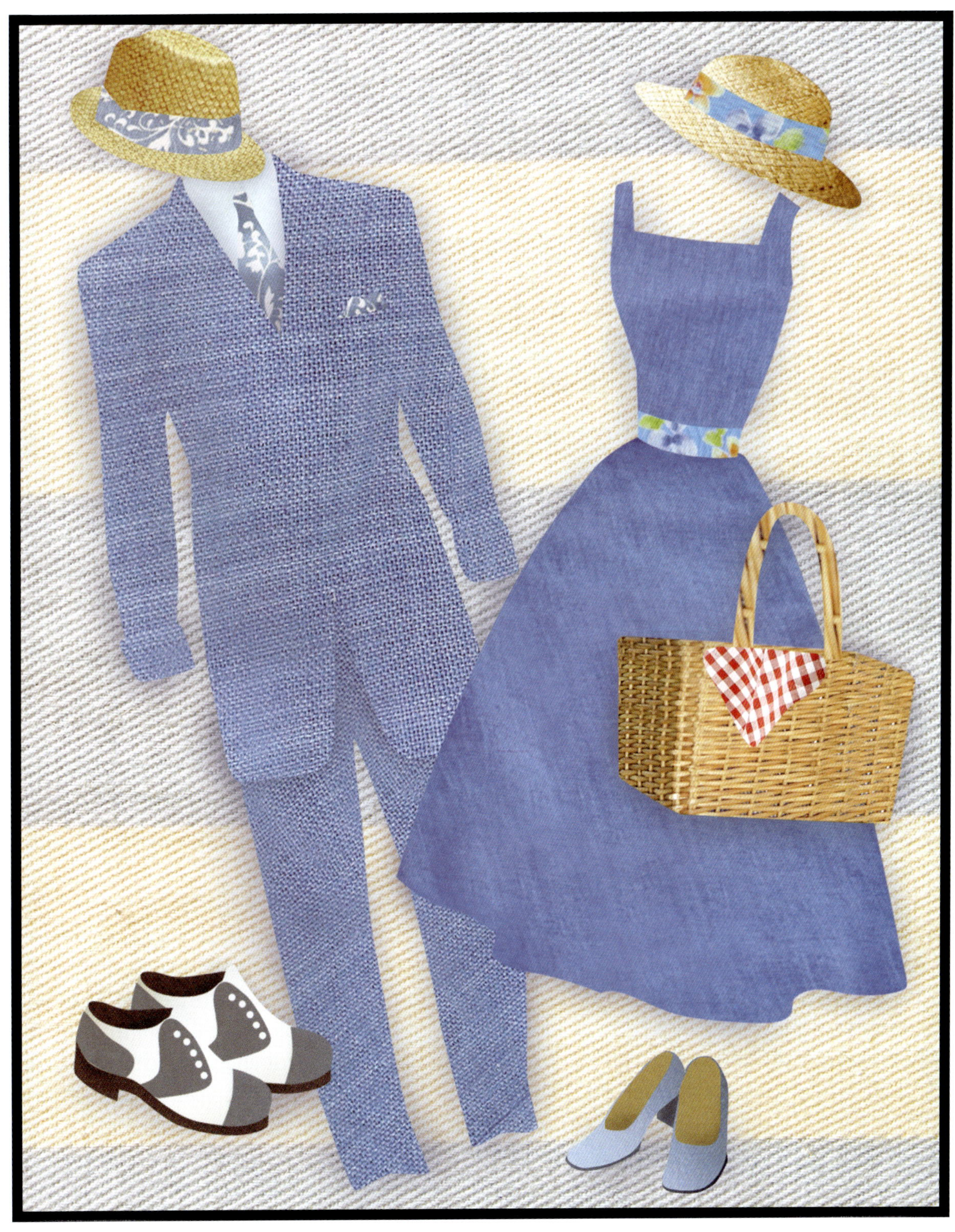

Why does Pheoby think that the man in Sanford is the better choice?

better 'bout yuh if you wuz maryin' dat man up dere in Sanford. He got somethin' tuh put long side uh whut you got and dat make it more better. He's endurable."

"Still and all Ah'd ruther be wid Tea Cake."

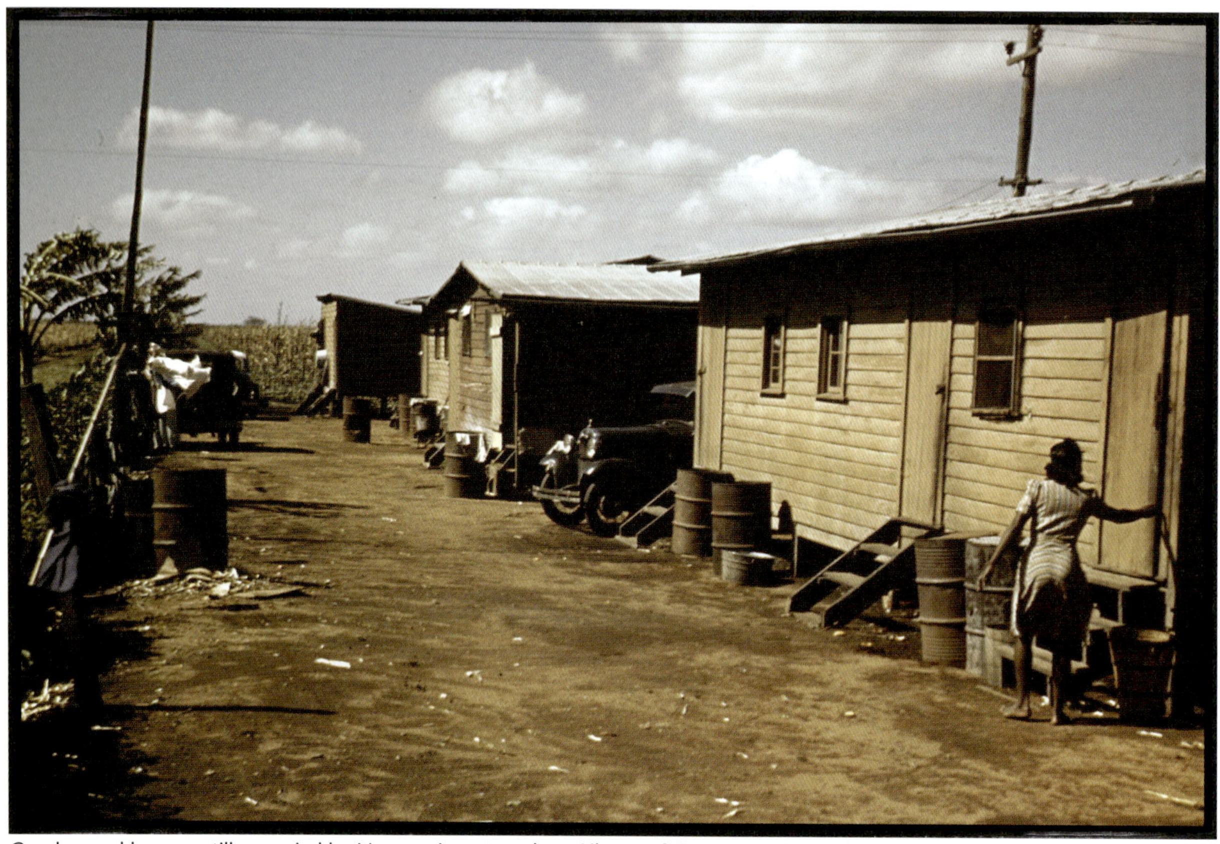

Condemned houses, still occupied by Negro migrant workers. Library of Congress, LC-DIG-fsqc-la34400.

"Well, if yo' mind is already made up, 'tain't nothin' nobody kin do. But you'se takin' uh awful chance."

"No mo' than Ah took befo' and no mo' than anybody else takes when dey gits married. It always changes folks, and sometimes it brings out dirt and meanness dat even de person didn't know thy had in 'em theyselves. You know dat. Maybe Tea Cake might turn out lak dat. Maybe not. Anyhow Ah'm ready and willin' tuh try 'im."

"Well, when you aim tuh step off?"

"Dat we don't know. De store is got tuh be sold and then we'se goin' off somewhere tuh git married."

"How come you sellin' out de store?"

"'Cause Tea Cake ain't no Jody Starks, and if he tried tuh be, it would be uh complete flom-muck. But de minute Ah marries 'im everybody is goin tuh be makin' comparisons. So us is goin' off somewhere and start all over in Tea Cake's way. Dis ain't no business proposition, and no race after property and titles. Dis is uh love game. Ah done lived Grandma's way, now Ah means tuh live mine."

"What you mean by dat, Janie?"

"She was borned in slavery time when folks, dat is black folks, didn't sit down anytime dey lak it. So sittin' on porches lak de white madam looked lak uh mighty fine thing tuh her. Dat's whut she wanted for me—don't keer whut it cost. Git up on uh high chair and sit dere. She didn't have time tuh think whut tuh do after you got up on de stool uh do nothin'. De object wuz tuh git dere. So Ah got up on de high stool lak she told me, but Pheoby, Ah done nearly **languished** tuh death

VOCABULARY IN PLACE

- **languish,** *v.* To waste away, become weak or feeble

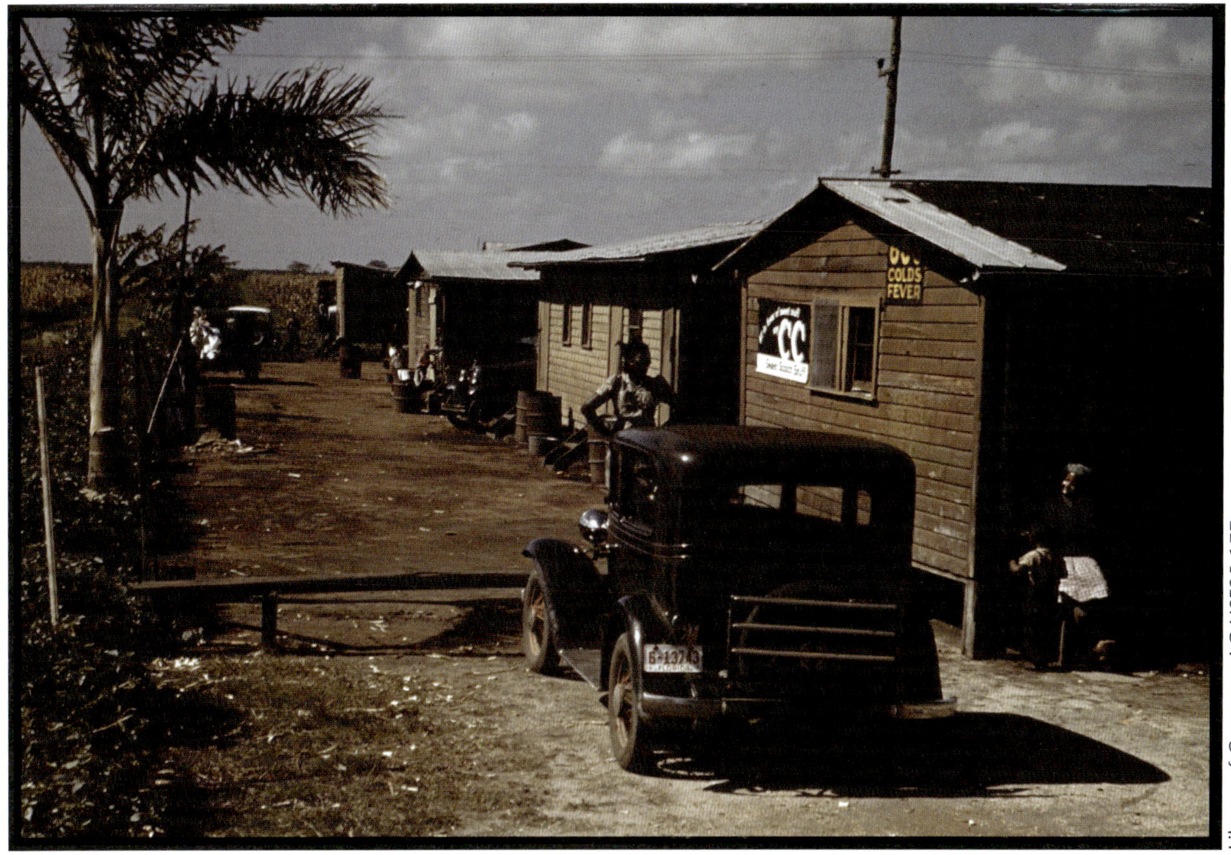

Library of Congress, LC-USF35-177.

up dere. Ah felt like de world wuz cryin' extry and Ah ain't read de common news yet."

"Maybe so, Janie. Still and all Ah'd love tuh experience it for just one year. It look lak heben tuh me from where Ah'm at."

"Ah reckon so."

"But anyhow, Janie, you be keerful 'bout dis sellin' out and goin' off wid strange men. Look whut happened tuh Annie Tyler. Took whut little she had and went off tuh Tampa wid dat boy dey call Who Flung. It's somethin' tuh think about."

"It sho is. Still Ah ain't Mis' Tyler and Tea Cake ain't no Who Flung, and he ain't no stranger tuh me. We'se just as good as married already. But Ah ain't puttin' it in de street. Ah'm telling' *you*."

"Ah jus lak uh chicken. Chicken drink water, but he don't pee-pee."

"Oh, Ah know you don't talk. We ain't shame faced. We jus' ain't ready tuh make no big kerflommuck as yet."

"You doin' right not tuh talk it, but Janie, you'se takin' uh mighty big chance."

"'Tain't so big uh chance as it seem lak, Pheoby. Ah'm older than Tea Cake, yes. But he done showed me where it's de thought dat makes de difference in ages. If people thinks de same they can make it all right. So in the beginnin' new thoughts had tuh be thought and new words said. After Ah got used tuh dat, we gits 'long jus' fine. He done taught me de maiden language all over. Wait till you see de new blue satin Tea Cake done picked out for me tuh stand up wid him in. High heel slippers, necklace, earrings, *everything* he wants tuh see me in. Some of dese mornin's and it won't be long, you gointuh wake up callin' me and Ah'll be gone." ■

How would you describe Janie's thoughts about Tea Cake?

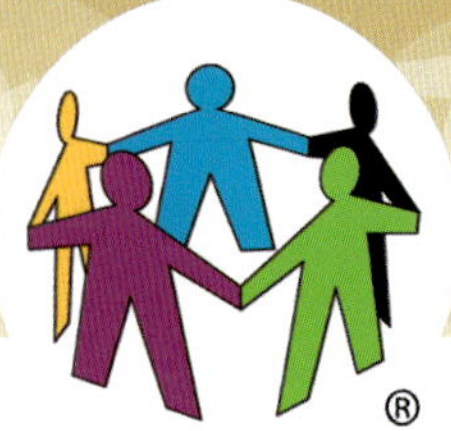

Understanding the Selection

Recalling

1. What did people in the town begin to notice after the picnic?
2. What, in particular, did Sam Watson notice about Janie?
3. What does Pheoby warn Janie about?
4. What does Janie tell Pheoby she is about to do?

Interpreting

1. Why would people be concerned about whom Janie is dating?
2. Why does Sam Watson want his wife, Pheoby, to talk to Janie?
3. Does Janie take Pheoby's warnings about Tea Cake seriously? Why, or why not?
4. Why does Janie think she and Tea Cake will be better off elsewhere?

Synthesizing

1. Explain why Janie believes that she and Tea Cake have a better chance at happiness than most people think they have. What does she believe is the most important aspect of a relationship, something more important than being of a similar age and class?

Delving Deeper

Understanding Literature

The Literature of Social Criticism. One important function served by literary works is that of **social criticsm**—exposing aspects of social life that are unpleasant or dangerous or counterproductive. In the 1930s, when Hurston was writing, many critics, influenced by the Marxism that was in the air, believed that literature should serve, primarily, the purpose of social criticism. Such critics attacked Hurston's work for not being sufficiently political and socially conscious. In recent years, however, Hurston's work has undergone considerable reevaluation. *Their Eyes Were Watching God* does, in fact, imply an important social criticism in that it attacks the tendency of people in communities to be gossipy and judgmental and to become involved in other people's private business. In the novel, Hurston upholds an ideal of romantic individualism embodied by her central character, Janie. Some critics would argue that such romantic individualism is the quintessential American character trait and that *Their Eyes Were Watching God* is thus a quintessentially American novel.

About the Author

Zora Neale Hurston (1891–1960) was the author of four published novels, a memoir, two collections of African-American folklore, and more than fifty short stories, essays, and plays. Her work was not always favorably received, and her books were out of print at the time of her death. In recent decades, however, she has been rediscovered by such writers as Alice Walker, and her most famous novel, *Their Eyes Were Watching God,* has become a staple of literature classes.

Hurston's childhood was spent in Eatonville, Florida, the first incorporated black town in America. Her father was a three-term mayor of the town. She attended Howard University and later, after going to New York City, studied anthropology under Franz Boas at Barnard. She did field work for Boas in Harlem and there became acquainted with Langston Hughes, Countee Cullen, and other notables of the Harlem Renaissance.

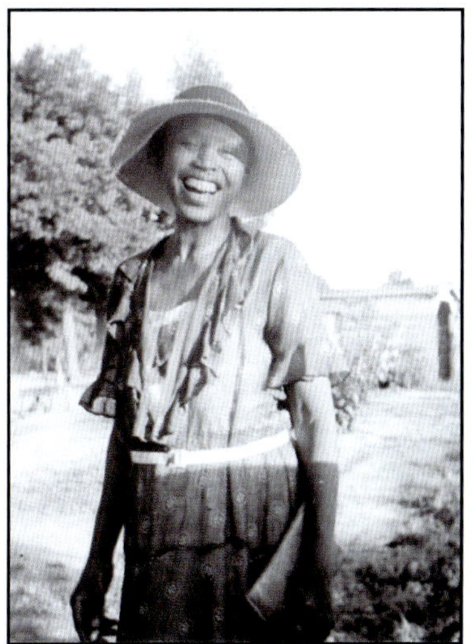

Hurston's interest in anthropology took her back to Florida, where she collected material for her book *Mules and Men.* Her travels to Jamaica and Haiti are reflected in *Tell My Horse.* Her interest in folklife inspired her to reclaim the South as the locus of her literary imagination.

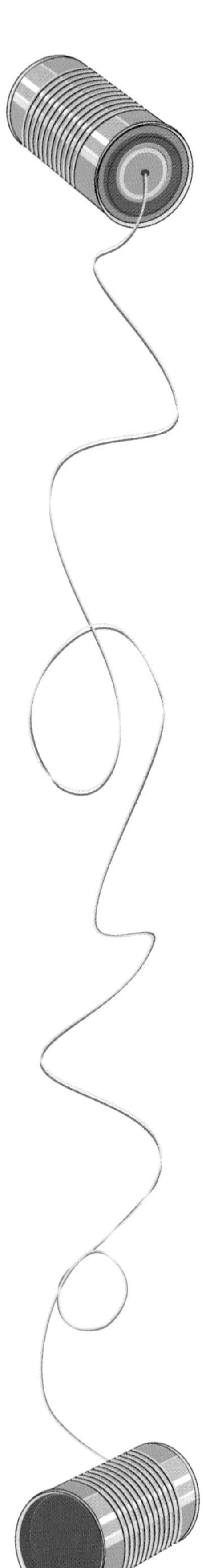

Unit 3

Speaking and Listening Skills: Giving a Speech

In Units 2 and 3 of this book, you have had the opportunity to encounter the work of some of the greatest orators, or public speakers, that this country has ever known—Frederick Douglass, Sojourner Truth, and Marcus Garvey. In Unit 4, you will encounter two men who can easily be called the greatest public speakers that the United States has ever produced—Malcolm X and Martin Luther King, Jr.

Public speaking is an ancient art form. For as long as there have been human societies, there has been the need for people to speak in public. There will be many, many occasions in your lifetime for you to do this. Mastering the skill of public speaking can make you a powerful and influential person. Public speaking is a skill, and it can be learned, just as one can learn how to ride a bicycle or how to play the piano.

The Elements of a Speech

When planning a speech, you need to give thought to each of the following elements of the speaking situation:

1. **Topic.** What are you going to speak about? Make sure that the topic is relevant and of interest to your audience.

2. **Purpose.** What do you want the speech to accomplish? Do you want to inform your audience? to entertain those in the audience? to move audience members to take some action?

3. **Audience.** Who will be in your audience? What do audience members already know about your subject? What will you have to explain to them? What will move them or interest them? What will appeal to them?

4. **Occasion.** On what occasion will you be speaking? How can you relate what you are saying to the occasion? What kind of speech does the occasion call for?

5. **Mode.** Should your speech be primarily one that entertains, informs, describes, tells a story, or persuades?

6. **Tone.** What should be the primary emotion communicated by the speech? How should the emotions communicated by the speech vary in the course of it?

7. **Delivery.** In what sort of space will the speech be delivered? How loudly will you have to speak to be heard clearly? Will you be able to walk around and interact with your audience? How can you vary your pace, pitch, tone, volume, stresses, facial expressions, body language, and proximity to your audience in order to make your performance (for every speech is a performance) engaging and interesting?

Preparing a Speech

Prepare a speech just as you would any extended piece of writing. Come up with a topic. Think about the topic, purpose, audience, occasion, mode, tone, and delivery of the speech. Make decisions about each of these. Do research on your topic. Draft the speech, making sure that you have a clear introduction, body, and conclusion. The introduction should be designed to grab the attention of your audience. Good ways to introduce a speech are by telling a story, posing an interesting question, telling a relevant joke, or sharing some startling or amazing or thought-provoking facts. Write out your speech in full and revise it. What you do once you have a final draft will depend upon the method of delivery that you plan to use.

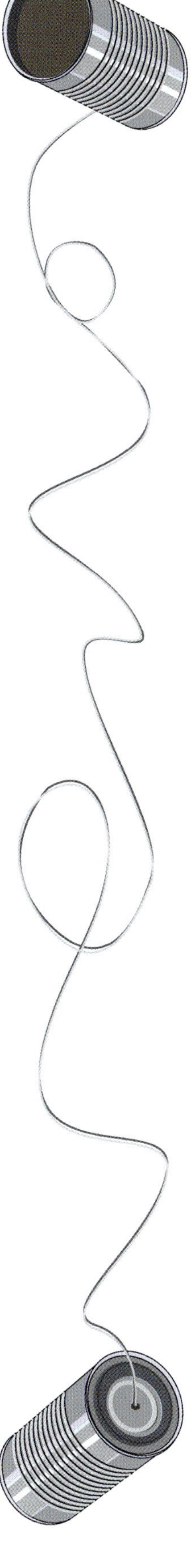

Choosing a Method of Delivery

NEVER simply read a speech from your transcript. Such reading aloud is DEADLY for an audience. Instead, follow one of these methods:

Memorization Method. Commit the entire speech to memory and practice it several times, preferably in front of an audience, to make sure that your memory of the whole is secure. Keep the transcript of the speech in front of you as you deliver it so that you will have something to fall back on if your memory momentarily fails you.

Notes Method. Write out the entire speech, but then work from your written version to produce note cards for the speech. Each note card will consist basically of an outline point from your speech. Do not simply copy parts of the speech onto the note cards. Instead, translate parts of the speech into corresponding phrases. Commit the speech to memory and use the note cards to jog your memory about the various parts of what you want to say.

Rehearsing Your Speech

Make sure to rehearse the speech thoroughly before delivering it. Thorough rehearsal is a good way to combat stage fright. Each time that you run through your speech, try to heighten, just a little bit, the variations of pace, pitch, tone, volume, stresses, facial expressions, body language, and proximity that will make your speech appealing.

Assignment: Choose one of the following topics, or a topic of your own, for a public speech:

Remembering . . . (one of the authors from Unit 3, such as Langston Hughes or Charles Chesnutt. The speech should be one that might be given on the anniversary of the author's death.)

The Importance of Participating in the Political System by Voting (emphasizing how hard it was for African Americans to win the right to vote in the first place)

Why Vigilante Justice Is Wrong (with emphasis on the sad history of lynching as detailed by Ida Wells-Barnett)

What It Means to Be Black in America Today (with reference to and comparison with "Of Our Spiritual Strivings" by W. E. B. Du Bois)

Follow the steps outlined above in Preparing a Speech, Choosing a Method of Delivery, and Rehearsing Your Speech.

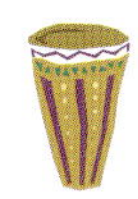
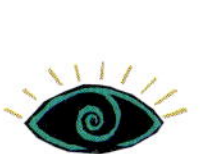
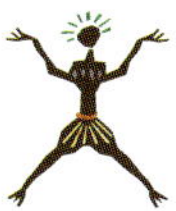
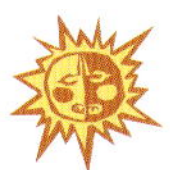
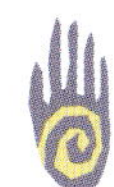
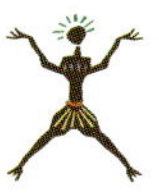
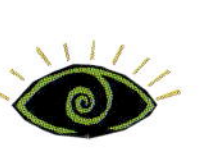
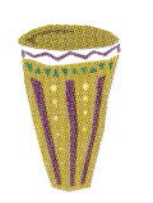

Focus on: The Birth of Uniquely American Music

Origins of the Blues

After the Civil War, a new voice began to be heard in the South. It sang of trials and troubles but in a spirit that raised up those who heard it and gave them hope. Music does that to people. It makes hard times easier to bear. To understand this music, it helps to imagine what the country was like at that time. First of all, in the South there was the devastation caused by the Civil War. Many people were homeless, and many were out of work. The nation as a whole was largely agricultural, and small cities were loosely connected by a sparse web of railroads, dirt roads, and rivers. Along these rails, roads, and rivers, recently emancipated African Americans traveled, looking for work and bringing with them their spirituals, work songs, and field hollers. According to Amiri Baraka, author of *Blues People,* many of these men and women carried with them instruments they picked up along the way, some of them discarded by former soldiers. With no formal training as musicians, they taught themselves to play these instruments. Rather than reading sheet music, they used the instruments to imitate the sounds of the human voice, including the distinctive "blue notes" of the field hollers (more about these later).

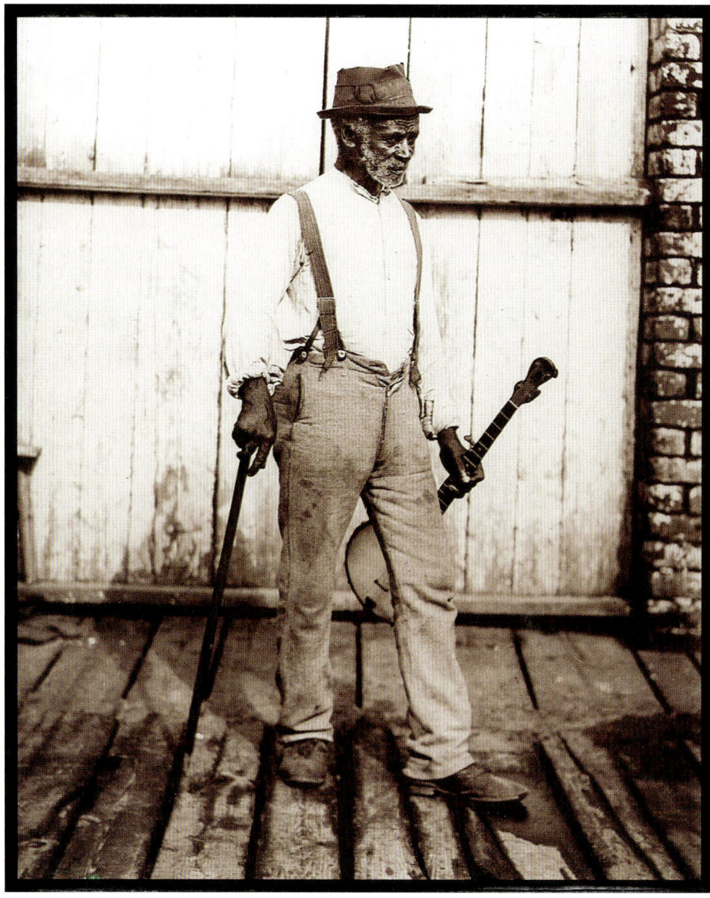

As freed slaves moved about the country in search of work, they transformed the musical traditions they knew into a new vehicle for self expression, **the blues.** This new music, which originated in rural areas, had no single known creator. It was truly a folk music, originating among singers now unknown. Whereas the spirituals and work songs had been primarily communal—sung by groups of people—the new music was at first solitary, sung by a single person without accompaniment or perhaps accompanied by a banjo or guitar.

The Content of Blues Songs. What makes a song "blues"? The answer is fairly complex. Having "the blues" has come to mean feeling down-hearted. Blues songs often dealt with life's troubles, such as problems in love, the lack of money, the difficulty of finding work, or the urge to move on to some better place. Often blues tunes implied a story. They told the woes of the singer, as in this song from the 1920s, wherein Richard Jones adopts a female perspective:

Trouble in Mind,
by Richard Jones

Trouble in mind, I'm blue,
But I won't be blue always,
Cause the sun's gonna shine
In my back door someday.

Now all you men's the same
But not a one enough to change
my name,
Cause that sun's gonna shine
In my back door someday.

I'm gonna lay my head
On that lonesome railroad line
And let the two nineteen
Ease my troubled mind.

Trouble in mind, I'm blue,
But I won't be blue always,
Cause that wind's gonna come
And blow my blues away.

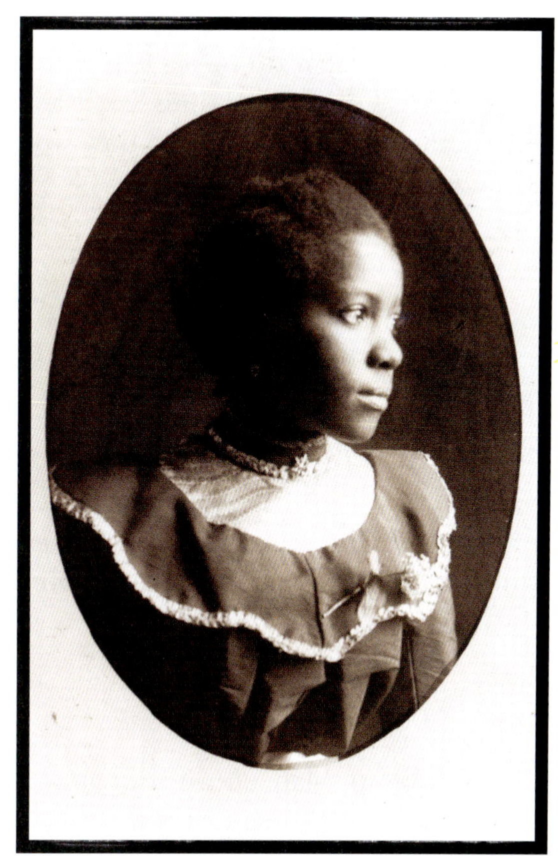

Young Woman, circa 1900. Library of Congress, LC-USZ62-124776.

The Structure of a Blues Tune. Early blues tunes varied considerably in structure, but eventually most took the form that has come to be known as **12-bar blues.** A 12-bar blues tune generally had several verses and a chorus that is repeated. Both the verses and the chorus were made up of 12 bars, or measures, with a particular chord progression. Blues tunes were unique in starting and ending on a dominant seventh chord. A blues in the key of A would have a progression like this:

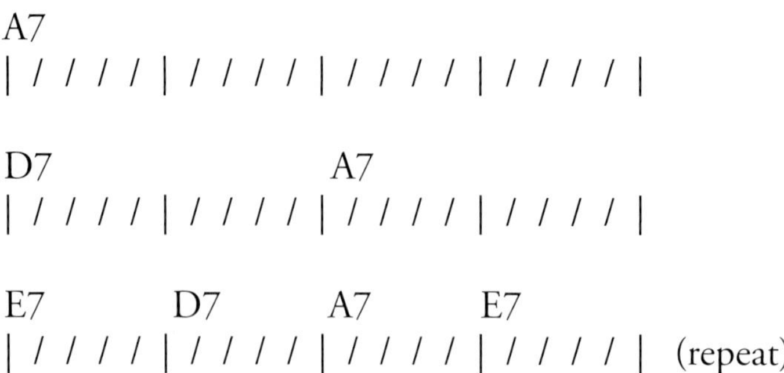

Of course, many variations were played on this basic pattern. Typically, in traditional call-and-response fashion, a 12-bar blues tune would begin with a repeated line (the call) that was followed by a third line (the response). Here is an example, written by an African-American survivor of the great Louisiana Flood of 1927. After this flood, African Americans were herded onto levees and held at gunpoint at the behest of local white farm owners so they wouldn't escape and head north to find work.

Woke up this morning, couldn't even get out my door.
Woke up this morning, couldn't even get out my door.
The levee broke and this town is overflowed.

—from "Broken Levee Blues"
by Alice Pearson

Note the use of this three-line, call-and-response structure in the following famous country blues tune by **Blind Willie McTell** (1901–1959):

Statesboro[1] Blues,
by Blind Willie McTell

Wake up, Mama, turn your lamp down low,
Wake up, Mama, turn your lamp down low;
Have you got the nerve to drive Papa McTell from your do'?

My mother died and left me reckless,
My Daddy died an, left me wild, wild, wild;
Mother died and left me reckless,
Daddy died an, left me wild, wild, wild;
No, I'm not good lookin, but I'm some sweet woman's angel child.

You're a mighty mean woman, do me this a-way,
You're a mighty mean woman, to me this a-way;

[1] **Statesboro.** A city in Georgia

Goin' to leave this town, pretty mama, goin' away to stay.

I loved a woman, better than I'd ever seen,
I once loved a woman, better than I ever seen;
Treated me like I was a king an' she was a dog-gone queen.

Sister tell your brother,
Brother tell your aunt,
I had to tell your uncle,
Uncle tell my cousin,
Cousin tell my friend,
Goin' up the country, Mama don't you want to go?
Missin' you bad gal, missin' one or two more.

Big Eighty[2] left Savannah,[3]
Lord, and didn't stop,
Y'ought to saw that colored
fireman when he got that
boiler hot,
You could reach over in the
corner, Mama, hand me my
travellin' shoes;
You know by that I've got them
Statesboro blues.

My sister got 'em,
Daddy got 'em,
Brother got 'em,
Mam' got 'em,
I got 'em,
Woke up this mornin', we had
them Statesboro blues;
I looked over in the corner,
grandma and grandpa had
'em too.

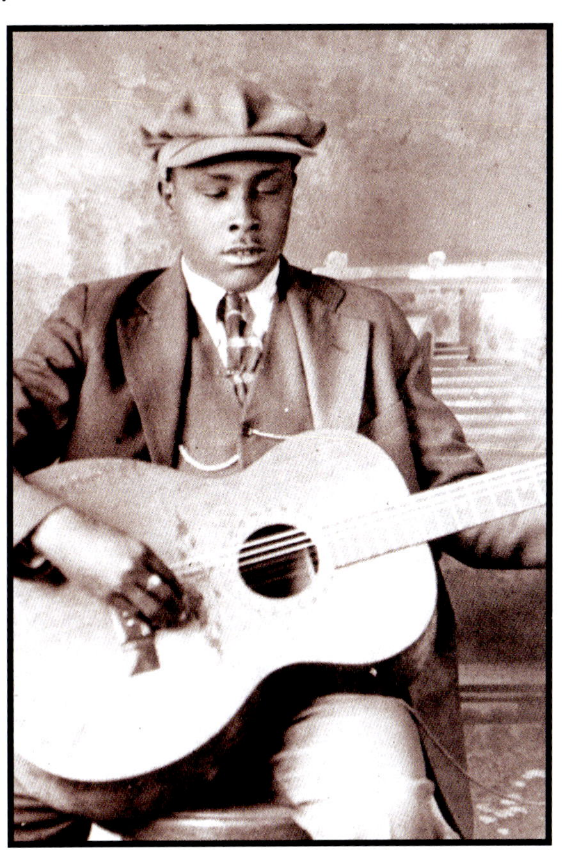

Blind Willie McTell. Twelve-string finger-picking blues guitarist.

The Blues Scale. In imitation of the human voice, in a manner borrowed from West African music, blues songs were built upon what was known as a **blues scale**, which contains a lowered, or flatted, third and seventh and an augmented, or raised, fourth, as follows:

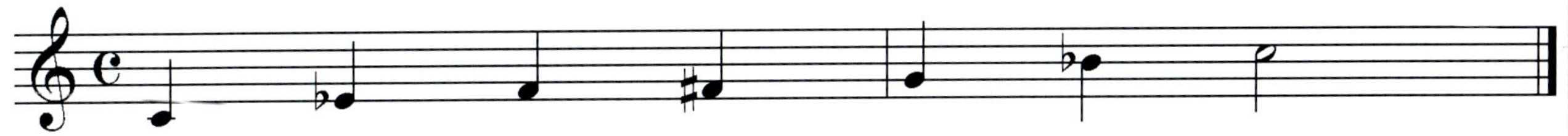

[2] **Big Eighty.** A train

[3] **Savannah.** A city in Georgia

(For readers who are musicians, this is the same as a minor pentatonic scale with an added augmented fourth.) The flatted third and seventh and the augmented fourth are known as **blue notes.** They give blues music its distinctive character. Blues performers often imitated the human voice by approaching individual notes indirectly. For example, a guitar player might slide up or down to a note, play one note and bend the string until the next higher note was reached, or play one note and then hammer on or pull off to sound another note. Slurring and bending notes was also common among blues horn players. These effects, combined with blue notes, gave the music its distinctively "bluesy" feel.

Instrumentation for the Blues. Like the music itself, many musical instruments used to play early blues had their origins in Africa. One such device, known as the **diddley bow,** is a single stringed instrument (technically, a type of chordophone) that recalls several related African instruments (See the picture on page 81). Common in the American South from the slavery era into the twentieth century, the diddley bow consists of a length of wire fastened to and stretched along the wall of a house or a portable length of fence picket. The instrument was played by plucking the string with a nail or a stick and sliding a glass bottle or cotton reel along its length to produce a whining pitch. Many blues musicians had their earliest musical training on the diddley bow and brought this sliding technique, sometimes referred to as "worrying" a note, to the guitar.

The legendary street singer and guitarist **Blind Lemon Jefferson** (1893–1929) is thought to have been the first (in 1926) to record the **slide guitar** style, fretting the guitar with a bottleneck or the blade of a knife. Altering the pitch of the strings in this **bottleneck slide style** became an important element of the blues and is still in use today. The slide style enabled a player to make the instrument imitate the effect of field hollers. On the piano, each note is discrete and notes cannot be slurred or bent, but early blues piano players overcame this difficulty by quickly alternating flanking white and black keys.

African-American musical variety shows of the vaudeville era often featured musicians blowing on various kinds of ceramic **jugs** with narrow necks, a practice that also had African precedents. The blues was played on such an instrument by buzzing one's lips near the opening of the jug without actually touching that opening. Doing so produced a bass tone that could be modified in pitch by tightening or loosening one's lips. As a bass instrument, the jug served in the rhythm section of an ensemble, alongside another principal jug band instrument, the

gut bucket, or **washtub bass,** which used a metal washtub as a resonator. Vaudeville shows featuring jug bands were a popular form of entertainment in such river cities as Memphis and Louisville in the early twentieth century until supplanted by swing jazz during the Depression era.

Early blues players favored string instruments like the guitar, the banjo, the harmonica, and the fiddle, in part because these instruments were inexpensive and easily carried. Over time, the piano, brass and woodwind instruments, basses, and drums were added to accompany blues singing. But whatever the instrument, it was always used, in part, to carry on a dialogue (again, often in call-and-response fashion) with the voice being accompanied.

Blues Styles and Places. Blues styles are often identified by geography as urban or rural, and among the country blues, there are further divisions by region. One of the most hauntingly powerful of blues styles emerged from the Mississippi Delta. **Delta blues** is characterized by passionate vocals and by the use of harmonicas and slide guitars. **Piedmont blues,** originating in the eastern United States in the lands adjacent to the Appalachian Mountains, is distinguished by an intricate finger-picking guitar style. Most varieties of country blues were performed by a solo singer, self-accompanied on the guitar, joined by an occasional **harmonica** or **washboard** percussion. Since the majority of the country blues musicians of note were self taught, each developed his own style of playing.

The advent of commercially available sound recordings in the 1920s led to a recording frenzy for African-American blues musicians. Despite their popularity, few blues artists received fair pay. Instead, their talents were exploited to enrich record companies. Fortunately, however, the rush to record so-called "race music artists" did produce a priceless archive of ground breaking music.

Blues Artists

Many people consider **Robert Johnson** (1911–1938) to have been the greatest of all the country blues artists. A legendary blues man, Johnson traveled widely and was enthusiastically received by audiences entranced by his virtuosity on the guitar and his stunning song writing. In his short life, he composed many of the greatest country blues tunes, ones that were subsequently "covered" in the 1960s and 70s by such rock-and-roll performers as Led Zeppelin, the Rolling Stones, Eric Clapton, Fleetwood Mac, and the Red Hot Chili Peppers. Johnson's compositions include many of the most famous of blues songs, including "Cross Road Blues," ".32-20 Blues," "Come on in My Kitchen," "Sweet Home Chicago," and "Love in Vain." Many legends surround this mysterious man, most of them untrue. He is said, for example, to have died from poisoning, but in fact died from pneumonia after recovering from poisoning. One thing is certain: His music strongly influenced and helped to shape the popular music of the late twentieth century. Here are the lyrics to his famous "Cross Road Blues":

Cross Road Blues,
by Robert Johnson

I went to the crossroad,
Fell down on my knee,
Went to the crossroad,
Fell down on my knee,

Asked the Lord above to have mercy,
Save poor Bob, if you please.

Uumh, standing at the crossroad,
I tried to flag a ride,
Standing at the crossroad,
I tried to flag a ride,
Didn't nobody seem to know me,
Everybody passed me by.

Uumh, the sun going down, boy,
Dark gonna catch me here,
Uumh, dark gonna catch me here,
I haven't got no loving sweet woman
That loves and feels my care.

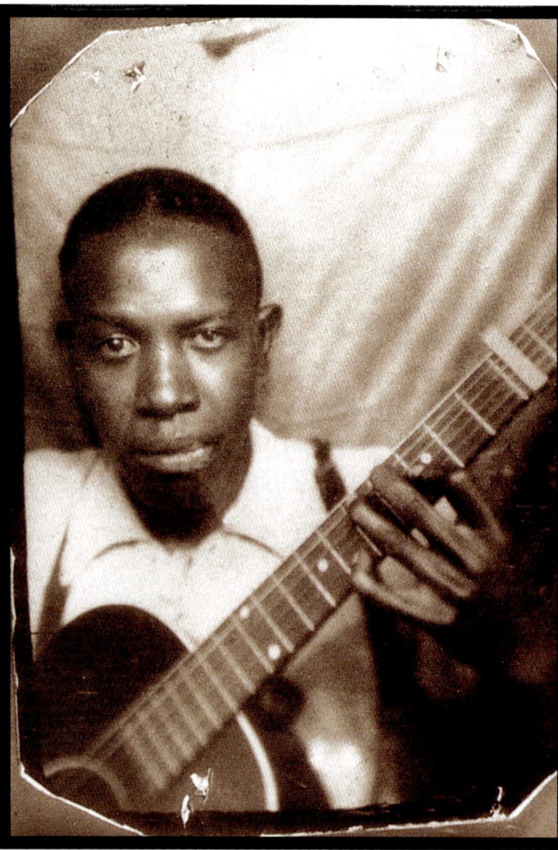

Robert Johnson. Legendary king of the Delta blues.

You can run, you can run,
Tell my friend, poor Willie Brown,
You can run,
Tell my friend, poor Willie Brown,
Lord, that I'm standing at the crossroad, babe,
I believe I'm sinking down.

One of the most interesting of the country blues artists was **Huddie Ledbetter** (1885–1949), whom folklorist **John Lomax** (1867–1948) discovered at Angola Prison in Louisiana. Called **Leadbelly** because he was famously tough, able to withstand most any punch, he was in and out of prison several times. He once won his freedom by composing this song as an appeal to the governor:

Please, Governor Neff, be good 'n' kind.
Have mercy on my great long time . . .
I don't see to save my soul.
If I don't get a pardon, try me on a parole . . .
If I had you, Governor Neff, like you got me,
I'd wake up in the mornin', and I'd set you free.

Another of Leadbelly's appeals for release, this time from Huntsville Prison in Texas, was included on the flip side of his signature song, "Goodnight Irene," which has become a standard of the folk music repertoire:

Goodnight, Irene,
by Huddie Ledbetter

Irene, Goodnight.
Irene, Goodnight.
Goodnight, Irene.
Goodnight, Irene.
I'll see you in my dreams.
Sometimes I live in the city.
Sometimes I live in the town.
Sometimes I take a great notion
To jump in the river and drown.

Last Saturday night I got
married,
Me and my wife settled down.
Now me and my wife are parted.
I'm gonna take another stroll
downtown.

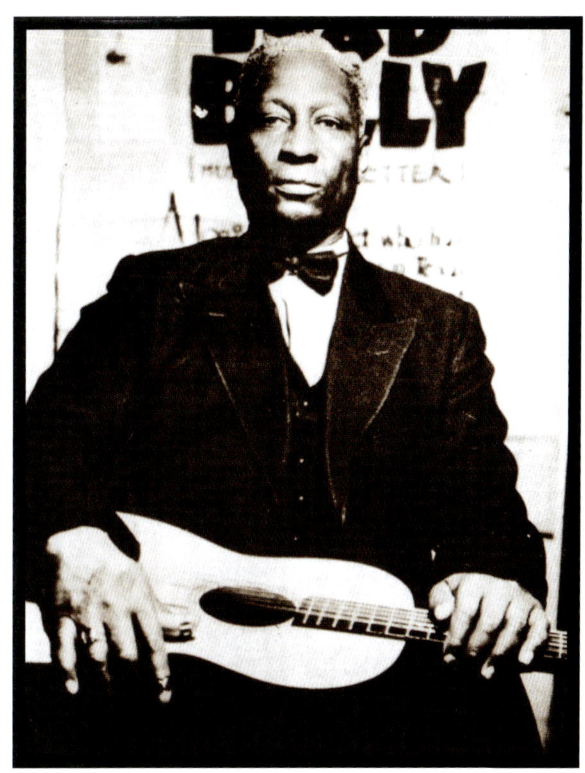

Huddie William Ledbetter (Leadbelly). Blues musician.

Stop ramblin',
stop your gamblin',
Stop stayin' out late at night
Go home to your wife and fam'ly.
There by your fireside bright.
She caused me to weep. She caused me to moan.
Caused me to leave my home.
But the very last words that I heard her say
Was please sing me one more song.

Irene, Goodnight.
Irene, Goodnight.
Good night, Irene. Goodnight, Irene.
I'll see you in my dreams.

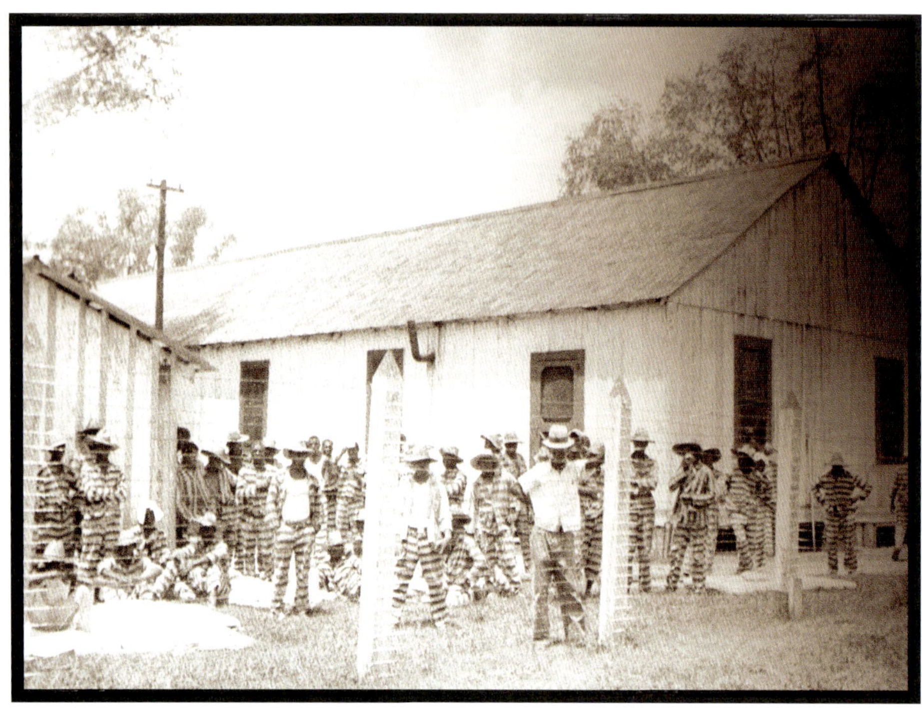

Prisoners in Angola, Louisisana. Huddie Ledbetter in the foreground. Library of Congress, LC-USZ61-1347.

Rural entertainment establishments located in remote parts of the Mississippi Delta country provided places where the blues could flourish. They were called **juke joints,** probably after a word in a West African language that meant wicked or disorderly.

Sometimes locales other than juke joints figured in the early history of the blues. **Dockery Plantation** in Cleveland, Mississippi, is considered by some to be the birthplace of the blues. A young resident employee of this plantation, **Charlie Patton** (1891–1934), proved himself to be an exceptional guitarist and master showman who influenced countless blues musicians. This lasting legacy earned him the title "Father of the Delta Blues." Future blues luminary **Chester Arthur Burnett,** better known as **Howlin' Wolf** (1910–1976), worked at Dockery Plantation in order to serve a musical apprenticeship under Patton. Numerous blues legends, such as **Eddie "Son" House** (1894–1970) and **Tommy Johnson** (1896–1956), were known to drop by the tenant quarters at Dockery to play along with the in-house musicians at parties and dances.

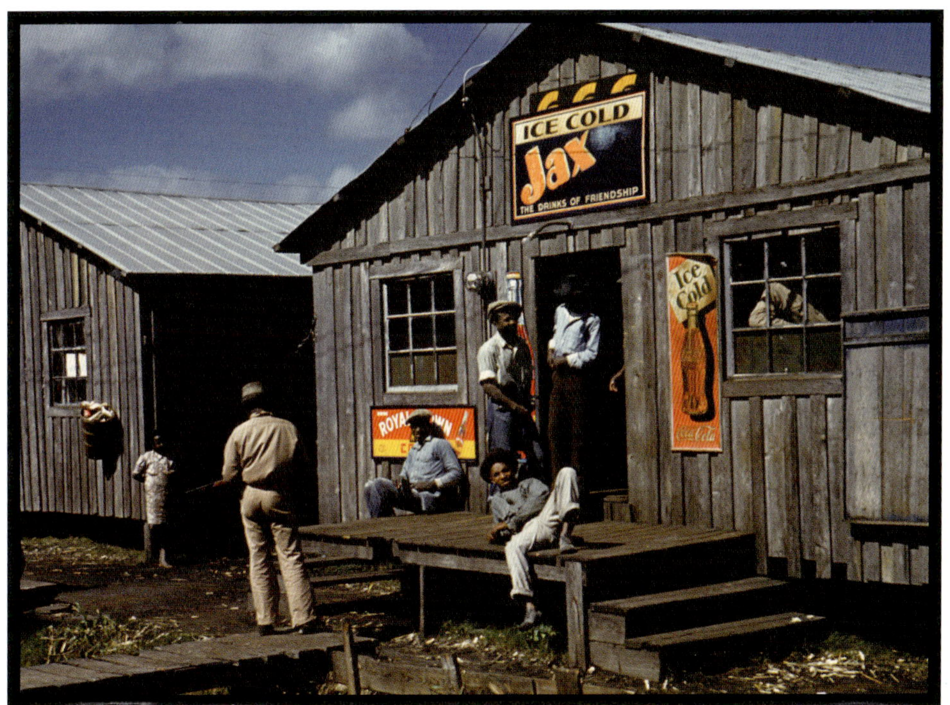

Migratory laborers outside of a "juke joint" during a slack session, Belle Glade, FL. Library of Congress, LC-D16-fsac-la34397.

Another historic locale was **Parchman Farm,** officially the Mississippi State Penitentiary. This large prison farm in the heart of blues country was infamous for its corruption, racism, and inhumane treatment of prisoners. Astonishingly, this hostile environment was proving ground for a long list of legendary blues men, including Son House and **Bukka White** (1896–1956). Folklorist **Alan Lomax** (1915–2002) went to Parchman Farm to document the blues tradition in a now famous series of recordings for the Library of Congress. The stunning emotion of Bukka White's coarse voice and his adroit guitar work are fortunately preserved for history along with the work of several other brilliant musicians. Fortunately, also, these recordings helped to expose the squalid conditions found at Parchman Farm.

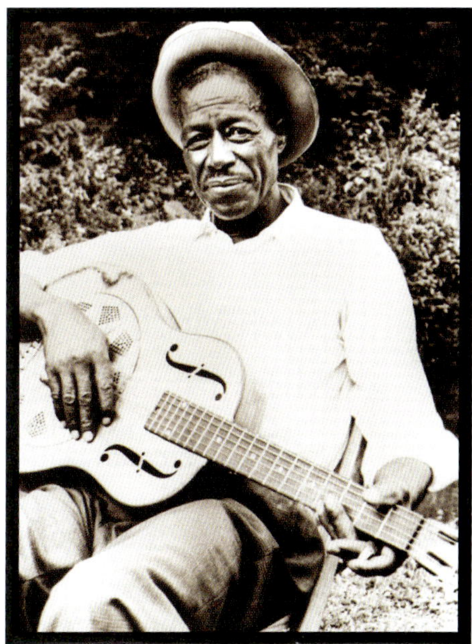
Son House. Blues musician, master of the slide guitar.

Outlaw Songs

Outlaw songs that emerged in the slavery era (See Unit 2, page 212) continued to be popular in the era following the Civil War and were adapted to the blues tradition. Often these songs dealt with folk anti-heroes based on real-life figures. The famous tune "Stagger Lee," for example, is probably based on Lee Sheldon, whose story is recorded in this account, which appeared in a St. Louis newspaper:

> "William Lyons, 25, a levee hand, was shot in the abdomen yesterday evening at 10 o'clock in the saloon of Bill Curtis, at Eleventh and Morgan Streets, by Lee Sheldon, a carriage driver. Lyons and Sheldon were friends and were talking together. Both parties, it seems, had been drinking and were feeling in exuberant spirits. The discussion drifted to politics, and an argument was started, the conclusion of which was that Lyons snatched Sheldon's hat from his head. The latter indignantly demanded its return. Lyons refused, and Sheldon withdrew his revolver and shot Lyons in the abdomen. When his victim fell to the floor, Sheldon took his hat from the hand of the wounded man and coolly walked away. He was subsequently arrested and locked up at the Chestnut Street Station. Lyons was taken to the Dispensary, where his wounds were pronounced serious. Lee Sheldon is also known as 'Stag' Lee."
>
> —*The St. Louis Globe Democrat,* December 28, 1895

Songs describing the murder circulated throughout the land. Stagger Lee soon became a folklore legend among African Americans as a rebellious anti-hero (for a visual interpretation of Stagger Lee, see Frederick Brown's painting by the same name in the Fine Art section). Mythically tough, bad men like Stagger Lee had acquired the same appeal as runaway slaves in the **antebellum,** or post-war, South, gaining lasting fame in song:

Stagger Lee

Police officer, how can it be?
You can 'rest everybody but cruel Stagger Lee.
That bad man, oh, cruel Stagger Lee.

Billy de Lyon told Stagger Lee, "Please don't take my life,
I got two little babies, and a darlin' lovin' wife."
That bad man, oh, cruel Stagger Lee.

"What I care about you little babies, your darlin' lovin' wife?
You done stole my Stetson hat, I'm bound to take your life."
That bad man, cruel Stagger Lee.

New Musical Venues: Medicine Shows and Vaudeville

As the nineteenth century progressed, musical traditions were still fostered in churches and juke joints, but new locations and new venues were added as well. One such venue was the **medicine show.** These shows, once prominent in rural American life, featured a salesman who traveled by horse and buggy, accompanied by musicians and entertainers. The salesman would set up his buggy as a stage, and the entertainers would draw the crowd's interest with magic tricks, storytelling, acrobatics, comedy, and music performances. Meanwhile, the salesman, or "doctor" would hawk such cure-alls as "snake oil" to the gathering throngs. Medicine shows and touring carnivals provided a livelihood for many African-American musicians and helped introduce a growing collection of popular acoustic folk blues songs to rural America.

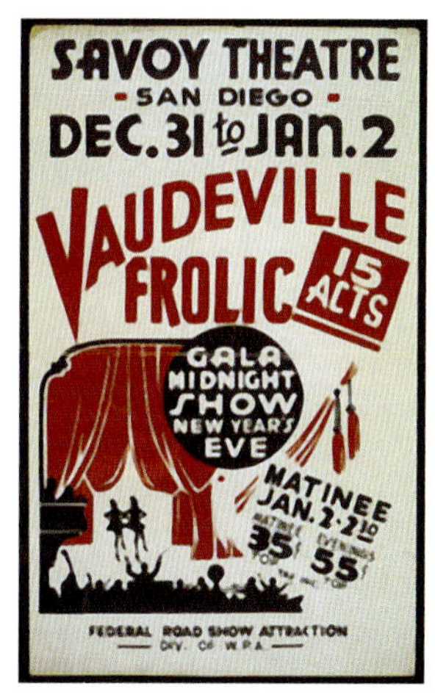

Poster for Federal Theatre Project presentation of "Vaudeville Frolic," circa 1936. Library of Congress, LC-USZC2-5546.

As early twentieth-century America became progressively more urbanized, medicine shows gave way to **vaudeville** variety entertainment, which could be staged in permanent theaters built in the nation's growing cities. The popular music of the vaudeville stage brought a professional quality to blues songs, which signaled the advent of entertainment as business and led the way for the Classic Blues. The word *vaudeville* may derive from the French phrase *voix de ville,* or "voice of the city." Or it might come from the *vau de Vire* valley in Normandy, France, a region renowned for popular satirical songs. Like the medicine show, vaudeville featured an assortment of performances that mixed song and dance, acrobats, pantomime, performing animals, and comedy. However, instead of ragtag bands of traveling entertainers, vaudeville houses offered more polished entertainment intended to appeal to the growing middle class.

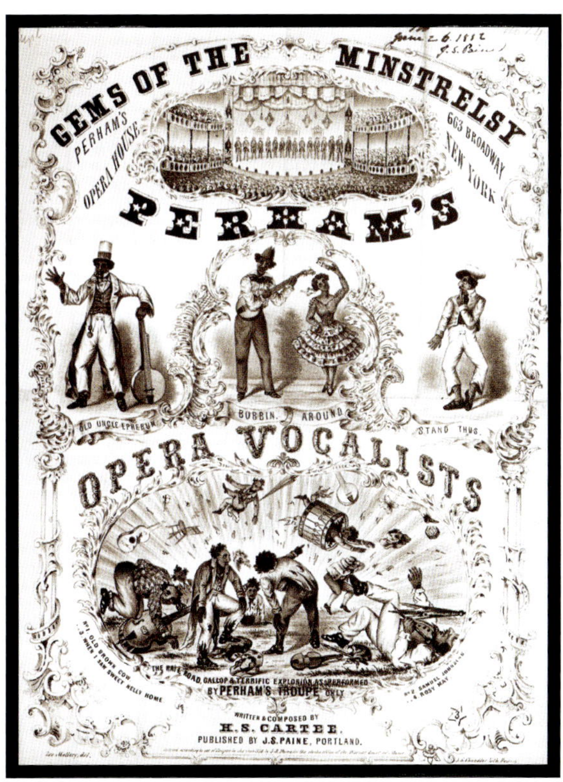

Poster for a minstrel show.

In the segregated era that followed emancipation, African Americans had to organize their own vaudeville houses, and in 1909 they formed the **Theater Owners Booking Association (T.O.B.A.)**, which served theaters in cities in the South and Midwest. At its height in the 1920s and 30s, the African-American vaudeville circuit included more than one hundred theaters. Since many theater owners were white, African-American entertainers were often poorly treated and underpaid. Among them the T.O.B.A. became derisively known as "Tough On Black Artists." Still, many top entertainers were pleased to perform for their fellow African Americans rather than opt for higher pay, Ma Rainey and Bessie Smith among them. Others, like the legendary dancer Bill "Bojangles" Robinson, were lured away from the T.O.B.A. circuit to perform in mainstream vaudeville.

Some big cities, like New York, Philadelphia, and Washington, developed important theaters that could book acts independently. The storied **Apollo Theater** in New York is the most famous of these. The development of affordable film entertainment as well as the Great Depression of the 1930s are said to have contributed to the demise or end of vaudeville. In New York, vaudeville was replaced by the superior artistry fostered by the **Harlem Renaissance.** This tremendous outpouring of original African-American literature, art, music, dance, and drama appropriated the Apollo stage and other venues to contribute a new vitality to American culture that still resonates today.

Classic Blues

Gertrude "Ma" Rainey (1886–1939) and the "Empress of the Blues," **Bessie Smith** (1894–1937), both grew to fame within the T.O.B.A. circuit and became stars in the genre of music that came to be called **classic blues.** Classic blues developed as African Americans migrated from the rural South to the big cities of the Midwest and the northeastern United States. There, blues took on an urban accent and eventually converged with the music known as jazz. Women vocalists came to the fore, and by the 1940s all major record labels featured a blues catalog, known in the parlance of the times as **race records.** Professional vocalists were accompanied by piano, guitar, or small jazz combos. Urban blues developed its own stars, including **Big Bill Broonzy** (c.1893–1958), **Lonnie Johnson** (c.1894–1970), **Tampa Red** (1904–1981), and **Memphis Minnie** (1897–1973). This urban strain, which lasted through World War II, eventually gave way to electric blues. The classic blues is masterfully represented in the famous song by **W. C. Handy** (1873–1958), "The St. Louis Blues." A woman's lament that her lover has been stolen away by a sophisticated city woman typifies the themes of the blues.The tune, closely associated with Bessie Smith, Louis Armstrong, and many other famous artists is so much a part of American culture that it even was adopted as the name for a hockey team. Handy, a sophisticated band leader, was largely responsible for introducing the blues form to a wide audience by means of his recordings of such tunes as

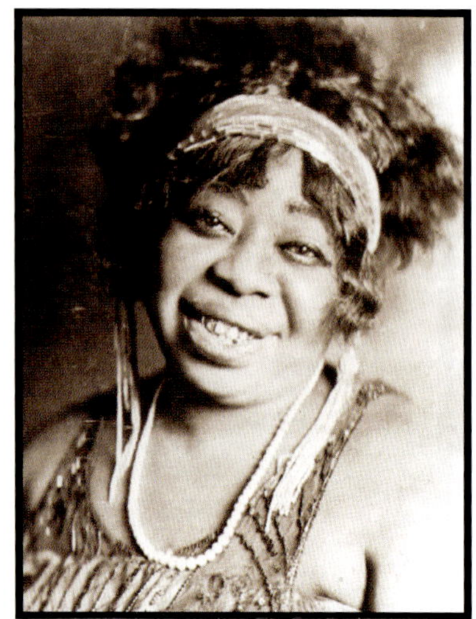

"Ma" Rainey. Classic blues vocalist.

"Memphis Blues." He even billed himself as "The Father of the Blues," though, of course, the blues had many fathers (and mothers!) who preceded him.

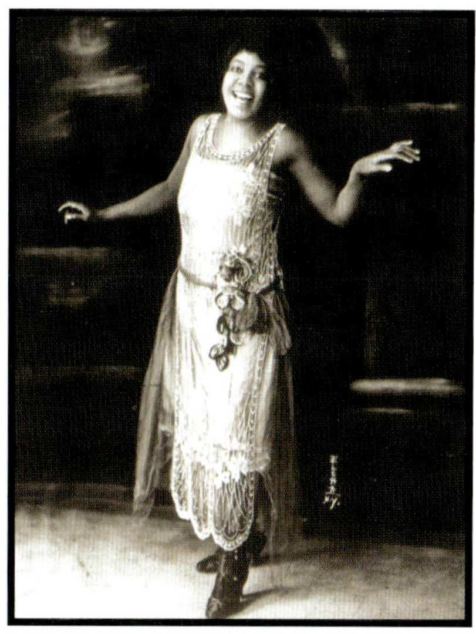
Bessie Smith. Classic blues vocalist

The St. Louis Blues,
by W. C. Handy

I hate to see the evenin' sun go down,
Hate to see the evenin' sun go down,
'Cause my baby, he done left this town.
Feelin' tomorrow like I feel today,
Feel tomorrow like I feel today,
I'll pack my trunk, make my getaway.

St. Louis woman with her diamond rings
Pulls that man around by her apron strings.
'Twant for powder and for store-bought hair
The man I love would not gone nowhere.

Got the St. Louis Blues, just as blue as I can be.
That man got a heart like a rock cast in the sea.
Or else he wouldn't have gone so far from me.

Been to the Gypsy to get my fortune told.
To the Gypsy done got my fortune told,
'cause I'm most wild 'bout my Jelly Roll.

Gypsy done told me "Don't you wear no black."
Yes, she done told me "Don't you wear no black.
Go to St. Louis, you can win him back."

I love that man like a schoolboy loves his pie.
Like a Kentucky col'nel loves his mint and rye.
I'll love my baby till the day I die.

Help me to Cairo, make St. Louis by myself.
Get to Cairo, find my old friend, Jeff.
Goin' to pin myself close to his side.
If I flag his train, I sure can ride.

Oh, ashes to ashes and dust to dust.
I said ashes to ashes and dust to dust.
If my blues don't get you, my jazzing must.

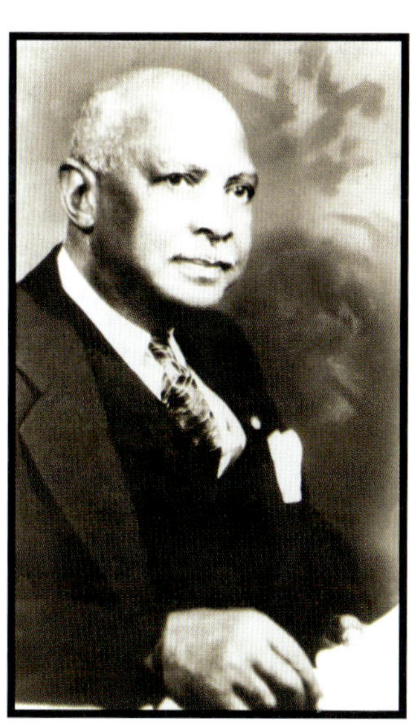
W. C. Handy. One of the first artists to record blues music, Handy billed himself as "The Father of the Blues."

Boogie Woogie

In the early twentieth century, rural African-American laborers entertained themselves in the ramshackle saloons of logging camps of the South and Midwest known as **barrelhouses.** Performers of this barrelhouse style often accompanied themselves on the piano and played in common 4/4 meter. This **barrelhouse music** became the basis of what would later be called **boogie woogie.** In boogie woogie, which was performed with two beats per measure, musicians developed a quicker-paced, entirely instrumental form of danceable piano blues.

The first generation of boogie woogie players followed the labor force to urban centers. The earliest record of the boogie woogie style dates to piano rolls from 1922. (Piano rolls were sheets of paper with holes punched into them that were used to play songs on mechanical player pianos.) Within a decade, the blues-based piano style would achieve formal recognition with the celebrated composition "Pinetop's Boogie Woogie," penned by the first significant exponent of the young genre, **Clarence 'Pinetop' Smith** (1904–1929). This recording, which included instructions for performing an accompanying dance, is significant as the first published tune with the expression "boogie woogie" in its title.

The qualities that came together to distinguish the boogie woogie include its blues chord progressions, vigorous tempo, and forceful, recurring eighth-note bass patterns. Underlying the tremendous verve of the boogie woogie were the vigorous, recurring "walking" left-hand bass lines running through various blues progressions, providing a powerful, percussive rhythmic foundation, usually eight beats per measure. Against this persistent pulse, the right hand played an improvised rhythmic and melodic accompaniment that is comparatively more liberated. An interesting tension came about through the combination of the left- and right-hand elements, which demonstrated remarkable independence, often achieving rhythmic contrast, or **polyrhythm**.

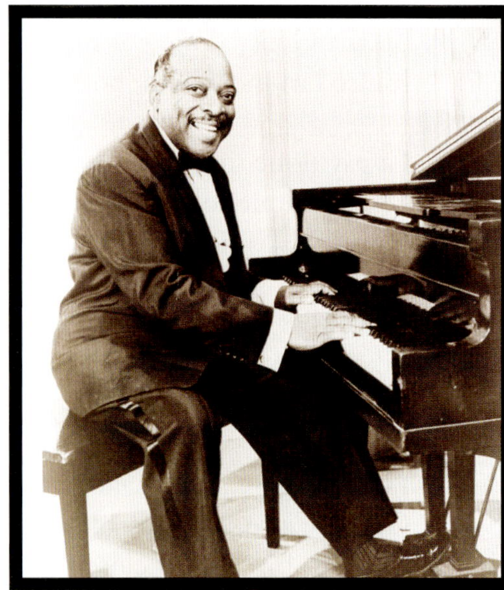

Count Basie. Pianist, composer, and band leader. Library of Congress, LC-USZ62-114733.

While record companies had flourished during the **Classic Blues era** of the 1920s, the **Great Depression** devastated the recording industry, causing many small production outfits to fold. Consequently, the boogie woogie style practically vanished from recordings by the early 1930s. However, during these early, lean years of the Depression, the boogie woogie would survive outside of the commercial mainstream in gatherings known as **rent parties** (parties to which admission was charged in order to raise money for rent). The phenomenon of rent parties thrived in the South Side neighborhoods of Chicago dating back prior to Prohibition. But Prohibition, which lasted from 1920 to 1933 and outlawed the sale of alcohol and the serving of alcoholic beverages in public places, encouraged rent parties and other ways to avoid the law. **Speakeasies**, for example, were underground venues where one had to "speak easy" or whisper "passwords" to gain entry.

To raise enough money to pay the rent, people would open up their apartments to friends and neighbors, charging a modest admission fee. The vigorous percussive rhythms of the boogie woogie made it an ideal music for rent parties, since it could be heard easily above the clamor of the raucous gathering. The best available piano players, well-versed in the crowd-pleasing style, were hired to perform, often for a guaranteed portion of the admission fee. The rent party phenomenon led to intense competitions between the piano players, each attempting to outperform the others by playing the most demanding musical pieces. Often the contests would last through the night and into the morning. If the rent party were successful, the audience was satisfactorily entertained, the musicians were paid for their performance, and the host raised enough money to cover the month's rent.

At rent parties, the boogie woogie style went underground and seemed destined to fade away, but one night in 1938 all that changed. Jazz producer **John Hammond** (1910–1987) decided to challenge the reigning musical format, swing jazz, by mounting a concert in New York's Carnegie Hall called "From Spirituals to Swing," which brought boogie woogie back into the public eye.

This concert aimed a spotlight on a number of overlooked African-American musical traditions and exposed them to new audiences. The momentous occasion presented the then obscure practitioners of the boogie woogie piano style—**Meade 'Lux' Lewis** (1905–1964) and **Albert Ammons** (1907–1949), both then earning a living as taxicab drivers in Chicago. Their performances launched a nationwide sensation. Within two weeks of their appearance at Carnegie Hall, Ammons and Lewis made the inaugural recordings for the fledgling **Blue Note Records** and joined with **Pete Johnson** (1904–1967) and his vocalist **Big Joe Turner** (1911–1985) to become resident musicians at various high-class nightclubs in New York City. Boogie woogie was alive and well.

Like most improvised musical forms, boogie woogie was not commonly transcribed[4] to sheet music. Despite the lack of a written legacy, however, it

[4] **transcribed.** Set down in written form

had an enduring influence on blues, rock 'n' roll, jazz, and other forms of popular music. Nevertheless, it remains sorely overlooked historically.

Perhaps due to its association with the newly popular swing jazz, the thumping rhythms of the boogie woogie solo piano style soon found their way into other instrumental formats. It became standard practice for jazz ensembles at the time to include a minimum of one boogie woogie tune in each performance set, Count Basie's "Boogie Woogie" being a popular choice. **William "Count" Basie** (1904–1985) was a great pianist and band leader of the big band era. He was associated with boogie woogie and the Kansas City style of jazz. His popular compositions included "Jumping at the Woodside" and "One O'Clock Jump."

Mostly an instrumental form, lyrics sometimes were added, as in the popular World War II-era tune, "Boogie Woogie Bugle Boy." Following World War II, the popularity of boogie woogie faded. Still its rollicking, percussive style can be said to have joined with blues and country music to form the basis many rhythm and blues and rock 'n' roll tunes. Boogie woogie is also a direct ancestor of the piano-based New Orleans rhythm and blues, as evidenced in the playing of **Henry Roeland Byrd "Professor Longhair"** (1918–1980) and **"Champion" Jack Dupree** (c.1908–1992). It is certainly an essential element of the **jump blues** sub-genre. Its rollicking rhythms are echoed in country music too, in many rockabilly and honky-tonk tunes.

Gospel Blues

Often the blues were seen as irreverent, something exclusively secular, to be avoided by devotees of religious music. But not always. Sometimes lyrics and melodies from the two genres were interchanged, and in this manner the **gospel blues** was born. In this sub-genre, the passion of the blues and religious music came together for a stunning emotional effect. Performed almost exclusively by street-corner evangelists, the singing employed the structure of the blues, but had an amazing emotional intensity. It more closely resembled field hollers and spirituals than secular blues music. Proponents of the style included the inimitable street singers **Blind Willie Johnson** (1902–1945) and the **Reverend Gary Davis** (1896–1972). Johnson, in particular, merits special mention, as both his raw emotional vocal power and virtuosic slide guitar playing remain unsurpassed in the gospel blues sub-genre. Johnson's rasping bass voice was so powerful, legend holds he was once arrested for inciting a riot in New Orleans by singing a passionate rendition of "If I had My Way I'd Tear This Building Down," the biblical account of Samson and Delilah set to song. His output includes other timeless classics such as "John the Revelator," "Nobody's Fault but Mine," and "Dark Was the Night (Cold Was the Ground)."

The blues was born in the juke joints, plantations, and prisons of the Mississippi Delta, but moved quickly to other places, following the great migration of workers to northern cities like Memphis, St. Louis, and Chicago. Although it had rural roots and produced many famous country blues performers like Leadbelly and Blind Lemon Jefferson, eventually, it took on an urban flavor and fused with the sophisticated and citified sounds of jazz.

Religious Music in the Post-Civil War Era

By the late nineteenth century there was an extraordinary outburst of African-American musical invention in the context of worship. Composed songs and written compositions became part of common worship practice among African Americans. Traditional spirituals were professionally arranged, cataloged, and published. Black universities contributed new energy to musical traditions.

Arranged Spirituals. At **Fisk University** in Nashville, Tennessee, spirituals were used in concert presentations made to international audiences. The concerts began in 1871 as an attempt to raise money for the university, which was saddled with mounting debt in the lean years following the Civil War. **The Fisk University Singers,** an even mix of men and women, most former slaves, were trained by the school treasurer. The first gender-mixed African-American musical group of fame, they were instrumental in moving spirituals from folk venues to the concert stage. Today, spirituals are common in the repertoires of concert vocal ensembles in the United States.

In their performances, the Fisk University Singers modified some characteristics of the spirituals. They retained the call-and-response format but minimized spontaneity, improvisation, and other hallmarks of African music in favor of exactness and reproducibility. They sang arranged spirituals ***a cappella*** (without musical accompaniment) and made notations for harmony according to European tradition. The singers enjoyed considerable acclaim, performing a repertoire of spirituals and popular tunes that included "Wade in the Water," "Were You There," "Steal Away to Jesus," and a number of works by the white composer Stephen Foster.

Fisk University was also influential in the development of **jubilee quartets.** These quartets featured unaccompanied singers, spanning in vocal pitch from tenor to bass. They showcased tight, barbershop harmonies distinguished by falsetto[5] tenors and pulsating bass singers. In line with the arranged spiritual tradition pursued by choirs, the jubilee quartets used transcribed

[5] **falsetto.** A male voice in an upper register beyond its usual range

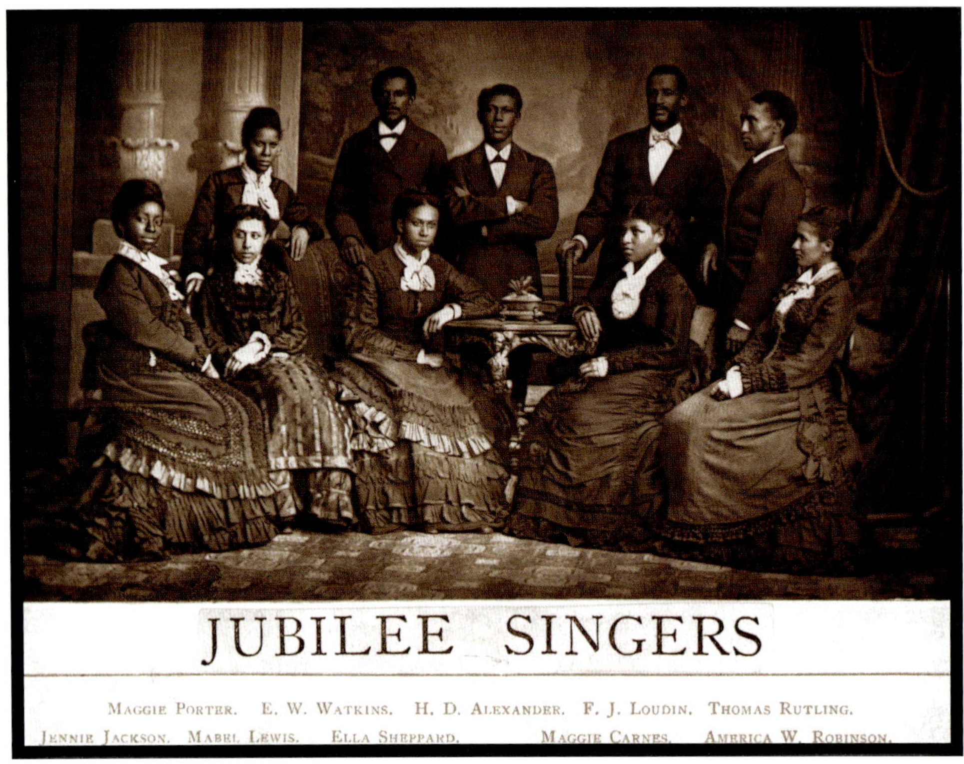

Jubilee Singers. The Jubilee Singers of Fisk University, who performed by invitation before Queen Victoria. Hulton-Deutsch Collection.

arrangements, synchronized movements, and a manner of song performance that stressed a controlled presentation derived from European choral techniques. The seminal group of all-male students known as the **Fisk Jubilee Quartet** inspired many other groups such as those at **Hampton Normal and Agricultural Institute** and **Tuskegee Institute.** Some of the earliest quartet recordings extant include the **Standard Quartette** (recorded in 1894), the **Dinwiddie Colored Quartet** (recorded in 1902), the **Fisk Jubilee Singers,** and the **Apollo Male Quartet** (recorded in 1912).

From Spirituals to Gospel. By the early 1930s, musical groups such as the **Golden Gate Quartet** added the rhythms of popular music to their unaccompanied jubilee-style performances of spirituals. This experimental style came to be known as **gospel music.** To spiritual lyrics, gospel singers added notes of protest, comedy, and wit for a combination far removed from conventional hymns. Gaining popularity in the 1930s and 40s via recordings, radio broadcasts, and frequent traveling, the Golden Gate Quartet was the most influential jubilee quartet in an era when the format was at the peak of its popularity. By including compositions by **Thomas A. Dorsey** (1899–1993) and other gospel tunesmiths in their performances, they solidified their reputation as legitimate singers of spiritual music. Jubilee ensembles such as the

Dixie Hummingbirds would go on to innovate, taking a more spontaneous and emotionally charged approach to the jubilee format, which came to be called **hard gospel.** Hard gospel progressively gained favor until it largely surpassed conventional jubilee singing and dominated popular practice in the **Golden Age of Gospel** of the 1950s.

Sanctified/Holiness. The jubilee style would not be confined to universities for long and quickly moved into African-American churches, which began to feature all-male quartets singing before audiences with a tradition of participation and "shouting out." The Pentecostal or "Sanctified" churches embraced the jubilee style with particular enthusiasm since it fit in with their passionate style of worship. **Sanctified singing** incorporated the shouts, percussive hand-clapping, and foot-stomping of African music so well known in the days of slavery. In the 1920s, Sanctified church performers began blending conventional spirituals with the blues. They also introduced jazz instruments into worship music. In Sanctified or Pentecostal churches, members of the congregation would spontaneously shout out, dance in exultation, and "give witness" to their faith and to the presence of the Holy Spirit.

Among the earliest musicians to introduce the Sanctified music of the Holiness movement to the masses was **Arizona Dranes.** This musician abandoned the *a cappella* performance format and used a percussive boogie woogie piano to accompany her intense soprano voice.

Classic Gospel. Thomas A. Dorsey introduced what is now considered the **Classic Gospel Era**, whereby instrumentation, often piano and organ, accompanied formerly *a cappella* vocals. Originally, religious and devotional music following the Civil War had sparse accompaniment or none at all. But Dorsey followed the Pentecostal and Holiness movements in composing for instruments, including the piano and organ, guitar, and drums. As in the music of the Sanctified churches, he used blue notes and syncopated rhythm schemes along with religious lyrics to form a riotous union of the sacred and secular. His lyrics, inspired by traditional spirituals and passages from the New Testament, addressed

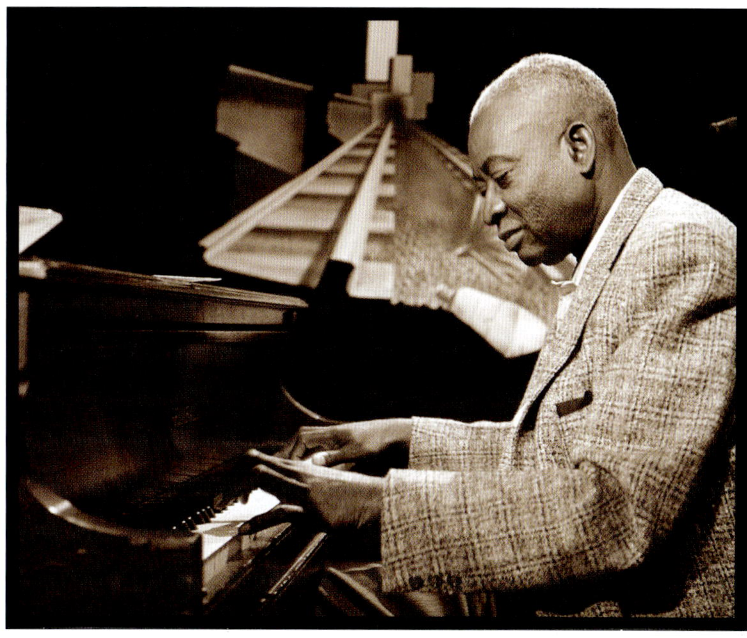

Thomas A Dorsey. The "Father of Gospel Music."

the trials of daily life. Although transcribed, Dorsey's music included flexible arrangements that provided opportunities for improvisation.

As a young man by the stage name of Georgia Tom, Dorsey wrote compositions and played piano for the legendary blues divas "Ma" Rainey and Bessie Smith. Some of Dorsey's early blues compositions had quite worldly themes and often ribald[6] lyrics. In later life, however, Dorsey became committed to religious music at the exclusion of all other styles; nonetheless, he wanted it to be lively. Dorsey faced hostility from more conservative church bodies who considered his music to be an improper expression of religious devotion. Despite opposition, he became a tireless advocate of gospel music, founding the **National Convention of Gospel Choirs and Choruses**, which continues to hold annual meetings to this day. He also established his own publishing company following the success of his sacred compositions "Precious Lord (Take My Hand)" and "Peace in the Valley." For his tremendous efforts to develop this daring new form of sacred music, Dorsey is regarded as the "Father of Gospel."

Within a church setting, gospel music is customarily performed in the call-and-response song form by a large choir and solo vocalists who improvise variations on the melody. This practice harkens back to traditional forms of congregational singing observed in the call-and-response pattern of field hollers. Soloists became more skilled as the musical style progressed and were able to perform with rapturous passion to convey, faithfully, the religious devotion of the music.

The Legacy of Gospel Music. Blues and original jazz were introduced into the gospel music created in the 1920s and 30s and brought to it a certain verve, or liveliness. Sometimes these influences were sent back out into the world again. In the 1930s, **Sister Rosetta Tharpe** (1915–1973) performed sacred songs in a night club, signaling a sea change. Gospel music began to be performed in concert halls, theaters, and other venues outside the church. Over time, the impact of the spirituals expanded even further, as many African-American singers, for example **Paul Robeson** (1898–1976), performed spirituals on stage and in motion pictures. These performances broke many barriers and were unprecedented both for their settings outside the church and for their solo aspect. Many people regard Robeson, concert singer, actor, and civil rights activist, to be one of the greatest solo gospel singers of all time, rivaled only by **Mahalia Jackson** (1911–1972).

Eventually gospel singers reached across other divides as well. Mahalia Jackson, **Brother Joe May** (1912–1972), **the Clara Ward Singers,**

[6] **ribald.** Characterized by vulgar, lewd humor

"Mother" Willie Mae Ford Smith (1904–1994), **James Cleveland** (1931–1991), and numerous others earned fame and broad appeal among listeners of all races.

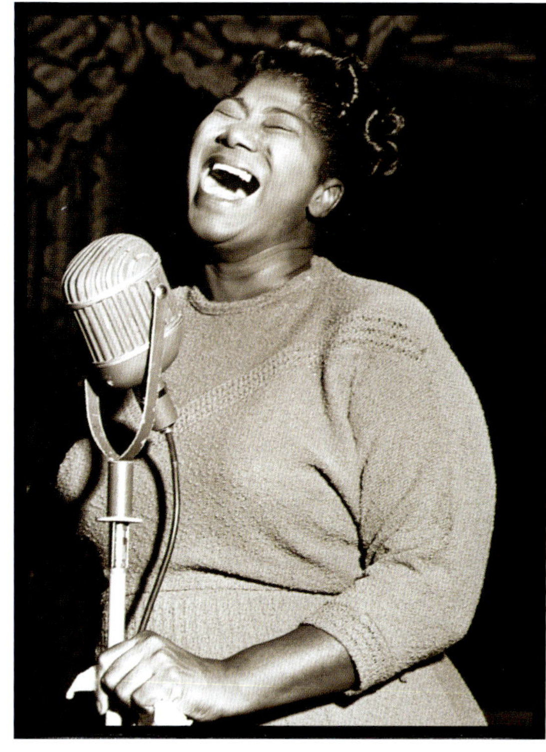

Mahalia Jackson. A legendary performer of gospel music.

Ragtime

First appearing in saloons of the South and the Midwest, **ragtime** grew to become the leading form of popular music from the late nineteenth century until the end of the First World War. Like its successor, jazz, it developed simultaneously in several places. Its rapid spread was made possible by the presence of African-American brass bands in almost every Southern city and by the circulation of this music on player pianos. A **player piano** was powered by foot pedals or by a simple motor that read a pattern of notes punched into metal spools. The spools produced at that time offered more ragtime than any other kind of music. Associated largely with the piano, ragtime nonetheless employed a variety of instruments and was often used as dance and even orchestral music.

It was favored by a new generation of African-American musicians seeking innovative self expression. Its greatest stylist, **Scott Joplin** (1868–1917), projected a new level of sophistication, aspiring as he did to produce a musical form to rival the classical music of Europe. His "Maple Leaf Rag" of 1899 became an enormous success, selling thousands of copies of sheet music. Greatly ambitious, Joplin composed a ragtime opera, *Treemonisha,* and fused the sonata form with African-American rhythms.

The term *ragtime* derived from the phrase *ragged time* used to describe syncopated rhythmic patterns. The use of a rhythm to contrast with the melody was known in its day as "ragging" a tune. The left hand played "oom-pah" bass patterns while the right hand played a contrasting melodic line. The **arpeggios,** or broken chords, of the right hand were decorative but not improvised as they were later in jazz. Sometimes jazz songs were labeled rags because of their syncopated rhythms, and indeed the terms *jazz* and *ragtime* were used interchangeably in the early years. Although ragtime was transcribed and arranged rather than improvised, its influence on jazz was profound. **Jelly Roll Morton** (1890–1941) can be viewed as a transitional figure, trailblazing a stride piano and jazz style, but carrying over some of ragtime's powerful rhythm.

In addition to the piano, ragtime bands featured a diversity of instruments. Guitar, bass, and drums were popular and later became the basis of many jazz combos. The banjo, as one part of a string instrumental group, was used in folk but not in classical ragtime. By the 1920s, ragtime had almost totally given way to jazz, but occasional revivals of ragtime music have taken place throughout the last century.

Jazz

In 1997, Congress declared **jazz** to be a national treasure, one worthy of preservation and support. Most people agree that it is an authentically American art form and that it bears the profound imprint of various African-American musical forms—spirituals, ragtime, and the blues among them. Like classical music, jazz embraces many subgenres and can serve many functions, ranging from unobtrusive background music to big band ensemble music made for dancing. While diverse, jazz music often has common traits: blue notes, collective and solo improvisation, rhythmic contrast or syncopation, swing rhythm, and the call-and-response song pattern.

Jazz is basically a metropolitan musical form and nowhere did it flourish more than in the city of New Orleans. A sophisticated port city with multinational influences, New Orleans was open to African-American music. Unlike the rest of America, it had three social divisions—black, white, and Creole (mixed race). Before **Reconstruction**, when racial divisions hardened, Creoles had high social standing and often professional status as musicians.

Some jazz traditions evolved from funeral practices, and New Orleans became famous for its jazz funerals, which were themselves derived from African funeral practices. The dead would be accompanied to the burial grounds by a procession of family members followed by a band of musicians known as the "first line." A crowd of dancing onlookers, known as the "second line," would also join the procession. En route, the band, often sponsored by one of New Orleans's many mutual assistance guilds or burial societies, would play solemn hymns or dirges. Later, the music would change to more jubilant tunes like "When the Saints Come Marching In" or "Oh, Didn't He Ramble." These sent the dancers, bedecked with umbrellas and handkerchiefs, into an exuberant mode. The second line echoed the earlier tradition brought from Africa, one that joined audience and performer. The jazz funeral marches, which developed a competitive edge, became training grounds where lead instrumentalists crafted their skills of improvisation and drummers fashioned rhythms that were translated into the characteristic "swing" of jazz.

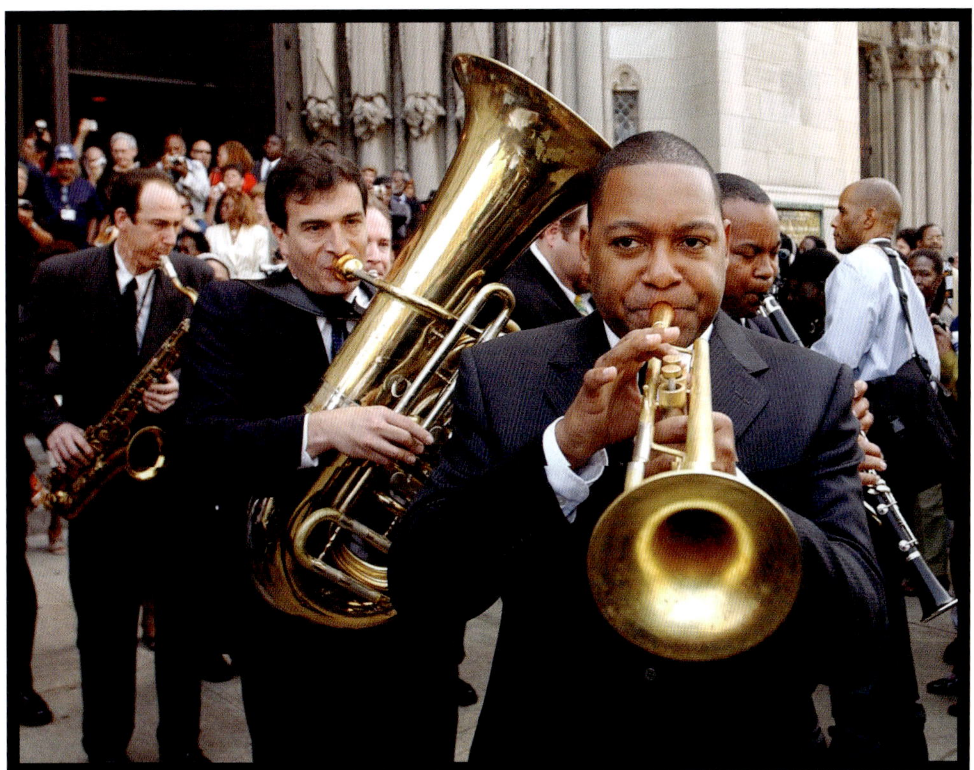

Wynton Marsalis leads funeral procession for jazz great Lionel Hampton. The jazz funeral tradition is still alive and well.

Storyville. From 1896 to 1917, in the district of New Orleans known as Storyville, jazz flourished alongside nightlife (and sometimes illegal activities). The forbidden haunts of Storyville provided settings for late night playing sessions where jazz music came into its own. Storyville was shut down by order of the U.S. Navy towards the close of World War I, sending jazz musicians up the Mississippi River in search of employment. In this way, jazz spread to port cities such as Memphis and St. Louis, as well as to major metropolitan areas like Chicago and New York. New Orleans, the birthplace of jazz, and other big cities gave us the jazz legends that follow.

Charles "Buddy" Bolden (1877–1931). Born in New Orleans, the cornetist Charles "Buddy" Bolden was the first star of jazz. Bolden formed his first band in 1895, and by 1900 was the most popular musician in his hometown.

Ferdinand "Jelly Roll" Morton (1890–1941). The first major composer of jazz, Jelly Roll Morton was born Ferdinand Joseph Lamothe into a Creole community of New Orleans in 1890. He later assumed the surname "Morton" by anglicizing the family name of his stepfather, Mouton. A skilled and versatile piano player, Jelly Roll Morton was proficient in both ragtime and jazz styles. Arrogant, extroverted, and given to hyperbole, he often boasted he had invented jazz in 1902. At the time, some found his boasting offensive, but today, his achievements as a musical innovator are widely admired.

Sidney Bechet (1897–1959). The first great soloist of jazz, Sidney Bechet (Beh-shay) was born in New Orleans to a musical Creole family in 1897. On the clarinet and later, on the soprano saxophone, Bechet displayed an unrivaled sense of melody. He would ornament his playing with a quivering effect that could be described in musical terms as a fast or wide vibrato. This technique gave a warm, vocal-like quality to his playing. A precocious talent, even as a teenager, he was featured in some of the top bands in his native New Orleans. Bechet, the first major figure from New Orleans to make lengthy sojourns across the South, became the first significant ambassador for jazz. His wanderlust led him on junkets throughout Europe where he was one of the earliest jazz men to achieve fame and the first to receive critical attention.

Louis Armstrong (c.1900–1971). Louis Armstrong, also known as **Satchmo** and **Pops,** was raised by his mother in severe poverty in New Orleans. Although poor, he was enriched by exposure to the city's familiar brass bands, funeral parades, ragtime, and church music of the day. His first musical employment involved blowing a tin horn to announce the arrival of a junk wagon as it rolled through Storyville selling coal to residents on cold evenings. As an eight year-old boy, he performed in the streets, earning pennies by singing with a barbershop quartet.

In 1913, Armstrong was jailed for eighteen months at the Colored Waifs Home for Boys (a reform school/orphanage) for shooting off an old pistol on New Year's Eve. The pride of the reformatory was the band. He obtained his first musical training under the Home's bandmaster and progressed rapidly from tambourine to bugle to cornet. Ultimately, he was promoted to band leader. One particular incident, fondly recalled by Armstrong in his autobiography, described the day the institution's band marched through Louis's old neighborhood. The residents, charmed to see young Louis leading the way with an entertainer's confidence, celebrated his return by donating money to purchase new instruments and uniforms for the boy's home.

Discharged from the reformatory in 1914, Louis spent the next few years working as a longshoreman and selling coal. Intermittently, he played with a number of musical ensembles around New Orleans, honing his prodigious talent. The first well-known musician to recognize Louis's gifts was **Joe 'King' Oliver** (1885–1938), who provided him music in exchange for his running errands. The experience playing in nightclubs and parades as apprentice to Oliver enabled Louis to build an impressive blues-based repertoire. When Oliver moved to Chicago, he appointed Louis to lead the band he had once led with **Edward 'Kid' Ory** (1886–1973), a band widely regarded as the finest in New Orleans.

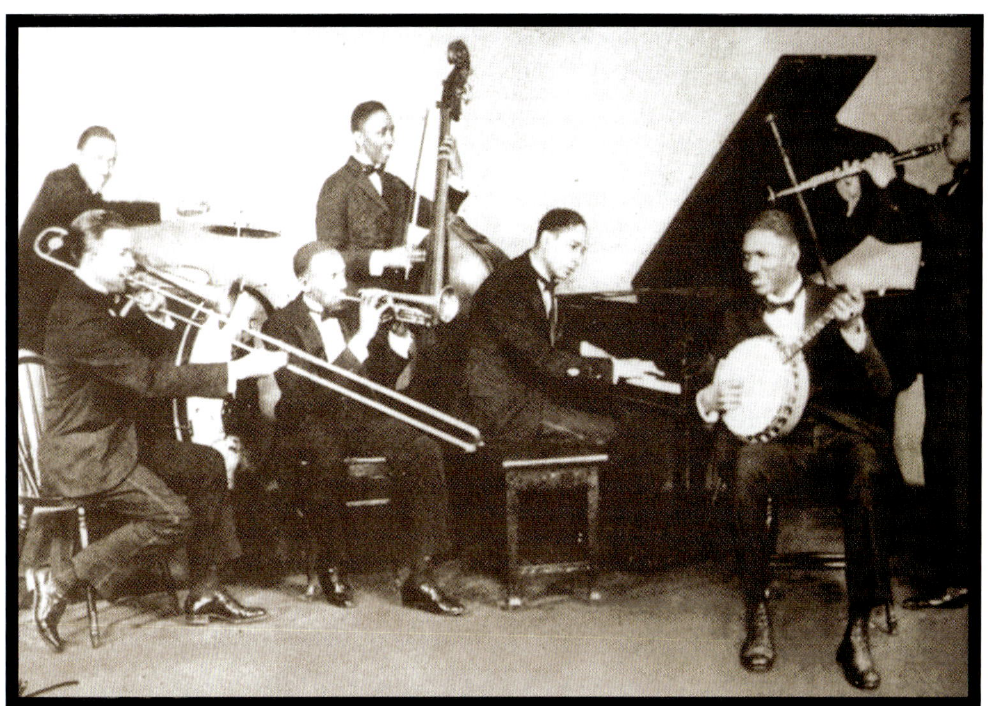

Jelly Roll Morton, seated at the piano, claimed to be the inventor of jazz music. He was certainly one of its early proponents.

For nearly three years, Armstrong played with the **Fate Marable Orchestra** on the Streckfus Steamboat Line. **Fate Marable** (1890–1947) is significant in the annals of early jazz. Besides Armstrong, he trained many other distinguished early jazz musicians, including band leader **'King' Oliver,** clarinetist **Johnny Dodds** (1892–1940), drummer **Warren "Baby" Dodds** (1898–1959), banjoist and guitarist **Johnny St. Cyr** (1890–1966), and trumpeter **Red Allen** (c.1906–1967), among others.

Louis's stint with Marable taught him to read a musical score, which, in turn, enabled him to transcribe arrangements of New Orleans jazz. Playing on the riverboats gave Louis experience of the world as well as of music, but he wanted to sing as well as play. Disappointed that Marable refused to allow him to sing, Louis left the Steamboat band in late 1921 and returned to New Orleans to resume playing in 'Kid' Ory's band.

Besides his considerable skill as a leader, Marable was a celebrated player of the piano and the **steam calliope,** a cumbersome pipe organ powered by the steam emanating from the riverboat's boiler. The calliope would often get so hot and wet from the condensation of the steam, it was necessary to wear a raincoat and gloves to play it. The greatest virtue of the steam calliope was the volume of its sound, which enabled it to be heard from a great distance. It was used to broadcast a riverboat's arrival to port.

Soon thereafter, Louis was invited to join band leader Louis "King" Oliver's New Orleans-style jazz band in Chicago, where night life flourished despite a recent ban on alcoholic beverages under Prohibition. Chicago, in fact, had become the new center for jazz musicians, many imported from New Orleans. In addition to Armstrong, Oliver's band featured clarinetist Johnny Dodds and his brother 'Baby,' a percussionist who introduced a higher level of refinement and rhythmic drive to jazz when he brought the notion of swing rhythm to jazz drumming.

The traditional New Orleans Dixieland jazz style was too confining for an imaginative talent of Armstrong's caliber. In search of more musical freedom and more opportunity to solo, Louis left Oliver's band in 1924 for a position in the **Fletcher Henderson Orchestra.** At the time, this orchestra was New York's most celebrated African-American band. It is now considered the first **big band** in the history of jazz.

Despite its fine reputation, the Fletcher Henderson Orchestra was comparatively stodgy and rigid. Louis changed all that with his alluring, lyrical tone, his talent for melodic paraphrase, and his rhythmic swinging quality. Early recordings show his famous band mate, **Coleman Hawkins** (1904–1967), as a rather leaden performer. After Louis joined the band, Hawkins's fluid tenor saxophone solos showed the power of Armstrong's influence.

Even though Armstrong's stint with the Fletcher Henderson Orchestra lasted only one year, it initiated a stylistic revolution that ultimately affected the entire swing music subgenre. While the band continued to rely on written arrangements, Henderson's chief arranger, Don Redman, was able to incorporate some of Armstrong's musical conceptions, including a looser beat and lengthier solos. Despite his outstanding playing, Louis was still not permitted to sing beyond a few phrases in "Everybody Loves My Baby (But My Baby Don't Love Nobody But Me)." Convinced his singing and instrumental talents were being underutilized, Louis returned to Chicago in late 1925.

Back in Chicago, Armstrong was encouraged by his wife to seek more musical autonomy. With a small ensemble, known as the **Hot Five,** Armstrong made recordings for **OKeh Records.** The Hot Five, branded the **Hot Seven** after the addition of tuba and drums, made dozens of recordings over a three-year period. The sidemen on the sessions varied, and the number of musicians in a given recording session did not always equal five or seven. Besides his piano-playing wife, **Lillian Hardin** (1898–1971), Armstrong engaged fellow New Orleans natives such as clarinetist Johnny Dodds, banjoist Johnny St. Cyr, and trombonist "Kid" Ory to round out the band.

The recordings, which showcased Armstrong at length, were a watershed in jazz music—a stylistic leap that remains unmatched, its solos sculpted with startling originality. Armstrong expanded the customarily brief two- and four-bar solo breaks to considerably longer durations. In doing this, he single-handedly supplanted the polyphonic group embellishment of New Orleans jazz with solo improvisation and individual expression, which would be hallmarks of jazz forever after. In search of a brighter tone, Armstrong switched from the cornet to the trumpet over the course of the Hot Five and Hot Seven recording sessions.

Armstrong's vocalized improvisations—swinging, wordless, nonsense syllables known as **scat singing**—were created with a melodic quality that matched that of his trumpet solos. "Heebie Jeebies," recorded in 1926, is a masterpiece of scat singing and made the style immediately popular. The recording also demonstrated Armstong's fluency as a vocalist. This new jazz vocal technique thrilled his fellow musicians, who blatantly copied Armstrong's style. After introducing his scat phrases, Armstrong soon demonstrated his skill with written lyrics. During the **Swing Era,** Louis became well-established as a vocalist, trumpet player, and big band leader.

Armstrong's singing had a permanent impact on the jazz repertoire, forming a lasting association between jazz and popular music. Although many traditional jazz tunes had been derived from popular tunes, numerous jazz

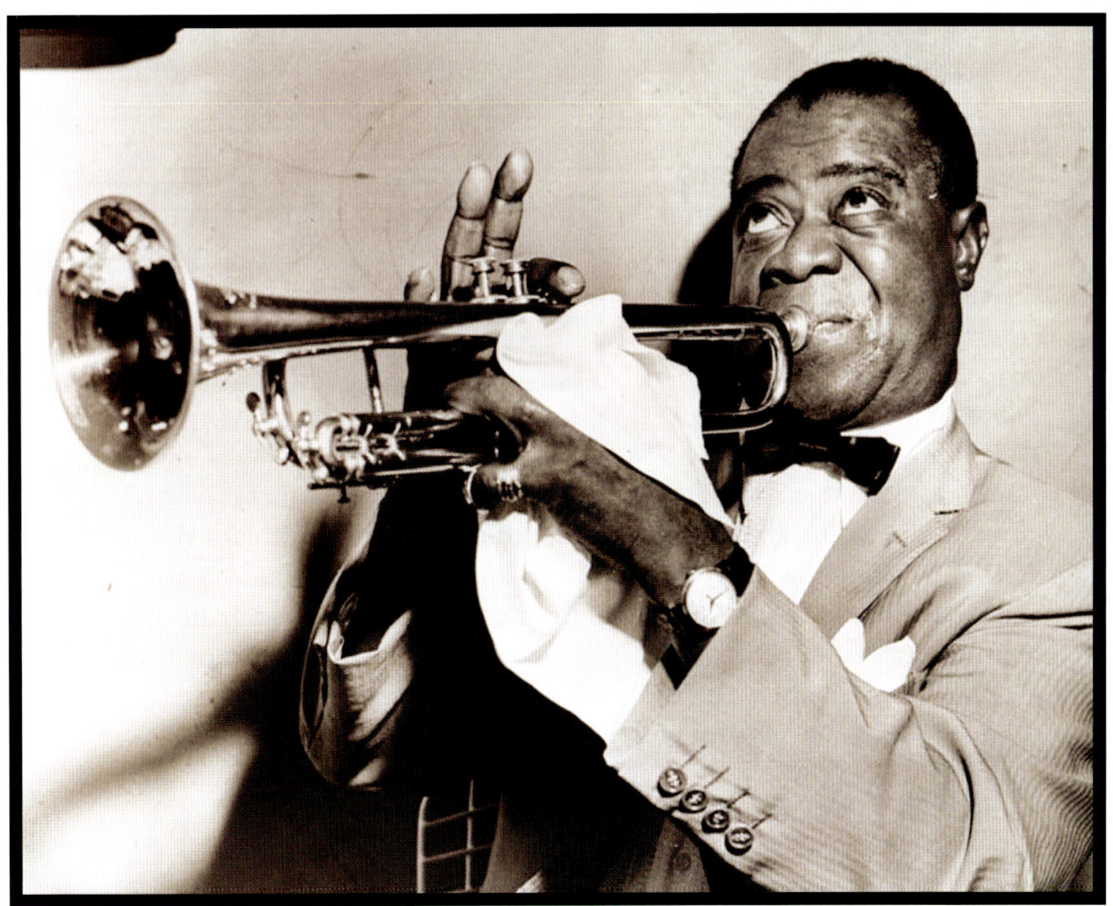

Louis Armstrong, king of the jazz trumpeters. Library of Congress, LC-USZ62-127236

enthusiasts of Armstrong's era felt that performing popular songs would somehow debase a jazz musician's reputation. Armstrong proved that, instead of diluting jazz, tunes from the famous New York song writing area known as **Tin Pan Alley** and from other sources of popular music expanded the idiom's potential. Armstrong showed that it is often interpretation and style, rather than the structure of the song, that determines the music's appeal and quality. Armstrong's flair for theatrics and his rhythmic genius helped him to refashion many an ordinary tune into an unforgettable masterpiece. Many people credit Armstrong with the invention, or at least with the widespread popularization, of so-called **swing time,** in which (in a 4/4 piece) the second and fourth beats are emphasized, rather than the first and third, as in traditional Western music.

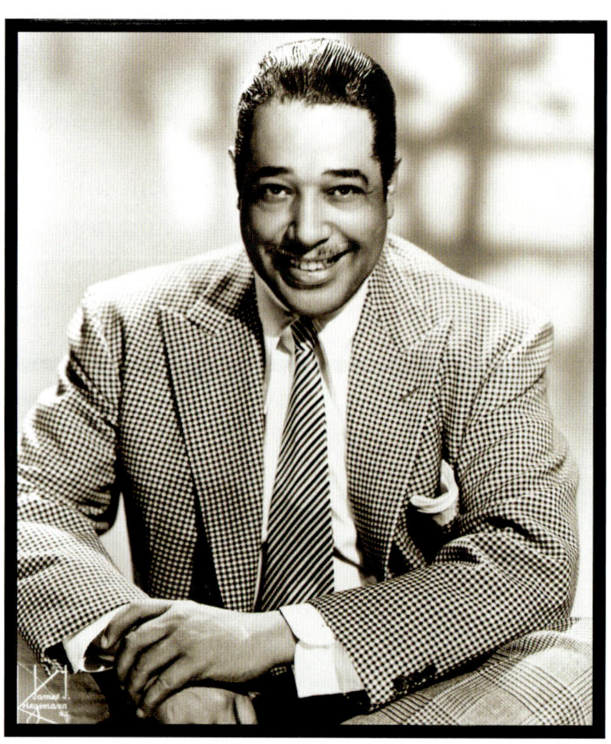
Duke Ellington. Composer, pianist, and band leader Library of Congress, LC-USZ62-125934.

Edward Kennedy "Duke" Ellington (1899–1974). It is impossible in a brief survey such as this one to do justice to, or even to mention, all of the great African-American performers and composers who made jazz the most popular music of the early twentieth century and the most enduring and important of the many contributions that African-Americans have made to the music of the world. But of all these musicians, perhaps the most influential and widely admired around the world is Duke Ellington. A phenomenally gifted pianist, composer, arranger, and orchestra leader, Ellington took jazz music to unprecedented heights. Ellington himself did not much care for the term *jazz,* for he considered himself, rightly so, to be beyond such narrow categorization. As an orchestra leader, he toured widely in the United States and abroad, and he appeared in many films. Nicknamed "Duke" because of his elegant dress and sophisticated style, Ellington composed, by himself and with others such as **Billy Stayhorn,** a vast number of works in many, many genres, including popular songs, blues songs, film scores, operas, musical comedies, and orchestral suites. Among the most famous of his recordings are "Black & Tan Fantasy,"

"It Don't Mean a Thing If It Ain't Got That Swing," "Sophisticated Lady," "In a Sentimental Mood," "Caravan," "Cotton Tail," "Take the 'A' Train," and "Satin Doll." Ellington performed with most of the major jazz artists of his day, including Louis Armstrong, Cab Calloway, Ella Fitzgerald, Tony Bennett, Dizzy Gillespie, Miles Davis, and John Coltrane. He won numerous Grammy Awards, received the President's Gold Medal from Lyndon Johnson, and was presented the Presidential Medal of Freedom by Richard M. Nixon.

Billie Holiday (1915–1959).
Some jazz legends used powerful lyrics to express their outrage at racism. One of the most famous of these is by the immortal jazz singer Billie Holiday, called **"Lady Day"** in reverent memory. Her rendition of "Strange Fruit," composed by Lewis Allen, remains the most stunning indictment of lynching made in any art form.

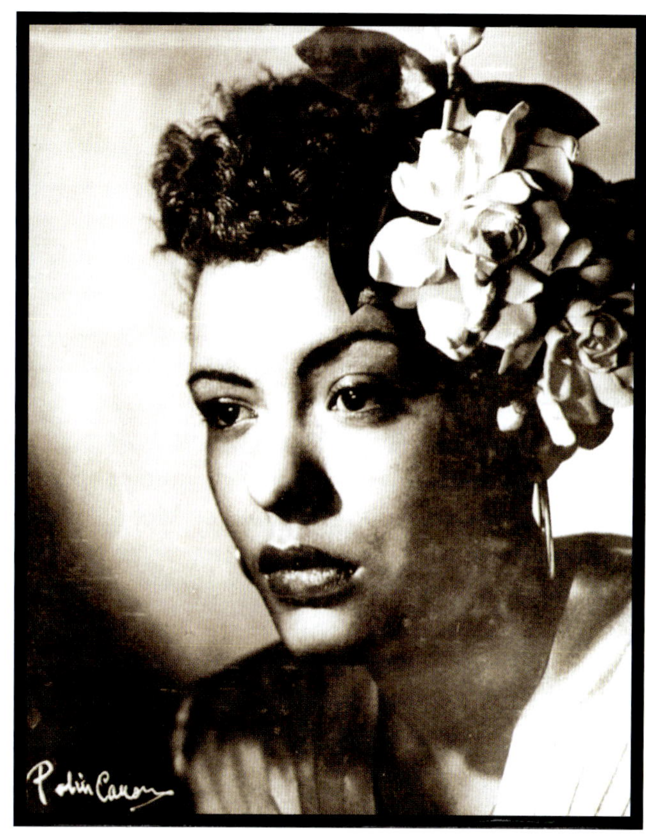
Billie Holiday. One of the greatest of female jazz vocalists

Strange Fruit,
by Lewis Allen

Southern trees bear strange
  fruit.
Blood on the leaves AND
Blood at the root.
Black body swinging in the
  Southern breeze,
Strange fruit hanging from the
  poplar trees.
Pastoral scene of the gallant South,
The bulging eyes and the twisted mouth.
Scent of magnolia sweet and fresh,
And the sudden smell of burning flesh!
Here is a fruit for the crows to pluck,
For the rain to gather,
For the wind to suck,
For the sun to rot,
For a tree to drop.
Here is a strange and bitter crop.

Other celebrated jazz standards performed by Billie Holiday include "God Bless' the Child," "Summertime," "I'm a Fool to Want You," "Body and Soul," "The Man I Love," and "But Beautiful."

Ella Fitzgerald (1917–1996). Sometimes referred to as **"The First Lady of Song,"** Ella Fitzgerald is considered one of the greatest of female jazz vocalists, rivaled only by Billie Holiday and Sarah Vaughan. She had an astonishing three-octave vocal range, a voice of amazing purity of tone, a mastery of the swing and scat singing styles, and an ebullience that captivated audiences. Her vast output of recordings included just about every great jazz standard, including such hits as "Anything Goes," "Mack the Knife," "How High the Moon," "Stormy Weather," "I Can't Give You Anything but Love," "Cry Me a River," and "Someone to Watch over Me."

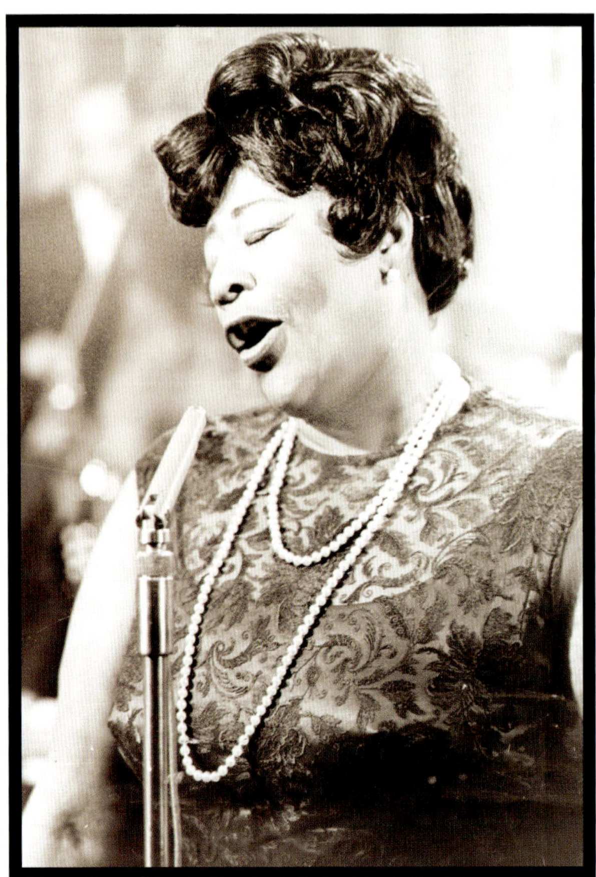

Ella Fitzgerald. Jazz vocalist. Library of Congress, LC-USZ62-114744.

Sarah Vaughan (1924–1990). Singing across an astonishing vocal range with a beautiful vibrato, Sarah Vaughan (See page 704) made many of the finest recordings ever done by a female jazz artist. Like Ella Fitzgerald, she recorded many of the great jazz standards, including such great tunes as "Tenderly" and "Misty."

Nat "King" Cole (1919–1965). A piano player and singer with a beautiful, fluid, lyrical voice, Nat "King" Cole first achieved fame with his recording of "Sweet Lorraine" in 1940. Over his long career, he had many, many hit songs, including "The Christmas Song," Nature Boy," "Mona Lisa," and the tune most widely associated with his name, "Unforgettable."

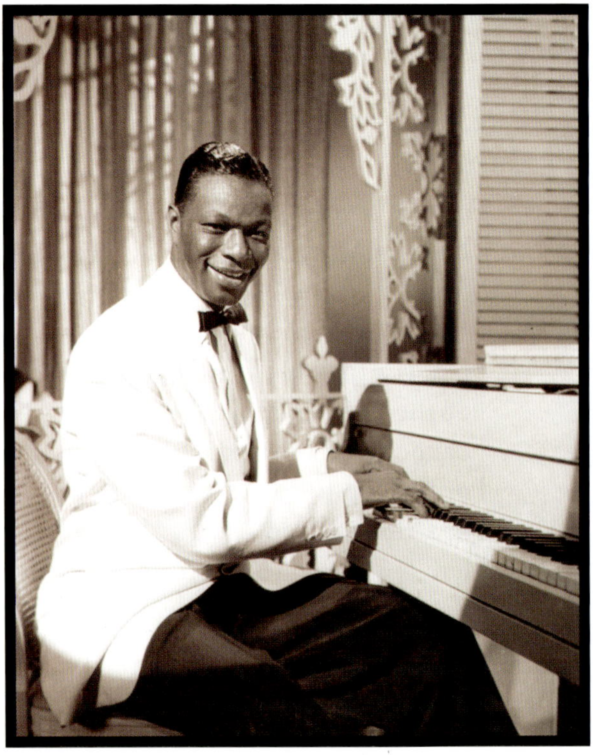

Nat "King" Cole. Pianist, vocalist, and songwriter

Art Tatum (1909–1956). Born in Toledo, Ohio, Art Tatum didn't let his near blindness get in the way of becoming one of the greatest pianists of all time. His virtuoso improvisation was so impressive that Fats Waller once said to his audience, when he saw Tatum walk into the club where Waller was playing, "I only play the piano, but tonight God is in the house."

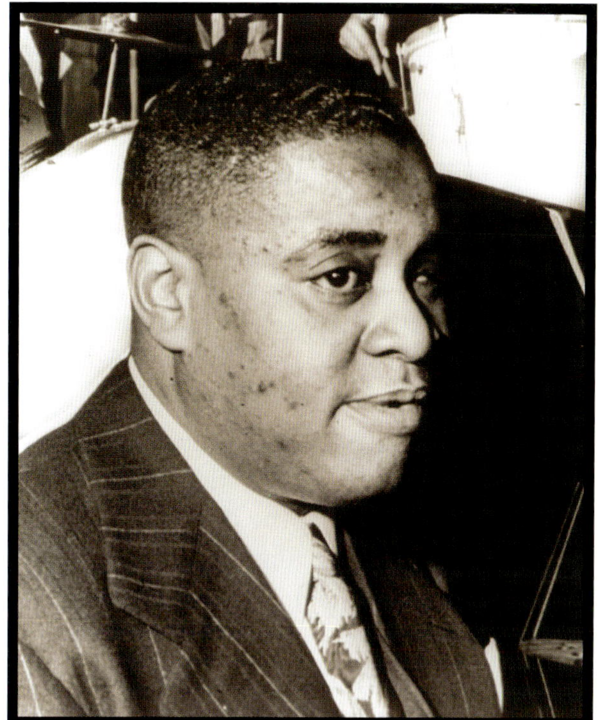
Art Tatum. The greatest of the early jazz pianists
Library of Congress, LC-USZ62-67705.

Other great African-American jazz musicians of the early twentieth century include the following:

James Hubert "Eubie" Blake (1887–1983). Pianist and songwriter

James P. Johnson (1894–1955). Pianist and originator of the stride piano style, characterized by alternating bass notes and chords with the left hand while playing melodies and improvisations with the right

Fletcher Hamilton Henderson, Jr. (1897–1952). Band leader and composer

Lionel Leo Hampton (1908–2002). Vibraphonist and band leader

Charlie Christian (1916–1942). The first great soloist on the electric (amplified) guitar

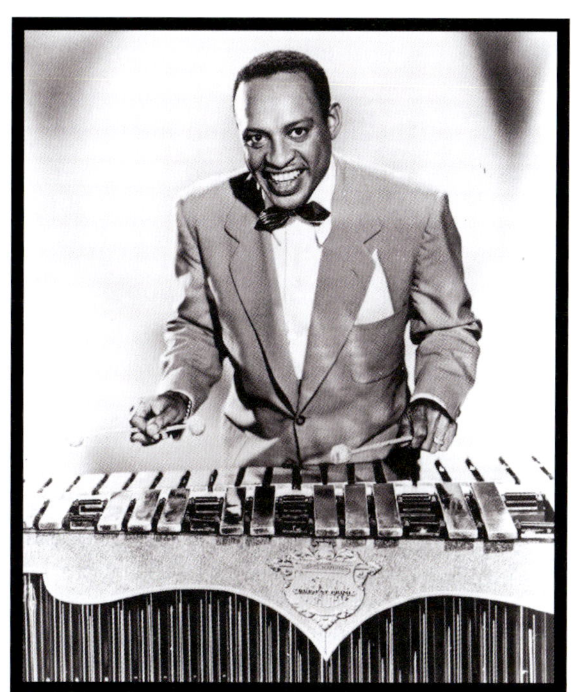
Lionel Leo Hampton. Vibraphonist and band leader.
Library of Congress, LC-USZ62-132945.

The Golden Age of African-American Dance

The Cakewalk and the Origins of the Chorus Line. The late nineteenth century saw the **cakewalk** become a nationwide craze. This high-stepping promenade with origins in slave dances (See Unit 2) became popularized following its inclusion in "The Creole Show," a theatrical production that played in Boston and New York, and through such popular performers as **Charles E. Johnson** and **Dora Dean.** Turn-of-the-century renditions of the cakewalk harkened back to the ring shout. Male and female dance partners lined up in a circular formation with interlocked arms and took abbreviated skipping steps interspersed with high kicks. This innovative high-kicking would become a staple of chorus lines on Broadway forever after. The cakewalk not only influenced Broadway but was also the first of a succession of dance crazes with their roots in African-American dance forms.

Swing Dance. After the Civil War, a succession of migrations brought great numbers of African Americans from rural areas in the South to cities in the North. These people brought with them the dances of southern juke joints. In those places, dances formerly performed by slaves, such as the **bamboula,** the **buzzard lope,** the **cakewalk,** the **calenda,** the **jig,** the **pigeon wing,** the **strut,** and the **ring dance,** were being adapted, transformed, and modernized. The dances of the juke joints developed into the forerunners of what would come to be known, in the North, as **swing dance**—the wildly energetic style of dance performed in clubs to the sounds of jazz and popular music from the 1920s through the 1940s. Some of the popular swing dances that emerged in this way during the early part of the twentieth century included the **turkey trot, ballin' the jack,** the **fox trot,** the **Charleston,** the **black bottom,** the **lindy hop,** and the **jitterbug.** These dances made so-called **swing jazz** the most popular music of the first half of the twentieth century, creating a frenzy that drew young people, black and white alike, into the clubs to kick up their heels. Some of these dances, the lindy hop and the jitterbug in particular, can still be seen in clubs today, and these dances were precursors, of course, to the varieties of dance that young people did from that era to the present, just as jazz and blues were the precursors of rock 'n' roll. It is no exaggeration to say that American popular dance, from the turkey trot at the turn of the twentieth century to the **breakdance** and **hip hop** styles at the turn of the twenty-first, were largely the creations of unnamed and unknown African Americans. When Elvis Presley shocked America and started a craze for rock 'n' roll with his gyrations on the *Ed Sullivan Show* in the 1950s, he was simply imitating what Broadway star **Earl "Snake Hips" Tucker** had done decades earlier, and Tucker was simply building upon inherited dance motifs that went all the way back to West Africa.

Tap Dance. The creativity unleashed in the aftermath of the Civil War also led to the development of one of the most innovative forms of American vernacular dance, **tap dance,** a dance style distinguished by percussive foot work in rhythmic patterns. While early dancers sounded out syncopated rhythms with wooden-soled shoes, later tappers affixed metal plates to their shoes, creating a distinctive rhythmic clacking sound.

Tap had its roots in the late 1800s, when early figures such as **Master Juba** (a stage name for William Henry Lane. See page 215), and his mentor, **"Uncle" Jim Lowe,** developed a unique form blending British folk dances (in particular, the Irish Jig and English Clog) with African derived dance movements and rhythms. Receiving top billing as a minstrel show artist at a time when white dancers dominated the scene, Master Juba paved the way for black dance artists, who gradually came to have a place in minstrel shows, vaudeville, and, later, Broadway. As they found their way into the spotlight, these early artists began to hammer out the tap form.

Minstrel comedian and dancer **Billy Kersands,** for instance, became famous for his performance of the **Virginia Essence,** an African-American vernacular form that evolved into **soft shoe,** a variety of tap performed with leather-soled shoes, in a smooth, elegant style. Other traveling entertainers, such as **The Bohee Brothers** (James and George) and an all-black roadshow act, **Black Patti's Troubadours,** also helped to popularize African-American dance forms that influenced tap. It wasn't long before tap dance hopped from the nightclub to the Broadway stage. From there, tap—almost literally—flew to the big screen, where flash acts, such as **The Berry Brothers** and **The Nicholas Brothers** combined jazz and tap dance with ad-lib acrobatics, such as knee-drops, splits, and flips.

No doubt, the single most important center for the development of tap dance, however, was the legendary **Hoofer's Club.** Although tap reached its height of popularity when it transitioned from theater to film, the now Hollywood-favored art form bubbled forth from this small site, a 15-ft-square

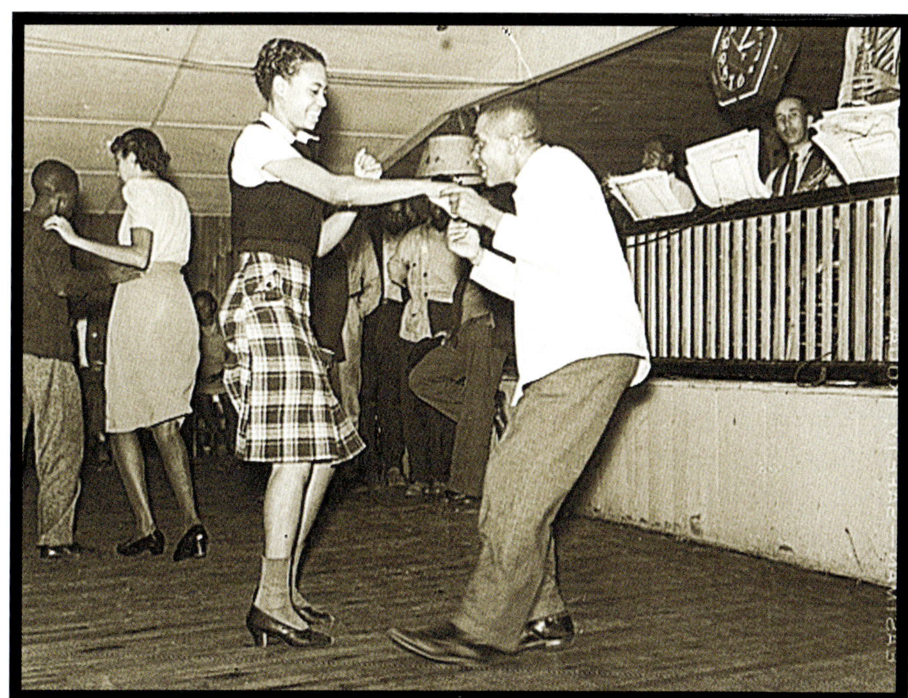

Jitterbugging in a juke joint. Library of Congress, LC-USF34-052589-D.

basement room in the back of a Harlem establishment known as The Comedy Club. Adjacent to the Lafayette Theater (See the Map of Harlem on page 220), the Hoofer's Club was set aside by proprietor Lonnie Hicks for tap dancers to practice their art, create new moves, inspire each other, and do what they did best—compete. In improvised dance "challenges," they tried to outdo each other; and "stealing steps," where one dancer copied another and added his own embellishments, was par for the course.

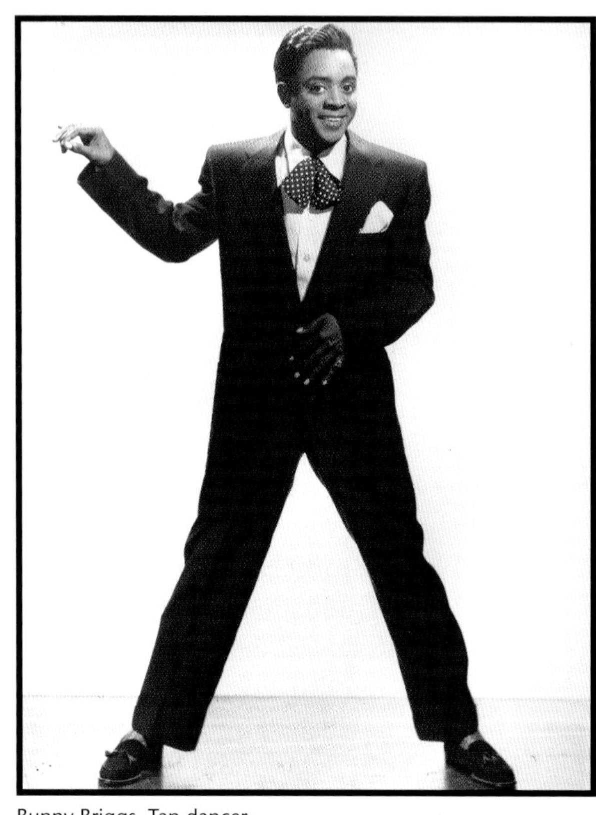
Bunny Briggs. Tap dancer.

Many celebrated tap dancers, known affectionately as "hoofers," graced the Hoofer's Club. One of the earliest, **King Rastus Brown,** was known for rhythmic variations on the Time Step. **Bill "Bojangles" Robinson,** perhaps the most renowned tap dancer due to his movie fame, also frequented the Hoofer's Club, although legend has it that he preferred to play pool. Robinson, who began as a vaudeville dancer and later wowed Broadway in such shows as *Blackbirds,* broke through social barriers and was instrumental in translating tap dance to the big screen. In such films as *The Little Colonel* (1935), in which he performed with Shirley Temple, Bojangles popularized tap and became famous for an elegant staircase dance that influenced many who followed him, including others of movie fame such as Fred Astaire and Gene Kelly. He was also known for bringing tap dance "up on the toes" with a lightness that didn't forget to swing.

Other Hoofer's Club regulars added their own innovations to tap. Among the many notables, **John Bubbles** (a stage name for John William Sublett), originally part of the theater duo **Buck and Bubbles** with partner **Ford Lee "Buck" Washington,** invented many new steps and combinations and added rhythmic complexity for which he earned the epithet "the father of rhythm tap." One of the youngest of the Hoofer's Club greats, **Baby Laurence,** drew inspiration from jazz artists such as Art Tatum and Charlie Parker and made his own imprint on the form. Friend and amiable rival **Bunny Briggs,** who danced with Duke Ellington's band, also built upon the creative interplay between tap dance and jazz music.

Concert Dance Innovators. In the 1920s, **Charles H. Williams** formed the **Hampton Institute Creative Dance Group,** which pioneered serious stage dance based on themes taken from spirituals and African sources. During the 1920s, black musical theater became extremely popular in New York because of the success of "Shuffle Along," by **Noble Sissle** and **Eubie Blake,** in 1921, and "Running Wild," which featured the dance known as the Charleston, in 1923. In the early 1930s, **Feral Benga** and **Josephine Baker** became huge sensations on concert stages in France. In 1931, **Hemsley Winfield** and **Edna Guy** appeared in a New York performance of what was billed as the first all-black serious dance recital in America. Both performers formed dance companies, and Winfield went on to become the first African American to take a leading role in a production at the Metropolitan Opera.

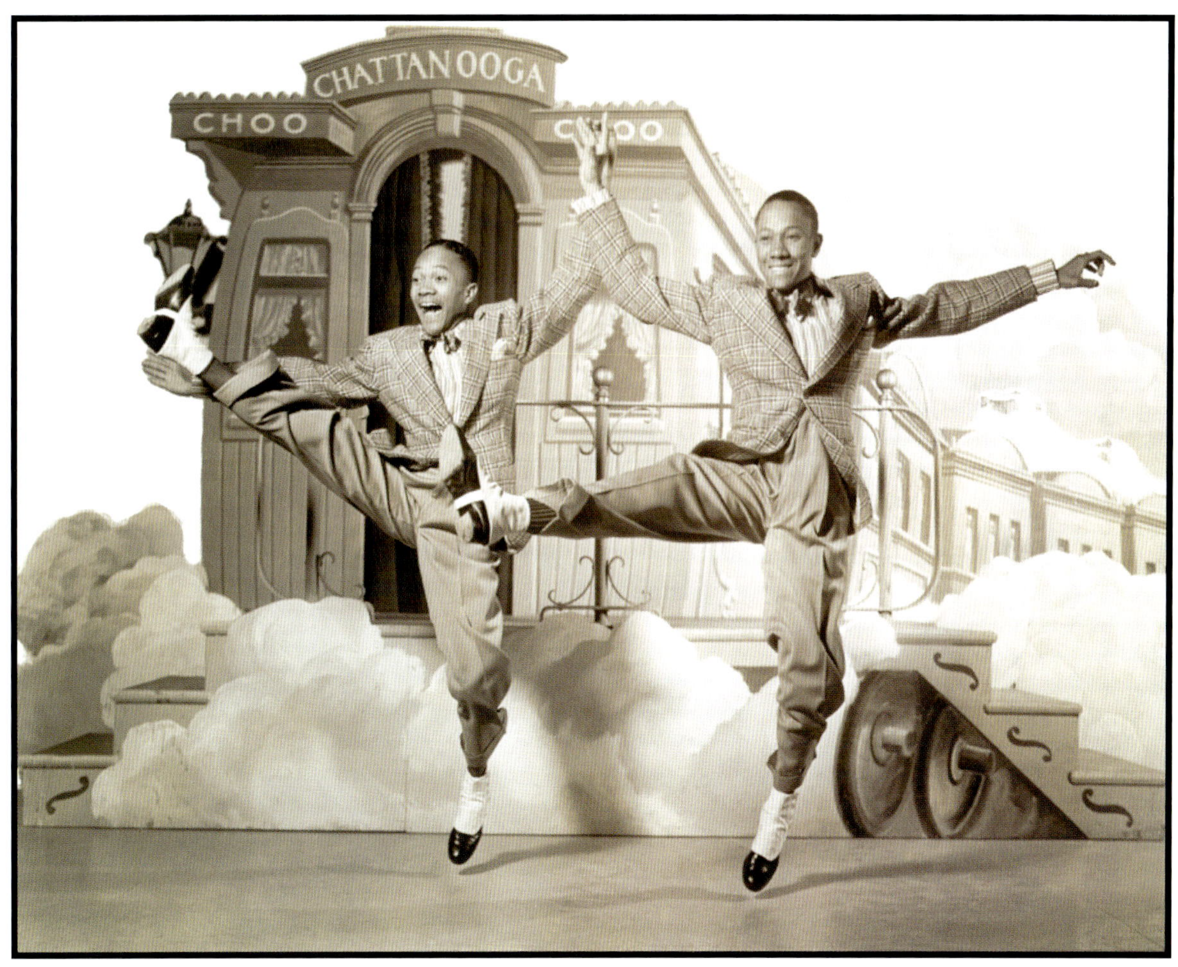

The Nicholas Brothers. Fayard and Harold Nicholas, tap dancers and stars in countless stage shows and motion pictures

Also in the early 1930s, **Katherine Dunham** (1909–2006) formed the **Ballet Negre** and a dance school in Chicago. A genius and an innovator, Dunham studied anthropology and dance, receiving a B.A. degree from the University of Chicago and an M.A. from Northwestern University. Performing fieldwork in the West Indies, she researched the links between Caribbean and African dance. An acclaimed dancer and influential choreographer, she drew inspiration from African-Caribbean themes and forms in such works as *L'Ag'Ya.* Dunham also founded the **Katherine Dunham Dance Company** and the **Dunham School of Dance and Theater,** choreographed for the Metropolitan Opera, and worked as a Civil Rights activist.

Another highly influential dancer, **Pearl Primus** (1919–1994) created and performed in dances known for their astonishing athleticism and their social protest content. Her choreography included interpretations of such poetry as Langston Hughes's "The Negro Speaks of Rivers" (See page 355) and Lewis Allen's powerful lyric about lynching, "Strange Fruit" (See page 467). Studying dance in West and Central Africa and in the Caribbean, she blended African and Caribbean styles with modern dance and ballet. Receiving a Ph.D. in Dance Education from New York University, she became a professor of Ethnic Studies. She also founded a dance company that evolved into a school for dancers, the **Pearl Primus Dance Language Institute.**

Talley Beatty (b. 1923), a member of Katherine Dunham's troupe from 1937 to 1943, performed on Broadway, appearing in such shows as "Cabin in the Sky" and "Showboat" with Pearl Primus. In the 1950s and '60s, he collaborated with jazz legend Duke Ellington. He formed his own dance company and choreographed for numerous American and international dance companies, including the Boston Ballet and the Bat-Sheva Company of Israel. ■

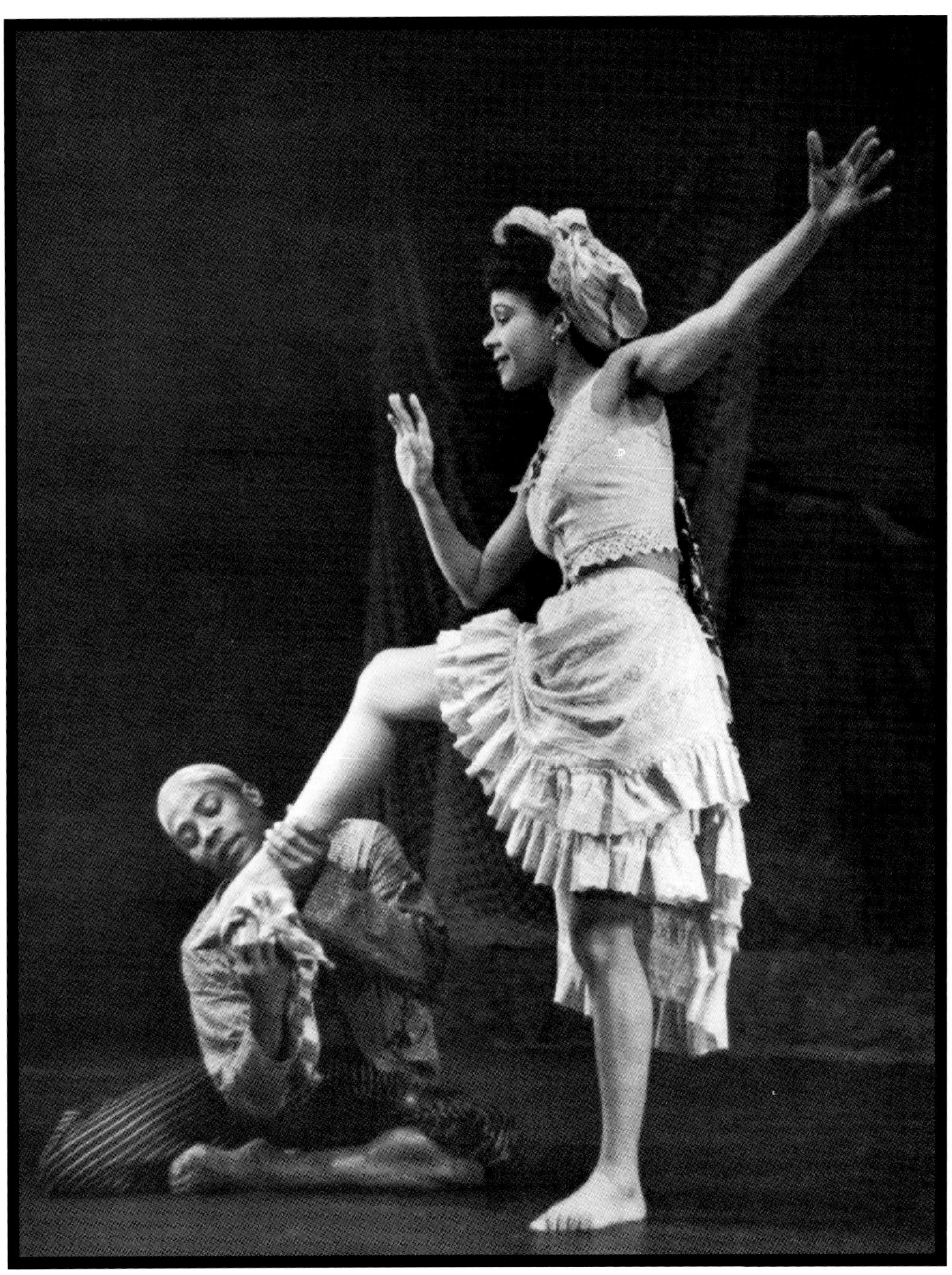

Katherine Dunham in a performance of her work *L'Ag'Ya.*

Robert Hayden Dudley Randall

MARGARET WALKER Mari Evans

Gwendolyn Brooks

AMIRI BARAKA

Eloise Greenfield

Sonia Sanchez Maya Angelou

Lucille Clifton Nikki Giovanni

Waverly Turner Carmichael

Rita Dove NTOZAKE SHANGE

Derek Walcott Jay Wright

Toni Cade Bambara Michael Harper

Dorothy West RALPH ELLISON

TONI MORRISON

Martin Luther King, Jr.

Malcolm X Lorraine Hansberry

Wynton Marsalis

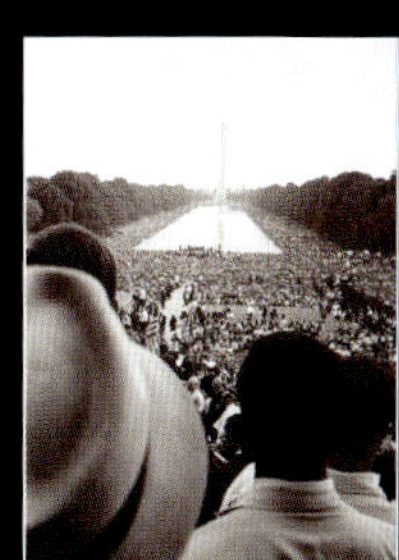

Unit 4
Civil Rights and Beyond

"When the history books are written in future generations, the historians will have to pause and say, 'There lived a great people — a black people — who injected new meaning and dignity into the veins of civilizations.'"

—The Reverend Dr. Martin Luther King, Jr.

of had lived by hustling and crime. I would be startled to catch myself thinking in a remote way of my earlier self as another person.

The things I felt, I was pitifully unable to express in the one-page letter that went every day to Mr. Elijah Muhammad. And I wrote at least one more daily letter, replying to one of my brothers and sisters. Every letter I received from them added something to my knowledge of the teachings of Mr. Muhammad. I would sit for long periods and study his photographs.

I've never been one for inaction. Everything I've ever felt strongly about, I've done something about. I guess that's why, unable to do anything else, I soon began writing to people I had known in the hustling world, such as Sammy the Pimp, John Hughes, the gambling-house owner, the thief Jumpsteady, and several dope peddlers. I wrote them all about Allah and Islam and Mr. Elijah Muhammad. I had no idea where most of them lived. I addressed their letters in care of the Harlem or Roxbury bars and clubs where I'd known them.

I never got a single reply. The average hustler and criminal was too uneducated to write a letter. I have known many slick, sharp-looking hustlers, who would have you think they had an interest in Wall Street; privately, they would get someone else to read a letter if they received one. Besides, neither would I have replied to anyone writing me something as wild as "the white man is the devil."

Why did people in Malcolm's old neighborhoods think he was crazy?

What certainly went on the Harlem and Roxbury wires was that Detroit Red was going crazy in stir,[1] or else he was trying some hype to shake up the warden's office.

During the years that I stayed in the Norfolk Prison Colony, never did any official directly say anything to me about those letters, although, of course, they all passed through the prison censorship.[2] I'm sure, however, they monitored what I wrote to add to the files which every state and federal prison keeps on the conversion of Negro inmates by the teachings of Mr. Elijah Muhammad.

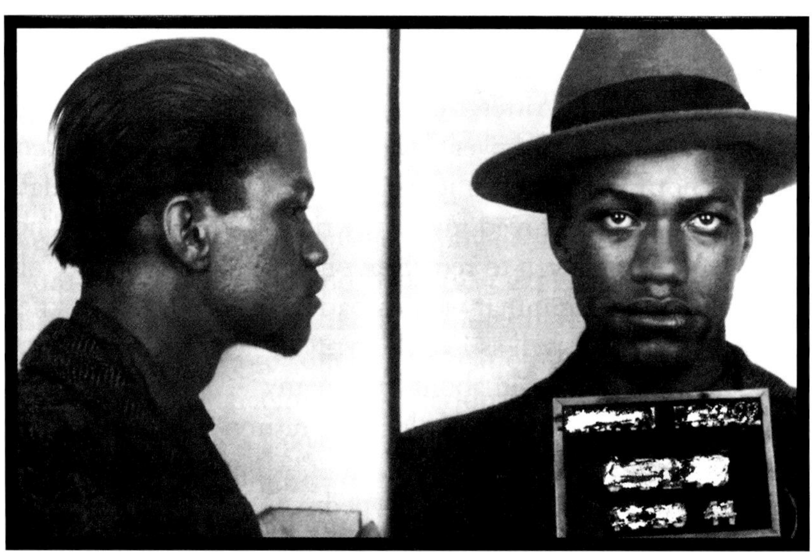

1944 Police Mugshot of Malcolm X.

But at that time, I felt that the real reason was that the white man knew that he was the devil.

Later on, I even wrote to the Mayor of Boston, to the Governor of Massachusetts, and to Harry S. Truman. They never answered; they probably never even saw my letters. I hand-scratched to them how the

[1] **Detroit Red . . . in stir.** Detroit Red was his street name. "In stir" means *in prison.*

[2] **censorship.** A *censor* is an official or officer who examines written or other communications (in this case, personal mail) and removes information deemed objectionable or undesirable. The *censorship* is the office or group charged with censoring.

white man's society was responsible for the black man's condition in this wilderness of North America.

It was because of my letters that I happened to stumble upon starting to acquire some kind of a homemade education.

I became increasingly frustrated at not being able to express what I wanted to convey in letters that I wrote, especially those to Mr. Elijah Muhammad. In the street, I had been the most **articulate** hustler out there—I had commanded attention when I said something. But now, trying to write simple English, I not only wasn't articulate, I wasn't even functional. How would I sound writing in slang, the way I would *say* it, something such as "Look, daddy, let me pull your coat about a cat, Elijah Muhammad—"

Many who today hear me somewhere in person, or on television, or those who read something I've said, will think I went to school far beyond the eighth grade. This impression is due entirely to my prison studies.

It had really begun back in the Charlestown Prison, when Bimbi first made me feel envy of his stock of knowledge. Bimbi had always taken charge of any conversation he was in, and I had tried to **emulate** him. But every book I picked up had few sentences which didn't contain anywhere from one to nearly all of the words that might as well have been in Chinese. When I just skipped those words, of course, I really ended up with little idea of what the book said. So I had come to the Norfolk Prison Colony still going through only book-reading motions. Pretty soon, I would have quit even these motions, unless I had received the motivation that I did.

I saw that the best thing I could do was get hold of a dictionary—to study, to learn some words. I was lucky enough to reason also that I should try to improve my penmanship. It was sad. I couldn't even write in a straight line. It was both ideas together that moved me to request a dictionary along with some tablets and pencils from the Norfolk Prison Colony school.

Why did Malcolm ask for a dictionary? What did he do with it?

I spent two days just **riffling** uncertainly through the dictionary's pages. I'd never realized so many words existed! I didn't know *which* words I needed to learn. Finally, just to start some kind of action, I began copying.

In my slow, painstaking, ragged handwriting, I copied into my tablet everything printed on that first page, down to the punctuation marks.

I believe it took me a day. Then, aloud, I read back, to myself, everything I'd written on the tablet. Over and over, aloud, to myself, I read my own handwriting.

I woke up the next morning, thinking about those words—immensely proud to realize that not only had I written so much at one time, but I'd written words that I never knew were in the world. Moreover, with a little effort, I also could remember what many of these words meant. I reviewed the words whose meanings I didn't remember. Funny thing, from the dictionary first page right now, that "aardvark" springs to my mind. The dictionary had a picture of it, a long-tailed, long-eared, burrowing African mammal, which lives off termites caught by sticking out its tongue as an anteater does for ants.

I was so fascinated that I went on—I copied the dictionary's next page. And the same experience came when I studied that. With every succeeding page, I also learned of people and places and events from history.

VOCABULARY IN PLACE

- **articulate, *adj.*** Expressing oneself easily in clear and effective language
- **emulate, *v.*** To strive to equal or excel; imitate
- **riffle, *v.*** To thumb through (the pages of a book)

Actually the dictionary is like a miniature encyclopedia. Finally the dictionary's A section had filled a whole tablet—and I went on into the B's. That was the way I started copying what eventually became the entire dictionary. It went a lot faster after so much practice helped me to pick up handwriting speed. Between what I wrote in my tablet, and writing letters, during the rest of my time in prison I would guess I wrote a million words.

I suppose it was inevitable that as my word-base broadened, I could for the first time pick up a book and read and now begin to understand what the book was saying. Anyone who has read a great deal can imagine the new world that opened. Let me tell you something: from then until I left that prison, in every free moment I had, if I was not reading in the library, I was reading on my bunk. You couldn't have gotten me out of books with a wedge. Between Mr. Muhammad's teachings, my correspondence, my visitors—usually Ella and Reginald—and my reading of books, months passed without my even thinking about being imprisoned. In fact, up to then, I never had been so truly free in my life.

Why did Malcolm feel "truly free," even though he was in prison?

The Norfolk Prison Colony's library was in the school building. A variety of classes was taught there by instructors who came from such places as Harvard and Boston universities. The weekly debates between inmate teams were also held in the school building. You would be astonished to know how worked up convict debaters and audiences would get over subjects like "Should Babies Be Fed Milk?"

Available on the prison library's shelves were books on just about every general subject. Much of the big private collection that Parkhurst[3] had willed to the prison was still in crates and boxes in the back of the library—thousands of old books. Some of them looked ancient: covers faded, old-time parchment-looking binding. Parkhurst, I've mentioned, seemed to have been principally interested in history and religion. He had the money and the special interest to have a lot of books that you wouldn't have in general circulation. Any college library would have been lucky to get that collection.

As you can imagine, especially in a prison where there was heavy emphasis on rehabilitation, an inmate was smiled upon if he demonstrated an unusually intense interest in books. There was a sizable number of well-read inmates, especially the popular debaters. Some were said by many to be practically walking encyclopedias. They were almost celebrities. No university would ask any student to devour literature as I did when this new world opened to me, of being able to read and *understand.*

Why did Malcolm emphasize the word understand, *but not the word* read?

I read more in my room than in the library itself. An inmate who was known to read a lot could check out more than the permitted maximum number of books. I preferred reading in the total isolation of my own room.

When I had progressed to really serious reading, every night at about ten p.m. I would be outraged with the "lights out." It always seemed to catch me right in the middle of something engrossing.

Fortunately, right outside my door was a corridor light that cast a glow into my room. The glow was enough to read by, once my eyes adjusted to it. So when "lights out" came, I would sit on the floor where I could continue reading in that glow.

At one-hour intervals the night guards paced past every room. Each time I heard the

[3] **Parkhurst.** A millionaire who donated his book collection to the prison library, to whom Malcolm also alluded in Chapter 10 of his autobiography

approaching footsteps, I jumped into bed and feigned sleep. And as soon as the guard passed, I got back out of bed onto the floor area of that light-glow, where I would read for another fifty-eight minutes—until the guard approached again. That went on until three or four every morning. Three or four hours of sleep a night was enough for me. Often in the years in the streets I had slept less than that.

What did Elijah Muhammad stress about history? What does this mean?

The teachings of Mr. Muhammad stressed how history had been "whitened"—when white men had written history books, the black man simply had been left out. Mr. Muhammad couldn't have said anything that would have struck me much harder. I had never forgotten how when my class, me and all of those whites, had studied seventh-grade United States history back in Mason, the history of the Negro had been covered in one paragraph, and the teacher had gotten a big laugh with his joke, "Negroes' feet are so big that when they walk, they leave a hole in the ground."

This is one reason why Mr. Muhammad's teachings spread so swiftly all over the United States, among *all* Negroes, whether or not they became followers of Mr. Muhammad. The teachings ring true—to every Negro. You can hardly show me a black adult in America—or a white one, for that matter—who knows from the history books anything like the truth about the black man's role. In my own case, once I heard of the "glorious history of the black man," I took special pains to hunt in the library for books that would inform me on details about black history.

I can remember accurately the very first set of books that really impressed me. I have since bought that set of books and have it at home for my children to read as they grow up. It's called *Wonders of the World*. It's full of pictures of archeological finds, statues that depict, usually, non-European people.

I found books like Will Durant's *Story of Civilization*. I read H. G. Wells' *Outline of History*. *Souls Of Black Folk* by W. E. B. Du Bois gave me a glimpse into the black people's history before they came to this country. Carter G. Woodson's *Negro History* opened my eyes about black empires before the black slave was brought to the United States, and the early Negro struggles for freedom.

J. A. Rogers' three volumes of *Sex and Race* told about race-mixing before Christ's time; about Aesop[4] being a black man who told fables; about Egypt's Pharaohs; about the great Coptic[5] Christian Empires; about Ethiopia, the earth's oldest continuous black civilization, as China is the oldest continuous civilization.

Mr. Muhammad's teaching about how the white man had been created led me to *Findings In Genetics* by Gregor Mendel.[6] (The dictionary's G section was where I had learned what "genetics" meant.) I really studied this book by the Austrian monk. Reading it over and over, especially certain sections, helped me to understand that if you started with a black man, a white man could be produced; but starting with a white man, you never could produce a black man—because the white gene is recessive. And since no one disputes that there was but one Original Man, the conclusion is clear.

During the last year or so, in the *New York Times*, Arnold Toynbee used the word

4 **Aesop.** A Greek fabulist traditionally considered the author of *Aesop's Fables*, which include "The Tortoise and the Hare"

5 **Coptic.** A Copt is an Egyptian belonging to or descended from the people of ancient or pre-Islamic Egypt. The Coptic Church is the Christian church of Egypt.

6 **Gregor Mendel.** (1822–1884) Austrian botanist and founder of the science of genetics. Conducting experiments with plants, especially garden peas, he discovered the principle of the inheritance of characteristics through the combination of genes from parent cells.

"bleached" in describing the white man. (His words were: "White (i.e. bleached) human beings of North European origin. . .") Toynbee also referred to the European geographic area as only a peninsula of Asia. He said there is no such thing as Europe. And if you look at the globe, you will see for yourself that America is only an extension of Asia. (But at the same time Toynbee is among those who have helped to bleach history. He has written that Africa was the only continent that produced no history. He won't write that again. Every day now, the truth is coming to light.)

What "truth is coming to light" every day, according to Malcolm?

I never will forget how shocked I was when I began reading about slavery's total horror. It made such an impact upon me that it later became one of my favorite subjects when I became a minister of Mr. Muhammad's. The world's most monstrous crime, the sin and the blood on the white man's hands, are almost impossible to believe. Books like the one by Frederick Olmstead[7] opened my eyes to the horrors suffered when the slave was landed in the United States. The European woman, Fannie Kimball, who had married a Southern white slaveowner, described how human beings were degraded. Of course I read *Uncle Tom's Cabin*. In fact, I believe that's the only novel I have ever read since I started serious reading.

Parkhurst's collection also contained some bound pamphlets of the Abolitionist Anti-Slavery Society of New England. I read descriptions of atrocities, saw those illustrations of black slave women tied up and flogged with whips; of black mothers watching their babies being dragged off, never to be seen by their mothers again; of dogs after slaves, and of the fugitive slave catchers, evil white men with whips and clubs and chains and guns. I read about the slave preacher Nat Turner,[8] who put the fear of God into the white slavemaster. Nat Turner wasn't going around preaching pie-in-the-sky and "non-violent" freedom for the black man. There in Virginia one night in 1831, Nat and seven other slaves started out at his master's home and through the night they went from one plantation "big house" to the next, killing, until by the next morning fifty-seven white people were dead and Nat had about seventy slaves following him. White people, terrified for their lives, fled from their homes, locked themselves up in public buildings, hid in the woods, and some even left the state. A small army of soldiers took two months to catch and hang Nat Turner. Somewhere I have read where Nat Turner's example is said to have inspired John Brown to invade Virginia and attack Harper's Ferry nearly thirty years later, with thirteen white men and five Negroes.

I read Herodotus,[9] "the father of History," or, rather, I read about him. And I read the histories of various nations, which opened my eyes gradually, then wider and wider, to how the whole world's white men had indeed acted like devils, pillaging and raping and bleeding and draining the whole world's non-white people. I remember, for instance, books such as Will Durant's story of Oriental civilization, and Mahatma Gandhi's[10] accounts of the struggle to drive the British out of India.

---

[7] **Frederick Olmstead.** (1822–1903) American landscape architect famous for designing urban parks, including New York's Central Park. Malcolm refers here to Olmstead's book *Journeys and Explorations in the Cotton Kingdom* (1861), which helped spur the antislavery movement.

[8] **Nat Turner.** Leader of a major slave rebellion in 1831. See page 104.

[9] **Herodotus.** (484 BC–circa 425 BC) Greek historian known for his book *The Histories,* which details (with significant controversy as to its accuracy) the cultures, customs, and conflicts of many different peoples in the ancient world

[10] **Mahatma Gandhi.** (1869–1948) Political and spiritual leader during India's struggle with Great Britain for home rule; an advocate of passive resistance

Book after book showed me how the white man had brought upon the world's black, brown, red, and yellow peoples every variety of the sufferings of exploitation. I saw how since the sixteenth century, the so-called "Christian trader" white man began to ply the seas in his lust for Asian and African empires, and plunder, and power. I read, I saw, how the white man never has gone among the non-white peoples bearing the Cross in the true manner and spirit of Christ's teachings—meek, humble, and Christ-like.

What conclusions did Malcolm draw with regard to history and slavery?

I perceived, as I read, how the **collective** white man had been actually nothing but a **piratical** opportunist who used Faustian[11] **machinations** to make his own Christianity his initial wedge in criminal conquests. First, always "religiously," he branded "heathen" and "pagan" labels upon ancient non-white cultures and civilizations. The stage thus set, he then turned upon his non-white victims his weapons of war.

I read how, entering India—half a *billion* deeply religious brown people—the British white man, by 1759, through promises, trickery and manipulations, controlled much of India through Great Britain's East India Company. The parasitical British administration kept tentacling[12] out to half of the subcontinent. In 1857, some of the desperate people of India finally mutinied—and, excepting the African slave trade, nowhere has history recorded any more unnecessary **bestial** and ruthless human carnage than the British **suppression** of the non-white Indian people.

Over 115 million African blacks—close to the 1930's population of the United States—were murdered or enslaved during the slave trade. And I read how when the slave market was **glutted,** the cannibalistic white powers of Europe next carved up, as their colonies, the richest areas of the black continent. And Europe's chancelleries[13] for the next century played a chess game of naked **exploitation** and power from Cape Horn to Cairo.

Ten guards and the warden couldn't have torn me out of those books. Not even Elijah Muhammad could have been more eloquent than those books were in providing indisputable proof that the collective white man had acted like a devil in virtually every contact he had with the world's collective non-white man. I listen today to the radio, and watch television, and read the headlines about the collective white man's fear and tension concerning China. When the white man professes ignorance about why the

---

11 **Faustian.** After Faust (Faustus), a German magician who, according to legend, sold his soul to the devil in exchange for knowledge. *Faustian* refers to a bargain in which someone willingly violates moral or ethical values for material gain.

12 **parasitical . . . tentacling.** A reference to British colonialism in India. *Parasitical* means taking advantage of others and offering nothing in return (like a plant or organism that lives on another but contributes nothing to its host's survival). *Tentacling* means extending tentacles (or influence) in all directions.

13 **chancelleries.** Official places of business for embassies or consulates

VOCABULARY IN PLACE

- **collective,** ***adj.*** Relating to a number of people acting as a group
- **piratical,** ***adj.*** Characteristic of pirates
- **machination,** ***n.*** A crafty scheme or cunning design for the accomplishment of a sinister end
- **bestial,** ***adj.*** Beastly; marked by brutality
- **suppression,** ***n.*** The act of restricting or prohibiting
- **glutted,** ***past part.*** Filled to capacity; no longer profitable
- **exploitation,** ***n.*** Utilization of another for selfish purposes

Chinese hate him so, my mind can't help flashing back to what I read, there in prison, about how the blood forebears of this same white man raped China at a time when China was trusting and helpless. Those original white "Christian traders" sent into China millions of pounds of opium. By 1839, so many of the Chinese were addicts that China's desperate government destroyed twenty thousand chests of opium. The first Opium War was promptly declared by the white man. Imagine! Declaring *war* upon someone who objects to being narcotized![14] The Chinese were severely beaten, with Chinese-invented gunpowder.[15]

The Treaty of Nanking made China pay the British white man for the destroyed opium; forced open China's major ports to British trade; forced China to abandon Hong Kong; fixed China's import tariffs so low that cheap British articles soon flooded in, maiming China's industrial development.

After a second Opium War, the Tientsin Treaties legalized the ravaging opium trade, legalized a British-French-American control of China's customs. China tried delaying that Treaty's ratification; Peking was looted and burned.

"Kill the foreign white devils!" was the 1901 Chinese war cry in the Boxer Rebellion. Losing again, this time the Chinese were driven from Peking's choicest areas. The vicious, arrogant white man put up the famous signs, "Chinese and dogs not allowed."

Red China[16] after World War II closed its doors to the Western white world. Massive Chinese agricultural, scientific, and industrial efforts are described in a book that *Life* magazine recently published. Some observers inside Red China have reported that the world never has known such a hate-white campaign as is now going on in this non-white country where, present birth-rates continuing, in fifty more years Chinese will be half the earth's population. And it seems that some Chinese chickens will soon come home to roost, with China's recent successful nuclear tests.

Let us face reality. We can see in the United Nations a new world order being shaped, along color lines—an alliance among the non-white nations. America's U.N. Ambassador Adlai Stevenson complained not long ago that in the United Nations "a skin game" was being played. He was right. He was facing reality. A "skin game" *is* being played. But Ambassador Stevenson sounded like Jesse James accusing the marshal of carrying a gun. Because who in the world's history ever has played a worse "skin game" than the white man?

Why did Malcolm see a "new world order" forming in the United Nations?

Mr. Muhammad, to whom I was writing daily, had no idea of what a new world had opened up to me through my efforts to document his teachings in books.

When I discovered philosophy, I tried to touch all the landmarks of philosophical development. Gradually, I read most of the old philosophers, Occidental and Oriental.[17] The Oriental philosophers were the ones I came to prefer; finally, my impression was that most Occidental philosophy had largely been borrowed from the Oriental thinkers. Socrates, for instance, traveled in Egypt. Some sources even say that Socrates was initiated into some of the Egyptian mysteries.

---

14 **narcotized.** Drugged

15 **Chinese-invented gunpowder.** The Chinese are credited with inventing gunpowder, though Europeans perfected its use as a weapon.

16 **Red China.** Communist China, after the Chinese civil war and communist revolution, which began in the 1920s and was completed following World War II

17 **Occidental and Oriental.** *Occident,* from the French word for the direction of the setting sun, refers to the countries of Europe and the western hemisphere; the *Orient* is the countries of Asia (especially east Asia, the direction of the rising sun).

Obviously Socrates got some of his wisdom among the East's wise men.

I have often reflected upon the new vistas that reading opened to me. I knew right there in prison that reading had changed forever the course of my life. As I see it today, the ability to read awoke inside me some long dormant craving to be mentally alive. I certainly wasn't seeking any degree, the way a college confers a status symbol upon its students. My homemade education gave me, with every additional book that I read, a little bit more sensitivity to the deafness, dumbness, and blindness that was afflicting the black race in America. Not long ago, an English writer telephoned me from London, asking questions. One was, "What's your alma mater?"[18] I told him, "Books." You will never catch me with a free fifteen minutes in which I'm not studying something I feel might be able to help the black man.

Yesterday I spoke in London, and both ways on the plane across the Atlantic I was studying a document about how the United Nations proposes to insure the human rights of the oppressed minorities of the world. The American black man is the world's most shameful case of minority oppression. What makes the black man think of himself as only an internal United States issue is just a catch-phrase, two words, "civil rights." How is the black man going to get "civil rights" before first he wins his *human* right? If the American black man will start thinking about his *human* rights, and then start thinking of himself as part of one of the world's great peoples, he will see he has a case for the United Nations.

According to Malcolm, how must the black man make a case for the United Nations?

I can't think of a better case! Four hundred years of black blood and sweat invested here in America, and the white man still has the black man begging for what every immigrant fresh off the ship can take for granted the minute he walks down the gangplank.

But I'm digressing. I told the Englishman that my alma mater was books, a good library. Every time I catch a plane, I have with me a book that I want to read—and that's a lot of books these days. If I weren't out here every day battling the white man, I could spend the rest of my life reading, just satisfying my curiosity—because you can hardly mention anything I'm not curious about. I don't think anybody ever got more out of going to prison than I did. In fact, prison enabled me to study far more intensively than I would have if my life had gone differently and I had attended some college. I imagine that one of the biggest troubles with colleges is there are too many distractions, too much panty-raiding, fraternities, and boola-boola and all of that. Where else but in a prison could I have attacked my ignorance by being able to study intensely sometimes as much as fifteen hours a day?

Schopenhauer, Kant, Nietzsche,[19] naturally, I read all of those. I don't respect them; I am just trying to remember some of those whose theories I soaked up in those years. These three, it's said, laid the groundwork on which the Fascist and Nazi[20] philosophy was built. I don't respect them because it seems to me that most of their time was spent arguing about things that are not really important. They remind me of so many of the Negro "intellectuals," so-called, with whom I have come in contact—they are always arguing about something useless.

---

18 **alma mater.** The school or college one has attended

19 **Schopenhauer, Kant, Nietzche.** Eighteenth- and nineteenth-century philosophers

20 **Fascist and Nazi philosophy.** Fascism is a political ideology that supports centralization of authority under a dictator and suppression of opposition. Nazism was a variety of Fascism instituted in Germany under the leadership of Adolf Hitler and his cronies.

Spinoza impressed me for a while when I found out that he was black. A black Spanish Jew. The Jews **excommunicated** him because he advocated a pantheistic doctrine,[21] something like the "allness of God," or "God in everything." The Jews read their burial services for Spinoza, meaning that he was dead as far as they were concerned; his family was run out of Spain, they ended up in Holland, I think.

I'll tell you something. The whole stream of Western philosophy has now wound up in a cul-de-sac. The white man has perpetrated upon himself, as well as upon the black man, so gigantic a fraud that he has put himself into a crack. He did it through his elaborate, **neurotic** necessity to hide the black man's true role in history.

And today the white man is faced head on with what is happening on the Black Continent, Africa. Look at the artifacts being discovered there, that are proving over and over again, how the black man had great, fine, sensitive civilizations before the white man was out of the caves. Below the Sahara, in the places where most of America's Negroes' foreparents were kidnapped, there is being unearthed some of the finest craftsmanship, sculpture and other objects, that has ever been seen by modern man. Some of these things now are on view in such places as New York City's Metropolitan Museum of Art. Gold work of such fine tolerance and workmanship that it has no rival. Ancient objects produced by black hands . . . refined by those black hands with results that no human hand today can equal.

History has been so "whitened" by the white man that even the black professors have known little more than the most ignorant black man about the talents and rich civilizations and cultures of the black man of millenniums ago. I have lectured in Negro colleges and some of these brainwashed black Ph.D.'s, with their suspenders dragging the ground with degrees, have run to the white man's newspapers calling me a "black fanatic." Why, a lot of them are fifty years behind the times. If I were president of one of these black colleges, I'd hock the campus if I had to, to send a bunch of black students off digging in Africa for more, more and more proof of the black race's historical greatness. The white man now is in Africa digging and searching. An African elephant can't stumble without falling on some white man with a shovel. Practically every week, we read about some great new find from Africa's lost civilizations. All that's new is white science's attitude. The ancient civilizations of the black man have been buried on the Black Continent all the time.

Why were white men so busy digging in Africa? What should black colleges have done, according to Malcolm?

Here is an example: a British anthropologist named Dr. Louis S.B. Leakey is displaying some fossil bones—a foot, part of a hand, some jaws, and skull fragments. On the basis of these, Dr. Leakey has said it's time to rewrite completely the history of man's origin.

This species of man lived 1,818,036 years before Christ. And these bones were found in Tanganyika.[22] In the Black Continent.

21 **Spinoza . . . pantheistic doctrine.** Baruch (or Benedict) Spinoza (1632–1677), Dutch philosopher. He espoused a pantheistic doctrine advocating the belief that the universe and God are one.

22 **Tanganyika.** Modern Tanzania (renamed after it achieved independence from Britain in 1961)

VOCABULARY IN PLACE

- **excommunicate,** ***v.*** To exclude from membership in a church or other group
- **neurotic,** ***adj.*** Overanxious; obsessive

It's a crime, the lie that has been told to generations of black men and white men both. Little innocent black children, born of parents who believed that their race had no history. Little black children seeing, before they could talk, that their parents considered themselves inferior. Innocent black children growing up, living out their lives, dying of old age—and all of their lives ashamed of being black. But the truth is pouring out of the bag now.

Two other areas of experience which have been extremely formative in my life since prison were first opened to me in the Norfolk Prison Colony. For one thing, I had my first experiences in opening the eyes of my brainwashed black brethren to some truths about the black race. And, the other: when I had read enough to know something, I began to enter the Prison Colony's weekly debating program—my baptism into public speaking.

I have to admit a sad, shameful fact. I had so loved being around the white man that in prison I really disliked how Negro convicts stuck together so much. But when Mr. Muhammad's teachings reversed my attitude toward my black brothers, in my guilt and shame I began to catch every chance I could to recruit for Mr. Muhammad.

You have to be careful, very careful, introducing the truth to the black man who has never previously heard the truth about himself, his own kind, and the white man. My brother Reginald had told me that all Muslims experienced this in their recruiting for Mr. Muhammad. The black brother is so brainwashed that he may even be repelled when he first hears the truth. Reginald advised that the truth had to be dropped only a little bit at a time. And you had to wait a while to let it sink in before advancing the next step.

Why did Malcolm have to be careful when "introducing the truth to the black man"?

I began first telling my black brother inmates about the glorious history of the black man—things they never had dreamed. I told them the horrible slavery-trace truths that they never knew. I would watch their faces when I told them about that, because the white man had completely erased the slaves' past, a Negro in America can never know his true family name, or even what tribe he was descended from: the Mandingo, the Wolof, the Serer, the Fula, the Fanti, the Ashanti, or others. I told them that some slaves brought from Africa spoke Arabic, and were Islamic in their religion. A lot of these black convicts still wouldn't believe it unless they could see that a white man had said it. So, often, I would read to these brothers selected passages from white men's books. I'd explain to them that the real truth was known to some white men, the scholars; but there had been a conspiracy down through the generations to keep the truth from black men.

I would keep close watch on how each one reacted. I always had to be careful. I never knew when some brainwashed black imp, some dyed-in-the-wool Uncle Tom,[23] would nod at me and then go running to tell the white man. When one was ripe—and I could tell—then away from the rest, I'd drop it on him, what Mr. Muhammad taught: "The white man is the devil."

How did others respond to Malcom's views?

That would shock many of them—until they started thinking about it.

This is probably as big a single worry as the American prison system has today—the way the Muslim teachings, circulated among

[23] **imp . . . Uncle Tom.** An *imp* is a mischievous child or childlike person. *Uncle Tom,* after the title character of Harriet Beecher Stowe's novel, is an offensive term for a black person regarded as being humiliatingly subservient to white people.

all Negroes in the country, are converting new Muslims among black men in prison, and black men are in prison in far greater numbers than their proportion in the population.

The reason is that among all Negroes the black convict is the most perfectly preconditioned to hear the words, "the white man is the devil."

You tell that to any Negro. Except for those relatively few "integration"-mad so-called "intellectuals," and those black men who are otherwise fat, happy, and deaf, dumb, and blinded, with their crumbs from the white man's rich table, you have struck a nerve center in the American black man. He may take a day to react, a month, a year; he may never respond, openly; but of one thing you can be sure—when he thinks about his own life, he is going to see where, to him, personally, the white man sure has acted like a devil.

And, as I say, above all Negroes, the black prisoner. Here is a black man caged behind bars, probably for years, put there by the white man. Usually the convict comes from among those bottom-of-the-pile Negroes, the Negroes who through their entire lives have been kicked about, treated like children—Negroes who never have met one white man who didn't either take something from them or do something to them.

You let this caged-up black man start thinking, the same way I did when I first heard Elijah Muhammad's teachings: let him start thinking how, with better breaks when he was young and ambitious he might have been a lawyer, a doctor, a scientist, anything. You let this caged-up black man start realizing, as I did, how from the first landing of the first slave ship, the millions of black men in America have been like sheep in a den of wolves. That's why black prisoners become Muslims so fast when Elijah Muhammad's teachings filter into their cages by way of other Muslim convicts. "The white man is the devil" is a perfect echo of that black convict's lifelong experience.

I've told how debating was a weekly event there at the Norfolk Prison Colony. My reading had my mind like steam under pressure. Some way, I had to start telling the white man about himself to his face. I decided I could do this by putting my name down to debate.

Standing up and speaking before an audience was a thing that throughout my previous life never would have crossed my mind. Out there in the streets, hustling, pushing dope, and robbing, I could have had the dreams from a pound of hashish and I'd never have dreamed anything so wild as that one day I would speak in coliseums and arenas, at the greatest American universities, and on radio and television programs, not to mention speaking all over Egypt and Africa and in England.

But I will tell you that, right there, in the prison, debating, speaking to a crowd, was as exhilarating to me as the discovery of knowledge through reading had been. Standing up there, the faces looking up at me, things in my head coming out of my mouth, while my brain searched for the next best thing to follow what I was saying, and if I could sway them to my side by handling it right, then I had won the debate—once my feet got wet, I was gone on debating. Whichever side of the selected subject was assigned to me, I'd track down and study everything I could find on it. I'd put myself in my opponent's place and decide how I'd try to win if I had the other side; and then I'd figure a way to knock down those points. And if there was any way in the world, I'd work into my speech the devilishness of the white man.

What effect did public speaking have on Malcolm's character?

"Compulsory Military Training—Or None?" That's one good chance I got unexpectedly, I remember. My opponent flailed the air about the Ethiopians throwing rocks and spears at Italian airplanes,[24] "proving" that compulsory military training was needed. I said the Ethiopians' black flesh had been spattered against trees by bombs the Pope in Rome had blessed, and the Ethiopians would have thrown even their bare bodies at the airplanes because they had seen that they were fighting the devil incarnate.

They yelled "foul," that I'd made the subject a race issue. I said it wasn't race, it was a historical fact, that they ought to go and read Pierre van Paassen's *Days of Our Years*, and something not surprising to me, that book, right after the debate, disappeared from the prison library. It was right there in prison that I made up my mind to devote the rest of my life to telling the white man about himself—or die. In a debate about whether or not Homer had ever existed, I threw into those white faces the theory that Homer only symbolized how white Europeans kidnapped black Africans, then blinded them so that they could never get back to their own people. (Homer and Omar and *Moor*, you see, are related terms; it's like saying Peter, Pedro, and *petra,* all three of which mean rock.) These blinded Moors the Europeans taught to sing about the Europeans' glorious accomplishments. I made it clear that was the devilish white man's idea of kicks. Aesop's *Fables*—another case in point. "Aesop" was only the Greek name for an Ethiopian.

Another hot debate I remember I was in had to do with the identity of Shakespeare. No color was involved there; I just got intrigued over the Shakespearean dilemma. The King James translation of the Bible is considered the greatest piece of literature in English. Its language supposedly represents the ultimate in using the King's English. Well, Shakespeare's language and the Bible's language are one and the same. They say that from 1604 to 1611, King James got poets to translate, to write the Bible. Well, if Shakespeare existed, he was then the top poet around. But Shakespeare is nowhere reported connected with the Bible. If he existed, why didn't King James use him? And if he did use him, why is it one of the world's best kept secrets?

I know that many say that Francis Bacon[25] was Shakespeare. If that is true, why would Bacon have kept it secret? Bacon wasn't royalty, when royalty sometimes used the *nom de plume*[26] because it was "improper" for royalty to be artistic or theatrical. What would Bacon have had to lose? Bacon, in fact, would have had everything to gain.

In the prison debates I argued for the theory that King James himself was the real poet who used the *nom de plume* Shakespeare. King James was brilliant. He was the greatest king who ever sat on the British throne. Who else among royalty, in his time, would have had the giant talent to write Shakespeare's works? It was he who poetically "fixed" the Bible—which in itself and its present King James version has enslaved the world.

When my brother Reginald visited, I would talk to him about new evidence I found to document the Muslim teachings. In either volume 43 or 44 of the Harvard Classics, I read Milton's *Paradise Lost*. The devil, kicked out of Paradise, was trying to regain possession. He was using the forces of Europe, personified by the Popes, Charlemagne, Richard the Lionhearted, and

---

24 **Ethiopians . . . Italian airplanes.** Italy, under Fascist dictator Benito Mussolini, invaded Ethiopia in 1935 without warning, using vastly superior modern military power, including chemical weapons, to defeat the Ethiopian army. Ethiopian emperor Haile Selassie pleaded for help from the international community but was largely ignored. The Ethiopians staged a heroic defense against overwhelming odds for seven months before final defeat.

25 **Francis Bacon.** (1561–1626) English philosopher, essayist, statesman, and jurist (legal scholar)

26 ***nom de plume.*** Penname (French)

other knights. I interpreted this to show that the Europeans were motivated and led by the devil, or the personification of the devil. So Milton and Mr. Elijah Muhammad were actually saying the same thing.

I couldn't believe it when Reginald began to speak ill of Elijah Muhammad. I can't specify the exact things he said. They were more in the nature of implications against Mr. Muhammad—the pitch of Reginald's voice, or the way that Reginald looked, rather than what he said.

It caught me totally unprepared. It threw me into a state of confusion. My blood brother, Reginald, in whom I had so much confidence, for whom I had so much respect, the one who had introduced me to the Nation of Islam. I couldn't believe it! And now Islam meant more to me than anything I ever had known in my life. Islam and Mr. Elijah Muhammad had changed my whole world.

Reginald, I learned, had been suspended from the Nation of Islam by Elijah Muhammad. He had not practiced moral restraint. After he had learned the truth, and had accepted the truth, and the Muslim laws, Reginald was still carrying on improper relations with the then secretary of the New York Temple. Some other Muslim who learned of it had made charges against Reginald to Mr. Muhammad in Chicago, and Mr. Muhammad had suspended Reginald.

When Reginald left, I was in torment. That night, finally, I wrote to Mr. Muhammad, trying to defend my brother, appealing for him. I told him what Reginald was to me, what my brother meant to me.

I put the letter into the box for the prison censor. Then all the rest of that night, I prayed to Allah. I don't think anyone ever prayed more sincerely to Allah. I prayed for some kind of relief from my confusion.

Who visited Malcolm? Was it a real person? Did he know who it was?

It was the next night, as I lay on my bed, I suddenly, with a start, became aware of a man sitting beside me in my chair. He had on a dark suit. I remember. I could see him as plainly as I see anyone I look at. He wasn't black, and he wasn't white. He was light-brown-skinned, an Asiatic cast of countenance, and he had oily black hair.

I looked right into his face.

I didn't get frightened. I knew I wasn't dreaming. I couldn't move, I didn't speak, and he didn't. I couldn't place him racially—other than that I knew he was a non-European. I had no idea whatsoever who he was. He just sat there. Then, suddenly as he had come, he was gone.

Soon, Mr. Muhammad sent me a reply about Reginald. He wrote, "If you once believed in the truth, and now you are beginning to doubt the truth, you didn't believe the truth in the first place. What could make you doubt the truth other than your own weak self?"

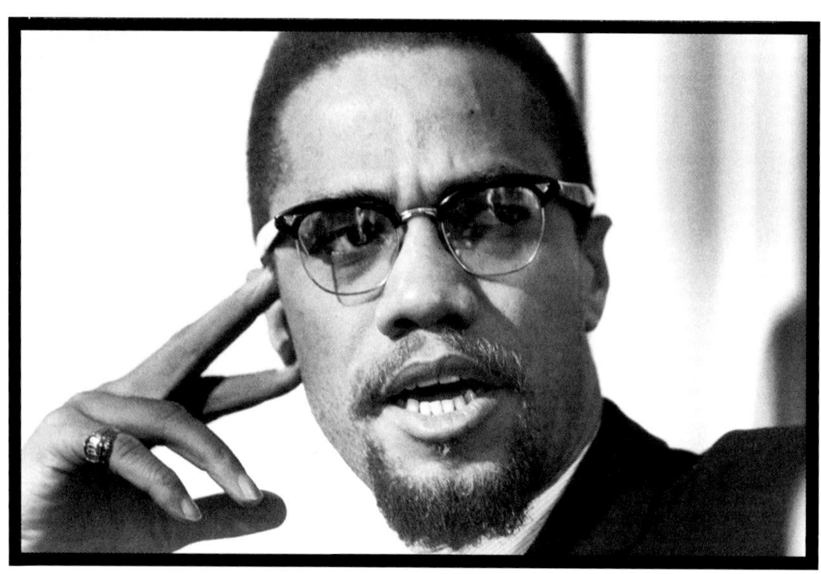

That struck me. Reginald was not leading the disciplined life of a Muslim. And I knew that Elijah Muhammad was right, and my blood brother was wrong. Because right is right, and wrong is wrong. Little did I then realize the day would come when Elijah Muhammad would be accused by his own sons as being guilty of the same acts of immorality that he judged Reginald and so many others for.

What happened to Reginald? What explanation did Malcolm give?

But at that time, all of the doubt and confusion in my mind was removed. All of the influence that my brother had wielded over me was broken. From that day on, as far as I am concerned, everything that my brother Reginald has done is wrong.

But Reginald kept visiting me. When he had been a Muslim, he had been **immaculate** in his attire. But now, he wore things like a T-shirt, shabby-looking trousers, and sneakers. I could see him on the way down. When he spoke, I heard him coldly. But I would listen. He was my blood brother.

Gradually, I saw the chastisement of Allah—what Christians would call "the curse"—come upon Reginald. Elijah Muhammad said that Allah was chastising Reginald—and that anyone who challenged Elijah Muhammad would be chastened by Allah. In Islam we were taught that as long as one didn't know the truth, he lived in darkness. But once the truth was accepted, and recognized, he lived in light, and whoever would then go against it would be punished by Allah.

Mr. Muhammad taught that the five-pointed star stands for justice, and also for the five senses of man. We were taught that Allah executes justice by working upon the five senses of those who rebel against His Messenger, or against His truth. We were taught that this was Allah's way of letting Muslims know His sufficiency to defend His Messenger against any and all opposition, as long as the Messenger himself didn't **deviate** from the path of truth. We were taught that Allah turned the minds of any defectors into a turmoil. I thought truly that it was Allah doing this to my brother.

One letter, I think from my brother Philbert, told me that Reginald was with them in Detroit. I heard no more about Reginald until one day, weeks later, Ella visited me; she told me that Reginald was at her home in Roxbury, sleeping. Ella said she had heard a knock, she had gone to the door, and there was Reginald, looking terrible. Ella said she had asked, "Where did you come from?" And Reginald had told her he came from Detroit. She said she asked him, "How did you get here?" And he had told her, "I walked."

I believed he *had* walked. I believed in Elijah Muhammad, and he had convinced us that Allah's chastisement upon Reginald's mind had taken away Reginald's ability to gauge distance and time. There is a dimension of time with which we are not familiar here in the West. Elijah Muhammad said that under Allah's chastisement, the five senses of a man can be so **deranged** by those whose mental powers are greater than his that in five minutes his hair can turn snow white. Or he will walk nine hundred miles as he might walk five blocks.

In prison, since I had become a Muslim, I had grown a beard. When Reginald visited me, he nervously moved about in his chair; he told me that each hair on my beard was a snake. Everywhere, he saw snakes.

VOCABULARY IN PLACE

- **immaculate,** ***adj.*** Impeccably clean, spotless
- **deviate,** ***v.*** To turn aside from a course or path; stray
- **deranged,** ***adj.*** Disordered; mentally disturbed

He next began to believe that he was the "Messenger of Allah." Reginald went around in the streets of Roxbury, Ella reported to me, telling people that he had some divine power. He graduated from this to saying that he was Allah.

He finally began saying he was *greater* than Allah.

Authorities picked up Reginald, and he was put into an institution. They couldn't find what was wrong. They had no way to understand Allah's chastisement. Reginald was released. Then he was picked up again, and was put into another institution.

Reginald is in an institution now. I know where, but I won't say. I would not want to cause him any more trouble than he has already had.

I believe, today, that it was written, it was meant, for Reginald to be used for one purpose only: as a bait, as a minnow to reach into the ocean of blackness where I was, to save me.

I cannot understand it any other way.

After Elijah Muhammad himself was later accused as a very immoral man, I came to believe that it wasn't a divine chastisement upon Reginald, but the pain he felt when his own family totally rejected him for Elijah Muhammad, and this hurt made Reginald turn insanely upon Elijah Muhammad.

It's impossible to dream, or to see, or to have a vision of someone whom you never have seen before—and to see him exactly as he is. To see someone, and to see him exactly as he looks, is to have a pre-vision.

I would later come to believe that my pre-vision was of Master W. D. Fard,[27] the Messiah, the one whom Elijah Muhammad said had appointed him—Elijah Muhammad—as His Last Messenger to the black people of North America.

My last year in prison was spent back in the Charlestown Prison. Even among the white inmates, the word had filtered around. Some of those brainwashed black convicts talked too much. And I know that the censors had reported on my mail. The Norfolk Prison Colony officials had become upset. They used as a reason for my transfer that I refused to take some kind of shots, an inoculation or something.

The only thing that worried me was that I hadn't much time left before I would be eligible for parole-board consideration. But I reasoned that they might look at my representing and spreading Islam in another way: instead of keeping me in they might want to get me out.

I had come to prison with 20/20 vision. But when I got sent back to Charlestown, I had read so much by the lights-out glow in my room at the Norfolk Prison Colony that I had astigmatism[28] and the first pair of the eyeglasses that I have worn ever since.

I had less maneuverability back in the much stricter Charlestown Prison. But I found that a lot of Negroes attended a Bible class, and I went there.

Conducting the class was a tall, blond, blue-eyed (a perfect "devil") Harvard Seminary student. He lectured, and then he started in a question-and-answer session. I don't know which of us had read the Bible more, he or I, but I had to give him credit; he really was heavy on his religion. I puzzled and puzzled for a way to upset him, and to give those Negroes present something to think and talk about and circulate.

Finally, I put up my hand; he nodded. He had talked about Paul.

---

27 **W. D. Fard.** An alias of Wallace Fard Muhammad (circa 1885–circa1934), founder of the Temple of Islam, which later became the Nation of Islam. There is controversy surrounding his true identity, with some sources saying he had as many as 38 aliases.

28 **astigmatism.** A visual defect that prevents light rays from focusing clearly at one point on the retina, resulting in blurred vision

I stood up and asked, "What color was Paul?" And I kept talking, with pauses, "He had to be black . . . because he was a Hebrew . . . and the original Hebrews were black . . . weren't they?"

He had started flushing red. You know the way white people do. He said "Yes."

I wasn't through yet. "What color was Jesus . . . he was Hebrew, too . . . wasn't he?"

Both the Negro and the white convicts had sat bolt upright. I don't care how tough the convict, be he brainwashed black Christian, or a "devil" white Christian, neither of them is ready to hear anybody saying Jesus wasn't white. The instructor walked around. He shouldn't have felt bad. In all of the years since, I never have met any intelligent white man who would try to insist that Jesus was white. How could they? He said, "Jesus was brown."

I let him get away with that compromise.

Exactly as I had known it would, almost overnight the Charlestown convicts, black and white, began buzzing with the story. Wherever I went, I could feel the nodding. And anytime I got a chance to exchange words with a black brother in stripes, I'd say, "My man! You ever heard about somebody named Mr. Elijah Muhammad?" ■

About the Author

Alex Haley (1921–1992) ghostwrote *The Autobiography of Malcolm X*—Malcolm dictated his story and Haley wrote. This was a fine choice on Malcolm's part since Haley is one of the best writers of the late twentieth century. He is well known for his Pulitzer-winning novel, *Roots: The Saga of an American Family,* which was made into a major television miniseries and has been translated into nearly 40 languages. (See page 503 for Malcolm's biography.)

Malcolm X Quotations

"Education is our passport to the future, for tomorrow belongs to the people who prepare for it today."

"Without education, you're not going anywhere in this world."

"Our objective is complete freedom, justice and equality by any means necessary."

"Truth is on the side of the oppressed."

"Dr. King wants the same thing I want—freedom!"

"Stumbling is not falling."

"I'm for truth, no matter who tells it. I'm for justice, no matter who it's for or against."

"In the past, I permitted myself to be used . . . to make sweeping indictments of all white people, the entire white race, and these generalizations have caused injuries to some whites who perhaps did not deserve to be hurt. Because of the spiritual enlightenment, which I was blessed to receive as a result of my recent pilgrimage to the holy city of Mecca, I no longer subscribe to sweeping indictments of any one race. . . . I must repeat that I am not a racist nor do I subscribe to the tenets of racism. I can state in all sincerity that I wish nothing but freedom, justice and equality, life, liberty and the pursuit of happiness for all people."

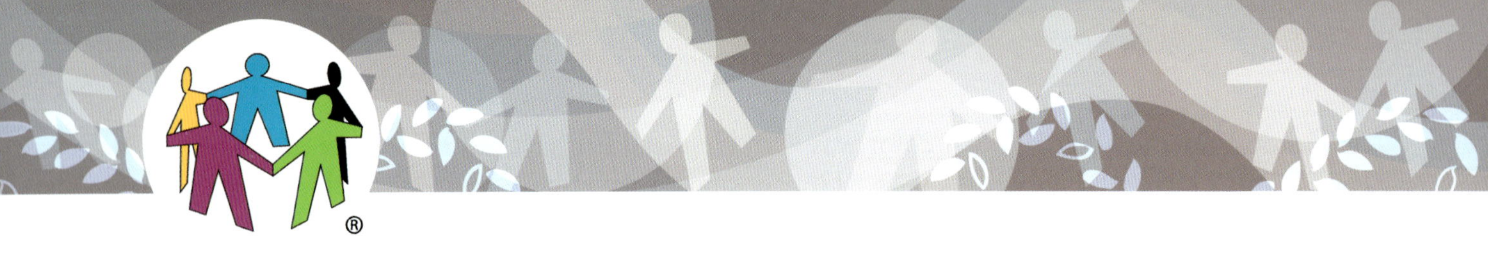

Understanding the Selection

Recalling

1. According to Elijah Muhammad, what did the black prisoner symbolize?
2. What was the hardest test Malcolm ever faced?
3. What did Malcolm do in order to improve his vocabulary and knowledge?
4. Prior to expanding his knowledge of words and history, what did Malcolm do, while reading, when he came to an unfamiliar word?
5. In what did Malcolm see "a new world order being shaped"?
6. What did Malcolm find as exhilarating as "the discovery of knowledge through reading"?

Interpreting

1. Did Malcolm agree with Elijah Muhammad's ideas about white society? Use a quotation from the text to support your answer.
2. Why was praying so difficult for Malcolm?
3. What does this reveal about his personality? How did he change after he started this project?
4. What is the difference between *reading* and *understanding,* according to Malcolm?
5. What evidence did he offer to substantiate this argument? What connection does he draw between civil rights and human rights?
6. What made Malcolm a skilled debater? Why did he enjoy debating so much?

Synthesizing

1. What did Elijah Muhammad mean when he wrote that "history had been 'whitened'"? Give at least three examples from the text that show that Malcolm agreed with Mr. Muhammad.
2. What was the single most important factor in Malcolm X's personal transformation?

Delving Deeper

Writing

Expository Essay. The word *essay* comes from the French word *essai,* "a trial or attempt." That means that the essay writer is free to explore new ideas, and the final product does not have to be exhaustive (the writer does not have to worry about including every single detail about the subject). However, the essay does have to be well organized; many essay writers, regardless of their level of expertise, create an outline before they write in order to organize and prioritize the essay's main ideas and examples.

In an **expository essay,** the writer's job is to explain something to the reader. A good expository essay demonstrates the writer's knowledge and experience in the subject area, about which, it is assumed, the reader knows little or nothing.

Write your own expository essay in which you explain the **main idea,** or purpose, behind Chapter 11, "Saved," from *The Autobiography of Malcolm X.* What was the author's main idea in this chapter, and how did he prove his point? Demonstrate your understanding of the chapter by including at least five examples or quotations from the text. Assume that your readers are familiar with Malcolm X but not with this chapter of his autobiography.

About the Author

Malcolm X (1925–1965) was one of the most influential political activists of the twentieth century. He was born Malcolm Little in Omaha, Nebraska. In 1931, his father was murdered, probably by white supremacists, and his mother subsequently was committed to a mental institution. At the age of 16 Malcolm moved to Boston, where he became involved in petty crime. While serving a prison sentence for burglary, he joined the Nation of Islam. In 1952, after his release from prison, he changed his last name to X, a common practice among Black Muslims who considered their forebears' names to be "slave names."

Malcolm X soon became spokesman for the Nation of Islam, using his powerful and persuasive speaking style to communicate a message of black pride, separation from whites, and self-defense, which contradicted the nonviolent methods espoused by many other civil rights activists of the time. In 1964, after leaving the Nation of Islam, Malcolm X made a pilgrimage to the Muslim holy city of Mecca. There he met Muslims of many different races and wrote, "There were tens of thousands of pilgrims, from all over the world. They were of all colors. . . . But we were all participating in the same rituals, displaying a spirit of unity and brotherhood." On his return home he formed the Organization of Afro-American Unity, whose view was that racial harmony could be achieved peaceably. Malcolm X was shot to death while giving a speech on February 21, 1965, in New York City.

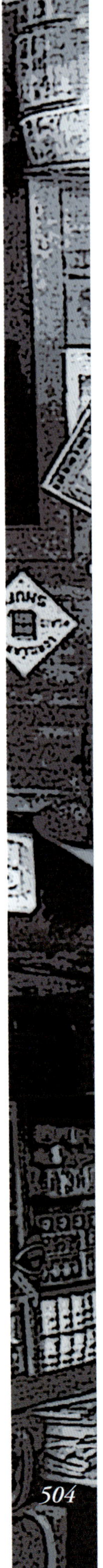

Prereading

I Know Why The Caged Bird Sings

by Maya Angelou

I Know Why the Caged Bird Sings is the first of several autobiographical works by Maya Angelou. An **autobiography** is the story of a person's life as told by that person. The book covers Angelou's childhood years up through age sixteen and traces the years during which she went back and forth between the small town of Stamps, Arkansas, where her grandmother lived, and St. Louis and San Francisco, the urban environments favored by her mother.

Chapter 2. We encounter Angelou at age five being cared for by her grandmother, called Momma, and by her crippled Uncle Willie, who together run the only black-owned grocery store in wholly segregated Stamps. Although they lived very frugally in the midst of the Great Depression, as store owners, the family was considerably better off than most in the community. Later in the book, it is revealed that Momma was even able to loan money to a white dentist. He later repaid her kindness by refusing to treat Maya for a terrible toothache. Such treatment, unfortunately, was typical for most African Americans in the rural South. Throughout the book, Angelou takes great pains to show that the image of field hands happily singing while they picked cotton was quite simply a myth constructed by white people to alleviate their guilt.

Chapter 16. We see the author at age ten as she goes to work in the kitchen of an affluent but racially prejudiced white woman. In this home Angelou is mentored by a kindly black servant called Miss Glory. The narrative dramatizes the difference between Miss Glory's approach to her life and Angelou's more rebellious attitudes. Both chapters presented here emphasize Angelou's deep affection for her brother, Bailey. One year older than Maya, Bailey provides his sister with her most stable and meaningful relationship.

Both chapters also advance some of the story's larger themes—the incredible endurance and ingenuity of poor rural African Americans in the South; the durable bonds of family and community; the attachment to learning in the face of deprived and impoverished schools; and, most of all, the struggle that one awkward, lonely girl faced to become one of the nation's most revered literary figures.

from I Know Why The Caged Bird Sings

by Maya Angelou

Chapter 2

When Bailey was six and I a year younger, we used to rattle off the times tables with the speed I was later to see Chinese children in San Francisco employ on their abacuses.[1] Our summer-gray pot-bellied stove bloomed rosy red during winter, and became a severe disciplinarian threat if we were so foolish as to indulge in making mistakes.

Uncle Willie used to sit, like a giant black Z (he had been crippled as a child), and hear us testify to the Lafayette County Training Schools' abilities. His face pulled down on the left side, as if a pulley had been attached to his lower teeth, and his left hand was only a mite bigger than Bailey's, but on the second mistake or on the third hesitation his big overgrown right hand would catch one of us behind the collar, and in the same moment would thrust the **culprit** toward the dull red heater, which throbbed like a devil's toothache. We were never burned, although once I might have been when I was so terrified I tried to jump onto the stove to remove the possibility of its remaining a threat. Like most children, I thought if I could face the worst danger voluntarily, and *triumph*, I would forever have power over it. But in my case of sacrificial effort I was thwarted. Uncle Willie held tight to my dress and I only got close enough to smell the clean dry scent of hot iron. We learned the times tables without understanding their grand principle, simply because we had the capacity and no alternative.

The tragedy of lameness seems so unfair to children that they are embarrassed in its presence. And they, most recently off nature's mold,[2] sense that they have only narrowly missed being another of her jokes. In relief at the narrow escape, they **vent** their emotions in impatience and criticism of the unlucky cripple.

Momma related times without end, and without any show of emotion, how Uncle Willie had been dropped when he was three years old by a woman who was minding him. She seemed to hold no **rancor** against the baby-sitter, nor for her just God who allowed the accident. She felt it necessary to explain over and over again to those who knew the story by heart that he wasn't "born that way."

In our society, where two-legged, two-armed strong Black men were able at best to eke out only the necessities of life, Uncle Willie, with his starched shirts, shined shoes and shelves full of food, was the whipping

[1] **abacuses.** An *abacus* is an ancient manual computing device consisting of a frame holding parallel rods strung with movable counters.

[2] **off nature's mold.** New to the world. *Mold* refers to a frame or model around which something is formed or shaped.

VOCABULARY IN PLACE

- **culprit,** *n.* One guilty of a fault or crime
- **vent,** *v.* To express one's thoughts, especially forcefully
- **rancor,** *n.* Bitter, long-lasting resentment

boy and butt of jokes of the underemployed and underpaid. Fate not only disabled him but laid a double-tiered barrier in his path. He was also proud and sensitive. Therefore he couldn't pretend that he wasn't crippled, nor could he deceive himself that people were not **repelled** by his defect.

Only once in all the years of trying not to watch him, I saw him pretend to himself and others that he wasn't lame.

Coming home from school one day, I saw a dark car in our front yard. I rushed in to find a strange man and woman (Uncle Willie said later they were schoolteachers from Little Rock) drinking Dr. Pepper in the cool of the Store. I sensed a wrongness around me, like an alarm clock that had gone off without being set.

I knew it couldn't be the strangers. Not frequently, but often enough, travelers pulled off the main road to buy tobacco or soft drinks in the only Negro store in Stamps. When I looked at Uncle Willie, I knew what was pulling my mind's coattails. He was standing erect behind the counter, not leaning forward or resting on the small shelf that had been built for him. Erect. His eyes seemed to hold me with a mixture of threats and appeal.

I dutifully greeted the strangers and roamed my eyes around for his walking stick. It was nowhere to be seen. He said, "Uh . . . this this . . . this . . . uh, my niece. She's . . . uh . . . just come from school." Then to the couple—"You know . . . how, uh, children are . . . th-th-these days . . . they play all d-d-day at school and c-c-can't wait to get home and pl-play some more."

The people smiled, very friendly.

He added, "Go on out and pl-play, Sister."

The lady laughed in a soft Arkansas voice and said, "Well, you know, Mr. Johnson, they say, you're only a child once. Have you children of your own?"

Uncle Willie looked at me with an impatience I hadn't seen in his face even when he took thirty minutes to loop the laces over his high-topped shoes. "I . . . I thought I told you to go . . . go outside and play."

Before I left I saw him lean back on the shelves of Garret Snuff, Prince Albert and Spark Plug chewing tobacco.

"No, ma'am . . . no c-children and no wife." He tried a laugh. "I have an old m-m-mother and my brother's t-two children to l-look after."

I didn't mind his using us to make himself look good. In fact, I would have pretended to be his daughter if he wanted me to. Not only did I not feel any loyalty to my own father, I figured that if I had been Uncle Willie's child I would have received much better treatment.

The couple left after a few minutes, and from the back of the house I watched the red car scare chickens, raise dust and disappear toward Magnolia.

Uncle Willie was making his way down the long shadowed aisle between the shelves and the counter-hand over hand, like a man climbing out of a dream. I stayed quiet and watched him lurch from one side, bumping to the other, until he reached the coal-oil tank. He put his hand behind that dark recess and took his cane in the strong fist and shifted his weight on the wooden support. He thought he had pulled it off.

I'll never know why it was important to him that the couple (he said later that he'd never seen them before) would take a picture of a whole Mr. Johnson back to Little Rock.

He must have tired of being crippled, as prisoners tire of penitentiary bars and the

VOCABULARY IN PLACE

- **repelled,** ***past part.*** Compelled to turn away from; kept away

guilty tire of blame. The high-topped shoes and the cane, his uncontrollable muscles and thick tongue, and the looks he suffered of either contempt or pity had simply worn him out, and for one afternoon, one part of an afternoon, he wanted no part of them.

I understood and felt closer to him at that moment than ever before or since.

With whom did she fall in love?

During these years in Stamps, I met and fell in love with William Shakespeare. He was my first white love. Although I enjoyed and respected Kipling, Poe, Butler, Thackeray and Henley, I saved my young and loyal passion for Paul Lawrence Dunbar, Langston Hughes, James Weldon Johnson and W. E. B Du Bois' "Litany at Atlanta." But it was Shakespeare who said, "When in disgrace with fortune and men's eyes." It was a state with which I felt myself most familiar. I pacified myself about his whiteness by saying that after all he had been dead so long it couldn't matter to anyone any more.

Bailey and I decided to memorize a scene from *The Merchant of Venice*, but we realized that Momma would question us about the author and that we'd have to tell her that Shakespeare was white, and it wouldn't matter to her whether he was dead or not. So we chose "The Creation" by James Weldon Johnson instead.[3]

---

[3] **"The Creation" . . . James Weldon Johnson.** (1871–1938) Popular African-American poet. See page 328.

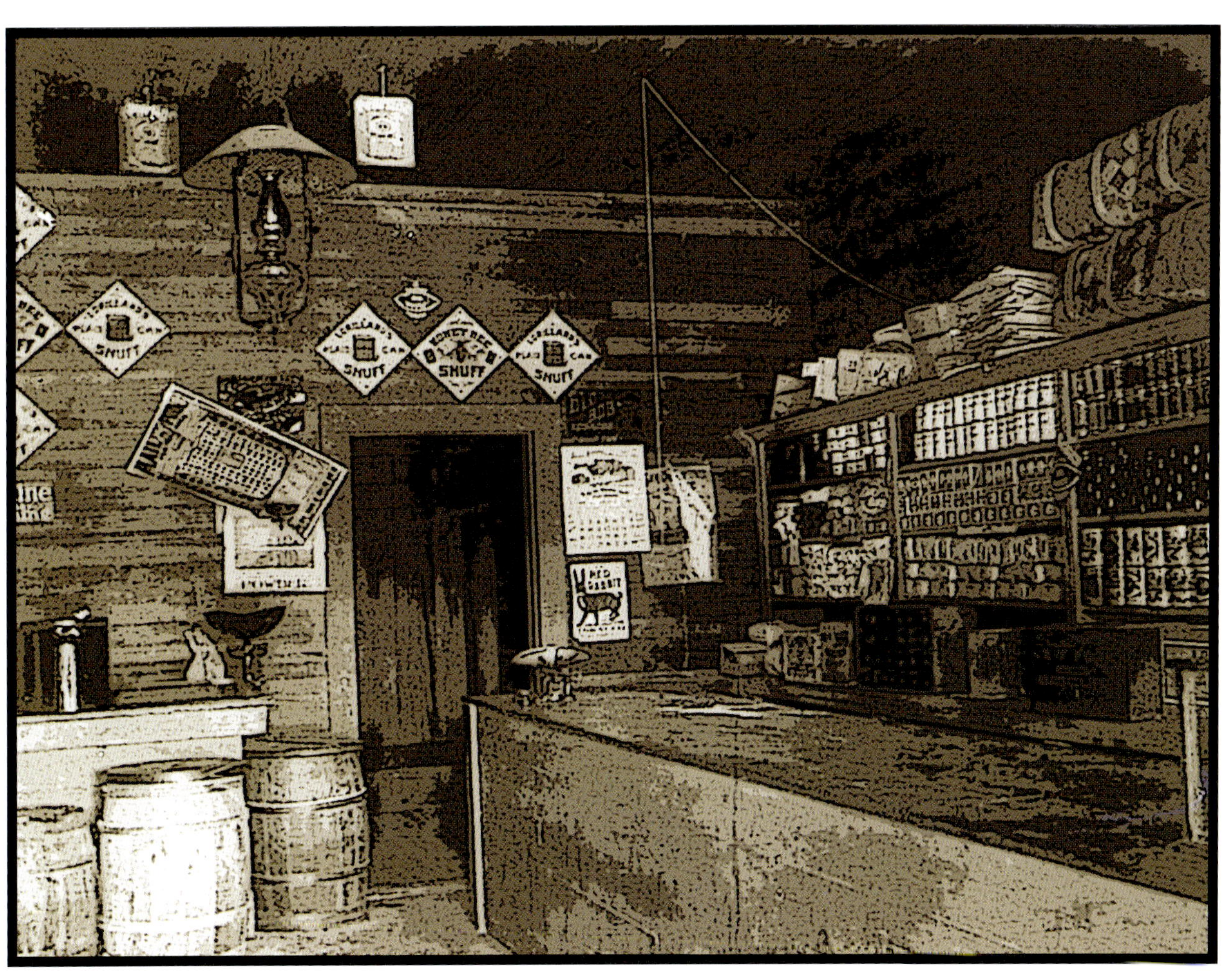

Understanding the Selection

Recalling

1. How old was Angelou in this chapter?
2. When Uncle Willie drilled Maya and Bailey on the school lessons, how did he punish them for wrong answers?
3. How did Uncle Willie come to have a problem with his legs?
4. When the couple from Little Rock visited the store, how did Uncle Willie behave?
5. What authors did Maya and her brother like to read, and which work did they choose to memorize?

Interpreting

1. Do you think her reactions, to lameness for example, were realistic for her age? Why, or why not?
2. Do you think that Uncle Willie was really trying to help the children despite his harsh methods? Explain.
3. Why was Momma, as Maya's grandmother was called, so insistent on explaining the cause of Willie's being crippled?
4. What did Uncle Willie do in order to try to hide his condition from visitors? What did this fact reveal about Uncle Willie?
5. Although Maya wanted to memorize scenes from Shakespeare's *Merchant of Venice,* explain why she chose James Weldon Johnson's "The Creation" instead.

Synthesizing

1. How did the narrator come to empathize with Uncle Willie?
2. Describe the values related to learning and literature held by Uncle Willie, Maya, and Bailey. Was Maya expected to take her education seriously?

Chapter 16

Recently a white woman from Texas, who would quickly describe herself as a liberal, asked me about my hometown. When I told her that in Stamps my grandmother had owned the only Negro general merchandise store since the turn of the century, she exclaimed, "Why, you were a debutante."[1] Ridiculous and even ludicrous. But Negro girls in small Southern towns, whether poverty-stricken or just munching along on a few of life's necessities, were given as extensive and irrelevant preparations for adulthood as rich white girls shown in magazines. Admittedly the training was not the same. While white girls learned to waltz and sit gracefully with a tea cup balanced on their knees, we were lagging behind, learning the mid-Victorian[2] values with very little money to indulge them. (Come and see Edna Lomax spending the money she made picking cotton on five balls of ecru tatting thread.[3] Her fingers are bound to snag the work and she'll have to repeat the stitches time and time again. But she knows that when she buys the thread.)

We were required to embroider and I had trunkfuls of colorful dishtowels, pillowcases, runners and handkerchiefs to my credit. I mastered the art of crocheting and tatting, and there was a lifetime's supply of dainty doilies[4] that would never be used in sacheted dresser drawers. It went without saying that all girls could iron and wash, but the finer touches around the home, like setting a table with real silver, baking roasts and cooking vegetables without meat, had to be learned elsewhere. Usually at the source of those habits. During my tenth year, a white woman's kitchen became my finishing school.

Mrs. Viola Cullinan was a plump woman who lived in a three-bedroom house somewhere behind the post office. She was singularly unattractive until she smiled, and then the lines around her eyes and mouth which made her look perpetually dirty disappeared, and her face looked like the mask of an **impish** elf. She usually rested her smile until late afternoon when her women friends dropped in and Miss Glory, the cook, served them cold drinks on the closed-in porch.

The exactness of her house was inhuman. This glass went here and only here. That cup had its place and it was an act of **impudent** rebellion to place it anywhere else. At twelve o'clock the table was set. At 12:15 Mrs. Cullinan sat down to dinner (whether her husband had arrived or not). At 12:16 Miss Glory brought out the food.

It took me a week to learn the difference between a salad plate, a bread plate and a dessert plate.

Mrs. Cullinan kept up the tradition of her wealthy parents. She was from Virginia. Miss Glory, who was a descendant of slaves that had worked for the Cullinans, told me her history. She had married beneath her (according to Miss Glory). Her husband's family hadn't had their money very long and what they had "didn't 'mount to much."

As ugly as she was, I thought privately, she was lucky to get a husband above or beneath her station. But Miss Glory wouldn't let me say a thing against her mistress. She

---

[1] **debutante.** A young woman making a formal debut into society. The woman's remark was sarcastic or derisive.

[2] **mid-Victorian.** Relating to the nineteenth-century Victorian Age, when value was placed on ornamentation and display of wealth, as well as strict moral and social standards

[3] **ecru tatting thread.** *Ecru* is a light yellow or yellowish brown color. *Tatting* is fancy handmade lace.

[4] **doilies.** Small ornamental mats, usually of lace or linen

VOCABULARY IN PLACE

- **impish**, *adj.* Mischievous
- **impudent**, adj. Brash, sassy, not respectful

was very patient with me, however, over the housework. She explained the dishware, silverware and servants' bells.

The large round bowl in which soup was served wasn't a soup bowl, it was a tureen. There were goblets, sherbet glasses, ice-cream glasses, wine glasses, green glass coffee cups with matching saucers, and water glasses. I had a glass to drink from, and it sat with Miss Glory's on a separate shelf from the others. Soupspoons, gravy boat, butter knives, salad forks and carving platter were additions to my vocabulary and in fact almost represented a new language. I was fascinated with the **novelty,** with the fluttering Mrs. Cullinan and her Alice-in-Wonderland[5] house.

What "new language" did Maya learn?

Her husband remains, in my memory, undefined. I lumped him with all the other white men that I had ever seen and tried not to see.

On our way home one evening, Miss Glory told me that Mrs. Cullinan couldn't have children. She said that she was too delicate-boned. It was hard to imagine bones at all under those layers of fat. Miss Glory went on to say that the doctor had taken out all her lady organs. I reasoned that a pig's organs included the lungs, heart and liver, so if Mrs. Cullinan was walking around without those essentials, it explained why she drank alcohol out of unmarked bottles. She was keeping herself **embalmed.**

When I spoke to Bailey about it, he agreed that I was right, but he also informed me that Mr. Cullinan had two daughters by a colored lady and that I knew them very well. He added that the girls were the spitting image of their father. I was unable to remember what he looked like, although I had just left him a few hours before, but I thought of the Coleman girls. They were very light-skinned and certainly didn't look very much like their mother (no one ever mentioned Mr. Coleman).

My pity for Mrs. Cullinan preceded me the next morning like the Cheshire cat's smile. Those girls, who could have been her daughters, were beautiful. They didn't have to straighten their hair. Even when they were caught in the rain, their braids still hung down straight like tamed snakes. Their mouths were pouty little cupid's bows. Mrs. Cullinan didn't know what she missed. Or maybe she did. Poor Mrs. Cullinan.

For weeks after, I arrived early, left late and tried very hard to make up for her **barrenness.** If she had had her own children, she wouldn't have had to ask me to run a thousand errands from her back door to the back door of her friends. Poor old Mrs. Cullinan.

Then one evening Miss Glory told me to serve the ladies on the porch. After I set the tray down and turned toward the kitchen, one of the women asked, "What's your name, girl?" It was the speckled-faced one. Mrs. Cullinan said, "She doesn't talk much. Her name's Margaret."

"Is she dumb?"

"No. As I understand it, she can talk when she wants to but she's usually quiet as a little mouse. Aren't you, Margaret?"

I smiled at her. Poor thing. No organs and couldn't even pronounce my name correctly.

"She's a sweet little thing, though."

"Well, that may be, but the name's too long. I'd never bother myself. I'd call her Mary if I was you."

---

5 **Alice in Wonderland.** A reference to the famous tea party scene in the book by Lewis Carroll

VOCABULARY IN PLACE

- **novelty,** ***n.*** Something new and unusual
- **embalmed,** ***past part.*** Treated with chemicals so as to preserve for burial
- **barrenness,** ***n.*** Inability to have children

I fumed into the kitchen. That horrible woman would never have the chance to call me Mary because if I was starving I'd never work for her. I decided I wouldn't pee on her if her heart was on fire. Giggles drifted in off the porch and into Miss Glory's pots. I wondered what they could be laughing about.

Whitefolks were so strange. Could they be talking about me? Everybody knew that they stuck together better than the Negroes did. It was possible that Mrs. Cullinan had friends in St. Louis who heard about a girl from Stamps being in court and wrote to tell her. Maybe she knew about Mr. Freeman.[6]

My lunch was in my mouth a second time and I went outside and relieved myself on the bed of four-o'clocks.[7] Miss Glory thought I might be coming down with something and told me to go on home, that Momma would give me some herb tea, and she'd explain to her mistress.

I realized how foolish I was being before I reached the pond. Of course Mrs. Cullinan didn't know. Otherwise she wouldn't have given me the two nice dresses that Momma cut down, and she certainly wouldn't have called me a "sweet little thing." My stomach felt fine, and I didn't mention anything to Momma.

That evening I decided to write a poem on being white, fat, old and without children. It was going to be a tragic ballad. I would have to watch her carefully to capture the essence of her loneliness and pain.

Why did she decide to write a poem?

The very next day, she called me by the wrong name. Miss Glory and I were washing up the lunch dishes when Mrs. Cullinan came to the doorway. "Mary?"

Miss Glory asked, "Who?"

Mrs. Cullinan, sagging a little, knew and I knew. "I want Mary to go down to Mrs. Randall's and take her some soup. She's not been feeling well for a few days."

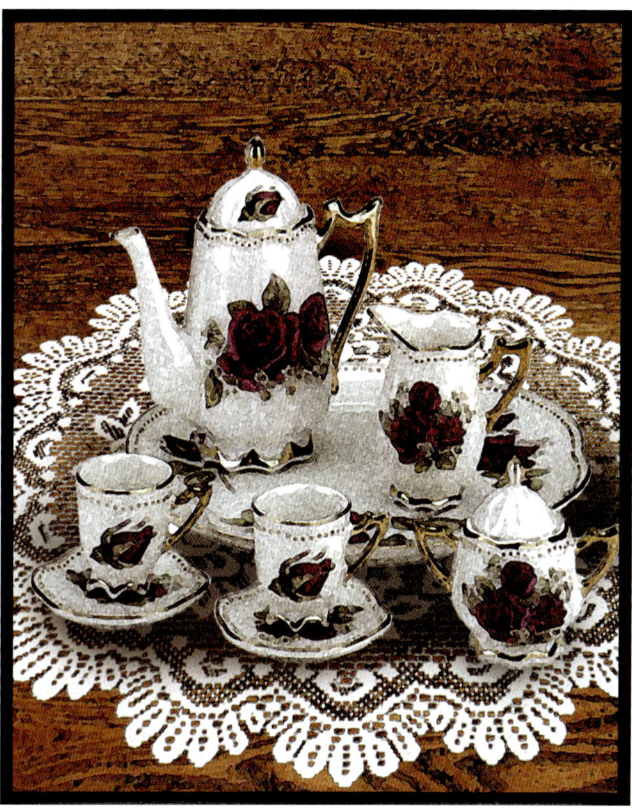

Miss Glory's face was a wonder to see. "You mean Margaret, ma'am. Her name's Margaret."

"That's too long. She's Mary from now on. Heat that soup from last night and put it in the china tureen and, Mary, I want you to carry it carefully."

Every person I knew had a hellish horror of being "called out of his name." It was a dangerous practice to call a Negro anything that could be loosely construed as insulting because of the centuries of their having been called niggers, jigs, dinges, blackbirds, crow, boots and spooks.

[6] **knew about Mr. Freeman.** In an earlier chapter, the author relates a story of being abused. Her family took the culprit to court, and Maya testified against him. Here, she was worried that news of this incident, which happened in St. Louis, might have reached Stamps, Arkansas.

[7] **four-o'clocks.** Funnel-shaped, variously colored flowers that open in the late afternoon

Miss Glory had a fleeting second of feeling sorry for me. Then as she handed me the hot tureen she said, "Don't mind, don't pay that no mind. Sticks and stones may break your bones, but words . . . You know, I been working for her for twenty years."

She held the back door open for me. "Twenty years. I wasn't much older than you. My name used to be Hallelujah. That's what Ma named me, but my mistress give me 'Glory,' and it stuck. I likes it better too."

I was in the little path that ran behind the houses when Miss Glory shouted, "It's shorter too."

For a few seconds it was a tossup over whether I would laugh (imagine being named Hallelujah) or cry (imagine letting some white woman rename you for her convenience). My anger saved me from either outburst. I had to quit the job, but the problem was going to be how to do it. Momma wouldn't allow me to quit for just any reason.

"She's a peach. That woman is a real peach." Mrs. Randall's maid was talking as she took the soup from me, and I wondered what her name used to be and what she answered to now.

For a week I looked into Mrs. Cullinan's face as she called me Mary. She ignored my coming late and leaving early. Miss Glory was a little annoyed because I had begun to leave egg yolk on the dishes and wasn't putting much heart in polishing the silver. I hoped that she would complain to our boss, but she didn't.

Then Bailey solved my dilemma. He had me describe the contents of the cupboard and the particular plates she liked best. Her favorite piece was a casserole shaped like a fish and the green glass coffee cups. I kept his instructions in mind, so on the next day when Miss Glory was hanging out clothes and I had again been told to serve the old biddies on the porch, I dropped the empty serving tray. When I heard Mrs. Cullinan scream, "Mary!" I picked up the casserole and two of the green glass cups in readiness. As she rounded the kitchen door I let them fall on the tiled floor.

I could never absolutely describe to Bailey what happened next, because each time I got to the part where she fell on the floor and screwed up her ugly face to cry, we burst out laughing. She actually wobbled around on the floor and picked up shards of the cups and cried, "Oh, Momma. Oh, dear Gawd. It's Momma's china from Virginia. Oh, Momma, I sorry."

Miss Glory came running in from the yard and the women from the porch crowded around. Miss Glory was almost as broken up as her mistress. "You mean to say she broke our Virginia dishes? What we gone do?"

Mrs. Cullinan cried louder, "That clumsy . . . Clumsy little . . . "[8]

Old speckled-face leaned down and asked, "Who did it, Viola? Was it Mary? Who did it?"

Everything was happening so fast I can't remember whether her action preceded her words, but I know that Mrs. Cullinan said, "Her name's Margaret, —— it, her name's Margaret!"

An expletive has been here deleted. —Eds.

And she threw a wedge of the broken plate at me. It could have been the hysteria which put her aim off, but the flying crockery caught Miss Glory right over her ear and she started screaming.

I left the front door wide open so all the neighbors could hear.

Mrs. Cullinan was right about one thing. My name wasn't Mary. ■

---

[8] **Mrs. Cullinan** . . . . Racist epithets have been here deleted by the editors. Mrs. Cullinan's use of racist epithets shows just how despicable a character she is.

The Wisdom of Maya Angelou

Maya Angelou is one of the most widely respected and beloved of American writers. One of the reasons why she is so highly regarded is that she has lived a full, rich, interesting life, and she has learned much from her experiences. To learn from experience is the very definition of wisdom. Read these gems culled from Angelou's work and see if you agree that they represent the voice of experience.

On the necessity of working hard to learn the craft of writing: "Some critics will write 'Maya Angelou is a natural writer'—which is right after being a natural heart surgeon."

On the importance of work: "Nothing will work unless you do."

On the value of struggle: "The fact that the adult American Negro female emerges as a formidable character is often met with amazement, distaste, and even belligerence. It is seldom accepted as an inevitable outcome of the struggle won by survivors and deserves respect if not enthusiastic acceptance."

On the value of attitude: "I love to see a young girl go out and grab the world by the lapels."

On the importance of a sound upbringing: "Living a life is like constructing a building: If you start wrong, you'll end wrong."

On the importance of realism: "If you don't like something, change it. If you can't change it, change your attitude. Don't complain."

On the importance of recognizing our common humanity: "We allow our ignorance to prevail upon us and make us think we can survive alone, alone in patches, alone in groups, alone in races, even alone in genders."

On the tendency of people to rationalize: "The needs of society determine its ethics."

On learning from history and experience: "History, despite its wrenching pain, cannot be unlived; however, if faced with courage, [it] need not be lived again."

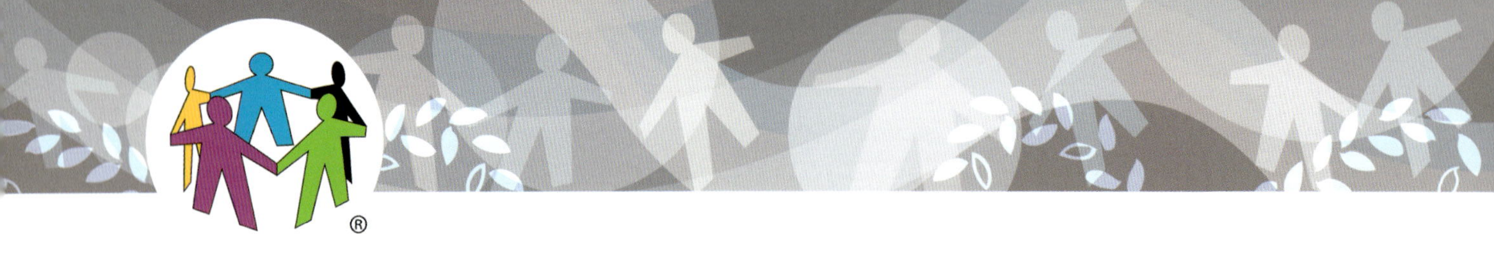

Understanding the Selection

Recalling

1. What did the self-described liberal white woman from Texas say when Maya told about her hometown?
2. What were some of the skills young African-American girls in Stamps were expected to master?
3. At age ten, where did Maya learn about the intricate aspects of table setting and silver polishing? Who taught Maya how to perform these tasks?
4. Marguerite's family called her Maya, but what did Mrs. Cullinan call her at first and then later?
5. What did Maya do to try to get fired from her job?

Interpreting

1. Why did Maya say that the woman's statement was "ridiculous" and "ludicrous"?
2. Did Maya think that the various needlework skills she was expected to learn were important and useful? Why, or why not?
3. How was this person's attitude toward her job different from Maya's?
4. Why did Mrs. Cullinan call Maya "Mary," and why was this insulting to Maya?
5. Why couldn't she simply quit?

Synthesizing

1. What was Maya expected to tolerate as a result of her social status?
2. From what you learned of her upbringing in Chapter 2, how might Maya's family values have affected her actions in Chapter 16?

Delving Deeper

Writing

An Autobiographical Sketch. *I Know Why the Caged Bird Sings* is an **autobiography,** meaning that the author is writing the story of her own life. Try your hand at writing an autobiographical sketch of your own. Model your work on the fine writing of Maya Angelou. Choose an incident from your life that taught you an important or valuable lesson. Make a list of the events that occurred, and write a sentence that states clearly the lesson that you learned. Make another list of concrete details that you can mention in your piece that will make it vivid and interesting to your readers. Write a piece consisting of four of five paragraphs. The first three or four paragraphs should tell the story. The concluding paragraph should explain the lesson that you learned from your experience. Write a rough draft. Revise it with the goal of making it more vivid and interesting to readers (one can always make improvements in this regard). Then make a final draft and proofread it carefully.

A Dramatization. A **narrative,** as you probably know, is writing or speech that tells a story. **Fiction** is narrative writing about imaginary events. **Biography** and **autobiography** are types of narrative writing about actual events. One of the characteristics of good narrative writing is that the writer provides details that are concrete and vivid enough for the characters and settings of the work to become clear in the reader's mind. When reading a narrative, you should be able to see the settings and watch the characters in your mind's eye. Some narratives are especially vivid and translate well to the stage. The act of transforming a narrative into a drama that can be acted out is called **dramatization.**

Read a few pages of *A Raisin in the Sun,* on page 677. Pay close attention to the conventions for writing drama. Notice how writers of drama, known as **playwrights,** use **stage directions** to describe the setting and, on occasion, the motions and ways of speaking of the characters. Notice how the **characters' names** are treated and that the bulk of a drama is made up of **dialogue,** what the characters say, which is placed after the characters' names. Choose a scene from one of the two chapters of *I Know Why the Caged Bird Sings* and try your hand at dramatizing it, or rewriting it in the form of a stage play. Follow the conventions for stage directions, character names, and dialogue that were followed in *A Raisin in the Sun.* Make sure that you put nothing in your dramatization that cannot actually be performed on a stage.

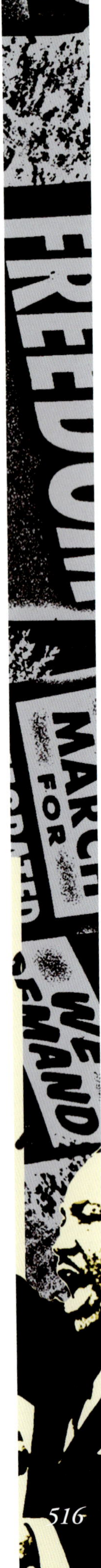

Prereading

from "Letter from Birmingham Jail"

by The Reverend Dr. Martin Luther King, Jr.

The following excerpt contains the first three pages of Dr. King's letter, which in its entirety is roughly twenty pages in length. This letter is an example of Dr. King's remarkable gift for **rhetoric** (the art of persuasion). In it, he laid out—in terms that should have been crystal clear to his critics—his philosophy of nonviolent protest and his justifications for disrupting business as usual in Birmingham.

The letter reveals King's deep skill and understanding of classic rhetoric; he draws on his audience's own background knowledge, evoking such historical figures as Socrates and the Apostle Paul, and applying those ancient examples to the modern world and to the human suffering that King's fellow clergymen—while they admitted that there was a civil rights problem—failed fully to comprehend.

King and fellow protesters had come to Birmingham, Alabama, with the goal of desegregating the city's businesses. If successful, this would have been a small victory on the road to complete desegregation of public facilities. **The Birmingham Campaign,** as it came to be known, involved several stages, including sit-ins and large-scale marches aimed at disrupting local businesses and forcing officials and citizens to confront civil rights issues.

Birmingham officials responded by obtaining an **injunction,** or court order, to stop the protesters. King and his followers defied the injunction, however, on the grounds that it was unconstitutional; when protests resumed, King was arrested and imprisoned for eleven days.

Soon after King's arrest, a group of white clergymen released a letter criticizing King for taking to the streets as opposed to keeping civil rights issues in the courts. King saw fit to write a response and so composed the brilliant "Letter from Birmingham Jail," which was published two months after his release from prison in *The New Leader,* a political magazine.

"Letter from Birmingham Jail" will give readers insight into King's fundamental beliefs and the basic issues at play in the era of the Civil Rights Movement.

Letter from Birmingham Jail

by The Reverend Dr. Martin Luther King, Jr.

MY DEAR FELLOW CLERGYMEN:

While confined here in the Birmingham city jail, I came across your recent statement calling my present activities "unwise and untimely." Seldom do I pause to answer criticism of my work and ideas. If I sought to answer all the criticisms that cross my desk, my secretaries would have little time for anything other than such correspondence in the course of the day, and I would have no time for constructive work. But since I feel that you are men of genuine good will and that your criticisms are sincerely set forth, I want to try to answer your statement in what I hope will be patient and reasonable terms.

I think I should indicate why I am here in Birmingham, since you have been influenced by the view which argues against "outsiders coming in." I have the honor of serving as president of the Southern Christian Leadership Conference, an organization operating in every southern state, with headquarters in Atlanta, Georgia. We have some eighty-five affiliated organizations across the South, and one of them is the Alabama Christian Movement for Human Rights. Frequently we share staff, educational, and financial resources with our **affiliates**. Several months ago the affiliate here in Birmingham asked us to be on call to engage in a nonviolent direct-action program if such were deemed necessary. We readily consented, and when the hour came we lived up to our promise. So I, along with several members of my staff, am here because I was invited here. I am here because I have organizational ties here.

What reasons did Dr. King give for his presence in Birmingham?

But more basically, I am in Birmingham because injustice is here. Just as the prophets of the eighth century B.C.[1] left their villages and carried their "thus saith the Lord" far beyond the boundaries of their home towns, and just as the Apostle Paul left his village of Tarsus and carried the gospel of Jesus Christ to the far corners of the Greco-Roman world, so am I compelled to carry the gospel of freedom beyond my own home town. Like Paul, I must constantly respond to the Macedonian call for aid.[2]

Moreover, I am **cognizant** of the interrelatedness of all communities and states. I cannot sit idly by in Atlanta and not be concerned about what happens in Birmingham. Injustice anywhere is a threat

[1] **prophets of the eighth century B.C.** A reference to the early Hebrew prophets of the Old Testament, including the major prophet Isaiah and such minor prophets as Micah and Hosea.

[2] **Macedonian call for aid.** The Apostle Paul dreamed that a man from Macedon (north of Greece) came to him asking for help. The last of the great Macedonian empire had finally crumbled under Roman might, and Paul traveled to Macedon, where he preached the Gospel for the first time on European soil.

VOCABULARY IN PLACE

- **affiliate,** ***n.*** A person or organization associated with another as a subordinate, subsidiary, or member
- **cognizant,** ***adj.*** Fully informed, conscious, aware

to justice everywhere. We are caught in an inescapable network of mutuality,[3] tied in a single garment of destiny. Whatever affects one directly, affects all indirectly. Never again can we afford to live with the narrow, **provincial** "outside agitator" idea. Anyone who lives inside the United States can never be considered an outsider anywhere within its bounds.

You **deplore** the demonstrations taking place in Birmingham. But your statement, I am sorry to say, fails to express a similar concern for the conditions that brought about the demonstrations. I am sure that none of you would want to rest content with the superficial kind of social analysis that deals merely with effects and does not grapple with underlying causes. It is unfortunate that demonstrations are taking place in Birmingham, but it is even more unfortunate that the city's white power structure left the Negro community with no alternative.

In any nonviolent campaign there are four basic steps: collection of the facts to determine whether injustices exist; negotiation; self-purification; and direct action. We have gone through all these steps in Birmingham. There can be no **gainsaying** the fact that racial injustice engulfs this community. Birmingham is probably the most thoroughly segregated city in the United States. Its ugly record of brutality is widely known. Negroes have experienced grossly unjust treatment in the courts. There have been more unsolved bombings of Negro homes and churches in Birmingham than in any other city in the nation. These are the hard, brutal facts of the case. On the basis of these conditions, Negro leaders sought to negotiate with the city fathers. But the latter consistently refused to engage in good-faith negotiation.

Why did Dr. King point out the injustices that took place in Birmingham?

Then, last September, came the opportunity to talk with leaders of Birmingham's economic community. In the course of the negotiations, certain promises were made by the merchants—for example, to remove the stores' humiliating racial signs. On the basis of these promises, the Reverend Fred Shuttlesworth and the leaders of the Alabama Christian Movement for Human Rights agreed to a **moratorium** on all demonstrations. As the weeks and months went by, we realized that we were the victims of a broken promise. A few signs, briefly removed, returned; the others remained.

What promise was broken?

As in so many past experiences, our hopes had been blasted, and the shadow of deep disappointment settled upon us. We had no alternative except to prepare for direct action, whereby we would present our very bodies as a means of laying our case before the conscience of the local and the national community. Mindful of the difficulties involved, we decided to undertake a process of self-purification. We began a series of workshops on nonviolence, and we repeatedly asked ourselves: "Are you able to accept blows without retaliating?" "Are you able to endure the ordeal of jail?" We decided to schedule our direct-action program for the Easter

[3] **mutuality.** The condition of having mutual or reciprocal interests; what happens to one happens to the other

VOCABULARY IN PLACE

- **provincial,** *adj.* Narrow, self-centered
- **deplore,** *v.* To strongly dislike or disapprove of; detest
- **gainsay,** *v.* To declare false; deny
- **moratorium,** *n.* A suspension of an activity

season, realizing that except for Christmas, this is the main shopping period of the year. Knowing that a strong economic-withdrawal program[4] would be the by-product of direct action, we felt that this would be the best time to bring pressure to bear on the merchants for the needed change.

According to Dr. King, what did "direct action" seek to do?

You may well ask, "Why direct action? Why sit-ins, marches, and so forth? Isn't negotiation a better path?" You are quite right in calling for negotiation. Indeed, this is the very purpose of direct action. Nonviolent direct action seeks to create such a crisis and foster such a tension that a community which has constantly refused to negotiate is forced to confront the issue. It seeks so to dramatize the issue that it can no longer be ignored. My citing the creation of tension as part of the work of the nonviolent-resister may sound rather shocking. But I must confess that I am not afraid of the word "tension." I have earnestly opposed violent tension, but there is a type of constructive, nonviolent tension which is necessary for growth. Just as Socrates[5] felt that it was necessary to create a tension in the mind so that individuals could rise from the bondage of myths and half-truths to the **unfettered** realm of creative analysis and objective appraisal, so must we see the need for nonviolent **gadflies** to create the kind of tension in society that will help men rise from the dark depths of prejudice and racism to the majestic heights of understanding and brotherhood.

The purpose of our direct-action program is to create a situation so crisis-packed that it will inevitably open the door to negotiation. I therefore concur with you in your call for negotiation. Too long has our beloved Southland been bogged down in a tragic effort to live in monologue rather than dialogue.

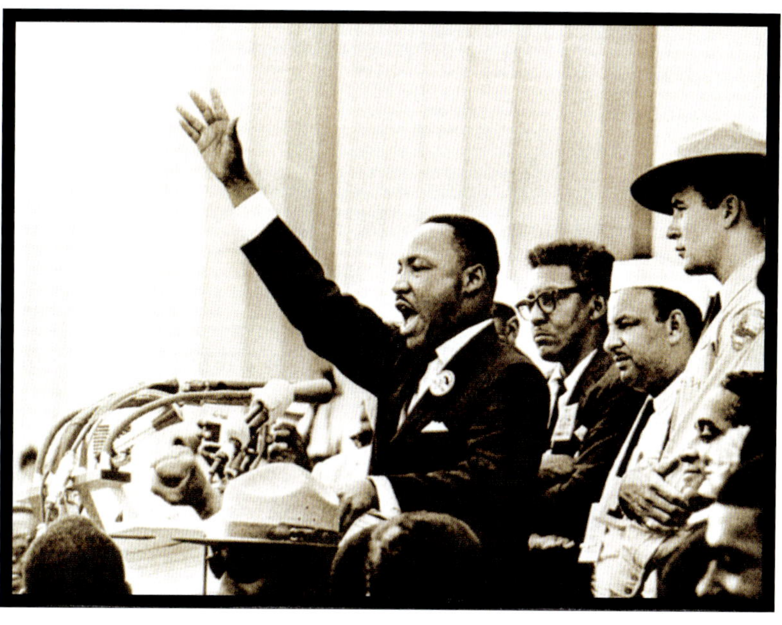

[4] **economic-withdrawal program.** King and fellow demonstrators hoped to increase the impact of their protest by disrupting shopping and other economic activity, not by violence, but by organization and sheer strength of numbers.

[5] **Socrates.** Greek philosopher (circa 470–399 BCE)

VOCABULARY IN PLACE

- **unfettered,** ***past part.*** Free from restrictions or bonds
- **gadfly,** ***n.*** A persistent irritating critic; a nuisance

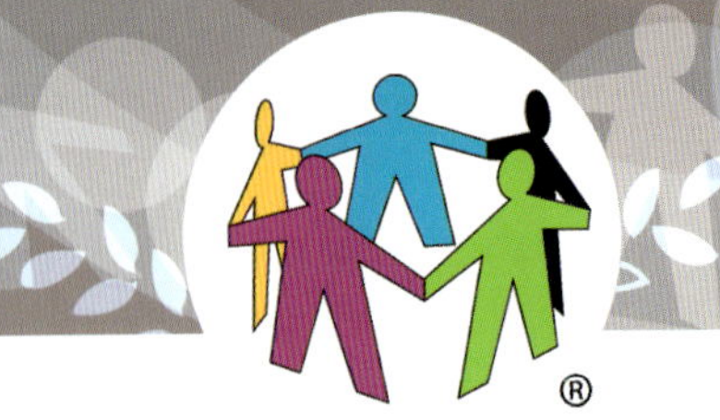

Understanding the Selection

Recalling

1. What reasons did Dr. King give for being in Birmingham? Why was he in jail?
2. According to Dr. King, what "is a threat to justice everywhere"?
3. Did Dr. King think that it was unfortunate that the march took place in Birmingham?
4. Identify at least two "hard, brutal facts" that Dr. King put forth in order to prove that the protest in Birmingham was justified.
5. Why did Dr. King and his supporters choose the Easter season as the time to stage their protest?
6. What was the purpose of direct action?

Interpreting

1. Why did he compare himself to the ancient prophets of the eighth century and to the Apostle Paul?
2. Why couldn't he sit "idly by in Atlanta" while injustice occurred in Birmingham?
3. Why did the "Negro community" have no choice but to protest, according to Dr. King? Provide a quote from the text to support your answer.
4. What was the result of previous negotiations with officials in Birmingham?
5. What response did he hope to receive from merchants, officials, and other whites in the city?
6. How, according to Dr. King, would direct action lead to negotiations?

Synthesizing

1. Did Dr. King want to provoke tension and confrontation in the white community? Explain using quotations from the text to support your answer.
2. Based on your reading of the "Letter from Birmingham Jail," do you think Dr. King and other participants in the Birmingham Campaign were justified in their anger and action? Do you agree with Dr. King's philosophy of nonviolent direct action?

Delving Deeper

History Connection

Nonviolent Direct Action. Dr. Martin Luther King, Jr., is remembered for his speeches and writings. He is remembered as a leader, a motivator, and a source of hope for millions. But his most important legacy, in terms of his impact on American society and democracies all over the world—wherever people feel the need to rise up and protest—lies in his patient, calculated, determined effort to force change through nonviolent direct action. He and other activists not only made their presence known and their voices heard; they also sought to have a direct impact on society by staging their protests in the right places at the right times.

Direct action requires serious organization and planning. Write a one-page report in which you define *direct action,* describe the four steps necessary for a successful nonviolent protest, and explain what Dr. King and his followers did in order to carry out each of these steps. Also, try to identify one issue in today's world that you believe should be addressed through direct action. You may use outside sources (e.g. a newspaper or encyclopedia) in your report; if you use Dr. King's words in your paper, you must use quotation marks and cite your source.

About the Author

Dr. Martin Luther King, Jr., (1929–1968) was born in Atlanta, Georgia, to a schoolteacher mother and a Baptist minister father. He attended Morehouse College in Atlanta and the Crozer Theological Seminary in Chester, Pennsylvania, where he earned a Ph.D. He returned to the segregated South to become a pastor in Montgomery, Alabama.

In 1955 King organized a boycott of Montgomery's bus service after Rosa Parks was arrested for refusing to give up her seat on a city bus to a white woman. The boycott lasted over a year before the Supreme Court declared that bus segregation was unconstitutional. In 1957 King became president of the Southern Christian Leadership Conference, a major civil rights advocacy group. In 1959 he traveled to India to study the life of Mahatma Gandhi. King returned to the U.S. convinced that nonviolence and civil disobedience—the practice of peacefully but firmly resisting unfair laws—were the best methods for fighting segregation.

King wrote six books, including *Stride toward Freedom* (1958) and *The Measure of a Man* (1959). He is best known for his stirring "I Have a Dream" speech in 1963. He was awarded the Nobel Peace Prize the following year. With the passage of the Civil Rights Act of 1964, King turned his attention to ending poverty in the United States. He was assassinated in 1968 while in Memphis, Tennessee, to support a strike for garbage workers.

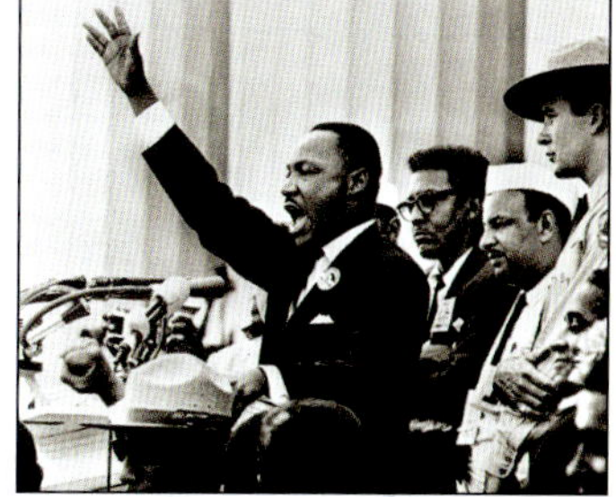

Prereading

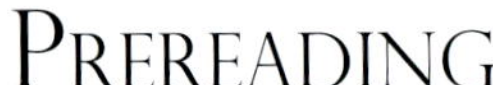

"I Have a Dream"

by The Reverend Dr. Martin Luther King, Jr.

On August 28, 1963, a Baptist preacher from Georgia—a poet and scholar, a warrior practicing peaceful civil disobedience, the embodiment of courage, the leader and brightest star of the Civil Rights Movement—grasped what he knew would be his finest moment and one of the defining events of an era, in the presence of a quarter-million followers. The speech he delivered will be remembered, celebrated, cited, and quoted more often than any other work in this book.

The setting for this speech, the steps of the Lincoln Memorial, was appropriate for two reasons. First, as Dr. King and his supporters knew quite well, Lincoln's shadow provided a fitting reminder of the promise of the Emancipation Proclamation and the failure of the American political and legal system to deliver fully on the principles set forth in the Declaration of Independence and the Constitution. Second, the Lincoln Memorial was a proper setting because, insofar as great American speeches are concerned, Lincoln's Gettysburg Address—which King evokes in the second sentence of his speech—is the only American speech that can claim parity with King's in historical terms.

As pure **rhetoric** (the art of using language effectively and persuasively), King's speech truly has no rivals. This speech came in the middle of what would prove to be one of the worst and most momentous years in American history. Police had brutally attacked King and his followers in Alabama, NAACP leader Medgar Evers had been murdered in Mississippi, and things only got worse after this speech. (See timeline on page 481.) Unfortunately, King's enemies and critics must not have listened to his speech that day, or their minds were too numb and their ears too deaf to truly hear and understand these words. For to comprehend this speech yet continue to support racial segregation is simply a failure to grasp the meaning of *freedom* and *human rights.*

King and his fellow civil rights activists—those 250,000 participants in the March on Washington who listened, awestruck, on that terribly hot summer day—had every reason to protest. The evidence is laid out in this speech; as King says, theirs was "legitimate discontent." Read slowly, and pay especially close attention, because these words still carry all the power, hope, and wisdom expressed by this preacher from Atlanta, who will remain, rightly, among the most revered of great Americans.

I Have a Dream

by The Reverend Dr. Martin Luther King, Jr.

I am happy to join with you today in what will go down in history as the greatest demonstration for freedom in the history of our nation.

Fivescore[1] years ago, a great American, in whose symbolic shadow we stand today, signed the Emancipation Proclamation. This momentous **decree** came as a great beacon light of hope to millions of Negro slaves who had been seared in the flames of **withering** injustice. It came as a joyous daybreak to end the long night of their captivity.

But one hundred years later, the Negro still is not free. One hundred years later, the life of the Negro is still sadly crippled by the **manacles** of segregation and the chains of discrimination. One hundred years later, the Negro lives on a lonely island of poverty in the midst of a vast ocean of material prosperity. One hundred years later, the Negro is still **languished** in the corners of American society and finds himself in exile in his own land.

And so we've come here today to **dramatize** a shameful condition.

In a sense we've come to our nation's capital to cash a check. When the architects of our republic wrote the magnificent words of the Constitution and the Declaration of Independence, they were signing a promissory note[2] to which every American was to fall heir. This note was the promise that all men, yes, black men as well as white men, would be guaranteed the **unalienable** rights of life, liberty, and the pursuit of happiness.

Who are the "architects" to whom King referred?

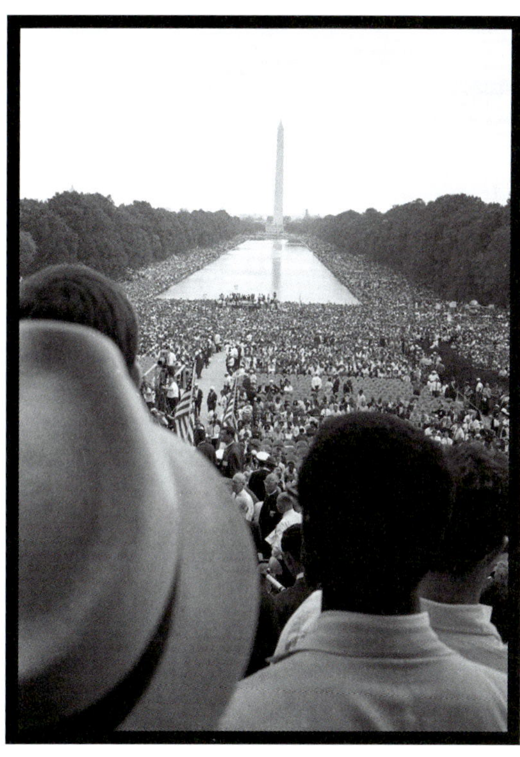

1 **fivescore.** One hundred (A *score* is equal to twenty.)

2 **promissory note.** A written promise to repay a debt

VOCABULARY IN PLACE

- **decree,** ***n.*** An authoritative order having the force of law
- **withering,** ***adj.*** Tending to overwhelm; devastating
- **manacle,** ***n.*** Something that confines or restrains
- **languished,** ***past part.*** Neglected; left to decay
- **dramatize,** ***v.*** To present in an emotional or forceful way
- **unalienable,** ***adj.*** Not to be taken away

It is obvious today that America has **defaulted** on this promissory note insofar as her citizens of color are concerned. Instead of honoring this sacred obligation, America has given the Negro people a bad check; a check which has come back marked "insufficient funds." We refuse to believe that there are insufficient funds in the great vaults of opportunity of this nation. And so we've come to cash this check, a check that will give us upon demand the riches of freedom and the security of justice.

We have also come to this **hallowed** spot to remind America of the fierce urgency of now. This is no time to engage in the luxury of cooling off or to take the tranquilizing drug of **gradualism.** Now is the time to make real the promises of democracy; now is the time to rise from the dark and desolate valley of segregation to the sunlit path of racial justice; now is the time to lift our nation from the quicksands of racial injustice to the solid rock of brotherhood; now is the time to make justice a reality for all of God's children.

It would be fatal for the nation to overlook the urgency of the moment. This **sweltering** summer of the Negro's legitimate discontent will not pass until there is an invigorating autumn of freedom and equality. Nineteen sixty-three is not an end, but a beginning. And those who hope that the Negro needed to blow off steam and will now be content, will have a rude awakening if the nation returns to business as usual. There will be neither rest nor tranquility in America until the Negro is granted his citizenship rights. The whirlwinds of revolt will continue to shake the foundations of our nation until the bright day of justice emerges.

Who was going to have a "rude awakening"? Why?

But there is something that I must say to my people who stand on the warm threshold which leads into the palace of justice. In the process of gaining our rightful place we must not be guilty of wrongful deeds. Let us not seek to satisfy our thirst for freedom by drinking from the cup of bitterness and hatred. We must forever conduct our struggle on the high plane of dignity and discipline. We must not allow our creative protest to **degenerate** into physical violence. Again and again we must rise to the majestic heights of meeting physical force with soul force.

What did King mean by the terms "creative protest" and "soul force"?

The marvelous new militancy[3] which has engulfed the Negro community must not lead us to a distrust of all white people, for many of our white brothers, as evidenced by their presence here today, have come to realize that their destiny is tied up with our destiny and they have come to realize that their freedom is **inextricably** bound to our freedom. We cannot walk alone.

And as we walk, we must make the pledge that we shall always march ahead. We cannot turn back. There are those who are asking the devotees of civil rights, "When will you be satisfied?" We can never be satisfied as long as the Negro is the victim of the

[3] **new militancy.** A reference to the emergent Black Power Movement whose members, including Malcolm X, emphasized separation from white society "by any means necessary"

VOCABULARY IN PLACE

- **default,** ***v.*** To fail to repay a debt or fulfill an obligation
- **hallowed,** ***adj.*** Sacred
- **gradualism,** ***n.*** Advancing toward a goal by slow stages
- **sweltering,** ***adj.*** Oppressively hot
- **degenerate,** ***v.*** To fall to an undesirable moral state
- **inextricably,** ***adv.*** So as to be impossible to untangle

unspeakable horrors of police brutality. We can never be satisfied as long as our bodies, heavy with the fatigue of travel, cannot gain lodging in the motels of the highways and the hotels of the cities. We can never be satisfied as long as the Negro's basic mobility is from a smaller ghetto to a larger one. We can never be satisfied as long as our children are stripped of their selfhood and robbed of their dignity by signs stating "for whites only." We can never be satisfied as long as a Negro in Mississippi cannot vote and a Negro in New York believes he has nothing for which to vote. No, no, we are not satisfied, and we will not be satisfied until justice rolls down like waters and righteousness like a mighty stream.

I am not unmindful that some of you have come here out of great trials and tribulations.[4] Some of you have come fresh from narrow jail cells. Some of you have come from areas where your quest for freedom left you battered by the storms of persecution and staggered by the winds of police brutality. You have been the veterans of creative suffering. Continue to work with the faith that unearned suffering is **redemptive.**

Why did Dr. King want his audience to believe that "unearned suffering is redemptive"?

Go back to Mississippi; go back to Alabama; go back to South Carolina; go back to Georgia; go back to Louisiana; go back to the slums and ghettos of our northern cities, knowing that somehow this situation can, and will be changed. Let us not **wallow** in the valley of despair.

I say to you today, my friends, that even though we face the difficulties of today and tomorrow, I still have a dream. It is a dream deeply rooted in the American dream. I have a dream that one day this nation will rise up and live out the true meaning of its creed—we hold these truths to be self-evident, that all men are created equal.[5]

I have a dream that one day on the red hills of Georgia, sons of former slaves and the sons of former slave owners will be able to sit down together at the table of brotherhood.

I have a dream that one day, even the state of Mississippi, a state sweltering with the heat of injustice, sweltering with the heat of oppression, will be transformed into an oasis of freedom and justice.

I have a dream that my four little children will one day live in a nation where they will not be judged by the color of their skin but by the content of their character. I have a dream today!

I have a dream that one day, down in Alabama, with its vicious racists, with its governor having his lips dripping with the words of interposition and nullification,[6] that one day, right there in Alabama, little black boys and black girls will be able to join hands with little white boys and white girls as sisters and brothers. I have a dream today!

I have a dream that one day every valley shall be **exalted,** every hill and mountain shall be made low, the rough places will be made

---

[4] **trials and tribulations.** Excessive and undue hardship

[5] **we hold . . . created equal.** A famous line from the Declaration of Independence

[6] **with its governor . . . interposition and nullification.** The governor in question is George C. Wallace, who—along with other elected officials in the South—attempted to block enactment of laws, backed by Supreme Court rulings, that called for desegregation of public institutions. *Interposition* is similar to interjection, or interruption; *nullification* is the declaration that something is void. Historically, these two words have been used to express the idea that a state has the right to nullify federal laws that it believes to be unconstitutional. This doctrine has virtually no support in mainstream politics today.

VOCABULARY IN PLACE

- **redemptive,** ***adj.*** Restoring honor or reputation
- **wallow,** ***v.*** To roll about clumsily, as if in mud; struggle
- **exalted,** ***adj.*** Elevated in rank or status

Why did Dr. King want every mountain to be made low? What did this have to do with Civil Rights?

plain, and the crooked places will be made straight and the glory of the Lord shall be revealed and all flesh shall see it together.[7]

This is our hope. This is the faith that I go back to the South with.

With this faith we will be able to hew out of the mountain of despair a stone of hope. With this faith we will be able to transform the jangling discords[8] of our nation into a beautiful symphony of brotherhood. With this faith we will be able to work together, to pray together, to struggle together, to go to jail together, to stand up for freedom together, knowing that we will be free one day.

Why did he want them to go to jail together?

This will be the day when all of God's children will be able to sing with new meaning—"my country 'tis of thee; sweet land of liberty; of thee I sing; land where my fathers died, land of the pilgrim's pride; from every mountain side, let freedom ring."

And if America is to be a great nation, this must become true.

So let freedom ring from the **prodigious** hilltops of New Hampshire.

Let freedom ring from the mighty mountains of New York.

Let freedom ring from the **heightening** Alleghenies of Pennsylvania.

Let freedom ring from the snow-capped Rockies of Colorado.

Let freedom ring from the curvaceous slopes of California.

But not only that.

Let freedom ring from Stone Mountain of Georgia.

Let freedom ring from Lookout Mountain of Tennessee.

Let freedom ring from every hill and molehill of Mississippi, from every mountainside, let freedom ring.

And when this happens—when we allow freedom to ring—when we let it ring from every village and every hamlet, from every state and every city, we will be able to speed up that day when all of God's children—black men and white men, Jews and Gentiles, Protestants and Catholics—will be able to join hands and to sing in the words of the old Negro spiritual, "Free at last, Free at last; thank God Almighty, we are free at last." ■

". . . and I've seen the Promised Land. I may not get there with you, but I want you to know tonight that we as a people will get to the Promised Land. So I'm happy tonight. I'm not worried about anything. I'm not fearing any man. Mine eyes have seen the glory of the coming of the Lord."

— from the "I've Been to the Mountaintop" speech, Memphis, April 3, 1968, the night before Dr. King was assassinated

VOCABULARY IN PLACE

- **prodigious,** ***adj.*** Impressively great in size
- **heightening,** ***adj.*** Rising

[7] **every valley . . . it together.** From Isaiah 40:4–5

[8] **jangling discords.** Irritating, disturbing arguments and disagreements

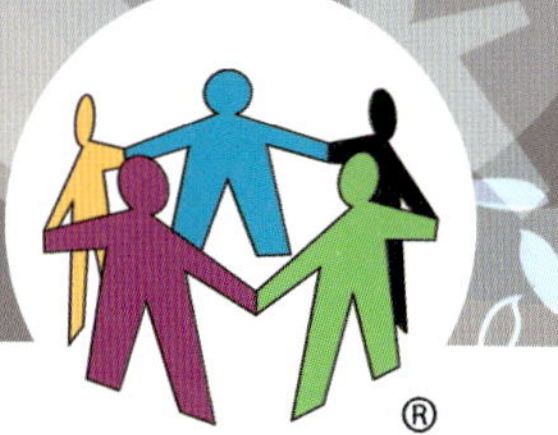

Understanding the Selection

Recalling

1. At what monument did Dr. King deliver his "I Have a Dream" speech?
2. According to Dr. King, what did the nation's Founding Fathers ("architects of our republic") promise to all Americans?
3. What "is not a beginning, but an end"?
4. Why should civil rights activists never be satisfied, according to Dr. King?
5. What did Dr. King urge his listeners to do when they returned home (to Mississippi, etc.)?

Interpreting

1. Why is this location significant with regard to his speech and the March on Washington?
2. What connection did Dr. King draw between cashing a check and the March on Washington?
3. Who "hoped that the Negro needed to blow off steam"? Why, according to Dr. King, would these people have a "rude awakening"?
4. Identify at least three reasons Dr. King gave why his followers should not be satisfied.
5. What faith did Dr. King want to "go back to the South with"? What would people be able to do with this faith?

Synthesizing

1. Dr. Martin Luther King, Jr., believed in the use of nonviolent protest to create social change. Why did he describe this type of protest as "creative"? What personal strengths would his followers need in order to accomplish their goals?
2. Why did Dr. King say that the March on Washington would go down as "the greatest demonstration for freedom in the history of our nation"?

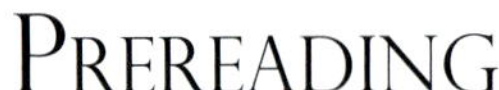

Prereading

"Speech at Tulane University"

by Wynton Marsalis

On August 29, 2005, after having made landfall in Florida and having crossed over the Gulf of Mexico, **Hurricane Katrina** pounded into Louisiana and Mississippi and other parts of the south central United States. Over 1,800 people died as a result of Katrina, and property damage from the storm reached 75 billion dollars, making it the costliest Atlantic hurricane ever. Levees broke in New Orleans, causing flooding in 80 percent of the city. The mayor of New Orleans at the time had ordered a complete evacuation, but many of the city's poorest inhabitants had been unable to get away in time and were among the hardest hit by the storm.

On **Martin Luther King Day**, 2006, the great jazz and classical trumpeter and composer **Wynton Marsalis,** who was born in New Orleans and attended **Tulane University,** spoke to students at Tulane about the storm. A true Renaissance man, Marsalis is not only one of the world's most gifted jazz and classical musicians but is also a great scholar of jazz history, a talented public speaker, and an activist. Marsalis took the occasion of the speech at Tulane to comment upon the legacy of Dr. King and of the Civil Rights Movement and to pose the question posed by Dr. King in the title of King's last book: *Where do we go from here?*

For Marsalis, the terrible disaster that was Hurricane Katrina provided a teachable moment—a time to reflect on the proper reaction to adversity. He called upon his listeners to take a cue from Dr. King and not to be complacent or apathetic. In particular, he spoke to a new generation of young people, represented by the students at Tulane, reminding them of the importance to freedom and democracy of the continued interest and active involvement of the young in civic and political affairs.

Speech at Tulane University

by Wynton Marsalis

Thank you Governor Blanco, Lieutenant Governor Landrieu, and especially President Cowen[1] for inviting me here tonight.

It's good to be home. It's especially good to be home in a time of crisis[2] because tough times force us to return to fundamentals. And there is nothing more fundamental than home. Many of you are visitors to New Orleans, but it won't take four years for the Crescent City[3] to be forever in your blood. So I feel in a way, that we are all home tonight.

I also feel a special honor in speaking to you on Martin Luther King, Jr.'s Day because it was Dr. King's tireless activism that fostered our modern way of relating to one another. Yes, we are here tonight empowered with the feeling that if we want to we can speak truthfully to one another.

We can work together. We can rely on one another because Dr. King's actions made his dream our reality, and this rebuilding of New Orleans gives us the perfect opportunity to see if we're ready to extend the **legacy** of Dr. King and the Civil Rights Movement.

Look around this room and realize that the final chapter of that movement still waits for a generation with the courage to write it. That's why I say we are all home tonight. We are all home because Dr. King led the charge to victory over **regressive,** ignorant traditions that had long gone unchallenged . . . because he was unwavering in presenting compelling arguments to make real the promises of the Constitution . . . because he never **succumbed** to hopelessness and showed us what one citizen can achieve when armed with an **evangelical** zeal for freedom and a first-class education, it is most fitting to re-open our city's finest institutions of higher education on the day we celebrate Dr. Martin Luther King, Jr. Though he is almost always reduced to a dreamer today, Dr. King was an achiever, a most powerful **exemplar** of action. His last book is entitled *Where Do We Go From Here: Chaos or Community?* It is a question that is most appropriate for us in this moment.

Dr. King worked in the shadow of slavery and discrimination. We are in the shadow of the worst natural disaster to ever befall America.[4]

VOCABULARY IN PLACE

- **legacy,** ***n.*** That which is left for later generations
- **regressive,** ***adj.*** Backward-leading
- **succumb,** ***v.*** To give in
- **evangelical,** ***adj.*** Characterized by a crusading enthusiam and a willingness to work toward gaining converts
- **exemplar,** ***n.*** Exceptionally fine example of something

[1] **Governor Blanco . . . President Cowen.** Kathleen Babineau Blanco, 55th Governor of Louisiana; Mitch Landrieu, Blanco's Lieutenant Governor; and Scott S. Cowen, 14th president of Tulane University

[2] **a time of crisis.** Shortly after Hurricane Katrina slammed into Florida, Louisiana, and Mississippi in 2005. See the Prereading.

[3] **Crescent City.** A nickname for New Orleans that comes from the shape of the Mississippi River as it winds though the city

[4] **worst . . . America.** At the time, Katrina was the most costly in dollar terms of any natural disaster in the country's history and the most deadly hurricane since the 1928 Okeechobee Hurricane.

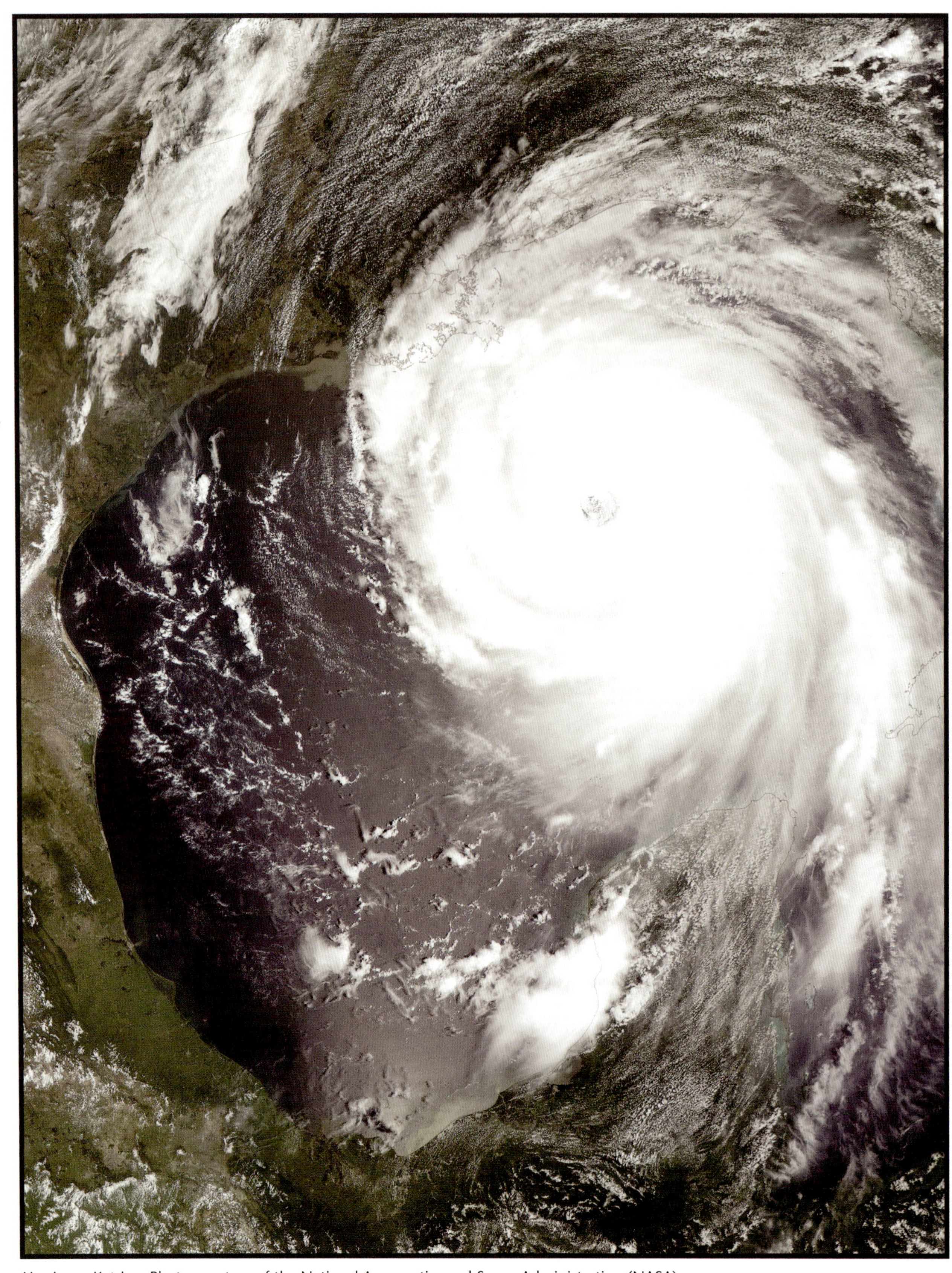

Hurricane Katrina. Photo courtesy of the National Aeronautics and Space Administration (NASA).

What better way to celebrate him than by rising to a challenge?

His challenge was to reverse 80 years of legalized **apartheid**—a **veritable** way of life in our land of freedom. Our challenge is merely to rebuild a great city in times of unbelievable political **callousness** and corruption. Even in these times there are still neighbors that will turn their backs on neighbors. Yes, this is Louisiana, and we are home tonight.

Through a tireless single-minded campaign to expose lies and **sanctioned** injustice, Dr. King never lost faith in the ability of humans to behave better. He didn't settle. He succeeded. Certainly his single-mindedness is what is required of us, at this time, to rebuild New Orleans. Don't settle. Succeed.

Catchy slogans aside, when we look around here, we see destruction, anguish, and uncertainty. Let's look deeper into ourselves and find possibility. That's why it's important to mark the reopening of New Orleans with the triumphant return of Tulane, Xavier, Loyola, and Dillard Universities. Through first-class education, a generation marches down the long uncertain road of the future with confidence. After all is said and done, education's purpose is to lead students to who they are, what they can be, and who they want to be. The best way to be, is to do. And when we pass on the best of what we do . . . that is quality education.

If we're lucky, we only have a good 80 years or so on this earth, and through education, those 80 are extended through the generations that follow. Look around: Paul Tulane put his life into this campus over 120 years ago. It's still here—inviting us tonight. I spent many a night as a high school student in the Tulane Library.

It's here for us now, and will be here for young people looking for knowledge to define themselves and their time long after we're all gone.

That's why it's important to address young people in the reopening of New Orleans—you have always been at the forefront of social change. In rebuilding, let's revisit the potential of American democracy and American glory when its citizens are mobilized to enlightened action. The soldiers in Martin Luther King's army were people demanding change—lawyers, clerks, politicians, housewives, businessmen, maids, clergymen. The ones on the frontlines were America's youth.

Young people, much like you, who felt empowered to better our nation . . . who understood that change required sacrifice . . . who were emboldened with a spirit of rightness and were determined to create change for the betterment of our country.

That is why, as I stand before you tonight, I say the best way to be, is to do. Don't settle for style. Succeed in substance. President Cowen said "don't come back if helping restore New Orleans is not in your DNA,"[5] and 91 percent of you Tulane students have returned. Most of you have returned at a time when many would have stayed away. And now that you are here, you have the opportunity to set a new tone, not only for New Orleans, but for our country. Remember, many a revolution started with

VOCABULARY IN PLACE

- **apartheid,** *n.* A political system, like that once found in South Africa, in which racial groups are separated and treated unequally
- **veritable,** *adj.* Being truly so called, real
- **callousness,** *n.* Lack of caring or compassion
- **sanctioned,** *past part.* Officially supported, as by law or by the actions of authorities

5 **DNA.** The complex molecule within cell nuclei that contains the genetic information that provides the blueprint for making an organism

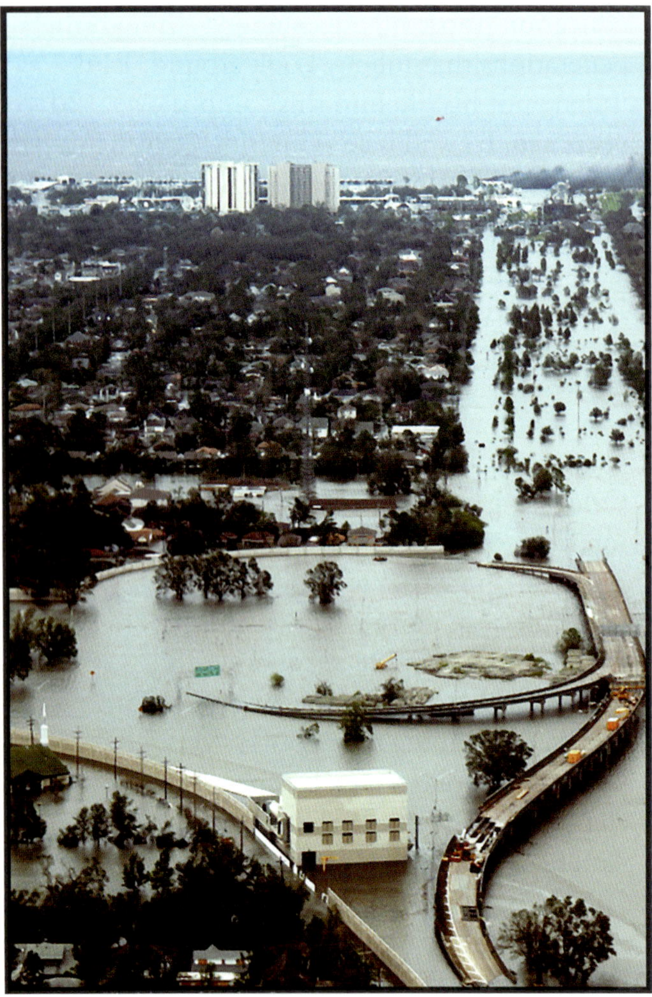

Flooding in New Orleans after Hurricane Katrina. Photo courtesy of the National Aeronautics and Space Administration (NASA).

the actions of a few. For example, only 56 men signed the Declaration of Independence of which Ben Franklin said, "We must all hang together, or assuredly we shall all hang separately." A few hanging together can lead a nation to change.

You know, we love to **patronize** young people with slogans like "the young will lead the way"—when actually, the young very seldom lead anything in our country today. It's been quite some time since a younger generation pushed an older one to a higher standard.[6]

My daddy thought—no, he expected—that my brothers and I and our generation would make the world a better place. He was correct in his belief because he had lived in an America of continual social progress. Depression followed by prosperity, segregation by integration, and so on.

And though I haven't quite pinpointed it, somewhere between my daddy's youth and mine, generational **aspirations** for a richer democracy changed to aspirations for a richer me—more wealth and more leisure time for a lower quality of work. Oh, and forget about our political process.

Voting became too much of a bore—let alone keeping an eye on how our tax dollars were being squandered or how our interests were being poorly served by our elected officials.

When did we begin to lose faith in our ability to effect change? Perhaps the demoralizing murders of John and Robert Kennedy, and MLK[7] scared the civic-minded young people of the 1960s right out of their idealism into despair and then, to **indifference.** Perhaps it was the 1980s when the "opportunity" inherent in the American Dream was distorted from the land of "we" to the land of "to hell with anybody else but me." Maybe the preoccupation with technological progress has overshadowed our concern with human progress. In any case, the result of this social inactivity is that generations are now named simply for the

VOCABULARY IN PLACE

- **patronize,** *v.* To treat someone in a condescending, parental manner
- **aspiration,** *n.* Hope, dream
- **indifference,** *n.* Lack of interest, concern, or involvement

[6] **some time . . . standard.** Marsalis is probably referring to the period of the late 1960s and early 1970s in which young people took political action related to women's rights, civil rights, and the Vietnam War.

[7] **MLK.** Dr. Martin Luther King, Jr.

last letters of the alphabet.[8] And these alphabet-named people are distinguished by the ability to manipulate new technology, buy new things with money they have not earned and be obsessed with the trivial lives of celebrities.

But I know you're more than that.

We have the tendency to make generations **unanimous.**[9] But in fact, there really have only ever been a few people in each generation who step out, are willing to put themselves on the line, and risk everything for their beliefs. Only a few act . . . the rest of us reap the benefits of their risk.

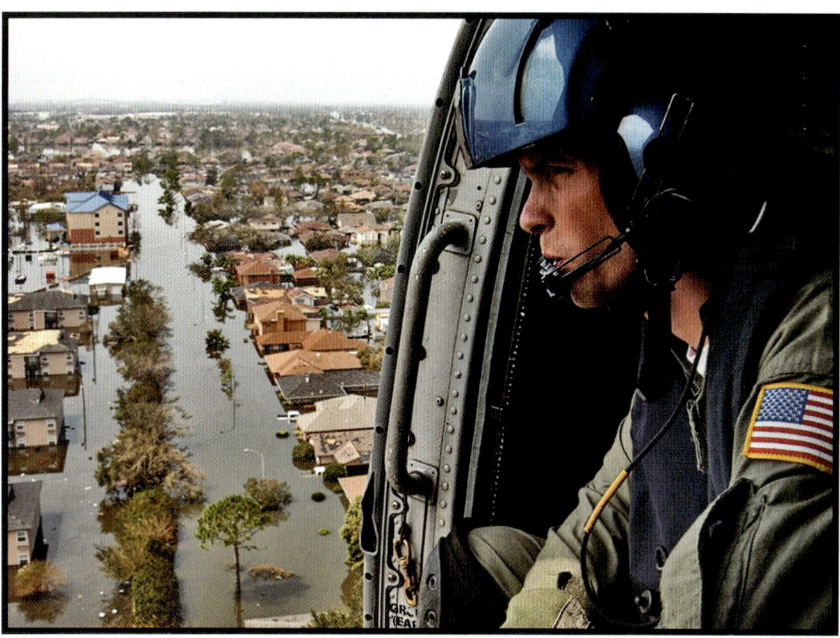

A Navy Helicopter Searches for Survivors. Photo courtesy of the the United States Navy.

Yes, I always laugh when people my age complain about their college-age and teenage kids by talking about how much better we were. I laugh because I have absolutely no idea what my generation did to enrich our democracy. What movement have we been identified with that forced our elders to keep their promises . . . that challenged their failures or built upon their successes? For me, we dropped the ball after the Civil Rights Movement. We entered a period of **complacency** and closed our eyes to the very public corruption of our democracy.

As we have seen our money squandered and stolen, our civic rights trampled, and the politics of **polarity** become the order of the day, we have held absolutely no one accountable. From us, you inherit an abiding helplessness.

If you realize the unfortunate consequences of inaction, hopefully you will understand even more the importance of holding both your elders and your peers accountable when it comes to the rebuilding of New Orleans. Stay up on the facts.

What, other than injustice, could be the reason that the **displaced** citizens of New Orleans cannot be accommodated by the richest nation in the world? You, along with the entire world, saw the bureaucratic fumbling and lack of concern inflicted on those very same citizens at the Superdome

VOCABULARY IN PLACE

- **unanimous,** ***adj.*** Done together, in one voice, without variation or difference
- **complacency,** ***n.*** The tendency to accept things as they are
- **polarity,** ***n.*** Sharp division into opposite parties or beliefs
- **displaced,** ***past part.*** Forced to leave (one's home)

[8] **letters of the alphabet.** A reference to the practice in the late twentieth century and early twenty-first century of naming generations after the final letters of the alphabet, as in "generation X" and "generation Y"

[9] **tendency . . . unanimous.** The habit of treating people of a particular age as though every person of that generation thought similarly

and the Convention Center.[10] Who is being held accountable now?

Take your example, not from my generation, but from generations—from those few inspired young people—who stood on the front lines and fought injustice throughout the course of our nation's history.

For example, in the first 20 years of the 1900s, youth supported the Progressive Movement to keep farmers from being shafted by big business, as well as the movements for women's suffrage, worker's rights, a League of Nations[11] and of course, keeping alcohol legal. The next 20 years would see the repeal of Prohibition,[12] and young people pushing for the establishment of Social Security, and unemployment insurance. Young people vowed to fight Fascism with the Lincoln Brigades[13] and also vowed not to fight old folks' wars by taking the Oxford Oath.[14] The 1940s began with young people fighting the "Good War."[15] The 50s saw young folks involved in tearing down the laws that supported segregation, challenging parental tastes and authority with rock-and-roll, and questioning **conformity** with the Beatniks.[16]

The 60s and 70s saw youth challenging Vietnam, the role of women, **rituals** of courtship, race relations, and the political process itself. Today, we still reap the benefits of these generations' successes and suffer losses from their failures.

The rebuilding of New Orleans is an important point in the history of the United States. Should my generation expect yours to be the watchdogs of this effort? Should we expect you to monitor how our leaders handle this responsibility to restore our city?

Well, my generation might not—because we have not been very good watchdogs ourselves. But I do. I expect you to be different than the example we've set for you.

Don't wish for someone else to do later what you can do now. When you perceive a problem, instead of speaking about it in dorm rooms or in hushed corners . . . put together a group of friends and be loud and public in your **dissent.**

When you notice inconsistencies between what is said by government officials and what is done, exercise your individual and collective power to take steps to remove them. Our form of democracy allows you to do that. Remember, the best way to be, is to do.

What are you going to do?

Well, when it comes to the rebuilding of New Orleans, start with the President.[17] He stood in Jackson Square and told the nation that he would rebuild New Orleans and fix the levees.

---

10 **Superdome . . . Convention Center.** Sites in New Orleans to which refugees from Hurricane Katrina fled

11 **League of Nations.** Precursor to the United Nations founded in 1920 to promote international cooperation and peace

12 **Prohibition.** Period from 1920 to 1933 in which the manufacture and sale of alcohol were prohibited in the United States under the 18th Amendment

13 **Lincoln Brigades.** One of a number of organizations of American volunteers who fought against the Fascists in the Spanish Civil War in the late 1930s

14 **Oxford Oath.** A resolution adopted by the Oxford University Student Union in 1933 not to fight "for king and country" to support imperialistic activity around the world

15 **"Good War."** World War II, considered by many a good or just war because it was waged against tyranny and Fascism

16 **Beatniks.** Members of the so-called "Beat Generation" of the 1950s and '60s who challenged conventional ways of living and thinking

17 **President.** George W. Bush, 43rd president of the United States

VOCABULARY IN PLACE

- **conformity,** ***n.*** Tendency to act in a conventional, accepted, traditional manner
- **ritual,** ***n.*** A ceremony or set of traditional actions
- **dissent,** ***n.*** Challenge to or disagreement with established authority or the status quo

When public outrage was at its highest and his popularity was nearing its lowest, let's remember that he put Karl Rove[18] in charge of the reconstruction effort. That was in September. Has anyone seen or heard from Karl Rove? Hmmm . . .

In the opening days of this New Year, the President **reiterated** that the levees will be fixed. Yes, money has been **appropriated.**

But is it enough? The task has been assigned. People have been put in charge. But are they going to take care of it? Are they waiting for people—like you—to stop paying attention?

Now is the time for your generation to reclaim the energy, optimism, and fire that is the real American spirit. I am confident that you students can, and will, make an incalculable contribution to the intelligent and compassionate rebuilding of our city and protection of our **dispersed** populace. In doing so, you will be using your collective power to redefine the soul of our nation.

You know, democracy is a can-do form. We always hear about the rights of democracy, but the major responsibility of it is participation. Throughout American history, we have seen causes for the betterment of democracy **invigorated** by young people unafraid to fight for the general welfare of all, even if it meant **alienation** from their own families.

Don't be disheartened by the destruction of the hurricane or by political **ineptitude** or even by the **apathy** of others. Remember, we are all home. That is why I urge you not to let this moment pass without sending a clear message to your peers and elders around the world, "New Orleans will be rebuilt, and it will be rebuilt with an intensity, with an intelligence, with an impatience and with a freshness that only serious minded young people can bring." One of the great lessons of the Civil Rights Movement—when the minds and hearts of enough citizens are focused on change America changes very quickly.

I know that the challenge of rebuilding may seem **insurmountable**. But we have a roadmap to success—the path of Dr. Martin Luther King, Jr. Because he didn't settle for "that's just the way things are," we don't have to. Because he led an intelligent assault on all sorts of sanctioned corruption, we too can use our intelligence to protect and **project integrity.**

Because he understood that all human beings are of one race long before the discovery of the DNA strain,[19] we can now live that reality. Because Dr. King was always about the business of making real the human **grandeur** outlined in the United States Constitution and Bill of Rights, we can still believe that our government can be of the

VOCABULARY IN PLACE

- **reiterate,** *v.* To repeat
- **appropriate,** *v.* To make available by legislative or other official action
- **dispersed,** *past part.* Spread out
- **invigorate,** *v.* To energize
- **alienation,** *n.* Isolation or estrangement from others
- **ineptitude,** *n.* Incompetence, lack of ability
- **apathy,** *n.* Lack of interest or concern
- **insurmountable,** *adj.* Not capable of being overcome
- **project,** *v.* To show outwardly
- **integrity,** *n.* Strict adherence to a moral or ethical code
- **grandeur,** *n.* Greatness

18 **Karl Rove.** Then Deputy Chief of Staff to President George W. Bush

19 **all human beings . . . DNA strain.** Recent studies of human DNA indicate that there is more variability in the genetic material (DNA) within so-called racial groups than there is, on average, between racial groups. This discovery lends scientific support to the idea that race is primarily a social construct with little physical basis, an idea that in turn supports the contention of Dr. King and others that all people are brothers and sisters, despite their superficial differences. (See also Science Connection, page 539.)

people, by the people, and for the people.[20] Let's concentrate our energies to that end.

You will hear that the most immediate concerns for New Orleans are the wetlands, the levees and the homes. But I'm here to tell you that the most immediate concern for New Orleans is the well-being of our displaced neighbors spread out in a **diaspora** all over the United States.

Look around the room . . . and I want you all to understand that there are forces all around you who wish to exploit division, rob you of your freedom, and tell you what to think. They are afraid of change . . . some of these forces are even within you.

But I'm here to tell you, when young folks are motivated to action, when they act with insight, soul and fire, they can **rekindle** the weary spirit of a slumbering nation. It's time somebody woke us up. ■

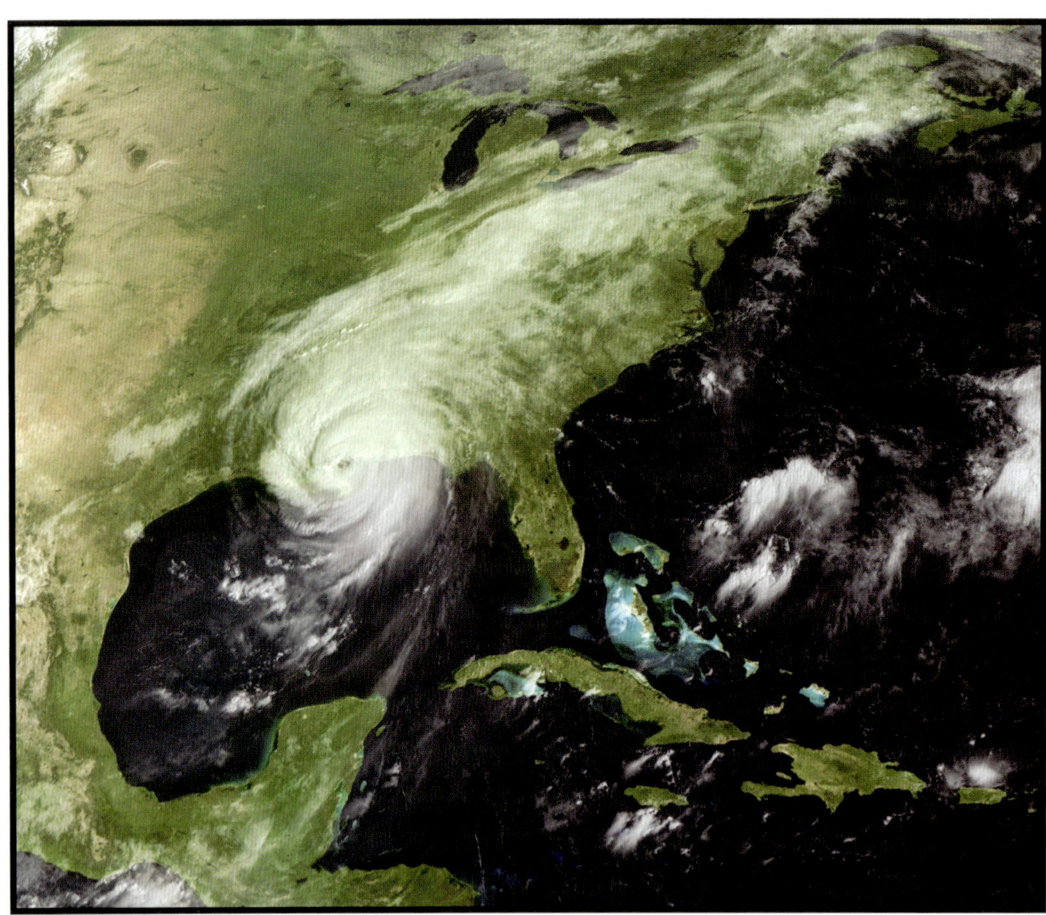

Hurricane Katrina Makes Landfall. Photo courtesy of the National Aeronautics and Space Administration (NASA).

VOCABULARY IN PLACE

- **diaspora,** *n.* A scattering of a people in places removed from their homeland
- **rekindle,** *v.* To light (a fire) again; metaphorically, to bring about a renewed interest or enthusiasm

20 **of the people . . . for the people.** Quotation from Lincoln's Gettysburg Address

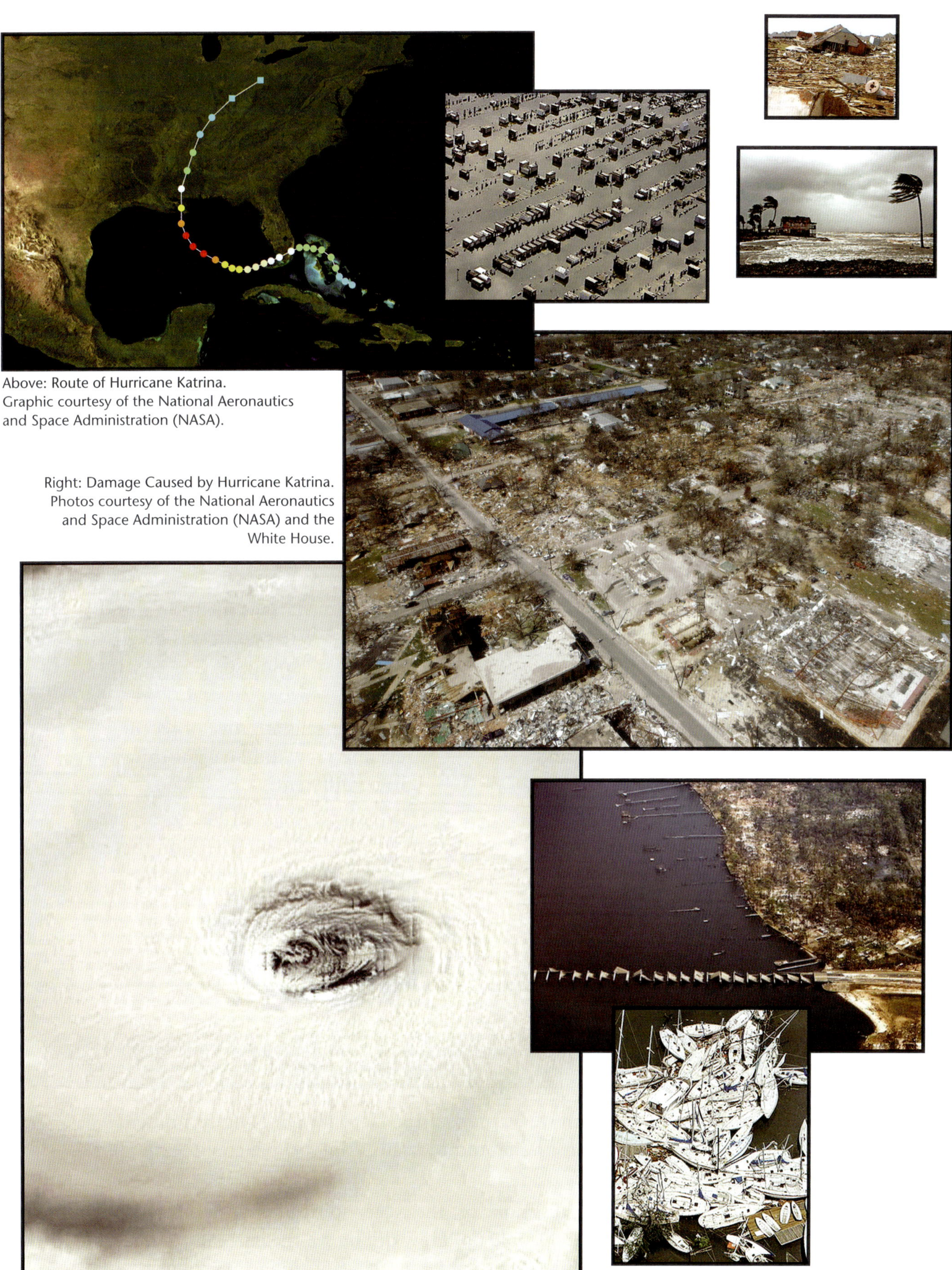

Above: Route of Hurricane Katrina. Graphic courtesy of the National Aeronautics and Space Administration (NASA).

Right: Damage Caused by Hurricane Katrina. Photos courtesy of the National Aeronautics and Space Administration (NASA) and the White House.

Above: The Eye of Hurricane Katrina. Photo courtesy of the National Aeronautics and Space Administration (NASA).

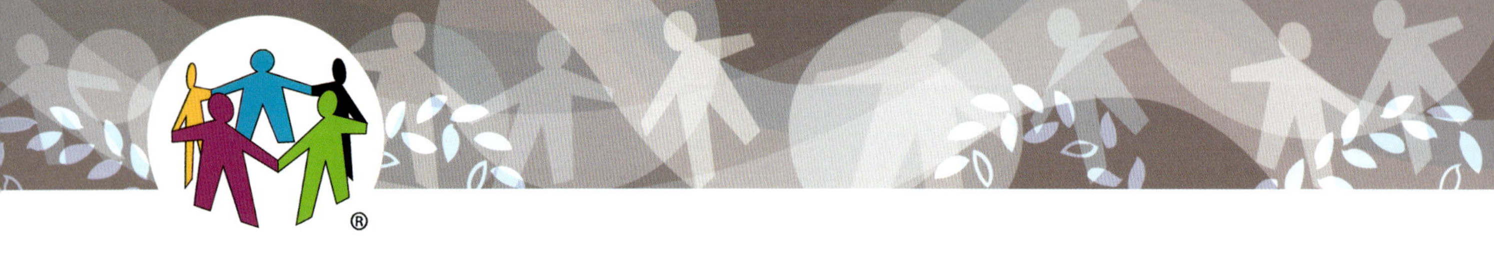

Understanding the Selection

Recalling

1. On what holiday did Wynton Marsalis give this speech? Where did he give it, and after what natural disaster?
2. To whom was Marsalis speaking?
3. How many people, according to Marsalis, signed the Declaration of Independence?
4. According to Marsalis, what happened between his father's generation and the time of the speech?
5. What examples did Marsalis give of people "who stood on the front lines and fought injustice"?

Interpreting

1. How did Marsalis connect the holiday with the recent events?
2. Do you think that he was aware of speaking to an audience beyond the immediate one in the room with him? Why, or why not?
3. Why did Marsalis mention this number? What point was he making by doing so?
4. Did Marsalis approve of recent events? How did he want things to be different?
5. Why did Marsalis mention these people? What did he want his audience to do?

Synthesizing

1. According to Marsalis, what can we learn from the fact that Dr. King combined zeal with a "first-class education"? What did Marsalis think people could learn from the memory of Dr. King?
2. At the end of this speech, Marsalis spoke of "the weary spirit of a slumbering nation" and called on somebody to wake people up. How did he see the current political situation? What did he think was wrong? How did he want things to change?

Delving Deeper

Science Connection

Genetics and Race: The New Scientific Consensus. In the course of his speech, Wynton Marsalis made reference to modern DNA studies that have shed enormous light on the concept of race. By studying human DNA, scientists have discovered that about 90 percent of the genetic variability among humans occurs in local populations (within, for example, the population of a small village), and only about 10 percent of the variability occurs between so-called racial groups. Furthermore, scientists have learned that most of the genetic variability among racial groups is related to a very few genes that govern very superficial matters such as the shape of the nose and skin pigmentation. All living humans had common ancestors a very short time ago, and so there simply has not been time enough for significant genetic variability to occur. The fact is that, beneath the skin, people are mostly alike, and the differences are greater within so-called racial groups than they are, on average, between racial groups.

So, as J. Craig Venter, one of the leading experts on the human genome has said, "Race is a cultural concept, not a scientific one."

About the Author

Wynton Marsalis (b.1961) is a renowned trumpet player, bandleader, and composer who is equally at home in the jazz and classical worlds. He was born into a great New Orleans musical family and showed considerable talent from an early age. (His father Ellis is a superb jazz pianist. Several of his brothers are musicians. His brother Branford is a very well-known and accomplished saxophone player.) Marsalis played with the New Orleans Philharmonic at the age of 14, studied at Tanglewood and at Juilliard, and in 1980 joined Art Blakey and the Jazz Messengers. He has made dozens of recordings and has won both the Pulitzer Prize for music (for his 1997 oratorio *Blood in the Fields)* and nine Grammy awards.

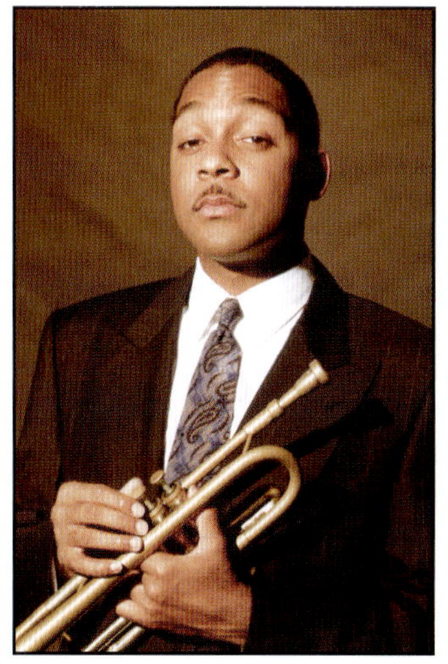

In addition to being one of the finest musicians alive today, Marsalis is also a tireless educator and promoter of jazz—someone who gives of his time and energy to teach young people about America's music. He was a major contributor to Ken Burns's film documentary series *Jazz* and serves as the artistic director of Jazz at the Lincoln Center.

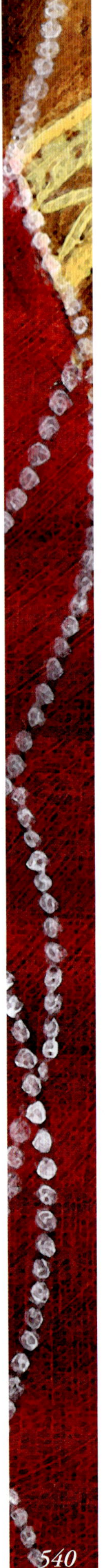

Prereading

"Frederick Douglass," "Those Winter Sundays," and "Homage to the Empress of the Blues"

by Robert Hayden

Robert Hayden possessed a rare ability to project his voice from the page, packing each carefully placed word with all the meaning and raw emotion that only a master of the English language can muster. Like many of his contemporaries, Hayden took a great deal of inspiration from the stories he heard while working for the Federal Writers' Project. These stories reached back to the foundations of African-American culture. He depicted the horror of the transatlantic slave trade in his celebrated poem "Middle Passage," and one of his most famous poems, "Runagate, Runagate," puts readers on the Underground Railroad. Robert Hayden had a profound sense of history, and he strove to imbue his readers with this same essential awareness.

Hayden's work is not simple, but the effort it takes to get to know one of his poems is always worth it. Please review the relevant notes below before reading each of the following short poems by this writer whose work easily places him high atop the list of great American writers.

Frederick Douglass. Readers should appreciate the **lyrical** (songlike) quality of Hayden's words and the crucial message that they convey: Frederick Douglass had an impact on all of our lives and continues to do so to this day. Critic Wilburn Williams, Jr., said it best when he wrote, "The poet emphasizes that the dead hero is still a vital force. The poem celebrates not a man who has been, but a man still coming into being."

Those Winter Sundays. In this elegant poem, Hayden shows his astonishing craftsmanship by choosing his words to convey precise emotion and sensory information. Young readers should relish his language and understand this message: do not take for granted the sacrifices that others make on your behalf, and do not mistake strictness for injustice or cruelty. Sometimes, people seem stern because they are simply tired and worn out, or because they love you so much.

Homage to the Empress of the Blues. You should read every poem at least twice. "Homage" is the sort of poem you should read carefully several times and discuss with other readers. Be sure to read the Reading of the Selection on page 545. You may be surprised by the doors through which this poem leads.

Frederick Douglass

by Robert Hayden

When it is finally ours, this freedom, this liberty, this beautiful
and terrible thing, needful to man as air,
usable as earth; when it belongs at last to all,
when it is truly instinct, brain matter, diastole, systole,[1]
reflex action; when it is finally won; when it is more
than the **gaudy** mumbo jumbo[2] of politicians:
this man, this Douglass, this former slave, this Negro
beaten to his knees, exiled, visioning a world
where none is lonely, none hunted, alien,
this man, superb in love and logic, this man
shall be remembered. Oh, not with statues' **rhetoric**,
not with legends and poems and wreaths of bronze alone,
but with the lives grown out of his life, the lives
fleshing his dream of the beautiful, needful thing.

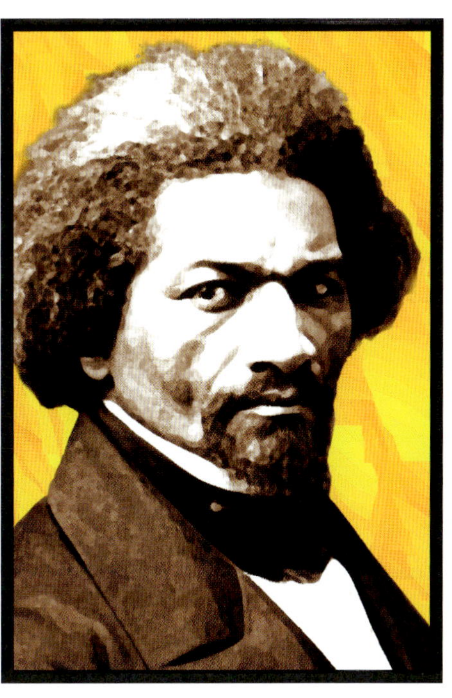

1 **diastole, systole.** During *diastole* the heart muscle (myocardium) relaxes and expands, filling the heart with blood. During *systole,* the myocardium contracts, forcing blood into the main blood vessels. These are examples of reflexes (over which you have no control).

2 **mumbo jumbo.** Language that is unnecessarily difficult to understand

VOCABULARY IN PLACE

- **gaudy,** ***adj.*** Showy in a tasteless or vulgar way
- **rhetoric,** ***n.*** Language that is overly elaborate or insincere
- **flesh,** ***v.*** To fill out; to give substance or detail to

Those Winter Sundays

by Robert Hayden

Sundays too my father got up early
and put his clothes on in the blueblack cold,
then with cracked hands that ached
from labor in the weekday weather made
banked fires blaze. No one ever thanked him.

I'd wake and hear the cold splintering, breaking.
When the rooms were warm, he'd call,
and slowly I would rise and dress,
fearing the **chronic** angers of that house,

Speaking **indifferently** to him,
who had driven out the cold
and polished my good shoes as well.
What did I know, what did I know
of love's **austere** and lonely offices?[1]

[1] **offices.** Duties

VOCABULARY IN PLACE

- **chronic,** ***adj.*** Constant, always returning
- **indifferently,** ***adv.*** Without concern or interest
- **austere,** ***adj.*** Unadorned, bleak; also stern or severe

Homage to the Empress of the Blues[1]

by Robert Hayden

Because there was a man somewhere in a candystripe silk shirt,
gracile[2] and dangerous as a jaguar and because a woman moaned
for him in sixty-watt gloom and mourned him Faithless Love
Twotiming Love Oh Love Oh Careless Aggravating Love,

She came out on the stage in yards of pearls, emerging like
a favorite scenic view, flashed her golden smile and sang.

Because grey laths[3] began somewhere to show from underneath
torn hurdygurdy lithographs of dollfaced heaven;[4]
and because there were those who feared alarming fists of snow[5]
on the door and those who feared the riot-squad of statistics,[6]

She came out on the stage in ostrich feathers, beaded satin,
and shone that smile on us and sang.

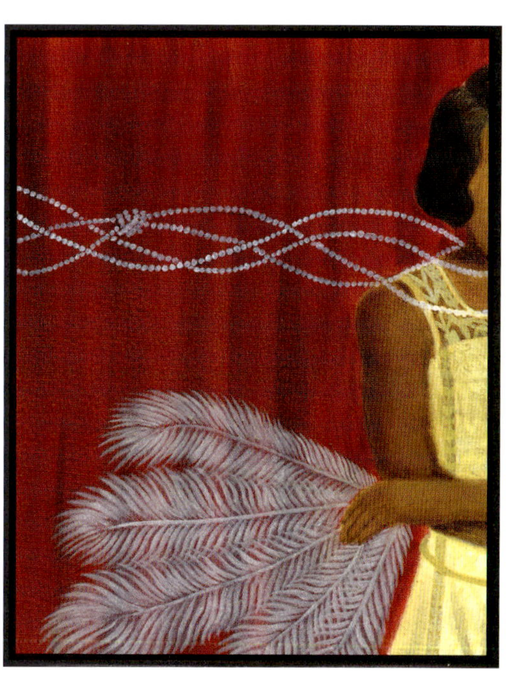

---

1 **Empress of the Blues.** Bessie Smith (1894–1937), American blues singer

2 **gracile.** Slender

3 **laths.** Slats of wood used as support in the substructure of a plaster wall

4 **Torn hurdygurdy . . . heaven.** A *hurdygurdy* was an illegal dancehall. A *lithograph* is an art print, or poster. The poem's speaker refers to torn pictures of (doll-faced) female dancers such as might have hung on the walls of a now dilapidated dance hall.

5 **fists of snow.** This is a reference either to white policemen (or Revenue agents) coming to close down an illegal nightclub, or to bill collectors knocking on the door.

6 **Riot-squad of statistics.** Probably refers to the high statistical probability one had—as an African American at the time—of being jailed, denied rights, or worse in a prejudiced society

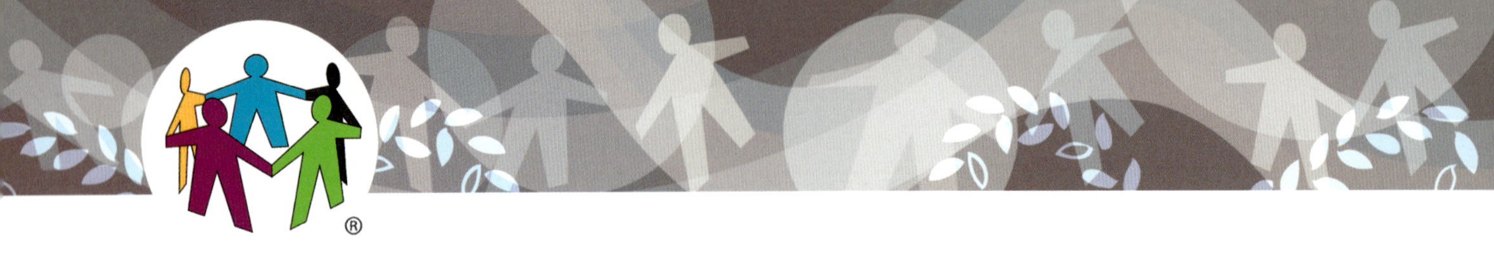

Understanding the Selection

Recalling

1. What is the "beautiful and terrible thing" described in lines 1–2 of "Frederick Douglass"?
2. According to the speaker, how will Frederick Douglass be remembered?
3. In "Those Winter Sundays," what did the speaker's father do every Sunday?
4. According to the speaker, what was the general mood in the house? How did he speak to his father?
5. For whom does the woman in the opening stanza of "Homage to the Empress of the Blues" mourn? Is the woman in line 5 the same woman in lines 1–4?

Interpreting

1. How can this thing be both beautiful and terrible? Why is it as important to man as air?
2. How does this differ from the kinds of memorials that other famous people often receive?
3. What does the speaker mean by the phrase "blueblack cold"? Why is it significant that his father did this on "Sundays too"?
4. How did the speaker feel about living in this house? How does he feel now about the way he spoke to his father?
5. What connection is there between the singer and the characters and events in the first stanza?

Synthesizing

1. Select at least three lines or phrases in Hayden's poetry that you find to be most interesting, confusing, or unique. Share them with the class. Does anyone else have a different interpretation of the same lines?
2. Which two of these three poems are most closely related? How many similarities can you find between them? Hint: Look at **theme** and **structure.**

Delving Deeper

A Reading of the Selection

Homage to the Empress of the Blues. In this justly celebrated poem, Robert Hayden attempts both to explain why Bessie Smith, the Empress of the Blues, was so meaningful to African Americans and to give us a glimpse into the significance and function of blues music in black culture. The opening stanza presents the traditional reading of the blues. The music exists because it expresses the heartache that people feel when they are subjected to "Faithless Love Twotiming Love . . . Careless Aggravating Love." In the second stanza, seeing Bessie on stage in her finery makes people forget about all that; it transforms all that sadness into something celebratory. The third stanza goes further. Because everything decays, like the broken walls and the torn photos in what used to be a hurdygurdy, because "the man" will come knocking on the door, and because the statistics are all stacked against them (death rates, crime and poverty statistics, etc.), people need the blues, they need Bessie in all of her finery, smiling and singing. Bessie's music, the blues, is cathartic. That is, it transforms pain into something beautiful.

About the Author

Robert Hayden (1913–1980) was an accomplished and highly acclaimed poet who composed no less than eleven volumes of poetry between 1940 and 1985. Born in Detroit, Michigan, Hayden was raised by foster parents and, intermittently, by his birth mother. His passion for literature was ignited early on, and he devoured books of all kinds, in part to escape from a violent home life. Hayden received a B.A. from Detroit City College (now Wayne State University) and an M.A. from the University of Michigan, pausing en route to work for the Federal Writers' Project, through which he researched African-American history and folklore.

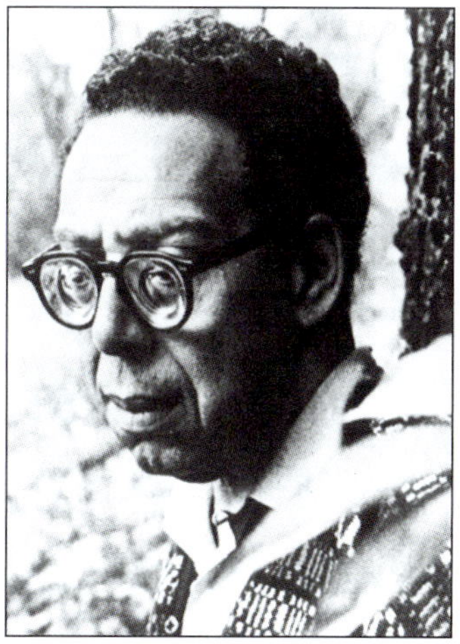

For over twenty-five years, Hayden taught English at the University of Michigan and Fisk University. He published numerous works, including *A Ballad of Remembrance* (1962), *Words in the Mourning Time* (1970), *Angle of Ascent* (1975), and *American Journal* (1978). Committed to the Baha'i religion, Hayden moved beyond his early focus on African-American history and experience to a more symbolic exploration of human liberation. A major influence in modern poetry, he was elected to the American Academy of Poets in 1975 and served as poetry advisor to the Library of Congress.

Prereading

"Booker T. and W. E. B."

by Dudley Randall

The poem "Booker T. and W. E. B." deals in a tongue-in-cheek manner with one of the most important controversies of the early twentieth century. The controversy involved two great African-American leaders with very different views of the proper road ahead for African Americans in the post-slavery era. **Booker T. Washington** (1856–1915) was born into slavery and struggled mightily to get an education. He served as principal of the Tuskegee Institute in Alabama and took the position that blacks could better themselves by concentrating first on achieving economic security. He advised young people to study the agricultural and vocational trades and became associated with an "assimilationist" point of view. **W. E. B. Du Bois** (1868–1963) attended Fisk and Harvard Universities and became one of the first African Americans to receive a Ph.D. A founding member of the NAACP and a leading intellectual of his day, Du Bois urged young people to educate themselves in the professions and the liberal arts, to take pride in their unique racial identity, to demand civil rights, and not to accept assimilation or second-class status. In *The Souls of Black Folk,* Du Bois states his position with regard to Booker T. Washington quite clearly:

> *Mr. Washington distinctly asks that black people give up, at least for the present, three things,—*
>
> *First, political power,*
> *Second, insistence on civil rights,*
> *Third, higher education of Negro youth,—*
>
> *and concentrate all their energies on industrial education, the accumulation of wealth, and the conciliation of the South. . . . As a result of this tender of the palm-branch, what has been the return?*
>
> *In these years there have occurred:*
>
> 1. *The disfranchisement of the Negro.*
> 2. *The legal creation of a distinct status of civil inferiority for the Negro.*
> 3. *The steady withdrawal of aid from institutions for the higher training of the Negro.*

Behind the particular issue that separated the two men lies a fundamental difference in character between the pragmatic compromiser and the man with high ideals. As you read this poem, ask yourself, "With which man do I agree?" and "Who, in Randall's poem, gets the last word?"

Booker T. and W. E. B.

by Dudley Randall

"It seems to me," said Booker T.,
"It shows a mighty lot of **cheek**
to study chemistry and Greek
When Mister Charlie needs a hand
To hoe the cotton on his land,
And when Miss Ann looks for a cook,
Why stick your nose inside a book?"

"I don't agree," said W. E. B.,
"If I should have the drive to seek
Knowledge of chemistry or Greek,
I'll do it. Charles and Miss can look
Another place for hand or cook.
Some men rejoice in skill of hand,
And some in **cultivating** land,
But there are others who maintain
The right to cultivate the brain."

"It seems to me," said Booker T.,
"That all you folks have missed the boat
Who shout about the right to vote,
And spend vain days and sleepless nights
In uproar over civil rights.
Just keep your mouths shut, do not **grouse,**
But work, and save, and buy a house."

"I don't agree," said W. E. B.,
"For what can property **avail**
If dignity and justice fail.
Unless you help to make the laws,
They'll steal your house with **trumped-up** clause.
A rope's as tight, a fire as hot,
No matter how much cash you've got.
Speak soft, and try your little plan,
But as for me, I'll be a man."

"It seems to me," said Booker T.—

"I don't agree,"
Said W. E. B. ■

VOCABULARY IN PLACE

- **cheek,** *n.* Impertinence; insulting boldness
- **cultivate,** *v.* 1. To grow crops; 2. To improve, to make more refined or sophisticated
- **grouse,** *v.* To complain
- **avail,** *v.* To help, be of advantage to
- **trumped-up,** *adj.* Falsified, said of false charges or purposefully incorrect readings of legal documents or statutes

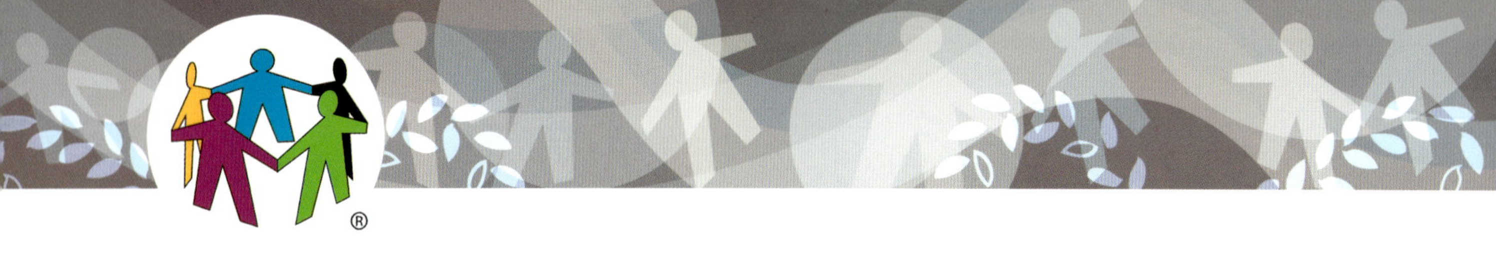

Understanding the Selection

Recalling

1. According to the first stanza of the poem, what did Booker T. not think African Americans should study? What should they do instead?
2. What, according to the second stanza of the poem, did W. E. B. think African Americans should "cultivate" instead of land?
3. According to the last line of the third stanza, what did Booker T. think African Americans should work to do?

Interpreting

1. What Washington actually claimed was that young African Americans should give themselves to agricultural and vocational studies. Given the way in which this idea is presented in Randall's poem, do you think he agrees with Washington? Why, or why not?
2. W. E. B. Du Bois was an intellectual and a university professor. In what way was his life consistent with the point of view expressed in the second stanza?
3. Why does W. E. B., in the fourth stanza, not agree? Why did he think that economic security was not enough?

Synthesizing

1. With whom do you think the poet, Dudley Randall, agrees? Why?
2. With whom do you agree? Which man, Booker T. Washington or W. E. B. Du Bois, had the correct view for African Americans of the post-slavery era? Is it possible that both men were right? (You may refer to the selections on pages 268 and 240.)

Delving Deeper

Understanding Literature

Pun. A **pun** is a play on words. The word *cultivate,* as you can see by looking at the vocabulary box on page 547, has two different meanings. What two meanings are used in stanza 2? What did Booker T. Washington want young people to learn to cultivate? What did W. E. B. Du Bois want them to learn to cultivate? Which, in your mind, is more important to learn?

Theme. A **theme** is a main idea in a literary work, the message that the work teaches. Consider these lines from the poem: "Speak soft, and try your little plan, / But as for me, I'll be a man." What implied criticism of Booker T. is made in these lines? How, according to the W. E. B. character in the poem, would a man behave? What would he do? What would he not accept?

About the Author

Dudley Randall (1914–2000) was made Detroit's poet laureate in 1981. He published his first poem at the age of thirteen and five volumes of poetry during his life. Just as importantly, he gave other black writers an opportunity to publish by founding, in 1965, the Broadside Press, which published ninety titles and printed half a million books, many of them important works in the Black Arts Movement.

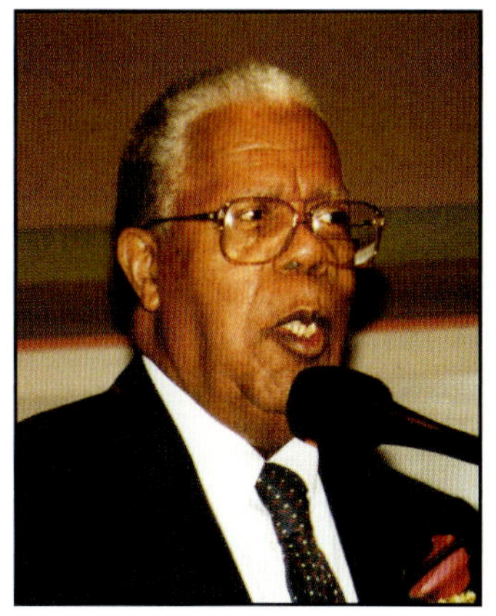

Randall was born in Washington, D.C., and moved to Detroit in 1920 at around the age of six. He published his first poem in the *Detroit Free Press.* He was first influenced primarily by English poets and later by the African-American poets Jean Toomer and Countee Cullen. In 1949 and 1951 he received college degrees in English and in library science. He worked as a librarian at two universities.

Much of Randall's work deals with suffering and with events in the Civil Rights Movement. His poem "Coral Atoll," for example, deals with service in World War II, and his poem "The Ballad of Birmingham" deals with four little girls killed in the bombing of a black church. Two of his poems, set to music by Jerry Moore, became anthems of the Civil Rights Era.

Prereading

The Poetry of Margaret Walker

by Margaret Walker

Margaret Walker's impressive writing career began in the late days of the Harlem Renaissance and continued through, and well beyond, the Black Arts Movement of the 1960s. The groundbreaking poetry collection *For My People* (1942) established Walker as a gifted intellectual, a leading figure in America's literary culture, and an early, influential voice in the Civil Rights and Feminist Movements that blossomed in the 1950s and '60s.

For My People. The title poem of Walker's first book is also her single most famous work. This is **free verse** poetry at its finest, where the poet makes and sticks to her own rules. Walker's compelling, inventive imagery flows across the page like a river of folklore and memory. Please consider the following points (See also A Reading of the Selection on page 557):

1. There are ten stanzas, each with its own theme and imagery.
2. The speaker's voice, mood, and tone change over the course of the poem. The first few stanzas recount the long, tiring years that African Americans have endured and celebrate the simple pleasures of daily life. The last four verses shift to a bitter voice that chastises blacks and whites alike before leaving the listener with a hopeful call to action.
3. Notice Walker's use of **repetition, alliteration** (repetition of consonant sounds at the beginnings of words), and **parallelism** (repetition of grammatical forms).

The Ballad of the Free. A **ballad** is a poem that tells a story, often one of folk origin and intended to be sung. The verse structure and language in a ballad tend to be fairly simple, and there is usually a refrain. Walker's "Ballad of the Free," which focuses on prominent leaders of slave rebellions, reflects the African-American folk tradition, in which she became interested through her work with the Federal Writers' Project of the 1930s.

For Malcolm X. This emotionally charged sonnet praises and mourns Malcolm X (See biography on page 503). Malcolm X had as many enemies as he had friends and followers, as history's movers and shakers often do. He was a man of great strength of spirit and mind, and though his words stirred controversy in his day, he will forever be counted among the African-American community's most admired and cherished figures.

For My People

by Margaret Walker

For my people everywhere singing their slave songs repeatedly: their dirges and their ditties
and their blues and jubilees,[1] praying their prayers nightly to an unknown god,
bending their knees humbly to an unseen power;

For my people lending their strength to the years, to the gone years and the now years and
the maybe years, washing ironing cooking scrubbing sewing mending hoeing
plowing digging planting pruning patching dragging along never gaining never
reaping never knowing and never understanding;

For my playmates in the clay and dust and sand of Alabama
backyards playing baptizing and preaching and doctor and jail and
soldier and school and mama and cooking and playhouse and
concert and store and hair and Miss Choomby and company;

For the cramped bewildered years we went to school to learn to know the reasons why and
the answers to and the people who and the places where and the days when, in
memory of the bitter hours when we discovered we were black and poor and small
and different and nobody cared and nobody wondered and nobody understood;

For the boys and girls who grew in spite of these things to be Man and
Woman, to laugh and dance and sing and play and drink their wine
and religion and success, to marry their playmates and bear children
and then die of consumption and anemia and lynching;[2]

For my people **thronging** 47th Street in Chicago and Lenox Avenue in New York and
Rampart Street in New Orleans,[3] lost **disinherited dispossessed** and happy people filling
the **cabarets** and taverns and other people's pockets needing bread and shoes and milk
and land and money and something—something all our own;

VOCABULARY IN PLACE

- **throng,** *v.* To crowd into; fill
- **disinherited,** *adj.* Denied a natural right or privilege
- **dispossessed,** *adj.* Deprived of possession
- **cabaret,** *n.* A nightclub that provides short programs of live entertainment (especially song and dance)

1 **dirges . . . jubilees.** A *dirge* is a slow funeral hymn. A *ditty* is a simple, festive song. *Blues* is a variety of indigenous African-American music. A *jubilee* is a celebration.

2 **consumption . . . lynching.** *Consumption* and *anemia* are diseases often linked to poverty. *Lynching* presented a constant, horrific threat to all African Americans, especially during the century after the Civil War.

3 **47th Street . . . New Orleans.** Well-known African-American neighborhoods

For my people walking blindly spreading joy, losing time being lazy,
sleeping when hungry, shouting when burdened, drinking when hopeless,
tied and shackled and tangled among ourselves by the unseen creatures
who tower over us **omnisciently** and laugh;

For my people blundering and groping and **floundering** in the dark of
churches and schools and clubs and societies, associations and councils and
committees and conventions, distressed and disturbed and deceived and devoured
by money-hungry glory-craving leeches, preyed on by **facile** force of state and fad
and novelty, by false prophet and holy believer;

For my people standing staring trying to fashion a better way from confusion,
from **hypocrisy** and misunderstanding, trying to fashion a world that will hold
all the people, all the faces, all the adams and eves and their countless generations;

Let a new earth rise. Let another world be born. Let a bloody peace be written in the sky.
Let a second generation full of courage issue forth; let a people loving freedom come
to growth. Let a beauty full of healing and a strength of final clenching[4]
be the pulsing in our spirits and our blood. Let the **martial** songs be written,
let the dirges disappear. Let a race of men now rise and take control. ■

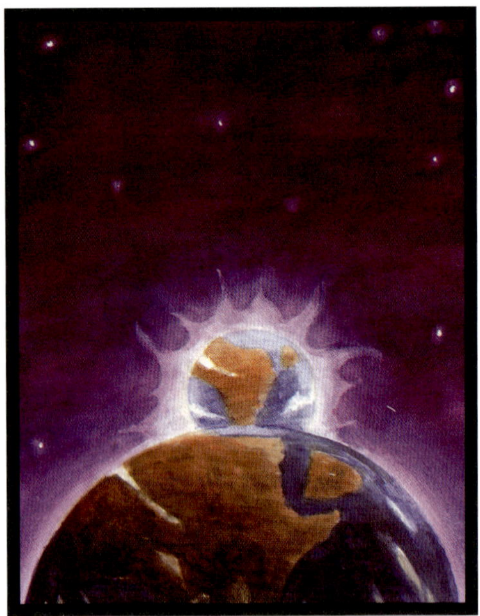

VOCABULARY IN PLACE

- **omnisciently,** ***adv.*** With knowledge of everything
- **flounder,** ***v.*** To move or act clumsily or in confusion
- **facile,** ***adj.*** Lacking sincerity or depth
- **hypocrisy,** ***n.*** Falseness; the act of professing (claiming) beliefs or virtues that one does not actually possess or practice
- **martial,** ***adj.*** Relating to or suggestive of war

4 **strength of final clenching.** The final clenching of the fists before death, or a reference to the strength that one may muster in a life-and-death struggle

The Ballad of the Free

by Margaret Walker

Bold Nat Turner[1] *by the blood of God*
Rose up Preaching of Virginia's sod;
Smote[2] *the land with his passionate plea*
Time's done come to set my people free.

The serpent is loosed and the hour is come
The last shall be first and first shall be none
The serpent is loosed and the hour is come

Gabriel Prosser[3] *looked at the sun,*
Said, "Sun, stand still till the work is done.
The world is wide and the time is long
And man must meet the avenging wrong."

The serpent is loosed and the hour is come
The last shall be first and first shall be none
The serpent is loosed and the hour is come

Denmark Vesey[4] *led his band*
Across the hot Carolina land.
The plot was foiled, the brave men killed,
But Freedom's cry was never stilled.

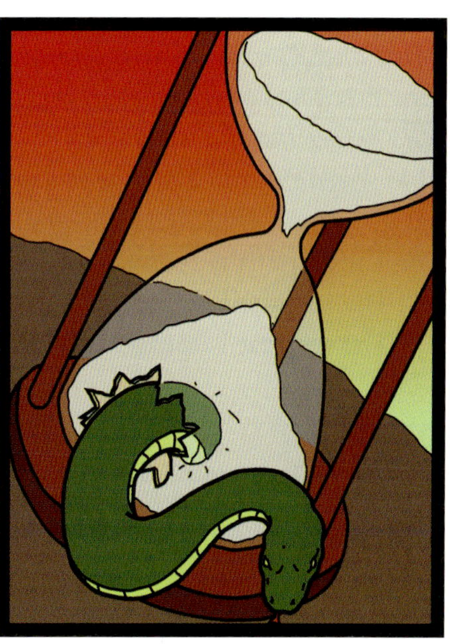

[1] **Nat Turner.** (1800–1831) Leader of a slave rebellion in Virginia. See also page 104.

[2] **smote.** Viciously struck

[3] **Gabriel Prosser.** (1775–1800) Leader of a slave rebellion, Prosser organized an army and planned to take over Richmond, Virginia. As his army gathered, an incredible rainstorm swept the city, causing the worst flooding in memory and thwarting the rebellion.

[4] **Denmark Vesey.** (1767–1822) A remarkable native of West Africa who was brought as a slave to America and was able to purchase his own freedom. He became a prosperous carpenter in Charleston, South Carolina. Vesey hated slavery and slaveholders. He developed a complex plan to take over Charleston that involved as many as 9,000 enslaved people and white collaborators. Vesey was betrayed and put to death shortly before carrying out his plans.

The serpent is loosed and the hour is come
The last shall be first and first shall be none
The serpent is loosed and the hour is come

Toussaint L'Ouverture[5] *won*
All his battles in the tropic sun,
Hero of the black man's pride
Among those hundred who fought and died.

The serpent is loosed and the hour is come
The last shall be first and first shall be none
The serpent is loosed and the hour is come

Brave John Brown[6] *was killed but he*
Became a **martyr** *of the free,*
For he declared that blood would run
Before the slaves their freedom won.

The serpent is loosed and the hour is come
The last shall be first and first shall be none
The serpent is loosed and the hour is come

Wars and Rumors of Wars have gone,
But Freedom's army marches on.
The heroes' list of dead is long,
And Freedom still is for the strong.

The serpent is loosed and the hour is come
The last shall be first and first shall be none
The serpent is loosed and the hour is come ■

---

1 **Toussaint L'Ouverture.** (1743–1805) Leader of the Haitian Revolution (1804), in which enslaved Haitians rose up, expelled the French from Haiti, and founded the first black republic and the first nation of self-liberated slaves. L'Ouverture died in a French prison, but he did lead one of the only successful slave rebellions in history, a fact that (as many American slaveholders and politicians feared) served to inspire enslaved people in the United States (including Gabriel Prosser and Denmark Vesey).

2 **John Brown.** (1800–1859) Militant white Abolitionist who carried out several violent and successful raids to free slaves in Kansas and Missouri. He was captured and executed after his famous raid on the federal armory at Harper's Ferry, Virginia (in what is now West Virginia).

VOCABULARY IN PLACE

- **martyr,** ***n.*** One who suffers death for a belief, cause, or principle

For Malcolm X

by Margaret Walker

All you violated ones with gentle hearts;
You violent dreamers[1] whose cries shout heartbreak;
Whose voices echo clamors of our cool capers,[2]
And whose black faces have hollowed pits for eyes.
All you gambling sons and hooked children and bowery bums[3]
Hating white devils and black **bourgeoisie,**
Thumbing your noses at your burning red suns,[4]
Gather round this coffin and mourn your dying swan.[5]

Snow-white Moslem head-dress[6] around a dead black face!
Beautiful were your sand-papering words against our skins!
Our blood and water pour from your flowing wounds.
You have cut open our breasts and dug scalpels in our brains.
When and Where will another come to take your holy place?
Old man mumbling in his **dotage,** or crying child, unborn? ■

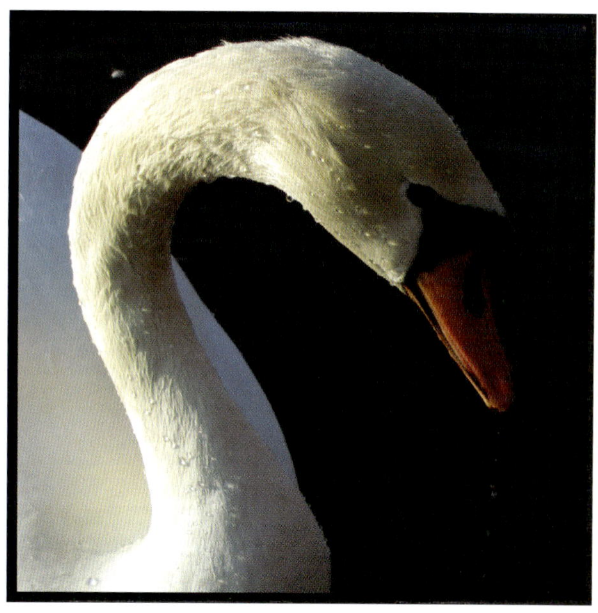

1 **violated ones . . . violent dreamers.** Those with gentle hearts represent those who practice nonviolent methods of protest, as opposed to those violent dreamers who espouse a militant approach.

2 **echo clamors of cool capers.** A *clamor* is a loud outcry or expression of discontent. *Cool* means indifferent, and *caper* may refer to a crime, plot, or prank. The line suggests admiration on the part of the downtrodden for those who do what they can only dream about.

3 **bowery bums.** The Bowery is a neighborhood in lower Manhattan (New York City) once known for its poverty.

4 **thumbing your . . . red suns.** Sunsets are traditional symbols of the end of life. To be someone who thumbs his or her nose at the end of life, someone who lives a lifestyle that "burns" up his or her life, is to be heedless of the consequences.

5 **dying swan.** According to legend, one variety of swan is mute throughout its life but sings a single, heart-breakingly beautiful note just before its death. The legend is false but here provides a metaphor for the voice that Malcolm X's death gave to all dispossessed people.

6 **Moslem head-dress.** A reference to the customary Muslim death shroud

VOCABULARY IN PLACE

- **bourgeoisie,** ***n.*** The middle class
- **dotage,** ***n.*** A deterioration of mental faculties; senility

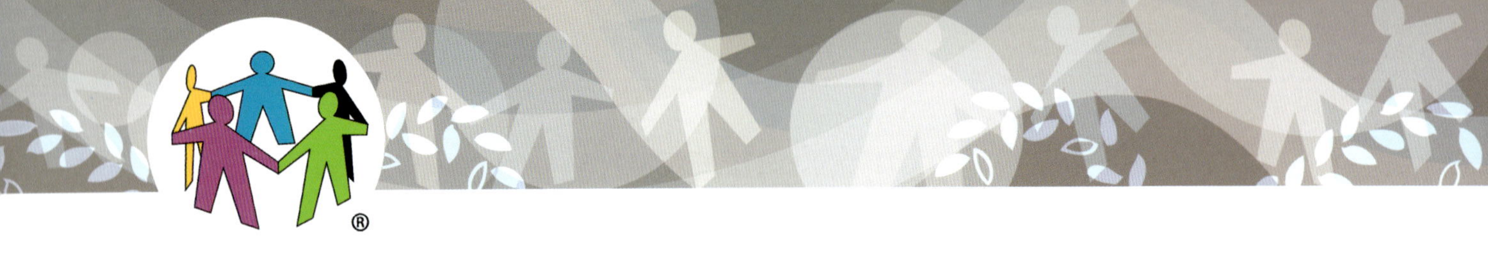

Understanding the Selection

Recalling

1. Which stanza in "For My People" focuses on strength and work?
2. Which years were "cramped and bewildered" (stanza 4)? What did the children discover in the "bitter hours"?
3. What did people do in Chicago, New York, and New Orleans?
4. What desires or wishes does the speaker express in the last stanza of "For My People"?
5. What is a ballad?
6. What do all the men named in "Ballad of the Free" have in common, aside from having led slave rebellions?
7. What does the speaker of "For Malcolm X" want people to do?

Interpreting

1. What does the speaker mean by the phrase "maybe years" (line 6)? What do "my people" never know or understand (line 7)?
2. Why were these "bitter" hours?
3. How can they be "lost disinherited dispossessed" yet "happy"?
4. Describe the speaker's tone (e.g., happy, angry, etc.) in the last stanza.
5. Identify at least two characteristics of "Ballad of the Free" that qualify it as a ballad.
6. Were any of the men named in the poem free? Why do you think this poem is titled "Ballad of the Free"?
7. With regard to mood and tone, how do the first 8 lines (the **octet**) differ from the last 6 lines (the **sextet**)?

Synthesizing

1. In the final stanza of "For My People," how do the **tone** (the emotion of the speaker) and the **mood** (the emotion created in listeners) differ from the other stanzas?
2. What is the purpose of the refrain in "Ballad of the Free"? How does it relate to the poem's other verses and the overall theme?
3. Is "For Malcolm X" a true Italian sonnet? (See page 399.)

Delving Deeper

A Reading of the Selection

For My People. As noted in the Prereading on page 550, each stanza of this poem has a distinct subject and main idea. Below are words or phases that summarize the topic of each stanza. Create a chart on a separate sheet of paper. Reread the poem, jotting down at least two key quotations (words or phrases) that reflect each stanza's subject. Examples of possible answers are provided for the first two stanzas.

Stanza 1: Music and religion
Stanza 1 Examples: "singing slave songs repeatedly," "praying . . . to an unknown god"
Stanza 2: Constant toil, strength, oppression
Stanza 2 Examples: "washing ironing cooking scrubbing," "dragging along never gaining"
Stanza 3: Simple daily pleasures, home
Stanza 4: Schooling, confusion
Stanza 5: Joys contrasted with poverty, racism
Stanza 6: Community, culture
Stanza 7: Negative traits, vices
Stanza 8: Ignorance, exploitation
Stanza 9: Civil rights struggles
Stanza 10: Hope and call to action

About the Author

Margaret Walker (1915–1998) published five volumes of poetry, one novel, and two books of essays and memoirs. She won the Yale Younger Poets award for her first book of poetry, *For My People* (1942), and the Houghton Mifflin Literary Award for her novel *Jubilee* (1966), a slave narrative based on her grandmother's memories.

Walker was the daughter of a Methodist minister and a music teacher in Birmingham, Alabama. When she was very young, her parents encouraged her to read poetry and philosophy. After she spent two years at New Orleans University, Langston Hughes read her poetry and urged her to come to the North for more training. Walker graduated from Northwestern University in 1935 and joined the Federal Writers' Project in Chicago during the Great Depression. She worked in poor urban areas, which gave her new insight and informed much of her future work.

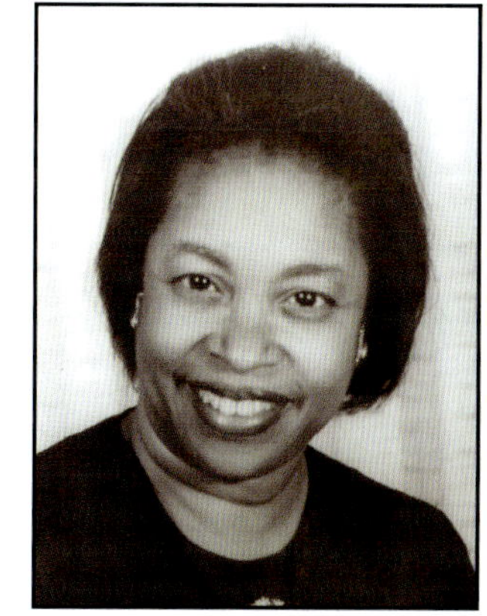

She earned a master's in creative writing from the University of Iowa in 1940 and married Firnist Alexander in 1943. She adopted his last name, but she continued to use "Margaret Walker" as her penname. In 1949 she moved with her family back to the South, where she felt most at home, and became an English professor at Jackson State University. She remained active in public life long after her retirement in 1968.

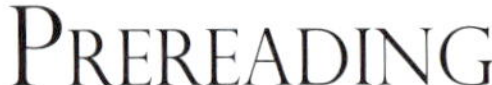

Prereading

"We Real Cool" and "Rudolph Is Tired of the City"

by Gwendolyn Brooks

Gwendolyn Brooks was that rare person—a poet who became extremely influential at the national level. One reason for her influence was that when the Black Arts Movement took place in the 1960s and '70s she was already an established artist. So, the fact that she joined the movement and became one of its leading figures lent the entire undertaking a certain credibility. Brooks also received many national honors. She won the Pulitzer Prize for *Annie Allen* (1949), was appointed to the American Academy of Arts and Letters, and served as poetry consultant to the Library of Congress.

Despite her impact at the national level, Brooks created a body of work that is, in one sense, extremely local. The textures of Chicago city life give her poetry its stunning authenticity and grittiness, and she is intimately associated with the life and literature of that city. These two poems, "We Real Cool" and "Rudolph Is Tired of the City," present portraits of some of the people of Brooks's Chicago—portraits of young people in a pool hall and of a young man with a dream. As you read, think about the differences between the characters depicted in the two poems. Also, notice the precise manner in which Brooks arranges her words on the page, thus using structure to convey meaning.

We Real Cool

by Gwendolyn Brooks

The Pool Players
Seven at the Golden Shovel.[1]

We real cool. We
Left school. We

Lurk late. We
Strike straight.[2] We

Sing sin. We
Thin gin.[3] We

Jazz June. We
Die soon. ■

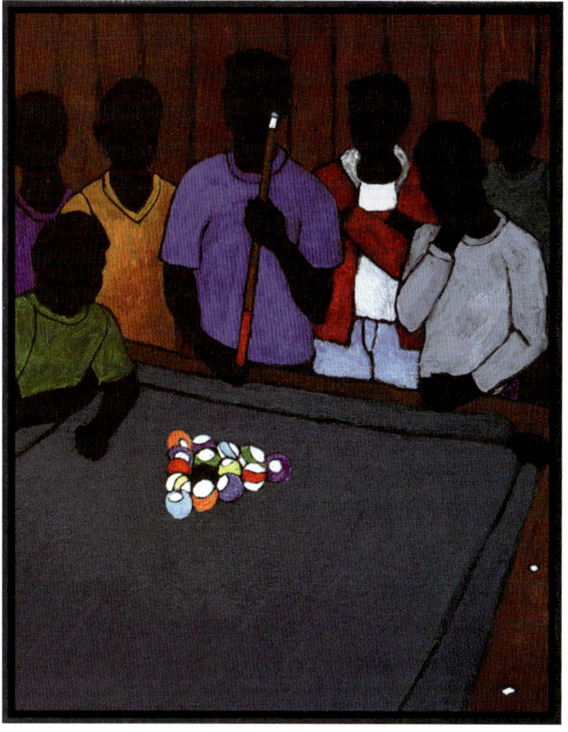

[1] **The Golden Shovel.** The name of the pool hall. Note that the name *Golden Shovel* suggests an attractive thing that could be used to bury a person.

[2] **Strike straight.** Strike the pool balls; possibly an allusion to fighting

[3] **Thin gin.** The expression suggests mixing the gin with other beverages, thus watering it down.

VOCABULARY IN PLACE

- **lurk,** *v.* To lie or wait in concealment, as a person in ambush

Rudolph Is Tired of the City

by Gwendolyn Brooks

These buildings are too close to me.
I'd like to PUSH away.
I'd like to live in the country,
And spread my arms all day.

I'd like to spread my breath out, too—
As farmers' sons and daughters do.

I'd tend the cows and chickens.
I'd do the other chores.
Then, all the hours left I'd go
A-SPREADING out-of-doors. ■

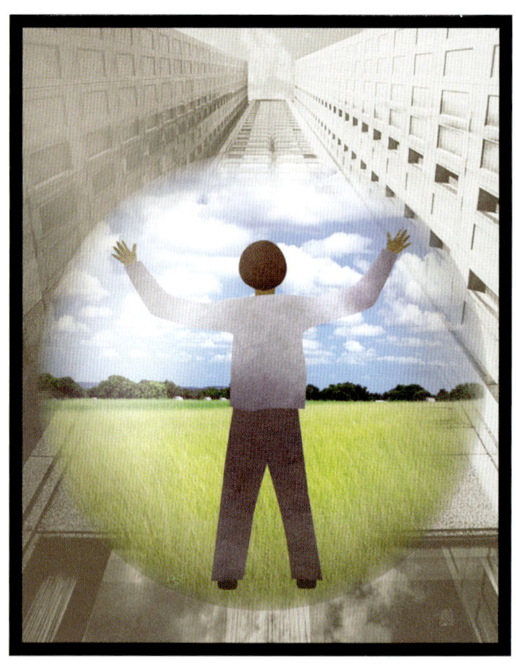

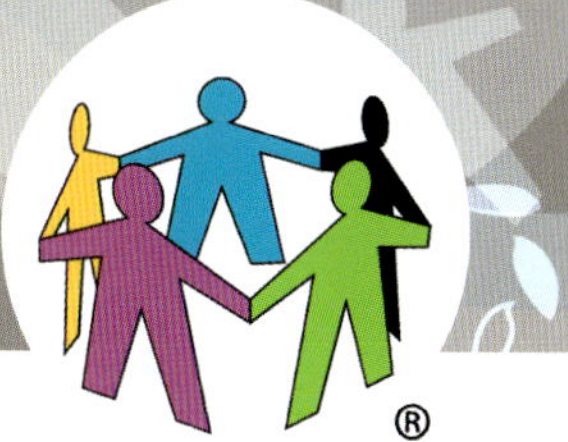

Understanding the Selection

Recalling

1. What activity brings the young men to the Golden Shovel?
2. What phrases do the young men use to describe themselves?
3. With what musical form do the "players" associate their way of life?
4. What complaint does Rudolph have at the beginning of the poem?

Interpreting

1. Is this a "respectable" activity? What is slightly sinister about the name *Golden Shovel?*
2. What do these young men think is "cool"? Is it a good thing that they left school? What negative connotations do the terms *lurk* and *strike* and *sin* have?
3. Jazz is a form of music that is cool, hip, not straight, improvised, sometimes wild and exuberant. June is the height of summer, a very brief period before fall. What might the pool players' lives be like if they "Jazz June"?
4. Of what does Rudolph dream? What physical action is mentioned in each of the three stanzas?

Synthesizing

1. How do the characters in "We Real Cool" and "Rudolph Is Tired of the City" differ from one another? Which have the most possibility and hope in their lives, the pool players or Rudolph? Why?
2. What view of city life does Brooks express in these poems? Do you think that this is positive or negative?

Prereading

"Narcissa," "Tommy," and "The Bean Eaters"

by Gwendolyn Brooks

Finally, what makes Gwendolyn Brooks a poet of lasting merit is her accurate, sensitive portrayals of people. Often, these portrayals take the form of "slices of life," moments captured with particular fidelity, or accuracy. The poems that follow are all of this kind. They are snapshots from three moments across the span of life.

Tommy. As you read this poem, think about the language that Brooks has used in it. What makes this language particularly appropriate for this poem?

Narcissa. How old do you think the main figure in this poem is? Why do you think that? What do you learn about her? How does she differ from the other girls mentioned at the beginning of the poem?

The Bean Eaters. Often, when poets write about elderly people or about children, they **sentimentalize** them (describe them in a nostalgic or emotional way). In this poem, Brooks certainly does not create a sentimental portrait. What aspects of her portrayal of these two elderly people are grittily realistic? Nonetheless, what overall attitude does she create in your mind, as a reader, toward the two people?

Tommy

by Gwendolyn Brooks

I put a seed into the ground
And said, "I'll watch it grow."
I watered it and cared for it
As well as I could know.

One day I walked in my back yard,
And oh, what did I see!
My seed had popped itself right out,
Without consulting me. ■

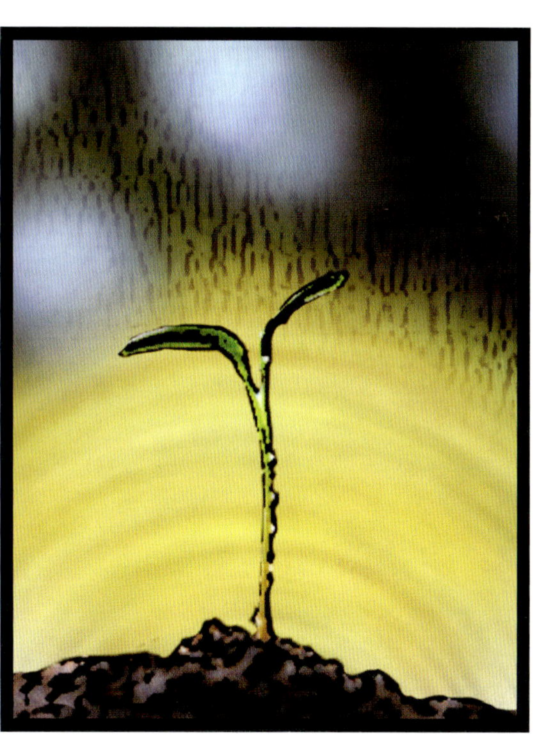

Narcissa[1]

by Gwendolyn Brooks

Some of the girls are playing jacks.
Some are playing ball.
But small Narcissa is not playing
Anything at all.

Small Narcissa sits upon
A brick in her back yard
And looks at tiger-lilies,
And shakes her pigtails hard.

First she is an ancient queen
In **pomp** and purple veil.
Soon she is a singing wind.
And, next, a nightingale.[2]

How fine to be Narcissa,
A-changing like all that!
While sitting still, as still, as still
As anyone ever sat! ■

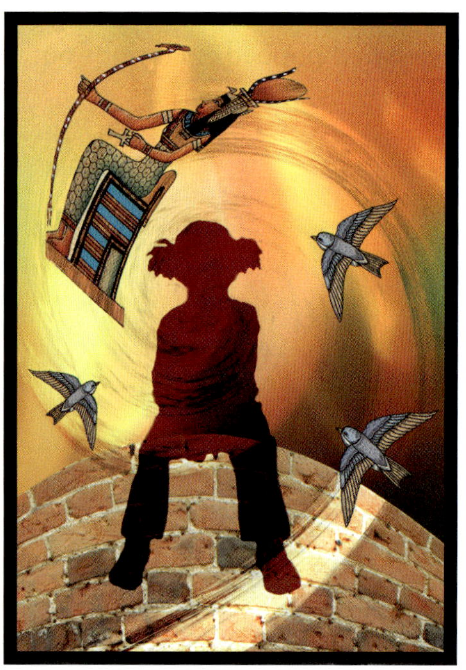

[1] **Narcissa.** In Greek mythology, Narcissus was a beautiful youth who fell in love with his own reflection in a pool and pined away for it. For his self-absorption, he was punished by being turned into a flower. The name suggests reflectiveness and self-absorption.

[2] **nightingale.** A European bird known for its melodious song

VOCABULARY IN PLACE

- **pomp,** ***n.*** Splendor, magnificence

The Bean Eaters

by Gwendolyn Brooks

They eat beans mostly, this old yellow pair.
Dinner is a casual affair.
Plain chipware on a plain and creaking wood,
Tin flatware.

Two who are Mostly Good.
Two who have lived their day,
But keep on putting on their clothes
And putting things away.

And remembering . . .
Remembering, with twinklings and twinges,[1]
As they lean over the beans in their rented back room that
is full of beads and receipts and dolls and cloths,
tobacco crumbs, vases and **fringes.** ■

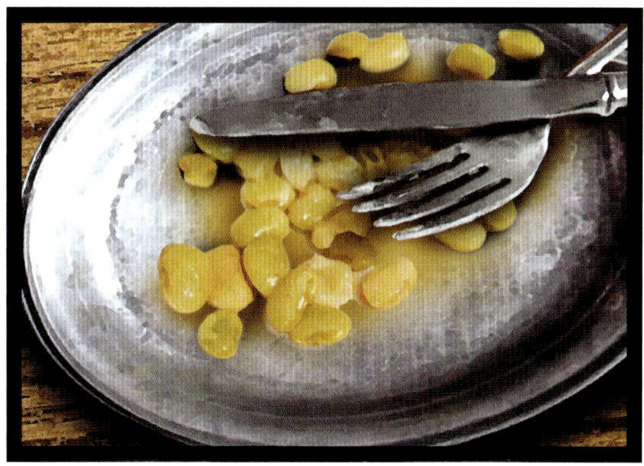

[1] **twinklings and twinges.** Intervals of both happy memories and physical pain of old age

VOCABULARY IN PLACE

• **fringe,** ***n.*** An outer edge, margin, or periphery

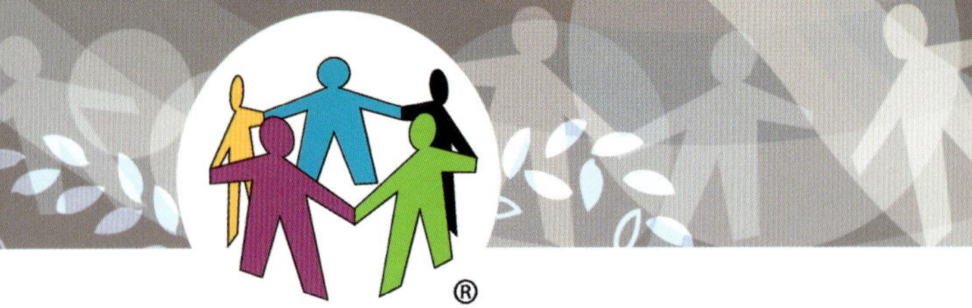

Understanding the Selection

Recalling

1. In the poem "Tommy" what did the speaker do with the seed?
2. What eventually happened to the seed?
3. What are the girls in the poem "Narcissa" doing?
4. Who and what does Narcissa imagine herself to be?
5. What kind of dinnerware does the couple in "The Bean Eaters" use?
6. The speaker does not describe the couple as good or bad. What description does she give of them?
7. What is the room full of?

Interpreting

1. What does the fact that the young boy said he'd watch the seed grow tell us about him?
2. The author wrote that the seed popped out of the ground without consulting Tommy. What does she mean?
3. Do you think Narcissa wants to do what the other girls are doing?
4. Why would Narcissa prefer daydreaming to playing with other kids?
5. What does this fact tell us about the couple?
6. How might this description be related to their "remembering, with twinklings and twinges"?
7. What details in the poem suggest poverty?

Synthesizing

1. Narcissa is in her own world as she is sitting on the brick in her backyard. Why might people want to imagine being something that they are not? Is that kind of daydreaming harmful or helpful to a young person, in your opinion? Explain.
2. There is a popular saying that "Nobody is perfect." What version of this idea appears in Brooks's "The Bean Eaters"? Do you agree that "Mostly Good" is good enough?

Delving Deeper

A Reading of the Selection

The Bean Eaters. As in much of Gwendolyn Brooks's poetry, the details in "The Bean Eaters" are rich with suggestion. The two old people eat beans so often that they can be identified as "the bean eaters." They eat from plain chipware, with tin flatware (not silver), on plain and creaking wood. Their home is a rented back room, stuffed full of the debris from a lifetime. They have lived their day. They are past their prime. To some extent, they just go through the motions. That is, they keep putting on their clothes and putting things away.

All in all, it isn't a glamorous or pretty picture. Oddly enough, however, most readers come away from the poem with a feeling of great sympathy and warmth toward the two people pictured here. Perhaps this is because they recognize that after a long life, to have someone be able to describe you as "Mostly Good" is probably as close to perfect as it gets. These people are human, and their very humanity, their less-than-perfectness, is appealing.

About the Author

Gwendolyn Brooks (1917–2000) was the first African American to win the Pulitzer Prize. She was still a child when she published her first poem, "Eventide."

Born in Topeka, Kansas, Brooks came to Chicago as a very young child and lived there all of her life. She attended white, black, and integrated schools on the South Side of the city. Her mother was a strong influence on her writing.

Her first poem was published in *American Childhood* magazine in 1930. Langston Hughes noticed her work and encouraged her to read modern poetry by Ezra Pound, T. S. Eliot, and E. E. Cummings. He also told her to write as often and as much as she could. She later said, "I felt that I had to write. Even if I had never been published, I knew that I would go on writing, enjoying it and experiencing the challenge."

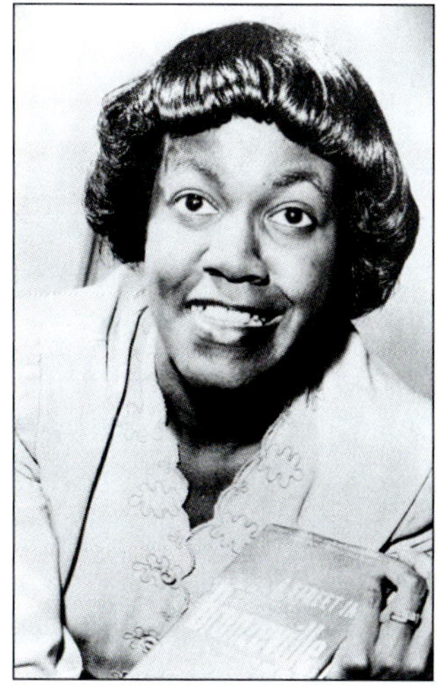

During a long lifetime, Brooks won many, many honors. She is remembered for many great works including the poetry collections *A Street in Bronzeville* (1945), *Annie Allen* (1949), and *The Bean Eaters* (1960); a novel, *Maude Martha* (1953); and a two-volume autobiography, *Report from Part One* (1972) and *Report from Part Two* (1997).

Prereading

"Ka'ba"

by Amiri Baraka

This poem was published in Baraka's book *Black Magic* (1969) during a time of tremendous social anxiety and unrest. American society was fractured along cultural and generational lines. Many black leaders, activists, and artists—angered by the assassinations of beloved leaders, frustrated by hollow political promises, and disgusted by continued racism and racist violence in society—were eager for social revolution. The **Black Arts Movement** (1965–1975) grew out of the **Black Power Movement,** whose proponents encouraged African Americans to improve their communities by building their own social, political, and economic institutions, as opposed to integrating into "white" America. This movement was greatly influenced by earlier **Black nationalism** leaders such as Marcus Garvey. (See page 284.) Leaders like Malcolm X encouraged black people to celebrate their African cultural heritage and history, and it was during this time that African Studies departments began to emerge on American campuses. The Black Power Movement was splintered along philosophical lines, with many leaders emphasizing militancy as a justifiable defense against racist violence.

During the 1950s, Amiri Baraka (then Leroi Jones) was a central figure in the Greenwich Village arts scene, where he counted Allen Ginsburg and other **Beat Poets** as his close friends. By the mid-1960s, however, Baraka had denounced his old ties to white culture, and *Black Magic* represents his artistic exit from white society. In it, he calls on African Americans to rediscover pride in their heritage and to destroy, once and for all, the negative stereotypes that allow racist hatred to persist.

The title of the poem reflects Baraka's interest in Islam, to which many Black Power advocates converted. The **Ka'ba,** located in the holy city of Mecca, is the most sacred shrine in Islam. The shrine itself is a box-like, granite structure roughly five stories tall. It is always covered in a huge black fabric (which is replaced every year), and in one corner is embedded the sacred "Black Stone." Pilgrims to Mecca **circumambulate** (walk around) the shrine and face it during prayer. During the pilgrimage season the area around the shrine becomes a sea of humanity, teeming with tens of thousands of the faithful.

In this poem, Baraka alludes to the Ka'ba not only because of its deep, rich religious and cultural significance, but also because it suggests great crowds of people intermingling and unified by common experience and heritage.

Ka'ba[1]

by Amiri Baraka

A closed window looks down
on a dirty courtyard, and black people
call across or scream across or walk across
defying physics in the stream of their will

Our world is full of sound
Our world is more lovely than anyone's
tho we suffer, and kill each other
and sometimes fail to walk the air[2]

We are beautiful people
with african imaginations
full of masks and dances and swelling chants
with african eyes, and noses, and arms,
though we sprawl in grey chains in a place
full of winters, when what we want is sun.

We have been captured,
brothers. And we labor
to make our getaway, into
the ancient image, into a new

correspondence with ourselves
and our black family. We need magic
now we need the spells, to raise up
return, destroy, and create. What will be

the sacred words? ■

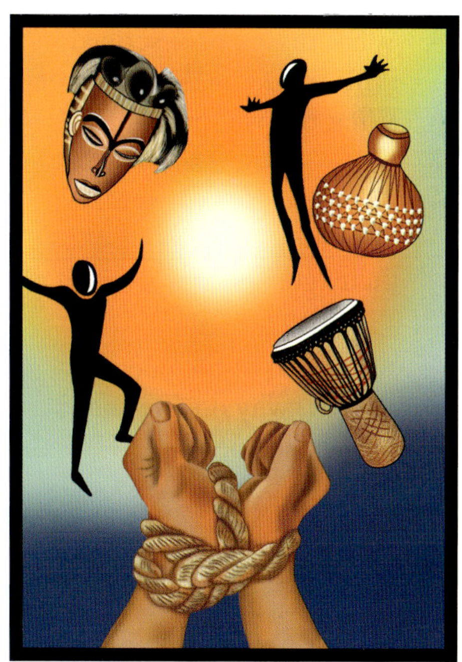

[1] **Ka'ba, (or Kaaba).** The most sacred shrine of Islam, located in the holy city of Mecca

[2] **walk the air.** Feel uplifted

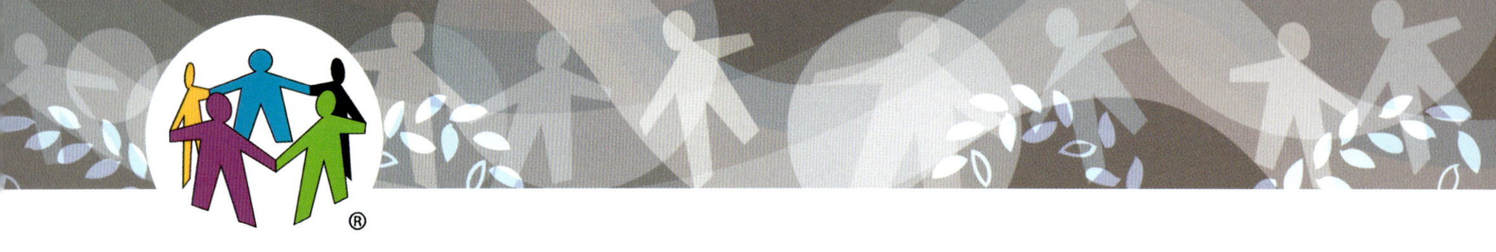

Understanding the Selection

Recalling

1. What setting does the speaker establish in the first stanza? What does he see, and from where is he watching? Use quotations from the text to justify your answer.
2. What is "our world" full of? How does "our world" compare to the world of others?
3. What things, as described in the third stanza, make "we" special? What do "we" have?
4. To where does the speaker encourage people to make their "getaway"?
5. According to the poem's speaker, why do "we" need magic and spells?

Interpreting

1. Where, or in what type of place, do you think that this poem is set?
2. To whom does the poem's speaker refer when he says "our" and "we"? How can "our world" be lovely, despite the presence of suffering and death?
3. Do the people in the courtyard literally have these things? What does the speaker mean?
4. What does the speaker mean by calling for a "new correspondence"?
5. Where does he want to "return"? What does he want to "destroy, and create"?

Synthesizing

1. Why do you think that the poet chose *not* to capitalize the word *african*?
2. How does the poem "Ka'ba" reflect the beliefs shared by Amiri Baraka and other black nationalists at the time? What does the poem's speaker want black people to do with regard to the past? white culture? and the future? Use examples from the poem to support your answer.

Delving Deeper

Understanding Literature

The Power of Art. Through the years, Amiri Baraka's views have evolved, but he has always been honest and forthright in his writing. Political and social events occur and fade into history, but the literature and art may live on to offer insight into events of the past, as well as fresh meaning for new generations of readers.

During the turbulent decade between 1965 and 1975, Baraka became a major voice for militant black nationalism, which in many ways came to represent the opposite of the nonviolent Civil Rights Movement of the 1950s and early '60s. Groups such as the **Nation of Islam** and the **Black Panthers** encouraged cultural separation of blacks and whites, and sometimes (though there were many internal philosophical conflicts) advocated separation through violence. A few years later, in the late '70s, Baraka rejected the notion of a violent separation and became focused, instead, on class struggles. Controversies old and new still surround his name, but in the end he will be remembered for his achievements as a scholar, educator, and activist, and for his total contribution to American arts and letters.

About the Author

Amiri Baraka (b.1934), prolific writer, poet, playwright, and editor, is best known for his work detailing the African-American experience. He has published over thirty plays, more than twenty-five books, and many collections of poetry.

Born Everett Leroy Jones, in Newark, New Jersey, he studied at Rutgers University before attending Howard University in Washington, D.C. He joined the Air Force in 1954, served for three years, and upon discharge moved to Greenwich Village in New York City. It was there that Baraka started writing, became involved with the Beat Movement, and established Totem Press, which published works by well-known Beat Poets.

Baraka published his critically acclaimed collection of poems *Preface to a Twenty Volume Suicide Note* (1961), under the name LeRoi Jones. He went on to write *Blues People: Negro Music in White America* (1963), an important work of musical history, and the influential black militant play *Dutchman* (1964), for which he won the Obie Award (for "off-Broadway" plays).

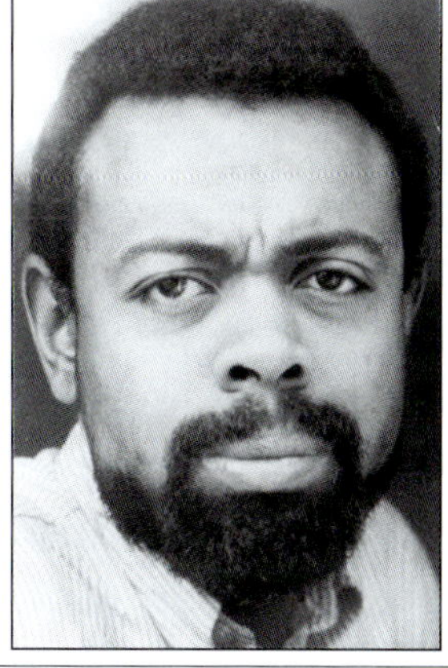

Baraka moved to Harlem after the death of Malcolm X in 1965, became a Black Nationalist, and converted to Islam. He changed his name to Imamu Amiri Baraka, and his new beliefs became common themes in his work. Later he became a Marxist and dropped the name Imamu. He continues to write, and he teaches at colleges and universities across the United States.

Prereading

"I Am a Black Woman"

by Mari Evans

In his essay "The Negro Artist and the Racial Mountain," written in 1926, Langston Hughes described how, in reaction to oppression, some African Americans in the early part of the twentieth century began to think of themselves not as having a distinct racial identity but rather as being simply Americans. No one can deny that for much of the twentieth century, throughout much of the United States, persons of African descent were treated as though they were inferior, as though they were second-class citizens. One way to deal with such treatment is to downplay one's racial identification, and it was that sort of reaction that disturbed Hughes, for he believed that African Americans should embrace their cultural uniqueness and that there was much in black culture and experience that was fascinating and wonderful and noble and worth celebrating in art.

Had Hughes lived to see the tumultuous 1960s and '70s, he would have witnessed a widespread reaction against the assimilationist attitudes that had so disturbed him. The sixties era was one of change and trouble in the United States. Students took to the streets to protest the Vietnam War. Women took to the streets to protest sexism, discrimination, and violence against women. Dr. Martin Luther King, Jr., and Malcolm X, each in their different ways, led a movement to achieve civil rights equality, and in the middle of all this turmoil, many African-American political leaders, artists, and intellectuals began to call for a renewal of racial pride. The **Black Power Movement** was born, and with it a parallel **Black Arts Movement.** From the mid-sixties to the mid-seventies, a kind of renaissance occurred in African-American political involvement and artistic creation, both perhaps summarized eloquently by the popular catch-phrase of the period: "**Black is Beautiful.**" Though the philosophies, methods, and aims of the members of the Black Power and Black Arts Movements differed considerably, the leaders of both movements shared in common the belief that young African Americans should take pride in their histories and in their unique gifts.

Mari Evans was one of the great writers of the Black Arts Movement. Her work captures eloquently the spirit of those times, and perhaps the most famous of her many works is the poem "I Am a Black Woman."

I Am a Black Woman

by Mari Evans

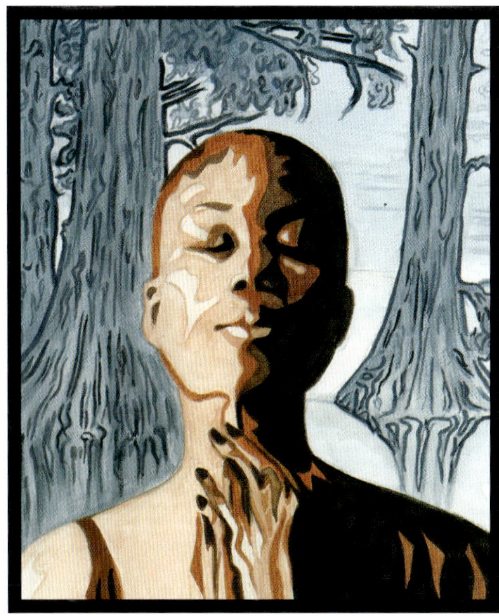

I am a black woman
the music of my song
some sweet **arpeggio** of tears
is written in a minor key
and I
can be heard humming in the night
Can be heard
humming
in the night

I saw my mate leap screaming to the sea[1]
and I/with these hands/cupped the lifebreath
from my issue in the canebrake[2]
I lost Nat's swinging body[3] in a rain of tears
and heard my son scream all the way from Anzio[4]
for Peace he never knew. . . . I
learned Da Nang and Pork Chop Hill[5]
in anguish
Now my nostrils know the gas
and these trigger tire/d fingers
seek the softness in my warrior's beard

I
am a black woman
tall as a cypress[6]
strong
beyond all definition still
defying place
and time
and circumstance
assailed
impervious
indestructible
Look
on me and be
renewed ■

[1] **my mate . . . the sea.** Enslaved persons being transported to the Americas via the infamous Middle Passage sometimes leapt to their deaths rather than endure the hardships of the journey, their homesickness, and their fears for the future.

[2] **canebrake.** A dense thicket of sugarcane, grown on plantations worked by enslaved persons in the British West Indies, Brazil, and elsewhere

[3] **Nat's swinging body.** Nat Turner led a slave rebellion, was captured, and was hanged. See page 104.

[4] **Anzio.** A town of central Italy on the Tyrrhenian Sea south-southeast of Rome. In World War II Allied troops landed at Anzio on January 22, 1944.

[5] **Da Nang and Pork Chop Hill.** Da Nang is a city in Vietnam, on the South China Sea, and was the site of much fighting during the Vietnam War. Pork Chop Hill was a site of much bloody fighting that occurred in 1953 during the Korean War.

[6] **cypress.** A kind of evergreen tree, especially common in swamps of the South

VOCABULARY IN PLACE

- **arpeggio,** ***n.*** The sounding of the tones of a chord in rapid succession rather than simultaneously

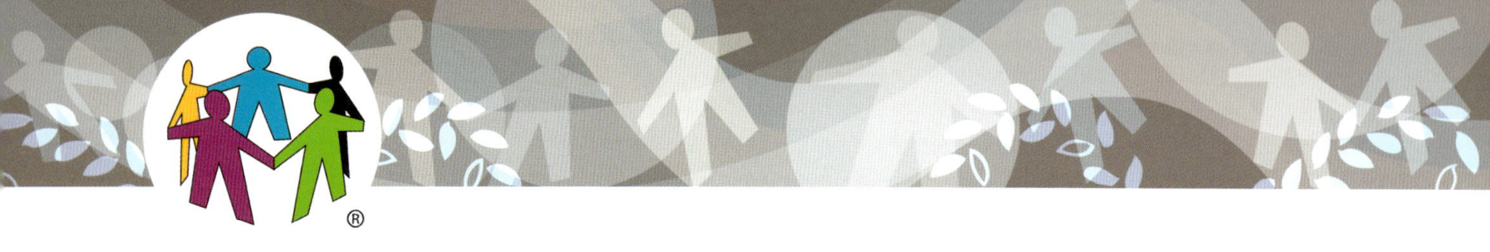

Understanding the Selection

Recalling

1. Who is the speaker of this poem, and what phrases does she use to describe her "song"?
2. What historical events are described in the second stanza of this poem?
3. At the present time of the poem, what do the speaker's "nostrils know"? How does she describe her fingers? What does she seek?
4. To what kind of tree does the speaker compare herself?

Interpreting

1. Why would this song be in a minor, not in a major, key? Why would the song be an "arpeggio of tears"?
2. What do these historical events have in common? What has been the fate of many of the African-American men whom the speaker cares about?
3. What is the emotional state of the speaker at this time?
4. What are the characteristics of this tree? What is the speaker saying about herself when she makes this comparison?

Synthesizing

1. Think of the adjectives that the speaker uses to describe herself at the conclusion of the poem. If the speaker stands for all black women, what is Mari Evans saying about these women?
2. What, according to the last line of the poem, can we learn from such women?

Delving Deeper

Understanding Literature

Metaphor. A **metaphor** is a figure of speech in which one thing is spoken of as though it were something completely different. For example, in one of the most famous of the spirituals, a constellation of stars is described as a drinking gourd. The popular name of this constellation, the Big Dipper, is also a metaphor. In the opening of "I Am a Black Woman," the speaker describes her poetry as a song that is a "sweet arpeggio of tears" that is "written in a minor key." The metaphor works particularly well because an arpeggio is a group of musical notes from a chord, in this case a minor chord. The notes are **discrete** (separated) and played in succession, one after another, just as tears are discrete and fall one after the other. In both cases, the tears and the song are sad. Metaphors work because the two parts of the metaphor—the writer's subject and the thing to which the subject is compared—have both similarities and obvious differences.

Understanding Literature

Simile. A **simile** is a type of metaphor in which two things are compared directly, often using *like* or *as*. The English language contains many, many conventional similes such as

quiet as a mouse	mad as a hatter	strong as a bull
hungry as a horse	tough as nails	tall as a tree

In the first part of this poem, the speaker describes herself as "humming / in the night." She also says that her song, though made of tears, is "sweet." In the second part of the poem, she describes many of the reasons that she might have for singing a sad song. She has inherited a history that includes the deaths of loved ones, leaping from a ship during the Middle Passage, being strangled rather than allowed to live under slavery on a sugarcane plantation, hanging like Nat Turner, and being killed in various wars. Despite this terrible history, in the concluding section of the poem, the speaker describes herself using the simile "tall as a cypress." What does the adjective "tall" suggest about the speaker? Is she literally tall, or is there another meaning that is implied by the use of this word? Remember that a cypress is an evergreen tree. What about this speaker is "evergreen"? In what ways is she, like a cypress tree, very strong and rooted? Also, cypress trees are common symbols in African-American poetry, often alluding to swamps in the deep South.

Prereading

"By Myself" and "Harriet Tubman"

by Eloise Greenfield

Eloise Greenfield has won numerous awards for her children's stories and poetry. "I love working with words," she once said. "Sometimes they come almost as if by magic. Other times, I feel a kind of pain in struggling to find the right ones. But I keep struggling because I want to do my best, and I want children to have the best."

In the hands of a writer as imaginative and energetic as Greenfield, words become food for the spirit. When you read a poem—aloud or silently—your mind and spirit take a big bite of those words and tear them right off the paper. And every time a poem is read, it changes the world in its own little way. Perhaps it makes you laugh or think of something you never even imagined. Perhaps it helps you to see your own life or your loved ones or the rest of the world in a whole new way.

Perhaps it simply makes you realize how much you can do with words. Eloise Greenfield's poetry is intended to teach and to provide adventures for the mind, and it is always fun to read. Think about the following things as you read or listen to the poems:

By Myself

1. Everyone has an imagination. What do you like to do with yours? What do you think about when you daydream?
2. How does Greenfield use **repetition,** and how does it affect the sound of the poem?
3. Does Greenfield use **punctuation** (periods, commas, etc.)?
4. What do the last three lines mean to you? How do they relate to the rest of the poem?

Harriet Tubman

1. Who was Harriet Tubman? What was the Underground Railroad? (See also History Connection, page 579.)
2. What do you notice about the speaker's voice and language?
3. Why do you think the speaker repeats the last line?
4. What similarities (if any) can you find between the styles in both of these poems?

By Myself

by Eloise Greenfield

When I'm by myself
And I close my eyes
I'm a twin
I'm a dimple in a chin
I'm a room full of toys
I'm a squeaky noise
I'm a gospel song
I'm a gong
I'm a leaf turning red
I'm a loaf of brown bread
I'm a whatever I want to be
An anything I care to be
And when I open my eyes
What I care to be
Is me ■

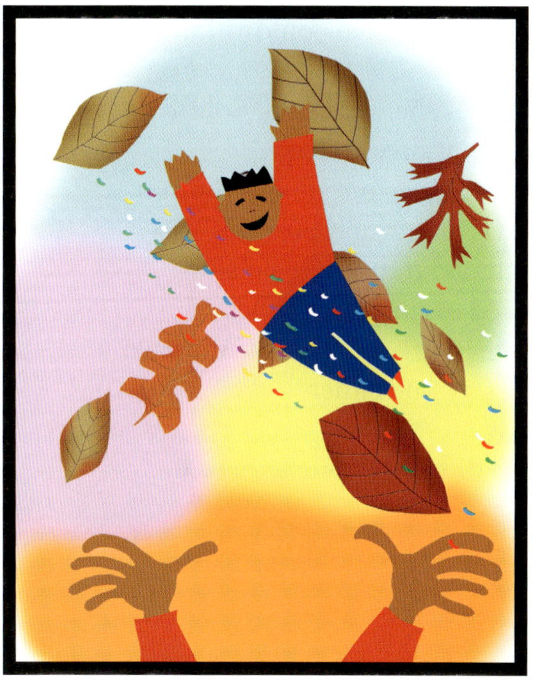

Harriet Tubman

by Eloise Greenfield

Harriet Tubman didn't take no stuff
Wasn't scared of nothing neither
Didn't come in this world to be no slave
And wasn't going to stay one either

"Farewell!" she sang to her friends one night
She was mighty sad to leave 'em
But she ran away that dark, hot night
Ran looking for her freedom

She ran to the woods and she ran through the woods
With the slave catchers[1] right behind her
And she kept on going till she got to the North
Where those mean men couldn't find her

Nineteen times she went back South
To get three hundred others
She ran for her freedom nineteen times[2]
To save Black sisters and brothers
Harriet Tubman didn't take no stuff
Wasn't scared of nothing neither
Didn't come in this world to be no slave
And didn't stay one either

And didn't stay one either ■

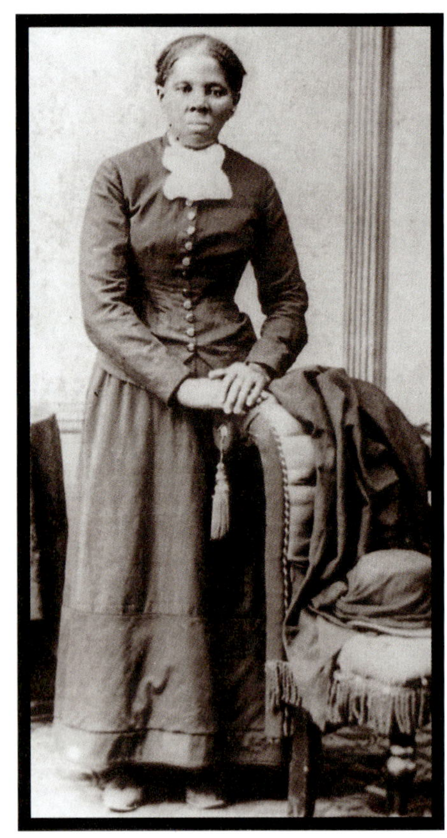

---

[1] **slave catchers.** Slave owners offered large rewards for the return of escaped, or fugitive, slaves, and so "slave catchers," or bounty hunters, were everywhere. The Underground Railroad helped the enslaved people escape and, of equal importance, provided safehouses and often new identification for fugitives.

[2] **nineteen times.** This is the number of return trips Tubman is known to have made to the South in order to help others escape to freedom. Tubman took incredible risks each time she returned, because the reward offered for her capture (or death) was much higher than those offered for other people.

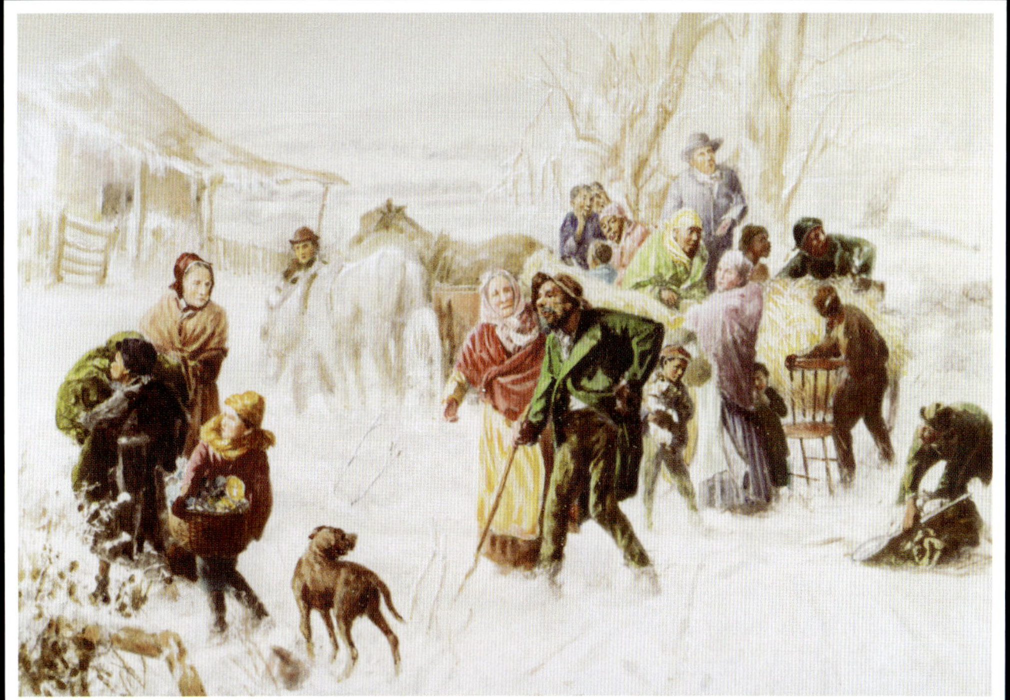

History Connection

The Underground Railroad. This famous system was established in the early 1800s by Abolitionists (those working to end slavery) to help enslaved persons escape from the South to safety in the North. It was not actually a railroad, but a vast network of people who escorted the slaves northward, provided safehouses, and helped to hide them from bounty hunters. Harriet Tubman was its most famous "conductor." (This topic is covered extensively in Unit 2 of *Grace Abounding*. See also Ann Petry, page 232.)

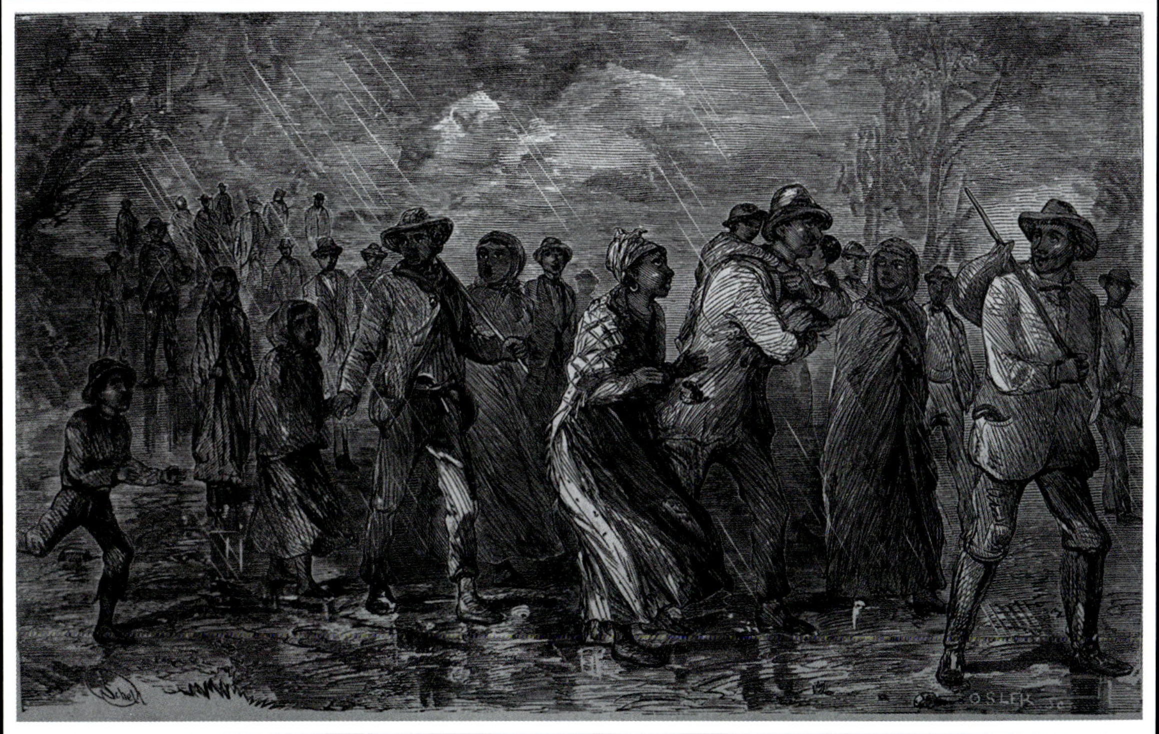

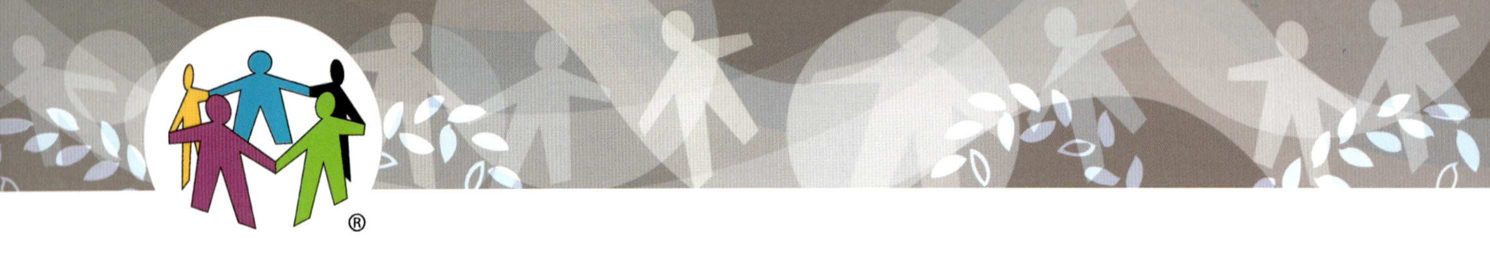

Understanding the Selection

Recalling

1. Give two examples of things that the speaker of "By Myself" becomes when she closes her eyes?
2. What word does the poet repeat most often in "By Myself"? How many times is this word repeated?
3. Who does the speaker want to be when she opens her eyes?
4. Was Harriet Tubman afraid of anything?
5. What did Harriet Tubman do on a "dark, hot night"? Why was she sad?
6. Why did she return to the South? How many times did she run for her freedom?

Interpreting

1. Does the speaker really become these things? What is she really doing when she closes her eyes?
2. Why do you think the poet chose to repeat this word so many times?
3. Does she like what she is when she opens her eyes? What does this tell you about the speaker?
4. What does the speaker of "Harriet Tubman" mean by the phrase "didn't take no stuff"? What kind of person was Tubman?
5. Was it easy to escape? Why or why not? Support your answer with a quotation from the text.
6. How do lines 5–16 provide proof of what the speaker says about Tubman in lines 1–4 and 17–21?

Synthesizing

1. In "By Myself," what is the main difference between what the speaker becomes when her eyes are open and what she becomes once they are closed?
2. Greenfield does not use any punctuation, such as periods or commas, in either of these poems. How does this affect your reading of the poem? Why do you think she chose not to use punctuation?

Delving Deeper

Writing

What Do You Imagine? Everyone uses his or her imagination once in a while. You probably do it a lot more often than you think. Just about any toy requires imagination in order for it to be fun. Some people like to play make-believe with their friends. You must use your imagination when you read in order to form pictures of the settings and characters in your mind. And all people, kids and grown-ups alike, like to imagine themselves as someone (or something) else from time to time. It's only natural.

Rewrite and personalize lines 3–10 of the poem "By Myself" by Eloise Greenfield. You will keep lines 1–2 and 11–15 just the way they are. You may change the **rhythm** or **number of beats** in each line to suit your needs. However, you must keep the same **rhyme scheme:** notice that lines 3–10 are divided into **rhyming couplets,** or pairs of lines in which the last word in each line rhymes. Your assignment is to write at least five new rhyming couplets that describe what you imagine when you close your eyes. Don't worry if you can't think of anything right away; just close your eyes and write whatever comes to mind. Imagine it!

About the Author

Eloise Greenfield (b.1929) was born in Parmele, North Carolina, the second of five children, and moved, as an infant, with her family to Washington, D.C. She studied piano as a child and was a lover of music, movies, and books. As a young wife and mother in her early twenties, while working as a clerk-typist at the U.S. Patent Office, Greenfield decided to pursue a more satisfying career in writing. After several years of rejection from publishers, Greenfield had her first poem published in the *Hartford Times* in 1962, and her first book was published in 1972. She is now the author of more than forty books of poetry, biography, children's stories, and juvenile fiction.

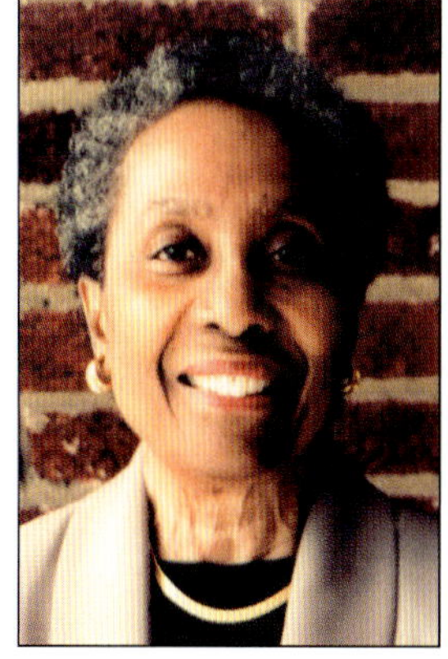

Greenfield has received numerous awards and honors, including the Coretta Scott King Award for the illustrated children's book *Africa Dream* and the Carter G. Woodson Award for her biography of Rosa Parks. Other award-winning titles include *Honey, I Love and Other Love Poems* and *Childtimes: A Three-Generation Memoir* (co-authored with her mother). She has received many more honors for her children's poetry. In 1999, Greenfield was inducted into the National Literary Hall of Fame for Writers of African Descent.

Eloise Greenfield enjoys working with and for young people. Through her work, she wants to give readers words that nourish the spirit, "words to love, to grow on."

Prereading

Poetry by Sonia Sanchez

From the publication of her first volume, *Home Coming* (1969), to the present, Sonia Sanchez has explored a vast array of issues and has honed the art of expressing herself in poetic form. In the 1960s, she was part of the **Black Arts Movement** and was one of the **Broadside Quartet,** a group of poets sponsored by Dudley Randall's **Broadside Press,** dedicated to publishing the works of black nationalist poets. In the 1970s, she became a spokesperson for the Nation of Islam, but she later left the organization. Sanchez has taught and lectured for nearly forty years and has traveled extensively, reading her poetry in countries as varied as Cuba, China, and Norway.

Despite the range of personal experience and the many different themes and styles that her poetry explores, certain features remain constant throughout Sanchez's work. One is a commitment to poetry as a political act. As with her fellow artists of the Black Arts Movement, Sanchez's poetry is revolutionary, not only because its content takes aim at social and cultural institutions that degrade black self-esteem, but also because the very way in which it is composed defies and rejects traditional ideas. Deliberately refusing to use Standard English and rejecting European poetic forms, Sanchez shows her love for black English. Through her poetry, she creates and expresses a new, African-American aesthetic—an artistic sense that is rooted in African-American experience.

Sanchez's poetry is often very direct and passionate. At times it asks the reader to confront the underbelly of life—those painful things many people would rather set aside or sweep under the rug. She is also known for delivering her poetry in a very moving and powerful way that evokes traditional African and African-American styles of performance. Read these poems first to yourself and then read them aloud. In what ways are the techniques of oral performance evident in the way in which she sets down her poetry on the written page?

for our lady[1]

by Sonia Sanchez

yeh.
            billie. if someone
had loved u like u
shud have been loved
ain't no telling what
kinds of songs
                        u wud have swung
gainst this country's wite mind.
or what kinds of lyrics
                                    wud have pushed us from
our blue / nites.
                        yeh.   billie.
if some blk / man
                        had reallee
made u feel
            permanentlee warm.
ain't no tellen
                    where the jazz of yo / songs.
                        wud have led us. ■

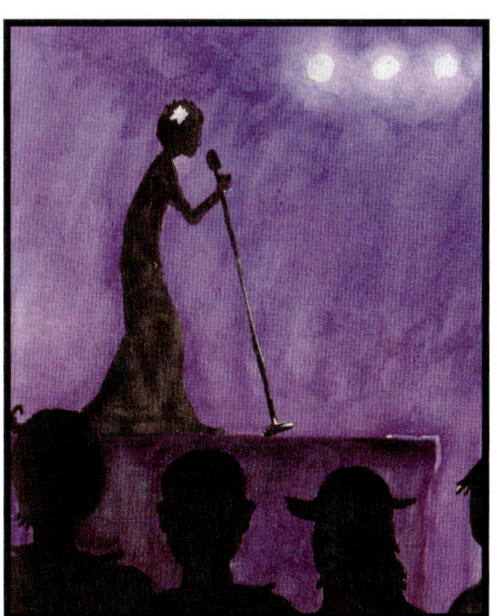

[1] **our lady.** A reference to Billie Holiday (1915–1959), also known as Lady Day, the African-American blues singer to whom the poem is addressed

to Kenny

by Sonia Sanchez

you are holy
young black God
as you reconstruct pyramids for our minds
as you interrupt our coca-cola lives
and turn them into a satellite[1]
of black stars.
you are what the prophets saw
young manchild[2]
ancient as memory. ■

WE CAN BE

by Sonia Sanchez

we can be anything we want
for we are the young ones
walken without footprints
moven our bodies in tune
to songs
echoen us. the beautiful
black ones.
recently born.
walken new
rhythms
leaven behind us a tap dancer's dream
of sunday nite ed sullivan shows.[3]
WE WILL BE
ALL that we want
for we are the young ones
bringen the world to a Black Beginnen. ■

---

[1] **satellite.** A celestial body that orbits a planet; a moon. Also, a subservient follower.

[2] **manchild.** A boy

[3] **ed sullivan shows.** Ed Sullivan (1901–1974) was a popular talk-show host in the 1950s and '60s

selected Haiku

by Sonia Sanchez

Haiku

did ya ever cry
Black man, did ya ever cry
til you knocked all over?

Haiku

if i had known, if
i had known you, i would have
left my love at home.

Haiku

come reluctant night
come to conscripted[1] black love
come and salute us.

Haiku

O this day like an
orange peeled against the sky
murmurs me and you.

[1] **conscripted.** Enrolled compulsorily; drafted

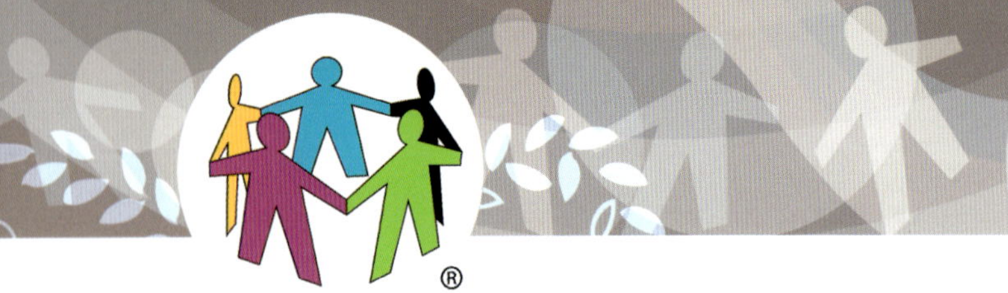

Understanding the Selection

Recalling

1. In "for our lady," what does the speaker say "billie" should have had?
2. Billie Holiday was a singer of jazz, or swing, tunes. The speaker of "for our lady" describes songs that are "swung" against what?
3. What term does the speaker of "To Kenny" use to describe the people's lives (line 4)?
4. Who, according to "We Can Be," is "bringen the world to a Black Beginnen"?
5. What moments are described by each of the haiku on page 585?

Interpreting

1. In what ways would such love have changed the nature of Billie's songs?
2. What two senses of the word *swung* is the speaker using? In what sense is the word referring to music? In what sense is it referring to a weapon? Can music be a weapon? Explain.
3. What do you think the speaker means by this?
4. What does the speaker of "We Can Be" expect of the young people of her generation?
5. What different emotional states are described in these poems?

Synthesizing

1. How do each of the poems by Sanchez relate to themes of black empowerment and celebration of the African-American cultural heritage and people?
2. What techniques does Sanchez use to render black urban vernacular? Identify 10 examples in which the poet deviates from Standard English. What effect does this have on you as a reader?

Delving Deeper

Understanding Literature

Haiku. A **haiku** is a traditional poem of Japanese origin that consists of a line of five syllables followed by a line of seven syllables, followed by another line of five syllables. Usually a haiku presents a single striking image that suggests a complex emotional state. Traditionally, haiku invoke some aspect of nature or the seasons. Here is an example of a traditional haiku:

> The aged tree stands
> Stoic, imperturbed by
> Everyday weather.

Do the haiku by Sonia Sanchez follow the traditional definition precisely? In what ways do the individual poems differ from traditional haiku both in form and content?

Try your hand at writing some haiku of your own. Leafing though a photobook can give you some ideas for subjects.

About the Author

Sonia Sanchez (b.1934), poet, playwright, novelist, lecturer, scholar, and activist, was prominent in the Black Arts Movement and has been hailed as one of the most important figures in late-twentieth-century African-American literature. Born in Birmingham, Alabama, Sanchez moved to Harlem as a young girl. She received a bachelor's degree from Hunter College in New York City and studied poetry for one year at New York University. In the 1960s she became active in the Civil Rights Movement and was influenced by the powerful speaking styles of such leaders as Malcolm X and Dr. Martin Luther King, Jr.

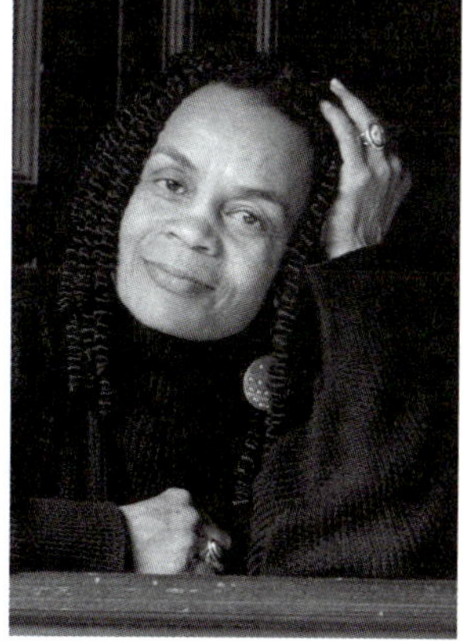

In addition to three children's books, seven plays, and many essays, Sanchez has published several volumes of poetry, including *Home Coming* (1969); *We a BaddDDD People* (1970); *Wounded in the House of a Friend* (1995); and *shAke Loose my sk*in (2000).

Since the 1960s, she has been instrumental in making Black Studies a university discipline. Sanchez has taught in many American universities and colleges, including Amherst College, San Francisco State University, Temple University, and the University of Pittsburgh. She has also traveled extensively, lecturing and reading her poetry in Africa, Australia, throughout the Caribbean, the People's Republic of China, Nicaragua, and Norway.

Prereading

"Life Doesn't Frighten Me" and "Woman Work"

by Maya Angelou

Maya Angelou is perhaps the best-known contemporary African-American poet and literary personality. Aside from her many popular poems, she has written six amazing autobiographies; has acted, directed, and written for movies and television; and is even a fine singer.

Readers and listeners of all ages love Angelou because, first and foremost, she knows how to have fun with words. Her children's poems are fun to read to oneself, but they are also intended to be read aloud.

Her work often focuses on issues of race and the unique experiences of African Americans. But her work also cuts across racial lines to remind all readers that—regardless of age, race, or nationality—we share common experiences, frustrations, needs, and dreams. Perhaps most importantly, her work tells us that we can find the courage to deal with those frustrations, to meet those needs, and to fulfill those dreams.

Life Doesn't Frighten Me. This poem wants to move fast with its short, vibrant lines and smooth rhymes. Pay attention to the poet's **rhyme scheme.** How does it change over the course of the poem? Is there any sort of pattern?

Overall, this comes across as a fun poem, though it touches on some serious issues and contains some not-so-fun images. Some of what the speaker hears and sees is real and very serious ("Tough guys in a fight," "Strangers in the park") and some is imaginary ("Lions on the loose"). Are any of the images in the poem familiar to you?

Woman Work. This poem speaks for countless women who have worked morning, noon, and night, all their lives, taking care of others. It seems that the speaker's work will never be done, for all of these tasks are of the sort that must be repeated day in, day out. (In the words of a well-known African-American proverb, "A cow doesn't stay milked.") As you read this poem, ask yourself, "Who or what takes care of the needs of this woman who spends all of her time caring for others?"

Life Doesn't Frighten Me

by Maya Angelou

Shadows on the wall
Noises down the hall
Life doesn't frighten me at all
Bad dogs barking loud
Big ghosts in a cloud
Life doesn't frighten me at all.

Mean old Mother Goose
Lions on the loose
They don't frighten me at all
Dragons breathing flame
On my counterpane
That doesn't frighten me at all.

I go boo
Make them shoo
I make fun
Way they run
I won't cry
So they fly
I just smile
They go wild
Life doesn't frighten me at all.

Tough guys in a fight
All alone at night
Life doesn't frighten me at all.

Panthers in the park
Strangers in the dark
No, they don't frighten me at all.

That new classroom where
Boys all pull my hair
(Kissy little girls
With their hair in curls)
They don't frighten me at all.

Don't show me frogs and snakes
And listen for my scream,
If I'm afraid at all
It's only in my dreams.

I've got a magic charm
That I keep up my sleeve,
I can walk the ocean floor
And never have to breathe.

Life doesn't frighten me at all
Not at all
Not at all.
Life doesn't frighten me at all. ■

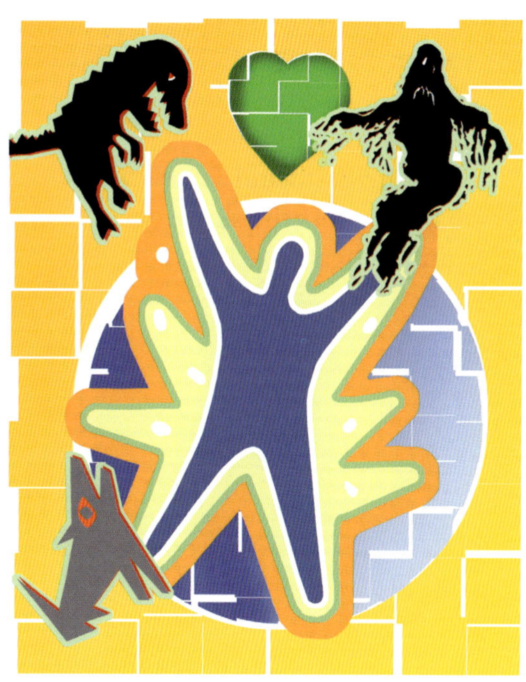

Woman Work

by Maya Angelou

I've got the children to **tend**
The clothes to mend
The floor to mop
The food to shop
Then the chicken to fry
The baby to dry
I got company to feed
The garden to weed
I've got the shirts to press
The tots to dress
The cane to cut[1]
I gotta clean up this hut
Then see about the sick
The cotton to pick.

Shine on me, sunshine
Rain on me, rain
Fall softly, dew drops
And cool my brow[2] again.

Storm, blow me from here
With your fiercest wind
Let me float across the sky
'Til I can rest again.

[1] **cane to cut.** Sugar cane grows in stalks that are cut down at harvest time.

[2] **brow.** Forehead

VOCABULARY IN PLACE

- **tend,** *v.* Care for

Fall gently, snowflakes
Cover me with white
Cold icy kisses and
Let me rest tonight.

Sun, rain, curving sky
Mountain, oceans, leaf and stone
Star shine, moon glow
You're all that I can call my own. ■

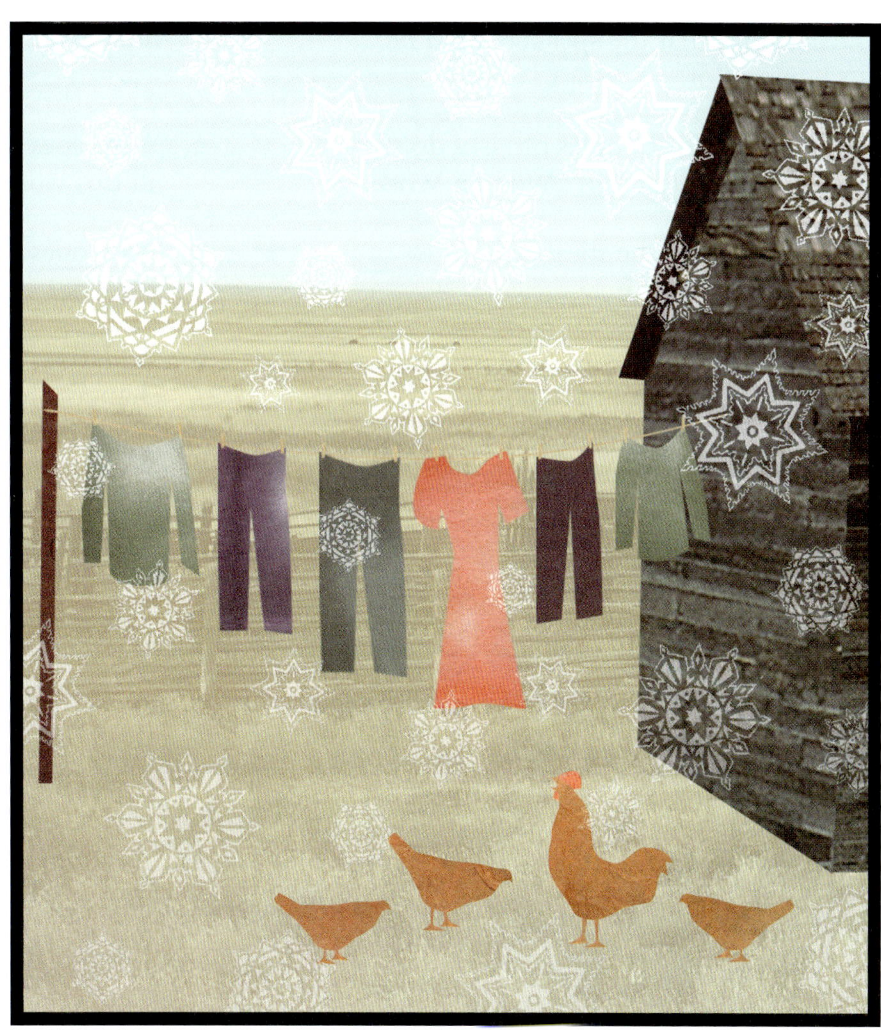

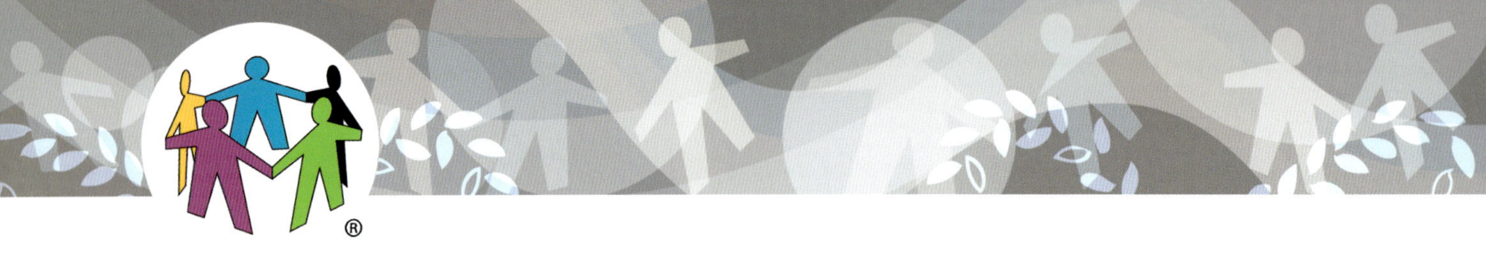

Understanding the Selection

Recalling

1. In "Life Doesn't Frighten Me," what does the speaker do to make the scary things go away?
2. When, according to the speaker, is the only time that she is "afraid at all"?
3. Give two examples of imaginary things and two examples of real things that the speaker could be afraid of.
4. Give five examples of tasks done by the speaker in "Woman Work."
5. How does the speaker want to cool down?
6. How do the first 14 lines differ from the rest of the poem?
7. What things can the speaker call her own?

Interpreting

1. Where do you think the poem's speaker lives? Give lines or quotations from the poem to support your answer.
2. In Lines 39 and 40, how is she able to "walk the ocean floor"? What is her magic charm?
3. Do you think that the speaker knows the difference between the imaginary and real things? Explain.
4. Why does the poem's speaker do all this work? Who needs her?
5. Why does she want the storm to blow her away?
6. Why does the poem's structure change after line 14?
7. Why can't the speaker call the sugarcane, cotton, garden, and other things "[her] own"?

Synthesizing

1. Are you afraid of anything? What kinds of things frighten you? What do you do when you are afraid? Have you overcome fears that you once had? How?
2. What is the speaker's relationship with nature? Give examples from the poem to support your answer.

Delving Deeper

Speaking and Listening

Cadence. People who have heard her never forget listening to Maya Angelou recite a poem. She has a distinctive voice, she seems to cherish every single word, and she has a wonderful sense of the beauty of the sounds of the language.

In poetry, the word **cadence** refers to the rhythmic order and "flow" of the words, as well as how one changes one's inflections (pitches) to express meaning. Working with a partner or in small groups, choose one of these poems and practice reading it aloud. Discuss the poem's rhythm: how many strong and weak beats are there in each line? Where should the speaker change his or her tone? How do repetition and rhyme shape the poem's sound? Which words deserve special emphasis? Experiment with various reading styles and practice until you are ready to recite to the whole class.

About the Author

Maya Angelou (b.1928) is among America's most popular poets and authors. She is best known for her many autobiographical works and collections of poems. Angelou was born Marguerite Johnson in St. Louis, Missouri, and spent much of her childhood shuttling between St. Louis and Stamps, Arkansas, where she lived with her grandmother. She studied music and dance and became involved with the Civil Rights Movement. In 1959 Angelou became the northern coordinator for the Southern Christian Leadership Conference, a civil rights group headed by Dr. Martin Luther King, Jr.

She became famous for the first of her six autobiographies, *I Know Why the Caged Bird Sings* (1969). (See page 504.) The book intimately chronicles the traumatic events of her childhood during the Great Depression and describes much of the racial discrimination she experienced. It was nominated for a National Book Award and later adapted for television. She has said of her work, "I speak to the black experience, but I am always talking about the human condition—about what we can endure, dream, fail at, and still survive." Her other autobiographies include *Gather Together in My Name* (1974), *All God's Children Need Traveling Shoes* (1986), and *A Song Flung Up to Heaven* (2002). Among her many poetry collections, *Just Give Me a Cool Drink of Water 'Fore I Die* (1971) was nominated for a Pulitzer Prize. Her work has also been nominated for the Tony and Emmy awards. Angelou has acted, written, and directed for stage and screen and has produced award-winning documentaries.

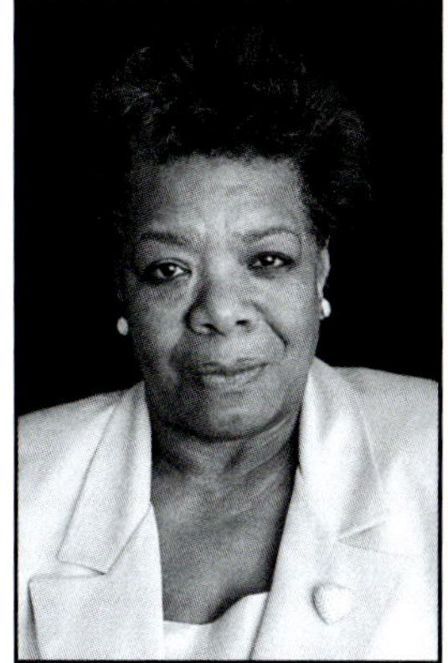

Prereading

The Poems of Nikki Giovanni

Many of Nikki Giovanni's best-known and most beloved poems deal with childhood and with such themes as cultural and personal identity and the importance of family and community. These works contrast sharply to much of her work during the **Black Arts Movement** of the 1960s, which fully reflects the militancy and pride expressed by the bold voices of that era.

Knoxville, Tennessee. This poem is a beautiful example of what is known as **imagist poetry,** poetry that uses words to portray sensory experience. The trick in an imagist poem is to present what the American poet T. S. Eliot called an **objective correlative**—a group of images that are the formula for an emotion. As you read "Knoxville, Tennessee," put yourself imaginatively into the scenes that Ms. Giovanni creates and imagine how it would feel to be present in this time from the speaker's memory.

Nikki-Rosa. There are many ways to measure wealth. This famous poem by Giovanni recounts her own childhood experiences growing up in Cincinnati, Ohio. As you read this poem, ask yourself, "In what sense was the speaker, though poor, actually quite wealthy?" and "Why is the speaker suspicious of what biographers might write about her?"

The Drum. This children's poem is based upon a single central metaphor. As you read it, ask yourself, "What does the drum represent? In what ways might the world be like a drum?" and "What resolution has the speaker made about how she is going to lead her life?"

Knoxville, Tennessee

by Nikki Giovanni

I always like summer
best
you can eat fresh corn
from daddy's garden
and okra
and greens
and cabbage
and lots of
barbecue
and buttermilk
and homemade ice-cream
at the church picnic
and listen to
gospel music
outside
at the church
homecoming
and go to the mountains with
your grandmother
and go barefooted
and be warm
all the time
not only when you go to bed
and sleep ■

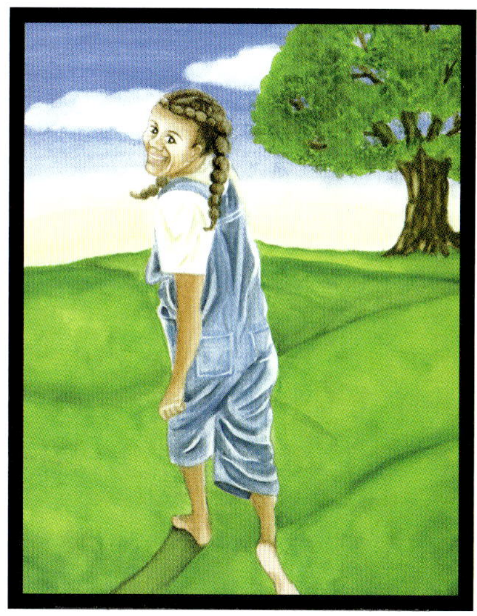

Nikki-Rosa

by Nikki Giovanni

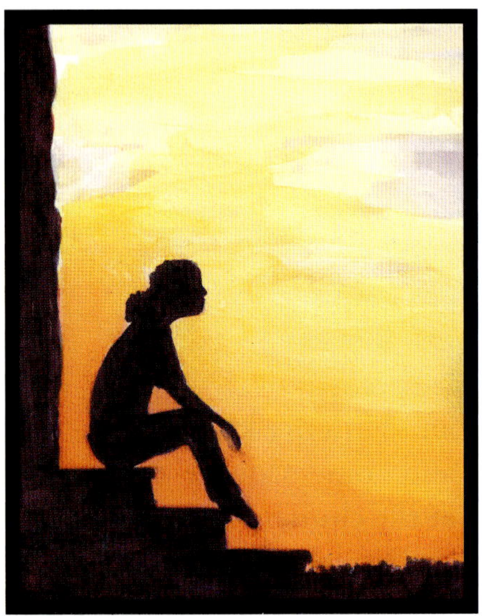

childhood remembrances are always a drag
if you're Black
you always remember things like living in Woodlawn[1]
with no inside toilet
and if you become famous or something
they never talk about how happy you were to
    have your mother
all to yourself and
how good the water felt when you got your bath
    from one of those
big tubs that folk in chicago barbecue in
and somehow when you talk about home
it never gets across how much you
understood their feelings
as the whole family attended meetings about Hollydale[2]
and even though you remember
your biographers never understand
your father's pain as he sells his stock
and another dream goes
and though you're poor it isn't poverty that
concerns you
and though they fought a lot
it isn't your father's drinking that makes any difference
but only that everybody is together and you
and your sister have happy birthdays and
very good christmasses
and I really hope no white person ever
    has cause to write about me
because they never understand Black
    love is Black wealth and
    they'll
probably talk about my hard childhood
    and never understand that
all the while I was quite happy ■

[1] **Woodlawn.** A suburb of Cincinnati, Ohio

[2] **Hollydale.** A community of African-American homes in Cincinnati, Ohio. The community enabled African Americans who otherwise could not afford to do so to build new homes.

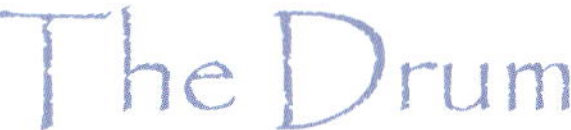

The Drum

by Nikki Giovanni

daddy says the world is
a drum tight and hard
and i told him
i'm gonna beat
out my own rhythm ■

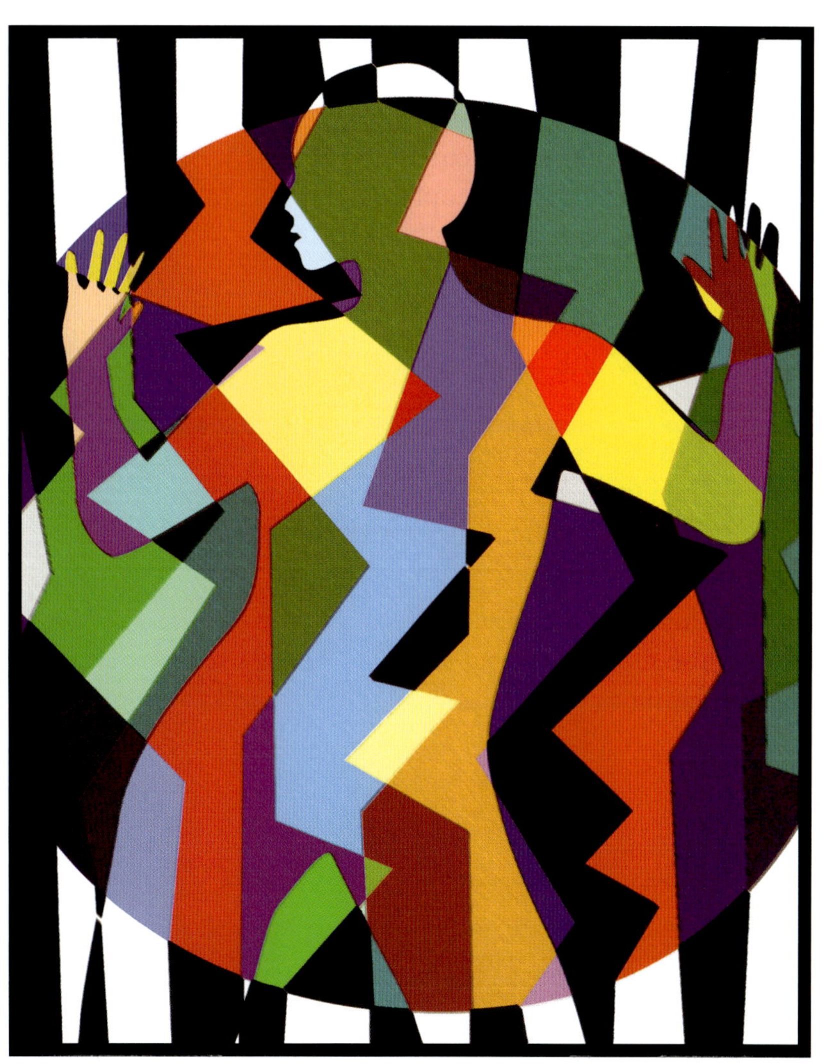

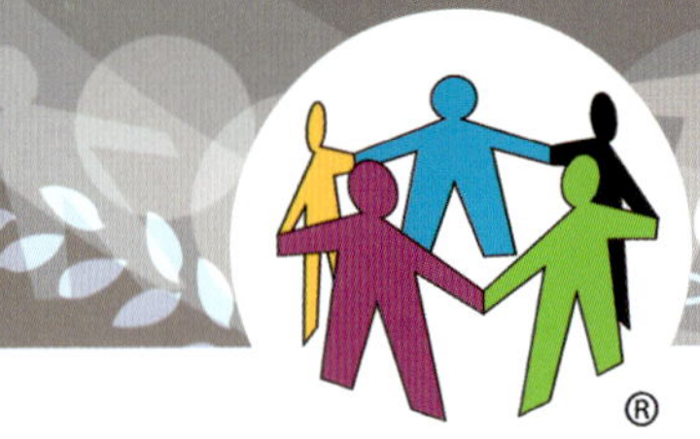

Understanding the Selection

Recalling

1. What images in "Knoxville, Tennessee" appeal to the sense of taste? to sight? to sound? to smell? to touch?
2. What does the speaker of "Nikki-Rosa" say at the beginning of the poem about the childhood memories of black people?
3. Of what, according to "Nikki-Rosa," does "Black wealth" consist?
4. What words are used in "The Drum" to describe both the drum and the world?
5. What does the speaker of "The Drum" say that she is going to do?

Interpreting

1. How do these images make the reader feel about the childhood being described?
2. What memories recounted in the poem show that this statement is not true?
3. What experiences recounted in the poem signal that Nikki's childhood was happy?
4. Does the speaker's father expect life to be easy? Why, or why not?
5. Does the speaker expect to grow up to be just like everybody else? Explain using a quote from the text to support your answer.

Synthesizing

1. Sociologists and psychologists will tell you that a warm, caring family life is important to the healthy development of a child. What sort of family life do you think the speaker of the first two poems had?
2. How would having such a family life help someone to feel confident enough to beat out his or her "own rhythm"?

Delving Deeper

Understanding Literature

Irony. An **irony** is a difference between appearance and reality, especially an unexpected or surprising difference. A **verbal irony** is a statement that implies its opposite. For example, if someone bumps into a table and spills his or her drink and if someone else says, "That was graceful," the comment is an example of (impolite) verbal irony. Nikki Giovanni begins the poem "Nikki-Rosa" with an ironic statement. She does not mean, literally, that childhood memories "are always a drag / if you're Black." She is referring to what biographers often have to say about famous people who had challenges in their childhoods such as poverty and discrimination. The rest of this poem is, of course, a refutation of that simplistic view. In what way does Giovanni refute that point of view? What conclusion does she draw about the importance of familial love?

About the Author

Nikki Giovanni (b.1945) was born in Knoxville, Tennessee, raised in Cincinnati, Ohio, and educated at Fisk and Columbia Universities. She is one of the most popular poets in America, having published over two dozen books, including volumes of poetry, children's books, and collections of essays.

Ms. Giovanni has received twenty-one honorary doctorates and has been named "Woman of the Year" by the magazines *Essence, Mademoiselle,* and *Ladies Home Journal.* She received the NAACP Image Award for literature in 1998, 2000, and 2003. She is an English Professor and the Gloria D. Smith Professor of Black Studies at Virginia Tech.

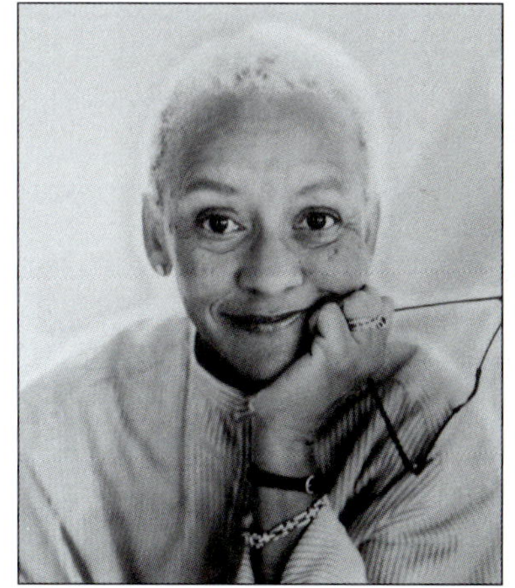

Giovanni made her name known in the 1960s as one of the leading voices in the Black Arts Movement. Her poetry collections include *Black Feeling, Black Talk* (1968), *Black Judgment* (1968), *Re: Creation* (1970), and *Love Poems* (1997). She has long been a prolific writer, speaker, and social critic. Her books of poetry for children include *Ego Tripping and Other Poems for Young People* (1993), *The Genie in the Jar* and *The Sun is So Quiet,* both published in 1996.

Prereading

"in the inner city" and "for deLawd"

by Lucille Clifton

Well respected as a writer of poetry and prose, Lucille Clifton has often been highly critical of white society. She is one of the most popular poets to emerge from the **Black Arts Movement** of the late 1960s and early 1970s. The influence of that movement is clearly evident in her work, which focuses on poverty and despair balanced by optimism and hope. Her work features women and youth and realistic insight into the African-American experience.

in the inner city. Clifton's poetry is often described as **minimalist,** simple in its form but complex in its meaning. Her minimalism is evident in "in the inner city," in which she uses a short **free verse style** to express love for her urban neighborhood, despite the many negative stereotypes that people often associate with poor, or depressed, urban areas. Clifton thought it was important to point out that—regardless of the struggles faced by its population—the inner city is still a place that people love to call home.

for deLawd. In "for deLawd" Clifton again deals with the subject of the inner city. This poem's speaker is a strong, independent woman and mother who copes with heartache and gets on with life, like her mother and her grandmother, and still goes on being herself, as well. Through this character the poet is able to comment on larger societal issues.

In Clifton's work the reader will consistently find representations of the pain, struggles, hope, and strength of people in the African-American community.

in the inner city

by Lucille Clifton

in the inner city
or
like we call it
home
we think a lot about uptown
and the silent nights
and the houses straight as
dead men
and the **pastel** lights
and we hang on to our no place
happy to be alive
and in the inner city
or
like we call it
home ■

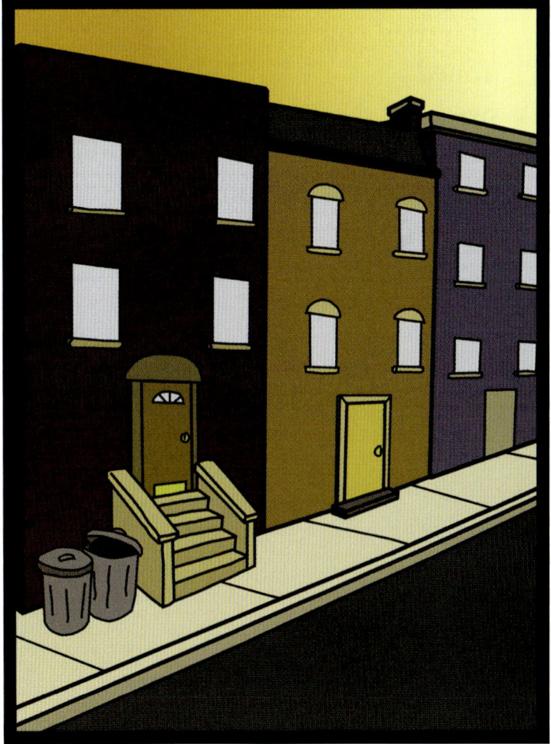

VOCABULARY IN PLACE

- **pastel,** ***adj.*** Light shade of any color

for deLawd

by Lucille Clifton

people say they have a hard time
understanding how I
go on about my business
playing my Ray Charles[1]
hollering at the kids—
seem like my Afro
cut off in some old image
would show I got a long memory
and I come from a line
of black and going on women
who got used to making it through murdered sons
and who grief kept on pushing
who fried chicken
ironed
swept off the back steps
who grief kept
for their still alive sons
for their sons coming
for their sons gone
just pushing ■

---

[1] **Ray Charles.** (1930–2004) A leading figure in R&B, soul, gospel, and blues music, the much-beloved singer and composer of songs such as "I Got a Woman"

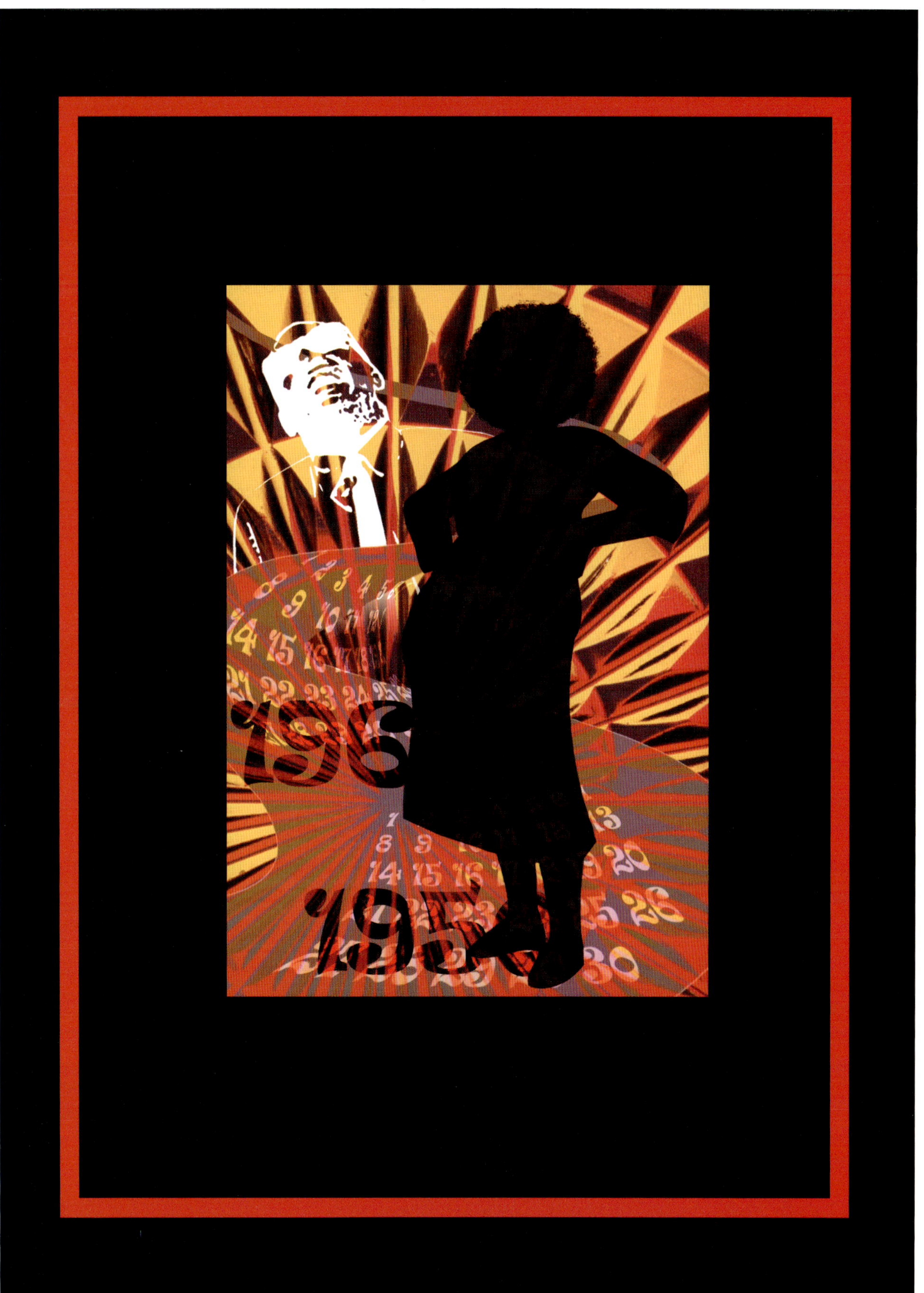

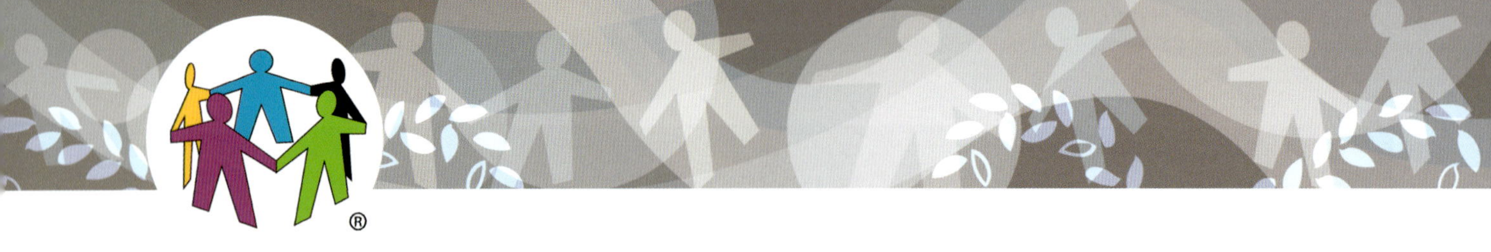

Understanding the Selection

Recalling

1. What do the people in the speaker's neighborhood call "the inner city"?
2. What type of neighborhood is being described? Is the speaker happy?
3. According to the speaker of "for deLawd," what do people have a hard time understanding?
4. What are some of the things that black and "going on" women do?
5. How is the speaker like the women before her?

Interpreting

1. What is life like "uptown"? Who lives there?
2. If life in the inner city seems hard, why do you think people still embrace it as home? What does the speaker mean when she says "hang on to our no place" in line 10?
3. What are your thoughts on the type of person the speaker is? Where does she live, and what does she have to deal with?
4. What does the speaker mean by "going on"?
5. Do you get the impression from this speaker that black women before her had it easy? Use evidence from the text to support your answer.

Synthesizing

1. How does Clifton's poetry serve to counter or dispel common negative stereotypes that people sometimes hold against inner-city residents?
2. Do the speakers in Clifton's poems think that white society understands them? Do they care?
3. Why do you think the poem is entitled "for deLawd"?

Delving Deeper

Writing

Who Cares What Other People Think? When it comes down to it, just about everyone "cares" what other people think or say about them. That is to say, if you know that someone else is talking about you, you almost surely care to hear what they have to say. Another simple fact of life is that humans tend to judge one another. Perhaps this is partly instinctive: through the course of human development the mind has learned to make quick judgments as a matter of survival. Also, people like to gossip and compare how others are living in relation to themselves and, at times, to point out things that other people are doing wrong.

To whom is the speaker in "in the inner city" comparing herself or her neighborhood? What do people say about the speaker in "for deLawd"? Does she care?

What do you think that other people say about you? Do you care? Answer this question in a journal entry or poem using anecdotes (examples) from your own life.

About the Author

Lucille Clifton (b.1936) was born Thelma Lucille Sayles, in Depew, New York, and moved to Buffalo with her family early in her life. Although neither of her parents were formally educated, they provided their large family with an appreciation of books, especially those by African Americans. Lucille entered college early, matriculating as a drama major at Howard University at age sixteen.

After transferring to Fredonia State Teachers College in 1955, Clifton worked as an actor and developed her signature-style "minimalist" poetry. Her work is distinguished for its short, free verse lines, usually in **iambic trimeter** with little rhyming. Clifton's images are sharp and concise, often in lowercase letters with little or no punctuation. The vocabulary of her poetry is also stark; she relies considerably on precise word choice and placement.

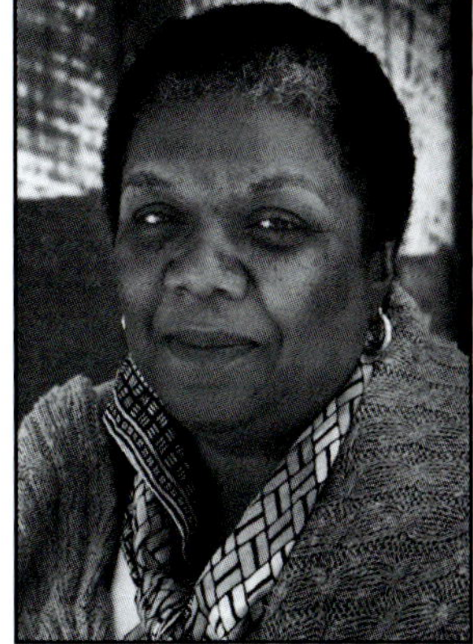

Clifton's first poetry collection, *Good Times* (1969), was very well received by critics. In the years since her debut she has taught at many American colleges and served as the Poet Laureate of Maryland from 1979 to 1985. She was nominated for the Pulitzer Prize in poetry in 1980, 1987, and 1991, and has won many prestigious poetry awards, including a National Book Award for *Blessing the Boats: New and Selected Poems, 1988–2000.* Other poetry collections include *Good Woman: Poems and a Memoir 1969–1980, The Terrible Stories* (1996), *The Book of Light* (1993), and *Mercy* (2004).

Prereading

"Parsley"

by Rita Dove

Critics have praised Rita Dove for her "economy of style," for using no more words than necessary. At first glance, Dove's bare-bones language and imagery conceal the profound and highly imaginative qualities of her work. Her poetry draws the reader into a carefully composed world, where powerful images await, ready to pounce from behind the poet's calm, calculated voice.

The poem "Parsley" was inspired by a horrific event that took place in the Dominican Republic, which shares an island with the nation of Haiti. Despite their geographic proximity, the two nations have very different histories and cultures: Dominicans have a Spanish heritage, while Haitians are of African descent and speak mainly French Creole. The history of the island is fascinating and complex, and references to Haitian history are scattered throughout *Grace Abounding.*

In 1937, the Dominican dictator, Rafael Trujillo, accused the Haitian government of aiding insurgent forces in the Dominican Republic. Whether such accusations were true or not, Trujillo responded by rounding up and slaughtering 20,000 Haitian migrant workers. He determined which workers were Haitian and which were Dominican by the fact that the Haitians could not pronounce the "rolling R" in the Spanish word *perejil,* for parsley.

"Parsley" is divided into two parts. The first part, written in the 19-line **villanelle** form (See the Handbook of Literary Terms), tells the story from the Haitian perspective. The second part, which does not follow a conventional form, is a meditation from Trujillo's own demented perspective as he decides how to identify and massacre the Haitian workers.

As you read the poem, notice Dove's use of repetition and variation of **imagery,** the smooth **rhythm** of her words, the way she establishes **mood,** and her use of a calm, steady **tone** to address this tragic and anger-provoking subject. Please refer to A Reading of the Selection on page 611 for an interpretation of the poem.

Parsley[1]

by Rita Dove

1. The Cane [2] Fields

There is a parrot imitating spring
in the palace, its feathers parsley green.
Out of the swamp the cane appears

to haunt us,[3] and we cut it down. El General[4]
searches for a word; he is all the world
there is. Like a parrot imitating spring,

we lie down screaming as rain punches through
and we come up green. We cannot speak an R—
out of the swamp, the cane appears

and then the mountain we call in whispers *Katalina.*[5]
The children gnaw their teeth to arrowheads.
There is a parrot imitating spring.

El General has found his word: *perejil.*
Who says it, lives. He laughs, teeth shining
out of the swamp. The cane appears

in our dreams, lashed by wind and streaming.
And we lie down. For every drop of blood
there is a parrot imitating spring.
Out of the swamp the cane appears.

---

[1] **Parsley.** On October 2, 1937, Rafael Trujillo (1891–1961), dictator of the Dominican Republic, ordered 20,000 blacks killed because they could not pronounce the letter *R* in *perejil,* the Spanish word for parsley.

[2] **Cane.** Sugarcane

[3] **to haunt us.** Haitians labored in the cane fields as slaves to the French. As migrant workers in the Dominican Republic, their status was little better than that of slaves. Therefore, the cane reminds them hauntingly of the slavery days.

[4] **El General.** Trujillo was also known as "El Jefe," which in Spanish means "The General" or "The Boss."

[5] ***Katalina.*** This is how the Spanish word *Katarina* sounds when the Haitians pronounce it because they cannot properly "roll" the letter *R.*

2. The Palace

The word the general's chosen is parsley.
It is fall, when thoughts turn
to love and death; the general thinks
of his mother, how she died in the fall
and he planted her walking cane at the grave
and it flowered, each spring **stolidly** forming
four-star blossoms. The general

pulls on his boots, he stomps to
her room in the palace, the one without
curtains, the one with a parrot
in a brass ring. As he paces he wonders
Who can I kill today. And for a moment
the little knot of screams[6]
is still. The parrot, who has traveled

all the way from Australia in an ivory
cage, is, **coy** as a widow, practising
spring. Ever since the morning
his mother collapsed in the kitchen
while baking skull-shaped candies
for the Day of the Dead,[7] the general
has hated sweets. He orders pastries
brought up for the bird; they arrive

dusted with sugar on a bed of lace.
The knot in his throat starts to twitch;
he sees his boots the first day in battle
splashed with mud and urine[8]
as a soldier falls at his feet amazed—
how stupid he looked!—at the sound
of artillery. *I never thought it would sing*
the soldier said, and died. Now

---

[6] **little knot of screams.** The parrot

[7] **Day of the Dead.** All Soul's Day, November 2. During this festival, which is based on Aztec traditions, friends and family of the dead move in procession to cemeteries carrying food and candles that are shaped to represent images of death, such as skulls.

[8] **mud and urine.** This suggests that the general was not on the front lines, where one's boots would be covered in blood, rather than mud. *Urine* suggests the general's fear.

VOCABULARY IN PLACE

- **stolidly,** ***adv.*** Having or revealing little emotion or sensibility
- **coy,** ***adj.*** Shy; tending to avoid social situations

the general sees the fields of sugar
cane, lashed by rain and streaming.
He sees his mother's smile, the teeth
gnawed to arrowheads. He hears
the Haitians sing without R's
as they swing the great machetes:
Katalina, they sing, *Katalina,*

mi madle, mi amol en muelte.[9] God knows
his mother was no stupid woman; she
could roll an R like a queen. Even
a parrot can roll an R! In the bare room
the bright feathers arch in a parody
of greenery,[10] as the last pale crumbs
disappear under the blackened tongue. Someone

calls out his name in a voice
so like his mother's, a startled tear
splashes the tip of his right boot.
My mother, my love in death.
The general remembers the tiny green sprigs
men of his village wore in their capes
to honor the birth of a son. He will
order many, this time, to be killed

for a single, beautiful word. ■

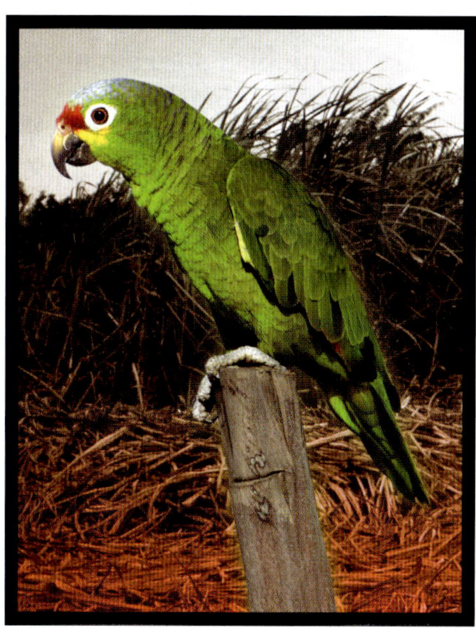

[9] **mi madle . . . en muelte.** In Spanish, the phrase should read "Mi madre, mi amor en muerte." This phrase is translated on line 67.

[10] **parody of greenery.** A *parody* is a literary or artistic work that pokes fun at another artistic work or style. The poem's speaker suggests that the parrot's intense greenness is, in a way, absurd, and seems to poke fun at, or belittle, other green things.

Prereading

The Poetry of Michael S. Harper

Already a major voice among late-twentieth-century poets, Michael Harper, as both poet and professor, has laid a promising foundation for the future of poetry. Harper gained recognition early on as a poet who successfully bridges the divide between the old and the new—between the themes, styles, and references of poetry's past and the highly sophisticated, specialized, and splintered world of modern poetry. His debut book, *Dear John, Dear Coltrane* (1970), is regarded as one of the very best collections of **jazz poetry**, in which the poet effectively converts the syncopated subtleties and style of jazz music into poetic verse. He is a poet's poet, highly regarded within the tight-knit poetry community, even by those who criticize him, from time to time, for upholding traditional Western literary conventions.

In fact, Harper's work celebrates the African-American experience and cultural identities, through which he interprets America's rich history. He also carries on the poet's custom of addressing and praising fellow poets, artists, and other memorable people. His work is imaginative and musical; it begs to be read aloud and performed. In the days of Countee Cullen and Langston Hughes, and for centuries prior, poems served as crucial transmitters and receptacles of the seminal ideas and linguistic styles of particular places and times. Poets were cultural go-betweens, distilling ideas and events into handy capsules to be shared and pondered. Modern poetry serves the same purpose, but its role is less prominent. Like other art forms, it has evolved greatly in the past half-century, becoming more sophisticated and refined. As a result, it appeals to a smaller, more specialized audience. This is not necessarily bad for poets or poetry, but it is unfortunate because it means that fewer people will ever read great poets such as Harper.

Slam poetry (improvised verse performed on stage) is one popular modern form, and rap lyricists are poets to one extent or another, but the written poem—the art produced to be read on a page and pondered—is, for the most part, appreciated only by those who seek it. It is no longer in the mainstream. However, poetry has evolved to such a point that a single written word or phrase within a poem can deliver a mountain of meaning(s) to any reader ready and willing to attend closely to the speaker's voice and perspective. Poetry may be crowded out by other media of modern life, but it is no less functional or necessary. It is still the product of a writer striving to capture the world, uniquely, in words.

See Understanding Literature for more information on Harper's poetry.

Br'er Sterling[1] and the Rocker

by Michael S. Harper

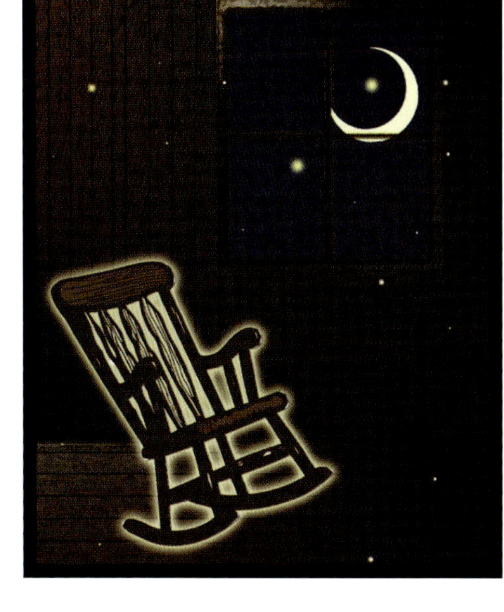

Any fool knows a Br'er in a rocker
is a boomerang **incarnate;** look at the blade
of the rocker, that wondrous crescent
rockin' in harness as poem.

To speak of poetry is the curled line straightened;
to speak of doubletalk, the tongue
gone pure, the **stoic** line a **trestle**
whistlin', a man a train comin' on:

Listen Br'er Sterling
steel-drivin' man, folk-said, folk-sayin',
that chair's a blues-harnessed star
turnin' on its earthy axis;[2]
Miss Daisy, latch on that star's arc,
hold on sweet mama; Br'er Sterling's rocker glows.

for Sterling A. and Daisy T. Brown
16 June 1973 ■

Michael S. Harper (left) and Sterling A. Brown (right), Rockefeller Library, Brown University (1974). Photo by Lawrence F. Sykes. (Used at the poet's request.)

---

[1] **Br'er Sterling.** Br'er means brother (dialect). The poem is dedicated to Sterling Brown, African-American poet (see page 402) and his wife, Daisy.

[2] **earthy axis.** Any of several definitions for *earthy* can be applied here: of, or consisting of the earth; characteristic of this world, worldly; hearty or uninhibited; unadorned or simple in style. This is an example of Harper's clever way with words; not only is the meaning of *earthy* left to interpretation, the phrase itself is also a twist on the common reference to the planet "turning on its earthly axis."

[3] **steel drivin' man.** A reference to folk hero John Henry

VOCABULARY IN PLACE

- **incarnate,** ***adj.*** Embodied in human form
- **stoic,** ***adj.*** Seemingly unaffected by pain or emotions; resilient
- **trestle,** ***n.*** A horizontal bar that acts as a support (in a bridge)

Use Trouble

by Michael S. Harper

For Jacob Armistead Lawrence[1]
1917–2000, in memorium

You told this to the children
when they confessed their works

were incomplete your dignity grace
a mapped space for trouble

your "migration" series at 23[2]
synaptic code[3] for having nothing

as you built off the backs of the poor
your symmetries where paint was talk

"gumbo yaya" Hayden[4] (your collaborator)
coined it about his native paradise valley

a nourishment of the Detroit ghetto[5]
while you were content with Harlem

a sixty-block walk to MoMA
for filial instruction

of the Italian Renaissance:[6]
now in Seattle they lay you down

those parts Indian of your heritage
in Chief Seattle's[7] words

"nothing is more sacred [ancient]
than the flow of blood in your veins
and in your tears"

migraines at gunpoint
bullet-ridden love song as migrants

to the highest plane
a vast battlefield of tones

over vegetation of the visible
where there is no insurance

yet in retrospective fantasy
to remake the spirit in your name

---

1 **Jacob Armistead Lawrence.** One of the most famous African-American painters of the twentieth century

2 **"migration" series at 23.** Lawrence's sixty-part mural, the "Migration Series," depicts the Great Migration of African Americans, specifically during the Great Depression. (See Gallery of African-American Art, page 772.) He was 23 years old when he finished the mural.

3 **synaptic code.** A *synapse* is the junction across which nerve impulses (signals) pass to a neuron, muscle cell, or gland. The poem's speaker suggests that the images in the mural externalize the mental (or emotional) state experienced by those who feel that they have nothing.

4 **"gumbo yaya" Hayden.** Gossip. *Gumbo yaya* is Creole patois (regional dialect or jargon) for "everybody talks." Hayden used the phrase in describing the social environment in his old neighborhood as well as the process and sources behind his poetry.

5 **paradise valley . . . Detroit ghetto.** During the first half of the twentieth century, Paradise Valley was a bustling commercial district and the center of African-American culture in Detroit with some seventeen jazz and blues venues.

6 **sixty-block . . . Italian Renaissance.** MoMA stands for Museum of Modern Art, which is in New York City. In 1935, Lawrence was mentored by a professor who, among other things, took him to an exhibit at the MoMA that greatly influenced the young artist. It is also true that Lawrence used to walk sixty blocks to receive instruction at the Metropolitan Museum of Art, where he studied the works of Italian Renaissance painters like Botticelli. In both cases, Lawrence followed a custom established during the Renaissance in which young artists served as apprentices to the masters. *Filial* refers to the relationship between parent and child.

7 **Chief Seattle.** (circa 1786–1866) Leader of the Duwamish, Suquamish, and other peoples of the Pacific Northwest. He is best remembered for a magnificent speech he delivered during treaty talks with the U.S. government in 1854.

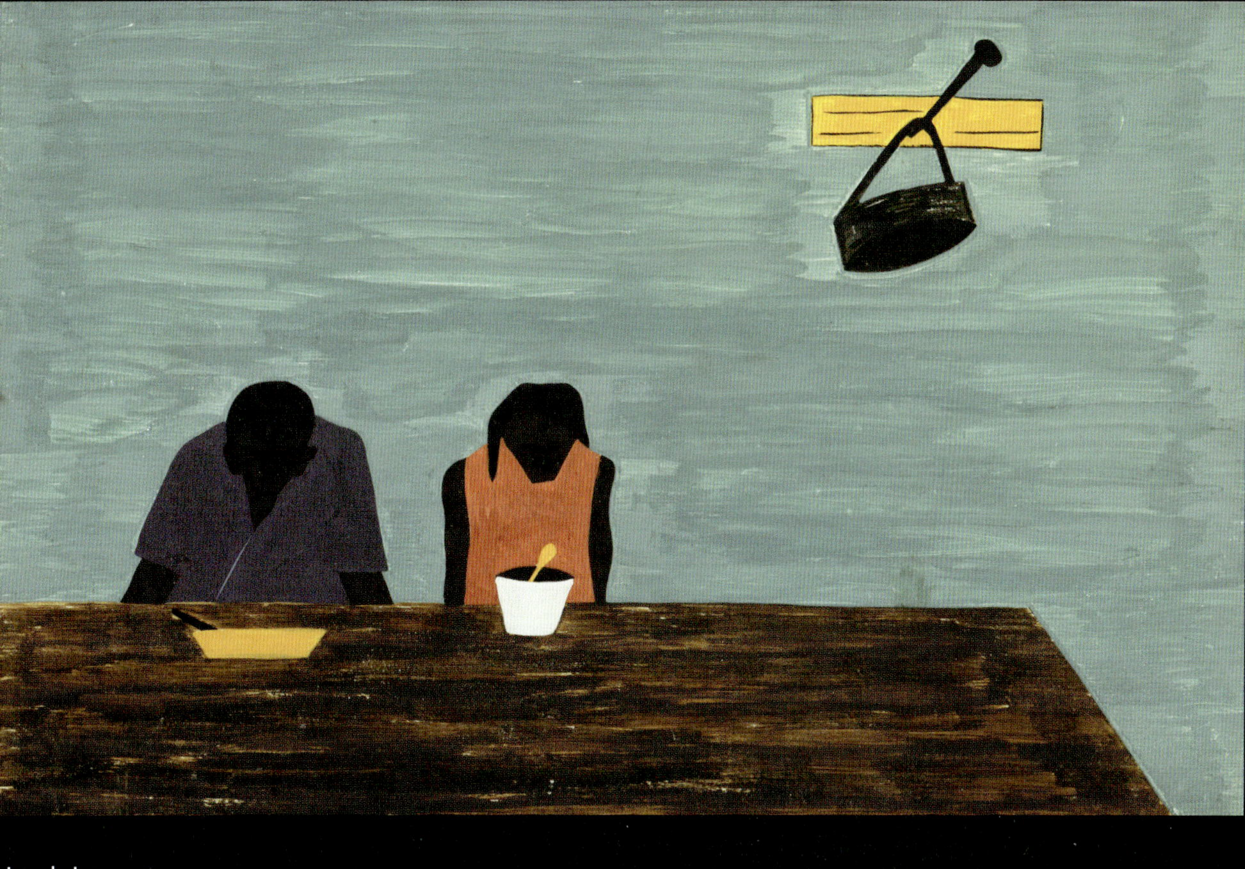

Jacob Lawrence
"Migration Series" (1940–41)
Panel 10, entitled "They were very poor"
See more art by Lawrence in the Gallery of African-American Art, page 772.

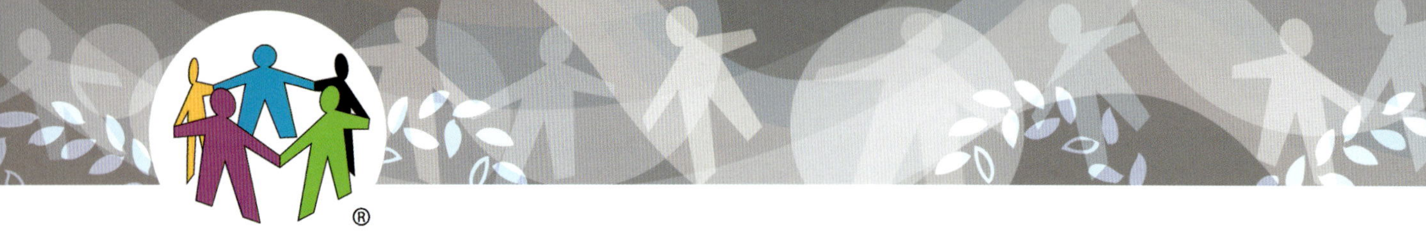

Understanding the Selection

Recalling

1. Who is a a "boomerang incarnate" in "Br'er Sterling and the Rocker"? What does a boomerang do?
2. What can poetry do to a straight line?
3. What hero does the speaker reference in line 10? What words are repeated in that same line? What is the chair, according to the speaker, in line 11?
4. In "Use Trouble," what was "a nourishment of the Detroit ghetto" (according to poet Robert Hayden)?

Interpreting

1. What is the speaker's attitude toward the Br'er in the rocker? Is it a good thing to be a "boomerang incarnate"? Why or why not?
2. What else can poetry do (lines 5–8)? Why do you think the poet used a colon at the end of line 8?
3. By alluding to folklore and the blues, what do you think the speaker is suggesting about Br'er Sterling and his poetry?
4. According to the speaker, where did Lawrence go to get his "nourishment"?

Synthesizing

1. Why is the person in the rocker like a boomerang? What might he be doing or talking and thinking about? Explain using a quotation from the text.
2. Harper uses poetry as a means to both praise and interpret the work of other artists, including musicians, painters, and fellow writers. Explain, using evidence from the poems, how he praises and interprets the works of Sterling Brown and Jacob Lawrence.

Delving Deeper

Understanding Literature

Evolution of Poetry. This is one of the last poetry selections in *Grace Abounding.* Whether you have read this anthology from the beginning or read only a few selections, it is important to take note of the evolution of poetry over the past two or three hundred years. **Evolution** is defined as "a gradual process in which something changes into a different and usually more complex or better form." Can it be said that the poetry of Michael Harper is "better" than that of Jupiter Hammon, Frances Harper, Paul Laurence Dunbar, Countee Cullen, or Langston Hughes? That will make an interesting discussion question, but there can be no definitive answer—in the end, the beauty of a poem is in the ear of the beholder. However, there is no doubt that poetry has changed by a steady, gradual process, punctuated by great waves of creative outpour, as in the **Harlem Renaissance** or **Black Arts Movement.** Poetry has also become far more complex: reader and writer alike approach poetry amidst the echoes of a vast choir of interconnected yet incredibly diverse voices—the "ancestors in the libraries," as Harper once called them.

Blues and Jazz Poetry. Harper's name will forever be linked to poet Sterling Brown, not only for the poem "Br'er Sterling and the Rocker," but also for the fact that Harper was heir to a distinctly African-American poetic style and form of which Brown is, if not the father, surely the best known progenitor. Blues and jazz musicians speak a language through their instruments, and that language, rooted in Africa's ancient past, has in fact only been defined and refined over the past hundred years or so. Harper, as well as Jay Wright, Robert Hayden, and others, express that same language—a language of the soul, of folklore and folk wisdom, and of the intricate web of human memory. Such poets do not seek to imitate blues and jazz music; they seek to extend it and to converse with it through its many modes and phases.

About the Author

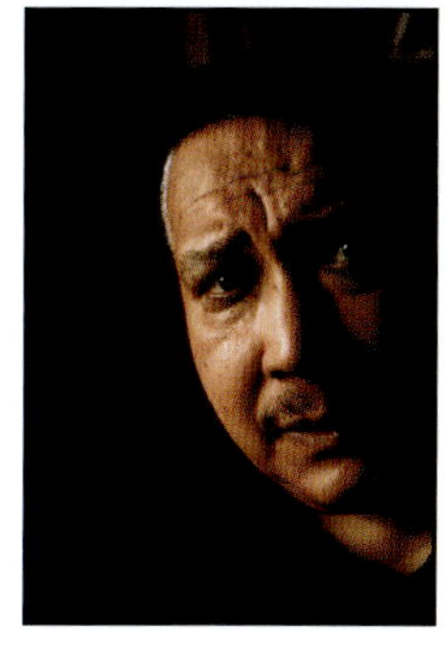

Michael S. Harper (b.1938), poet and professor in the Literary Arts Program at Brown University, has published no less than eight poetry collections since his first book of poetry, *Dear John Coltrane* (1970). The collection *Images of Kin* (1977) won the Melville-Cane Award and was nominated for the 1978 National Book Award. Harper was the first Poet Laureate of Rhode Island (1988–1993) and recipient of the National Endowment for the Arts Creative Writing Award. The highly regarded audio collection *Use Trouble* (2003) contains recordings of the poet reading twenty of his best-known poems.

Prereading

"Che," "The Season of Phantasmal Peace," "A Far Cry from Africa," and "A Map of the New World: I Archipelagoes"

by Derek Walcott

A poet with a painter's eye and great subtlety of thought and expression, Derek Walcott richly deserves the Nobel Prize in literature that he received in 1992. The press release issued by the Swedish Academy to announce the prize pointed out that Walcott draws his inspiration from three sources—from his Caribbean homeland, from the English language and literary tradition, and from his African heritage. The four poems included here are among Walcott's finest, but they by no means even begin to represent the richness of his work.

Che. Che Guevara (1928–1967) was a socialist revolutionary and guerrilla leader who helped Fidel Castro seize power in Cuba in 1959. Guevara left Cuba in 1965 to undertake revolutionary activities in the Congo and in Bolivia. He was captured and killed by the Bolivian army in 1967.

The Season of Phantasmal Peace. This poem takes place in October, the season when birds migrate. The speaker imagines the birds mythically lifting "the huge net of the shadows of the earth." The poem evokes, poignantly, the brevity and irreality of peace, which lasts for "one moment, like the pause / between dusk and darkness."

A Far Cry from Africa. This poem begins with a reference to an extended, bloody war that took place in Kenya in the 1950s. European settlers had forced the native Kikuyu people off their lands, and some Kikuyu responded by forming a militant opposition, the Mau Mau, which waged war against the British colonialists and those Kikuyu who supported them. Reflection on this event leads the speaker of the poem to think about his own troubled relationship with both the European and African parts of his heritage.

A Map of the New World: I *Archipelagoes.* According to ancient Greek myth, a Trojan prince, Paris, stole the beautiful Helen, wife of the Greek king Menelaus. In response, the Greeks raised an army, sailed for Troy, and laid siege to the city for ten years. The story of the siege of Troy is told in the ancient Greek epic poem the *Iliad,* attributed to the blind poet Homer. A second epic also attributed to Homer, the *Odyssey,* tells the story of the return home from Troy of one of the Greek heroes, Odysseus. At the beginning of Walcott's poem, Troy has been destroyed, and a boat sets sail from all of this destruction, seeking a harbor, or safe haven. The true harbor lies in the work of the imagination, which fashions of this terrible experience great art.

Che

by Derek Walcott

In this dark-grained news photograph, whose glare
is rigidly composed as Caravaggio's,[1]
the corpse glows candle-white on its cold altar—

its stone Bolivian[2] Indian butcher's slab—
stare till its **waxen** flesh begins to harden
to marble, to veined, white Andean[3] iron;
from your own fear, *cabron*,[4] its **pallor** grows;

it stumbled from your doubt, and for your pardon
burnt in brown trash, far from the **embalming** snows. ■

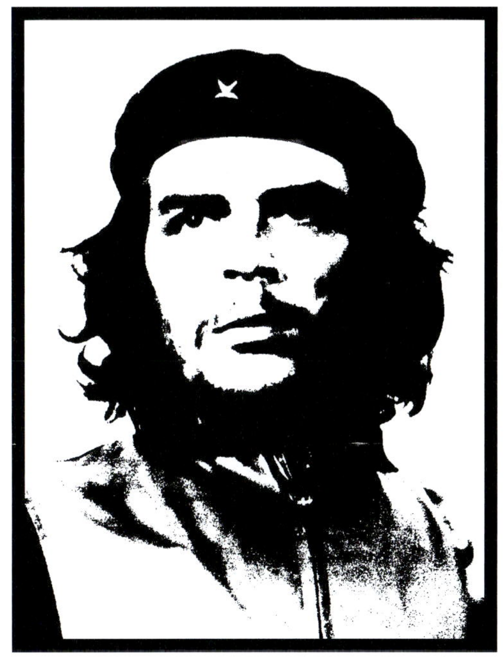

[1] **Caravaggio.** Michelangelo Merisi da Caravaggio (1573–1610), an Italian painter known for his realism and his use of *chiaroscuro,* a technique that emphasizes dramatic contrasts between darkness and light

[2] **Bolivian.** Bolivia, a country in South America, was the site of the killing of Che Guevara, who was involved in an attempted revolution there.

[3] **Andean.** Having to do with the Andes mountains

[4] **cabron.** Vulgar Spanish, literally a male goat; a derogatory term, sometimes used between intimates as a term of endearment

VOCABULARY IN PLACE

- **waxen,** ***adj.*** Like wax, lacking life
- **pallor,** ***n.*** Sickly whiteness
- **embalming,** ***part.*** Causing to be preserved in a manner that prevents decay

The Season of Phantasmal Peace

by Derek Walcott

Then all the nations of birds lifted together
the huge net of the shadows of this earth
in **multitudinous** dialects, twittering tongues,
stitching and crossing it. They lifted up
the shadows of long pines down trackless slopes,
the shadows of glass-faced towers down evening streets,
the shadow of a frail plant on a city sill—
the net rising soundless as night, the birds' cries soundless, until
there was no longer dusk, or season, **decline,** or weather,
only this passage of **phantasmal** light
that not the narrowest shadow dared to **sever.**

And men could not see, looking up, what the wild geese drew,
what the **ospreys** trailed behind them in silvery ropes
that flashed in the icy sunlight; they could not hear
battalions of starlings waging peaceful cries,
bearing the net higher, covering this world

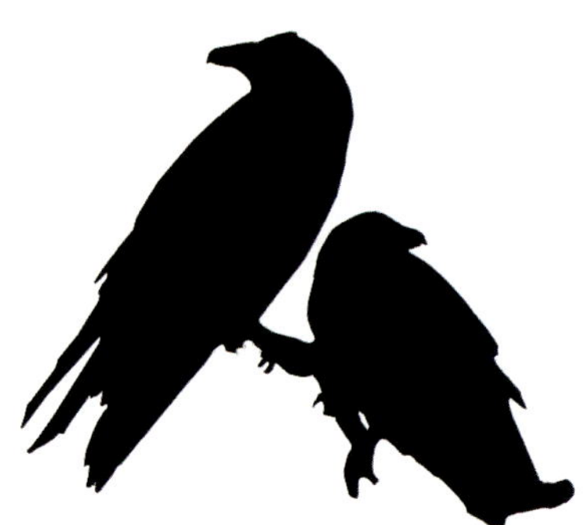

VOCABULARY IN PLACE

- **multitudinous,** ***adj.*** Very numerous
- **decline,** ***n.*** Sinking, or ending, as of the setting sun
- **phantasmal,** ***adj.*** Illusory, unreal, said of an apparition having no physical reality
- **sever,** ***v.*** To cut in two
- **osprey,** ***n.*** A large bird of prey
- **battalion,** ***n.*** A large body of troops

like the vines of an orchard, or a mother drawing
the trembling gauze over the trembling eyes
of a child fluttering to sleep;[1]
                                        it was the light
that you will see at evening on the side of a hill
in yellow October, and no one hearing knew
what change had brought into the raven's cawing,
the killdeer's[2] screech, the ember-circling chough[3]
such an immense, soundless, and high concern
for the fields and cities where the birds belong,
except it was their seasonal passing, Love,
made seasonless, or, from the high privilege of their birth,
something brighter than pity for the wingless ones
below them who shared dark holes in windows and in houses,
and higher they lifted the net with soundless voices
above all change, betrayals of falling suns,
and this season lasted one moment, like the pause
between dusk and darkness, between fury and peace,
but, for such as our earth is now, it lasted long. ■

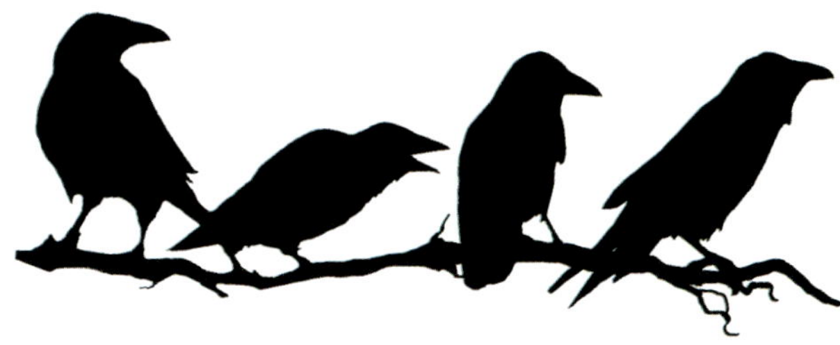

[1] **a mother . . . to sleep.** Perhaps a reference to using gauze, in a tropical region, to protect the eyes of a sleeping infant from insects

[2] **killdeer.** A New World bird, a type of plover, with a noisy call

[3] **chough.** An Old World bird similar to a crow, with a black body and red legs (pronounced /chuf/)

A Far Cry from Africa

by Derek Walcott

A wind is ruffling the **tawny pelt**
Of Africa. Kikuyu[1], quick as flies,
Batten upon the bloodstreams of the **veldt.**
Corpses are scattered through a paradise.
Only the worm, colonel of carrion,[2] cries:
"Waste no compassion on these separate dead!"
Statistics justify and scholars seize
The **salients** of colonial policy.
What is that to the white child hacked in bed?
To savages, expendable as Jews?[3]

Threshed out by beaters, the long rushes break
In a white dust of ibises[4] whose cries
Have wheeled since civilization's dawn
From the parched river or beast-teeming plain.
The violence of beast on beast is read
As natural law, but upright man
Seeks his **divinity** by inflicting pain.
Delirious as these worried beasts, his wars

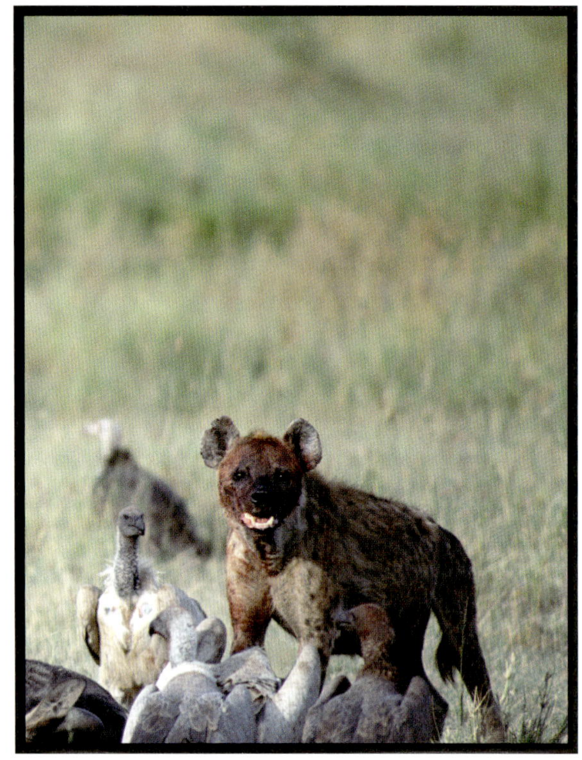

[1] **Kikuyu.** Tribal group in what is now Kenya

[2] **carrion.** Scavengers

[3] **expendable as Jews.** The speaker wonders whether the world will ignore this massacre as it ignored the Holocaust. (The phrase is ironic, not anti-Semitic.)

[4] **ibis.** Any of a number of storklike wading birds

VOCABULARY IN PLACE

- **tawny,** *adj.* A light brown to brownish orange
- **pelt,** *n.* Fur-covered skin
- **batten,** *v.* To eat until gorged, or full; fatten
- **veldt,** *n.* Any of the open grazing areas of central or southern Africa
- **salients,** *n.pl.* Facts that stand out, essential facts
- **divinity,** *n.* Godlike nature or appearance

Dance to the tightened **carcass** of a drum,
While he calls courage still that native **dread**
Of the white peace contracted by the dead.

Again **brutish** necessity wipes its hands
Upon the napkin of a dirty cause, again
A waste of our compassion, as with Spain,[5]
The gorilla wrestles with the superman.[6]
I who am poisoned with the blood of both,
Where shall I turn, divided to the vein?
I who have cursed
The drunken officer of British rule, how choose
Between this Africa and the English tongue I love?
Betray them both, or give back what they give?
How can I face such slaughter and be cool?
How can I turn from Africa and live? ■

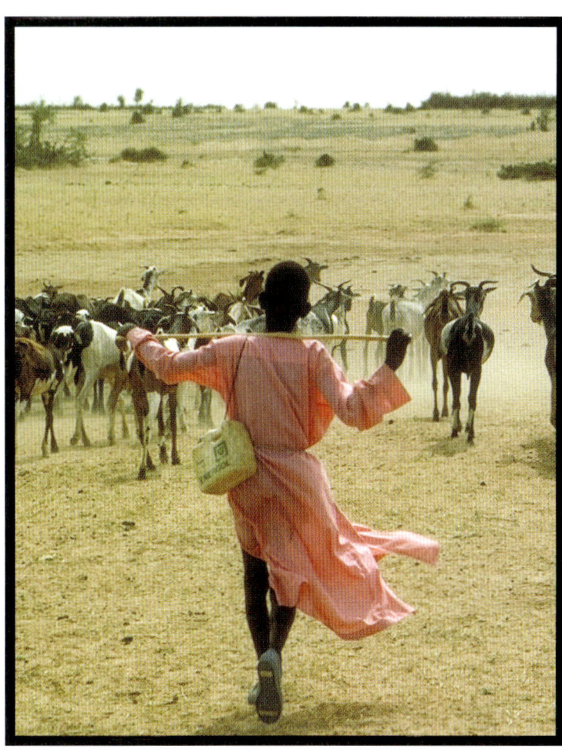

[5] **as with Spain.** A reference to the violent Spanish Civil War, fought between pro-Fascist and anti-Fascist forces

[6] **gorilla . . . superman.** Two stereotypical descriptions representing animal-like tribal peoples pitted against Europeans who, because of their technology-enhanced power, thought of themselves as superior, as "supermen"

VOCABULARY IN PLACE

- **carcass,** *n.* Dead body of an animal
- **dread,** *n.* Worry caused by fear
- **brutish,** *adj.* Uncivilized, savage

A Map of the New World: I Archipelagoes[1]

by Derek Walcott

At the end of this sentence, rain will begin.
At the rain's edge, a sail.

Slowly the sail will lose sight of islands;
into a mist will go the belief in harbours
of an entire race.

The ten-years war is finished.
Helen's[2] hair, a grey cloud.
Troy,[3] a white ashpit
by the drizzling sea.

The drizzle tightens like the strings of a harp.
A man with clouded eyes[4] picks up the rain
and plucks the first line of the *Odyssey.*[5] ■

---

[1] **Archipelago.** A sea containing a large number of scattered islands. The Aegean Sea, between Troy and Greece, is an archipelago.

[2] **Helen.** Wife of the Greek king Menelaus, stolen away by Paris, a Trojan prince; reputedly the most beautiful of all women

[3] **Troy.** City destroyed by the Greeks in the Trojan War

[4] **man with clouded eyes.** According to tradition, Homer, the Greek poet to whom the *Iliad* and the *Odyssey* are attributed, was blind. The *Iliad* tells the story of the Trojan War. See note 5 on the *Odyssey,* below. Ancient Greek poets recited their works accompanied by a harp or lyre.

[5] **Odyssey.** A Greek epic poem, traditionally attributed to Homer, that tells of the voyage home and strange adventures of the Greek hero Odysseus, who fought at Troy

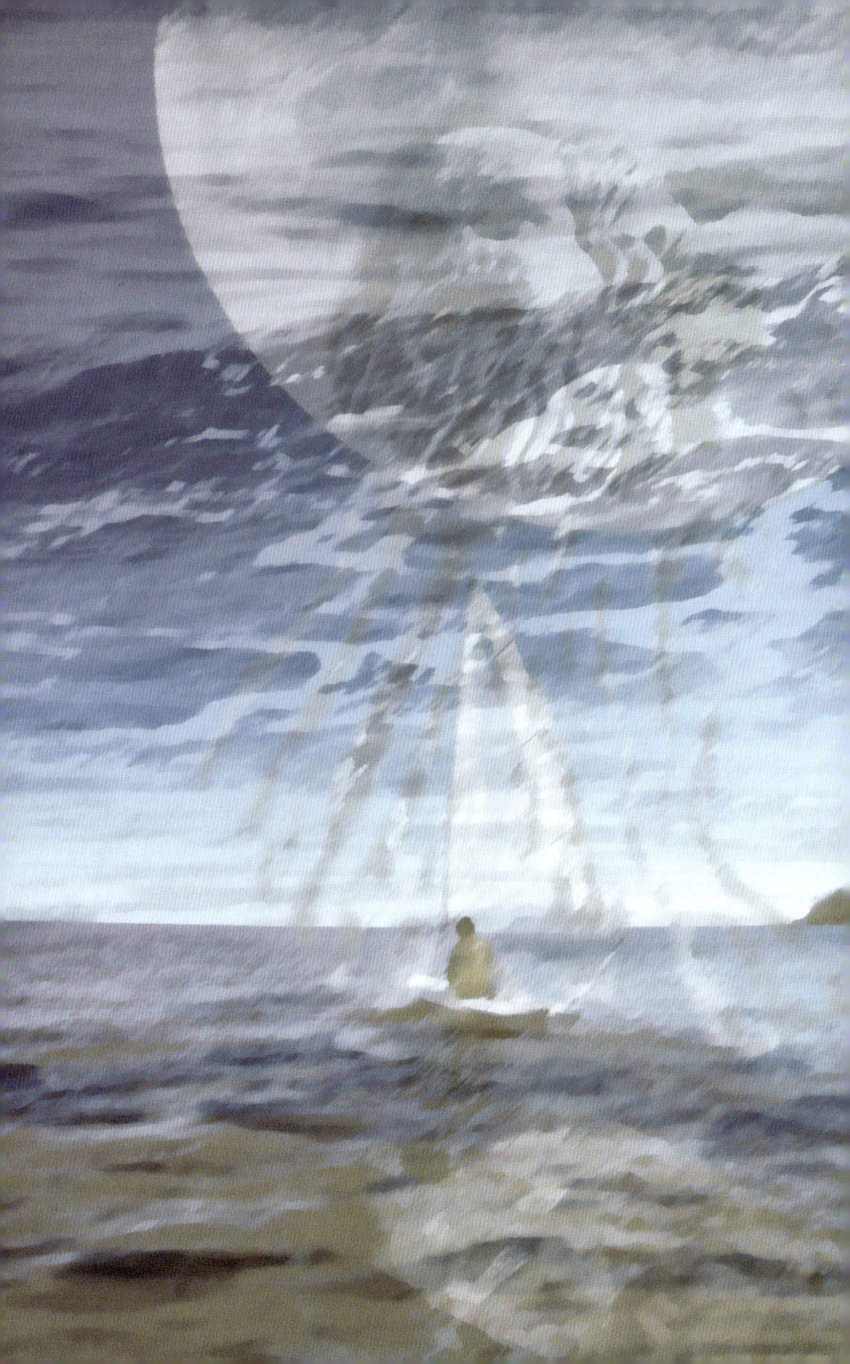

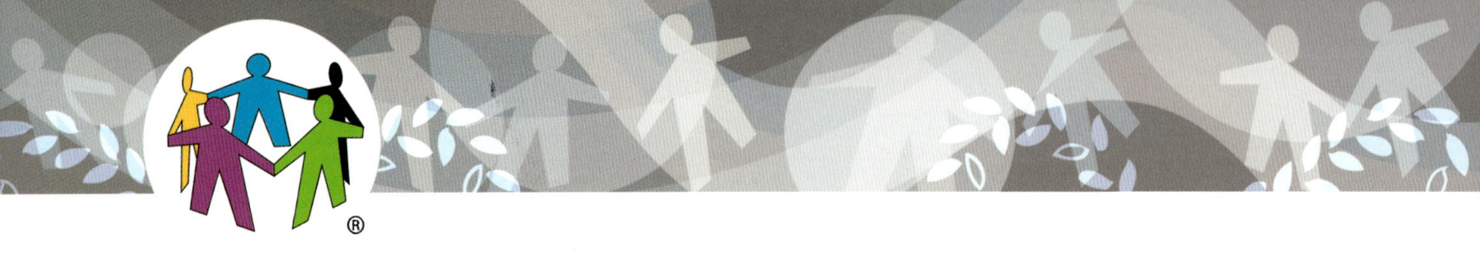

Understanding the Selection

Recalling

1. What does the speaker imagine Che's body becoming?

2. What is lifted up by all the nations of the birds in "The Season of Phantasmal Peace"?

3. What events and actions described in lines 1–25 horrify the speaker of "A Far Cry from Africa"? What does the speaker say of his own blood?

4. What, according to the first line of "A Map of the New World: I Archipelagoes" happens at the end of the first sentence?

Interpreting

1. Why might Che be stronger, more like iron, in death than in life? What does the person addressed in line 7 have to fear?

2. The word *phantasmal* means unreal. What is the speaker saying about this brief moment of peace? How long, according to line 33, did it last?

3. Walcott claims both European and African ancestry and influences. What about these events between Colonial and African peoples makes him unhappy with both?

4. In what way does a poet bring things into existence, as if by magic? Who "picks up the rain," so like the strings of a harp, and what does he produce?

Synthesizing

1. Each of these poems can be thought of as reflections on particular events—the appearance of a photograph of the dead Che in a newspaper, the migration of birds in the autumn, a bloody Colonial battle in Africa, the destruction of the city of Troy. What reflections does the speaker have about each of these events?

Delving Deeper

A Reading of the Selection

A Map of the New World: I Archipelagoes. A writer has the ability to bring a world into existence as if by magic: "At the end of this sentence, rain will begin." The rain appears in the imagination of the reader. So, at the end of the Trojan War, after all the devastation, in the midst of a rain that symbolizes the natural reaction to such calamity, the poet, Homer, picks up the rain (that is, responds emotionally to it and to the recent events), and plucks this emotion, like the strings of a harp, and creates the first lines of a poem about setting out from all that devastation onto a sea of perils and adventures. The "new world" is one of archipelagoes, islands created in the sea of the imagination. Out of the most horrific and tragic of experiences—the destruction and burning of the city of Troy—comes this, what is saved from the ruins, the art that experience makes possible.

About the Author

Derek Walcott (b.1930) was born in Castries, St. Lucia, an isolated Caribbean island. His father, an artist, died when Walcott was quite young. His mother, a teacher, was well read and taught her children to love poetry. Walcott was educated at the University College of the West Indies in Kingston, Jamaica, where he studied French, Latin, and Spanish. He lived for a time in Trinidad, studied theater in New York, worked as a teacher on several Caribbean islands, and also worked as a journalist and then as a professor of English at Boston University. He is an accomplished painter as well as a superb poet.

As a poet, he made his debut at the age of eighteen with *Twenty-Five Poems,* which was privately printed. His widespread recognition as a poet came with *In a Green Light* (1964). Other works include *Castaway* (1965), *The Gulf* (1969), *The Fortunate Traveler* (1981), *Midsummer* (1984), and the epic poem *Omeros* (1990). This last work takes its title from the Greek for *Homer* and recasts Homeric themes in a Caribbean setting. A self-described "mulatto of style," Walcott is a native English speaker and a speaker of West Indian Creole. He has written in both languages. In 1992, he received the Nobel Prize for Literature.

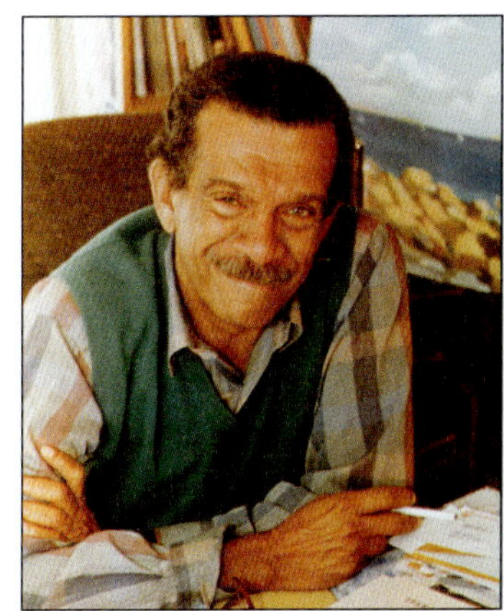

Prereading

"Benjamin Banneker Sends His Almanac to Thomas Jefferson"

by Jay Wright

The eminent literary critic and educator Harold Bloom grants Jay Wright status among a select few "major" poets alive today. Not every academic in the poetry establishment agrees with Bloom's theories about literature, but one thing is certain: Bloom knows poetry as well as anyone in the United States. When he hears or reads a poem, he instantly compares and contrasts it with the innumerable poems stored in his gifted mind. Praise from Bloom can make a poet's career.

Much of Wright's work deals with historical events and themes. This poem is a touching meditation on Banneker's accomplishments, his courage, and the challenge he faced when he sat down to write his letter to Thomas Jefferson. It is also an **apostrophe**, a work that addresses the absent Banneker, with sadness and with profound respect.

This poem is, of course, based on a true event, and readers are strongly encouraged to read Banneker's "Letter to Thomas Jefferson" on page 151, as well as Jefferson's brief reply on page 155. Wright's poem can certainly stand on its own, but the reader should have a minimum of background knowledge on the subject: Benjamin Banneker, an eighteenth-century African-American astronomer, published an almanac from 1792–1797 containing his own astronomical calculations and predictions. He gave Jefferson a copy of his manuscript in 1791 and composed an incredible letter encouraging the future president to reject notions that black people were intellectually inferior to whites and to work toward ending slavery.

All readers will benefit by first reading Banneker's letter and understanding the way in which he crafts his argument, tapping into Jefferson's own words and his insistence on natural human rights. Banneker's letter did not have its intended effect on Jefferson, but the Sable Astronomer, as he was known, would be glad to hear Wright's poem and to know that you remember him, as well.

Benjamin Banneker Sends His Almanac to Thomas Jefferson

by Jay Wright

Old now,
your eyes nearly blank
from plotting the light's
movement over the years,
you clean your Almanac
and place it next
to the heart of this letter.
I have you in mind,
giving a final brush and twist
to the difficult pages,
staring down the shape of the numbers
as though you would find a flaw
in their forms.
Solid, these calculations
verify your body on God's earth.
At night,
the stars submit themselves
to the remembered way you turn them;[1]
the moon **gloats** under your attention.
I, who know so little of stars,
whose only acquaintance with the moon
is to read a myth, or to listen
to the surge
of songs the women know,
sit in your marvelous reading[2]
of all movement,
of all relations.

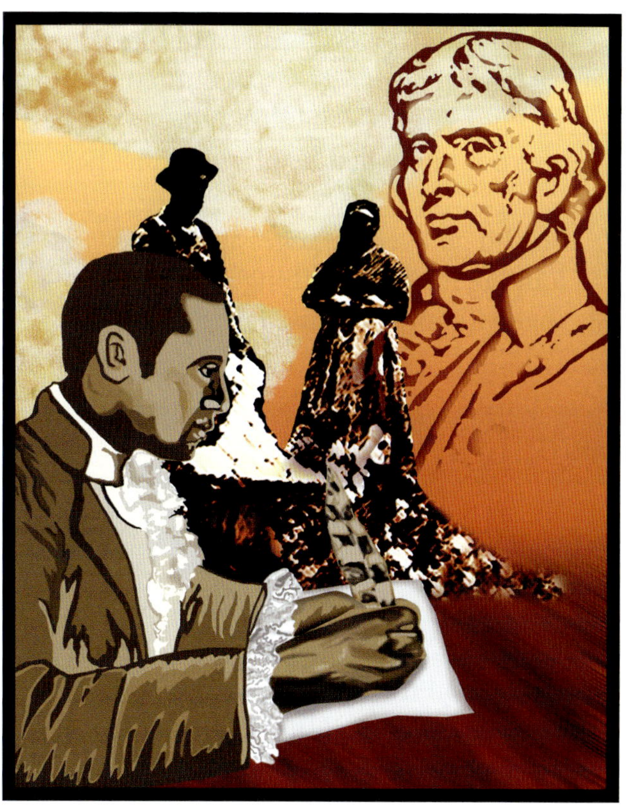

[1] **the stars . . . you turn them.** Banneker's calculations are so accurate that one might think he wields control over the stars.

[2] **reading.** Interpretation

VOCABULARY IN PLACE

• **gloat,** *v.* To feel or express great self-satisfaction

So you look into what we see
yet cannot see,
and shape and take a language
to give form to one or the other,
believing no form will escape,
no movement appear, nor stop,
without explanation,
believing no reason is only reason,
nor without reason.
I read all of this into your task,
all of this into the uneasy
reproof of your letter.[3]

Surely, there must be a flaw.
These perfect calculations fall apart.
There are silences
that no perfect number can retrieve,
omissions no perfect line could catch.
How could a man but challenge God's
impartial distributions?
How could a man sit among
the free and ordered movements
of stars, and waters, beasts and birds,
each movement seen or accounted for,
and not know God jealous,
and not know that he himself must be?

So you go over the pages again,
looking for the one thing
that will not reveal itself,
judging what you have received,
what you have shaped,
believing it cannot be strange
to the man you address.
But you are strange to him
—your skin, your tongue,
the movement of your body,
even your mysterious ways with stars.
You argue here with the man and God,
and know that no man can be right,
and know that no God will argue right.
Your letter turns on what the man knows,
on what God, you think, would have us
    know.
All stars will forever move under your gaze,
truthfully, leading you from line to line,
from number to number, from truth to
    truth,
while the man will read your soul's desire,
searcher, searching yourself,
losing the relations. ■

---

[3] **uneasy reproof of your letter.** A reference to the letter in which Banneker—delicately and respectfully, yet with force and frankness—criticized Jefferson for his stance on slavery

VOCABULARY IN PLACE

- **reproof,** *n.* The act of voicing disapproval; rebuke
- **omission,** *n.* Something intentionally left out or discarded
- **impartial,** *adj.* Unprejudiced, fair

About the Author

Jay Wright (b.1935), poet and playwright, was born in Albuquerque, New Mexico. His work often revolves around historical or spiritual themes, and he is sometimes called a "blues poet," meaning that his poetry reflects the language, rhythm, and mood of blues music (particularly with regard to dialect and setting). He received a MacArthur Fellowship in 1986 and the Bollingen Prize for poetry in 2005. His poetry collections include *The Homecoming Singer* (1971), *Dimensions of History* (1976), *Soothsayers and Omens* (1976), *The Double Invention of Komo* (1980), *Elaine's Book* (1986), and *Transfigurations: Collected Poems.*

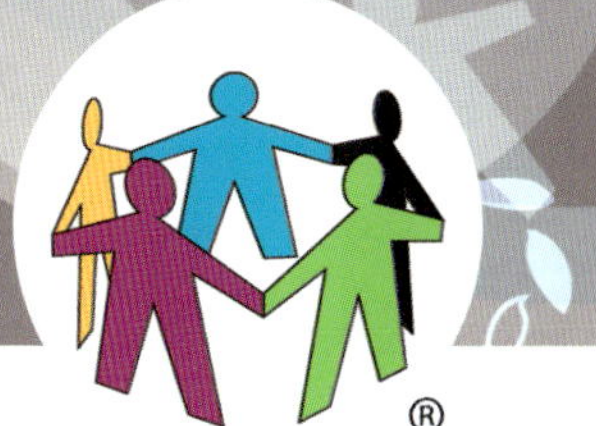

Understanding the Selection

Recalling

1. Whom is the speaker of the poem addressing? Why are this person's eyes "nearly blank"?
2. What does Banneker do to his Almanac?
3. What do Banneker's calculations do (lines 14–19)?
4. What does the speaker question in the second stanza (lines 40–52)?
5. According to the speaker, what does Banneker believe about his calculations and what Jefferson will think of them (lines 58–59)?
6. On what does Banneker's letter turn (line 67)?

Interpreting

1. Describe the speaker's tone. How does he feel about Banneker? What tone of voice would you use if you read the poem aloud?
2. What does the speaker mean when he refers to the "heart" of Banneker's letter?
3. Does the poem's speaker truly understand Banneker's calculations? Why does he praise Banneker so much?
4. How does the speaker's tone change in the second stanza? Why does Banneker go over the pages again (line 53)?
5. What does the speaker tell Banneker in line 60? Why is this so?
6. What do you think the speaker means in line 68?

Synthesizing

1. Where will the stars lead Banneker? Is Banneker the searcher, searching himself (line 73)? What will be lost (line 74)? Who will lose it, Banneker or "the man"?
2. Wright has a knack for slipping subtle, original, and imaginative phrases into his work, such as "remembered ways you turn them" (line 18). Select another line or phrase from the poem and explain why you think it is interesting or unique.

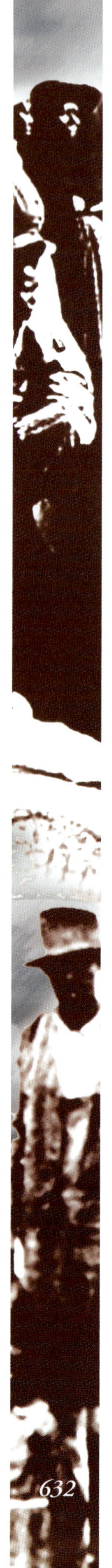

Prereading

"The Man Who Saw the Flood"

by Richard Wright

Wright could easily have been included in Unit 3 of *Grace Abounding,* since much of the subject matter of his writing occurred during the first three decades of the twentieth century, and many of his short stories appeared in the 1930s. However, Richard Wright's name became widely known only after the publication of the novels *Native Son* (1940) and *Black Boy* (1945), and his career peaked in 1947. So, his work spanned a period of incredible transition.

This story, first published in 1937 with the title "Silt," is one of a number by Richard Wright about the Mississippi flood of 1927. (See the History Connection on page 637.) Like many of Wright's stories, novels, and poetry, this one focuses on the hardships faced by African Americans in the deep South during the first half of the twentieth century.

Sharecropping, or tenant farming, became common throughout the South following the Civil War and remained a sad reality for poor people—black and white alike—through the 1950s and beyond. A sharecropper was required to give a large portion of his crop yields to the landlord, and often there was barely enough left over to enable the farmer and his family to scrape by.

In fact, more often than not, the sharecropper had to borrow money or equipment from the landlord or from another lender just to get started, and therein lies the great trap of sharecropping. The sharecropper's earnings from one year simply went to pay debts from the preceding year, and so the cycle of debt was unending and there was little hope for escape. To make matters worse, if a natural disaster wiped out the tenant's fields and equipment, he was still liable for all of his debts. This is the sort of no-win situation experienced by the family in "The Man Who Saw the Flood."

Richard Wright often wrote in the **vernacular,** that is, in the everyday language of a given region or group of people. The southern vernacular in the dialogue sections of this story reflects the kind of language that Wright listened to throughout his youth, growing up as the son of a sharecropper.

Hopelessness, abject poverty, and racism—Richard Wright was all too familiar with the hardships of the sharecropper's life where the steady love of family was one's most valuable possession.

The Man Who Saw the Flood

by Richard Wright

*When the flood waters **recede,** the poor folk along the river start from scratch.*

At last the flood waters had receded. A black father, a black mother, and a black child tramped through muddy fields, leading a tired cow by a thin bit of rope. They stopped on a hilltop and shifted the bundles on their shoulders. As far as they could see the ground was covered with flood **silt.** The little girl lifted a skinny finger and pointed to a mudcaked cabin.

"Look, Pa! Ain that our home?"

The man, round-shouldered, clad in blue, ragged overalls, looked with bewildered eyes. Without moving a muscle, scarcely moving his lips, he said: "Yeah."

For five minutes they did not speak or move. The flood waters had been more than eight feet high here. Every tree, blade of grass, and stray stick had its flood mark; caky, yellow mud. It clung to the ground, cracking thinly here and there in spider web fashion. Over the **stark** fields came a gusty spring wind. The sky was high, blue, full of white clouds and sunshine. Over all hung a first-day strangeness.

VOCABULARY IN PLACE

- **recede,** ***v.*** To move back
- **silt,** ***n.*** Sedimentary material consisting of very fine particles
- **stark,** ***adj.*** Barren; harsh or grim

"The henhouse is gone," sighed the woman.

"N the pigpen," sighed the man.

They spoke without bitterness.

"Ah reckon them chickens is all done drowned."

"Yeah."

"Miz Flora's house is gone, too," said the little girl.

They looked at a clump of trees where their neighbor's house had stood.

"Lawd!"

"Yuh reckon anybody knows where they is?"

"Hard t tell."

The man walked down the slope and stood uncertainly.

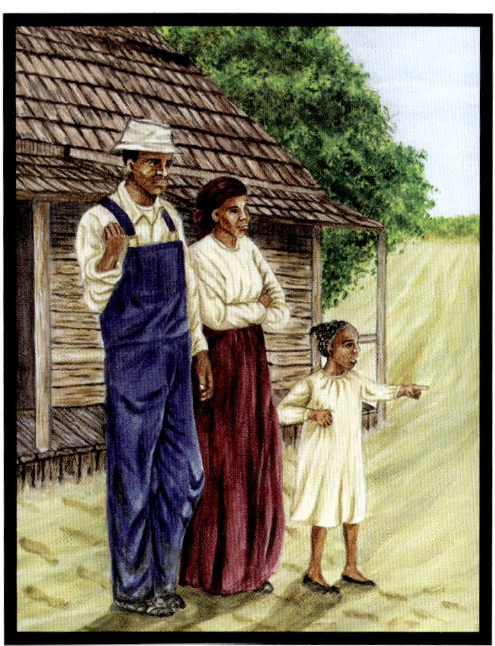

"There wuz a road erlong here somewheres," he said.

But there was no road now. Just a wide sweep of yellow, scalloped[1] silt.

"Look, Tom!" called the woman. "Here's a piece of our gate!"

The gatepost was half buried in the ground. A rusty hinge stood stiff, like a lonely finger. Tom pried it loose and caught it firmly in his hand. There was nothing particular he wanted to do with it; he just stood holding it firmly. Finally he dropped it, looked up, and said:

"C mon. Les go down n see whut we kin do." Because it sat in a slight depression, the ground about the cabin was soft and slimy.

"Gimme tha bag o lime,[2] May," he said.

With his shoes sucking in mud, he went slowly around the cabin, spreading the white lime with thick fingers. When he reached the front again he had a little left; he shook the bag out on the porch. The fine grains of floating lime flickered in the sunlight.

"Tha oughta hep some." He said.

"Now, yuh be careful, Sal!" said May. "Don yuh go n fall down in all this mud, yuh hear?"

"Yessum."

The steps were gone. Tom lifted May and Sally to the porch. They stood a moment looking at the half-opened door. He had shut it when he left, but somehow it seemed natural that he should find it open. The planks in the porch floor were swollen and warped. The cabin had two colors; near the bottom it was a solid yellow, at the top it was the familiar gray. It looked weird, as though its ghost were standing beside it.

The cow **lowed.**

"Tie Pat t the pos on the en of the porch, May."

May tied the rope slowly, **listlessly.** When they attempted to open the front door, it would not budge. It was not until Tom placed his shoulder against it and gave it a stout shove that it scraped back jerkily. The front room was dark and silent. The damp smell of flood silt came fresh and sharp to their nostrils. Only one-half of the upper window was clear, and through it fell a rectangle of dingy light. The floors swam in ooze. Like a mute warning, a wavering flood mark went high around the walls of the room. A dresser sat cater-cornered,[3] its drawers and sides bulging like a bloated corpse. The bed, with the mattress still on it, was like a giant casket forged of mud. Two smashed chairs lay in a corner, as though huddled together for protection.

"Les see the kitchen," said Tom.

"The stove's still good. We kin clean it."

"Yeah."

"But where's the table?"

"Lawd knows."

"It must've washed erway wid the rest of the stuff, Ah reckon."

They opened the back door and looked out.

They missed the barn, the henhouse, and the pigpen.

"Tom, yuh bettah try tha ol pump n see ef eny watah's there."

The pump was stiff. Tom threw his weight on the handle and carried it up and

[1] **scalloped.** Edged with a series of curved projections

[2] **lime.** Calcium oxide (compound of calcium and oxygen). In powder form, this substance can be spread around an affected area and used to control bacteria.

[3] **cater-cornered.** Diagonal; in a diagonal position. One of several variants of *catty-corner.*

VOCABULARY IN PLACE

- **low,** *v.* To call; to moo
- **listlessly,** *adv.* Lazily, without energy

down. No water came. He pumped on. There was a dry hollow cough. Then yellow water trickled. He coughed his breath and kept pumping. The water flowed white.

"Thank Gawd! We's got some watah."

"Yuh bettah boil it[4] fo yuh use it," he said.

"Yeah. Ah know."

"Look, Pa! Here's you ax," called Sally.

Tom took the ax from her. "Yeah. Ah'll need this."

"N here's something else," called Sally, digging spoons out of the mud.

"Waal, Ahma git a bucket n start cleanin," said May. "Ain no use in waitin, cause we's gotta sleep on them floors tonight."

When she was filling the bucket from the pump, Tom called from around the cabin. "May, look! Ah done foun mah plow!" Proudly he dragged the silt-caked plow to the pump. "Ah'll wash it n it'll be awright."

"Ahm hungry," said Sally.

"Now, yuh jus wait! Yuh et this mawnin," said May. She turned to Tom. "Now, whutcha gonna do, Tom?"

He stood looking at the mud-filled fields.

"Yuh goin back t Burgess?"

"Ah reckon Ah have to."

"Whut else kin yuh do?"

"Nothin," he said. "Lawd, but Ah sho hate t start all over wid tha white man. Ah'd leave here ef Ah could. Ah owes im nigh eight hundred dollahs. N we needs a hoss, grub, seed, n a lot mo other things. Ef we keeps on like this tha white man'll own us body n soul."

"But, Tom, there ain nothing else t do," she said.

"Ef we try t run erway they'll put us in jail."

"It coulda been worse," she said.

Sally came running from the kitchen. "Pa!"

"Hunh?"

"There's a shelf in the kitchen the flood didn't git!"

"Where?"

"Right up over the stove."

"But, chile, ain nothing up there," said May.

"But there's something on it," said Sally.

"C mon. Les see."

High and dry, untouched by the flood-water, was a box of matches. And beside it a half-full sack of Bull Durham tobacco. He took a match from the box and scratched it on his overalls. It burned to his fingers before he dropped it.

"May!"

"Hunh?"

"Look! Here's ma bacco n some matches!"

She stared unbelievingly. "Lawd!" she breathed.

Tom rolled a cigarette clumsily.

May washed the stove, gathered some sticks, and after some difficulty, made a fire. The kitchen stove smoked, and their eyes

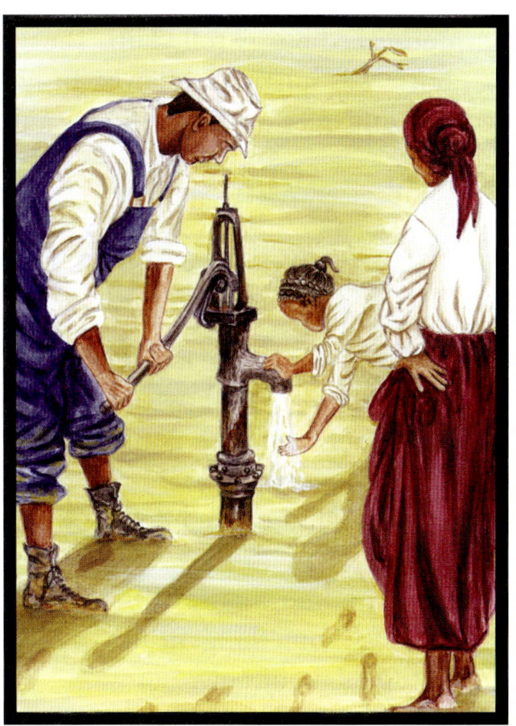

[4] **boil it.** Boiling purifies the water, which has probably been contaminated as a result of the flood.

smarted. May put water on to heat and went into the front room. It was getting dark. From the bundles they took a kerosene lamp and lit it. Outside Pat lowed longingly into the thickening gloam[5] and tinkled her cowbell.

"Tha old cow' hungry," said May.

"Ah reckon Ah'll have t be gittin erlong t Burgess."

They stood on the front porch.

"Yuh bettah git on, Tom, fo it gits too dark."

"Yeah."

The wind had stopped blowing. In the east a cluster of stars hung.

"Yuh goin, Tom?"

"Ah reckon Ah have t."

"Ma, Ah'm hungry," said Sally.

"Wait erwhile, honey. Ma knows yuh's hungry."

Tom threw his cigarette away and sighed.

"Look! Here comes somebody!"

"Thas Mistah Burgess now!"

A mud-caked buggy rolled up. The shaggy horse was splattered all over. Burgess leaned his white face out of the buggy and spat.

"Well, I see you're back."

"Yessuh."

"How things look?"

"They don look so good, Mistah."

"What seems to be the trouble?"

"Waal. Ah ain got no hoss, no grub, nothing. The only thing Ah got is tha ol cow there . . ."

"You owe eight hundred dollahs down at the store, Tom."

"Yessuh, Ah know. But, Mistah Burgess, can't yuh knock something off tha, seein as how Ahm down n out now?"

"You ate that grub, and I got to pay for it, Tom."

"Yessuh, Ah know."

"It's going to be a little tough, Tom. But you got to go through with it. Two of the boys tried to run away this morning and dodge their debts, and I had to have the sheriff pick em up. I wasn't looking for no trouble out of you, Tom . . . The rest of the families are going back."

Leaning out of the buggy, Burgess waited. In the surrounding stillness the cowbell tinkled again. Tom stood with his back against a post.

"Yuh got t go on, Tom. We ain't got nothing here," said May.

Tom looked at Burgess.

"Mistah Burgess, Ah don wanna make no trouble. But this is jus *too* hard. Ahm worse off now than befo. Ah got to start from scratch."

"Get in the buggy and come with me. I'll stake you with grub. We can talk over how you can pay it back." Tom said nothing. He rested his back against the post and looked at the mud-filled fields.

"Well," asked Burgess. "You coming?" Tom said nothing. He got slowly to the ground and pulled himself into the buggy. May watched them drive off.

"Hurry back, Tom!"

"Awright."

"Ma, tell Pa t bring me some 'lasses,"[6] begged Sally.

"Oh, Tom!"

Tom's head came out of the side of the buggy.

"Hunh?"

"Bring some 'lasses for Sal!"

"A wright!"

She watched the buggy disappear over the crest of the muddy hill. Then she sighed, caught Sally's hand, and turned back into the cabin. ■

---

5 **gloam.** (Archaic) Twilight, dusk

6 **'lasses.** Molasses

History Connection

The Flood of 1927. Beginning early in the nineteenth century, levees were built along the banks of the Mississippi River above the city of New Orleans to control flooding. Following the Civil War, the Confederate Colonel W. A. Percy returned home to Greenville, Mississippi, and lobbied the state government to build more levees to protect his family's farmlands. He built a massive farming empire based on black sharecropper labor. Over the coming decades, as the Percy empire spread, harsh, discriminatory Jim Crow laws were passed to keep African Americans from attaining any political power and to ensure that they would remain dependent workers. At the same time, the Army Corps of Engineers instituted a "levees only" policy to control flooding along the river, instead of depending on natural outlets and spillways. In the fall of 1926, heavy rains occurred along tributaries that fed into the Mississippi. The river rose to dangerous heights. More rains occurred in Mississippi and Louisiana in March and April, and on April 16, 1927, a 1,200-foot stretch of levee collapsed just below Cairo, Illinois, and nearly 200,000 acres of land were flooded. On April 21, a levee burst in Greenville, Mississippi, with similar disastrous results. The town and surrounding land turned into a raging sea. Thirteen thousand African Americans were stranded on the remaining unbroken levees, but the local Flood Relief Committee refused to evacuate these people, for fear that they would flee the region and be unavailable to work after the flood waters receded. Meanwhile, most whites were evacuated, and most relief supplies went to whites while blacks suffered horribly in makeshift camps established on the levees and patrolled by the National Guard. (Compare this information with Wynton Marsalis, *Speech at Tulane,* page 528.)

Plight of the American Sharecropper. (Students must complete this activity prior to beginning the Writing activity on page 639.) It started with "40 acres and a mule." That was Union General **William Tecumseh Sherman's** promise and the duty of the **Freedmen's Bureau** immediately following the Civil War. Forty thousand African Americans were granted this allotment of land in the South, but **Andrew Johnson** (U.S. President, 1865–1869) rescinded the land titles and returned the land to the original plantation owners.

Thereafter, poverty-stricken blacks (and whites) throughout the South found themselves with little choice other than to become tenants on the land, working themselves to the bone and getting almost nothing in return. This resembled a life of slavery in many ways. For decades, sharecroppers lived at the mercy of both the landlords and the law, always in debt with nowhere to turn, always toiling for someone else's profits. Black sharecroppers faced additional hardships in a society riddled with racism, hatred, and distrust, where those sworn to uphold the law sometimes joined ranks with lynch mobs.

Students should browse the hundreds of images available under the keyword "sharecropper" in the **Library of Congress** online image collection. Many of these images were collected by the Department of Agriculture simply for the purpose of documenting the depth of hardship suffered by these Americans. Here, students will also find the famous photographs of **Walker Evans,** whose work reveals that the human face of abject poverty is the same regardless of race.

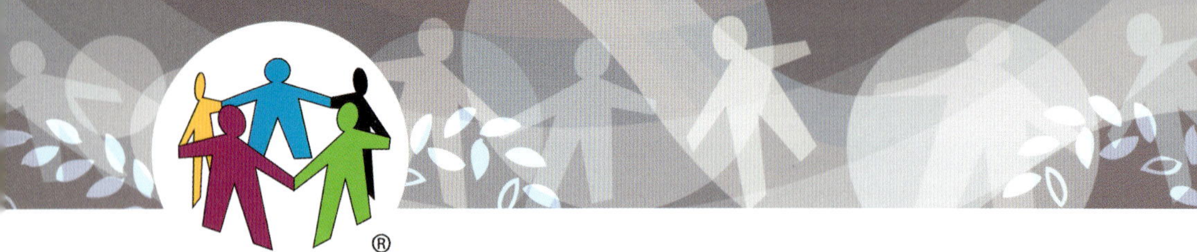

Understanding the Selection

Recalling

1. What has happened to the family's farm? Using details or descriptive words from the text, briefly describe changes that have occurred to their surroundings.
2. Does the family own the farm?
3. To whom does Tom owe money?
4. What does the little girl complain about twice during the story?
5. Why does Mr. Burgess come to the farm?

Interpreting

1. Did this family have much to lose in the first place? How do you know?
2. Why can't they simply leave their farm?
3. How is he going to pay it back?
4. How does the mother's response to the girl's complaints change over the course of the story? Provide specific examples from the text to support your answer.
5. Is Mr. Burgess sympathetic to the family's problems? Is he likely to give them much support? Explain your reasoning.

Synthesizing

1. Identify at least three things that the family finds that seem to give them some hope or relief. Which family member seems to be the most hopeful or encouraging? Find one quotation from the text to support your answer.
2. What do you think will happen to the family? Will things change for better, for worse, or not at all?

Delving Deeper

Writing

Sharecroppers During the Great Depression. Richard Wright published this story late in the Great Depression. He was not the only writer or artist at the time who focused on the plight of sharecroppers and other small farmers during those troubled years. In truth, though, sharecroppers had always lived in total poverty, and so the difficulties of the Depression made things worse, but sharecroppers could endure just about anything if it didn't kill them outright. That strength is evident in all the faces in the Library of Congress image collection. (See the History Connection on page 637.)

Browse through the collection of sharecropper images and choose one that you find particularly interesting, whether it is a portrait, a landscape, or other scene. Study the picture closely and take notes about specific details, including facial features, clothing, skin, and other important elements of the photo. Identify at least ten details that you feel are especially important or striking. Use your images to write a poem or song from the perspective of the person or people in the photo or an observer of the scene.

About the Author

Richard Wright (1908–1960) was born in Roxie, Mississippi, to a schoolteacher mother and a sharecropper father. When he was a small child, Wright moved to Memphis, Tennessee, with his mother. At eleven, when his mother became very ill, he went back to Mississippi, where he was raised by his grandmother, who was strict in the ways of her religion and believed that fictional literature was evil.

The young Richard Wright read voraciously, for a time, by borrowing a Memphis library card from a white friend since he was not allowed to have his own. At 19, Wright moved to Chicago and got a job as a postal clerk. He actually finished his first novel, *Lawd Today,* in 1935, though it was not published until 1963 (posthumously). The novel tells the story of a single day in the life of an angry black postal worker.

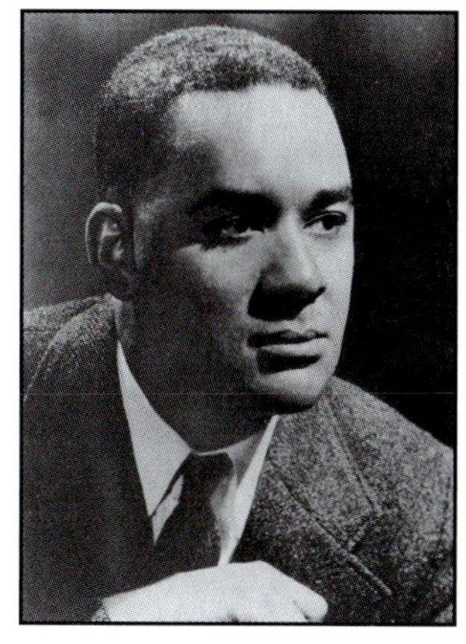

Wright published several short stories before publishing his novel *Uncle Tom's Children* (1938) to good reviews. His next novel, *Native Son* (1940), became a bestseller. This was followed by *Black Boy: A Record of Childhood and Youth* (1945). By 1947, he was the most famous published black writer in the United States. Still, he moved to France to live for the rest of his life in order to escape racial prejudice and the "Red Scare" of the 1950s.

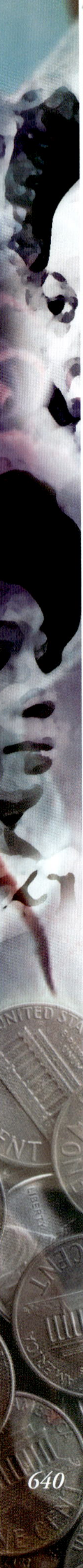

Prereading

"The Richer, the Poorer"

by Dorothy West

This well-known story lends its name to the title of a book that Dorothy West published when she was 85 years old: *The Richer, the Poorer: Stories, Sketches, and Reminiscences* (1995). This collection features short stories from the author's impressive seventy-year writing career and cherished memories of the Harlem Renaissance and Great Depression eras.

West's close friend Langston Hughes and other stars of the Harlem Renaissance used to call her "The Kid." That is because she moved to New York—and made a big splash in the literary and social circles of mid-1920s Harlem—when she was just nineteen. She never stopped writing, publishing at least sixty short stories in her life, in addition to her novels and other works.

"The Richer, the Poorer" is about two sisters who took different paths in life. Bess married a musician at a young age and set off to see the world. After a lifetime spent traveling and scratching out a meager living, Bess has nothing to show for it but a raggedy suitcase. Lottie, by contrast, has always been the cautious one, the penny-pincher focused almost entirely on earning and saving money. When Bess's husband dies, Lottie feels obligated to invite her penniless sister to come live with her.

The middle of the story focuses on Lottie's thoughts and feelings as she prepares for Bess's arrival. Lottie reminisces about the choices that they both have made in life, and she expresses frustration that she has to take her sister in. Lottie has always frowned upon her sister's carefree lifestyle, but she soon realizes, with regret, that perhaps it is she, not Bess, who has missed out on life.

This is a tidy little story that should provide readers and young writers with insight into the art of character development. West was a gifted storyteller who made each word count. Almost every paragraph has something special to offer, whether it is an important character detail or a tidbit from Dorothy West's own well of wisdom and experience.

The Richer, the Poorer

by Dorothy West

Over the years Lottie had urged Bess to prepare for her old age. Over the years Bess had lived each day as if there were no other. Now they were both past sixty, the time for summing up. Lottie had a bank account that had never grown lean. Bess had the clothes on her back, and the rest of her worldly possessions in a battered suitcase.

Lottie had hated being a child, hearing her parents' skimping and scraping. Bess had never seemed to notice. All she ever wanted was to go outside and play. She learned to skate on borrowed skates. She rode a borrowed bicycle. Lottie couldn't wait to grow up and buy herself the best of everything.

As soon as anyone would hire her, Lottie put herself to work. She minded babies, she ran errands for the old.

She never touched a penny of her money, though her child's mouth watered for ice cream and candy. But she could not bear to share with Bess, who never had anything to share with her. When the dimes began to add up to dollars, she lost her taste for sweets.

By the time she was twelve, she was clerking after school in a small variety store. Saturdays she worked as long as she was wanted. She decided to keep her money for clothes. When she entered high school, she would wear a wardrobe that neither she nor anyone else would be able to match.

VOCABULARY IN PLACE

- **frivolous,** ***adj.*** Silly, of little value
- **whim,** ***n.*** A sudden idea, a fancy; impulse

But her freshman year found her unable to indulge so **frivolous** a **whim,** particularly when her admiring instructors advised her to think seriously of college. No one in her family had ever gone to college, and certainly Bess would never get there. She would show them all what she could do, if she put her mind to it.

She began to bank her money, and her bankbook became her most private and precious possession.

In her third year of high school she found a job in a small but expanding restaurant, where she cashiered from the busy hour until closing. In her last year of high school the business increased so rapidly that Lottie was faced with the choice of staying in school or working full time.

She made her choice easily. A job in hand was worth two in the future.

Why didn't Lottie stay in school?

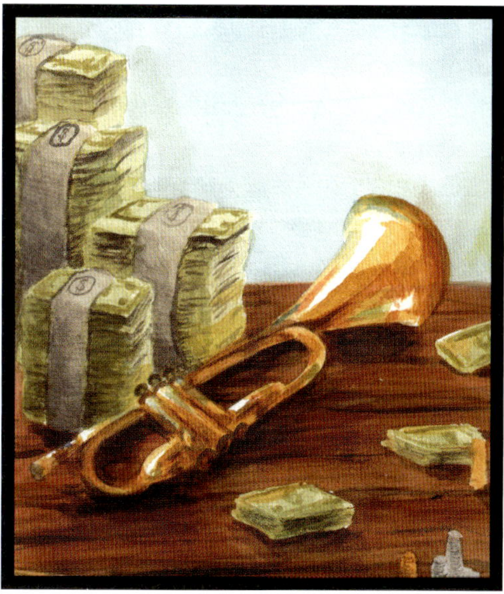

Bess had a beau[1] in the school band, who had no other ambition except to play a horn. Lottie expected to be settled with a home and family while Bess was still waiting for Harry to earn enough to buy a marriage license.

That Bess married Harry straight out of high school was not surprising. That Lottie never married at all was not really surprising either. Two or three times she was halfway persuaded, but to give up a job that paid well for a homemaking job that paid nothing was a risk she was incapable of taking.

Bess's married life was nothing for Lottie to envy. She and Harry lived like gypsies,[2] Harry playing in second-rate bands all over the country, even getting himself and Bess stranded in Europe. They were often in rags and never in riches.

Bess grieved because she had no child, not having sense enough to know she was better off without one. Lottie was certainly better off without nieces and nephews to feel sorry for. Very likely Bess would have dumped them on her doorstep.

That Lottie had a doorstep they might have been left on was only because her boss, having bought a second house, offered Lottie his first house at a price so low and terms so reasonable that it would have been like losing money to refuse.

She shut off the rooms she didn't use, letting them go to rack and ruin. Since she ate her meals out, she had no food at home, and did not encourage callers, who always expected a cup of tea.

Her way of life was **mean** and **miserly,** but she did not know it. She thought she lived **frugally** in her middle years so that she could live in comfort and ease when she most needed peace of mind.

The years, after forty, began to race. Suddenly Lottie was sixty, and retired from her job by her boss's son, who had no **sentimental** feeling about keeping her on until she was ready to quit.

She made several attempts to find other employment, but her dowdy[3] appearance made her look old and inefficient. For the first time in her life Lottie would gladly have worked for nothing, to have some place to go, something to do with her day.

Harry died abroad, in a third-rate hotel, with Bess weeping as hard as if he had left her a fortune. He had left her nothing but his horn. There wasn't even money for her passage home.

Lottie, trapped by the blood tie, knew she would not only have to send for her sister, but take her in when she returned. It didn't seem fair that Bess should reap the harvest of Lottie's lifetime of self-denial.

It took Lottie a week to get a bedroom ready, a week of hard work and hard cash. There was everything to do, everything to replace or paint. When she was through the room looked so fresh and new that Lottie felt she deserved it more than Bess.

She would let Bess have her room, but the mattress was so lumpy, the carpet so worn, the curtains so threadbare that Lottie's conscience pricked her. She supposed she would have to redo that room, too, and went about doing it with an eagerness that she mistook for haste.

---

[1] **beau.** Boyfriend (from French)

[2] **gypsies.** People inclined to a nomadic, unconventional way of life. From Gypsy (or Romany), a member of a people that arrived in Europe from northern India around the fourteenth century.

[3] **dowdy.** Shabby, lacking style

VOCABULARY IN PLACE

- **mean,** ***adj.*** Low in social status; humble
- **miserly,** ***adj.*** Characterized by a lack of generosity
- **frugal,** ***adj.*** Not wasteful, thrifty
- **sentimental,** ***adj.*** Influenced by emotion rather than reason

When she was through upstairs, she was shocked to see how **dismal** downstairs looked by comparison. She tried to ignore it, but with nowhere to go to escape it, the contrast grew more **intolerable.**

She worked her way from kitchen to parlor, persuading herself she was only putting the rooms to rights to give herself something to do. At night she slept like a child after a long and happy day of playing house. She was having more fun than she had ever had in her life. She was living each hour for itself.

There was only a day now before Bess would arrive. Passing her gleaming mirrors, at first with vague awareness, then with painful clarity, Lottie saw herself as others saw her, and could not stand the sight.

She went on a spending spree from the specialty shops to beauty salon, emerging transformed into a woman who believed in miracles.

She was in the kitchen basting[4] a turkey when Bess rang the bell. Her heart raced, and she wondered if the heat from the oven was responsible.

She went to the door, and Bess stood before her. Stiffly she suffered Bess's embrace, her heart racing harder, her eyes suddenly smarting from the onrush of cold air.

"Oh, Lottie, it's good to see you," Bess said, but saying nothing about Lottie's splendid appearance. Upstairs Bess, putting down her shabby suitcase, said, "I'll sleep like a rock tonight," without a word of praise for her lovely room. At the lavish table, top-heavy with turkey, Bess said, "I'll take light and dark, both," with no marveling at the size of the bird, or that there was turkey for two elderly women, one of them too poor to buy her own bread.

With the glow of good food in her stomach, Bess began to spin stories. They were rich with places and people, most of them lowly, all of them magnificent. Her face reflected her telling, the joys and sorrows of her remembering, and above all, the love she lived by that enhanced the poorest place, the humblest person.

Then it was that Lottie knew why Bess had made no mention of her finery,[5] or the shining room, or the twelve-pound turkey. She had not even seen them. Tomorrow she would see the room as it really looked, and Lottie as she really looked, and the warmed-over turkey in its second-day glory. Tonight she saw only what she had come seeking, a place in her sister's home and heart.

She said, "That's enough about me. How have the years used you?"

"It was me who didn't use them," said Lottie wistfully. "I saved for them. I saved for them. I forgot the best of them would go without my ever spending a day or a dollar enjoying them. That's my life story in those few words, a life never lived.

"Now it's too near the end to try."

Bess said, "To know how much there is to know is the beginning of learning to live. Don't count the years that are left us. At our time of life it's the days that count. You've too much catching up to do to waste a minute of a waking hour feeling sorry for yourself."

Lottie grinned, a real wide-open grin, "Well to tell the truth, I felt sorry for you. Maybe if I had any sense I'd feel sorry for myself, after all. I know I'm too old to kick up my heels, but I'm going to let you show me how. If I land on my head, I guess it won't matter; I feel giddy already, and I like it." ■

---

4 **basting.** Moistening with sauce or butter

5 **finery.** Fancy accessories, linens, and other adornments

VOCABULARY IN PLACE

- **dismal,** *adj.* Causing gloom or depression
- **intolerable,** *adj.* Impossible to tolerate or endure

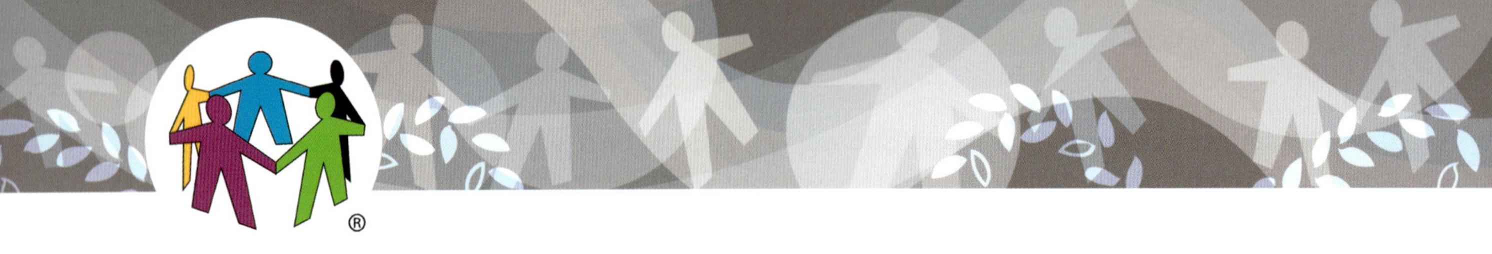

Understanding the Selection

Recalling

1. When did Lottie lose her taste for sweets?
2. Why didn't Lottie finish high school?
3. Why didn't Lottie get married? Were people surprised?
4. What does Lottie do to prepare for Bess's arrival?
5. Why does Lottie clean the upstairs of her house? Is it an easy job?
6. What is Bess seeking when she arrives at Lottie's house?

Interpreting

1. What did she decide was more important than sweets?
2. Do you think this was a wise choice, based on what you know about the end of the story?
3. Why would Lottie have had a problem working while caring for a family? Do you think that times have changed since this story was written? Why or why not?
4. Why is Lottie frustrated or annoyed, at first, by the fact that her sister is coming to live with her? Why is she resentful of Bess?
5. What change does Lottie undergo while she is cleaning the house? How is this different than the way she acted in years past?
6. Does Bess find what she is looking for?

Synthesizing

1. What drove Lottie to become obsessed with making money? What were her goals, intentions, or wishes? Use examples from the text to support your answer.
2. What does Bess mean when she says, "To know how much there is to know is the beginning of learning to live"?
3. What does the story's title mean in relation to the characters?

Delving Deeper

Writing

Character Analysis. Lottie and Bess possess distinct personalities, and each has her own set of positive and negative traits. Write a short essay in which you explain, using at least two quotations or examples from the text, what lesson each sister learned from the other.

About the Author

Dorothy West (1908–1998), a prolific short-story writer, novelist, essayist, and journalist, was born in Boston. In 1926 she traveled to New York, accompanied by her cousin, poet Helene Johnson (see page 396), to accept a prize from the Urban League's *Opportunity* magazine. From that moment forward, she was known as a shining young star and close friend of such leading African-American writers as Countee Cullen, Arna Bontemps, and Langston Hughes. In 1932 she traveled to Moscow with Hughes as part of a twenty-two-member group of African-American writers and artists led by the civil rights activist Louise Patterson. West wrote warmly of the experience in her book of stories and memoirs, *The Richer, The Poorer: Stories, Sketches, and Reminiscences* (1995), which was published the same year as her second and last novel, *The Wedding.*

During the Great Depression of the mid-1930s, West, like so many of her colleagues, joined the Works Progress Administration Federal Writers' Project, which existed to nurture artistic talent as well as to gather important stories, cultural information, and other data from America's diverse regions and communities.

Beginning in 1940, West became a regular contributor to the *New York Daily* in a time when a writer could make a decent living selling short stories. Her first novel, *Living Is Easy* (1948), was well received by critics, but it did not sell well. This did not deter West from pursuing her art. She was a truly great short-story writer, for not only were her works impeccably crafted, they also conveyed valuable lessons, revealed insight into life's joys and struggles, and helped raise awareness of racial inequality in America.

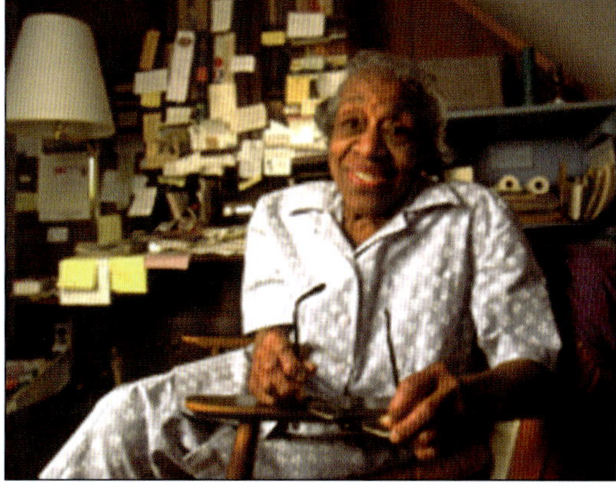

Prereading

"Everyday Use"

by Alice Walker

During the first three quarters of the twentieth century, a mass exodus took place in the United States, a movement of hundreds of thousands of poor African-American and white people from areas in the rural South to the big northern cities. This exodus was fueled largely by a desire to find jobs. Many young people also left rural areas to go to school in urban settings. The differences in rural culture and in education often created rifts within families—differences that drove families apart in ways that were permanent and irreparable.

The 1960s was a time of great turmoil in the United States—turmoil associated with heightened political consciousness. It was a time that saw the rise of the Black Power Movement and protests against the Vietnam War and in favor of civil rights and rights for women.

It is against this backdrop that Alice Walker sets her exquisite, tender tale of a visit home by a daughter who has been educated in the big city. The daughter has learned a lot of big city ways. She wears typical hippie garb, she is accompanied by a man who has taken a Muslim name, and she has herself taken on an African name as a sign of her lack of acceptance of her given name, inherited from the days of slavery.

As you read this story, think about **point of view**, the vantage point from which the story is told. This story is told by a simple country woman. What are this woman's values? What does she care about? What differences separate her from her daughter? Which of these characters, the mother or the daughter, has the more attractive personality and why? How would the story be different if told from the daughter's point of view?

Everyday Use

by Alice Walker

For your grandmama

I will wait for her in the yard that Maggie and I made so clean and wavy yesterday afternoon. A yard like this is more comfortable than most people know. It is not just a yard. It is like an extended living room. When the hard clay is swept clean as a floor and the fine sand around the edges lined with tiny, irregular grooves, anyone can come and sit and look up into the elm tree and wait for the breezes that never come inside the house.

Maggie will be nervous until after her sister goes: she will stand hopelessly in corners, homely and ashamed of the burn scars down her arms and legs, eying her sister with a mixture of envy and awe. She thinks her sister has held life always in the palm of one hand, that "no" is a word the world never learned to say to her.

You've no doubt seen those TV shows where the child who has "made it" is confronted, as a surprise, by her own mother and father, tottering in weakly from backstage. (A pleasant surprise, of course: What would they do if parent and child came on the show only to curse out and insult each other?) On TV mother and child embrace and smile into each other's faces. Sometimes the mother and father weep, the child wraps them in her arms and leans across the table to tell how she would not have made it without their help. I have seen these programs.

Sometimes I dream a dream in which Dee and I are suddenly brought together on a TV program of this sort. Out of a dark and soft-seated limousine I am ushered into a bright room filled with many people. There I meet a smiling, gray, sporty man like Johnny Carson[1] who shakes my hand and tells me what a fine girl I have. Then we are on the stage and Dee is embracing me with tears in her eyes. She pins on my dress a large orchid, even though she has told me once that she thinks orchids are tacky flowers.

In real life I am a large, big-boned woman with rough, man-working hands. In the winter I wear flannel nightgowns to bed and overalls during the day. I can kill

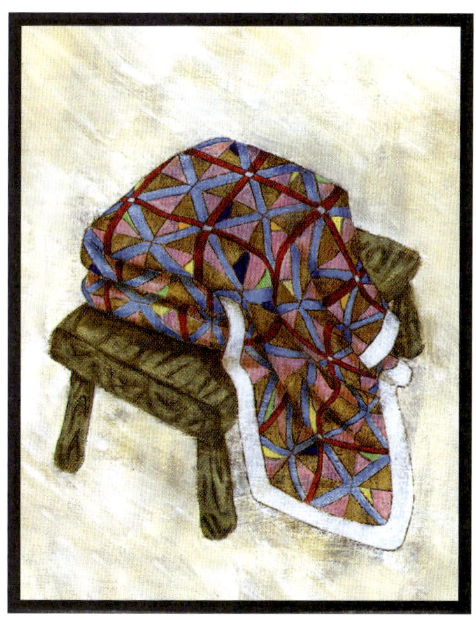

[1] **Johnny Carson.** Host of the NBC television program *The Tonight Show* from 1962 to 1992

and clean a hog as mercilessly as a man. My fat keeps me hot in zero weather. I can work outside all day, breaking ice to get water for washing; I can eat pork liver cooked over the open fire minutes after it comes steaming from the hog. One winter I knocked a bull calf straight in the brain between the eyes with a sledge hammer and had the meat hung up to chill before nightfall. But of course all this does not show on television. I am the way my daughter would want me to be: a hundred pounds lighter, my skin like an uncooked **barley** pancake. My hair glistens in the hot bright lights. Johnny Carson has much to do to keep up with my quick and witty tongue.

How does the narrator differ in "real life" from the way her daughter wants her to be?

But that is a mistake. I know even before I wake up. Who ever knew a Johnson with a quick tongue? Who can even imagine me looking a strange white man in the eye? It seems to me I have talked to them always with one foot raised in flight, with my head turned in whichever way is farthest from them. Dee, though. She would always look anyone in the eye. **Hesitation** was no part of her nature.

"How do I look, Mama?" Maggie says, showing just enough of her thin body enveloped in pink skirt and red blouse for me to know she's there, almost hidden by the door.

"Come out into the yard," I say.

Have you ever seen a lame animal, perhaps a dog run over by some careless person rich enough to own a car, **sidle** up to someone who is ignorant enough to be kind to him? That is the way my Maggie walks. She has been like this, chin on chest, eyes on ground, feet in shuffle, ever since the fire that burned the other house to the ground.

Why is Maggie so fearful?

Dee is lighter than Maggie, with nicer hair and a fuller figure. She's a woman now, though sometimes I forget. How long ago was it that the other house burned? Ten, twelve years? Sometimes I can still hear the flames and feel Maggie's arms sticking to me, her hair smoking and her dress falling off her in little black papery flakes. Her eyes seemed stretched open, blazed open by the flames reflected in them. And Dee. I see her standing off under the sweet gum tree[2] she used to dig gum out of; a look of concentration on her face as she watched the last dingy gray board of the house fall in toward the red-hot brick chimney. Why don't you do a dance around the ashes? I'd wanted to ask her. She had hated the house that much.

Why might Dee have hated the house?

I used to think she hated Maggie, too. But that was before we raised the money, the church and me, to send her to Augusta to school. She used to read to us without pity; forcing words, lies, other folks' habits, whole lives upon us two, sitting trapped and ignorant underneath her voice. She washed us in a river of make-believe, burned us with a lot of knowledge we didn't necessarily need to know. Pressed us to her with the serious way she read, to shove us away at just the moment, like dimwits, we seemed about to understand.

Dee wanted nice things. A yellow organdy[3] dress to wear to her graduation from high school; black pumps to match a green

2 **sweet gum tree.** A tree widely used to make furniture from which an aromatic resin is harvested

3 **organdy.** A stiff material made of silk or cotton

VOCABULARY IN PLACE

- **barley,** *n.* An edible grain
- **hesitation,** *n.* Pausing, as to think about something before acting
- **sidle,** *v.* Approach cautiously alongside rather than face to face

suit she'd made from an old suit somebody gave me. She was determined to stare down any disaster in her efforts. Her eyelids would not flicker for minutes at a time. Often I fought off the temptation to shake her. At sixteen she had a style of her own: and knew what style was.

I never had an education myself. After second grade the school was closed down. Don't ask me why: in 1927 colored asked fewer questions than they do now. Sometimes Maggie reads to me. She stumbles along good-naturedly but can't see well. She knows she is not bright. Like good looks and money, quickness passed her by. She will marry John Thomas (who has mossy teeth in an earnest face) and then I'll be free to sit here and I guess just sing church songs to myself. Although I never was a good singer. Never could carry a tune. I was always better at a man's job. I used to love to milk till I was hooked in the side in '49. Cows are soothing and slow and don't bother you, unless you try to milk them the wrong way.

Why does the narrator like to milk cows? What does this tell you about her personality?

I have deliberately turned my back on the house. It is three rooms, just like the one that burned, except the roof is tin; they don't make shingle roofs any more. There are no real windows, just some holes cut in the sides, like the portholes in a ship, but not round and not square, with rawhide holding the shutters up on the outside. This house is in a pasture, too, like the other one. No doubt when Dee sees it she will want to tear it down. She wrote me once that no matter where we "choose" to live, she will manage to come see us. But she will never bring her friends. Maggie and I thought about this and Maggie asked me, "Mama, when did Dee ever *have* any friends?"

She had a few. **Furtive** boys in pink shirts hanging about on washday after school. Nervous girls who never laughed. Impressed with her they worshipped the well-turned phrase, the cute shape, the **scalding** humor that erupted like bubbles in lye.[4] She read to them.

When she was courting Jimmy T she didn't have much time to pay to us, but turned all her faultfinding power on him. He *flew* to marry a cheap city girl from a family of ignorant flashy people. She hardly had time to **recompose** herself.

When she comes I will meet—but there they are!

Maggie attempts to make a dash for the house, in her shuffling way, but I stay her with my hand. "Come back here," I say. And she stops and tries to dig a well in the sand with her toe.

It is hard to see them clearly through the strong sun. But even the first glimpse of leg out of the car tells me it is Dee. Her feet were always neat-looking, as if God himself had shaped them with a certain style. From the other side of the car comes a short, stocky man. Hair is all over his head a foot long and hanging from his chin like a kinky mule tail. I hear Maggie suck in her breath. "Uhnnnh," is what it sounds like. Like when you see the wriggling end of a snake just in front of your foot on the road. "Uhnnnh."

Dee next. A dress down to the ground, in this hot weather. A dress so loud it hurts my

[4] **lye.** A caustic liquid obtained by allowing water to seep through wood ashes, widely used in soap-making

VOCABULARY IN PLACE

- **furtive,** ***adj.*** Secretive, given to hiding things, not trustworthy
- **scalding,** ***adj.*** Burning, harshly offensive
- **recompose,** ***v.*** To regain a sense of calm and well-being

eyes. There are yellows and oranges enough to throw back the light of the sun. I feel my whole face warming from the heat waves it throws out. Earrings gold, too, and hanging down to her shoulders. Bracelets dangling and making noises when she moves her arm up to shake the folds of the dress out of her armpits. The dress is loose and flows, and as she walks closer, I like it. I hear Maggie go "Uhnnnh" again. It is her sister's hair. It stands straight up like the wool on a sheep. It is black as night and around the edges are two long pigtails that rope about like small lizards disappearing behind her ears.

"Wa-su-zo-Tean-o!"[5] she says, coming on in that gliding way the dress makes her move. The short stocky fellow with the hair to his navel is all grinning and he follows up with "Asalamalakim,[6] my mother and sister!" He moves to hug Maggie but she falls back, right up against the back of my chair. I feel her trembling there and when I look up I see the perspiration falling off her chin.

"Don't get up," says Dee. Since I am **stout** it takes something of a push. You can see me trying to move a second or two before I make it. She turns showing white heels through her sandals, and goes back to the car. Out she peeks next with a Polaroid.[7] She stoops down quickly and lines up picture after picture of me sitting there in front of the house with Maggie cowering behind me. She never takes a shot without making sure the house is included. When a cow comes nibbling around the edge of the yard she snaps it and me and Maggie *and* the house. Then she puts the Polaroid in the back seat of the car, and comes up and kisses me on the forehead.

Is Asalamalakim really the man's name? What is he trying to do to Maggie's hand?

Meanwhile Asalamalakim is going through motions with Maggie's hand. Maggie's hand is as limp as a fish, and probably as cold, despite the sweat, and she keeps trying to pull it back. It looks like Asalamalakim wants to shake hands but wants to do it fancy. Or maybe he don't know how people shake hands. Anyhow, he soon gives up on Maggie.

"Well," I say. "Dee."

"No, Mama," she says. "Not 'Dee,' Wangero Leewanika Kemanjo!"[8]

"What happened to 'Dee'?" I wanted to know.

"She's dead," Wangero said. "I couldn't bear it any longer, being named after the people who oppress me."

Why did Dee change her name?

"You know as well as me you was named after your aunt Dicie," I said. Dicie is my sister. She named Dee. We called her "Big Dee" after Dee was born.

"But who was *she* named after?" asked Wangero.

"I guess after Grandma Dee," I said.

"And who was she named after?" asked Wangero.

"Her mother," I said, and saw Wangero was getting tired. "That's about as far back as I can trace it," I said. Though, in fact, I probably could have carried it back beyond the Civil War through the branches.

---

5 **Wa-su-zo-Tean-o.** A phrase in the Luganda language of Uganda, meaning "Good morning"

6 **Asalamalakim.** A corruption of the Arabic *as-salam alaykum,* meaning, "peace be with you"

7 **Polaroid.** A once very popular mass-market camera used to take instant snapshots

8 **Wangero Leewanika Kemanjo.** An assumed name that contains a number of corruptions of authentic African names. For example, *Wangero* is a corruption of the name *Wanjiru,* a clan name of the Kikuyu people of Kenya.

VOCABULARY IN PLACE

- **stout,** ***adj.*** Bulky, thickset

"Well," said Asalamalakim, "there you are."

"Uhnnnh," I heard Maggie say.

"There I was not," I said, "before 'Dicie' cropped up in our family, so why should I try to trace it that far back?"

He just stood there grinning, looking down on me like somebody inspecting a Model A car. Every once in a while he and Wangero sent eye signals over my head.

"How do you pronounce this name?" I asked.

"You don't have to call me by it if you don't want to," said Wangero.

"Why shouldn't I?" I asked. "If that's what you want us to call you, we'll call you."

"I know it might sound awkward at first," said Wangero.

"I'll get used to it," I said. "**Ream** it out again."

Well, soon we got the name out of the way. Asalamalakim had a name twice as long and three times as hard. After I tripped over it two or three times he told me to just call him Hakim-a-barber.[9] I wanted to ask him was he a barber, but I didn't really think he was, so I didn't ask.

"You must belong to those beef-cattle peoples down the road," I said. They said "Asalamalakim" when they met you, too, but they didn't shake hands. Always too busy: feeding the cattle, fixing the fences, putting up salt-lick shelters, throwing down hay. When the white folks poisoned some of the herd the men stayed up all night with rifles in their hands. I walked a mile and a half just to see the sight.

Hakim-a-barber said, "I accept some of their doctrines, but farming and raising cattle is not my style." (They didn't tell me, and I didn't ask, whether Wangero (Dee) had really gone and married him.)

We sat down to eat and right away he said he didn't eat collards and pork was unclean. Wangero, though, went on through the chitlins and corn bread, the greens and everything else. She talked a blue streak[10] over the sweet potatoes. Everything delighted her. Even the fact that we still used the benches her daddy made for the table when we couldn't afford to buy chairs.

"Oh, Mama!" she cried. Then turned to Hakim-a-barber. "I never knew how lovely these benches are. You can feel the rump prints," she said, running her hands underneath her and along the bench. Then she gave a sigh and her hand closed over Grandma Dee's butter dish. "That's it!" she said. "I knew there was something I wanted to ask you if I could have." She jumped up from the table and went over to the corner where the churn stood, the milk in it clabber[11] by now. She looked at the churn and looked at it.

"This churn top is what I need," she said. "Didn't Uncle Buddy whittle it out of a tree you all used to have?"

"Yes," I said.

"Uh huh," she said happily. "And I want the dasher,[12] too."

"Uncle Buddy whittle that, too?" asked the barber.

---

[9] **Hakim-a-barbar.** Dee's mother has misunderstood the name, which is probably the Arabic name Hakim al Baba. Many African-American Muslims assumed Islamic names.

[10] **talked a blue streak.** Spoke very quickly, basically about nothing (probably a reference to a lightning bolt)

[11] **churn . . . clabber.** A *churn* is a device for working milk to turn it into butter. *Clabber* is curdled milk from which butter is made.

[12] **dasher.** Plunger used in a churn to make butter

VOCABULARY IN PLACE

- **ream,** *v.* To squeeze

Dee (Wangero) looked up at me.

"Aunt Dee's first husband whittled the dash," said Maggie so low you almost couldn't hear her. "His name was Henry, but they called him Stash."

"Maggie's brain is like an elephant's," Wangero said, laughing. "I can use the churn top as a centerpiece for the **alcove** table," she said, sliding a plate over the churn, "and I'll think of something artistic to do with the dasher."

When she finished wrapping the dasher the handle stuck out. I took it for a moment in my hands. You didn't even have to look close to see where hands pushing the dasher up and down to make butter had left a kind of sink in the wood. In fact, there were a lot of small sinks; you could see where thumbs and fingers had sunk into the wood. It was beautiful light yellow wood, from a tree that grew in the yard where Big Dee and Stash had lived.

After dinner Dee (Wangero) went to the trunk at the foot of my bed and started **rifling** through it. Maggie hung back in the kitchen over the dishpan. Out came Wangero with two quilts. They had been pieced by Grandma Dee and then Big Dee and me had hung them on the quilt frames on the front porch and quilted them. One was in the Lone Star pattern. The other was Walk Around the Mountain. In both of them were scraps of dresses Grandma Dee had worn fifty and more years ago. Bits and pieces of Grandpa Jarrell's Paisley shirts. And one teeny faded blue piece, about the size of a penny matchbox, that was from Great Grandpa Ezra's uniform that he wore in the Civil War.

"Mama," Wangero said sweet as a bird. "Can I have these old quilts?"

I heard something fall in the kitchen, and a minute later the kitchen door slammed.

"Why don't you take one or two of the others?" I asked. "These old things was just done by me and Big Dee from some tops your grandma pieced before she died."

"No," said Wangero. "I don't want those. They are stitched around the borders by machine."

"That'll make them last better," I said.

"That's not the point," said Wangero. "These are all pieces of dresses Grandma used to wear. She did all this stitching by hand. Imagine!" She held the quilts securely in her arms, stroking them.

"Some of the pieces, like those lavender ones, come from old clothes her mother handed down to her," I said, moving up to touch the quilts. Dee (Wangero) moved back just enough so that I couldn't reach the quilts. They already belonged to her.

"Imagine!" she breathed again, clutching them closely to her bosom.

"The truth is," I said, "I promised to give them quilts to Maggie, for when she marries John Thomas."

She gasped like a bee had stung her.

"Maggie can't appreciate these quilts!" she said. "She'd probably be backward enough to put them to everyday use."

"I reckon she would," I said. "God knows I been saving 'em for long enough with nobody using 'em. I hope she will!" I didn't want to bring up how I had offered Dee (Wangero) a quilt when she went away to college. Then she had told me they were old-fashioned, out of style.

"But they're *priceless!"* she was saying now, furiously; for she has a temper.

VOCABULARY IN PLACE

- **alcove,** ***n.*** A nook or partly-closed extension in a room
- **rifle,** ***v.*** Look through something hurriedly, in a sloppy, haphazard manner

"Maggie would put them on the bed and in five years they'd be in rags. Less than that!"

"She can always make some more," I said. "Maggie knows how to quilt."

Dee (Wangero) looked at me with hatred. "You just will not understand. The point is these quilts, *these* quilts!"

"Well," I said, stumped. "What would *you* do with them?"

"Hang them," she said. As if that was the only thing you *could* do with quilts.

Maggie by now was standing in the door. I could almost hear the sound her feet made as they scraped over each other.

"She can have them, Mama," she said, like somebody used to never winning anything, or having anything reserved for her. "I can 'member Grandma Dee without the quilts."

I looked at her hard. She had filled her bottom lip with checkerberry[13] snuff and it gave her face a kind of dopey, hangdog look. It was Grandma Dee and Big Dee who taught her how to quilt herself. She stood there with her scared hands hidden in the folds of her skirt. She looked at her sister with something like fear but she wasn't mad at her. This was Maggie's portion. This was the way she knew God to work.

When I looked at her like that something hit me in the top of my head and ran down to the soles of my feet. Just like when I'm in church and the spirit of God touches me and I get happy and shout. I did something I never had done before: hugged Maggie to me, then dragged her on into the room, snatched the quilts out of Miss Wangero's hands and dumped them into Maggie's lap. Maggie just sat there on my bed with her mouth open.

"Take one or two of the others," I said to Dee.

But she turned without a word and went out to Hakim-a-barber.

"You just don't understand," she said, as Maggie and I came out to the car.

"What don't I understand?" I wanted to know.

"Your heritage," she said. And then she turned to Maggie, kissed her, and said, "You ought to try to make something of yourself, too, Maggie. It's really a new day for us. But from the way you and Mama still live you'd never know it."

She put on some sunglasses that hid everything above the tip of her nose and her chin.

Maggie smiled; maybe at the sunglasses. But a real smile, not scared. After we watched the car dust settle I asked Maggie to bring me a dip of snuff. And then the two of us sat there just enjoying, until it was time to go in the house and go to bed. ■

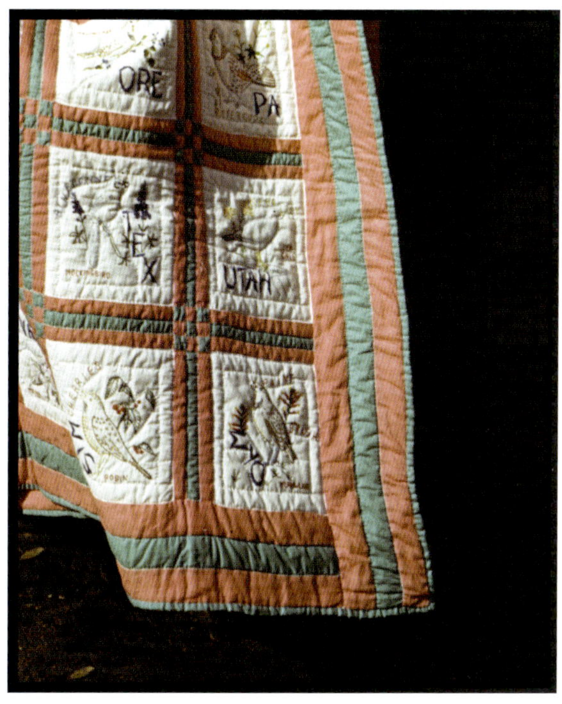

13 **checkerberry.** Wintergreen, a creeping evergreen plant with aromatic leaves

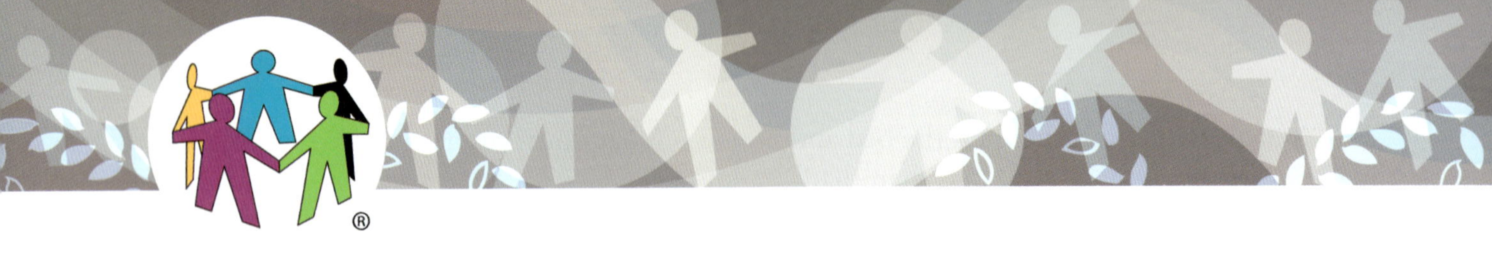

Understanding the Selection

Recalling

1. How is the narrator of this story related to Maggie and to Dee?
2. What name does Dee insist upon being called and why? How does the man who accompanies Dee introduce himself?
3. What does Dee want to do with the top and the plunger from the butter churn? What do the narrator and Maggie use these items for?
4. What does Dee want to do with the quilt? What would Maggie do with it?

Interpreting

1. How do these three characters feel toward one another? Cite evidence to support your answers.
2. What do these names reveal about Dee and her companion? In what way does their experience differ from that of the narrator and of Maggie?
3. Again, what differences between Dee on the one hand and the narrator and Maggie on the other are revealed by their different uses for these items?
4. What different perspective is revealed by these different ideas about how the quilt should be used?

Synthesizing

1. With whom do you as the reader of this story most sympathize, with Dee on the one hand or with the narrator and Maggie on the other? Why?
2. How would this story be different if it were told from Dee's point of view?
3. What does this story reveal about an unintended result of education on relations between children and their uneducated parents from rural areas?

Delving Deeper

Understanding Literature

Conflict. A **conflict** is a struggle in a literary work. Answer these questions about the conflict in "Everyday Use":

1. What conflict exists in this story between Dee on the one hand and Maggie and the narrator on the other with regard to what should happen with the quilt?
2. How does this conflict grow out of the different personalities of the three characters and their differing life experiences?
3. How is the conflict ultimately resolved, or ended?
4. How do you as the reader feel about this resolution of the conflict? With which characters do you have the most sympathy, and why?
5. What does this story have to teach us about the difference between being right on an abstract, general level and treating other people with ordinary, common decency and respect?

About the Author

Alice Walker (b.1944) was born in Eatonton, Georgia, and grew up in a sharecropping family. She was valedictorian of her high school class and went on to receive a B.A. degree from Sarah Lawrence College. She worked for a time registering voters and as a welfare department employee, but from her earliest years, her passion was for writing. Her first novel was published at the age of 26 and was followed by a short-story collection and a second novel. She became internationally famous, however, after the publication in 1983 of her novel *The Color Purple,* which was made into a highly successful movie. She has taught at a number of universities, including Jackson State College, Wellesley College, the University of Massachusetts, the University of California at Berkeley, and Brandeis University. She has received many honors and awards, including the Pulitzer Prize, a grant and fellowship from the National Endowment for the Arts, a Guggenheim Award, and an O'Henry Award. She has been alternately praised and censured for her strong stand on women's rights. Recent works by Walker include *The Temple of My Familiar* (1989) and *In Search of Our Mothers' Gardens: Womanist Prose* (1983).

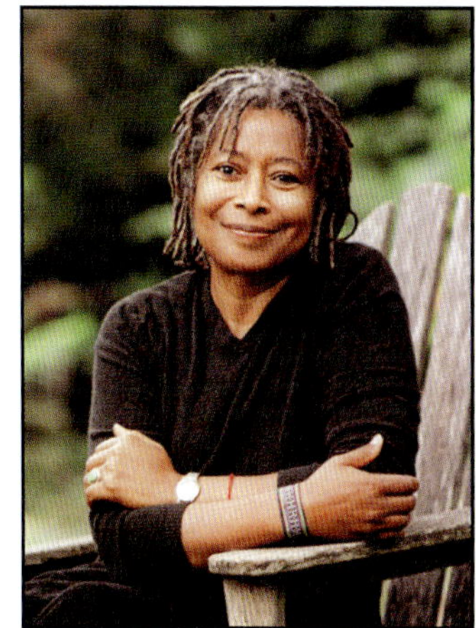

Prereading

"Geraldine Moore: The Poet"

by Toni Cade Bambara

Toni Cade Bambara was a wonderful storyteller whose short stories and novels often relate the hardships and unfair treatment faced by women in the African-American community. The short story "Geraldine Moore: The Poet" was written especially for children.

This is a fine short story about a single day in the life of a girl named Geraldine, who lives in a city neighborhood where people are mostly poor and down on their luck and must rely on one another in order to get by from day to day.

In Geraldine readers will find a strong, brave girl full of dreams, a girl who, unfortunately, seems to know more about the worry and responsibility of being an adult than about the joy and happiness of childhood.

From this story readers will also, perhaps, gain an understanding of poetry and the fact that sometimes poems are just floating around out there in the air, waiting to be pulled down and placed on paper.

Think about these points as you read the story:

1. How does the author illustrate Geraldine's personality and details about the setting in which she lives?
2. What is a poem? Do poems always have to be about happy or cheerful or beautiful subjects? Why do people write poems?
3. What kinds of challenges do Geraldine and her neighbors face?
4. In what ways do people sometimes sell themselves short? In what ways do the fear of failure and a lack of complete self-knowledge sometimes keep people from accomplishing things in their lives?

Geraldine Moore: The Poet

by Toni Cade Bambara

1
The Walk Home

Geraldine paused at the corner to pull up her kneesocks. The rubber bands she was using to hold them up made her legs itch. She dropped her books on the sidewalk and gave her legs a good scratch. But when she pulled the socks up again, two fingers poked through the top of the left one.

"That stupid dog," she **muttered,** grabbing her books. "First he chews up my gymsuit. Now it's my socks."

Geraldine kept muttering about Mrs. Watson's dog, which she took care of two days a week for a dollar. She passed the hot-dog man on the corner and waved. He shrugged, as if to say business was bad. Geraldine was not surprised. Nobody around here had hot-dog money.

Geraldine turned down her street, wondering what her sister Anita would have for her lunch. She was glad she didn't have to eat the free lunches in high school anymore. She hated the funny-looking tomato soup and the dried-out cheese sandwiches.

When Geraldine's mother first got sick and went away, Geraldine had been on her own. Miss Gladys next door came in on Thursdays to clean the apartment and make a meatloaf for Geraldine. But Geraldine never managed to get breakfast for herself. So she'd sit through classes scraping her feet to cover up the noise of her stomach growling.

Now Anita, her older sister, was living at home while her husband was in the Army. She usually fixed something good for lunch.

2
Kicked Out

Geraldine was almost home when she stopped dead. Right outside her building was a pile of furniture and boxes.

That wasn't anything new. She had seen people get put out of apartments before. But this time the ironing board looked familiar. And she recognized the ugly sofa standing on its arm. You could see the hole in the bottom, where Mrs. Watson's dog had gotten to it.

Why are there boxes outside the building?

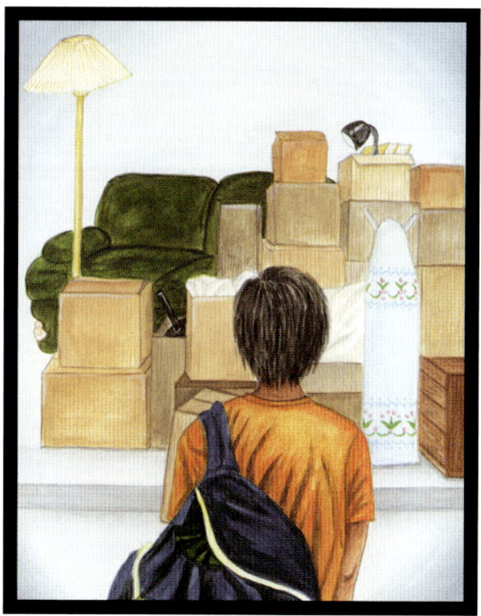

VOCABULARY IN PLACE

- **mutter,** *v.* To speak in a low tone; especially when complaining; grumble

Miss Gladys was sitting outside. "Well, Gerry," she said, "I guess you'll be staying with me for a while." She looked at the men carrying out a box of stuff. "Anita is upstairs. Go on up and get your lunch."

Upstairs, Geraldine went into the apartment. She found Anita in the kitchen.

"I don't know, Gerry," Anita said. "I just don't know what we're going to do. But everything is going to be all right as soon as Mama gets well." Anita's voice cracked as she set a bowl of soup before Geraldine.

"What's this?"

"It's tomato soup, Gerry."

Geraldine was about to say something. But when she looked at her sister, she saw that Anita was about to cry.

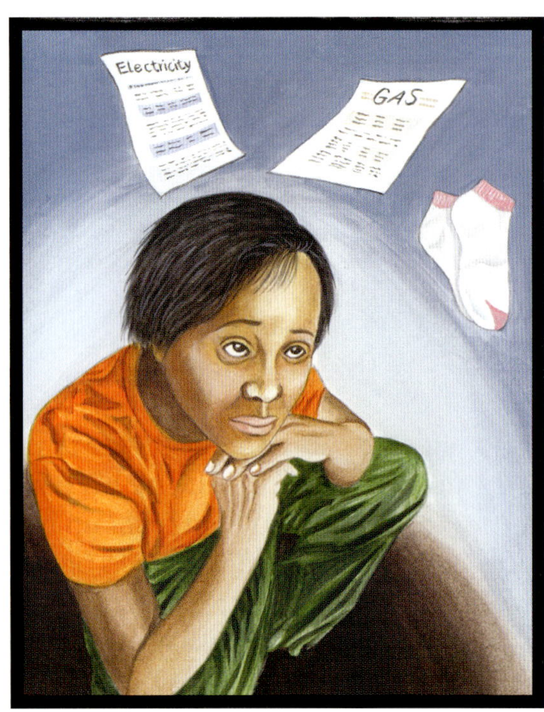

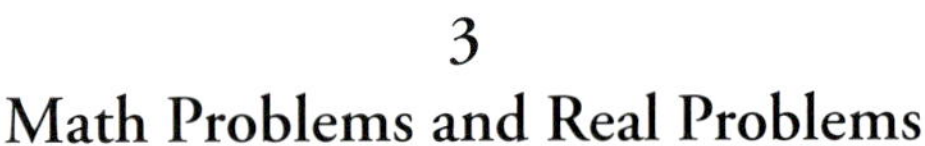

3
Math Problems and Real Problems

That afternoon, Mr. Stern, the geometry[1] teacher, drew squares and circles on the board. Geraldine sat at her desk, adding up figures in her notebook—the rent, the light bill, the gas bill, a new gymsuit, some socks . . .

What is Geraldine thinking about during class? Why?

Maybe she and Anita would move somewhere else. Maybe then she would have her own room.

"For your homework," Mr. Stern was saying, "set up your problems this way." He wrote *GIVEN:* in large letters, and then gave the first problem. Then he wrote *TO FIND:* and listed three things they should include in their answers.

Geraldine started to ask what squares and circles had to do with solving real problems. But she told herself, "You'd better not. Your big mouth got you in trouble last term."

In health class, Mrs. Potter kept saying, "The human body is a wonderful machine. Right now it is producing all the energy you will need to get through tomorrow."

Geraldine kept wondering, "How does my body know what it will need? I don't even know what I'll need to get through tomorrow."

As Geraldine walked to her English class, she remembered that she hadn't done the homework. Mrs. Scott had said to write it during lunch. There was nothing to it—a flower here, a raindrop there, and some words that rhymed. But the men carrying off the furniture had made her forget.

[1] **geometry.** The mathematical study of the measurements and relationships among angles, lines, shapes, points, and surfaces

4
The Assignment

"Now put away your books," Mrs. Scott was saying. "Today let's talk about poetry."

Mrs. Scott moved up and down the aisles, talking about her favorite poems. She got excited whenever she saw the homework of a student who had done the assignment.

"A poem is your own special way of saying what you feel and what you see," Mrs. Scott said.

For almost half an hour, she stood at the front of the room, reading poems and talking about poets. Geraldine drew pictures of houses and designs for curtains.

"If you haven't done your homework," Mrs. Scott said, "try it now. Try to express what it's like to be . . . to be alive in this . . . this wonderful world."

Mrs. Scott moved up and down the aisles again, looking at the students' work and saying, "That's nice," or "Keep trying." Finally she came to Geraldine's desk and stopped.

"I can't write a poem," Geraldine said loudly. And the whole class looked up.

"Why not?" Mrs. Scott asked, looking hurt.

"I can't write a poem, Mrs. Scott, because nothing lovely's been happening in my life. I haven't seen a flower since Mother's Day, and the sun don't even shine on my side of the street. No robins come to sing on my windowsill."

Geraldine thought of saying that her father doesn't even come to visit anymore, but changed her mind. "Just the rain comes," she went on, "and the bills come, and the men to move out our furniture. I'm sorry, but I can't write a pretty poem."

5
Geraldine's Poem

Teddy Johnson was about to laugh. But Mrs. Scott looked so serious that he changed his mind.

"You have just said a very poetic thing, Geraldine Moore," said Mrs. Scott. "'Nothing lovely's been happening in my life.'" She repeated it so quietly that the students had to lean forward to hear.

Mrs. Scott went to the board and stood there, staring at the chalk in her hand. Then she said, "Class, I'd like you to copy it down." And she wrote it just as Geraldine had said it, bad grammar and all:

Nothing lovely's been happening in
my life.
I haven't seen a flower since Mother's Day,
And the sun don't even shine on my side
of the street.
No robins come sing on my windowsill.
Just the rain comes, and the bills come,
And the men to move out our furniture.
I'm sorry, but I can't write a pretty poem.

Mrs. Scott stopped writing. But she kept her back to the class—even after the bell rang. Geraldine waited for her to turn around. Finally Geraldine stacked her books and started to leave. Then she saw Mrs. Scott's shoulders shake a little. ■

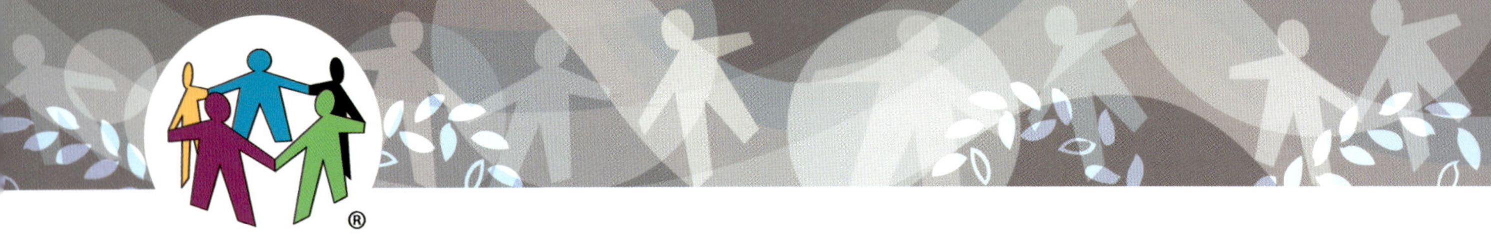

Understanding the Selection

Recalling

1. Is business good for the "hot-dog man" on Geraldine's street? How do you know?
2. Who is Miss Gladys? What does she do to help Geraldine?
3. What is Geraldine surprised to see outside her apartment building?
4. What does Geraldine think about during geometry class?
5. What was Geraldine's homework assignment in English class?
6. What does Mrs. Scott do when the bell rings?

Interpreting

1. What does this tell you about Geraldine's neighborhood?
2. Why is life so difficult for Geraldine? Where are her parents?
3. To whom does this stuff belong? What are Geraldine and her sister, Anita, going to do?
4. Does Geraldine think and worry about the same sort of matters that other kids her age are thinking about? Explain your answer.
5. Does Geraldine think that the assignment is too difficult? What, according to Geraldine, does one need to do in order to write a poem?
6. Why is Mrs. Scott doing this? Do you think Geraldine is surprised?

Synthesizing

1. Why is life so difficult for Geraldine? Find at least five difficulties mentioned in the text.
2. Why does Mrs. Scott think that Geraldine's excuse is actually a poem? Why does the teacher think that Geraldine's words are poetic? Do you agree with Mrs. Scott?
3. How could writing poetry help Geraldine deal with problems?

Delving Deeper

Writing

Setting and Character Development: It's in the Details. Perhaps you have heard the saying "show, don't tell" in an English or writing class; this is one of the first things you should think about when you sit down to write a story. What exactly does this saying mean? It means that, in a story, it is better to show your readers details about the setting and characters than to generalize about them.

By "showing" instead of "telling" you will help the reader to form a mental picture of the setting and a deeper understanding of the characters; also, your writing will be more interesting and memorable. When you write a story, you should think of yourself as a painter, not as an "explainer"—you must "paint a picture" with your words and let your audience draw its conclusions from details you provide.

Complete the following exercises in your notebook or on a separate piece of paper to see how Toni Cade Bambara "shows" instead of simply "tells."

1. Reread Part 1 of "Geraldine Moore: The Poet."
2. What does Part 1 tell you about Geraldine and her neighborhood? Does Geraldine have much money? What about other people in her neighborhood?
3. In Part 2, the narrator does not simply tell you that Geraldine has been evicted from her apartment. Instead, readers see things from Geraldine's point of view. How does the narrator "show" instead of "tell" what has happened?
4. In Part 3, does the narrator ever *tell* readers directly that Geraldine is not paying attention to the teachers? How does the narrator *show* this?

Notice that, in Part 1, the narrator does tell readers that "nobody around here had any hot-dog money." First, however, the narrator shows us the hot-dog vendor, whose situation provides direct proof of the fact that the people are poor. Sometimes it is necessary simply to tell readers, but a good writer always supports such statements with details or events.

Complete the following writing exercise and you will be one step closer to becoming a great story writer. Select two of the following fictional scenarios and write a short scene or sketch for each. *Show* readers the main idea without telling them directly. If possible, use at least two characters and include dialogue (characters speaking) and details about the setting.

1. It is cold outside and the roads are not safe.
2. Ethan is very nervous about crossing the street, even when there are no cars.
3. Kyle likes basketball more than anything else in the world.
4. Lexi has a beautiful singing voice.
5. This morning things were really crazy around my house.

Prereading

"Raymond's Run"

by Toni Cade Bambara

This story provides more proof of Bambara's status as a master of the short-story form. Anyone who reads "Raymond's Run" will learn a lot from the story's main character, Hazel Elizabeth Deborah Parker, better known as Squeaky. She is fast, very fast; and she can run the 50-yard dash as quickly as she can sum up someone's personality and motives. Squeaky does not take any guff from anyone, and those who try her patience soon learn that she is also very quick with words.

Squeaky has a special responsibility in life: her brother Raymond. Pay attention to this title character, and remember that, at its heart, this story is just as much about him as it is about Squeaky.

Bambara combines the everyday language and scenery of Squeaky's neighborhood on 151st Street with the craft and skill of an expert writer to create vivid, memorable characters and to pass on valuable lessons. Notice that the story is written in the **present tense.** (See also Understanding Literature, page 671.) This is unusual but by no means unheard-of in fiction. In this case, the present tense is just about the only way to keep up with the energetic and quick-witted central character.

Here are just a few of the themes that run through this great story:

1. This story is about how and why people get along or don't get along.
2. It is about the tendency of some children to gang up on or tease those who are vulnerable or choose to stand alone.
3. It is about competition, and how the desire to win and be the very best can have both a positive and negative impact on a person's character.
4. It is about smiles.
5. It is about jealousy and rivalry, good losers and bad winners, the bond between siblings, and the simple fact that not everyone likes to do what everyone else is doing.

Raymond's Run

by Toni Cade Bambara

I don't have much work to do around the house like some girls. My mother does that. And I don't have to earn my pocket money by hustling; George runs errands for the big boys and sells Christmas cards. And anything else that's got to get done, my father does. All I have to do in life is mind my brother Raymond, which is enough.

Sometimes I slip and say my little brother Raymond. But as any fool can see he's much bigger and he's older too. But a lot of people call him my little brother cause he needs looking after cause he's not quite right. And a lot of smart mouths got lots to say about that too, especially when George was minding him. But now, if anybody has anything to say to Raymond, anything to say about his big head, they have to come by me. And I don't play the dozens[1] or believe in standing around with somebody in my face doing a lot of talking. I much rather just knock you down and take my chances even if I am a little girl with skinny arms and a squeaky voice, which is how I got the name Squeaky. And if things get too rough, I run. And as anybody can tell you, I'm the fastest thing on two feet.

How did she get the name Squeaky?

There is no track meet that I don't win the first place medal. I used to win the twenty-yard dash when I was a little kid in kindergarten. Nowadays, it's the fifty-yard dash. And tomorrow I'm subject to run the quarter-meter relay all by myself and come in first, second, and third. The big kids call me Mercury[2] cause I'm the swiftest thing in the neighborhood. Everybody knows that—except two people who know better, my father and me. He can beat me to Amsterdam

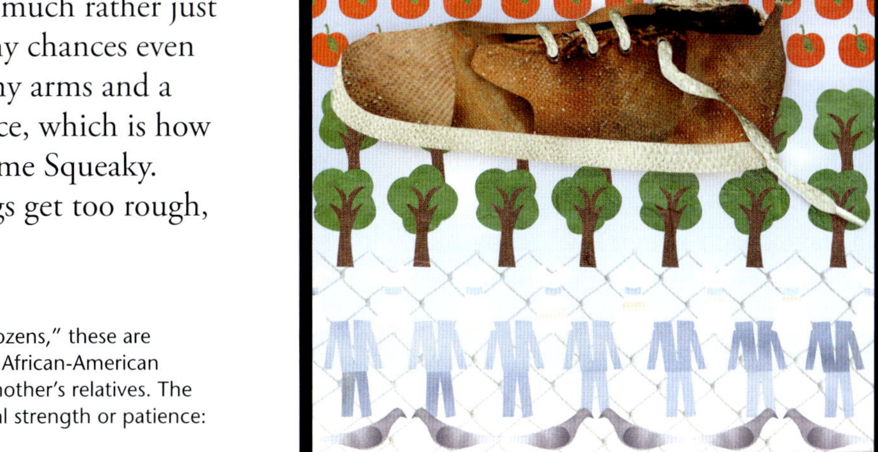

[1] **dozens.** Also known as the "dirty dozens," these are traditional oral games, primarily among African-American males, in which opponents insult one another's relatives. The object is to test an opponent's emotional strength or patience: the first person to get angry loses.

[2] **Mercury.** The god of trade and messenger of the gods in Roman mythology (equivalent to Hermes in Greek mythology). Mercury has wings on his sandals and is often pictured carrying a winged staff or wand.

Avenue with me having a two fire-hydrant headstart and him running with his hands in his pockets and whistling. But that's private information. Cause can you imagine some thirty-five-year-old man stuffing himself into PAL[3] shorts to race little kids? So far as everyone's concerned, I'm the fastest and that goes for Gretchen, too, who has put out the tale that she is going to win the first-place medal this year. Ridiculous. In the second place, she's got short legs. In the third place, she's got freckles. In the first place, no one can beat me and that's all there is to it.

I'm standing on the corner admiring the weather and about to take a stroll down Broadway so I can practice my breathing exercises, and I've got Raymond walking on the inside close to the buildings, cause he's subject to fits of fantasy and starts thinking he's a circus performer and that the curb is a tightrope strung high in the air. And sometimes after a rain he likes to step down off his tightrope right into the gutter and slosh around getting his shoes and cuffs wet. Then I get hit when I get home. Or sometimes if you don't watch him he'll dash across traffic to the island in the middle of Broadway and give the pigeons a fit. Then I have to go behind him apologizing to all the old people sitting around trying to get some sun and getting all upset with the pigeons fluttering around them, scattering their newspapers and upsetting the waxpaper lunches in their laps. So I keep Raymond on the inside of me, and he plays like he's driving a stage coach which is O.K. by me so long as he doesn't run me over or interrupt my breathing exercises, which I have to do on account of I'm serious about my running, and I don't care who knows about it.

Now some people like to act like things come easy to them, won't let on that they practice. Not me. I'll high-prance down 34th Street like a rodeo pony to keep my knees strong even if it does get my mother uptight so that she walks ahead like she's not with me, don't know me, is all by herself on a shopping trip, and I am somebody else's crazy child. Now you take Cynthia Procter for instance. She's just the opposite. If there's a test tomorrow, she'll say something like, "Oh, I guess I'll play handball this afternoon and watch television tonight," just to let you know she ain't thinking about the test. Or like last week when she won the spelling bee for the millionth time, "A good thing you got 'receive,' Squeaky, cause I would have got it wrong. I completely forgot about the spelling bee." And she'll clutch the lace on her blouse like it was a narrow escape. Oh, brother. But of course when I pass her house on my early morning trots around the block, she is practicing the scales on the piano over and over and over and over. Then in music class she always lets herself get bumped around so she falls accidentally on purpose onto the piano stool and is so surprised to find herself sitting there that she decides just for fun to try out the ole keys. And what do you know—Chopin's[4] waltzes just spring out of her fingertips and she's the most surprised thing in the world. A regular **prodigy.** I could kill people like that. I stay up all night studying the words for the spelling bee. And you can see me any time of day practicing running. I never walk if I can trot,

Why does Squeaky's mother sometimes pretend that she does not know Squeaky?

[3] **PAL.** A brand of clothing

[4] **Chopin.** *(Pronounced sho-pan)* Frederic François Chopin (1810–1849), Polish-born French composer and pianist of the Romantic Era

VOCABULARY IN PLACE

- **prodigy,** ***n.*** A person with exceptional talent or powers

and shame on Raymond if he can't keep up. But of course he does, cause if he hangs back someone's **liable** to walk up to him and get smart, or take his allowance from him, or ask him where he got that great big pumpkin head. People are so stupid sometimes.

So I'm strolling down Broadway breathing out and breathing in on counts of seven, which is my lucky number, and here comes Gretchen and her sidekicks: Mary Louise, who used to be a friend of mine when she first moved to Harlem from Baltimore and got beat up by everybody till I took up for her on account of her mother and my mother used to sing in the same choir when they were young girls, but people ain't grateful, so now she hangs out with the new girl Gretchen and talks about me like a dog; and Rosie, who is as fat as I am skinny and has a big mouth where Raymond is concerned and is too stupid to know that there is not a big deal of difference between herself and Raymond and that she can't afford to throw stones. So they are steady coming up Broadway and I see right away that it's going to be one of those Dodge City[5] scenes cause the street ain't that big and they're close to the buildings just as we are. First I think I'll step into the candy store and look over the new comics and let them pass. But that's chicken and I've got a reputation to consider. So then I think I'll just walk straight on through them or even over them if necessary. But as they get to me, they slow down. I'm ready to fight, cause like I said I don't feature a whole lot of chit-chat, I much prefer to just knock you down right from the jump and save everybody a lotta precious time.

"You signing up for the May Day[6] races?" smiles Mary Louise, only it's not a smile at all. A dumb question like that doesn't deserve an answer. Besides, there's just me and Gretchen standing there really, so no use wasting my breath talking to shadows.

Why does Squeaky say that Mary Louise's question is "dumb"?

"I don't think you're going to win this time," says Rosie, trying to signify with her hands on her hips all salty,[7] completely forgetting that I have whupped her behind many times for less salt than that.

"I always win 'cause I'm the best," I say straight at Gretchen who is, as far as I'm concerned, the only one talking in this

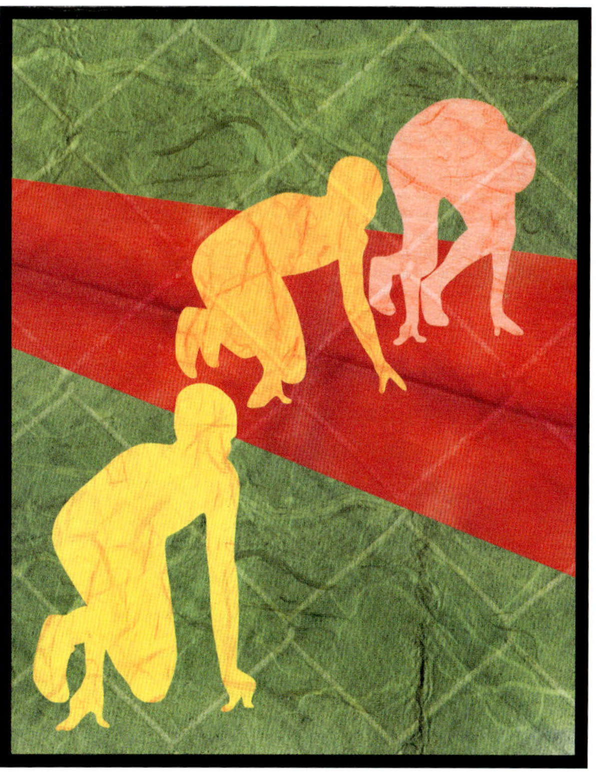

[5] **Dodge City.** A bustling frontier town in Kansas during the 1800s. The town was located at the start of the Santa Fe Trail. The city has been the setting of many western novels and movies and was the site of many gunfights and standoffs (to which the narrator refers).

[6] **May Day.** The first day of May, a traditional day for fairs or games

[7] **salty.** Sassy, witty

VOCABULARY IN PLACE

- **liable,** ***adj.*** Likely (often used with reference to an unfavorable outcome)

ventriloquist-dummy routine. Gretchen smiles, but it's not a smile, and I'm thinking that girls never really smile at each other because they don't know how and don't want to know how and there's probably no one to teach us how, cause grown-up girls don't know either. Then they all look at Raymond who has just brought his mule team to a standstill. And they're about to see what trouble they can get into through him.

Does Raymond really have a mule team? What are the girls going to do?

"What grade you in now, Raymond?"

"You got anything to say to my brother, you say it to me, Mary Louise Williams of Raggedy Town, Baltimore."

"What are you, his mother?" sasses Rosie.

"That's right, Fatso. And the next word out of anybody and I'll be *their* mother too." So they just stand there and Gretchen shifts from one leg to the other and so do they. Then Gretchen puts her hands on her hips and is about to say something with her freckle-face self but doesn't. Then she walks around me looking me up and down but keeps walking up Broadway and her sidekicks follow her. So me and Raymond smile at each other and he says, "Gidyap" to his team and I continue with my breathing exercises, strolling down Broadway toward the ice man on 145th with not a care in the world cause I am Miss Quicksilver[8] herself.

I take my time getting to the park on May Day because the track meet is the last thing on the program. The biggest thing on the program is the May Pole[9] dancing, which I can do without, thank you, even if my mother thinks it's a shame I don't take part and act like a girl for a change. You'd think my mother'd be grateful not to have to make me a white organdy[10] dress with a big satin sash and buy me new white-baby-doll shoes that can't be taken out of the box till the big day. You'd think she'd be glad her daughter ain't out there prancing around a May Pole getting the new clothes all dirty and sweaty and trying to act like a fairy or a flower or whatever you're supposed to be when you should be trying to be yourself, whatever that is, which is, as far as I am concerned, a poor Black girl who really can't afford to buy shoes and a new dress you only wear once a lifetime cause it won't fit next year.

How does Squeaky's mother expect her to behave? What does Squeaky consider to be her "self"?

I was once a strawberry in a Hansel and Gretel[11] pageant when I was in nursery school and didn't have no better sense than to dance on tiptoe with my arms in a circle over my head doing umbrella steps and being a perfect fool just so my mother and father could come dressed up and clap. You'd think they'd know better than to encourage that kind of nonsense. I am not a strawberry. I do not dance on my toes. I run. That is what I am all about. So I always come late to the May Day program, just in time to get my number pinned on and lay in the grass till they announce the fifty-yard dash.

I put Raymond in the little swings, which is a tight squeeze this year and will be impossible next year. Then I look around for Mr. Pearson, who pins the numbers on. I'm really looking for Gretchen if you want to know the truth, but she's not around. The park is jam-packed. Parents in hats and

---

8 **Quicksilver.** *Quicksilver* is another name for the element mercury, which becomes liquid and runny at room temperature.

9 **May Pole.** A pole decorated with colorful streamers that those celebrating May Day hold while dancing

10 **organdy.** A stiff transparent fabric of cotton or silk

11 **Hansel and Gretel.** A Grimm Brothers fairytale about a brother and sister who are lost in the woods and captured by a witch who lives in a gingerbread house

corsages and breast-pocket handkerchiefs peeking up. Kids in white dresses and light-blue suits. The parkees[12] unfolding chairs and chasing the rowdy kids from Lenox as if they had no right to be there. The big guys with their caps on backwards, leaning against the fence swirling the basketballs on the tips of their fingers, waiting for all these crazy people to clear out the park so they can play. Most of the kids in my class are carrying bass drums and glockenspiels[13] and flutes. You'd think they'd put in a few bongos[14] or something for real like that.

Why does Squeaky wish they had bongos? Why do you think they don't have them?

Then here comes Mr. Pearson with his clipboard and his cards and pencils and whistles and safety pins and fifty million other things he's always dropping all over the place with his clumsy self. He sticks out in a crowd because he's on stilts. We used to call him Jack and the Beanstalk to get him mad. But I'm the only one that can outrun him and get away, and I'm too grown for that silliness now.

"Well, Squeaky," he says, checking my name off the list and handing me number seven and two pins. And I'm thinking he's got no right to call me Squeaky, if I can't call him Beanstalk.

"Hazel Elizabeth Deborah Parker," I correct him and tell him to write it down on this board.

"Well, Hazel Elizabeth Deborah Parker, going to give someone else a break this year?" I squint at him real hard to see if he is seriously thinking I should lose the race on purpose just to give someone else a break. "Only six girls running this time," he continues, shaking his head sadly like it's my fault all of New York didn't turn out in sneakers. "That new girl should give you a run for your money." He looks around the park for Gretchen like a periscope in a submarine movie. "Wouldn't it be a nice gesture if you were . . . to ahhh . . ."

I give him such a look he couldn't finish putting that idea into words. Grownups got a lot of nerve sometimes. I pin number seven to myself and stomp away, I'm so burnt. And I go straight for the track and stretch out on the grass while the band winds up with "Oh, the Monkey Wrapped His Tail Around the Flag Pole," which my teacher calls by some other name. The man on the loudspeaker is calling everyone over to the track and I'm on my back looking at the sky, trying to pretend I'm in the country, but I can't, because even grass in the city feels hard as sidewalk, and there's just no pretending you are anywhere but in a "concrete jungle" as my grandfather says.

The twenty-yard dash takes all of two minutes cause most of the little kids don't know no better than to run off the track or run the wrong way or run smack into the fence and fall down and cry. One little kid, though, has got the good sense to run straight for the white ribbon up ahead so he wins. Then the second-graders line up for the thirty-yard dash and I don't even bother to turn my head to watch cause Raphael Perez always wins. He wins before he even begins by psyching[15] the runners, telling them they're going to trip on their shoelaces and fall on their faces or lose their shorts or something, which he doesn't really have to

12 **parkee.** People who spend most of their time in the park have a sense of ownership over it.

13 **glockenspiel.** A percussion instrument with a series of metal bars played with two light hammers

14 **bongos.** A pair of connected drums that are played by beating with the hands

15 **psyching.** Intimidating or undermining the confidence of

VOCABULARY IN PLACE

- **corsage,** ***n.*** A flower or small bouquet worn at the shoulder or on the wrist

do since he is very fast, almost as fast as I am. After that is the forty-yard dash which I use to run when I was in first grade. Raymond is hollering from the swings cause he knows I'm about to do my thing cause the man on the loudspeaker has just announced the fifty-yard dash, although he might just as well be giving a recipe for angel food cake cause you can hardly make out what he's saying for the static. I get up and slip off my sweat pants and then I see Gretchen standing at the starting line, kicking her legs out like a pro. Then as I get into place I see that ole Raymond is on line on the other side of the fence, bending down with his fingers on the ground just like he knew what he was doing. I was going to yell at him but then I didn't. It burns up your energy to holler.

Every time, just before I take off in a race, I always feel like I'm in a dream, the kind of dream you have when you're sick with fever and feel all hot and weightless. I dream I'm flying over a sandy beach in the early morning sun, kissing the leaves of the trees as I fly by. And there's always the smell of apples, just like in the country when I was little and used to think I was a choo-choo train, running through the fields of corn and chugging up the hill to the orchard. And all the time I'm dreaming this, I get lighter and lighter until I'm flying over the beach again, getting blown through the sky like a feather that weighs nothing at all. But once I spread my fingers in the dirt and crouch over the Get on Your Mark, the dream goes and I am solid again and am telling myself, Squeaky you must win, you must win, you are the fastest thing in the world, you can even beat your father up Amsterdam if you really try. And then I feel my weight coming back just behind my knees then down to my feet then into the earth and the pistol shot explodes in my blood and I am off and weightless again, flying past the other runners, my arms pumping up and down and the whole world is quiet except for the crunch as I zoom over the gravel in the track. I glance to my left and there is no one. To the right, a blurred Gretchen, who's got her chin jutting out as if it would win the race all by itself. And on the other side of the fence is Raymond with his arms down to his side and the palms tucked up behind him, running in his very own style, and it's the first time I ever saw that and I almost stop to watch my brother Raymond on his first run. But the white ribbon is bouncing toward me and I tear past it, racing into the distance till my feet with a mind of their own start digging up footfulls of dirt and brake me short. Then all the kids standing on the side pile on me, banging me on the back and slapping my head with their May Day programs, for I have won again and everybody on 151st Street can walk tall for another year.

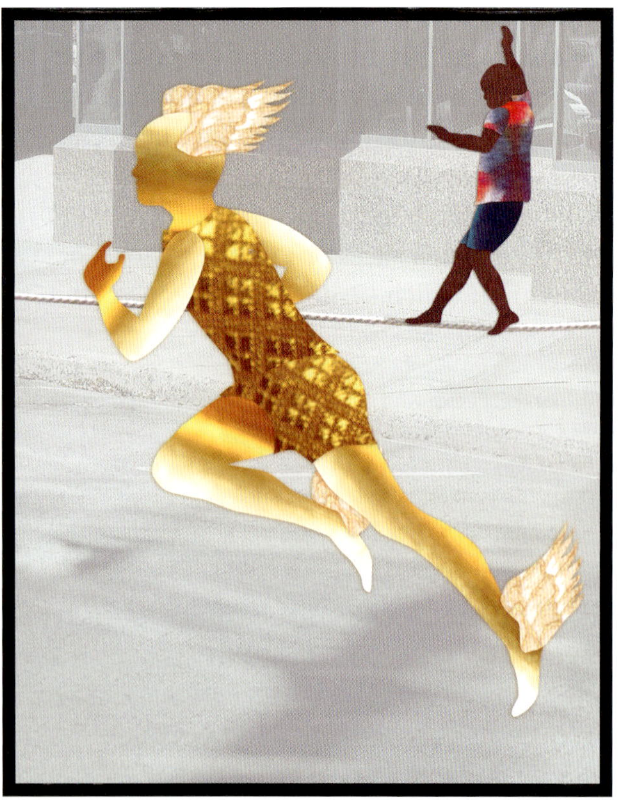

Why can the people "walk tall for another year"?

"In first place . . ." the man on the loudspeaker is clear as a bell now. But then he pauses and the loudspeaker starts to whine. Then static. And I lean down to catch my breath and here comes Gretchen walking back, for she's overshot the finish line too, huffing and puffing with her hands on her hips taking it slow, breathing in steady time like a real pro and I sort of like her a little for the first time. "In first place . . ." and then three or four voices get all mixed up on the loudspeaker and I dig my sneaker into the grass and stare at Gretchen who's staring back, we both wondering just who did win. I can hear old Beanstalk arguing with the man on the loudspeaker and then a few others running their mouths about what the stopwatches say. Then I hear Raymond yanking at the fence to call me and I wave to shush him, but he keeps rattling the fence like a gorilla in a cage like in them gorilla movies, but then like a dancer or something he starts climbing up nice and easy but very fast. And it occurs to me, watching how smoothly he climbs hand over hand and remembering how he looked running with his arms down to his side and with the wind pulling his mouth back and his teeth showing and all, it occurred to me that Raymond would make a very fine runner. Doesn't he always keep up with me on my trots? And he surely knows how to breathe in counts of seven cause he's always doing it at the dinner table, which drives my brother George up the wall. And I'm smiling to beat the band cause if I've lost this race, or if me and Gretchen tied, or even if I've won, I can always retire as a runner and begin a whole new career as a coach with Raymond as my champion. After all, with a little more study I can beat Cynthia and her phony self at the spelling bee. And if I bugged my mother, I could get piano lessons and become a star. And I have a big rep[16] as the baddest thing around. And I've got a roomful of ribbons and medals and awards. But what has Raymond got to call his own?

So I stand there with my new plans, laughing out loud by this time as Raymond jumps down from the fence and runs over with his teeth showing and his arms down to the side, which no one before him has quite mastered as a running style. And by the time he comes over I'm jumping up and down so glad to see him—my brother Raymond, a great runner in the family tradition. But of course everyone thinks I'm jumping up and down because the men on the loudspeaker have finally gotten themselves together and compared notes and are announcing "In first place—Miss Hazel Elizabeth Deborah Parker." (Dig that.) "In second place—Miss Gretchen P. Lewis." And I look over at Gretchen wondering what the "P" stands for. And I smile. Cause she's good, no doubt about it. Maybe she'd like to help me coach Raymond; she obviously is serious about running, as any fool can see. And she nods to congratulate me and then she smiles. And I smile. We stand there with this big smile of respect between us. It's about as real a smile as girls can do for each other, considering we don't practice real smiling every day, you know, cause maybe we too busy being flowers or fairies or strawberries instead of something honest and worthy of respect . . . you know . . . like being people. ■

16 **rep.** Reputation

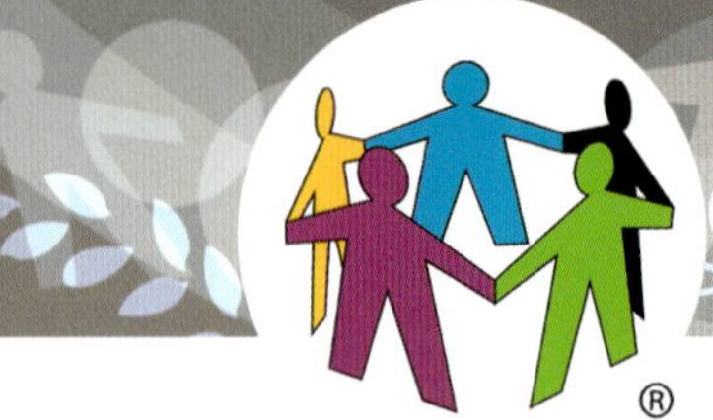

Understanding the Selection

Recalling

1. What is Squeaky's main responsibility in life?
2. How do other kids treat Raymond?
3. According to Squeaky, how is a girl expected to act when someone says "be yourself"?
4. According to Squeaky, do girls ever smile at each other?
5. Where did Squeaky live as a baby? What does her grandfather call the place they live now?
6. What "new plans" does Squeaky make near the end of the story?
7. Does Squeaky win the race? What does Gretchen do at the end?

Interpreting

1. Is this is an easy job? Explain using a quotation from the story to support your answer.
2. Does Squeaky stick up for her brother? Give an example.
3. Does Squeaky act like other girls? Is she ashamed of her own behavior? How do you know?
4. Why does Squeaky think that girls don't smile at each other?
5. Does Squeaky think about the country a lot? Does she like the city? Support your answer with examples from the text.
6. Why does she make these plans?
7. What does Squeaky think about Gretchen's smile?

Synthesizing

1. In general, what is Squeaky's attitude toward other kids? toward adults? Find at least two scenes or quotations from the story that illustrate Squeaky's feelings.
2. How does Squeaky's attitude about smiles change over the course of the story?
3. Does Squeaky feel bothered by having to care for her brother? What does Squeaky realize about her feelings for Raymond by the end of the story?

DELVING DEEPER

Writing

The Present Tense. Sometimes we all wish we could go back in time or jump into the future, but we all live in the present, and it is difficult to get away from that fact. Fiction stories, on the other hand, are usually written in the **past tense**, but not always! Toni Cade Bambara's "Raymond's Run" is written in the **present tense.** The action of the story occurs as the narrator experiences it, in *present* time. The present tense is uncommon in fiction as a matter of convention. Because stories are usually written in the past tense, most writers find it difficult to tell a story in the present tense. However, doing so can be interesting. Try your hand at writing in the present tense. Dig up a story you have previously written *or* select a favorite fairytale, myth, or other story written in the past tense. Rewrite a scene or two in the present tense. When you are finished, discuss the positives and negatives of writing in the present tense. Why do you think that most readers (and writers) prefer their stories to be written in the past tense?

About the Author

Toni Cade Bambara (1939–1995), writer, filmmaker, and social activist, created work inspired by unfairness in the treatment of women and by oppression of the black community. She was also an accomplished writer of fiction for young readers.

Bambara was born Miltona Mirkin Cade in Harlem, New York. This community inspired her work and was the setting of many of her stories. She was educated in New York, Italy, and France and worked for many years as a teacher.

In 1970 she edited a groundbreaking literary anthology called *The Black Woman.* The book promoted black awareness and feminism and became one of the most important collections of black female writers. Soon after, she changed her name to *Bambara,* an African tribal name from Mali, which she first found in a notebook belonging to her grandmother.

Bambara became well known for her use of African-American dialect and language in telling stories about ordinary people and events. She went on to write two collections of short stories, *Gorilla, My Love* (1972) and *The Sea Birds Are Still Alive* (1977), and novels, including *The Salt Eaters* (1980), for which she won the American Book Award. Bambara was later involved in filmmaking and helped make documentaries, including *The Bombing of Osage Avenue* (1986), which won an Academy Award. After her death, her long-time friend Toni Morrison edited her unfinished work *Those Bones Are Not My Child,* which was published in 1999.

Prereading

from *Beloved*

by Toni Morrison

This is one of the very best American novels from the last two decades of the twentieth century. It won the Pulitzer Prize in 1988 and was undoubtedly on the judges' minds when they gave Morrison the Nobel Prize in Literature five years later. One would have to search far and wide to find an unfavorable review of this book or just about anything else written by Toni Morrison. She is one of America's best storytellers, and *Beloved* represents an astonishing, superhuman display of skill and imagination.

Beloved has always appealed to a wide audience because of the range of issues and themes that it covers. Most people identify it first and foremost as a ghost story, and for those who enjoy this genre, it does not disappoint. If you have seen the movie, then you know that it is what horror fans call a real "spine-tingler." However, as all readers know, a movie, no matter how well-made, rarely delivers the same emotional, intellectual, and psychological punch as a good book—and this book will keep you up at night.

The novel is set in Ohio about three decades after the Civil War. As those who have read Units 2 and 3 of *Grace Abounding* know, the last half of the nineteenth century was a troubled time for many African Americans all around the country. Poverty, sharecropping, racist segregation, and the Ku Klux Klan worked against the black community.

The novel's central character is Sethe, a mother and former slave living with the torturous memory of her first daughter's death. The rest of the characters—Denver, Baby Suggs, Paul D., Halle, Sixo, Stamp Paid, and Amy Denver—represent parts of a tragic, horrifying past that, at times, is indistinguishable from the present.

The plot of the story is not linear; that is, it does not move in a straight line. Instead, pieces of the story emerge in a manner more akin to the tormented, disordered condition of the main characters' memories (and fears).

No mere synopsis can do justice to a great story. The following excerpt may be read by itself as a gripping example of Morrison's style, but it is best not to divulge too many details. Readers are encouraged to enjoy this passage for what it is: an intriguing glimpse into an amazing book that can be found in just about every major bookstore in the English-speaking world and beyond. Pick up a copy whenever you muster the courage and strength, for it will not allow itself to be taken lightly.

from Beloved

by Toni Morrison

There is a loneliness that can be rocked. Arms crossed, knees drawn up; holding, holding on, this motion, unlike a ship's, smooths and contains the rocker. It's an inside kind—wrapped tight like skin. Then there is a loneliness that roams. No rocking can hold it down. It is alive, on its own. A dry and spreading thing that makes the sound of one's own feet going seem to come from a far-off place.

Everybody knew what she was called, but nobody anywhere knew her name. Disremembered and unaccounted for, she cannot be lost because no one is looking for her, and even if they were, how can they call her if they don't know her name? Although she has claim, she is not claimed. In the place where long grass opens, the girl who waited to be loved and cry shame erupts into her separate parts, to make it easy for the chewing laughter to swallow her all away.

It was not a story to pass on.

They forgot her like a bad dream. After they made up their tales, shaped and decorated them, those that saw her that day on the porch quickly and deliberately forgot her. It took longer for those who had spoken to her, lived with her, fallen in love with her, to forget, until they realized they couldn't remember or repeat a single thing she said, and began to believe that, other than what they themselves were thinking, she hadn't said anything at all. So, in the end, they forgot her too. Remembering seemed unwise. They never knew where or why she crouched, or whose was the underwater face she needed like that. Where the memory of the smile under her chin might have been and was not, a latch latched and lichen attached its apple-green bloom to the metal. What made her think her fingernails could open locks the rain rained on?

It was not a story to pass on.

So they forgot her. Like an unpleasant dream during a troubling sleep. Occasionally, however, the rustle of a skirt hushes when they wake, and the knuckles brushing a cheek in sleep seem to belong to the sleeper. Sometimes the photograph of a close friend or relative—looked at too long—shifts, and something more familiar than the dear face itself moves there. They can touch it if they like, but don't because they know things will never be the same if they do.

This is not a story to pass on.

Down by the stream in back of 124 her footprints come and go, come and go. They are so familiar. Should a child, an adult place his feet in them, they will fit. Take them out and they disappear again as though nobody ever walked there.

By and by all trace is gone, and what is forgotten is not only the footprints but the water too and what is down there. The rest is weather. Not the breath of the disremembered and unaccounted for, but wind in the eaves, or spring ice thawing too quickly. Just weather. Certainly no clamor for a kiss.

Beloved. ■

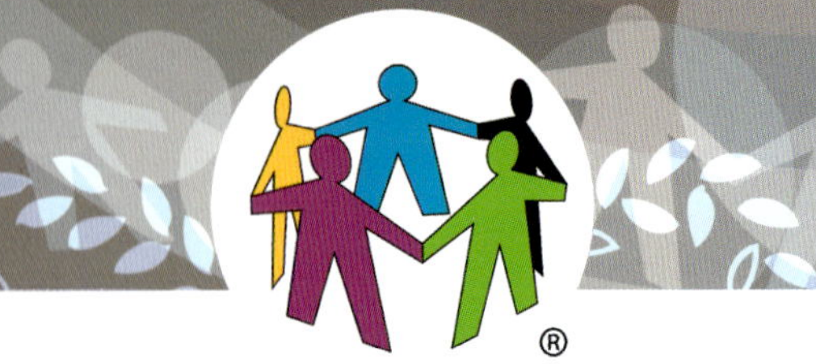

Understanding the Selection

Recalling

1. What are the two kinds of loneliness named? Describe them using quotations from the text.
2. Did people remember the girl's name?
3. What line does the narrator repeat in this passage?
4. Where did the girl appear? What did people do when they saw her?

Interpreting

1. Why are there two kinds of loneliness?
2. Why does the narrator choose to say that the girl is "disremembered" as opposed to simply "forgotten"?
3. Why is this line repeated?
4. What is the narrator's tone? What kind of voice do you think the narrator has?

Synthesizing

1. Do you think this passage is creepy or mysterious in any way? Why? Find at least one line or image that you find especially powerful or downright creepy.
2. What kind of mood does this passage convey? How do you feel while reading it? Reread the passage and, on a separate sheet of paper, copy at least ten words, phrases, or sentences that have a direct effect on the mood created by the writing.

Delving Deeper

Understanding Literature

Oprah's Book Club. Oprah Winfrey, celebrated talk-show host, businesswoman, and actress, starred in the movie *Beloved* (1998), but she was probably a big Toni Morrison fan long before that. In fact, Morrison's *Song of Solomon* was one of the first three picks for Oprah's Book Club in 1996; Morrison's novels *Sula, Paradise,* and *The Bluest Eye* were recommended later. These are all bestsellers, as are most of the titles on Oprah's book list.

Oprah Winfrey's accomplishments are impressive, her fortune stunning, and her fan base enormous. She has made a tremendous contribution to American popular culture and overcome social barriers and obstacles that used to (and often still do) keep black women from getting a foot in the door. She delighted publishers, writers, booksellers, and teachers everywhere when she started using her popular television talk-show to promote reading. She has, in fact, probably done more than any TV star in history to increase the number of readers and book sales in America. She brought countless people back to the joy of reading, reintroduced fans to classic American writers, and granted instant fame and success to many of the authors on her list.

About the Author

Toni Morrison (b.1931) is an author and essayist whose work deals primarily with black Americans struggling to find their identity within an unfair society. In 1993, Morrison became the first African American to win the Nobel Prize in Literature.

Born Chloe Anthony Wofford in Lorian, Ohio, Morrison grew up in a household where the telling of stories and folktales was a tradition. She attended Howard University in Washington, D.C., and Cornell University in New York. She has worked as a teacher and an editor ever since. Morrison's first novel, *The Bluest Eye* (1970), focuses on a black girl who wishes she has blue eyes because she does not recognize her own beauty, and set the tone for Morrison's subsequent writing. Often tragic and complex, her stories use poetic language, symbolism, and fantasy to describe the painful journeys her characters make toward salvation.

Her major titles include *Sula* (1974), *Song of Solomon* (1977), *Tar Baby* (1981), *Jazz* (1992), *Paradise* (1998), and *Love* (2003). Her 1987 novel *Beloved,* about a former slave who is haunted by the baby daughter she killed, won a Pulitzer Prize and was later adapted to film.

Prereading

from A Raisin in the Sun

by Lorraine Hansberry

A Raisin in the Sun first opened in 1959, a time of calm before the storm of the 1960s. For years, social resentments had been brewing beneath the contentment and complacency of the white American middle class, and these resentments were soon to erupt into the Civil Rights, Black Power, and Feminist Movements. In the late '50s, segregation still flourished in the South, where many state and local governments vehemently resisted legal efforts toward integration. It was also widespread in the North, where cities had been divided into white and black neighborhoods.

Hansberry powerfully confronts the problems of segregation and urban racial tensions in this drama about the Youngers, an African-American family living in a cramped apartment on Chicago's Southside. When Mama receives a long-awaited life insurance payment (owed her because of the death of her husband), much to the dismay of her son Walter, she puts a down payment on a new home in a white community. When a white man from the neighborhood "Improvement Association" attempts to prevent their move by buying them out, the family pulls together and, in the end, bravely determines to live in their new home.

Hansberry herself was no stranger to racial prejudice. When her own family moved from Southside Chicago to a predominately white neighborhood, white mobs gathered and expressed outrage at her family's presence. A brick thrown through a window of the new home nearly hit eight year-old Hansberry in the head. Her father took legal action, which ultimately went all the way to the Supreme Court, and the family kept their home. So, the events of *A Raisin in the Sun* are semi-autobiographical.

Visionary for its time, *A Raisin in the Sun* was the first drama to move beyond stereotypical presentations of black life to present starkly realistic African-American characters and to expose their human concerns. The title of the play is a reference to Langston Hughes's poem "Harlem [2]" (page 364), in which Hughes questions what happens when dreams are not realized. Do deferred dreams "wither like a raisin in the sun," as the poem suggests? Like Hughes's poem, Hansberry's drama protests the social and political forces that suppress African Americans' desires and prevent them from realizing their dreams. As you read the selection, think about what the characters' dreams are and what kinds of obstacles they face in achieving them.

from A Raisin in the Sun

by Lorraine Hansberry

Characters in Act I, Scene I

Ruth Younger, Pretty mom in her thirties

Travis Younger, Young son to Ruth and Walter

Walter Lee Younger (Brother), Ruth's husband; Travis's father

Beneatha Younger, Walter's younger sister

Lena Younger (Mama), Strong woman in her early sixties

Act I, Scene I

The YOUNGER *living room would be a comfortable and well-ordered room if it were not for number of indestructible contradictions to this state of being. Its furnishings are typical and undistinguished and their primary feature now is that they have clearly had to accommodate the living of too many people for too many years—and they are tired. Still, we can see that at some time, a time probably no longer remembered by the family (except perhaps for* MAMA), *the furnishings of this room were actually selected with care and love and even hope—and brought to this apartment and arranged with taste and pride.*

That was a long time ago. Now the once loved pattern of the couch upholstery has to fight to show itself from under acres of crocheted doilies and couch covers which have themselves finally come to be more important than the upholstery. And here a table or a chair had been moved to disguise the worn places in the carpet; but the carpet has fought back by showing its weariness, with depressing uniformity, elsewhere on its surface.

Weariness has, in fact, won in this room. Everything has been polished, washed, sat on, used, scrubbed too often. All pretenses but living itself have long since vanished from the very atmosphere of this room.

Moreover, a section of this room, for it is not really a room unto itself, though the landlord's lease would make it seem so, slopes backward to provide a small kitchen area, where the family prepares the meals that are eaten in the living room proper, which must also serve as dining room. The single window that has been provided for these "two" rooms is located in this kitchen area. The sole natural light the family may enjoy in the course of the day is only that which fights its way through this little window.

At left, a door leads to a bedroom which is shared by MAMA *and her daughter,* BENEATHA. *At right, opposite, is a second room (which in the beginning of the life of this apartment was probably a breakfast room), which serves as a bedroom for* WALTER *and his wife,* RUTH.

Time: Sometime between World War II and the present.

Place: Chicago's Southside.

At Rise: It is morning dark in the living room. TRAVIS *is asleep on the make-down bed at center. An alarm clock sounds from within the bedroom at right, and presently* RUTH *enters from that room and closes the door behind her. She crosses sleepily toward the window. As she passes her sleeping son she reaches down and shakes him a little. At the window she raises the shade and a dusky Southside morning light comes in feebly. She fills a pot with water and puts it on to boil. She calls to the boy, between yawns, in a slightly muffled voice.*

RUTH *is about thirty. We can see that she was a pretty girl, even exceptionally so, but now it is apparent that life has been little that she expected, and disappointment has already begun to hang in her face. In a few years, before thirty-five even, she will be known among her people as a "settled woman."*

She crosses to her son and gives him a good, final, rousing shake.

RUTH: Come on now, boy, it's seven thirty! (*Her son sits up at last, in a stupor of sleepiness*) I say hurry up, Travis! You ain't the only person in the world got to use a bathroom! (*The child, a sturdy, handsome little boy of ten or eleven, drags himself out of the bed and almost blindly takes his towels and "today's clothes" from drawers and a closet and goes out to the bathroom, which is in an outside hall and which is shared by another family or families on the same floor.* RUTH *crosses to the bedroom door at right and opens it and calls in to her husband*) Walter Lee! . . . It's after seven thirty! Lemme see you do some waking up in there now! (*She waits*) You better get up from there, man! It's after seven thirty I tell you. (*She waits again*) All right, you just go ahead and lay there and next thing you know Travis be finished an Mr. Johnson'll be in there and you'll be fussing and cussing round here like a mad man! And be late too! (*She waits, at the end of patience*) Walter Lee—it's time for you to get up!

(*She waits another second and then starts to go into the bedroom, but is apparently satisfied that her husband had begun to get up. She stops, pulls the door to, and returns to the kitchen area. She wipes her face with a moist cloth and runs her fingers through her sleep-disheveled hair in a vain effort and ties an apron around her housecoat. The bedroom door at right opens and her husband stands in the doorway in his pajamas, which are rumpled and* ***mismated.*** *He is a lean, intense young man in his middle thirties, inclined to quick nervous movements and* ***erratic*** *speech habits—and always in his voice there is a quality of* ***indictment***)

WALTER: Is he out yet?

RUTH: What you mean *out*? He ain't hardly got in there good yet.

WALTER: (*Wandering in, still more oriented to sleep than to a new day*) Well, what was you doing all that yelling for if I can't even get in there yet? (*Stopping and thinking*) Check coming today?

RUTH: They *said* Saturday and this is just Friday and I hopes to God you ain't going to get up here first thing this morning

VOCABULARY IN PLACE

- **mismated,** ***past part.*** Mismatched, without the proper mate
- **erratic,** ***adj.*** Lacking in steadiness or regularity
- **indictment,** ***n.*** Accusation of wrongdoing

and start talking to me 'bout no money—'cause I 'bout don't want to hear it.

WALTER: Something the matter with you this morning?

RUTH: No—I'm just sleepy as the devil. What kind of eggs you want?

Why does Ruth scramble the eggs? How does she feel toward Walter this morning?

WALTER: Not scrambled. (RUTH *starts to scramble eggs*) Paper come? (RUTH *points impatiently to the rolled up* Tribune *on the table, and he gets it and spreads it out and vaguely reads the front page*) Set off another bomb yesterday.[1]

RUTH: (*Maximum* ***indifference***) Did they?

WALTER: (*Looking up*) What the matter with you?

RUTH: Ain't nothing the matter with me. And don't keep asking me that this morning.

WALTER: Ain't nobody bothering you. (*Reading the news of the day absently again*) Say Colonel McCormick is sick.

RUTH: (*Affecting tea-party interest*) Is he now? Poor thing.

WALTER: (*Sighing and looking at his watch*) Oh, me. (*He waits*) Now what is that boy doing in that bathroom all this time? He just going to have to start getting up earlier. I can't be being late to work on account of him fooling around in there.

RUTH: (*Turning on him*) Oh, no he ain't going to be getting up no earlier no such thing! It ain't his fault that he can't get to bed no earlier nights 'cause he got a bunch of crazy good-for-nothing clowns sitting up running their mouths in what is supposed to be his bedroom after ten o'clock at night . . .

WALTER: That's what you mad about, ain't it? The things I want to talk about with my friends just couldn't be important in your mind, could they?

(*He rises and finds a cigarette in her handbag on the table and crosses to the little window and looks out, smoking and deeply enjoying this first one*)

RUTH: (*Almost matter of factly, a complaint too automatic to deserve emphasis*) Why you always got to smoke before you eat in the morning?

WALTER: (*At the window*) Just look at 'em down there . . . Running and racing to work . . . (*He turns and faces his wife and watches her a moment at the stove, and then, suddenly*) You look young this morning, baby.

RUTH: (*Indifferently*) Yeah?

WALTER: Just for a second—stirring them eggs. It's gone now—just for a second it was—you looked real young again. (*Then, drily*) It's gone now—you look like yourself again.

RUTH: Man, if you don't shut up and leave me alone.

WALTER: (*Looking out to the street again*) First thing a man ought to learn in life is not to make love to no colored woman first thing in the morning. You all some evil people at eight o'clock in the morning.

---

1 **Set off another bomb yesterday.** This may be a reference to the practice by whites of bombing vacant houses in white neighborhoods to prevent non-whites from moving in.

VOCABULARY IN PLACE

- **indifference,** ***n.*** The state or quality of lacking concern; apathy

(TRAVIS *appears in the hall doorway, almost fully dressed and quite wide awake now, his towels and pajamas across his shoulders. He opens the door and signals for his father to make the bathroom in a hurry*)

TRAVIS: (*Watching the bathroom*) Daddy, come on! (WALTER *gets his bathroom utensils and flies out to the bathroom*)

RUTH: Sit down and have your breakfast, Travis.

TRAVIS: Mama, this is Friday. (*Gleefully*) Check coming tomorrow, huh?

RUTH: You get your mind off money and eat your breakfast.

TRAVIS: (*Eating*) This is the morning we supposed to bring the fifty cents to school.

RUTH: Well, I ain't got no fifty cents this morning.

TRAVIS: Teacher say we have to.

RUTH: I don't care what teacher say. I ain't got it. Eat your breakfast, Travis.

TRAVIS: *I am* eating.

RUTH: Hush up now and just eat!

(*The boy gives her an* ***exasperated*** *look for her lack of understanding, and eats* ***grudgingly***)

TRAVIS: You think Grandmama would have it?

RUTH: No! And I want you to stop asking your grandmother for money, you hear me?

TRAVIS: (*Outraged*) Gaaaleee! I don't ask her, she just gimme it sometimes!

RUTH: Travis Willard Younger—I got too much on me this morning to be—

TRAVIS: Maybe Daddy—

RUTH: *Travis!*

(*The boy hushes abruptly. They are both quiet and tense for several seconds*)

TRAVIS: (*Presently*) Could I maybe go carry some groceries in front of the supermarket for a little while after school then?

RUTH: Just hush, I said. (*Travis jabs his spoon into his cereal bowl viciously, and rests his head in anger upon his fists*) If you through eating, you can get over there and make up your bed.

(*The boy obeys stiffly and crosses the room, almost mechanically, to the bed and more or less carefully folds the covering. He carries the bedding into his mother's room and returns with his books and cap*)

TRAVIS: (*Sulking and standing apart from her unnaturally*) I'm gone.

Why is Travis frustrated with his mother?

RUTH: (*Looking up from the stove to inspect him automatically*) Come here. (*He crosses to her and she studies his head*) If you don't take this comb and fix this here head, you better! (*Travis puts down his books with a great sigh of* ***oppression,*** *and crosses to the mirror. His mother mutters under her breath about his "slubbornness"*[2]) 'Bout to march out of here with that head looking just like chickens slept in it! I just don't know where you get your slubborn ways . . . And get your jacket, too. Looks chilly out this morning.

[2] **slubborness.** Ruth's made-up word combining *sloppiness* and *stubborness*

VOCABULARY IN PLACE

- **exasperated,** ***past part.*** Greatly annoyed
- **grudgingly,** ***adv.*** With reluctance or resentment; unwillingly
- **oppression,** ***n.*** A feeling that one is weighed down by unjust or cruel authority or power

TRAVIS: (*With* ***conspicuously*** *brushed hair and jacket*) I'm gone.

RUTH: Get carfare and milk money—(*Waving one finger*)—and not a single penny for no caps, you hear me?

TRAVIS: (*With* ***sullen*** *politeness*) Yes'm.

(*He turns in outrage to leave. His mother watches after him as in his frustration he approaches the door almost comically. When she speaks to him, her voice has become a very gentle tease*)

RUTH (*Mocking; as she thinks he would say it*) Oh, Mama makes me so mad sometimes, I don't know what to do! (*She waits and continues to his back as he stands stock-still in front of the door*) I wouldn't kiss that woman good-bye for nothing in this world this morning! (*The boy finally turns around and rolls his eyes at her, knowing the mood has changed and he is* ***vindicated;*** *he does not, however, move toward her yet*) Not for nothing in this world! (*She finally laughs aloud at him and holds out her arms to him and we see that it is a way between them, very old and practiced. He crosses to her and allows her to embrace him warmly but keeps his face fixed with masculine* ***rigidity.*** *She holds him back from her presently and looks at him and runs her fingers over the features of his face. With utter gentleness—*) Now—whose little old angry man are you?

TRAVIS: (*The masculinity and gruffness start to fade at last*) Aw gaalee—Mama . . .

RUTH: (*Mimicking*) Aw—gaaaaalleeeee, Mama! (*She pushes him, with rough playfulness and finality, toward the door*) Get on out of here or you going to be late.

TRAVIS: (*In the face of love, new aggressiveness*) Mama, could I *please* go carry groceries?

RUTH: Honey, it's starting to get so cold evenings.

WALTER: (*Coming in from the bathroom and drawing a make-believe gun from a make-believe holster and shooting at his son*) What is it he wants to do?

RUTH: Go carry groceries after school at the supermarket.

WALTER: Well, let him go . . .

TRAVIS: (*Quickly, to the ally*) I *have* to—she won't gimme the fifty cents . . .

WALTER: (*To his wife only*) Why not?

RUTH: (*Simply, and with flavor*) 'Cause we don't have it.

WALTER: (*To* RUTH *only*) What you tell the boy things like that for? (*Reaching down into his pants with a rather important gesture*) Here son—

(*He hands the boy the coin, but his eyes are directed to his wife's.* TRAVIS *takes the money happily*)

TRAVIS: Thanks, Daddy.

(*He starts out.* RUTH *watches both of them with murder in her eyes.* WALTER *stands and stares back at her with* ***defiance,*** *and suddenly reaches into his pocket again on an afterthought*)

VOCABULARY IN PLACE

- **conspicuously,** ***adv.*** In a way that attracts attention
- **sullen,** ***adj.*** Showing silent resentment; gloomy
- **vindicate,** ***v.*** To free from blame
- **rigidity,** ***n.*** The state of being inflexible; stiffness
- **defiance,** ***n.*** Bold resistance to an opposing force

WALTER: (*Without even looking at his son, still staring hard at his wife*) In fact, here's another fifty cents . . . Buy yourself some fruit today—or take a taxi cab to school or something!

TRAVIS: Whoopee—

(*He leaps up and clasps his father around the middle with his legs, and they face each other in mutual appreciation; slowly* WALTER LEE *peeks around the boy to catch the violent rays from his wife's eyes and draws his head back as if shot*)

WALTER: You better get down now—and get to school, man.

TRAVIS: (*At the door*) O.K. Good-bye.

(*He exits*)

WALTER: (*After him, pointing with pride*) That's *my* boy. (*She looks at him in disgust and turns back to her work*) You know what I was thinking 'bout in the bathroom this morning?

RUTH: No.

WALTER: How come you always try to be so pleasant!

RUTH: What is there to be pleasant 'bout!

WALTER: You want to know what I was thinking 'bout in the bathroom or not!

RUTH: I know what you was thinking 'bout.

WALTER: (*Ignoring her*) 'Bout what me and Willy Harris was talking about last night.

RUTH: (*Immediately—a refrain*) Willy Harris is a good-for-nothing loud mouth.

WALTER: Anybody who talks to me has got to be a good-for-nothing loud mouth, ain't he? And what you know about who is just a good-for–nothing loud mouth? Charlie Atkins was just a "good-for-nothing loud mouth" too, wasn't he! When he wanted me to go in the dry-cleaning business with him. And now—he's grossing a hundred thousand a year. A hundred thousand dollars a year! You still call *him* a loud mouth!

RUTH: (*Bitterly*) Oh, Walter Lee . . .

(*She folds her head on her arms over on the table*)

WALTER: (*Rising and coming to her and standing over her*) You tired, ain't you! Tired of everything. Me, the boy, the way we live—this beat-up hole—everything. Ain't you? (*She doesn't look up, doesn't answer*) So tired—moaning and groaning all the time, but you wouldn't do nothing to help, would you? You couldn't be on my side that long for nothing, could you?

RUTH: Walter, please leave me alone.

WALTER: A man needs for a woman to back him up . . .

RUTH: Walter—

WALTER: Mama would listen to you. You know she listen to you more than she do me and Bennie. She think more of you. All you have to do is just sit down with her when you drinking your coffee one morning and talking 'bout things like you do and—(*He sits down beside her and demonstrates* ***graphically*** *what he thinks her methods and tone should be*)—you just sip your coffee, see, and say easy like that you been thinking 'bout the deal Walter Lee is so interested in, 'bout the store and all, and sip some more coffee, like what you saying ain't really that important to you—And the next thing you know

VOCABULARY IN PLACE

- **graphically**, ***adv.*** With vivid detail and gestures

she be listening good and asking you questions and when I come home—I can tell her the details. This ain't no fly-by-night proposition, baby. I mean we figured it out, me and Willy and Bobo.

RUTH: (*With a frown*) Bobo?

WALTER: Yeah. You see, this little liquor store we got in mind cost seventy-five thousand and we figured the initial investment on the place be 'bout thirty thousand, see. That be ten thousand each. Course, there's a couple of hundred you got to pay so's you don't spend your life just waiting for them clowns to let your license get approved—

What is Walter's plan to make money?

RUTH: You mean graft?[3]

WALTER: (*Frowning impatiently*) Don't call it that. See there, that just goes to show you what women understand about the world. Baby, don't *nothing* happen for you in this world 'less you pay *somebody* off!

RUTH: Walter, leave me alone! (*She raises her head and stares at him vigorously—then says, more quietly*) Eat your eggs, they gonna be cold.

WALTER: (*Straightening up from her and looking off*) That's it. There you are. Man say to his woman: I got me a dream. His woman say: Eat your eggs. (*Sadly, but gaining in power*) Man say: I got to take hold of this here world, baby! And a woman will say: Eat your eggs and go to work. (*Passionately now*) Man say: I got to change my life, I'm choking to death, baby! And his woman say—(*In utter anguish as he brings his fists down on his thighs*)—Your eggs is getting cold!

RUTH: (*Softly*) Walter, that ain't none of our money.

WALTER: (*Not listening at all or even looking at her*) This morning, I was lookin' in the mirror and thinking about it . . . I'm thirty-five years old; I been married eleven years and I got a boy who sleeps in the living room—(*Very, very quietly*)—and all I got to give him is stories about how rich white people live . . .

RUTH: Eat your eggs, Walter.

WALTER: DAMN MY EGGS . . . DAMN ALL THE EGGS THAT EVER WAS!

RUTH: Then go to work.

WALTER: (*Looking up at her*) See—I'm trying to talk to you 'bout myself—(*Shaking his head with the repetition*)—and all you can say is eat them eggs and go to work.

RUTH: (*Wearily*) Honey, you never say nothing new. I listen to you every day, every night and every morning, and you never say nothing new. (*Shrugging*) So you would rather *be* Mr. Arnold than be his chauffeur. So—I would *rather* be living in Buckingham Palace.

WALTER: That is just what is wrong with the colored woman in this world . . . Don't understand about building their men up and making 'em feel like they somebody. Like they can do something.

RUTH: (*Drily, but to hurt*) There *are* colored men who do things.

WALTER: No thanks to the colored woman.

RUTH: Well, being a colored woman, I guess I can't help my-self none.

(*She rises and gets the ironing board and sets it up and attacks a huge pile of rough-dried clothes, sprinkling them in preparation for the ironing and then rolling them into tight fat balls*)

---

3 **graft.** Money or an advantage gained by immoral means

WALTER: (*Mumbling*) We one group of men tied to a race of women with small minds.

(*His sister* BENEATHA *enters. She is about twenty, as slim and intense as her brother. She is not as pretty as her sister-in-law, but her lean, almost intellectual face has a handsomeness of its own. She wears a bright-red flannel nightie, and her thick hair stands wildly about her head. Her speech is a mixture of many things; it is different from the rest of the family's insofar as education has* ***permeated*** *her sense of English—and perhaps the Midwest rather than the South has finally—at last—won out in her* ***inflection;*** *but not altogether, because over all of it is a soft slurring and transformed use of vowels which is the* ***decided*** *influence of the Southside. She passes through the room without looking at either* RUTH *or* WALTER *and goes to the outside door and looks, a little blindly, out to the bathroom. She sees that it has been lost to the Johnsons. She closes the door with a sleepy vengeance and crosses to the table and sits down a little defeated*)

BENEATHA: I am going to start timing those people.

WALTER: You should get up earlier.

BENEATHA: (*Her face in her hands. She is still fighting the urge to go back to bed*) Really—would you suggest dawn? Where's the paper?

WALTER: (*Pushing the paper across the table to her as he studies her almost* ***clinically,*** *as though he has never seen her before*) You a horrible-looking chick at this hour.

BENEATHA: (*Drily*) Good morning, everybody.

WALTER: (*Senselessly*) How is school coming?

BENEATHA: (*In the same spirit*) Lovely. Lovely. And you know, biology is the greatest. (*Looking up at him*) I dissected something that looked just like you yesterday.

WALTER: I just wondered if you've made up your mind and everything.

BENEATHA: (*Gaining in sharpness and impatience*) And what did I answer yesterday morning—and the day before that?

RUTH: (*From the ironing board, like someone disinterested and old*) Don't be so nasty, Bennie

BENEATHA: (*Still to her brother*) And the day before that and the day before that!

WALTER: (*Defensively*) I'm interested in you. Something wrong with that? Ain't many girls who decide—

WALTER *and* **BENEATHA:** (*In unison*) —"to be a doctor."

(*Silence*)

WALTER: Have we figured out yet just exactly how much medical school is going to cost?

RUTH: Walter Lee, why don't you leave that girl alone and get out of here to work?

BENEATHA: (*Exits to the bathroom and bangs on the door*) Come on out of there, please!

(*She comes back into the room*)

VOCABULARY IN PLACE

- **permeate,** ***v.*** To spread or diffuse through
- **inflection,** ***n.*** Pitch or tone of voice
- **decided,** ***adj.*** Definite
- **clinically,** ***adv.*** Analytically, without emotion

WALTER: (*Looking at his sister* ***intently***) You know the check is coming tomorrow.

BENEATHA: (*Turning on him with a sharpness all her own*) That money belongs to Mama, Walter, and it's for her to decide how she wants to use it. I don't care if she wants to buy a house or a rocket ship or just nail it up somewhere and look at it. It's hers. Not ours—*hers*.

WALTER: (*Bitterly*) Now ain't that fine! You just got your mother's interest at heart, ain't you, girl? You such a nice girl—but if Mama got that money she can always take a few thousand and help you through school too—can't she?

Why are Walter and Beneatha fighting? Are their dreams compatible?

BENEATHA: I have never asked anyone around here to do anything for me!

WALTER: No! And the line between asking and just accepting when the time comes is big and wide—ain't it!

BENEATHA: (*With fury*) What do you want from me, Brother—that I quit school or just drop dead, which!

WALTER: I don't want nothing but for you to stop acting holy 'round here. Me and Ruth done made some sacrifices for you—why can't you do something for the family?

RUTH: Walter, don't be dragging me in it.

WALTER: You are in it—Don't you get up and go work in somebody's kitchen for the last three years to help put clothes on her back?

RUTH: Oh, Walter—that's not fair . . .

WALTER: It ain't that nobody expects you to get on your knees and say thank you, Brother; thank you, Ruth; thank you, Mama—and thank you, Travis, for wearing the same pair of shoes for two semesters—

BENEATHA: (*Dropping to her knees*) Well—I *do*—all right? Thank everybody . . . and forgive me for ever wanting to be anything at all . . . forgive me, forgive me!

RUTH: Please stop it! Your mama'll hear you.

WALTER: Who the hell told you you had to be a doctor? If you so crazy 'bout messing 'round with sick people—then go be a nurse like other women—or just get married and be quiet . . .

BENEATHA: Well—you finally got it said. . . It took you three years but you finally got it said. Walter, give up; leave me alone—it's Mama's money.

WALTER: *He was my father, too!*

BENEATHA: So what? He was mine, too—and Travis' grandfather—but the insurance money belongs to Mama. Picking on me is not going to make her give it to you to invest in any liquor stores—(*Underbreath, dropping into a chair*)—and I for one say, God bless Mama for that!

WALTER: (*To* RUTH) See—did you hear? Did you hear!

RUTH: Honey, please go to work.

WALTER: Nobody in this house is ever going to understand me.

BENEATHA: Because you're a nut.

WALTER: Who's a nut?

VOCABULARY IN PLACE

- **intently,** ***adv.*** Purposefully; with concentration

BENEATHA: You—you are a nut. Thee is mad, boy.

WALTER: (*Looking at his wife and his sister from the door, very sadly*) The world's most backward race of people, and that's a fact.

BENEATHA: (*Turning slowly in her chair*) And then there are all those prophets who would lead us out of the wilderness—(WALTER *slams out of the house*)—into the swamps!

RUTH: Bennie, why you always gotta be pickin' on your brother? Can't you be a little sweeter sometimes? (*Door opens.* WALTER *walks in*)

WALTER: (*To* RUTH) I need some money for carfare.

RUTH: (*Looks at him, then warms; teasing, but tenderly*) Fifty cents? (*She goes to her bag and gets money*) Here, take a taxi.

(WALTER *exits.* MAMA *enters. She is a woman in her early sixties, full-bodied and strong. She is one of those women of a certain grace and beauty who wear it so* ***unobtrusively*** *that it takes a while to notice. Her dark-brown face is surrounded by the total whiteness of her hair, and, being a woman who has adjusted to many things in life and overcome many more, her face is full of strength. She has, we can see, wit and faith of a kind that keep her eyes lit and full of interest and expectancy. She is, in a word, a beautiful woman. Her bearing is perhaps most like the noble bearing of the women of the Hereros of Southwest Africa—rather as if she imagines that as she walks she still bears a basket or a vessel upon her head. Her speech, on the other hand, is as careless as her* ***carriage*** *is precise—she is inclined to slur everything—but her voice is perhaps not so much quiet as simply soft*)

MAMA: Who that 'round here slamming doors at this hour? (*She crosses through the room, goes to the window, opens it, and brings in a* ***feeble*** *little plant growing* ***doggedly*** *in a small pot on the window sill. She feels the dirt and puts it back out*)

RUTH: That was Walter Lee. He and Bennie was at it again.

MAMA: My children and they tempers. Lord, if this little old plant don't get more sun than it's been getting it ain't never going to see spring again. (*She turns from the window*) What's the matter with you this morning, Ruth? You looks right **peaked.** You aiming to iron all them things? Leave some for me. I'll get to 'em this afternoon. Bennie honey, it's too drafty for you to be sitting 'round half dressed. Where's your robe?

BENEATHA: In the cleaners.

MAMA: Well, go get mine and put it on.

BENEATHA: I'm not cold, Mama, honest.

MAMA: I know—but you so thin . . .

BENEATHA: (*Irritably*) Mama, I'm not cold.

MAMA: (*Seeing the make-down bed as* TRAVIS *has left it*) Lord have mercy, look at that poor bed. Bless his heart—he tries, don't he?

(*She moves to the bed* TRAVIS *has sloppily made up*)

VOCABULARY IN PLACE

- **unobtrusively,** ***adj.*** In a manner that is not obvious; inconspicuously
- **carriage,** ***n.*** Posture
- **feeble,** ***adj.*** Weak; lacking vigor
- **doggedly,** ***adv.*** With stubborn determination
- **peaked,** ***adj.*** Having a sickly appearance

RUTH: No—he don't half try at all 'cause he know you going to come along behind him and fix everything. That's just how come he don't know how to do nothing right now—you done spoiled that boy so.

MAMA: Well—he's a little boy. Ain't supposed to know 'bout housekeeping. My baby, that's what he is. What you fix for his breakfast this morning?

RUTH: (*Angrily*) I feed my son, Lena!

MAMA: I ain't **meddling**—(*Underbreath; busy-bodyish*) I just noticed all last week he had cold cereal, and when it starts getting this chilly in the fall a child ought to have some hot grits or something when he goes out in the cold—

RUTH: (*Furious*) I gave him hot oats—is that all right!

MAMA: I ain't meddling. (*Pause*) Put a lot of nice butter on it? (RUTH *shoots her an angry look and does not reply*) He likes lots of butter.

RUTH: (*Exasperated*) Lena—

MAMA: (*To* BENEATHA. MAMA *is **inclined** to wander conversationally sometimes*) What was you and your brother fussing 'bout this morning?

BENEATHA: It's not important, Mama.

(*She gets up and goes to look out at the bathroom, which is apparently free, and she picks up her towels and rushes out*)

MAMA: What was they fighting about?

RUTH: Now you know as well as I do.

MAMA: (*Shaking her head*) Brother still worrying hisself sick about that money?

RUTH: You know he is.

MAMA: You had breakfast?

RUTH: Some coffee.

MAMA: Girl, you better star eating and looking after yourself better. You almost thin as Travis.

RUTH: Lena—

MAMA: Un-hunh?

RUTH: What are you going to do with it?

MAMA: Now don't you start, child. It's too early in the morning to be talking about money. It ain't Christian.

RUTH: It's just that he got his heart set on that store—

MAMA: You mean that liquor store that Willy Harris want him to invest in?

RUTH: Yes—

MAMA: We ain't no business people, Ruth. We just plain working folks.

RUTH: Ain't nobody business people till they go into business. Walter Lee say colored people ain't never going to start getting ahead till they start gambling on some different kinds of things in the world—investments and things.

MAMA: What done got into you, girl? Walter Lee done finally sold you on investing.

RUTH: No. Mama, something is happening between Walter and me. I don't know what it is—but he needs something—something I can't give him any more. He needs this chance, Lena.

MAMA: (*Frowning deeply*) But liquor, honey—

RUTH: Well—like Walter say—I spec people

VOCABULARY IN PLACE

- **meddle**, *v.* To intrude or interfere
- **inclined**, *adj.* Disposed to a certain preference or opinion

going to always be drinking themselves some liquor.

MAMA: Well—whether they drinks it or not ain't none of my business. But whether I go into business selling to 'em *is*, and I don't want that on my ledger[4] this late in life. (*Stopping suddenly and studying her daughter-in-law*) Ruth Younger, what's the matter with you today? You look like you could fall over right there.

RUTH: I'm tired.

MAMA: Then you better stay home from work today.

RUTH: I can't stay home. She'd be calling up the agency and screaming at them, "My girl didn't come in today—send me somebody! My girl didn't come in!" Oh, she just have a fit . . .

MAMA: Well, let her have it. I'll just call her up and say you got the flu—

RUTH: *(Laughing)* Why the flu?

MAMA: 'Cause it sounds respectable to 'em. Something white people get, too. They know 'bout the flu. Otherwise they think you been cut up or something when you tell 'em you sick.

RUTH: I got to go in. We need the money.

MAMA: Somebody would of thought my children done all but starved to death the way they talk about money here late. Child, we got a great big old check coming tomorrow.

RUTH: (*Sincerely, but also self-righteously*) Now that's your money. It ain't got nothing to do with me. We all feel like that—Walter and Bennie and me—even Travis.

MAMA: (*Thoughtfully, and suddenly very far away*) Ten thousand dollars—

RUTH: Sure is wonderful.

MAMA: Ten thousand dollars.

RUTH: You know what you should do, Miss Lena? You should take yourself a trip somewhere. To Europe or South America or someplace—

MAMA: (*Throwing up her hands at the thought*) Oh, child!

RUTH: I'm serious. Just pack up and leave! Go on away and enjoy yourself some. Forget about the family and have yourself a ball for once in your life—

MAMA: (*Drily*) You sound like I'm just about ready to die. Who'd go with me? What I look like wandering 'round Europe by myself?

RUTH: Shoot—these here rich white women do it all the time. They don't think nothing of packing up they suitcases and piling on one of them big steamships and—swoosh!—they gone, child.

MAMA: Something always told me I wasn't no rich white woman.

RUTH: Well—what are you going to do with it then?

MAMA: I ain't rightly decided. (*Thinking. She speaks now with emphasis*) Some of it got to be put away for Beneatha and her schoolin'—and ain't nothing going to touch that part of it. Nothing. (*She waits several seconds, trying to make up her mind about something, and looks at* RUTH *a little tentatively before going on*) Been thinking that we maybe could meet the notes on a little old two-story somewhere, with a yard where Travis could play in the summertime, if we use part of the insurance for a down payment and everybody kind of pitch in. I could

---

[4] **ledger.** Record book (figurative)

maybe take on a little day work again, few days a week—

RUTH: (*Studying her mother-in-law* ***furtively*** *and concentrating on her ironing, anxious to encourage without seeming to*) Well, Lord knows, we've put enough rent into this here rat trap to pay for four houses by now . . .

MAMA: (*Looking up at the words "rat trap" and then looking around and leaning back and sighing—in a suddenly reflective mood—*) "Rat trap"—yes, that's all it is. (*Smiling*) I remember just as well the day me and Big Walter moved in here. Hadn't been married but two weeks and wasn't planning on living here no more than a year. (*She shakes her head at the dissolved dream*) We was going to set away, little by little, don't you know, and buy a little place out in Morgan Park. We had even picked out the house. (*Chuckling a little*) Looks right dumpy today. But Lord, child, you should know all the dreams I had 'bout buying that house and fixing it up and making me a little garden in the back—(*She waits and stops smiling*) And didn't none of it happen.

What had been Mama and Big Walter's dream? What happened?

(*Dropping her hands in a* ***futile*** *gesture*)

RUTH: (*Keeps her head down, ironing*) Yes, life can be a barrel of disappointments, sometimes.

MAMA: Honey, Big Walter would come in here some nights back then and slump down on that couch there and just look at the rug, and look at me and look at the rug and then back at me—and I'd know he was down then . . . really down. (*After a second very long and thoughtful pause; she is seeing back to times that only she can see*) And then, Lord, when I lost the baby—little Claude—I almost thought I was going to lose Big Walter too. Oh, that man grieved hisself! He was one man to love his children.

RUTH: Ain't nothin' can tear at you like losin' your baby.

MAMA: I guess that's how come that man finally worked hisself to death like he done. Like he was fighting his own war with this here world that took his baby from him.

RUTH: He sure was a fine man, all right. I always liked Mr. Younger.

MAMA: Crazy 'bout his children! God knows there was plenty wrong with Walter Younger—hard-headed, mean, kind of wild with women—plenty wrong with him. But he sure loved his children. Always wanted them to have something—be something. That's where Brother gets all these notions, I reckon. Big Walter used to say, he'd get right wet in the eyes sometimes, lean his head back with the water standing in his eyes and say, "Seem like God didn't see fit to give the black man nothing but dreams—but He did give us children to make them dreams seem worth while." (*She smiles*) He could talk like that, don't you know.

RUTH: Yes, he sure could. He was a good man, Mr. Younger.

MAMA: Yes, a fine man—just couldn't never catch up with his dreams, that's all.

VOCABULARY IN PLACE

- **furtively,** ***adv.*** Secretly
- **futile,** ***adj.*** Having no useful result; useless

(BENEATHA *comes in, brushing her hair and looking up to the ceiling, where the sound of a vacuum cleaner has started up*)

BENEATHA: What could be so dirty on that woman's rugs that she has to vacuum them every single day?

RUTH: I wish certain young women 'round here who I could name would take inspiration about certain rugs in a certain apartment I could also mention.

BENEATHA: (*Shrugging*) How much cleaning can a house need, for Christ's sakes.

MAMA: (*Not liking the Lord's name used thus*) Bennie!

RUTH: Just listen to her—just listen!

BENEATHA: Oh, God!

MAMA: If you use the Lord's name just one more time—

BENEATHA: (*A bit of a whine*) Oh, Mama—

RUTH: Fresh—just fresh as salt, this girl!

BENEATHA: (*Drily*) Well—if the salt loses its savor—[5]

MAMA: Now that will do. I just ain't going to have you 'round here reciting the scriptures[6] in vain—you hear me?

BENEATHA: How did I manage to get on everybody's wrong side by just walking into a room?

RUTH: If you weren't so fresh—

BENEATHA: Ruth, I'm twenty years old.

MAMA: What time you be home from school today?

BENEATHA: Kind of late. (*With enthusiasm*) Madeline is going to start my guitar lessons today.

(MAMA *and* RUTH *look up with the same expression*)

MAMA: Your *what* kind of lessons?

BENEATHA: Guitar.

RUTH: Oh, Father!

What kind of lessons is Beneatha taking? Why do Ruth and Mama scold her?

MAMA: How come you done taken it in your mind to learn to play the guitar?

BENEATHA: I just want to, that's all.

MAMA: (*Smiling*) Lord, child, don't you know what to do with yourself? How long it going to be before you get tired of this now—like you got tired of that little play-acting group you joined last year? (*Looking at Ruth*) And what was it the year before that?

RUTH: The horseback-riding club for which she bought that fifty-five-dollar riding habit that's been hanging in the closet ever since!

MAMA: (*To* BENEATHA) Why you got to flit so from one thing to another, baby?

BENEATHA: (*Sharply*) I just want to learn to play the guitar. Is there anything wrong with that?

MAMA: Ain't nobody trying to stop you. I just wonders sometimes why you had to flit so from one thing to another all the time. You ain't never done nothing with all that camera equipment you brought home—

BENEATHA: I don't flit! I—I experiment with different forms of expression—

RUTH: Like riding a horse?

BENEATHA:—People have to express themselves one way or another.

5 **if the salt loses its savor.** A reference to Matthew 5:13

6 **scriptures.** The Bible

MAMA: What is it you want to express?

BENEATHA: (*Angrily*) Me! (MAMA *and* RUTH *look at each other and burst into* ***raucous*** *laughter*) Don't worry—I don't expect you to understand.

MAMA: (*To change the subject*) Who you going out with tomorrow night?

BENEATHA: (*With displeasure*) George Murchison again.

MAMA: (*Pleased*) Oh—you getting a little sweet on him?

RUTH: You ask me, this child ain't sweet on nobody but herself—(*Underbreath*) Express herself!

(*They laugh*)

BENEATHA: Oh—I like George all right, Mama. I mean I like him enough to go out with him and stuff, but—

RUTH: (*For* ***devilment***) What does *and stuff* mean?

BENEATHA: Mind your own business.

MAMA: Stop picking at her now, Ruth. (*A thoughtful pause, and then a suspicious sudden look at her daughter as she turns in her chair for emphasis*) What *does* it mean?

BENEATHA: (*Wearily*) Oh, I just mean I couldn't ever really be serious about George. He's—he's so shallow.

RUTH: Shallow—what do you mean he's shallow? He's *Rich!*

MAMA: Hush, Ruth.

BENEATHA: I know he's rich. He knows he's rich, too.

RUTH: Well—what other qualities a man got to have to satisfy you, little girl?

BENEATHA: You wouldn't even begin to understand. Anybody who married Walter could not possibly understand.

MAMA: (*Outraged*) What kind of way is that to talk about your brother?

BENEATHA: Brother is a flip—let's face it.

MAMA: (*To* RUTH, *helplessly*) What's a flip?

RUTH: (*Glad to add kindling*) She's saying he's crazy.

BENEATHA: Not crazy. Brother isn't really crazy yet—he—he's an elaborate neurotic.[7]

MAMA: Hush your mouth!

BENEATHA: As for George. Well. George looks good—he's got a beautiful car and he takes me to nice places and, as my sister-in-law says, he is probably the richest boy I will ever get to know and I even like him sometimes—but if the Youngers are sitting around waiting to see if their little Bennie is going to tie up the family with the Murchisons, they are wasting their time.

RUTH: You mean you wouldn't marry George Murchinson if he asked you someday? That pretty, rich thing? Honey, I knew you was odd—

BENEATHA: No I would not marry him if all I felt for him was what I feel now. Besides, George's family wouldn't really like it.

MAMA: Why not?

BENEATHA: Oh, Mama—the Murchisons

[7] **elaborate neurotic.** An emotionally unstable person

VOCABULARY IN PLACE

- **raucous,** ***adj.*** Rough-sounding and harsh
- **devilment,** ***n.*** Devilish behavior; mischief

are honest-to-God-real-*live*-rich colored people, and the only people in the world who are more snobbish than rich white people are rich colored people. I thought everybody knew that. I've met Mrs. Murchison. She's a scene!

MAMA: You must not dislike people 'cause they well off, honey.

BENEATHA: Why not? It makes just as much sense as disliking people 'cause they are poor, and lots of people do that.

RUTH: (*A wisdom-of-the-ages manner. To* MAMA) Well, she'll get over some of this—

BENEATHA: Get over it? What are you talking about, Ruth? Listen, I'm going to be a doctor. I'm not worried about who I'm going to marry yet—if I ever get married.

MAMA *and* **RUTH:** *If!*

Does Beneatha want to marry George Murchinson? How does she feel about marriage?

MAMA: Now, Bennie—

BENEATHA: Oh, I probably will . . . but first I'm going to be a doctor, and George, for one, still thinks that's pretty funny. I couldn't be bothered with that. I am going to be a doctor and everybody around here better understand that!

MAMA: (*Kindly*) 'Course you going to be a doctor, honey, God willing.

BENEATHA: (*Drily*) God hasn't got a thing to do with it.

MAMA: Beneatha—that just wasn't necessary.

BENEATHA: Well—neither is God. I get sick of hearing about God.

MAMA: Beneatha!

BENEATHA: I mean it! I'm just tired of hearing about God all the time. What has He got to do with anything? Does he pay tuition?

MAMA: You 'bout to get your fresh little jaw slapped!

RUTH: That's just what she needs, all right!

BENEATHA: Why? Why can't I say what I want to around here, like everybody else?

MAMA: It don't sound nice for a young girl to say things like that—you wasn't brought up that way. Me and your father went to trouble to get you and Brother to church every Sunday.

BENEATHA: Mama, you don't understand. It's all a matter of ideas, and God is just one idea I don't accept. It's not important. I am not going out and be immoral or commit crimes because I don't believe in God. I don't even think about it. It's just that I get tired of Him getting credit for all the things the human race achieves through its own stubborn effort. There simply is no blasted God—there is only man and it is he who makes miracles!

(MAMA *absorbs this speech, studies her daughter and rises slowly and crosses to* BENEATHA *and slaps her powerfully across the face. After, there is only silence and the daughter drops her eyes from her mother's face, and* MAMA *is very tall before her*)

MAMA: Now—you say after me, in my mother's house there is still God. (*There is a long pause and* BENEATHA *stares at the floor wordlessly.* MAMA *repeats the phrase with precision and cool emotion*) In my mother's house there is still God.

BENEATHA: In my mother's house there is still God.

(*A long pause*)

Why does Mama scold Beneatha so harshly? What position does she hold in the family?

MAMA: (*Walking away from* BENEATHA, *too disturbed for triumphant posture. Stopping and turning back to her daughter*) There are some ideas we ain't going to have in this house. Not long as I am at the head of this family.

BENEATHA: Yes, ma'am.

(MAMA *walks out of the room*)

RUTH: (*Almost gently, with profound understanding*) You think you a woman, Bennie—but you still a little girl. What you did was childish—so you got treated like a child.

BENEATHA: I see. (*Quietly*) I also see that everybody thinks it's all right for Mama to be a **tyrant.** But all the tyranny in the world will never put a God in the heavens!

(*She picks up her books and goes out*)

RUTH: (*Goes to* MAMA's *door*) She said she was sorry.

MAMA: (*Coming out, going to her plant*) They frightens me, Ruth. My children.

RUTH: You got good children, Lena. They just a little off sometimes—but they're good.

MAMA: No—there's something come down between me and them that don't let us understand each other and I don't know what it is. One done almost lost his mind thinking 'bout money all the time and the other done commence to talk about things I can't seem to understand in no form or fashion. What is it that's changing, Ruth?

RUTH: (*Soothing, older than her years*) Now . . . you taking it all too seriously. You just got strong-willed children and it takes a strong woman like you to keep 'em in hand.

MAMA: (*Looking at her plant and sprinkling a little water on it*) They spirited all right, my children. Got to admit they got spirit—Bennie and Walter. Like this little old plant that ain't never had enough sunshine or nothing—and look at it . . .

(*She has her back to* RUTH, *who has had to stop ironing and lean against something and put the back of her hand to her forehead*)

RUTH: (*Trying to keep* MAMA *from noticing*) You . . . sure . . . loves that little old thing, don't you? . . .

MAMA: Well, I always wanted me a garden like I used to see sometimes at the back of the houses down home. This plant is close as I ever got to having one. (*She looks out of the window as she replaces the plant*) Lord, ain't nothing as dreary as the view from this window on a dreary day, is there? Why ain't you singing this morning, Ruth? Sing that "No Ways Tired." That song always lifts me up so—(*She turns at last to see that* RUTH *has slipped quietly into a chair, in a state of semiconsciousness*) Ruth! Ruth honey—what's the matter with you . . . Ruth!

Curtain

VOCABULARY IN PLACE

- **tyrant,** *n.* A ruler who exercises power in a harsh, cruel manner

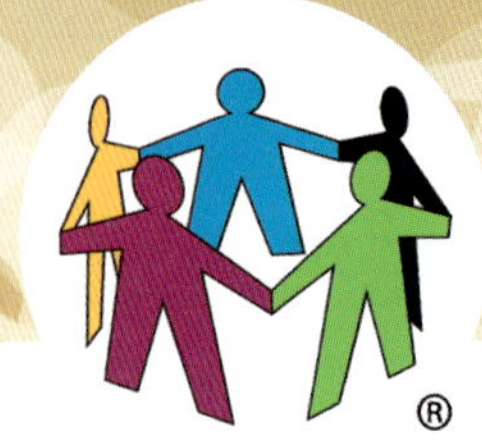

Understanding the Selection

Recalling

1. What does the Youngers' apartment look like?
2. What does Walter give his son, Travis, before Travis leaves for school?
3. What does Walter want to do with the life insurance money?
4. What description does Mama give of her late husband?
5. What does the plant that Mama carries into the living room look like?

Interpreting

1. What kind of living conditions do the Youngers currently face?
2. Why does Walter do this? What is Walter's attitude toward money, and how does this attitude differ from Ruth's?
3. How do Mama and Ruth feel about Walter's dream?
4. What saying of Big Walter's does Mama quote? How does this saying relate to the central conflict brewing in Act I?
5. Why does she care for the plant so much? What does it seem to represent?

Synthesizing

1. What dream does each major character in Act I have? In what way are these dreams "deferred," or put on hold?
2. What strengths does this family show, despite all the disagreements and tensions?

Delving Deeper

Speaking and Listening

Reading with Flair. Drama, perhaps like no other form, is well suited to conveying the range of emotions involved in human relationships. When reading a drama aloud, therefore, it is important to read with expression, for this emotional force is not just an embellishment or minor detail. It is essential for conveying the play's meaning. Working in pairs, practice reading aloud the dialogue that Mama and Ruth have when Walter has exited and before Beneatha returns (pages 686–689). Choose a role and try to put yourself in your character's shoes. How does your character feel at this point? What is her **motivation,** the cause of her actions and feelings? Using variations in your pitch, tone, volume, and physical gestures, try to convey what your character is feeling.

About the Author

Lorraine Hansberry (1930–1965) was a woman ahead of her time. She wrote essays on feminism, was an activist for peace and for black causes, and produced a great deal of writing before her life was tragically cut short by cancer at the age of 35. When her acclaimed drama *A Raisin in the Sun* opened in 1959, Hansberry became the first black author to have a play produced on Broadway. She also received the prestigious New York Drama Critics Circle Award and was the youngest African American to earn this honor.

Born in Chicago's Southside, Hansberry grew up in a prominent middle-class family that was active in the fight against racial segregation. After briefly attending the University of Wisconsin, she moved to New York, where she worked as a reporter and, eventually, as associate editor for Paul Robeson's radical black newspaper, *Freedom.*

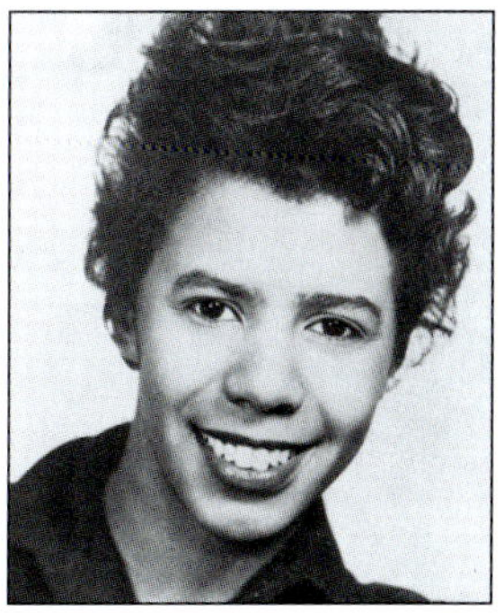

In addition to *A Raisin in the Sun,* for which she also composed a screenplay, Hansberry published an essay on Simone de Beauvoir; a drama, *The Sign in Sidney Brustein's Window* (1964); a book for the influential Student Nonviolent Coordinating Committee (SNCC) called *The Movement: Documentary of a Struggle for Equality* (1964); and letters for *The Ladder* magazine. After Hansberry's death, her husband, Robert Nemiroff, edited and published her books *Les Blances, What Use are Flowers?* and *The Drinking Gourd.* He also edited *To Be Young, Gifted and Black,* a compilation of her unfinished plays, letters, and autobiographical writings.

Prereading

"lady in blue"

by Ntozake Shange

With the rise of the **Black Arts Movement**, African-American theatres emerged as important community centers, geared toward both artistic expression—in the form of poetry, dance, drama, and music performances—and political activity, including community meetings and lectures. Ntozake Shange's *for colored girls who have considered suicide/ when the rainbow is enuf* is an important work that grew out of this close interconnection between the literary, the political, and the artistic. Originally workshopped at Woodie King's New Federal Theatre in Manhattan, the play eventually hit Broadway and won several awards, including an Obie Award and an Outer Circle Award.

for colored girls is often called a **choreopoem.** The name refers to the fact that in performance the actors' movements are choreographed in the manner of a dance that reflects and builds upon the poetry that functions as the play's dialogue. The play interweaves poetry, music, and dance as seven African-American women, dressed in the colors of a rainbow (plus brown), perform twenty poems, narrating the struggles they have faced throughout their lives. As they relate their individual stories, these women form a collage of voices that also expresses the ability of black women to survive hardships and gives voice to hope and determination. Their voices also serve as a protest, speaking out against the denial of African-American women's voices in American culture.

Although *for colored girls* is rooted in performance, it is also literary, and Shange wished to carve out a space for African-American women in the world of literature. Her training as a dancer shines through in the way she crafts her poetry. Pay attention to the ways in which Shange's poetry defies the conventions of the English language. In what ways do her words show movement? In what ways do the letters and words move you through the poem? How does Shange use language to convey the emotions felt by the "lady in blue"?

lady in blue

by Ntozake Shange

one thing i dont need
is any more apologies
i got sorry greetin me at my front door
you can keep yrs
i dont know what to do wit em
they dont open doors
or bring the sun back
they dont make me happy
or get a mornin paper
didnt nobody stop usin my tears to wash cars
cuz a sorry

i am simply tired
of collectin
    i didn't know
    i was so important toyou'
i'm gonna haveta throw some away
i cant get to the clothes in my closet
for alla the sorries
i'm gonna tack a sign to my door
leave a message by the phone
    'if you called
    to say yr sorry
    call somebody
    else
    i dont use em anymore'
i let sorry / didn't meanta / & how cd i know abt that
take a walk down a dark & musty street in Brooklyn
i'm gonna do exactly what i want to
& i wont be sorry for none of it
letta sorry soothe yr soul / i'm gonna soothe mine

you were always inconsistent
doin something & then bein sorry
beatin my heart to death
talking bout you sorry
well
i will not call
i'm not goin to be nice
i will raise my voice
& scream & holler
& break things & race the engine
& tell all yr secrets bout yrself to yr face
& i will list in detail
    everyone of my wonderful lovers
& their ways
i will play oliver lake[1]
loud
& i wont be sorry for none of it ■

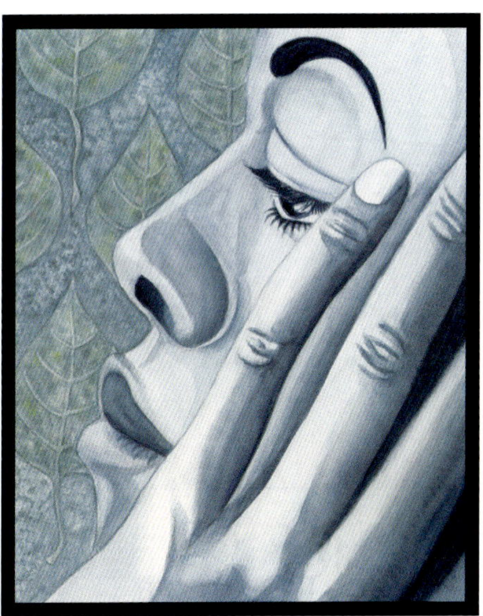

[1] **oliver lake.** (b.1942) Poet, painter, and performance artist

Understanding the Selection

Recalling

1. What does the "lady in blue" not need anymore?
2. What does she let "take a walk down a dark & musty street in Brooklyn"?
3. What is she going to do instead of listening to apologies?

Interpreting

1. What things does she say that apologies won't do?
2. What does this image say about her attitude?
3. Why might these things soothe her soul?

Synthesizing

1. What adjectives would you use to describe the attitude of the "lady in blue"? If you were going to perform this poem, what would you do with the tempo and volume of your voice at various points within the poem? What would be your tone of voice in various parts of the poem? Explain.

Delving Deeper

Understanding Literature

Blocking. When directors work with actors on a play, they **block** the scenes, meaning that they show the actors roughly where and how to move throughout the play. Usually, the director will relate a movement to a piece of dialogue, saying, for example, "Move downstage center on the line beginning with 'I am simply.'" Within that framework, actors then refine the movements to fit the characters that they are playing. In *for colored girls,* however, Shange introduced some innovations. Rather than speaking dialogue, the actors recite poetic narrative; and rather than getting their movements from a blocking rehearsal, the actors—both the woman reciting and the other women of the rainbow that support her—perform choreographed dance movements coordinated with the rhythms of the poetry. Working in groups of three, reread "lady in blue." How would you describe the overall mood of the selection? What rhythms might work well to accompany this scene? If you were acting out this role, how would you convey the poem's emotional message through your body? What kinds of dance movements might work in this scene?

About the Author

Ntozake Shange (b.1948) is a poet, playwright, novelist, dancer, and educator. Shange was born Paulette Williams in Trenton, New Jersey, to Paul T. Williams, a surgeon, and Eloise Williams, a psychiatric social worker and educator. When she was eight years old, her family moved to St. Louis, Missouri, and Paulette was bused to a formerly segregated school. The racism she experienced there propelled her interest in writing. She graduated with honors from Barnard College in 1970. In 1971 she changed her name to Ntozake Shange, meaning "she who comes with her own things" (ntzoke) and "she who walks like a lion" (shange) in **Xhosa,** the Zulu language. Receiving a master's degree in American Studies at the University of California at Los Angeles, she taught at various colleges in California. During this time, she joined Halifu Osumare's dance company and collaborated with Paula Moss on poetry, music, and dance that became the basis of *for colored girls.* Shange has published many other plays, including *Spell #7* (1979), *A Photograph: Lovers-in-Motion* (1979), as well as poetry collections, children's books, and novels, including *If I Can Cook You Know God Can* (1998).

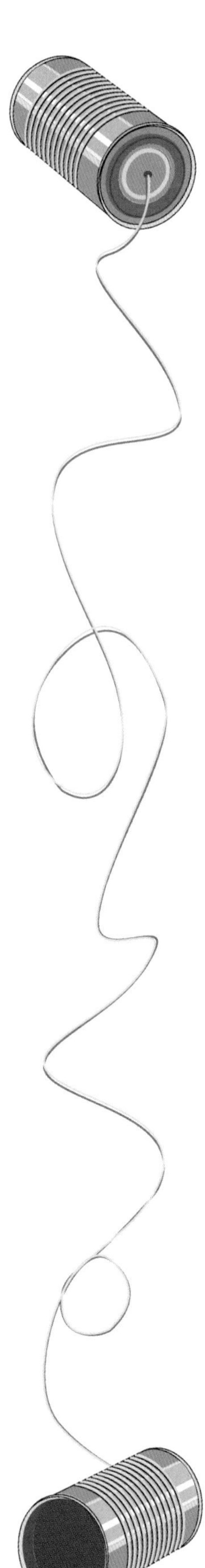

Unit 4

Speaking and Listening Skills: Debate

A **debate** is a formal process by which teams of speakers support, in front of an audience, opposing points of view with regard to some proposition.

The Debate Proposition, or Resolution

A **debate proposition**, also known as a **resolution**, is simply a statement about which there can be disagreement. People usually distinguish between three types of debate proposition:

A **proposition of fact** is a statement about what was the case in the past, is the case in the present, or will be the case in the future. Here are some examples:

RESOLVED: That the major dance crazes in the cities of the North in the first half of the twentieth century were largely creations of African-American emigrants from the South.

RESOLVED: That the major uniquely American musical forms were created by African Americans.

RESOLVED: That an African American will become president of the United States within the next twenty-five years.

A **proposition of value** is a statement that judges or evaluates something. Here are some examples:

RESOLVED: That the greatest poetry being produced during the 1920s and 1930s in the United States was being written by African Americans.

RESOLVED: That the best art by African Americans is that which deals with African-American themes, characters, and experiences.

A **proposition of policy** is a statement about some course of action that should be taken. Here are some examples:

RESOLVED: That the governments of former slave states should institute reparation payments for descendants of enslaved persons in those states.

RESOLVED: That every American college should have an African-American Studies department.

How a Debate Is Conducted

The debaters are divided into two teams. The **affirmative team** assumes the burden of proving the proposition to be true. The affirmative team may also define the central terms in the proposition. The **negative team** assumes the burden of **rejoinder**—that is, of demonstrating the weaknesses in the arguments presented by the affirmative team. It may also challenge the definitions of key terms provided by the affirmative team. To prove the proposition, the affirmative team must present **evidence** to support the proposition. Obviously, in order to gather such evidence, members of the affirmative team must do a great deal of research to gather relevant information. The affirmative team presents its case in **constructive speeches.** The negative team presents its refutation of the constructive case in **rebuttal speeches.** Both the affirmative team and the negative team conduct **cross-examinations** of the speakers on the other teams. The cross-examination is conducted by the opposing team. There are many possible formats for a formal debate. A common debate format is as follows:

First Affirmative Constructive Speech (8 minutes)
  Cross-Examination by the Negative Team (3 minutes)
First Negative Constructive Speech (8 minutes)
  Cross-Examination by the Affirmative Team (3 minutes)
Second Affirmative Constructive Speech (8 minutes)
  Cross-Examination by the Negative Team (3 minutes)
Second Negative Constructive Speech (8 minutes)
  Cross-Examination by the Affirmative Team (3 minutes)
First Negative Rebuttal Speech (4 minutes)
First Affirmative Rebuttal Speech (4 minutes)
Second Negative Rebuttal Speech (4 minutes)
Second Affirmative Rebuttal Speech (4 minutes)

At the end of the debate, a decision is made by the audience or by the judges based on which team presented the best case.

Assignment: Hold a debate in class on one of the propositions presented above or on a proposition decided upon by your teacher and class. Follow the format for debate given above.

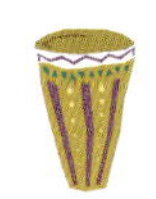 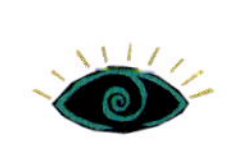 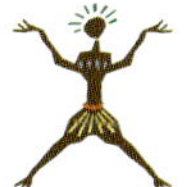 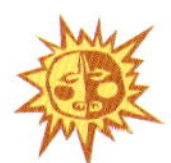 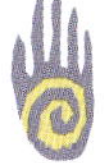 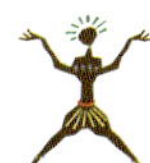 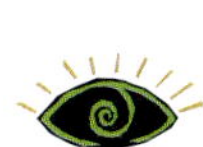 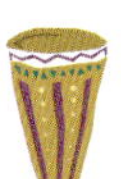

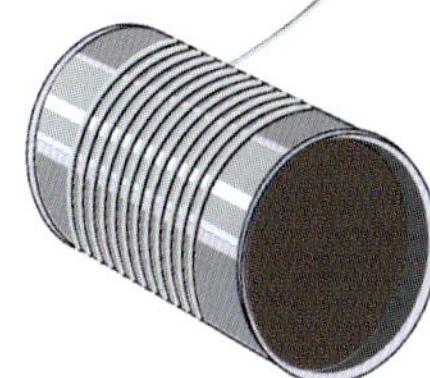

Unit 4 Writing

Critical and Expository Writing

1. **A Comparison/Contrast Essay. Topic 1:** Reread Dudley Randall's "Booker T. and W. E. B." Then reread the lessons on Booker T. Washington and W. E. B. Du Bois on pages 240 and 268. Write an **essay** in which you compare and contrast the points of view of Washington and Du Bois. Refer to the Randall poem in your introduction. In the body of the essay, present Washington's point of view in one paragraph and Du Bois's point of view in the next paragraph. Then conclude with a paragraph in which you take stock of this famous disagreement and present your point of view about which man was right and why. Topic 2: During the early years of their work as leaders of the Civil Rights Movement, Malcolm X and Martin Luther King, Jr., had very different views regarding what the methods and goals of the Civil Rights Movement should be. Reread the selections on pages 484 and 516. Then do some additional research on both men. Finally, write an essay in which you compare and contrast their points of view. Conclude your essay with a paragraph in which you present your own opinion about which person had the right view for African Americans at the time.

2. **A Close Critical Reading.** Choose a poem from this unit that is particularly complex and rich. Possibilities include "Homage to the Empress of the Blues," by Robert Hayden; "Map of the New World: Archipelagos," by Derek Walcott; and "Benjamin Banneker Sends His Almanac to Thomas Jefferson," by Jay Wright. Write an essay in which you present a close, line-by-line reading (interpretation) of the poem for an audience of high-school students.

3. **A Research Report on a Topic Related to African-American Studies.** Choose one of the following topics for a ten- to twelve-page research report:

   Three Slave Narratives
   Origins of the Blues
   Nat Turner and Denmark Vesey—Slave Rebellions in the United States
   The Tuskegee Airmen
   Ida Wells-Barnett and the Campaign against Lynching
   The Role of Religion in the Thought of Martin Luther King and Malcolm X
   The Lack of Genetic Basis for the Idea of Race

Creative Writing

1. **An Imaginary Dialogue.** Write an imaginary historical dialogue in which Malcolm X and Martin Luther King, Jr., discuss with one another their differing views of the struggle for Civil Rights in America. Incorporate in your dialogue material from the selections on pages 484 and 516.

2. **Haiku.** Reread the haiku by Sonia Sanchez on page 585. A traditional haiku presents a snapshot of a scene in very concrete, vivid language. A **haiku** is supposed to follow a rigid format consisting of a five-syllable line followed by a seven-syllable line followed by another five-syllable line. Try your hand at writing some haiku. Write one or two haiku of the traditional variety—ones that present scenes from nature. Then try creating some nontraditional haiku that follow the haiku form but that treat off-beat, contemporary topics (such as, for example, a scene from a video game or a political issue facing America today).

3. **An Interior Monologue. An interior monologue** is a short piece (usually one or two paragraphs long) that presents the thoughts of a character. Choose any character from Unit 4, such as the daughter in *A Raisin in the Sun* or the sharecropper in "The Man Who Saw the Flood" or the little girl from *I Know Why the Caged Bird Sings* and write an interior monologue presenting his or her thoughts about a subject. Try to capture in your monologue the speech and personality of the character.

Unit 4

Focus on: The Triumph of African-American Music

Background: Swing Jazz and Jazz Standards

Bebop: Bird, Dizzy, and Monk

"'Round Midnight," by Thelonius Monk
and Bernie Hanighen

Miles Davis and Cool Jazz

John Coltrane

"A Love Supreme," by John Coltrane

Other Jazz Greats and Idioms: Hard Bop, Soul Jazz, Free Jazz, Jazz Fusion, Smooth Jazz

The Evolution of the Blues

What the Blues Became: Varieties of Popular Music

From the 1950s to the Present

Early R&B and Rock 'n' Roll
Jimi Hendrix

Motown
"What's Going On," by Marvin Gaye, Al Cleveland,
and Renaldo Benson

Soul

"When a Man Loves a Woman," by Percy Sledge

Funk

Special Feature: Bob Marley and the Wailers

Hip Hop/Rap

The Legacy of African-American Music

Modern African-American Dance: Selected Developments

Modal jazz makes use of scales other than the standard major and minor ones, particularly of scales built off other degrees of the major and minor scales. So, for example, if a musician plays the notes of a major scale but begins and ends on the third note of the scale, the result is a type of modal scale known as the Phrygian. Davis innovated by not writing out the music for *Kind of Blue* beforehand but instead giving his players chord progressions and modal scales to play against these progressions. Davis went on through a long career to dabble in other styles of jazz, including so-called **fusion** (which blends jazz with rock 'n' roll) and so-called **free jazz** (which breaks all the rules of traditional musicality). Other not-to-be missed recordings by Davis include his albums ***Milestones*** (1958), ***Sketches of Spain*** (1960), and ***Someday My Prince Will Come*** (1961).

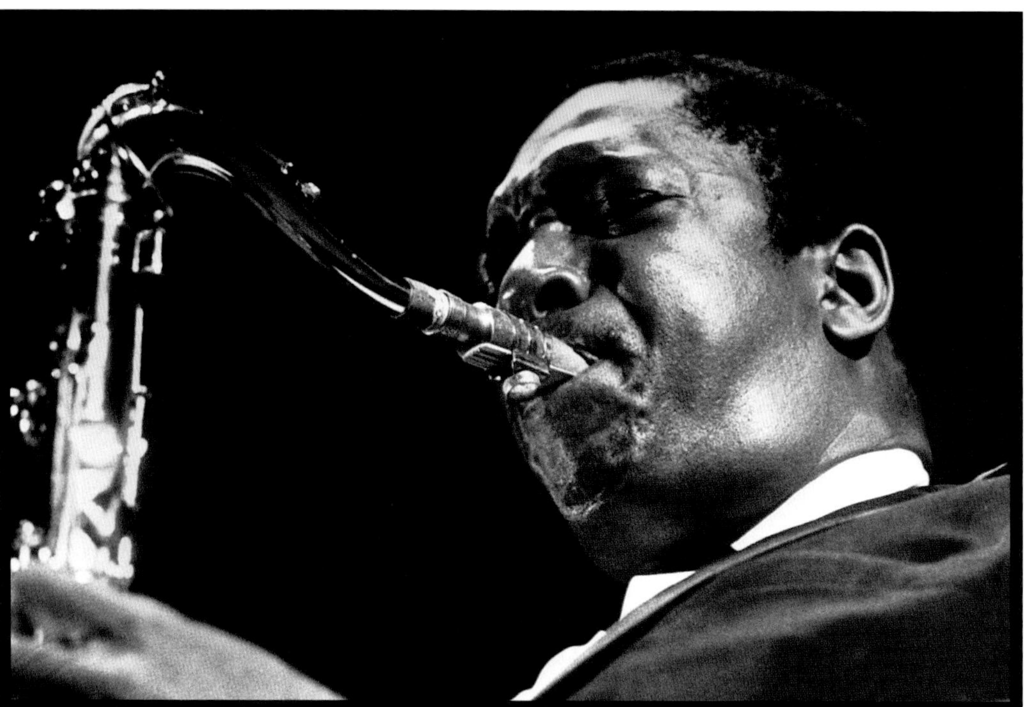

John Coltrane. Jazz saxophonist

John Coltrane

Of the many great jazz musicians of the mid-twentieth century, only one other can be said to have equaled Parker and Davis in influence on the subsequent development of jazz music, and that was the great tenor and soprano saxophonist **John Coltrane** (1926–1967), commonly referred to simply as **Trane.** A master of the modal jazz style, Coltrane recorded with many of the greats, including Davis, Monk, Hartman, and Ellington. He practiced relentlessly, mastered the complexities of music theory (including unusual scales and harmonic theory), and, in a short life, reinvented his playing many times. Early on, he mastered the bebop style. He then became one of the great performers in what is known as the **hard bop** style, which combines bebop with elements of gospel and rhythm and blues. He carried improvisation to new heights of intensity and complexity, not to mention length. It wasn't uncommon for Coltrane to improvise on a single simple tune such as "**My Favorite Things**" or "**Inchworm**" for forty minutes or more. Not-to-miss recordings by Coltrane include *Giant Steps* (1959), *My Favorite Things* (1960), *Duke Ellington and John Coltrane* (1962), and *John Coltrane and Johnny Hartman* (1963). In his early thirties, Coltrane experienced a profound religious conversion and began to search spiritually in an intense and profound way. One of the results was his great album, *A Love Supreme* (1964), a highly experimental recording that includes these lyrics, themselves a refined improvisation on a few themes:

A Love Supreme,
by John Coltrane

I will do all I can to be worthy of Thee O Lord.
It all has to do with it.
Thank you God.
Peace.
There is none other.
God is. It is so beautiful.
Thank you God. God is all.
Help us to resolve our fears and weaknesses.
Thank you God.
In You all things are possible.
We know. God made us so.
Keep your eye on God.
God is. He always was. He always will be.
No matter what . . . it is God.
He is gracious and merciful.
It is most important that I know Thee.
Words, sounds, speech, men, memory, thoughts,
fears and emotions—time—all related . . .
all made from one . . . all made in one.
Blessed by His name.
Thought waves—heat waves—all vibrations—
all paths lead to God. Thank you God.
His way . . . it is so lovely . . . it is gracious.
It is merciful—Thank you God.
One thought can produce millions of vibrations
and they all go back to God . . . everything does.
Thank you God.

Have no fear . . . believe . . . Thank you God.
The universe has many wonders. God is all.
His way . . . it is so wonderful.
Thoughts—deeds—vibrations, etc.
They all go back to God and He cleanses all.
He is gracious and merciful . . . Thank you God.
Glory to God . . . God is so alive.
God is.
God loves.
May I be acceptable in Thy sight.
We are all one in His grace.
The fact that we do exist is acknowledgement
of Thee O Lord.
Thank you God.
God will wash away all our tears . . .
He always has . . .
He always will.
Seek Him everyday. In all ways seek God everyday.
Let us sing all songs to God.
To whom all praise is due . . . praise God.
No road is an easy one, but they all
go back to God.
With all we share God.
It is all with God.
It is all with Thee.
Obey the Lord.
Blessed is He.
We are all from one thing . . . the will of God . . .
Thank you God.
I have seen God—I have seen ungodly—
none can be greater—none can compare to God.
Thank you God.
He will remake us . . . He always has and He
always will.
It is true—blessed be His name—Thank you God.
God breathes through us so completely . . .
so gently we hardly feel it . . . yet,
it is our everything.
Thank you God.
ELATION—ELEGANCE—EXALTATION—
All from God.
Thank you God. Amen

Other Jazz Greats and Idioms: Hard Bop, Soul Jazz, Free Jazz, Jazz Fusion, Smooth Jazz

It is impossible in a brief treatment like this one to do justice to the incredible wealth of jazz music from the mid-to-late twentieth century. Other great African-American jazz musicians in the **cool jazz** style were saxophonist and prolific composer **Wayne Shorter** (b. 1933) and pianist and composer **John Lewis** (1920–2001), leader of **The Modern Jazz Quartet** and composer of the jazz classic **"Django,"** a tribute to the great Gypsy jazz guitarist Django Reinhardt. During his long career, Shorter has composed many jazz standards

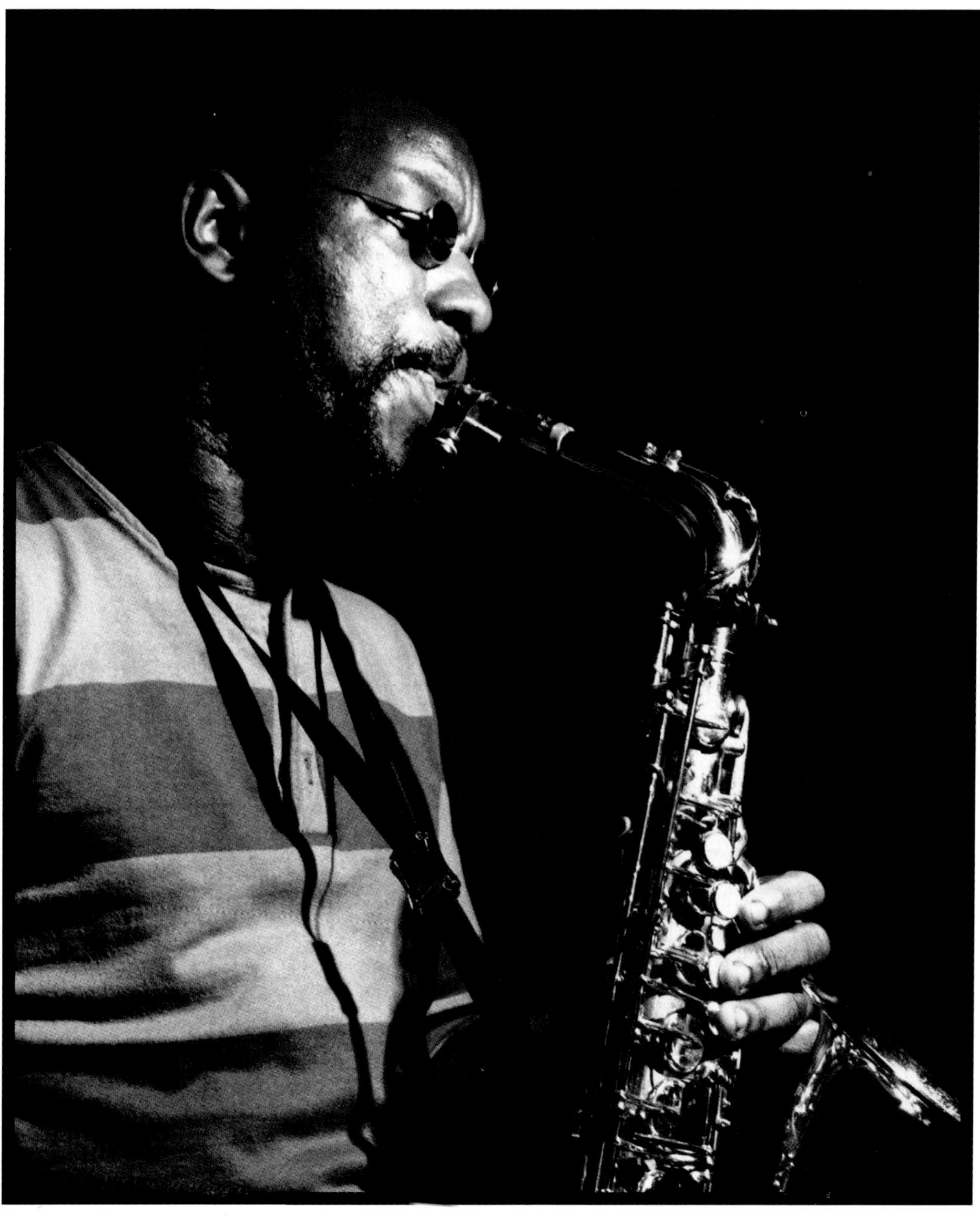

Ornette Coleman. His radical musical innovations created the genre known as free jazz.

and has made major contributions in just about every jazz idiom. Other great **hard bop** players include saxophonist **Sonny Rollins** (b. 1930), trumpeter **Clifford Brown** (1930–1956), bassist **Charlie Mingus** (1922–1973), drummer **Art Blakey** (1919–1990), and saxophonist **Dexter Gordon** (1923–1990). Mingus was also a leading figure in the development of **soul jazz,** which drew on blues, gospel, and rhythm and blues sources; often made use of the organ as a jazz instrument; and made more use than hard bop of repetitive riffs, or themes. Other great

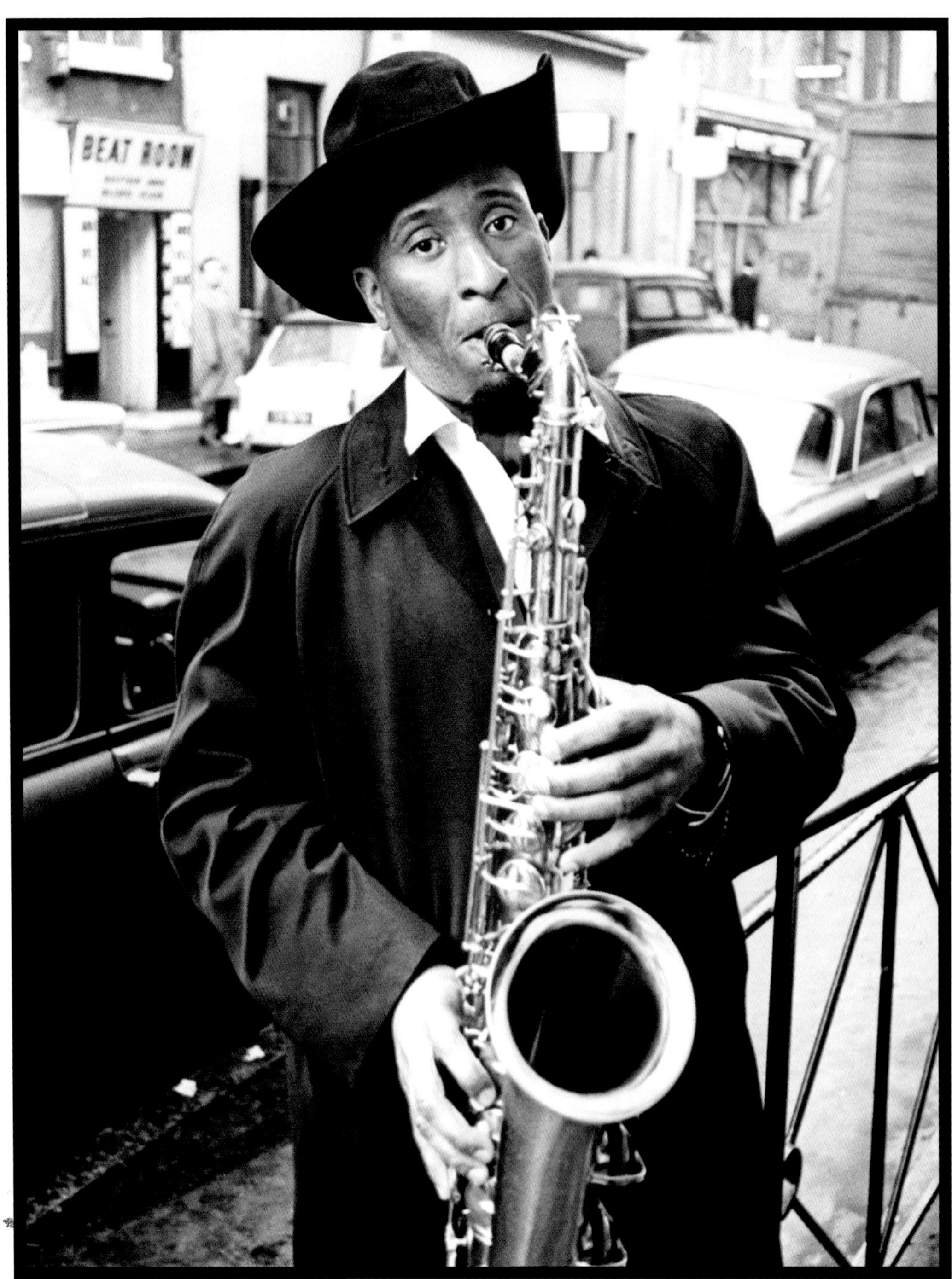

Sonny Rollins. Jazz saxophonist

players of soul jazz include organist **Ramsey Lewis** (b. 1935) and guitarist **Grant Green** (1935–1979). Saxophonist and composer **Ornette Coleman** (b. 1930) is widely considered the creator and chief exponent of **free jazz,** which violates many traditional tenets of musicality, playing freely with time signatures and tonality, for example. Pianist and composer **Herbie Hancock** is one of the great innovators of soul jazz and fusion. **Jazz fusion** draws heavily on influences outside the jazz idiom, including blues, rock-and-roll, funk, and soul. Another great jazz fusion player is bassist **Stanley Clarke** (b. 1951). Guitarist **George Benson** (b. 1943) is perhaps the greatest performer of so-called **smooth jazz,** which borrows heavily from New Age Music and is typified by its return to easily listenable melody. Not-to-be-missed recordings in these genres include *Clifford Brown & Max Roach* (1954), Sonny Rollins's *Saxophone Colossus* (1956), Art Blakey and the Jazz Messengers' *A Night in Tunisia* (1957), Charles Mingus's *Ah Um* (1959), Ornette Coleman's *Shape of Jazz to Come* (1959), Grant Green's *Ballads* (1961), John Lewis's *Evolution,* (1964), Wayne Shorter's *JuJu* (1965), George Benson's *White Rabbit* (1971), and Dexter Gordon's *Sophisticated Giant* (1977) .

The Evolution of the Blues

In the early part of the twentieth century, millions of African Americans left the rural South and moved to cities in the North in what has been called **The Great Migration.** As people moved north, they took their music with them. It is sometimes said, tongue-in-cheek but with some truth to it, that the blues was born in the Delta and then moved up the river to Memphis, St. Louis, and Chicago. After World War II, Chicago became a mecca for blues artists, and the availability of amplified instruments (especially electric guitars) made possible the creation of a new, gritty sound known variously as **Chicago blues** or **electric blues.** Great performers in this genre included **Big Walter Horton** (1918–1981), **B. B. King** (b. 1925); **Freddie King** (1934–1976), **Jimmy Reed** (1925–1976), **Magic Sam** (1937–1969), **Koko Taylor** (b. 1935), **Little Walter** (1930–1968), **Muddy Waters** (1915–1983), **Junior Wells** (1934–1998), and **Sonny Boy Williamson II** (1899–1965). Other great electronic blues artists included **Bo Diddley** (b. 1928), **John Lee Hooker** (1917–2001), **Elmore James** (1918–1963), **Etta James** (b. 1938), **J. B. Lenoir** (1929–1967), **Junior Wells** (1934–1998), and **T-Bone Walker** (1910–1975). In other developments related to the blues, the boogie-woogie and stride piano forms developed into **piano blues,** often played solo or with a small rhythm section. The piano blues artists of note include **Champion Jack Dupree** (1909–1992), **Leroy Carr** (1905–1935), **Fats Domino** (b. 1928), and **Otis Spann** (1930–1970). Also popular in the late 1940s was a style known as **jump blues,** usually involving a lead saxophone and other horns in front of a rhythm section consisting of piano, bass, and drums. Exponents of the jump blues included **Louis Jordan** (1908–1975), **Big Joe Turner** (1911–1985), and **Roy Brown** (1925–1981).

In recent years, there has been a resurgence of interest in traditional country blues styles. One of the greatest of the contemporary players of such traditional blues music is **Corey Harris** (b. 1969), a talented young guitarist and singer who is also a great scholar of blues history.

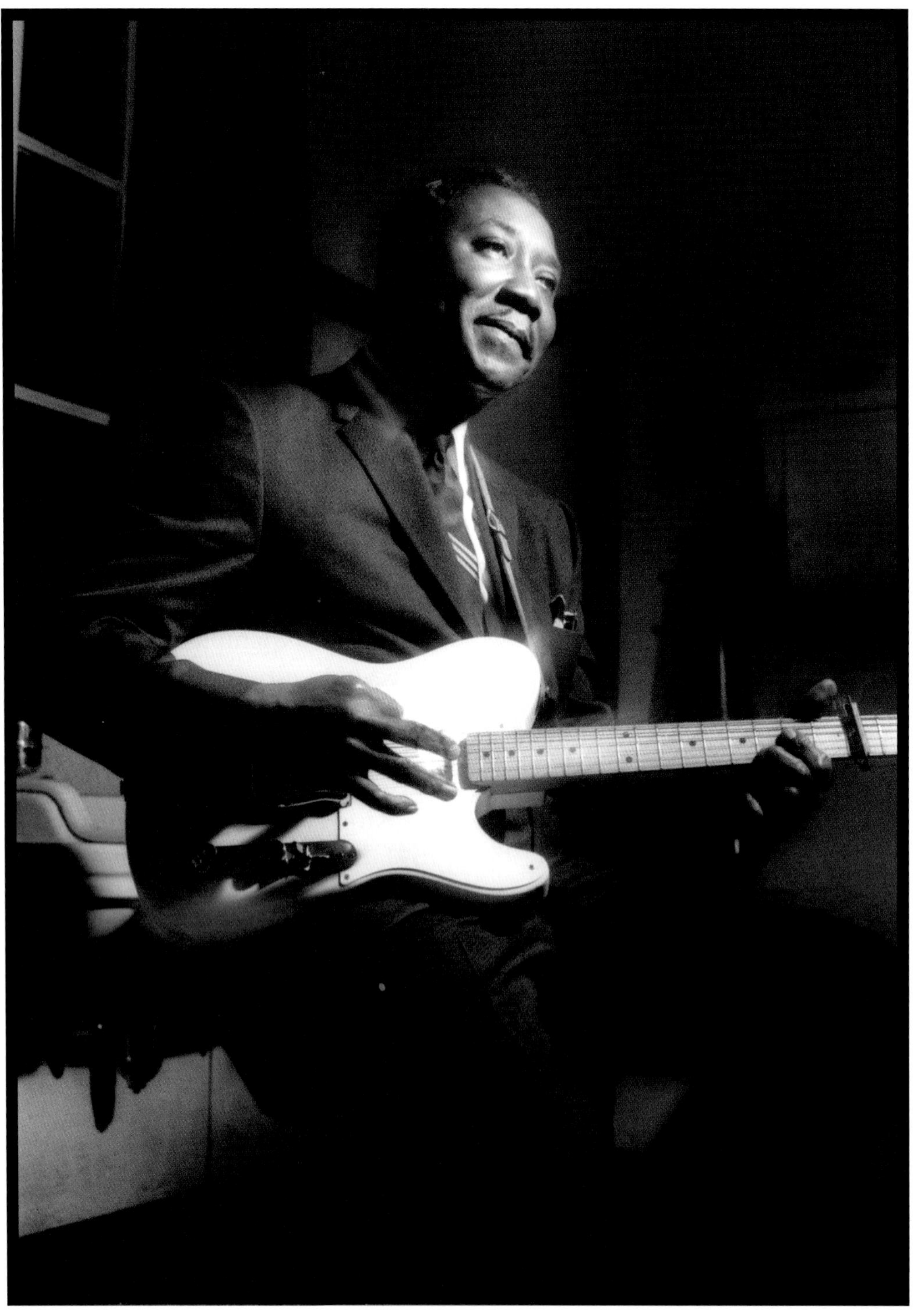

Muddy Waters. One of the originators of electronic blues

What the Blues Became: Varieties of Popular Music from the 1950s to the Present

Early R & B and Rock 'n' Roll. An astonishing diversity of music sprang from roots in blues, jazz, and gospel during the 1950s. In 1949, *Billboard,* a music trade magazine, began using the term **rhythm and blues** (now commonly shortened to **R & B**) to describe popular African-American music. The term has been used from that day forth as a catch-all phrase to cover every bit of popular music by African Americans that can't clearly be placed in another specific category. From the perspective of today, a number of the early R & B songs, such as **"Rocket 88"** (1951), **"Sh-Boom"** (1954), and **"Ain't That a Shame"** (1955) are clearly rock 'n' roll tunes, and the rock 'n'

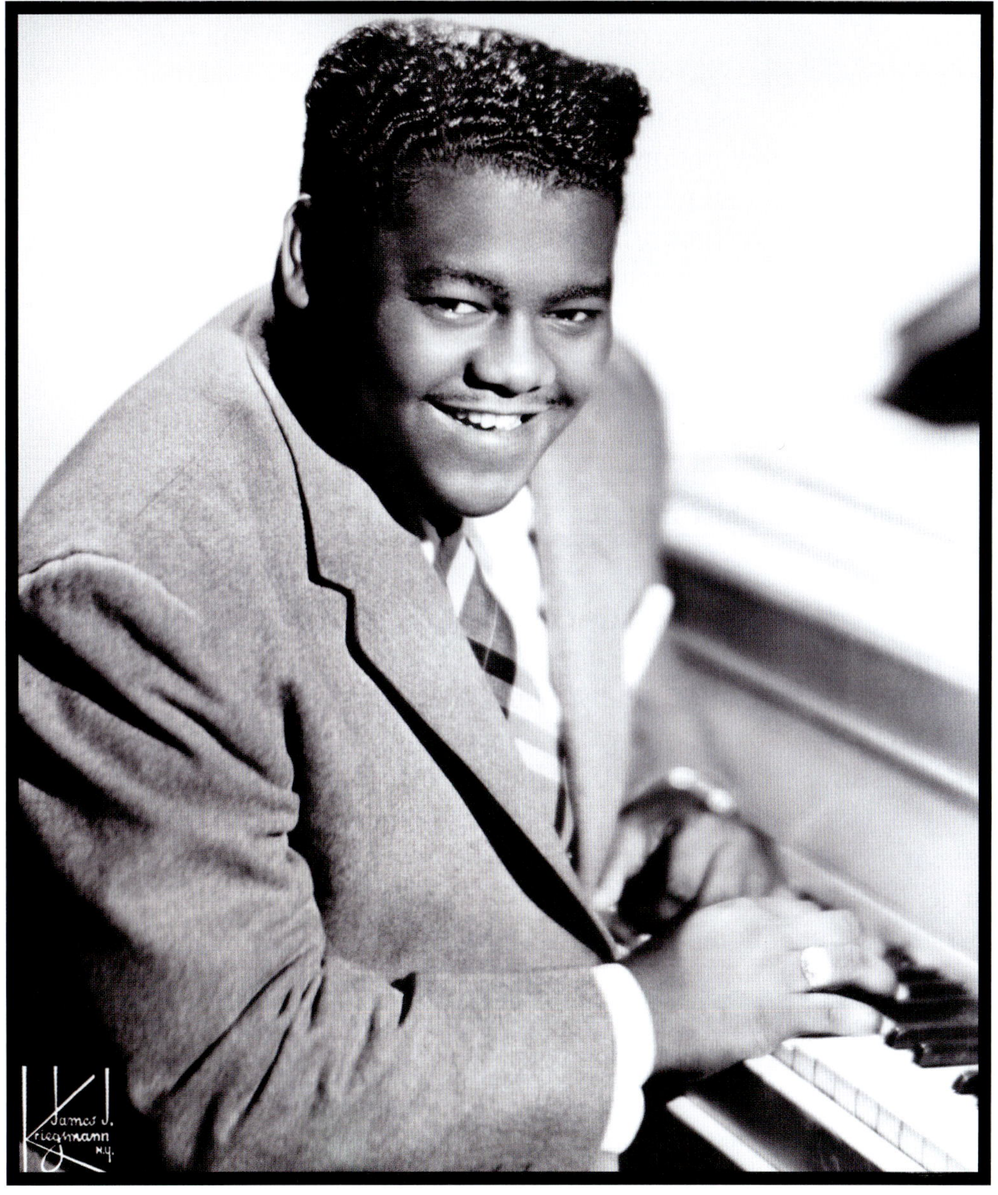

Fats Domino. Piano rhythm and blues player and rock 'n' roll pioneer

roll phenomenon that dominated popular music in the late twentieth century clearly owed its origins primarily to blues and boogie-woogie. "Rocket 88," often called the first rock 'n' roll song, was written and recorded by **Ike Turner** (b. 1931) and his band the **Kings of Rhythm** under the name Jackie Brenston and His Delta Cats.

Rock 'n' roll was popularized in the United States in two waves. First, a number of country-and-blues-inspired **rockabilly** artists, such as Bill Haley and the Comets, Jerry Lee Lewis, and Buddy Holly became tremendously successful. These artists were followed by the musicians of the so-called **British Invasion**—the Beatles, the Rolling Stones, Herman's Hermits, Cream, and so on. Both rockabilly and the British invasion owed much to the blues tradition. Both varieties of early rock 'n' roll were commonly written in 12-bar format (See page 439) with dominant (B7) chords in the tonic. A typical 1950s rock 'n' roll tune was simply blues or boogie-woogie played up-tempo with a backbeat (stress on the second and fourth beats in tunes played in 4/4 time). When lead guitar came to dominate rock 'n' roll instrumentation, the lines played by those lead guitarists were typically based on blues scales (See page 441). When white artist Jerry Lewis had an enormous hit in 1957 with "Whole Lotta Shakin' Going On," it was a tune co-authored by an African American, **Dave "Curly" Williams.** Elvis Presley was singled out by his record producer specifically for the purpose of serving as a vehicle for taking the black rhythm and blues sound to white audiences. The British Invasion rockers all cut their teeth on material by African-American rhythm and blues artists such as **Little Richard** (b. 1932), author of such hits as "**Long Tall Sally**" and "**Tutti Frutti,**" and **Chuck Berry** (b. 1926).

If anyone can claim to be **the father of rock 'n' roll,** Berry can. In and out of trouble with the law from an early age, Berry nonetheless drew upon blues roots to produce a fully synthesized, hard-driving, electric sound characterized by innovative, up-tempo lead guitar licks. He recorded hit after hit in the 1950s, including "**Maybelline**" (1955), "**Johnny B. Goode**" (1955), and "**Roll Over Beethoven,**" and the success of these songs led just about every rock 'n' roll wannabe to copy his style. Rock 'n' roll legends such as Keith Richards of the Rolling Stones and John Lennon of the Beatles frankly acknowledged their debt to Berry. These British Invasion groups also reached back further into the blues tradition, covering (doing their own recordings of) such older blues numbers as Robert Johnson's "**Love's in Vain**" (recorded by the Rolling Stones), Willie Dixon's "**You Shook Me**" (recorded by Led Zeppelin), Robert Johnson's "**Cross Road Blues**" and Charlie Patton's "**Spoonful**" (recorded by Cream, featuring guitarist Eric Clapton).

Many rock 'n' roll purists believe that this music reached its zenith in the work of guitarist and songwriter **Jimi Hendrix** (1942–1970), whose dazzling lead guitar work and brilliant song writing have rarely been equaled in the rock 'n' roll genre. Hendrix owed a great debt to the blues, and one of his all-time finest recordings is of the traditional 12-bar blues tune **"Red House."** (See the special section on the next page for more about Jimi Hendrix.)

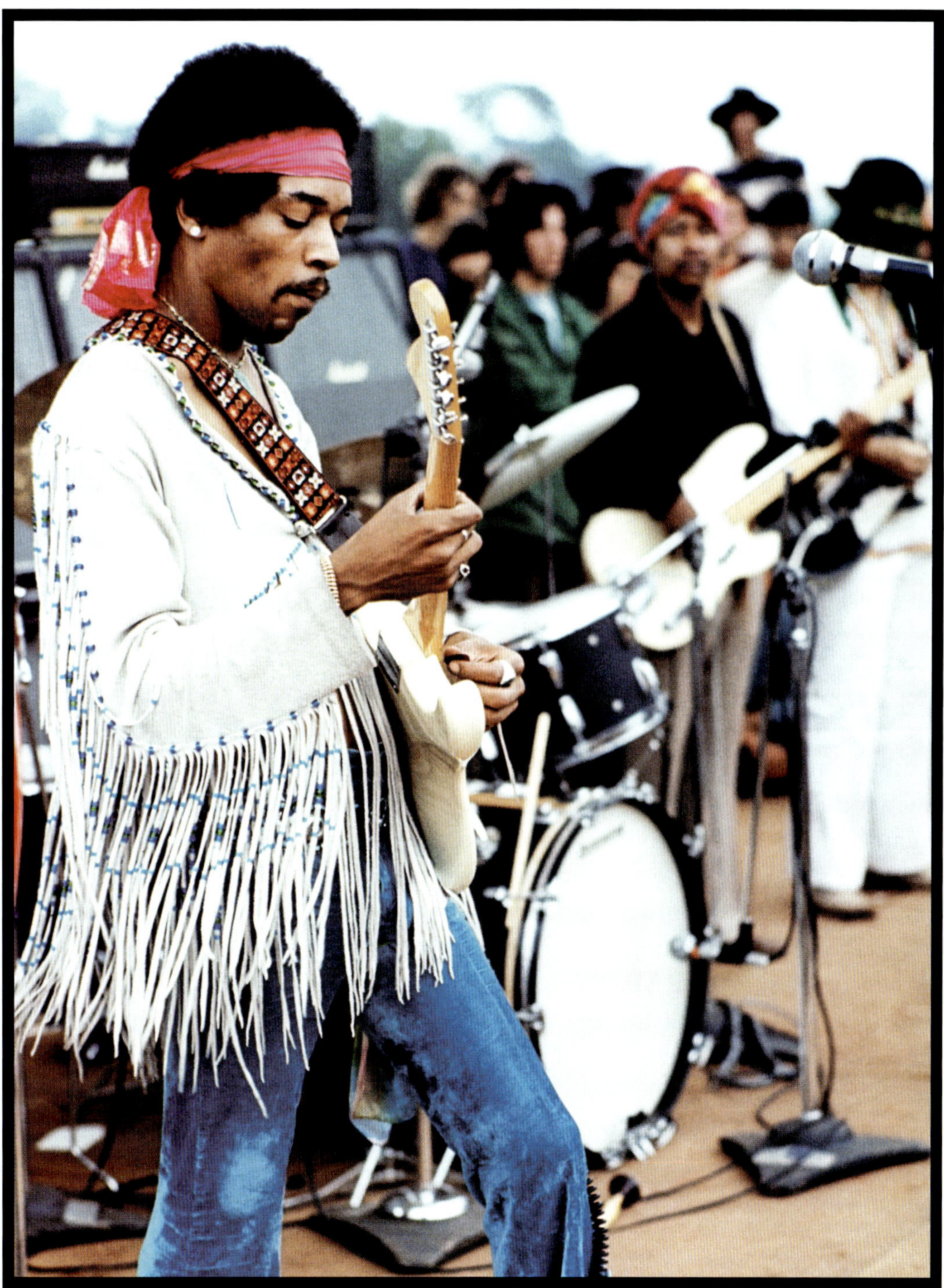

Jimi Hendrix. Undisputed king of rock 'n' roll lead guitar

Jimi Hendrix (1942–1970)

Jimi Hendrix is one of the most influential musicians and songwriters in rock 'n' roll history. He is remembered for his superhuman guitar talent as well as for his electrifying stage presence. In 2003, *Rolling Stone* magazine named Hendrix the number one rock 'n' roll guitarist of all time. This feat is all the more impressive since Hendrix was active as a professional musician only from 1967 to his tragic death in 1970.

Hendrix's father took note of his son's interest in music when he saw the boy strumming a broomstick in the style of Elvis Presley. When Hendrix was fourteen, he found his first guitar, a beat-up old acoustic with one string, in the garbage. For weeks he strutted around with the guitar slung over his shoulder and experimented, as much as was humanly possible, with that single old string. Eventually, his father bought him his first electric guitar, which was built for a right-handed player. Hendrix was left-handed, and so he restrung the guitar and played it upside-down; he did this with every guitar he owned thereafter.

He was fired midway through his first professional gig (in the basement of a synagogue) for his rambunctious behavior. Of course, this same behavior would eventually help to earn him a massive following. His three-man group, *The Jimi Hendrix Experience,* first swept the British music world in 1967–68, and though his popularity steadily climbed in the United States during that time, it was not until his appearance at the Woodstock Music Festival in 1969 that he established himself as one of the most important rock icons of the 1960s.

Describing his innovative music, Hendrix said that he blended "earth," rooted in blues and jazz traditions, with "space," the high-pitched, psychedelic, distortion-fed sounds that he created through his improvisation and experimentation with electronics and recording techniques. He was a brilliant lyricist, as well. His most famous and enduring songs include "The Wind Cries Mary," "Purple Haze," "Voodoo Chile," and "Red House."

Motown. Any overview of late-twentieth-century popular music would be woefully inadequate if it left out the extremely influential sound created by music producer **Berry Gordy, Jr.** (b. 1924) at **Motown** records, a Detroit label, the name of which came from a combination of the words *motor* and *town*. Employing rich, large-scale arrangements with a heavily gospel-influenced style, Gordy and the Motown studios turned out hit after hit from the 1960s through the 1980s, including **"Shop Around"** (1960), by **Smokey Robinson and the Miracles; "Please Mr. Postman"** (1961), by the **Marvelettes; "Heat Wave"** (1963), by **Martha and the Vandellas; "My Girl"** (1965), by the **Temptations; "I Can't Help Myself"** (1965), by the **Four Tops; "You Can't Hurry Love"** (1966), by **Diana Ross and the Supremes; "I Heard It through the Grapevine"** (1968), by **Marvin Gaye** (also recorded by **Gladys Knight and the Pips**); **"ABC"** (1970), by the **Jackson 5; "I Wish"** (1977), by **Stevie Wonder;** and **"Endless Love"** (1981), by Diana Ross and **Lionel Ritchie.**

For the most part, Motown music was apolitical, though the same could not be said of every artist who got his or her start with Motown.

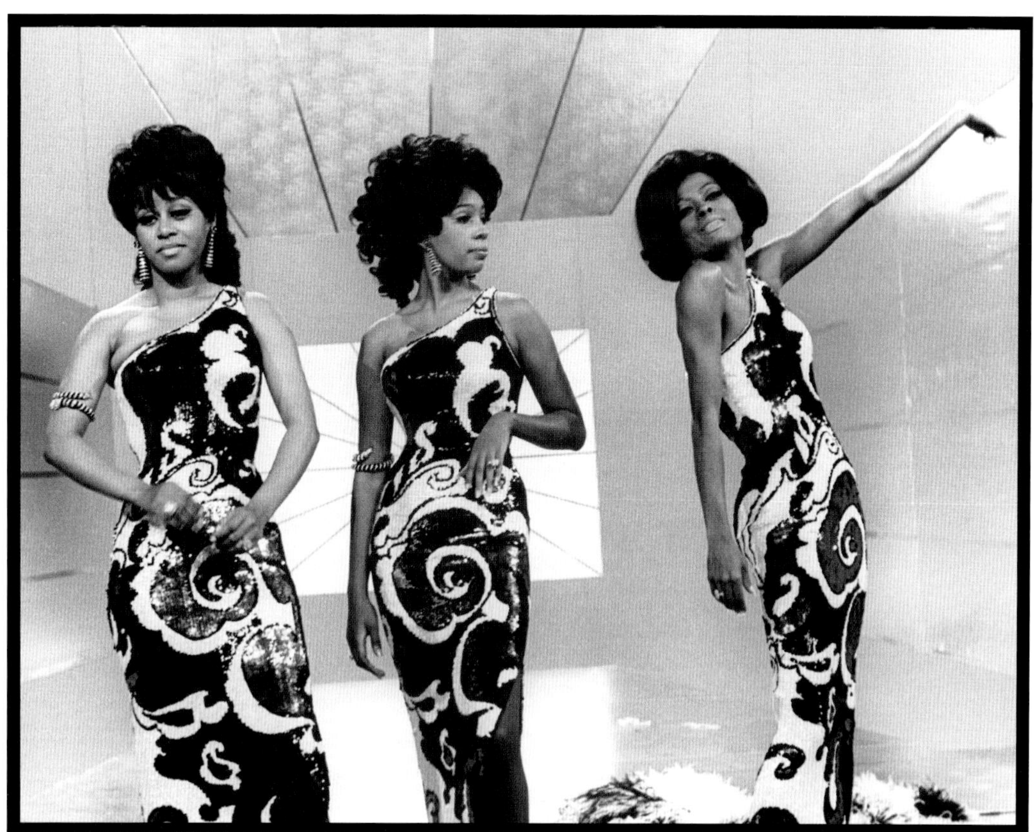

The Supremes. Motown superstars

Working with Al Cleveland and Renaldo Benson, Marvin Gaye created a huge hit with the following social protest song written and recorded in 1970, during the Vietnam War:

What's Going On,
by Marvin Gaye, Al Cleveland, and Renaldo Benson

Mother, mother,
There's too many of you crying,
Brother, brother, brother,
There's far too many of you dying.
You know we've got to find a way
To bring some lovin' here today, yeah.

Chorus:
Picket lines and picket signs:
Don't punish me with brutality.
Talk to me so you can see,
Oh, what's going on?

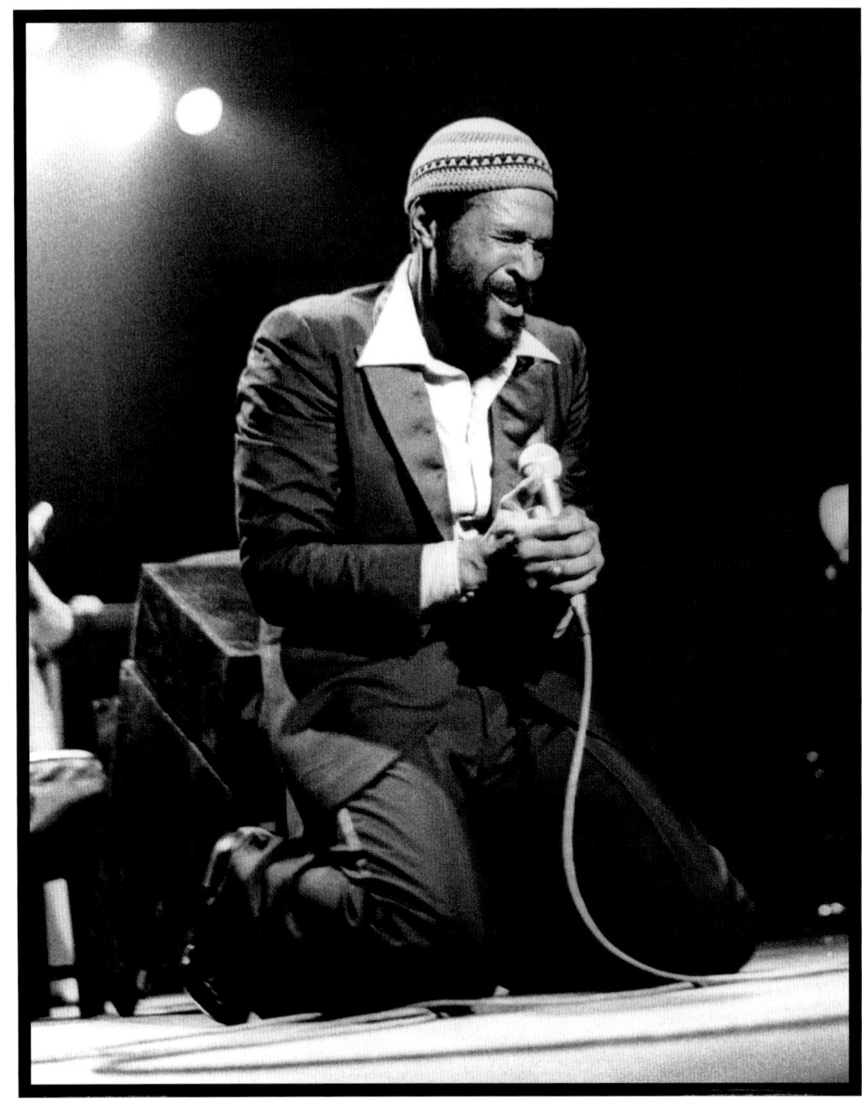

Marvin Gaye. One of the greatest of the Motown/soul singers and songwriters

What's going on?
Yeah, what's going on?
Ah, what's going on?

Father, father
We don't need to escalate
You see, war is not the answer
For only love can conquer hate
You know we've got to find a way
To bring some lovin' here today.
Chorus

Mother, mother,
Everybody thinks we're wrong
Oh, but who are they to judge us

Simpy 'cause our hair is long.
Oh you know we've got to find a way
To bring some understanding here today, oh.
Chorus

Soul. The late 1950s and 60s saw the emergence of a new style also derived from previous gospel, blues, and rhythm and blues. **Soul music** was characterized by its often languid emotion and by incorporation of a strongly gospel feel into secular music. It's a difficult music to define, but one knows it when one hears it. Soul music has been defined and redefined by its practitioners. Some of the best soul artists include **Sam Cooke** (1931–1964), **Ray Charles** (1930–2004), **James Brown** (b. 1933), **Otis Redding** (1941–1967), **Al Green** (b. 1946), **Percy Sledge** (b. 1941), **Aretha Franklin** (b. 1942), **James Carr** (1942–2001), **Eddie Floyd** (b. 1935), **Johnnie Taylor** (1937–2000), **Sly and the Family Stone, Curtis Mayfield** (1942–1999), **Isaac Hayes** (b. 1942), **Stevie Wonder**

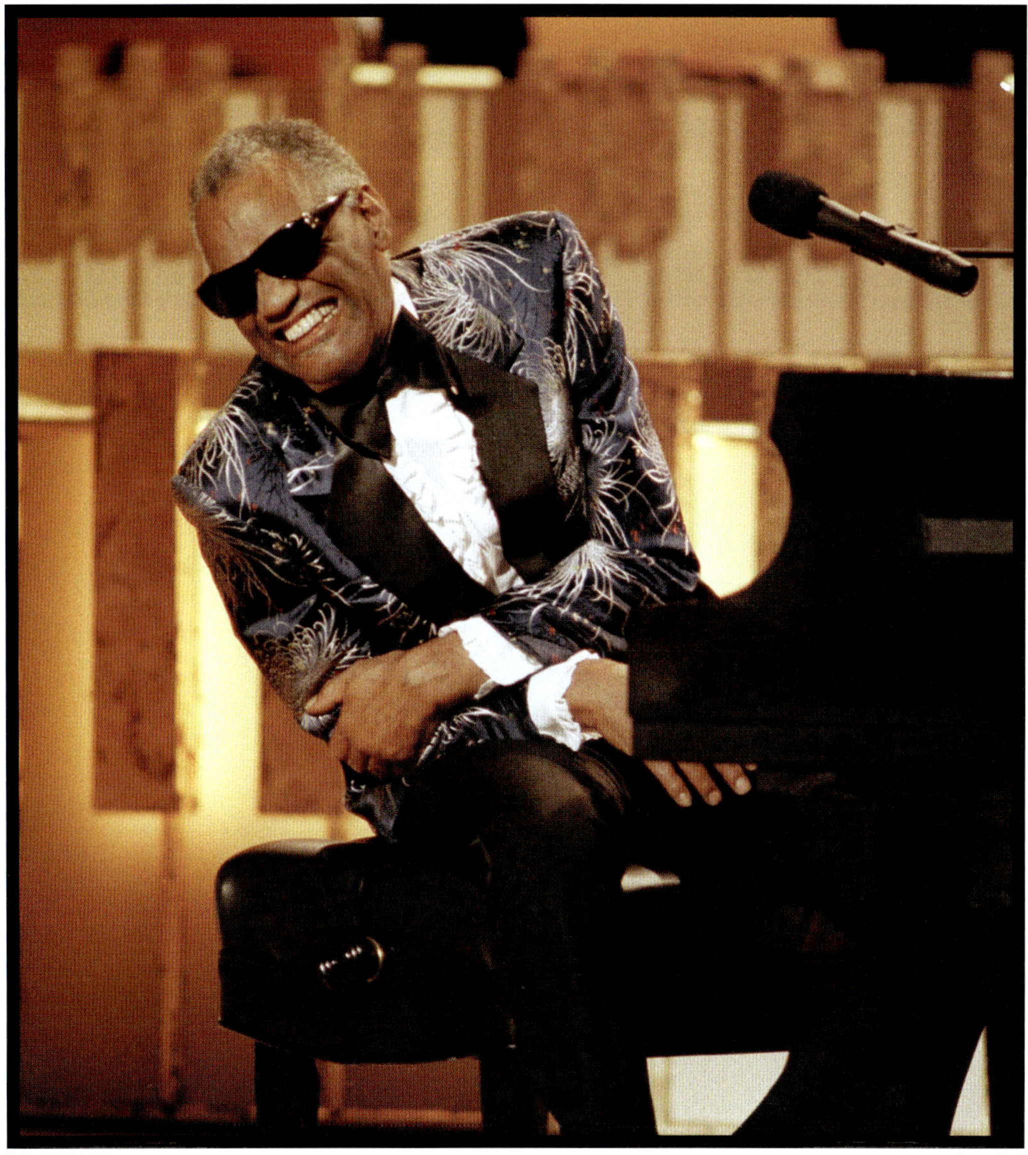

Ray Charles. Brilliant soul and rhythm and blues pianist, vocalist, and songwriter

(b. 1950), **The Staple Singers, Jerry Butler** (b. 1939), and the **Chi-Lites.** Percy Sledge's "**When a Man Loves a Woman**" remains a classic of the soul music genre:

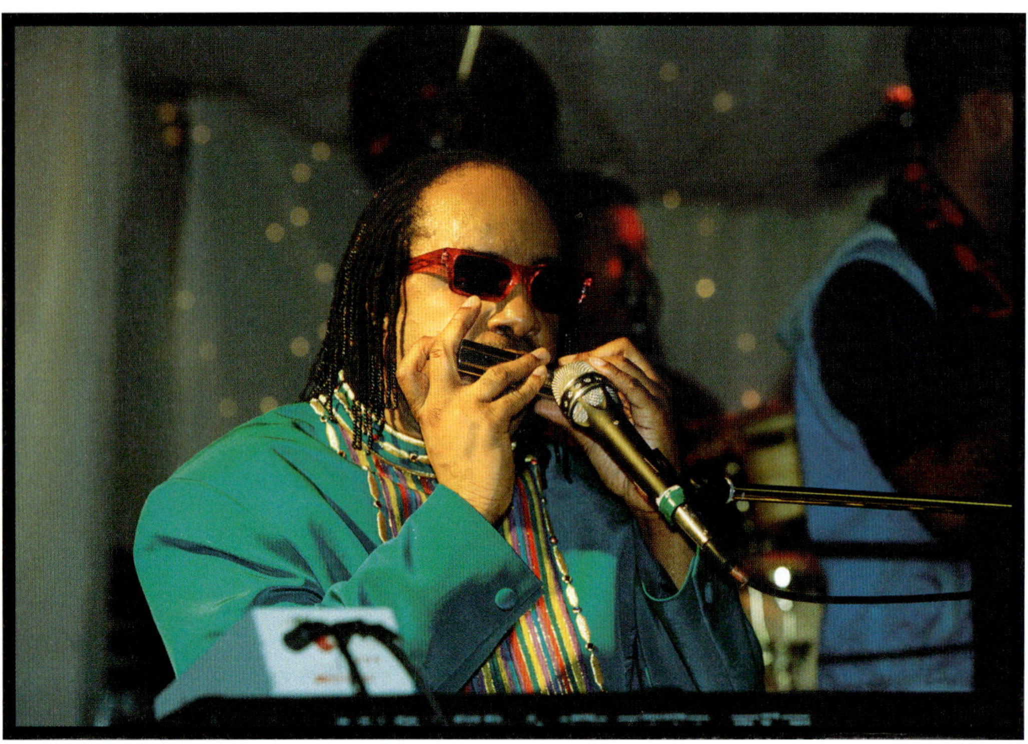

Stevie Wonder. Soul singer, pianist, and songwriter

When a Man Loves a Woman,
by Percy Sledge

When a man loves a woman,
Can't keep his mind on nothin' else.
He'd trade the world for a good thing he's found.

If she is bad, he can't see it.
She can do no wrong.
Turn his back on his best friend if he puts her down.

When a man loves a woman,
He'll spend his very last dime,
Trying to hold on to what he needs.

He'd give up all his comforts
And sleep out in the rain
If she said that's the way it ought to be.

Well, this man loves you, woman.
I gave you everything I have
Trying to hold onto your precious love.
Baby, please don't treat me bad.

When a man loves a woman,
Deep down in his soul
She can bring him such misery.

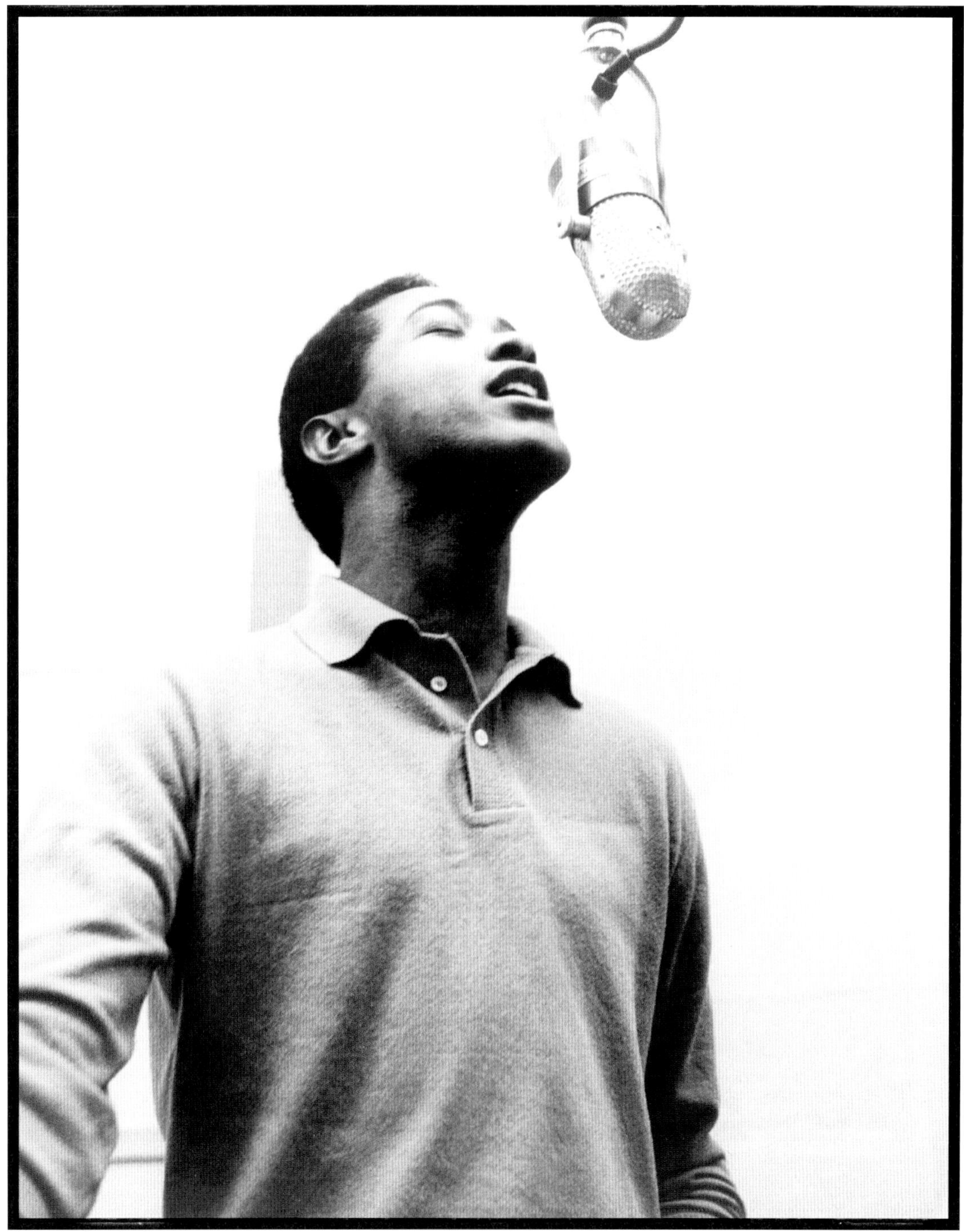

Sam Cooke. Soul singer

If she is playing him for a fool,
He's the last one to know.
Loving eyes can never see.

When a man loves a woman,
He can do her no wrong.
He can never hug some other girl.

Yes, when a man loves a woman,
I know exactly how he feels,
'Cause baby, baby, I'm a man.

When a man loves a woman . . .

Of course, musicians cannot always be pigeon-holed into particular categories. Curtis Mayfield's "**Superfly**" and Isaac Hayes's "**Shaft,**" for example, are clearly within the funk genre. A great rhythm and blues artist like **Tina Tuner** (b. 1939) has done some tunes that are clearly soul. James Brown worked in both the soul and funk genres, and Aretha Franklin has recorded tunes in just about every category of twentieth-century popular music.

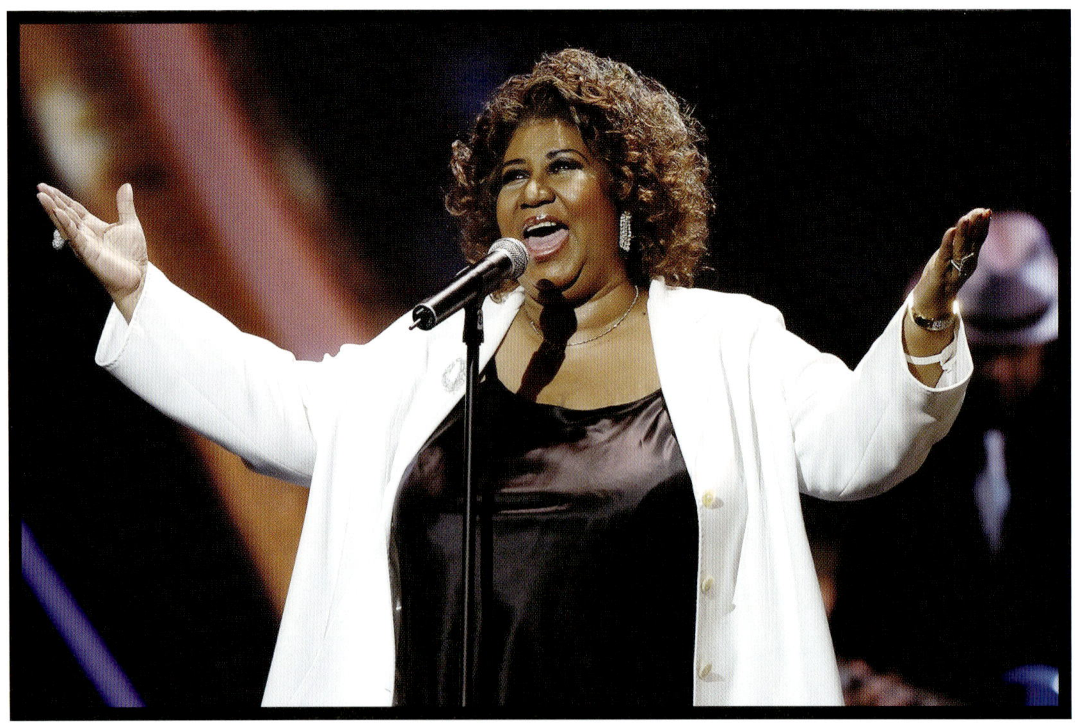

Aretha Franklin. An R & B and soul artist of enormous range and power

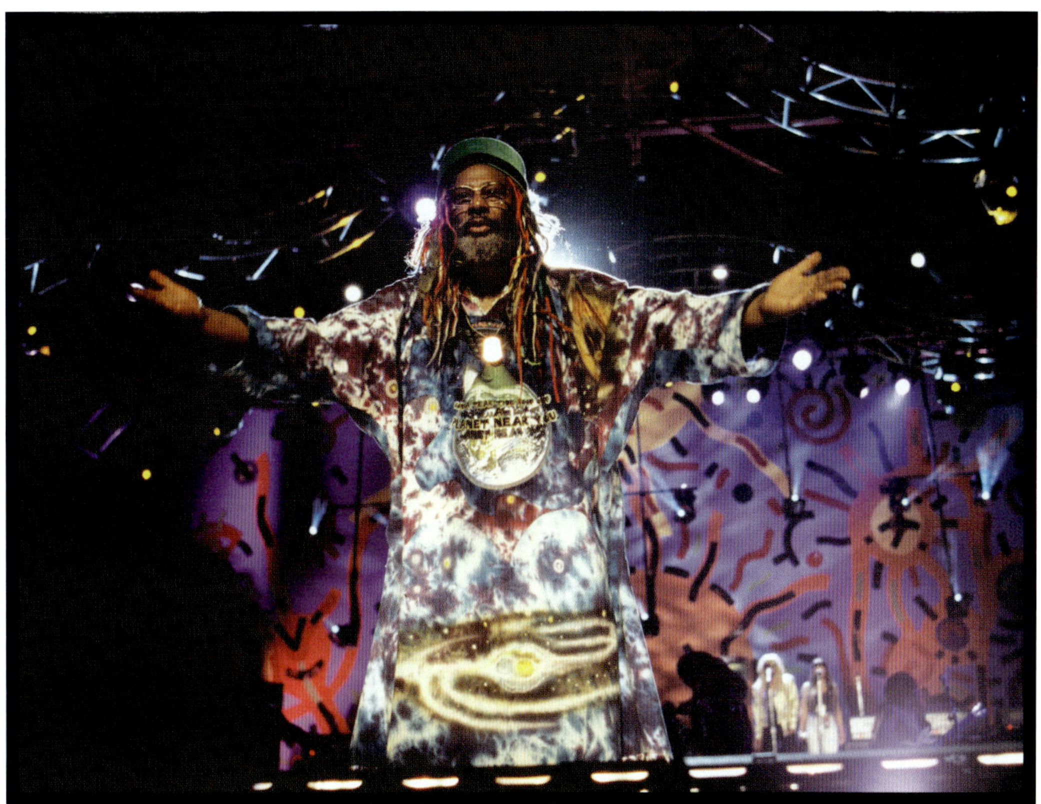

George Clinton. The creator of P-funk

Funk. In the mid 1960s, soul music took an exciting direction in the form of **funk,** which was pioneered by James Brown in such tunes as "**Papa's Got a Brand New Bag**" (1965) and "**Say It Loud, I'm Black and I'm Proud**" (1968). Funk is typified by strong, sometimes complex, syncopated rhythms; percussive guitar; heavy bass; horns used for rhythmic accentuation; and sometimes shouted or chanted vocals. Funk is an extremely danceable music. One of the greatest innovators in this genre was **George Clinton** (b. 1941), originator of so-called **P-funk,** or **funkadelic,** which blended elements of funk with jazz and 1960s psychedelic music. Classic George Clinton recordings include "**Loopzilla**" (1982), "**Atomic Dog**" (1982), and "**Do Fries Go with That Shake?**" (1986). Other funk artists include **Earth, Wind, and Fire, Tower of Power, Kool & the Gang, The Commodores,** and the **Bar-Kays.**

Disco. The 1970s and 80s saw the emergence of a very popular variety of highly produced (some would say "overproduced") dance music known as **disco** (from the word *discothéque,* meaning "dance club"). Among the most successful of African-American artists of the disco era were **Donna Summer** (b. 1948), whose hits included "**Love to Love You, Baby**" (1975); "**I Feel Love**" (1977), "**Could It Be Magic?**" (1976), and "**Bad Girls**" (1979); and **Gloria Gaynor** (b. 1949), whose hits included "**Never Can Say Goodbye**" (1974) and "**I Will Survive**" (1979).

Bob Marley and the Wailers

This anthology contains, with few exceptions, the work of African-American writers and artists—that is, people born in or who emigrated (forcibly or not) to the United States. When necessary, as in the case of Jamaican hero Marcus Garvey, the editors have included the works and biographies of non-Americans who have had a direct and substantial influence on American culture. **Bob Marley** (1945–1981) is one such artist whose influence on Americans and on worldwide pop culture is unquestionable.

Indeed, Bob Marley's music—or, rather, the music of **Bob Marley and the Wailers**—is now so widespread that most people don't even think about its creator when they hear his songs in a television commercial or in the background in the shopping mall. His songs are catchy; just about every human ear on earth finds his music to be (at least) acceptable, if not wonderful. Marley's music will endure far longer than that of most musicians. If, in a hundred years, his name is forgotten, his spirit will still linger in the backbeat of whatever evolves beyond reggae, hip hop, or rock 'n' roll.

But Bob Marley, in essence, does not belong to the world. The world's people do not all celebrate his name in the same way. He did sing of racial harmony and of peace, but his special audience, the people to whom his heart sang, were the offspring of Africa, wherever they lived, but especially those who came off those slave ships, beginning some 400 years ago. One of the most important facts about his music, a fact usually lost on listeners and marketers, is the underlying source, the root of so many of his songs: injustice, barbaric greed, and exploitation exerted upon black people by white, a cold fact that began in earnest during the fifteenth century, or earlier.

This man could move a crowd like a prophet, and that is how he was and is, by some, identified. He was an amazing performer, a poet, a gifted musician, and a true icon for millions of people. His music lifted and still lifts people, and makes change, but not in a striking, revolutionary manner. Marley's music soothes souls and affirms optimism, and it endures in the inner ear and stays inside those who love it.

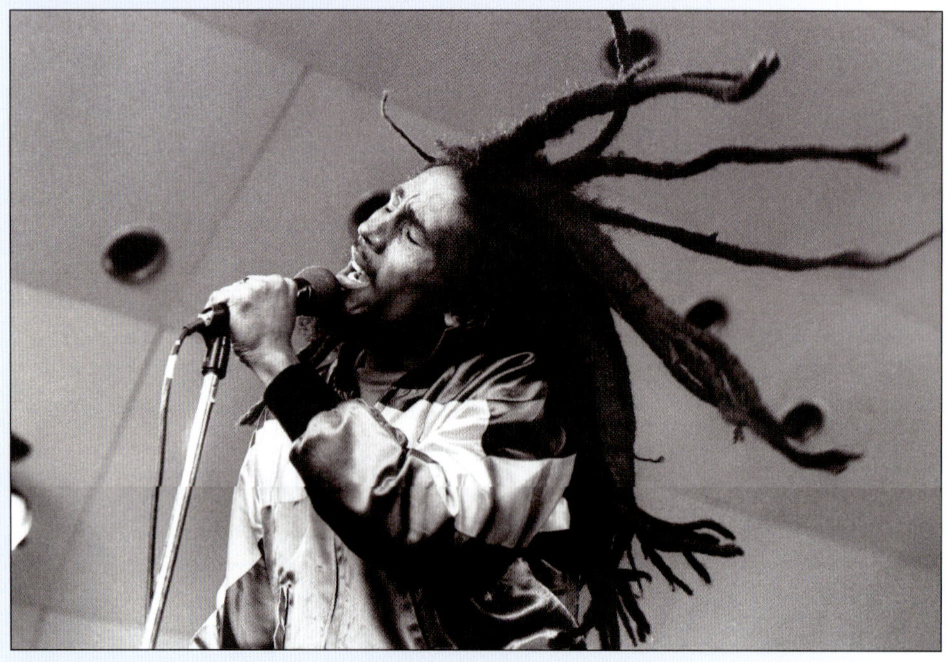

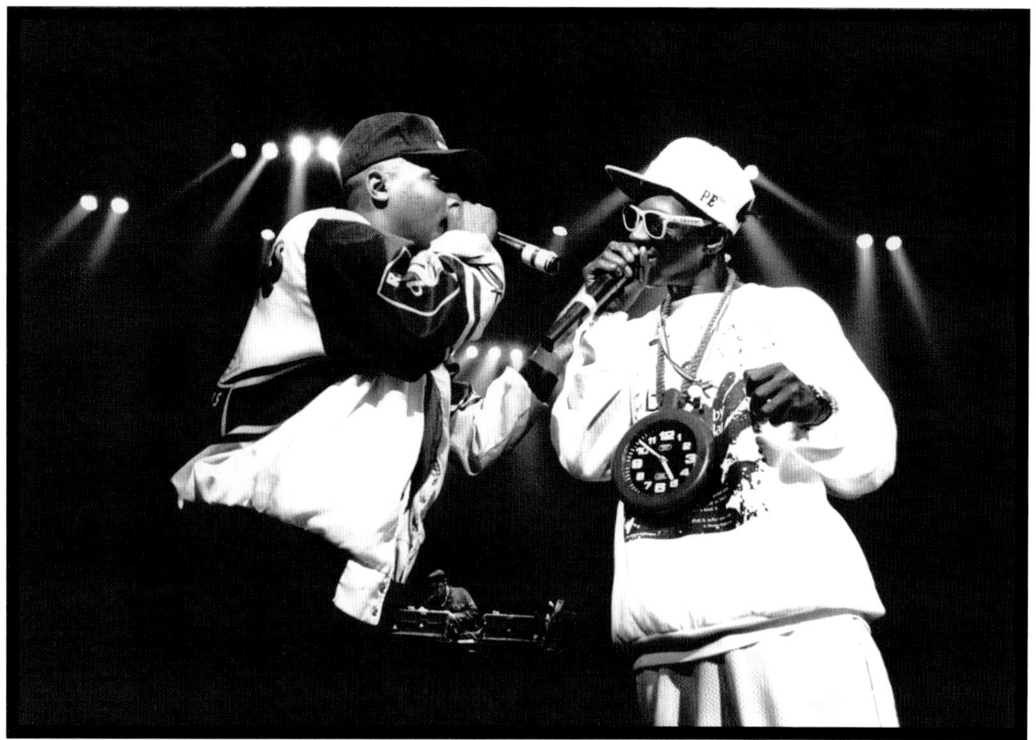

Public Enemy. A very popular hip hop group in the 1980s

Hip Hop/Rap. The club/disco scene brought the DJ to the fore. DJs carry out many functions. They choose music carefully to control the mood of their audiences and the atmosphere at a party or in a club, they do audio mixing, they sometimes add percussive elements to the music they play by "scratching" records, and they sometimes ad-lib between songs or even over the tops of tracks. Out of the speaking, or **MCing,** done by DJs grew **rapping,** which involved, generally, verbally brilliant improvisation over the top of a rhythm track consisting primarily of bass and synthesized percussion. **Hip hop** music combines all of these elements—mixing and remixing, quoting from other artists and even other musical traditions, and spoken vocals (intermixed at times with sung vocals) involving extensive use of rhyme, alliteration, puns, metaphor, and other word play. The content of hip hop music is often confrontational and expresses an outsider stance with regard to the larger white culture and thus can be seen as an extension of the tradition of **signification** (See the note on page 168) that goes all the way back to West African sources and early spirituals and work songs. To ancient West African roots can also be traced the common tendency of hip hop to tell stories and to serve as a vehicle for the transmission of and commentary on culture. The exact origins of hip hop are obscure and hotly debated. Many people trace its origins to the work of **DJ Kool Herc** (b. 1955), a Jamaican DJ who improvised raps over reggae sides in the Bronx, New York, in the early 1970s. From this beginning, and with help from such early hip hop innovators as **The Sugarhill Gang, Grandmaster Flash, Kurtis Blow, The**

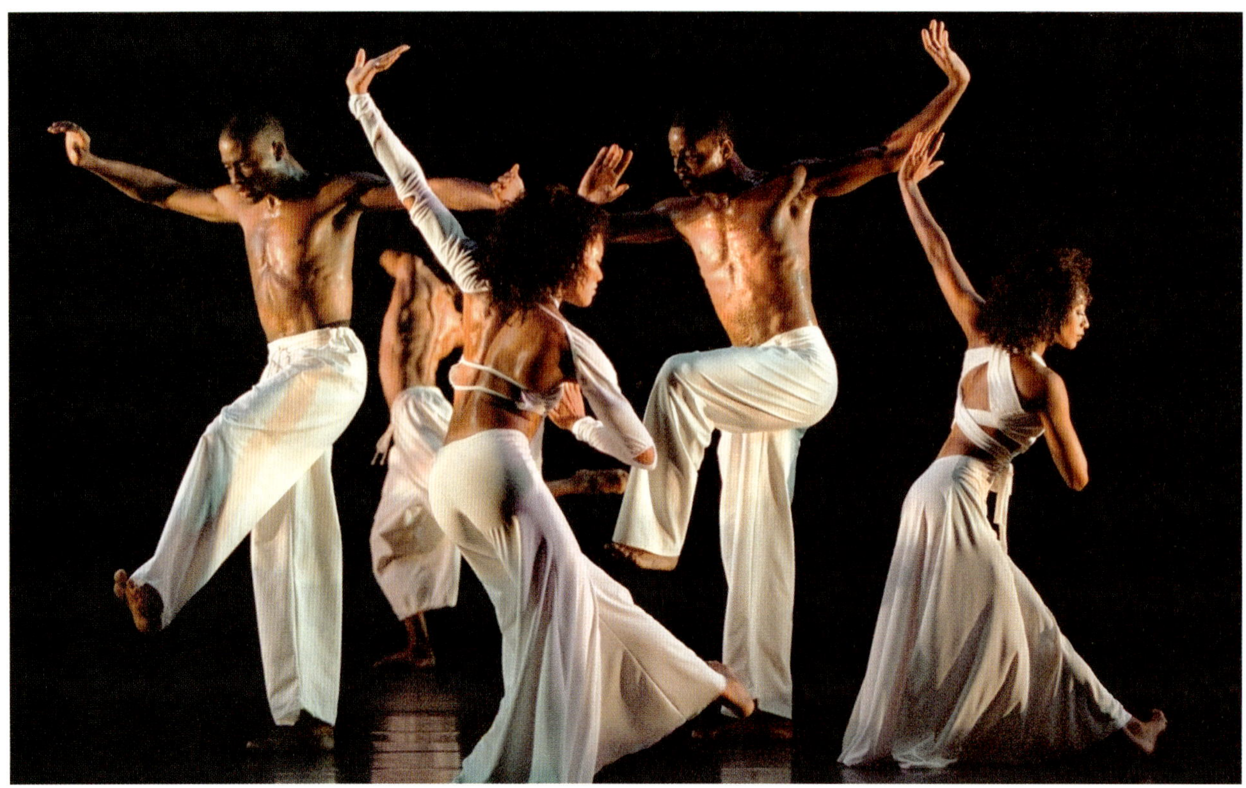

Alvin Ailey American Dance Theater troupe performing *Grace* (1999).

that she would be required to perform in white face, she promptly refused. She went on to become the first African-American *prima ballerina* for the Metropolitan Opera in New York and made numerous guest appearances with other companies. As a teacher at the School of American Ballet in New York City and Manhattanville College, she also inspired and trained many aspiring dancers.

Other prominent ballet dancers include **Geoffrey Holder** (b.1930) and **Carmen de Lavallade,** both dancers with the Metropolitan Opera who also appeared in Hollywood films, and **Virginia Alma Fairfax Johnson** (b.1950), a prima ballerina in the Dance Theatre of Harlem.

In addition to concert hall forms of dance, African-American contributions to urban-derived dance forms, such as **tap, break dance, popping,** and **hip hop,** deserve mention. Although popular interest in tap dance declined in the 1960s (for a discussion of earlier developments in tap history, see Unit 3, page 470), this form flourished outside the media's eye and, by the late twentieth century, had grown in popularity once again through the efforts of such figures as **Gregory Hines** (1946–2003) and **Savion Glover** (b.1973). Urban dances have also made their way to theater performances. The **Rennie Harris Puremovement Company**, founded by **Rennie Harris** (b.1963) in 1991 is dedicated exclusively to hip hop and has performed throughout the U.S. and abroad. The all-female company **Urban Bush**

Women, founded in 1984 by **Jawole Willa Jo Zollar** (b.1950), also interweaves urban dance with live music, vocals, literary readings, and other dance styles in performances that explore and educate about the history, spiritual traditions, and literary heritage of African Americans.

There are also many African-American dance companies dedicated to preserving and performing traditional African dances. **Charles Rudolph Davis** (b.1937), founder of the **Chuck Davis Dance Company,** studied African dance styles in Senegal, Guinea, and the Ivory Coast and is a leading proponent of African dance in America. Davis also founded the **African American Dance Ensemble** and the **Alayanfe Children's Dance Company** in Durham, North Carolina, and created the **DanceAfrica Festival**, celebrated yearly at the Brooklyn Academy of Music (BAM).

Additional performing ensembles devoted to African dance include **KanKouran West African Dance Company; Ko-Thi Dance Company; Dinizulu and His African Dancers, Drummers, and Singers; Muntu Dance Theater of Chicago; Universal African Dance and Drum Ensemble;** and **BAM/Restoration DanceAfrica Ensemble.**

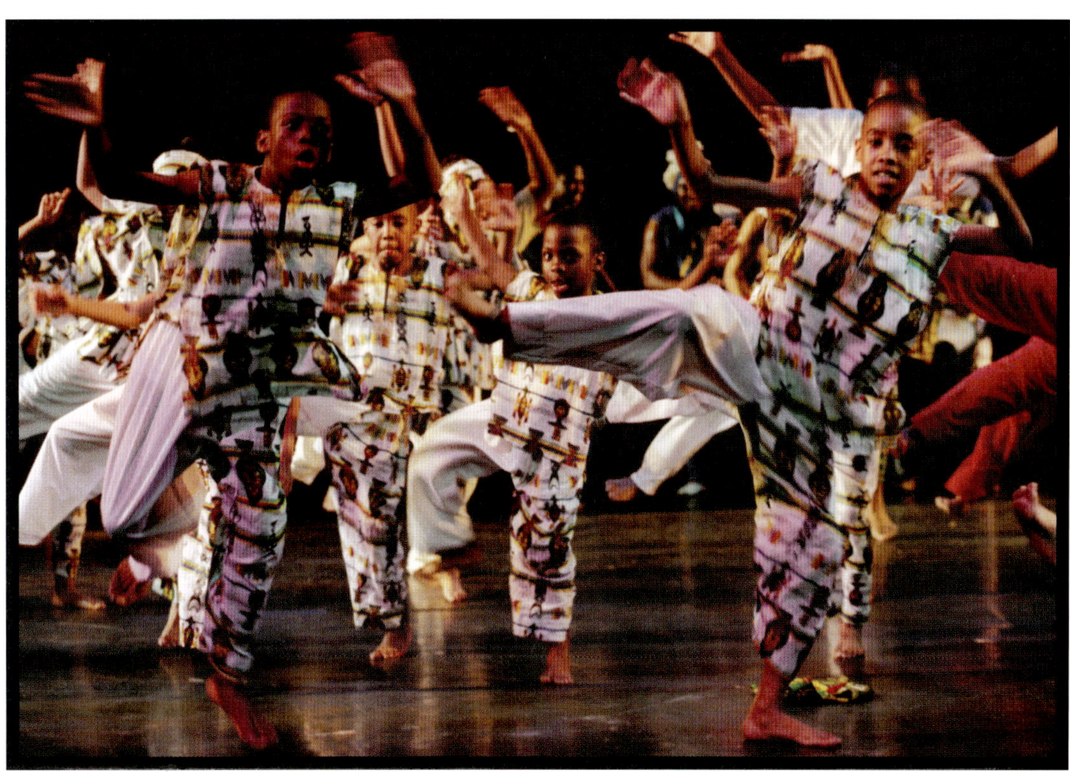

Restoration DanceAfrica Ensemble performing at the DanceAfrica Festival held at the Brooklyn Academy of Music (1998).

The Legacy of African-American Music

Together, the music sections appearing at the end of each of the units in this book provide a brief introduction to the legacy of African-American music. They were not designed to be comprehensive, for they cannot do justice to the astonishing contributions of African Americans to the music of this country and of the world. Although they contain the names of many famous musicians, by necessity many important names have been omitted. Nevertheless, this brief survey conveys just how essential, how formative, African-American contributions have been to American and world musical culture. The forms that our dances take, the structures that we give our songs, the most important genres of popular music, the scales that rock 'n' roll guitarists play when they improvise, the attitude toward the subject of discourse adopted by contemporary slam poets and rap composers/performers—these are but a few of the many, many debts that we owe to African-Amerian musicians. What a legacy of genius! Certainly, it is not exaggeration to say that most of the music that we think of as essentially American had its roots in African-American culture. And it is no overstatement to say that this music has, in turn, become the popular music of just about the entire world. The editors and authors of this text

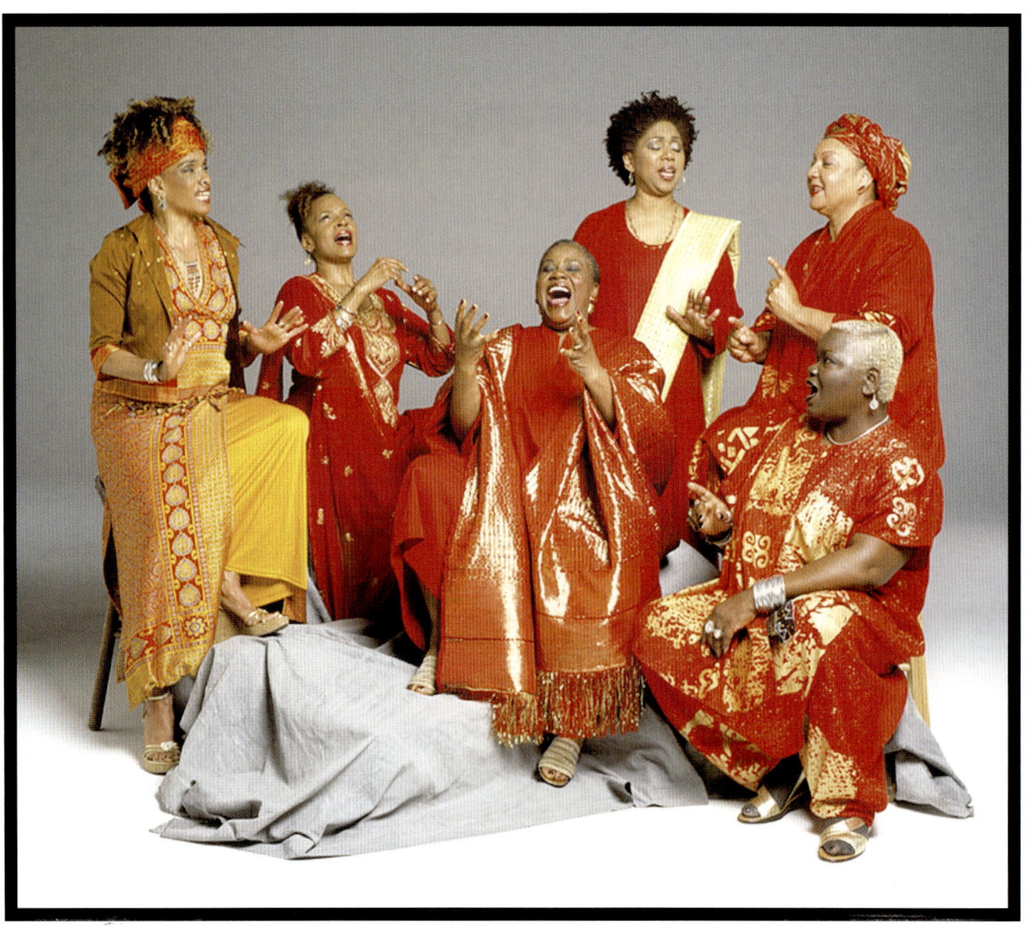

Sweet Honey in the Rock. Vocal ensemble dedicated to keeping alive African-American roots music.

hope that after reading these brief surveys of African-American music, you will turn and listen anew to this music. Listen with ears that hear African drums in the distance. Listen with renewed appreciation for the innovativeness and brilliance of African-American popular music and with new reverence for its African sources and inspiration.

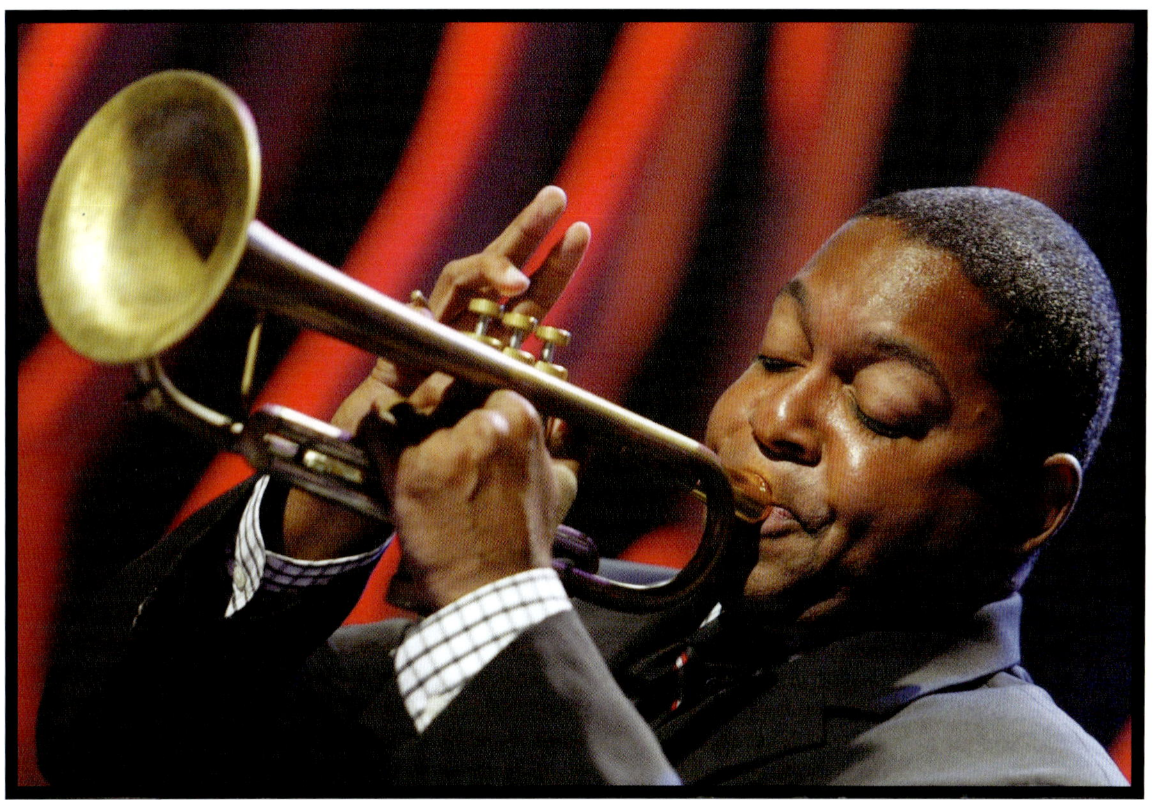

Wynton Marsalis is a supremely talented and innovative trumpet player in his own right, but if pressed to do so, he can also play magnificently in the styles of all the great jazz trumpet players before him. He is not only a gifted player. He is also an eloquent teller of the story of the African-American musical legacy.

Edmonia Lewis LOUIS DELSARTE

Rex Goreleigh EDWARD MITCHELL BANNISTER

Aaron Douglas Hale Woodruff

AUGUSTA SAVAGE James VanDerZee

Sargent Claude Charles Sallee

Hilda Wilkinson Brown Sam Gilliam

Jacob Lawrence Lois Mailou Jones

GORDON PARKS William E. Smith William Artis

James A. Porter Horace Pippin

Hughie Lee-Smith James Hampton

RICHARD DEMPSEY JOHN BIGGERS

LEV T. MILLS Charles Alston

Alma Thomas Elizabeth Catlett

Romare Bearden Frank Bowling

Rex Goreleigh

DEREK WALCOTT

David Driskell Frederick Brown

Franklin White IRENE CLARK

AUGUSTA SAVAGE Richard Mayhew

Charles White Hilda Wilkinson Brown

Henry O. Tanner George Wilson

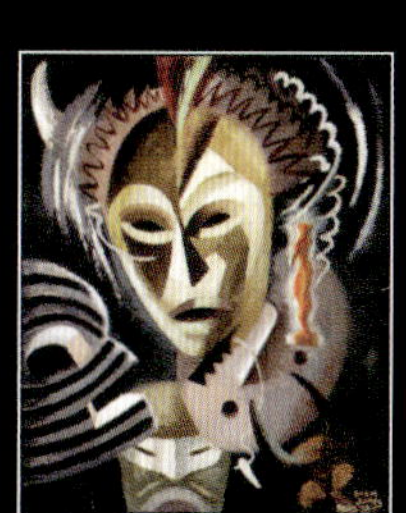

Unit 5
Gallery of African-American Art

"Thus it is the bounden duty of black America to begin this great work of the creation of Beauty, of the preservation of Beauty, of the realization of Beauty."

—W. E. B. Du Bois

Hagar, 1875

Edmonia Lewis
Marble
Smithsonian American Art Museum

Edmonia Lewis (circa1843–circa1909)

Edmonia Lewis's father was a free African American, and her mother was a Chippewa Indian. Both died when she was nine, and she was raised mainly by her mother's tribe. As a young woman at Oberlin College, she was attacked by a racist mob who falsely accused her of poisoning two white people. She was acquitted in court and soon after, with encouragement from Abolitionist William Lloyd Garrison, she moved to Boston. There she studied sculpture and came into contact with many of the most prominent writers and artists of her day. Later, she moved to Italy and set up a sculpture studio there. Her sculptures were often politically charged and provocative, especially for a black woman in her place and time. Her 1867 sculpture *Forever Free,* for instance, depicted a black man holding a broken chain with a white man kneeling at his feet. The sensitively carved sculpture *Hagar* (also called *Hagar in the Wilderness)* depicts a Biblical character, the Egyptian handmaiden of Abraham's wife, Sarah. In Islamic tradition, Hagar and her son by Abraham, Ishmael, were the founders of the lineage of Arab peoples. Hagar and Ishmael were also traditionally believed to be ancestors of a number of African kings.

Thinking about the Art

1. Critics and art fans like to discuss Lewis's somewhat ironic choice of white marble as her primary medium. What is ironic about this choice? Why might Lewis have chosen white marble as her medium, given her subject?
2. Edmonia Lewis's Hagar is in the **neoclassical** style. It shares many similarities with Greek and Roman sculpture of the Classical Age. Look at some Greek and Roman sculpture online or in the library. What similarities can you find between Hagar's work and ancient Greek and Roman antecedents?

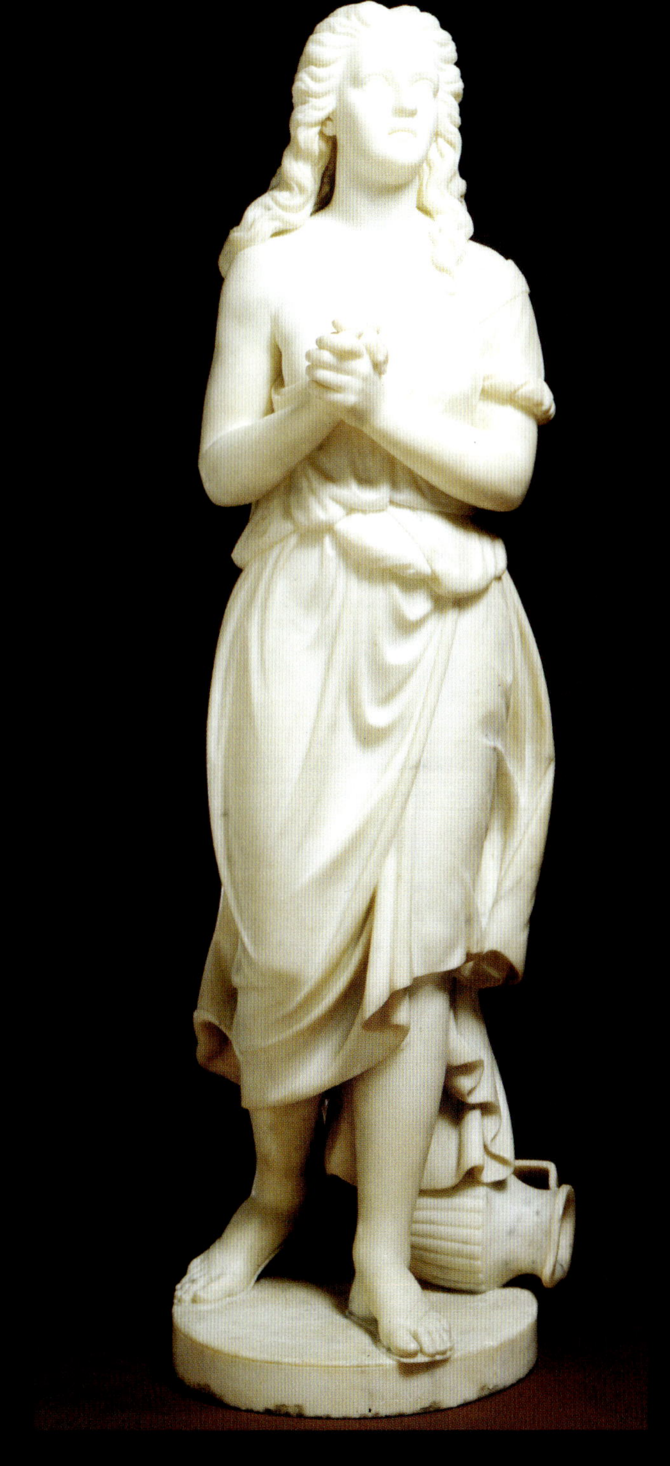

Woman Walking Down Path, 1882

Edward Mitchell Bannister
Oil on Canvas
Smithsonian American Art Museum

Edward Mitchell Bannister (1828–1901)

The first African-American painter to achieve national recognition, Edward Mitchell Bannister expressed in his work a deep, spiritual love of nature. He was born in Canada and moved to Boston in 1848, where he learned to paint. He later moved to Rhode Island and joined a growing community of landscape artists influenced by the rustic, serene styles developed by painters of France's **Barbizon School.** Bannister's work has both Romantic and Realistic elements. **Romantic** works tend to idealize and glorify the natural and to express the emotions experienced by an individual. **Realistic** works attempt to show external realities as they are, in precise, accurate detail. Bannister won the first-place medal at the Philadelphia Centennial Exposition in 1876. His *Woman Walking Down the Path* is one of the great masterworks of American painting. Few artists have so evocatively captured a moment and a mood.

Thinking about the Art

1. What time of day is depicted in this work? What elements of the painting suggest the time of day and season of the year?
2. What aspects of this painting are Realistic? What aspects are Romantic? Why do you think the artist chose to make the figure so small and ill defined? What does this fact suggest about the relationship between the individual and nature? What mood does the painting suggest to you?
3. Bannister's style is sometimes described as **"painterly"** because the medium in which he worked is quite evident. What qualities of this painting make it "painterly"?

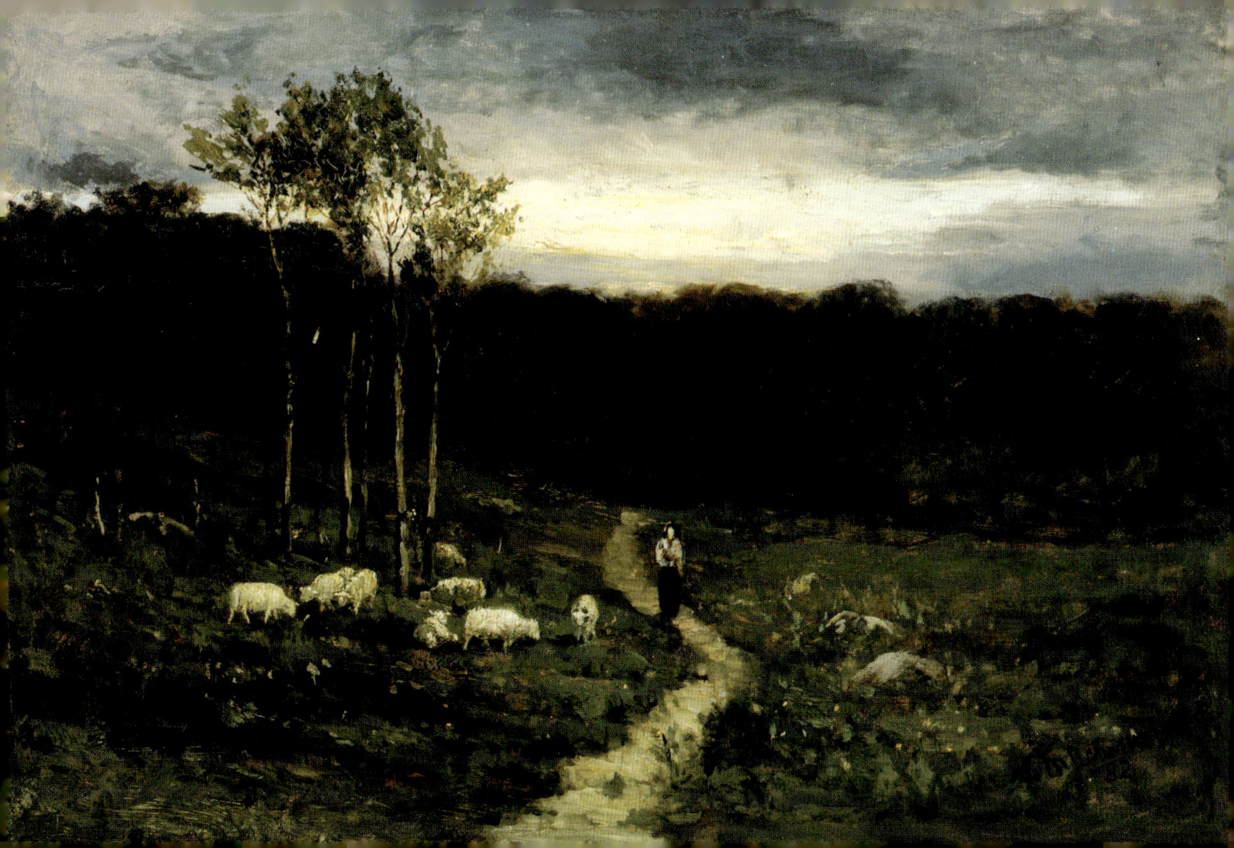

The Banjo Lesson, 1893

Henry O. Tanner
Oil on Canvas
Hampton University Museum

Henry Ossawa Tanner (1859–1937)

Henry Ossawa Tanner is perhaps the most renowned African-American painter of the nineteenth century. He became interested in art at a young age and began painting while recuperating from a serious illness. In 1880 he enrolled in the prestigious Pennsylvania Academy of Fine Arts, where he trained under one of America's greatest painters, Thomas Eakins. After selling his small gallery in Philadelphia, Tanner moved to the mountains of North Carolina, where he photographed and sketched African-American subjects. Upon traveling to Europe, however, Tanner was captivated by the art scene in Paris and soon enrolled in the *Academie Julian.* Thereafter he produced many of his most famous works, including *The Banjo Lesson, The Thankful Poor* (1894), and *Daniel in the Lion's Den* (1895). He returned to Philadelphia briefly but was discouraged by the racial prejudice in America and so returned to Paris for the rest of his life.

The Banjo Player. This is one of the most beloved of American paintings because of its sensitive treatment of a moving subject—the transmission of culture from one generation to another.

Thinking about the Art

1. What are the figures in this painting doing? What relation might they have? What is the time of day? Are these figures rich or poor? In what sense are they rich despite their surroundings?
2. In this painting, Tanner makes use of a technique known as **chiaroscuro,** in which there are great contrasts in **value** (that is, between areas of darkness and light). How does this contrast between darkness and light mirror the painting's subject and theme?

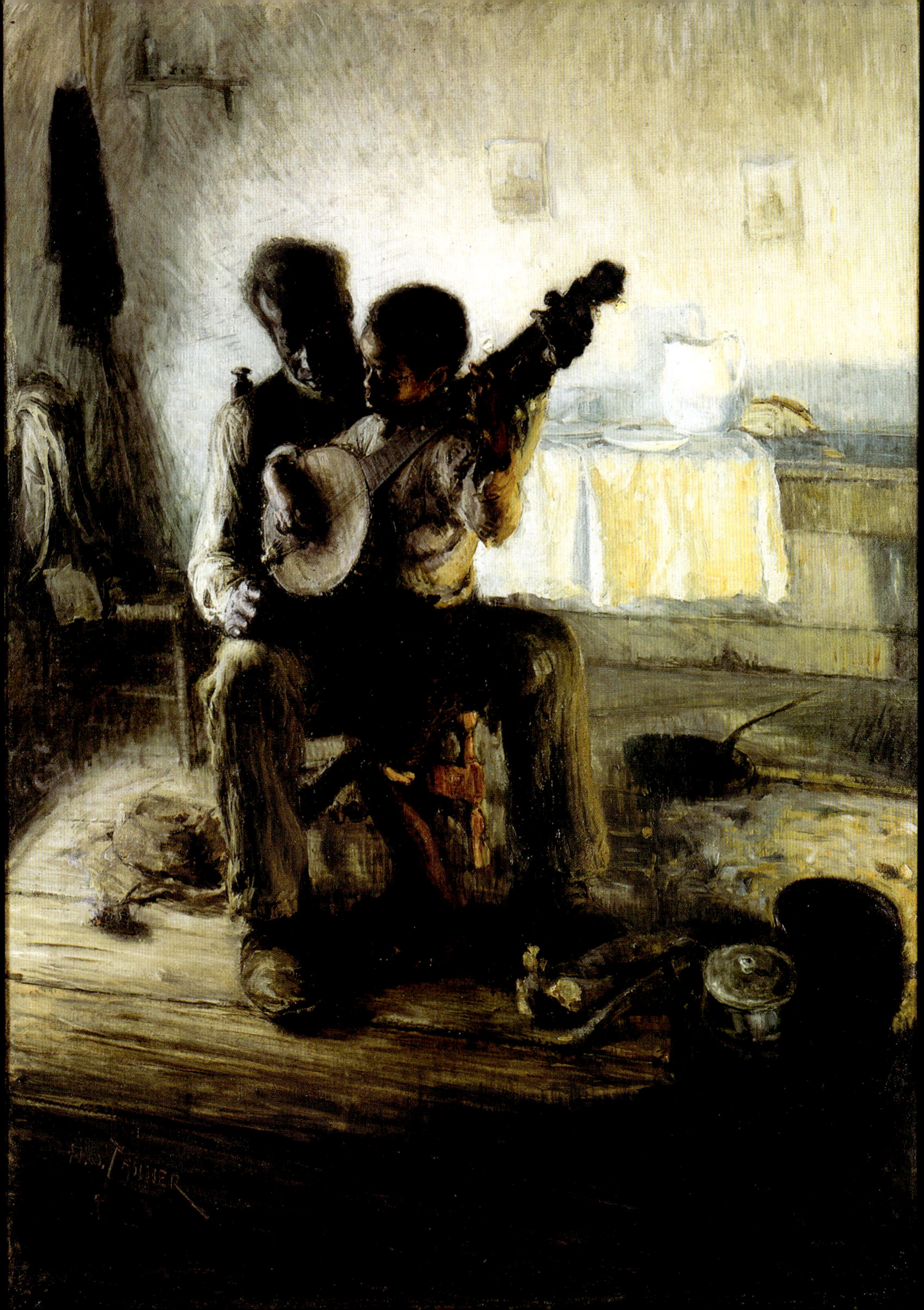

The Good Shepherd, 1920

Henry O. Tanner
Oil on canvas
The Newark Museum

The Wreck, circa 1913

Henry O. Tanner
Oil on Canvas
Smithsonian American Art Museum

Henry Ossawa Tanner (1859–1937)

The Good Shepherd. In this painting Tanner again shows himself a master of the manipulation of light and color. Notice that the painting is almost monochromatic but contains just enough color of just the right hues to give the whole a gemlike, Byzantine quality appropriate to its Middle-Eastern subject. The painting is based upon Christ's parable of the Good Shepherd, in Matthew 18:12, in which Christ poses this question: if a shepherd has a hundred sheep and one becomes lost, will he not leave the others and go into the mountains to search for and save the lost one?

The Wreck. This painting is strongly **expressionist** in that it makes use of thick, heavy brush strokes. It is also **minimalist** (though it predates by many decades the minimalist movement in American art) in that it presents only the essence of its subject. It is a powerful evocation of the decay to which all things come, set against a background of water turned golden by the last rays of sunlight, again evocative of an ending.

Thinking about the Art

1. How does the painting *The Good Shepherd* make you feel? How is this mood created by the painting consistent with the painting's title? In Christian thought, Christ is often referred to as *The Good Shepherd* who cares for his flock. He is also called "The King." Why, then, are gemlike colors appropriate for this sensitive portrayal of the shepherd caring for a lost lamb (returning him to the fold)? Of what might the light behind the good shepherd be a symbol?

2. What is there about the way in which *The Wreck* is painted that suggests the subject of the painting—a wreckage? In other words, how is the style of the painting expressive of its subject?

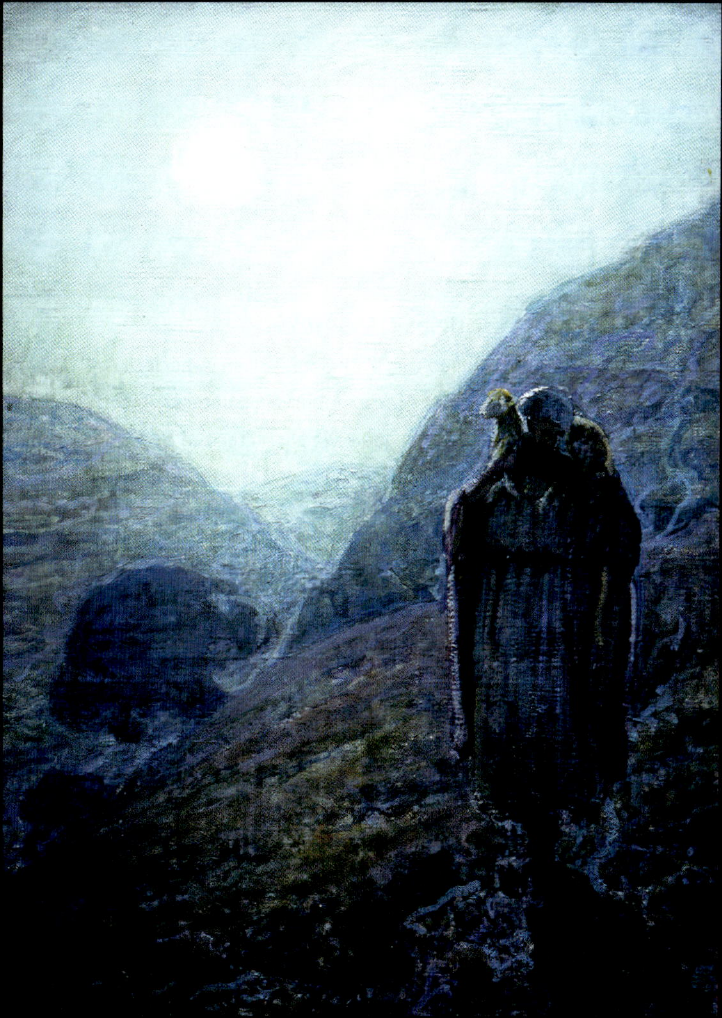

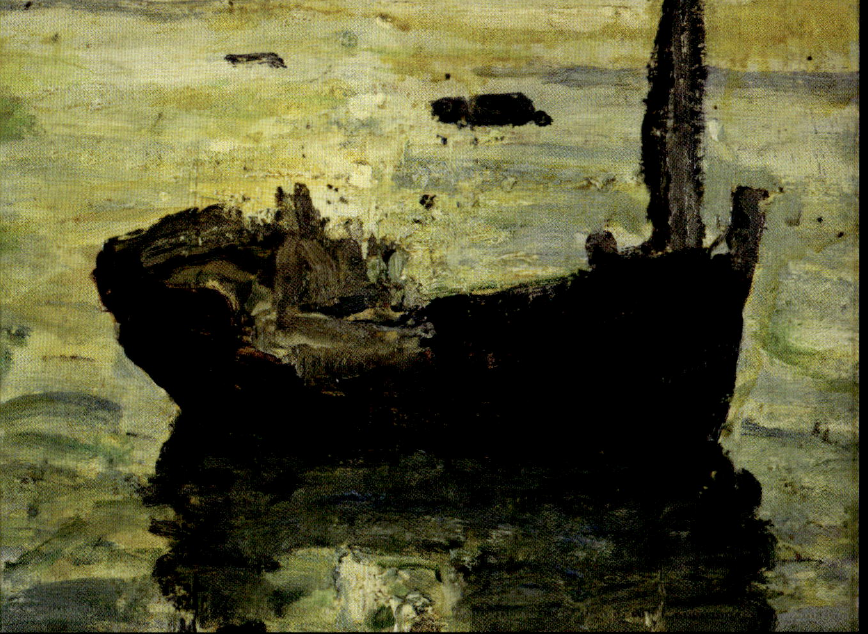

Couple in Raccoon Coats, 1932

James VanDerZee
Gelatin silver print

James VanDerZee (1886–1983)

Couple in Raccoon Coats. This photograph represents the height of sophistication in the 1930s. It shows an obviously affluent young couple dressed in the fur coats favored by jazz-era hipsters and posing with a shiny new Cadillac convertible roadster.

Thinking about the Art

1. In what way does the car, in the **foreground** (or front) of this picture differ from the brownstone buildings in the **background?** How does the fuzziness of the brownstones affect, by contrast, the impact of the car on the viewer? Why would the photographer have sought such a contrast in this shot?

2. What does this photograph suggest about life in Harlem at the height of the jazz era?

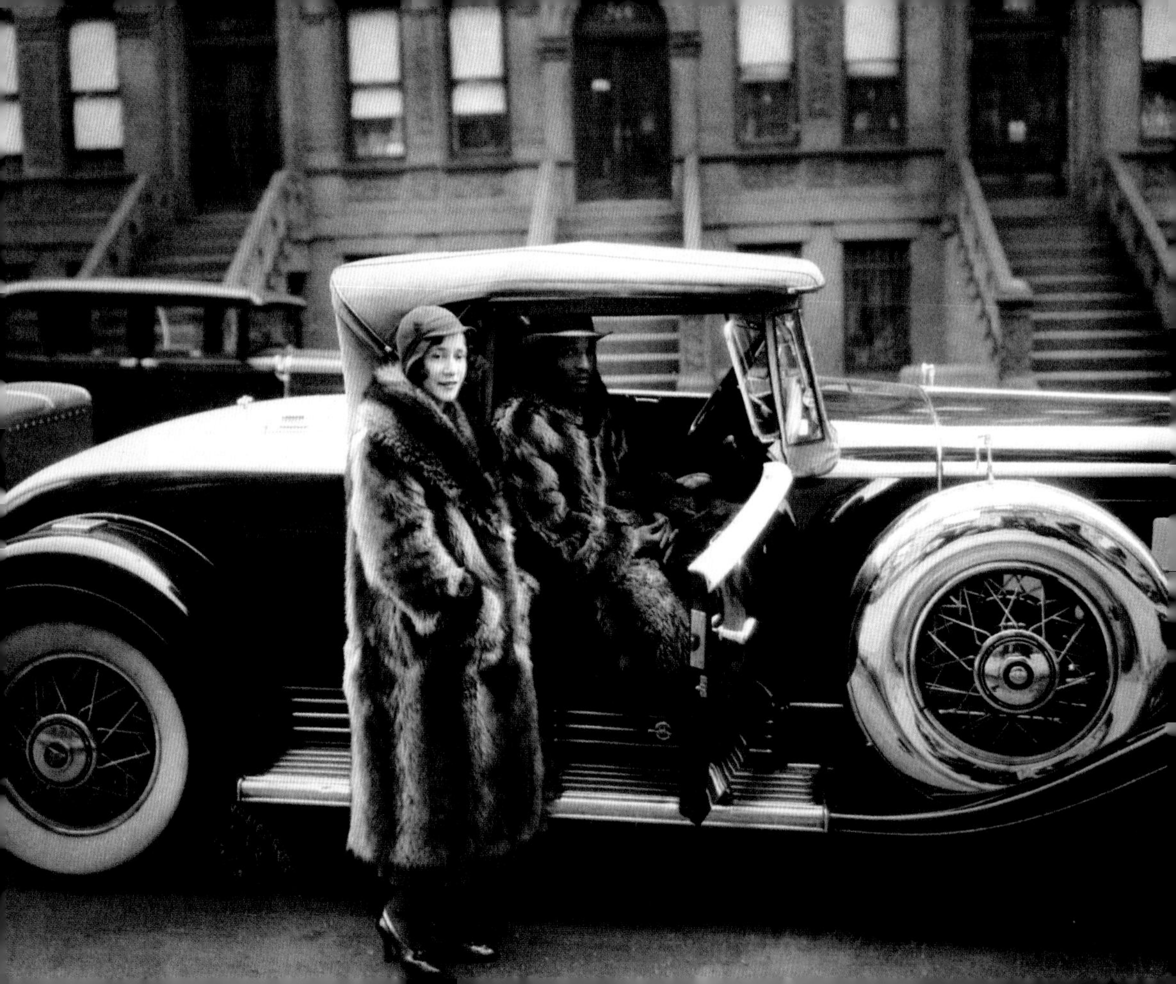

Gamin, 1929

Augusta Savage
Painted Plaster
Howard University Gallery of Art

Augusta Savage (1892–1962)

Sculptor and educator Augusta Savage was among the countless artists, especially from the South, who found new hope and self-understanding in Harlem. She enrolled at Cooper Union in 1921 and focused, like no other artist, on the African-American physiognomy. Physiognomy is the study of facial features and expressions as a reflection of personal character. In 1929 Savage won a Rosenfeld Fellowship for *Gamin*, a bust of her nephew. After attending the *Académie de la Grande Chaumière* in Paris, she returned to Harlem, where she opened the Savage Studio of Arts and Crafts. She was the first director of the Harlem Community Arts Center and devoted much of her life to teaching her fellow Harlem residents about art.

Thinking about the Art

1. Is this a portrait of an upper-class or a working-class boy? How can you tell?
2. What aspects of the sculpture seem particularly realistic and not romanticized? (For definitions of these terms, see page 742.)
3. What sort of expression does the boy have on his face? What emotions do you imagine that he is feeling? What kind of personality do you think he might have? How does this impression of the boy contrast with the realism of the portrait? Some have described this work as a particularly sensitive portrayal of a particularly sensitive boy. What makes this work a "sensitive portrayal"?

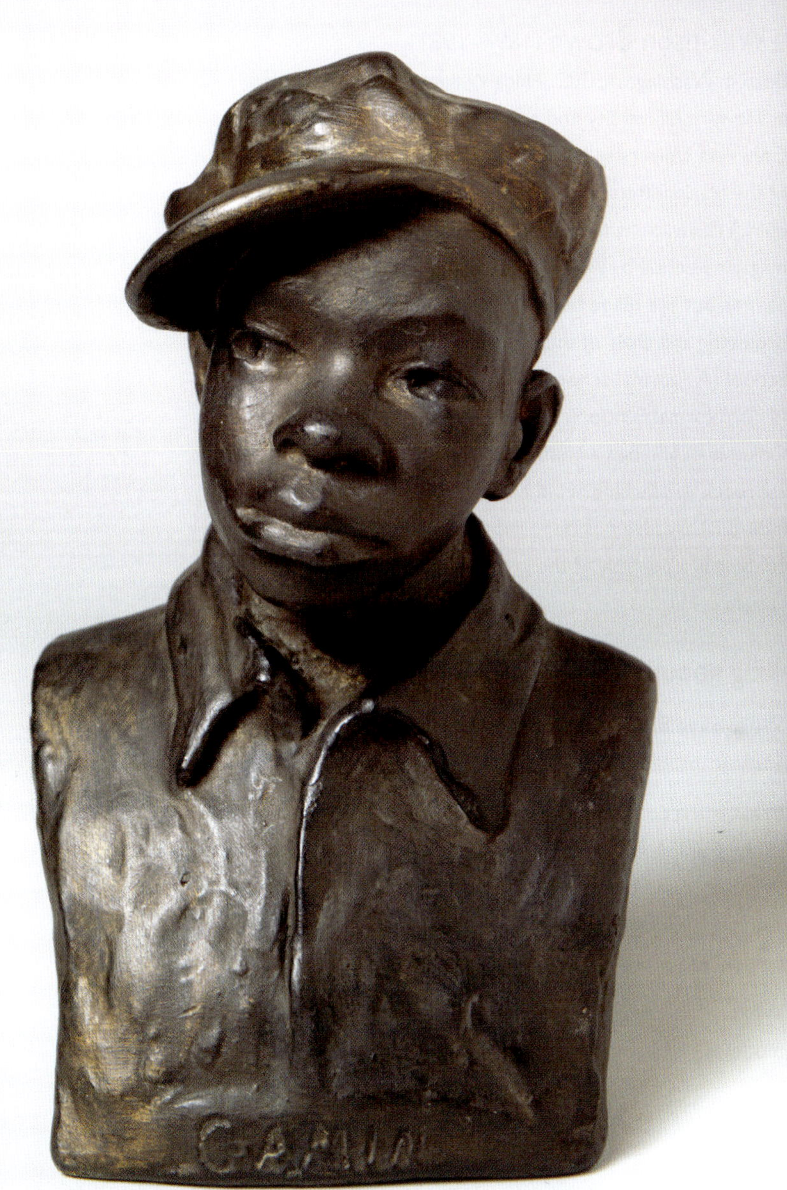
GAMIN

Young Man Studying, circa1932

Hilda Wilkinson Brown
Oil on Canvas
Howard University Gallery of Art

Hilda Wilkinson Brown (1894–1981)

Born in Washington, D.C., Hilda Wilkinson Brown studied at Howard University and earned a master's degree from Columbia University, which she attended in the early days of the Harlem Renaissance. Her early artistic work included quirky illustrations for *The Brownies Book,* a children's magazine edited by W. E. B. Du Bois. Brown was a talented painter, but she made her living, and her greatest impact, as a professor and chair of the arts department at Miner Normal School (A "normal school" was a teacher's college. The Minor Normal School is now the University of the District of Columbia.) She had a tremendous influence over the modern approach to teaching art in elementary schools, encouraging individual creativity as opposed to imitation. *Young Man Studying* is a portrait of the great Harlem Renaissance poet Langston Hughes.

Thinking about the Art

1. Why would Brown have entitled her painting *Young Man Studying* instead of, say, "Portrait of Langston Hughes"?
2. What is the color palette of this painting? What two parts of the painting are most detailed and most vivid in color? What do these two parts have in common? What does this commonality say about the subject of the portrait? Can a person be a work of art?
3. What is the young man in the portrait doing? What kind of model is he to young African Americans?

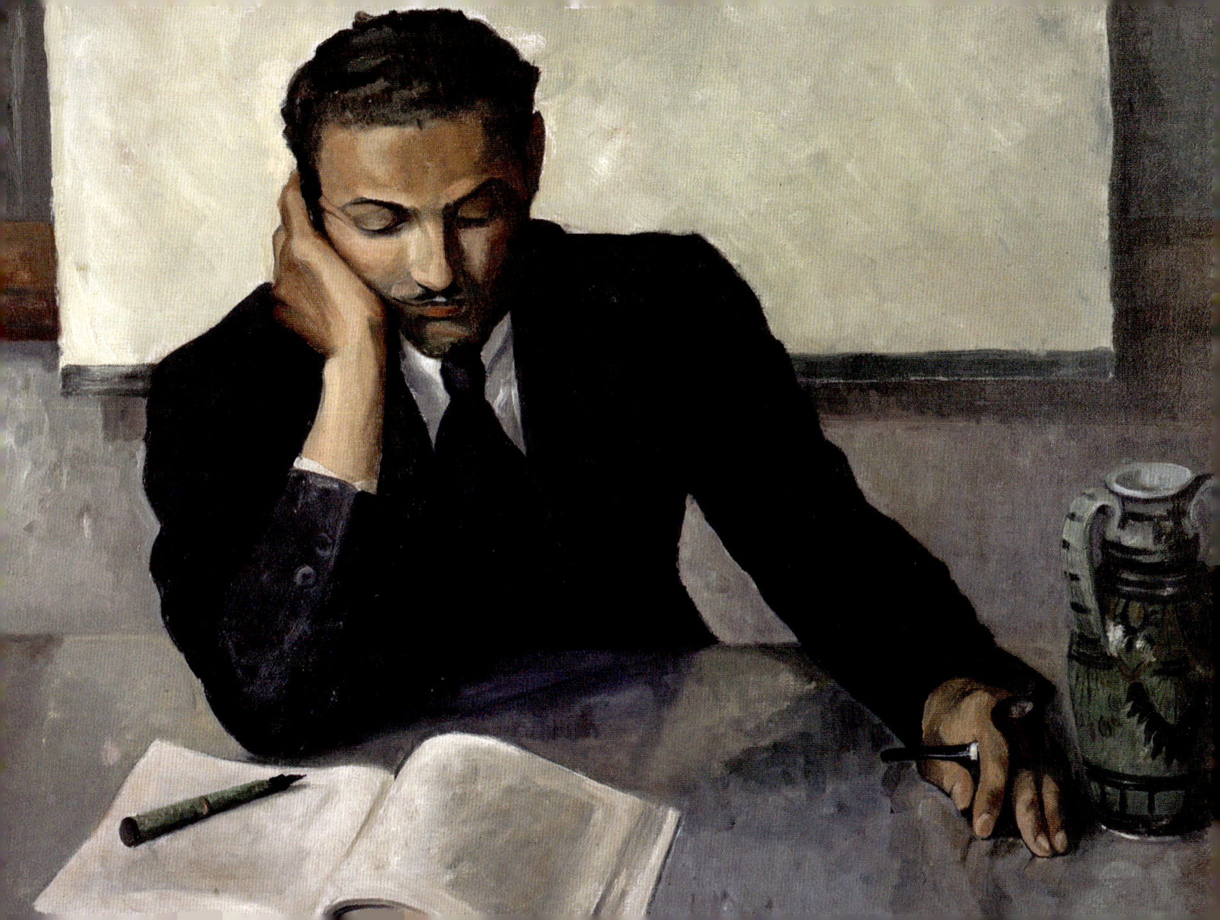

Mask, circa 1930
Sargent Claude Johnson
Copper on Wood Base
Smithsonian American Art Museum

Singing Saints, 1940
Sargent Claude Johnson
Lithograph
California African American Museum

Sargent Claude Johnson (1888–1967)

Printmaker, sculptor, and ceramist Sargent Claude Johnson was one of the first African-American modern artists. Though he worked with a variety of media and themes, Johnson's work focuses on the human form and on the African-American cultural heritage. His most famous works were produced during the Harlem Renaissance, and he had several major exhibitions in New York. He said of his work, "It is the pure American Negro I am concerned with, aiming to show the natural beauty and dignity in that characteristic lip and that characteristic hair, bearing and manner; and I wish to show that beauty not so much to the white man as to the Negro himself."

Thinking about the Art

1. Johnson had a lifelong interest in the characteristic beauty of people of African descent and drew inspiration from the deep well of African art, particularly African sculpture. Go online or to the library and look at some of the great traditional sculpture of Benin, West Africa. What similarities do you see between that work and Johnson's "Mask"?
2. One aspect of African art that had enormous influence on Western art in the twentieth century was its **stylization**—its tendency to simplify the human face and form to geometric shapes. What simple shapes are used to render the face in *Mask?* Do you agree that the sculpture succeeds in showing "natural beauty and dignity," as Johnson wanted his work to do? Why, or why not?
3. In what ways are the figures in *Singing Saints* not realistic? What abstract geometric shapes dominate this piece? Notice that the pattern of the one musician's sleeve is like the staves of a musical score or the strings of an instrument. Notice also that the hat of the figure on the left is shaped like the instrument held by the figure on the right. In what way has Johnson shown these singers becoming wholly one with their music?

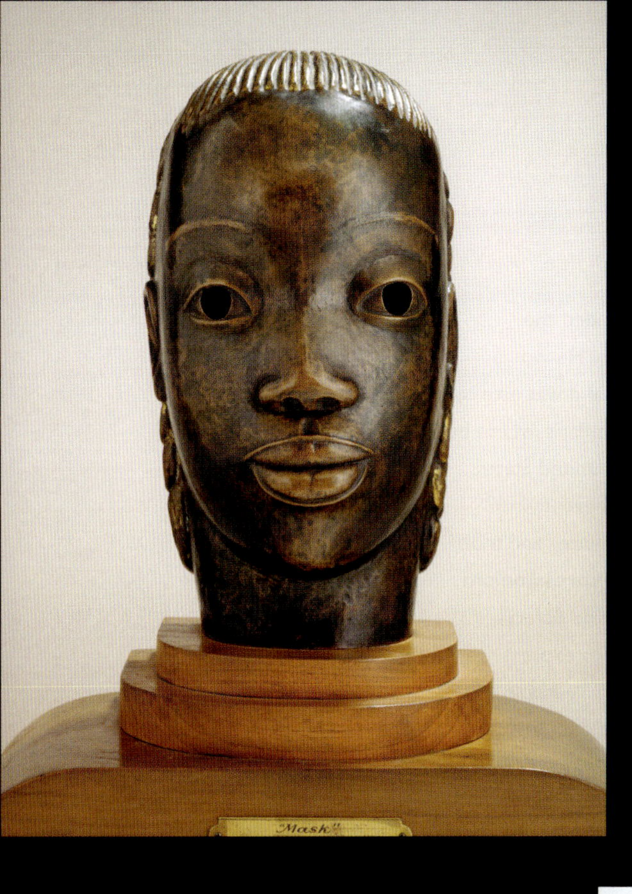
"Mask"

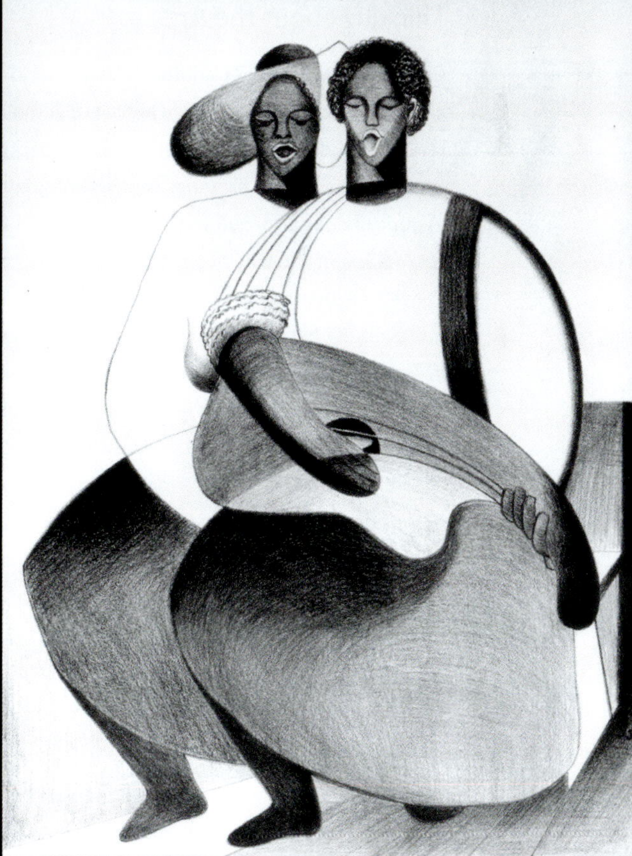

Returning Home, 1935

Hale Woodruff
Linocut
Howard University Gallery of Art

Hale Woodruff (1900–1980)

Hale Woodruff was born in Tennessee and attended the John Herron Art Institute in Indianapolis, Indiana. He won a prestigious Harmon Foundation award in 1926 and was able to enroll in the *Académie de la Grande Chaumière* in Paris, where he remained for four years. After returning to the United States, he produced large murals based on themes and events from African-American history, such as the *Amistad* mutiny and trial. In the mid-1930s he began to favor **abstract expressionism,** which de-emphasized representation of real-world objects and emphasized abstract color and forms used to express the artist's inner experiences and feelings. *Returning Home* is representative of Woodruff's transitional period between the **representational** and abstract expressionist styles. Many of his works are on permanent display in major art collections around the United States.

Thinking about the Art

1. One of the subjects of traditional Chinese and related Japanese painting is monks or pilgrims climbing up a mountainside with stylized clouds and/or ocean waves in the background. The overall effect in such paintings is of serenity. In this linocut, Woodruff does a tongue-in-cheek, cartoonlike American reinvention of the traditional subject, showing a stocky person in heels negotiating some rickety stairs leading up to some even more rickety buildings shaped like a mini mountain range. But if Woodruff's *Returning Home* were simply a **parody,** a work intended to poke fun at its subject, then it would not be the great work that it is. Instead, like Edwin Arlington Robinson's classic American poem "Mr. Flood's Party," Woodruff's work evokes both humor and pathos. What elements of the work are humorous? What elements make you feel empathy for the character depicted?
2. What elements of this picture are representational? What elements have been abstracted?

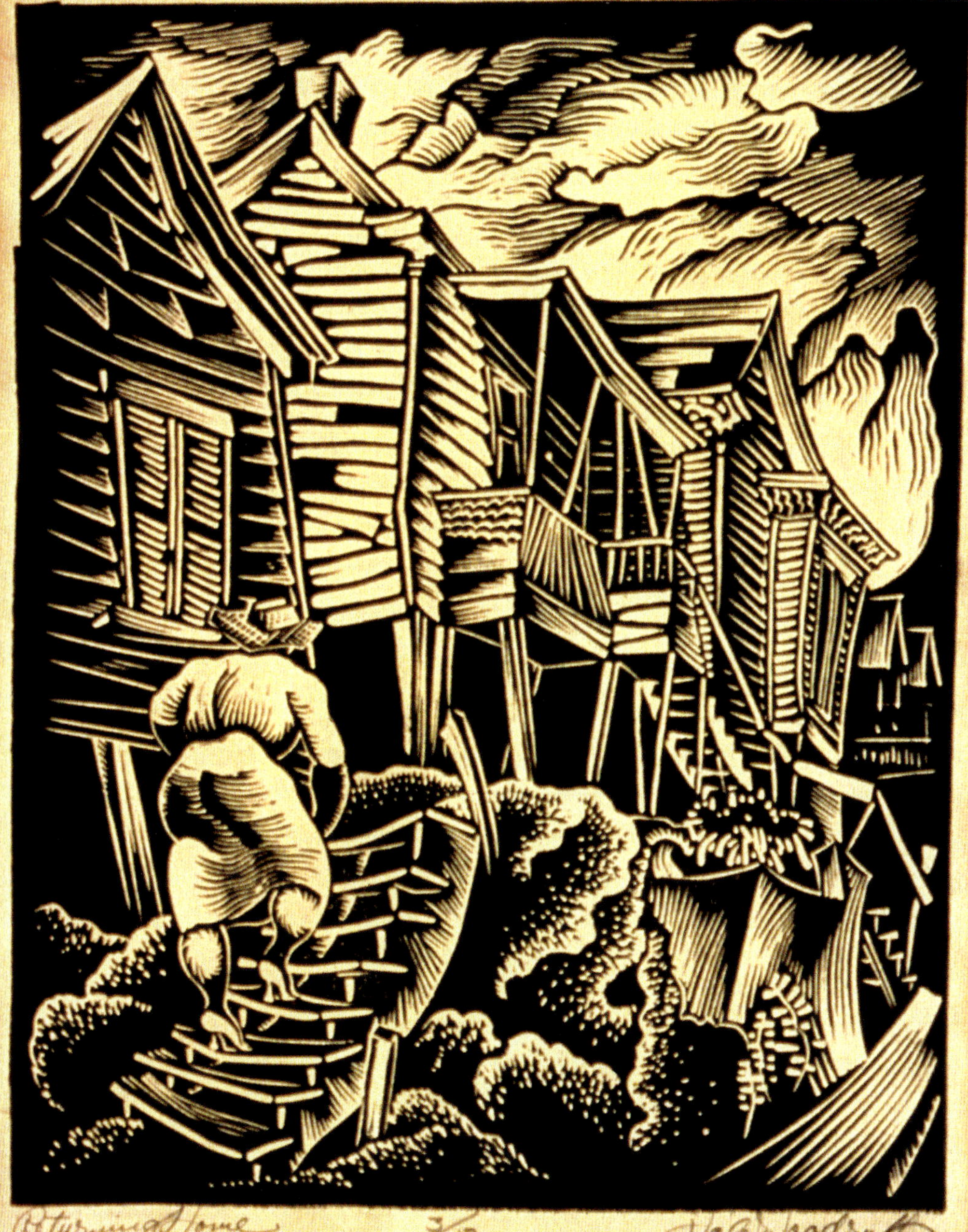

Returning Home
3/10
Hale Woodruff

Poor Man's Cotton, 1944

Hale Woodruff
Watercolor on Paper
The Newark Museum

Hale Woodrufff (1900–1980)

Poor Man's Cotton. The Reverend Dr. Martin Luther King, Jr., once wrote that "If a man is called to be a streetsweeper, he should sweep streets even as Michelangelo painted, or Beethoven composed music, or Shakespeare wrote poetry. He should sweep streets so well that all the hosts of heaven and earth will pause to say, here lived a great streetsweeper who did his job well." King's words make a fine gloss on this exciting work by Hale Woodruff. It is entitled "Poor Man's Cotton," and indeed, the cotton being worked in this painting is meager and not likely to provide bountifully for those doing the work, but there is nothing poor or meager about the depiction. The vivid colors, dramatic angles, and energetic bodily movements in the painting give it an astonishing richness that tells us something of the richness of the interior lives of the people depicted.

Thinking about the Art

1. When colors are intense or vivid, they are called **saturated**. When they are washed out and so not intense they are called **desaturated.** Are the colors in this painting saturated or desaturated? What is the emotional effect of the use of such colors?

2. Consider the use of line in this painting. How do the straight lines of the hoes differ from the lines used in the bodies of the figures? How do the lines of the hoes help to create the illusion of motion in the figures? How are the figures arranged in relation to one another? Again, how does this arrangement help to create the illusion of motion?

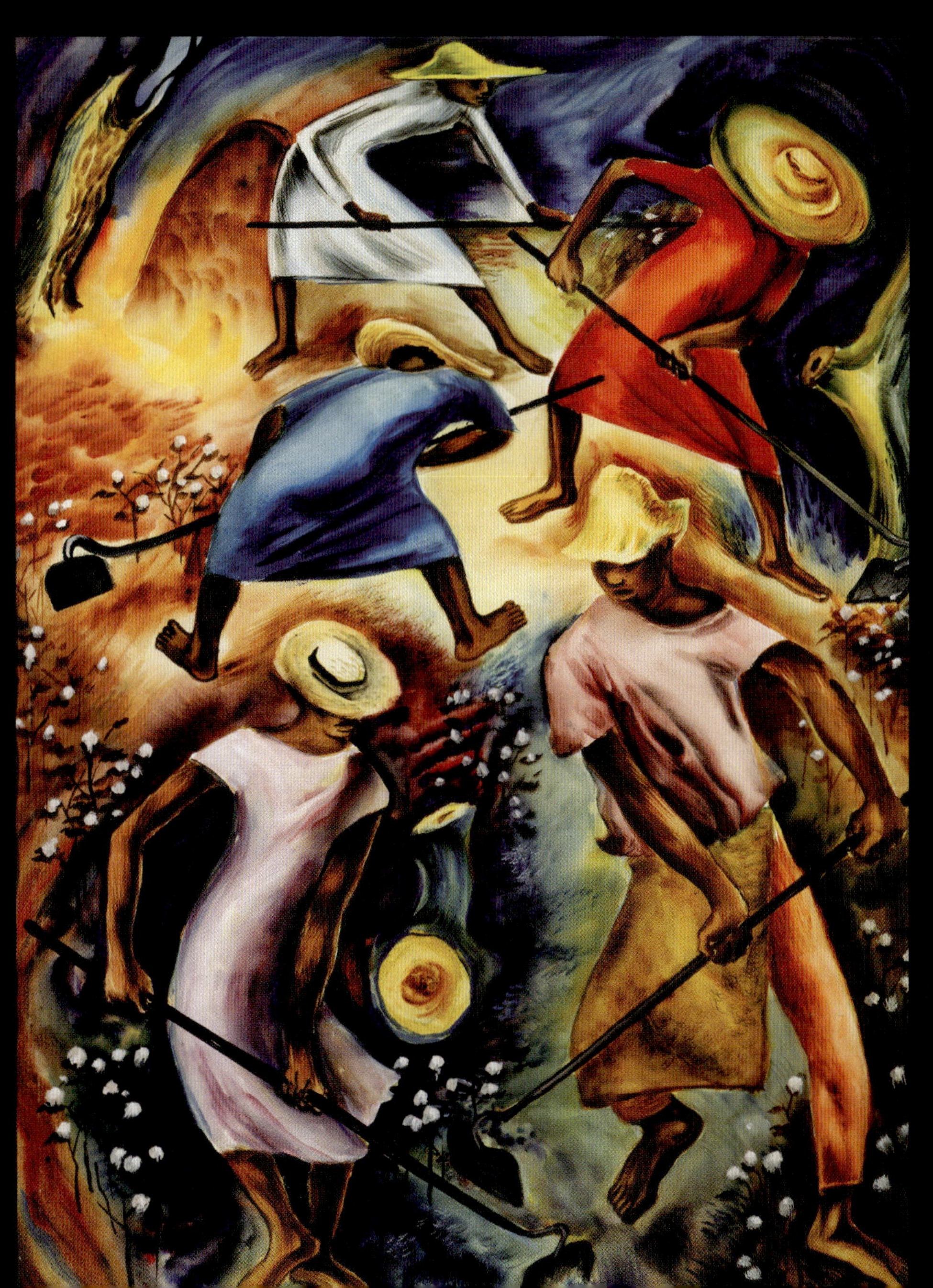

Swingtime, 1937

Charles Sallee
Aquatint and Etching
Howard University Gallery of Art

Charles Sallee (b.1913)

Charles Sallee is a versatile and prolific artist. He is best known for the murals he painted in Cleveland under a commission from the Works Progress Administration. While these works depicted Cleveland's diverse neighborhoods, most of Sallee's other artwork focused on the African-American experience, which he expressed most often in the form of realistic portraits, life scenes, and still lifes. His paintings are noted for their realism and for their subtle use of color, but his etchings and black-ink prints are far more numerous and representative of his true passion. He made his living as an interior designer, a career to which his creative, artistic mind was well suited, and some of his finest work still graces executive offices in Cleveland. Sallee continues to sketch since retiring, and his work can be seen at the Smithsonian American Art Museum, at the Cleveland Art Museum, and in many smaller public and private collections.

Thinking about the Art

1. A widely followed guideline for good **composition,** or layout, is the so-called **rule of thirds.** Imagine that lines are drawn across the work, dividing it into three equal parts vertically and three equal parts horizontally. The point of major focus in the composition should be placed at one of the intersecting lines. What is the point of major focus in this work? Does it lie on one of these intersecting lines? How does the artist use **value** (darkness and light) to emphasize this focal point even more? Explain.
2. How does the artist use curved lines to suggest the idea of dance (of swinging)? In what parts of the composition does the artist use straight lines to form a contrast with and so to accentuate the curved lines of the figures?
3. Who is the focal point of this work? How does the arrangement of the figures emphasize the focal point of the work?

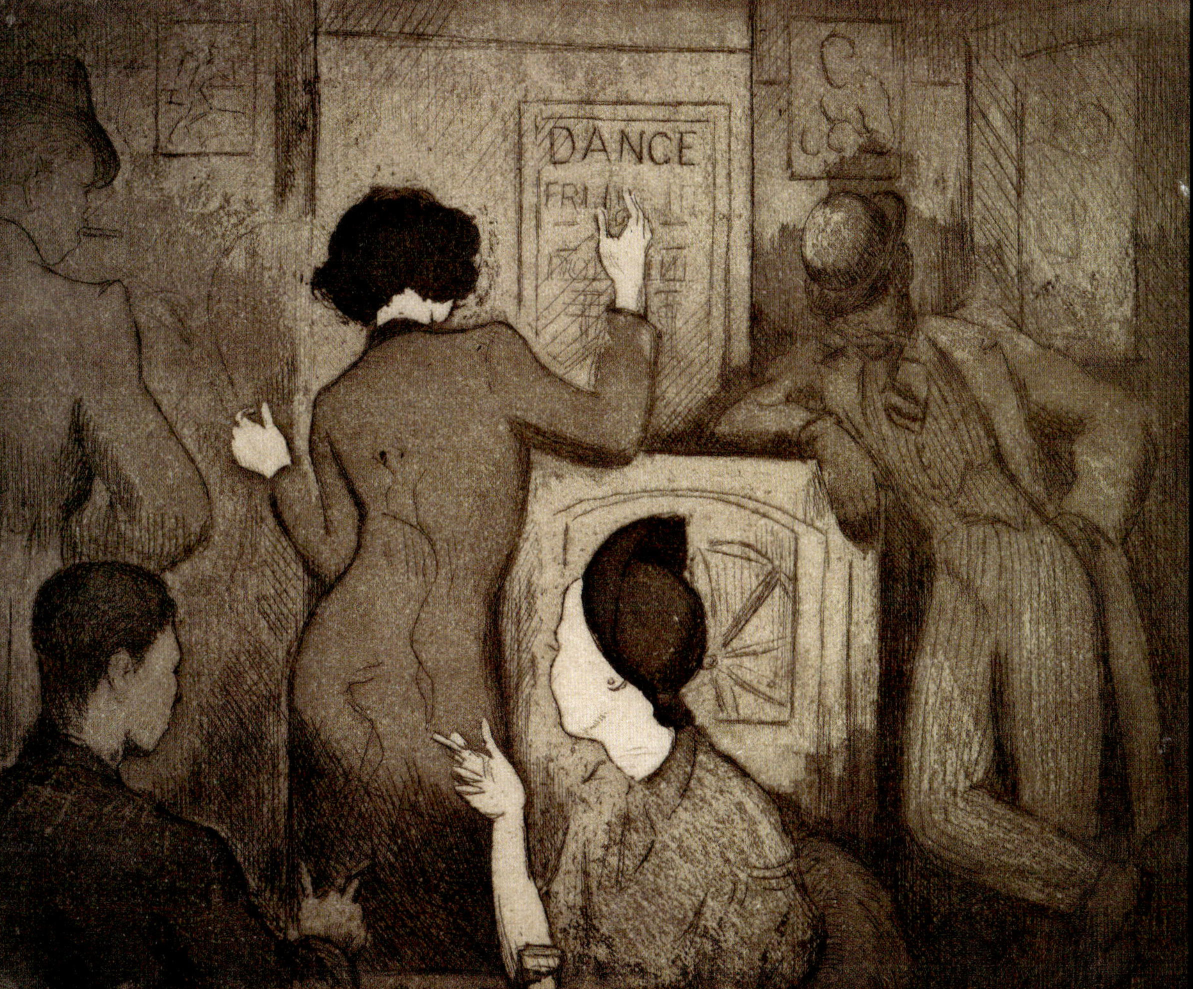
DANCE

Les Fetiches, 1938

Lois Mailou Jones
Oil on Linen
Smithsonian American Art Museum

Lois Mailou Jones (1905–1998)

Lois Mailou Jones joined the faculty of Howard University in 1930 and, aside from a year spent studying in Paris in 1937, she continued teaching and influencing young black artists until her retirement from Howard in 1977. During those many years she also became one of America's top African-American artists. Renowned art historian James Porter said of Jones, "She has a commanding brush that does not allow a nuance of the poetry to escape. Sensuous color delicately adjusted to mood indicates [her] artistic perceptiveness." Working with different styles, techniques, and subjects, Jones evolved over her long career from doing colorful **impressionist** landscapes and portraits to producing **cubist** works with African themes. Elizabeth Catlett (page 808) and David Driskell (page 816) are two of her best-known students. Her work is housed in several major institutions, including the National Museum of American Art, the Corcoran Gallery, the Museum of Fine Arts in Boston, the Brooklyn Museum of Art, and the Howard University Gallery of Art. *Les Fetiches* was the first of a number of African-inspired works done by Jones while she was living and studying in Paris. The painting features five African masks, a white pendant (or perhaps a bone or tooth), and red statuette. A *fetiche,* or fetish, is an object believed to have magical or spiritual powers. The objects pictured in this painting are all fetishes, or ritual objects, of the kind used in Animist African religious practices (and practices in the Americas derived from those).

Thinking about the Art

1. What has the painter done to make these objects appear to be animated or inspirited instead of simply flat and lifeless?
2. What is the emotional response triggered by looking at these objects? Does the painter intend for the viewer to feel comfortable, or did she have something else in mind?

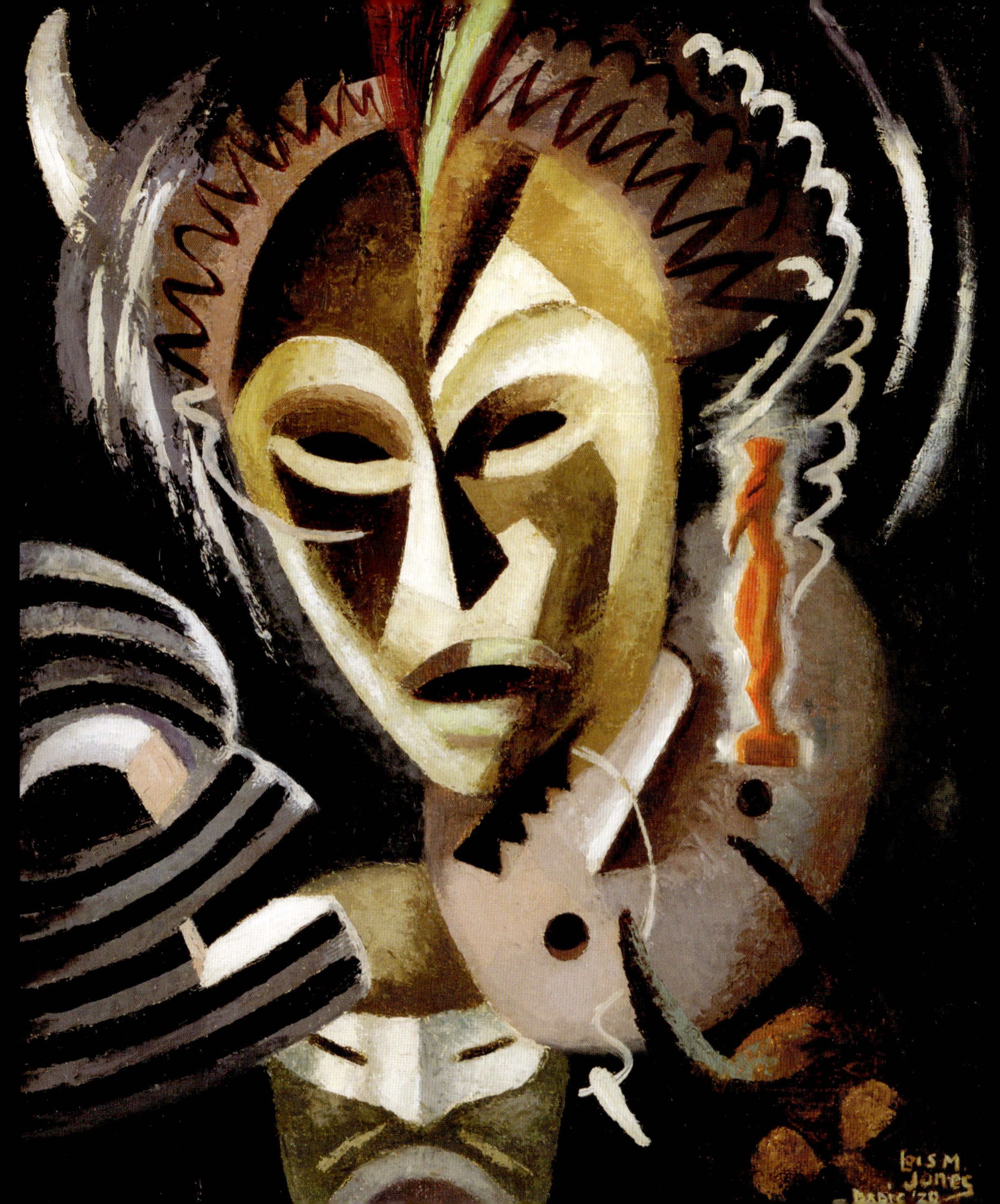
Lois M.
Jones

Portrait, 1996
Lois Mailou Jones
Color Lithograph
Paul R. Jones Gallery/University Museums

Jazz Combo, 1996
Lois Mailou Jones
Color Lithograph
Paul R. Jones Gallery/University Museums

Lois Mailou Jones (1905–1998)

The two works depicted here are among a group done by Jones to illustrate a collection of poems by Léopold Sédar Senghor, poet, teacher, first president of Senegal, and proponent of the concept of **négritude,** a Harlem Renaissance-influenced celebration of the common identity and inheritance of all black peoples of the African Diaspora.

Thinking about the Art

1. What traditional and modern elements are juxtaposed in Jones's portrait of Senghor? Reread the note above about Senghor. Why might the painter have included representations from traditional Senagalese art in her portrait of this man?
2. What two art forms are celebrated in Jones's "Jazz Combo"?
3. How are the color palettes of the two works pictured here similar? In what ways are they different? What makes each color palette particularly appropriate for the subject being portrayed?

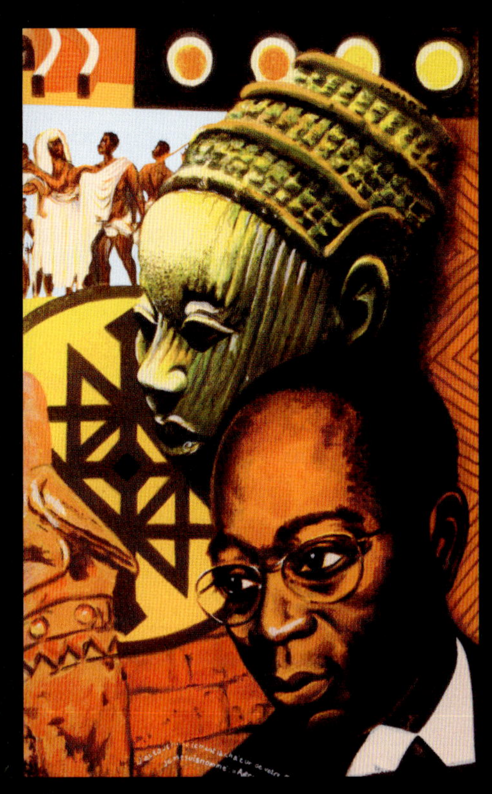

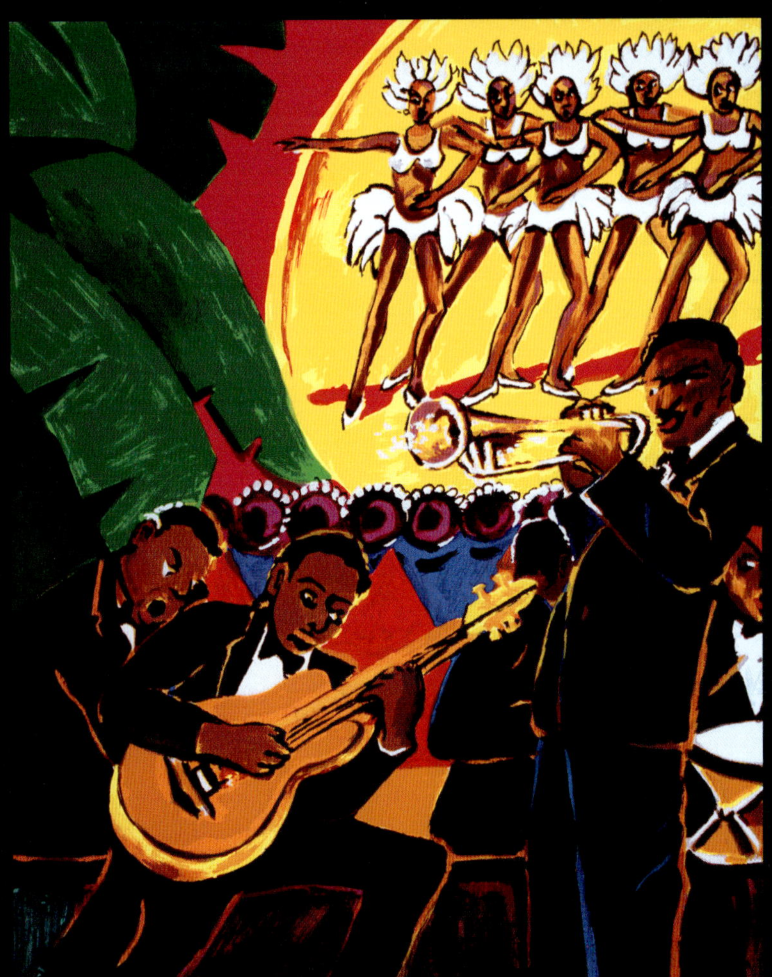

The Migration of the Negro

Panel 3

Caption: In every town Negroes were leaving by the hundreds to go North and enter into Northern industry.

1940–1941
Jacob Lawrence
Casein tempera on hardboard
The Phillips Collection

Panel 15

Caption: Another cause [for the Great Migration] was lynching. It was found that where there had been a lynching, the people who were reluctant to leave at first left immediately after this.

1940–1941
Jacob Lawrence
Casein tempera on hardboard
The Phillips Collection

Jacob Lawrence (1917–2000)

One of the greatest artists of the twentieth century, Jacob Armstead Lawrence produced work that combined social realism with spareness bordering on abstraction. He is best remembered for the great works that he did on historical themes, including series of paintings dealing with Toussaint L'Overture, Harriet Tubman, and John Brown. His most celebrated series is his masterful *The Migration of the Negro,* which consists of sixty fairly small panels, half of which tell the story of what drove people from the South during the Great Migration, and the other half of which tell about what people encountered when they came to the North. The abstraction of Lawrence's style, which includes silhouetted figures, is mimicked by the understated matter-of-factness of his captions and is reinforced by the generally somber color palette of the series. The spareness and small size of each frame contrasts with and, by virtue of this contrast, heightens the dramatic nature of the scene portrayed.

Thinking about the Art

1. Panel 3: Where are these people headed and what do they carry? What do the birds in the painting symbolize?
2. Panel 15: What is the subject of this panel? What has the painter left out? Why might this be called a **minimalist** treatment of its subject? How does this treatment affect the impact of the painting on the viewer?

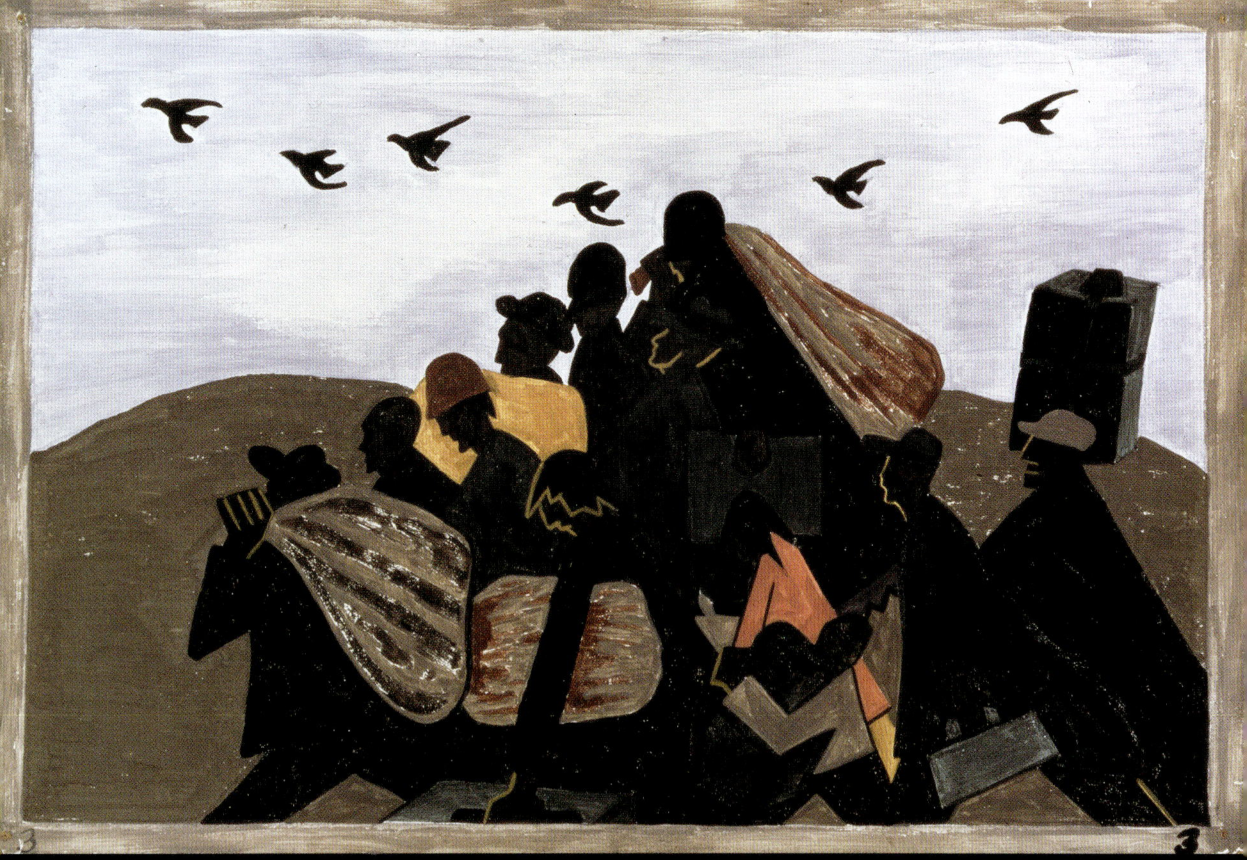

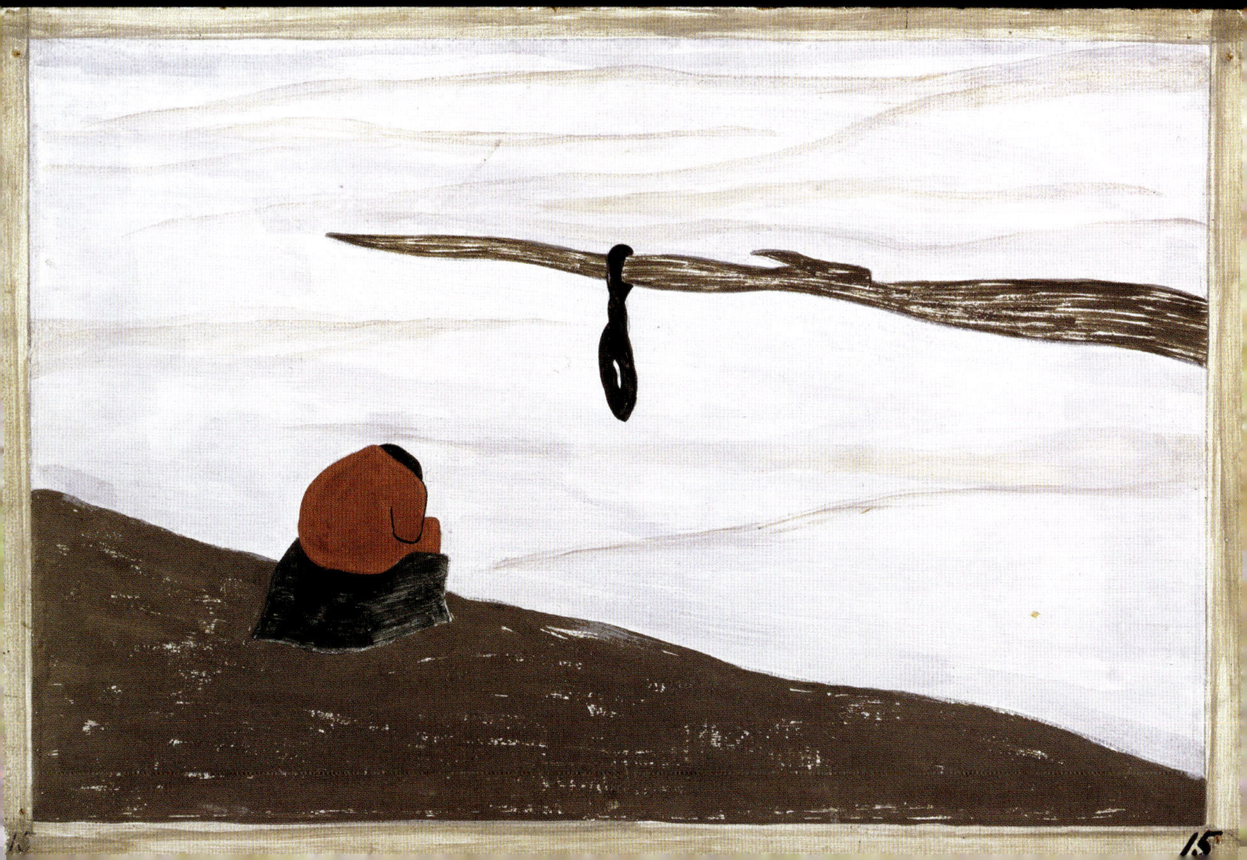

The Migration of the Negro

Panel 10

Caption: They were very poor.

1940–1941
Jacob Lawrence
Casein tempera on hardboard
Museum of Modern Art

Panel 58

Caption: In the North the Negro had better educational facilities.

1940–1941
Jacob Lawrence
Casein tempera on hardboard
Museum of Modern Art

Panel 10. This is one of the most powerful of the many powerful individual works in the *Migration of the Negro* series. When he was a young man training as an artist in Harlem, Lawrence used to walk sixty blocks to the Metropolitan Museum of Art to learn from the Old Masters. But none of them could have taught him this—his breathtaking use of color and empty space to evoke poverty and hardship. Have any faces ever painted looked so weighed down? And yet, even in the midst of such penury, there are touches of vibrant color suggesting—and this suggestion is always to be found in Lawrence's work—possibility, hope, spiritedness.

Panel 58. Compare the colors in this panel with those used in Panel 15. Consider also the geometric shapes in this panel and the poses of the bodies. Every aspect of the work is chosen for effect.

Thinking about the Art

1. What elements in this panel suggest extreme poverty? What elements in this panel suggest the boldness of the human spirit even under extreme conditions?
2. Why did the painter use brighter colors in this panel than in, say, Panel 15? What emotions does the stance of each girl suggest? Why has the painter arranged his figures so as to make them successively taller, higher? What is he saying about education?

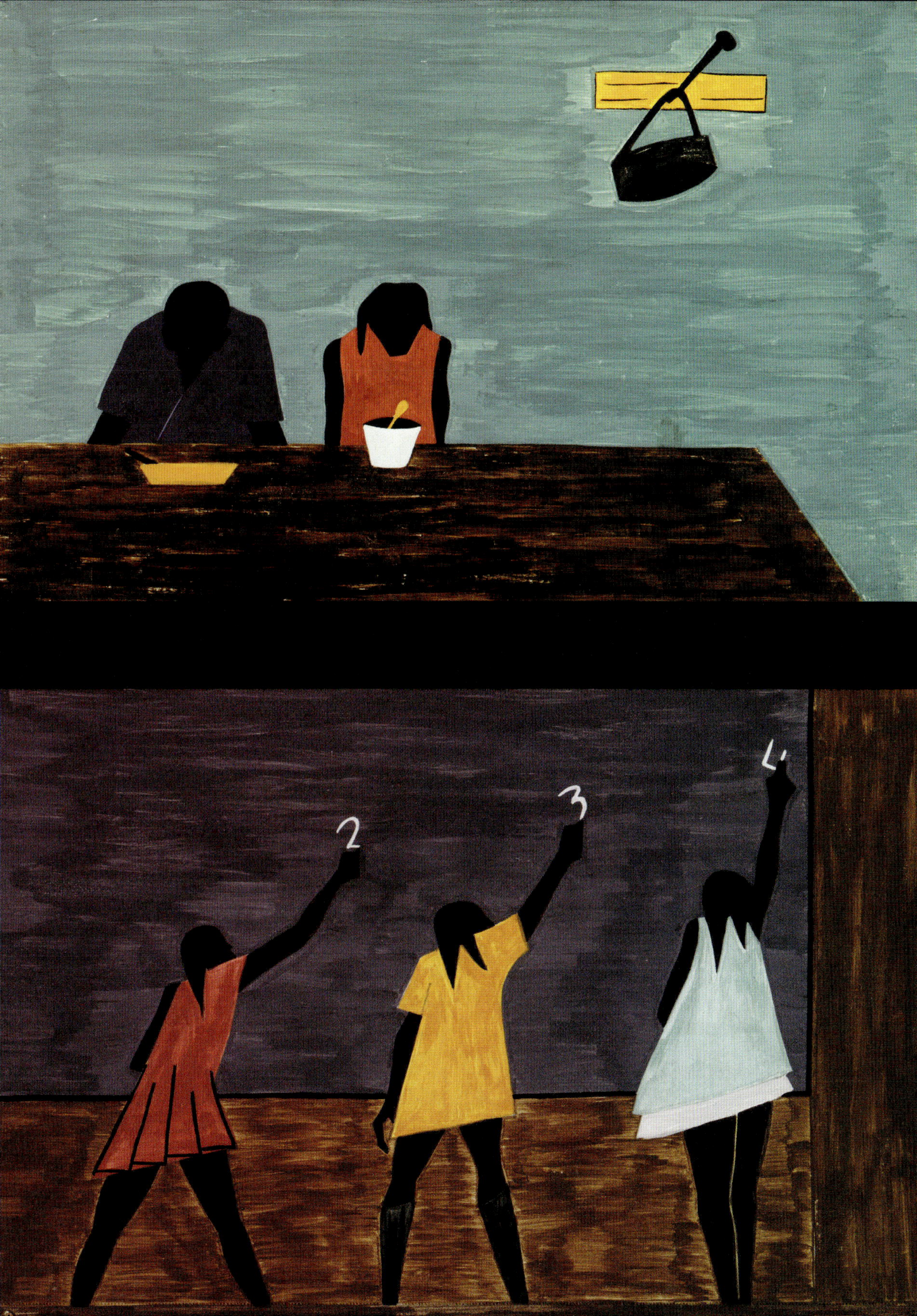

Char Woman with Mop and Broom by American Flag, 1942
Gordon Parks
Photograph

Family in Apartment, 1942
Gordon Parks
Photograph

Football Practice, 1943
Gordon Parks
Photograph

Forging Class, 1943
Gordon Parks
Photograph

Gordon Parks (1912–2006)

Gordon Parks was a pioneer of modern photography. He is best known for the photo essays and cover images he created for *Life* magazine. He was also an accomplished poet, musician, novelist, and activist. In 1971 he made a foray into film and directed *Shaft,* which is mandatory viewing in most film schools and media-studies departments. Parks once said of his work that "the subject matter is so much more important than the photographer." But it takes a gifted photographer to recognize and capture great subject matter. Parks exhibited talent from the very first time he took a photo (with a seven-dollar camera that he bought more or less on a whim). His work with the Farms Security Administration, for *Vogue* and *Life* magazines, and on an astonishing variety of projects provides windows into the African-American experience from the waning days of the Harlem Renaissance to the early days of the twenty-first century. He also recognized and took advantage of photography's special power to affect and shape cultural and political conscience and consciousness.

Charwoman with Mop. In the 1940s Parks participated in a large Farm Security Administration project to document the lives of the poor. The subject of this photograph, taken as part of that project, was Mrs. Ella Watson, who was employed as a charwoman, or janitor, in a federal office building in Washington, D.C.

Family in Apartment. This photograph is of a family living in the southwest section of Washington, D.C., in 1942.

Football Practice. This photograph is of football players at practice at Bethune-Cookman College in Daytona Beach, Florida.

Forging Class. This photograph is of students learning to forge metal at Bethune-Cookman College in Daytona Beach, Florida.

Thinking about the Art

1. Look up the Grant Wood painting *American Gothic* in the library or on the Internet. What similarities can you find between Wood's painting and Gordon Parks's photograph *Charwoman with Mop?* What makes this photograph ironic?
2. How well off is the family in *Family in Apartment?* How can you tell? What might the lamp in the middle of the table symbolize?
3. How has Parks composed *Football Practice* and *Forging Class* to emphasize, reinforce, and heighten the actions he is capturing on film?

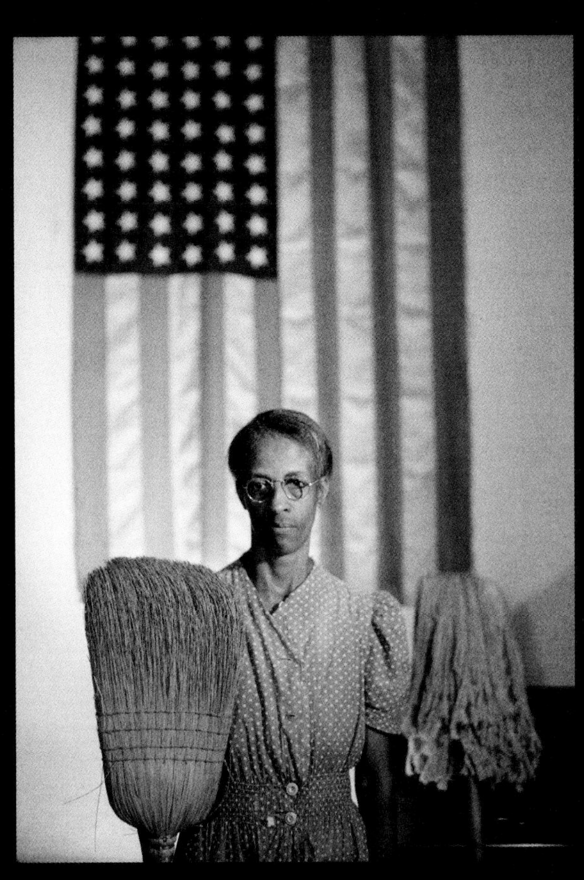

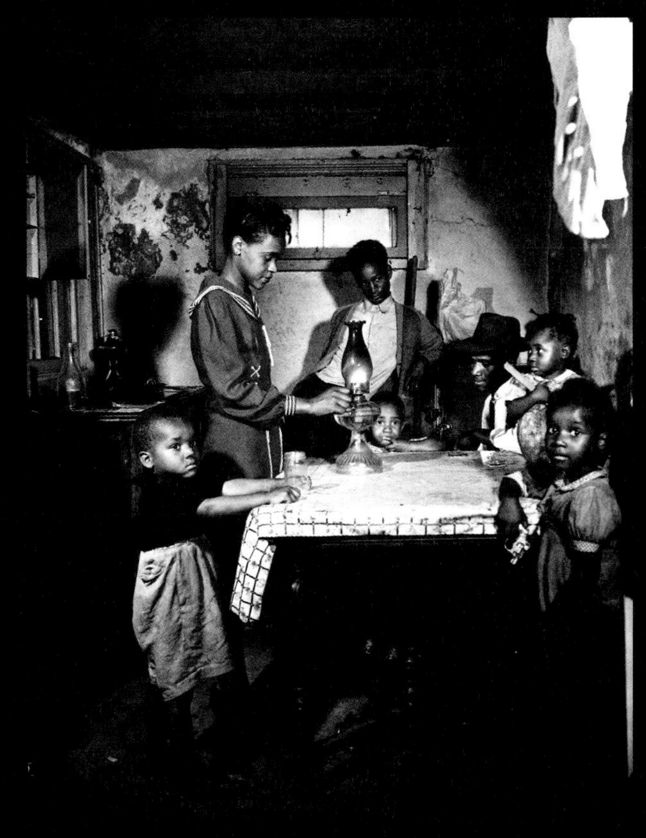

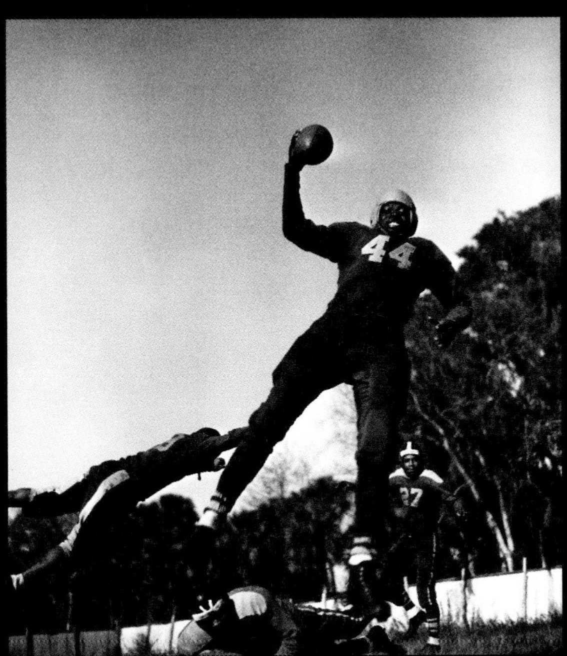
44

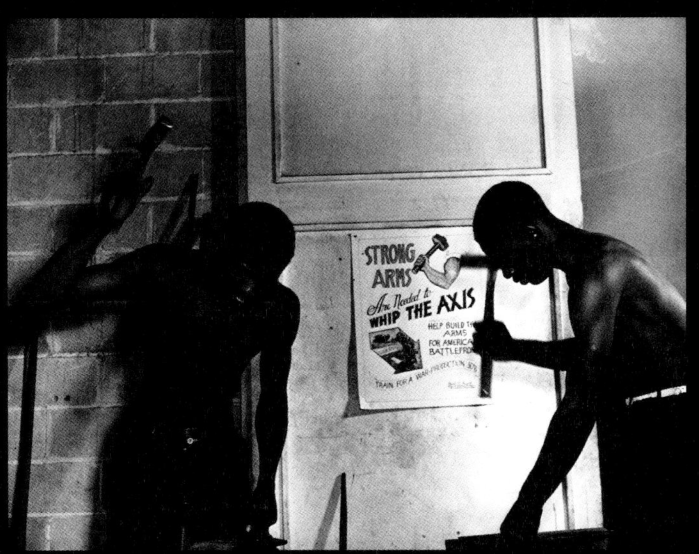
STRONG ARMS
Are Needed to
WHIP THE AXIS
HELP BUILD
ARMS
TRAIN FOR A WAR PRODUCTION JOB

Photographer GP, 1999
Douglas Kirkland
Paper collage
The Studio Museum of Harlem

Queenie, 1943
Gordon Parks
Photograph
The Studio Museum of Harlem

Ethel Shariff in Chicago, 1963
Gordon Parks
Photograph
(Pictured in photo by Kirkland)

Woman and Dog, 1943
Gordon Parks
Photograph

Photographer GP. In this portrait, Kirkland posed Parks with one of Parks's photographs, entitled "Ethel Shariff in Chicago," which was taken in 1963. Ethel Shariff was the leader of the women's corps of the Black Muslims and the daughter of the Black Muslim spiritual leader Elijah Muhammad.

Queenie. This photograph of a student worker was taken at Bethune-Cookman College in Daytona Beach, Florida, in 1943. Notice the wartime propaganda poster in the background.

Woman and Dog in Window. This photograph of a woman and her dog was taken in Harlem, New York, in 1943.

Thinking about the Art

1. What emotions are captured in the faces of the women in these photographs?
2. How does the photograph of Queenie make you feel about work and workers?
3. At what is the woman in *Woman and Dog in Window* looking? Where is the dog looking? What instant has the photographer captured?

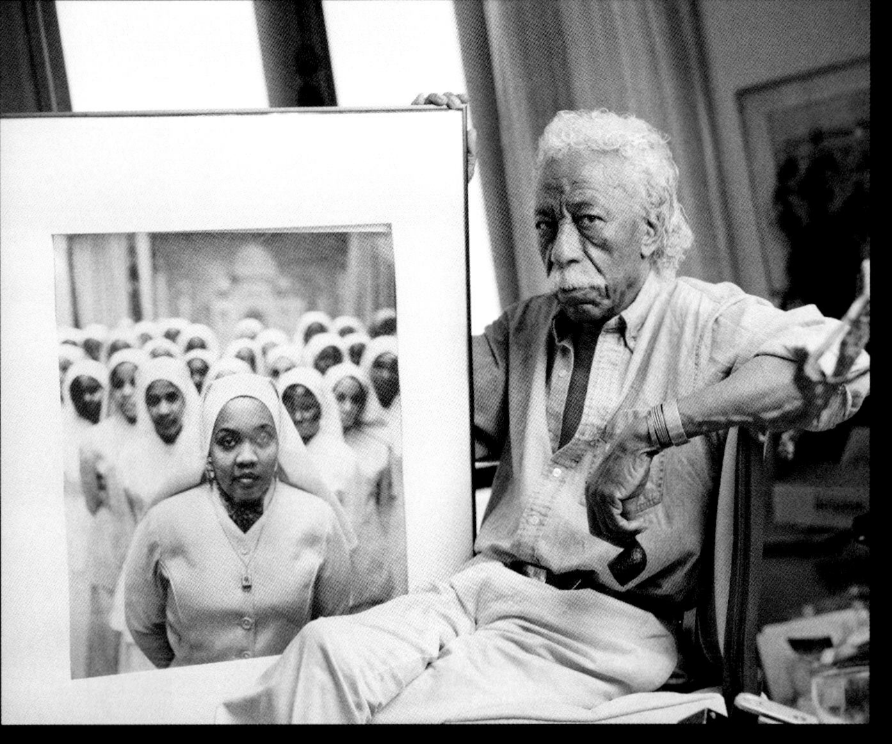

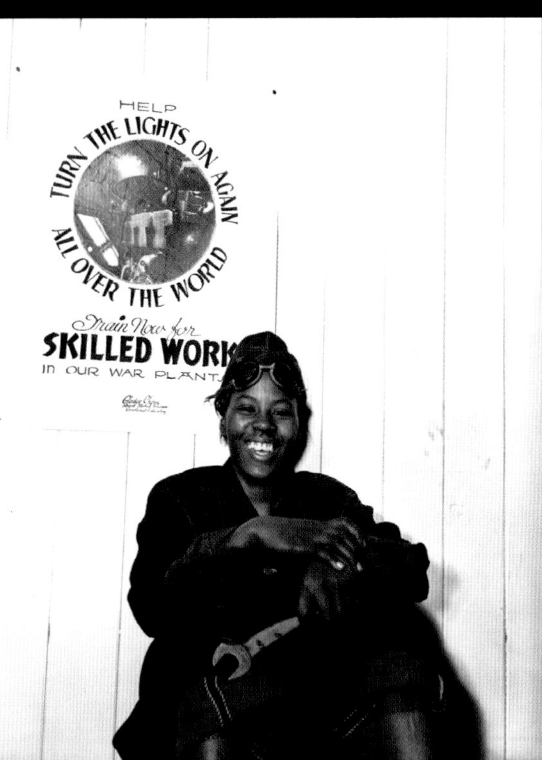
HELP
TURN THE LIGHTS ON AGAIN
ALL OVER THE WORLD
Train Now for
SKILLED WORK
IN OUR WAR PLANTS

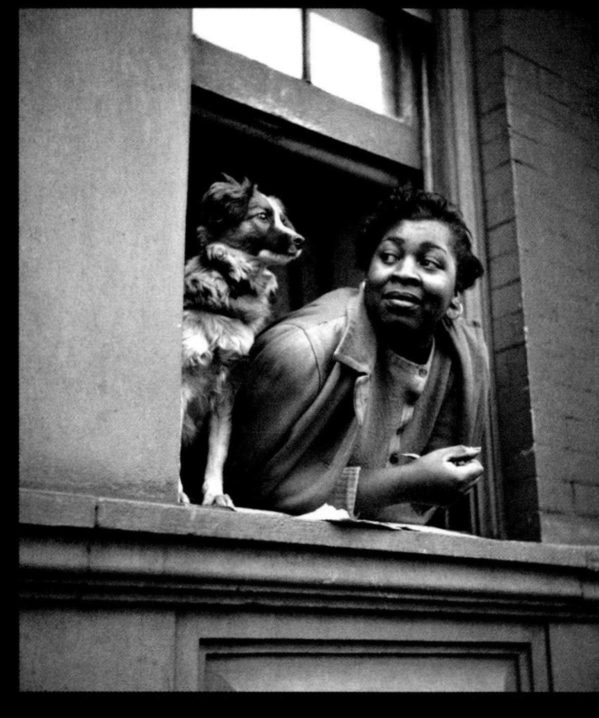

Mr. Prejudice, 1943

Horace Pippin
Oil on Canvas
Philadelphia Museum of Art

Horrace Pippin (1888–1946)

Horace Pippin was a well-known "primitive" or "outsider" artist, meaning that his work had the look and feel of folk art and reflected his lack of formal training. His art was intuitive, based solely on expression and composed of vibrant colors and flat shapes. In addition to painting, Pippin developed an unusual etching style in which he used a hot poker to draw on wood. He began producing serious art around the age of forty and is known to have produced about 150 oil paintings, drawings, and etchings. Pippin's subjects included images of trench warfare (he was severely wounded in the First World War) and of African-American history, religion, and daily life. His work was featured in an exhibit at New York's Museum of Modern Art when he was fifty, after which he took formal lessons for the first time and produced some of his best work, including *Mr. Prejudice.*

Thinking about the Art

1. At the time when this painting was made, the United States was at war, and black soldiers were fighting and dying for their country alongside whites. At the same time, back in the United States, the Ku Klux Klan and Jim Crow were in full force. How does this painting show these two opposing forces occurring in America at the time?

2. The "V" symbol was commonly used in Britain and the United States during World War II as a a sign for victory. What is "Mr. Prejudice" doing to victory in this painting? How is Liberty (represented by the statue) reacting?

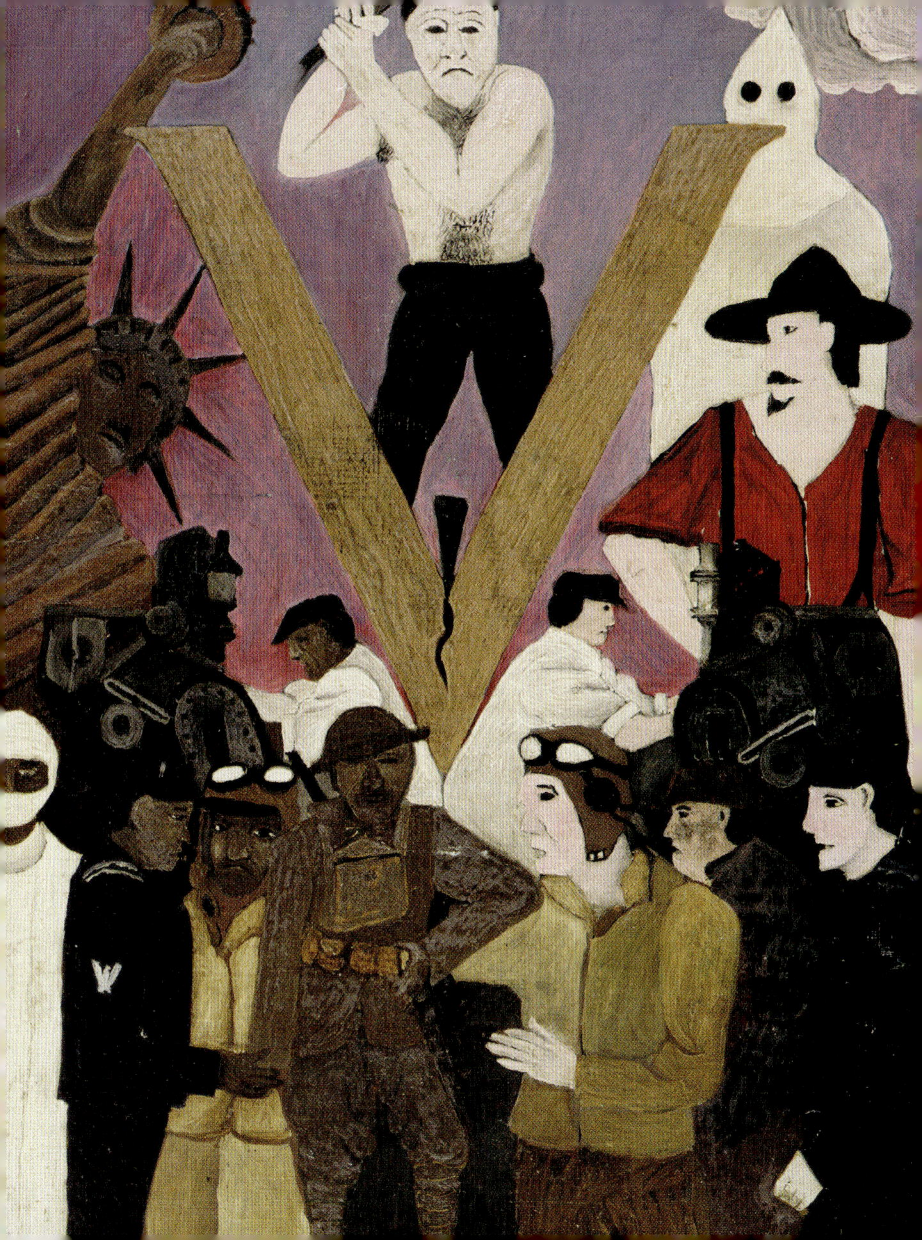

Dr. George Washington Carver, circa 1945

William H. Johnson
Paper collage
Smithsonian American Art Museum

William H. Johnson (1901–1970)

One of the most versatile and popular painters of his time, William H. Johnson moved from humble roots in South Carolina to New York's National Academy of Design. From there he went on to study in Paris and to travel through Europe, where he painted impressionist landscapes. Johnson worked in numerous media and styles and often focused on historical, social, and political themes. He produced his most original and memorable works in the mid-1940s, having developed what is known as a "conscious naiveté." He intentionally gave his work the same "primitive" or "outsider" feel that made folk artists like Horace Pippin famous. However, unlike a true "primitive" painter, Johnson brought all of his training and experience to the canvas or wooden board upon which he painted, resulting in a distinct elegance and vitality. The wonderful painting at right depicts scenes from the life of the great scientist of the Tuskegee Institute.

Thinking about the Art

1. Dr. George Washington Carver was a great inventor who found many uses for agricultural products important to the South. What agricultural products are featured in this painting? In what part of the painting is he shown at work in his laboratory?

2. In addition to being a great scientist, Dr. Carver was a painter who exhibited at the 1893 World's Fair. He was also the inventor of a number of formulae for paints and dyes. What part of the painting depicts these things? Dr. Carver worked with Henry Ford and developed a synthetic rubber. What part of this painting celebrates that accomplishment?

3. Dr. Carver was an advisor to three presidents. In what part of this painting is he shown greeting Franklin D. Roosevelt? In what part is his school, the Tuskegee Normal and Industrial Institute, shown? In what part is he shown caring for a child?

4. Late medieval and early Renaissance painters introduced **perspective,** the technique of making a scene look realistic by making foreground objects larger than more distant, background objects. Does this painting use perspective? What other aspects of the painting make it look primitive? Why would a cultivated, trained artist like Johnson use a consciously primitive style to celebrate a folk hero like Dr. Carver?

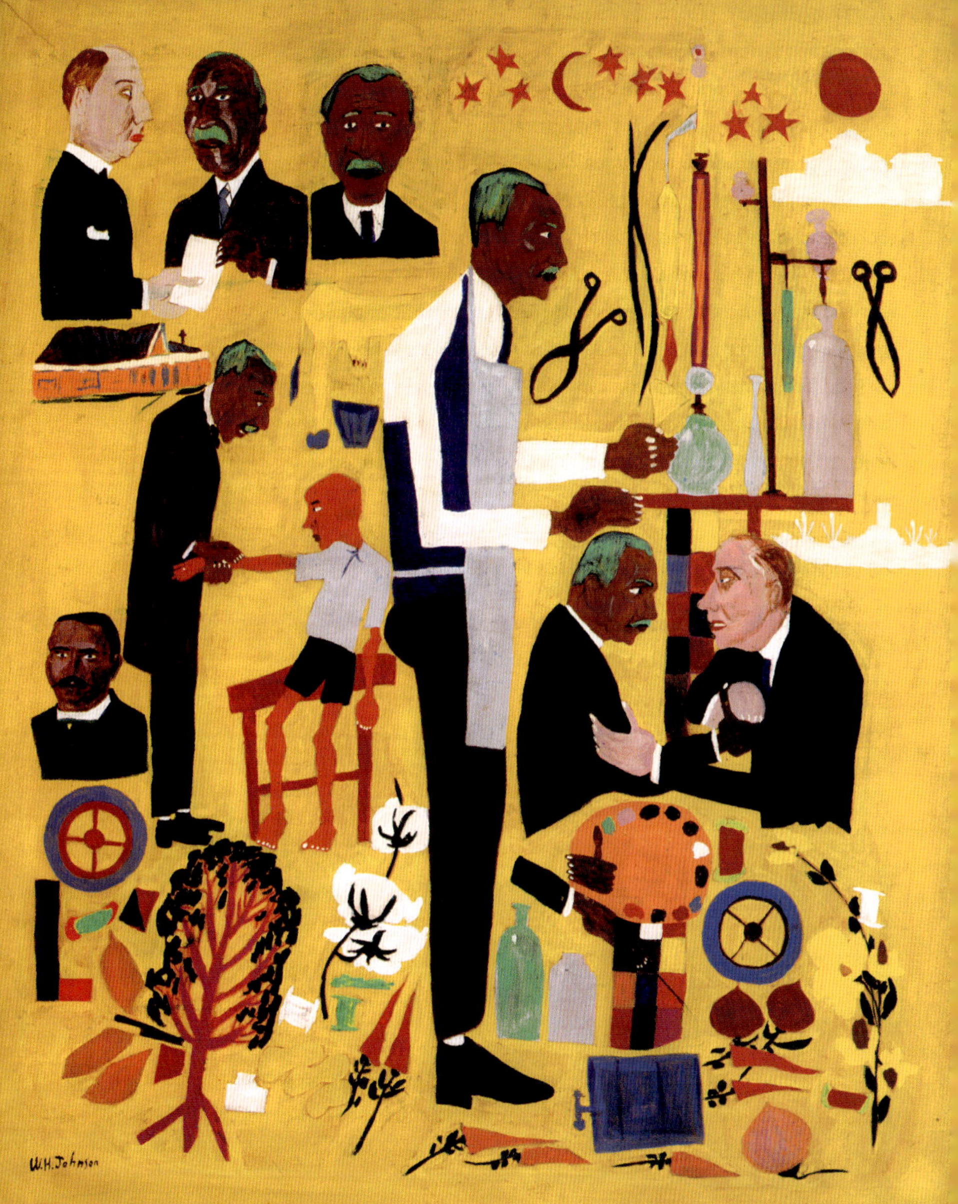
W.H. Johnson

Can Fire in the Park, 1946

Beauford Delaney
Oil on canvas
Smithsonian American Art Museum

Beauford Delaney (1901–1979)

During the Harlem Renaissance, Beauford Delaney developed a reputation as a fine portrait artist, working primarily in pastel colors. He gradually shifted his focus to street scenes and mastered the **impasto** technique of applying thick layers of paint to create a textured, pasty look. *Can Fire in the Park* was one such painting and features the rich colors and the black outlines characteristic of his work during this period. Over time, his works became increasingly **abstract** (nonrepresentational) and **expressionist** (emphasizing the medium to express emotion), perhaps due to his burgeoning cynicism regarding race relations in America. Delaney visited Paris in the early 1950s and, like so many artists, was so enraptured by the city that he remained there for the rest of his life.

Thinking about the Art

1. The great expressionist painter Vincent Van Gogh once said, "Instead of trying to render what I see before me, I use color in a completely arbitrary way to express myself powerfully." In Paris in 1905, at the *Salon d'automne,* paintings by Henri Matisse, André Derain and others were exhibited together. The paintings took a bold new approach to color, using highly saturated, intense colors that did not appear in nature. The viewing public was outraged by this abandonment of realism, and one critic dubbed these painters ***Les Fauves,*** the wild beasts. What similarities does *Can Fire in the Park* have with Fauvist painting? How does the use of black in the painting intensify its unnatural colors?
2. What are the street people in this painting doing? Why do they have to do this? In this painting, Delaney has chosen to make the figures indistinct, faceless. Why? What is he saying about these people?

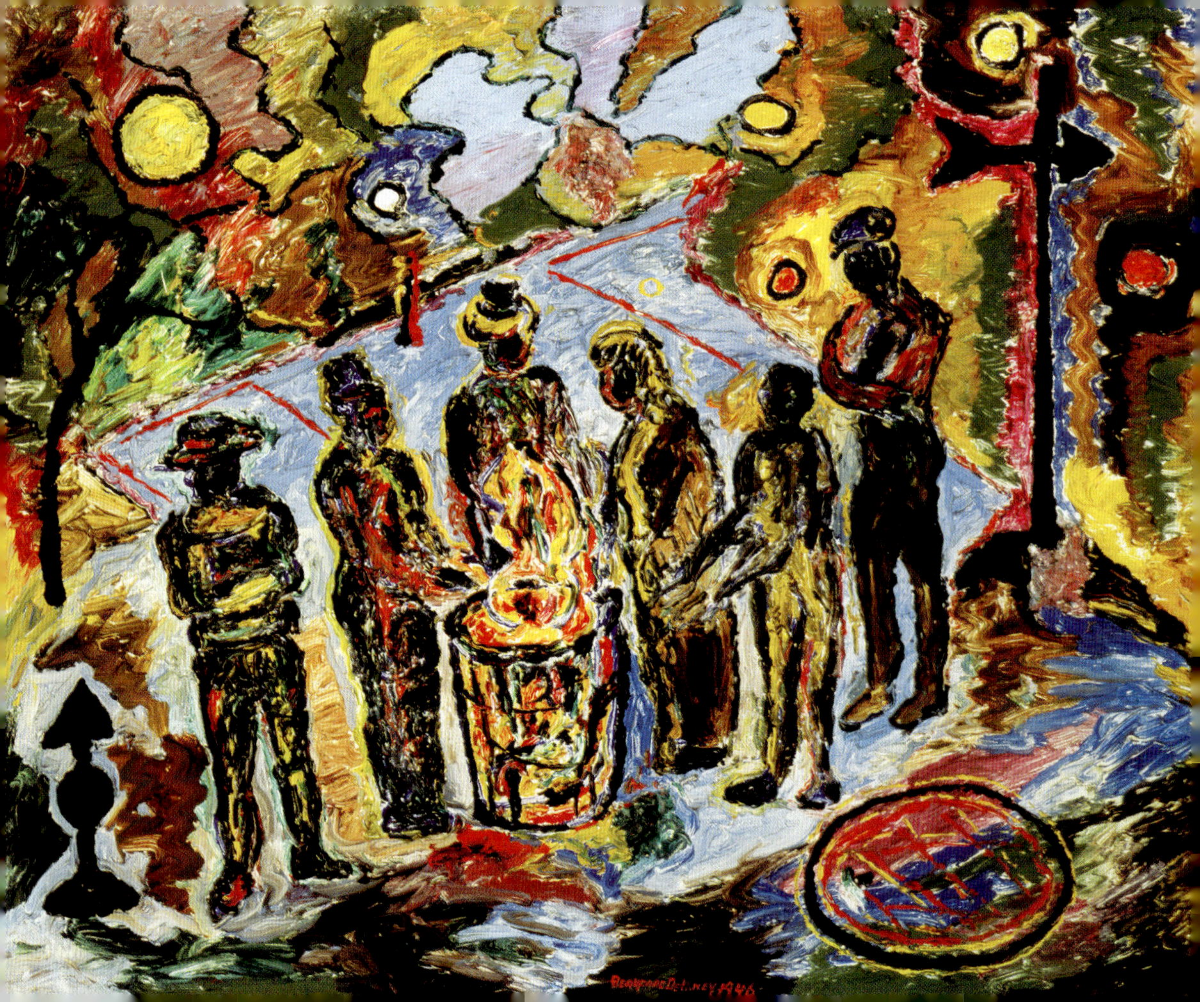

On a Cuban Bus, 1946

James A. Porter
Oil on Canvas
Howard University Gallery of Art

James A. Porter (1905–1971)

Every African-American artist or art student has known the name James A. Porter since 1943, when he published his influential *Modern Negro Art.* It is because of this book and because he influenced young minds for more than forty years as chairman of the outstanding art department at Howard University that Porter is remembered as the "father of African-American art history." His accomplishments as an artist were also impressive. He was a great portrait artist and a master at depicting the human form. *On a Cuban Bus* was part of a series of scenes from daily life that Porter painted after trips to Haiti and Cuba. As in all of his works featuring human subjects, Porter captures with striking sensitivity the intricacies of the human face and the subtle, poignant details that we so often overlook in daily life.

Thinking about the Art

1. How did the artist manage to communicate through a purely visual medium the soulfulness of the song being performed by the guitarist and singer?

2. Porter is considered a **realist,** someone who captured details from real life in his work. What aspects of the portrayal of the singer suggest that he is a professional entertainer? What details can you make out in the landscape outside the bus? How did the artist convey the crowding typical of third-world public transportation? Why would this be an amazing trip despite the crowding and despite having to share the ride with farm animals?

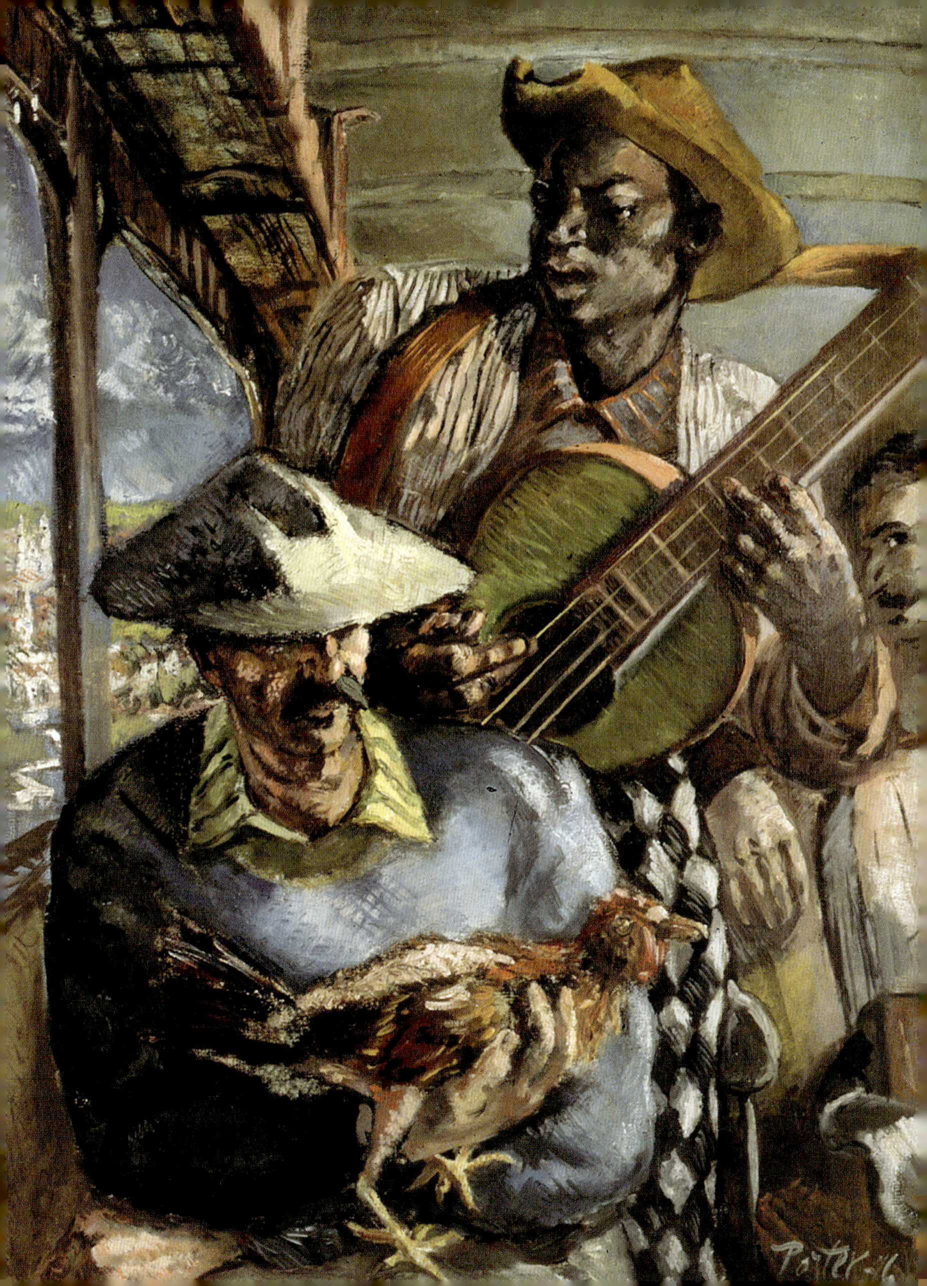

Bust of Miss Coleman, 1946

William Artis
Terra Cotta with a Wood Base
Howard University Gallery of Art

William Artis (1914–1977)

William Artis moved to New York in 1927, at the height of the Harlem Renaissance, and studied sculpture at the Savage Studio of Arts and Crafts. His work was displayed in the Harmon Foundation exhibition when he was just nineteen. Artis was active in community arts and education programs through the 1950s, during which time he earned his Bachelors and Masters in Fine Arts degrees from Syracuse University. He went on to become an art professor. He was clearly influenced by his mentor, Augusta Savage (See page 756), and especially by her mastery of physiognomy, the study of the human face as a reflection of character and mood. Artis's frequent use of **terra cotta** (a lightly fired, often reddish earthenware), as opposed to bronze or other dark, textured media, added to the distinct expressiveness of his work. His sculptures treat African-American subjects with neoclassical clarity and grace.

Thinking about the Art

1. One of the most exquisitely beautiful of American portrait sculptures, this work by Artis embodies Greek and neoclassical concepts of ideal proportion but shows those adapted to the portrayal of the face of a woman of African descent. Measure from the base of the neck to the chin, from the chin to the top of the nose, and from the top of the nose to the top of the hair. Notice that the distances are about the same. What other regularities of measurement and form do you see in this work? In what ways have the features been simplified, stylized, and idealized to intensify their beauty?

2. One critic has written, "If you have any questions about whether 'Black is beautiful,' all you have to do is look at the work of Sargent Johnson, Augusta Savage, or William Artis. What about this work proves the critic's point?

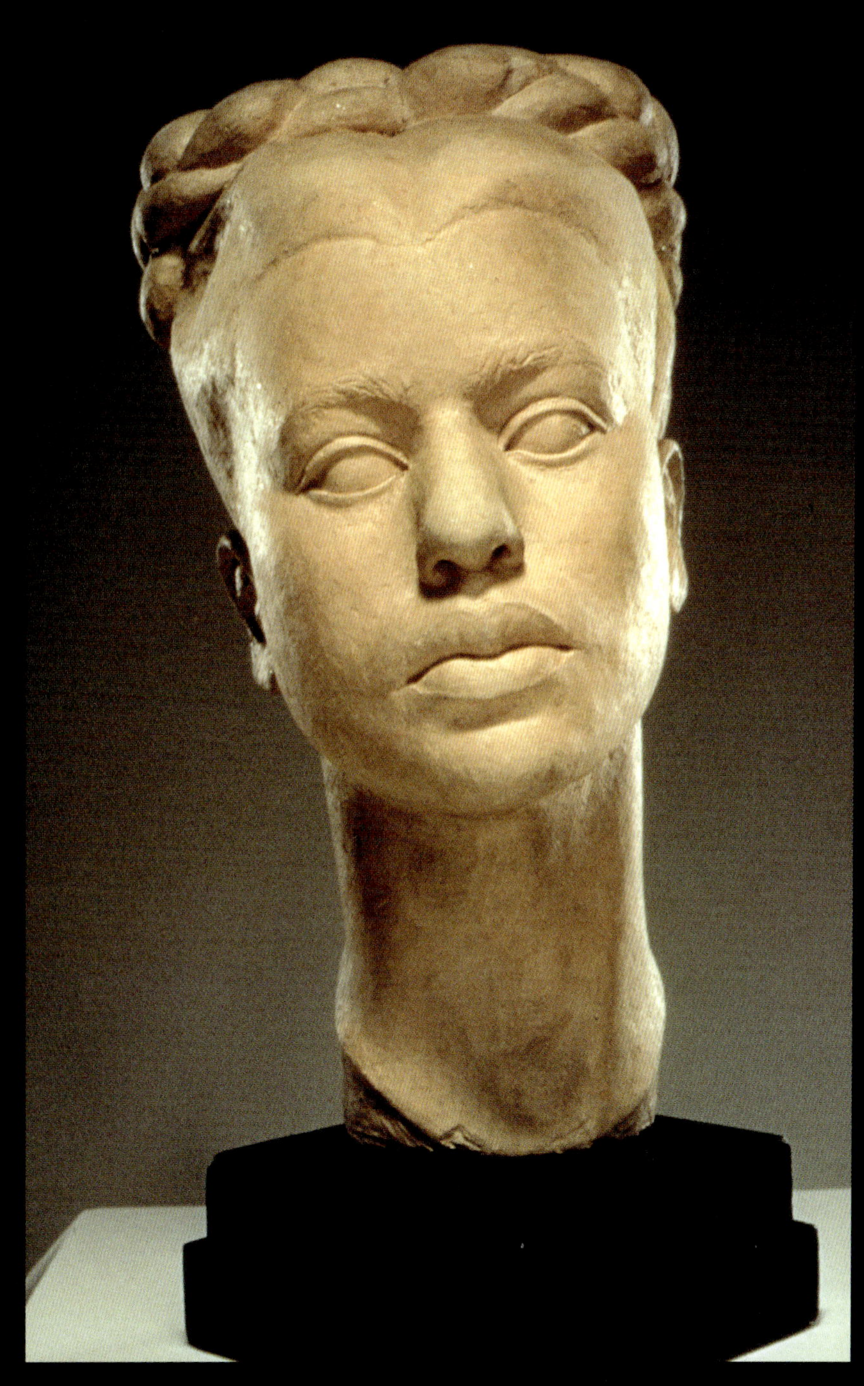

The Throne of the Third Heaven of the Nations Millennium General Assembly, 1950–1964

James Hampton
Gold and silver tinfoil, Kraft paper, plastic over wood furniture, paperboard, glass, etc.
Smithsonian American Art Museum

James Hampton (1909–1964)

Those who knew James Hampton viewed him as a quiet, solitary, religious fellow of little pretension. He was employed as a janitor for the General Services Administration in Washington, D.C. It was not until after his death that his sister opened the doors to a small garage near his apartment, and the world discovered the James Hampton whose single masterwork, created over fourteen years, almost defies classification. The piece is symmetrical, consists of 180 individual objects, and spans 10½ x 27 x 14½ feet. It represents the chancel in a church, within which one might find an altar, chairs, offertory tables, and various objects of religious devotion, constructed from an array of objects too numerous to list here, and all reflecting the artist's inventiveness and "passionate and highly personal religious faith," as one essayist wrote. Atop the seven-foot throne are the words "FEAR NOT." Panels on the left and right refer to the New and Old Testaments, respectively, and various other inscriptions suggest that Hampton was preparing for the Second Coming. His work is on display at the National Museum of American Art, where one can get a truer sense of this remarkable creation. A millennium is a period of a thousand years. Some interpretations of the Book of Revelation in the Bible suggest that in the final times there will be a period of rule by the Antichrist followed by a climactic Battle of Armaggedon and then a thousand-year rule by Christ on earth. This work may be a depiction of the throne of "Christ the king."

Thinking about the Art

1. What aspects of this work suggest kingliness and unimaginable wealth? Why is it ironic that the work was constructed of such materials as tin foil and wood scraps?
2. Along what axis is this work symmetrical? Why would achieving this effect have been so time consuming? (The work took Hampton a good portion of a lifetime to complete.)
3. Critics have compared this work to prophetic works such as the Book of Revelation and the poetry of William Blake. Why?

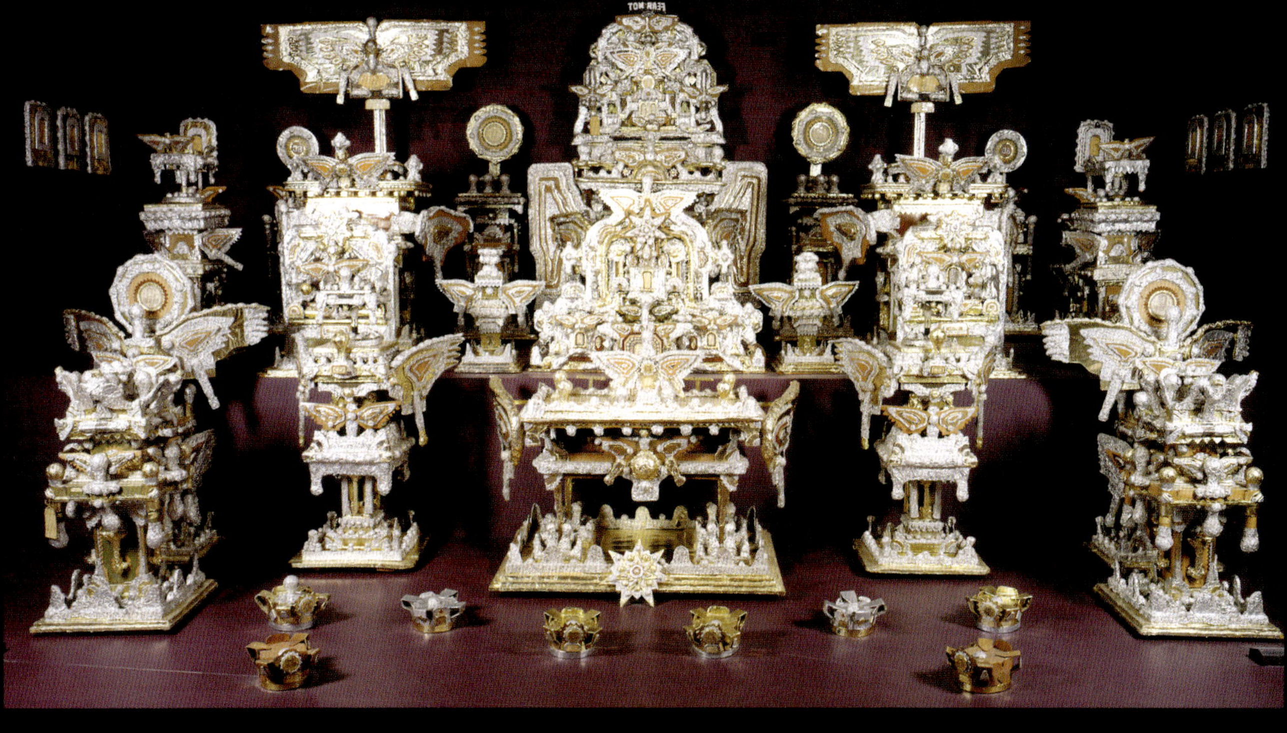
FEAR NOT

Boy With Tire, 1952

Hughie Lee-Smith
Oil on Panel
The Detroit Institute of Arts

Hughie Lee-Smith (1915–2000)

Urban decay was the primary subject of Hughie Lee-Smith's work, but he brought much more to the canvas than such a dreary theme may suggest. He brought poetry to every crack in the sidewalk and broken windowpane. His color tones and depictions of motion leave strong impressions on the mind, and though his works always appear simple at a glance, something will always cause the viewer to stop and ponder. Lee-Smith's human subjects are part of the environment, but they are also, often, the main source of optimism—as shown in the bright yellow shirt and the facial expression of the young man in this painting. Lee-Smith received several major prizes in his lifetime and was elected a member of the National Academy of Design. His works are valued components of many prestigious public and private collections throughout the United States.

Thinking about the Art

1. In this painting, the artist has made use of strong vertical lines. What parts of the painting make use of strong verticals?
2. What time of day is pictured here? How do you know?
3. **Symmetry** is balance across a dividing line or around a center. Imagine a line drawn from the upper left-hand corner of this painting to the bottom right-hand corner. How has the artist arranged objects in the painting to balance on either side of that imaginary line?

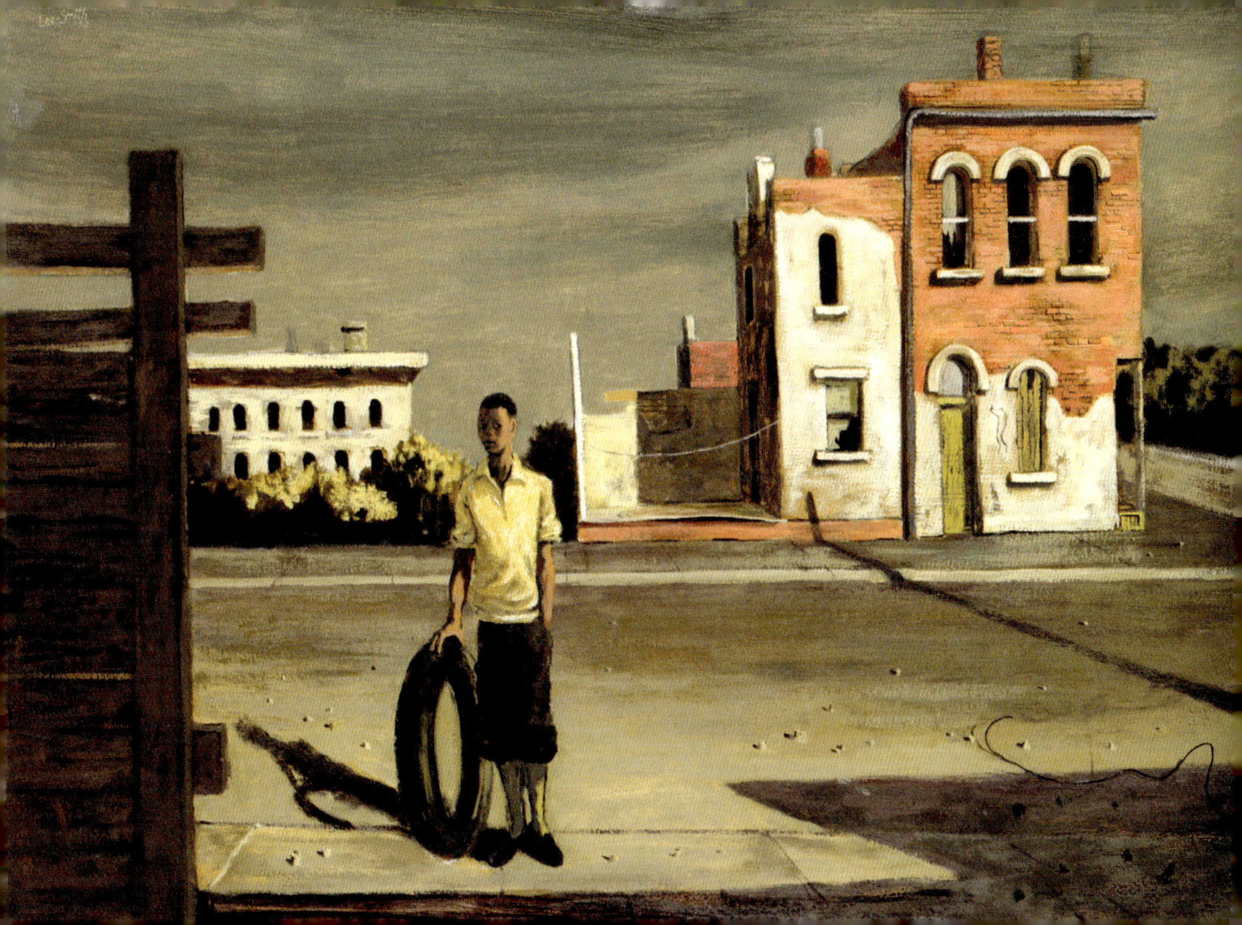
Lee-Smith

Details from

The History of Negro Education in Morris County, Texas, 1955

John Biggers
Mural
Paul Pewitt Elementary School, Omaha-Naples, Texas

John Biggers (1924–2001)

John Biggers was a painter, sculptor, and educator whose art depicted African culture and the African-American experience. A **social realist,** he is best remembered for his dramatic murals. His work is characterized by exquisite detail and earthy tones, as well as by impassioned movement and expression. Biggers infused his work with images of Africa and African-American history and folk culture. Several of Biggers's famous murals are located in Texas, mainly in African-American communities. *The History of Negro Education in Morris County, Texas* (1955) is 22 1/2 x 60 feet and tells the story behind the first all-black high school in the county. The man in the top panel is Principal P.Y. Gray, to whom the mural was dedicated by the citizens who commissioned the artist. Note the strong, exaggerated size of Gray's hand, in which he holds corn kernels. Biggers had a personal affection for this mural and was inspired, in his words, by the "spirituality, cooperation, and industriousness of this and other black communities."

Thinking about the Art

1. Of what might the kernels (seeds) in the hands of the principal be a symbol?
2. What different types of industry, or work, are depicted in these frames from Biggers's mural? What practical arts are the children in the top frame being taught?

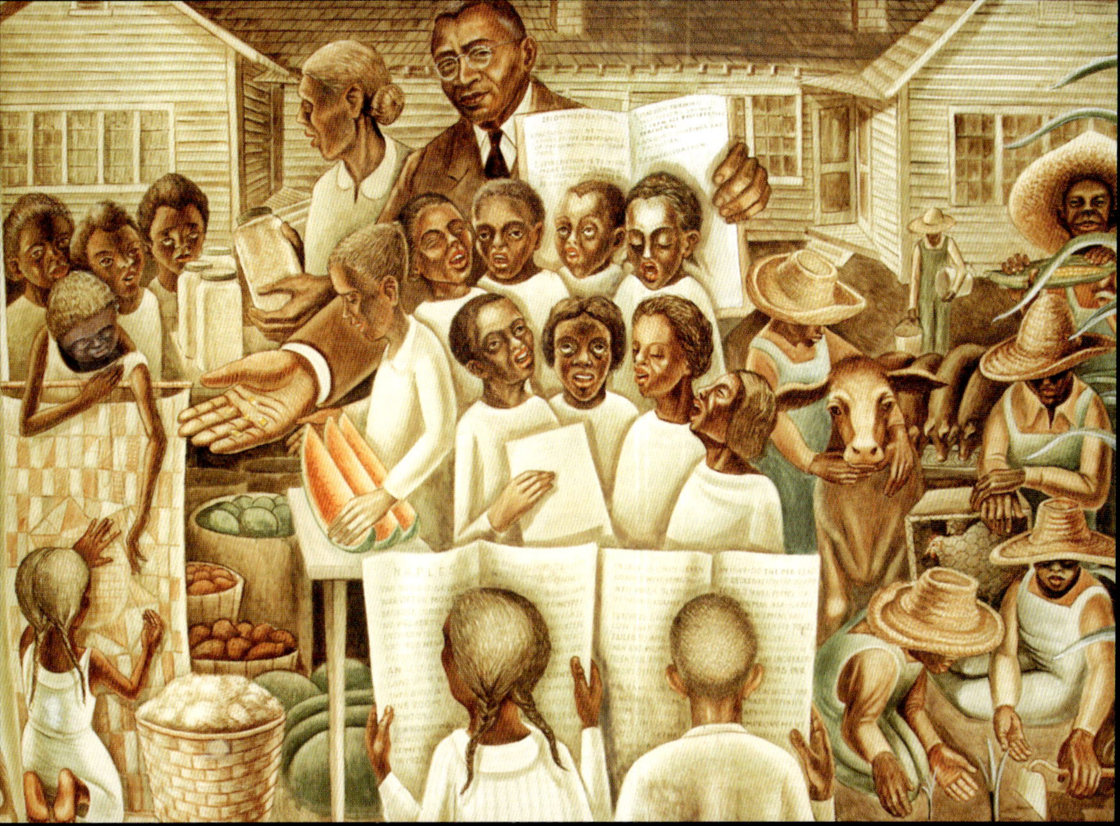

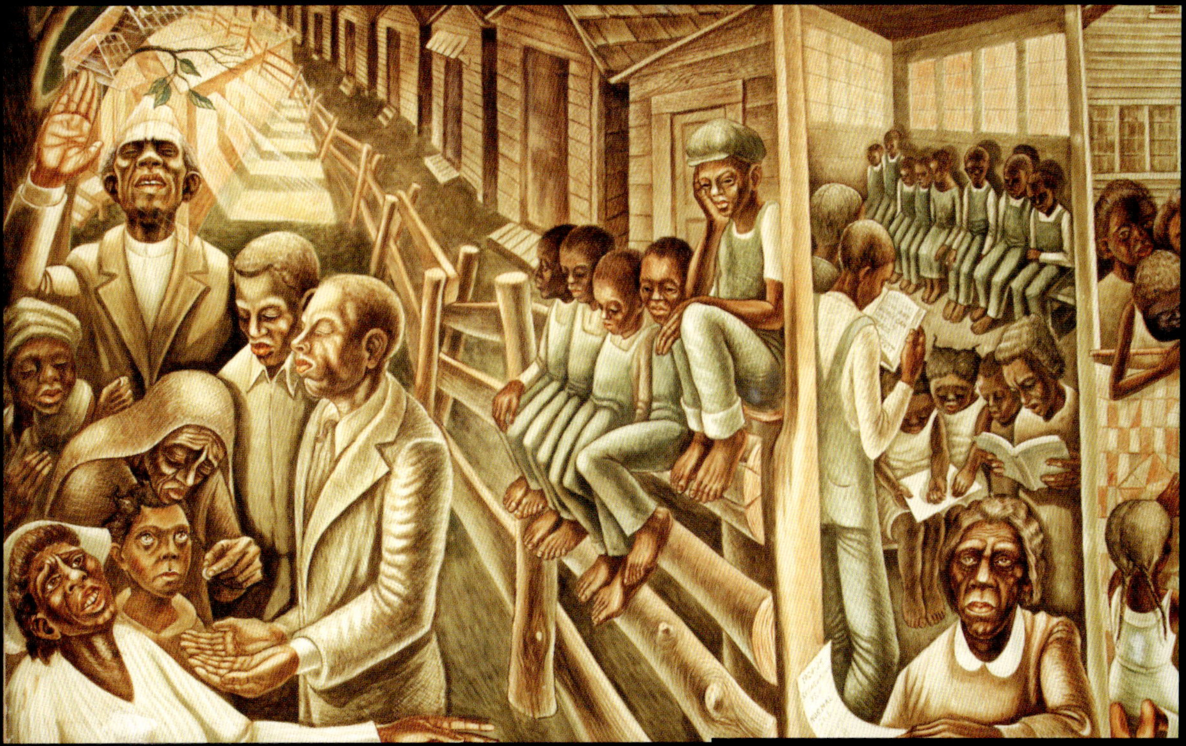

Details from

The History of Negro Education in Morris County, Texas, 1955

John Biggers
Mural
Paul Pewitt Elementary School, Omaha-Naples, Texas

John Biggers (1924–2001)

John Biggers was strongly influenced by the work of muralist Diego Rivera and worked in Rivera's **social realist** style. In this part of Biggers's mural are pictured children arriving at a new high school by bus, a visionary man holding a book, and workers planting. The words printed on the book read, on the left, "By proper guidance our children can be led to enter profitable economic and social enterprises" and, on the right, "Education pays in terms of law abiding citizenship." Such use of inscriptions within murals is also found in the work of Rivera.

Thinking about the Art

1. A **symbol** is something that stands for something beyond itself. For example, a rose is a conventional symbol of beauty or love. Biggers makes considerable use of symbolism in this mural. Look at the panel at the top of this page and at the two panels on the preceding page. Locate the following symbolic objects: kernels (or seeds), a tree of life, books, and a quilt. Of what might these be symbols?
2. What vision for the future do you think that the man holding the book has? How do you know?
3. What other aspects of the lives of these people are depicted in the mural, aside from schooling?

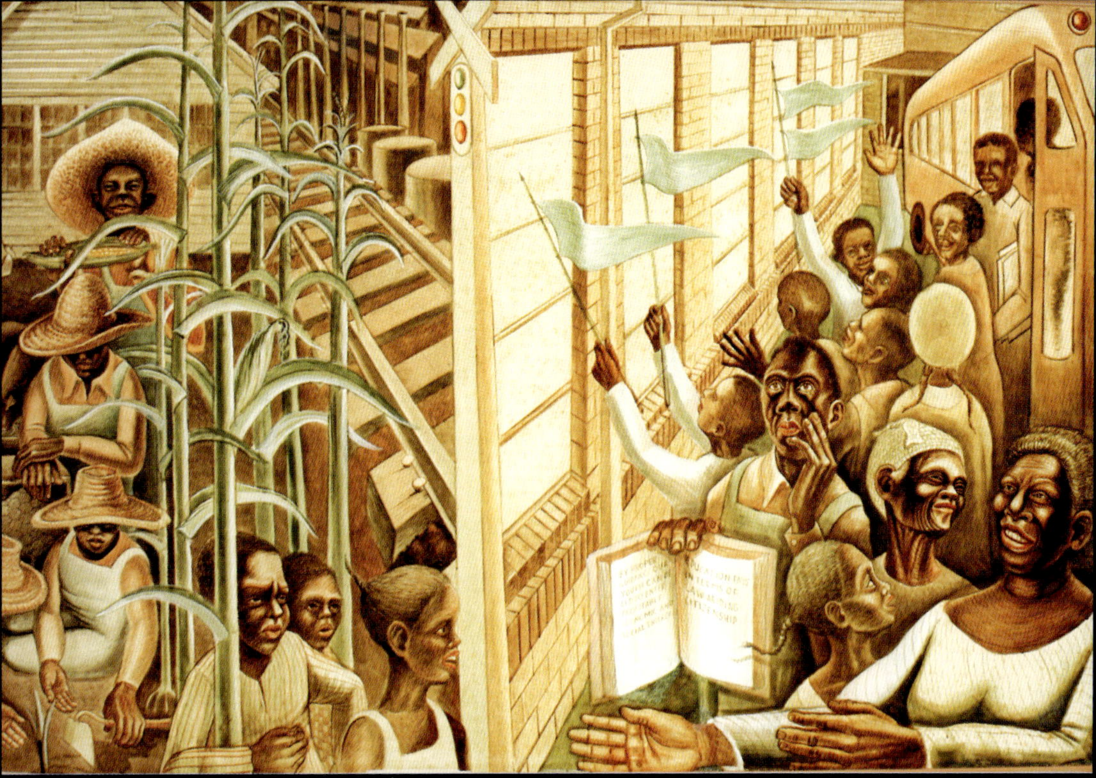

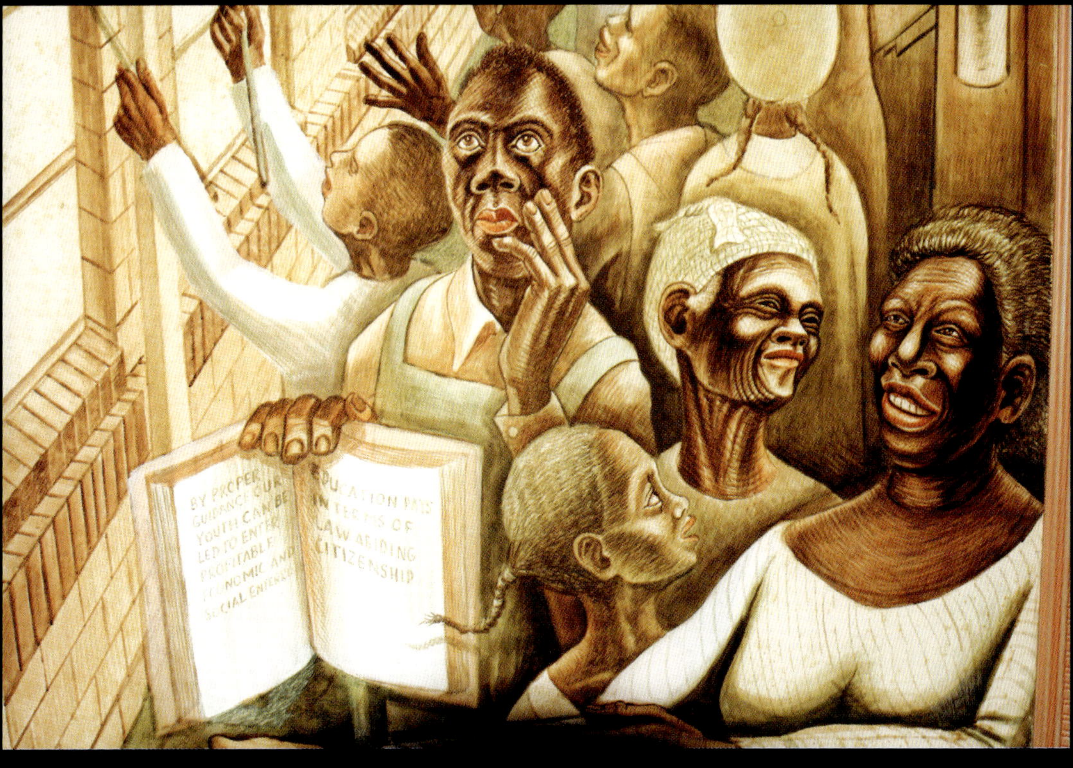

Circus in Bogota, s.a., 1960

Richard Dempsey
Oil on Board
Dorothy Porter Wesley Research Center

Richard Dempsey (1909–1987)

Painting was Richard Dempsey's lifelong pastime, and he continued to work his day job with the federal government even after his name was known from coast to coast. After winning a Julius Rosenwald Fellowship in 1946, he painted well-received portraits of prominent figures like Duke Ellington and Thurgood Marshall. It is his abstract expressionist work, however, that reveals Dempsey's extraordinary talent and artistic vision. **Abstract expressionism** was a dominant movement in Western art from the mid-to-late twentieth century. Practioners of abstract expressionism held the view that art should be nonrepresentational and improvisational. Like the expressionist work of the early twentieth century, the abstract art of Dempsey's time sought to convey or evoke inner experiences. Much of Dempsey's work centers on African-American people and in particular on his reaction to the history of slavery. A large portion of Dempsey's body of work reflects his extensive travels through Haiti, Cuba, Africa, Jamaica, and Colombia (where he was inspired to paint *Circus in Bogota).*

Thinking about the Art

1. Although this is a fairly abstract work, one can still make out some representational elements. What things do you see in the painting that suggest a traveling circus?
2. Wassily Kandinsky, the great Russian abstract expressionist, wrote in his book *Concerning the Spiritual in Art* about how abstract lines, shapes, and colors can create emotional effects. How would you describe the color scheme in this painting? What kinds of shapes predominate? What emotions do these colors and shapes suggest to you?

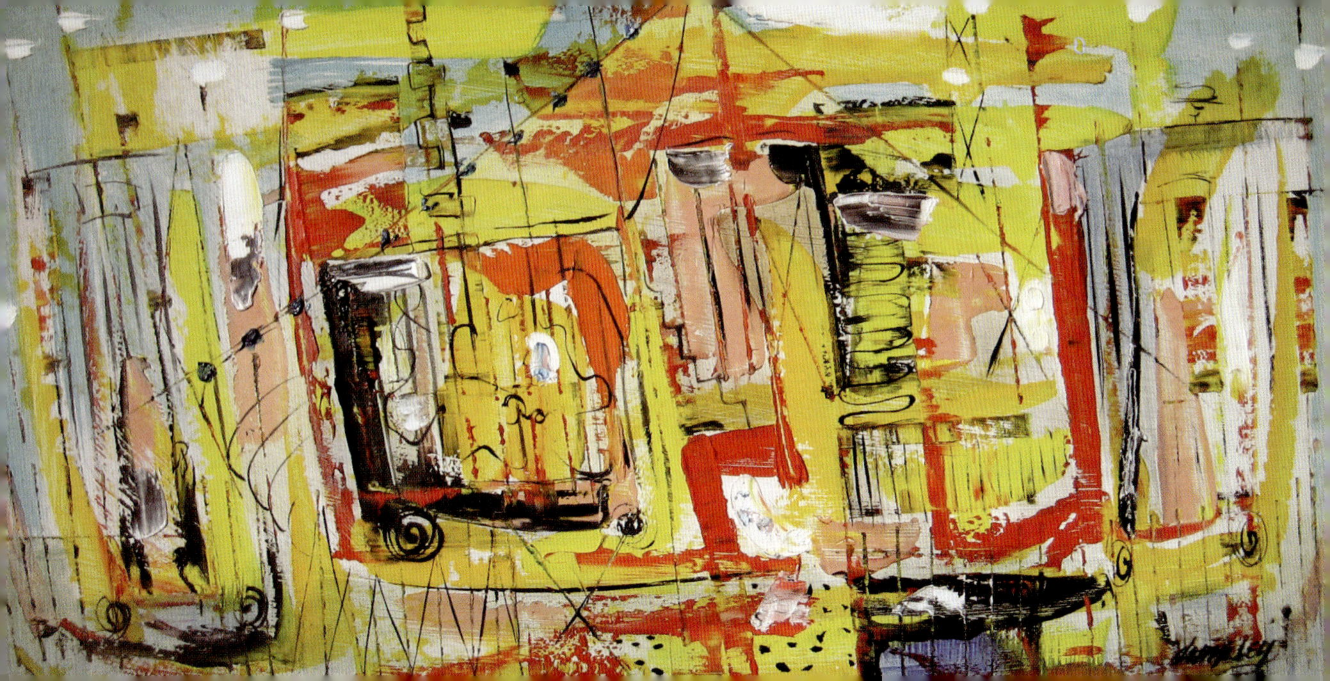

Gemini I, 1969

Lev T. Mills
Etching
Paul R. Jones Gallery/University Museums

Lev T. Mills (b.1940)

Lev T. Mills is a printmaker, graphic artist, and mixed media artist and describes himself as a **constructionist,** meaning that he "create[s] by building up ideas, tearing them down and rebuilding again until the subject matter, design and color have been integrated into a unified visual statement." Since 1970, when Mill received his first major recognition in the form of an award from the Ford Foundation, his art has evolved as he experiments with different materials. His works generally revolve around African-American cultural identities and sociopolitical themes. He is also known for his spectacular tile designs and for a light sculpture he designed for Hartsfield-Jackson International Airport in Atlanta. He studied in London and Paris and became a professor of art at Spelman College in Atlanta in 1978. His works are housed in many fine collections in Europe and the United States.

Thinking about the Art

1. *Gemini I* was the first, unmanned test flight of the Gemini space program. The name suggests visionary accomplishment. What kind of vision is this girl having? What appears in her imagination? Why has the artist featured her eyes so prominently? In what sense might she be ready to take flight?

2. The name of this painting also suggests the Gemini constellation associated with the twin brothers from classical mythology, Castor and Pollux. Notice that the images at the top (presumably in the girl's imagination) are both very positive (the "Black is beautiful" sign) and very negative (people running, a necklace that is also nooselike, a young man hiding behind a wall). What complex, mixed, "twin" feelings do these images suggest? What mood is suggested by the expression on the girl's face?

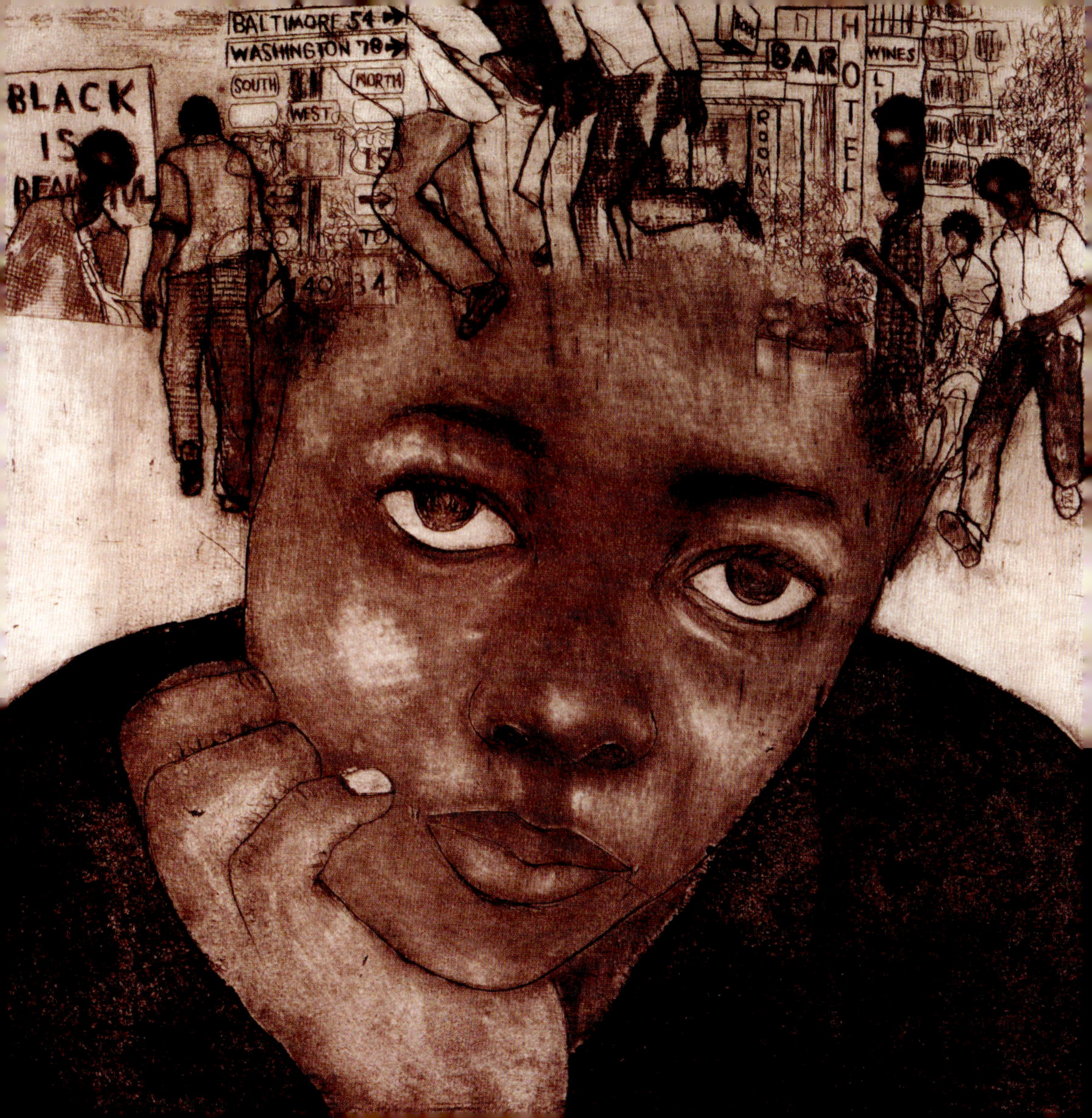
BLACK
IS
BALTIMORE 54
WASHINGTON 78
SOUTH
NORTH
WEST
US 15
TO
40
34
BAR
HOTEL
WINES
ROOMS

Eclipse, 1970

Alma Woodsey Thomas
Acrylic on Canvas
Smithsonian American Art Museum

Alma Woodsey Thomas (1891–1978)

Alma Woodsey Thomas was the first African-American woman to earn a master's degree from Columbia University. She is often classified among the **color field** painters of the 1960s who broke from the emotional and personal abstract expressionism of the previous decade, focusing instead on the fundamental elements of abstract art—large, solid areas of color, two-dimensional imagery, and spatial ambiguity. Color field artists sought to remove the individual and nature from the canvas, leaving pure, monumental images on large and sometimes irregularly shaped canvases. Thomas, however, did bring a great deal of personal flair to the canvas; her work, which she called "Alma's stripes," was largely inspired by the changes she observed, day in and day out, in the garden outside her apartment in Washington, D.C. Her pieces are typified by vibrant colors, mosaic-like patterns, and lines that define geometric shapes.

Thinking about the Art

1. Notice that most of this work is made up of colors that could appear in a flame. What is the artist's subject? Why are such colors appropriate to this subject?
2. A **mosaic** is a design or picture made with pieces of broken pottery, glass, or stone. How is this work both like and unlike a traditional mosaic?
3. One cannot look directly at an eclipse without damaging one's eyesight. But one can, of course, look at this painting. What is the artist telling us, here, about the power of art?

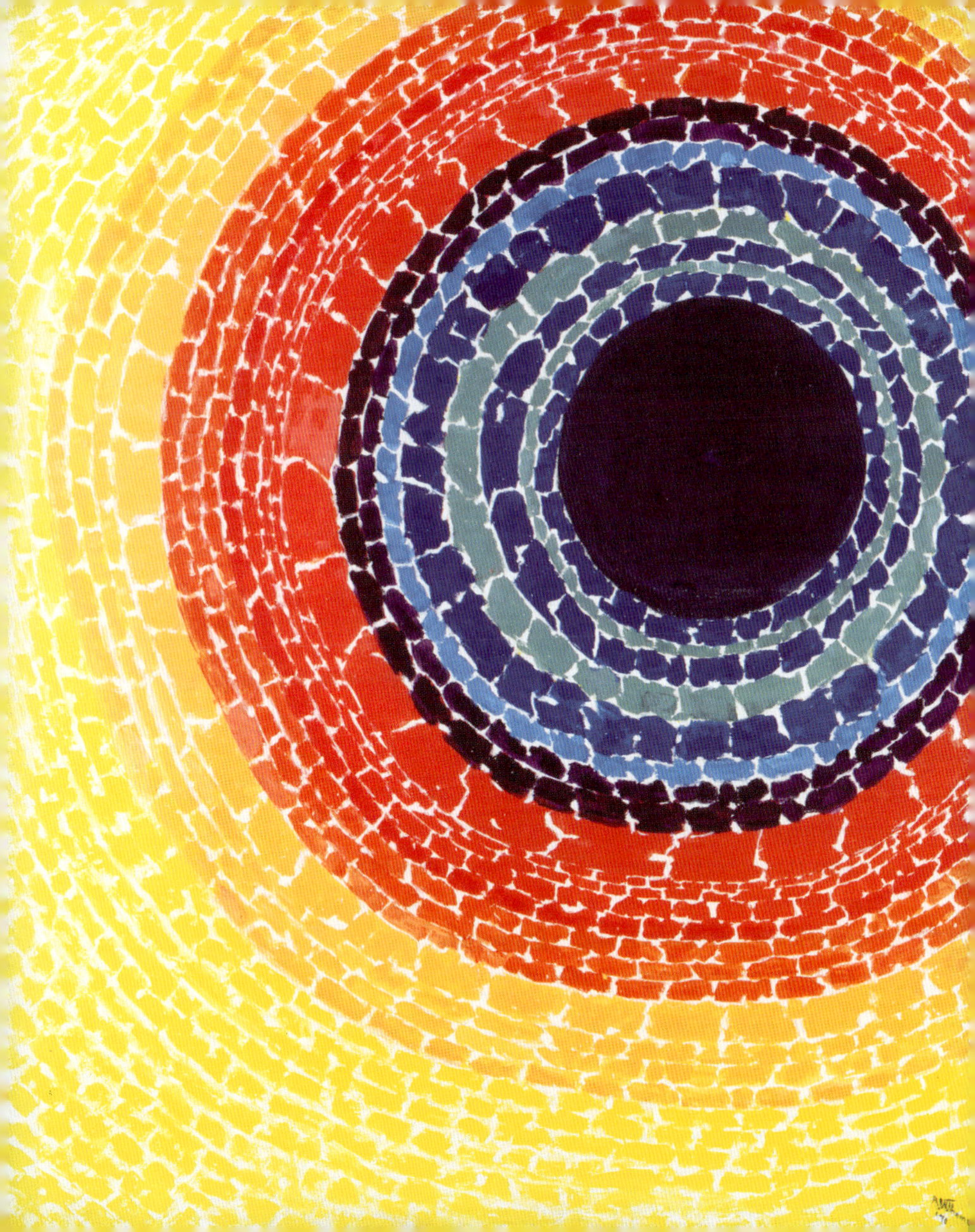

M. L. K. Jr., 1970

Charles Alston
Bronze
National Portrait Gallery, Smithsonian

Charles Alston (1907–1977)

Charles Alston was a painter, sculptor, illustrator, and teacher during the Harlem Renaissance. He worked in the Harlem Community Art Center, directed the Harlem Art Workshop, and was a supervisor for the Works Progress Administration during the Depression. He mentored Jacob Lawrence (See page 772) and other notable African-American artists. Alston also produced art for book and record covers and for magazines such as *Fortune* and *The New Yorker.* He is known for creating abstract works with dramatic outlines and bold colors, but he worked in a number of other styles over the course of his career. The sculpture *M. L. K., Jr.,* reveals Alston's remarkable perceptiveness, capturing as it does both the determination and the deep concern of this great leader, who carried the troubles and aspirations of a people on his shoulders but never faltered under the weight.

Thinking about the Art

1. As you know from the photographs you have seen of Dr. Martin Luther King, Jr., he was a very handsome, charismatic man whose smile could light up a room. Interestingly, the artist has chosen here to portray Dr. King not in an upbeat, hopeful mood and not in a stylized or "beautified" way. What emotions are displayed on the face in this portrait? What aspects of the portrait make it grittily realistic?

2. Some critics have said that Alston chose to portray Dr. King not as an idealized leader but as Everyman. Do you agree? Why, or why not? Would the portrayal of himself as Everyman have appealed to Dr. King, based on what you know of him? Why, or why not?

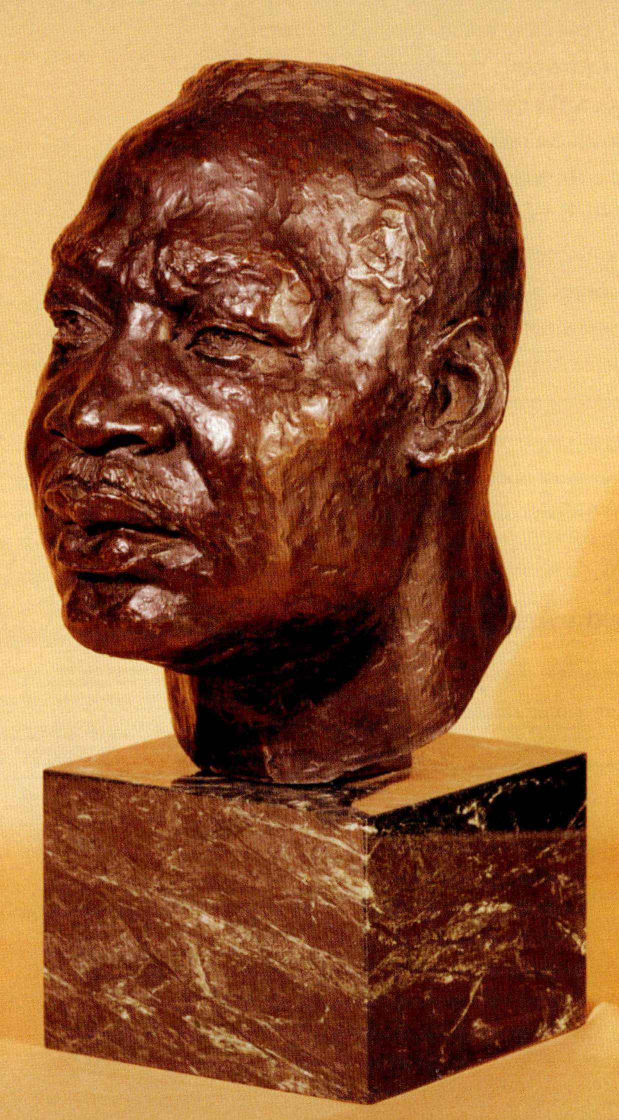

Sharecropper, 1970

Elizabeth Catlett
Woodcut

Elizabeth Catlett (b.1915)

Elizabeth Catlett graduated with honors from Howard University and went on to become the first student to complete the requirements for a Master of Fine Arts at the University of Iowa. She devoted her life and work to the goal of raising black self-awareness after she and her husband, fellow artist Charles White (See page 822) traveled South and experienced the harsh realities of racist segregation, from which she had been somewhat sheltered during her middle-class upbringing. She became well-known during the Black Arts Movement of the 1960s and '70s, when much of her work reflected African and militant images. She sculpts in many media, including stone, wood, and terra cotta, and her sculptural imagination is evident in all of her work, including *Sharecropper,* her most popular piece. Catlett later moved to Mexico and has become one of that country's most popular artists.

Thinking about the Art

1. What does the simple detail of the pin tell you about this woman's worldly circumstances?

2. What does the treatment of the woman's hair tell you about her age?

3. Notice that the hat is radial and halolike. Notice as well how the colors accentuate the woman's face, which almost glows, and that the two colors, green and brown, suggest plants and the earth. In what way is a sharecropper "of the earth"? What do you think the artist's attitude was toward her subject? Why?

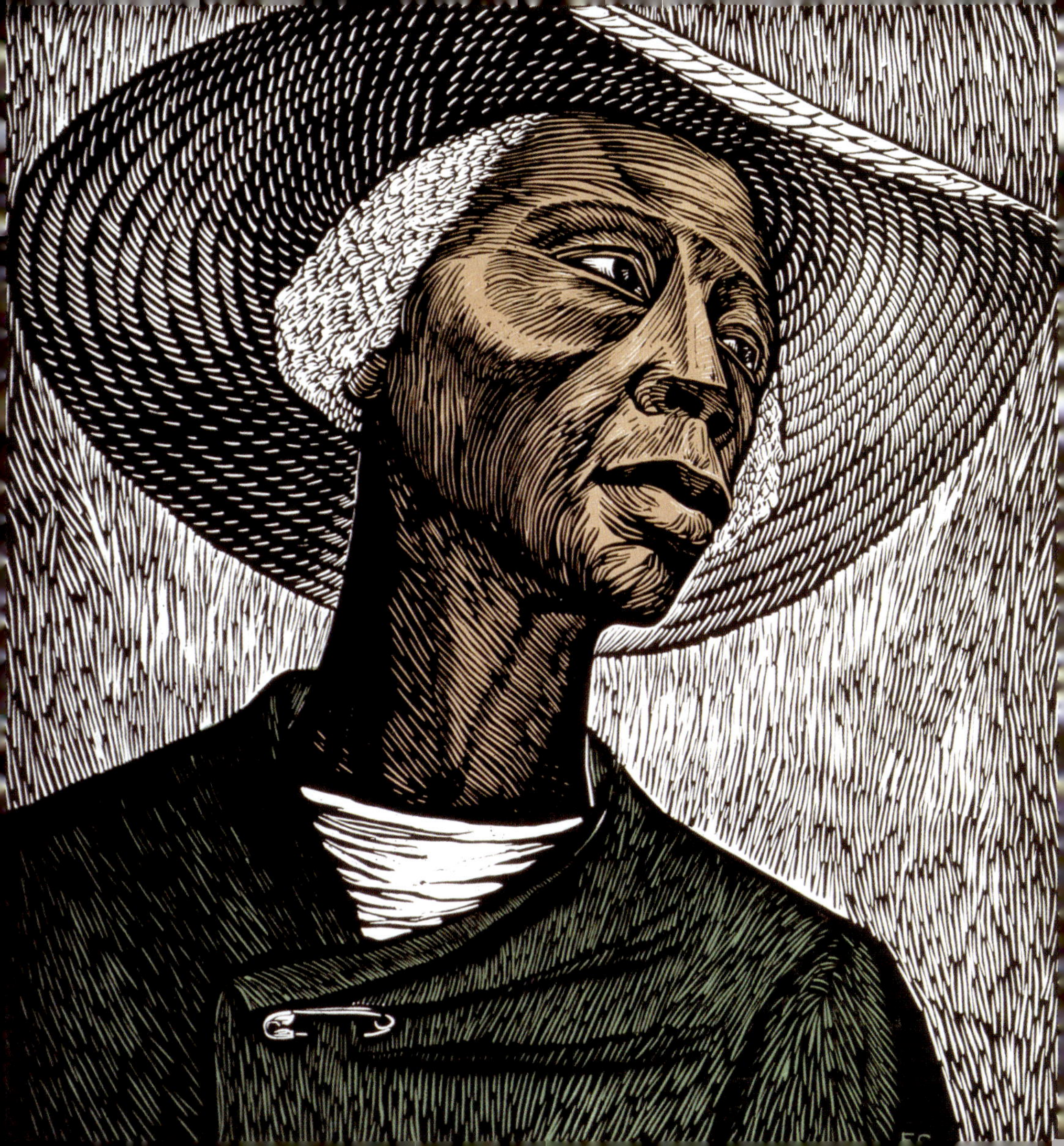

Where Is Lucienne?, 1970

Frank Bowling
Synthetic Polymer on Canvas
Private Collection

Frank Bowling (b.1936)

Born in Guyana and trained in Britain, Frank Bowling splits his time between New York and London. He has become one of the most celebrated and widely collected artists of African descent in the world. His art has received many awards, his work has been displayed in more than one hundred major solo and group exhibitions, and his paintings are included in over thirty important public and private collections, including permanent exhibits at the Metropolitan Museum of Art in New York and at the Tate Gallery in London. He is one of the foremost abstract painters alive today. His works are often highly textural and make optimal use of sometimes minimal color. He is well known for a series of highly textured, nearly **monochromatic** (one-color) works known as *The White Paintings.* In *Where Is Lucienne?,* warm, flowing oranges and yellows beckon the viewer toward the rich layers of the painting, and closer inspection reveals the earth's continents with Africa at the center. If one looks closer, beneath the primary field of colors, more details and images emerge, including (if one looks just below West Africa), the faint image of a human face.

Thinking about the Art

1. This is a highly abstract work, but it hides within it some representational images and invites (both through its title and its composition) the viewer to seek these out. What representational images can you see in the work? Look for, among other things, a wading bird, a human face, a crescent moon, Africa, South and Central America, and a river scene.
2. What details in this painting suggest travel, adventure, and mystery?

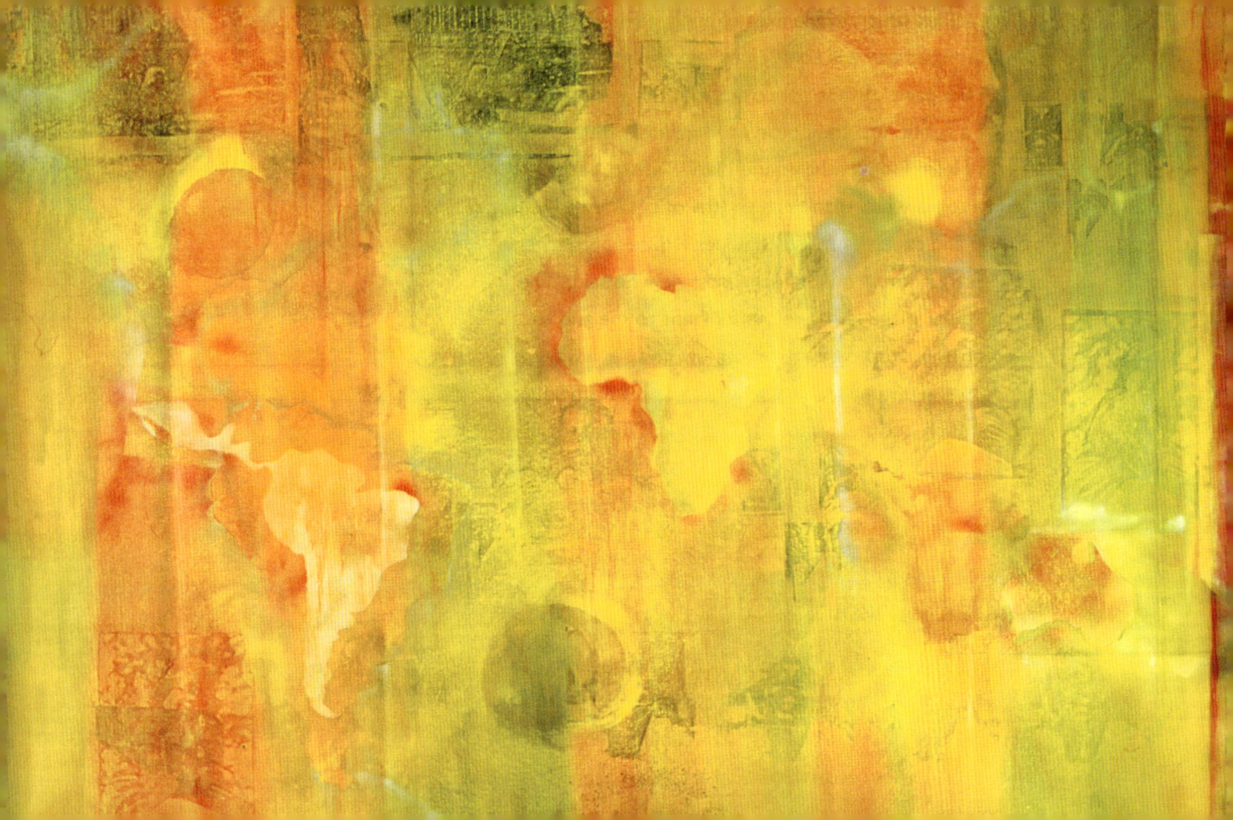

Blue Lizard, 1970

Irene Clark
Silk Screen
Howard University Gallery of Art

Irene Clark (1927–1984)

Irene Clark was born in Washington, D.C. and trained at the Art Institute of Chicago. In the mid-1940s she worked in a well-known decorative arts and design studio run by William McBride. Clark remained active in Chicago for most of her career, though she also studied at the San Francisco Art Institute. Her work is Afrocentric and intentionally primitive. Her works are reminiscent of African-American folk art and incorporate the symbology and themes of traditional African arts and crafts, but they also show a refinement that suggests her professional training and experience.

Thinking about the Art

1. A **fetish** is an object with supposed magical power. **Totemism** is a traditional religious practice, found in Africa and in many other parts of the globe, in which clans, or groups of people, associate themselves with particular animals. What aspects of this painting suggest a traditional African fetish, such as a ceremonial mask or sculpture with religious significance? What aspects of the work suggest totemism?
2. What mood is conveyed by this work? How is this mood connected to the predominate use of the color blue?
3. What do the concentric circles represent?

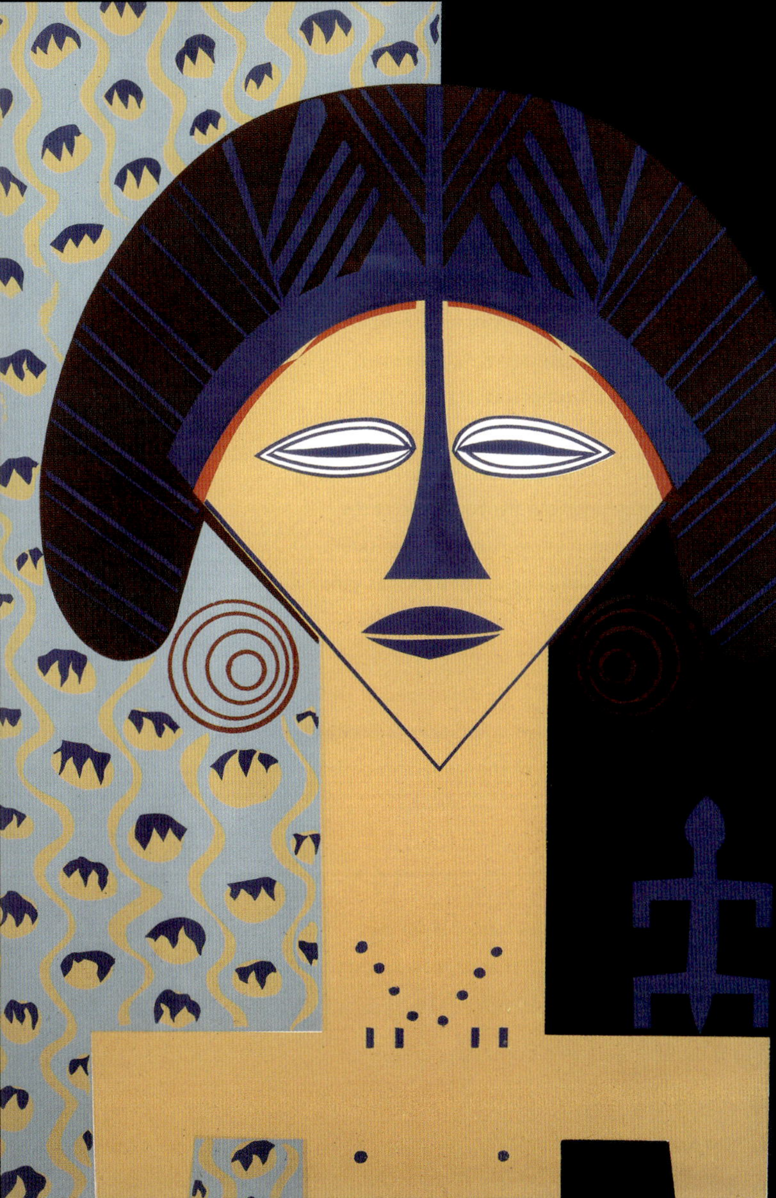

Woman in Interiors, 1973

David Driskell
Acrylic on canvas and paper
Paul R. Jones Gallery/University Museums

David Driskell (b. 1931)

Artist, scholar, curator, educator, collector, and writer David Driskell is among the world's top authorities on African-American art. Like so many artists, he counts Howard University professor and art historian James A. Porter (See page 788) as his main influence. Driskell's first major exhibition, "Two Centuries of Black American Art," held in 1976 at the Los Angeles County Museum of Art, spawned unprecedented interest in African-American art history. His work since then has brought numerous artists and their works to the attention of collectors around the world. Driskell specializes in African-American figures and creates art in a variety of media. *Woman in Interiors* reflects Driskell's interest in **collage,** the art of assembling diverse images (and often materials) in order to create a unified whole. Colors and lines are used to bring the elements together. The work also shows the influence of **cubism,** a style developed in the early twentieth century by Pablo Picasso and Georges Braque that involved geometric disintegration of the subject in order to show simultaneous views of it.

Thinking about the Art

1. How does the artist show simultaneous views of various interiors associated with this woman? What aspects of these interiors are somewhat disturbing?
2. What symbols in the painting suggest domestic pursuits?
3. Use your hand or a piece of paper to block off one side of the woman's face and then the other. What different expressions are portrayed? What do you think the artist means to convey about this woman's emotional state? How does the collagelike presentation of her figure contribute to conveying this conception of her? How might her state be related to these interiors? In what sense can a person be simultaneously "in interiors," that is, in more than one interior at the same time?

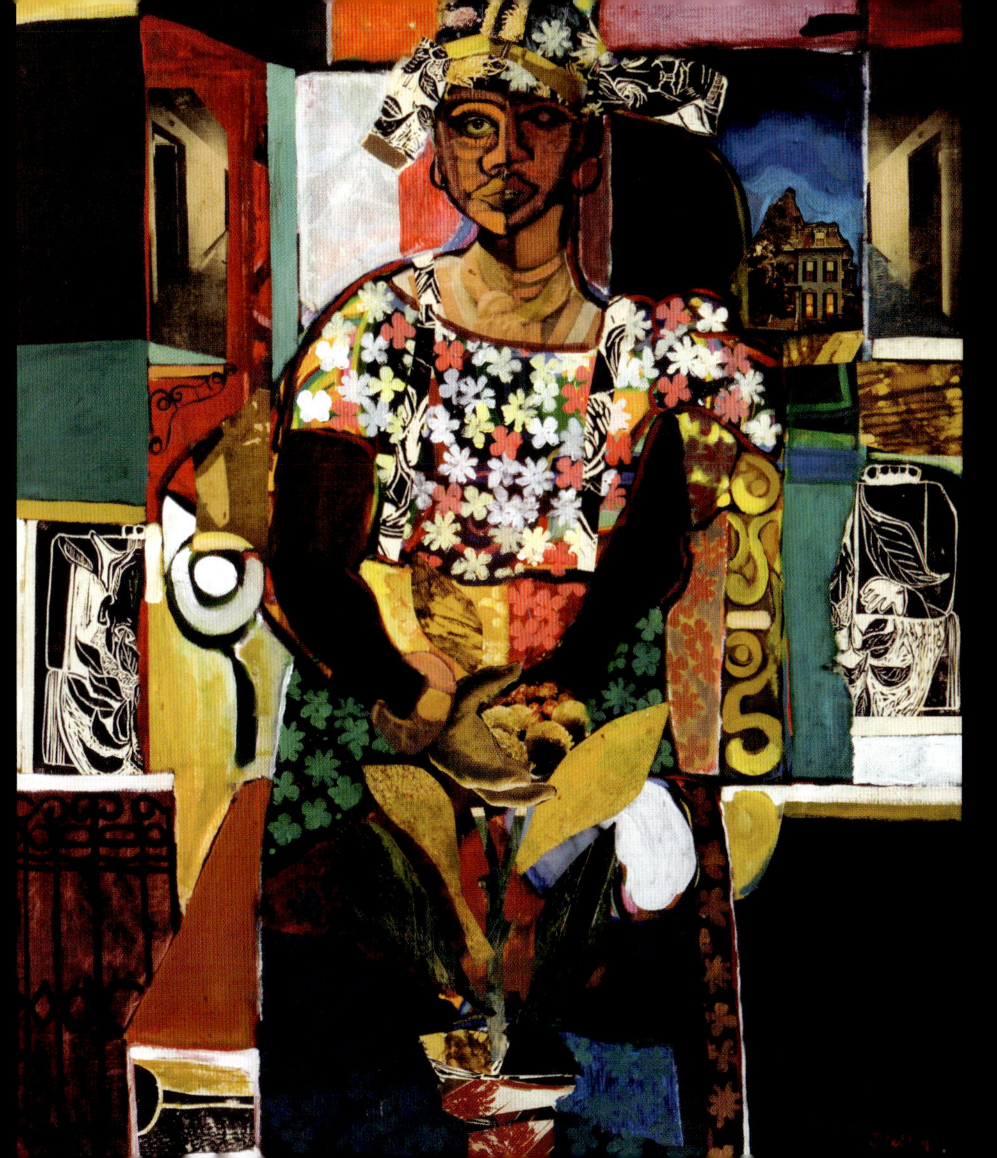

Roots Odyssey, 1976

Romare Bearden
Screen print
Library of Congress

Romare Bearden (1911–1988)

Using photographs and fragments of paper, Romare Bearden created a remarkable sense of unity in his works despite his sometimes haphazard and whimsical juxtapositions of incongruous objects. His themes and images refer predominantly to aspects of African-American life—jazz musicians, family gatherings, urban and rural circumstances, and cultural rituals—yet his work expresses a strong sense of universal experience. Bearden insisted that his works were paintings, not collages, because he used the techniques and materials of collage to create the rhythms, surfaces, tones, and moods associated with painting. His parents' home in Harlem was a frequent meeting place for many of the great artists, writers, and thinkers of the Harlem Renaissance, and he became a true Renaissance man himself—a celebrated visual artist, a musician, and a social activist who helped found the Spiral group to promote African-American art (shortly before the 1963 March on Washington). He also, at one period in his life, was employed as a social worker, and he always retained a social consciousness in his work. In addition to these many accomplishments, he designed sets, costumes, and programs for acclaimed dance companies, the Alvin Ailey American Dance Theater and Nanette Bearden's Contemporary Dance Theatre. He received in his lifetime many honorary degrees, was a founder of the Black Academy of Arts and Letters, and was elected to the National Institute of Arts and Letters. In 1987 he was presented with the National Medal of Arts by President Ronald Reagan.

Thinking about the Art

1. What symbol does Bearden use in this painting to suggest that his subject is *Americans* of African descent?
2. What is portrayed in the bottom left-hand corner of this work? The birds have the color of doves (traditional symbols of peace), but not the shape. What kinds of birds are suggested by the shapes of these birds? Why might such birds be associated in color and design, with the sails of the ship?
3. What symbol in this work suggests the "rising" of an African or Afrocentric consciousness? How might the emergence of such consciousness help one to come to a kind of peace with regard to the horrifying history of slavery?

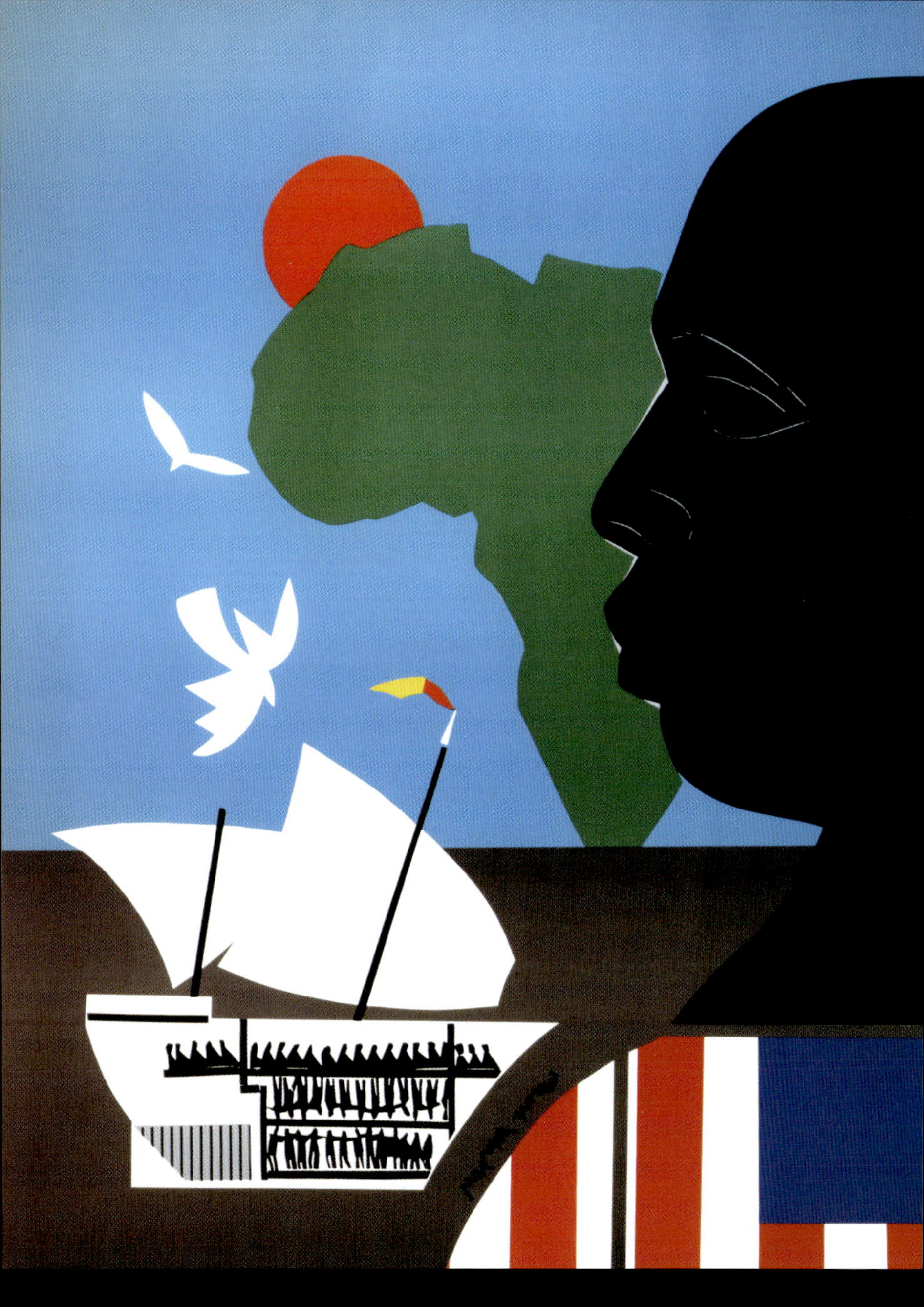

New Orleans: Ragging Home (1974)

Romare Bearden
Collage
North Carolina Museum of Art

Ragging Home. This beautiful work is a collage (an assemblage) of plain, painted, and printed papers, to which has been applied acrylic, lacquer, graphite, and marker. The work is mounted on Masonite. It depicts a New Orleans-style jazz funeral. In the early days of jazz music, the terms ragtime and jazz were used interchangeably, and ragging was another term for playing New-Orleans-style Dixieland jazz. Funerals were one of the great venues for early jazz music. Bearden himself was an accomplished jazz musician and composer. (For more on jazz funerals, see page 460.)

Thinking about the Art

1. Given that this is a portrayal of a jazz funeral, in what sense is the word *home* used in the title? Who is going "home"?

2. Dixieland jazz has been described by more than one person as "a joyful noise" or as "a riot of sound." In what ways does the positioning of the players/dancers in this jazz funeral procession reflect the style of the music being played? Is this an orderly, stately procession? In what sense is their procession "ragged"?

3. Notice that the figures in this work have a spectral, or ghostlike quality. What has the artist done to give his figures this quality? Why is this characteristic of the figures appropriate to this work? In ancient times, people used to set an empty place at the feasting table for death. This custom was known as a *memento mori,* or reminder of death, and the purpose was to have people remember that their time on this earth is short and they should live well and enjoy themselves while they have a chance. A jazz funeral is a kind of simultaneous festival and reminder of death. What aspects of this painting, such as the movement of the figures and the colors used, suggest gaiety and good times? What aspects suggest death? In what way is this work a *memento mori,* just as a jazz funeral is?

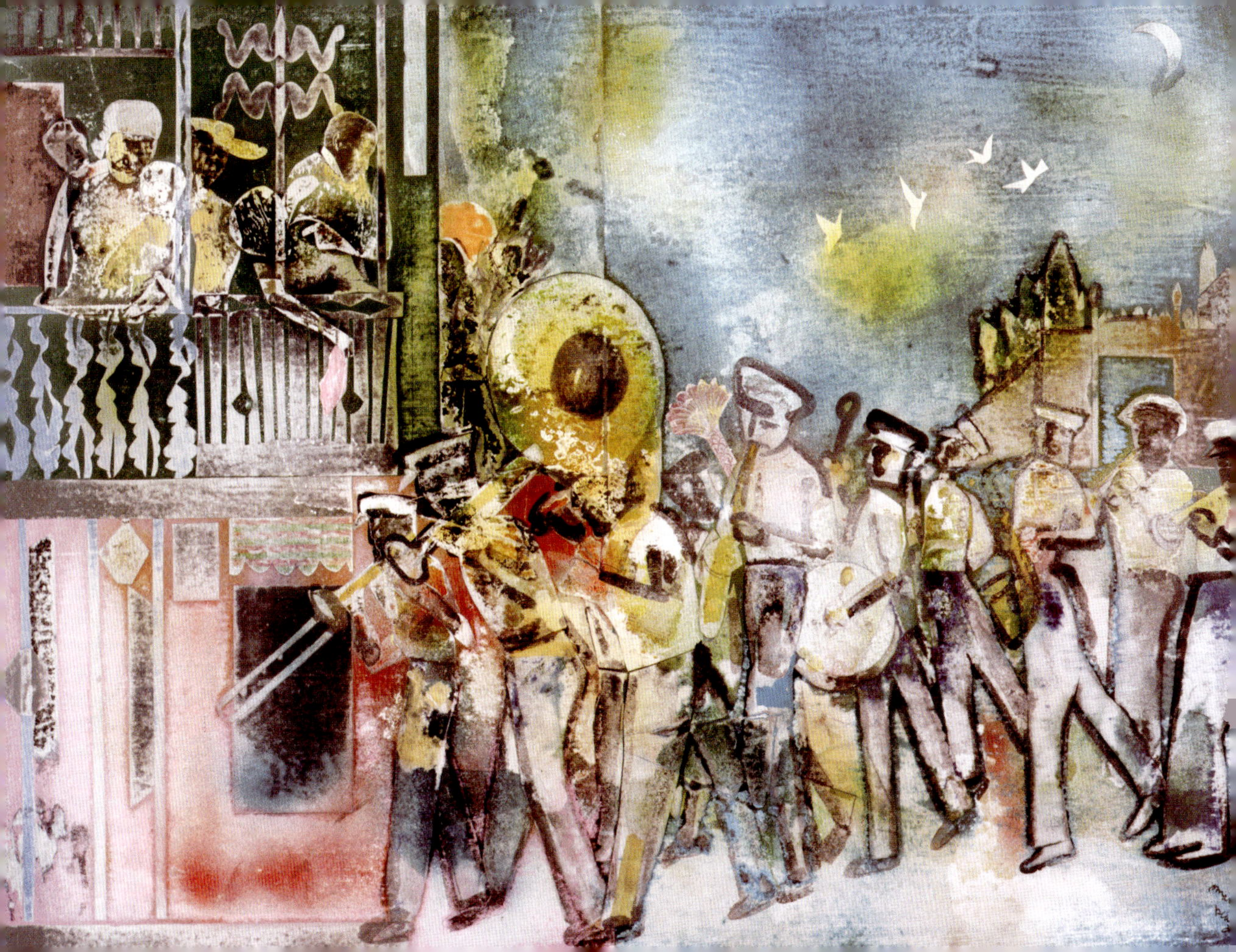

John Henry, 1975

Charles White
Oil Wash
Paul R. Jones Gallery/University Museums

Charles White (1918–1979)

Alain Locke's monumental anthology *The New Negro* (See page 290) first opened Charles White's eyes to the fact that Africans' and African-Americans' cultural and social contributions have been largely overlooked and suppressed through the centuries. White dedicated his art to undoing the prejudice and negative stereotypes to which black people have been subjected in America. Following the Second World War, most artists turned to abstract expressionism and other styles that broke from traditional realism. White, however, focused on historical and social themes, and though his work was often highly stylized and original, maintained a fast hold on realism. In White's rendering, *John Henry*, the legendary "steel drivin' man," is the very face of quiet courage, defiance, and determination. (For more on John Henry, see page 211.) White was famous for his ability to capture the unmistakable yet subtle details in the human expression that reveal everything about a person at a moment in time.

Thinking about the Art

1. White is known as a **social realist** painter, one whose work is representational and treats themes of social and political import. What aspects of this painting are realistic? What aspects are not realistic but cubist? (Hint: The **cubists** of the early twentieth century often made use of geometric shapes and incorporated words, collagelike, into their compositions.)

2. What aspects of this portrayal of John Henry are heroic, larger than life? What message do you think White meant to communicate about this man to audiences in general and to African-American audiences in particular?

3. What is the general shape of the background material at the top of this work? Why might the artist have chosen to create such a shape and to relate it to this figure of John Henry?

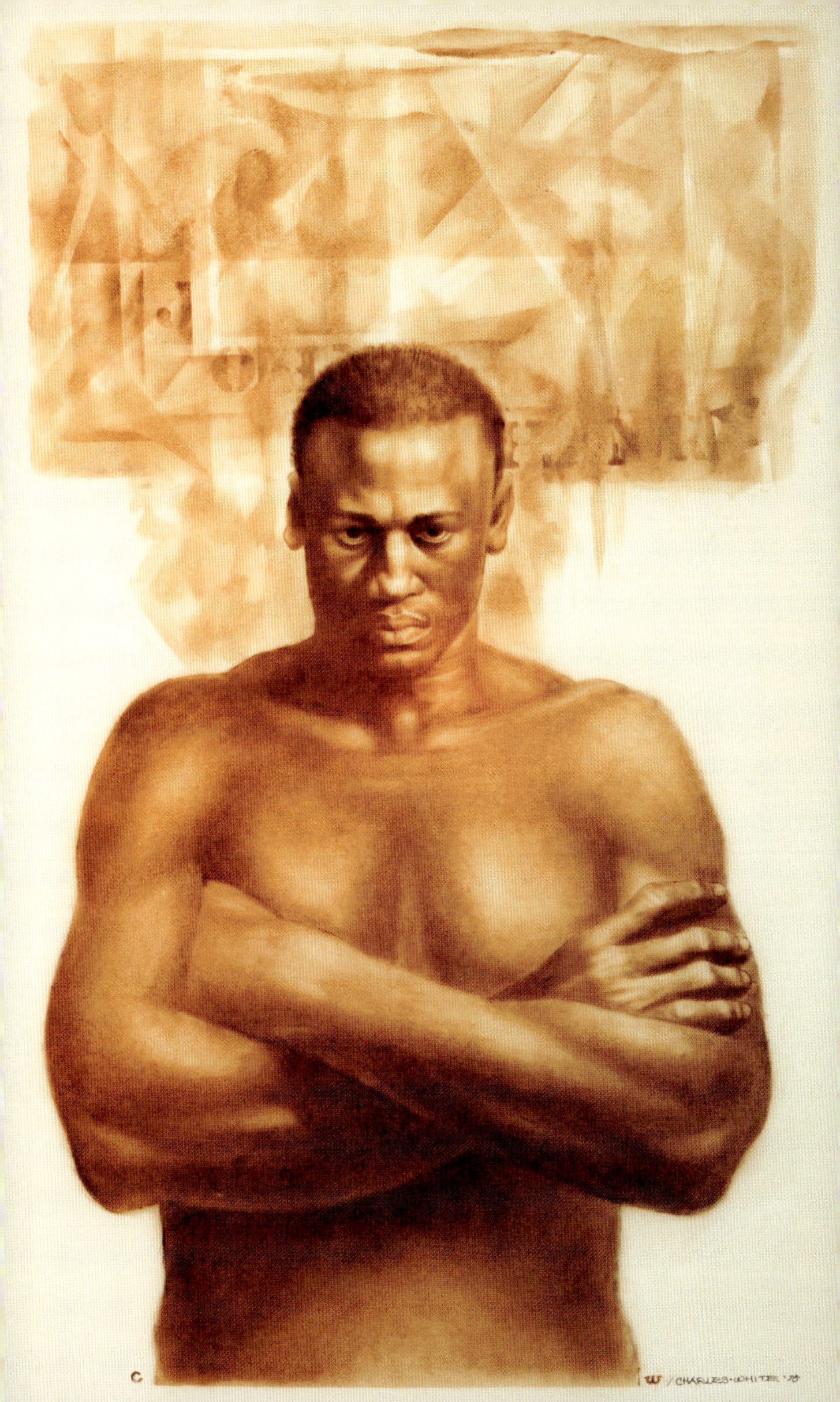
CHARLES·WHITE

Jumping Rope, 1975

George Wilson
Oil on Canvas
Howard University Gallery of Art

George Wilson

Thinking about the Art

1. How would you describe the color palette and the degree of distinctness of the figures (and particularly the faces) in this work? What emotional effect is created by these techniques?

2. Of what races are the figures in this painting? What does the painting suggest about the meaning of race to children?

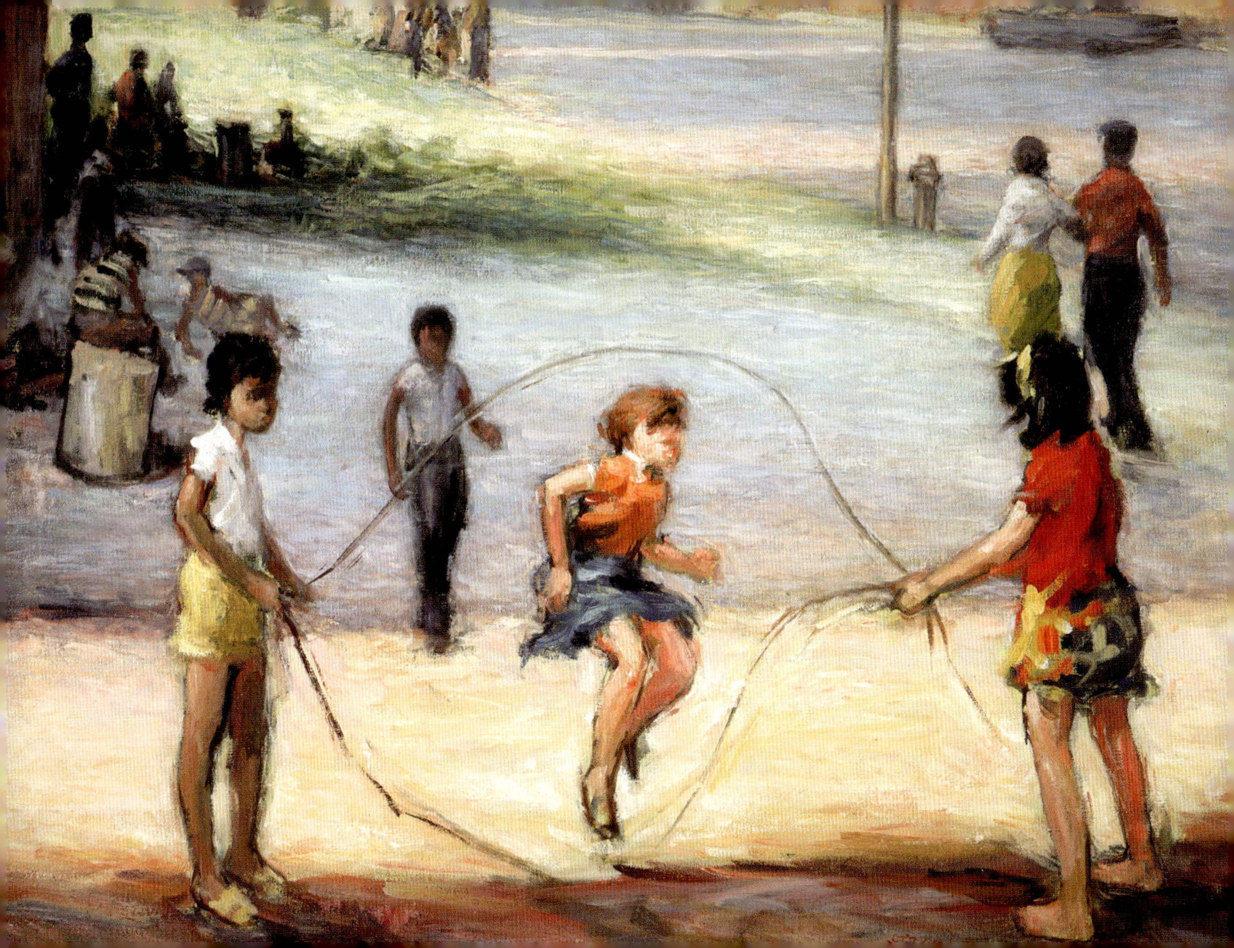

Open Cylinder, 1979

Sam Gilliam
Oil on Canvas, cut and pieced
Smithsonian American Art Museum

Sam Gilliam (b.1933)

One of the most celebrated and influential African-American artists of the late twentieth century, Sam Gilliam is known for his improvisational and experimental techniques using a vast array of media. Some of his most acclaimed works have been large installations in public spaces. In his early days, Gilliam was associated with the **color field** painters, who sought to purge painting of representation by filling canvases with large, unbroken areas of color. Gilliam's work quickly evolved from there. In the mid-1960s he became interested in manipulating canvas, which artists ordinarily stretch and frame before applying paint. Gilliam started by staining and folding canvases. Eventually he hit upon suspending large, unstretched pieces of canvas in the manner of drapes. *Open Cylinder,* which is part of Gilliam's *Wild Goose Chase* series, consists of two panels to which have been glued geometric patterns cut from other thickly layered canvases.

Thinking about the Art

1. It has been said that some of Gilliam's work suggests highly patterned West African textiles or the "crazy quilts" (quilts that do not follow a particular pattern but that are pieced together in an irregular arrangement from odd pieces of material) done by African-American quilters from the deep South. What elements of *Open Cylinder* recall those sorts of patterns?
2. Which of the orange shapes in Open Cylinder appears to have one corner tucked beneath a section of white? How does this effect give the flat surface of the painting a feeling of dimensionality?
3. Which two orange shapes seem to be falling off the edges of fields of white? In which direction does the arrowlike shape seem to be going? How has the artist suggested movement in this painting even though he is dealing with flat, immobile patterns?

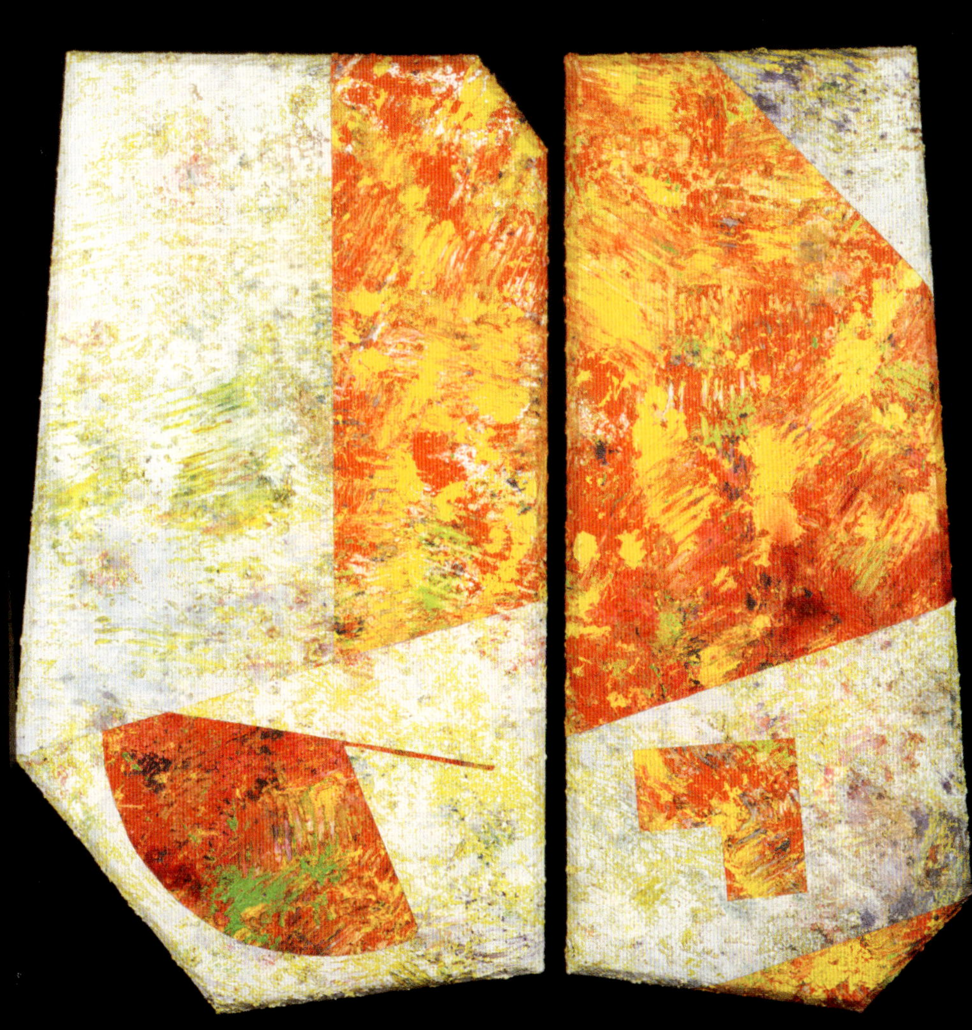

Red Barn, 1980

Rex Goreleigh
Watercolor
Paul R. Jones Gallery/University Museums

Rex Goreleigh (1902–1987)

A **realist** painter specializing in representational scenes from African-American rural life, Rex Goreleigh is perhaps best remembered by the many young artists whose lives he touched as an instructor in Harlem, Chicago, North Carolina, and New Jersey. While waiting tables in New York during the early '30s, Goreleigh met famed muralist Diego Rivera, who invited Goreleigh to watch him at work. Goreleigh later said that this experience put him "on the road to becoming an artist." His career spanned more than fifty years, though most of his best-known works were produced after 1960. He specialized in watercolors, using a narrow palette of **primary colors** (the basic colors on the color wheel) supplemented by earthy tones.

Thinking about the Art

1. What are the predominant colors in this painting? What effect does the use of such colors have on the viewer?
2. What is the focal point of this painting? How complicated are the shapes and textures used to render the barn? How do the shapes used to render the barn differ from those used to render the grass, the trees, and the water?
3. What effect does the use of primary colors and simple geometric shapes have on you as a viewer? The artist has purposefully striven for a childlike simplicity in this work, but what aspects of the work show that it is far more sophisticated than something a typical child could do?

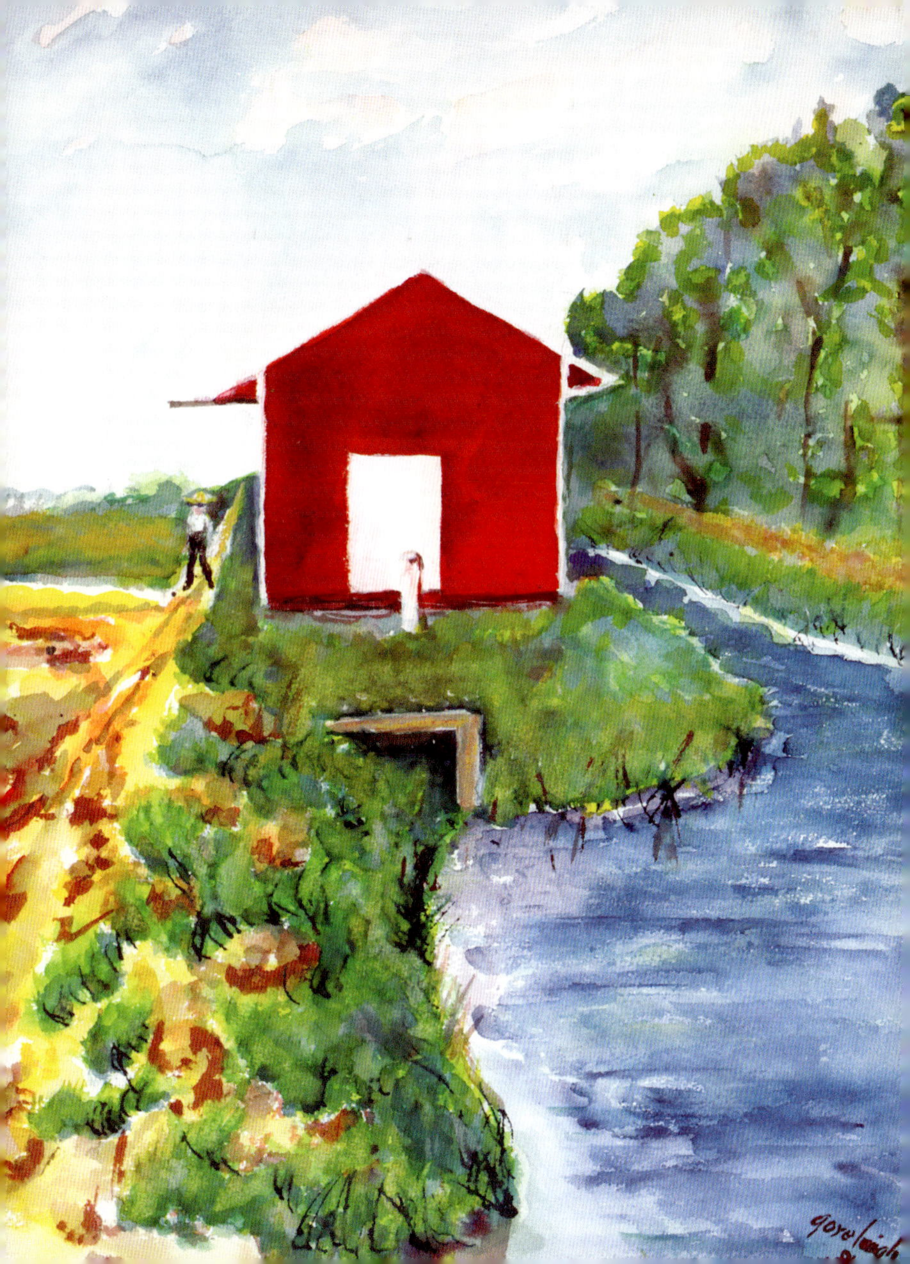

Stagger Lee, 1983

Frederick Brown
Oil on Canvas
Smithsonian American Art Museum

Frederick Brown (b.1945)

Born in rural Georgia, Frederick Brown moved with his family to Chicago early in life and fell in love with that city's jazz and blues scene. Schooled in the style of **abstract expressionism,** which he called "a very beautiful, lyrical language," Brown is best known for *Portraits of Music I Love,* nineteen colorful, larger-than-life, stylized portraits of famous blues and jazz artists; the portraits were part of a larger project exhibited by Brown in 1987. The painting *Stagger Lee* reflects Brown's interest in American icons. Stagger Lee (also known as Stack O'Lee or Stackerlee), was a real historical figure who murdered a man named Billy Lyons during an argument in St. Louis in 1895. The story of the killing has been retold by countless blues musicians over the past century. Stagger Lee is always portrayed as a villain, but he is also an antihero and is often given the odd sort of reverence reserved in American folk culture for outlaws such as Jesse James. In his painting, Brown does not indulge in such sentimental romanticizing. Far from it. Instead, Brown addresses the complex and mixed perceptions of good and evil in America by placing Stagger Lee on the canvas alongside grotesque versions of Lincoln, a Native American, and other figures and images from the American (mainly urban) landscape. (For more on Stagger Lee, see page 448.)

Thinking about the Art

1. What is the overall emotional effect of this painting? Would you want to meet the group of people depicted in this painting? Why, or why not?

2. Notice that the demonic characters presented with Stagger Lee incorporate partial motifs from American culture generally. One has a Native American headdress and a pipe (a peace pipe?). One has a partial Lincoln beard and a stovepipe hat. The "Lincoln" figure seems to be wearing clerical vestments and a cross. One figure has a pocket protector and a tie. These figures are far from attractive or comforting. Some have bared teeth, and their skeletal hands are poised for horrific action. It's a rogues' gallery. Notice that there are lots of iconic American images in the background—television sets, airplanes, skyscrapers, crosses, dogs and pigs, stoplights, crosses, and row houses. What is the artist saying about American culture in general and the kinds of people it produces? What indictment is he making of American society?

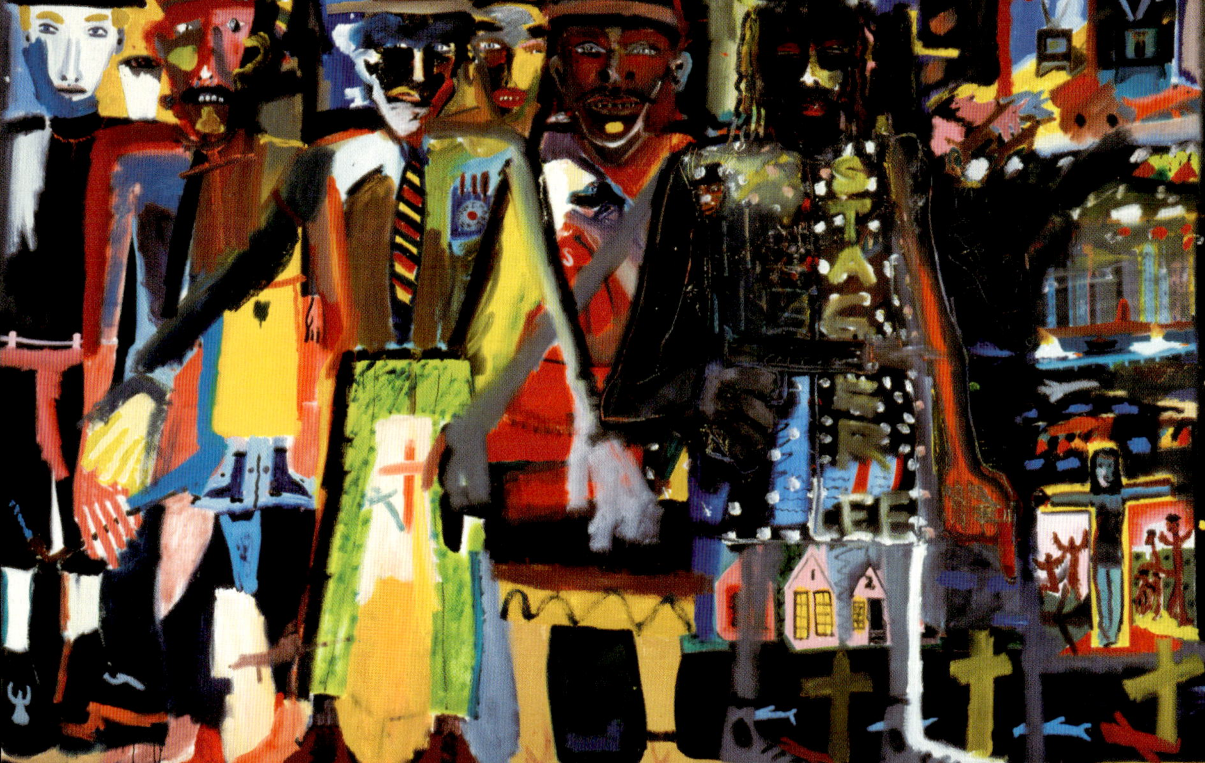
STAGER
LEE

Summer Serenade, 1992
Richard Mayhew
Oil on Canvas
ACA Galleries

Vista, 2004
Richard Mayhew
Watercolor on Canvas
ACA Galleries

Richard Mayhew (b.1924)

Born in Amityville, New York, of African-American and Native American parents, Richard Mayhew was deeply influenced by what he learned from his paternal grandfather about Native American "nature lore." In keeping with Native American traditions, Mayhew creates paintings of natural scenes that show nature both imbued with an astonishing spirituality and suspended in time. Mayhew attended Columbia University. He was a member of the Art Students League in New York and of the Spiral group of New York African-American intellectuals interested in creating artwork that promoted African-American social and political agendas. He has taught at Brooklyn Museum Art School, at Smith College, and at Pennsylvania State University and has had major exhibitions at the Brooklyn Museum, the Minneapolis Institute of Arts, the High Museum of Art, the Newark Museum, and the Studio Museum in Harlem. He uses intensely saturated colors and indistinct forms that create in viewers feelings of serenity and wonder. He says of his **abstract expressionist** work, "Many of my so-called landscapes are very abstract because they are very free-form; I am involved with the spiritual feeling of space. Just to work with figures would be very limiting because that would identify a particular place or situation. The paintings look like landscapes but that is not necessarily my preoccupation in painting." He does both large-scale oil paintings and small-scale watercolors.

Thinking about the Art

1. What is unusual about the color palette used in each of these paintings? How does it differ from the color palette of a more conventional landscape painter such as, say, Edward Mitchell Bannister? (See page 742.)
2. Critics have said that Mayhew's work is done "just on the edge of abstraction." Do you agree? Why, or why not?
3. Mayhew says that landscape is not necessarily his preoccupation. What is he preoccupied with? What elements of his work are most salient (stand out)? How do you think the artist wants us to relate to and feel about nature?

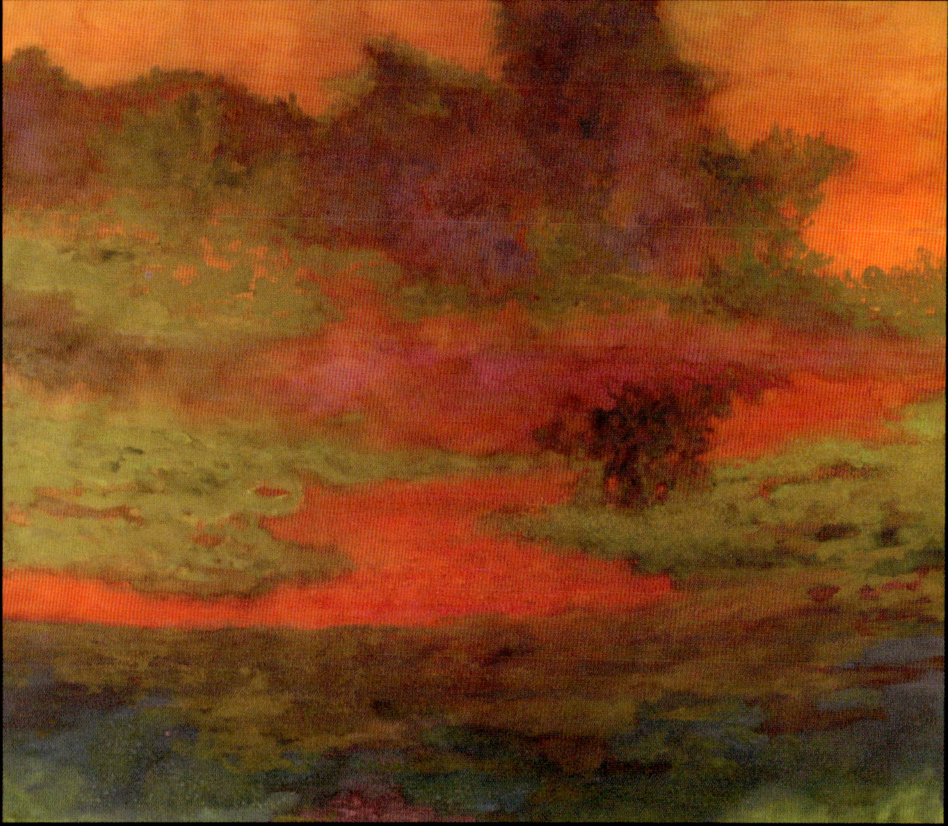

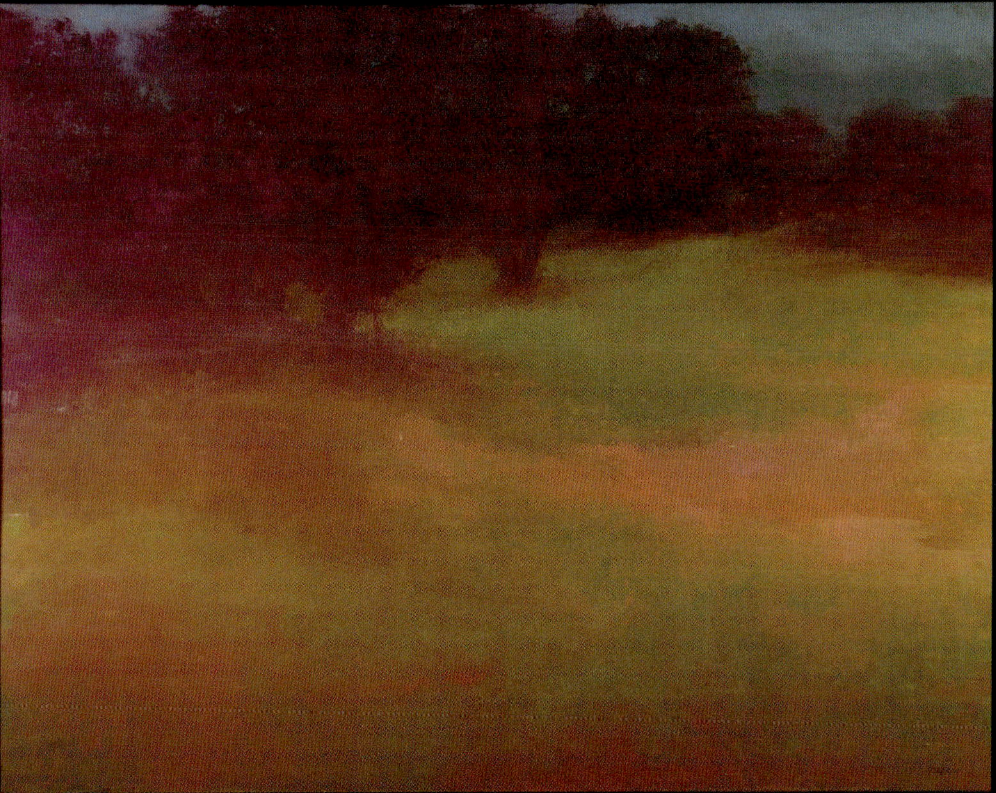

Breakers, Becune Point, 1995

Derek Walcott
Oil on Canvas Board

Derek Walcott (b. 1930)

A child of St. Lucia who has become a citizen of the world, Derek Walcott draws upon three cultural currents in his work—Caribbean, Western European, and African. A winner of the Nobel Prize in Literature for his exquisite poetry (See page 618), Walcott is also an accomplished, award-winning painter. He produces beautiful, tranquil landscapes and seascapes and scenes of island life that capture the breathtaking colors and light that make the Caribbean so spectacular. (For a biography of Walcott, see page 627.)

Thinking about the Art

1. What two families of colors are used in this painting? Look very closely at the rocks and the waves. How many distinct colors has the artist used to render each?

2. What is the weather like in this painting? How has the painter captured the restlessness of this windy day? What kinds of boats can you see way out on the horizon? How can you tell that they are moving very fast? Why, despite all this motion, does the painting suggest serenity? Buddhists often speak of cultivating a state of "mindfulness" that is simultaneously tranquil and very alert and active. In what way is this painting suggestive of the state that Buddhists call mindfulness?

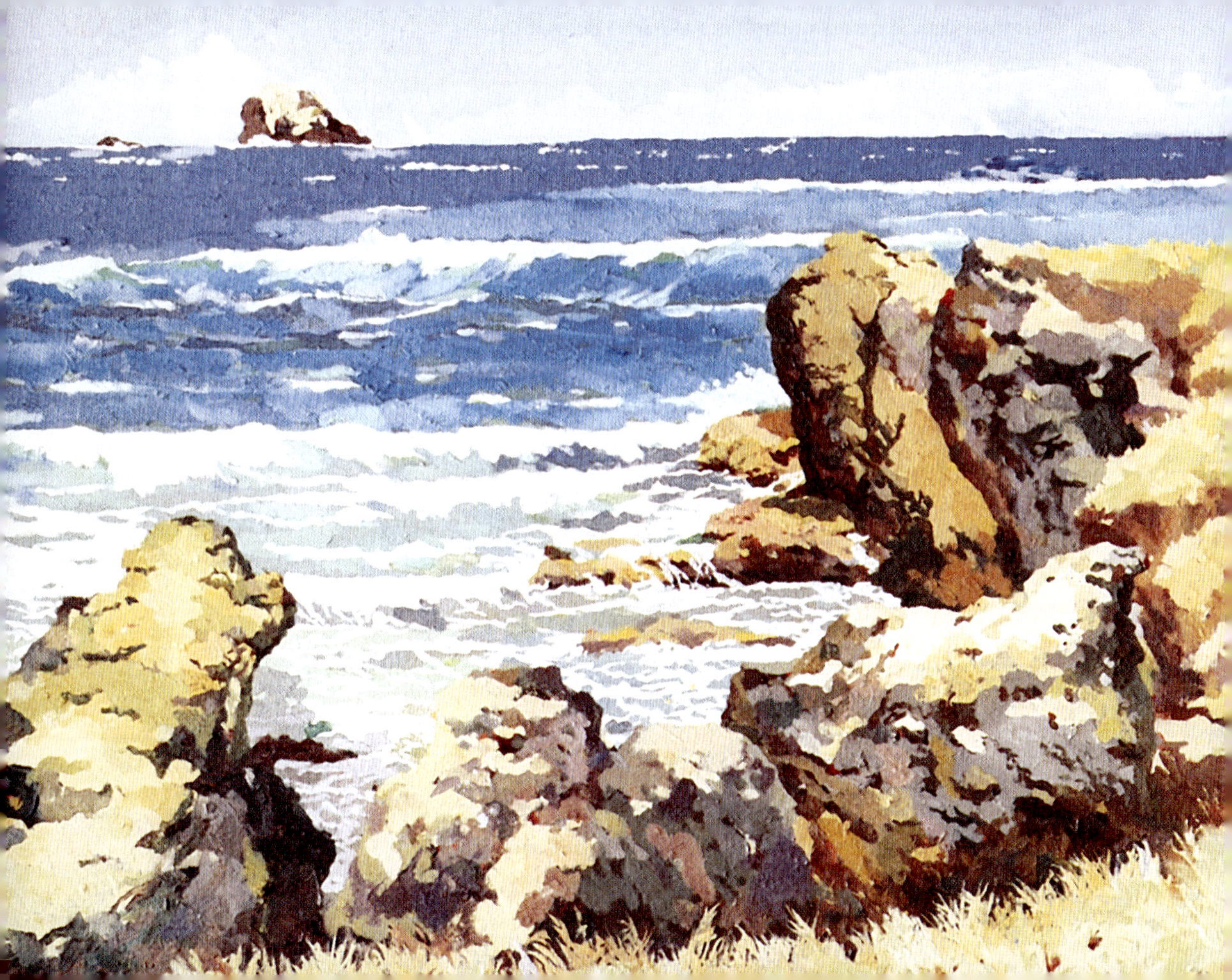

Reflections, 2002
Louis Delsarte
Oil on Canvas

The Search, 2002
Louis Delsarte
Mixed Media Collage

Louis Delsarte (b. 1944)

Delsarte is an artist and educator who is best known for his **figurative expressionism** (incorporating the human figure into abstract expressionism). He uses African-American themes and said of his work, "I do things that deal with the family, the dance, the celebrations of rituals. . . . It's very hard for me to paint ugliness or war or destruction or death." Born and raised in Brooklyn, Delsarte became interested in painting murals after taking his first classes at the Brooklyn Art Museum. He has been commissioned for numerous public murals, and his paintings are included in many significant collections. Viewing a Delsarte painting one can almost hear the jazz, gospel, mambo, and reggae music that so influenced the artist, who unites in his work the tangible, the sensual, and the abstract. Delsarte has a B.F.A. from the Pratt Institute and an M.F.A. from the University of Arizona and has taught at several universities. Delsarte says of his own work that it is spiritual in nature, that it documents life and provides a channel through which ancestors can communicate. His work is dreamlike, visionary, and often surrealistic. (The **surrealists** were a school of painters that included Giorgio de Chirico, Salvador Dali, René Magritte, Joan Miró, and Yves Tanguy. They sought to liberate the mind by rejecting the pedestrian and the rational in favor of expression of the subconscious mind through fantastic, dreamlike imagery.) Delsarte was also strongly influenced by the textural qualities and use of light in **impressionist** painting such as that done by Claude Monet.

Thinking about the Art

1. Where is the woman sitting in *Reflections?* What seems to be her state of mind? What aspects of the painting give it a dreamy and thoughtful quality?

2. *The Search* is a fantastically complicated painting that suggests some sort of legendary, mythical, dreamlike story. What sort of landscape is pictured here? What is the relation between the figures and the landscape? What aspects of the painting seem particularly strange or fantastic? What figure in the painting seems to be running away? What figures seem to be searching methodically? What aspects of the painting suggest frantic movement? What is the time of day, and how do you know? Why might the horses be rearing up?

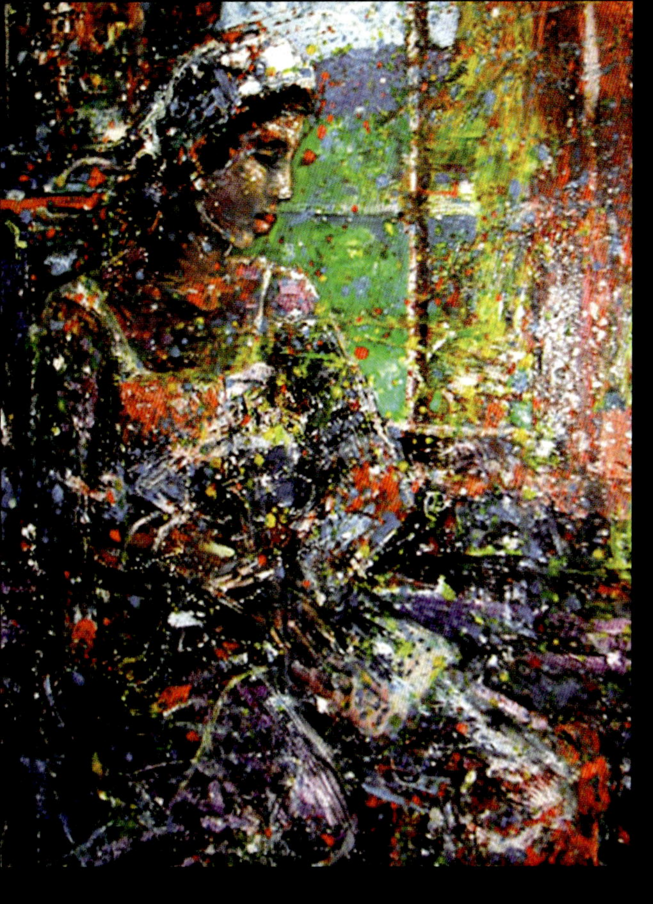

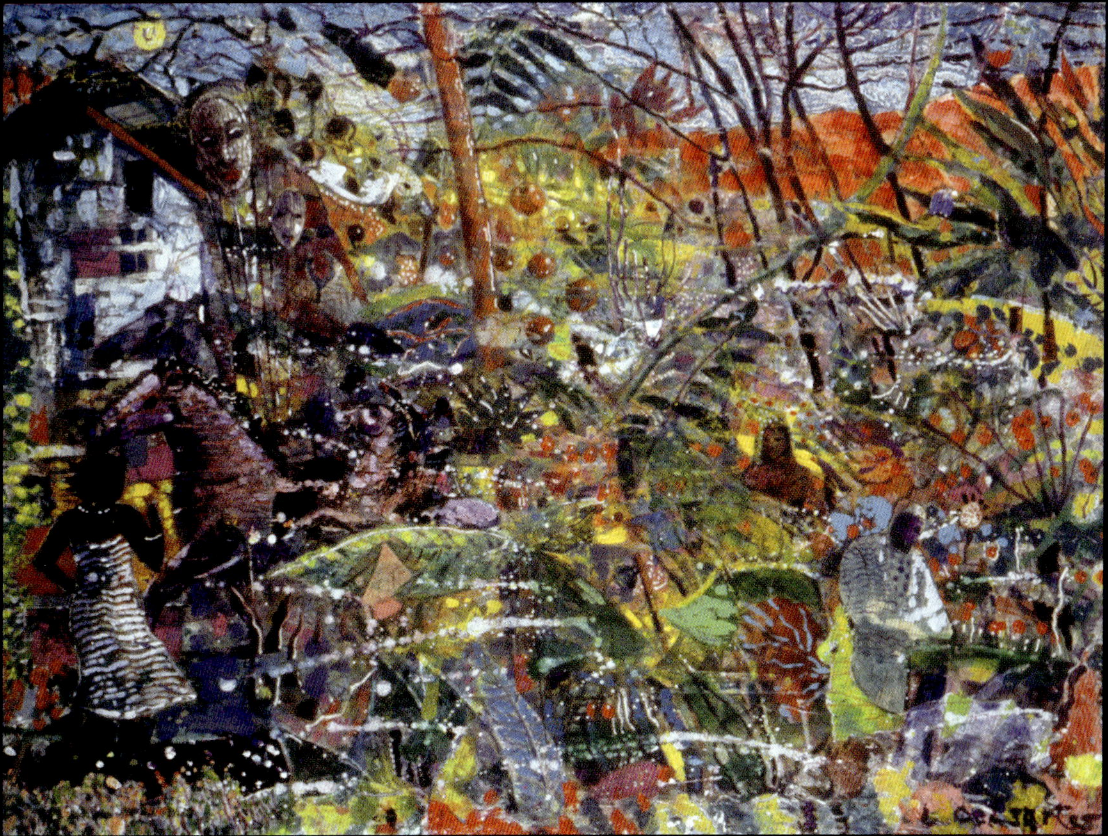

Credits and Acknowledgments

Text Credits

Continued from page ii

From *How Many Spots Does a Leopard Have? and Other Tales* by Julius Lester. Copyright © 1989 by Julius Lester. Reprinted by permission of Scholastic Inc.

"Talk" from *The Cow-Tail Switch and Other West African Stories* by Harold Courlander and George Herzog. © 1947, 1974 by Harold Courlander. Reprinted by permission of Henry Holt and Company, LLC.

"Great Hymn to the Aten" by Pharaoh Amenhotep IV (Akhenaten), translated by William van den Dungen. Used by permission of William van den Dungen.

From *Sunjata* by Bamba Suso and Banna Kanutte, pp. 24-29 (Penguin Books, 1999). Text and notes copyright © Gordon Innes, 1974 and 1999. Introduction and additional material copyright © Lucy Durán and Graham Furniss, 1999. Reproduced by permission of Penguin Books Ltd.

"The Knee-High Man," from *The Knee-High Man and Other Tales* by Julius Lester, copyright © 1972 Julius Lester. Used by permission of Dial Books for Young Readers, A Division of Penguin Young Readers Group, A Member of Penguin Group (USA) Inc., 345 Hudson Street, New York, NY 10014. All rights reserved.

"The Headless Hant" from Bundles of Troubles and Other Tarheel Tales, ed. W. C. Hendricks, 1943.

Used courtesy of New York Life Insurance Company, sponsor of the educators' website www.jimcrowhistory.org <http://www.jimcrowhistory.org/>; authored by Ronald Davis, Ph.D., California State University, Northridge.

"Flight" reprinted by the permission of Russell & Volkening as agents for the author. Copyright © 1955 by Ann Petry, renewed in 1983 by Ann Petry.

Text of Telegram sent to the Disarmament Conference "Speech on Disarmament Conference Delivered at Liberty Hall, November 6, 1921" by Marcus Garvey from *The Philosophy and Opinions of Marcus Garvey,* edited by Amy Jacques Garvey.

"The New Negro" by Alain Locke. Reprinted with the permission of Scribner, an imprint of Simon & Schuster Adult Publishing Group, from *The New Negro: Voices of the Harlem Renaissance* by Alain Locke. Copyright 1925 by Albert & Charles Boni, Inc.

"The Negro Artist and the Racial Mountain" by Langston Hughes, originally published in *The Nation,* June 1926. Copyright 1926 by Langston Hughes. Reprinted by permission of Harold Ober Associates Incorporated.

"The Creation," from *God's Trombones* by James Weldon Johnson, copyright 1927 The Viking Press, Inc., renewed © 1955 by Grace Nail Johnson. Used by permission of Viking Penguin, a division of Penguin Group (USA) Inc.

"Lift Every Voice and Sing," from *Saint Peter Relates An Incident* by James Weldon Johnson, copyright 1917, 1921, 1935 by James Weldon Johnson, copyright renewed © 1963 by Grace Nail Johnson. Used by permission of Viking Penguin, a division of Penguin Group (USA) Inc.

"The Black Finger" by Angelina W. Grimké from *Selected Works of Angelina Weld Grimké* edited by Carolivia Herron, 1991.

"The Tropics of New York" and "If We Must Die" by Claude McKay. Courtesy of the Literary Representative for the Works of Claude McKay, Schomburg Center for Research in Black Culture, The New York Public Library, Astor, Lenox and Tilden Foundations.

"Dream Variations," "April Rain Song," "Jazzonia," "Daybreak in Alabama," "Song for a Dark Girl," "Mother to Son," "Harlem," "Dreams," and "I, Too" from *The Collected Poems of Langston Hughes* by Langston Hughes, copyright © 1994 by The Estate of Langston Hughes. Used by permission of Alfred A. Knopf, a division of Random House, Inc.

"Heritage" and "Fantasy" by Gwendolyn Bennett. Courtesy of the Literary Representative for the Works of Gwendolyn B. Bennett, Schomburg Center for Research in Black Culture, New York Public Library, Astor, Lenox and Tilden Foundations.

Reprinted by permission of GRM Associates, Inc., Agents for the Estate of Ida M. Cullen. "Incident," "A Song of Praise," "Yet Do I Marvel," and "Heritage" from the book *Color* by Countee Cullen. Copyright © 1925 by Harper & Brothers; copyright renewed 1953 by Ida M. Cullen.

Reprinted by permission of GRM Associates, Inc., Agents for the Estate of Ida M. Cullen. "Scottsboro, Too, Is Worth Its Song" from *The Medea and Some Poems;* copyright © 1935 by Harper & Brothers; copyright renewed 1963 by Ida M. Cullen.

"November Cotton Flower" and "Cotton Song" from *Cane* by Jean Toomer. Copyright 1923 by Boni & Liveright, renewed 1951 by Jean Toomer. Used by permission of Liveright Publishing Corporation.

"Magalu" by Helene Johnson. Permission granted by Abigail McGrath.

"Sonnet to a Negro Harlem" by Helen Johnson. Reprinted by permission of Abigail McGrath.

All lines from "Ma Rainey" from *The Collected Poems of Sterling A. Brown,* edited by Michael S. Harper. Copyright 1932 by Harcourt Brace & Co. Copyright renewed 1960 by Sterling A. Brown. Reprinted by permission of HarperCollins Publishers.

"The Day-Breakers," "Southern Mansion," "A Black Man Talks of Reaping" by Arna Bontemps from *Personals.* Copyright © 1963 by Arna Bontemps. Reprinted by permission of Harold Ober Associates Incorporated.

Their Eyes Were Watching God by Zora Neale Hurston. Copyright 1937 by Harper & Row, Publishers, Inc.; renewed © 1965 by John C. Hurston and Joel Hurston. Reprinted by permission of HarperCollins Publishers.

"Trouble In Mind" by Richard M. Jones, 1937.

"Statesboro Blues" by Willie McTell, 1929.

"Crossroad Blues" by Robert Johnson. Words and Music by Robert Johnson. Copyright © (1978), 1990, 1991 Lehsem 11, LLC and Claud L. Johnson. Administered by Music & Media International, Inc. International Copyright Secured. All Rights Reserved.

"Goodnight, Irene" by Huddie Ledbetter and John A. Lomax, published by Ludlow Music, Inc.

"Strange Fruit" by Billie Holiday and Lewis Allen.

"Saved" copyright © 1964 by Alex Haley and Malcolm X. Copyright © 1965 by Alex Haley and Betty Shabazz, from *The Autobiography of Malcolm X* by Malcolm X and Alex Haley. Used by permission of Random House, Inc.

From *I Know Why The Caged Bird Sings* by Maya Angelou, copyright © 1969 and renewed 1997 by Maya Angelou. Used by permission of Random House, Inc.

"Letter from Birmingham Jail" and "I Have a Dream" by Martin Luther King Jr. Reprinted by arrangement with the Estate of Martin Luther King Jr., c/o Writers House as agent for the proprietor New York, NY. Copyright 1963 Martin Luther King Jr., copyright renewed 1991 Coretta Scott King.

Speech by Wynton Marsalis, January 17, 2006 at Tulane University in New Orleans. Copyright © 2006 by Wynton Marsalis. Reprinted with permission of Wynton Marsalis.

"Frederick Douglass," "Homage to the Empress of the Blues," and "Those Winter Sundays." Copyright © 1966 by Robert Hayden from *Collected Poems of Robert Hayden* by Robert Hayden, edited by Frederick Glaysher. Copyright © 1985 by Emma Hayden. Used by permission of Liveright Publishing Corporation.

"Booker T. and W.E.B." by Dudley Randall. Reprinted by permission of the Dudley Randall Estate.

"For My People," "The Ballad of the Free," and "For Malcolm X" from *This is My Century: New and Collected Poems* by Margaret Walker Alexander, 1989. Used by permission of the University of Georgia Press.

"We Real Cool," "The Bean Eaters," "Tommy," "Rudolph Is Tired of The City," and "Narcissa" from *Bronzeville Boys and Girls* by Gwendolyn Brooks. Copyright © 1956 by Gwendolyn Brooks Blakely. Reprinted by Consent of Brooks Permissions.

"Ka'Ba" by Amiri Baraka. Reprinted by permission of SLL/ Sterling Lord Literistic, Inc. Copyright by Amiri Baraka.

"I Am A Black Woman" from I *Am A Black Woman* by Mari Evans, published by Wm. Morrow & Co., 1970, by permission of the author.

"By Myself" and "Harriet Tubman" from *Honey, I Love and Other Love Poems* by Eloise Greenfield, 1978.

"for our lady" by Sonia Sanchez from *We a BaddDDD People,* Broadside Press 1970. Reprinted by permission of Sonia Sanchez.

"WE CAN BE" and "to Kenny" from *It's A New Day,* by Sonia Sanchez, 1971. Reprinted by permission of Sonia Sanchez.

"did ya ever cry..." 1968, "if i had known, if..." 1969, "come reluctant night...," "O this day like an orange..." from *Love Poems* by Sonia Sanchez, 1973. Reprinted by permission of Sonia Sanchez.

"Life Doesn't Frighten Me" and "Woman Work" copyright © 1978 by Maya Angelou, from *And Still I Rise* by Maya Angelou. Used by permission of Random House, Inc.

"Knoxville, Tennessee" and "Nikki-Rosa" from *Black Feeling, Black Talk, Black Judgment* by Nikki Giovanni. Copyright © 1968, 1970 by Nikki Giovanni. Reprinted by permission of HarperCollins Publishers, William Morrow.

"the drum" from *Spin a Soft Black Song,* Revised Edition by Nikki Giovanni, illustrated by George Martins. Copyright © 1971, 1985 by Nikki Giovanni. Reprinted by permission of Hill and Wang, a division of Farrar, Straus and Giroux, LLC.

Lucille Clifton, "in the inner city" and "for deLawd" from *Good Woman: Poems and a Memoir 1969-1980.* Copyright © 1987 by Lucille Clifton. Reprinted with the permission of BOA Editions, Ltd.

"Parsley" from *Museum,* Carnegie Mellon University Press, © 1983 by Rita Dove. Reprinted by permission of the author.

"Br'er Sterling and the Rocker" by Michael S. Harper. *Callaloo* - Volume 21, Number 4, Fall 1998, pp. 883. © Charles H. Rowell. Reprinted with permission of The Johns Hopkins University Press.

"Use Trouble" by Michael Harper originally published in *The American Scholar,* 2000, forthcoming *Use Trouble,* Illinois, 2007. Reprinted by permission of the author.

"Archipelagoes" from "Map of the New World," "A Far Cry from Africa," "Che," and "Season of Phantasmal Peace" from *Collected Poems, 1948-1984* by Derek Walcott. Copyright © 1986 by Derek Walcott. Reprinted by permission of Farrar, Strauss and Giroux, LLC.

"Benjamin Banneker Sends His 'Almanac' to Thomas Jefferson," originally published i*n Soothsayers and Omens* (Seven Woods Press, 1976), © 1976 by Jay Wright. Reprinted in *Transfigurations: Collected Poems* (Louisiana State University Press, 2000), © 2000 by Jay Wright. Reprinted by permission of the author.

"The Man Who Saw the Flood," pp. 102-108, from *Eight Men* by Richard Wright. Copyright 1940, © 1961 by Richard Wright; renewed © 1989 by Ellen Wright. Introduction © 1996 by Paul Gilroy. Reprinted by permission of HarperCollins Publishers.

From "The Richer, The Poorer" from *The Richer, The Poorer* by Dorothy West, copyright © 1995 by Dorothy West. Used by permission of Doubleday, a division of Random House, Inc.

"Everyday Use" from *In Love and Trouble: Stories of Black Women,* copyright © 1973 by Alice Walker, reprinted by permission of Harcourt Inc.

"Geraldine Moore: the Poet" by Toni Cade Bambara. Reprinted by permission of Karma Bambara.

"Raymond's Run," copyright © 1971 Toni Cade Bambara, from *Gorilla, My Love* by Toni Cade Bambara. Used by permission of Random House, Inc.

From *Beloved* by Toni Morrison, copyright © 1987 by Toni Morrison. Used by permission of Alfred A. Knopf, a division of Random House, Inc.

From A *Raisin In The Sun* by Lorraine Hansberry, copyright © 1958 by Robert Nemiroff, as an unpublished work. Copyright © 1959, 1966, 1984 by Robert Nemiroff. Used by permission of Random House, Inc.

"lady in blue." Reprinted with permission of Scribner, an imprint of Simon & Schuster Adult Publishing Group, from *For Colored Girls Who Have Considered Suicide When The Rainbow Is Enuf* by Ntozake Shange. Copyright © 1975, 1976, 1977 by Ntozake Shange.

"'Round Midnight." Words by Bernie Hanighen. Music by Cootie Williams and Thelonious Monk. © 1944 (Renewed) Warner Bros. Inc. and Thelonious Music. Lyrics Reprinted by Permission of Alfred Publishing Co., Inc. All Rights Reserved.

"A Love Supreme" by John Coltrane, 1964.

"What's Going On" by Marvin Gaye, Al Cleveland & Renaldo Benson, 1971. Words and Music by Marvin Gaye, Al Cleveland and Renaldo Benson. © 1970, 1971, 1972 (Renewed 1998, 1999, 2000) Jobete Music Co., Inc. All Rights Controlled and Administered by EMI April Music Inc. and EMI Blackwood Music Inc. on behalf of Jobete Music Co., Inc. and Stone Agate Music (A Division of Jobete Music Co., Inc.) All Rights Reserved. International Copyright Secured. Used by Permission.

"When a Man Loves a Woman." Lyrics and Music by Calvin Lewis and Andrew Wright. © 1966 (Renewed) Pronto Music, Inc., Mijac Music and Quinvy Music Publishing Co. All Rights Administered by Warner-Tamerlane Publishing Corp. All Rights Reserved. Reprinted by permission of Alfred Publishing Co., Inc.

Image Credits

T – Top	**L – Left**
B – Botttom	**R – Right**
C – Center	

Cover	Douglas, Aaron, *The Creation,* Howard University Gallery of Art, Washington, DC
iv	Library of Congress, Prints and Photographs, LC-USZ62-16225
vi	Lev T. Mills, *Gemini I,* 1981, color serigraph, 28"h x 22"w, Image courtesy of University Museums, University of Delaware. Paul Jones Collection.
xii	Courtesy of Parish Gallery-Georgetown.
38	© Ruggero Vanni/Corbis
46	Robert Harding World Imagery/Bruno Morandi/Getty Images
55	Library of Congress, Prints and Photographs, LC-USZ62-54026
57	The Granger Collection, New York
60	The Granger Collection, New York
69	The Granger Collection, New York
75	© Gideon Mendel/Corbis
76	© Bob Sacha/Corbis
77	© Charles & Josette Lenars/Corbis
78	© David Sutherland/Corbis
83	Robert Harding World Imagery/Bruno Morandi/Getty Images
87	Library of Congress, Prints and Photographs, LC-USZ62-89701
89	Library of Congress, Prints and Photographs, LC-USZ62-41837
91	The Granger Collection, New York
92	Library of Congress, Prints and Photographs, LC-USZ62-103293
95	Library of Congress, Prints and Photographs, LC-USZ62-125169
99	The Granger Collection, New York

105	Library of Congress, Prints and Photographs, LC-USZ62-58152
129	Library of Congress, Prints and Photographs, LC-USZ62-15887
134	Library of Congress, Prints and Photographs, LC-USZ62-125297
137	Library of Congress, Prints and Photographs, LC-USZ62-125348
145	Library of Congress, Prints and Photographs, LC- USZ62-16225
149	Library of Congress, Prints and Photographs Division, LC-DIG-ppmsca-08978
155	The Granger Collection, New York
177	Library of Congress, Prints and Photographs, LC-USZ62-56850
183	Library of Congress, Prints and Photographs, HABS, VA, 16-LONI.V,1J-
185	Library of Congress, Prints and Photographs, LC-USZ62-118946
195	Library of Congress, Prints and Photographs, LC-USZC4-1561
203	Library of Congress, Prints and Photographs, LC-USZ62-103393
205	Library of Congress, Prints and Photographs, LC-USF34-032707-D
207	Library of Congress, Prints and Photographs, LC-USZ62-118809
208	Library of Congress, Prints and Photographs, LC-USZ62-38540
209	Library of Congress, Prints and Photographs, LC-USZ62-23008
214	The Granger Collection, New York
218	Library of Congress, Prints and Photographs Division, LC-DIG-cwpb-04079
219	Harlem Couple, The Granger Collection, New York, Photo by James VanDerZee, © Donna Mussenden VanDerZee.
222	Library of Congress, Prints and Photographs Division, LC-DIG-cwpbh-04424
223	Library of Congress, Prints and Photographs Division, LC-USZ62-1848
224	© Bettmann/Corbis
225	Library of Congress, Prints and Photographs Division, LC-USZ62-13017
226	© Bettmann/Corbis
227	© Bettmann/Corbis
228	© Corbis
231	The Granger Collection, New York
239	The Granger Collection, New York
249	Library of Congress, Prints and Photographs, LC-USZ62-94863
251	Library of Congress, Prints and Photographs, LC-USZ62-119897
259	Library of Congress, Prints and Photographs, LC-USZ62-86372
267	Library of Congress, Prints and Photographs, LC-USZ62-107756
277	Library of Congress, Prints and Photographs, LC-DIG-ggbain-07435
279	Special Collections & Archives, W. E. B. Du Bois Library, University of Massachusetts, Amherst
283	Special Collections & Archives, W. E. B. Du Bois Library, , University of Massachusettes, Amherst
286	Marcus Garvey, The Granger Collection, New York, Photo by James VanDerZee, © Donna Mussenden VanDerZee.
289	Library of Congress, Prints and Photographs, LC-USZ62-109626
294	© Bettmann/Corbis
297	© Lucien Aigner/Corbis
301	© Bettmann/Corbis
303	The Granger Collection, New York
305	Library of Congress, Prints and Photographs Division, LC-USZc2-1124
307	Prints and Photographs Division, Schomburg Center for Research in Black Culture, New York Public Library, Astor, Lenox and Tilden Foundations
313	© Bettmann/Corbis
317	SCHOMBURG CENTER / Art Resource, NY
327	Library of Congress, Prints and Photographs, LC-USZ62-108239
335	Library of Congress, Prints and Photographs, Visual Materials from the NAACP Records, LC-USZ62-36619
341	University of North Carolina Library from "Documenting the South."
345	Library of Congress, Prints and Photographs Division, LC-B811-3569
347-*T*	The Granger Collection, New York
347-*C*	General Research & Reference Division, Schomburg Center for Research in Black Culture, New York Public Library, Astor, Lenox and Tilden Foundations
347-*B*	Moorland-Spingarn Research Center, Howard University
353	Library of Congress, Prints and Photographs, LC-USZ62-105919
371	The Granger Collection, New York
375	National Archives photo no. 69-N-23339-D
377	National Archives photo no. 69-N-23339-D

389 Library of Congress, Prints & Photographs Division, Carl Van Vechten Collection, LC-USZ62-42529

395 © Bettmann/Corbis

399-*L* Library of Congress, Prints & Photographs, LC-USZ62-47605

399-*R* Library of Congress, Prints & Photographs, LC-USZ62-104495

401 Schlesinger Library, Radcliffe Institute, Harvard University.

407 Library of Congress, Prints and Photographs, LC-USZ62-134555

413 Library of Congress, Prints and Photographs, Carl Van Vechten Collection, LC-USZ62-6356

425 The Granger Collection, New York

430 Library of Congress, Prints and Photographs, LC-DIG-fsac-1a34400

431 Library of Congress, Prints and Photographs, LC-USF35-177

433 Library of Congress, Prints and Photographs, LC-USZ62-62394

438 Prints and Photographs Division, Schomburg Center for Research in Black Culture, New York Public Library, Astor, Lenox and Tilden Foundations

439 Library of Congress, Prints and Photographs, LC-USZ62-124776

441 Hulton Archive/Frank Driggs Collection/Getty Images

444 The Granger Collection, New York

445 The Granger Collection, New York

446 Library of Congress, Prints and Photographs, LC-USZ61-1347

447-*T* Library of Congress, Prints and Photographs, LC-DIG-fsac-1a34396

447-*B* © Dick Waterman

449-*T* Library of Congress, Prints and Photographs, LC-USZC2-5546

449-*B* © Bettmann/Corbis

450 The Granger Collection, New York

451-*T* Hulton Archive/Frank Driggs Collection/Getty Images

451-*B* The Granger Collection, New York

452 Library of Congress, Prints and Photographs, LC-USZ62-114733

456 © Hulton-Deutsch Collection/Corbis

457 © Ted Williams/Corbis

459 © Underwood & Underwood/Corbis

461 © Reuters/Corbis

463 The Granger Collection, New York

465 Library of Congress, Prints and Photographs, LC-USZ62-127236

466 Library of Congress, Prints and Photographs, NYWT & S Collection, LC-USZ62-125934

467 The Granger Collection, New York

468-*T* Library of Congress, Prints and Photographs, NYWT & S Collection, LC-USZ62-114744

468-*B* The Granger Collection, New York

469-*T* Library of Congress, Prints and Photographs, LC-USZ62-67705

469-*B* Library of Congress, Prints and Photographs, NYWT & S Collection, LC-USZ62-132945

471 Library of Congress, Prints and Photographs, LC-USF34-052589-D

472 Courtesy of the Rusty Frank Archive

473 © Bettmann/Corbis

475 © Hulton-Deutsch Collection/Corbis

477 Library of Congress, Prints and Photographs, LC-U9-10363-5

478-*T* Library of Congress, Prints and Photographs, LC-USW33-029184-C

478-*B* Library of Congress, Prints and Photographs, LC-USE6-D-004362

479-*T* Library of Congress, Prints and Photographs, LC-U9-1027B-11

479-*B* Library of Congress, Prints and Photographs, LC-U9-10364-37

480-*T* Library of Congress, Prints and Photographs, LC-USZ62-120275

480-*CL* Library of Congress, Prints and Photographs, LC-USZ62-7449

480-*CR* Library of Congress, Prints and Photographs, LC-USZ62-98170

480-*B* Library of Congress, Prints and Photographs, LC-USZ62-126826

481-*line 1* Library of Congress, Prints and Photographs, LC-DIG-ppmsca-08102

481-*line 2 left* Library of Congress, Prints and Photographs, LC-USZ62-134151

481-*line 2 right* Library of Congress, Prints and Photographs, LC-USZ6-1847

481-*line 3* Library of Congress, Prints and Photographs, LC-USZ62-1315695

481-*line 4* © Christian Simonpietri/Sygma/Corbis

481-*line 5 left* Library of Congress, Prints and Photographs, LC-DIG-ppmsca-03191

481-*line 5 right* © Henry Diltz/Corbis

482-*T* © Bettmann/Corbis

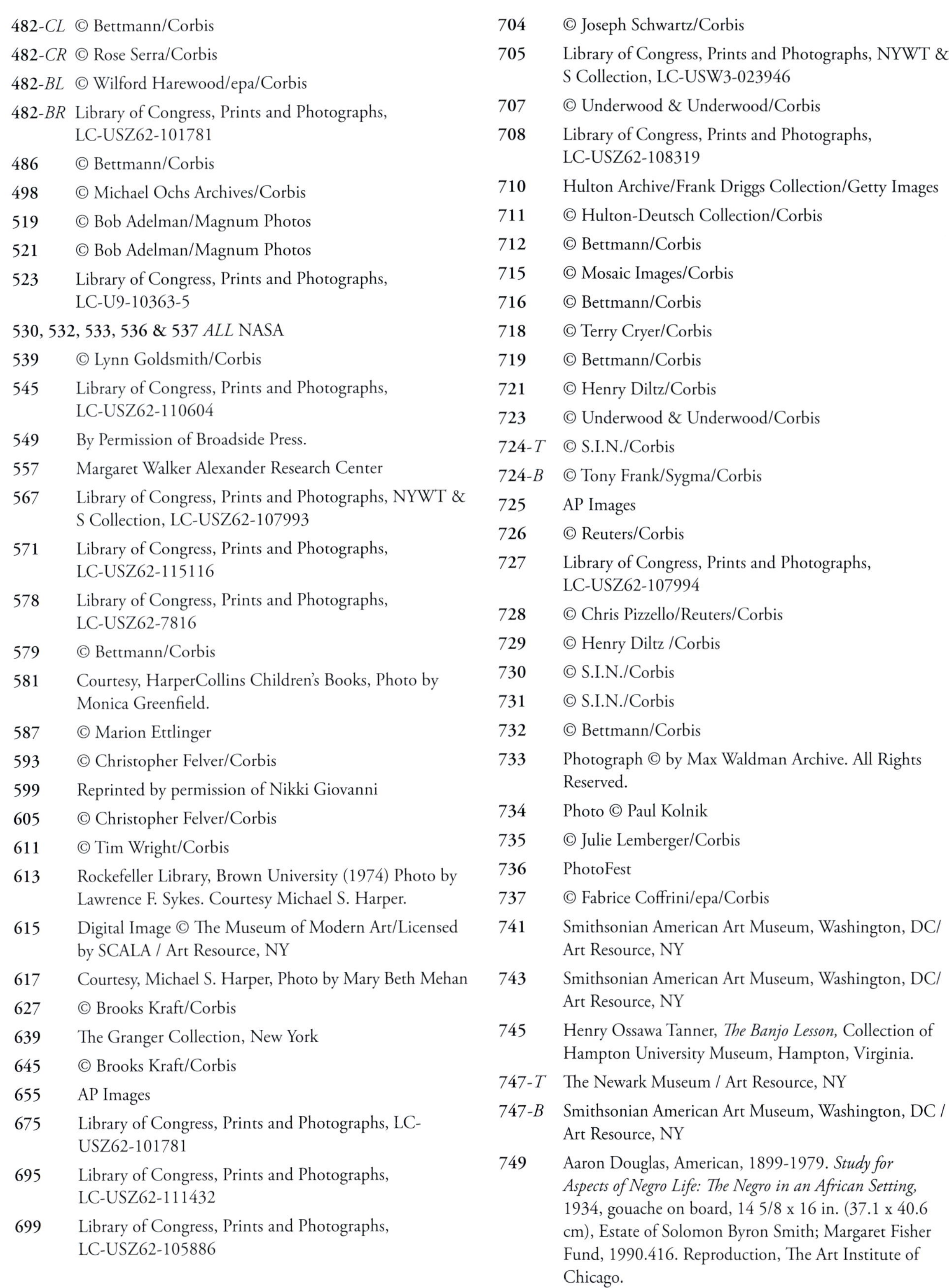

482-*CL* © Bettmann/Corbis

482-*CR* © Rose Serra/Corbis

482-*BL* © Wilford Harewood/epa/Corbis

482-*BR* Library of Congress, Prints and Photographs, LC-USZ62-101781

486 © Bettmann/Corbis

498 © Michael Ochs Archives/Corbis

519 © Bob Adelman/Magnum Photos

521 © Bob Adelman/Magnum Photos

523 Library of Congress, Prints and Photographs, LC-U9-10363-5

530, 532, 533, 536 & 537 *ALL* NASA

539 © Lynn Goldsmith/Corbis

545 Library of Congress, Prints and Photographs, LC-USZ62-110604

549 By Permission of Broadside Press.

557 Margaret Walker Alexander Research Center

567 Library of Congress, Prints and Photographs, NYWT & S Collection, LC-USZ62-107993

571 Library of Congress, Prints and Photographs, LC-USZ62-115116

578 Library of Congress, Prints and Photographs, LC-USZ62-7816

579 © Bettmann/Corbis

581 Courtesy, HarperCollins Children's Books, Photo by Monica Greenfield.

587 © Marion Ettlinger

593 © Christopher Felver/Corbis

599 Reprinted by permission of Nikki Giovanni

605 © Christopher Felver/Corbis

611 © Tim Wright/Corbis

613 Rockefeller Library, Brown University (1974) Photo by Lawrence F. Sykes. Courtesy Michael S. Harper.

615 Digital Image © The Museum of Modern Art/Licensed by SCALA / Art Resource, NY

617 Courtesy, Michael S. Harper, Photo by Mary Beth Mehan

627 © Brooks Kraft/Corbis

639 The Granger Collection, New York

645 © Brooks Kraft/Corbis

655 AP Images

675 Library of Congress, Prints and Photographs, LC-USZ62-101781

695 Library of Congress, Prints and Photographs, LC-USZ62-111432

699 Library of Congress, Prints and Photographs, LC-USZ62-105886

704 © Joseph Schwartz/Corbis

705 Library of Congress, Prints and Photographs, NYWT & S Collection, LC-USW3-023946

707 © Underwood & Underwood/Corbis

708 Library of Congress, Prints and Photographs, LC-USZ62-108319

710 Hulton Archive/Frank Driggs Collection/Getty Images

711 © Hulton-Deutsch Collection/Corbis

712 © Bettmann/Corbis

715 © Mosaic Images/Corbis

716 © Bettmann/Corbis

718 © Terry Cryer/Corbis

719 © Bettmann/Corbis

721 © Henry Diltz/Corbis

723 © Underwood & Underwood/Corbis

724-*T* © S.I.N./Corbis

724-*B* © Tony Frank/Sygma/Corbis

725 AP Images

726 © Reuters/Corbis

727 Library of Congress, Prints and Photographs, LC-USZ62-107994

728 © Chris Pizzello/Reuters/Corbis

729 © Henry Diltz /Corbis

730 © S.I.N./Corbis

731 © S.I.N./Corbis

732 © Bettmann/Corbis

733 Photograph © by Max Waldman Archive. All Rights Reserved.

734 Photo © Paul Kolnik

735 © Julie Lemberger/Corbis

736 PhotoFest

737 © Fabrice Coffrini/epa/Corbis

741 Smithsonian American Art Museum, Washington, DC/ Art Resource, NY

743 Smithsonian American Art Museum, Washington, DC/ Art Resource, NY

745 Henry Ossawa Tanner, *The Banjo Lesson,* Collection of Hampton University Museum, Hampton, Virginia.

747-*T* The Newark Museum / Art Resource, NY

747-*B* Smithsonian American Art Museum, Washington, DC / Art Resource, NY

749 Aaron Douglas, American, 1899-1979. *Study for Aspects of Negro Life: The Negro in an African Setting,* 1934, gouache on board, 14 5/8 x 16 in. (37.1 x 40.6 cm), Estate of Solomon Byron Smith; Margaret Fisher Fund, 1990.416. Reproduction, The Art Institute of Chicago.

751 Howard University Gallery of Art, Washington, DC

753-*L* Satin and Pearls, 1932. Photo by James VanDerZee, © Donna Mussenden VanDerZee.

753-*R* Father's Day, 1929. Photo by James VanDerZee, © Donna Mussenden VanDerZee.

755 Harlem Couple, The Granger Collection, New York, Photo by James VanDerZee, © Donna Mussenden VanDerZee.

757 Smithsonian American Art Museum, Washington, DC/ Art Resource, NY

759 Howard University Gallery of Art, Washington, DC

761-*T* Smithsonian American Art Museum, Washington, DC / Art Resource, NY

761-*B* Collection of California African American Foundation, Courtesy of California African American Museum.

763 Howard University Gallery of Art, Washington, DC

765 The Newark Museum/Art Resource, NY, Courtesy the Estate of Hale Woodruff

767 Howard University Gallery of Art, Washington, DC

769 Smithsonian American Art Museum, Washington, DC / Art Resource, NY

771-*TR* Jones, Lois Mailou, *Portrait,* 1996, color lithograph, 16"h x 13"w, Image courtesy of University Museums, University of Delaware. Copyright Lois Mailou Jones Pierre-Noel Trust.

771-*BL* Jones, Lois Mailou, *Jazz Combo,* 1996, color lithograph, 16"h x 13"w, Image courtesy of University Museums, University of Delaware. Copyright Lois Mailou Jones Pierre-Noel Trust.

773-*T* Lawrence, Jacob, *The Migration of the Negro Panel no. 3,* 1940-1941, Casein tempera on hardboard, 12 x 18 in.; 30.48 x 45.72 cm. Acquired 1942. The Phillips Collection, Washington, DC.

773-*B* Lawrence, Jacob, *The Migration of the Negro Panel no. 15,* 1940-1941, Casein tempera on hardboard, 12 x 18 in.; 30.48 x 45.72 cm. Acquired 1942. The Phillips Collection, Washington, DC.

775-*T, B* Digital Image © The Museum of Modern Art/Licensed by SCALA / Art Resource, NY

777 Howard University Gallery of Art, Washington, DC

779-*TL* Gordon Parks, photographer, Library of Congress, Prints and Photographs, LC-USF34-T013407-C

779-*TR, BR, BL* © Corbis

781-*T* © Douglas Kirkland/Corbis

781-*BL, BR* © Corbis

783 The Philadelphia Museum of Art/Art Resource, NY

785 Smithsonian American Art Museum, Washington, DC/ Art Resource, NY

787 Smithsonian American Art Museum/Art Resource, NY

789 Howard University Gallery of Art, Washington, DC

791 Howard University Gallery of Art, Washington, DC

793 Smithsonian American Art Museum, Washington, DC / Art Resource, NY

795 *Boy with Tire,* 1952, Hughie Lee-Smith. Gift of Dr. S. B. Milton, Dr. James A. Owen, Dr. B. F. Seabrooks and Dr. A. E. Thomas, Jr. Photograph © 1988 The Detroit Institute of Arts. Art © Estate of Hughie Lee-Smith/ Licensed by VAGA, New York, NY

797 & 799-*ALL* John Biggers, *The History of Negro Education in Morris County, Texas.* Art © John T. Biggers Estate/ Licensed by VAGA, New York, NY. Estate Represented by Michael Rosenfeld Gallery. Photography by Jennifer Whatley, Omaha, TX, for Core Knowledge Foundation.

801 Constance Porter Uzelac, Executive Director, for Dorothy Porter Wesley Research Center, Inc. Photo by Milan Uzelac. Used by permission.

803 Lev T. Mills, *Gemini I,* 1981, color serigraph, 28"h x 22"w, Image courtesy of University Museums, University of Delaware. Paul Jones Collection.

805 Smithsonian American Art Museum, Washington, DC/ Art Resource, NY

807 National Portrait Gallery, Smithsonian Institution/Art Resource, NY

809 Art © Elizabeth Catlett/Licensed by VAGA, New York, NY

811 Frank Bowling, *Where is Lucienne?* Photo: Joe Grant. Used by permission of Spencer A. Richards for Frank Bowling.

813 Howard University Gallery of Art, Washington, DC

815 Howard University Gallery of Art, Washington, DC

817 David Driskell, *Woman in Interiors,* mixed media, 48"h x 40"w, Image courtesy of University Museums, University of Delaware, Used by permission of the artist, David C. Driskell.

819 Romare Bearden, *Roots Odyssey,* Library of Congress, Prints and Photographs Division, Ben and Beatrice Goldstein Foundation Collection, LC-USZC4-6169. Art © Romare Bearden Foundation/ Licensed by VAGA, New York, NY

821 Image: © North Carolina Museum of Art/Corbis Artwork: © Romare Bearden Foundation/VAGA, New York

823 White, Charles, *John Henry,* 1975, oil wash, 31"h x 24"w, Image courtesy of University Museums, University of Delaware

825 Howard University Gallery of Art, Washington, DC

827 Smithsonian American Art Museum, Washington, DC/ Art Resource, NY

829 Goreleigh, Rex, *Red Barn,* 1981, watercolor, 28"h x 22"w, Image courtesy of University Museums, University of Delaware.

831 Smithsonian American Art Museum, Washington, DC/ Art Resource, NY

833-*ALL*Courtesy of ACA Galleries, New York.

835 "Breakers, Becune Point, 1995" from *Tiepolo's Hound* by Derek Walcott. Copyright © 2000 by Derek Walcott. Reprinted by permission of Farrar, Straus and Giroux, LLC.

837-*ALL*Courtesy of Parish Gallery, Georgetown

Handbook of Literary and Critical Terms

abstract 1. Adjective. Not representational. See *abstraction, abstract expressionism, representation,* and *criticism.* 2. Noun. A summary. See *summary.*

abstraction In the visual arts, the tendency away from representation of objects as they appear in real life and toward stylization or the use of pure color, line, value, and form. See *representation, abstract expressionism,* and *criticism.*

abstract expressionism An artistic movement of the twentieth century that did away with representation of real-world objects and figures in favor of the use of pure color, line, value, shape, and other so-called abstract elements to express or convey emotional effects. Sam Gilliam's *Open Cylinder* (See page 826) is an example of abstract expressionism.

act A major division of a play. Both Roman and Elizabethan plays (including those of Shakespeare) were divided into five acts. In modern theater, plays most commonly have three acts, as does Lorraine Hansberry's *A Raisin in the Sun* (See page 676).

action An event or sequence of events that occurs in a literary work. In drama, action refers to events that occur on stage as opposed to events that happen off-stage or before or after the events covered in the play. Sometimes a dramatist will make an event that occurred before the present action of a play part of the play's action by introducing a *flashback* scene. In the literary form known as the epic, the action sometimes begins *in medias res* (Latin for "in the middle of things"). West African griots could begin their epic tales *in medias res* because their audiences were already intimately familiar with the stories they were telling. See *flashback.*

actor One who performs the role of a character in a drama.

adaptation A presentation of a work of art in another form or medium. Alice Walker's novel *The Color Purple,* Zora Neale Hurston's *Their Eyes Were Watching God,* and Toni Morrison's *Beloved,* for example, were all adapted for film.

adage See *proverb.*

aesthetics The philosophical study of beauty, having as its goal the development of principles to guide the creation, interpretation, and evaluation of works of art. Commonly accepted aesthetic principles change from age to age. As a result, what is considered beautiful at one time may not be considered beautiful at another. The Greek philosopher Aristotle considered art to be most beautiful when it most closely imitated life or nature. Followers of another Greek philosopher, Plato, believed, in sharp contrast, that beauty could be found by rising above accidental, natural, earthly things and seeking sublime, eternal, idealized forms. Differing ideas about beauty give rise to differing schools of aesthetic thought.

Neoclassicists hold that beauty derives from order, harmony, proportion, and balance, features that characterize Greek and Roman classical art and architecture.

Romantics favor the intense expression of emotion and nature in a wild state rather than in a controlled state. To a romantic, for example, an uncut forest is preferable to an ordered garden.

Realists believe that art should imitate life and show the human capacity both for good and for evil. *Social Realists* believe that art should imitate and portray the real life struggles and aspirations of common people.

Naturalists tend to emphasize in their work the idea that people's lives are governed by forces or circumstances beyond their control.

Sterling A. Brown (See page 403) developed an aesthetic based upon African-American folk language and customs.

Alain Locke (See page 290) helped to define and nurture the aesthetic vision of the Harlem Renaissance; he encouraged artists to use their work to transform society and to create self-awareness, including collective self-awareness of what it was to be, in his terms, "the New Negro."

W. E. B. Du Bois (See page 268) developed a Marxist aesthetic based upon using art to achieve social and political purposes and articulated this aesthetic of art as propaganda in his essay "Criteria of Negro Art."

Henry Louis Gates, Jr. (See page 168) developed an aesthetic and theory of African-American literary criticism based upon the principle of *signification,* or duality of vision and expression.

Léopold Senghor (See page 770) developed an aesthetic called *négritude* based upon celebration of the common inheritance of peoples of the African Diaspora.

See *criticism, neoclassicism, naturalism, realism,* and *romanticism.*

aim The primary intention that the writer of a work tries to achieve. The aim of a piece of writing, for example, might be to persuade, to inform others, or to express oneself. One aim of most works of art is to move the audience or the reader. Tragedy, claims Aristotle, aims to move the audience to terror and pity as it witnesses the fall of a once great person through some fault of his or her own. Comedy, on the other hand, aims to have the reader or viewer rejoice at the success of the hero or main character. The term *aim* is most often used in the discussion of nonfiction informative or persuasive writing. The aim of Langston Hughes's "The Negro Artist and the Racial Mountain," for example, was to convince people that a specifically African-American art is possible and desirable. The aim of Harriet Jacobs's *Incidents in the Life of a Slave Girl* was to demonstrate to people the horrors of slavery and so convince them to support its abolition. See *mode*.

allegory A work in which each element represents or stands for something else. It is possible to read Lorraine Hansberry's play *A Raisin in the Sun* as an allegory in which each of the characters in the Younger family represents a commonly unrealized aspiration, or dream, of African Americans at the midpoint of the twentieth century.

alliteration The repetition of initial consonant sounds. Robert Hayden uses alliteration when he describes Frederick Douglass as being "superb in love and logic."

allusion A reference in a writing, speech, or work of art to another work or to an external person, place, object, or event. In his speech "What to the Slave Is the Fourth of July?" (See page 122), Frederick Douglass likens asking an ex-slave to speak at a Fourth of July celebration to the Babylonians asking their captives, the Israelites, to sing one of the songs of Zion. Douglass thus makes an allusion to the Biblical story of the Babylonian captivity of the Jews. Derek Walcott's "Map of the New World: I Archipelagoes," on page 624, makes allusions to the destruction of the ancient city of Troy by the Greeks and to Odysseus, a Greek warrior who encountered many adventures on his way back home from Troy. Dr. Martin Luther King, Jr.'s "I Have a Dream" speech, on page 523, contains numerous allusions to the Bible.

ambiguity A statement that has more than one meaning, or speech that can be interpreted in more than one way so that the meaning cannot be clearly resolved. For example, the statement "Yolanda cannot bear children" might mean that Yolanda doesn't like children or that she is not able to give birth to them. Writers often make intentional use of ambiguity. For example, in Mari Evans's "I Am a Black Woman," on page 572, the word *tire/d* is ambiguous. It can mean either "rubberlike," like an automobile tire, or "exhausted."

analogy A comparison of two things that shows how they are alike. The comparison is explicitly or directly made, not just implied. In the statement "He ran like a gazelle," the speed of the runner is compared to that of a gazelle. The title of the spiritual "Sometimes I Feel Like a Motherless Child" is an analogy, comparing the speaker to a child without a mother.

analysis A thought process in which one breaks a subject into parts and then examines the relationships among the parts and the relationships of the parts to the whole. In the literary analysis of a play, for example, one might examine how the plot is developed in its various parts—the exposition, the inciting incident, the rising action, the climax, the falling action, the resolution, and the dénouement. The two final parts of the plot show how the conflict is resolved and how all the characters introduced have been affected. For an example of analysis of a period in African-American history, see Preface to *The New Negro,* by Alain Locke, on page 290.

anapest A poetic foot consisting of two unstressed syllables, followed by one stressed syllable. The rhythm of this triple meter is sounded *da, da, dah,* as in the word *interrupt* or the phrase *on the loose.* The third foot in the last line of "The Day Breakers," by Arna Bontemps, on page 409, is an anapest:

´ ˘ ˘ ´ ˘ ˘ ´ ˘ ´

Beating | a way | for the ris | ing sun.

See *meter.*

anecdote A brief story, usually one that demonstrates a specific point or teaches a specific lesson. Writers sometimes use anecdotes to introduce essays. In his essay "The Negro Artist and the Racial Mountain," on page 314, Langston Hughes told an anecdote about an African-American woman who paid to hear someone sing Andalusian folk songs but who would not pay to hear someone sing African-American folk songs. He told the anecdote to make the point that some African-Americans in his time had insufficient pride in or respect for their own cultural achievements. In the phrase *anecdotal evidence,* the word *anecdote* implies knowledge derived from hearsay (that is, from a story that someone told) rather than from verifiable sources.

antagonist A character in a story who is in conflict with the main character, or protagonist. In the West African oral epic *Sunjata*, the antagonist, Sumanguru, is destroyed because the sister of the protagonist, Sunjata

Keita, coaxes from Sumanguru the secret of his vulnerability. See *character.*

antihero A character who lacks the qualities usually associated with heroes, such as courage, compassion, grace, intelligence, vigor, beauty, or virtue, but who is nonetheless attractive to audiences, often because of his or her defiance of authority. The heroes of the so-called "outlaw songs" like "Po' Lazarus" and "Stagger Lee" are antiheroes. (See pages 212 and 447.)

antithesis The rhetorical technique of drawing a strong contrast between words or ideas. Speakers and writers often emphasize the contrast by using parallel verbal structures, as in the sentence "What we're saying today is that you're either part of the solution or you're part of the problem" (an often-repeated statement by Leroy Eldridge Cleaver, one of the leaders of the Black Power Movement of the 1960s).

aphorism A brief saying that makes a point, usually a moral or philosophical one. An aphorism that is retained in a language for a long time can come to be called a *proverb* or an *adage* and be an expression of folk wisdom. "A hyena cannot smell its own stench" is an aphorism from Kenya. See *maxim.*

apology A defense or justification of some point of view or course of action. When used in its literary sense, the word *apology* does *not* imply belief that one has done something wrong. For example, Martin Luther King's "Letter from a Birmingham Jail" (See page 516) is an apology for breaking a discriminatory law based on the contention that the law was unjust.

apostrophe A literary technique in which a person, place, or thing is directly addressed even though it is not present. Sometimes the thing or phenomenon is addressed as if it were a person. "The Great Hymn to the Aten" on page 38 is an apostrophe to the sun. "Bre'r Sterling and the Rocker," by Michael Harper, on page 612, is an apostrophe addressed to the poet Sterling Brown and to his wife, Daisy.

apposition A word, phrase, or clause that renames something using different words. In the title *Narrative of the Life of Frederick Douglass, An American Slave,* the phrase *An American Slave* is an apposition.

archaic language Language that is ancient or dated. Compare, for example, the archaic but beautiful language of the King James Bible

The earth was without form and void, and darkness was upon the face of the deep; and the Spirit of God was moving over the face of the waters.

with the more modern, informal language of James Weldon Johnson's "The Creation," on page 328:

As far as the eye of God could see
Darkness covered everything,
Blacker than a hundred midnights
Down in a cypress swamp.

archetype An inherited and perhaps unconscious ancestral memory or motif that appears again and again in dreams, thoughts, or cultural artifacts like literary works and paintings. The psychologist Carl Jung believed that archetypes formed an inherited "collective unconscious" with considerable influence on human behavior. More generally, archetypes are familiar patterns in a culture that people can easily identify. So, for example, the call-and-response format might be considered archetypal for people of the African Diaspora. It has deep roots in the culture and appears again and again in many forms, from West African ceremonies to contemporary blues songs. A poem like Hughes's "A Negro Speaks of Rivers," on page 354, is a celebration of archetypal memories. Countee Cullen's "Heritage," on page 382, presents a speaker who cannot escape his archetypal memories of Africa.

argument 1. A prose summary of the theme or meaning of a poem or play. 2. In nonfiction pieces, the case made by the author for accepting a particular point of view or adopting a particular course of action. Thus one might speak of the argument made by Sojourner Truth for the equality of women in "Ar'n't I a Woman," on page 144.

art deco An artistic movement of the 1920s and '30s that involved the use of bold but nonprimary colors and of geometric shapes, particularly zigzags, triangles, concentric circles, and fluted forms. Aaron Douglas's paintings, such as the one on the cover of this book, are examples of art deco.

article A brief work of nonfiction created for a periodical such as a newspaper or magazine or for a collection of works such as an encyclopedia. Sometimes *article* is used interchangeably with *essay,* although the latter term suggests a more serious or involved treatment of a subject. George Schuyler's "Negro-Art Hokum" and Langston Hughes's "The Negro Artist and the Racial Mountain" were both articles written for the June 1926 edition of the *Nation* magazine (See page 314).

aside A statement made by a character in a play but not meant to be heard by other characters. In the past, such a statement was sometimes directed to the audience, but in modern practice might be simply the character talking to himself or herself and being overheard by the audience. Walter's line "We one group of men tied to a race of women with small minds," from Act I of *A Raisin in the Sun* (See page 684) can be delivered as an aside to suggest that Walter would not dare say such a thing in a voice loud enough for his wife to hear it.

assonance The repetition of vowel sounds followed by different consonant sounds, especially in stressed syllables. Consider, for example, these lines from James Weldon Johnson's "Lift Ev'ry Voice and Sing," on page 332:

Lift ev'ry voice and sing,
Till earth and heaven ring,
Ring with the harmonies of Liberty;

Examples of assonance in these lines include the vowel sound in *Lift*, in *Till*, and in the first syllable of *Liberty*, as well as the vowel sounds in *Sing* (or *Ring)* and the last vowel sound in *harmonies*. Most people readily recognize rhyme and alliteration when they see or hear these, but assonance is less commonly recognized though it often contributes greatly, as in Johnson's lines, to creating the musicality of a verse or prose passage.

autobiography The story of a person's life as written or told by that person. *The Narrative of the Life of Frederick Douglass, An American Slave*, Jacobs's *Incidents in the Life of a Slave Girl*, Malcolm X and Haley's *Autobiography of Malcolm X*, and Angelou's *I Know Why the Caged Bird Sings* are examples of autobiographies. Sometimes the term *memoir* is used interchangeably with *autobiography*, but the term *memoir* connotes a less intimate sharing of one's life with a greater emphasis on public events.

background 1. In the visual arts, the part of a work of art that appears to be distant from the viewer, behind the material in the foreground. 2. In a literary work, anything that has happened before the current action or any part that explains the history of a character before the current action.

ballad A narrative poem, often one meant to be sung, conventionally using quatrains, or four-line stanzas, and an *abcb* rhyming pattern. Commonly, ballads have simple rhymes, frequent refrains, and alternating lines of three and four stresses. *Folk ballads*, popular since early medieval times, were passed down orally by wandering troubadours. *Literary ballads* are written down and, although they sometimes use sophisticated techniques, are still basically imitations of folk ballads. "John Henry," on page 211, is an example of a popular American folk ballad. Margaret Walker's "Ballad of the Free," on page 553, is a literary ballad. It borrows from the folk ballad tradition in its format and in its treatment of a number of individuals whose stories have received folk ballad treatment in the past. However, Walker's poem differs from a traditional ballad in that it does not tell a single story but rather shows connections of meaning that tie together a number of stories.

bibliography A list of works used or cited by the author as sources, usually presented alphabetically by the author at the end of a work. Arthur Schomburg's "The Negro Digs Up His Past," on page 304, is not itself a bibliography, though an impressive bibliography of early African American cultural contributions could be prepared based upon the works and creators whom Schomburg mentions in his essay.

biographical criticism The interpretation or evaluation of a work of art based upon information about the life of the artist. So, for example, a reading of Langston Hughes's "The Negro Speaks of Rivers" (See page 354) as the poet's reaction to seeing the Mississippi on a trip south to see his father would be an example of biographical criticism. See *criticism*.

biography An account of a person's life written by someone other than the person. Ann Petry's *Harriet Tubman: Conductor on the Underground Railroad*, excerpted on page 232, is an example of a work that is part biography and part historical fiction. It is fictional to the extent that some parts of the work—some of the specific dialogue, for example—were created by the author and not simply reported.

blank verse Unrhymed verse with a regular (but not necessarily strict) metrical pattern, typically iambic pentameter. An iambic pentameter line consists of five feet, and each foot contains two syllables with the heavier stress on the second syllable. (dee *dum*, dee *dum*, dee *dum*, dee *dum*, dee *dum*). Blank verse is one of the most common forms in English language poetry. "Frederick Douglass," by Robert Hayden, on page 541, is written in blank verse.

blues A variety of indigenous American music that treats as its subject matter various troubles and tribulations and that typically makes use of bent notes, a blues scale, and a call-and-response structure. (See pages 438 and 717.)

cacophony Harsh or unpleasant sound. Sometimes writers purposefully use cacophony for effect, as in these lines from Paul Laurence Dunbar's poem "Sympathy."

I know why the caged bird beats his wing
Till its blood is red on the cruel bars

The sounds in these lines are intentionally cacophonous and so mirror the subject. The hard *c* sounds create a degree of harshness, as does the use of three strongly stressed words together—*caged, bird,* and *beats.* The *b* sounds onomatopoetically mimic the beating of the wings against the cage. The harshness of the language is called for by the subject—frustration and a frantic desire to escape caused by feelings of confinement or lack of freedom that are in turn the result of encounters with racism.

cæsura The major pause in a line of poetry. In most metrical, or rhythmic, poetry, there is one place in each line where there is a natural break, or pause, the cæsura. Vertical lines indicate the cæsuras in the lines below. The lines are from Derek Walcott's beautiful, moving poem "The Season of Phantasmal Peace," on page 620.

Then all the nations of birds | lifted together
the huge net | of the shadows of this earth
in multitudinous dialects, | twittering tongues,
stitching and crossing it. | They lifted up
the shadows of long pines | down trackless slopes.

canon A group of literary or religious works considered authentic or worthy enough to be read and taught by future generations. There has been much debate in the last few decades concerning what works should be considered canonical and therefore worthy of inclusion in school curricula. In previous centuries, there was often disagreement over whether the Western (that is, the European and American) literary canon should include works by modern authors, in addition to works by the classical authors of Greece and Rome. In contemporary times, arguments over the canon often deal with the relative degree of inclusion in the canon of works by women, members of minority groups, and writers from non-Western cultures. Some people would argue that debates about the canon are preposterous because the canon is established by readers. If a book or poem continues to be read by many people, then (or so the argument goes), it is canonical. Others would argue that the canon is established not by ordinary readers but by the judgments of professionals, such as editors of anthologies and professors of literature, who make decisions about what works to promote and what to pass over. In some societies (the former Soviet Union was one), works were considered canonical only if they received official sanction, which was granted only if those works adhered to a particular political ideology or view of history. Many people believe that politics should have nothing to do with such decisions, that a work should be considered canonical only if it clearly has great artistic merit, regardless of the social or political merit of its ideas. A perusal of the masterworks included in *Grace Abounding* should provide ample evidence that African Americans have produced many works that, because of their merit as works of art, deserve inclusion in the canon. And, of course, many of these works are ones that have not, in the past, received due attention. In other words, they are great works that in the past were not considered canonical by the makers of school curricula. See *classic.*

caricature A piece of writing, work of art, or performance that exaggerates certain qualities in order to satirize or ridicule. Minstrel shows of the nineteenth and early twentieth centuries presented extremely offensive caricatures of African Americans. In works of visual art, caricatures typically exaggerate facial or bodily features. Such caricatures are found, for example, in political cartoons. The figures in Frederick Brown's painting *Stagger Lee,* on page 832, are caricatures done for thematic effect. The exaggerations and distortions of these characters reinforce the overall message of the work—that our culture promotes violence.

catalog A literary technique that involves providing a list of people or things. James Weldon Johnson's poem "The Creation," on page 328, contains several catalogs that reflect the abundance of God's creativity, such as this catalog of objects in nature:

Then the green grass sprouted,
And the little red flowers blossomed,
The pine tree pointed his finger to the sky,
And the oak spread out his arms,
The lakes cuddled down in the hollows of the
ground,
And the rivers ran down to the sea;

catastrophe The conclusion of a play, in particular, the final action in a tragedy, the part that depicts the fall of the hero. In the catastrophe, the conflict of the play is finally resolved. See *plot.*

catharsis A purging or release of emotions as a result of an intensely emotional experience, such as viewing or reading a tragic play or novel. The term *catharsis* was used by the Greek philosopher Aristotle to describe the effect of tragedy, which he said should inspire pity and fear in the audience. To read a catalog of horrors such as those depicted in slave narratives like Douglass's *Narrative of the Life of Frederick Douglass* or Harriet Jacobs's *Incidents in the Life of a Slave Girl* (See pages 114 and 130) or like those detailed in the work on lynching by Ida Wells-Barnett (See page 260) is at first to feel anger and outrage. But a great effect is accomplished if that anger, that outrage, is transformed by catharsis into a quiet determination to fight racism and to work toward ensuring that such events are not allowed to occur again.

character A person (or sometimes an animal) who figures in the action of a literary work. *Major characters* are players significantly involved in the conflict, and *minor characters* play lesser roles. Characters are often referred to as rounded, full, multidimensional, or one-dimensional. If a character is *rounded, full,* or *multidimensional,* that means that he or she is adequately developed and gives the impression of being complex, like a person in real life. If a character is *one-dimensional,* he or she is not fully developed. This could be a failure on the part of the author or, in other cases, could be intentional, as in satire. A *stock character* is one found over and over in many works, such as the absent-minded professor or the cruel stepmother. Short-story writers and screenwriters often have to include one-dimensional or stock characters because of the limits of the length of their media. Many works, such as novels, plays, and biographies, show how characters change over time in reaction to conflict. A conflict, for example, might lead the hero of a story to some new knowledge or to some spectacular triumph or failure. A character who changes is a *dynamic character.* One who does not change is a *static character.*

characterization The collection of techniques used to create a character. A writer can depict a character in several ways. The writer can have one character, or perhaps a narrator, directly comment on another character's behavior. The writer can show a character reacting to certain situations or to other characters. The writer can convey the ideas and feelings of a character by means of dialogue or internal monologues or asides. A writer can also create character through descriptions, as of clothing, bodily movements, and facial expressions, or by providing background information or direct assessments of characters. A great fiction writer like Charles Chesnutt or Richard Wright or Zora Neale Hurston can convey character deftly with a few well-chosen details.

chiaroscuro In painting, a technique that emphasizes contrasts in value, that is, between darkness and light.

chiasmus A rhetorical technique in which the order of words or phrases is reversed, often for ironic effect as in "You should eat to live, not live to eat" or "You can weather change, but you can't change the weather." Frederick Douglass makes use of chiasmus frequently in his *Narrative,* as when he says of a cruel overseer, "He was just the man for such a place, and it was just the place for such a man."

chorus See *refrain.*

chronicle A systematic record of historical events, often one that strives to narrate the facts of history without much comment or interpretation. Ida Wells-Barnett's *A Red Record: Tabulated Statistics and Alleged Causes of Lynching in the United States, 1892–1893–1894* (See page 260) contains a chronicle of incidents of lynching over a three-year period.

chronological order The arrangement of events in order of their occurrence, the most common way of organizing narrative material, especially nonfiction. Beginning a narrative in the middle (See *medias res*) is a disruption of chronological order. Short stories such as Alice Walker's "Everyday Use" (See page 646), novels such as William Wells Brown's *Clotelle: A Tale of the Southern States* (See page 192), and plays such as Lorraine Hansberry's *A Raisin in the Sun* (See page 676) are typically organized in chronological order but also often contain flashbacks that treat material before the present time in the story or foreshadowing that treats material after the present time in the story. Contemporary writers like Toni Morrison (See page 672) often play with time and vary from chronological order in order to achieve particular effects.

classic 1. A work of literature, art, or architecture from ancient Greece or Rome. 2. A work of literature that is believed to be central to a particular literary tradition, one that is judged to be part of the canon. Recognized classics of African-American literature include most of the works in *Grace Abounding,* such as *The Souls of Black Folk* and "The Negro Speaks of Rivers." See *canon.*

classicism Techniques or aesthetic principles derived from the study of works by Greek and Roman writers and artists of the classical era. Features that define the classical style in both the visual arts and in literature include clarity, order, moderation, restraint, simplicity, harmony, proportion, and unity. The great African-American sculptor Edmonia Lewis (See page 740) is known for the classicism of her style. The poetry of Derek Walcott (See page 618), though rich in imagery, shows classical elements in the clarity and precision of its language and in its frequent use of understatement. Classicism is most often contrasted with romanticism. See *romanticism.*

cliché A tired or trite expression that once might have been striking or colorful but has lost its impact because of overuse. "Clear as a bell" or "beyond a shadow of a doubt" are examples of clichés. Good writers avoid obvious clichés, though it is almost impossible to write without use of some so-called dead metaphors such as *nightfall* or *foot of a hill,* terms that people commonly use without even being aware that these are metaphorical clichés. Sometimes artistic images can become cliché if they are too well known. The farmer and his wife in Grant Wood's painting *American Gothic,* for example, are so well known as to have become cliché, and the photographer Gordon Parks made *allusions* to this cliché in his portrait photograph of a charwoman (See page 778). See *dead metaphor.*

climax The point of highest interest in a novel, play, short story, or narrative poem, the point at which the conflict reaches its greatest intensity. (The term is sometimes, but incorrectly, used to refer to the *crisis,* the point when something decisive happens to influence the outcome for the central character or to the *resolution,* the point in a story when the central conflict is resolved.) The climax of the *Sunjata* (See page 46) occurs when the final battle against the villain, Sumanguru, takes place. The term *climax* comes from the Greek word for *ladder* and suggests a conflict rising to its highest point. See *plot.*

coherence The effect achieved when the ideas or details in a work are presented in a rational progression. Coherence is achieved by arranging ideas or details in a sensible sequence and by connecting them with transitions. See *transition.*

collage 1. A literary work that brings together disparate materials, such as snatches of dialogue or song, quotations, foreign words, allusions, materials from myth or folklore, graphic elements, news clips, and so forth. The collage technique is frequently used in modern poetry. Michael Harper's "Use Trouble," on page 614, for example, brings together unlikely elements—a praise name in Creole patois, brain science, Italian Renaissance masters, the words of Chief Seattle, weapons, vegetation, and so on to create a coherent whole—an appreciation of the work of painter Jacob Lawrence. 2. The term *collage* as applied to literary works is adapted from the term as used in the visual arts to describe artworks created by juxtaposing and overlaying varying materials. The artist Romare Bearden was a master of collage. He sometimes combined collage and painting techniques in a single work, as in his *New Orleans: Ragging Home* (See page 820), and he sometimes painted in such a way as to imitate collage, as in *Roots Odyssey* (See page 818).

colloquialism The use of informal or everyday language. The poet Sterling Brown (See page 402) and the novelist Zora Neale Hurston (See page 427) were masters of the use of colloquial language for literary effect. See *vernacular.*

color field painting Painting like that of such artists as Mark Rothko or Helen Frankenthaler that makes use of large swaths of uninterrupted color.

comedy A literary work, especially a play, with a happy or successful ending, one in which the main characters avoid disaster or defeat. Originally, in Greek drama, comedies were rowdy affairs presented during festivals celebrating Dionysus, the god of merriment. Later, the term *comedy* came to be associated with happy endings, but not necessarily with rollicking humor. Today, in everyday speech, the term is typically used in its earlier sense to refer to any work that is intentionally funny or outrageous.

commonplace book A collection of quotations derived from various sources. A superb commonplace book could be made containing quotations from materials in *Grace Abounding.*

complication The stage in a plot after the introduction of the central conflict in which that conflict is developed and brought to its point of greatest intensity. In the scene from William Wells Brown's *Clotelle,* on page 192, the conflict is that a young man's beloved is being sold at auction. The complication is the period in the story when the bidding is taking place. See *plot.*

composition 1. A piece of writing. 2. A musical work created by a particular composer or group of composers. 3. In the visual arts, the arrangement of materials within a work, as, for example, the balancing of objects in a painting on either side of a line of symmetry. See *symmetry.*

conceit An elaborate or unusually clever or strained analogy or metaphor, often an extended comparison. Michael Harper's description of Sterling Brown in a rocking chair in "Br'er Sterling and the Rocker," on page 613, is an example of a conceit:

Any fool knows a Br'er in a rocker
is a boomerang incarnate;

concrete A word or phrase that describes something that can be perceived by one or more of the senses. *Clank, cloud, rose,* and *silky* are concrete words. *Justice, hatred, honor,* and *frivolity* are abstract words that describe things that cannot be perceived, directly, by the five senses. In her poem "Magalu," on page 397, Helene Johnson shows herself to be a master of the use of concrete language:

A vulture bears away a foolish jackal.
The flamingo is a dash of pink
Against the dark green mangroves,
Her slender legs rivalling her slim neck.
The laughing lake gurgles delicious music in
its throat
And lulls to sleep the lazy lizard

concrete universal A particular object, person, or action that is meant to suggest a general concept. So, for example, when Countee Cullen writes in his poem "Incident" (See page 378) about a child experiencing a racist incident, the poem is about a single child and about a single incident, but it is also meant to suggest a universal truth, applicable to all people who have experienced such incidents. The concept of the concrete universal is related to the general idea that a writer should show and not tell. That is, good writers present specific, concrete instances that suggest broad, general ideas.

conflict A struggle between two forces or characters in a literary work. The conflict is worked out through the stages of the plot—the complication, climax, falling action, and resolution. The event that introduces the central conflict is called the *inciting incident.* The event that ends the central conflict is called the *resolution.* The main character usually struggles against another character or against nature, society, fate, or some aspect of himself. In the case of the struggle against self, the conflict is *internal* rather than *external.* Nikki Giovanni's poem "Nikki-Rosa," on page 596, describes, in part, an external conflict between the speaker and those outside her who would present stereotypical representations of her experiences. Derek Walcott's poem "A Far Cry from Africa," on page 622, presents an internal conflict between the speaker's need for identification with the cultures of his heritage and his distaste for aspects of those cultures and their histories.

connotation An association attached to an expression as opposed to its literal meaning. Consider, for example, these lines from Helene Johnson's "Magalu," on page 397:

The flamingo is a dash of pink
Against the dark green mangroves,
Her slender legs rivalling her slim neck.

The words *slender* and *slim* are more positive in their connotations than are, say, the words *scrawny* or *skinny.*

consonance The repetition in stressed syllables of identical consonant sounds preceded by different vowel sounds. In the words *linger, languor,* and *longer,* for example, the consonant sound spelled *ng* is preceded by three different vowel sounds. In the following line by poet Paul Lawrence Dunbar, the words *When* and *sun* provide an example of consonance:

When the sun is bright on the upland slopes

convention An arbitrary element in language, in a literary work, or in any other work of art that is accepted by the reader or audience because it is traditional. The capitalization of names, for example, is a convention in written English. It is conventional for a ballad to be divided into four- or six-line stanzas. Many poets of the Black Arts Movement commonly violated, intentionally, many conventions of written English, as in these lines from Ntozake Shange's *for colored girls* (See page 696):

one thing i dont need
is any more apologies
i got sorry greetin me at my front door
you can keep yrs

The poet has intentionally violated the conventions of capitalizing the pronoun *I* and words at the beginnings of sentences, using apostrophes in contractions, and using end marks at the ends of sentences. She has also used unconventional spellings such as *greetin* for *greeting* and *yrs* for *yours.* Some common conventions of literature include writing stories in the past tense and, in the presentation of a play on a stage, imagining that the fourth wall of a room has been removed so that the audience can see the action taking place within. See *dramatic convention.*

couplet A pair of rhyming poetic lines of the same metric length that form a complete unit. These lines from Claude McKay's "Outcast" (See page 351) are a couplet:

For I was born, far from my native clime,
Under the white man's menace, out of time.

See *stanza.*

crisis The point in a story, a play, or any other narrative work at which an event occurs that turns the action decisively in favor of or against the main character. In Toni Cade Bambara's story "Raymond's Run," on page 662, the crisis occurs when the main character sees her brother Raymond running beside her. This event determines the emotional fate of the character. Whether she wins or loses the race will make no difference because she has won something much better than a race: she has won a new-found respect for her little brother. See *plot.*

critic One who practices *criticism,* the interpretation and evaluation of a work of art, such as a story or a painting, based on careful attention to its details and on certain principles or guidelines. See *criticism.*

criticism 1. The interpretation and evaluation of a work of art, such as a story or a painting, based on careful attention to its details. 2. The development or application of general principles to govern such interpretation or evaluation. Literary works and other artistic creations can be viewed from many different perspectives. A particular perspective, along with its associated principles, is called a *school of criticism:*

Biographical criticism looks at the ways in which the lives of artists affect their work.

Deconstructionist criticism attempts to approach a work from a vantage point that denies or varies the binary, or two-part, oppositions that underlie conventional readings of the work. In societies with democratic institutions, for example, people tend to think in terms of the binary opposition *democratic/nondemocratic.* However, a work produced in a society with no experience of democratic institutions would not typically be read or understood in those terms, as either supporting or opposing democracy. So, a reading of the work that dealt with its implications for democracy would be a deconstruction of the conventions imposed upon the work by the culture in which it was produced. Similarly, a reading of a work that conventionally is seen as dealing with democratic values from a cultural stance that is nondemocratic would also be a deconstruction of the work. Deconstructionist criticism is a variety of *postmodernism.*

Didactic criticism deals with the moral lessons that can be learned from works of art.

Feminist, or *gender, criticism* looks at the influence on a work of ideas about gender and gender relations.

Formal criticism looks at a work in terms of its genre, or type, or in terms of its structural characteristics, such as its rhyme scheme or plot structure.

Freudian criticism draws upon the work of Sigmund Freud, the founder of psychoanalysis, and looks at the actions of characters or at works of art as a whole as expressions of unconscious desires, as wish fulfillments, or as workings out of unresolved conflicts, often conflicts from childhood.

Historical criticism looks at the effects on works of art of historical events.

Jungian criticism, based on the work of psychologist Carl Jung, looks at those aspects of works of art that are believed to be archetypal, or related to unconscious images, symbols, associations, or concepts that are part of the common psychological inheritance of human beings. (See *archetype.)*

Marxist criticism, based upon the work of political philosopher Karl Marx, looks at works as shaped by material economic forces, especially as shaped by or as reflecting struggles between members of different economic or social classes.

Mimetic criticism views works of art as being more or less perfect imitations of nature or reality.

New Criticism attempts to interpret and evaluate works of art based upon elements in the works themselves rather than on external information such as the biographies of artists or the historical circumstances in which a work was created.

Rhetorical, or *pragmatic, criticism* looks at a work in terms of its effects on an audience.

Reader-response criticism views a work as having meaning only as a result of the interaction between the work and the subjective, personal experience that the person experiencing the work brings to it.

Romantic, or *expressive, criticism* views a work of art as being primarily an expression of its creator's ideas, beliefs, values, feelings, or spirit.

Structuralist criticism views a work in terms of the binary, or two-part, oppositions that are part of the culture in which the work was produced or in which it is being evaluated or interpreted. So, for example, a structuralist approach to the *Sunjata* might look at the work in terms of its treatment of clan membership or nonmembership (a binary category important in West African culture).

Textual criticism attempts to analyze various existing versions of a work, such as alternate printed versions and author's manuscripts, to arrive at a definitive version.

See *aesthetics, biographical criticism, romantic criticism,* and *textual criticism.*

cubism An artistic movement of the early twentieth century characterized by the reduction and fragmentation of natural forms into abstract and geometrical forms, often forms viewed simultaneously from several different perspectives. Masters of cubism included Pablo Picasso and Georges Braque. For an example of cubism, see the background in Charles White's portrait of John Henry, page 822.

dactyl A poetic foot consisting of a strongly stressed syllable followed by two weakly stressed syllables, as in the words *merrily, prominent,* and *notable.* The third foot in the following line by Langston Hughes is an example of a dactyl: See *meter.*

˘ ´ ˘ ´ ´ ˘ ˘ ´ ˘
The rain | makes still | pools on the | side walk.

dead metaphor A metaphor so familiar that its original metaphorical meaning has been lost or is rarely thought of when the expression is used. *Bed of a river* is an example of a dead metaphor. When Booker T. Washington writes, "I worked long enough to earn money for my *breakfast*," he is using a dead metaphor. A *fast* is a time in which one does not eat. It is metaphorically "broken" when one takes the morning meal. Other examples of dead metaphors include *nightfall* (night does not literally fall) and *seize the moment* (one does not literally grab, or seize, a moment).

deconstructionist criticism See *criticism*.

definition An explanation of the meaning of a word or phrase. There are many varieties of definition. One can define a term, for example, by reference to a thing in the world named by the word. This is called *ostensive* or *referential definition*. For example, one can define *platypus* by pointing to such an animal or by showing a picture of one. One can also define a word by example or illustration. So, for example, one might define the term *conifer* by giving examples of conifers: they include cedars, pines, and firs. Dictionaries typically define terms by placing them in a group (a genus, or class) and then showing how the things described by the word differ from other things in that group. This method is called *genus and differentia definition*. For example, the word *blues* might be defined as a type of American folk music (genus) characterized by use of the blues scale, bent or slurred notes, a 12-bar or similar organization, and lyrics that deal with woes or troubles (differentia).

denotation That part of the meaning of a word that includes only what the word specifically refers to, as opposed to any associations, or *connotations*, that the word might also have. Good writers choose from among the words that they might use those that have appropriate associations, or connotations, in addition to their denotations. So, for example, the words *stingy* and *thrifty* both have the denotation "careful about spending money." However, *stingy* suggests a negative evaluation of this character trait, whereas *thrifty* suggests a positive evaluation of the same trait. In slave narratives, people often wrote about their "masters." By doing so, of course, they were using the denotative meaning "an owner of a slave," but few of the authors of slave narratives would have accepted the connotations that a word like *master* has—the connotations of superiority and legitimate authority, for example.

dénouement See *plot*.

desaturation In the visual arts, use of a color that is not intense, that looks light or washed out. See *saturation*.

description A type of writing that presents a portrait, in words, of some subject, using sensory details to show how the subject looks, feels, smells, sounds, or tastes. Chapter XXII of Harriet Jacobs's *Incidents in the Life of a Slave Girl*, on page 137, begins with a vivid description of the small space in which she was confined for many years. Her description is concrete enough to enable the reader to picture the scene in his or her mind. See *mode*.

dialect A version of a language spoken by people of a particular place or social group. Dialects differ in their lexicon (in the words they contain) and in details of their pronunciation, grammar, and usage. There are many regional dialects in American English. There are also dialects spoken by members of different socioeconomic and ethnic groups. Zora Neale Hurston used rural Southern dialect to make the characters in *Their Eyes are Watching God* seem realistic and believable. In the early part of the twentieth century, many white editors encouraged African-American authors to write "dialect pieces," to conform to stereotypes about how African-American writing was supposed to sound. Some poets, like Paul Laurence Dunbar, wrote masterfully both in dialect and in Standard English.

dialogue Conversation involving two or more persons in a play, novel, short story, or dramatic or narrative poem. A novel uses dialogue, narration, and description to depict action and character. A play uses dialogue and stage directions.

diary A daily record of a person's experiences, activities, thoughts, and feelings. Many writers keep diaries that they expect to be published or that they mine for material to be used in their work.

diction 1. Word choice. Because the English language is so large and has borrowed so widely from other languages, writers in English can vary their diction considerably to suit particular occasions, audiences, and tones. So, for example, a writer might speak very formally of the *attire* or *apparel* at a fancy dinner or very informally of the *threads* or *duds* worn by hippies in the 1960s. A character's diction can reveal quite a lot about him or her. It might show, for example, that a character is blunt, conceited, sophisticated, naive, old-fashioned, hip, or diplomatic. It might reveal the character's social class or his or her profession. Precise diction, or word choice, is one of the characteristics of good writing. So, for example, Arna Bontemps did not write, "A dry leaf brushes against the wall." Instead, he wrote, "A dry leaf trembles on the wall." The words *trembles on* help to create the mood of his poem "Southern Mansion" (See page 410). 2. The degree of clarity and distinctness of a person's pronunciation in speech or in singing. The singer Paul Robeson (See page 458) was known for his superb diction. See *register* and *style.*

didactic criticism See *criticism.*

didactic poem A verse whose central aim is to teach a lesson. Langston Hughes's "Harlem [2]" (See page 364) is a didactic poem. So is Phillis Wheatley's "On Being Brought from Africa to America" (See page 175).

dimeter See *meter.*

drama A story told through characters played by actors. Dramas make use of *dialogue* (the words of the characters) and *stage directions* (notes that the author provides to describe scenes or the movements and speech of characters). In addition, dramas involve *spectacle*—what the audience sees, including costumes, make-up, stage sets, music, sound effects, and lighting. Lorraine Hansberry's *A Raisin in the Sun,* on page 676, is an example of a drama. Some great contemporary African-American dramatists include Charles Fuller, Charles Dordone, Anna Deaver Smith, and August Wilson.

dramatic convention An unrealistic or artificial element of a dramatic presentation that is accepted by the audience as if it were natural. For example, there should be a fourth wall when a stage setting depicts a room, but an audience accepts without question the dramatic convention of the removal of the fourth wall so that the audience can see the action. Similarly, an audience accepts a curtain's closing as indicating the end of a period of time in the story unfolding on stage. Acceptance of dramatic conventions involves, in the words of the English poet Samuel Taylor Coleridge, "a willing suspension of disbelief." See *convention.*

dramatic monologue A poem that presents the voice of a single speaker who tells or suggests a story. Ntozake Shange's verse play *for colored girls* is made up of a number of dramatic monologues. The selection from that play entitled "lady in blue" (See page 696) is one example.

dramatis personae A Latin phrase for the characters in a literary work, mostly used to refer to the list of characters in a play. See, for example, the list at the beginning of *A Raisin in the Sun,* on page 676.

dynamic character See *character.*

dystopia An imaginary world that is extremely unpleasant, the opposite of a utopia. Kevin Willmott's *CSA: The Confederate States of America* is a mock documentary film that tells the story of what might have happened had the South won the Civil War and if slavery had consequently been extended throughout the country. The film presents a dystopia in which racism underlies U.S. foreign policy from that point on.

editorial A short piece of writing intended to persuade that appears in a newspaper, magazine, or other periodical. Frederick Douglass wrote many editorials for his newspaper *The North Star* in order to advance the cause of abolition. See *periodical.*

effect The general impression or emotional impact made by a work of art or some portion thereof. See *objective correlative.*

elaboration In writing, the technique of expanding upon a subject, after it has been introduced, by any of a number of means, such as giving examples or illustrations, telling a story that proves the point, comparing or contrasting, analyzing the parts of the subject, or making analogies to similar things or circumstances.

elegy A long, formal poem lamenting death or loss. Rita Dove's "Parsley," on page 606, is an elegy for the victims of a massacre that occurred in the Dominican Republic.

end rhyme Rhyme that occurs at the ends of lines of verse. This stanza from Arna Bontemps's "A Black Man Talks of Reaping" (See page 411) contains end rhyme:

I scattered seed enough to plant the land
In rows from Canada to Mexico
But for my reaping only what the hand
Can hold at once is all that I can show.

end-stopped line A line of verse in which both the sense, or meaning, and the grammatical unit are complete at the end of the line. The opposite of the end-stopped line is the *run-on line* in which the meaning is carried over to the next line or the next several lines. The following lines by the poet Countee Cullen are run-on, although there is a major pause after the first line.

Now, will the poets sing, —
Their cries go thundering
Like blood and tears
Into the nations' ears,
Like lightning dart
Into the nation's heart.

The following lines by the poet Waverly Turner Carmichael (See page 339) are end-stopped:

Hear me as I cry to Thee;
Keep me, Jesus, keep me;
May I that bright glory see;
Keep me, Jesus, keep me.

See *run-on line.*

enjambment See *run-on line.*

epic A long, serious story, often told in verse, that depicts the actions of gods and heroes and that presents a portrait of an entire culture, including its values and ways of life. The *Sunjata* (See page 46) is an epic poem from Mali, West Africa. In his poem "Map of the New World: I Archipelagoes," on page 624, Derek Walcott draws upon material from the *Iliad* and the *Odyssey*, two great epics from classical Greece.

epigram A brief, witty saying. The Reverend Dr. Martin Luther King, Jr.'s statement "A man can't ride your back unless it's bent" is an example of an epigram. See *aphorism* and *maxim.*

epigraph A short inscription, often a quotation, used at the beginning of a literary work or at the beginning of one of its sections, often to establish the theme of the work. At the beginning of his first autobiography, Frederick Douglass quoted these lines from a poem by John Greenleaf Whittier as an epigraph:

What, ho!—our countrymen in chains!
The whip on woman's *shrinking flesh!*
Our soil still reddening with the stains,
Caught from her scourging, warm and fresh!
What! mothers from their children riven!
What! God's own image bought and sold!
Americans *to market driven,*
And barter'd as the brute, for gold!

epithet A word or phrase used to describe something characteristic of that person, making him or her easily identifiable. Epithets are a common feature of West African praise poems. So, for example, in the *Sunjata* (See page 46), the person who fired the arrow that killed Sumanguru is referred to with the epithet "arrow on the forehead Faa Ganda." In the "Great Hymn to the Aten," on page 38, the pharaoh Akhenaten refers to the Aten using a number of epithets, including "Lord of eternity," "giver of breath," "Lord of all," and "sole God without equal." See *praise poem.*

epilogue A concluding section or declaration, usually brief and usually summing up the larger meaning of the work.

epiphany In literary usage, a moment of sudden insight. In his confession, Nat Turner described an epiphany in which he understood what his mission in life was to be—to lead a slave rebellion (See page 104).

episode A self-contained section of a literary work. "The Slave Auction," on page 192, is an episode from William Wells Brown's novel *Clotelle: A Tale of the Southern States.*

eponym A person or character whose name is the source of a word. For example, either Colonel Charles Lynch or William Lynch is the eponym of the word *lynching* (See page 267).

essay A brief nonfiction composition, usually on a single subject. A good essay is characterized by coherence and clarity but is not expected to be an exhaustive treatment of its subject. The word *essay* derives from a French word meaning "a trial or an attempt." The word still retains some of this connotation, and so it is expected that an essay will be a reasonably brief and sometimes tentative exploration of a subject. Arthur Schomburg's "The Negro Digs Up His Past," on page 304, and Langston Hughes's "The Negro Artist and the Racial Mountain," on page 314, are examples of essays.

euphemism An indirect or polite word or phrase used in place of a word or idea that might be considered unpleasant or crude or offensive. "The peculiar institution" is a euphemism often used in the past to describe slavery in the American South.

euphony A pleasing, harmonious sound. Euphony can be achieved by using various literary techniques, such as rhythm, rhyme, parallelism, or the repetition of vowel and consonant sounds. Euphony is the opposite of cacophony, or harsh sound. Notice how all of these techniques are used to create euphony in these lines from Gwendolyn Bennet (See page 372):

I want to see the slim palm trees,
Pulling at the clouds
With little pointed fingers. . . .

I want to see lithe Negro girls,
Etched dark against the sky
While sunset lingers.

exposition 1. A kind of nonfiction writing that presents factual information, also known as *informative writing.*

2. In a work of fiction, the part of the story that presents background information such as details of the setting or basic information about the characters. In this sense, the term is typically used to refer to any material presented in a story before the *inciting incident* (the incident that introduces the central conflict). See *mode.*

expository writing See *exposition.*

expressionism A twentieth-century movement in art, drama, and literature that reacted against realism and exaggerated aspects of the medium of the art in order to portray (or express) emotions, particularly those brought on by the irrational and confusing elements of modern life. Beauford Delaney's "Can Fire in the Park," on page 786, is painted in an expressionist style. Notice the thick textures of the paint, the obvious brush strokes, and the thick outlines, all of which draw attention to the medium and add to the overall emotional effect.

expressive criticism See *romantic criticism.*

extended metaphor A figure of speech in which one thing is described as though it were something else and in which several points of comparison are made. Billie Holiday's song "Strange Fruit" is an example of an extended metaphor, in which bodies of people who have been lynched are compared to fruit.

falling action See *plot.*

Fauves, Les In French, literally "the wild beasts." A term applied to a group of painters, including Henri Matisse and Andre Dérain, who made unnaturally bold use of color and otherwise departed from the tenets of realism.

Fauvism See *Fauves, Les.*

feet See *meter.*

feminist criticism See *criticism.*

fiction Prose writing, especially short stories and novels, in which the author presents imagined events or people.

field holler A variety of indigenous American song created and sung by individuals working in fields as enslaved persons or sharecroppers. The field holler was one of the precursors of the blues. Field hollers can be distinguished from work songs because the former were sung by individuals, while the latter were sung by groups. Some field hollers, however, made use of call and response, wherein an individual would sing the main part of the holler and the group would sing a refrainlike response. (See page 207.)

figurative language Language that suggests more than what is conveyed by the literal meanings of the words. Types of figurative language include metaphors and similes. See *figures of speech.*

figures of speech Also called *tropes,* expressions that have more than a literal meaning. Besides metaphor and simile, figures of speech include hyperbole, personification, synaesthesia, synecdoche, and understatement. See *figurative language.*

first-person point of view See *narrator* and *point of view.*

flashback A literary device that depicts an event that took place before the action being currently described. A mystery, for example, might clue the reader in by flashing back to the actual scene of a crime already committed and in the process of being solved. A writer or speaker often uses the technique of the flashback to provide the reader or listener with background information. So, for example, when Bamba Suso, the griot who tells the selection from the *Sunjata* included in this text (See page 46), pauses to tell about Sunjata Keita's peculiar birth (how he was carried by two mothers), this is an example of a flashback.

flash fiction See *short short.*

focus See *rule of thirds.*

foil A character who contrasts with another character. Such a contrast often emphasizes key traits of the central character, important to the theme of the story. For example, in the selection from Maya Angelou's *I Know Why the Caged Bird Sings* (See page 504), Miss Glory serves as a foil for the main character. Miss Glory patiently bears the insulting behavior of Mrs. Cullinan, whereas the central character reacts against this behavior in a dramatic way (by breaking some dishes). The contrast between the main character and Miss Glory helps to emphasize the characteristics of each.

folk song An anonymous song that is passed down orally from generation to generation. "John Henry," on page 211, and "Stagger Lee," on page 448, are examples of folk songs.

folktale A brief story passed down orally through many generations. "All Stories Are Anansi's," on page 14, and "The Headless Hant," on page 164, are folk tales from West Africa and the United States, respectively.

foot A unit of rhythm in a poetic line, consisting of stressed and unstressed syllables. See specific types of feet: *anapest, dactyl, iamb, spondee,* and *trochee.* See *meter.*

foreground 1. In the visual arts, that part of a work that appears to be closest to the viewer. 2. In a work of literature, the present action, as opposed to the background. See background, sense 2.

foreshadowing The act of presenting material that suggests what will happen later in a story. This can be spoken material or perhaps music or sound effects that hint at some ominous or happy event to come later in the plot. At the beginning of Nat Turner's confession, Turner tells a brief story about a miraculous event that occurred when he was a child. This story foreshadows the unusual events that are going to occur later in his story.

foreword. See *preface.*

formal criticism See *criticism.*

free verse Poetry that does not use regular rhyme and does not divide the verses into conventional stanzas with standard meters. Free verse does, however, include some metrical effects and many other poetic techniques designed to make it musical, including alliteration, assonance, and consonance. James Weldon Johnson's "The Creation," on page 328, and Mari Evans's "I Am a Black Woman," on page 572, are examples of free verse. See *alliteration, assonance, consonance,* and *meter.*

full character See *character.*

gender criticism See *criticism.*

genre A category of literary work. Genres of literature can be defined in terms of structure and type of language used. *Novel, short story, poem, ballad, lyric, narrative poem, dramatic poem, essay, drama, tragedy,* and *comedy* are all examples of genres in this sense. Genres of literature can also be defined in terms of content. *Autobiography, biography, spiritual, outlaw song, praise song, fable, detective story, adventure story, mystery, slave narrative, romance, western,* and *science fiction* are all genres in this sense.

griot A traditional West African singer and storyteller who performs accompanied by traditional instruments such as the kora or balafon. Also known as a *jali.* See the *Sunjata,* page 46.

haiku A traditional Japanese poem containing three lines with five syllables in the first line, seven in the second, and five in the third. It is intended to present a precise image that will arouse a specific emotion in the reader. Here is an example of a haiku.

In the pink twilight
Each star wakes from slumber.
Tossing silver rays.

See the selected haiku from *Love Poems,* by Sonia Sanchez, on page 585. Note that Sanchez takes some liberties with the traditional haiku form.

Harlem Renaissance A dynamic period during the 1920s and '30s, of intense creative activity among African-American writers, musicians, poets, and visual artists living in or connected with the Harlem neighborhood of New York City. The period is also called the Jazz Age because the growth of jazz, particularly among African-American musicians, ran parallel with the growth of other art forms. Important figures of the Harlem Renaissance include Gwendolyn Bennett, Sterling Brown, Arna Bontemps, Countee Cullen, Aaron Douglas, Langston Hughes, Zora Neale Hurston, Alain Locke, Claude McKay, Arthur Schomburg, and Jean Toomer.

heptameter See *meter.*

heroic epic An epic whose main purpose is to relate the feats of a great hero and illustrate what cultural values are represented by this hero. Homer's *Iliad,* for example, tells the story of the brave but impetuous Achilles, hero of the Trojan War, and the *Odyssey* relates the adventures of the wily Odysseus, who makes his difficult way home from the Trojan War by using his intelligence more than his strength. The *Sunjata,* a West African heroic epic (See page 46), tells the story of Sunjata Keita, the legendary "Lion King" who founded the Mali Empire.

hexameter See *meter.*

historical criticism See *criticism.*

hue In the visual arts, the color of a given element, for example, vermilion, teal, or burnt sienna.

hymn A religious song or verse of worship or praise. Akhenaten's "Great Hymn to the Aten," on page 38, and Waverly Turner Carmichael's "Keep Me, Jesus, Keep Me," on page 339, are examples of hymns.

hyperbole An exaggeration made for effect. Frederick Douglass used hyperbole (and a series of metaphors) when he wrote, "It is not light that is needed, but fire; it is not the gentle shower, but thunder. We need the storm, the whirlwind, and the earthquake."

iamb A poetic foot containing one weakly stressed syllable, followed by one strongly stressed syllable, as in the words *destroy, awake,* and *insist.* Poetry consisting mostly of iambs is called *iambic.* The following line by Alice Dunbar Nelson (See page 343) is written in iambic pentameter: See meter.

˘ ´ ˘ ´ ˘ ´ ˘ ´ ˘ ´
I sit | and sew— | a use | less task | it seems.

See *meter.*

iambic pentameter See *meter.*

Iambic tetrameter See *meter.*

image A word or phrase that describes how something looks, tastes, feels, smells, or sounds. For examples of poems that make exceptional use of imagery, see "The Tropics in New York," by Claude McKay, on page 350, and "Magalu," by Helene Johnson, on page 396.

imagism A twentieth-century literary movement that involved creating very brief works that presented vivid images intended to evoke particular states in the reader.

impasto In the visual arts, the application of thick layers of paint to a canvas or other surface.

impressionism A style of painting that originated in France in the 1870s and that was characterized by the attempt to reproduce the immediate visual impression created by a scene, typically a natural scene, and involving the use of primary colors and small brush strokes to give the impression of reflected light.

inciting incident See *plot.*

informative writing See *exposition.*

introduction See *preface.*

inversion A poetic technique in which the normal order of words is changed. In Dunbar's poem "Symphony," on page 324, the poet inverts the normal word order in the line "But a plea, that upward to Heaven he flings—." The normal order would be "He flings a plea upward to heaven."

irony A difference between what is said and what is meant or between what something is and what it appears to be. *Verbal irony* occurs when what is intended is the opposite of what is said. *Dramatic irony* occurs when the reader or viewer knows something that is hidden from a character in the story. *Situational irony* occurs when an event takes place that is extremely surprising because it contradicts expectations, logic, or common sense.

jali See *griot.*

jazz A sophisticated variety of indigenous American music involving the use of swing rhythms and improvisation. There are many subgenres of jazz, including Dixieland, bebop, hard bop, cool jazz, hot jazz, and free jazz. (See pages 460 and 704.)

journal A record of day-to-day activities, sometimes used interchangeably with *diary.* The term *journal* implies a record of public activities, whereas the term *diary* implies a record of personal, subjective responses to events.

jubilee See *spiritual.*

Jungian criticism See *criticism.*

lithograph A print produced by lithography, a printing process in which the image to be printed is rendered on a flat surface, such as a sheet of aluminum, and treated to retain ink while the nonimage areas are treated to repel ink.

limited point of view See *narrator* and *point of view.*

linocut In the visual arts, a work produced by etching lines onto a linoleum block, inking the block, and then pressing paper against it. See *woodcut.*

lyric poem A non-narrative poem with musical qualities, usually one that is short, is written in stanzas, and expresses the emotions of a speaker. Paul Laurence Dunbar's "We Wear the Mask," on page 322, Georgia Douglas Johnson's "The Heart of a Woman," on page 344, and Langston Hughes's "Song for a Dark Girl," on page 368, are examples of lyric poems.

magical realism Fiction that combines both realistic and fantastic, unrealistic elements. Tony Morrison's novel *Beloved* (See page 672) is an example of magical realism.

Marxist criticism See *criticism.*

maxim A short, pithy statement or aphorism believed to contain wisdom or insight into human nature. A maxim might suggest a good rule of conduct, as in Maya Angelou's "Nothing will work unless you do" (See page 513).

medias res, in A Latin phrase meaning "in the middle of things," referring to the narrative and dramatic convention of beginning the action at some point in the middle of a story. This convention is commonly followed in epic poetry and in many contemporary novels and plays.

metaphor A figure of speech in which one thing is spoken of or written about as if it were another thing. The implied comparison is often surprising and meant to point to some feature of the subject that might not otherwise be noticed. In Dunbar's poem "We Wear the Mask," on page 322, the opening lines "We wear the mask that grins and lies, / It hides our cheeks and shades our eyes,—", the speaker is not referring to real masks; rather the mask is a metaphor for a happy face that one puts on, for pretending not to be hurt when one is actually suffering greatly. A metaphor results whenever the reader or listener is invited to make an indirect comparison, as in "He is a snake." In the type of metaphor known as the *simile,* an indirect comparison is made using *like* or *as:* "He is like a snake." In an *analogy,* a comparison is directly made. One thing is said to share a characteristic of another but is not directly identified with the other: "He is as mean as a snake." A *personification* is a type of metaphor in which a nonhuman thing is described as being in some way human or humanlike. See *simile, dead metaphor, mixed metaphor,* and *personification.*

meter A regular pattern of stressed and lightly stressed (sometimes called "unstressed") syllables. A unit of stressed and lightly stressed syllables is called a *foot.*

An *iambic foot,* or *iamb,* has a weak stress followed by a strong stress, as in the words *undo* and *afraid.*

An *anapestic foot,* or *anapest,* has two weak stresses followed by one strong stress, as in *in a pinch* or *understand.*

A *trochaic foot,* or *trochee,* has a strong stress followed by a weak stress, as in *fever* or *Help me!*

A *dactylic foot,* or *dactyl,* has a strong stress followed by two weak stresses, as in *feverish* or *subtlety.*

A *spondaic foot,* or *spondee,* has two strong stresses, as in *baseball* or *drop dead.*

A *pyrrhic foot,* or *pyrrhic,* has two weak stresses. The existence of pyrrhic feet is controversial, as some experts in scansion, the analysis of meters, insist that every foot must have at least one strong stress.

The following terms are used to describe lines with varying numbers of feet:

monometer: one foot to a line
dimeter: two feet to a line
trimeter: three feet to a line
tetrameter: four feet to a line
pentameter: five feet to a line
hexameter: six feet to a line (also called *Alexandrine)*
heptameter: seven feet to a line
octameter: eight feet to a line

A description of the meter of a poem includes which kind of foot predominates as well as the number of feet occurring in most of the lines. In English the most common meters are *iambic tetrameter* and *iambic pentameter.*

metonymy A figure of speech in which the name of an object is replaced by the name of a thing associated with that object. Calling a monarch *the crown* is an example of metonymy, as is using *Wall Street* to stand for the whole world of financial trading.

mimetic criticism See *criticism.*

minimalism A movement in late-twentieth-century art that involved extreme simplifications of content and form.

minor character See *character*

mixed metaphor An expression or passage that uses more than one metaphor, back to back, to describe a single subject. Describing a subject using a number of different metaphors is fine when the metaphors are not meant to be thought of simultaneously or when they do not contradict one another. Thus it is fine for Langston Hughes to compare a dream deferred to, in turn, a raisin in the sun, an open sore, and an explosion. Problems can occur when metaphors are mixed and not clearly presented in such a way as to be thought of separately. Consider, for example, the following example of badly mixed metaphors: *"Our staff is swamped with work, and the battle axe of a department manager is trying to load us down right up to the gills."* This sentence employs the metaphorical verb *swamped,* compares the department manager to a military weapon, compares the workers to fish, and then suggests that these fish are being loaded like a container or perhaps a beast of burden. And it is clear from the sentence that the writer doesn't know up from down. One cannot imagine what it is like to be a loaded-down (or up) fish swamped by an axe. The metaphors break down when thought of together, and so the sentence fails.

mode A form or type of writing. Common modes of writing include *exposition* (or *informative writing), persuasion, description,* and *narration. Expository writing* presents information. *Persuasive writing* attempts to convince people to adopt a belief or to take a course of action. *Descriptive writing* paints a picture of something in words. *Narrative writing* tells a story. Some teachers of writing also distinguish a mode that they call *expressive writing*—writing that has as its main purpose conveying the feelings of the writer. See *aim.*

modernism A general, somewhat vague term for a movement in the arts, including poetry, literature, philosophy, architecture, and the fine arts that began in the early twentieth century (or some say at the end of the nineteenth century) and that was characterized by an embrace of the irrational and the experimental. Modernism encompasses many other artistic movements, among them surrealism and primitivism. The essence of modernism lay in the desire to "make it new," that is, to innovate. Langston Hughes was modernist in his attempt to capture the rhythms of jazz in free verse. Romare Bearden was modernist in his combination of painting with collage.

mood The emotion created in the reader by the overall tone of a literary work. Mood is established by the use of atmospheric details, language, characterization, plot, pacing, and other literary techniques. The word comes from the Anglo-Saxon word *mód,* meaning heart or spirit. For example, the mood of Langston Hughes's "Song for a Dark Girl," on page 368, could be described as despairing.

monochromatic Consisting of or using only one color, typically various shades of that color.

monometer See *meter.*

mosaic 1. A design or picture made with pieces of broken glass, pottery, stone, or other material. 2. A literary work done in imitation of a mosaic, for example, one that is made up of bits and pieces gathered from various sources.

motif An element that recurs frequently within a work of literature or among a collection of literary works. Motifs common to folktales include three wishes; the transformation of an animal into a human (or vice versa); the grateful dead; the beautiful, endangered princess; and the cruel stepmother. The romance tradition often included the motif of a hero on a quest or subjected to some difficulty, or trial. Both "All Stories Are Anansi's," on page 14, and "Tug of War," on page 26, make use of the motif of the trickster character who uses guile to overcome physically stronger opponents.

motivation A force that moves a character to think, feel, or act in a certain way. In the selection from Alice Walker's "Everyday Use," on page 646, the main character is motivated by a desire to protect the interests of the daughter who has remained home with her. See *motive.*

motive A feeling that moves a character to act in a certain way. See *motivation.*

multidimensional character See *character.*

Muse One of a number of characters from Greek and Roman myth believed to inspire or guide the creation of various arts and sciences. The Muses were the nine daughters of Zeus and Mnemosyne, or Memory. They are listed below along with their spheres of influence.

- Calliope (epic poetry)
- Clio (history)
- Euterpe (lyric poetry/music)
- Melpomene (tragedy)
- Terpsichore (choral dance)
- Erato (love poetry)
- Polyhymnia (hymns and sacred poems)
- Urania (astronomy)
- Thalia (comedy)

The words *amuse* and *amusement* are remnants in our vocabulary of the belief in muses.

myth A story that explains events or objects in the natural world, such as how the world came to be or why parts of it are as they are. Myths are often religious in nature and describe the actions of the gods. "All Stories Are Anansi's," on page 14, is an example of a myth that explains the origins of Anansi stories.

narration 1. What a narrator does. See *narrator.* 2. Writing that tells a story. See *mode.*

narrative poem A poem that tells a story. "The Signifying Monkey," on page 168, and "The Creation," on page 328, are examples of narrative poems.

narrator The assumed voice that tells a story. In a work of fiction, the narrator can be a main character or minor character who tells the story in the *first person,* using pronouns like *I, we,* and *me.* Or the narrator can be someone outside the narrative who tells it in the *third person,* using pronouns like *he, she,* and *they.* A third-person narrator can be *omniscient.* When a story is told from a *third-person omniscient point of view,* the narrator knows all and can, for example, report what is going on in all the characters' minds, including how they feel about events and about one another. When a story is told from a *limited point of view,* either in the first person or in the third person, the narrator knows only his or her mind and has no privileged knowledge of the internal states of other characters. In a first-person narrative, the storyteller can be *reliable* or *unreliable.* An *unreliable narrator* is one that cannot be trusted, often one who misinterprets events and misunderstands the motives of the other characters. Usually, in modern drama, there is no narrator, and the action of the play advances entirely through dialogue. There are some exceptions among modern dramas, however, such as the play *Our Town,* which makes use of a narrator who comes on stage and comments on the action. See *point of view.*

naturalism A literary movement of the late nineteenth and early twentieth century that produced works that portrayed people's lives as being determined by forces of heredity or environment over which the people themselves had little or no control. Influenced by the work of Charles Darwin, naturalist writers depicted human beings with what was regarded as scientific realism and often showed life at its most challenging. Richard Wright's story "The Man Who Saw the Flood," on page 632, is an example of naturalism. See *aesthetics.*

neoclassicism A revival of the techniques and aesthetic principles that held sway in the classical world of Greece and Rome. Interest in these techniques and principles was particularly strong during the period called the Enlightenment and was felt in literature and the fine arts as well as in architecture. The influence of neoclassicism can be seen in the federal architecture of the new American republic as well as in the writings of Franklin and Jefferson. Neoclassicists value harmony, moderation, proportion, simplicity, wit, and unity. Neoclassical writers focused primarily on social life and social interactions instead of on the subjective emotional states of individuals, and they often dealt with moral or ethical themes in a didactic, or teacherly, manner. Edmonia Lewis's *Hagar,* on page 740, is a fine example of neoclassical sculpture by an African-American artist. The poems of Jupiter Hammon (See page 172) and Phillis Wheatley (See page 175) are neoclassical in both subject and style.

New Criticism See *criticism.*

nonfiction Prose writing that concerns real events. Types of nonfiction include the essay, the autobiography, the biography, news, speeches, and editorials.

nonsense verse A kind of amusing, light verse, that contains elements that are absurd or apparently meaningless.

novel A long work of narrative fiction written in prose. Although there were some earlier precedents, the form gained prominence in the eighteenth century, at the time in which *Gulliver's Travels* and *Robinson Crusoe* were written. *Clotelle: A Tale of the Southern States,* excerpted on page 192, is one version of the first novel ever published by an African-American writer.

novella A short novel. *Their Eyes Were Watching God,* by Zora Neale Hurston (See page 426), is sometimes referred to as a novella.

objective correlative A term coined by the American poet T. S. Eliot in an essay on *Hamlet* to describe the use of a set of images that work together to create a particular emotional response in the reader or audience. See *effect.*

octameter See *meter.*

octave An eight-line stanza. See *sonnet* and *stanza.*

octet An eight-line stanza. See *sonnet* and *stanza.*

off rhyme See *slant rhyme.*

omniscient point of view See *narrator* and *point of view.*

one-dimensional character See *character.*

onomatopoeia The use of words or phrases that imitate the sounds to which they refer. Words like *buzz, rattle, moan,* and *click* are onomatopoeic words. Certain letter combinations can also create sounds that mimic the subject being described. The word *humming,* from Mari Evans's "I Am a Black Woman" (See page 573) is onomatopoetic:

and I
can be heard humming in the night

oral tradition The passing of ideas, customs, stories, poems, and motifs from generation to generation by word of mouth. Many African-American spirituals, like "Follow the Drinking Gourd," are products of the oral tradition. So are many early field hollers, work songs, and blues songs. Common products of the oral tradition include folktales, fairy tales, fables, proverbs, legends, myths, riddles, parables, and ballads. "The White Man and the Snake," on page 25, and "Tar Baby," on page 160, are examples of works from the oral traditions of West Africa and the United States, respectively.

oxymoron Statements or terms that are self-contradicting. *Sweet sorrow, small crowd,* and *working vacation* are examples. Typically, an oxymoron presents a contradiction that makes sense at a deeper level. The phrase *wise fool,* for instance, might be used to indicate that wisdom sometimes appears like foolishness to those who are not wise or that it is wise to cultivate a state of frivolity (or foolishness).

palindrome A word, phrase, or statement that reads the same backward as forward. Examples include the words *radar, civic,* and *level.* The statements *I prefer pi; Madam, I'm Adam;* and *Able was I ere I saw Elba* are also palindromes. The latter statement refers to the exile of the emperor Napoleon on the island Elba.

parable A short narrative with human characters that teaches a moral lesson, a psychological reality, or a general truth. Christ uses many parables in the gospels to instruct his disciples. Such parables include "The Prodigal Son" and "The Good Samaritan." Parables are similar to fables in their use of stories for moral instruction, but differ in that fables use animal characters. The story "Hercules and the Wagoner," discussed on page 261, is an example of a parable.

paradox A contradictory statement, idea, or occurrence. Some paradoxes seem sensible on the surface but are actually self-contradictory. For example, if a student says, "All students are liars," one can conclude that, if she is telling the truth, then she is lying. But if she is lying, then she is telling the truth. Paradoxes appear quite commonly in literature, as in Shakespeare's famous line from *Julius Caesar,* "Cowards die many times before their deaths." A paradox can sometimes be identified as an oxymoron or as an irony. In "What to the Slave Is the Fourth of July?" (See page 122), Frederick Douglass asserts that it is a paradox to ask a former slave to speak on a day that celebrates freedom when many of his brothers and sisters are still enslaved. In his poem "Yet Do I Marvel," Countee Cullen asserts that it is a paradox to be born African American and a poet:

Yet do I marvel at this curious thing:
To make a poet black, and bid him sing!

See *oxymoron* and *irony.*

parallelism A rhetorical technique in which a writer underscores the equal value of two ideas by expressing them using similar grammatical structures. Careful attention to parallel structure is often the key to effective writing. Consider the difference between the following sentences. The first uses proper parallelism. The second doesn't: (1) Mary, a good speaker, uses diction that is clear, precise, and colorful. (2) Mary likes to write poems and play music. Parallelism is used in these lines from Huddie Ledbetter's song "Goodnight, Irene":

Sometimes I live in the city.
Sometimes I live in the town.
Sometimes I take a great notion
To jump in the river and drown.

paraphrase A rewriting of a passage in different words. A paraphrase differs from a summary or an abstract in that it may be as long as, or even longer than, the original. Paraphrase is a useful tool for studying poetry. A paraphrase may help to clarify some aspects of the meaning of the original work. However, any paraphrase necessarily distorts the original in some respects because the meaning and effect of a poem depend upon its exact wording and rhythms. See *summary.*

parody An artistic work that humorously imitates characteristic features of another work or type of work. Hale Woodruff's *Returning Home,* on page 762, is in part a parody of a certain kind of Chinese and Japanese landscape painting.

pathetic fallacy The attribution of human emotions or other characteristics to nonhuman things. The Victorian critic John Ruskin coined the term as a derisive one to apply to excessively sentimental verse. Romantic poetry often attributes human characteristics to objects in nature. Langston Hughes indulges in the pathetic fallacy in "April Rain Song" (See page 360) when he writes, "Let the rain kiss you" and "Let the rain sing you a lullaby" and in "Dream Variations," (See page 358) when he describes night coming "tenderly." See *personification.*

pen name See *pseudonym.*

pentameter See *meter.*

periodical A newspaper, journal, magazine, or any other publication that is produced on a regular, or periodical, basis. William Lloyd Garrison's newspaper *The Liberator* and Frederick Douglass's *The North Star* were abolitionist periodicals. *The Crisis, Opportunity: A Journal of Negro Life,* and *The New York Amsterdam News* were some important African-American periodicals of the Harlem Renaissance.

persona The qualities of personality and character that are displayed through a person's actions and speech. In literature, the persona or outward aspect conveyed by a speaker or character may or may not reveal the totality of his or her inner life. Paul Laurence Dunbar's famous poem "We Wear the Mask" (See page 322) is about the fact that racism sometimes causes those people who are subjected to it to put on personae that do not reflect how they actually feel and think.

perspective In the visual arts, the technique of creating realism by making objects in the foreground larger than objects in the background, as they appear to a viewer in real life. See *foreground* and *background.*

personal essay A short work of nonfiction prose, usually one on a topic of particular interest to the writer. Often a personal essay deals with or springs from a significant personal experience that the writer has had. The chapter in this text from Frederick Douglass's *Narrative* (See page 114) can be read as a personal essay on the subject of the importance to an enslaved person of learning to read. The tone of a personal essay is often informal and intimate. Personal essays are typically written in the first person.

personification A figure of speech in which animals, abstract ideas, or inanimate objects are given human traits and described as if they were somehow human. In Countee Cullen's poem "Scottsboro, Too, Is Worth Its Song," the poet portrays the nation as a deaf person. Traditional tales, such as the Anansi and Br'er Rabbit stories, often make use of a variety of personification in which animals speak and behave like humans. This type of personification is called *anthropomorphism,* from Greek words meaning *human* and *form.*

persuasion See *mode.*

persuasive writing See *mode.*

plagiarism The act of using material derived from the work of another without noting the source.

plot A series of events related to the central conflict in a work of fiction, either a novel, short story, play, or narrative poem. A plot can be *analyzed,* or broken down into its various elements, so that one can look at the relationships among the elements and determine how the story progresses from the introduction of the conflict to its resolution. A plot is typically analyzed into the following parts::

- the *exposition*, which introduces the characters and establishes the tone, mood, and setting
- the *inciting incident,* which introduces the central conflict and thereby sets the plot into motion
- the *rising action,* or *complication,* during which the conflict develops up to its most intense point, the climax
- the *climax,* often the most suspenseful point in the action, the point at which the conflict is brought to its highest intensity
- the *crisis,* or *turning point,* often the same as the climax, during which something happens that decisively determines the future course of events
- the *falling action,* all the incidents that follow the climax, up to the resolution
- the *resolution,* or point at which the central conflict is ended or brought to a conclusion
- the *catastrophe,* the point in a tragedy that marks the final downfall of the tragic hero
- the *dénouement,* any events that follow the resolution and that tie up loose ends, explaining, for example, what happens to the characters as a result of the resolution

The elements described above are not a formula, and plot development can be quite varied. The action doesn't always follow chronologically. Sometimes information is given in flashbacks. Sometimes the story begins in the middle of the action (*in media res*). Sometimes the inciting incident is not revealed until near the end of the action. Sometimes the dénouement is left out altogether. These are but a few possible variations on a conventional plot structure. Some plots are episodic and don't really involve the usual building to a climax. The author, however, is usually aware of the elements of a conventional plot and knows when he or she is ignoring them to achieve some effect. See *episode, flashback, foreshadowing,* and *media res.*

poetic license The right claimed by a writer to make use of artistic elements and conventions that do not conform to reality. In her biography of Harriet Tubman, Ann Petry took poetic license when she invented some of the dialogue and descriptions to make her story more vivid and realistic (See page 232). Readers are said to accept instances of poetic license by making a "willing suspension of disbelief."

point of view The vantage point from which a story is told. Stories that are written in the *first person* use words such as *I, my, we,* and *us,* whereas stories told in the *third person* use *he, she, it,* and *they, them,* and *their.* In first person stories, the narrator may be a participant in the action or an observer of it. In some narration, the storyteller's point of view is *limited.* He or she knows only his own inner thoughts and not those of the other characters. In third-person narratives, the speaker may be *omniscient,* that is, he or she may be privy to the interior life of all the characters. The voice of the narrator is not necessarily the same as the voice of the author. The author can assume a different persona in telling the story. See *narrator* and *persona.*

pragmatic criticism Also called *rhetorical criticism,* an evaluation or interpretation of a literary work that concentrates on how it achieves its effect on the audience. See *criticism.*

praise poem A traditional African verse form, the purpose of which is to praise, or celebrate, a person, often containing elaborate praise names and information on the person's lineage, or ancestry, as well as on his or her accomplishments and personal characteristics.

précis See *summary.*

preface A statement made before the beginning of a literary work (from the Latin *prefatia,* to speak beforehand). A preface can serve any of a number of different purposes. For example, it might serve as an introduction to the themes of the work, as an explanation of the work's origins or structure, or as a critical interpretation or evaluation. The essay by Alain Locke on page 290 is the preface to an important and influential anthology called *The New Negro.* This anthology helped to determine the canon of important authors of the Harlem Renaissance. See also the "Preface by the Author" to Harriet Jacobs's *Incidents in the Life of a Slave Girl* on page 132. The term *preface* is sometimes used interchangeably with *introduction* or *foreword.* See *canon* and *Harlem Renaissance.*

prologue An introduction to a literary work, one that sets the scene or that specifically introduces the themes and characters. A prologue comes before the formal beginning of the action of a novel or play or before the first stanza of a poem.

prose All writing that is not poetry or drama. Prose includes both fiction and nonfiction. Interestingly, everyday spoken language is actually closer to poetry than to prose, since it depends on numerous rhythmic techniques; very tight, elliptical structures; spoken and hinted allusions; and verbal tricks that prevail in poetry more than in prose.

prose poem A work of prose, usually short, that makes such extensive use of poetic language that it blurs the already vague line between prose and poetry. Many passages in Frederick Douglass's autobiography, such as his famous apostrophe to the ships in the Chesapeake Bay, sailing free while he is bound, might be considered a prose poem. (See page 108 in the Core Knowledge edition of the *Narrative of the Life of Frederick Douglass, An American Slave.*) Fenton Johnson's "The Banjo Player," on page 336, can be considered a prose poem, as can Margaret Walker's "For My People," on page 551.

prosody The study of versification or poetic structure. The objects of this study include *meter, rhyme, rhythm* and *stanza form* as well as other effects that create the sounds of poetry, such as *alliteration, assonance,* and *onomatopoeia.* See the separate entries for the italicized terms.

protagonist The main character in a literary work, the one who undergoes a struggle, or conflict. A protagonist sometimes struggles against another character, the *antagonist.* See *antagonist, character,* and *conflict.*

proverb A traditional saying, used widely within in a culture, that expresses some commonly held truth. A proverb is often a pithy expression of folk wisdom. "You can catch more flies with honey than with vinegar" and "The early bird catches the worm" are examples of proverbs. See "The Origin of African Proverbial Wisdom," on page 8, and "African Proverbial Wisdom," on page 10.

psalm A lyrical hymn of praise, meant to be sung or chanted. The Old Testament of the Bible contains an entire book called the Book of Psalms, and psalms are also found in the Islamic tradition. Waverly Turner Carmichael's "Keep Me, Jesus, Keep Me," on page 339, is a psalm that has much in common in mood, tone, and imagery with the psalms of the Bible.

pseudonym A name assumed by a writer, also called a *pen name* or a *nom de plume.* Some writers of slave narratives published their work under pseudonyms in order to protect themselves and their family members. They also often changed the names of characters in their narratives for the same reason. Many African-American writers, artists, and activists of the Black Power and Black Arts Movements assumed pseudonyms to express their rejection of identification with slave histories and identities. So, for example, LeRoy Jones took the name *Amiri Baraka,* Malcolm Little took the name *Malcolm X,* and Paulette Williams took the name *Ntozake Shange.*

psychological fiction A type of fiction that emphasizes the inner life of its characters, often fiction that presents extreme, disturbed, or anguished states of mind. Richard Wright's *Invisible Man* is an example of psychological fiction.

pun A play on words, usually one that exploits a double meaning for comic effect, as in the poetic line, "And in those eyes the lovelight lies / And lies —and lies—and lies!" Puns were widely used in Shakespeare's day and up through the eighteenth century, even in very serious poetry. Now they are typically considered a low form of humor, suitable for knock-knock jokes and the like: *Question*: "What is a popular instrument for fish?" *Answer*: "a bass guitar." The title of Arna Bontemps poem "The Day-Breakers," on page 408, is a pun. It refers, simultaneously, to people who are up at break of day, to people who are by their actions bringing about "a new day," and to people who are up in the daytime, breaking soil with their tools.

pyrrhic foot See *meter.*

quatrain See *ballad* and *stanza.*

quintain See *stanza.*

rap An improvised, heavily rhymed verse that is chanted or sung, an integral product of hip-hop culture. See page 731.

Reader-response criticism An approach to the interpretation and evaluation of literature taken by people who hold that a work has no meaning until it is read and responded to by the reader. People who hold this point of view believe that the meaning of a work derives from the interplay between the text and the person reading it. Different readers bring different background experiences and understandings to the text, and so the meaning of the text changes from reader to reader. See *criticism.*

realism The attempt in art to portray life in an accurate manner. In the novel, this attempt at realistic depiction was achieved by attention to setting, to atmosphere, to the details of social customs and class (especially to the customs of the lower and middle classes), and to other features of the material world. Although realism saw its first flowering in the eighteenth century in writers like Jane Austen, the full development of the realistic novel is considered to have occurred in the latter part of nineteenth century in the works of writers like Charles Dickens and George Eliot in England and Emile Zola, Honoré Balzac, and Gustave Flaubert in France. Realism was also a movement in the visual arts and can be seen in the works of artists like Goya and Millet. Masters of realistic fiction in the United States include Charles W. Chesnutt (See page 414), Zora Neale Hurston (See page 426), Dorothy West (See page 640), Alice Walker (See page 646), Ralph Ellison, Nella Larsen, and Alex Haley.

redundancy Needless repetition of words or ideas. The phrase *firmly committed* is redundant because commitment implies firmness. Redundancy is something to be avoided in effective writing.

refrain One or more lines that are repeated in a song or poem; also known as a *chorus.* Many spirituals, ballads, and other folk songs contain refrains, and refrains are often used in poetry in imitation of songs. Here is the refrain from "Go Down, Moses":

Go down, Moses,
Way down in Egypt's land.
Tell ole Pharaoh,
Let My People Go.

register The level of formality of speech or writing, varying from highly formal to informal to intimate. See *colloquialism, diction, vernacular,* and *style.*

Renaissance The period from the fourteenth to the early seventeenth century when Europe was making the transition from the medieval to the modern world. The word *renaissance* means "rebirth," and the period was characterized by rebirth of interest in the ancient classical world as well as by new interest in the sciences and in individual freedom. The period saw a great flowering in the arts, including architecture, a flowering that displayed a reverence for the aesthetic beliefs of classical Greece and Rome. *The Harlem Renaissance* and *The Chicago Renaissance* are, of course, names derived from this name for a period in European cultural history. See *Harlem Renaissance.*

representation In the visual arts, the attempt to portray objects, people, scenes from nature, and other subjects as they appear to be in real life. Representation is in keeping with Aristotle's idea that art should be mimetic—that it should imitate nature. Representational works are said to be examples of realism and are at the opposite extreme from works that are abstract. See *abstraction* and *criticism.*

resolution See *plot.*

reversal A dramatic turn of events in a drama or narrative, particularly an event during which a major character's fortunes change from good to bad or *vice versa.* See *plot.*

review A written or spoken evaluation of a work of art, a literary work, or a performance, usually one that appears in a periodical or on a broadcast program. See *periodical.*

rhetoric The art of persuasive speech or writing, including the use of eloquent or effective language to influence audiences and move them to action. Rhetoric employs both logical arguments and appeals to the emotions. Frederick Douglass, Sojourner Truth, W. E. B. Du Bois, Marcus Garvey, Malcolm X, and Martin Luther King, Jr., were all masters of the art of rhetoric.

rhetorical criticism See *pragmatic criticism.*

rhetorical question A figure of speech in which a question is asked for effect. A rhetorical question is not expected to be answered because the answer is obvious or is implied by the way the question is asked. When Sojourner Truth asks, "Ar'n't I a Woman?" (See page 144) and when Frederick Douglass asks, "Must I undertake to prove that the slave is a man?" (See page 125), these questions are not meant to be answered because their answers are obvious. It is the very obviousness of the answers that make the questions powerful rhetorically.

rhyme The repetition of sounds at the ends of words. Rhyme is more than decoration. In oral traditions, it serves as an aid to memory. Rhyme also helps to establish unity in a poem and to delight and surprise the reader with intriguing patterns of sound. The following terms identify some of the important types of rhyme:

- *end rhyme,* rhyming words that appear at the ends of lines
- *internal rhyme,* rhyming words used within lines
- *exact rhyme,* a rhyme ending with exactly the same sounds (plain/rain)
- *slant rhyme,* or *off rhyme,* rhyming sounds that are similar but not identical (rot/rock)
- *sight rhyme,* similarity in spelling but not in sound (love/move)
- *masculine rhyme,* a rhyme with the stress on the final syllable (sublime/crime)
- *feminine rhyme,* a rhyme with the stress on the penultimate or second to last syllable (picky/sticky)

These lines from Phillis Wheatley's "To Maecenas" end with a slant rhyme:

But I less happy, cannot raise the song,
The fault'ring music dies upon my tongue.

rhythm The pattern of stresses or beats in a line of verse or prose. See *meter.*

romance A term first used to describe stories believed to have been told by the Romans that later was used to describe first medieval stories about knights and their ladies and, even later, prose fiction in general because many medieval romances were told in prose rather than in poetry. Various types of stories are classified as romances: stories of knightly adventures, stories set in exotic locations full of mysterious events, stories that involve fantasy and other unrealistic elements, and finally stories that deal primarily with the subject of love.

romantic criticism An approach to the interpretation and evaluation of works of art taken by people who are interested primarily in the spirit, ideas, and emotions of the work's creator. An interpretation of Richard Wright's *Native Son* that focuses on the author's concern for the deprivation and injustice faced by the central character and (by extension) by other impoverished, misunderstood African Americans would be an example of romantic criticism. Also called *expressive criticism.*

romanticism A literary and artistic movement that flowered in the first third of the nineteenth century and that favored emotion and imagination over reason; the individual over society or the community; liberty over authority and order; wilderness over the contained landscape; and ordinary people over aristocrats. It was, in some ways, a dismissal of the ideas emphasized in the Enlightenment, during which time logic and reason were seen as the basis for dealing with one's life and with society's problems. Romantics typically favor revolutionary means for changing unjust conditions rather than gradual application of new laws and new programs. In its literary expression, romanticism often explored the theme of freedom and the relationships of people to nature. American transcendentalism, a kind of idealism embraced by Emerson, Thoreau, and others, is a form of romanticism. It viewed human beings as part of nature and nature as being filled with the divine spirit. Langston Hughes, with his frequent use of dream images and images from nature, could be considered a romantic poet. "Magalu," by Helene Johnson (See page 396), is a poem very much in the romantic tradition because it expresses strong emotion and celebrates nature and a natural, native culture as opposed to an artificial, imposed one.

rounded character See *character.*

rule of thirds In the visual arts, a rule for achieving focus (that is, directing the attention of the viewer). The visual field, such as the canvas, is divided into three parts horizontally and vertically by imaginary lines. An object that is to receive focus is placed at one of the places where the imaginary vertical and horizontal lines cross. See *composition,* sense 3.

rule of threes In literature, the tendency of writers to present material in threes. The motif of three wishes, found in folktale traditions around the world, is an example of the rule of threes. See *motif.*

run-on line A line of verse in which the meaning and the grammatical structure are carried over to the next line or lines. The act of carrying over the statement beyond the line's end is called *enjambment.* These lines from the third stanza of Countee Cullen's poem "Heritage" (See page 380) are mostly run-on lines.

Africa? A book one thumbs
Listlessly, till slumber comes.
Unremembered are her bats
Circling through the night, her cats
Crouching in the river reeds,
Stalking gentle flesh that feeds
By the river brink: no more
Does the bugle-throated roar
Cry that monarch claws have leapt
From the scabbard where they slept.

Note that running on the lines helps the poet achieve several effects: the flow of the opening lines, the surprise of encountering the crouching cats, and the suddenness of the bared claws. This technique also avoids the dull repetitiveness of sound that comes from the use of end-stopped lines. See *end-stopped line.*

satire Humorous speech or writing that makes fun of human failings, often with an intent to improve human behavior or correct social ills. During the Enlightenment, satire was especially conceived of as a way to expose the folly of human beings and to encourage more humane behavior. Gwendolyn Brooks's poem "We Real Cool" (See page 558) can be read as a satire on the "cool" young men who hang out at a pool parlor and mistakenly think that they have life all figured out.

saturation In the visual arts, the degree of intensity of a color, from very light to very intense.

scansion The art and science of analyzing the meters of poems. See *meter.*

scene A brief section of a literary work that presents an action taking place in a single setting at a single time. The acts of full-length dramas are usually divided into scenes, often requiring changes in the stage set.

science fiction Imaginative fiction containing fantastic or unrealistic elements and drawing upon scientific principles, discoveries, or laws. Often science fiction deals with worlds distant in time or space. Sometimes science fiction writers construct alternative societies in order to point out flaws in our current society, to warn about a possible dystopian future, or to express a hope that future scientific advances will improve our lot. Science fiction is similar to fantasy in that both types of work contain highly unrealistic elements, but fantasy is not based in science as science fiction is. See *dystopia.*

sentimentality An emotional response that is more than what is called for by the situation, especially a disproportionate show of emotion that is suspected of not being genuine. *Sentimentality* is a negative term, implying that those who engage in it are phoney or that they have a poorly developed sense of what is worthy of strong emotional response. The eighteenth and early nineteenth century produced novels called *sentimental novels* that took an overly optimistic, unrealistic view of the human condition. In the visual arts, sentimentality might be said to characterize pictures that are prettified, such as those that present cute animals and insistently pleasant scenes of family life. In music, sentimentality might be exemplified by tinkling piano keys playing corny melodies or by swelling strings meant to express deep emotion. See *cliché.*

septastich See *sonnet* and *stanza.*

sestet See *sonnet* and *stanza.*

set A collection of objects and painted backdrops that furnish the stage and constitute the physical environment in which the action of a play occurs.

setting The time and place in which the action of a literary work occurs. Setting can be central to the theme and action of the story on both a literal and a symbolic level. The settings of many of August Wilson's plays are the taverns, parlors, and streets of the Hill District of Pittsburgh. These settings lend an air of believability to his action and an air of earthy dignity to his characters. In fiction, setting is revealed by concrete descriptions and use of details that suggest time and place. As in drama, setting in fiction can contribute to the mood and atmosphere of the story, as well as help define the political, social, and moral world inhabited by the characters.

Shakespearean sonnet See *sonnet.*

short short An extremely brief short story, sometimes called *flash fiction.* This recently defined genre is popular in literary magazines and often is a retelling of a single anecdote or incident, although there are also short shorts that revel in packing as much plot as possible into a few sentences.

sight rhyme See *rhyme.*

simile An analogy in which one thing is compared to another using one of the prepositions *like* or *as.* A simile is a kind of metaphor. In James Weldon Johnson's "The Creation" (See page 328), the poet describes God kneeling in the dust to form man from the earth as being "like a mammy bending over her baby." See *metaphor.*

slang Extremely colloquial speech not suitable for formal occasions. Slang is often associated with a particular group, frequently with the young, who adopt new expressions as a sort of code for use among themselves. The use of the word *bad,* for example, to refer to something good is an example of slang. Slang also can be associated with particular activities, like skateboarding, surfing, or playing jazz. For example, the terms *head* used to refer to a verse in a song and *bridge* used to refer to the chorus are examples of jazz slang. Although considered nonstandard, slang, and colloquial language in general, are often used by writers to give their work authenticity. Zora Neale Hurston, for example, in *Their Eyes are Watching God,* used the slang and other colloquial speech of rural Southern blacks in the 1930s. When Robert Hayden wrote in "Homage to the Empress of the Blues," on page 543, of "torn hurdygurdy lithographs," he was using a slang term, *hurdygurdy,* for an illegal tavern, or speakeasy.

slant rhyme See *rhyme.*

slave narrative An autobiographical story written by an enslaved person or by a formerly enslaved person. *The Interesting Life of Olaudah Equiano*, by Olaudah Equiano; *Narrative of the Life of Frederick Douglass, an American Slave,* by Frederick Douglass; and *Incidents in the Life of a Slave Girl,* by Harriet Jacobs, are all examples of slave narratives. See pages 54, 96, 114, and 130. (Note: Strictly speaking, there were no slaves; there were people who were enslaved. However, the term *slave narrative* has been and continues to be widely used to refer to works by enslaved persons about their experiences in bondage.)

social realism See *aesthetics.*

sonnet A fourteen-line poem that can follow a number of different rhyme schemes. The *Elizabethan,* or *Shakespearean, sonnet* is composed of three quatrains and a final couplet, often rhyming *abab cdcd efef gg.* The *Petrachan,* or *Italian, sonnet,* employed notably by the fourteenth-century Italian poet Petrarch, is divided into two parts, an *octave,* or eight-line stanza, rhymed *abbaabba,* and an *sestet,* or six-line stanza, rhymed *cdecde.* Many variations on these rhyme schemes are possible. Examples of sonnets in *Grace Abounding* include Claude McKay's "Outcast," on page 351, and Robert Hayden's "Frederick Douglass," on page 540.

sorrow song See *spiritual.*

source A work used by an author to develop or document his or her material. One must document one's sources in order to avoid plagiarism. See *plagiarism.*

speaker The voice that tells a lyric poem, a voice assumed by the author. Since poems are meant primarily to be spoken rather than read, the voice that the author assumes in a poem, which is not necessarily the poet's own voice, is called the *speaker.* The speaker in the poem "We Real Cool" (See page 558) is not the author, Gwendolyn Brooks, but a swaggering young pool player.

spectacle All of the sensory elements—the sights, sound effects, music, lighting, costumes, and movements—that accompany the action of a play. See *drama.*

spiritual A variety of indigenous American folk song created by enslaved African Americans and treating themes of freedom and escape using images, symbols, actions, characters, and other elements from Judeo-Christian religion. Also known as *jubilees* or *sorrow songs,* the spirituals were typically written in what has come to be known as *the code,* a set of symbolic correspondences between circumstances described in the Bible and the circumstances of the lives of the enslaved. For example, the river Jordan might stand for the Ohio River, which separated slave states from free states. (See page 202.)

spondee See *meter.*

stage Any space in which the action of a drama is performed. In the Middle Ages, traveling performers would often use the beds of wagons. Such wagons were forerunners of the *thrust stage,* a platform that extends out into the audience. The open area around the thrust stage was called *the pit,* and in Shakespeare's time, this is where the common people, the *groundlings,* stood to watch performances. The more affluent members of the audience were seated in balconies above the action. The modern *proscenium stage* is usually closed on three sides, effecting the pretense that it is a room missing a fourth wall. Modern theater frequently experiments with a stage placed in the middle of the audience. Such a set-up is called *theater in the round,* a return on a smaller scale to the arenas or coliseums of the classical world of Greece and Rome.

stage directions Notes included in the text of a play to describe elements of the spectacle, such as the stage set and the lighting, or to indicate how the author wants the dialogue to be delivered or the action to be performed. See *spectacle* and *dialogue.*

stanza A recurring pattern into which poetic lines are organized, similar to the paragraph in prose writing. Some types of stanzas include the *couplet* (two lines); the *tercet* or *triplet* (three lines); the *quatrain* (four lines); the *quintain* (five lines); the *sestet* (six lines); the *septastich* (seven lines); and the *octave* or *octet* (eight lines). Langston Hughes's "Song for a Dark Girl" (See page 368) is written in quatrains.

static character See *character*.

stereotype An oversimplified and unexamined conception or image, usually a fixed but unjustified and unjustifiable opinion about members of some group. When used in drama, stereotypical characters are called *stock characters.* Examples include the cruel landlord, the mad scientist, and the laconic, virtuous cowboy. The ways in which stereotypes injure people and distort reality is a frequent theme in African-American literature. Frederick Douglass, for example, in his *Narrative,* exposes the absurdity of the stereotype of slaves being happy because they sang songs while working in the fields. This stereotype, promulgated by apologists for slavery, was also notably attacked by W. E. B. Du Bois and Amiri Baraka.

stock character See *character*.

stream-of-consciousness A technique in writing that attempts to imitate the free flow of thought and emotion of the mind at work. Stream-of-consciousness passages record images, thoughts, and feelings in an intentionally disordered manner in order to reflect the random associations that people make when thinking. Masters of the stream-of-consciousness technique include modern writers like James Joyce and Virginia Woolf. The famous opening of Ralph Ellison's novel *Invisible Man* contains much stream-of-consciousness material.

stress See *meter.*

structuralist criticism See *criticism*.

style The manner in which something is said or written. A writer's style depends on many elements of his or her work, including diction, or choice of words, and sentence structure, or arrangement of those words grammatically to form sentences. A good writer develops a distinctive style, one recognizably different from that of other writers. Turn, for example, from a passage by W. E. B. Du Bois (See page 268) to a passage by Zora Neale Hurston (See page 426) and note how different the styles are. Style can be *elevated* or *high* (suitable for formal occasions); *middle* (suitable for ordinary occasions); or *low* (suitable for extremely informal or intimate occasions). Low style would include the use of colloquial and slang expressions.

stylization In art, the tendency to move away from complex representation toward simplified shapes and lines. Stylization in art from Africa was one of the great influences on the development of abstract expressionism. See *abstract expressionism.*

subplot A plot developed in addition to the main plot, one subordinate to it.

summary A rewriting of an original work in fewer words in an attempt to capture the essence of its meaning and organization. Also called an *abstract* or *précis.*

suspense A feeling of expectation, often characterized by dread or anxiety, created in the mind of the reader or viewer. Suspense is created by raising questions in the reader or viewer's mind, the primary one being, "What is going to happen next?"

symbol A word, object, character, or place that suggests something beyond itself. A flag, for example, can be the symbol of a country or of an organization. A stop sign symbolizes the need for a full stop. A *cultural* or *conventional symbol* is one that is traditionally and widely understood to signify a particular association. Examples of conventional symbols include a rose as a symbol of love or beauty, a dove as a symbol of peace, an owl as a symbol of wisdom, and the color purple as a symbol of royalty. Sometimes, instead of using conventional symbols, writers create *personal symbols,* ones unique to their work. In August Wilson's *Piano Lesson,* for example, the piano represents the characters' longing for beauty, so the decision about whether to sell it is a crucial one. The use of symbols is extremely important in both literature and in the visual arts because symbols enable an artist to call up very complex ideas in an economical way. The graphic on page 387, for example, shows three figures, one closing its eyes, one covering its mouth, and one stopping its ears. This graphic is a representation of a conventional idea—one should "see no evil, speak no evil, and hear no evil." However, when paired with the poem about people turning a deaf ear to the plight of the Scottsboro Nine, the graphic becomes a powerful symbol of the whole history of suppressing justice and paying no attention to suffering. An essay of several pages explaining the details of this history would not have as powerful an effect as this simple, symbolic graphic.

symmetry In the visual arts, correspondence of form or constituent configuration on opposite sides of a dividing line or plane or about a center or an axis of rotation. So, for example, a painter might place a large object on the left side of an imaginary line running down the center of his or her canvas and make the work symmetrical by placing another large object on the right side to create a balanced, symmetrical composition. See *composition,* sense 3.

synaesthesia A figure of speech in which two or more different senses are combined. Calling a genre of music *the blues* is an example of synaesthesia.

synecdoche A figure of speech in which the name of a part of something is used to stand for the whole. In the phrase *Give me a hand* the word *hand* is meant to stand for the whole idea of help. In the command *Render unto Caesar,* the name *Caesar* was meant to stand for the whole nation state of which Caesar was the head.

syntax The patterns by which words are arranged into phrases, clauses, and sentences. English syntax ordinarily calls for words in a sentence to follow a subject-verb-object pattern, but writers, especially poets, often change this normal order to achieve variety and a distinctive voice. Countee Cullen, in his poem "Scottsboro, Too, Is Worth Its Song" (See page 387), might have written, "The poets will sing now," but he varied the syntax and wrote, instead, "Now will the poets sing." Notice that the change in syntax makes a big difference. The line with the inverted syntax is much more poetic. Cullen's arrangement of the syntax places emphasis on the first word, *Now*. See *inversion*.

tall tale A story, usually humorous and lighthearted in tone, that contains highly exaggerated elements and that features superhuman characters, often ones who carry out extraordinary tasks. From the American folklore tradition, Paul Bunyan, Johnny Appleseed, and Pecos Bill are examples of heroes from tall tales. Though based on an actual event, the song "John Henry" (See page 211) has characteristics of the tall tale.

tercet See *stanza.*

terra cotta 1. A lightly fired, hard, waterproof, typically reddish-brown ceramic clay used in pottery and sculpture. 2. A work produced using this material.

terza rima The Italian term for a three-line stanza used notably in Dante's *Divine Comedy.* The rhyme scheme is *aba, bcb, cdc, ded,* and so forth.

tetrameter See *meter*.

textual criticism The analysis of existing manuscript and printed versions of a work to establish an original or authentic text, often an attempt to establish the definitive text that a writer would have approved for use by posterity. See *criticism*.

theater of the absurd A type of twentieth-century drama that presents illogical or unrealistic scenes and improbable characters in order to emphasize the distorted and inhumane features of modern life and the aimlessness of human endeavors.

theme A central idea in a literary work. A woman's search for her authentic self in the face of severe social sanctions is the theme of Zora Neale Hurston's novel *Their Eyes Were Watching God* (See page 426).

thesis The main idea of a work of nonfiction prose. Arthur Schomburg's thesis in "The Negro Digs Up His Past," on page 304, was that there was a significant body of valuable cultural creations by African Americans waiting to be discovered and preserved.

third-person point of view See *narrator* and *point of view.*

tragedy A serious work of drama that traditionally follows the fate of a hero as he falls from a high status to his doom through some flaw in his character. The characteristics of tragedy were famously described by the Greek philosopher Aristotle, who had in mind the tragic works of Greek dramatists such as Sophocles and Euripedes. Many works by William Shakespeare, such as *Hamlet, Macbeth, Othello,* and *King Lear,* are tragedies. Tragedies by Sophocles, Euripedes, and Shakespeare dealt with the downfalls of important, powerful people. In modern times, tragedies often deal with the fates of ordinary people. In fact, playwrights like Arthur Miller, Eugene O'Neill, and August Wilson are insistent in their belief that ordinary people should be able to claim our attention and that their downfalls should elicit the same terror and pity that would be engendered by the fall of, say, a king.

transcendentalism See *romanticism.*

transition A word, phrase, sentence, or paragraph used to connect ideas and to show the relationships among them. Words such as *however, therefore, in addition,* and *in contrast* are typically used as transitions. Repeated nouns and pronouns, as well as repeated grammatical forms, can serve to tie ideas together and so function as transitions. Use of transitions helps to improve the *coherence* of a piece of writing—the connectedness of its ideas.

trimeter See *meter.*

triplet See *stanza.*

trochee See *meter.*

trope See *figure of speech.*

turning point See *plot.*

understatement An ironic mode of speaking or writing in which something important is spoken of or written about as if it were trivial, presenting, for example, a broken leg as if it were just a scrape. Comedy often relies on understatement.

unity Applied to a literary or artistic work, the sense that all the parts of the work form a whole and that each part is necessary to achieving the effect achieved by the whole. Some classically oriented critics have in the past asserted that a work of literature should obey the *three unities*—1. that it should deal with one main action, 2. that the action should occur in a single place, and 3. that the action should occur in a single time.

utopia An idealized world in which people work cooperatively and happily for the greatest good. The term comes from the title given to a work by the sixteenth-century English saint Thomas More. The word comes from the Greek for "no-place." See *dystopia.*

value In the visual arts, the relative darkness or lightness of an element in a work.

vernacular The speech of the common people. Up until the last two centuries or so, educated European discourse was conducted in Latin, and the vernacular referred to native languages used in everyday conversations and transactions. Since Latin is no longer a spoken language, the term *vernacular* is now used to refer to the ordinary, everyday speech of the middle and working classes, and especially to informal varieties of such speech, including colloquialisms and slang. See *colloquialism* and *slang.*

villanelle A complex, nineteen-line verse form, originally French, whose rhyme scheme is *aba aba aba aba abaa.* The first line is repeated as lines 6, 12, and 18. The third line is repeated as lines 9, 15, and 19. At the end of the poem, the first and third lines appear as a rhymed couplet. The beginning of Rita Dove's "Parsley" (See page 606) is a villanelle.

woodcut In the visual arts, a work produced by etching lines onto a wooden block, inking the block, and then pressing paper against it. See *linocut.*

work song A variety of indigenous African and African-American folk song created for singing by a group of workers. Work songs were common among enslaved persons in the United States and among sharecroppers and inmates of prison work farms. Work songs often made use of call-and-response elements and so-called blue notes and were one of the precursors of the blues. Work songs were communal, sung by a group, as opposed to field hollers, which were sung by individuals. (See page 207.)

Glossary of vocabulary from the selections

A

abhor, *v.* To regard with horror or hatred, to detest
abhorrence, *n.* Loathing; hatred
abode, *n.* A dwelling-place; house
abomination, *n.* Detestable or loathsome thing or act
academician, *n.* Teacher in a university, professor
acclaim, *n.* Fame
accrue, *v.* To increase or accumulate
adduce, *v.* To cite as evidence or proof
adoration, *n.* Profound love or regard, worship
adverse, *adj.* Harmful or unfavorable
affability, *n.* The state of being easy and pleasant
affiliate, *n.* A person or organization associated with another as a subordinate, subsidiary, or member
affirm, *v.* To declare to be true
affirmative, *adj.* Positive
affirmatively, *adv.* Positively, said of a speech that supports a given proposition
agitate, *v.* To arouse interest in
agitation, *n.* The stirring up of public interest
alcove, *n.* A nook or partly closed extension in a room
allay, *v.* To reduce the intensity of; relieve
alluring, *adj.* Inviting or tempting
anecdote, *n.* A short account of an interesting or funny event
antagonism, *n.* Actively-expressed opposition, or hostility
anthem, *n.* A song of praise
antidote, *n.* A cure, usually for poison
antiquarian, *n.* A scholar or lover of old things
aperture, *n.* An opening, such as a hole, gap, or slit
apprehend, *v.* To capture
apprehension, *n.* Fearful anticipation of the future
apt, *adj.* Quick to learn and understand
ardent, *adj.* Passionate; displaying strong enthusiasm
arpeggio, *n.* The sounding of the tones of a chord in rapid succession rather than simultaneously
arrant, *adj.* Completely such; thoroughgoing
articulate, *adj.* Expressing oneself easily in clear and effective language
ascend, *v.* To move upward; rise up; to climb
ascertain, *v.* To determine
ascribe, *v.* To attribute to a specified cause
aspiration, *n.* Hope, dream
assail, *v.* To attack verbally, as with ridicule or censure
assiduous, *adj.* Diligent, unceasing, persistent
atone, *v.* To show remorse or regret for one's past actions
attainment, *n.* Achievement
august, *adj.* Inspiring awe or admiration
austere, *adj.* Unadorned; bleak; stern or severe
austerity, *n.* The quality of being stern or disciplinary
avail, *v.* To be of use or advantage to; to help
avarice, *n.* Greed; a great desire for wealth
avert, *v.* To turn aside
avowed, *past part.* Expressed

B

bales, *n.pl.* Bundles
barley, *n.* An edible grain
battalion, *n.* A large body of troops, consisting of two or more companies
batten, *v.* Eat until gorged or full; fatten
benediction, *n.* A blessing; an expression of good will
benevolence, *n.* Kindness, generosity
benighted, *adj.* Intellectually or morally ignorant
bequeath, *v.* To leave or give personal property by will
bestial, *adj.* Beastly; marked by brutality
betoken, *v.* To be or give a sign to
betroth, *v.* To promise to marry or give in marriage
bewilder, *v.* Confuse
blight, *n.* 1. Something that impairs growth or withers hopes and ambitions. 2. A disease in plants.
bombastic, *adj.* Pretentious, inflated
bounteous, *adj.* Abundant or overflowing
bourgeoisie, *n.* The middle class
boycott, *n.* Concerted action to keep from using or buying some product or dealing with some organization in order to bring about change
braggadocio, *n.* Exaggerated boasting
brethren, *n.* Brothers (poetic)
brute, *n.* Animal
brutish, *adj.* Uncivilized, primitive, beastly
bulwark, *n.* Something serving as a defense or safeguard
burly, *adj.* Strong, massive

C

cabalistic, *adj.* Having a hidden or secret meaning; occult
calabash, *n.* A large gourd used as a vessel, jar, or bowl
candor, *n.* Sincerity and openness
canker, *v.* To infect with corruption or decay
capitulation, *n.* Surrender
caprice, *n.* An inclination to change one's mind impulsively
carcass, *n.* Dead body of an animal
caste, *n.* A social class separated from others according to hereditary rank, profession, or wealth
censure, *n.* Expression of strong disapproval; harsh criticism
chamber, *n.* Room
chaos, *n.* Confusion, disarray
chastisement, *n.* Punishment

chastity, ***n.*** Purity
chattel, ***n.*** An article of movable personal property, such as a cow or wagon
cheek, ***n.*** Impertinence; insulting boldness
chime in, ***v.*** To break into a conversation
chronic, ***adj.*** Constant, always returning
cognizant, ***adj.*** Fully informed, conscious, aware
collective, ***adj.*** Relating to a number of people acting as a group
comeliness, ***n.*** The state of being attractive
competent, ***adj.*** Adequate for the purpose; capable
compliance, ***n.*** Acquiescence, act of yielding to the will of another person
concede, ***v.*** To agree with
conceive, ***v.*** To become pregnant with
concurrent, ***adj.*** In accordance with; in harmony with
conduce, ***v.*** To contribute to or lead to a specific result
consign, ***v.*** To give to the care of another; transfer
consolation, ***n.*** Something that makes up for grief or sorrow
console, ***v.*** To comfort
conspire, ***v.*** To join or act together
constable, ***n.*** A police officer
consternation, ***n.*** Paralyzing dismay or fear
constrain, ***v.*** To require or compel
contingency, ***n.*** An unforeseen event or condition
contravene, ***v.*** To act or be counter to; violate
contrive, ***v.*** To plan with cleverness
convey, ***v.*** To transport
copious, ***adj.*** Plentiful
coroner, ***n.*** A public officer whose job it is to investigate the causes of people's deaths
corsage, ***n.*** A flower or small bouquet worn at the shoulder or on the wrist
countenance, ***n.*** Facial expression
coy, ***adj.*** Shy; tending to avoid social situations
credulity, ***n.*** The tendency to believe too readily; gullibility
credulous, ***adj.*** Ready to believe, especially on slight or uncertain evidence
cultivate, ***v.*** 1. To grow crops. 2. To improve, to make more refined or sophisticated.
cutaneous, ***adj.*** Having to do with the skin

D

dart, ***v.*** To move about quickly
deck, ***v.*** To decorate
decline, ***n.*** Sinking, or ending, as of the setting sun
decree, ***n.*** An authoritative order having the force of law
default, ***v.*** To fail to repay a debt or fulfill an obligation
deficiency, ***n.*** Incompleteness or inadequacy
defray, ***v.*** To undertake the payment of; to pay
degenerate, ***v.*** To fall to an undesirable moral state
dejected, ***past part.*** Extremely sad, despairing
delta, ***n.*** A triangle-shaped area of land created by alluvial deposits (materials carried downstream) left at the mouth of a river
denunciation, ***n.*** Condemnation, censure
deplore, ***v.*** To strongly dislike or disapprove of; detest
depravity, ***n.*** Moral corruption
deranged, ***adj.*** Disordered; mentally disturbed
descend, ***v.*** To come down from a higher place to a lower
despondency, ***n.*** Depression from loss of hope or confidence
despotism, ***n.*** Nation ruled by a tyrant, someone with absolute power and authority
deviate, ***v.*** To turn aside from a course or path; stray
devout, ***adj.*** Worshipful, pious
diabolic, ***adj.*** Devilish; characteristic of the devil
diligently, ***adv.*** In an attentive and thorough manner
dire, ***adj.*** Warning of or having dreadful consequences
disapprobation, ***n.*** Condemnation; moral disapproval
disassociate, ***v.*** To separate out; disunite
discomfiture, ***n.*** Frustration, disappointment, or embarrassment
discourse, ***n.*** A formal, lengthy discussion; speech
disinherited, ***past part.*** Denied a natural right or privilege
disparagement, ***n.*** A lowering of esteem, discouragement
disparity, ***n.*** Differences
dispatch, ***n.*** A story sent out by reporters or news services
dispel, ***v.*** 1. To drive away. 2. To rid one's mind of.
dispose, ***v.*** To arrange
disposition, ***n.*** A bestowal or transfer to another
dispossessed, ***adj.*** Deprived of possession
distinct, ***adj.*** Clearly differing from one another
divest, ***v.*** 1. To deprive or rid oneself of, as rights or property. 2. To free of.
divinity, ***n.*** Godlike nature or appearance
dogged, ***adj.*** Stubbornly determined; tenacious
doleful, ***adj.*** Full of grief; sad
dotage, ***n.*** A deterioration of mental faculties; senility
dowry, ***n.*** Money or property brought by a bride to her husband on the occasion of their marriage
dramatize, ***v.*** To present in an emotional or forceful way
dread, ***n.*** Worry caused by fear
drench, ***v.*** To wet thoroughly
dyspeptic, ***adj.*** Relating to or having disturbed digestion or indigestion

E

ecstasy, ***n.*** Extreme joy
elate, ***v.*** To make proud or joyful
elicit, ***v.*** To draw or provoke
embalming, ***v.*** Treating (a corpse) with preservatives in order to prevent decay
embodied, ***past part.*** Given form and substance
emigration, ***n.*** Movement out of one country or area in transit to another
eminently, ***adv.*** Remarkably, to an unusual degree
emulate, ***n.*** To strive to equal or excel; imitate
endowment, ***n.*** A natural gift, ability, or quality
equivocate, ***v.*** Falsify; avoid direct, straightforward, complete

statement

eradicate, *v.* To tear up by the roots; wipe out

evince, *v.* To show or determine clearly

exalted, *adj.* Elevated in rank or status

excommunicate, *v.* To exclude from membership in a church or other group

exploitation, *n.* Utilization of another for selfish purposes

exquisite, *adj.* Lovely, especially in an unusually fine or delicate way

exuberance, *n.* A feeling of unrestrained joy. Also, the state of being lavish or extravagant.

exultation, *n.* Great joy

F

facile, *n.* Lacking in sincerity or depth

fain, *adv.* Happily or gladly

fair, *adj.* Of light color

fare, *v.* To move toward a goal

fell, *v.* To cut down

fertility, *n.* Power to give birth or to generate, said literally of children and figuratively of ideas

fervently, *adv.* In a manner that shows great affection

fetter, *v.* To chain or shackle

fidelity, *n.* Loyalty, faithfulness

flay, *v.* To cut

flesh, *v.* To fill out; to give substance or detail to

flounder, *v.* To move or act clumsily or in confusion

flute, *v.* To produce a flutelike tone

foment, *v.* To promote the growth of; incite

ford, *n.* The shallow part of a body of water

forlorn, *adj.* Sad or lonely from being deserted or abandoned

fortified, *adj.* Surrounded by walls and trenches and/or protected by armed guards for security reasons

fowl, *n.* Bird

fringe, *n.* An outer edge, margin, or periphery

frisk, *v.* To move briskly and playfully

fugitive, *n.* One who flees; a run-away

furtive, *adj.* Secretive, given to hiding things, not trustworthy

futile, *adj.* Useless; having no useful result

G

gainsay, *v.* To declare false; deny

gaudy, *adj.* Showy in a tasteless or vulgar way

gaunt, *adj.* Thin and bony; haggard

gazelle, *n.* A small, swift antelope

glee, *n.* Joy; jubilant delight

glibly, *adv.* Showing little thought, preparation, or concern

glutted, *adj.* Filled to capacity; no longer profitable

gradualism, *n.* Advancing toward a goal by slow stages

grievous, *adj.* Causing or characterized by severe pain, suffering, or sorrow

grouse, *v.* To complain

guile, *n.* Sinister cunning in attaining a goal; artful deception

H

habituated, ***past part.*** Accustomed to

hallowed, *adj.* Sacred

harbinger, *n.* One that signals the approach of something

haughty, *adj.* Scornfully or condescendingly proud

heart-rending, *adj.* Causing anguish or deep distress (rend, *v.* to tear apart)

heathen, *n.* A person or group that is considered uncivilized, irreligious, or unenlightened

heathen, *adj.* Non-Christian; also, uncivilized or barbaric

heightening, *n.* Rising

heinous, *adj.* Shockingly evil; abominable

hermit, *n.* A person who has withdrawn from society

hesitation, *n.* Pausing, as to think about something before acting

hitherto, *adj.* Up to this time

holocaust, *n.* Great destruction resulting in the extensive loss of life, especially by fire

hover, *v.* To hang in the air

husbandry, *n.* The practice or act of breeding and raising livestock

hypocrisy, *n.* Falseness; the act of professing (claiming) beliefs or virtues that one does not actually possess or practice

I

idleness, *n.* Laziness

imbibe, *v.* To absorb into the mind

imitable, *adj.* Worthy of imitation

impertinence, *n.* Rudeness

impertinent, *adj.* Exceeding the limits of good manners

implicitly, *adv.* Without doubt, unquestionably

impose, *v.* To force something upon someone else

impudence, *n.* Insolence, impertinence, shamelessness

impudent, *adj.* Marked by contemptuous boldness or disregard for others

imputation, *n.* A suggestion or accusation

incarnate, *adj.* Embodied in human form

incendiarism, *n.* Arson, the setting of an unlawful fire

incessantly, *adv.* Continuously, without stopping

incongruous, *adj.* Contradictory, incompatible

inconsolable, *adj.* Impossible or difficult to comfort

incontinence, *n.* The act of being unfaithful or unchaste; lack of restraint

inculcate, *v.* To impress upon the mind of another by frequent instruction or repetition

indifferently, *adv.* Without concern or interest

indispensable, *adj.* Absolutely necessary, essential

induce, *v.* To lead or persuade

indelible, *adj.* Permanent

inestimable, *adj.* Of immeasurable value; priceless

inextricably, *adv.* In a manner that is impossible to untangle

inglorious, *adj.* Not famous; obscure; shameful

inherent, *adj.* Essential, built-in, inborn

innate, *adj.* Possessed at birth; inborn

inquest, *n.* A formal inquiry by a public official or institution,

such as a grand jury or a legislative committee
inquisitive, *adj.* Questioning and reflective
inscrutable, *adj.* Difficult to understand; unfathomable
instigator, *n.* A person who stirs others to action
insurrection, *n.* Open revolt against civil authority or government
intelligentsia, *n.* Members of the intellectual elite
inter, *v.* To place in a grave or tomb; bury
interminable, *adj.* Endless; being or seeming to be without end
intolerable, *adj.* Unbearable
invocation, *n.* A prayer or other saying used to seek guidance or inspiration from a higher power; a prayer used at the beginning of a religious service
irascible, *adj.* Easily angered
ire, *n.* Anger, wrath
ironic, *adj.* Contradictory in a surprising or humorous way

J

jubilee, *n.* A festival or celebration
juncture, *n.* A point in time, especially a critical point

K

keen, *adj.* Intense, piercing
ken, *n.* Range of vision
kindred, *n.* Relations, family members, or, metophorically, others of the same tribe or community

L

lacerate, *v.* To tear, wound
lament, *n.* Expression of grief
lamentation, *n.* The act of expressing grief; mourning
languid, *adj.* Lacking energy; weak
languish, *v.* To become weak
latent, *adj.* Present or potential but not evident or active
laudatory, *adj.* Expressing praise
leisure, *n.* Freedom from time-consuming duties, responsibilities, or activities
liable, *adj.* Likely. Often used with reference to an unfavorable outcome.
listless, *adj.* Lacking energy or disinclined to exert effort
lithe, *adj.* Marked by effortless grace; supple or flexible
loathe, *v.* To dislike greatly
loathsomeness, *n.* Nastiness
lofty, *adj.* Elevated in character; exalted or dignified
lurid, *adj.* Shining with the glare of fire
lurk, *v.* To lie or wait in concealment, as a person in ambush

M

machination, *n.* A crafty scheme or cunning design for the accomplishment of a sinister end
malice, *n.* A desire to harm others or to see others suffer
manacle, *n.* Something that confines or restrains
manifestation, *n.* Outward show
mariner, *n.* Sailor
martial, *adj.* Of, relating to, or suggestive of war
martyr, *n.* One who dies for a belief, cause, or principle
miscreant, *n.* Wrongdoer
monarchy, *n.* Nation ruled by a king or queen
monotony, *n.* Sameness
moratorium, *n.* A suspension of an activity
multitudinous, *adj.* Extremely varied
mutter, *v.* To speak in a low tone, especially when complaining; grumble

N

naught, *n.* Nothing
neurotic, *adj.* Overanxious; obsessive
nominal, *adj.* In name only; half-hearted, uncommitted
nourish, *v.* To feed and otherwise provide for
novel, *adj.* Strikingly new; unusual

O

obdurate, *adj.* 1. Not giving in to persuasion. 2. Hardened in wickedness.
obeisance, *n.* A gesture of the body that expresses deference or homage
ominous, *adj.* 1. Menacing; threatening. 2. Foreshadowing evil.
omission, *n.* Something left out or not included
omniscient, *adj.* Knowing everything
orator, *n.* Public speaker
ordained, *past part.* Predestined
orthodox, *adj.* Standard or traditional
osprey, *n.* A large bird of prey
outlandish, *adj.* Bizarre, strikingly unfamiliar

P

pacify, *v.* Restore calm or establish peace in
pallid, *adj.* Pale; lacking intensity of color
pallor, *n.* Extreme or unnatural paleness
palpitate, *v.* To beat rapidly
panoply, *n.* The arms and armor of a warrior
parity, *n.* Equality, as in amount, status, or value
pastel, *adj.* Light shade of any color
pedigree, *n.* A line of ancestors; a lineage
peevish, *adj.* Discontented or querulous; annoyed
pelt, *n.* Fur-covered skin
peremptorily, *adv.* Not allowing contradiction or refusal
persistence, *n.* The state or quality of holding firmly to a purpose or goal despite obstacles or setbacks
personification, *n.* A person typifying a certain quality or idea; embodiment
peruse, *v.* To read or examine with care
pestilential, *adj.* Infected with contagious disease; deadly
phantasmal, *adj.* Illusory, unreal, said of an apparition having no physical reality
pillage, *v.* To rob of goods by force; plunder
pious, *adj.* Deeply religious; devout

piratical, ***adj.*** Characteristic of pirates
pitiable, ***adj.*** Arousing or deserving of pity; pathetic
plaintive, ***adj.*** Sad
plaintively, ***adv.*** In a sad or distressed manner
plume, ***n.*** A feather, especially a large showy one
polemic, ***n.*** An aggressive attack on someone else's opinions
pomp, ***n.*** Splendor, magnificence
portent, ***n.*** An indication of something important or calamitous about to occur; an omen
potent, ***adj.*** Possessing strength; powerful
precaution, ***n.*** An action taken in advance to protect against danger
precipitate, ***v.*** To cause or bring on abruptly
presumptuous, ***adj.*** Boldly arrogant or offensive
pretension, ***n.*** Ostentatious display; pretentiousness (demanding a position of distinction, especially when unjustified)
pretentious, ***adj.*** Claiming or demanding a position of merit, usually unjustified
prevail, ***v.*** To persuade someone to do something
procure, ***v.*** To obtain or acquire
prodigious, ***adj.*** Impressively great in size
prodigy, ***n.*** A person with exceptional talent or powers
profusion, ***n.*** Abundance or extravagance
propriety, ***n.*** Appropriateness
providential, ***adj.*** As if through divine intervention
provincial, ***adj.*** Limited in perspective; narrow and self-centered
provocation, ***n.*** The act of inciting anger or resentment
prowess, ***n.*** Superior skill or ability
puerile, ***adj.*** Childish and silly
pulpit, ***n.*** An elevated platform

Q

quackery, ***n.*** The act of pretending to be a physician or dispensing medicine or medical advice without training
quibble, ***v.*** To evade the essential aspects of an issue by raising trivial distinctions and objections

R

radiant, ***adj.*** Giving off rays (of light)
range, ***v.*** To wander or roam over a large area
rapture, ***n.*** Joy
ream, ***v.*** To squeeze
reap, ***v.*** To gather or harvest
rebuke, ***v.*** To criticize sharply
rebuke, ***n.*** Sharp criticism
recompose, ***v.*** To regain a sense of calm and well-being
reconnoiter, ***v.*** To inspect or check an area
reconsecrate, ***v.*** To solemnly rededicate to a service or goal
rectitude, ***n.*** Moral uprightness; righteousness
redemptive, ***adj.*** Restoring honor or reputation
refined, ***adj.*** Polite, purified; free form vulgarity
refinement, ***n.*** Sophistication; improvement
refrain, ***v.*** To prevent oneself from doing something
reign, ***v.*** To rule or govern
rejuvenated, ***past part.*** Refreshed or reborn
remonstrate, ***v.*** To plead in protest; to present an objection
rend, ***v.*** To tear apart violently; to shred
render, ***v.*** To make
reproach, ***n.*** 1. Criticism, disapproval. 2. A cause of blame or disgrace.
reticent, ***adj.*** Restrained in expression; silent
retrospectively, ***adv.*** In a way that contemplated the past
revile, ***v.*** To abuse verbally
rhetoric, ***n.*** Language that is overly elaborate or insincere
riffle, ***v.*** To thumb through (the pages of a book)
rifling, ***pres. part.*** Looking through something hurriedly, in a sloppy, haphazard manner
roguery, ***n.*** Mischievous behavior or an act of mischief
roseate, ***adj.*** Rose-colored
rouse, ***v.*** To excite to anger or to action
row, ***n.*** An altercation or fight

S

sable, ***adj.*** Dark, black
sacrilegious, ***adj.*** Blasphemous, irreligious
salience, ***n.*** Facts that stand out; essential facts
salutation, ***n.*** Greeting
saucy, ***adj.*** Insolent, flippant
saunter, ***v.*** To walk at a leisurely pace; stroll
savant, ***n.*** A learned person; a scholar
scalding, ***adj.*** Burning; harshly offensive
scowl, ***v.*** To make a face that shows extreme dissatisfaction
scruple, ***n.*** An uneasy feeling arising from conscience; qualm
sentinel, ***n.*** Guard
serf, ***n.*** An agricultural worker
servitude, ***n.*** The state of being a servant or slave
sever, ***v.*** Cut in two
shackles, ***n.*** Manacles and chains
sham, ***n.*** Something that is not genuine, a fake
sidle, ***v.*** Approach cautiously alongside rather than face to face
singularity, ***n.*** Uniqueness
slight, ***n.*** A deliberate discourtesy; the act of treating something as if it has little importance
smug, ***adj.*** Showing excessive self-satisfaction
solicitous, ***adj.*** Full of desire; eager
stark, ***adj.*** Harsh, unadorned, not fruitful, meager
steal, ***v.*** To sneak quietly; to creep
stolid, ***adj.*** Showing or feeling little emotion
stout, ***adj.*** Burly, strong
stratagem, ***n.*** A clever underhanded scheme for achieving an objective
subconsciously, ***adv.*** In a manner not readily recognized because the thought wells up from the depths of the mind
subterfuge, ***n.*** A deceptive stratagem or device; a trick
succor, ***v.*** To give assistance to in time of difficulty or distress; to help
summons, ***n.*** A call from an authority to appear or do

sunder, *v.* To divide or separate
superb, *adj.* Magnificent; impressive
superstition, *n.* A belief that is not based in reason or scientific understanding, especially one that involves magic or the supernatural
suppression, *n.* The act of restricting or prohibiting something
sustain, *v.* To maintain or keep in existence
swagger, *n.* Literally, a cocky walk; figuratively, an expression of excessive self-assuredness
sweltering, *adj.* Oppressively hot
sycophancy, *n.* Servile flattery (A sycophant is a person who attempts to win favor by flattering influential people)

T

tawny, *adj.* A light brown to brownish orange
tedious, *adj.* Extremely tiresome
tempest, *n.* A violent windstorm, frequently accompanied by rain, snow, or hail
tend, *v.* To care for
throng, *v.* To crowd into; fill
throng, *n.* A crowd of people
tillage, *n.* The cultivation of land
timorous, *adj.* Full of apprehensiveness; nervous
toil, *v.* To work
tone, *n.* Manner or style of speaking
transaction, *n.* An interchange, especially one involving a purchase or barter
travail, *n.* Work, especially of a painful or laborious nature; toil
treacherous, *adj.* Untrustworthy, dangerous, unreliable
trifling, *adj.* Insignificant
trumped-up, *adj.* Falsified, said of false charges or purposefully incorrect readings of legal documents or statutes
tumultuous, *adj.* Noisy and disorderly

U

unabated, *adj.* Continued at full strength or force
unalienable, *adj.* Not to be taken away
unavailing, *adj.* Ineffectual or useless; futile
uncouth, *adj.* Crude, unrefined; awkward or clumsy
unequivocal, *adj.* Admitting no doubt; unambiguous
unfaltering, *adj.* Steady in purpose of action; confident
unfetter, *v.* To set free or keep free from restrictions or bonds
unremittant, *adj.* Unceasing, persistent
unspeakable, *adj.* Beyond description; inexpressibly bad
urchin, *n.* Mischievous, playful youngster

V

vain, *adj.* Pointless; to no avail
veldt, *n.* Any of the open grazing areas of central or southern Africa
verbiage, *n.* An excess of words; wordiness
vicinity, *n.* A nearby, surrounding, or adjoining place; a neighborhood
vicissitude, *n.* A sudden or unexpected change
vile, *adj.* Unpleasant or objectionable; disgusting
vindicate, *v.* To provide justification or support for
vogue, *n.* Fashion

W

wallow, *v.* To roll about clumsily, as if in mud; struggle
waxen, *adj.* Like wax, lacking life
weaver, *n.* A person who makes cloth or rugs for a living
wheeze, *v.* To breathe hoarsely or with difficulty
wile, *n.* A trick intended to deceive or ensnare
winged, *adj.* Soaring as if with wings; elevated or sublime
withering, *adj.* Tending to overwhelm; devastating
wrath, *n.* Forceful, often vindictive anger; vengeance
wretched, *adj.* Miserable, unhappy, distressed

Z

zeal, *n.* Enthusiastic devotion to a cause
zealously, *adv.* With enthusiastic devotion to a cause

Subject Index

Index of Prominent Africans and African Americans Appearing in *Grace Abounding*

Index of Authors, Titles, and First Lines

"Roman type in quotation marks" = First line **Boldface type** = Author *Italic type* = Title

Index of Terms and Concepts for Cultural Studies

Literary Terms

Writing Exercises and Strategies

Speaking and Listening

Drama

Music and Dance

(Terms for types of music, such as blues and soul jazz, can be found in the Subject Index.–Ed.)

Art

Common Literary Allusions, Phrases, and Interesting Etymologies

(Students can expect to encounter these again at some point in their reading lives. All allusions are defined in footnotes or texts of Grace Abounding. *Numerous scriptural references appear throughout the book and are footnoted and cited wherever they appear. This index can be used as the basis of a number of language arts exercises in the classroom. –Ed.)*

Scriptural References

Index of Illustrations